THE *Virgin* ENCYCLOPEDIA OF

NINETIES MUSIC

edited and compiled by

COLIN LARKIN

IN ASSOCIATION WITH MUZE UK

Dedicated to the founder dewds

First published in Great Britain in 2000 by
VIRGIN BOOKS
an imprint of Virgin Publishing Ltd
Thames Wharf Studios, Rainville Road, London W6 9HT
www.virgin-books.com

A catalogue record for this book is available from the British Library

ISBN 0-7535 0427 8

muze

Written, edited and produced by
MUZE UK Ltd
to whom all editorial enquiries should be sent
Suite 16, Arcade Chambers, 28 High Street, Brentwood, Essex CM14 4AH, England

check us out at **www.muze.com**

Editor In Chief: Colin Larkin. colin@muze.co.uk
Production Editor: Susan Pipe. sue@muze.co.uk
Research Editor: Nic Oliver. nic@muze.co.uk
Pogo Team Coach: Neal Goddard. nealg@uk.muze.com
Typographic Design Consultant: Roger Kohn
Special thanks to Trev Huxley, and Paul Zullo of Muze Inc.,
and to Rob Shreeve and David Gould of Virgin Publishing.

Typeset by Fork 'n' Spoon Studio
Printed and bound in Great Britain by Butler & Tanner Ltd, Frome and London

INTRODUCTION

An opinion generally shared by music writers and critics is that the 'now' decade is there to be trashed. As music enters subsequent decades and ageism creeps in, it appears inferior to what preceded it.

Therefore, we have the glorious 60s, followed by the not quite as good 70s. The latter decade started with glam, went flat in the middle and perked up a bit after 1977. My personal view is that the 80s were generally static, computerised and mind numbingly dull. I could never say that in one of my books, especially the Eighties Encyclopedia! I just put it down to the fact that I was another 10 years older and was entering my curmudgeonly phase of life.

Fortunately, the music of the 90s pulled me and many of my colleagues out of the armchair. I truly believe it ranks second only to the 60s as the best ever decade for popular music. Indie, Dance and Hip-Hop are exciting and fertile genres that have borrowed a pinch of reggae, a sprig of metal and a shake of latin and lounge music. There has been so much good stuff, and even though much of it has been derivative, the basic five chord song is still very much alive. My own slightly narrow and subjective list would include the likes of Blur, Oasis, Teenage Fanclub and Stereophonics from the UK, and Foo Fighters, New Radicals, Fastball, Goo Goo Dolls and Eels from the USA. Other high points have been Erykah Badu, Macy Gray, Robbie Williams and yes, Shania Twain. There are tons more of course but there is nothing more boring than an editor listing his favourites. Recent Blues, Country and Jazz can be found in the recently published specialist titles. We have tried to give a broad spread to cover most of the top artists from every genre. And we even found room for Peter Andre! Ultimately you have already made up your own minds, and I hope to goodness that we have managed to fit them all in. If not I know you will let me know. At the usual address please.

Other titles already in your favourite store are:
The Virgin Encyclopedia Of Fifties Music
The Virgin Encyclopedia Of Sixties Music
The Virgin Encyclopedia Of Seventies Music
The Virgin Encyclopedia Of Eighties Music
The Virgin Encyclopedia Of Popular Music (Concise)
The Virgin Encyclopedia Of Indie & New Wave
The Virgin Encyclopedia Of The Blues
The Virgin Encyclopedia Of R&B And Soul
The Virgin Encyclopedia Of Reggae
The Virgin Encyclopedia Of Country Music
The Virgin Encyclopedia Of Dance
The Virgin Encyclopedia Of Heavy Rock
The Virgin Encyclopedia Of Jazz
The Virgin Encyclopedia Of Stage & Film Musicals
The Virgin All-Time Top 1000 Albums
The All-Time Top 1000 Albums Mini-Guide

ALBUM RATING

Due to public demand we now rate all albums. All new releases are reviewed either by me, Nic Oliver, or by our team of contributors. We also always take into consideration the review ratings of the leading music journals, newspapers and reliable critics' opinions.

Our system is slightly different to most 5 Star reviews in that we grade according to the artist in question's work.

★★★★★

Outstanding in every way. A classic and therefore strongly recommended. No comprehensive record collection should be without this album.

★★★★

Excellent. A high standard album from this artist and therefore highly recommended.

★★★

Good. By the artist's usual standards and therefore recommended.

★★

Disappointing. Flawed or lacking in some way.

★

Poor. An album to avoid unless you are a completist.

ENTRY STYLE

Albums, EPs (extended play 45s), newspapers, magazines, television programmes, films and stage musicals are referred to in italics. All song titles appear in single quotes. The further reading section at the end of each entry has been expanded to give the reader a much wider choice of available books. These are not necessarily recommended titles but we have attempted to leave out any publication that has little or no merit.

We have also started to add videos at the ends of the entries. Again, this is an area that is expanding more quickly than we can easily cope with, but there are many items in the videography and further items in the filmography, which is another new section we have decided to include. For a more comprehensive list see the muze.com web site. Release dates in keeping with albums attempt to show the release date in the country of origin. We have also tried to include both US and UK titles where applicable.

PLAGIARISM

In maintaining the largest text database of popular music in the world we are naturally protective of its content. We license to approved licensees only. It is both flattering and irritating to see our work reproduced without credit. Time and time again over the past few years I have read an obituary, when suddenly I realise the author has used our text as the base.

Music websites are also using our data. If you are not licenced by MUZE UK or MUZE Inc., you should immediately remove our text from your site. I refer specifically to the many unofficial fan based music sites. Yes, we are flattered that you think our text is the best available, but what you are doing is illegal and infringes copyright.

Record companies have lifted chunks of text without credit. They know who they are and will continue to pay through the courts for such bare-faced theft. Finally, it has come to our notice that other companies attempting to produce their own music guides blatantly use our material as a core. Flattering this might also be, but highly unfair. We have therefore dropped a few textual 'depth charges' in addition to the original ones. Be warned, our busy lawyers have already started litigation.

ACKNOWLEDGEMENTS

Our in-house editorial team is small and efficient. The EPM Database is now well over 10 years old and needs only regular food, attention and love. Thanks to my MUZE UK team for their continuing efficiency: Susan Pipe and Nic Oliver run an almost trouble free office. Regular outsiders continue to work with us: Jon Staines, Salsri Nyah, Alex Ogg, Big John Martland, Bruce Crowther, Dave Gil De Rubio (down by the schoolyard), and new boys Eddie Houghton, Dominic Chadwick (who supplied some updates), Mark Keresman and David Hemingway.

Other past contributors' work may appear in this volume and I acknowledge with thanks once again the past work of Karen Glossop, Brian Hogg, Simon Williams, John Eley, Dave Laing, Spencer Leigh, David MacDonald

and Jeff Tamarkin. Please do not be offended if I have left out your name, it is a minefield to try and remember which entries have not been completely rewritten over the years.

Thank you Mike (remember you're a womble) Kaye, our brilliant software developer. Pete Bassett and his Quite Greats and as always Johnny 'the leprechaun' Rogan. Thanks for the co-operation of our colleagues at Virgin Publishing under the firm (but fair) guidance of Rob Shreeve, in particular to the highly amiable David Gould and the shamelessly organized and part-time lap dancer Roz Scott.

Thanks to John Burton for continuing to send press cuttings and to Johnny Black, Pete Frame, Chris Charlesworth and Peter Doggett for simply existing. To Fred and Dawn Nelson, Kathleen Dougherty and Dave and Sabe.

Thanks to a few record company press offices and PR companies. The ones that bother with us are Murray Chalmers at Parlophone, Matt at Polydor, Dorothy Howe, Alan Robinson at Castle, Richard Wootton, Julia Honeywell at Ace, Sue and Dave Williams at Frontier, Pat Tynan at Koch International and finally to the marginally agreeable Stuart Batsford at Warner ESP. Stuart is one of only a handful, working at a major record label, who is not only passionate about music but highly knowledgeable (and hopelessly opinionated).

Thanks to all my MUZE Inc. colleagues, some I can even call my friends, at the office on 304 Hudson Street in New York City. In particular to Marc Miller, Mad Gary Geller, Raisa Howe, Adam Silver, Phil 'born to run' Fletcher, Matt 'operetta' Puccini, Stephen 'petty officer' Hughes and the chief mullet hunter Scott Lehr. At the ever expanding MUZE UK operations centre I get help from Neal Goddard, Stephanie Jones, Doug Taylor Johnson and the highly agreeable Jon 'able seaman' Staines.

In no order whatsoever, Robin 'testosterone' Altman, Peter Rivera (and the Raiders), Paul Parriera (and the Raiders),Philip (PHIL) Sidel, Paul Marino, Paul Perez, Michael Kennedy. Not to ignore: Jennifer Lyn Rose, Phil Antman, Jim 'you failure' Allen, Stephen Parker, Terry 'grape' Vinyard, Amanda 'high sweedie' Denhoff, Jannett Diaz, Ed 'gentleman' Moore, the continually impressive Bill 'the haircut' Schmitt, Michael Doustan, Jeanne Petras, Ejay, Gail 'oh, my, God!' Niovitch, Sandra 'not forgotten' Levanta, Bernadette Elliott, Kal Dogin, Silvia Kessel and all the other Klugettes.

And to the original founding dewds Paul 'King Biscuit' Zullo and Trev 'Easy Rider' Huxley. May your dreams come true.

Finally to my consistently amazing tin lids; Marbella, Hitchcock and Tim, and my leap year sweetheart, Kelly.

Colin Larkin, February 2000

A Guy Called Gerald

Gerald Simpson's solo career has failed to ignite as many predicted, although he remains a maverick and influential presence on the UK's dance music scene. Simpson, who once sold copies of the left-wing newspaper *Socialist Worker* on the streets of Manchester, England, first recorded with the Scratchbeat Masters (who included Nicky Lockett, the future MC Tunes) before joining the Hit Squad. The latter mutated into the seminal 808 State, but Simpson left following a dispute over writing credits for what would prove to be the group's breakthough hit, 'Pacific State'. His most notable contribution to the UK's fledgling dance scene was 'Voodoo Ray', which reached number 55 in April 1989 before re-entering at number 12 two months later. Those statistics barely reflect the reverence with which it came to be regarded on the club scene. Simpson was subsequently offered the chance to remix for Cabaret Voltaire and Turntable Orchestra, and signed a major label deal with Sony Records for the release of *Automanikk*. The label rejected the follow-up and Simpson was released from his contract. He retreated to his home studio, the 'Machine Room', where he continued to record club-orientated material at a prolific rate. He put together a tape to accompany a book by Trevor Miller entitled *Trip City*, and set up his JuiceBox/JuiceGroove Records label. The hardcore breakbeats on *28 Gun Bad Boy* and *Black Secret Technology*, the latter featuring a pre-fame Finlay Quaye on vocals, found favour as acid house was displaced by the new sound of jungle. With his name once again prominent on the UK dance scene, Simpson signed a contract with Island Records. His run of bad luck with major labels continued, however, when Island was taken over by PolyGram Records. The new owners dropped A Guy Called Gerald shortly before a new album was due to be released. An unperturbed Simpson carried on with his busy recording and DJing schedule.
● ALBUMS: *Hot Lemonade* (Rham 1988)★★★, *Automanikk* (Columbia 1990)★★★, *28 Gun Bad Boy* (JuiceBox 1993)★★★, *Black Secret Technology* (JuiceBox 1995)★★★★.
● COMPILATIONS: various artists *Juice Box Concentrate* (JuiceBox 1998)★★★, *The John Peel Sessions* (Strange Fruit 1999)★★★, *Cyrogenix: A Decade In Dance* (MP3.Com 1999)★★★★.

A House

A witty, intelligent post-punk pop band from Dublin, Eire, led by lyricist Dave Couse (vocals), with Fergal Bunbury (guitar) and Martin Healy (bass). The band was originally signed by Geoff Travis for his Warner Brothers Records-backed Blanco y Negro label in 1987, on the strength of their debut single 'Kick Me Again Jesus' and support slots with the Waterboys. However, their debut album failed commer-cially. Still tied to a two-album contract, the band then recorded *I Want Too Much*, which was highly acclaimed for bright, defiant songs such as 'The Patron Saint Of Mediocrity'. However, many considered that the album signalled the end of the band, but they subsequently regrouped. Keith Cullen had recently set up the Setanta Records label (also home to Frank And Walters and Into Paradise) and invited them to join the roster. Their 'new' career started with an EP, *Doodle*, then the controversial 'Endless List' single. This attracted the wrath of feminists who noted that, of the dozens of names recounted by Couse in a spoken tribute to individuals who had furthered humanity, none were female. The result was a second 'list', this time composed entirely of women. *I Am The Greatest* followed in October 1991, but its impact was deadened by distribution problems (BBC Radio 'playlisted' it, but, unable actually to get the record into the shops, the band had to request that the BBC *not* play it). It was produced by Edwyn Collins on a shoestring budget ('He isn't really a producer as such, he just comes up with ideas and gets the drinks in'), and proved another superb showcase for Couse's lyrical aptitude and affecting vocals. Re-released and re-promoted, it eventually entered the UK Top 50. *Wide Eyed And Ignorant* was an accomplished collection of songs, with the production credits shared this time between Collins and Phil Thornalley. *No More Apologies*, however, was a disappointingly mediocre swansong for such an interesting band.
● ALBUMS: *On Our Big Fat Merry Go Round* (Blanco y Negro 1988)★★, *I Want Too Much* (Blanco y Negro 1990)★★★, *I Am The Greatest* (Setanta 1991)★★★, *Wide Eyed And Ignorant* (Setanta/Parlophone 1994)★★★, *No More Apologies* (Setanta 1996)★★.
● COMPILATIONS: *Live In Concert* (Strange Fruit 1998)★★★.

A Man Called Adam

This mellow house outfit, formed in the late 80s in north London, England, first began life as a 10-piece jazz band. Clubgoers, however, came to know them through the distinctive vocals of Sally Rodgers, and the layered Chicago house sounds promulgated by musician Steve Jones. Paul Daley, later half of Leftfield, was also an early collaborator, alongside future members of the Sandals. Their debut releases were 'A.P.B.' and 'Earthly Powers' for Acid Jazz Records, but after a short spell with Ritmo Records (for whom they released 'Musica De Amor') they moved on to Big Life Records. Their spatial and rhythmic experiments were immediately successful, despite an apparent awkwardness with lyrical construction. Easily the best representation of the band was their minor chart success, 'Barefoot In The Head', which remained a highly respected club song well into the 90s. It was followed by 'I Want To Know', which was remixed by Steve Anderson of Brothers In Rhythm and Graeme Park, and became a major club hit. However, by 1993 their relationship with Big Life had soured and, following a spate of unsuccessful big budget remixes of their work, they were unceremoniously dropped from the label. The duo eventually responded with the formation of the Other Records label, which began in 1994 with the jazz-tinged disco of 'I Am The Way'. Subsequent releases included 'Love Comes Down' and 'Easter Song', and tracks by their dub alter ego, Beachflea.
● ALBUMS: *The Apple* (Big Life 1991)★★★.

A Tribe Called Quest

This US male rap outfit originally comprised Q-Tip (b. Jonathan Davis, 20 November 1970, New York, USA), DJ Ali Shaheed Muhammad (b. 11 August 1970, Brooklyn, New York, USA), Jarobi and Phife Dog (b. Malik Taylor, 10 April 1970, Brooklyn, New York, USA). They formed at school in Manhattan, New York, where they started out as part of the Native Tongues Posse, with Queen Latifah and the Jungle Brothers, and were given their name by Afrika Baby Bambaataa of the Jungle Brothers. Following their August 1989 debut, 'Description Of A Fool', they had a hit with 'Bonita Applebum' a year later, which was apparently based on a real person from their school. Their biggest success came the following year with the laid-back 'Can I Kick It?', typical of their refined jazz/hip-hop cross-match. A UK Top 20 single, it was later used extensively in television advertisements. Q-Tip also appeared on Deee-Lite's August 1990 hit, 'Groove Is In The Heart'. As members of the Native Tongues Posse they were promoters of the Afrocentricity movement, which set out to make US Africans aware of their heritage, a theme emphasized in the group's music. While their debut, *People's Instinctive Travels And The Paths Of Rhythm*, was more eclectic, and even self-consciously jokey, *The Low-End Theory* (recorded as a trio following the departure of Jarobi) saw them return to their roots with a more bracing, harder funk sound. They were helped considerably by jazz bass player Ron Carter (who had worked with Miles Davis and John Coltrane), whose contribution rather dominated proceedings. Tracks such as 'The Infamous Date Rape' stoked controversy, while samples from Lou Reed, Stevie Wonder and Earth, Wind And Fire were used in a frugal and intelligent manner. By *Midnight Marauders* there were allusions to the rise of gangsta rap, although they maintained the optimism predominant on their debut. Q-Tip appeared in the 1993 movie *Poetic Justice* opposite Janet Jackson, and helped to produce Tony! Toni! Toné! (whose Raphael Wiggins made an appearance on *Midnight Marauders*), Nas, Shyheim and labelmate Shaquille O'Neal. They received the Group Of The Year award at the inaugural *Source Magazine* Hip Hop Award Show in 1994, before being pulled off the stage by the arrival of 2Pac and his Thug Life crew, attempting to steal some publicity. Two years elapsed before *Beats, Rhymes And Life* debuted at number 1 on the *Billboard* album chart. Their lyrics on this album addressed issues with greater philosophy than the crude banter of their past recordings. Q-Tip's conversion to the Islamic faith may have had some bearing on this style. *The Love Movement*, which debuted at US number 3 in October 1998, was another mature, stylish collection of material that lacked the spark of their earlier work. It proved to be their final recording as the individual members elected to concentrate on solo work.

● ALBUMS: *People's Instinctive Travels And The Paths Of Rhythm* (Jive 1990)★★★, *The Low-End Theory* (Jive 1991)★★★★, *Revised Quest For The Seasoned Traveller* remix album (Jive 1992)★★, *Midnight Marauders* (Jive 1993)★★★, *Beats, Rhymes And Life* (Jive 1996)★★★★, *The Love Movement* (Jive 1998)★★★.

● COMPILATIONS: *The Anthology* (Jive 1999)★★★★.

A+

b. Andre Levins, 1983, Hempstead, New York, USA. Another in a long line of 'child rappers', including Da Youngsta's and Shyheim, A+ was just 13 years old at the time of his debut, *The Latch-Key Child*. The first artist signed to Kedar Entertainment (headed by Kedar Massenburg, manager of D'Angelo), he stated his intention was to '. . . grab all the latch-key kids and bring them in. I want to let them know that they don't have to live like that.' As a testament to this 'far-sightedness', his record company provided a full-time tutor during the record's promotion. The album included contributions from Q-Tip (A Tribe Called Quest), Prodigy (Mobb Deep) and AZ. A+ initially fostered hopes of becoming a professional football player, but soon began imitating Leaders Of The New School and Onyx in high-school talent contests. He won a national competition sponsored by Def Jam Records in 1995, where he was spotted by Massenburg. His debut single, 'All I See', saw many hip-hop commentators compare his lucid microphone skills to those of Method Man of the Wu-Tang Clan. After a two year hiatus, A+ returned with the international hit 'Enjoy Yourself', which reached UK number 5 in February 1999. The single was an effective introduction to the rapper's adoption of a laid back, swingbeat-influenced style on *Hempstead High*.

● ALBUMS: *The Latch-Key Child* (Kedar/Universal 1996)★★★, *Hempstead High* (Kedar/Universal 1999)★★★★.

Aaliyah

b. Aaliyah Dani Haughton, 16 January 1979, Brooklyn, New York, USA, but grew up in Detroit, Michigan. Pronounced Ah-Lee-Yah ('highest, most exalted one' in Swahili), this female artist initially came to attention as part of the 'new jill swing' movement in the mid-90s. Her early career was fostered by R. Kelly and 1994's debut *Age Ain't Nothing But A Number* included the US Top 10 singles 'Back & Forth' and 'At Your Best (You Are Love)'. She travelled to Kelly's home in Chicago for the sessions while she was still a student at the Detroit High School of the Performing Arts. She remained a 'straight A's' student throughout the first stage of her recording career, persevering with her education despite commercial success. After marrying Kelly, Aaliyah released 1996's superior follow-up, *One In A Million*, on which she worked with hotshot producer Timbaland. Soundtrack work followed, with contributions to *Anastasia* ('Journey To The Past') and *Dr. Dolittle* ('Are You That Somebody?'). Aaliyah also began filming her screen debut in Andrzej Bartkowiak's *Romeo Must Die*.

● ALBUMS: *Age Ain't Nothing But A Number* (Blackground/Atlantic 1994)★★★, *One In A Million* (Atlantic 1996)★★★.

Abdul, Paula

b. 19 June 1962, San Fernando, California, USA. After spending much of her childhood in dance schools and troupes, Paula Abdul secured a role in the L.A. Lakers basketball cheerleaders team and at 17 became their choreographer. Spotted by the Jacksons, she was employed to assist them on dance routines for their live dates on the *Victory* tour. Abdul's big break came when she landed a job choreographing a young Janet Jackson's videos for *Control*. Their immediate success focused attention on Abdul's dance talents and she quickly found herself much in demand from a string of other artists (including ZZ Top, Duran Duran and the Pointer Sisters) seeking a high MTV profile. The inevitable move to her own singing career brought immediate fame. Stylistically in the mould of her former pupil, Janet Jackson, her third single, 'Straight Up', went to number 1 in the US in 1988, and was followed by three other chart-topping singles: 'Forever Your Girl', 'Cold Hearted' and 'Opposites Attract'. The latter's popularity was enhanced by the video's depiction of the singer duetting with a cartoon character, MC Skat Cat. Abdul's debut, *Forever Your Girl*, triumphed on both sides of the Atlantic, reaching number 1 in the USA, staying there for 10 weeks, and peaking at number 3 in the UK. A follow-up collection of remixes, *Shut Up And Dance*, issued in early 1990, marked time until *Spellbound* was released in 1991. The latter gave Abdul another US chart-topping album and spawned two US number 1 singles in 'Rush, Rush' and 'The Promise Of A New Day'. Her popularity in Europe, although quite substantial ('Straight Up', 'Opposites Attract' and 'Rush, Rush' were all UK Top 10 singles), was nonetheless no match for her image in the USA, being every young girl's role model as the all-singing, all-dancing trouper. Abdul's choreography work in the movies and her marriage to actor Emilio Estevez also helped maintain her high profile, although the couple were divorced in May 1994. She returned in 1995 (after a long absence owing to a lawsuit filed by a former backing singer) with the minor hit single 'My Love Is For Real', which preceded *Head Over Heels*. Abdul made her acting debut in January 1997 with the television movie, *Touched By Evil*. She subsequently signed a recording deal with Mercury Records.

● ALBUMS: *Forever Your Girl* (Virgin 1988)★★★, *Shut Up And Dance (The Dance Mixes)* (Virgin 1990)★★, *Spellbound* (Virgin 1991)★★★, *Head Over Heels* (Virgin 1995)★★.

● VIDEOS: *Compilation* (Virgin Vision 1988), *Skat Strut/Opposites Attract* (Virgin Vision 1991), *Captivated: The Video Collection '92* (Virgin Vision 1992).

Above The Law

Gangsta rappers from Pomona, California, USA, whose ultra-violent lyrics betrayed a keen nose for breezy rhythm tracks, largely sampled from 70s soul. They also utilized live keyboards, bass and guitar to back the rhymes of the self-styled 'hustlers', Cold 187um (b. Gregory Hutchinson), KM.G. The Illustrator (b. Kevin Gulley), Total K-oss (b. Anthony Stewart) and original member Go Mack (Arthur Goodman). Their debut album consisted of two quite separate themes on the Mega and the Ranchin' sides. The first dealt with graphic, unpleasant street violence narratives, while the second observed leering sexual scenarios. It was an unappetizing mix, despite the presence of Eazy-E on 'The Last Song' (both he and Dr. Dre chaired production while they were still on speaking terms), and some otherwise attractive instrumental work. The follow-up, *Vocally Pimpin'*, at least boasted improved studio technique, but their second long-playing set, produced by Cold 187um, did not fare as well. Cold 187um went on to produce Kokane's 1994 debut *Funk Upon A Rhyme*. The trio attempted greater lyrical depth on 1994's *Uncle Sam's Curse*, and although not altogether successful the grooves were still imaginative. Newly signed to Tommy Boy Records, they were still plugging away with the same formula on *Time Will Reveal* and *Legends*, the latter included a reworking of Luther Vandross' 'Promise Me'. In the late 90s, they set up their own West World imprint.

● ALBUMS: *Livin' Like Hustlers* (Ruthless 1990)★★★, *Vocally Pimpin'* mini-album (Ruthless 1991)★★, *Black Mafia Life: The Album* (Ruthless 1992)★★★, *Uncle Sam's Curse* (Ruthless 1994)★★, *Time Will Reveal* (Tommy Boy 1996)★★★, *Legends* (Tommy Boy 1997)★★★.

Ace Of Base

Ace Of Base achieved their breakthrough in 1993 with the worldwide number 1, 'All That She Wants'. The comparisons to a fellow Swedish band seemed obvious - two female vocalists, one blonde, one brunette, and two male musicians, playing catchy dance-inflected pop music. The band, who originally recorded as Tech Noir, was formed by Malin Berggren (b. 31 October 1970; vocals), Jenny Berggren (b. 19 May 1972; vocals), Jonas Berggren (b. 21 March 1967; programming/songwriting) and Ulf Ekberg (b. 6 December 1970; programming/songwriting). Before their breakthrough the sisters sang in church choirs in their native Gothenburg, while brother Jonas and close friend Ekberg perfected their expertise in new technology. Their chart-friendly combination of pop and reggae was further revealed on 'Wheel Of Fortune', 'Happy Nation', 'Waiting For Magic' and the hugely popular 'The Sign' (US number 1/UK number 2), while their debut album went to number 1 in six countries, selling over 21 million copies. They enjoyed further worldwide success with 'Don't Turn Around', a cover version of Aswad's pop-reggae standard. Their second album, *The Bridge*, was released at the end of 1995 and saw the band move away from reggae basslines to encompass more mature, considered songwriting. While 'Ravine' expressed their Christianity, 'Experience Pearls' saw them move in the direction of sophisticated Euro pop. It was far from the unholy music experience some critics imagined, despite the band's continued inability to negotiate English-language lyrics with anything approaching subtlety. They debuted at UK number 5 in August 1998 with the catchy 'Life Is A Flower', and enjoyed transatlantic chart success with a cover version of Bananarama's 'Cruel Summer' (US number 10/UK number 8). The attendant album was a disappointingly bland affair. The following year's singles compilation provided the perfect way to enjoy their innocuous Euro pop.

● ALBUMS: *Happy Nation* (Mega/London 1993)★★★, *The Sign* US only (Arista 1993)★★★, *The Bridge* (Mega/London/Arista 1995)★★★, *Flowers* (UK) *Cruel Summer* (US) (London/Arista 1998)★★.

● COMPILATIONS: *The Singles Of The 90s* (Polydor 1999)★★★.

● VIDEOS: *Happy Nation: Home Video* (Mega 1993), *The Sign: Home Video* (Arista 1994).

Acetone

Based in California, Los Angeles, USA, introspective guitar rock trio Acetone comprises Richie Lee (bass/vocals), Mark Lightcap (guitar/vocals), Steve Hadley (drums). The three members first came together in 1987 while Lee was studying painting at Cal Arts in Valencia, California. Here he met Lightcap, a compositional music student and tuba player, while Hadley was an acquaintance of Lee's from Newport Beach. The trio originally played together behind a succession of singers in the surf/garage-inspired Spinout, before they began recording on their own in 1992 as Acetone. On the strength of a demo tape they were signed to the Vernon Yard label, a subsidiary of Virgin Records. The 1993 debut, *Cindy*, was a laboured drone-rock album that betrayed the band's Velvet Underground influences. A tour of America with the UK's similarly inclined the Verve followed, but failed to generate much interest. By 1994's *I Guess I Would*, a mini-album of country cover versions recorded in Nashville, the trio had changed tack and were exploring their roots rock affinities. Of particular note was an extended version of

Kris Kristofferson's 'Border Lord'. These influences found their way onto the band's second full-length album, *If You Only Knew*. Marking a great step forward in the band's use of dynamics, the album seamlessly merged acoustic melodies into their atmospheric psychedelic soundscape. After being dropped by Vernon Yard in 1997, the band relocated to the independent Vapor Records label. Their eponymous 1997 album benefited from a sparse, introspective production that saw them bracketed alongside 'sleep-rock' bands such as Spiritualized and the Verve.

● ALBUMS: *Cindy* (Vernon Yard 1993)★★, *I Guess I Would* mini-album (Vernon Yard 1995)★★★, *If You Only Knew* (Vernon Yard 1996)★★★, *Acetone* (Vapor 1997)★★★.

Acheron

Based in Florida, USA, Acheron came to prominence as part of the Satanic black metal movement of the early 90s. The band's leader, guitarist and vocalist Vincent Crowley, founded the anti-Christian youth movement, the Order of the Evil Eye. Musically, the band displayed obvious death-metal roots, with their rapid hammering guitars and guttural vocal style. However, they distinguished themselves from the increasing number of Satanic metal acts appearing during the early 90s by the authenticity of their material. Much of this derives from the involvement of the Reverend Peter Gilmore, a priest in the notorious Church of Satan, who contributed not only advice on the infernal content of the lyrics, but also provided the atmospheric keyboard introductions that link the songs on Acheron's albums. *Hail Victory* constitutes an expanded version of *Satanic Victory*, adding eight songs and nine intros to the original.

● ALBUMS: *Rites Of The Black Mass* (Turbo 1992)★★, *Satanic Victory* (Turbo 1994)★★★, *Hail Victory* (Turbo 1994)★★★, *Lex Talionis* (Turbo 1995)★★★, *Those Who Have Risen* (Full Moon 1998)★★★.

Adams, Bryan

b. Bryan Guy Adams, 5 November 1959, Kingston, Ontario, Canada. Bryan Adams has grown to be the most popular mainstream Canadian rocker of the late 80s and 90s. His solo career commenced in 1978 (having previously worked with Sweeney Todd, who released one album, 1977's *If Wishes Were Horses*) when he began writing songs with Jim Vallance, a former member of Prism, who was keen to retire from live work but not from songwriting. Some of these early collaborations were recorded by Loverboy, Bachman-Turner Overdrive, Bonnie Tyler fand others. In 1979, Adams signed a contract with A&M Records' Rondor Music, assembling a band that included Vallance on drums, plus Ken Scott (lead guitar) and Dave Taylor (bass). Their debut single, 'Let Me Take You Dancing', was followed by a self-titled album (which featured a cameo from Jeff 'Skunk' Baxter of Steely Dan), although neither charted. He spent 1982 touring with Foreigner (whose Lou Gramm guested on the forthcoming album), the Kinks and Loverboy. The resultant *You Want It, You Got It* scraped into the lower regions of the US charts. A third album, *Cuts Like A Knife*, released in 1983, was Adams' breakthrough, reaching number 8 and going platinum in the USA (although it did not chart in the UK until three years later). It saw Vallance leave, to be replaced by Mickey Curry, though he maintained his songwriting partnership with Adams. The first single from the album, 'Straight From The Heart', also made the US Top 10 with the help of MTV air-

play, and two follow-up singles, 'Cuts Like A Knife' and 'This Time', reached the Top 20 and Top 30, respectively. Adams' fourth album, *Reckless*, was issued towards the end of 1984 and topped the *Billboard* album chart. It also gave him his first major UK chart placing, reaching number 7, while the singles 'Run To You' (US number 6/UK number 11) and 'Somebody' (US number 11/UK number 35) further established Adams as a hitmaker. He enjoyed a US number 1 in mid-1985 with 'Heaven', the b-side of which was 'Diana', a tribute to the UK princess, which helped to create the tabloid headline 'Princess Di Flirts With Canadian Rock Star'. Adams was introduced by actor Jack Nicholson at the July 1985 Live Aid concert in Philadelphia, though UK audiences had to cope with transmission problems. He also co-wrote (with Vallance) and helped to perform the Canadian benefit record for Ethiopia, 'Tears Are Not Enough'. The defiant and cele-bratory 'Summer Of '69' returned him to the Top 10 in the US and he ended a successful year by duetting with Tina Turner on 'It's Only Love' (though there was one further, bizarre release in December, when he coupled the festive 'Christmas Time' with 'Reggae Christmas'). His fifth album, *Into The Fire*, released in March 1987, became a Top 10 hit in both the USA and UK, boasting songs of a more political bent, informed by Adams' charity work and tours in support of Amnesty International. It also saw the final effort of the Adams/Vallance songwriting partnership, and the end of a five-album tenure with producer Bob Clearmountain. 'Heat Of The Night' provided Adams with his fifth US Top 10 hit, although subsequent single releases fared less well. Indeed, the late 80s proved a comparatively tranquil time for the artist, as he took stock of his career and waited for a window in producer Mutt Lange's diary. He did, however, contribute to records by Mötley Crüe, Belinda Carlisle, Charlie Sexton and others. In 1988, he guested at the Nelson Mandela birthday party concert at Wembley Stadium in London, and in 1990 appeared with Roger Waters and others at the special Berlin performance of *The Wall*. All this was eclipsed, how-ever, by his contribution to the 1991 Kevin Costner movie, *Robin Hood: Prince Of Thieves*. '(Everything I Do) I Do It For You' was a phenomenal chart success, topping the UK sin-gles listings for an incredible 16 weeks, the longest run since Frankie Laine's 18-week domination with 'I Believe' in 1953; it also sold three million copies and hit the number 1 posi-tion in the USA, becoming the bestselling single of that year. The follow-up, 'Can't Stop This Thing We Started' (US number 2/UK number 11), and another powerful ballad, 'Thought I'd Died And Gone To Heaven' (US number 13/UK number 8), were also commercial successes. The aforemen-tioned singles featured on his hugely successful 1991 album, *Waking Up The Neighbours*, which underwent no less than 18 months in production before topping the UK charts. 'Please Forgive Me' extended Adam's run of UK/US Top 10 successes in late 1993. It was followed by 'All For Love', a collaboration with Sting and Rod Stewart for the 1993 movie *The Three Musketeers*, which became another major hit on both sides of the Atlantic (US number 1, UK number 2). In 1994, he undertook a major tour of South-East Asia (in the process becoming the first Western hard rock artist to visit Vietnam since the end of the war) and bought a house in London. His latter-day commercial breakthrough may have diminished his stature in the eyes of those fans who once made up the main constituency of his followers, but as a performer and songwriter the greater body of his work remains firmly within the rock tradition. Those who do subscribe to the fact that he is a 'rocker' must have been perplexed by the Spanish tempo and lightweight Lange/Adams/Kamen song, 'Have You Ever Really Loved A Woman?' (from the movie *Don Juan de Marco*), which topped a number of charts around the world in the summer of 1995. Adams' finances may have been secure but his credibility as a hard-edged rocker was debatable, as the groover from Vancouver was now much smoother. The *18 'Til I Die* album attempted to restore his rocker image with limited success. *On A Day Like Today* and 'When You're Gone', a high profile duet with Melanie C. from the Spice Girls that reached UK number 3 in December 1998 and spent 10 weeks in the Top 10, helped re-establish his commercial profile.

● ALBUMS: *Bryan Adams* (A&M 1980)★★★, *You Want It, You Got It* (A&M 1981)★★★, *Cuts Like A Knife* (A&M 1983)★★, *Reckless* (A&M 1984)★★★★, *Into The Fire* (A&M 1987)★★★, *Live! Live! Live!* (A&M 1989)★★, *Waking Up The Neighbours* (A&M 1991)★★★, *18 'Til I Die* (A&M 1996)★★, *Unplugged* (A&M 1997)★★★, *On A Day Like Today* (A&M 1998)★★★.

● COMPILATIONS: *So Far So Good* (A&M 1993)★★★★, *The Best Of Me* (A&M 1999)★★★★.

● VIDEOS: *Reckless* (A&M 1984), *So Far So Good And More* (A&M 1994), *MTV Unplugged* (Vision Video 1998).

● FURTHER READING: *Bryan Adams: The Inside Story*, Hugh Gregory. *The Illustrated Biography*, Sandy Robertson. *Bryan Adams: A Fretted Biography*, Mark Duffett. *Bryan Adams: Everything He Does*, Sorelle Saidman.

Adams, Oleta

This fine soul singer had a typical gospel upbringing in Yakima, Washington, USA. Adams formed her own trio in the 80s and recorded two self-funded albums for a Kansas label that sold poorly. She was singing cabaret in a hotel bar in Kansas when she was discovered by Roland Orzabal and Curt Smith of Tears For Fears in 1985. In 1987, they invited her to sing on two tracks, 'Woman In Chains' and 'Badman's Song', on their much vaunted *The Seeds Of Love*. She went on to join the band as a semi-permanent third member, both live and in the studio. This led to her own contract with Tears For Fears' Phonogram label, and Orzabal was on hand to produce her solo *Circle Of One*, which topped the UK chart and reached the US Top 20. Her first single from it, 'Rhythm Of Life', was originally written by Orzabal for *The Seeds Of Love*, but was eventually omitted. Her biggest hit to date came with the Brenda Russell song, 'Get Here', which broke into both the UK and US Top 5 in early 1991. The follow-up *Evolution* was less successful. Her third album, *Moving On*, reversed the trend of smooth balladry to funky, up-tempo, dance-orientated numbers, including a powerful cover version of Elton John's 'Don't Let The Sun Go Down On Me'. Adams moved into the gospel market with 1997's *Come Walk With Me*, but whatever style of music she attempts, her voice is consistently outstanding.

● ALBUMS: *Circle Of One* (Fontana 1990)★★★, *Evolution* (Fontana 1993)★★, *Moving On* (Fontana 1995)★★★, *Come Walk With Me* (Harmony 1997)★★★.

● COMPILATIONS: *The Very Best Of Oleta Adams* (PolyGram 1998)★★★★.

Adams, Yolanda

b. Houston, Texas, USA. One of the fastest-rising stars of 90s gospel music, Yolanda Adams began her recording career in 1987. She had previously worked as a fashion model before joining the Southeast Inspirational Choir as a soloist. She toured and recorded widely with the choir from the age of 13 onwards. During this time her talent was recognized by Thomas Whitfield, who offered her the opportunity to record a solo album. *Just As I Am* duly followed in 1987, attracting widespread critical praise, strong sales and a Grammy award. Subsequent recognition included three Stellar awards for her 1993 album, *Save The World*, the second of her albums for Tribute Records. Spending 61 weeks in the *Billboard* gospel chart, it included a contemporary Christian standard in 'The Battle Is The Lord's'. The R&B-orientated *More Than A Melody* featured another strong single in 'Gotta Have Love', as well as a song written specially for her by Bebe Winans, 'What About The Children?'. Adams' stunning 1996 concert set ably captured the intensity of her live performances. Following another strong collection, 1998's *Songs From The Heart*, Adams signed to Elektra Records in an attempt to consolidate her crossover appeal. The attendant *Mountain High ... Valley Low* received glowing reviews.

● ALBUMS: *Just As I Am* (Sound Of Gospel 1987)★★★★, *Through The Storm* (Tribute 1991)★★★, *Save The World* (Tribute 1993)★★★★, *More Than A Melody* (Tribute 1995)★★★, *Yolanda - Live In Washington* (Tribute 1996)★★★★, *Songs From The Heart* (Verity 1998)★★★★, *Mountain High ... Valley Low* (Elektra 1999)★★★★.

● COMPILATIONS: with the Southeast Inspirational Choir *Yolanda Adams At Her Very Best* (Paula 1993)★★★★, *The Best Of Yolanda Adams* (Verity 1999)★★★★.

Adamski

b. Adam Tinley, England. Adamski's first recordings were cut at the age of 11 as a member of the Stupid Babies, a preteen punk duo (with his brother) immortalized on the Fast Products *Earcom 3* sampler. He was also a member of Diskord Datkord in 1987, who released one single - a cover version of X-Ray Spex's 'Identity' (his brother subsequently formed Garden Of Eden). Adamski went on to record as a keyboard player on instrumental dance records. His solo breakthrough came with the release of 'N-R-G', which reached number 12 in the UK charts in January 1990. Unfortunately, legal action from Lucozade, who claimed the single plagiarized their advertising slogan, forced him to donate £5,000 of his royalties to charity. He replied with April's massive dancefloor hit and UK number 1, 'Killer'. This tautly orchestrated electronic piece was enhanced by the emotive vocals of guest vocalist Seal. September's follow-up, 'The Space Jungle', which derived from 'All Shook Up', was hammered by the critics, but still reached UK number 7. While his former vocalist went on to national adoration, Adamski slipped from view, although he did enjoy a minor hit with 'Flashback Jack' at the end of 1990. An epitaph, of sorts, was offered on the *Naughty* track, 'Take The Money And Run': 'I've been chewed up and spat out by the restrictions of dance'. Many critics judged such petulance as sour grapes following his commercial decline. The same year he joined with Elton John to remix 'Medicine Man' for charity, but was not sighted for some time afterwards. He went on to form remix team the Jet Slags with Mr Monday, working on projects including Bump's 'I'm Rushin''. He signed a new deal with ZTT Records and returned in July 1998 with a new single, 'One Of The People', and the attendant *Adamski's Thing*. The album eschewed the hardcore sound of the earlier records for a mellow house vibe influenced by Adamski's visits to Ibiza.

● ALBUMS: *Liveandirect* (MCA 1989)★★, *Dr. Adamski's Musical Pharmacy* (MCA 1990)★★, *Naughty* (MCA 1992)★★, *Adamski's Thing* (ZTT/Uptown 1998)★★★.

● VIDEOS: *Liveandirect* (MCA 1990).

Adamson, Barry

b. 1 June 1958, Moss Side, Manchester, England. The original bass player for Magazine, and also a member of Visage and Nick Cave's Bad Seeds, Adamson's solo output has largely been in the field of instrumental music intended for films. These ventures have allowed him to plough a much deeper artistic furrow, and anything from scat jazz to sinister, electronic instrumentals can and have found their place on his recordings. His debut EP, *The Man With The Golden Arm*, which included the first of his spectacular cover versions of *James Bond* film themes, was released on Mute Records in 1988. The title track was also included on Adamson's debut album, *Moss Side Story*, the soundtrack to a non-existent film noir about the Manchester suburb, which presaged his later scores. The recording featured newscasts sharing space with sampled sound effects, plus excellent musicianship from a noble cast including Marcia Schofield (the Fall), Diamanda Galas and various former colleagues from the Bad Seeds. *Delusion* allowed Adamson to garnish a real film with his music, and since then his services have remained in constant demand by a variety of directors (some critics have even labelled him a 90s Ennio Morricone). Similarly, his seductive mood pieces and instrumentals also stand on their own without any visual, situation-specific stimuli. The excellent *Soul Murder*, dominated by Adamson's trademark keyboard stabs and surges, earned him a surprise Mercury Prize nomination in 1992, a feat he also repeated with *The Negro Inside Me*. Ultimately less compelling, this album nevertheless confirmed him as one of the most unlikely success stories of the 90s. *Oedipus Schmoedipus* was another superb album, featuring Pulp's Jarvis Cocker on 'Set The Controls For The Heart Of The Pelvis'. Following an enforced absence for major hip surgery, Adamson returned to recording to provide music for David Lynch's *Lost Highway* and release *As Above, So Below*, on which he handled his own vocals for the first time.

● ALBUMS: *Moss Side Story* (Mute 1989)★★★, *Delusion: Original Motion Picture Soundtrack* (Mute 1991)★★★, *Soul Murder* (Mute 1992)★★★★, *The Negro Inside Me* (Mute 1993)★★★, *A Prayer Mat Of Flesh* (Mute 1995)★★★, *Oedipus Schmoedipus* (Mute 1996)★★★★, *As Above, So Below* (Mute 1998)★★★.

● COMPILATIONS: *The Murky World Of Barry Adamson* (Mute 1999)★★★★.

Add N To (X)

This UK trio comprising, Ann Shenton, Stephen Clayton and Barry Smith, produce a disconcerting fusion of electronica and lo-fi rock dubbed *avant hard*. Smith's background included work as a DJ on pirate station Radio Stalin in Prague. He met Shenton in 1993, adopting the Add N To (X) moniker (taken from a mathematical formula) in 1994 when

they added Theremin expert Clayton to the line-up. The trio released a low-key debut, *Vero Electronics*, in 1996, and played live shows with Stereolab drummer Andy Ramsay and High Llamas' bass player Rob Hallam. They released the acclaimed *On The Wires Of Our Nerves* on the Satellite label in 1998. The album's cover illustrated the trio's fascination with the man/machine interface, while the contents demonstrated their mastery of a diverse range of pioneering electronic music forms ranging from Varése, Robert A. Moog and Wendy Carlos, through experimental German rock (Can) and English art rock (Roxy Music). Their use of vocoders and vintage analogue synths also earned comparisons to American pioneers Suicide. Tracks such as 'Sound Of Accelerating Concrete' and 'The Orgy Of Bubastis' were as wilfully difficult as the latter's work, but the album also included the highly accessible single 'King Wasp'. The trio signed to Mute Records shortly afterwards, releasing *Avant Hard* the following year.

● ALBUMS: *Vero Electronics* (Blow Up 1996)★★★, *On The Wires Of Our Nerves* (Satellite 1998)★★★★, *Avant Hard* (Mute 1999)★★★.

Afghan Whigs

From Cincinnati, Ohio, USA, and original stalwarts of the Sub Pop Records empire, Afghan Whigs gained prominence as favoured proponents of grunge, although the traditional nature of much of their recorded output has progressively belied this tag. Their *Uptown Avondale* EP, for example, was a collection of classic soul cover versions, while as early as 1990's *Up In It*, they were bastardizing country rock on tracks such as 'Son Of The South'. The band originally comprised Rick McCollum (b. 14 July 1965, Kentucky, USA; guitar), Steven Earle (b. 28 March 1966, Cincinnati, USA; drums) and John Curley (b. 15 March 1965, Trenton, New Jersey, USA; bass), alongside the distinctive vocals ('I think Camel cigarettes are a big influence on my voice') of frontman Greg Dulli (b. 11 May 1965, Ohio, USA; vocals/guitar). With his origins in Hamilton, a steel-town 30 miles outside Cincinnati, Dulli abandoned his film course in an attempt to pick up acting parts (apparently making it into the last 50 at the auditions for *The Breakfast Club*'s 'weirdo'). He first met bass player Curley in jail, where they were being held overnight for, respectively, urinating in front of a police officer and drug-dealing. When Afghan Whigs provoked the interest of the major labels, Dulli insisted that he produce their records and direct their videos (in fact, before signing, Dulli had handled band management). Elektra Records agreed to his conditions, and to financing a movie project. Their major label debut, *Gentlemen*, concerned familiar Afghan Whigs subjects: alienation and the seedier side of life. One of the songs, 'My Curse', was so personal that Dulli could not sing it himself - instead employing Marcy Mays of Scrawl. Marketing the album also became the subject of a College Music Journal seminar. Earle was subsequently replaced by Paul Buchignani. In 1994, Dulli was part of the supergroup who recorded a soundtrack for *Backbeat*, the Stuart Sutcliffe biopic, singing as John Lennon. Other band members were Mike Mills (R.E.M.), Don Fleming (Gumball), Dave Grohl (Nirvana; Foo Fighters) and Thurston Moore (Sonic Youth). Dulli also covered Barry White's 'Can't Get Enough Of Your Love' for the soundtrack to *Beautiful Girls*. *Black Love* confirmed the soul influence, and featured cover versions of Marvin Gaye's 'Let's Get It

On' and the Who's 'Quadrophenia'. Decamping to New Orleans to record the major label follow-up, Dulli overcame his personal demons to produce a seamless fusion of his musical influences. *1965* proved to be one of 1998's outstanding releases, a sexually charged and funky collection of songs that earned the band an almost universal round of critical plaudits. In December, Dulli was beaten up and temporarily left in a coma after a concert in Austin, Texas.

● ALBUMS: *Big Top Halloween* (Ultrasuede 1988)★★★, *Up In It* (Sub Pop 1990)★★★, *Congregation* (Sub Pop 1992)★★★, *Gentlemen* (Sub Pop/Elektra 1993)★★★, *What Jail Is Like* mini-album (Sub Pop/Elektra 1994)★★, *Black Love* (Sub Pop/Elektra 1996)★★★★, *1965* (Columbia 1998)★★★★★.

Afro-Celt Sound System

A bold attempt to fuse modern dance music styles with ethnic rhythms from the African and Celtic traditions, Afro-Celt Sound System is the brainchild of Grammy-nominated producer Simon Emmerson. He brought together a diverse team of musicians, including members of Baaba Maal's band, N'Faly Kouyate (kora, balaphon, vocals), Moussa Sissokho (djembe, talking drum), Jo Bruce (b. 9 February 1969, d. 8 October 1997) (son of Jack Bruce), James McNally (of the Pogues), Irish traditional singer Iarla O'Lionaird, Breton harp player Myrdhin, Martin Russell (keyboards), Davy Spillane (uilleann pipes) and Ronan Browne (uilleann pipes), (who toured with the phenomenally successful *Riverdance* show), to record together over a week in July 1995. With artwork from Jamie Reid (famed for his Sex Pistols graphics), the album, *Volume One Sound Magic*, embraced many disparate sounds, from jungle to trip-hop and ambient trance, underpinned by the performers' Celtic and African heritage. Before its release in 1996 the same band appeared at the 1995 WOMAD Festival (they repeated the performance the following year). Their success was marred by the tragic death of Bruce in October 1997. A second volume appeared in 1999, with O'Lionaird joined by Sinead O'Connor on the title track.

● ALBUMS: *Volume One Sound Magic* (Real World 1996)★★★★, *Volume 2: Release* (Real World 1999)★★★★.

Afro-Cuban All Stars

A Cuban big band, specially assembled by Juan de Marcos González of Sierra Maestra to participate in a two-week recording session at Egrem studios, Havana, in March 1996. The line-up spanned three generations of Cuban musicians, from 80-year-old flute player Richard Egües, to 14-year-old percussionist Julienne Oviedo Sanchez. *A Toda Cuba Le Gusta* (All Of Cuba Loves It) was recorded in the first six days of the session, following which the debut album by Rubén González (the All Stars' 77-year-old pianist) and Ry Cooder's *Buena Vista Social Club* were both also completed. Cooder adds stinging blues guitar to 'Alta Songo', one of the stand-out tracks on *A Toda Cuba Le Gusta*. Other non-Cuban elements include a baroque classical piano solo within a son (i.e., Cuban song style) arrangement on 'Clasiqueando Con Ruben', and the closing 'Elube Chango', which is sung in the Yoruba language of Nigeria. However, much of the album joyously echoes and updates the sound of the great Cuban 'orquestras' of the 40s and 50s (in which the older members of the group all played), using classic songs from that era as well as newer tunes that suit the overall feel. To coincide with the release of the album, the All Stars undertook a well-received 40-date tour of Europe in the spring of 1997. A second collection was released in October 1999.

● ALBUMS: *A Toda Cuba Le Gusta* (World Circuit 1997)★★★★, *Distinto, Diferente* (World Circuit 1999)★★★.

After 7

After 7, comprising brothers Kevon and Melvin Edmonds (both b. Indianapolis, Indiana, USA) alongside long-time friend Keith Mitchell, became one of the most successful urban R&B/soul acts in the USA of the early 90s. The brothers met Mitchell at Indiana University where he and Kevon were pursuing business studies degrees, and were also members of the Indiana University Soul Review. Melvin joined them after touring with the group Deele and working in the studio with Shalamar. After 7's self-titled debut album was released in 1989 and documented what was already a potent live repertoire, based on 50s doo-wop harmonies combined with 90s hip-hop rhythms. It produced two US Top 10 singles, 'Ready Or Not' and 'Can't Stop', and accrued a host of awards (including a Grammy nomination for Best Soul Group). The trio waited three years and toured with artists including M.C. Hammer, Gladys Knight and Whitney Houston before releasing the follow-up collection, *Takin' My Time*, which achieved gold status. Further exposure came through soundtrack commissions for the movies *Sugar Hill* ('Gonna Love You Right') and *The Five Heartbeats* ('Nights Like This') and for the television programme *Beverly Hills 90210* ('Not Enough Hours In The Night'). After contributing to the trio's debut, third brother Kenny 'Babyface' Edmonds returned to provide production assistance on *Reflections*, also writing three of the songs and singing on 'Honey (Oh How I Need You)'. The following year, Babyface and Kevon Edmonds joined forces with the Jodeci brothers K-Ci And JoJo in Milestone, recording the hit ballad 'I Care About You'. Kevon Edmonds released his debut solo album in October 1999.

● ALBUMS: *After 7* (Virgin 1989)★★★★, *Takin' My Time* (Virgin 1992)★★★, *Reflections* (Virgin 1995)★★.

● COMPILATIONS: *The Very Best Of After 7* (Virgin 1996)★★★.

Aguilera, Christina

b. 18 December 1980, Staten Island, New York, USA. Aguilera was one of several American teen pop stars to rise to huge popular acclaim in the late 90s. Of Irish and Ecuadorian descent, her mother played violin and piano professionally while her father's position in the military resulted in the family travelling extensively around the world. Finally settling in Wexford, Philadelphia, Aguilera began performing at school talent shows, before making her first professional appearance at the age of eight on the nationally syndicated *Star Search* show. When she was 10 she sang the national anthem for the Pittsburgh Steelers and Pirates. She joined [Walt] Disney's *Mickey Mouse Club* at the age of 12, appearing alongside future pop stars JC Chasez and Justin Timberlake of 'N Sync, and Britney Spears. Aguilera spent two years with the *Mickey Mouse Club* before moving to Japan to record 'All I Wanna Do', a hit duet with local pop star Keizo Nakanishi. Back in the USA in early 1998, Aguilera recorded 'Reflection' for the soundtrack of Disney's full length animation *Mulan*. Her rapid ascent to stardom continued when she signed to RCA Records shortly afterwards. Her debut album was recorded with a host of leading songwriters and producers. 'Genie In A Bottle', a lightweight swingbeat number with an infectious hookline, went to the top of the US charts in July 1999. Written by UK-based songwriter Pam Sheyne, the single stayed at the top for 5 weeks, making it the biggest selling US single of the year. The other tracks on Aguilera's self-titled debut included upbeat dance anthem 'Love Will Find A Way', soulful ballad 'So Emotional', and the requisite Diane Warren blockbuster, 'I Turn To You'. The album entered the US album chart at number 1 in September. A month later 'Genie In A Bottle' entered the UK singles chart at number 1. Aguilera returned to the top of the US charts in January 2000 with 'What A Girl Wants'.

● ALBUMS: *Christina Aguilera* (RCA 1999)★★★.

Air

Purveyors of delightfully retro electronic space pop, former architect Nicolas Godin (bass, guitar, vocoder, percussion) and mathematician Jean-Benoit Dunckel (keyboards, clavinet, synthesizer) both come from Versailles, France. They initially met at college, where Godin joined Dunckel in indie rock band Orange, alongside future producer Alex Gopher. After a period spent concentrating on their respective studies, Dunckel and Godin reunited as Air and began forging a new electronic direction, signing to the Paris-based Virgin Records offshoot Source. They released several singles, including the *Modular Mix* EP in November 1995 and the *Casanova 70* EP in July 1996. These early tracks, since disowned by Godin and Dunckel, were collected on the *Premiers Symptomes* compilation, and helped to bring the duo to the attention of European DJs. They also embarked on remix work for Depeche Mode and Neneh Cherry. Godin and Dunckel then decamped to an abandoned eighteenth-century chateau outside Paris to record the new material that appeared on their debut, *Moon Safari*. Produced on an eight-track console, the 10 songs on the album were a striking mixture of dance music loops and pop melodies, moving from lush instrumentals to effortless electro-pop with vocals by Godin and Paris-based American singer Beth Hirsch. The album's retro feel was heightened by Dunckel and Godin's use of mini-Moog and vocoder, and the romantic themes of space travel and stargazing. The first single, 'Sexy Boy', reached UK number 13 in February 1998. The follow-up, 'Kelly Watch The Stars', was a homage to *Charlie's Angels* actress Jaclyn Smith. *Moon Safari* won the UK's *Muzik* magazine's award for Best Album in October 1998. They also composed the original score for Sophie Coppola's *The Virgin Suicides*.

● ALBUMS: *Moon Safari* (Source/Virgin 1998)★★★★.
● COMPILATIONS: *Premiers Symptomes* (Source/Virgin 1997)★★★.

Air Liquide

German experimental outfit comprising Walker (b. Ingmar Koch, Germany) and Jammin' Unit (b. Cem Oral), with lyrical input provided by expatriate American Mary S. Applegate. Koch is a half-German, half-Hungarian music graduate from the University of Köln, where he specialized in electronic composition. Previously he had worked for the euro house labels Hype! and Technoline. The strangely named Jammin' Unit is a half-Turkish, half-Finnish musician who had recorded *avant garde* and experimental music

for over a decade. He is also a professional sound engineer who runs Air Liquide's Ocean Blue studios, alongside Koch. The duo met on the fertile German underground dance music scene. They set up the Structure Records label, whose releases encompassed everything from acid house and ambient, to hardcore and techno. This unlikely collaboration was informed by mutual tastes in underground exotica, German progressive rock, hip-hop and electronica, which was wonderfully captured by the release of 'If There Was No Gravity'. This combined the wide-eyed wonder of Applegate's delivery with an unsettling ambient production from her partners. The subsequent album, licensed to Rising High Records in the UK, was similarly fêted, and preceded a collaboration with that label's Caspar Pound on The New London School Of Electronics project. Koch also provided a set for the unrelated but phonetically similar New Electronica series, and records solo as Walker (the best example of which is 'Don't Fuck With Cologne' for DJ.Ungle Fever). Jammin' Unit's solo excursions, meanwhile, include 'Flower Swing' for the same label, which is one of some 14 labels that originated from the original Structure set-up. Koch also runs the Liquid Sky club in Cologne, which originally started life as a fashion store. In addition to the prolific output on their own labels, the pair also record for the New York based Sm:)e Communications label. In 1996, EMI Records resurrected their Harvest Records label to release a series of Air Liquide-related albums.

● ALBUMS: *Nephology* (Blue/Rising High 1993)★★★★, *The Increased Difficulty Of Concentration* (Sm:)e 1994)★★★, *Black* (SM:)e 1995)★★★, *Red* (Sm:)e 1995)★★★, *Sonic Weather Machine* (Rising High 1996)★★★, *Liquid Air* (Harvest 1997)★★★.

Alabama 3

A highly eclectic and original project, Alabama 3 are the genre-bending creation of a motley crew of underground club veterans based in Brixton, London. They were formed around singer/songwriter Larry Love (b. Robert Spragg), a native of South Wales. Spragg began working as a DJ in the late 80s, and recorded *Mahalia*, a gospel techno record released under the Shed moniker, in the early 90s. He began working on the Brixton scene with Piers Marsh, whose experimental sampling of blues music helped formulate the newly named Alabama 3's sound. The loose collective played several sets in Northern Italy and Brixton, and soon began to attract a loyal following. The One Little Indian Records' subsidiary Elemental signed the group for the UK and European markets in January 1996, while Geffen Records snapped up the US rights in September. The singles 'Ain't Goin' To Goa' and 'Woke Up This Morning' followed in November and spring 1997 respectively. They served as an excellent introduction to the band's heady fusion of traditional American popular music forms, including country, gospel and blues, with contemporary dance music grooves. An appearance on the soundtrack to the Cameron Diaz/Ewan McGregor movie *A Life Less Ordinary* provided further valuable exposure for their uneven debut, *Exile On Coldharbour Lane*. They appeared at Primal Scream's Brixton all-nighter in February 1998 and supported Chumbawamba on their US tour the following month. A re-released 'Ain't Goin' To Goa' peaked at number 40 on the UK singles chart.

● ALBUMS: *Exile On Coldharbour Lane* (Elemental 1997)★★★.

Albini, Steve

b. USA. Though he first rose to prominence as a musician, Albini's most high-profile work has come as a producer in the 90s. His first band was the caustic Big Black - powered by Albini's monolithic guitar playing, which took punk rock to its logical conclusion. That band's work is worth assessing in terms of Albini's later production work, in particular the low mixing of the vocals that became a feature of his subsequent output. After Big Black he formed Rapeman - an impressive band whose short career was continually overshadowed by the 'offence' its name caused. In the meantime, Albini was establishing a second career as a producer. Artists including the Pixies, Wedding Present, PJ Harvey and Nirvana all prospered from his employment. Although he often insisted he was merely a 'good engineer', the evidence of records such as *Surfer Rosa* (Pixies), *In Utero* (Nirvana) and *Rid Of Me* (PJ Harvey) argued against such modesty. He also remained one of American underground music's most controversial figures, attacking figures in the mainstream such as Urge Overkill (another of his previous production assignments) and many others for what he considered a lack of integrity. Another tenet of his Big Black days - that of a preference for vinyl over CD, which he once famously christened 'the rich man's eight-track', was maintained. He continued to insist that most of his productions were completed merely to 'pay the rent', and he took particular relish in charging exorbitant fees for artists signed to major record labels, allowing him to work with favoured artists (Scrawl, Jesus Lizard, etc.) for comparatively trivial sums. After the demise of Rapeman he regularly stated to the press how much he missed being part of a band, and it therefore came as little surprise when he formed the typically uncompromising Shellac in 1993. Two albums followed, fitted in around Albini's busy production schedule.

Ali, Tatyana

b. 24 January 1979, New York City, New York, USA. The multi-talented Ali's first taste of stardom was as a child actress, appearing at the age of four in America's highly popular children's television programme *Sesame Street*. Further roles included an appearance on Broadway in the Pulitzer prize winning *Fences* with Billy Dee Williams, and a highly successful television spot on *Star Search* when she was seven. Her breakthough came with the role of Ashley in *The Fresh Prince Of Bel-Air*, the American television sitcom which made a star of lead actor Will Smith. Ali began filming as an 11-year old, and developed into a mature young actress through the show's six seasons. Ali was convinced to sign to her co-star's production company Will Smith Enterprises following a cameo vocal performance in the show. Signed to MJJ, she recorded an album of sophisticated modern R&B/pop, employing several talented writers and producers including Rodney Jenkins, Shawn Stockman (Boyz II Men) and Narada Michael Walden. 'Daydreamin'' was a US/UK number 6 hit single in late 1998, and was followed by February 1999's UK number 3 single 'Boy You Knock Me Out', which featured a rap from Will Smith and a sample from Bobby Caldwell's 'What You Won't Do For Love'. *Kiss The Sky* was less successful on the charts. Ali has continued to balance her musical career with further acting roles and a college education.

● ALBUMS: *Kiss The Sky* (MJJ/Epic 1998)★★★.

Alice In Chains

Formed in 1987 in Seattle, USA, by Layne Staley (b. 22 August 1967, Kirkland, Washington, USA; vocals) and Jerry Cantrell (b. 18 March 1966, Tacoma, Washington, USA; vocals, guitar) with Mike Starr (bass) and Sean Kinney (b. 27 June 1966, Seattle, Washington, USA; drums), Alice In Chains developed a sound that mixed Black Sabbath-style riffing with Staley and Cantrell's unconventional vocal arrangements and strong songwriting. Cantrell had drifted from his home in Tacoma to Seattle, homing in on a musician's collective entitled the Music Bank. He brought in the rhythm section of Kinney and Starr, before Staley was recruited from a local funk metal act. After dispensing with their early moniker, 'Fuck', they became Alice In Chains, a name invented by Staley for 'a parody heavy metal band that dressed in drag'. The band won a major recording contract despite some record executives being scared off by Staley's aggressive performance at an early showcase. *Facelift* received excellent reviews, but took off slowly, boosted by US touring with Van Halen, the difficult opening slot on the US Clash Of The Titans tour, featuring Slayer, Anthrax and Megadeth, and European dates with Megadeth and the Almighty. 'Man In The Box' became an MTV favourite, and the album went gold in the autumn of 1991, just as Nirvana's success began to make Seattle headline news. The band released the gentler five-track *Sap* EP, featuring guests from Heart, Soundgarden and Mudhoney, before recording their second full album. *Dirt* was a dark, cathartic work with many personal lyrics, including 'Rooster', which described Cantrell's father's Vietnam War experiences and became a live centrepiece. However, critical attention focused on a sequence of songs referring to Staley's past heroin problems, descending from the initial high of 'Junkhead' ('We are an elite race of our own/The stoners, junkies and freaks'), through depths of addiction, to the realization of the need to break away from dependency in 'Angry Chair' ('Little boy made a mistake/Pink cloud has now turned to gray'). Despite the controversy, *Dirt* was deservedly acclaimed, and was the critics' album of the year in many metal magazines, entering the US charts at number 6. 'Would?' became a hit, boosted by an appearance playing the song in the movie *Singles*, and the band supported Ozzy Osbourne in the USA, with Staley in a wheelchair for the early dates, having broken his foot, before Starr's departure. Ex-Ozzy Osbourne bass player Michael Inez (b. 14 May 1966, San Francisco, California, USA) stepped in, and the band embarked on a sell-out tour of Europe and the USA. The cancellation of European stadium shows supporting Metallica in mid-1993, owing to exhaustion, led to speculation about a setback in Staley's recovery, but Alice In Chains returned in fine style, contributing to the *Last Action Hero* soundtrack and playing superbly on the third Lollapalooza tour. In early 1994, *Jar Of Flies* became the first EP to top the US album charts, debuting at number 1. Staley put together a side-project, Mad Season, with Pearl Jam's Mike McCready and Barrett Martin from Screaming Trees, amid rumours that Alice In Chains had split. These rumours were exacerbated by the return of Staley's misfortunes in August 1994 when gigs, including Woodstock II, were cancelled, as a result of further 'health problems'. Amid continuing rumours of drug abuse the band managed a further album in 1995 that boasted some excellent moments. In 1996, the band performed their first concert in over three years, performing for MTV on an *Unplugged* special. Rumours about the band's future resurfaced in the late 90s with the release of Cantrell's solo debut and two compilation sets.

● ALBUMS: *Facelift* (Columbia 1990)★★★, *Sap* mini-album (Columbia 1992)★★★, *Dirt* (Columbia 1992)★★★★, *Jar Of Flies* mini-album (Columbia 1993)★★★★, *Alice In Chains* (Columbia 1995)★★★, *MTV Unplugged Live* (Sony 1996)★★★.
Solo: Jerry Cantrell *Boggy Depot* (Columbia 1998)★★.
● COMPILATIONS: *Nothing Safe: The Best Of The Box* (Columbia 1999)★★★★, *Music Bank* 3-CD box set (Columbia 1999)★★★.
● VIDEOS: *Live Facelift* (SMV 1994), *Nona Weisbaum* (Columbia 1995), *The Nona Tapes* (SMV 1996), *MTV Unplugged* (SMV 1996).

Alisha's Attic

The daughters of Brian Poole, leader of the 60s UK beat group Brian Poole And The Tremeloes, Shellie (b. 20 March 1972, Barking, Essex, England) and Karen Poole (b. 8 January 1971, Chadwell Heath, Essex, England) grew up in Dagenham, Essex. Alisha's Attic were signed to Mercury Records in 1995 after their demo tape was passed to Howard Berman. He was so enamoured of the tape's contents that he telephoned the duo's management company and immediately offered them a recording contract, on their own terms. In 1996, the sisters entered the studio with producer David A. Stewart to work on sessions for their debut single, 'I Am I Feel'. To promote it they embarked on their first national tour, with a full supporting band. They achieved an instant breakthrough in the UK charts, 'I Am I Feel' reaching number 14 and follow-up single 'Alisha Rules The World' reaching number 12. The sisters had spent over eight years writing songs together, ensuring a large stockpile of material for their credible debut album. 'The Incidentals', a number 13 single in September 1998, introduced the more cohesive *Illumina*. The album benefited considerably from Mark Plati's production work, but stalled at number 15 in the charts.

● ALBUMS: *Alisha Rules The World* (Mercury 1996)★★★, *Illumina* (Mercury 1998)★★★.

All Saints

The fact that All Saints' initial media exposure was accompanied by a teaser caption stating 'Don't mention the Spice Girls', is highly illuminating - add to this the fact that London Records' marketing of their first single stated 'sexier than the Spice Girls, smarter than the Spice Girls, sassier than the Spice Girls', and the marketing intentions for this London-based all-female vocal quartet were readily obvious. Their debut, 'I Know Where It's At', was released in August 1997. Some credibility was lent to their subsequent debut album by the involvement of Neneh Cherry and Massive Attack producer Cameron McVey. The quartet were also keen to insist that they had formed as early as 1993, originally as a duo featuring songwriters Shaznay Tricia Lewis (b. 14 October 1976) and Melanie Blatt (b. 25 March 1976; who had also sung with the short-lived Drive). Taking their name from the street in which their London recording studio was based, they signed with ZTT Records and released one unsuccessful single, 'If You Wanna Party'. By 1995 they had been joined by Canadian-born sisters Nicola Marie (b. 7 December 1975) and Natalie Jane Appleton (b. 14 May 1973). They were eventually signed by London Records in

November 1996. Recorded in Washington and London, the predominantly mid-paced collection of songs that comprised their debut album held few surprises and betrayed little sign of invention beyond the central principle of cloning a successful formula. The single 'Never Ever' was a hugely successful UK number 1, however, and also climbed to number 4 in the US later in the year. The follow-up single, pairing cover versions of the Red Hot Chili Peppers' 'Under The Bridge' and LaBelle's 'Lady Marmalade', was another UK chart-topper in May 1998. They achieved a third consecutive UK number 1 in September 1998 with 'Booty Call', but their fourth single 'War Of Nerves' stalled at number 7 in December. The quartet has rarely been out of the media spotlight since and their new single 'Pure Shores', produced by William Orbit and featured on the soundtrack of the Leonardo DiCaprio movie, *The Beach*, debuted at number 1 on the UK chart in February 2000.

● ALBUMS: *All Saints* (London 1997)★★★, *The Remix Album* (London 1998)★★.
● VIDEOS: *The Video* (London 1998).

All Seeing I

This quirky UK electronic outfit comprises; Dean Honer, Jason Buckle and DJ Parrot (b. Richard Barratt), the latter a mainstay of Sheffield, England's dance music scene since the mid-80s. After a spell as a DJ at the Jive Turkey club, Parrot worked with Richard H. Kirk of Cabaret Voltaire, recording material for Warp Records under the title Sweet Exorcist. The pioneering 1990 tracks 'Testone' and 'Clonk', the former featuring a video by Pulp's Jarvis Cocker, helped define the 'bleep' sound, a home-grown reaction against the vocal house music that was hugely popular in the south. Parrot went on to production work before, at the instigation of Cocker, starting his own Earth Records label in the mid-90s. Buckle, meanwhile, had recorded tracks for Warp using the moniker Rubber Johnny, and also worked on the Rephlex Records label under his own name. He also shared a house with Essex native Honer, who met Parrot during production sessions for Sheffield electronic outfit Add N To (X). The trio subsequently formed the All Seeing I, releasing 1997's debut single 'I Walk'. Their commercial breakthrough came about when they sampled a live recording of jazz drummer Buddy Rich and his 13 year-old daughter Cathy covering Sonny And Cher's 1967 hit, 'The Beat Goes On'. Ironically, the track was released on the Earth label at the same time as Sonny Bono died in a skiing accident. The single became a big radio hit and translated into UK chart success in March 1998 when it reached number 11. The trio then began recording an album in collaboration with several other Sheffield musicians, including suave 70s cabaret crooner Tony Christie, Phil Oakey of 80s pop stars the Human League, and maverick singer-songwriter *baby*bird. Christie's stylish performance of 'Walk Like A Panther', Cocker's wry tribute to Sheffield ('the old home town still looks the same/like a derelict man who died out of shame/like a jumble sale left out in the rain/it's not good, it's not right'), reached UK number 10 in January 1999. *Pickled Eggs And Sherbert* proved to be a delightful tribute to Sheffield, mixing cheesy MOR and pop melodies with quirky, electronic interludes. 'First Man In Space', that also reached the UK Top 30, featured a suitably plaintive vocal performance from Phil Oakey. Stephen Jones, aka *baby*bird, contributed a biting performance of his own 'Plastic Diamond', while Cocker stepped up to the microphone himself on 'Drive Safely Darlin''. In a bizarre turn of events, Honer, Buckle and Parrot were asked to produce Britney Spears cover version of 'Beat Goes On', which featured on the American teen sensation's debut album.

● ALBUMS: *Pickled Eggs And Sherbert* (ffrr 1999)★★★★.

All-4-One

This doo-wop styled modern vocal quartet comprises school friends Jamie Jones (b. 26 November 1974, Palmdale, California, USA) and Alfred Nevarez (17 May 1973, Mojave, California, USA), alongside Tony Borowiak (b. 12 October 1972, California City, California, USA) and Delious Kennedy (b. 21 December 1970). None of the singers received any formal vocal training, but gained valuable experience singing in their local church choirs. All-4-One was formed in the recording studio, where the members were gainfully employed singing jingles for local radio stations. They were signed to the Los Angeles-based label Blitzz (with distribution through Atlantic Records) on the strength of an impromptu arrangement of what would prove to be their debut single, a cover version of the Tymes' 1963 US chart-topper 'So Much In Love'. Released in January 1994, the single reached the *Billboard* Top 5. The real breakthrough came with the group's second single, a cover version of John Michael Montgomery's country hit 'I Swear'. The song topped the US Hot 100 singles chart for an astonishing 11 weeks, and was 1994's biggest-selling US single. 'I Swear' was also a huge international hit, reaching UK number 2, and won the 1995 Grammy for Best Pop Performance By A Duo Or Group With Vocal, as well as being nominated for Song Of The Year. The quartet's self-titled debut album, released in April 1994, featured the hot production team of David Foster, Tim O'Brien and Gary St. Clair. A lush blend of doo-wop harmonies and modern R&B rhythms, the album went on to sell over five million units. The quartet subsequently embarked on an extensive world tour, which demonstrated their live prowess and showcased their exquisite vocal harmonies. *And The Music Speaks* was released in June 1995, premiered by the US Top 5 hit single 'I Can Love You Like That'. The album also included a cover version of the Dubs' 1957 doo-wop hit 'Could This Be Magic', second single 'I'm Your Man', and another Montgomery number, 'These Arms'. The quartet also contributed 'One Summer Night' to the soundtrack of *My Family*, and a cover version of 'Tapestry' to the Carole King tribute *Tapestry Revisited: A Tribute To Carole King*. They ended the year with the seasonal *An All-4-One Christmas*. 'Someday', taken from Walt Disney's *The Hunchback Of Notre Dame* soundtrack album, was released as a single in May 1996. Later in the year they contributed 'I Turn To You' to the *Space Jam* soundtrack. After a four year recording hiatus, the quartet returned in June 1999 with *On And On*. Retaining the Foster/O'Brien production team, and featuring added contributions from guitarist Nile Rodgers (ex-Chic), the album marked a strong comeback. It also included the Dianne Warren/Foster collaboration, 'One Summer Night'.

● ALBUMS: *All-4-One* (Blitzz 1994)★★★, *And The Music Speaks* (Blitzz 1995)★★★★, *An All-4-One Christmas* (Blitzz 1995)★★, *On And On* (Blitzz 1999)★★★.

● VIDEOS: *And The Music Speaks* (Penthouse 1995).

Allen, Mark

Like many involved with the psychedelic trance scene Allen was switched on to the sound while in Goa in 1991. On returning to the UK he trained as a solicitor and began to DJ as part of the legendary Pagan sound system, which also featured the DJs Yazz, Chrisbo and Loll and whose parties graduated from a squat in Brixton to Linford Studios. Following another trip to India in the early 90s, Allen decided to pursue a career in music and, with Phil Ross and Janice Duncan, began Return To The Source at the Rocket in London. It has since become the most successful trance club in the UK, often featuring Tsuyoshi Suzuki. (During the mid- to late 90s, Return To The Source put on events throughout Europe and further afield, including New York, Sydney and Mount Fuji in Japan. In October 1997, Return To The Source helped to organize Earthdance, which featured such artists as Banco De Gaia, Hallucinogen, Medicine Drum and System 7, and was part of a global event organized to raise money in support of the Tibetan issue.) In 1995, Allen began to record with Chrisbo, Simon Maine and John Ford as Minefield. While working at Return To The Source, Allen met Tim Healey (DJ Squid) and in 1996 the pair formed Quirk. Their album *Machina Electrica & Fornax Chemica* was released on Matsuri Productions in 1998 to an enthusiastic response. Allen has also collaborated on various projects with the Green Nuns Of The Revolution, Andy Guthrie and Nick Taylor (Snake Thing) and compiled a number of mix CDs, including the first *Deck Wizards* album (Psychic Deli 1995) and Return To The Source's *Shamanic Trance Vol. 2* (Positiva 1998). He has continued to co-promote and DJ at Return To The Source around the world.

Almighty

This Scottish hard rock quartet was formed in 1988 by vocalist and guitarist Ricky Warwick (husband of Vanessa, hostess of *Headbanger's Ball* on MTV), guitarist Tantrum, bass player Floyd London and drummer Stumpy Munroe. Along with Little Angels, Quireboys and the Dogs D'Amour, the Almighty spearheaded a revival in UK heavy rock during the late 80s, drawing their inspiration from bands such as the Cult, Ramones and Motörhead. Signing to Polydor Records in 1989, they released *Blood, Fire And Love* to widespread critical acclaim. The title was changed from *Blood, Fire And Roses* to avoid any possible confusion with Guns N'Roses. This was swiftly followed by a perfunctory live mini-album, which included a cover version of the Bachman-Turner Overdrive's standard, 'You Ain't Seen Nothin' Yet'. *Soul Destruction* reaffirmed the development in the band's songwriting abilities. It spawned the UK Top 40 hit 'Free 'N' Easy', and gained them recognition throughout Europe. However, internal tensions led to the dismissal of Tantrum, with Canadian Peter Friesen, whom the band had met during his time in Alice Cooper's band, filling the gap. The band broke from recording sessions to open the 1992 Donington Festival with a fiery performance, a recording of which was released with initial copies of *Powertrippin'*. Mark Dodson's production gave the band a heavier sound, drawing Metallica and Soundgarden comparisons, yet retaining the Almighty's characteristic aggressive delivery, while a more mature lyrical approach enhanced the band's already strong songwriting platform. Single success with 'Addiction' was followed by heavy touring as the band supported Iron Maiden across Europe, played stadium dates with Metallica, and took on a gruelling club trek to lay the groundwork in the USA. On their return, the Almighty headlined one of the most acclaimed UK tours of 1993 with the Wildhearts and Kerbdog in tow. However, despite a UK Top 5 placing for *Powertrippin'*, the band were faced with demands for new material from Polydor within four months of its release. This led to a parting of the ways, with the Almighty sacking manager Tommy Tee and signing to Chrysalis Records in early 1994. Relocated in London, the debut album for their new label was produced by Chris Sheldon (responsible for Therapy?'s *Troublegum*) and spawned two UK Top 30 singles, 'Wrench' and 'Jonestown Mind'. *Just Add Life* included two co-writing ventures between Warwick and former members of the Ruts. The band issued an anti-government single in 1996, 'All Sussed Out', which urged fans not to vote Conservative at the next general election. Warwick left in 1996 and the band folded soon afterwards.

● ALBUMS: *Blood, Fire And Love* (Polydor 1989)★★★, *Blood, Fire And Love - Live* (Polydor 1990)★★, *Soul Destruction* (Polydor 1991)★★★, *Powertrippin'* (Polydor 1993)★★★, *Crank* (Chrysalis 1994)★★★, *Just Add Life* (Chrysalis 1996)★★.

● VIDEOS: *Soul Destruction Live* (PolyGram Music Video 1991).

Aloof

One of the few dance music acts able to transfer their music to a live arena, the Aloof were formed in London, England, in 1990. Their prime mover is DJ Dean Thatcher, who has been a member of many recording outfits, particularly through his activities at Cowboy Records and Flaw Records, the latter co-run with Red Snapper's Richard Thair. Singer Ricky Barrow adds another unusual facet in that he gives the band a recognizable lead vocal presence where so many other dance acts utilize guest performers. The rest of the band comprises Jagz Kooner and Gary Burns, both sound engineers who have also worked with Sabres Of Paradise. From their inception (originally just as a duo of Kooner and Thatcher), they set out to use a broad palate of musics to inform and expand the dance beats, with Jamaican dub the most easily detectable. After recruiting the other members, their debut single was picked up for wider distribution by ffrr Records, but they passed on any further options. By 1993, they had reached something of an impasse, leading to Thair and Thatcher setting up Flaw Records in 1993. The original intention was to release Aloof records, but the label also became a home for Thair's Red Snapper. The Aloof also made the most of their new outlet, releasing three singles in 1994, followed by their debut album, *Cover The Crime*, which was picked up for distribution by East West Records in 1995. Buoyed by a new major label contract, they embarked on a nationwide tour that culminated in an appearance at the Glastonbury Festival in June 1995. The follow-up *Sinking* was assured and hypnotic, although the negativity of the lyrics belied the rich overall sound. A third album was released in 1998, after which the Aloof returned to independent label status for *This Constant Chase For Thrills*.

● ALBUMS: *Cover The Crime* (Flaw 1994)★★★, *Sinking* (East West 1996)★★★, *Seeking Pleasure* (East West 1998)★★★, *This Constant Chase For Thrills* (Screaming Target 1999)★★★.

Altern 8

Hardcore ravers from Stafford, England, Altern 8 comprised Mark Archer and Chris Peat, and was an offshoot of their Nexus 21 project. Of the two, Archer was the house music aficionado, while Peat was a former music technology student with an interest in computers. They crashed the UK charts in 1991 with 'Infiltrate 202' and 'Activ8 (Come With Me)', two chaotic slices of overground techno, the latter reaching number 3. They were aided in their chart aspirations by the circulation of fictitious press stories concerning their alleged activities, which included promoting the decongestant Vicks Vapo Rub, which, it was claimed, heightened the effects of the Ecstasy drug; playing shows in a hot-air balloon and dispensing to the crowd Christmas cakes laced with Ecstasy; and standing as candidates for the 1993 General Election. Their live 'events' were also designed as eye-catching performances, where the band donned RAF chemical warfare suits and dust-masks. They were aided by their resident dancers Crez and John Parkes, and, in the case of their gig at Stafford Bingley Hall, an actual shaman. His job was to cleanse the venue of its 'rock 'n' roll' past', prior to performance. Additional vinyl outings included the *Overload* EP (1990), 'Frequency' (10,000 copies of which were on sale for a single day only), and another UK Top 10 hit, 'Evapor 8'. The protagonists long maintained that this was a temporary diversion from their main project, Nexus 21, and confirmed this by releasing a 'final' Altern 8 single, 'Everybody', in June 1993. Mark Archer has gone on to form Slo-Moshun, a duo of Archer and Danny Taurus from Stoke-on-Trent. They released 'Bells Of NY', one of the biggest club hits of early 1994, breaking the main Top 30 on the back of its house/hip-hop undulations. However, some of the Altern 8 methodology remained - this time the scam was to trick everyone into thinking it was a US import. Their second single was 'Help My Friends'.

● ALBUMS: *Full On ... Mask Hysteria* (Network 1992)★★★.

Ama, Shola

b. March 1979, London, England. A rising star of the UK R&B scene, Shola Ama grew up listening to her mother's Aretha Franklin and Gladys Knight records while still at school. She was first spotted by Kwame of the UK jazz-funk group D-Influence when she was just 15 years old. Kwame overheard her humming a tune on the westbound Piccadilly line platform at Hammersmith, and invited her to audition for him right there and then. Two songs, one by Mariah Carey and one by Mary J. Blige, convinced him of her potential. He signed her to his London independent label FreakStreet, who released Ama's debut single, 'Celebrate', in 1995. Although there were encouraging reviews, particularly for her mature, strident voice, the single faltered through lack of distribution. Kwame addressed this impasse by securing an agreement with WEA Records that would ensure more widespread distribution. Ama enjoyed two UK Top 5 hit singles in 1997 with 'You Might Need Somebody' and 'You're The One I Love'. She also co-wrote several songs on her debut album, in collaboration with members of D-Influence, songwriter Paul Waller, and some of America's top-flight producers. In February 1998, she was voted Best Female Artist at the BRIT Awards. She also collaborated with Craig Armstrong on 'Someday I'll Find You', her contribution to the Noël Coward tribute album, *Twentieth Century Blues*. Ama was less successful in reproducing the winning urban R&B formula of her debut on 1999's *In Return*.

● ALBUMS: *Much Love* (FreakStreet 1997)★★★, *In Return* (FreakStreet 1999)★★★.

Amos, Tori

b. Myra Ellen Amos, 22 August 1963, North Carolina, USA. Amos was compared early in her career to everyone from Kate Bush to Joni Mitchell. She began playing the piano aged two-and-a-half, and was enrolled in Baltimore's Peabody Institute as a five-year-old prodigy. Legend has it that she was formally ejected for 'playing by ear' the songs of John Lennon and the Doors, following six years study. After failing an audition to gain re-entry, Amos concentrated on the bar circuit of Washington, DC, which she continued to do throughout her high-school years, gradually moving to better venues and adding her own material. In 1980, aged 17, she released (under her real name, Ellen Amos) her first single 'Baltimore'/'Walking With You' on the MEA label (named after her own initials). She favoured cover versions such as Joni Mitchell's 'A Case Of You', Billie Holiday's 'Strange Fruit' and Bill Withers' 'Ain't No Sunshine', later staples of her 90s live set. Amos then adopted the first name Tori, after a friend's boyfriend's remark that she 'didn't look much like an Ellen, more like a Tori'. Still the dozens of demo tapes she had recorded since her early teens (mostly sent out by her doting father) failed to give her a break, and she switched tack to front pop-rock band Y Kant Tori Read (a play on words that referred to her previous expulsion from the conservatory). Musicians in the band included guitarist Steve Farris (ex-Mr. Mister), Matt Sorum (future Cult and Guns N'Roses drummer), Vinny Collauta (Frank Zappa), Peter White (co-writer to Al Stewart) and Kim Bullard (ex-Poco), but the production and material (largely co-composed between Bullard and Amos) did her few favours. Amos lowered her profile for a while after this undignified release, though she did appear on albums by Stewart, Canadian songwriter Ferron and Stan Ridgway. As she remembers, 'After the trauma I crumbled. I was very confused about why I was doing music.' Nevertheless, she persevered in writing her own songs, and eventually a tape of these reached Atlantic Records' co-chairman, Doug Morris. Though he saw the germ of her talent, he decided that her current sound was to the taste of the average American-FM listener, and sent Amos instead to the UK (and East West Records) so that she might enjoy a better reception. Amos moved to London in February 1991 and started playing small-scale gigs around the capital. Her 'debut' EP, *Me And A Gun*, was released in October 1991, and tackled the emotive and disturbing topic of her rape by an armed 'fan' as she drove him home after a gig. An acclaimed debut album, *Little Earthquakes*, followed in January 1992, although the comparisons to Kate Bush continued (not helped by a similar cover design). Much of the following year was spent writing and recording a second album with co-producer and partner Eric Rosse. The result, *Under The Pink*, included a guest appearance from Trent Reznor (Nine Inch Nails), and was recorded in his new home - the house where in 1969 Sharon Tate was murdered by Charles Manson's followers. The first single lifted from it, 'Cornflake Girl', reached number 4 in the UK charts in January 1994. The follow-up, 'Pretty Good Year', reached number 7 in March, and with the album topping the UK

chart Amos confirmed she was now a commercial force. She was heralded in the press, alongside Polly Harvey (PJ Harvey) and Björk, as part of a new wave of intelligent, literate female songwriters. This was cemented with the release of the sexually charged *Boys For Pele*. Quite apart from having a baby pig suckling on her breast on the cover, the lyrics were a powerful combination of artistic and erotic liberation. Armand Van Helden's remix of 'Professional Widow' gained a huge club following and secured Amos a UK number 1 hit. Several of the songs on the follow-up, *From The Choirgirl Hotel*, were informed by Amos' recent miscarriage. The album proved to be her most mature and musically adventurous to date, Amos recording with a full band for the first time. A prolific songwriting burst led to the release of the double *To Venus And Back* the following year.

● ALBUMS: as Y Kant Tori Read *Y Kant Tori Read* (Atlantic 1988)★★, *Little Earthquakes* (East West 1992)★★★★, *Under The Pink* (East West 1993)★★★★, *Boys For Pele* (East West 1996)★★★★, *From The Choirgirl Hotel* (East West 1998)★★★★, *To Venus And Back* (East West 1999)★★★.

● VIDEOS: *Little Earthquake* (A*Vision 1992), *Tori Amos: Live From New York* (Warner Music Vision 1997), *The Complete Videos 1991-1998* (Warner Music Vision 1999).

● FURTHER READING: *All These Years: The Illustrated Biography*, Kalen Rogers.

Anathema

Formed in Liverpool, England, in the summer of 1990, by brothers Danny (guitar) and Vinny Cavanagh (vocals), doom metal band Anathema owe much to early 70s Black Sabbath, most notably their low, ominous riffs. Combined with this is the influence of 90s death metal, particularly the abrasive guitar and vocals. Perhaps the oddest element of Anathema's sound is their poetic romanticism, most evident in their lyrics. Earlier recordings featured the occasional use of the angelic tones of a female vocalist, Ruth, to complement lead singer Darren White. The results of this odd hybrid were surprisingly effective and Anathema built up a strong cult following among doom metal fans. Their four-track demo, *An Illiad Of Woes*, was released in November 1990 under their original name, Pagan Angel. A second demo, *All Faith Is Lost*, recorded at MA Studios, was released in July 1991. In its wake, they cut a limited edition single, 'They Die'/'Crestfallen', for the Swiss label Witchunt. Eventually, the band earned a contract with the musically sympathetic Peaceville Records, initially contributing one track, 'Lovelorn Rhapsody', to the *Volume 4* compilation. The *Crestfallen* EP was sufficiently well received to warrant an album the following year. However, in 1995 White left the band to form Blood Divine, leaving behind the mini-album *Pentecost III* as his epitaph. Although only five tracks long, it has a full 40 minutes duration. Bass player Duncan Patterson and drummer Shaun Steels left following the release of 1998's *Alternative 4*, and were replaced by Dave Pybus and John Douglas. Slow, melancholy and heavy, Anathema boast a depth often missing from standard heavy metal.

● ALBUMS: *Serenades* (Peaceville 1993)★★★, *Pentecost III* mini-album (Peaceville 1995)★★★, *The Silent Enigma* (Peaceville 1995)★★★, *Eternity* (Peaceville 1996)★★★, *Alternative 4* (Peaceville 1998)★★★★, *Judgement* (Music For Nations 1999)★★★.

Andre, Peter

b. Peter James Andrea, 27 February 1973, Harrow, London, England. Andre moved to Australia at the age of 10, where he successfully launched his career as a teen pop star in 1992. By the mid-90s he had returned to England and in 1995 he saw his debut single, 'Turn It Up', reach the UK Top 70. His follow-up, 'Mysterious Girl', failed to make much of an impression despite the extensive broadcasts of its video (which held the number 1 request slot on cable television programme *The Box* long after it had disappeared from the charts). It was not until April 1996 and 'Only One' that Andre reached the UK Top 20. 'Mysterious Girl' then became a huge summer hit when re-released to capitalize on the previous single's success, while Andre embarked on a promotional personal appearance tour of UK venues as well as return trips to Australia and New Zealand. The two follow-up singles, 'Flava' and 'I Feel You', both went on to top the UK singles chart as Andre established himself as the country's newest teen idol. Desperate to be regarded as a serious R&B singer, Andre then enlisted the heavyweight help of Coolio, Montell Jordan and the Fugees for 1997's decidedly lightweight *Time*. 'Kiss The Girl', taken from the soundtrack of the movie *Little Mermaid*, debuted at number 9 in the UK singles chart in August 1998.

● ALBUMS: *Natural* (Mushroom 1996)★★★, *Time* (Mushroom 1997)★★.

● VIDEOS: *Live At Wembley* (PolyGram Video 1997).

Andrews, Jessica

b. Huntingdon, Tennessee, USA. Andrews tasted her first success in the fourth grade when her rendition of Dolly Parton's 'I Will Always Love You' won the competition at her school talent show. She started taking singing engagements at local fairs and carnivals as well as bars. News of her talent reached Nashville producer Byron Gallimore (Tim McGraw, Jo Dee Messina), who immediately took her into the studio. With Gallimore's backing she won over representatives of DreamWorks Nashville label, who offered her a contract. Her first notable release was 'I Will Be There For You', included on *The Prince Of Egypt – Nashville* compilation. It was followed in March 1999 by debut album *Heart Shaped World*. This saw her celebrated, alongside such artists as LeAnn Rimes and Lila McCann, as part of a new wave of teenagers rejuvenating contemporary country music.

● ALBUMS: *Heart Shaped World* (DreamWorks Nashville 1999)★★★.

Angel, Dave

b. David Gooden, 13 May 1966, Chelsea, London, England. Based in Clapham, south London, techno DJ and recording artist Dave Angel's father was a professional jazz musician. As a result, he grew up listening to Charlie Parker and Miles Davis, and became a jazz session drummer by the age of 14. However, his background was also one of stifling poverty, his father buying him his first drum-kit the day the electricity was cut off. He released his debut single in 1989, shortly after returning from a nine-month prison term for possession of cannabis. He had recorded a bassline on a standard tape deck, and in a moment of inspiration, mixed it against a nearby copy of the Eurythmics' 'Sweet Dreams (Are Made Of This)'. Once approval had been given from RCA Records, who licensed the record, it was released as a white label, before Angel moved to Dave Dorrell's Love label

for 'Never Leave'. He began his career in earnest with two strong EPs, *Royal Techno* and *Of The Highest Order*. The critically acclaimed *Family* EP followed in 1993, before *Third Voyage* EP (originally released in April 1991). His debut album was released in association with the Island Records' offshoot, Blunted, in 1995. A second and final long-player followed for Island in 1997, following which Angel recorded a mix compilation for React Music. More popular in Germany than his homeland, Angel continues to DJ at the Orbit club and to remix for various clients, including Sun Electric's 'En-Trance', Katana for Eastern Bloc and the *Seas Of Tranquillity* EP for his own label, Rotation Records.

● ALBUMS: *Tales Of The Unexpected* (Blunted/Island 1995)★★★, *Globetrotting* (4th & Broadway/Island 1997)★★★.

● COMPILATIONS: with Daren Emerson *Mixmag Live! Vol. 13: Techno Fruit* (Mixmag 1995)★★★, *Classics* (R&S 1996)★★★, *39 Flavours Of Tech Funk* (React 1998)★★★★, *X-MIX-4 - Beyond The Heavens* (Studio !K7 1998)★★★.

Annihilator

This heavy metal band is a vehicle for the talents of classically trained Canadian guitarist Jeff Waters (b. Ottawa, Canada). Annihilator set the underground scene alight with a demo entitled 'Phantasmagoria', before relocating to Vancouver and releasing their debut, *Alice In Hell*. This was a *tour de force* of intricate thrash, with all the guitars and bass parts played by Waters, who also produced and wrote the material, with Randy Rampage (vocals, ex-D.O.A.) and Ray Hartmann (drums); the line-up was augmented by Anthony Greenham (guitar) and Wayne Darley (bass) after the recording. The sizzling guitar work helped the record to become, at the time, the best-selling debut in the history of Roadrunner Records. The band subsequently suffered from an unstable line-up, with Greenham being replaced almost immediately by Dave Scott Davis, while Rampage departed when touring was complete, with ex-Omen frontman Coburn Pharr stepping in. *Never, Neverland* was another excellent effort, displaying rather more lyrical maturity than the debut, and a new version of 'Phantasmagoria'. Band stability remained an issue, and Davis' departure on the eve of a European tour as guests of Judas Priest caused problems due to the sheer complexity of the material, but the band nevertheless managed to produce creditable performances. After a lengthy break, Annihilator returned with new guitarist Neil Goldberg and another vocalist, Aaron Randall. *Set The World On Fire*, though less well received by the metal press than previous offerings, revealed some promising progression beyond thrash boundaries into more melodic spaces, and sold well. The remixed and unreleased tracks compilation *Bag Of Tricks* was the band's last release for Roadrunner. *King Of The Kill* saw Waters take over lead vocals and featured Randy Black (drums), later adding Dave Davis (guitar) and Cam Dixon (bass). *Refresh The Demon* was poor, but Waters bounced back with *Remains*, which introduced an exciting new industrial direction.

● ALBUMS: *Alice In Hell* (Roadrunner 1989)★★★, *Never, Neverland* (Roadrunner 1990)★★★, *Set The World On Fire* (Roadrunner 1993)★★, *King Of The Kill* (Music For Nations 1994)★★★, *Refresh The Demon* (Music For Nations 1996)★★, *In Command (Live 1989-1990)* (Roadrunner 1996)★★★, *Remains* (Music For Nations 1997)★★★, *Criteria For A Black Widow* (Roadrunner 1999)★★★.

● COMPILATIONS: *Bag Of Tricks* (Roadrunner 1994)★★★.

Anointed

A mixed-gender gospel trio masterminded by producers Mark Heimermann and Chris Harris, the Anointed's sound blends traditional church-singing with pop and R&B nuances. Their broad appeal was confirmed in 1996 when singles from their third album were serviced by Myrrh Records not just to gospel, but also Contemporary Christian and R&B stations. The group originally comprised four singer-songwriters, all born in Ohio. Steve Crawford, his sister Da'dra Crawford-Greathouse, Mary Tiller and Denise 'Nee-C' Wallis began performing together in their home-town of Columbus in the early 90s. They had soon secured a contract with the local independent label Brainstorm, at that time distributed by Word Records. Crawford-Greathouse, reflecting on the group's debut, noted that '[it was] really heavy R&B gospel, because that was pretty much our surroundings growing up.' They then switched to the Nashville-based gospel label Myrrh. *The Call*, with an accent on pop melodies to ensnare the Contemporary Christian audience, proved their breakthrough album. It collected three Gospel Music Association Dove Awards, a Stellar Award for Best Performance By A Group Or Duo, Contemporary, and a Grammy nomination for Best Contemporary Soul Gospel Album. The attendant EP, 'In God's Hands Now', also received significant mainstream exposure, as the quartet supported Groove Theory on a national promotional tour. Tiller departed in January 1996 prior to the release of *Under The Influence*, though this did not seem to impede their commercial ascendancy. In November the trio embarked on the multi-artist Christian music Christmas tour dubbed 'Emmanuel'. Their major label debut for Sony Records found the trio working with R&B producers Tony Rich and Keith Crouch in an attempt to corner the crossover market.

● ALBUMS: *Spiritual Love Affair* (Brainstorm 1993)★★, *The Call* (Myrrh 1995)★★★, *Under The Influence* (Myrrh 1996)★★★, *Anointed* (Sony 1999)★★★.

Another Level

A UK male vocal quartet whose urban R&B flavoured pop proved a big success on the UK charts in the late 90s. The band, comprising former Brit School alumni Dane Bowers (b. 29 November 1979) and Wayne Williams (b. 20 January 1977) alongside Bobak Kianoush (b. 1 November 1978) and Mark Baron (b. 18 August 1974), were keen not to be misinterpreted as another manufactured boy band. Their demo was originally heard by US rapper Jay-Z, who in turn passed it onto the newly formed Northwestside label (which had recently been granted the non-US license for distributing artists on Jay-Z's Roc-A-Fella Records). The band were signed by Northwestside in March 1997, and were eagerly marketed as purveyors of slick UK urban R&B with great crossover potential. Their debut single 'Be Alone No More', featuring a cameo performance from Jay-Z, climbed to UK number 6 in March 1998. Their big breakthrough came with a cover version of Silk's 1993 US number 1 hit 'Freak Me', which topped the UK charts in July 1998. 'Guess I Was A Fool' reached number 5 in November, and by the end of the year the band were confirmed as having sold more UK singles in 1998 than any newcomers apart from B*Witched and LeAnn Rimes. Their self-titled debut was released in November, entering the UK charts at number 22. Reasserting

their street credentials, the band collaborated with Ghostface Killah of the Wu-Tang Clan on 'I Want You For Myself', a UK number 2 hit single in January 1999. 'From The Heart', taken from the soundtrack to the film *Notting Hill*, entered the UK charts at number 6 in June. The band collaborated with US rapper TQ on the follow-up single, 'Summertime', which reached number 7 in August. 'Bomb Diggy' also broke into the Top 10 in November.

● ALBUMS: *Another Level* (Northwestside 1998)★★★, *Nexus ...* (Northwestside 1999)★★★.

Ant And Dec

(see PJ And Duncan)

Anthony, Marc

b. Marco Antonio Muñiz, 16 September 1969, New York City, New York, USA. One of the leading salsa stars of the late 90s, Anthony began his career as a session vocalist for pop and dance acts. His Puerto Rican parents boasted a strong Latin music heritage and named their son after a Mexican singer. Under his new name, Anthony worked as a songwriter and backing vocalist for pop acts including Menudo and the Latin Rascals. He subsequently collaborated with house producer Little Louie Vega, who featured the singer on the Latin-flavoured club hit 'Ride On The Rhythm' and *When The Night Is Over*. In 1992, Vega and Anthony opened for Latin bandleader Tito Puente at New York's Madison Square Garden. Seeking new inspiration from the music of Puente, Rubén Blades and Juan Gabriel, Anthony performed at the Latin music convention Radio y Musica, his first step on the road to salsa stardom. He released his Spanish-language debut, *Otra Nota*, in 1993, and achieved his first taste of mainstream success performing the hit duet 'Vivir Lo Nuestro' with singer La India. Subsequent tours throughout the Americas, including an opening slot for Blades, established Anthony as one of the hottest new stars in salsa. His excellent 1995 collection, *Todo A Su Tiempo*, was nominated for a Grammy. The more traditional-sounding follow-up, *Contra La Corriente*, was promoted by a sell-out solo concert at Madison Square Garden. Anthony also appeared alongside Blades in Paul Simon's 1998 flop stage musical, *The Capeman*, which closed after only 68 regular performances. Rebounding from that failure, Anthony began working on his English language debut with a crew of leading producers, including Rodney Jerkins and Walter Afanasieff. Released in September 1999, and promoted by the huge radio hit 'I Need To Know', the self-titled collection was a clear attempt to emulate the crossover success of Jennifer Lopez and Ricky Martin, at the risk of angering his traditional salsa fans. Anthony had already appeared with Lopez on the duet 'No Me Ames', taken from her *On The 6* collection. During a busy year, Anthony appeared alongside Nicolas Cage in Martin Scorsese's *Bringing Out The Dead*.

● ALBUMS: with Little Louie Vega *When The Night Is Over* (Atlantic 1991)★★★, *Otra Nota* (Sony Discos 1993)★★★, *Todo A Su Tiempo* (Sony Discos 1995)★★★★, *Contra La Corriente* (Sony Discos 1997)★★★, *Marc Anthony* (Columbia 1999)★★★.

● COMPILATIONS: *Desde Un Principio: From The Beginning* (Sony Discos 1999)★★★.

● FILMS: *Natural Causes* (1994), *Hackers* (1995), *Big Night* (1996), *The Substitute* (1996), *Bringing Out The Dead* (1999).

Anthony, Mike

The UK Saxon sound system from Lewisham, London, has spawned a number of revered performers, including Phillip Papa Levi, Daddy Colonel, Maxi Priest and Tippa Irie. Priest enjoyed initial hits with Barry Boom, who nurtured Anthony's recording career in the late 80s. Anthony performed in the lovers rock style and enjoyed a reggae Top 10 hit with 'Crash Crash', swiftly following that success with 'Glide Gently', which showcased his smooth vocals. Numerous hits ensued, including 'Cruising In Love', 'Open Your Heart' and, with the illustrious Fashion Records label producer Gussie Prento, 'Still Your Number One'. In 1991, Anthony topped the reggae chart for an extensive period with his cover version of David Ruffin's 'Walk Away From Love'. The song had been a reggae hit in the 70s for Ken Boothe, which inspired Anthony to emulate the Studio One veteran (producer Lloyd Charmers, motivated by Anthony's unprecedented success, eventually re-released Boothe's version). Anthony followed this success with 'No Halfway Love', which reaffirmed his popularity. Throughout the 90s he has consistently enjoyed Top 10 placings in the UK reggae charts, with notable hits including 'Spread Love', 'Don't Play Games', 'Sexy Eyes', 'Call Me' and Top Cat's 'rude boy mix', 'This Time I Know', which was released as part of a joint venture between Gussie P and Nine Lives.
● ALBUMS: *Short Of Nothing* (Merger 1992)★★, *Back 4 More* (Gussie P 1996)★★★★.

Apache Indian

b. Steve Kapur, 11 May 1967, Birmingham, West Midlands, England. The 'Don Raja' of UK Asian raggamuffin, Apache Indian came to represent a cross-cultural fusion of musics that both baffled and excited pundits and punters alike in the mid-90s. Apache Indian grew up in Handsworth, Birmingham, in the 70s - an era when the city was being celebrated as a kind of UK reggae melting pot through the efforts of Steel Pulse, and others, whose *Handsworth Revolution* album first put it on the musical map. Although he was of Indian parentage, Apache associated with reggae sound systems in the early 80s, sporting dreadlocks and an abiding love of Bob Marley. By the mid-80s, locks trimmed to a sharp fade, he was known locally on the mic as a dancehall rapper, and in 1990 he cut his first single, 'Movie Over India', as a white label, later picked up by UK reggae distributors Jet Star. A compelling, catchy ragga tune, with a few elements of bhangra, the preferred music of many UK Asians, the record was a huge hit in both the reggae and bhangra markets. Two more cult hits followed, 'Chok There' and 'Don Raja', before the majors became interested in him. Island Records finally lured him into a contract, and 1993's *No Reservations* was cut in Jamaica and included Sly Dunbar, Bobby Digital and Robert Livingstone producing. Critically acclaimed, it saw Apache move away from the frothier elements of his distinctive ragga-reggae and towards a role as social commentator and Anglo-Asian representative. This approach was exemplified in the three crossover hits, 'Arranged Marriage', 'Boom Shack A Lak' (from 1993's *Nuff Vibes* EP) and 'Movin' On', the latter a cry of resistance against the election of a BNP member to a council seat in Tower Hamlets, London. Apache's assimilation into the mainstream music business continued apace, although he drew some flak from the more traditional elements in the reggae business, who may have been displeased at the apparent ease with which he conquered the pop charts, and he subsequently began to lose his ragga audience. His propensity for winning awards (Best Newcomer in the UK Reggae Industry Awards 1990, a short list entry for the Mercury Prize in 1993 and a nomination for four BRIT Awards in 1994) and his open, friendly personality made him a media favourite throughout 1993. Subsequent albums were artistically disappointing, and, crucially, commercial success also began to elude Apache Indian. By 1997's *Real People* his association with Island had come to an end.
● ALBUMS: *No Reservations* (Island 1993)★★★★, *Make Way For The Indian* (Island 1995)★★★, *Real People* (Coalition 1997)★★.

Aphex Twin

b. Richard D. James, 18 August 1971, Ireland, but raised in Truro, Cornwall, England. During the 90s James, under a variety of names, has become one of the leading exponents of 'intelligent techno', 'ambient techno' and other terms invented to describe his brand of electronic music. As a child he was not interested in music, but instead amused himself 'making noises and banging on things'; later he began recording his efforts on tape and consequently began building and customizing his own synthesizers. While DJing at parties and raves he sometimes included in his sets the odd original tune such as 'Didgeridoo'; 'I wanted to have some tracks to finish the raves I used to play in Cornwall, to really kill everybody off so they couldn't dance any more'. He eventually released the *Aphex Twin* EP and 'Analogue Bubblebath' on the Exeter-based Mighty Force label in 1991. His breakthrough came the following year when he released 'Didgeridoo' on R&S Records. Much of his work from around this time such as 'Phloam' and 'Isopropanol' was built from incredibly abrasive sounds but a different style by which he became more widely known emerged on the album *Selected Ambient Works '85 - '92*. In the same year, Warp Records included his 'Polygon Window', credited to the Diceman, on their *Artificial Intelligence* compilation. This track opened *Surfing On Sine Waves* which James released the following year under the name Polygon Window as part of Warp's Artificial Intelligence series. Like much of the work on these albums, much of the music sounded quite unique and followed little of the dancefloor trends of the time, but the press soon managed to invent the term 'ambient techno'. However, some of the tracks were anything but ambient and 'Quoth' (which was also released as a single in 1993) with its coarse kick drum sound actually had more in common with much hard techno. Even so, on a number of more introspective tunes, notably 'If It Really Is Me' with its forlorn melodies and 'Quino - phec', James managed to create a barren Eno-like texture. The *On* EP in November 1993 followed his signing to Warp on a permanent basis and the next year he released the eagerly awaited *Selected Ambient Works Vol. 2*. In 1995, Aphex Twin released the album *I Care Because You Do* and the EPs, *Ventolin* and *Donkey Rhubarb* and as AFX two *Hangable Auto Bulb* EPs. These were followed the next year by *Richard D. James Album* on which his usual combination of caustic noises and forlorn textures were set beside more varied rhythms than usual, showing the influence of drum 'n' bass. As one of the few modern artists to establish an individual sound, James is often hailed as electronic music's most experimental individual. He has also become associated with deliberately obscure DJ sets in which he has been known to put sandpaper on the turntable, and his Rephlex Records label has promoted the work of similarly esoteric artists. However, it seems after a number of albums that much of his work tends to revolve around the same ideas. Hysteria in the press may also have obscured his tendency towards self-indulgence. Other names under which he has released material include Caustic Window, GAK, Blue Calx and PCP.

● ALBUMS: *Selected Ambient Works '85 - '92* (R&S 1992)★★★★, as Polygon Window *Surfing On Sine Waves* (Warp 1993)★★★, *Selected Ambient Works Vol. 2* (Warp 1994)★★, *I Care Because You Do* (Warp 1995)★★★, *Richard D. James Album* (Warp 1996)★★★.

● COMPILATIONS: as Caustic Window *Compilation* (Rephlex 1998)★★★.

● VIDEOS: *Come To Viddy* (Warp 1997).

Aphrodite

b. Gavin King. Although Roni Size and Goldie are perhaps the most famous sons of the drum 'n' bass scene, King is its unsung hero. He is a record label boss, globe-trotting DJ, recording artist and producer and remixer, working with high-profile artists including A Tribe Called Quest, Ice Cube, the Jungle Brothers, Nine Inch Nails and Moby. King first began making his own tracks when he could not afford to buy enough records to compile his own mix-tapes. Using a very basic Omega computer, he recorded extra tracks to supplement the tapes. He used to play these mix-tapes to people at his local record store. One of these people was the DJ-producer Mickey Finn, and the two subsequently began to work together. King's first release was the *Cellar 4* EP but he first experienced commercial success as Urban Shakedown with Finn. Released in 1992, 'Some Justice' was a prototype jungle single. It combined the positivism of acid house (with its 'We'll live as one' refrain) with heavy sub-bass and infectious synthesiser melodies. The track established a blueprint for future jungle releases and entered the UK national Top 40, despite some problems in clearing the sample of Ce Ce Rogers' 'Someday'. It was Aphrodite and Mickey Finn's (as Urban Takeover) remix of the Jungle Brothers' 'Jungle Brother' that exposed the team to a much wider audience. Their reworking brought together New York hip-hop beats with the new jungle sound, entered the UK Top 40 and caught the imagination of US hip-hop fans. Aphrodite and Mickey Finn established their own record label, Aphrodite Recordings and a sister label, Urban Takeover, in 1993. Since then, they have released a string of respected and popular drum 'n' bass singles. King would rather remain prolific than produce technically precise but uninspired music. He takes a similar approach to his Djing, often playing his own roughly produced dub plates, including his own versions of the themes from the television programme *Bonanza* and the movie *2001*. His own hip-hop-infused form of drum 'n' bass has become known as 'jump-up'. In 1999, the major record label V2 signed Aphrodite for the single 'BM Funkster' and *Aphrodite*. The album featured remixes of older, classic tracks from the Aphrodite Recordings label, such as 'Woman That Rolls', 'King Of Beats' and 'Rincing Quince' alongside new material. It demonstrated a range of influences including breakbeats, soul, jazz, dub, funk and the ever-present hip-hop.

● ALBUMS: *Aphrodite* (V2 1999)★★★★.

Apollo 440

This wildly eclectic Liverpool, England-based crew features Trevor Gray (keyboards/vocals), Howard Gray (backing vocals) and Noko (vocals/guitar/keyboards, ex-Luxuria). Inspired by the acid house scene, they initially recorded for their own Stealth Sonic label. Following the release of early singles 'Blackout', 'Destiny' and club favourite 'Lolita', Apollo 440 soon became more widely known for their remix work, numbering U2, Liz Francis ('Rhythm Of Life'), EMF and Pop Will Eat Itself among their clients. Further notoriety came with their sample of Emerson, Lake And Palmer on their 1993 single, 'Astral America'. They have also recorded as Fast ('Fast' - Stealth 1992, a pure adrenaline rush at 155 bpm). They made the UK Top 10 in February 1997 with the Van Halen-sampling 'Ain't Talkin' About Dub', and debuted at number 4 the following August with the theme to the movie *Lost In Space*. In the late 90s they were joined by the colourful figure of Mary Millington (ex-Gaye Bykers On Acid), and enjoyed another crossover hit in September 1999 with 'Stop The Rock'.

● ALBUMS: *Millennium Fever* (Stealth Sonic 1994)★★★, *Electro Glide In Blue* (Stealth Sonic/Epic 1997)★★★, *Gettin' High On Your Own Supply* (Stealth Sonic/Epic 1999)★★★.

Apple, Fiona

b. Fiona Apple Maggart, 13 September 1977, New York, USA. Growing up in a dysfunctional New York family, Fiona Apple soon discovered the impetus to articulate frustrations that would eventually result in widespread comparisons to Alanis Morissette for her 1996 debut, *Tidal*. As a child she was introduced to the Beatles by her stepfather, while her mother educated her in jazz standards. By the age of 11 she was writing her own songs, as a means of coping with self-imposed isolation caused by her shyness and lack of confidence about her appearance, and a rape ordeal at the age of 12. She found solace in the poetry of Maya Angelou, which she maintains to be her biggest influence. She took her first step on the road to international success when Clean Slate Records owner Andy Slater overheard her demo tape (recorded on a cheap tape recorder in her bedroom) at a Christmas party in 1993. He quickly signed her to the label, but allowed her a full two years of writing and recording before her debut album was released in July 1996. *Tidal* made an immediate impact, entering the *Billboard* Top 100 while Apple built up encouraging reviews by opening for Chris Isaak on tour. She was subsequently asked to appear on a November 1996 edition of *Saturday Night Live* - a booking that carries a *de facto* nod of approval from the music industry's left-field cognoscenti. The album's attendant single, the haunting 'Shadowboxer', also earned rave reviews, and was playlisted on several Top 40 radio stations. In 1997, Apple won the Best New Artist accolade at the MTV Awards. Her relationship with magician David Blaine raised her media profile, although the couple split up while Apple was recording her sophomore collection. The title of this album runs to an astonishing 90 words, but is commonly abbreviated as *When The Pawn ....* When all the fuss regarding its title had died down, the album proved to be another challenging collection of singer-songwriter material, albeit less accessible than her debut.

● ALBUMS: *Tidal* (Clean Slate/Work Group 1996)★★★, *When The Pawn ...* (Clean Slate/Epic 1999)★★★.

Apples In Stereo

Led by vocalist/guitarist Robert Schneider, Denver, Colorado, USA-based Apples In Stereo are one of a crop of allied bands, known as the Elephant 6 Recording Company and including the Olivia Tremor Control and Neutral Milk Hotel, who have spent their career trying to recreate the sonic abandon of classic 60s songwriting. The Beach Boys are by some way the band's most obvious reference point. Backed by Schneider's girlfriend Hilary and a bass player, the band (originally known as the Apples) released a series of acclaimed EPs for SpinART Records in the mid-90s that were eventually compiled on *Science Faire*. Their debut album proper was *Fun Trick Noisemaker*, on which Schneider pretended to be 'in a studio orbiting 12,000 miles above Earth'. Their major-label debut revealed the method behind their madness, containing instantly memorable psychedelic pop songs. The follow-up, *Her Wallpaper Reverie*, was even more magical and a confirmation, if any was needed, of what a fertile musical breeding ground the Elephant 6 scene is proving to be.

● ALBUMS: *Fun Trick Noisemaker* (spinART 1996)★★★, *Tone Soul Evolution* (spinART/Warners 1997)★★★, *Her Wallpaper Reverie* (spinART/Warners 1999)★★★★.

● COMPILATIONS: *Science Faire* (spinART 1996)★★★.

Aqua

Maverick Danish pop quartet Aqua could hardly have earned a higher profile than that achieved by their third UK single, 'Barbie Girl'. A tribute-cum-pastiche of the American toy favoured by pre-adolescent girls, it received extensive television and radio airplay as it climbed and eventually topped the UK charts in late 1997. Conversely, their debut, 'Roses Are Red', did not possess the same novelty value and caused barely a ripple of attention, although it had been a huge success in Denmark (topping the charts, achieving platinum sales and earning a Danish Grammy nomination). The follow-up, 'My Oh My', also went straight to number 1 in Denmark. Part of the reason for the success of 'Barbie Girl' was its amusing video, which featured lead singer Lene G. Nystrom (b. 2 October 1973, Tønsberg, Norway) dressed in a succession of Barbie outfits, with band member René Dif (b. 17 October 1967, Copenhagen, Denmark) playing male doll Ken. The band was formed in 1994, though the production and writing nucleus of Claus Norreen (b. 5 June 1970, Charlottenlund, Denmark) and Soren Rasted (b. 13 June 1969, Blovstrød, Denmark) had been together since 1989 as members of Joyspeed. In this incarnation they enjoyed a solitary success in the Danish charts with 'Itsy Blitzy'. 'Barbie Girl' successfully prepared the international market for 1997's *Aquarium*, a more stylistically varied album than might have been expected. The band enjoyed further success in 1998 when 'Doctor Jones' and 'Turn Back Time' both debuted at number 1 in the UK charts. 'My Oh My' ended their remarkable sequence when it stalled at number 6 in August.

● ALBUMS: *Aquarium* (Universal 1997)★★★.

● VIDEOS: *The Official Aqua Video Diary* (Universal Music 1998).

Arab Strap

Arab Strap was originally a one-man band, the brainchild of Aidan Moffat, who cobbled together 'self-indulgent wank' with two drums and a kazoo in his bedroom in Falkirk, Scotland. Nearby, Malcolm Middleton was doing similarly onanistic things with a guitar, under the name the Laughing Stock. Having vaguely known each other for five years, the pair decided to unite as Arab Strap (the name of a device Moffat found in a sex toy catalogue) in the summer of 1995, with the addition of David Gow (drums) and Gary Miller (bass). Within a few months they had been signed up by Glasgow's Chemikal Underground Records although their sound bore little resemblance to the current vogue for wall-of-sound guitars, relying more on the literary renaissance of urban Scotland typified by Irvine Welsh's *Trainspotting*. The duo's debut single, 'The First Big Weekend', consisted of little more than a guitar, a drum machine and Moffat's deliberately banal cameo of *The Simpsons*, strawberry tonic wine and the Scottish football team losing to England in the 1996 European championships. Arab Strap's selective live appearances and the ensuing album maintained the downbeat, minimalist tone. Occasional folky tinges give their music a veneer of user-friendliness, but a certain lyrical bluntness ('tell me you want me in your cunt/tell me you know sure what you want') indicates that Moffat may not qualify as a guest presenter for *Top Of The Pops* quite yet. *Philophobia* featured more bleakly humorous tales of love and lust set to minimalist music, with stand-out tracks including 'Packet Of Three' and 'New Birds'. An oddly compelling live album followed before the release of the band's fourth album, *Elephant Shoe*.

● ALBUMS: *The Week Never Starts Round Here* (Chemikal Underground 1996)★★★, *Philophobia* (Chemikal Underground 1998)★★★, *Mad For Sadness* (Go! Beat 1999)★★★, *Elephant Shoe* (Go! Beat 1999)★★★.

Archer, Tasmin

b. Bradford, Yorkshire, England. Singer-songwriter Archer became the first UK woman to have a solo UK number 1 since Bonnie Tyler's 'Total Eclipse Of The Heart' in 1983, when 'Sleeping Satellite' topped the charts at the end of 1992. Although seemingly an overnight success, Archer had actually spent several years perfecting her songwriting craft ('Sleeping Satellite' was a four-year-old song). Part-time employment as a clerk at a magistrates court and as a sewing machine operator preceded her attempt at stardom. Eventually finding work at a Bradford studio, Archer made tea and cleaned toilets as well as helping out on backing vocals. Here she met future songwriting partners John Hughes (guitar), and John Beck (keyboards). Over five years they worked together (originally under the title the Archers) until they had built up a strong song catalogue that would allow Archer immediately to capitalise on the success of 'Sleeping Satellite'. The follow-up single, 'In Your Care', was a biting indictment of child abuse, and the debut album also covered topics such as urban decay alongside more conventional ballads. Too long had elapsed for her second album to make any significant impression on an impatient and fickle market that had moved on, even with the support of Elvis Costello's Attractions.

● ALBUMS: *Great Expectations* (EMI 1992)★★★, *Bloom* (EMI 1996)★★.

● VIDEOS: *When It Comes Down To It* (EMI 1993).

Arena, Tina

b. Philopina Lidia Arena, 1 November 1967, Melbourne, Australia. Singer-songwriter Arena (a Sicilian name pronounced ah-rey-nah) had her first brush with fame on the Australian television show *Young Talent Time*. Having become a stalwart of the show (as 'Tiny Tina'), she made an abortive attempt at starting a solo career with 'Turn Up The Beat' in 1985. In 1989, she tried again with the single 'I Want Your Body'. A faceless pop-dance composition that accompanied a similarly unconvincing debut album, *Strong As Steel*, it reached number 2 in the Australian charts. Sadly, it also severely affected Arena's credibility, and in December 1991 she moved to Los Angeles, California, USA. An unknown there, she managed to meet local songwriters and also found time to work on her own songs. These compositions, which eventually appeared on her 1995 comeback album, *Don't Ask*, were a major stylistic improvement on those of her debut. Cultivating an audience among Melbourne's vibrant gay population (which had proved so instrumental in Kylie Minogue's rise), there was still little about *Don't Ask* to excite critics. Launched internationally with a sequence of promotional visits to the UK, she discovered the market already inundated with photogenic dance-pop singers - not least her own compatriots. 'Chains' still managed to become a worldwide hit, reaching the Top 10 in the UK and breaking into the *Billboard* Top 40 in America. On the back of further hit singles, *Don't Ask* went on to sell over three million copies worldwide, making Arena the biggest-selling Australian female artist of all time, although she failed to conquer the lucrative American market. *In Deep* was another huge success in Australia, promoted by the single 'Burn', which reached number 2 in her home chart. The album was not issued in the US until two years later. In June 1998, she reached the UK Top 30 with the title song of Andrew Lloyd Webber and Jim Steinman's *Whistle Down The Wind*.

● ALBUMS: *Strong As Steel* (Columbia 1989)★★, *Don't Ask* (Columbia 1995)★★★, *In Deep* (Columbia 1997)★★.

Armstrong, Craig

b. Shettleston, Scotland. Armstrong is a musical Renaissance man, having worked in the classical, jazz, experimental electronics, pop and dance music fields. He trained at London's Royal Academy Of Music and won the UK's Young Jazz Musician Of The Year in 1981. In the mid-80s, he was involved in the Scottish pop scene and was briefly a member of Texas (writing some of their material), Big Dish and Hipsway. In the 90s, he went on to score the strings on Massive Attack's second album *Protection*, as well as working with artists including Madonna, Tina Turner, U2 and Luciano Pavarotti. It is perhaps as the writer of film scores that Armstrong is better known, having won a British Academy Of Film And Television Award (BAFTA) and an Ivor Novello Award for his work on Baz Luhrmann's film adaptation of *Romeo And Juliet*. He has also scored music for the movies *Goldeneye*, *Mission: Impossible* and *Plunkett & Macleane*. The UK's *Guardian* newspaper described him as 'a John Barry for the millennium . . .'. His debut album was released on Massive Attack's record label, Melankolic, in 1999.

● ALBUMS: *The Space Between Us* (Melankolic/Virgin 1999)★★★.

Arnold

London-based Arnold were signed to Creation Records in 1996, when label boss Alan McGee broke his own 'no more signings' promise after hearing their roughly recorded demo. Mark Saxby (guitar), Phil Payne (bass) and Phil Morris (vocals) had previously played in generic indie band Patio, but following the death of their friend and lead singer Rob in 1996, they elected to carry on playing music and renamed themselves Arnold. Recording an eight-track demo in a Kent barn, their tuneful but melancholic songs attracted the ear of McGee, who signed the band and insisted the demo tapes be released. *The Barn Tapes* was a mellow and largely acoustic mini-album, the outstanding tracks 'Face' and '2 Chairs' capturing the rootsy charm of the band, while not disguising the downbeat tone of Saxby's lyrics. Persevering with their determinedly low-key approach, the band returned to the barn in Kent to record further material for their forthcoming debut album, which was introduced by the edgy sound of their new single, 'Twist'. The band released another fine album, *Hillside*, the following year. They were dropped by Creation in summer 1999.

● ALBUMS: *The Barn Tapes* mini-album (Creation 1997)★★★, *Hillside* (Creation 1998)★★★★.

Arrested Development

This rap collective came from Atlanta, Georgia, USA, and were headed by Speech (b. Todd Thomas, 25 October 1968, Milwaukee, Wisconsin, USA; lead vocals). He originally met DJ Headliner (b. Timothy Barnwell, 26 July 1967, New Jersey, USA) while they were studying at the Art Institute Of Atlanta. Speech, then known as DJ Peech, had already formed Disciples Of Lyrical Rebellion, a proto-gangsta outfit that evolved into Secret Society. They soon switched musical tack to a more community-conscious act, changing the name to Arrested Development and gradually picking up new members. These included Aerle Taree (b. Taree Jones, 10 January 1973, Wisconsin, USA; vocals/clothes design), Montsho Eshe (b. Temelca Garther, 23 December 1974, Georgia, USA; dancer), and Rasa Don (b. Donald Jones, 22 November 1968, New Jersey, USA; drums). They developed an Afrocentric outlook, and all moved into the same house while maintaining their own daytime jobs. Afterwards, spiritualist Baba Oje (b. 15 May 1932, Laurie, Mississippi, USA), whom Speech had known as a child, was added as the group's symbolic head man. Influenced heavily by Sly And The Family Stone, when Arrested Development arrived on 1992's music scene they brought an intriguing blend of charisma and wisdom. While most modern rap uses urban dystopia as its platform, this group drew on a black country narrative as well as more universal themes. Speech penned a regular column for the *20th Century African* newspaper and took his views on race issues on lecture tours. Cited by many critics as the most significant breakthrough of 1992, singles 'Tennessee', 'People Everyday' and 'Mr. Wendal' confirmed their commercial status by enjoying lengthy stays in the US and (for the latter two) UK Top 10. Their debut album (titled after the length of time it took them to gain a record contract after formation) also embraced a number of issue-based narratives, in particular 'Mama's Always On The Stage', a feminist treatise, and 'Children Play With Earth', an exhortation for children to get back in touch with the natural world that surrounds them. After contributing 'Revolution' to the soundtrack of Spike Lee's *Malcolm X*, they released *Unplugged*, taken from their set at New York's Ed Sullivan Theatre in December 1992, featuring an expanded 17-person line-up. The same year also brought two Grammy awards for Best New Artist and Best Rap Duo Or Group. Speech's first production project, with fellow southern funk-rappers Gumbo, also met with critical approval. A second album, *Zingalamaduni*, Swahili for 'beehive of culture', emerged in 1994, once again extending their audience beyond the hip-hop cognoscenti. As well as introducing new vocalist Nadirah, plus DJ Kwesi Asuo and dancer Ajile, it saw the departure of Taree, who had gone back to college. The album was a commercial failure, and the members of the band went their separate ways at the end of 1995. Speech released a disappointing solo album in 1996.

● ALBUMS: *3 Years, 5 Months, And 2 Days In The Life Of ...* (Chrysalis 1992)★★★★, *Unplugged* (Chrysalis 1993)★★★, *Zingalamaduni* (Chrysalis 1994)★★★.

● COMPILATIONS: *The Best Of Arrested Development* (Chrysalis 1998)★★★.

Ash

A highly touted young guitar band from Downpatrick, County Down, Northern Ireland, who first began to make headway into the mainstream in 1994. Playing sprightly, youthful punk-pop, the members' average age was only 17 when they released their debut record. Rick 'Rock' McMurray (b. 11 July 1975, Larne, Co. Antrim, Northern Ireland; drums), Tim Wheeler (b. 4 January 1977, Downpatrick, Co. Down, Northern Ireland; vocals/guitar) and Mark Hamilton (b. 21 March 1977, England; bass) were still studying for their A-levels when that single, 'Jack Named The Planets', was released in a limited edition of 1,000 copies. Both radio and press were immediately wooed by their snappy, commercial sound. Their appeal easily translated to an American alternative climate, where every A&R executive was searching for a new Green Day, and tantalizing offers followed to sign with either Warner/Reprise Records (who eventually attained their signatures) or Interscope Records. The band elected to fly to Los Angeles and let their hosts squabble and indulge them beyond any expectations that a young UK indie band had a right to entertain. In the UK, they signed to Infectious Records, though they first had to negotiate a series of prolonged discussions between record label executives, parents and headmasters. Following a seven-song mini-album in late 1994, their topical fourth single, 'Kung Fu', featured a cover picture of Manchester United's Eric Cantona executing his famous 'kung fu' assault on a Crystal Palace fan. It was recorded in Wales with Oasis producer Owen Morris: 'We wanted to write a really crap Ramones song and it was meant to be the b-side but it turned out too good', they surmised. In its wake, 'Girl From Mars' became a major national hit, debuting at number 11 in the UK charts. It was followed by 'Angel Interceptor', a term lifted from the animated children's series *Captain Scarlet*, but which apparently referred to 'missing someone sexually.' Their long-playing debut proper came in 1996 during which they graced the UK Top 10 with the singles 'Goldfinger' and 'Oh Yeah'. Titled *1977*, many considered this to be a dedication to the punk scene that evidently remained their pivotal influence, yet in actuality, it referred to Wheeler and Hamilton's year of birth, the same

year that *Star Wars* was released and Elvis Presley died. It rose straight to number 1 in the UK charts. By that time, the band had opted for a more elaborate sound, inspired by recent listening to Phil Spector and the Beach Boys. However, other recognizable themes remained, such as science-fiction television, with another tribute to *Star Wars* on 'Darkside Lightside'. They added a new member in August 1997 when guitarist Charlotte Hatherley (b. Charlotte Franklin Hatherley, 20 June 1979) joined from Nightnurse, and returned to the UK Top 10 in October with the title song of the movie *A Life Less Ordinary*. Introduced by the frenetic single 'Jesus Says', 1998's *Nu-Clear Sounds* saw the band move towards a harder-edged alternative sound with considerable maturity.

● ALBUMS: *Trailer* mini-album (Infectious 1994)★★★, *1977* (Infectious 1996)★★★★, *Live At The Wireless* (Death Star 1997)★★★, *Nu-Clear Sounds* (Infectious 1998)★★★★.

● FURTHER READING: *Ash 1977-97*, Charles Porter.

Asian Dub Foundation

Asian Dub Foundation was formed in 1993 at the Community Music centre in Farringdon, London, England, which had been established by jazz drummer John Stevens. The inaugural sound system line-up featured two of the centre's teachers, Dr Das (b. Aniruddha Das; bass) and Pandit G (b. John Pandit; DJ/mixer), and one of their students, Master D (b. Deedar Zaman; vocals). Chandrasonic (b. Steve Chandra Savale; guitar), Bubble-E (dancer), and Sun-J (DJ/keyboards) had been added to the line-up by 1995. The band perform a combination of ragga, garage punk and traditional Indian ragas, which has proved especially popular on the festival circuit where they have built a huge following. They have performed twice at the Essential Roots day festivals, sharing the same stage as Bunny Wailer, Buju Banton, Augustus Pablo and Lee Perry. In 1995, following the previous year's *Conscious* EP, the band released *Facts & Fictions*, which clearly demonstrated the influence of Jamaican dub on their sound. They continued touring, proving especially popular in Europe where their follow-up, *R.A.F.I. (Real Areas For Investigation)*, was released in France. This album dealt with issues relating to the Indian diaspora, including miscarriages of justice and a chance to redress items of historical interest ignored by the historians. The band enjoyed media interest when Primal Scream acknowledged them as the best live act in England, and a major label contract with London Records soon followed. The band's credibility with the indie genre was further enhanced when they collaborated with Primal Scream on the protest single 'Free Saptal Ram'. A variety of television appearances followed to promote the single, 'Change'. Their second album was then remixed and re-released as *Rafi's Revenge*, paying lip service to the Pakistani-born Bollywood singer Mohamed Rafi.

● ALBUMS: *Facts & Fictions* (Nation 1995)★★★, *R.A.F.I.* (Virgin France 1997)★★★★, *Rafi's Revenge* (London/Slash 1998)★★★★.

Astral Projection

The roots of this pioneering Israeli trance outfit lie in the group SFX, formed in 1989 by Lior Perlmutter and Avi Nissim, who had already made a name for himself as an acid house DJ. After two years of recording and playing in Israel's underground clubs, they had their first release,

'Monster Mania', on the Belgian label Music Man Records. During the early 90s Perlmutter spent some time in the USA working as an engineer, and SFX consequently brought out four singles on X-Rave Records. Later, Yaniv Haviv, whom Perlmutter had known since childhood, and Guy Sabbag joined SFX back in Israel and in 1994 all four formed Trust In Trance Records. Their debut album, *Trust In Trance Vol. 1*, was released on that label through Phonokol Records later that year, after which Sabbag left to pursue his own interests. At this point Perlmutter, Nissim and Haviv opened their Dance City studio, where they began recording their second album as Astral Projection. *Trust In Trance Vol. 2* entered the Israeli album chart at number 2 and became popular with a number of European DJs; two tracks in particular, 'Mahadeva' (released as a single on Transient Records in 1996) and 'Power Gen', were favourites of Danny Rampling and Paul Oakenfold. Released in the UK through TIP Records, *Trust In Trance* was their most successful album yet and helped them to break into the European market. It was supported by the singles 'Enlightened Evolution' and 'People Can Fly' and by over 30 live shows throughout Israel and Europe. The following year the group switched to Transient Records for *The Astral Files*, which contained some new material as well as a number of remixes from the previous album. After its release, Haviv left to work on his own material. *Dancing Galaxies* presented a collection of new material in the same vein as before, but was perhaps the most focused and consistent of all their albums to date. Astral Projection are known as the original and best exponents of the Israeli style of psychedelic trance, which they have distilled to its finest point while others have moved on to a new approach. Rather than the sparsely arranged abstract noises employed by many of their contemporaries, the group's sound relies on layered riffs based around Eastern-sounding scales, thick synth pads and heavy reverbs, while the solid four-on-the-floor drum patterns reflect none of the tendencies towards more varied, funky breakbeats. Towards the end of the 90s, this style came under criticism from some areas as being formulaic and clumsy, as a large number of artists attempted to recreate the sound. However, few managed to match Astral Projection's economy, remarkably consistent production and logical, organic arrangements, which together created one of the most unique and identifiable sounds in their field. The duo reasserted their supremacy in the trance field with the release of 1999's *Another World*, which received a very enthusiastic reception from most areas of the dance music press.

● ALBUMS: *Trust In Trance Vol. 1* (Smart 1994), *Trust In Trance Vol. 2* (Smart 1995), *Trust In Trance* (TIP 1996)★★★, *The Astral Files* (Transient 1997)★★★, *Dancing Galaxies* (Transient 1997)★★★★, *Another World* (Transient 1999)★★★★.

Atari Teenage Riot

This caustic punk collective make music that rails against the rise of the fascist right in their native Germany, with lyrics such as 'Put a bullet straight through a Nazi's head.' From Berlin, frontman Alec Empire grew up with punk and was in bands from the age of 12, but when acid house music arrived in 1988, he became interested in club sounds instead. He began DJing in the late 80s and released solo politically minded techno tunes for the Force Inc label. Slightly bored with the pulpit life of the DJ, he joined Carl Crack (b. Switzerland) and Hanin Elias (b. Spain) so he could play live again. Together they signed to Phonogram Records as Atari Teenage Riot, but were dropped after two singles. Though heavily hyped, their records failed to sell in the anticipated quantities, despite an unlikely techno cover version of Sham 69's 'If The Kids Are United'. Nic Endo was added to the line-up in 1997 to bolster the band's ferocious sound. Empire founded the Digital Hardcore label to release extreme music from bands such as Shizuo, Ec8or and Christoph De Babalon. He has continued to release his own material as part of the Atari collective, and as a prolific solo artist under his own name or a multitude of pseudonyms (including The Jaguar, PJP, The Destroyer, Deathfunk, Safety Pin Sex).

● ALBUMS: *Delete Yourself* (DHR 1995)★★★, *The Future Of War* (DHR 1997)★★, *60 Second Wipe Out* (DHR 1999)★★★.

● COMPILATIONS: *Burn, Berlin, Burn!* (DHR 1997)★★.

ATB

b. Andreas Tanneberger, Freiberg, Germany. Recording under the abbreviation ATB, Tanneberger, who had worked as a remixer for acts such as the Outhere Brothers and Haddaway, came to fame in July 1999 when his melodic trance single '9pm (Till I Come)' became a UK number 1 hit. The single was distinctive for its infectious melody and its synthesized slide guitar sound. Its feel-good ambience and funky percussion and bassline made it a perfect candidate to become the summer's Ibiza anthem, and to cross over into the mainstream charts as Stardust's 'Music Sounds Better With You' had done in 1998. It had already received a great deal of radio airplay across continental Europe and had proved massively popular in the clubs. The track was featured on ATB's full-length debut and numerous club-based compilations, and spawned various inferior imitations. In the UK, the track was licensed from Germany's Kontor Records by Ministry Of Sound Recordings. He also mixed their 1999 compilation *Clubber's Guide To Trance* and played a live DJ set at the club itself.

● ALBUMS: *Movin' Melodies* (Sound Of Ministry/Radikal 1999)★★★.

● COMPILATIONS: *Clubber's Guide To Trance* (MOS 1999)★★★.

Atkins, Juan

b. 12 September 1962, Detroit, Michigan, USA. Atkins attended Belleville High School until 1980, where he met Derrick May and Kevin Saunderson, his future compatriots in the revolutionising of techno. He acquired his love of dance music listening to the various mix shows on the radio, and in particular those of the Detroit DJ The Electrifying Mojo. Inspired by the emergence of synthesizer technology, Atkins first came to prominence in the early 80s with Cybotron, an electro outfit he formed with Rick Davis. The duo achieved some success, most notably with the 1982 track 'Clear', which established the basic sound of what would later be termed techno. Branching out from Cybotron, Atkins concentrated on Deep Space Soundworks, a music collective he had formed with May and Saunderson in 1981. The three men also founded Detroit's Music Institute, which quickly became the focal point for the city's underground club movement. From 1985 Atkins started working solo as Model 500, releasing polished, minimalist, hi-tech gems such as 'No UFO's', 'The Chase' and 'Night Drive' on his own Metroplex label (home to the first releases by many of the

Detroit stars), which were pivotal in the development of techno (most of these were later reissued on Belgian label R&S Records' *Classics* compilation). Atkins' reputation took off in the late 80s, when the new Detroit dance movement reached the shores of Europe, and was frequently invited to remix tracks for artists as diverse as Inner City, Coldcut, Fine Young Cannibals, Seal and the Style Council. During the exploitative early 90s Atkins remained justifiably aloof, with his own artistic output somewhat limited, although during this period he continued to work in conjunction with Mike Banks and Underground Resistance, helping to produce Underground Resistance's *Galaxy 2 Galaxy* and the Red Planet series of releases. In 1992, he reopened his Metroplex label, and when Model 500 signed to R&S, releases such as *Classics* and the brilliant EP *Sonic Sunset* received the attention they deserved. With the album *Deep Space*, Atkins treated a new generation of dance enthusiasts to his typically highly crafted compositions. More recently, a second compilation of his earlier, Metroplex-based work under the name Infiniti was released by Tresor Records. Although at times sounding formulaic, the compilation does include 'Game One' (produced with Orlando Voorn), one of Atkins' most memorable records, capturing his classically minimal yet warm style. In a prolific period between 1998 and 1999, Atkins recorded new Infiniti and Model 500 albums.

● ALBUMS: as Model 500 *Deep Space* (R&S 1995)★★★, as Infiniti *Skynet* (Tresor 1998)★★★, as Model 500 *Mind And Body* (R&S 1999)★★★.

● COMPILATIONS: as Model 500 *Classics* (R&S 1993)★★★★, as Infiniti *The Infiniti Collection* (Tresor 1996)★★★, *Wax Trax! MasterMix: Volume 1* (TVT 1998)★★★★.

Audioweb

Formed in Manchester, England, in 1991, originally as the Sugar Merchants, Audioweb are led by fast-talking but honey-voiced singer Martin 'Sugar' Merchant, previously a prominent member of the Saxon sound system reggae entourage and a collaborator with Maxi Priest. The rest of the band comprises guitarist Robin File and bass player Sean McCann, both originally from Dover, Kent, and drummer Maxi. The band's sound, a mix of hip-hop and hard step reggae rhythms with searing post-punk guitar, was one of the more interesting prototypes developed during the mid-90s. In particular, Merchant's versatility as a vocalist, alternating between ragga chatting and an affecting falsetto, gave the band a unique musical stamp. Despite this, an appetite for more traditional and conservative fare post-Oasis reduced their potential impact. A series of support slots to bands as diverse as Garbage, Cast, Northern Uproar and Mansun acquainted them with a larger concert following and improved their visibility. Their biggest breakthrough came in 1997 with a cover version of the Clash's 'Bankrobber', which reached the UK Top 20. By this time they had released a series of singles - 'Into My World', 'Sleeper' and 'Yeah' - that highlighted their varied stylistic reference points. They also cemented the impression that their experimental, confrontational style gave them an edge over their more orthodox indie-rock peers. They returned to the UK Top 30 in 1998 with the impressive 'Policeman Skank (The Story Of My Life)'.

● ALBUMS: *Audioweb* (Mother 1996)★★★, *Fireworks City* (Mother 1998)★★★.

Autechre

Sean Booth (b. Rochdale, Yorkshire, England) and Rob Brown (b. Torquay, Devon, England) are one of the UK's most dedicated techno acts, remaining at the cutting edge of the genre throughout the 90s with a series of innovative releases that have eschewed the more commercial aspects of dance music. Having first started mixing tapes at school, the duo's early demos of tracks such as 'Crystel' and 'The Egg' brought them to the attention of Warp Records, who included them on a compilation set. Their 1993 debut album was one of the most effective releases on Warp's 'Artificial Intelligence' series. Reflecting their stated disapproval of structured music, the duo have continued to champion a free-form style that echoes the experimental edge of modern jazz, arguably reaching a creative peak with 1995's *Tri Repetae*. They also record material as part of the mysterious Gescom, and run their own Skam label.

● ALBUMS: *Incunabula* (Warp/Wax Trax! 1993)★★★★, *Amber* (Warp/Wax Trax! 1994)★★★, *Tri Repetae* (Warp/Wax Trax! 1995)★★★★, *Chiastic Slide* (Warp 1997)★★★, *LP5* (Warp/Nothing 1998)★★★★, *Peel Session* (Warp/Nothing 1999)★★★.

Auteurs

Truculent UK indie stars the Auteurs are spearheaded by the imposing figure of Luke Haines (b. 7 October 1967, Walton-On-Thames, Surrey, England; vocals/guitar), alongside Glenn Collins (b. 7 February 1968, Cheltenham, Gloucestershire, England; drums) and Haines' girlfriend, Alice Readman (b. 1967, Harrow, Middlesex, England; bass). Both Haines and Readman had previously performed in 'shambling' band the Servants between 1987 and 1991, while Collins had worked with Dog Unit and Vort Pylon (they were joined by cellist James Banbury in 1993). Together they took their new name from the film term (which initially appeared in the *Cahiers Du Cinema* journal and generally denotes director, or more literally, 'author'). Their debut public appearance came at the Euston Rails Club in London in April 1992, and it was December of that year before their first vinyl emerged ('Showgirl'). This instantly saw them transported to the head of the post-Smiths bed-sit/student throne, with Haines' impressive use of language (instructed by film, music and theatre) the focal point. Irrespective of the fact that they were tempestuously dispensed with as support to The The in 1993, their live performances were erratic, and sometimes awful. At least their debut album (recorded on a budget of £10,000 as an unsigned band) saw Haines confirm their arrival with a strong body of songs. Although it failed to ignite commercially, the critical reception was lavish, and the band missed out on the 1993 Mercury Prize by just one vote. *Now I'm A Cowboy* continued the pattern of press eulogy and public indecisiveness, on a set soaked with Haines' class obsessions ('The Upper Classes', etc.), though negotiations to enlist the services of Vanessa Paradis to duet on 'New French Girlfriend' broke down. The promotional touring arrangements were also inconvenienced by Haines having to spend much of the end of 1994 recuperating after a fall in Spain that broke both his ankles. *After Murder Park* was produced by Steve Albini, whose previous credits include Nirvana's *In Utero* and the Pixies' *Surfer Rosa*. Haines then put the Auteurs on hold and released an uneven album as Baader-Meinhof. He later formed Black Box Recorder with singer Sarah Nixey and guitarist John Moore (ex-Jesus And Mary Chain), before re-forming the Auteurs for *How I Learned To Love The Bootboys*.

● ALBUMS: *New Wave* (Hut 1993)★★★★, *Now I'm A Cowboy* (Hut 1994)★★★, *After Murder Park* (Hut 1996)★★★, as Baader-Meinhof *Baader-Meinhof* (Hut 1996)★★, *How I Learned To Love The Bootboys* (Hut 1999)★★★.

AZ

b. Anthony Cruz, Brooklyn, New York, USA. Rapper AZ made his debut on Nas' debut, *Illmatic*, guesting on the track 'Life's A Bitch'. Raised in the same Queensbridge housing project that spawned Mobb Deep, Mic Geronimo and Nas, he instantly made headway in the *Billboard* R&B, rap and pop charts in 1995 with 'Sugar Hill'. The single referred to the suburban district so beloved of the black middle-class which had given its name to rap's first proper record label. Like Nas before him, AZ's concerns were firmly rooted in the ghetto life and his attempts to break free from it ('No more cuttin' grams or wrapping grands up in rubber bands'). It prefaced *Doe Or Die*, released in October, which confirmed AZ as one of the 90s most gifted new rappers. In 1997, he collaborated with Foxy Brown, Nas and Dr. Dre as part of the hugely suc-cessful rap 'supergroup', the Firm. *Pieces Of A Man*, taking its title from Gil Scott-Heron's classic early 70s album, was a strong sophomore effort with funky production from Dr. Dre and Trackmasterz adding commercial appeal to excellent tracks such as the single 'What's The Deal'.

● ALBUMS: *Doe Or Die* (EMI 1995)★★★★, *Pieces Of A Man* (Noo Trybe/Virgin 1998)★★★★.

B*Witched

Irish quartet comprising Sinead O'Carroll (b. 14 May 1978, Dublin, Eire), Lindsay Armaou (b. 18 December 1980, Athens, Greece), Edele (b. 15 December 1979, Dublin, Eire) and Keavy Lynch (b. 15 December 1979, Dublin, Eire), the twin sisters of Shane Lynch from Boyzone. B*Witched burst onto the UK music scene in 1998, hijacking a portion of the market previously owned by the Spice Girls with a skilfully marketed brand of youthful and vibrant pop music. Dance student O'Carroll first met Keavy Lynch in the garage where the latter was working as a trainee car mechanic. With the addition of Armaou, who Keavy met at a kick boxing class, and Edele Lynch they formed B*Witched. The quartet met up in O'Carroll's Dublin flat to write songs and record low budget demos, before signing up with producer Ray Hedges' Glow Worm label. Hedges' previous credits included Boyzone, Bros and Ant And Dec, and his experience helped attract the attention of Epic Records, who snapped up both the group and the label. Epic eagerly promoted the group's exuberant blend of pop, hip-hop and traditional Irish music. Their debut single, 'C'est La Vie', was an immediate success, entering the UK singles chart at number 1 in June 1998. The follow-ups, 'Rollercoaster' (September) and 'To You I Belong' (December) also topped the UK singles chart, the latter dethroning Cher's 'Believe' after its seven week tenure at the top. Their debut album, co-written with Hedges, entered the UK album chart at number 3 in November and notched up double-platinum status. They cemented their position in the record books in March 1999, when 'Blame It On The Weatherman' became their fourth successive UK number 1, making them the first act in UK chart history to go straight in at number 1 with their first four singles. At the same time, 'C'est La Vie' climbed to number 9 in America and their album entered the *Billboard* Top 20. Their phenomenal chart run in the UK was ended when 'Jesse Hold On', debuted at number 4 in October. The attendant *Awake And Breathe* received a lukewarm critical and commercial response.

● ALBUMS: *B*Witched* (Epic 1998)★★★★, *Awake And Breathe* (Epic 1999)★★★.

B., Anthony

b. Anthony Keith Blair, Trelawny, Jamaica, West Indies. Anthony B. shot to fame in 1996 when his hugely contro-versial single, 'Fire Pon Rome', became one of the biggest hits of the year, in spite of the presence of a blanket radio ban. When he followed its success with further hits, 'Raid Di Barn' and 'Hurt The Heart', it was clear that a major new dancehall star had been born. The artist, who wisely decided against issuing his records under the name 'Tony Blair', had grown up in rural Jamaica, weeding cane-fields as part of a poor family. There he memorized songs from the radio, his greatest influences being Peter Tosh and Bob Marley. A large number of critics, in fact, suggested comparisons with Tosh when Anthony B. broke through in the 90s. He moved to Kingston in his teens at the height of dancehall reggae's pop-ularity, but while appreciating the musical vitality of the scene, he was disappointed by the 'slack' lyrics and lack of 'positivity'. His efforts to launch a solo career temporarily thwarted, he eventually returned to his village. However, his perseverance was rewarded when he came to the attention of producer/writer Richard 'Bello' Bell, owner of the Startrail studio complex and label founded in 1989 in Miami. The label had moved to Kingston in the early 90s after enjoying commercial success with Beres Hammond and Cutty Ranks, and Anthony B. became their second major project there, following the breakthrough of Everton Blender. He later recorded a successful single, 'I'm Gonna Tell You', with the Mystic Revealers, and released the powerful 'Nah Vote Again' at the height of the country's national elections. The excellent *Seven Seals* delivered some fine conscious reggae cuts, including 'Conscious Entertainer' and 'Mr. Heartless'.

● ALBUMS: *So Many Things ...* (Greensleeves 1996)★★★, *Real Revolutionary* (VP 1996)★★★★, *Universal Struggle* (Charm 1998)★★★★, with Sizzla *2 Strong* (Star Trail 1999)★★★★, *Seven Seals* (VP 1999)★★★★.

B., Howie

b. Howard Bernstein. Glasgow, Scotland-based producer Howie B. shot to fame in 1994 as one of the most favoured exponents of trip-hop, even although he himself remained suspicious of the term. Renowned for his productions of the scene's leading artists, Tricky and the Mo' Wax Records roster, he had previously worked with acts as diverse as Soul II Soul, Massive Attack, Goldie and Siouxsie And The Banshees. In 1994, he founded Pussyfoot Records and was engaged in a number of projects, including the *One Hell Of A Storm* set, which saw poets and musicians such as Lemn Sissay, Malika B and Haji-Mike join together for a dubbed-up funk session. Bernstein's impressive contribution was a collaboration with the poet Patience Agbabi on 'There's Gonna Be One Hell Of A Storm'. He then joined Mat Ducasse for 1994's *No 1.*, credited to Skylab. This exhibited the influence of spaghetti westerns and classical and ambient music, and in interviews, Howie B. readily admitted the influence of David Byrne and Brian Eno's *My Life In The Bush Of Ghosts* on the album. After this he worked simultaneously on several projects, including work with the Stereo MC's singer Cath Coffey and Japan's Major Force West, and also on Björk's *Post*. In 1995, he worked on U2's *Passengers* project, produced remixes for Annie Lennox, Simply Red and New Order and added samples to U2's *Pop*. His success as a remixer led to a multi-album deal with Polydor Records, although this output has not always reflected his talents. 'Take Your Partner By The Hand', a track from *Turn The Dark Off* featuring ex-Band singer Robbie Robertson, was a big club in 1997.

● ALBUMS: *Music For Babies* (Polydor 1996)★★★, *Turn The Dark Off* (Polydor 1997)★★★★, *Snatch* (Polydor 1999)★★★.

B.G.

This New Orleans, Louisiana, USA-based rapper's prodigious output saw him rack up four albums for the city's Cash Money Records label before he turned 18 years old. The B.G. (aka Baby Gangsta) signed to Cash Money at the age of 11, having been inspired to start rapping by the unsolved murder of his father on the streets of New Orleans. He enjoyed strong word of mouth sales in his local area, as like many southern rappers his records were denied widespread exposure on mainstream radio. His albums, beginning with the autobiographical *True Story*, documented the gangsta/playa lifestyle favoured by New Orleans' rappers, allied to smooth G-funk backing tracks which echoed the sound of the city's other leading rap label, No Limit Records. The prolific rapper also appeared alongside labelmates Juvenile, Lil Wayne and Young Turk as a member of the Hot Boy$, who debuted with 1997's *Get It How U Live!!* Cash Money's lucrative distribution deal with Universal Records in 1998 brought the label's artists to a wider audience for the first time. As a result, B.G.'s new release, *Chopper City In The Ghetto*, crossed over into the US Top 10 in May. The sophomore Hot Boy$ collection, *Guerrilla Warfare*, reached number 5 later in the year.

● ALBUMS: *True Story* (Cash Money 1993)★★★, *It's All On U, Vol. 1* (Cash Money 1996)★★★, *It's All On U, Vol. 2* (Cash Money 1997)★★, *Chopper City* (Cash Money 1997)★★★, *Chopper City In The Ghetto* (Cash Money/Universal 1999)★★★.

b.l.o.w.

Something of a mid-90s supergroup, hard rock outfit b.l.o.w. was formed in 1994 by Dave Gooding (vocals, ex-No Sweat), brothers Bruce (b. 10 May 1968, Berwick-upon-Tweed, Scotland; guitar) and Jimmy Dickinson (keyboards, both ex-Little Angels), Mark Richardson (drums) and final recruit, Nick Boyes (bass). Based in Surrey, England, their first demo exceeded expectations, even given their pedigree, and included a more psychedelic/pop-influenced approach than might have been anticipated. A cover version of Peter Tosh's 'Legalise It' typified their eclectic and much-admired live set throughout 1994. This style was partly a conscious decision on behalf of the former Little Angels members, who wanted a more fluid environment for their songwriting and performances. In the summer of 1995, Mark Richardson departed to assume the vacant drummer's position in Skunk Anansie, after he was recruited during a drunken exchange at that year's *Kerrang!* magazine awards ceremony.

● ALBUMS: *Man And Goat Alike* mini-album (Cottage Industries 1995)★★★, *Pigs* (Cottage Industries 1996)★★★.

Babes In Toyland

This hardcore rock trio spearheaded a new wave of US female bands at the turn of the 90s. Their origins can be traced back to 1987, when Kat Bjelland (b. Katherine Bjelland, 9 December 1963, Woodburn, Oregon, USA; vocals/guitar) moved to Minneapolis. Previously, she had played in a band, Sugar Baby Doll, with Courtney Love (Hole) and Jennifer Finch (L7) in San Francisco. The trio was completed by Michelle Leon (bass) and Lori Barbero (b. 27 November 1961, Minneapolis, Minnesota, USA; drums/vocals). They first came to prominence at the legendary singles club at Sub Pop Records, then made a lasting impression on a European support tour with Sonic Youth. A debut album, produced by Jack Endino, was recorded live with the vocals overdubbed. Soon afterwards, WEA Records A&R representative Tim Carr saw the band live in Minneapolis and was impressed. After signing to the label, they recorded the 1992 mini-album *To Mother*. Bjelland, meanwhile, was busy defending the band within the media, who were attempting to categorize them alongside other all-girl bands to create a convenient 'movement': 'Men and women play their instruments to a completely different beat. Women are a lot more rhythmic - naturally - than men. It doesn't even have anything to do with music, it all has to do with timing.' In 1992, Leon left and was replaced by Maureen Herman (b. 25 July 1966, Chicago, Illinois, USA). *Fontanelle* received excellent reviews throughout the rock and indie press, and a support tour with Faith No More brought them further plaudits, as they signed with their first manager, Debbie Gordon. However, when the band took a break in 1993, press speculation suggested their imminent demise. Lori Barbero formed her own label, Spanish Fly, home of Milk, while Bjelland worked with her husband Stuart Gray, singer with Australian noise outfit Lubricated Goat, on two projects, Crunt and KatSu. Babes In Toyland reconvened in time for the Lollapalooza tour and in 1995 *Nemesisters* was a powerful return to form, with memorable cover versions of Sister Sledge's 'We Are Family' and Eric Carmen's 'All By Myself' sitting well alongside strong original compositions such as 'Memory' and 'Scherezadian 22'. Herman was replaced by Dana Cochrane in late 1996. Her former bandmates have subsequently concentrated on other projects, with Babes On Toyland put on extended hiatus.

● ALBUMS: *Spanking Machine* (Twin Tone 1990)★★, *To Mother* mini-album (Reprise/WEA 1991)★★, *The Peel Sessions* (Strange Fruit 1992)★★★, *Fontanelle* (Reprise/WEA 1992)★★★★, *Painkillers* (Reprise/WEA 1993)★★★, *Nemesisters* (Reprise/WEA 1995)★★★★.

● FURTHER READING: *Babes In Toyland: The Making And Selling Of A Rock And Roll Band*, Neal Karlen.

Baby D

After playing with a variety of bands and working as session musicians, Baby D were formed in 1990 in north-west London, England. Featuring Baby D (vocals), MC Nino (keyboards/vocals), Claudio Galdez (keyboards/vocals) and Dice (writer/producer), they released their first single, 'Daydreaming', in January 1991. Though it failed to reach the national charts, it rose to number 27 in the dance music charts. Their first major success came in December 1993 when 'Destiny' reached number 69 in the UK charts. 'Casanova', released in July 1994, was a similar minor success, but their fortunes changed substantially with the release of 'Let Me Be Your Fantasy' in November 1994. This rose to number 1 in the UK charts, and sold just short of half a million copies. It had originally topped dance charts two years prior to its mainstream breakthrough. The follow-up single was a retitled cover version of the Korgis' 'Everybody's Gotta Learn Sometime'. By this time, original member Dice had left the band, though he still helped out in a production capacity. Before the release of '(Everybody's Got To Learn Sometime) I Need Your Loving', it emerged that another band, NRG, intended to record it, leading to a struggle for the publishing rights. Baby D's version eventually climbed to number 3 in the UK charts in June 1995. 'So Pure' reached the same position in January 1996, and was followed by their debut album.

● ALBUMS: *Deliverance* (Systematic 1996)★★★.

Baby Doc

b. London, England. One of the UK and Europe's leading hard house DJ/artist/producers, Baby Doc has established a reputation for delivering outstanding live shows as far afield as Europe, Australia and South Africa. Baby Doc also records as Hellfire Club, releasing several tracks on React Music. He also has his own label, Shine Records, set up with his long-term recording partner SJ. He first began releasing tracks on the labels Prolekult and Dream Inn before his debut, *In Worship Of False Idols* (TEC), which featured the vocals of SJ – who has also released such club classics as 'Fever' and 'I Feel Divine' on React. Positiva Records signed Baby Doc and released 'La Batteria', a huge club hit. He has worked with respected names in the dance music field such as Carl Cox, and has remixed the work of artists including Iggy Pop, Pet Shop Boys, Cher and Marc Almond. His remix of the Age Of Love's trance classic 'Age Of Love' was extremely popular with clubbers and critics alike, as were his mixes of Hardfloor's acid classic 'Hardtrance Acperience' and NRG's 'Never Lost His Hardcore'. In 1998, Baby Doc (along with SJ) toured Israel, Australia, Spain and South Africa as part of the 'Quadrophoria Experience' with Judge Jules, Sash!, Sonique and Rob Playford. Baby Doc has twice appeared at the huge Dance Valley festival in Amsterdam, Netherlands, playing the main stage in 1999. A live recording, *Live From Dance Valley 99*, was released in September 1999. *Never A DJ*, a mixed compilation of his own work, was based on his sets in Australia. Baby Doc has his own studio, Hellfire Studios Ltd, where he has collaborated with Trade resident DJs, Pete Wardman and Fat Tony.

● COMPILATIONS: *Never A DJ - Live In Australia* (React Music 1999)★★★★.

babybird

b. Stephen Jones, 16 September 1962, Sheffield, England. Like Alice Cooper, *baby*bird has been both man and band (but without the dismembered corpses). In the first incarnation, Stephen Jones recorded over 400 songs as four-track demos, going on to release several dozen of them across four self-released albums, between July 1995 and August 1996. The albums quickly acquired a cult following, as well as critical acclaim, with comparisons ranging from Leonard Cohen to fellow Sheffielder Jarvis Cocker of Pulp, taking in Scott Walker and even surreal UK comic Eddie Izzard en route. The simple, almost childlike instrumentation of the albums was complemented by Jones' wayward, cracked vocals and deliriously sordid lyrics. In 1996, Jones signed to Chrysalis Records' offshoot label Echo and assembled a real live band for the first time, comprising Huw Chadbourne (b. 7 December 1963; keyboards), Robert Gregory (b. 2 January 1967; drums), John Pedder (b. 29 May 1962; bass) and Luke Scott (b. 25 August 1969; guitar), with which line-up he recorded *Ugly Beautiful*, a major label debut received with mixed emotions by some critics who felt it lacked the lo-fi immediacy of the four-track albums, but lapped up by the public on the back of the single 'You're Gorgeous', which reached number 3 in the UK charts in October 1996. The latter was immediately seized upon by lazy television producers as a soundtrack for any footage of supermodels, completely missing the ironic gender-reversal lyrics ('You took me to a rented motor car/and filmed me on the bonnet'). *baby*bird also went out on tour, where Jones proved himself to be an able performer, especially when dealing with hecklers, but a raw singer, his voice seizing up on several occasions. Despite these glitches, Jones managed the transition from self-appointed 'young man in the bedroom with beautiful ideas for the future' to Top 10 icon with great aplomb, sticking out like a sore larynx in the mid-90s pop landscape. The commercial failure of May 1998's wilfully difficult 'Bad Old Man' (UK number 31), taken from his second major label album *There's Something Going On*, indicated that Jones' dalliance with the charts may have been a brief one.

● ALBUMS: *I Was Born A Man* (Baby Bird 1995)★★★, *Bad Shave* (Baby Bird 1995)★★, *Fatherhood* (Baby Bird 1995)★★★, *The Happiest Man Alive* (Baby Bird 1996)★★★, *Ugly Beautiful* (Echo 1996)★★★, *Dying Happy* (Baby Bird 1997)★★, *There's Something Going On* (Echo 1998)★★★.

● COMPILATIONS: *Greatest Hits* US only (Baby Bird 1997)★★★.

Babyface

b. Kenneth Edmonds, 10 April 1959, Indianapolis, Indiana, USA. Babyface's achievements as a songwriter and producer throughout the late 80s and 90s, especially with L.A. Reid, sometimes overshadowed his own efforts as a performer, which go back to the mid-70s with the funk outfit Manchild. His early solo efforts showed a sophisticated, adult-orientated strain of urban soul, going against the current grain of rap-influenced explicitness and raunchy swingbeat; wisely, perhaps, as his light, pleasant voice could not really compare to earthier singers such as R. Kelly. It was not until 1995, when the single 'When Can I See You' won a Grammy, that he could claim the commercial success that had been heaped on his own protégés such as Boyz II Men (Edmonds wrote and produced the massive US chart-topper, 'End Of The Road'), Bobby Brown and Toni Braxton. In fact, since the split with Reid, Babyface's main success has been as a producer and writer of movie soundtracks, with *The Bodyguard* and *Waiting To Exhale* both going multi-platinum. Expectations were high for his 1996 solo album, which should have sealed his claim to be taken seriously as a contemporary soul performer. Unfortunately, *The Day* turned out to be something of a back-slappers' showcase; guest spots by the likes of Stevie Wonder, Eric Clapton, LL Cool J, Mariah Carey and even Shalamar could not obscure the fact that the songs Babyface kept for himself were simply not as strong as those he provided for other members of the R&B royalty.

● ALBUMS: *Lovers* (Solar 1987)★★, *Tender Lover* (Solar 1989)★★, *A Closer Look* (Solar 1991)★★, *For The Cool In You* (Epic 1993)★★★, *The Day* (Epic 1996)★★, *MTV Unplugged NYC 1997* (Epic 1997)★★, *Christmas With Babyface* (Epic 1998)★★★.

Babylon Zoo

Formed in Wolverhampton, West Midlands, England, the 90s pop band Babylon Zoo are the creation of their singer, writer and producer, Jas Mann (b. Jaswinder Mann, 24 April 1971, Dudley, West Midlands, England). A precocious young man, he decided to concentrate on music after being expelled from art school and failing trials for Warwickshire County Cricket Club. His first band, the Sandkings, enjoyed minor success in UK indie circles in the early 90s and supported the Stone Roses and Happy Mondays on tour, but the other members did not share his 'vision'. His new creation, Babylon Zoo, was signed to Phonogram Records after Clive Black heard their first three-track demo tape in May 1993. When Black moved to Warner Brothers Records in 1993, he took Mann's contract with him. An album had been prepared and sleeves for a single, 'Fire Guided Light', were printed, but Babylon Zoo's debut was put on hold again when Black moved once more to EMI Records in 1995. However, promotional copies of 'Spaceman' had already been distributed, and it was chosen to tie in with a new Levis jean advertisement. The advertisement concentrated on the speeded-up vocal section at the beginning and end of the song (actually the product of the Arthur Baker remix). When released as a single on 15 January 1996, after the band had been signed to a seven-album contract with EMI, it entered the UK chart at number 1 - becoming the fastest-selling debut record in UK chart history. Appearances on UK television's *Top Of The Pops* featured several backing musicians, but these were seen as a mere sideshow compared to their leader. The original musicians who worked with him had been sacked for 'their aggressiveness towards females'. *The Boy With The X-Ray Eyes* was produced at Mann's New Atlantis Productions music/artwork/video centre and included new-age tracts such as the self-explanatory 'Is Your Soul For Sale?' and 'I'm Cracking Up I Need A Pill'. Towards the end of 1996, 'Spaceman' was approaching UK sales of 1 million and was the biggest-selling single of the year. The

comparative failure of the album and follow-up singles did, however, pose questions about their future survival. Mann's full-on adoption of glam rock on the follow-up *King Kong Groover*, appeared too late to cash in on the attendant furore surrounding Todd Haynes' genre tribute, *Velvet Goldmine*. Irony or no irony, 'All The Money's Gone' stalled at UK number 46 in February 1999.

● ALBUMS: *The Boy With The X-Ray Eyes* (EMI 1996)★★, *King Kong Groover* (EMI 1998)★★★.

Back To The Planet

This sprawling collective became a fixture on the UK festival circuit in the early 90s thanks to their potent blend of dance music, ska and punk traditions. Based in Camberwell, London, members include Fil 'the Girl' Walters (b. 31 January 1970, Dartford, Kent, England; vocals), Carl Hendrickse (b. 28 January 1970, London, England; bass), Fraggle (b. David Fletcher, 5 August 1968, Kent, England; guitars), Henry Nicholas Cullen (b. 10 October 1969, Lewisham, London, England; drums) and Guy McAfter (b. 27 May 1969; keyboards). Together they create an enchanting cocktail of simple but effective goodtime music whose lyrics are often overtly political. Their recordings were originally only available on cassette, notably 1991's album-length *Warning The Public* which sold 5,000 copies at gigs alone. The band also built up a loyal live following through their appearances at various festivals, including the notorious Castlemorton rave. Their first vinyl release was the 12-inch 'The Revolution Of Thought', though 1993 singles 'Teenage Turtles' (a *New Musical Express* Single Of The Week) and 'Please Don't Fight' looked most likely to see them accepted by a hesitant media. Signed to London Records subsidiary Parallel, after a minor bidding war among the majors, they began the new year headlining the *New Musical Express*' On Into 93 showcase gig and gracing the cover of that magazine. However, the liaison with a major record label did not work out, and after just a year the band were again recording independently on their own Arthur Mix label. The mail-order *A Potted History* collected their previous cassette only releases. Predictably, by the arrival of *Messages After The Bleep*, the mainstream music media had moved on.

● ALBUMS: *Mind And Soul Collaborators* (Parallel 1993)★★★, *Messages After The Bleep* (Arthur Mix 1995)★★★.

● COMPILATIONS: *A Potted History* (Arthur Mix 1995)★★.

Backstreet Boys

Formed in Orlando, Florida, USA, in the mid-90s, white vocal quintet the Backstreet Boys comprises Kevin Scott Richardson (b. 3 October 1972, Lexington, Kentucky, USA), Nicholas Gene Carter (b. 28 January 1980, Jamestown, New York, USA), Brian 'B-rok' Littrell (b. Brian Thomas Littrell, 20 February 1975, Lexington, Kentucky, USA), A.J. McLean (b. Alexander James McLean, 9 January 1978, West Palm Beach, Florida, USA) and Howie D. (b. Howard Dwaine Dorough, 22 August 1973, Orlando, Florida, USA). Managed by former New Kids On The Block tour manager Johnny Wright and his wife Donna, they began their careers by making a breakthrough in Europe rather than their domestic market. Their success began in 1995 when the single 'We've Got It Goin' On' became a substantial hit in Germany, and eventually charted in the rest of mainland Europe. The band's first UK success came in June 1996, when 'Get Down (You're The One For Me)' reached number 14. Reissues of their earlier singles broke them into the UK Top 10 for the first time, with 'We've Got It Goin' On' reaching number 3 in August, and 'I'll Never Break Your Heart' climbing to number 8 in November (the previous year they had stalled at number 54 and 42 respectively). Their self-titled debut album repeated this success, although it was only made available in Europe, as was the 1997 follow-up, *Backstreet's Back*. The latter featured a cover version of P.M. Dawn's 'Set Adrift On Memory Bliss', but was otherwise another suite of teenage-orientated love songs and ballads. 'Everybody (Backstreet's Back)' became another huge hit, and was instrumental in breaking the group in the US when it reached number 4 in June 1998. Further huge hits followed with 'Quit Playing Games (With My Heart)' and 'As Long As You Love Me'. Their self-titled US debut, compiling tracks from the European albums, went on to become the third best-selling record of 1998 in that country. They topped the UK singles chart in May 1999 with a new single, 'I Want It That Way', which also proved an enduringly popular US Top 10 radio hit. *Millennium* was a predictable success, topping the US album charts at the start of June 1999 and selling two million copies in just over three weeks.

● ALBUMS: *Backstreet Boys* (Jive 1995)★★★, *Backstreet's Back* (Jive 1997)★★★, *Millennium* (Jive 1999)★★★.
● VIDEOS: *Live In Concert* (MVD Video 1998), *All Access Video* (Jive Video 1998), *Night Out With The Backstreet Boys* (Jive Video 1998), *Homecoming: Live In Orlando* (Jive Video 1999).

Backyard Babies

These Swedish sleaze rockers finally began to reap international success in the late 90s. The band, formed by four high school friends, came together in Nässjö, Sweden in 1987. Nicke Borg, Dregen (guitar), Peder Carlsson (drums) and Johan Blomquist (bass) were briefly joined by singer Tobbe, before Borg was switched from bass to handle vocals. The band recorded several demo tapes and toured extensively throughout Sweden, before releasing a self-financed 12-inch single, 'Something To Swallow', in 1991. They continued to tour before signing a deal with Megarock Records two years later. Premiered by the single 'Electric Suzy', their debut album, *Diesel And Power* garnered the band praise for their energetic update of the sleazy glam rock sound of fellow Scandinavians Hanoi Rocks. Following the release of the album the band remained quiet for an 18-month period, with Dregen forming the Hellacopters with Nicke Andersson of Entombed. In 1997, with Dregen back on board, the Backyard Babies returned to the international live circuit, supporting US hardcore outfit Social Distortion. They then signed a deal with MVG Records and set about recording their sophomore album. *Total 13* appeared in January 1998, and gained the band further plaudits from critics won over by their aura of rock 'n' roll decadence. The limited edition single '(Is It) Still Alright To Smile?' featured ex-Wildhearts singer Ginger on the b-side, a cover version of Faster Pussycat's 'Babylon'.

● ALBUMS: *Diesel And Power* (Megarock 1994)★★★, *Total 13* (MVG 1998)★★★★, *Safety Pin & Leopard Skin* (Coalition 1998)★★★.

Bad Livers

A startling bluegrass trio from Austin, Texas, USA, the Bad Livers' career has done much to deflate criticisms about that particular musical strand being obsolete. Mark Rubin (double bass/tuba), Danny Barnes (banjo/guitar) and Ralph White III (fiddle/accordion) boasted influences spanning Cajun, heavy metal, punk and gospel. Rubin and Barnes started out in the Dallas bluegrass band Killbilly. After recruiting White, they became first the Danny Barnes Trio, then Bad Livers. Early performances at the Saxon club in Austin brought Paul Leary of the Butthole Surfers in the audience. Liking what he heard, Leary insisted on producing the trio's 1992 debut, and also secured them a recording contract with his label, Touch & Go Records (via the subsidiary outlet Quarterstick). This kinetic collection of songs included a cover version of a Butthole Surfers track, as well as Reno And Smiley's 'I Know You're Married'. They then travelled to the UK for a month's tour, confounding audiences and contributing to an album by the Rockingbirds. *The Golden Years* EP featured cover versions of Motörhead and Johnny Cash songs, although the trio were keen to point out that they saw both as legitimate musical reference points, and maintained that they had not been included for novelty value. *Horses In The Mines*, a humorous and bizarre collection of songs featuring a guest appearance by bluesman Steve James, was mastered at the Beatles' Abbey Road Studios. Rubin then spent several months collaborating with Santiago Jiminez Jnr., before work began on a third Bad Livers album, *Hogs On The Highway*. However, its release was delayed because of a move to a new label, Sugar Hill Records. Although Ralph White III contributed to the record, he had left by the time of its release because of the band's demanding touring schedule. His replacement was Bob Grant (mandolin/guitar). The follow-up, *Industry And Thrift*, saw the band honing their zany brand of bluegrass to near perfection.

● ALBUMS: *Delusions Of Banjer* (Quarterstick 1992)★★★, *Horses In The Mines* (Quarterstick 1994)★★★, *Hogs On The Highway* (Sugar Hill 1997)★★★, *Industry And Thrift* (Sugar Hill 1998)★★★★.

Badly Drawn Boy

b. Damon Gough, Manchester, England. Gough established a cult following on the strength of two EPs, *EP1* and *EP2* on his own label, Twisted Nerve. He runs the label with Andy Votel, a recording artist on the Manchester-based Grand Central label. The releases provoked something of an A&R bidding war before Gough signed to XL Records for a reputedly six-figure sum. He had also contributed 'Nursery Rhyme' to U.N.K.L.E.'s 1998 release, *Psyence Fiction*. The track was considered by many to be one of the album's highlights. Badly Drawn Boy's sound has a sparse, lo-fi quality and the music features repetitive guitar melodies, strong percussion and Gough's ethereal vocals. His live shows are notoriously amateurish, Gough sometimes forgetting lyrics or playing material that he has not finished writing. The performances are considered brilliantly original by some and a sham by others. His fourth EP, *It Came From The Ground* was released in April 1999, accompanied by live performances in Liverpool and London. A further EP, *Once Around The Block*, was released in August.

Badmarsh

b. Yemen. This DJ and producer grew up in east London, England, and consequently absorbed a range of musical styles from various cultures as a child (his name is Urdu for scoundrel or trickster). While he was working for a reggae label that hired sound systems and PAs to clubs, he came into contact with dance music and began to DJ. With his brother, he ran a pirate radio station in Walthamstow called Ali FM and later played house at Labyrinth. It was a natural progression to begin making his own music, and as Easy Mo he released a number of house tracks on his own label, Pure Vibes. In the mid-90s he turned towards drum 'n' bass and signed to Outcaste Records, where he worked on various projects that reflected his multicultural background. After the promo 'I Am That Type Of Badmarsh', he contributed to Nitin Sawhney's second album, *Displacing The Priest* (1996), and as Badmarsh And Shri he worked with the multi-instrumentalist Shrikanth Sriram for 1998's *Dancing Drums*. Here the pair blended funky, busy breakbeats and dubby grooves with traditional Indian instruments and Shri's nimble bass guitar playing. Some tracks, such as the excellent reworkings of Shankar's 'Dancing Drums', employ Indian-sounding melodic ideas, while others, notably 'Gharana' and '130 Steps', focus more on rhythm and percussion. The album also contains an excellent version of the Dave Pyke Set's late 60s sitar-led track 'Mathar', while the title track was featured on Outcaste's *Untouchable Outcaste Beats* compilation in 1997. At the same time, Shri continued to work as a solo artist and released some material with Ubiquity Records and a second promo on Outcaste, 'I Am That Type Of Badmarsh II'. He has DJed and performed in various countries around the world, including the USA and France.

● ALBUMS: as Badmarsh And Shri *Dancing Drums* (Outcaste 1997)★★★★.

Bainbridge, Merril

b. Melbourne, Australia. Bainbridge, the subject of frequent comparisons to artists such as Tori Amos and Juliana Hatfield, became a singer-songwriter in her mid-teens. After teaching herself the piano she was discovered performing on the folk circuit by Koyoko Mashita of Sapphire Music. Mashita sent a three-track demo of her songs to BMG subsidiary Gotham Records, the label established by singer John Farnham and producer Ross Fraser. Bainbridge's debut, *The Garden*, was released in July 1995. Taken from it, 'Mouth' became the first self-penned debut record by an Australian woman to top the Australian sales chart. 'Mouth' also achieved another first, with the longest stay at number 1 ever achieved by a woman during its six-week residency at the top, eventually selling over 75,000 copies. The song topped the charts in several Asian territories, and broke Bainbridge in America, reaching number 4 on the *Billboard* Hot 100 in 1997. *The Garden* achieved gold sales in the USA, where it was released through Universal Records. *Between The Days*, was released in October 1998.

● ALBUMS: *The Garden* (Gotham/Universal 1995)★★★, *Between The Days* (Gotham/Universal 1998)★★★.

Baka Beyond

The punningly named Baka Beyond is a collaboration between former Outback guitarist Martin Cradick and the denizens of Cameroon's rain forests, the Baka pygmies.

Using their traditional rhythmic patterns alongside Western technology and musicianship, *Spirit Of The Forest* managed to amalgamate these disparate sources into a series of haunting soundscapes. That it sustained its emotive dynamism was undoubtedly due to the sensitivity of Cradick's approach, with the Bakas viewed as co-writers rather than merely creative adjuncts: 'They've got an incredible, special awareness of sound. They have all these interlocking rhythms and melodies and things. When they are playing their music, they are part of the forest.' Cradick's interest in the Baka people dated back to the late 80s when he saw a documentary on their activities, and, indeed, a previous Outback album was titled *Baka*. He was particularly inspired by their use of the limbindi (a bow made with branch and creeper, played on the chin), and resolved to investigate further. This was made possible with the aid of a grant from Oxford's Pitt Rivers Museum. Previously Cradick and wife Sue Hart had busked through the Andes and played with the Berbers of Morocco. With Cradick on guitar, mandolin and ngende, Jerry Soffe on bass, Paddy Le Mercier on violin/flutes and Hart on vocals, *Spirit Of The Forest* was the result of a six-week residency in 1992 with the Baka people, later edited together in the studio. The recordings were instigated by Cradick playing a guitar or mandolin (easier to carry through the dense undergrowth) riff from which the Bakas would devise a rhythm and harmony. As if to distance himself from the accusations of cultural imperialism that accompanied the success of Deep Forest, a companion album was released at the same time, *Heart Of The Forest*, with the music of the Baka people committed to tape in its original, unreconstructed form - a strategy originally pioneered by Peter Gabriel. A subsequent 1995 album, *The Meeting Pool*, while still using the Baka Beyond name, relied only on the rhythmic and melodic structures inspired by the Bakas. This allowed Cradick free reign to shape songs that transcended cultural reference points. *Journey Between* spread its wings even further, utilising the rhythm section from Ghanaian band Kakasitsi.

● ALBUMS: *Spirit Of The Forest* (Hannibal 1993)★★★, *Heart Of The Forest* (Hannibal 1993)★★★, *The Meeting Pool* (Hannibal 1995)★★★, *Journey Between* (Hannibal 1998)★★★.

Ball, Edward

b. 23 November 1959, Chelsea, London, England. A founder-member of the Television Personalities, Ed Ball's distinguished career on the periphery of the music industry was intimately linked with the rise of Creation Records. Ball's compositions throughout the 80s and 90s were some of the UK's most distinctive - from TVP's spin-off band the Times' infamous 'I Helped Patrick McGoohan Escape', to house staples such as *Palatial* and *Give Me Some Love* (credited to Love Corporation). The latter two albums were remixed by Danny Rampling and Andy Weatherall, respectively, though perhaps Ball's greatest moment in terms of dance music had already arrived with the acid house love song, 'Manchester'. He also included a notable reworking of New Order's 'Blue Monday' ('Lundi Bleu') for the French market on the Times' *Pure* album. Another of his many guises is the Teenage Filmstars, whose singles included 'Star' and 'Rocket Charms'. While an intern with the Television Personalities and Whaam! Records he also recorded a single as O Level. He was part of a Creation triumvirate with Alan McGee and

Dick Green who recorded as Biff Bang Pow!, and he has also released material with Tippa Irie and Denise Johnson. He also periodically joined Creation acts the Boo Radleys and Idha as auxiliary live keyboard player, before recording the romantically suicidal *If A Man Ever Loved A Woman*, in 1995. In 1996, now known as Edward Ball, he hit the UK charts with the lively 'Mill Hill Self Hate Club'. The subsequent album, *Catholic Guilt*, was a gem, packed with some highly commercial pop songs, and deserving of a wider audience. With a much fuller production than the sparse *If A Man Ever Loved A Woman*, the album benefited from the assistance of Andy Bell (ex-Ride) and Nick Heyward (newly signed to Creation). Even record company boss Alan McGee and his secretary added backing vocals, which did not detract from the excellence of the record and its highlights - 'The Mill Hill Self Hate Club', 'Controversial Girlfriend', and the sparkling and brassy 'Trailblaze'. Further work under the Teenage Filmstars and the Times monikers followed, although Creation's well-documented business problems and commercial fall from grace may put this artist's future in doubt.

● ALBUMS: *Welcome To The Wonderful World Of Ed Ball* (Creation 1995)★★, *If A Man Ever Loved A Woman* (Creation 1995)★★★, *Catholic Guilt* (Creation 1997)★★★★.

● COMPILATIONS: *Why Do I Need A Gun, I'm Chelsea* (Creation 2000)★★★.

Banco De Gaia

With a background in classical music, heavy metal, folk, jazz and bhangra, Toby Marks formed Banco De Gaia in Leamington Spa in 1989 after absorbing sounds he heard while travelling around the world. For the first six years he worked closely with the producer and sound engineer Andy Guthrie. Along with bands such as Transglobal Underground and Loop Guru, Banco De Gaia began performing live at Megadog and Whirl-Y-Gig events, which benefited from a more broad-minded and eclectic feel than most clubs, often featuring a heady world/dance fusion. Marks first released material on tapes, with *Freeform Flutes And Fading Tibetans* appearing on his own World Bank label. Following tracks on a number of compilations, including Planet Dog Records' *Feed Your Head*, he released 'Desert Wind' in November 1993, followed by the albums *Maya* and *Last Train To Lhasa*. Banco De Gaia's varied melodies, rhythms and textures blend techno, hip-hop, ambience, dub and rock with samples of traditional music from around the world, particularly the Middle East and Asia. Tracks such as 'Last Train To Lhasa' and 'Amber' encapsulated Banco's moderate-paced, melodic sound, while 'Kuos' and 'Data Inadequate' presented a more percussive, four-on-the-floor side; 'China', complete with storyteller, provided some moments of blissful ambience. *Live At Glastonbury* was more upbeat than the studio sets, with less ambient tracks and different mixes. The 1997 release *Big Men Cry* was perhaps the weakest of all, at times sounding rather like Pink Floyd, but still featured some memorable moments, particularly 'Drippy' and 'Drunk As A Monk'. In live performances since *Big Men Cry*, Marks has worked with a live band including percussion, drums, bass guitar, saxophone and flute, sometimes edging towards a rock sound. *The Magical Sounds Of Banco De Gaia* attempted to update Marks' sound for the late 90s with the introduction of some more club-orientated beats.

● ALBUMS: *Maya* (Planet Dog 1994)★★★, *Last Train To Lhasa*

(Planet Dog 1995)★★★★, *Live At Glastonbury* (Planet Dog 1996)★★★★, *Big Men Cry* (Planet Dog 1997)★★★, *The Magical Sounds Of Banco De Gaia* (Gecko 1999)★★★.

Bandulu

Formerly members of the Infonet Records network, which they helped establish alongside founder Chris Abbott, Bandulu are John O'Connell and former graffiti artists/breakdancers Jamie Bissmire and Lucien Thompson. In the early 90s, they established their headquarters at Bissmire's parents' home in Muswell Hill, north London. Influenced by Detroit techno, New York electro and Chicago house, Bandulu additionally added tribal percussion, sampling and 'real' instruments (guitars, drums, etc.) to their potential musical sources. Retrospectively, the trio have claimed their primary influence on forming in 1990 to be the creative decline of dance music at that time. 'It was all Kylie Minogue, all pop music. So we just decided to each put £50 in a pot and go into a studio', claimed O'Connell. Bandulu's early singles, such as 'Phaze-In-Version', were widely categorized within the fledgling trance movement, though the execution was more intricate and more flexible than that of many of their peers who relied more on simple repetition. Their debut release was 'Better Nation', followed by 'Internal Ocean' at the end of 1992. They also record under aliases such as ECC (Earth Coincidence Control), Sons Of The Subway, Koh Tao, Escobar, Shy Man and Thunderground. As the latter they include 'fourth member' Lewis Keogh, the Orb's resident DJ. With Bandulu he remixed the Orb's 'U.F.Orb'. hunderground is also the name of the club night they host at London's Bass Clef venue. With a discernible debt to the experimental electronic music of Philip Glass and Laurie Anderson, Bandulu have nevertheless forged their own identity in the dance world. In the summer of 1994, they released another widely admired single, 'Presence', followed by a second studio album. In 1995, they signed to Warner Brothers Records' subsidiary Blanco y Negro, for whom their debut release was the promotional-only EP *Running Time*. This was accompanied by live appearances at the Orbit Club's 5th Birthday party, the Omen in Germany and the Ministry Of Sound's celebratory night at Wembley Stadium. In March 1996, they released a further EP, *Troubleshooter*, which prefaced their major label debut, *Cornerstone*. This included nods to prevailing dance trends, such as jungle in 'Selah' and hard house in 'Jester'. It was promoted with a series of live appearances, although critics judged these shows to be inferior to the efforts of peers such as Orbital and the Prodigy in translating dance to a performance art medium.

● ALBUMS: *Guidance* (Infonet 1992)★★★, *Antimatters* (Infonet 1994)★★★, *Cornerstone* (Blanco y Negro 1996)★★★.

Banton, Buju

b. Mark Myrie, 1973, Kingston, Jamaica, West Indies. Banton was raised in Denham Town and began to learn the craft of the DJ at the age of 13 with the Rambo Mango and Sweet Love sound systems. The name Buju, meaning breadfruit, was given to him by his mother when he was a baby because of his chubbiness. DJ Clement Irie introduced him to Robert Ffrench, who produced his 1986 debut single 'The Ruler'. In 1987, he worked with Red Dragon, Bunny Lee and Winston Riley, the latter successfully remixing several of his tracks.

As his voice matured its rich growl was likened to Shabba Ranks. Several hits that established Banton as the most exciting newcomer in 1991 were written with Dave 'Rude Boy' Kelly, resident engineer at Donovan Germain's Penthouse Studio. Some of their lyrics drew controversy, such as 'Love Mi Browning', which describes Banton's fondness for light-skinned girls. 'Women Nuh Fret', 'Batty Rider', 'Bogle Dance' and 'Big It Up' (the first release on Kelly's Mad House label) set dancehall fashions. Several hits on Penthouse, Soljie, Shocking Vibes, Bobby Digital and Exterminator confirmed Banton's prominence and coincided with the release of *Mr. Mention* on Penthouse. 'Boom Bye Bye' for Shang was certainly the most infamous of these singles because of its aggressive homophobia. National television exposure in the UK caused a wave of media hostility and criticism. Nevertheless, the reggae charts were dominated by Banton's hits, often in combination with other Penthouse artists, including Wayne Wonder, Beres Hammond, Marcia Griffiths and Carol Gonzales. Later in 1991, Banton signed a major contract with Mercury Records. By 1993, his lyrics had more frequently begun to address cultural issues. 'Tribal War' (featuring star guest performers) was a reaction to Jamaica's political conflicts, 'Operation Ardent' took exception to Kingston's curfew laws, and 'Murderer' dealt with the shooting of his friend and fellow DJ, Pan Head. This element of harsh reality in juxtaposition with Banton's crude lyrical seduction of women has helped confirm his world-class status. In 1996, *Til Shiloh* (meaning 'forever') was ranked in *Spin* magazine's Top 20 albums of the year. The album, featuring a full studio band, was instrumental in moving dancehall away from synthesized music. The following year's *Inna Heights* received equal praise and helped establish Banton as one of the leading reggae artists of the late 90s.

● ALBUMS: *Stamina Daddy* (Techniques 1991)★★★, *Mr. Mention* (Penthouse 1991)★★★★, *Voice Of Jamaica* (Mercury 1993)★★★, *Til Shiloh* (Loose Cannon 1995)★★★★, *Inna Heights* (Jet Star 1997)★★★★.

Barenaked Ladies

Taking their name from a childhood slang term for a naked woman, the Barenaked Ladies are, in fact, five strapping lads from Scarborough, near Toronto, Canada. They were formed in 1988 by songwriters Steven Page (b. 22 June 1970, Scarborough, Ontario, Canada; guitar/vocals) and Ed Robertson (b. 25 October 1970, Ontario, Canada; guitar/vocals) while they were students. Brothers Jim Creeggan (b. 12 February 1970; bass/keyboards) and Andrew Creeggan (b. 4 July 1971; congas) and Tyler Stewart (b. 21 September 1967; drums) were soon added to the line-up. The band set off on an intensive series of club dates; word of their prowess soon spread and their first release, a five-song EP, proved a big hit. Their debut album, *Gordon*, subsequently sold more than half a million copies in their native Canada, outselling acts such as U2 and Michael Jackson. Their melodic pop, with its strong harmonies and string-driven acoustics, has led to them being unfairly dubbed the Fat Canadian Housemartins. Despite their undeniable debt to the British band, the Barenaked Ladies - who cite the Beach Boys and the Proclaimers among their influences - have carved out a distinctive sound. Songs such as 'Be My Yoko Ono' and 'If I Had A Million Dollars' are particular

crowd favourites. Live, their self-deprecating humour, catchy songs and high energy make for a thoroughly entertaining show, captured on 1996's *Rock Spectacle*. They bounced back into the commercial spotlight in 1998 when *Stunt* entered the US charts at number 3 in July, and continued generating huge sales on the back of October's infuriatingly catchy chart-topper, 'One Week'.

● ALBUMS: *Gordon* (Sire 1992)★★★★, *Maybe You Should Drive* (Sire 1994)★★★, *Born On A Pirate Ship* (Reprise 1996)★★★★, *Rock Spectacle* (Reprise 1996)★★★, *Stunt* (Warners 1998)★★★★.

Barker, Sally

b. 19 September 1959, Barrow upon Soar, Leicestershire, England. One of the newer generation of folk performers, Barker has a strong blues-based voice that she accompanies with some impressive guitar work. Her influences are wide and varied, and include Bessie Smith, John Martyn and Aretha Franklin. She worked as half of a duo called Sally And Chris, with bass player Chris Watson, performing folk-blues in pubs and clubs in the Midlands. Later, the duo went on to support Steeleye Span, Gordon Giltrap and Roy Harper. After a brief foray into radio and television, Barker moved to London in May 1986 and continued to work as a soloist. In 1987, she won the National Songsearch Competition and began touring in a support capacity to acts such as Fairport Convention, Taj Mahal and Roy Harper. Her first album contained cover versions of songs that had previously featured in her live act. The second release illustrated the ongoing development of her maturing musical potential, and in 1990, she supported both Bob Dylan and Robert Plant in Germany. In December of the same year, she formed the acclaimed Poozies, playing a mixture of Cajun, folk, blues and country. The line-up featured harpist Mary McMaster and Patsy Seddon from Sileás, Jenny Gardner (fiddle) and Karen Tweed (accordion). Barker left the band in 1995. She continues to work both the folk clubs and festivals, but it is evident that her appeal actually extends far beyond the boundaries of folk music.

● ALBUMS: *In The Spotlight* (Old Dog 1988)★★★, *This Rhythm Is Mine* (Old Dog 1990)★★★, *Beating The Drum* (Hypertension/Ariola 1992)★★★, *Favourite Dish* (Hypertension 1996)★★★, *Passion And The Countess* (Rideout 1998)★★★.

Barlow, Gary

b. 20 January 1971, Frodsham, Cheshire, England. Formerly lead singer with the most successful 'boy band' of the 90s, Take That, Barlow began his musical apprenticeship at the age of 12 as pianist in a Frodsham social club. By the age of 14 he had moved on to the cabaret circuit, supporting artists such as Ken Dodd. His first attempt at launching a solo career came two years later, but publishing companies could not at this time see the potential in his compositions, which already included later Take That staple 'A Million Love Songs'. However, he was then contacted by Nigel Martin-Smith, who was in the process of piecing together a UK version of New Kids On The Block. That band was Take That, a teen-pop phenomenon that enjoyed a series of number 1 singles and albums, with Barlow as chief songwriter. Barlow launched his second solo career in 1996 at almost exactly the time that another former member of Take That, Robbie Williams, released his first single. There was certainly acrimony between the two parties. In a magazine article printed

shortly before the release of both songs, Williams labelled Barlow: 'Clueless . . . really fucking dated . . . selfish, stupid and greedy.' A victory for Barlow was widely predicted in the press - Barlow was the musical brains behind Take That, a natural pop songwriter who had undergone music training. He was able to release one of his own compositions while Williams had to rely on a cover version of George Michael's 'Freedom'. Barlow won the race to the UK number 1 spot, his 'Forever Love' (hardly the most outstanding example of his songwriting) reaching the top in its first week of release. Williams' song was released at the end of July 1996 while Barlow put the finishing touches to the tracks for his debut. The album was completed, only for Barlow to set about re-recording most of it, as well as splitting from his manager. One year later, with six new tracks and with a new executive producer in Arista Records' Clive Davis, *Open Road* was finally released to muted reviews. Barlow's frustration at having his career on hold must have been considerable, especially as Williams' career was spectacularly revived by the enormous success of his 'Angels' single. Barlow returned to the UK singles chart in July 1999 with 'Stronger'. The song disappeared after a short stay, however, and with *Twelve Months & Eleven Days* also failing cynics were left to ponder if it was back to gigs at the Frodsham social club.
● ALBUMS: *Open Road* (RCA 1997)★★★, *Twelve Months & Eleven Days* (RCA 1999)★★.

Basehead

Playing a cut-and-paste combination of rap, R&B, reggae and funk, Basehead, aka dcBasehead, from Maryland, Washington, USA, comprises Michael Ivey (b. 5 February 1968, Pittsburgh, Pennsylvania, USA; vocals, guitar, writer, producer), joined, originally for touring purposes only, by DJ Unique (b. Paul Howard), guitarist Keith Lofton (b. 9 May 1967, Washington, USA), drummer Brian Hendrix (b. 29 July 1968, Pittsburgh, Pennsylvania, USA) and bass player Bill Conway (b. 29 November 1967, Washington, USA). Ivey's sound has been loosely categorized as both 'slacker rap' and 'intelligent hip-hop'. A student of film at Howard University, Ivey recorded Basehead's debut album on his basic home set-up with minimal help from Hendrix and Howard. Originally released by small independent concern Emigre in 1991, *Play With Toys*' highly inventive grooves and stoned charm attracted strong reviews and extensive airplay, with Ivey fêted as one of hip-hop's most imaginative talents. 'There are hip-hop elements in there, but if a hardcore hip-hop fan bought it, they might be disappointed', was his frank description of the album. The follow-up *Not In Kansas Anymore* was equally enthralling, and featured Ivey's full touring band on several tracks. In 1994, Ivey put together the B.Y.O.B collective, with shared songwriting and vocal contributions. He reassembled Basehead in 1996, releasing the spiritually inclined *Faith*.
● ALBUMS: *Play With Toys* (Emigre/Imago 1991)★★★★, *Not In Kansas Anymore* (Imago 1993)★★★, as B.Y.O.B *B.Y.O.B* (13/Rykodisc 1994)★★★, *Faith* (Imago 1996)★★★.

Basement Jaxx

Basement Jaxx is a respected, UK-based DJing and production duo, comprising Felix Buxton and Simon Ratcliffe. Setting out to rediscover the original feeling of early Chicago house music they began by holding illegal parties in Brixton,

south London in 1994. Since then, starting in Ratcliffe's bedroom studio, they have gone on to release the club classic 'Fly Life', an unusual blend of ragga and house, and the Ibiza anthem, 'Samba Magic', besides various remixes, white labels and dub plates. Their unique cocktail of influences (rap, funk, ragga, disco and garage, all given a deep house twist) has been described as 'punk garage'. It has found a devoted audience in their native London and beyond (especially in Japan, Canada, Australia and the USA) where their DJing skills have been in demand. Their Basement Jaxx club nights in London never fail to fill venues. In 1998, Basement Jaxx signed to highly successful XL Records (home of the Prodigy). Their first single for the label, 'Red Alert', released in April 1999, received much praise and radio airplay in the UK and US and broke into the UK Top 5. The single's critical and commercial success was repeated by the follow-up, 'Rendezvous', and the attendant *Remedy*. The duo's faces were rarely *not* on the cover of hip music and style magazines during 1999 and many pundits were naming them as the saviours of truly inventive dance music. *Remedy* featured in most music critics 'best of' polls at the end of the year.
● ALBUMS: *Remedy* (XL Records 1999)★★★★.

Bassomatic

Bassomatic was a pseudonym adopted by William Orbit (b. William Wainwright, England), a leading mixer, writer and composer who came to prominence in September 1990 with the UK number 9 hit single and techno anthem, 'Fascinating Rhythm'. This was included on a debut set that also featured the services of Sharon Musgrave, percussionist Fergus and MC Inna One Step, the title of which was a reference to Pink Floyd's 'Set The Controls For The Heart Of The Sun'. In the process, Bass-O-Matic spearheaded a movement in the dance music scene that rediscovered elements of music from yesteryear, finding much in sympathy with the trance like state of 90s house. The album actually included a cover version of the Pink Floyd track, as well as another single, 'In The Realm Of The Senses'. A year later Orbit unveiled a follow-up, this time utilizing vocalist Sindy (ex-Well Red) and rappers Glory and Divine. It proved another competent and intoxicating collection, with Orbit's keen sense of rhythm carrying the album through from deep house to more pop-orientated cuts.
● ALBUMS: *Set The Controls For The Heart Of The Bass* (Virgin 1990)★★★, *Science And Melody* (Virgin 1991)★★★.

Baxter, Blake

From Detroit, Michigan, USA, Baxter is a first-generation Detroit hero of 'Ride 'Em Boy' and 'Forever And A Day' fame, whose early recordings (with their edgy experimentation) provided a guiding light to the Aphex Twin, the Chemical Brothers and others. His early funk-inspired material appeared on the leading Chicago underground house labels DJ International and KMS Records. Closely involved with the seminal *Techno: The New Dance Sound Of Detroit* compilation, he subsequently severed his links with the city's 'Big Three' (Juan Atkins, Derrick May and Kevin Saunderson) and moved on to the Detroit independent Incognito. He released 'Sexuality' and the *Crimes Of The Heart* EP for the latter, which prefaced a debut album in early 1990. He also provided Jeff Mills/Mad 'Mike Banks'

Underground Resistance with a rare outside production in 1991 with 'Prince Of Techno'. Skilled as both a drummer and DJ, he recorded for several European labels in the 90s after relocating to Berlin, including 1992's 'One More Time' and 'Brothers Gonna Work It Out' for Logic Records (the latter was later sampled to great effect by the Chemical Brothers). He also recorded with Orlando Voom as the Ghetto Brothers, and set up his own Mix Records and Phat Joint labels. Later mix projects, which showed an increasing fascination with hip-hop, appeared on the Disko B label. The superb Globus mix album offers as good an introduction as any to this unsung pioneer.

● ALBUMS: *The Underground Lives* (Incognito 1990)★★★, *The Project* (Tresor 1992)★★★, *The Vault* (Disko B 1995)★★★★, *The H Factor* (Disko B 1998)★★★.

● COMPILATIONS: *Globus Mix, Vol. 2: A Decade Underground* (EFA 1998)★★★★.

BBM

The potential was greater than the sum of the parts. The power trio of the 90s could have been BBM, had the fiery members stayed together long enough. Gary Moore (b. 4 April 1952, Belfast, Northern Ireland; vocals, guitar), Jack Bruce (b. John Symon Asher, 14 May 1943, Glasgow, Lanarkshire, Scotland; bass, vocals) and Ginger Baker (b. Peter Baker, 19 August 1939, Lewisham, London, England; drums) decided to create a semi-skimmed version of 60s supergroup Cream in the autumn of 1993. Their lone album was highly derivative of some of the songs on Cream's *Disraeli Gears* and *Wheels Of Fire*. 'Waiting In The Wings' owed a debt to the melody and lyrics of 'White Room', even though long-time lyricist Pete Brown was overlooked for this project. 'City Of Gold' was uncannily similar to 'Crossroads' and 'Why Does Love (Have To Go Wrong)?' oozed likeness to 'We're Going Wrong'. Those that had pined for a Cream reunion were somehow placated by this album, and Gary Moore proved quite acceptable with the Gibson Les Paul sound. All three sounded better than ever, and had they been able to continue they could have courted heavy metal and blues in the same way many late 60s bands did. Rumour had it that they had a blistering argument at the end of a media-only performance at London's Marquee Club. No encores were forthcoming at this or any other gig and the band effectively folded, leaving one pretty good album as a legacy.

● ALBUMS: *Around The Next Dream* (Virgin 1994)★★★.

Beastie Boys

Former hardcore trio who initially found international fame as the first crossover white rap act of the 80s, and later earned critical plaudits for their eclectic approach in a musical genre not known for its experimental nature. After forming at New York University, original guitarist John Berry departed after the release of the hardcore *Polly Wog Stew* EP, leaving Adam Yauch (b. 15 August 1967, Brooklyn, New York, USA), Mike Diamond (b. 20 November 1965, New York, USA), drummer Kate Schellenbach and guitarist Adam Horovitz (b. 31 October 1966, New York City, New York, USA), recently recruited from The Young And The Useless (one single, 'Real Men Don't Use Floss'), to hold the banner. Horovitz, it transpired, was the son of dramatist Israel Horovitz, indicating that far from being the spawn of inner-city dystopia, the Beasties all came from privileged middle-class backgrounds. In 1983, the new line-up released the *Cooky Puss* EP, which offered the first evidence of them picking up on the underground rap phenomenon and the use of samples. 'Beastie Revolution' was later sampled for a British Airways commercial, earning them $40,000 in royalties. Schellenbach soon departed reducing the crew to the core trio of Yauch, Diamond and Horovitz, now going by the hip-hop monikers of MCA, Mike D and King Adrock respectively. Friend and sometime member Rick Rubin quickly signed them to his fledgling Def Jam Records. They did not prove hard to market. Their debut album revealed a collision of bad attitudes, spearheaded by the raucous single '(You Gotta) Fight For Your Right (To Party!)', and samples of everything from Led Zeppelin to the theme to *Mister Ed*. There was nothing self-conscious or sophisticated about the lyrics, Diamond and Yauch reeling off complaints about their parents confiscating their pornography or telling them to turn down the stereo. Somehow, however, it became an anthem for pseudo-rebellious youth everywhere, reaching US number 7 in December 1986, and UK number 11 in February 1987. *Licensed To Ill* became the first rap album to top the US pop charts at the end of November 1986, and reached number 7 in the UK charts the following January. By the time follow-up singles 'No Sleep Till Brooklyn' (number 14, May 1987) and 'She's On It' (number 10, July 1987) charted in the UK, the Beastie Boys had become a media *cause célèbre*. Their stage shows regularly featured caged, half-naked females, while their Volkswagen pendants resulted in a crime wave, with fans stealing said items from vehicles throughout the UK. A reflective Horovitz recalled that this never happened in the USA, where they merely stole the car itself. More disturbing, it was alleged that the trio derided terminally ill children on a foreign jaunt. This false accusation was roundly denied, but other stories of excess leaked out of the Beastie Boys camp with grim regularity. There was also friction between the trio and Def Jam, the former accusing the latter of withholding royalties, the latter accusing the former of withholding a follow-up album. The trio went their separate ways after finishing a fraught tour, with Yauch and Diamond working on solo projects and Horovitz appearing in Hugh Hudson's movie *Lost Angels*. By the time they reassembled on Capitol Records in 1989, the public, for the most part, had forgotten about them. Rap's ante had been significantly raised by the arrival of Public Enemy and NWA, yet *Paul's Boutique* remains one of the genre's most overlooked pieces, a complex reflection of pop culture that is infinitely more subtle than their debut. Leaving their adolescent fixations behind, the rhymes plundered cult fiction (Anthony Burgess' *A Clockwork Orange*) through to the Old Testament. It was co-produced by the Dust Brothers, who subsequently became a hot production item, but stalled at number 14 in the US album chart, and number 44 in the UK. Moving to California and setting up their own G-Son studio, *Check Your Head* saw them returning, partially, to their thrash roots, reverting to a guitar, bass and drums format, aided by the keyboard playing of Mark Nishita (Money Mark). The album proved popular, reaching US number 10 in May 1992. In the meantime, the Beasties had invested wisely, setting up their own magazine and label, Grand Royal, whose first release was the *In Search Of Manny* EP by Luscious Jackson (featuring the

Beastie Boys' original drummer Schellenbach). Other signings included The Young And The Useless, DFL (Horovitz's hardcore punk project), DJ Hurricane (also of the Afros), Noise Addict and Moistboyz. However, in 1993 Horovitz pleaded guilty to a charge of battery on a television cameraman during a memorial service for River Phoenix. He was put on two years' probation, ordered to undertake 200 hours' community service and pay restitution costs. His connections with the Phoenix family came through his actress wife Ione Sky. He himself had undertaken roles in underground movies *The Santa Anna Project* and *Roadside Prophets*, and also appeared in a television cameo for *The Equalizer*. By this time, both he and Diamond had become Californian citizens, while Yauch had become a Buddhist, speaking out in the press against US trade links with China because of the latter's annexation of Tibet. In 1994, Yauch set up the Milarepa Fund to raise funds and public awareness of the situation in Tibet, and organized the hugely successful Tibetan Freedom Concerts from 1996 to 1998. *Ill Communication* was another successful voyage into inspired Beastie thuggism, featuring A Tribe Called Quest's Q-Tip, and a second appearance from rapper Biz Markie, following his debut on *Check Your Head*. An eclectic mix of hardcore, hip-hop and funk, the album debuted at number 1 on the US album chart. The trio then released the hardcore *Aglio E Olio EP*, which contained eight songs blasted out in only 11 minutes, followed by *The In Sound From Way Out!*, a space-filler of b-sides and instrumental cuts from their previous two albums. The long-awaited *Hello Nasty* (a title inspired by their agent's telephone greeting), their first full studio album in four years, was a return to a more sparse, hip-hop-dominated sound after the funky feel of *Ill Communication*. The album debuted at US number 1 in August 1998, staying at the top for three weeks. It also became their first UK chart-topper.

● ALBUMS: *Licensed To Ill* (Def Jam/Columbia 1986)★★★, *Paul's Boutique* (Capitol 1989)★★★★, *Check Your Head* (Capitol 1992)★★★★, *Ill Communication* (Grand Royal 1994)★★★★, *Root Down EP* (Grand Royal 1995)★★, *Aglio E Olio EP* (Grand Royal 1995)★★★, *The In Sound From Way Out!* (Grand Royal 1996)★★, *Hello Nasty* (Grand Royal 1998)★★★★.

● COMPILATIONS: *Some Old Bullshit* (Capitol 1994)★★★, *The Sounds Of Science* (Grand Royal 1999)★★★★.

● VIDEOS: *Sabotage* (1994), *The Skills To Pay The Bills* (1994).

● FURTHER READING: *Rhyming & Stealing: A History Of The Beastie Boys*, Angus Batey.

Beatnuts

This Latino hip-hop crew from New York established their name in the late 80s with remix credits for Prime Minister Pete Nice, Naughty By Nature, Da Lench Mob and Cypress Hill, and also produced Chi-Ali, Da Youngsta's and Fat Joe. Originally comprising Psycho Les (b. Lester Fernandez) and Junkyard JuJu (b. Jerry Tineo), lyricist Fashion (b. Berntony Smalls) was added when they began recording their own material, which kicked off with 1993's *Intoxicated Demons* EP. Although featuring a light touch and plenty of humour, this did not mask the level of innovation and insight, with samples drawn from their direct environment (i.e. children talking) rather than movie themes and old funk records. The release of the debut EP had been delayed when Fashion was arrested on a drug-related charge and imprisoned for six months. Before joining the other two, he had recorded 'Let The Horns Blow' with members of De La Soul and Chi-Ali in 1991. The trio's self-titled debut offered a further healthy dose of their twisted world view, with an increasingly hostile edge replacing the humour. Fashion subsequently left, converting to Islam and changing his name to Al Tariq. JuJu and Psycho Les continued to work behind the boards, returning to the studio to record the highly inventive long-players, 1997's *Stone Crazy* and, two years later, *A Musical Massacre*.

● ALBUMS: *Intoxicated Demons* mini-album (Combat 1993)★★★★, *The Beatnuts* (Violator/Relativity 1994)★★★, *Stone Crazy* (Relativity 1997)★★★, *A Musical Massacre* (Relativity 1999)★★★.

Beats International

This studio team of musicians was formed by Norman Cook (b. Quentin Cook, 31 July 1963, England; ex-Housemartins) following the break-up of his former employers. Its basic composition was Cook (bass), Linda Layton (b. Belinda Kimberley Layton, 7 December 1970, Chiswick, London, England; vocals), Lester Noel (b. Lester John Noel, 3 September 1962, Paddington, London, England; vocals, ex-Grab Grab The Haddock; North Of Cornwallis), Andy Boucher (keyboards) and MC Wildski (rap). However, to these personnel could be added a range of occasional members ranging from Billy Bragg to Definition Of Sound to Captain Sensible. The first Beats International single, 'For Spacious Lies', gathered numerous rave reviews, and was much closer to traditional pop fare than subsequent releases. It included a contribution from Noel, who had met Cook when North Of Cornwallis supported the Housemartins on tour. Beats International shot to prominence in the UK when 'Dub Be Good To Me' hit number 1 in the UK charts in February 1990. Controversy followed it shortly afterwards, as the audience placed the bassline as a note-for-note lift from the Clash's 'Guns Of Brixton'. In truth, the song also borrowed heavily from the S.O.S. Band's 'Just Be Good To Me'. This 'creative theft' may have diminished royalty cheques, but the interpretation of various styles and even passages of music proved a deliberate strategy in Beats International's armoury. Although the subsequent 'Burundi Blues' single, a delicate mix of soul, jazz and African music, failed to repeat the success, Cook was heavily in demand as a remixer for a variety of projects, ranging from Aztec Camera to the Jungle Brothers. The incredibly eclectic debut album charted at number 17, while the follow-up concentrated heavily on ska and reggae rhythms and included a disastrous version of 'In The Ghetto'. Cook disbanded Beats International in order to put together his new band, the acid jazz-styled Freak Power, and concentrate on further production work. He has also recorded as Pizzaman, and enjoyed major chart success in the late 90s as Fatboy Slim.

● ALBUMS: *Let Them Eat Bingo* (Go! Discs 1990)★★★, *Excursion On The Version* (Go! Discs 1991)★★★.

Beautiful South

This highly literate adult pop band arose from the ashes of the Housemartins. The line-up features vocalists Paul Heaton (b. 9 May 1962, Birkenhead, Lancashire, England) and David Hemmingway (b. 20 September 1960, England) from Hull's self-proclaimed 'Fourth Best Band'. In reference to their previous dour northern image, Heaton sarcastically named his new band the Beautiful South, recruiting Sean

Welch (bass), Briana Corrigan (b. Londonderry, Northern Ireland; vocals, ex-Anthill Runaways), former Housemartins roadie David Stead (drums) and Heaton's new co-writer, David Rotheray (guitar). Continuing an association with Go! Discs Records, their first single was the ballad 'Song For Whoever', which gave them instant UK chart success (number 2, June 1989). After the rejection of the original sleeve concept for their debut album (featuring a suicidal girl with a gun in her mouth), *Welcome To The Beautiful South* emerged in October 1989 to a positive critical reception. 'A Little Time' became their first number 1 the following year. A bitter duet between Corrigan and Hemmingway, it was supported by a memorable video that won the Best Music Video award at the 1991 BRIT Awards. Lyrically, Heaton had honed his songwriting to a style that allowed the twists and ironies to develop more fully: 'I find it difficult to write straightforward optimistic love songs . . . I throw in a row, a fight, get a few knives out . . .' Though giving the band their least successful chart position to date (number 43), 'My Book' provided one of Heaton's most cutting lyrics (including a hilarious reference to the soccer player Peter Beardsley) and also saw Jazzie B. of Soul II Soul sue for the slight use of the 'Back To Reality' refrain. Always a writer able to deal with emotive subjects in an intelligent and forthright manner, Heaton's next topic was lonely alcoholism in 'Old Red Eyes Is Back', the first fruit of a protracted writing stint in Gran Canaria. However, Corrigan became a little unsettled at some of the subject matter expressed in Heaton's lyrics (notably '36D', a song about *The Sun* newspaper's 'Page 3' topless models, which was open to a variety of interpretations) and left the band after *0898: Beautiful South*. Her replacement, Jacqueline Abbot, was introduced on a cover version of Fred Neil's 'Everybody's Talkin'', and more fully on the band's fourth studio album, *Miaow*. However, its success was dwarfed by the singles collection, *Carry On Up The Charts*, which dominated the listings in late 1994 and early 1995. 'Rotterdam', taken from the album *Blue Is The Colour*, continued their run of hit singles at the end of 1996. 'Perfect 10' was another success, entering the UK charts at number 2 in September 1998 and staying in the Top 10 for several weeks. The band's most adventurous single to date, it proved to be an apt taster for the diverse styles found on the chart-topping *Quench*.

● ALBUMS: *Welcome To The Beautiful South* (Go! Discs 1989)★★★, *Choke* (Go! Discs 1990)★★★, *0898: Beautiful South* (Go! Discs 1992)★★★, *Miaow* (Go! Discs 1994)★★★, *Blue Is The Colour* (Go! Discs 1996)★★★, *Quench* (Go! Discs 1998)★★★.

● COMPILATIONS: *Carry On Up The Charts: The Best Of The Beautiful South* (Go! Discs 1994)★★★★.

● VIDEOS: *The Pumpkin* (PolyGram Music Video 1992), *Carry On Up The Charts* (PolyGram Music Video 1995).

● FURTHER READING: *Last Orders At The Liars' Bar: The Official Story Of The Beautiful South*, Mike Pattenden.

Beck

b. Beck Hansen, 8 July 1970, Los Angeles, California, USA. Beck Hansen rose swiftly to prominence in 1994 with his exhilarating marriage of folk (Lead Belly, Woody Guthrie) and guitar noise. As a child he loitered around his bluegrass street musician father, living with his office-worker mother and half-brother in some of Los Angeles' worst addresses, picking up on the city's nascent hip-hop scene as a break-dancer. He also spent time in Kansas with his grandmother and Presbyterian preacher grandfather, and with his other grandfather, the artist Al Hansen, in Europe. His guitar-playing, however, was primarily inspired by the blues of Mississippi John Hurt, which he would deliver with improvised lyrics while busking. After dropping out of school at 16 he moved to New York, though he was unable to join in with the local punk scene. On his return to Los Angeles he played his first gigs in-between sets at clubs such as Raji's and Jabberjaw. His music was now a potpourri of those diverse early influences - street hip-hop, Delta blues, Presbyterian hymns, punk with scat lyrics - and the whole was beginning to take shape as he released his first single, 'MTV Makes Me Want To Smoke Crack', the title of which would be made ironic by his future success in that very medium. This was followed by a 12-inch for Los Angeles independent Bong Load Custom Records, entitled 'Loser', produced with hip-hop technician Karl Stephenson. Those who might try retrospectively to read something sardonic into this title should be reminded that Beck was, at the time, living in a rat-infested shed: 'I was working in a video store doing things like alphabetizing the pornography section for minimum wage'. When 'Loser' was finally released after a year's delay in the summer of 1993, critics fell over themselves to cite it as an anthem for doomed youth. Vaulted into the pop charts, Beck was suddenly viewed as a baby-faced saviour for the 'slacker' generation, a platform he was most unwilling to mount: 'I never had any slack. I was working a $4-an-hour job trying to stay alive. I mean, that slacker kind of stuff is for people who have the time to be depressed about everything.' The major labels swooped for his signature. Geffen Records won possibly the most competitive chase for an artist in a decade, though not before David Geffen had telephoned Beck at home, and the artist had already set in motion two more independent records - 'Steve Threw Up' for Bong Load and a 10-inch album, *A Western Harvest Field By Moonlight*, on Fingerpaint Records. Despite this, the contract with Geffen was highly unusual in that it allowed Beck to record and release material for other companies should he wish - a right he took delight in exercising. The *Mellow Gold* debut album for Geffen was only one of three albums scheduled for release in 1994. The second, *Stereo Pathetic Soul Manure*, appeared on LA's Flipside independent, and the third, a collaboration with Calvin Johnson of Beat Happening, emerged on K Records. *Odelay* was his next major release in the spring of 1996, and was an outstanding record of great depth and multiple layers. The album reaped numerous Album Of The Year awards in the music press and spawned five successful singles, including 'Where It's At' and a Noel Gallagher (Oasis) remix of 'Devil's Haircut'. His major label follow-up *Mutations* was originally planned for release on Bong Load, but its downbeat charms were still impressive for what was effectively a stopgap collection. Beck returned to the mix-and-match style of *Odelay* on 1999's soul-influenced *Midnite Vultures*, which confirmed him as one of America's most original musical talents.

● ALBUMS: *A Western Harvest Field By Moonlight* 10-inch album (Fingerpaint 1993)★★, *Golden Feelings* (Sonic Enemy 1993)★★, *Mellow Gold* (Geffen 1994)★★★★, *Stereo Pathetic Soul Manure* (Flipside 1994)★★, *One Foot In The Grave* 1993 recording (K Records 1995)★★, *Odelay* (Geffen 1996)★★★★, *Mutations* (Geffen 1998)★★★, *Midnite Vultures* (Geffen 1999)★★★★.

Bedhead

Bedhead, from Dallas, Texas, USA, were regularly name-checked by peers such as the Breeders, Luna, Come, Seam and the UK's Stereolab on their arrival in the mid-90s. They specialized in a mature form of alternative guitar pop song-writing that eschews all notions of bombast in favour of lo-fi subtlety and craft. Cover versions of songs by Joy Division ('Disorder') and the Stranglers ('Golden Brown') also indicated their versatility. Their self-titled 1995 EP was recorded live in a church in front of a stereo microphone and issued with a similar absence of fanfare. Guitarist Bubba Kadane acted as spokesman for the band (comprising his brother Matt Kadane, bass player Kris Wheat and drummer Trini Martinez), but otherwise they shunned interviews and avoided using real names, refusing to have their photographs taken as it 'leads to preconceptions'. *Transaction De Novo*, produced by Steve Albini, was their strongest set to date. Unfortunately it proved to be their swansong, although a 10-inch single, 'Lepidoptera', appeared posthumously.

● ALBUMS: *WhatFunLifeWas* (Trance Syndicate 1994)★★★, *Bedheaded* (Rough Trade 1996)★★★, *The Dark Ages EP* (Trance Syndicate 1996)★★★, *Transaction De Novo* (Trance Syndicate 1997)★★★★.

Bega, Lou

b. David Loubega, 13 April 1975, Munich, Germany. This global pop sensation brought some much needed style and humour to the charts in the summer of 1999 with his reworking of Perez Prado's 1949 hit, 'Mambo No. 5'. Bega's Ugandan father went to Germany in the early 70s to study biochemistry, and stayed in the country after meeting his Sicilian wife in a youth hostel. Lou showed an early interest in soul music, but it was his discovery of Cuban mambo music while living in Miami that influenced his future musical direction. He adopted a distinctive visual image, part Cab Calloway and part Kid Creole, with his white suit, polka dot handkerchief, spats and Borsalino hat topped off by a snazzy pencil moustache. Bega subsequently signed to RCA Records and released his debut single, 'Mambo No. 5', a cartoonish update of the old Prado song. The single, with an irritatingly catchy chorus listing several of Bega's ex-girl-friends, stayed at the top of the German charts for over 10 weeks and reached number 1 on most European charts. The song crossed over to the top of the UK charts in August 1999, and reached number 3 in the USA a month later. The attendant *A Little Bit Of Mambo* relied on glossy production values to mask Bega's limited repertoire. A second single, 'A Girl Like You', was predictably less successful.

● ALBUMS: *A Little Bit Of Mambo* (BMG 1999)★★.

Bell Biv DeVoe

On their arrival on the music scene in 1989, this trio of former New Edition members, Ricky Bell (b. 18 September 1967, Boston, Massachusetts, USA), Michael Bivins (b. 10 August 1968, Boston, Massachusetts, USA) and Ronnie DeVoe (b. 17 November 1967, Boston, Massachusetts, USA), heralded a new development in American urban music, infusing their hip-hop-inflected rhymes with a more stylish and less brutal timbre. The hybrid became known as Ghetto Swing. Their debut singles, 'Poison' and 'Do Me!', both made US number 3, and the album that followed was similarly successful, earning over three million sales. In 1991, at the ini-

tiation of Motown Records president Joe Busby, Bivins was asked to become A&R executive for his own record company - Biv Entertainment - to be licensed through Motown. Signings included Another Bad Creation and Boyz II Men, both of whom found almost immediate success. Bell and DeVoe would oversee a similar set-up through PolyGram Records, established in 1992. The second Bell Biv DeVoe album included a New Edition reunion on 'Word To The Mutha!'. Bivins has produced for MC Brains in addition to the aforementioned Another Bad Creation and Boyz II Men, and put together the East Coast Family hip-hop project. After the release of *Hootie Mack*, and the attendant 'Gangsta' single, the trio launched their own range of clothes through Starter merchandising. All three members participated in 1996's full-blown New Edition reunion.

● ALBUMS: *Poison* (MCA 1990)★★★★, *WBBD-Bootcity!* remix album (MCA 1991)★★★, *Hootie Mack* (MCA 1993)★★★.

Belle And Sebastian

Formed at an all-night café in Glasgow, Scotland in early 1996, and named after a cult 60s television show, Belle And Sebastian appear to have taken a few hints from the Residents as far as publicity goes. The core of the band, songwriter Stuart Murdoch (vocals/guitar/piano) and Stuart David (bass), refuse to release photographs or any information about individual members beyond their names. Despite this self-effacement (or gimmick, if you prefer), Belle And Sebastian, also comprising Stevie Jackson (guitars, harmonica, vocals), Richard Colburn (drums), Chris Geddes (keyboards/guitar), Isobel Campbell (cello) and Sarah Martin (violin/stylophone), started packing out their Scottish gigs within months of their formation. Their string-based sound owes much to the Tindersticks, who headlined their first London gig, at the ICA, but also carries hints of country music and early 80s bed-sitter favourites such as Felt. After the limited edition, mail-order-only *Tigermilk* sold out within a month of its May 1996 release, with the enthusiastic backing of Radio 1 disc jockey Mark Radcliffe, the band were signed to London independent Jeepster Records. Within 10 days a second album had been completed. The band's dark tones and Murdoch's quirky, sometimes Morrissey-esque lyrics, allegedly written on Glasgow buses, found favour in alternative circles as far afield as San Francisco and especially France, where *Les Inrockuptibles* magazine placed them above Oasis in their end of 1996 poll. In 1997, the band released the *Dog On Wheels*, *Lazy Line Painter Jane* and *3 ... 6 ... 9 ... Seconds Of Light* EPs, the latter breaking into the UK Top 40 in October. Part-time trumpeter Mick Cooke was also made a full-time member of the band at this point. With their ever increasing success on the US independent charts the band were able to finalise an American deal with Matador Records, releasing *The Boy With The Arab Strap* the following year. The album entered the UK album chart at number 12 in September, and earned the band a BRIT Award for Best British Newcomer. Stuart David (as Looper) and Isobel Campbell (as the Gentle Waves) also released solo records. The following year, David had his debut novel, *Nalda Said*, published.

● ALBUMS: *Tigermilk* (Electric Honey 1996)★★★, *If You're Feeling Sinister* (Jeepster/Enclave 1996)★★★, *The Boy With The Arab Strap* (Jeepster/Matador 1998)★★★.

Belle, Regina

b. 17 July 1963, Englewood, New Jersey, USA. Belle first considered a career in the music business in her teenage years, after being inspired to sing by the gospel music greats Shirley Caesar and Inez Andrews. Both her mother and father were gospel singers and encouraged her to follow the same path - they were initially resistant to the idea that she should become involved in secular music. Further exposure to shows such as *American Bandstand* and *Soul Train* encouraged her to take up an instrument, and while at high school she learned trombone, tuba and steel drums, playing along to R&B and jazz standards as part of the school band. Her performance of the Emotions' 'Don't Ask My Neighbours' at a high-school concert won her $25, encouraging her to take up semi-professional employment singing at fashion shows and weddings (often with the band Private Property). She secured a scholarship to the prestigious Manhattan School Of Music to study voice and opera, and then Rutgers University. There she became the first vocalist to sing with the music department's jazz ensemble - a jazz influence has remained detectable in much of her subsequent output. At the same time she began to perform on the Greenwich Village folk circuit, attracting the attention of New York disc jockey Vaughn Harper. Through his recommendation and a subsequent viewing of Belle singing the black national anthem, 'Lift Every Voice And Sing', she joined the Manhattans, an opening act to Dionne Warwick, Gladys Knight and Patti LaBelle. Spending two years touring with the Manhattans, she appeared on the Bobby Womack-produced single, 'Where Did We Go Wrong' (a duet with Gerald Alston of the band). She also contributed to their 1986 Columbia Records album, *Back To Basics*. A year later she was signed to the label as a solo artist. *All By Myself* received immediate acclaim, particularly for the minor hit singles 'Show Me The Way' and 'So Many Tears'. It was promoted by tours with Guy, the O'Jays and the Whispers. *Stay With Me* included the number 1 R&B hits 'Baby Come To Me' and 'Make It Like It Was' (written by a member of the Winans). It earned Belle her first RIAA gold award, and also included a duet with James 'J.T.' Taylor of Kool And The Gang, 'All I Want Is Forever'. The early 90s were spent on more domestic concerns. She married and started a family. It was 1993 before she returned to the mainstream music scene. *Passion* included the major international hit 'A Whole New World ('Aladdin's Theme')', from the movie *Aladdin*, a duet with Peabo Bryson that won four Grammy Awards including Song Of The Year, Record Of The Year, Best Pop Performance By A Duo Or Group and Best Song Written Specifically For A Motion Picture Or For Television. It was also a US number 1 hit. *Reachin' Back* featured assistance from Gerald LeVert, Keith Thomas, and producers Thomas McElroy and Denzil Foster. On this record, Belle attempted to recreate the atmosphere of vintage Philly soul. Material chosen included the Delfonics' 'Didn't I (Blow Your Mind This Time)', Teddy Pendergrass' 'Love TKO' and the Spinners' 'Could It Be I'm Falling In Love'. *Believe In Me*, moved in a different direction, introducing contemporary hip-hop rhythms to her set.

● ALBUMS: *All By Myself* (Columbia 1987)★★, *Stay With Me* (Columbia 1989)★★★, *Passion* (Columbia 1993)★★★★, *Reachin' Back* (Columbia 1995)★★★, *Believe In Me* (MCA 1998)★★★.

● COMPILATIONS: *Baby Come To Me: The Best Of Regina Belle* (Sony 1997)★★★★.

Belly

Based in Newport, Rhode Island, USA, Belly was the brainchild of the mercurial Tanya Donelly (b. 14 August 1966, Newport, Rhode Island, USA; vocals/guitar). Donelly, along with half-sister Kristin Hersh, was a founding member of Throwing Muses. She was able to write the occasional song within that band, but inevitably felt constrained; when Hersh took time out to start a family, Donelly left amicably after recording *The Real Ramona*. She had already worked with the Breeders, a female punk-pop supergroup featuring Kim Deal (Pixies) and Josephine Wiggs (Perfect Disaster). However, this too was primarily someone else's band and Donelly finally moved on to Belly. They originally formed in December 1991 with brothers Thomas (b. 20 May 1966, USA; lead guitar) and Chris Gorman (b. Christopher Toll Gorman, 29 August 1967, USA; drums) and bass player Fred Abong (ex-Throwing Muses). He was replaced by Leslie Langston (ex-Throwing Muses), who in turn was replaced by Gail Greenwood (b. 3 October 1960, USA), who had had stints with the all-female band the Dames and hardcore outfit Boneyard. She also worked as a freelance illustrator, designing Aerosmith's fan club Christmas cards. Belly debuted with the EPs *Slow Dust* and then *Gepetto*, which preceded the album *Star*. Recorded in Nashville, *Star* featured a confident Donelly welding perverse, abusive and uplifting lyrics to a smothering mesh of guitar and sweet vocals. In its wake, the *Feed The Tree* EP gave them unlikely daytime airplay and a first chart hit, before the album soared to number 2 in the UK charts. Included on it was a version of 'Trust In Me' (from *The Jungle Book*), a song that summed up the band's appeal: a clash of the nice and the nasty. *King* was recorded at the end of 1994 in Nassau, Bahamas, with producer Glyn Johns, and featured writing contributions from Tom Gorman and Greenwood for the first time. For Donelly's part, the lyrics switched to a first person focus, though when pressed for a summary she described the album as 'just pop rock like everything else'. The band went belly up in late 1995. Donelly embarked on a solo career, while Greenwood joined L7.

● ALBUMS: *Star* (Sire/4AD 1993)★★★, *King* (Sire/4AD 1995)★★.

Beltram, Joey

b. 6 November 1971, Queens, New York, USA. Widely considered to be one of the gurus of New York hardcore, Beltram's 1988 release 'Energy Flash' (Transmat Records) was a milestone of the genre, providing a bassline that has re-emerged countless times (not least on Beltram's own recordings). By the age of 16 he was recording as Code 6 and Lost Entity for New York labels such as Nu Groove Records. At school he had saved his dinner money in order to buy records at the end of the week to make mix tapes. He certainly boasts eclectic tastes in dance music, at the last count owning over 60,000 records. The follow-up single, 1992's 'Mentasm', was credited to Second Phase, a collaboration with Mundo Muzique, and was one of several *nom de plume* that include Final Exposure ('Vortex', on Plus 8), Disorder ('Panic'/'Groove Attack', on Rhythmatic Rage) and Program 2 ('The Omen', on R&S Records). He has also recorded in a less frenetic house vein. His work on Cutting Records (Vice Tribe's 'Something Unreal') is a good example of this, while under his own name he has also provided a three-track EP (Beltram Presents ... Odyssey Nine - 'Drums Of Orbit') for

Visible, which dabbled in trance, and the long-player *Aonox*, which demonstrated an ambient influence. He also produced the *Caliber* EP for Warp Records, which saw many critics drawing comparisons to the mighty 'Energy Flash'. His remixes include Orbital's 'Oolaa' and the Smarte's 'Sesame's Treet', for US consumption.

● ALBUMS: *Aonox* (Visible 1994)★★★, *Places* (Tresor/Logic 1995)★★★, *Close Grind* (Novamute 1996)★★★.

● COMPILATIONS: *Classics* (R&S 1996)★★★★, *Joey Beltram Live* (Logic 1997)★★★★, *Re: Releases 1989-1991* (Trax 1998)★★★, *The Sound Of 2AM: A DJ Mix* (Moonshine 1999)★★★★.

Ben Folds Five

Formed in North Carolina, USA, Ben Folds Five take their name from leader Ben Folds (b. Chapel Hill, North Carolina, USA; piano/vocals). However, the band is a trio rather than the quintet that the name implies, the line-up completed by Robert Sledge (bass) and Darren Jessee (drums). A rock band without a lead guitarist is certainly something unique, but Ben Folds Five fit the bill so well that most listeners fail to notice the absence of the guitar. Immediately it was apparent that Folds intended to create something a little different from the usual perception of the pianist/singer-songwriter: 'The one thing I knew when I started out was that I didn't want to be the singer-songwriter at the piano. Everybody wants you to be like Billy Joel or Elton John or somebody, and that just doesn't interest me.' He formed the trio after originally working as a percussionist on Nashville sessions for Christian pop artists. He also spent time playing bass in a Broadway production of *Buddy*. After returning to North Carolina and recruiting local musicians Jessee and Sledge, the Ben Folds Five made their debut with a fine self-titled album for Caroline Records in 1996. This displayed the band's offbeat, ever-inventive style, and captured the imagination of critics throughout Europe and the USA. The follow-up *Whatever And Ever Amen* used wry humour to temper its sad tales of broken relationships. Tracks such as 'Brick' and 'Song For The Dumped', meanwhile, presented contrasting viewpoints from both sides of the gender war. *Naked Baby Photos* collected unreleased and live material. In 1998, Folds collaborated with the band's producer, Caleb Southern, and John Marc Painter on the side project, Fear Of Pop. Ben Folds Five returned with *The Unauthorized Biography Of Reinhold Messner*, another challenging but rewarding collection. This was an album that, aside from the typically catchy single 'Army', demanded concentration.

● ALBUMS: *Ben Folds Five* (Caroline 1996)★★★★, *Whatever And Ever Amen* (Epic 1997)★★★★, *The Unauthorized Biography Of Reinhold Messner* (Epic 1999)★★★.

● COMPILATIONS: *Naked Baby Photos* (Caroline 1997)★★★.

Benét, Eric

b. Milwaukee, Wisconsin, USA. Along with Rahsaan Patterson, D'Angelo and Tony Rich, Benét is representative of the current revival of the singer-songwriter tradition in modern urban soul. After gaining valuable experience as a featured singer with touring bands, Benét formed his own self-titled trio with his sister and his cousin George Nash Jnr. Having developed his own songwriting, he signed with Warner Brothers Records as a solo artist, writing and co-producing his acclaimed 1997 debut *True To Myself*. Heavily influenced by Stevie Wonder, Al Green and Sly Stone, the album's highlights varied from the slow-burning, confessional title-track and the romantic balladry of 'I'll Be There', to the funky groove of 'Spiritual Thang' and the cover version of Stone's 'If You Want Me To Stay'. Following an acclaimed US support slot for Erykah Badu, Benét visited the UK to join Shola Ama and D-Influence on the 1998 Rhythm Nation Tour. Wyclef Jean was among many big name contributors to 1999's mature sophomore set, *A Day In The Life*, which featured the R&B number 1 hit duet with Tamia, 'Spend My Life With You'.

● ALBUMS: *True To Myself* (Warners 1997)★★★★, *A Day In The Life* (Warners 1999)★★★★.

Bennett, Martyn

b. 1971, Newfoundland, Canada. Multi-instrumentalist Bennett can trace his family back to the Isle of Skye and Wales, and he was raised among Scottish-speaking immigrants on the island of Newfoundland. He returned to Scotland when he was six, where he was brought up surrounded by the sound of traditional Celtic folk songs. He was enrolled in a specialist music school as a teenager, leading to a classical education in violin and piano at the Royal Academy Of Music And Drama in Glasgow where he played in a symphony orchestra. At the same time Bennett continued to absorb traditional music structures, teaching himself the ancient Ceol Mor technique of bagpipe playing. In the early 90s, Bennett was drawn to Glasgow's burgeoning rave scene, and began hatching the idea of mixing house and hip-hop beats with traditional folk tunes. He developed these ideas busking in Edinburgh, playing folk dance reels over house and hip-hop backing tapes for a joke. The ideas took more serious form when Bennett was commissioned to work on several European theatre productions, beginning with the score for Billy Marshall's *The Haunting*. This in turn led to work on television and movie scores, and a bizarre one-off job as personal piper for the Tanzanian President when he visited Edinburgh. Bennett returned to more traditional live work supporting Wolfstone on a US tour and appearing at the Edinburgh Hogmanay in 1995 and 1996. The Scottish indie label Eclectic Records released his self-titled debut in 1996, with Bennett drawing praise for his bold fusion of modern dance rhythms with roots music from Celtic, Asian and Scandinavian sources. The album attracted the attention of Rykodisc Records, who released the follow-up, *Bothy Culture*, in 1997, a hugely impressive album which fine-tuned Bennett's multi-cultural approach to modern folk music.

● ALBUMS: *Martyn Bennett* (Eclectic 1996)★★★, *Bothy Culture* (Rykodisc 1997)★★★★.

Bentley Rhythm Ace

Richard March (b. 4 March 1965, York, Yorkshire, England; ex-Pop Will Eat Itself) and Mike Stokes began recording together in the mid-90s. In 1996, the pair sent a four-track demo of their work to Skint Records and consequently signed to that label as Bentley Rhythm Ace, taking the name from an old drum machine. Later that year the band gained widespread attention when they released a demo, which included the track 'Bentley's Gonna Sort You Out!', as the EP *This Is Carbootechnodisco*. This was followed by the *Last Train To Bentley On C* EP (1996) and the single 'Midlander' (1997), which prompted attention from the major labels.

They eventually signed to Parlophone Records and released the album *Bentley Rhythm Ace* in 1997. During the same period the pair toured around the UK, played at various festivals around Europe, and visited the USA at the end of the year. Their sound combines a variety of prominent sampled beats with bass guitar, synth patterns and riffs. However, unlike much of the big beat movement, with which they have often been associated, Bentley Rhythm Ace have a unique style on account of the range of influences that can be heard in the music, and the notoriously bizarre samples that highlight their eccentric sense of humour.

● ALBUMS: *Bentley Rhythm Ace* (Skint/Parlophone 1997)★★★.

Berg, Matraca

b. 3 February 1964, Nashville, Tennessee, USA. The song 'Appalachian Rain', on 90s country singer Berg's first album, is about an unmarried mother moving away to have her baby, and she explained, 'It is what happened to my mom; and in the song I tried to deal with how she must have felt, and what I wished had happened to my father.' Berg is one of the few country singers to have been born in Nashville and her mother, Icee Berg, who died when Matraca was 20, was a songwriter and backing vocalist. Matraca Berg and Bobby Braddock wrote a US country number 1 for T.G. Sheppard and Karen Brooks, 'Faking Love', and she followed it with another chart-topper, 'The Last One To Know' for Reba McEntire. Her songs, usually for female artists, include 'Eat At Joe's', 'Diamonds And Tears', 'Hey Cinderella', 'Give Me Some Wheels' (all recorded by Suzy Bogguss), 'Walk On' (Linda Ronstadt), 'Wrong Side Of Memphis', 'Everybody Knows' (Trisha Yearwood), 'Black Water Bayou' (Tanya Tucker), 'Wild Angels', 'Cryin' On The Shoulder Of The Road' (Martina McBride), 'You Can Feel Bad' (Patty Loveless), 'Strawberry Wine', 'We Danced Anyway' (Deana Carter) and 'Calico Plains' (Pam Tillis). Her 1990 debut, *Lying To The Moon*, included some minor country hits. The title track has the makings of a country standard, having also been recorded by Trisha Yearwood. Strangely, Berg moved to RCA Records' pop division for her second album, which was much more melancholy. In 1997, she won the Country Music Association Song Of The Year Award for 'Strawberry Wine', co-written with Gary Harrison for Deana Carter. She released a debut album for her new label Rising Tide the same year. A prolifically successful country songwriter, her own recording career tends to have become overshadowed by the success of others.

● ALBUMS: *Lying To The Moon* (RCA 1990)★★★, *Bittersweet Surrender* (RCA 1991)★★★, *The Speed Of Grace* (RCA 1993)★★★, *Sunday Morning To Saturday Night* (Rising Tide 1997)★★.

● COMPILATIONS: *Lying To The Moon And Other Stories* (RCA 1999)★★★★.

Berryhill, Cindy Lee

b. California, USA. An evocative singer-songwriter with a penchant for literary themes stretching from progressive science fiction to the beat poets, Berryhill's initial career choice was the theatre. After joining a San Diego vaudeville troupe, she attended the Lee Strasberg Theatre Institute in Los Angeles. Later, she formed her first punk band in the early 80s, the Stoopids, who only ever recorded privately distributed cassettes. Her experience on the Los Angeles punk scene was later revisited in songs such as 'Ballad Of A

Garage Band' on her debut album, but she felt that the whole movement, and her subsequent disenchantment with it, was a contributing factor in her nervous breakdown. It was the mid-80s before she recovered her strength and resolve, at that time pursuing a more folk rock-orientated direction. In 1987 she made her solo debut by contributing a song to *The Radio Tokyo Tapes Vol. 3* cassette, alongside artists such as Henry Rollins and the Minutemen. That song, 'Damn, Wish I Was A Man', was also included on her 1988 debut album, *Who's Gonna Save The World*. Having established a growing reputation for her intelligent, frequently sarcastic songs, she recorded *Naked Movie Star* the following year, with Patti Smith associate Lenny Kaye as producer. Despite the innovative use of jazz players and some trademark Kaye experimentation, it failed to produce adequate sales and Berryhill relocated to New Mexico, before having her entire worldly possessions stolen while in transit to San Diego. Several years passed before she was approached by local label Cargo Records while working at a city bookstore. They invited her to record a CD. The ensuing album was called *Garage Orchestra*, which is also the name of her backing band. The most noteworthy track was 'Song To Brian', a tribute to Brian Wilson, whose music had become an increasing influence. A follow-up collection was delayed when boyfriend Paul Williams (author and Bob Dylan biographer) was involved in a motorcycle crash and suffered a serious brain injury. *Straight Outta Marysville*, its title a pun on NWA's famed debut, again featured strong songs, particularly 'Unknown Master Painter', which some critics interpreted as self-analogy for this talented artist who still plies her trade in relative obscurity. The follow-up live album was recorded before a handful of fans in a San Francisco living room.

● ALBUMS: *Who's Gonna Save The World* (New Routes 1988)★★★, *Naked Movie Star* (Awareness 1989)★★★, *Garage Orchestra* (Unique Gravity 1995)★★★, *Straight Outta Marysville* (Demon 1996)★★★, *Living Room 16* (Griffith Park 1999)★★★★.

Beta Band

John MacLean (sampling), Robin Jones (drummer) and Steve Mason (vocals) formed this highly acclaimed UK art rock band while studying at college in Edinburgh, Scotland. With the addition of English bass player Richard Greentree they teamed up with Oasis associate Brian Cannon and began building a strong word-of-mouth reputation. Produced by Nick McCabe of the Verve, their debut EP *Champion Versions* appeared in July 1997. The EP's four tracks set the standard for future releases, revealing an approach to record production far removed from the pop-based format of most indie music. An eclectic mix of alternative and kraut rock styles with ambient dub and samples, the band's sound eschewed conventional music categories in preference for a bold, experimental approach. *The Patty Patty Sound* EP featured another wildly diverse fusion of sounds, although the 15-minute progressive rock jam 'The Monolith' came dangerously close to vacuous noodling. June 1998's *Los Amigos Del Beta Bandidos* saw the band decamping to a deserted Cornish tin mine for recording. Collected together on one album, *The 3 E.P.s* broke into the UK Top 40 in October 1998. In December, while the band were still recording material for an album, Mason released the solo EP *King Biscuit Time "Sings" Nelly Foggit's Blues In Me And The Pharaohs*. Their self-titled debut employed a diverse range of musical styles to no coherent effect, although the results were often charming. Promotion was not helped by the band members claiming the album was 'rubbish'.

● ALBUMS: *The 3 E.P.s* (Regal 1998)★★★★, *The Beta Band* (Regal 1999)★★★.

Bibb, Eric

b. 16 August 1951, New York City, New York, USA. Based in Sweden, singer-songwriter and guitarist Bibb is, with Corey Harris and Alvin Youngblood Hart, at the forefront of the 90s country blues revival. The son of famous 60s folk revivalist Leon Bibb, there was a constant stream of musical visitors to his father's house during his childhood, including Odetta, Pete Seeger, Judy Collins and Bob Dylan. Meeting the cream of the folk revival created a lasting impression on the young Bibb, who first started to learn the guitar when he was eight. Keen to explore different countries, Bibb then left New York to busk and travel in Europe, staying in Paris before moving to Stockholm for 10 years. Returning to New York briefly in the 80s, he finally settled in Sweden with his family. Regular touring with slide guitar player Göran Wennerbrandt built up his live reputation, and he supported country blues legend Taj Mahal. He recorded two albums for the Opus 3 label, with production duties handled by Wennerbrandt. His songs are both social and spiritual, reflecting the influence of the original country blues singers, but tackle modern-day problems and issues rather than lapsing into nostalgic authenticity. After signing to Warner Brothers Records' Code Blue outlet, Bibb indicated that his new material would reflect a more diverse range of musical influences, which was subsequently borne out by the excellent *Me To You* and *Home To Me*.

● ALBUMS: *Spirit & The Blues* (Opus 3 1995)★★★, *Good Stuff* (Opus 3 1997)★★★, *Me To You* (Code Blue 1997)★★★★, *Home To Me* (Code Blue 1999)★★★.

Big Bad Voodoo Daddy

The most immediately successful exponents of the retro jive/swing boom that swept the southern Californian marketplace in the late 90s, Big Bad Voodoo Daddy established their reputation with a weekly residency at the Derby dancehall in Los Angeles. Though they had been around for some time, their profile increased substantially when they made a cameo appearance in the 1996 independent movie, *Swingers*. The band had been founded in Ventura, California, in 1989 by vocalist and guitarist Scotty Morris, an established session musician in the area. His first exposure to big band swing came, aged nine, when he heard Cab Calloway's 'Minnie The Moocher' sung during a *Betty Boop* cartoon. Big Bad Voodoo Daddy finally gave him the chance to pursue the style further, after he had become disillusioned with the local music scene. The group grew from a trio to eventually include Dirk Shumaker (bass/vocals), Kurt Sodergren (drums/percussion), Karl Hunter (saxophones), Glen 'The Kid' Marhevka (trumpet/vocals), Andy 'Lucious' Rowley (saxophone/vocals), Jeff Harris (trombone) and Josh Levy (piano/vocals). They played dates throughout the west coast, and released two albums on their own Big Bad Records. Their biggest break, however, came when they took over the Wednesday night residency at the Derby from previous incumbents the Royal Crown Revue, in 1995. The director of *Swingers*, Jon Favreau, became a regular visitor

and befriended the band. Their signature tune, 'You & Me & The Bottle Makes Three Tonight (Baby)', was included on the movie soundtrack, while 'Cruel Spell' was featured in the same year's *Party Of Five*. The attention focused on the swing revival by the success of *Swingers* led to the band being contacted by producer Brad Benedict, of Capitol Records' *Ultra-Lounge* compilation series. As a result, Benedict was inspired to start up the EMI/Capitol Records' subsidiary Coolsville, with Big Bad Voodoo Daddy's third album (their second to be self-titled) becoming its first release. The album featured several winning Morris originals, including 'You & Me & The Bottle Makes Three Tonight (Baby)' and 'Mr. Pinstripe Suit', and a perfunctory cover version of Calloway's 'Minnie The Moocher'. The album went on to achieve gold sales and be nominated for a 1999 Grammy Award. The follow-up, *This Beautiful Life*, was released in October 1999.

● ALBUMS: *Big Bad Voodoo Daddy* (Big Bad 1994)★★★, *Whatchu' Want For Christmas?* (Big Bad 1995)★★★, *Big Bad Voodoo Daddy* (Coolsville/Capitol 1998)★★★★, *This Beautiful Life* (Coolsville/Capitol 1999)★★★.

Big Bub

b. Frederick Lee Drakeford, New Jersey, USA. Big Bub resumed his solo career in 1997 after spending several years as a successful soul and R&B producer for artists including Mary J. Blige, Boy George, Keith Sweat, BLACKstreet and Bobby Brown. He first built his reputation in the late 80s as a member of Today, a band who, with the help of Teddy Riley, were pivotal in the development of 'new jack swing' (aka swingbeat). His debut solo album followed in 1992, and is best remembered for the inclusion of the single 'Tellin' Me Stories', a song discussing the problems of coping with a drug-addicted girlfriend, at a time when matters of conscience were not uppermost in the minds of most R&B songwriters. Afterwards, Drakeford concentrated on production and writing, his biggest successes including a co-writing credit for Bobby Brown's 'My Prerogative', and material for Heavy D, Johnny Gill, Horace Brown and others. After a brief stint as an A&R director for Motown Records, he elected to enter the fray as a solo artist once again. His second album, *Timeless*, saw him reunited with producer Teddy Riley, while lead-off single 'Need Your Love' featured rappers Heavy D and Queen Latifah. Also included was an update of the Commodores' 'Zoom', which featured on the soundtrack to *Hoodlum*.

● ALBUMS: *Big Bub Comin' At Ya* (East West 1992)★★★, *Timeless* (Kedar Entertainment 1997)★★★.

Big Head Todd And The Monsters

Formed at high school in Boulder, Colorado, USA, in 1986, the band put together two albums and several single releases to little outside interest. Gradually, however, songwriter Todd Park Mohr (vocals/guitar), Rob Squires (bass) and Brian Nevin (drums) earned a groundswell of support after financing the band from their own pockets. *Midnight Radio*, with cover artwork by Chris Mars of the Replacements, one of their most vociferous fans, began to take that 'buzz' to a national level, but despite the breakthrough the band remained with their own label for its release. Finally signing to Giant Records through the auspices of Irving Azoff in 1993, they made their major label debut with *Sister Sweetly*, produced with David Z (Prince, Fine Young Cannibals, BoDeans) at Paisley Park studios, where strong musical frameworks emboldened songs such as 'Broken Hearted Saviour' and 'True Groove Thing'. Guitarist Leo Kottke contributed to 'Soul For Every Cowboy', while the band, on the back of an 18-month US tour, had three singles in the *Billboard* AOR Top 10, performed enthusiastically on the *David Letterman* and *Today* shows, and supported Robert Plant. *Strategem* [sic] was disappointing, despite unveiling further gritty displays of rural blues rock on tracks such as 'Neckbreaker' (inspired by fourteenth-century mystic St. John Of The Cross) and 'Angel Leads Me On'. *Beautiful World* was a more satisfying collection, although it failed to achieve the crossover success many expected.

● ALBUMS: *Another Mayberry* (Big Records 1989)★★★, *Midnight Radio* (Big Records 1990)★★★, *Sister Sweetly* (Giant 1993)★★★, *Strategem* (Giant 1995)★★, *Beautiful World* (Giant 1997)★★★, *Live Monsters* (Giant/Reprise 1998)★★★.

Big Mountain

Big Mountain evolved from a San Diego, Californian reggae band, the Rainbow Warriors, in the mid-80s. They toured the USA playing gigs to the uninitiated, introducing a diluted form of reggae to American ears. The multicultural line-up, featuring Quino (vocals), Gregory Blakney (drums), Jerome Cruz (guitar), Lance Rhodes (drums, percussion), Manfred Reinke (keyboards) and Lynn Copeland (bass), released 1992's *Wake Up* on the Quality label. A revamped line-up, featuring Quino, Copeland, Santa Davis (drums), James McWhinney (percussion), Billy Stoll (keyboards), Michael Hyde (keyboards), and leading Jamaican session player Tony Chin (lead guitar), convened to record their second album. In 1994, they released a version of Peter Frampton's 'Baby, I Love Your Way', which when featured in the movie *Reality Bites* became an international bestseller, peaking at UK number 2 and US number 6. The single also featured a Spanish version, enabling the band to enjoy successful sales in the South American market. The hit was followed by 'Sweet Sensual Love', performed in both English and Spanish, although it only reached number 51 in the UK pop chart. *Unity* followed, selling over a million copies worldwide. The band's accomplishment led to successful appearances at Jamaica's 1994 and 1995 Reggae Sunsplash festivals. They have since been unable to match the success of their first hit, but have continued to record with a number of Jamaica's top sessionmen, including Sly And Robbie and Handel Tucker. In 1995, 'Caribbean Blue' failed to make an impression in either the reggae or pop charts. *Free Up* featured singer-songwriter Sheryl Crow on co-writing credits.

● ALBUMS: *Wake Up* (Quality 1992)★★★★, *Unity* (Giant 1994)★★★★, *Resistance* (Giant 1995)★★★★, *Free Up* (Giant 1997)★★★.

● COMPILATIONS: *The Best Of Big Mountain* (Giant 1999)★★★★.

Bikini Kill

Pioneers of the 90s radical feminist musical movement named Riot Grrrl, USA's Bikini Kill were widely perceived to be the transatlantic cousins of UK band Huggy Bear - an impression confirmed when they joined that band for a 1993 shared album that was one of the movement's most celebrated documents. Hailing from Olympia, Washington, and featuring the haranguing voice of Kathleen Hanna alongside

Billy Karren (guitar), Tobi Vail (drums) and Kathi Wilcox (bass), Bikini Kill believed that indie rock was just as sexist as mainstream rock. Their tactics in attempting to create a new artistic platform included asking men to make way for women at the front of their concerts. Musically they resembled some of the late 70s punk pioneers, particularly the Slits. The Huggy Bear collaboration was followed later in the same year by *Pussy Whipped*. This included direct takes on sexual politics that spared no blushes. 'Rebel Girl', the band's anthem, which had previously been recorded twice, once in single form with Joan Jett as producer, made a third appearance. The band recorded one further album before disbanding in 1998. While the initial spark of Riot Grrrl has died down, Bikini Kill remains its most vibrant legacy.

● ALBUMS: *Bikini Kill* (K Records 1992)★★★, *Bikini Kill* mini-album (Kill Rock Stars 1993)★★★, with Huggy Bear *Yeah Yeah Yeah* (Kill Rock Stars 1993)★★★, *Pussy Whipped* (Kill Rock Stars 1993)★★, *Reject All American* (Kill Rock Stars 1996)★★★.

● COMPILATIONS: *The Tape Version Of The First Two Albums* (Kill Rock Stars 1994)★★★, *The Singles* (Kill Rock Stars 1998)★★★.

Billie

b. Billie Paul Piper, 22 September 1982, Swindon, Wiltshire, England. Teenage pop sensation Billie was groomed for stardom from an early age, training at London's prestigious Sylvia Young Theatre School (whose other alumni has included members of the Spice Girls and All Saints and television personalities Nick Berry, Denise Van Outen and Samantha Janus). A bit part in *EastEnders* was followed by the prominent use of Piper as the face of a *Smash Hits* advert in August 1997. This high-profile campaign was instrumental in Virgin Records subsidiary Innocent signing the 15-year old Piper. She recorded tracks for her debut album while still studying at school, but the hard work paid off when her debut single 'Because We Want To' went straight in at UK number 1 in July 1998. Her follow-up 'Girlfriend' also debuted at number 1 in October, making Billie the first UK female solo artist to have two number 1s in the same year since Cilla Black in 1964. The success of her first two singles meant that November's number 16 placing for her debut album was viewed as something of a disappointment. 'She Wants You' failed to attain the UK Christmas number 1 slot, debuting at number 3 in December. The album's title-track, a more adult-orientated swingbeat number, reached the same position in March 1999.

● ALBUMS: *Honey To The B* (Virgin 1998)★★★.

Binary Finary

Binary Finary (Matt, Ricky Grant, Woody and Tony) aroused massive interest from the press and public with their unmistakable trance anthem, '1998'. It was originally released on Aquarius Records, before being signed to EMI Records' dance music offshoot, Positiva Records and consequently becoming a massively successful single. The track is the epitome of the surging, melodic trance that has been the soundtrack to the late 90s' 'Mitsubishi [a type of strong ecstasy tablet] Revolution' in European clubs, such as the UK's Gatecrasher. '1998' took dance floors by storm, with its powerful chord changes, heart-stopping breakdown and dramatic crescendos. The track has been featured on numerous mix compilations and has proved a favourite with many notable DJs such as Paul Van Dyk (who remixed the track),

Paul Oakenfold and Judge Jules. Positiva re-released the track as '1999' in that year, in a two-disc format, featuring remixes from Van Dyk, Matt Darey, Gouryella (DJ Tiesto and Ferry Corsten) and Kaycee. It proved a crossover success, reaching number 11 in the UK charts. Binary Finary performed live at numerous club events and festivals in 1998 and 1999, including Glastonbury Festival, Cream's Creamfields and in Ibiza, before beginning work on an eagerly-awaited album.

Biohazard

The mean streets of Brooklyn, New York, USA, saw the formation of Biohazard in 1988 by Evan Seinfeld (bass/vocals), Billy Graziadei (guitar/vocals), Bobby Hambel (guitar) and Danny Schuler (drums). The harsh realities of urban life provide constant lyrical inspiration for this socially and politically aware hardcore band. Modest beginnings supporting the likes of the Cro-Mags and Carnivore at the famous L'Amour club led to an independent debut, *Biohazard*. Constant touring built such a cult following that the band were able to sign to Roadrunner Records for one album, and then secure a major contract with Warner Brothers Records in 1992. *Urban Discipline* was recorded in under two weeks on a tiny budget, but proved to be the band's breakthrough album. Blisteringly heavy, with lyrics to match - 'Black And White And Red All Over' was an anti-racism tirade, intended to dispel a mistakenly applied fascist label stemming from the debut's 'Howard Beach', which concerned a racially motivated Brooklyn murder - the album drew massive praise, as did wild live shows during heavy touring with Kreator in Europe and Sick Of It All in the USA. The band also recorded a well-received track with rappers Onyx for the *Judgement Night* soundtrack. The Warners debut, *State Of The World Address*, was recorded in seven weeks, and demonstrated that major label status did not mean any compromising on Biohazard's part. The album featured a furiously heavy Ed Stasium production and an aggressive performance that attracted a succession of rave reviews. The band embarked on a successful US tour with Pantera and Sepultura as album sales took off. However, a second appearance at the Donington Festival came to a controversially premature end, owing to the stage management's safety worries over Biohazard's penchant for encouraging their audience to join them on stage *en masse*. Further European touring, including several festival dates, was problem-free, with the band reaffirming a deserved reputation for their ferocious live shows, before returning to the USA for dates with House Of Pain and Danzig. Hambel was sacked from the band in November 1995 prior to the recording of *Mata Leáo*. His replacement was Rob Echeverria (b. 15 December 1967, New York, USA; ex-Helmet). *No Holds Barred*, a fierce live album recorded in Europe, was followed by the band's PolyGram Records debut, *New World Disorder*.
● ALBUMS: *Biohazard* (Maze 1990)★★, *Urban Discipline* (Roadrunner 1992)★★★, *State Of The World Address* (Warners 1994)★★★, *Mata Leáo* (Warners 1996)★★, *No Holds Barred* (Roadrunner 1997)★★★, *New World Disorder* (Mercury 1999)★★★.

Bis

Formed in Edinburgh, Scotland, Bis comprises Manda Rin (b. 22 March 1977, Thornliebank, Scotland; vocals, keyboards, bass) and brothers Steve Sci-Fi (b. 20 March 1976; vocals,

guitar) and John Disco (b. 21 August 1978; guitar). The band was formed at school when the brothers were 11, before they enlisted fellow school friend Rin in 1994. They were supported by the fanzine community (notably *All About Dee*) from their inception - Rin and Sci-Fi also being fanzine editors of *Funky Spunk* and *Paper Bullets*, respectively. They made a dramatic commercial breakthrough in 1996 when they became the first unsigned band to appear on the BBC Television programme *Top Of The Pops*. They made a second appearance a week later as 'Kandy Pop' entered the UK Top 30. Previously they had released a limited edition of the *Transmissions On The Teen-C Tip!* EP, featuring the Bikini Kill-inspired 'Kill Yr Boyfriend'. Supports to Super Furry Animals, Garbage and Bikini Kill themselves followed, though in performance the band's lo-fi pop approach did not translate well to large venues. They signed to Wiiija Records in June 1996 and released their debut long-player the following year. By time they were facing increasingly hostile criticism from a music press which has continued to ignore the band's subsequent releases.
● ALBUMS: *The New Transistor Heroes* (Wiiija 1997)★★★, *Social Dancing* (Wiiija 1999)★★.

Biz Markie

b. Marcel Hall, 8 April 1964, Harlem, New York, USA. This member of Marley Marl's posse delivered his tales of nose-picking, bad breath and other niceties in a jerky manner that came close to self-parody, but found a niche market in adolescent circles. His progress was aided by an unlikely US Top 10 hit single, 'Just A Friend', in 1990, which helped the attendant *The Biz Never Sleeps* achieve gold sales. Resolutely old school, he nevertheless brought a sense of humour and undoubted rhyming talents to hip-hop. His 1993 album featured 'Let Me Turn You On' over a sample of 'Ain't No Stoppin' Us Now', on which he actually sang. The set's title, *All Samples Cleared!*, was more than an unjustified whinge at copyright laws. Each and every sample was cleared by the relevant artist's representatives, after Markie had previously come under threat of imprisonment. This stemmed from his sampling of Gilbert O'Sullivan's 1972 ballad 'Alone Again (Naturally)' on *I Need A Haircut*. Judge Kevin Thomas Duff awarded punitive damages, ruling that 'sampling is theft under criminal law', giving all rap artists cause for concern and changing the way hip-hop albums were prepared for release. Markie later appeared as a guest vocalist for the Beastie Boys, who were early supporters of his human beatbox style.
● ALBUMS: *Goin' Off* (Cold Chillin'/Warners 1988)★★, *The Biz Never Sleeps* (Cold Chillin'/Warners 1989)★★★, *I Need A Haircut* (Cold Chillin'/Warners 1991)★★★, *All Samples Cleared!* (Cold Chillin'/Warners 1993)★★★.
● COMPILATIONS: *Biz's Baddest Beats* (Cold Chillin'/Warners 1994)★★★.
● FILMS: *The Meteor Man* (1993).

Björk

b. Björk Gudmundsdóttir, 21 November 1965, Reykjavik, Iceland. The former Sugarcubes vocalist, armed with a remarkable, keening vocal presence, has crossed over to huge success via her club-orientated material. The success of *Debut* culminated in awards for Best International Newcomer and Best International Artist at the 1994 BRIT

Awards. However, she had made her 'debut' proper as far back as 1977, with an album recorded in her native territory as an 11-year old prodigy (including cover versions of pop standards by the Beatles and others). It was only the start of a prodigious musical legacy. Her next recording outfit was Tappi Tíkarrass (which apparently translates as 'Cork that bitch's arse'), who recorded two albums between 1981 and 1983. A more high-profile role was afforded via work with KUKL, who introduced her to future Sugarcubes Einar Örn and Siggi. The band's two albums were issued in the UK on the Crass label. Björk returned to Iceland after the Sugarcubes' six-year career, partially to pay off debts, recording a solo album in 1990 backed by a local be-bop group. She re-emerged in 1993 with *Debut* and a welter of more house-orientated material, including four hit singles. These chiefly came to prominence in the dance music charts (Björk having first dipped a toe in those waters with 808 State on *Ex:El*) via their big-name remixers. The most important of these were Underworld and Bassheads ('Human Behaviour'), Black Dog ('Venus As A Boy'), Tim Simenon of Bomb The Bass ('Play Dead', which was used on the soundtrack to *The Young Americans*) and David Morales, Justin Robertson and Fluke ('Big Time Sensuality'). Björk appeared at the 1993 BRIT Awards duetting with PJ Harvey, while in 1994 she co-wrote the title track to Madonna's album *Bedtime Stories*. Released in 1995, *Post* was an impressive and even more eclectic album, ranging from the hard techno beats of 'Army Of Me' to the shimmering 'Hyperballad'. Now an unwilling media star, Björk made the headlines following her attack on an intrusive reporter, and through her liaison with jungle artist Goldie. Following a desultory remix album, Björk released her third solo set, the self-produced *Homogenic*. Though she received critical plaudits for her seemingly tireless musical invention, the album was also notable for lyrics revealing a more personal side to the singer, reflecting on her troubled year.

● ALBUMS: *Björk* (Fàlkinn 1977)★★★, with Trió Gudmundar *Gling-Gló* (Smekkleysa 1990)★★★, *Debut* (One Little Indian 1993)★★★★, *Post* (One Little Indian 1995)★★★★, *Telegram* remix album (One Little Indian 1996)★★★, *Homogenic* (One Little Indian 1997)★★★★.
● COMPILATIONS: *The Best Remixes From The Album, Debut, For All The People Who Don't Buy White-Labels* (One Little Indian 1994)★★.
● VIDEOS: *Björk* (Propaganda 1994), *Vessel* (PolyGram Music Video 1994), *Live In Shepherd's Bush* (One Little Indian 1998), *Volumen* (One Little Indian 1998).
● FURTHER READING: *Post: The Official Björk Book*, Penny Phillips. *Björkgraphy*, Martin Aston.

Black Box

One of the leading exponents of a wave of Italian house music that flourished on the dancefloors of the late 80s and early 90s, Black Box comprised three Italian studio musicians (Daniele Davoli, Mirko Limoni and Valerio Semplici), collectively known as Groove Groove Melody. Based in the Regio D'Emillia area of northern Italy, and made frequent use of 'singer' Katrin (b. Catherine Quinol, Paris, France, of Guadelope descent). Semplici was a clarinet teacher and played in the La Scala Classical Music Orchestra in Milan. Davoli was a well-known Italian club DJ (known as DJ Lelewel), largely at the Marabu Starlight Club, while Limoni was the computer and keyboard whizz kid of the trio and had previously engineered for Italian pop act Spagna. The

Groove Groove Melody team were established as one of the top two production outfits in Italian dance music, churning out more than a dozen singles a year in their native country. Katrin was spotted by Spagna's guitarist at a club, and, after introductions, featured as vocalist on 'Ride On Time'. The single became the first of a series of Italian house records to crossover to the UK charts, staying at number 1 for six weeks in 1989. Controversy reigned when it was realized that the single had sampled the voice of singer Loleatta Holloway from the 'Love Sensation' single she made with Dan Hartman in the late 70s. An agreement was eventually worked out with Salsoul (who owned the rights) as both companies benefited from 800,000 UK sales. The Groove Groove Melody team were also behind the production of Starlight's 'Numero Uno' and Mixmaster's 'Grand Piano', another prime example of 'Italo-house', and another crossover hit. Under seven or more pseudonyms, they turned out numerous further records. However, as Black Box, their hits included 'I Don't Know Anybody Else', 'Everybody Everybody' (the last of the 'Ride On Time' trilogy), 'Strike It Up', and 'Fantasy', a revamp of the Earth, Wind And Fire hit, all of which featured an uncredited Martha Wash on vocals and broke them into the US market. They were also responsible for, among other remixes, ABC's 1991 comeback single, 'Say It'. Their mid-90s singles, 'Not Anyone', 'I Got The Vibration', and 'Native New Yorker', enjoyed limited chart success.

● ALBUMS: *Dreamland* (Deconstruction/RCA 1990)★★★, *Remixed Reboxed Black Box/Mixed Up* (Deconstruction/RCA 1991)★★★.
● COMPILATIONS: *Hits & Mixes* (Camden 1998)★★★.
● VIDEOS: *Video Dreams* (BMG Video 1990).

Black Crowes

Exposed to a wide variety of music from an early age by their musician father, brothers Chris (b. Christopher Mark Robinson, 20 December 1966, Atlanta, Georgia, USA; vocals) and Rich Robinson (b. Richard S. Robinson, 24 May 1969, Atlanta, Georgia, USA; guitar) formed the band under the name Mr. Crowe's Garden in 1984. A procession of six bass players and three drummers passed through before the band stabilized with Johnny Colt (b. 1 May 1966, Cherry Point, USA; bass) and Steve Gorman (b. 17 August 1965, Muskegon, Michigan, USA; drums, ex-Mary My Hope). His predecessor, Jeff Sullivan, went on to join Drivin' N' Cryin'. Jeff Cease joined the band as a second guitarist in 1988 from the Nashville band Rumble Circus, to augment and toughen both the songs and the live sound. As the Black Crowes, they were signed to the Def American label by George Drakoulias. Given the heavy nature of other members of the label's roster, such as Slayer and Danzig, the purist rock 'n' roll style of the Crowes was a stark contrast. Drakoulias produced their 1990 debut, *Shake Your Money Maker*, a remarkably mature album from such a young band, blending soul and uncomplicated R&B in a manner reminiscent of vintage Rolling Stones and Humble Pie. Another influence was made obvious by the stirring cover version of Otis Redding's 'Hard To Handle'. The record's highlight was 'She Talks To Angels', an emotive acoustic ballad about the frailties of a drug addict, featuring a superb vocal and highly accomplished lyric from Chris Robinson. The album was released to critical acclaim, and the band went on the road, supporting first Steve Stevens' Atomic Playboys, and then

Junkyard in the USA, plus a handful of UK dates as head-liners or opening for the Dogs D'Amour. Their live performances drew further Stones comparisons, the band's image being very much rooted in the 70s, and with Chris Robinson's thin frame dominating the stage like a young Mick Jagger. With heavy radio and MTV airplay exposing the Crowes to a wider audience, the first single, 'Jealous Again', reached number 75 in the *Billboard* charts, and the band were invited to fill the prestigious support slot for the final leg of Aerosmith's 'Pump' tour on their return to the USA. Canadian keyboard player Ed Harsch, recommended by former Green On Red member Chuck Leavell, who had played on the album, joined the band in early 1991. The band were invited on another high-profile tour as guests of ZZ Top, but their uncompromising attitude led to ZZ Top's management demanding that the Crowes leave the tour following a home-town show in Atlanta, owing to Chris Robinson's persistent, if oblique, criticism of the corporate sponsorship of the tour. Somewhat ironically, the band fired the support act for their subsequent headline shows after discovering that they had made advertisements for a similar major company.

By this stage, the band had achieved a considerable level of chart success, and they joined the European Monsters Of Rock tour, opening at the prestigious Donington Festival in England and culminating in a massive free show in Moscow. Prior to these dates, the band were forced to take a five-week break (their longest in 22 months of touring) when Chris Robinson collapsed, suffering from exhaustion, following an acoustic showcase at Ronnie Scott's club in London. The singer recovered to undertake the tour, plus a UK trek to complete the band's world tour. This ended with further controversy, with Colt and vocalist Robinson becoming embroiled in a fight with a member of the crowd at the Edinburgh Playhouse. Almost immediately after the tour, the band parted company with Jeff Cease, replacing him with former Burning Tree guitarist/vocalist Marc Ford. Rather than rest on their laurels, the band went straight into pre-production for their second album, completing basic tracks in only eight days. Borrowing from the title of an old hymn book, *The Southern Harmony And Musical Companion* was released in the spring of 1992, again to positive reviews. The musical progression of the band, and of the brothers as songwriters, was obvious, with more complex arrangements than the debut, a much greater expanse of sound and the use of female backing singers. New recruit Ford provided superb guitar solos, with one particularly notable lead on 'Sometimes Salvation'. With both the album and opening single 'Remedy' (US number 48, UK number 24) a success, the Black Crowes returned to the road for the High As The Moon tour - a free show in Toronto's G Rose Lord Park drew a 75,000 crowd, with people entering the park at a rate of 1,000 per minute at one point. In 1994, *Amorica* was finally released. A previously completed album (*Tall*) had been scrapped, with only five songs retained, and producer Jack Puig had been brought in to rectify matters. Live shows saw the debut of percussionist Chris Trujillo, and the band achieved another UK success with 'High Head Blues/A Conspiracy' reaching number 25 in February 1995. *Three Snakes And One Charm* was hampered by the numerous personnel changes which interrupted the recording process. Marc Ford left the band in August 1997, and was soon fol-lowed by Johnny Colt; the latter was replaced in early 1998 by Sven Pipien (ex-Mary My Hope). *By Your Side* marked a welcome return to the sleazy rock 'n' roll style of their earlier albums.

● ALBUMS: *Shake Your Money Maker* (Def American 1990)★★★, *The Southern Harmony And Musical Companion* (Def American 1992)★★★★, *Amorica* (American 1994)★★★, *Three Snakes And One Charm* (American 1996)★★★, *By Your Side* (Columbia 1999)★★★.

● COMPILATIONS: *Sho' Nuff* (American 1998)★★★.

● VIDEOS: *Who Killed That Bird On Your Windowsill ... The Movie* (Warner Brothers Video 1993).

● FURTHER READING: *The Black Crowes*, Martin Black.

Black Dog Productions

Ken Downie joined up with Ed Handley and Andy Turner, who themselves formed Plaid, in 1988 to form Black Dog Productions, a secretive east London techno crew, communicating with the outside world from the infamous Black Dog Towers, and determinedly obscuring their identities. After attempting to persuade Larry Heard to remix their first tracks (he turned them down on the grounds that the music was 'too weird'), Black Dog released their first record, the *Virtual* EP, on Black Dog Records a year later. With the subsequent *Age Of Slack* and *Black Dog* EPs, despite their limited distribution (in part, the result of the distributor melting down half of the 1,000 copies of *Black Dog*), Black Dog had attracted a strong and loyal fanbase. With the inspirational use of breakbeats (at the time being hijacked by the 'happy hardcore' brigade) and melodies, in these early recordings Black Dog created some of their finest work, and indeed some of the finest abstract techno to emerge from the UK. They continued in style with the *Parallel Squelch* EP, released on the newly formed GPR label, attracting the interests of Warp Records and R&S Records. In 1993, Black Dog released their debut album, *Bytes*, as part of Warp's Artificial Intelligence series. Certainly one of the highlights of the series, the album highlighted their subtle sense of songwriting propriety, and attracted the attention of numerous artists, resulting in remix and production work for artists such as Nicolette and Björk. *Temple Of Transparent Balls*, on GPR, followed a year later, although much of the work had been produced prior to *Bytes*, and had been spilt between Ken Downie on the one hand, and the pairing of Ed Handley and Andy Turner on the other. *Spanners*, the third and last album featuring the original band line-up, was released in 1995. Sounding more accomplished, the album occasionally lacks the raw feel of some of their earlier cuts, although the sheer inventiveness of the synthetic sounds and percussion still manages to entrance the listener. Following *Spanners*, Handly and Turner departed to concentrate on Plaid, leaving Downie to continue working alone under the Black Dog name. The first 'solo' Black Dog album, *Music For Adverts (And Short Films)*, was released on Warp in 1996. A collaborative EP with Israeli singer Ofra Haza followed in 1999.

● ALBUMS: *Bytes* (Warp 1993)★★★★, *Temple Of Transparent Balls* (GPR 1993)★★★, *Spanners* (Warp 1995)★★★★, *Music For Adverts (And Short Films)* (Warp 1996)★★★, with Ofra Haza *Babylon* (Warners 1999)★★★.

● COMPILATIONS: *Parallel* (GPR 1995)★★★★.

Black Grape

There was no lack of media interest in the post-Happy Mondays pursuits of singer Shaun Ryder (b. 23 August 1962) and 'dancer' Bez (b. Mark Berry). However, save for a solitary guest appearance with Intastella, by the end of 1994 it appeared that Ryder had lost his muse permanently. The ecstatic reviews that greeted Black Grape's debut album, *It's Great When You're Straight, Yeah!*, soon silenced such doubts. However, the germination of Black Grape had apparently occurred only weeks after the dissolution of the Happy Mondays, with demo recordings conducted in Ryder's bedroom. The band he put together was initially named simply the Mondays, and included Kermit (b. Paul Leveridge), a veteran of Manchester hip-hop act Ruthless Rap Assassins, plus ex-Paris Angels guitarist 'Wags' (b. Paul Wagstaff), second guitarist Craig Gannon (ex-Smiths) and Martin Smith of Intastella. However, by the time Black Grape had taken their new name and moved to Rockfield Studios in Wales to record their debut album, both Smith and Gannon had departed, to be replaced by Cypress Hill collaborator Danny Saber, who took on a co-writing role, Ged Lynch (drums) and Stephen Lironi (ex-Altered Images, songwriter to Rose Royce, among others, and husband of Clare Grogan). The title of the album partly expressed Ryder's decision to turn away from hard drug abuse, and this was indeed a comparatively sober effort given the artist's past reputation. However, his much-publicized 'cut-up' lyrics were present, along with his trademark scat coupling of meaningless phrases used primarily for their phonetic value. The real plus, however, came in the contribution of Kermit, whose growling raps balanced the slurring Ryder delivery perfectly. The band was rewarded with a UK number 1 album, which also figured as one of the albums of the year among a number of respected rock critics. During an eventful 1996, the band toured regularly and lost the services of dancer Bez, while Kermit announced his own side-project, Man Made, in early 1997. With new vocalist Carl 'Psycho' McCarthy on board, the long-awaited *Stupid, Stupid, Stupid* was released to mixed reviews, although there was no denying the lyrical verve of Ryder on tracks such as 'Dadi Waz A Badi' and 'Squeaky'. Soon afterwards, both Kermit and Psycho left, reducing the band to the duo of Ryder and Saber, and the inevitable split followed. Ryder re-formed the Happy Mondays in 1999.

● ALBUMS: *It's Great When You're Straight ... Yeah* (Radioactive 1995)★★★★, *Stupid, Stupid, Stupid* (Radioactive 1997)★★★.

● VIDEOS: *The Grape Tapes* (Radioactive 1997).

● FURTHER READING: *Shaun Ryder: Happy Mondays, Black Grape And Other Traumas*, Mick Middles. *High Life 'N' Low Down Dirty: The Thrills And Spills Of Shaun Ryder*, Lisa Verrico. *Freaky Dancin'*, Bez.

Black Moon

Brooklyn-based rappers, whose entrance on the New York scene was rewarded with sales of over 200,000 of their debut cut, 'Who Got Da Props?'. Black Moon, who comprise 5ft Excellerator, DJ Evil Dee and Buckshot, signed with Nervous Records' offshoot, Wreck, despite stern competition, in 1991 (there were certainly offers on the table from major companies). Black Moon (signifying Brothers Lyrically Acting Combining Kickin' Music Out On Nations) also kept a firm handle on the management of their own affairs, setting up their own production and management companies, Beat Minerz (Evil Dee and his brother Mr. Walt) and Duck Down (Buckshot and Big Dru Ha). The latter also looked after the affairs of Wreck's second signing, Smif N Wessun, fellow members of the Brooklyn-based Boot Camp Clik of MCs. Musically, Black Moon are a throwback to rap's old school, with Evil Dee's bleak bass and beatbox underpinning Buckshot and 5ft's considered raps for minimalist impact. Their debut album was afforded a strong critical reaction, no less than KRS-One himself noting it to be '. . . the phattest shit I've heard in a long time'. Instantly heralded as a defining example of east coast crime rap, it included further classics in their second single 'How Many MC's', and 'Buck Em Down'. The trio embarked on a national tour with Das-EFX but then remained dormant for several years due to legal and personal problems. Buckshot worked with Special Ed and Master Ace, as the Crooklyn Dodgers, on the title track to Spike Lee's 1994 movie, *Crooklyn*. A remix album, featuring two new tracks, was released in 1996 before the trio finally returned in 1999 with their much delayed sophomore set, *War Zone*. The album, released on Duck Down Records, saw the trio on fine form on old school classics such as 'This Is What It Sounds Like (Worldwind)' and 'Two Turntables And A Mic'.

● ALBUMS: *Enta Da Stage* (Wreck 1993)★★★★, *Diggin' In Dah Vaults* remixes (Wreck/Nervous 1996)★★★, *War Zone* (Duck Down 1999)★★★.

Black Sheep

Rap duo comprising Andre 'Dres' Titus (b. Sanford, North Carolina, USA) and William 'Mista Lawnge' McLean (b. 11 December 1970, Sanford, North Carolina, USA), who are based in the Bronx, New York, though they actually met in North Carolina in 1983. Titus' father, an army officer, was stationed there, while McLean's mother had relocated to the state while he was in school. He was sharing the bill with Sparkie Dee at a gig when her DJ, Red Alert, advised him that if he ever moved back to the capital, he should contact him. He did just that in 1985, linking up with the Jungle Brothers and A Tribe Called Quest, before telephoning Titus to invite him to join a band. Finally together, they arrived from a similar angle to the Native Tongues Posse, of which they were members, but doused their Afrocentricity in humour. Their self-produced debut album made the *Billboard* Top 30 in 1991, mainly on the back of the excellent single, 'The Choice Is Yours', the video for which brought them an MTV award. The album that housed it was filled with spoken interludes, heightened accents and ramshackle comedy. By the advent of their second long-playing set, the duo had toughened up slightly, but kept their musical stance sprightly. The album was prefaced by a single, 'No Way, No How'. They had also set up their own label operation, One Love Records, the first signing to which was a crew entitled Legion.

● ALBUMS: *A Wolf In Sheep's Clothing* (Mercury 1991)★★★, *Non Fiction* (Mercury 1994)★★★.

Black Star

Brooklyn-based MCs Mos Def (b. Dante Beze) and Talib Kweli are key players in the new school of hard-hitting underground rappers. Alongside artists such as Company Flow, Jurassic 5 and Canibus, and the pioneering underground label Rawkus Records, they constitute an informal reaction to hip-hop's twin bugbears, the commercialism of

Puff Daddy and the negativity of gangsta rap. Def rapped from an early age, forming Urban Thermo Dynamics (UTD) with his brother and sister, although he also developed an acting career. He joined the influential Native Tongues Posse, making a guest appearance on De La Soul's 1996 set *Stakes Is High*. He released the 'The Universal Magnetic' and 'Body Rock' singles, the latter featuring Q-Tip from key Native Tongues artists A Tribe Called Quest. Kweli worked in the African-American bookstore Nkiru Books on St. Mark's Place, and performed with DJ Hi-Tek as one half of Reflections Eternal. As a Rawkus recording artist, Kweli also appeared on the label's seminal *Lyricist Lounge Volume 1* compilation. He teamed up with Mos Def, performing free gigs at Nkiru, and collaborating on the Reflections Eternal cut 'Fortified Live'. Their Black Star venture was named after the early twentieth-century visionary Marcus Garvey's Black Star Line shipping company, which intended to return all black people back to their ancestral African home. The duo's debut single, 'Definition', was an underground hit. The attendant self-titled album eschewed the negativity of gangsta rap for a highly intelligent and searching examination of black culture, harking back to the classic era of rap epitomised by Public Enemy and KRS-1. The album's sparse, hard-hitting rhythms were also in marked comparison to the overblown productions of Puff Daddy, which dominated the rap mainstream. Def released his solo debut, *Black On Both Sides*, the following October.

● ALBUMS: *Mos Def & Talib Kweli Are Black Star* (Rawkus 1998)★★★★.

Black, Clint

b. 4 February 1962, Long Branch, New Jersey, USA. Black was born in New Jersey when his father was working there, but the family soon headed back to their home of Houston, Texas. Black was playing the harmonica at the age of 13 and the guitar at 15. He spent several years playing country music in Houston clubs, and his career took off when he met local musician Hayden Nicholas. They wrote 'Straight From The Factory' as soon as they met and forged a lasting songwriting partnership. Their demos impressed Bill Ham, the manager of ZZ Top, who quickly secured a contract with RCA Records. Most unusually, Black reached number 1 on the US country chart with his first record, 'A Better Man', which he had written about his own broken romance. The title track from his 1989 debut *Killin' Time* was also a number 1 record. The album was a multi-million-seller. *Put Yourself In My Shoes* included another number 1 single, 'Loving Blind'. In both vocal and songwriting ability, the obvious comparison is with Merle Haggard, and one that Black is happy to acknowledge. Managerial disputes halted his recording career after the release of *Put Yourself In My Shoes*, but his superstar status was affirmed in 1992 with the belated appearance of *The Hard Way*, which spawned a number 1 single ('We Tell Ourselves'), and showed heartening signs that Black was unwilling to rest on his artistic laurels. He also duetted with Roy Rogers, reaching the charts with 'Hold On Partner', and recorded 'No Time To Kill' with Wynonna. Black sang 'A Run Of Bad Luck' on the *Maverick* soundtrack album and enjoyed further hits with 'We Tell Ourselves', 'Burn One Down' and 'Life Gets Away'. In 1995, he recorded a Christmas album with a difference, eschewing traditional material in favour of his own songs. *Nothin' But*

The Taillights saw Black supported by high-quality guest musicians including Alison Krauss, Mark Knopfler and Chet Atkins. Black produced himself for the first time on the highly eclectic follow-up *D'Lectrified*.

● ALBUMS: *Killin' Time* (RCA 1989)★★★, *Put Yourself In My Shoes* (RCA 1990)★★★★, *The Hard Way* (RCA 1992)★★★★, *No Time To Kill* (RCA 1993)★★★, *One Emotion* (RCA 1994)★★★★, *Looking For Christmas* (RCA 1995)★★, *Nothin' But The Taillights* (RCA 1997)★★★, *D'Lectrified* (RCA 1999)★★★.

● COMPILATIONS: *Clint Black* (RCA 1993)★★, *The Greatest Hits* (RCA 1996)★★★★.

● VIDEOS: *Summer's Comin'* (RCA 1995).

● FURTHER READING: *A Better Man*, R.D. Brown.

● FILMS: *Maverick* (1994), *Cadillac Jack And Ponder* (1997).

Black, Frances

Irish folk singer Frances Black found instant success in 1994 with her debut solo album, a number 1 success in Ireland, but had spent several years in less celebrated musical activity before the breakthrough. Her first recording came in 1986 as a contributor to *The Black Family Album* with her renowned sibling, Mary Black, before work with Arcady, and a duet with Kieran Goss. *Talk To Me*, completed with help from musicians James Blennerhassett, Artie McGlynn and Nollaig Casey, plus Ray Dodds and Graham Henderson of Fairground Attraction, featured new songs written expressly for her by Nanci Griffith and Mark Nevin, alongside standards drawn from the repertoires of Donagh Long, Christy Hennessy and John Lennon. Its success came as a surprise to Black. The album was dedicated to her mother and her sister, Fran Byrne, and there was a small role for sister Mary on the album, although not one so ostentatious as to deflect critics from her own emerging talent as a song interpreter. The album's success earned her a major record label deal with Sony, the fruits of which were evident on 1998's *Don't Get Me Wrong*.

● ALBUMS: *Talk To Me* (Dara 1994)★★★, with Kieran Goss *Frances Black And Kieran Goss* (Transatlantic II 1995)★★★, *Don't Get Me Wrong* (Sony 1998)★★★.

Black, Frank

b. Charles Thompson IV, 1965, Long Beach, California, USA. This US vocalist/guitarist led the Boston-based Pixies under the name Black Francis. When that band underwent an acrimonious split in 1993, Francis embarked on a solo career as Frank Black. His self-titled debut featured assistance from Nick Vincent (drums) and Eric Drew Feldman (guitar/saxophone). The latter, formerly of Captain Beefheart's Magic Band, also produced the set, which featured cameos from fellow Beefheart acolyte Jeff Morris Tepper and ex-Pixies guitarist Joey Santiago. *Frank Black* showed its creator's quirky grasp of pop, from the abrasive 'Los Angeles' to the melodic 'I Hear Ramona Sing'. It also contained a version of Brian Wilson's 'Hang On To Your Ego', which the Beach Boys' leader recast as 'I Know There's An Answer' on *Pet Sounds*. A sprawling double set, *Teenager Of The Year*, ensued, but critical reaction suggested the artist had lost his incisive skills and a year later it was announced he had been dropped by 4AD Records. A new release on Epic Records, preceded by the highly commercial single 'Men In Black' (UK number 37), failed to heighten his reputation and followers continued to revert to praising his work with the

Pixies. Backed by the Catholics (Lyle Workman, Dave McCaffrey and Scott Boutier), Black returned to indie cultdom with the rough and ready double whammy of *Frank Black And The Catholics* and *Pistolero*.

● ALBUMS: *Frank Black* (4AD 1993)★★★, *Teenager Of The Year* (4AD 1994)★★★★, with Teenage Fanclub *Frank Black & Teenage Fanclub* (Strange Fruit 1995)★★★, *The Cult Of Ray* (Epic 1996)★★★, *Frank Black And The Catholics* (Play It Again Sam 1998)★★★, *Pistolero* (Play It Again Sam 1999)★★★.

Blackhawk

When Henry Paul, the lead singer of the southern rock band the Outlaws, moved to Nashville, Tennessee, USA, the rest of the band elected not to join him. He formed the 90s country band Blackhawk with Van Stephenson (guitar) and Dave Robbins (keyboards), who were both session musicians and songwriters. The duo had written Willie Nelson's 1983 US country hit 'All My Life' and several singles for Restless Heart. Stephenson had also made the solo albums *Suspicious Heart* and *Righteous Anger*, and had enjoyed a US Top 40 hit with 'Modern Day Delilah' in 1984. Blackhawk took their name from the Stutz Blackhawk, an American pre-war sports car, and their chart-topping single, 'Goodbye Says It All', was heavily promoted on CMT. Following the platinum success of their first album, they developed into a touring band. Heavily influenced by Restless Heart, their records are as much middle-of-the-road rock as country.

● ALBUMS: *Blackhawk* (Arista 1994)★★★, *Strong Enough* (Arista 1995)★★★, *Love & Gravity* (Arista 1997)★★★, *The Sky's The Limit* (Arista 1998)★★★.

● VIDEOS: *Almost A Memory Now* (Arista 1996).

BLACKstreet

Among the most highly rated of the new generation of urban R&B bands, BLACKstreet is the brainchild of gifted musician and producer Teddy Riley (b. Edward Theodore Riley, New York City, New York, USA). The band, formed in Los Angeles, California, USA, originally comprised songwriters Riley and Chauncey Hannibal (b. New Jersey, USA), with Levi Little and David Hollister as additional vocalists. The quartet made their self-titled debut for Interscope Records in 1994. This well-received collection, dominated by hip-hop rhythms, provided a compulsive rhythmic soundtrack to the summer of 1994, selling over one million copies and featuring the hit single 'Before I Let You Go'. For the follow-up, Hollister and Little were replaced by Mark Middleton (b. New York, USA) and Eric Williams (b. New Jersey, USA), and the musical accent changed from hip-hop to pure R&B. The only exception was the brilliant single, 'No Diggity' (a Grammy winning US chart-topper and UK Top 10 single), which featured a guest rap from Dr. Dre. More arresting was 'The Lord Is Real', a vocal track which borrowed heavily from the gospel tradition, and a completely restyled version of the Beatles' 'Can't Buy Me Love'. The album went on to sell over six million copies. The same year they were featured on New Edition's reunion tour, and in 1997 performed a highly rated *MTV Unplugged* special. The band also appeared on the single 'Take Me There' (US number 14, January 1999), taken from the soundtrack to the *Rugrats* movie, alongside Mya, Ma$e and Blinky Blink. The heavily anticipated *Finally* was released in March, and was the first album to feature Middleton's replacement, Terrell Philips.

The record included the hit singles 'Can You Feel It' (including a sample of the Jacksons' song of the same name) and 'Girlfriend/Boyfriend'.

● ALBUMS: *BLACKstreet* (Interscope 1994)★★★, *Another Level* (Interscope 1996)★★★★, *Finally* (Interscope 1999)★★★.

Blake, Perry

This Sligo, Eire native appeared on the music scene in the late 90s as a maverick but highly original singer-songwriter. Blake developed his songs over several years, performing to a mixed response at various clubs in Dublin, but created enough of an impression for Polydor Records to sign him up in 1996. He opted out of recording his debut album with the in-demand Howie B., choosing to use producer Ross Cullum (Enya) instead. His self-titled album was recorded at Cullum's London studio, with Graham Murphy handling programming and arranging duties. Blake's debut single, 'The Hunchback Of San Francisco', was released in Autumn 1997, and was voted single of the week by Jo Whiley on her BBC Radio One lunchtime show. The lush, romantic 'Genevieve (Pilot Of Your Thighs)' was released as a follow-up in March 1998, earning critical plaudits from the European music press. Blake was particularly acclaimed in France, where he was viewed as a natural heir to the European tradition of pop melancholy epitomised by singers such as Jacques Brel and Scott Walker. Following a low-key semi-acoustic tour, Blake teamed up with fellow Sony artist, French singer Helena Noguerra, on a bizarre version of 'All Shook Up'.

● ALBUMS: *Perry Blake* (Polydor 1998)★★★★.

Blender, Everton

b. Everton Dennis Williams, Clarendon, Jamaica, West Indies. The 90s saw a revival of the popularity of conscientious dancehall singers, notably Garnett Silk, with whom Blender initially performed on the Destiny Outernational Sound System, and Luciano. He began performing in the mid-80s, inspired by Sugar Minott, Dennis Brown and Tenor Saw. He initially performed as Bubbaroo, cultivating his vocal skills and subsidizing his developing career through various postings in and around Clarendon. Blender was introduced to Richard Bell who produced his debut, 'Create A Sound', in 1993, followed by 'Ethiopia Calling' in combination with Kulcha Knox, 'Ghetto Youths', 'Family Man' and, over a dub version of the popular Sleng Teng rhythm, 'Man Is Unjust'. At the 1993 Reggae Sunsplash Festival he preceded his long-time sparring partner Garnett Silk on the same stage. Both artists demonstrated that they had a promising future, although regrettably Silk's was curtailed owing to his untimely demise. Shortly after the tragedy Blender released *Lift Up Your Head* in the USA where, in the ensuing months, the compilation of roots classics made a significant impact. Hailed as one of reggae's fastest-rising stars Blender augmented his position with a number of hits, including the Jack Scorpio-produced 'Blen' Dem'. Numerous hits followed, including 'Dem A Fight', 'Give Me Your Loving', 'Piece A Di Blender', 'Bob Marley' and with DJ President Brown, 'Blow Your Nose, Not Your Mind'. The production skills of Anthony Red Rose and Anthony Malvo featured on the Swell Headed rhythm were demonstrated on the hit 'Live Up', with a chorus comparable to that of his debut. His recording success was acknowledged when he was invited to play at the 1995 Reggae Sunsplash Festival in St. Anns, where he performed an acclaimed set. He performed most of his hits, along with 'World Corruption', 'Mistaken Identity' and 'Bring The Kutchie Come'. He repeated his accomplishment when he appeared at the Reggae Sumfest Festival on International Night Part One, alongside Buju Banton, Mikey Spice, Garnett Silk's brother, Aaron Silk, Nadine Sutherland, *et al.* Blender has maintained his popularity accompanied by predictions that he is destined for a long and prolific career. The Jamaican success of 'World Corruption' led to an album of the same name featuring writing collaborations with Garnett Silk's sidekick Anthony Rochester for the tracks 'Material Girl' and 'Coming Harder'. In 1999, Blender enjoyed a hit single with 'Ghetto People Sing', included on *Rootsman Credential*.

● ALBUMS: *Lift Up Your Head* (Heartbeat 1994)★★★, *Blend Dem* (Pow Wow 1995)★★★, *World Corruption* (Greensleeves 1996)★★★★, *Rootsman Credential* (Heartbeat 1999)★★★★.

● COMPILATIONS: *A Piece Of The Blender* (Heartbeat 1996)★★★★.

Blessid Union Of Souls

Formed in Cincinnati, Ohio, USA, modern rock quintet Blessid Union Of Souls broke through in 1995 with the US hit singles 'I Believe' and 'Let Me Be The One'. As a consequence, the band's debut album of that year, *Home*, became an international bestseller. Led by songwriters Eliot Sloan (b. USA; vocals) and Jeff Pence (b. USA; guitar), the band also includes Eddie Hedges (percussion), C.P. Roth (keyboards), Tony Clark (bass) and production collaborator Emosia. After intensive touring following their debut, the band enrolled the expertise of writers Tommy Sims and Shelley Peiken to help with new compositions for their self-titled follow-up set, issued on EMI-affiliated Capitol Records. Peiken's contribution, 'Peace And Love', and Sims' 'Light In Your Eyes', were among the strongest tracks on *Blessid Union Of Souls*, which the band conceptualized as a canon of 'rural soul' songs. As Sloan told the press: 'We're not just straightforward pop, but country-flavoured, rock, and spiritual - all that pretty much meshes into one.' However, the critical reaction that greeted the first single lifted from the album, 'I Wanna Be There', was less encouraging than expected. Another change of labels saw the band issuing *Walking Off The Buzz* on Push/V2 Records. The album was premiered by the highly catchy single 'Hey Leonardo (She Likes Me For Me)'.

● ALBUMS: *Home* (EMI 1995)★★★★, *Blessid Union Of Souls* (Capitol 1997)★★★, *Walking Off The Buzz* (V2 1999)★★★.

Blige, Mary J.

b. Mary Jane Blige, 11 January 1971, Atlanta, Georgia, USA. Blige was signed to Uptown Records by their head of A&R, Sean 'Puffy' Combs. After being promoted by her record company as 'The original queen of hip-hop and soul', Mary J. Blige's debut album sold over two million copies (many of the best songs being written for her by POV). The hip-hop quotient was represented by bass-driven rhythms, the soul stylings including her affecting voice. Guest appearances from rappers Grand Puba and Busta Rhymes were merely a bonus on this accomplished piece of work. When she journeyed to England for live shows in 1993 she was widely criticised for overpricing a set that was merely six songs long, but quality rather than quantity remains the keynote to Blige's career. *My Life* was an edgy, raw set that dealt with

the break-up of her relationship with K-Ci Hailey of Jodeci. According to her publicity handout, *Share My World*, her first album away from mentor Combs, marked 'her personal and musical rebirth'; rebirth or not, it was certainly another excellent album. *Mary* featured guest appearances from the artists including, Lauryn Hill, Eric Clapton, George Michael, Elton John and, on the tense personal drama of 'Not Lookin'', her ex-lover Hailey.

● ALBUMS: *What's The 411?* (Uptown 1992)★★★★, *What's The 411? - Remix Album* (Uptown 1993)★★★, *My Life* (Uptown 1994)★★★, *Share My World* (MCA 1997)★★★★, *The Tour* (MCA 1998)★★, *Mary* (Universal 1999)★★★★.

Blind Melon

A US pop-rock band comprising Glen Graham (b. Columbus, Mississippi, USA; drums), Shannon Hoon (b. Lafayette, Indiana, USA, d. 21 October 1995, New Orleans, Louisiana, USA; vocals), Rogers Stevens (b. West Point, Mississippi, USA; guitar), Christopher Thorn (b. Dover, Pennsylvania; guitar) and Brad Smith (b. West Point, Mississippi, USA; bass), Blind Melon entered the US mainstream in 1993. One of their major claims to fame was introducing the phenomenon of the 'bee girl'. Back in their home base of Columbus, Mississippi, Graham was passing round a snap of his sister, Georgia, appearing in a school play. The band elected to use the shot, which presented young Georgia as an awkward, publicity-shy youngster adorned in a bee-suit, on their debut album. The image would also reappear in the video for their second single, 'No Rain', in June 1992. Directed by Sam Bayer (responsible for Nirvana's 'Smells Like Teen Spirit'), the Bee Girl was portrayed by 10-year-old Heather DeLoach. MTV played the clip relentlessly, helping to boost the fortunes of their album. The young girl became a huge cult icon, beloved of various rock stars including Madonna, while Blind Melon profited greatly from their association with her. Their album had been shipped for several months and was languishing outside the US charts, but it soon re-entered and went on to reach number 3. However, success had not been as instantaneous as many assumed. Smith had long been a dedicated musician, playing drums, baritone saxophone and guitar, the last of which he taught to Stevens. The two had left Columbus in 1989 for Los Angeles, where they met first Hoon, a small-town mischief-maker who had left his sporting ambitions behind when he became involved in the drugs scene, and Thorn, who had formerly played in a local heavy metal band, R.O.T. Together they scoured Hollywood for a drummer and found fellow Mississippi refugee Graham. A demo tape was recorded, and, without their consent, circulated to the major record companies, who began queuing up for their services. This despite the fact that they had an armoury of just five songs. It was Atlantic Records who eventually requested their signatures. They were put to work in a Los Angeles studio, but were distracted by the presence of Hoon's old Indiana friend, Axl Rose, who was recording *Use Your Illusion* with Guns N'Roses. Hoon was invited to add backing vocals, and appeared in the video to 'Don't Cry'. After a support tour to Soundgarden the band relocated to Durham, North Carolina, to find space and time to finish writing their debut set, before teaming with producer Rick Parashar in Seattle. Afterwards, events overtook them, and by November 1993 *Rolling Stone* magazine was parading them, naked, on their cover. Two years' touring fol-

lowing, including dates at Woodstock II in America and the Glastonbury Festival in England. The pressure to repeat the success of the debut with *Soup* was obvious, but when it finally emerged it was far less accessible than many expected. Recorded in New Orleans during bouts of drug-related non-activity, Hoon confessed in interviews that he could not actually remember making the record. In truth he had passed some of the time between albums in a rehabilitation clinic. The new songs included 'St. Andrew Fall', which concerned suicide, and 'Skinned', about serial killer Ed Gein, who dressed in the skins of his female victims. Some of the effect of this track's lurid subject matter was alleviated by the presence of a kazoo solo. It was generally known that Hoon had unsuccessfully fought heroin addiction for some time, but neither the band nor his family could prise him away for long enough periods for him to complete his rehabilitation programme. He died from a heroin overdose, his body discovered in the band's bus. The final album, *Nico* (named after Hoon's stepdaughter), was released in 1997. It was a sad and patched-together affair that the remaining members felt morally obliged to release.
● ALBUMS: *Blind Melon* (Capitol 1993)★★★★, *Soup* (Capitol 1995)★★, *Nico* (Capitol 1997)★★.
● VIDEOS: *Letters From A Porcupine* (Capitol 1996).

Blink-182

Based in San Diego, California, USA, Blink-182's highly melodic and entertaining thrash rock achieved mainstream success in the late 90s. The band were originally formed by Mark Hoppus (b. 15 March 1972, USA; bass/vocals), who had moved to San Diego to study, and Tom DeLonge (b. 13 December 1975, USA; guitar/vocals). Hoppus and DeLonge were joined by drummer Scott Raynor, and began a non-stop gigging schedule on the local punk circuit. The self-released *Fly Swatter* EP appeared in 1993, and was followed by the cassette only 'Buddha' demo, released by Filter Records in a run of less than a 1,000 (the material was re-issued in a slightly different format three years later by Kung Fu Records). Several of the songs from the demo tape subsequently appeared on the band's full-length debut, *Cheshire Cat*, which was released by the Grilled Cheese label in 1994. Shortly afterwards the trio were forced to adopt the new moniker Blink-182 following the threat of legal action by an Irish techno outfit already recording as Blink. Despite the enforced name change, the trio's popularity continued to grow owing to support slots with several leading punk bands including No FX and Pennywise, and their ubiquitous presence on the skating and snow boarding scenes. They also developed a reputation for stripping off during live shows. A steady flow of singles and EPs confirmed both the trio's penchant for gloriously immature scatological lyrics, and their ability to craft great tunes.

Their commercial breakthrough arrived with 1997's *Dude Ranch*. The album included the endearing hit 'Dammit (Growing Up)', which enjoyed constant radio play alongside material by other hardcore bands, including the Offspring, Green Day and Smash Mouth. Following the release of *Dude Ranch*, founding member Raynor was replaced by Travis Barker (b. 14 November 1975, USA). Barker appeared on the band's major label debut, *Enema Of The State*, which debuted in the US Top 10 in June 1999 and went on to sell over a million copies in barely two months. The album was helped by another highly catchy radio hit, 'What's My Name Again?'
● ALBUMS: *Cheshire Cat* (Grilled Cheese/Cargo 1994)★★★, *Dude Ranch* (Cargo 1997)★★★, *Enema Of The State* (MCA 1999)★★★.

Block, Brandon

b. England. In the late 90s, Block found UK Top 5 chart success in the guise of the Blockster with 'You Should Be...', a revamped house version of the Bee Gees disco classic 'You Should Be Dancing', but he has been a stalwart behind the decks ever since the acid house explosion of 1988. Back then he could be found playing at Broadway Boulevard in Ealing, London. He moved on to his own Sunday night at Haven Stables in Ealing, which was a popular fixture until it ended in 1991. His DJing career really took off in collaboration with Flying Records, promoting Queens in Colnbrook, Berkshire in 1990. In the same year, he first visited the Spanish island of Ibiza, where he became an essential part of the summer's festivities. Over the years, Block's residencies have included: Up Yer Ronson in Leeds, F.U.B.A.R. at the Milk Bar in London, Club For Life in London, Malibu Stacey in London and Scream in Plymouth. He regularly plays at all the major clubs in the UK and internationally, and performed at the hand-over party in Hong Kong in 1997. He has recorded two successful mix compilation albums for the Fantazia label and has had a highly successful radio show on the UK's Kiss 100 with Alex P. Like his colleague, Block's reputation for hell-raising both in front and behind the decks precedes him. He has had to tone down his hedonism in recent years, as a matter of self-preservation, if nothing else. However, like Alex P, Block's DJing avoids snobbery and pretension. His only criteria in choosing and mixing tracks is whether or not his audience will get their hands in the air and feet stomping. In March 1999, Ministry Of Sound released *Dance Nation 6*, a compilation mixed by 'Tall' Paul Newman and Brandon Block.
● COMPILATIONS: with 'Tall' Paul Newman *Dance Nation 6* (MOS 1999)★★★★.

Bloom, Luka

b. Barry Moore, 23 May 1955, Newbridge, Eire. Folk-singer and guitarist Moore, and brother of the legendary Christy Moore, has made a career for himself, despite considerable hardship. He recorded several albums under his own name before developing 'carpal tunnel syndrome', which halted the finger-picking guitar style that he had thus far favoured. Forced to adapt to an open-string approach, he relocated to New Jersey, USA, before relaunching his career as Luka Bloom - adapting the first name from Suzanne Vega's song about child abuse, and the surname from Leopald Bloom, the character in James Joyce's novel *Ulysses*. He displayed a bountiful Celtic soul on *Riverside*, particularly in 'This Is For Life', a defiant tale of sweethearts torn apart and put in an English prison. Elsewhere, 'Gone To Pablo' discussed the suicide of Picasso's second wife. His third album impressed with its sinewy way with a tune and reflective lyrics, while 1994's *Turf* included some of his best songs, such as 'Cold Comfort', 'Right Now' and 'Sanctuary'. Now resident in Ireland once more, Bloom returned to the studio to record the acclaimed *Salty Heaven*.
● ALBUMS: *Luka Bloom* (Mystery/Warners 1988)★★★★, *Riverside* (Reprise 1990)★★★, *The Acoustic Motorbike* (Reprise 1992)★★★, *Turf* (Reprise 1994)★★★★, *Salty Heaven* (Shanachie 1999)★★★★.

Blues Traveler

New York, USA blues-rock quartet Blues Traveler are led by singer and harmonica player John Popper (b. Cleveland, Ohio, USA). Some of the interest in the band in the mid-90s arose from the fact that Popper was a close friend of Eric Schenkman and Chris Barron, putting the pair (who subsequently formed the Spin Doctors) in contact with each other. Like the latter band and another set of friends, Phish, Blues Traveler share an appetite for extended jams, and at their best, the spontaneous musicianship that flows through their live sets can be inspired. Popper first sought to play harmonica after being inspired by the movie *The Blues Brothers*, while at school in Connecticut. He initially intended to become a comedian; his physical appearance has prompted comparisons with actor John Belushi. When Popper moved to Princeton, New Jersey, to attend high school, he met drummer Brendan Hill, the duo calling themselves 'The Blues Band' by 1985. They were eventually joined by the younger, sports-orientated guitarist Chan Kinchla until a knee injury cut short that career. He moved instead to New York, with Hill and Popper. Bass player Bobby Sheehan (d. 20 August 1999, New Orleans, Louisiana, USA) joined in 1987. Playing low-key gigs at Nightingale's in the East Village, they eventually honed their organic rock into something a little more structured, changing their name to Blues Traveler at the end of the 80s. Recording and selling demo tapes at gigs eventually brought a high-profile visitor to one of their gigs, Bill Graham. Through his influence they found themselves on bills with the Allman Brothers Band and Carlos Santana. Interest from A&M Records followed and the band recorded their debut at the end of 1989, for release early the following year. The band had been befriended at an early stage by Blues Brothers keyboard player Paul Shaffer, who, since his five minutes of celluloid fame, had become bandleader and arranger for the David Letterman television show. Letterman's sponsorship of the band stretched to over a dozen appearances in their first four years of existence, and was paramount in establishing their no-nonsense appeal. The appearances on *Letterman* were part of a huge promotional push that included over 800 gigs in three years. The only setback came in autumn 1992 when Popper was involved in a motorcycle accident which left him with major injuries. *Save His Soul*'s release was consequently delayed, but the incident necessitated a long hiatus from touring, until he took the stage again in April 1993 in a wheelchair. He continued in this vein for a second HORDE tour (Horizons Of Rock Developing Everywhere), an alternative to the Lollapalooza events, with Big Head Todd And The Monsters, among others. A third stint was later undertaken with the Allman Brothers Band, whose Chuck Leavell joined Paul Shaffer in contributing to *Four*. The group then appeared at Woodstock '94, but, true to form, they were unable to stay the whole weekend because of gig commitments elsewhere. They remain a phenomenon in their homeland; *Four* was still in the US charts with 4 million sales two years after its release. *Straight On Till Morning* was eagerly anticipated after the huge success of *Four* and the band managed to get the balance right between rock and blues. The blues harp playing was noticeably spectacular and the longer tracks such as 'Make My Way' and 'Yours' highlighted the band at their best, unlike the throwaway pastiche of 'Felicia' and 'Canadian Rose'. Popper recorded the solo *Zygote* in 1999, but also had to undergo emergency angioplasty. In August, Sheehan was found dead in his New Orleans home.

● ALBUMS: *Blues Traveler* (A&M 1990)★★, *Travelers And Thieves* (A&M 1991)★★★, *On Tour Forever* bonus disc given away free with copies of *Travelers And Thieves* (A&M 1992)★★★, *Save His Soul* (A&M 1993)★★, *Four* (A&M 1994)★★★★, *Live From The Fall* (A&M 1996)★★, *Straight On Till Morning* (A&M 1997)★★★.

Bluetones

Formed in Hounslow, London, England, in 1990, melodic guitar pop band the Bluetones spent the next four years practising in garages. They consist of Scott Morriss (b. 10 October 1973; bass), Eds Chesters (drums), Adam P. Devlin (b. 17 September 1969; guitar) and Mark James Morriss (b. 18 October 1971; vocals, brother of Scott), and their patience was rewarded in 1995 when they became the toast of the UK's music press. Mark Morriss said of their music: 'What we do is a continuation of what went on in the 60s without the flower-power bullshit. Good tunes. And over-lapping melodies; the best lyrics in the world don't mean anything without a nice tune.' They quickly established a strong fanbase - no less than three fanzines were dedicated to the Bluetones before they had released their third single. They contributed to a compilation EP, released on the Fierce Panda label, and this led to an appearance on Channel 4 television's *The White Room*. Superior Quality Records then signed the band and the Bluetones' debut single, 'Are You Blue Or Are You Blind?', entered the UK Top 40 in June 1995. It was followed in October 1995 by 'Bluetonic' (the track that had originally appeared on the Fierce Panda EP as 'No. 11'), and the band completed its first headlining UK tour supported by their protégés Hooker. The band also joined the Cardigans, Heavy Stereo and Fluffy on the well-publicized *New Musical Express* Brat Bus Tour. The third single, 'Slight Return', was their biggest hit, while *Expecting To Fly* (named after a classic Buffalo Springfield song), produced by Hugh Jones, reached number 1 in the UK album charts in February 1996. Many pundits predicted greater things for the band, although ultimately their lack of originality may be a stumbling block. *Return To The Last Chance Saloon* attempted to make a clean break from the style of their debut, but with limited success. The album was also met by a worryingly indifferent commercial response.

● ALBUMS: *Expecting To Fly* (Superior Quality 1996)★★★★, *Return To The Last Chance Saloon* (Superior Quality 1998)★★★.

Blur

'When our third album comes out our position as the quintessential English band of the 90s will be assured.' A typical bullish statement that could have been made by any number of UK indie bands in 1990 - but from the mouth of Damon Albarn of Blur it amounts to prophecy. Blur were formed in London while Albarn (b. 23 March 1968, Whitechapel, London, England; vocals), Alex James (b. 21 November 1968, Bournemouth, Dorset, England; bass) and Graham Coxon (b. 12 March 1969, Rinteln, Hannover, Germany; guitar) were studying at Goldsmiths College. Coxon had first seen Albarn when he played a debut solo gig at Colchester Arts Centre in 1988. Also in that audience was future Blur drummer Dave Rowntree (b. 8 May 1964, Colchester, Essex, England). Albarn's desire to make music was encouraged by his father, who moved in circles that exposed his son to artists such as Soft Machine and Cat Stevens, while his mother was a stage designer for Joan Littlewood's theatre company at Stratford. Rowntree's father was sound engineer for the Beatles at the BBC, and had taken lessons on the bagpipes. When the four members convened in London (the first person James saw in halls of residence was Coxon), they formed a band - initially entitled Seymour - and started out on the lower rungs of the gig circuit by playing bottom of the bill to New Fast Automatic Daffodils and Too Much Texas at Camden's Dingwalls venue. A year and a dozen gigs later, the quartet had signed to Food Records, run by ex-Teardrop Explodes keyboard player David Balfe and *Sounds* journalist Andy Ross, whose suggestion it was that they change their name to Blur. They earned a reputation with venue promoters for haphazardly implemented onstage stunts. Playing vibrant 90s-friendly pop with a sharp cutting edge, Blur's debut release, 'She's So High' (which had initially ensured that Seymour were signed when included on their first demo tape), sneaked into the Top 50 of the UK chart. With the band displaying a justifiably breezy confidence in their abilities, there was little surprise when the infectious 'There's No Other Way' reached number 8 in the UK charts in the spring of 1991. This success continued when *Leisure* entered the UK charts at number 2 - a mere two years after formation. However, a relatively fallow period followed when 'Popscene' failed to rise above number 34 in the UK charts. As the 'baggy' and 'Madchester' movements died, the band were viewed with the same hostility that now greeted bands such as Rain or the Mock Turtles, as audiences looked away from the Byrds-fixated guitar pop of the period. Blur seemed set to disappear with the same alacrity with which they had established themselves, although their names were kept alive in press columns by their 'expert liggers' status. *Modern Life Is Rubbish* was presented to their record company at the end of 1992 but rejected, Balfe insisting that Albarn should go away and write at least two more tracks. The resultant songs, 'For Tomorrow' and 'Chemical World', were the album's singles. When it finally emerged in 1993, its sales profile of 50,000 copies failed to match that of its predecessor or expectations, but touring and a strong headlining appearance at the Reading Festival rebuilt confidence. The 'new' model Blur was waiting in the wings, and saw fruition in March 1994 with the release of 'Girls & Boys', the first single from what was to prove the epoch-making *Parklife*. This set wantonly upturned musical expectations, borrowing liberally from every great British institution from the Beatles, the Small Faces and the Kinks to the Jam and Madness, topped off by Albarn's knowing, Cockney delivery. At last there seemed to be genuine substance to the band's more excessive claims. With the entire music media their friends again, Blur consolidated their position with a live spectacular in front of 8,000 fans at London's Alexandra Palace; meanwhile, the album gained a Mercury Music Prize nomination, and they went on to secure four trophies, including Best Band and Album, at the 1995 BRIT Awards. Subsequently, the UK press attempted to concoct an Oasis versus Blur campaign when both bands released singles on the same day. In the event, Oasis won the chart battle (with 'Country House') but remained diplomatically silent; however, it was Oasis who took over the headlines on a daily basis. Following the lukewarm reception given to *The Great*

Escape, Blur quietly retreated to Iceland to work on new material. The result of their labour was 'Beetlebum', another number 1 single, in January 1997, and *Blur*, a UK number 1 album. The harder sound (evident on the thrashy 'Song 2') and more downbeat subject matter ('Death Of A Party') recalled some of their earlier singles, and proved beyond any doubt that they remained a major force in UK pop. With its obvious debts to American alternative rock bands such as Sonic Youth and Pavement, the album also broke Blur in the US. In 1998, Coxon launched his own label, Transcopic, and released his solo debut. The band returned in March 1999 with the UK number 2 single, 'Tender'. The chart-topping *13* marked the end of their long association with producer Stephen Street, with all but one of the tracks on the album overseen by William Orbit.

● ALBUMS: *Leisure* (Food 1991)★★★★, *Modern Life Is Rubbish* (Food 1993)★★★, *Parklife* (Food 1994)★★★★, *The Great Escape* (Food 1995)★★★, *Live At The Budokan* (Food 1996)★★★, *Blur* (Food 1997)★★★★, *Bustin' + Dronin'* remixes (Food 1998)★★, *13* (Food 1999)★★★★.

Solo: Graham Coxon *The Sky Is Too High* (Transcopic 1998)★★★.

● COMPILATIONS: *10th Anniversary Box Set* (Food 1999)★★★.

● VIDEOS: *Star Shaped* (1993), *Showtime* (PMI 1995).

● FURTHER READING: *Blurbook*, Paul Postle. *An Illustrated Biography*, Linda Holorney. *Blurbook*, Paul Postle. *Blur: The Illustrated Story*, Paul Lester. *Blur: The Whole Story*, Martin Roach. *Blur: The Great Escape*, Paul Moody. *Blur In Their Own Words*, Mick St Michael. *3862 Days: The Official History*, Stuart Maconie.

BMX Bandits

Formed in Bellshill, Lanarkshire, Scotland, in 1985, this idiosyncratic band revolves around Duglas Stewart (ex-Faith Healers and Pretty Flowers). Stewart chose the name 'BMX Bandits' because he assumed the band would last for one gig, but it quickly became one of the prime components of the 'anorak' or 'C86' movement. However, despite an early, naïve image - Stewart sometimes passed sweets out to his audience - the singer has proved himself a wry lyricist, akin to idol Jonathan Richman. The band's debut single, 'E102', was issued on 53rd & 3rd in 1986. Sean Dickson (keyboards), Jim McCulloch (guitar), Billy Wood (vocals) and Willie McArdle (drums) joined Stewart for this release, although within months, the first of a host of line-up changes was underway. Dickson formed the Soup Dragons, which McCulloch later joined, and the Bandits were buoyed by the arrival of Joe McAlinden (vocals/guitar/saxophone) and Norman Blake (guitar/vocals, ex-Faith Healers). Both musicians were involved in another band, the Boy Hairdressers, but were part of the reshaped line-up featured on *C-86*, mischievously dubbed so by Stewart when his band was denied a spot on the compilation tape of that name. Gordon Keen (guitar) and Francis MacDonald (drums) completed the 'new' Bandits, which was aurally moving away from its early, jejune sound. Eugene Kelly (ex-Vaselines) joined the quintet for *Star Wars*, issued by a label based in Japan where the Bandits enjoyed a cult following. It showed the band's increased musical maturity, although individual commitments to other projects defied convention. Blake found success with Teenage Fanclub, McAlinden had formed Superstar while Kelly and Keen forged Captain America, later known as Eugenius. The Bandits joined Creation Records in 1993, but attendant publicity announced that the last-named pair would no longer feature in the band. *Life Goes On* was another excellent set, boosted by the inclusion of the memorable 'Serious Drugs'. The Bandits supported southern soul singer-songwriter Dan Penn on a rare live appearance prior to completing *Gettin' Dirty*. By this point a new line-up of Stewart, Francis MacDonald, Finlay MacDonald, John Hogarty and Sishil K. Dade (ex-Soup Dragons) had emerged. 'It's the first time the BMX Bandits have been a group, rather than friends backing me', Duglas opined. The results were their finest album to date. *Theme Park* was an equally strong follow-up, but since its release the band has fragmented into solo projects.

● ALBUMS: *C-86* (1990)★★★, *A Totally Groovy Live Experience* (Avalanche 1990)★★★, *Star Wars* (Vinyl Japan 1992)★★★, *Gordon Keen And His BMX Bandits* mini-album (Sunflower 1992)★★★, *Life Goes On* (Creation 1994)★★★★, *Gettin' Dirty* (Creation 1995)★★★★, *Theme Park* (Creation 1996)★★★★.

● COMPILATIONS: *C-86 Plus* (Vinyl Japan 1992)★★★.

Boards Of Canada

This enigmatic electronica duo Mike Sandison (b. 14 July 1971, Scotland) and Marcus Eoin (b. 27 May 1973, Scotland) reportedly derive their collaborative moniker from the National Film Board of Canada whose nature/socio-political documentaries they (supposedly) watched as infants, when both sets of parents relocated to Alberta, Canada to work. These grainy films influence the mood and ambience of their early singles 'Hi-Scores' and 'Aquarius' (on the Skam imprint), and their long-players *Twoism* (of which only 100 copies were pressed) and *Music Has The Right To Children*. Much of their output could appropriately be utilized as soundtrack material for natural history programming. With their lovely melodies and hip-hop derived crunchy percussion, Boards Of Canada certainly draw inspiration from like-minded Warp Records labelmates (Autechre, Plaid), yet the duo imbue their own downtempo music with a curious sense of nostalgia and child-like wonderment. On one track, a treated child's voice seems to be declaring 'I love you, Mum.' This poignant deployal of infant speech seems engineered to trigger a sense of loss - both Sandison and Eoin have acknowledged an acute nostalgia for their childhoods, maintaining that the main source of their music is a refusal to accept adulthood. Advert soundtracks, corporate jingles and the production aesthetics of late 60s and early 70s folk artists have also been asserted as overt influences. The duo claim to litter their music with subliminal messages. Though cut through with a slightly sinister undercurrent, Boards Of Canada's music is sometimes cute and always endearing - descriptions not normally applied to techno recordings. Now based in the Pentland Hills, Scotland where they apparently live and record in a refurbished nuclear bunker, Sandison and Eoin are notably part of a wider arts collective *Music70*, who create short films, animations and paintings with no commercial impetus.

● ALBUMS: *Twoism* (Music70 1995)★★★★, *Music Has The Right To Children* (Warp/Skam 1998)★★★★.

Body Count

The Ice-T (b. Tracy Marrow, 16 February 1958, Newark, New Jersey, USA) spin-off metal/hardcore band, who achieved notoriety with the inclusion of the track 'Cop Killer' on their 1992 debut for Warner Brothers Records. Other songs included titles such as 'KKK Bitch' and 'Bowels Of The Devil', but it was 'Cop Killer' that effectively ended Ice-T's tenure with his record company, and made him public enemy number one within the American establishment. Body Count made their debut during the inaugural Lollapalooza US festival tour in 1991, preceding the release of the album. The line-up was completed by Ernie-C (guitar), D-Roc (guitar), Mooseman (bass) and Beatmaster V (drums), whom Ice-T knew from Crenshaw High School in South Central Los Angeles. Although occasionally suffering from the misogynistic street language common to much US west coast rap, their material contained forceful anti-drug and anti-racism themes, particularly 'Momma's Gotta Die Tonight', which addressed the issue of institutionalized bigotry being passed down through successive generations. The band continued touring, and were offered the opening slot on the Guns N'Roses/Metallica North American trek, exposing them to a more mainstream audience. In the meantime, the Los Angeles Police Department were taking extreme exception to 'Cop Killer', a song they viewed as dangerous and inflammatory ('I got my twelve gauge sawed off/I got my headlights turned off/I'm 'bout to bust some shots off/I'm 'bout to dust some cops off'). The fury aimed at Ice-T, now officially number 2 in the FBI National Threat list, came thick and fast. Actor Charlton Heston read out the lyrics to 'KKK Bitch' to astonished shareholders at Time Warner's AGM. 'Cop Killer' also appeared in Warners' blockbuster movie *Batman Returns*, which consequently faced calls for boycotts. Among the other opponents were Oliver North, President George Bush, and the Texas police force, who called for a nationwide boycott of Time Warner, including their Disneyland complex, thereby threatening to wipe millions off Warners' share value. The pivotal moment came when death threats were received by record company employees, and the U-turn was made. The track was eventually replaced with a spoken word message from former Dead Kennedys frontman and noted anti-censorship lobbyist, Jello Biafra. Undeterred, Ice-T has resolved to continue in authority-tackling mode, and Body Count persist as an ongoing musical concern. Indeed, further albums for new label Virgin Records offered greater musical depth.

● ALBUMS: *Body Count* (Sire 1992)★★★, *Born Dead* (Virgin 1994)★★★, *Violent Demise: Last Days* (Virgin 1997)★★★.

● FURTHER READING: *The Ice Opinion*, Ice-T and Heidi Seigmund.

Bogguss, Suzy

b. Suzy Kay Bogguss, 30 December 1956, Aledo, Illinois, USA. Bogguss grew up in a farming family that loved music but had diverse tastes: her father favoured country music, her mother big bands, and her brothers and sister the 60s hits. Bogguss gained a degree in art, but sang in clubs and coffee-houses to earn extra money. She included country songs in her repertoire such as 'I Want To Be A Cowboy's Sweetheart' and 'Night Rider's Lament'. After five years of touring in a van, she secured a residency at a restaurant in Nashville. A tape made in 1986 to sell at Dolly Parton's Dollywood impressed Capitol Records. Both 'I Don't Want To Set The World On Fire' and Merle Haggard's 'Somewhere Between' did reasonably well on the US country charts and her first album had an appealing mixture of old and new songs. Bogguss sang 'Happy Trails' with Michael Martin Murphey on his *Cowboy Songs* set, and she and Lee

Greenwood had a US country hit with the duet 'Hopelessly Yours'. Her strategy paid off when she won the Horizon Award for the most promising artist at the 1992 Country Music Association Awards ceremony. *Something Up My Sleeve* built upon her success and contained some excellent radio-friendly songs that were able to cross over to mainstream appeal. 'Hey Cinderella', for example, falls comfortably into both pop and country genres, while the sparkling Matraca Berg and Gary Harrison song 'Diamonds And Tears' is pure country rock. Her admiration for Chet Atkins led to him to being jointly billed for *Simpatico* and sharing centre stage on the video for the engaging 'One More For The Road'. *Give Me Some Wheels* broke a three-year hiatus, and was an accomplished set whose title track was co-written with Berg and Harrison. The follow-up, *Nobody Love, Nobody Gets Hurt*, featured the stand-out track, 'Somebody To Love', co-written with Berg and husband Doug Crider.

● ALBUMS: *Somewhere Between* (Liberty 1988)★★, *Moment Of Truth* (Liberty 1990)★★, *Aces* (Liberty 1991)★★, *Voices In The Wind* (Liberty 1992)★★★, *Something Up My Sleeve* (Liberty 1993)★★★★, with Chet Atkins *Simpatico* (Liberty 1994)★★★, *Give Me Some Wheels* (Capitol 1996)★★★★, *Nobody Love, Nobody Gets Hurt* (Capitol 1998)★★★, *Its A Perfect Day* (Intersound 1999)★★★.

● COMPILATIONS: *Greatest Hits* (Liberty 1994)★★★★.

Bolland, C.J.

b. Christian Jay Bolland, 18 June 1971, Yorkshire, England. DJ and techno maestro Bolland moved with his family to Antwerp, Belgium at an early age, where his parents ran a club. Widely respected on the Euro techno circuit, Bolland initially worked at the influential R&S Records label, specializing in hard-edged rave tunes. He recorded as the Project ('Do That Dance'), Sonic Solution ('Music'), Space Opera and released the *Ravesignal 1, 2* and *3* EPs, the latter including the club favourite 'Horsepower'. However, *The 4th Sign* in 1993 saw him dispense with his other former *noms de plume*. It included the new dancefloor techno anthem 'Carmague'. His busy remixing schedule has included work for the Orbital, the Prodigy, Tori Amos, and Baby Ford. Following another album for R&S, Bolland signed a multi-album deal with Internal Records. *The Analogue Theatre* included the club hit 'Sugar Is Sweeter'. Bolland has also released an album as part of Studio !K7's *DJ-Kicks* series.

● ALBUMS: *The 4th Sign* (Apollo/R&S 1993)★★★★, *Electronic Highway* (R&S 1995)★★★, *The Analogue Theatre* (Phuture Trax/Internal 1996)★★★★, *DJ-Kicks* (Studio !K7 1998)★★★.

Bolton, Michael

b. Michael Bolotin, 26 February 1954, New Haven, Connecticut, USA. Bolton became one of the most successful rock balladeers of the late 80s and early 90s. He grew up listening to soul artists such as Stevie Wonder, Ray Charles and Marvin Gaye before recording his first single (under his real name) for Epic Records in 1968. Among the backing musicians on Bolotin's first solo album for RCA Records were Bernard Purdie, David Sanborn and Muscle Shoals session musician Wayne Perkins. Critics made frequent comparisons between Bolotin and Joe Cocker. In the late 70s, Bolotin became lead singer with hard rock band Blackjack. However, despite the presence of top producers Tom Dowd (Allman Brothers Band and Eric Clapton) and Eddy Offord (Yes), their two albums for Polydor Records sold poorly.

After the band split, guitarist Bruck Kulick played with Billy Squier, while drummer Sandy Gennaro joined the Pat Travers Band and bass player Jim Haslip became a session musician. Bolotin himself turned to songwriting and to a new solo recording contract with Columbia Records. Initially, he had greater success as a composer, providing Laura Branigan with the 1983 hit 'How Am I Supposed To Live Without You', co-written with Doug James. He started using the more accessible name Bolton in 1983. As a solo performer, he persevered with a heavy rock approach and it was not until he shifted to a soul-ballad style on *The Hunger* that he had his own first Top 20 single, 'That's What Love Is All About', in 1987. From that point Bolton had a series of blue-eyed soul hits that included a new US chart-topping version of 'How Am I Supposed To Live Without You' in 1990, as well as 'How Can We Be Lovers' (US number 3) and the 1991 successes 'Love Is A Wonderful Thing' (US number 4), 'Time, Love And Tenderness' (US number 7) and his second US chart-topper, a cover version of 'When A Man Loves A Woman'. He also enjoyed a brief, and unexpected, songwriting collaboration with Bob Dylan, but by the middle of the 90s his career had peaked. In 1995, he resurfaced with a hit single, 'Can I Touch You ... There?', and a greatest hits package. After the commercial failure of *All That Matters*, Bolton reappeared in the late 90s performing quasi-operatic material.

● ALBUMS: as Michael Bolotin *Michael Bolotin* (RCA 1975)★★, as Michael Bolotin *Every Day Of My Life* (RCA 1976)★★, with Blackjack *Blackjack* (Polydor 1979)★★, with Blackjack *Worlds Apart* (Polydor 1980)★★, *Michael Bolton* (Columbia 1983)★★, *Everybody's Crazy* (Columbia 1985)★★, *The Hunger* (Columbia 1987)★★★, *Soul Provider* (Columbia 1989)★★★, *Time, Love And Tenderness* (Columbia 1991)★★, *The One Thing* (Columbia 1993)★★, *This Is The Time - The Christmas Album* (Columbia 1996)★, *All That Matters* (Columbia 1997)★★★, *My Secret Passion: The Arias* (Sony Classical 1998)★★.

● COMPILATIONS: *Timeless - The Classics* (Columbia 1992)★★★, *Greatest Hits 1985-1995* (Sony 1995)★★★, *The Early Years* (RCA 1997)★★, *Timeless - The Classics, Vol. 2* (Columbia 1999)★★.

● VIDEOS: *Soul Provider; The Videos* (CMV Enterprises 1990), *This Is Michael Bolton* (1992), *Decade: Greatest Hits 1985-1995 The Videos* (SMV 1995).

Bomb The Bass

Early pioneers of the UK's house scene, Bomb The Bass is a collective front for Tim Simenon (b. Brixton, London, England; of Malay Chinese and Scottish parents). After attending a course in studio engineering he shot to prominence in 1988 with 'Beat Dis', which reached the UK Top 5. Both 'Megablast' and 'Say A Little Prayer' were also UK Top 10 hits, the latter featuring Maureen Walsh, who went on to her own solo career, beginning with a cover version of Sister Sledge's 'Thinking Of You' for Urban. Simenon then worked with Neneh Cherry (producing her hits 'Buffalo Stance' and 'Manchild'). After completing work on his new studio he took up production duties for an album by Prince sidekick Cat. Co-production on Adamski's 'Killer' and the Seal single 'Crazy' followed. However, feeling aggrieved at the lack of credit and financial recompense he gained from these ventures, he returned to Bomb The Bass. His timing was less than apt, as the 1991 Gulf War made continued use of the name indelicate. He reverted to his own name for the single 'Love So True', co-written with bass player Doug Wimbush

(Tackhead) and vocalist Loretta Heywood. By this time he was also working extensively with guitarist Kenji Suzuki, in addition to a myriad of guest vocalists. Bomb The Bass returned in 1995 with a new album, *Clear*, their finest and most eclectic collection to date, which featured vocal contributions from maverick English writer Will Self. Simenon also unveiled his own label, Stoned Heights, distributed through Island Records. He has subsequently concentrated on building up the label's roster of artists.

● ALBUMS: *Into The Dragon* (Rhythm King 1988)★★★, *Unknown Territory* (Rhythm King 1991)★★★, *Clear* (Stoned Heights 1995)★★★★.

● COMPILATIONS: *Beat Dis: The Very Best Of* (Camden 1999)★★★.

● VIDEOS: *Don't Make Me Wait* (Weinerworld 1988).

Bon Jovi, Jon

b. John Francis Bongiovi, 2 March 1962, Perth Amboy, New Jersey, USA. The highly photogenic lead singer of soft rockers Bon Jovi established himself as a respected actor and solo artist in the late 90s. For a period from the late 80s to the mid-90s, Bon Jovi was one of the biggest-selling acts in the world, thanks to the multi-platinum success of *Slippery When Wet* and *New Jersey*. The singer actually began his recording career way back in 1980, recording several tracks as John Bongiovi at his cousin Tony's Power Station recording studio (this material was eventually released in 1997 as *The Power Station Years*). Fame and fortune soon followed with Bon Jovi the band, before the singer took time out in 1990 to record the solo *Blaze Of Glory*. This quasi-soundtrack collection was inspired by the movie *Young Guns II*, in which Bon Jovi also made a brief appearance. The singer's Western-themed songs failed to stretch a stellar cast of backing musicians including Elton John and Jeff Beck, but the album was a commercial success and the title track reached the top of the US singles chart. Bon Jovi the band returned in 1992 with *Keep The Faith*, which unveiled a new, mature rock sound. Following the release of *These Days* in 1995, the singer elected to concentrate on his acting career. His natural good looks led to starring roles in amiable but lightweight fare such as *Moonlight And Valentino* and *The Leading Man*. In 1997, he released a second solo album, *Destination Anywhere*, on which he completed his rehabilitation into a mature, Bruce Springsteen-styled rock artist. The album, which included the minor hit singles 'Midnight In Chelsea' and 'Janie, Don't Take Your Love To Town', augured well for his future as a solo artist.

● ALBUMS: *Blaze Of Glory* (PolyGram 1990)★★, *Destination Anywhere* (PolyGram 1997)★★★.

● COMPILATIONS: as John Bongiovi *The Power Station Years 1980-1983* (Masquerade 1997)★★.

● FILMS: *The Return Of Bruno* (1988), *Young Guns II* (1990), *Moonlight And Valentino* (1995), *The Leading Man* (1996), *Destination Anywhere* (1997), *Row Your Boat* (1998), *Little City* (1998), *No Looking Back* (1998), *Homegrown* (1998).

Bonamy, James

b. Florida, USA. Contemporary country singer James Bonamy gravitated to the honky tonk scene through the auspices of his father, a fan of Johnny Paycheck and Merle Haggard. However, when he began to attend high school he invested much of his time in sports, at which he achieved great proficiency, while his listening tastes changed to those

of Bon Jovi *et al*. Despite this, he maintained in an interview with *Country Music People*: 'The songs are laid out the same, and what they're saying is pretty close, too.' However, as he surmised, 'It's country music I was raised on, so that's the music I came back to.' His first steps into the music industry also came while at college. In his first year at the University of Alabama in Birmingham, he gained a spot on local radio. However, it was not until he left academia and took a job at an Orlando gift store back in his home state that he began to take his musical ambitions more seriously. There he sat in with numerous house bands, before relocating to Nashville and a job at the Opryland Theme Park as a summer singer. After months of auditions he finally secured a recording contract with Epic Records. His debut album, *What I Live To Do*, immediately spawned the Top 30 country hit 'She's Got A Mind Of Her Own'. However, Bonamy's career had still not taken off by the time he released the follow-up *Roots And Wings*, a rather unimaginative and lacklustre collection.

● ALBUMS: *What I Live To Do* (Epic 1996)★★★, *Roots And Wings* (Epic 1997)★★★.

Bone Thugs-N-Harmony

Based in Cleveland, Ohio, USA, Bone Thugs-N-Harmony were one of the most successful rap outfits to break into the mainstream in 1995. Formed in 1993 by Layzie Bone, Bizzy Bone, Krayzie Bone, Wish Bone and Flesh-N-Bone, they were signed and nurtured by the founder of Ruthless Records, the late Eazy-E. Their initial impact was astounding, even within a musical genre associated with a fast turnover of star acts. Their 1994 debut EP, *Creeping On Ah Come Up*, spent over 70 weeks on *Billboard*'s Top 200 album chart, and sold well over four million units. The following year's *E. 1999 Eternal* went to number 1, selling over 330,000 copies in its first week of release. The quintet's popularity could be attributed to their appealing blend of vocal harmonies and tough street raps, as featured on the single '1st Of Tha Month'. Much of Stevie Wonder's smooth R&B harmony style was brilliantly mixed with DJ Uneek's hardcore beats, and even if their gangsta rapping became tiresome, the strength of tracks such as 'Budsmokers Only' and 'East 1999' managed to put it into the background. The quintet returned in 1997 with the overindulgent *The Art Of War*, which stretched its lyrical and musical conceits far too thinly over the double disc's 70 minutes playing time. The individual members have subsequently concentrated on solo work, with Bizzy Bone and Krayzie Bone both releasing commercially and critically successful albums.

● ALBUMS: *E. 1999 Eternal* (Ruthless 1995)★★★★, *The Art Of War* (Ruthless 1997)★★.
Solo: Bizzy Bone *Heaven'z Movie* (Loud 1998)★★★. Krayzie Bone *Thug Mentality 1999* (Loud 1999)★★★.

● COMPILATIONS: *The Collection: Volume One* (Ruthless 1998)★★★★.

● VIDEOS: *The Collection Volume 1* (Epic Music Video 1998).

Boo Radleys

The Boo Radleys took an arduous route to the popular acclaim that they always anticipated and their talents demanded. Formed in 1988 in Liverpool by Sice (b. Simon Rowbottom, 18 June 1969, Wallasey, Merseyside, England; guitar/vocals), Martin Carr (b. 29 November 1968, Thurso, Highland Region, Scotland; guitar), Timothy Brown (b. 26

February 1969, Wallasey, Merseyside, England; bass) and Steve Drewitt (b. Northwich, England; drums), they took their name from a character in the novel *To Kill A Mockingbird*. Sice and Carr had played out fantasies of pop stardom as children - waving to imagined fans and fielding self-composed interview questions - with the Beatles the cornerstone of their reference points. Carr's first venture into rock music was as a failed critic, writing two reviews for the *Liverpool Quiggins Market* paper. After several years of sporadic activity the Boo Radleys quietly released *Ichabod And I* on a small independent label. The album showcased the band's talent for guitar-blasted melodies, where timeless tunes were bolstered with up-to-date effects pedals, in truth, a fairly accurate revision of Dinosaur Jr's caustic blueprint. The British music press were unusually late to arrive on the scene, only paying attention after disc jockey John Peel had championed the quartet on BBC Radio 1. In the summer of 1990, drummer Steve Drewitt left to join Breed and was replaced by Robert Cieka (b. 4 August 1968, Birmingham, West Midlands, England), just as the Boo Radleys signed to Rough Trade Records. Within six months the band had started to fulfil their commercial potential by entering the Top 100 of the UK charts with an EP, *Every Heaven*. However, when the Rough Trade ship went down, the Boo Radleys needed Creation Records' intervention to continue. Their new record company's vision (hard critical commentary of the Boo Radleys at the time included corrupting their name to 'Do Baddleys') was rewarded with *Everything's Alright Forever*, which broke them firmly out of the indie ghetto. Songs such as 'Lazy Day', which predicted their later optimistic direction, were actually inspired by Sice's reading of the Manson murders, while other moments simply gloried in guitar-led musical abandon. *Giant Steps* saw the band abandon their previous standing as 'mediocre indie stalwarts' by producing a set that retraced the grandeur of Merseybeat, dripping with poise, attitude and melody, bringing them several Album Of The Year awards in the UK press. Surprisingly, the stakes were further raised by *Wake Up*, now without any of the usual chaotic experimentalism, the latter replaced instead by sweeping vistas of orchestrated pop. The buoyant, positive mood, epitomised by the glorious Top 10 hit single 'Wake Up Boo!', was only darkened by the occasional barbed lyric of '4am Conversation' or 'Wilder'. 'Joel' even attempted to pre-empt critics with the line: 'All I want is harmony, Like some outmoded 60s throwback'. An evident attempt to wrest chart domination away from newcomers Oasis or the rejuvenated Blur, *Wake Up* sacrificed nothing apart from a previous inaccessibility. Despite an avowed intention to become chart fixtures, the album was recorded in Wales amid much catastrophe and artistic abandon'. The spirit of the Boo Radleys obviously lived on despite the new commercial climate in which found themselves. This feeling was captured in the follow-up, *C'Mon Kids*, the band's most challenging album. A commercial failure, it saw the Boo Radleys almost wilfully pushing themselves onto the fringes of the music scene once more. Sice also released a solo album as Eggman, revealing a hidden melodic talent. *Kingsize* was predictably another critical success and commercial failure, and shortly afterwards, in January 1999, the band announced they were splitting up to concentrate on solo projects.

● ALBUMS: *Ichabod And I* (Action 1990)★★, *Everything's Alright Forever* (Creation 1992)★★★, *Giant Steps* (Creation 1993)★★★★, *Wake Up* (Creation 1995)★★★, *C'mon Kids* (Creation 1996)★★★★, *Kingsize* (Creation 1998)★★★.
Solo: Eggman *First Fruits* (Creation 1996)★★★.
● COMPILATIONS: *Learning To Walk* (Rough Trade 1994)★★★.

Boo, Betty

b. Alison Moira Clarkson, 6 March 1970, Kensington, London, England. Born of Scottish and Malayan parents, Clarkson began her career in a rap trio, the She-Rockers, and later appeared as part of a duo called Hit 'N' Run. Guesting on vocals for the Beatmasters' 'Hey DJ, I Can't Dance To That Music You're Playing', she was credited as Betty Boop (until lawyers representing the cartoon character of the same name stepped in!). In launching her own bid for stardom with 'Doin' The Do', again aided by the Beatmasters, Betty earned her first UK Top 10 single in May 1990. This was bettered a few months later with one of the brightest pop singles of the year, 'Where Are You Baby', which was also accompanied by one of the best pop videos of 1990. A mixture of bubbling pop and engaging videos won Betty many pop awards that same year. The artist ran into trouble in 1991 when, on a tour of Australia, she was discovered to be miming to backing tapes, resulting in promoters tearing up contracts for future live dates on the Antipodean tour, and prompting a speedy return to the UK. After signing to WEA Records, her low profile and silence were broken in July 1992 when she released the single 'Let Me Take You There' (UK number 12), but subsequent singles 'I'm On My Way' (UK number 44) and 'Hangover' (UK number 50) experienced diminishing returns. Boo has not recorded since she left WEA in 1993.

● ALBUMS: *Boomania* (Rhythm King 1990)★★★.
● VIDEOS: *Boomania: The Boomin' Vids* (Virgin Vision 1990).

Boo-Yaa T.R.I.B.E.

Of Samoan descent, Boo-Yaa T.R.I.B.E. were born and bred in the Los Angeles neighbourhood of Carson, where their father was a Baptist minister. Life was tough, evidence of which exists in their choice of name (slang for a shotgun being discharged). Running with the Bloods gang, every member of the clan had endured a stretch in prison, and one of their brothers, Robert 'Youngman' Devoux, was shot dead before the family turned musical. The brothers freely admit to having had involvement with drug production and brokering, as well as gun running. Ultimately they took the death of their kin as a sign from God, and headed for Japan to escape the gang warfare, staying with their Sumo wrestler cousin. There they subsisted by working as a rap/dance outfit in Tokyo, which convinced them their success could be imported back to LA. Island Records were the first to see a potential market for a sound that fused gangster imagery with hardcore hip-hop, and obtained their signatures. They appeared in Michael Jackson's Walt Disney movie *Captain EO* as breakdancers, as well as the television shows *Fame* and *The A-Team*. The line-up of the T.R.I.B.E. (Too Rough International Boo-Yaa Empire) boasts lead rapper Ganxsta Ridd (aka Paul Devoux), EKA, Rosco, Ganxsta OMB, the Godfather (aka Ted Devoux), and Don-L. Some members of the Los Angeles Police Department still harboured suspicions that the Tribe was merely a front for their continued illicit activities, but powerful singles such as 'Psyko Funk' represented a genuine, bullying rap presence. Their second album, 1994's *Doomsday*, featured further gangland narratives such as 'Kreepin' Through Your Hood' and 'Gangstas Of The Industry', the latter a put-down of rank commercialism and fake posturing for profit. In 1995, the Tribe set up their own Samoan Mafia Records and released *Occupation Hazardous*. Another low-key album followed two years later, but it is as an incendiary live outfit that the Boo-Yaa T.R.I.B.E. continue to impress.

● ALBUMS: *New Funky Nation* (4th & Broadway 1990)★★★, *Doomsday* (Bullet Proof 1994)★★★, *Occupation Hazardous* (Samoan Mafia 1995)★★★, *Angry Samoans* (Bullet Proof 1997)★★★.

Boredoms

Based in Yamatsuka, Japan, the Boredoms have borrowed liberally from the US hardcore punk tradition to forge their own climatic rock music. A septet comprising Yoshimi P-We, YY, God Mana, Human Rich Vox Y, Hila Y, Eye Y and No. 1 Y, the band's records combine the musical assault of hardcore with the experimental distorted song structures of the Butthole Surfers. *Onanie Bomb Meets The Sex Pistols*, compiling the first two Japanese releases, featured impenetrable noise and sequences of communal belching. Even more extreme was 1989's *Soul Discharge*, released on Kramer's Shimmy-Disc label, which featured song titles including 'JB Dick + Tin Turner (sic) Pussy Badsmell' and 'Bubblebop Shot'. The music that supported such lyrics offered unremitting musical chaos, akin to Extreme Noise Terror crossed with American no wave and art rock. *Pop Tatari* was once analogized as the 'least commercially viable album released by a major label since *Metal Machine Music*', the Lou Reed album. The band's subsequent records have been comparatively accessible, attracting a cult audience in America and Europe, helped by their notorious stage show. Away from the main band Eye performs with Hanatarash, and worked with John Zorn on 1996's *Nani Nani*.

● ALBUMS: *Anal By Anal* (Trans 1986)★★, *Osorezan To Stooges Kyo* (Selfish 1988)★★, *Onanie Bomb Meets The Sex Pistols* (Warners 1988)★★, *Soul Discharge* (Shimmy Disc 1989)★★, *Pop Tatari* (Warners/Reprise 1992)★★, *Wow-2* (Avant 1993)★★★, *Super Roots* mini-album (Warners/Reprise 1993)★★, *Chocolate Synthesizer* (Warners/Reprise 1994)★★★, *Super Roots 2* mini-album (Warners 1994)★★, *Super Roots 3* (Warners 1994)★★, *Super Roots 5* (Reprise 1995)★★, *Super Roots 6* (Reprise 1996)★★★, *Super æ* (Birdman 1998)★★★.

Bortolotti, Gianfranco

One of dance music's most colourful ambassadors in the golden period of the late 80s and early 90s, Bortolotti was the name behind many 'Italo-house' classics as manager of Media Records. Bortolotti had originally found himself in the DJ world to supplement his university days. He was initially influenced by DJ Pierre (not the US DJ), learning his craft from him, and when the latter's career began, actually helped in distributing records. His involvement grew until he too recouped the rewards of a couple of minor hit singles, reinvesting the money in a home studio and founding the Media label. The success of Media allowed Bortolotti to invest in no less than 10 studios - the main complex in Brescia, North Italy, was built on the Motown Records principle, churning out hits at a rate other factories ship beans. Cappella's breakthrough hit, 'Heylom Halib', introduced the

insistent rhythms, zany samples, tinkling piano and memorable choruses and catch phrases. This in turn predicted the wave of Italo-house hits (Black Box's 'Ride On Time', Starlight's 'Numero Uno', Mixmaster's 'Grand Piano') that dominated the late 80s dance scene. Media continued to release a unabated flow of hits through acts such as the 49ers ('Touch Me'), Fargetta ('The Music Is Movin''), East Side Beat, Clubhouse, Clock, DJ Professor and RAF. Just as Berry Gordy might have envisioned had he enjoyed access to the technology, the Media set-up ran along strictly businesslike lines, with three main producers (DJ Pierre, DJ Professor or RAF) working on their own floor. Each record was mixed between 15 and 20 times to suit individual territories, an astoundingly efficient and economic approach to making music.

● COMPILATIONS: various artists *Power Of The Media* (Media 1994)★★★.

Bottle Rockets

A US quartet comprising Uncle Tupelo associate Brian Henneman (guitar/vocals), Tom Parr (guitar/vocals), Tom Ray (bass) and Mark Ortmann (drums), Bottle Rockets formed in Festus, Missouri, USA, in 1992. Henneman, Parr and Ortmann had originally played together in covers band Chicken Truck, alongside Parr's brother Bob. Henneman's appearance on Uncle Tupelo's *March 16-20, 1992* brought about a recording deal with independent label East Side Digital. The band's ramshackle self-titled debut was recorded in five days with producer John Keane. *The Brooklyn Side* followed in 1994, and featured a distinctive, carefree blend of roots rock and barfly country songs expertly produced by Eric Ambel. Local reviews were strong, but the band were disgruntled to learn during sessions for a follow-up collection, *24 Hours A Day*, that their future was in serious doubt. Tag, the record label that had signed them and redistributed *The Brooklyn Side*, had been taken over by Atlantic Records. Nevertheless, they proceeded with the recording at Echo Park, the Bloomington, Indiana studio owned by John Mellencamp's guitarist Mike Wanchic. Eventually Atlantic agreed to pick up their contract, and the group's natural vivacity ensured that neither the despondency nor the anxiety of the times was reflected in the finished product. Ambel again served as producer on the album, which featured two hidden tributes to Mellencamp. 'When I Was Dumb' employed a guitar riff from Mellencamp's 'Hurts So Good', while 'Indianapolis' mentioned Mellencamp by name. Throughout the album there was a discernible ethos of spontaneous joking and humorous asides, typified by songs such as 'Perfect Far Away' and 'One Of You', a 'drunken ballad'. The band signed with Austin, Texas-based independent label Doolittle Records shortly afterwards. They released the *Leftovers* EP, which comprised tracks recorded during the *24 Hours A Day* sessions, in November 1998. The popular radio single 'Nancy Sinatra' premiered the following August's *Brand New Year*, which also featured new bass player Robert Kearns (ex-Cry Of Love).

● ALBUMS: *Bottle Rockets* (East Side Digital 1993)★★★, *The Brooklyn Side* (East Side Digital/Tag 1994)★★★, *24 Hours A Day* (Atlantic 1997)★★★, *Brand New Year* (Doolittle 1999)★★★.

Bounty Killer

b. Rodney Price, 12 June 1972, Riverton City, Jamaica, West Indies. Coming from a dancehall background, his father ran the Black Scorpio Sound System, and it was not long before he picked up the microphone himself. He soon became known performing on other sound systems, including Stereo Two and Metromedia. His first recording session was in the spring of 1992 at King Jammy's studio when he sang 'Watch The Gun', produced by Uncle T. After singing a number of other rhythms, Uncle T's brother King Jammy recognized Bounty Killer's potential and 'Fat And Sexy' was the resulting hit. Many ragga hits related to guns and Killer's contribution to the list is considerable: 'New Gun', 'Cop A Shot', 'Kill Fe Fun' and 'New Gun Gal Say Yes'. The flurry of gun-related hits continued unabashed and in 1993 the inevitable clash took place with his main rival, Beenie Man. In 1994, Killer recorded a number of singles that moved the subject matter away from guns, including, with Chuck Turner, 'Run Around Girl' and 'Roots Reality And Culture'. His big hit 'Down In The Ghetto' described how guns and drugs reached the ghettos sanctioned by corrupt government officials: 'Down in the ghetto where the gun have a ting - and the politician is the guns them a bring - hey - and the crack and the coke them a support the killing - me check it out the whole a dem ah the same ting'. The singer also contributed to tracks by Colin Roach ('I'll Be Back') and Junior Reid ('This World's Too Haunted'). He also appeared on 'No, No, No (World A Respect)' by seasoned Studio One performer Dawn Penn, alongside fellow veterans Dennis Brown and Ken Boothe. Bounty Killer's growing popularity resulted in a prominent UK tour, and in the spring of 1995 his single with Sanchez, 'Searching', enjoyed a long stay on the reggae chart. He continued to record many hits throughout 1995, including 'Book Book', 'Cellular Phone', 'Smoke The Herb', 'Mama', 'No Argument' and 'Fear No Evil'. By the end of 1995 the continuing feud with Beenie Man was resolved through RJR's disc jockey Richard Burgess, who invited the two to the station where a truce was announced. In the summer of 1996 Bounty's inimitable style enhanced the dancehall mix of the Fugees' chart-busting version of Roberta Flack's 'Killing Me Softly'. During the late 90s, he released the albums *Next Millennium* and *The 5th Element*, and started up his own Pricele$$ Records label.

● ALBUMS: *Jamaica's Most Wanted* (Greensleeves 1993)★★★★, *Down In The Ghetto* (Jammys 1994)★★★★, with Beenie Man *Guns Out* (Greensleeves 1994)★★★, *No Argument* (Greensleeves 1995)★★★, *My Xperience* (Blunt/Virgin 1996)★★, *Ghetto Gramma* (Greensleeves 1997)★★, *Next Millennium* (TVT 1998)★★★★, *The 5th Element* (TVT 1999)★★★.

Boyz II Men

This versatile close-harmony teenage soul quartet enjoyed an almost unprecedented level of success during the early 90s, beginning with the US Top 3 debut single 'Motownphilly'. They comprise Wanya 'Squirt' Morris (b. 29 July 1973, Philadelphia, Pennsylvania, USA), Michael 'Bass' McCary (b. 16 December 1972, Philadelphia, Pennsylvania, USA), Shawn 'Slim' Stockman (b. 26 September 1972, USA) and Nathan 'Alex-Vanderpool' Morris (b. 18 June 1971, USA). The four men met at the Philadelphia High School Of Creative And Performing Arts, forming the band in 1988. Michael Bivins of Bell Biv DeVoe took the quartet under his

wing and brought them, fittingly, to Motown Records. Their debut album was one side dance, one side ballad, and was a huge seller in the USA. By the middle of 1993 the album was still high on the US chart with sales of over seven million copies. The previous autumn, the soundtrack song 'End Of The Road' topped the US charts for a mammoth 13 weeks and provided the quartet with a UK chart-topper. Their winning formula was repeated with uncanny accuracy in 1994, the follow-up album (imaginatively titled *II*) becoming a huge hit. It spawned three of the best-selling singles in US chart history, with 'I'll Make Love To You' (at the top for 14 weeks), 'On Bended Knee' (at the top for 6 weeks) and 'One Sweet Day' (with Mariah Carey, number 1 for an astonishing 16 weeks). *Evolution* featured all-star contributions from Sean 'Puffy' Combs, Keith Crouch, Babyface and Jimmy Jam And Jerry Lewis. The quartet also set up their own label, Stonecreek.

● ALBUMS: *Cooleyhighharmony* (Motown 1991)★★★, *II* (Motown 1994)★★★★, *Remix, Remake, Remember* (Motown 1996)★★★★, *Evolution* (Motown 1997)★★★.

● VIDEOS: *Then II Now* (Motown Video 1994).

Boyzone

Considered by many to be the natural inheritors of Take That's 'boy band' throne, Boyzone are a quintet of unaffected young Irish men tailored for mainstream success by Polydor Records and their manager, promoter Louis Walsh. After auditions Mikey Graham (b. 15 August 1972, Dublin, Eire) and Keith Duffy (b. 4 October 1974, Dublin, Eire) were recruited from their jobs as mechanics, Shane Lynch (b. 3 July 1976, Dublin, Eire) from an architecture course, while Ronan Keating (b. 3 March 1977, Dublin, Eire) and Stephen Gately (b. 17 March 1976, Dublin, Eire) were enlisted directly from school. They were rapidly rehearsed and groomed, and signed with Polydor in 1994. Their first single, a cover version of the Osmonds' 'Love Me For A Reason', was produced for them by Take That collaborator Mike Hedges. It became an instant success on release in December 1994, peaking at number 2 in the UK charts and selling 700,000 copies. It also became a Top 10 hit in most European countries. The band's debut album, *All Said And Done*, was released in August 1995 and sold over one million copies worldwide. As well as 'Love Me For A Reason', it included three other hit singles, 'Key To My Life', 'So Good' and their Christmas 1995 cover version of Cat Stevens' 'Father And Son'. With the demise of Take That in 1996 and the rise of numerous 'boy bands', Boyzone moved to the head of the pack, with further hit singles including 'Coming Home Now' and a cover version of the Bee Gees' 'Words', their first UK number 1. In 1997, they teamed up with French boy band Alliage for a cover version of the Detroit Spinners' 'Working My Way Back To You', reaching number 3 in the French charts, and reached UK number 2 in December 1997 with their cover version of Tracy Chapman's 'Baby Can I Hold You'. 'All That I Need' topped the charts in May 1998, a feat repeated in August by the Andrew Lloyd-Webber/Jim Steinman-penned 'No Matter What', taken from the musical *Whistle Down The Wind*. The latter also became the band's first million-selling single. The band's next single, 'I Love The Way You Love Me', stalled at number 2 in December. *A Different Beat* and *Where We Belong* followed in the footsteps of their debut album by entering the UK charts at number 1, although both albums indicated that the band's strength remains as a singles act. The band's charity single, a cover version of Billy Ocean's 'When The Going Gets Tough', topped the UK singles chart for two weeks in March 1999. Keating worked hard to establish himself away from the band, recording solo material and presenting the prime-time UK talent show *Get Your Act Together*. He also enjoyed success as a manager/promoter, with his protégés Westlife topping the UK charts in May with their debut single, 'Swear It Again'. Boyzone followed them to the top the same month with their new single, 'You Needed Me', their popularity seemingly unaffected by Gately publically declaring his homosexuality shortly afterwards. Keating's cover version of Keith Whitley's country hit 'When You Say Nothing At All', taken from the soundtrack of *Notting Hill*, topped the UK charts in August. Boyzone's weak Christmas single, 'Every Day I Love You', stalled at number 3 in December.

● ALBUMS: *All Said And Done* (Polydor 1995)★★★, *A Different Beat* (Polydor 1996)★★★, *Where We Belong* (Polydor 1998)★★.

● COMPILATIONS: *By Request* (Polydor 1999)★★★.

● VIDEOS: *Said And Done* (VVL 1995), *Live At Wembley* (Vision Video 1996), *Live: Where We Belong* (VVL 1998), *By Request: Their Greatest Hits* (Vision Video 1999), *Boyzone Dublin: Live By Request* (Vision Video 1999).

BR5-49

Regarded by many as the most exciting country rock-inspired band in Nashville since Jason And The Scorchers, BR5-49 arrived in 1996 with a provocative manifesto. As Chuck Mead (b. 22 December 1960, Nevada, Montana, USA; guitar/vocals) told the press: 'I don't want it to be seen as some kind of planned competition to stamp out new country. But that'd be nice, because it sucks.' Mead had formerly played as a child in the Family Tree, a gospel hillbilly band made up of relatives, then Kansas roots rock group the Homestead Grays (one EP, *Big Hits*, and a CD, *El Supremo*, in 1991). The other members of BR5-49 are Gary Bennett (b. 9 October 1964, Las Vegas, Nevada, USA; acoustic guitar/vocals), Shaw Wilson (drums), Smilin' Jay McDowell (b. 11 June 1969, Bedford, Indiana, USA; slap bass) and Donnie Herron (dobro/mandolin/fiddle). Since its formation in 1994, the band has built a widespread reputation for its uninhibited, ferocious, good-time honky tonk. As well as cover versions of standards by Hank Williams, Bob Wills, Carl Perkins and Faron Young, originals such as '18 Wheels And A Crowbar', 'Do Something Even If It's Wrong' and 'Me And Opie Down By The Duck Pond', when combined with the band's exhaustive four-hour live sets, place them firmly in the 50s tradition of hillbilly music. Taking their name from the phone number used for Junior Sample's used car lot in the comedy television show *Hee Haw*, the band made their debut with a typically enthralling live set for Arista Records in 1996. This was quickly followed later in the year by their full-length debut. Among the treats on display here was 'Little Ramona (Gone Hillbilly Nuts)', Bennett's evocative account, with reference to the Ramones, of former hardcore punk friends now turned on to 50s hillbilly records. The record also included cover versions of two staples of that period, 'I Ain't Never' and 'Crazy Arms'. *Big Backyard Beat Show* was another fine collection demonstrating the band are maturing into seasoned performers.

● ALBUMS: *Live At Robert's* mini-album (Arista 1996)★★★, *The Number To Call Is ... BR5-49* (Arista 1996)★★★★, *Big Backyard Beat Show* (Arista 1998)★★★★.

Brad

The involvement of Pearl Jam guitarist Stone Gossard in this project inevitably and unfairly saw Brad tagged as Gossard's solo outing, when in reality, it was a collaboration with two old friends, Pigeonhed/Satchel vocalist and keyboard player Shawn Smith and Satchel drummer Regan Hagar, plus bass player Jeremy Toback. The band was originally called Shame, but Los Angeles musician Brad Wilson held a copyright on the name and was not prepared to give it up - hence, the band cheekily named themselves Brad. They entered the studio with only the album opener, 'Buttercup', written, and wrote, recorded and mixed *Shame* in just 17 days. The result was an enthralling and atmospheric work, blending funk, rock, jazz and soul with a melancholy lyrical air, and the fact that much of the material stemmed from studio jams gave the album a loose, laid-back feel. Gossard produced a largely understated performance that complemented Smith's piano and organ lines, backed by a solid, economical groove from the rhythm section, while Smith's smoky, soulful vocals added another dimension to the band, and drew comparisons with Prince and Stevie Wonder amid a heap of deserved critical praise. The players reconvened for a less vital second album in 1997, although tracks such as 'Upon My Shoulders' and 'The Day Brings' confirmed Smith's reputation as one of the finest singers of the 90s.

● ALBUMS: *Shame* (Epic 1993)★★★★, *Interiors* (Epic 1997)★★★.

Brainiac

Formed in Dayton, Ohio, USA, maverick art rock band Brainiac played their first gig together at Rightstate University in March 1992. Immediately the band became a legend in their area by dabbling in the urban netherworlds depicted in their songs. Following a splendidly adventurous debut album produced by Girls Against Boys keyboard player Eli Janney, Gary Gersch, managing director of Geffen Records, launched a £2 million offer for their services. Brainiac's response, allegedly, was to tell him to 'fuck off'. Instead they continued touring with Jesus Lizard and Shudder To Think as well as Girls Against Boys, and befriended R.E.M.'s Michael Stipe in Hollywood. Comprising Tim Taylor (b. 1969, USA, d. 23 May 1997; vocals), Tyler Trent (drums), Michelle O'Dean (guitar) and Juan Monasterio (bass), the band went on to establish a reputation as one of America's most forthright and entertaining live acts, while their ambition and irreverence was confirmed by the arrival of a second album in 1994: 'Too many American bands dress like lumberjacks and tell the kids "we're with you". Which means fuck. It's boring. The kids want something they can aspire to or make fun of.' O'Dean left in 1995 and was replaced by John Schmersal, who changed the overall sound of the band to become more challenging. They supported Beck on tour in 1997 and released the *Electro-Shock For President* mini-album, before Taylor was killed in a car crash in Ohio in May of that year.

● ALBUMS: *Smack Bunny Baby* (Grass 1993)★★★, *Bonsai Superstar* (Grass 1994)★★★, *Hissing Prigs In Static Couture* (Touch & Go 1996)★★★.

Bran Van 3000

This sprawling, highly eclectic Canadian outfit were formed by Montreal-based video director James 'Bran Man' Di Salvio, whose CV includes work for Branford Marsalis and Sarah McLachlan. His extensive record collection also ensured work as a part-time DJ, but it was not until the late 90s that he decided to pursue a recording career. Di Salvio hooked up with Canadian dance music veteran 'EP' Bergen, who had released an album on TOX Records as far back as 1992. Musical director Di Salvio and co-producer Bergen were joined in the initial line-up of Bran Van 3000 (the origin of the name is dubious) by vocalists Sara Johnston and Jayne Hill, but gradually recruited a large cast of Montreal musicians for recording and touring purposes. Experienced rapper Steve 'Liquid' Hawley, guitarist Nick Hynes, bass player Gary McKenzie, drummer Rob Joanisse, and vocalist Stéphane Moraille were brought on board to augment the band's sample-heavy mixture of sprightly indie pop melodies, club beats, trip-hop sprawl, and cheesy lounge music. Their debut *Glee* was originally released in spring 1997 on the Audioworks label, but the following year's international release contained several new songs and different versions of many tracks owing to licensing problems. 'Drinking In LA' featured Moraille's soulful vocal chorus juxtaposed with Di Salvio's ranting verses. 'Afrodisiak' and 'Everywhere' were equally tuneful standouts amid the general chaos, which reached surreal heights on a cover version of Slade's 'Cum On Feel The Noize'. 'Drinking In LA', which had originally stalled outside the UK Top 30 in summer 1998, reached number 3 when re-released in the UK in August 1999 thanks to its prominent use in a Rolling Rock beer advertisement.
● ALBUMS: *Glee* (Audioworks/Capitol 1997)★★★.

Brand New Heavies

Simon Bartholomew and Andy Levy are the central duo behind Ealing, London, England-based band the Brand New Heavies, alongside drummer Jan Kincaid and (initially) keyboard player Ceri Evans. They had already suffered one failed contract with Acid Jazz Records, who tried to launch them as a 'rare groove' outfit, before they joined with US label Delicious Vinyl. The latter's management put them in touch with N'Dea Davenport (b. Georgia, USA), who had previously provided backing vocals for George Clinton, Bruce Willis and appeared in videos for Young MC and Madonna's former band the Breakfast Club. Word spread throughout the USA of their liaison, and soon hip-hop teams picked up on the band. They were sampled heavily on a number of early 90s rap records, before inviting members of that community to provide guest raps on their second album, *Heavy Rhyme Experience: Vol. 1*. These included Black Sheep, Gang Starr, Grand Puba, Main Source, Kool G. Rap, Ed.Og, Master Ace, Tiger and Pharcyde. Ceri Evans left the band in January 1992 to undertake production work for Alison Limerick and Galliano, recording solo as Sunship ('Muthafuckin''/'The 13th Key', for Dorado Records). Their huge success in the US with the single 'Never Stop' was soon mirrored in the UK, with the singles 'Dream On Dreamer' and 'Midnight At The Oasis' reaching the Top 20 in 1994. Soul singer Siedah Garrett became the new front-person in 1997 after Davenport's departure the previous year for a solo career. They enjoyed further chart success the same year when

their cover version of James Taylor's 'You've Got A Friend' broke into the UK Top 10.
● ALBUMS: *Brand New Heavies* (Acid Jazz 1990)★★★, *Heavy Rhyme Experience: Vol. 1* (ffrr 1992)★★★★, *Brother Sister* (ffrr 1994)★★★, *Original Flava* (Acid Jazz 1995)★★, *Excursions: Remixes & Rare Grooves* (Delicious Vinyl 1996)★★, *Shelter* (London 1997)★★★.
● COMPILATIONS: *Dream Come True: The Best Of The Acid Jazz Years* (Music Club 1998)★★★, *Trunk Funk: The Best Of The Brand New Heavies* (ffrr 1999)★★★.

Brand Nubian

From the Bronx, New York, and led by Grand Puba (b. Maxwell Dixon, New Rochelle, New York, USA; ex-Masters Of Ceremony), Brand Nubian's 1990 debut, *One For All*, was as cool, classy and unaffected as hip-hop comes. Joined by Lord Jamar (b. Lorenzo Dechelaus, 17 September 1968, New Rochelle, New York, USA), Derek X (b. Derrick Murphy, 29 December 1968, New Rochelle, New York, USA) and DJ Alamo (the latter two cousins), Puba's Muslim-influenced lyrics were backed by samples of James Brown and Roy Ayers, ensuring the musical backing was never less than interesting. In 1991, Puba left to go solo, taking DJ Alamo with him, but Brand Nubian elected to continue as a three-piece unit with the addition of DJ Sincere (and with Derek X now known as Sadat X). Their first album following his defection was *In God We Trust*, which focused on their intensely held beliefs with tracks such as 'The Meaning Of The 5%', 'Allah And Justice' and 'Ain't No Mystery'. The album title referred to a significant element of 5% Nation (a sectarian branch of the Nation of Islam) doctrine. 'We represent ourselves as god', said Lord Jamar, 'and we're not trusting any mystery in the sky to help us with what we have to do. When a religion teaches you to depend on something else instead of being self-sufficient, then that becomes the downfall of people.' There were signs of a creative impasse on 1994's *Everything Is Everything*, a disappointingly unfocused and messy album, with laboured beats failing to raise the interest level. Sadat X released a solo album in 1996, before the original line-up regrouped for 1998's strong comeback album, *Foundation*, which featured collaborations with Busta Rhymes and Common.
● ALBUMS: *One For All* (Elektra 1990)★★★★, *In God We Trust* (Elektra 1992)★★★, *Everything Is Everything* (Elektra 1994)★★, *Foundation* (Arista 1998)★★★.

Brandy

b. Brandy Norwood, 11 February 1979, McComb, Mississippi, USA. Among the best of the 90s crop of R&B's 'new jill swingers', Brandy is actually much less sex and violence-obsessed than most of her peers. Her career in entertainment began early - at the age of 15 she was nominated for a Youth In Film Award for her portrayal of schoolgirl Denesha in the ABC television situation comedy *Thea*. Her breakthrough in music followed quickly. Her self-titled debut album, produced by Keith Crouch and the Somethin' For The People collective, reached number 6 in the R&B album charts, selling over 1.3 million copies. It included the successful crossover single, 'I Wanna Be Down'. That song was then transformed in an alternative version marketed specifically at rap fans. The 'Hyman Rhythm Hip Hop Remix' featured guest rhymes from Queen Latifah, MC Lyte and Yo Yo. Released on the b-side of the follow-up single, 'Baby', it helped the a-side become one of the fastest-selling R&B number 1s in recent US chart history. Both single and album won awards at the inaugural Soul Train Lady of Soul Awards in Los Angeles in 1995. Regarded as a comparatively wholesome performer, she was also named spokeswoman for the 1996 Sears/Seventeen Peak Performance Scholarship Program and tour, which supports the efforts of young women to achieve specific goals. In 1996 her brother, Ray-J, made his recording debut for Elektra Records. Brandy also appears in the hugely popular TV show *Moesha*, and her second album was recorded during breaks from filming. Her spiky duet with fellow soul singer Monica on 1998's 'The Boy Is Mine' was a huge-selling US number 1, spending 13 weeks at the top of the *Billboard* Hot 100 and becoming the all-time number one female duet in US chart history. The single also reached number 2 in the UK and sold over 3 million copies worldwide. The attendant number 2 album, *Never S-A-Y Never*, was disappointingly bland, but follow-up single, 'Top Of The World' (featuring a guest appearance from Ma$e) was another transatlantic hit single (UK number 2, October 1998). 'Have You Ever?', written by Diane Warren, topped the Hot 100 in January 1999. The same year, Brandy made her acting debut in the horror movie *I Still Know What You Did Last Summer*.

● ALBUMS: *Brandy* (Atlantic 1994)★★★, *Never S-A-Y Never* (Atlantic 1998)★★★.

● FURTHER READING: *Brandy … An Intimate Look*, Karu F. Daniels.

● FILMS: *I Still Know What You Did Last Summer* (1999).

Braxton, Toni

b. 7 October 1968, Severn, Maryland, USA. Braxton, with her four sisters, was signed to Arista Records in 1990 as the Braxtons. It was their 'The Good Life' single that brought them to the attention of producers L.A. And Babyface, who provided her with solo successes such as 'Another Sad Love Song' and 'You Mean The World To Me'. Though she has been widely described as the 'new Whitney Houston' (a fate that befalls many female vocalists), her vocal talent also found an audience in dance music circles, causing her debut album to sell more than two million copies, and she won a Grammy for Best New Artist in 1993. *Secrets* repeated the success of her debut, particularly in her homeland (eight million sales) where she threatens to make Whitney Houston appear to be 'the old Toni Braxton'. Her biggest hit to date came with 'Unbreak My Heart', which seemed to be a permanent fixture on the charts in 1996, reaching number 2 in the UK. She won Female Rhythm & Blues Artist Of The Year at the 1997 *Billboard* Music Awards. Surprisingly, in light of her previous commercial success, Braxton filed for bankruptcy in January 1998 following litigation with her record company.

● ALBUMS: *Toni Braxton* (Arista 1994)★★★, *Secrets* (Arista 1996)★★★.

● VIDEOS: *The Home Video* (Arista 1994).

Breeders

Restless with her subordinate role in Boston, USA guitar band the Pixies, bass player Kim Deal (b. 10 June 1961, Dayton, Ohio, USA; guitar, vocals, synthesizers) forged this spin-off project with Throwing Muses guitarist Tanya Donelly (b. 14 August 1966, Newport, Rhode Island, USA). The name Breeders, a derogatory term used by homosexuals

to describe heterosexuals, had been the name of a band Deal fronted prior to the Pixies, with her twin sister Kelley. Kim and Donelly initially undertook sessions with Muses drummer David Narciso, but these sessions were abandoned. Now joined by bass player Josephine Wiggs (b. Josephine Miranda Cordelia Susan Wiggs, 26 February 1965, Letchworth, Hertfordshire, England) from British act the Perfect Disaster, the Breeders recorded *Pod* in Edinburgh during a Pixies tour of Britain. Britt Walford from Kentucky hardcore band Slint, drummed on the record under the pseudonym Shannon Doughton. Distinctively 'engineered' by Steve Albini, the tenor of the album leant towards Deal's work with her parent band with plangent guitars, menacing melodies and uncompromized lyrics. The harrowing 'Hellhound' took the view of an aborted foetus, 'Iris' graphically detailed menstruation, while their reading of the Beatles' 'Happiness Is A Warm Gun' expressed the tension only implicit in the original. A four-track EP, *Safari*, which featured a thrilling version of the Who's 'So Sad About Us', followed. Here the band was augmented by Kelley Deal (guitar/vocals), but despite critical and commercial acclaim, the Breeders remained a sideline. However, following the Pixies' bitter split in the wake of *Trompe Le Monde*, Kim Deal rekindled the band in 1993. Tanya Donelly had already left the Muses to form Belly and was thus unavailable. However, Wiggs, who left Perfect Disaster during the Breeders' first inception, abandoned Honey Tongue, a band she formed with Jon Mattock from Spiritualized, to rejoin the Deal twins. Jim MacPherson (b. James Carl Macpherson, 23 June 1966, Dayton, Ohio, USA; drums), formerly of the Raging Mantras, completed the line-up featured on *Last Splash*. Less abrasive than its predecessor, this engaging set revealed Kim Deal's growing maturation as a songwriter, encompassing mock C&W ('Driving All Night'), grunge-styled instrumentals ('Roi') and ballads ('Do You Love Me Now?'). The future of the band was in doubt during 1996 while Kelley Deal underwent a drug rehabilitation programme. She departed and worked with the Last Hard Men in late 1996, before forming the Kelley Deal 6000. Wiggs also left to concentrate on the Josephine Wiggs Experience. Kim Deal, meanwhile, formed the Amps, who released *Pacer* in October 1995. A short Breeders tour in December 1996 featured the Amps line-up (Deal, Nate Farley, Luis Lerma) and Carrie Bradley. The new Breeders line-up, with Macpherson replaced by Brainiac drummer, Tyler Trent, entered the studio to work on an abortive new album. Rumours of Kim Deal reuniting with the original band have continued to circulate ever since, although the only material to have surfaced is a cover version, 'Collage', recorded for *The Mod Squad* soundtrack.

● ALBUMS: *Pod* (4AD 1990)★★★, *Last Splash* (4AD 1993)★★★, *Live In Stockholm* (Breeders' Digest 1995)★★★.

Brian Jonestown Massacre

This prolific American retro-psychedelic band are led by the provocative Anton Newcombe (guitar/vocals), and named after the Rolling Stones' dead guitarist and the 1978 mass suicide in Jonestown, Guyana. Formed in Newcombe's hometown of San Francisco, California, USA in 1990, other key members include Matt Hollywood (bass) and Joel Gion (tambourine and self-styled 'Spokesman For The Revolution'). Highly prolific, they have released seven albums of original material in only three years on

Newcombe's own Tangible label, with distribution through 60s specialists Bomp Records. Newcombe's musical vision was based on replicating the successive musical phases of the Rolling Stones, paying particular interest to 1967's psychedelic rock era. Following two earlier singles, the line-up of Newcombe, Hollywood, Gion, Dean Taylor (guitar), Mara Regal (organ), Dawn Thomas (accordion) and Brian Glaze (drums) released *Methodrone* in August 1995. Despite an affinity with the spaced out drone rock of more contemporary bands such as Spaceman 3 and My Bloody Valentine, the retro distorted fuzz guitars rooted the band firmly in the mid- to late 60s. A compilation of earlier recordings preceded the minor classic *Their Satanic Majesties 'Second Request*, arguably a more coherent take on psychedelic rock than the Rolling Stones album from which the title was taken. *Take It From The Man!* followed in June, and from the Union Jack on the cover to the music within gloriously revived mid-60s UK R&B as it mutated into rock. Standout tracks included '(David Bowie I Love You) Since I Was Six' and 'Straight Up And Down'. In the liner notes to the album, Newcombe recounted how the ghost of Brian Jones came to him in the studio and asked him to make the record. The low budget (allegedly $17.36) *Thank God For Mental Illness* was released in October. An all-acoustic recording, the reference points this time were the country blues of earlier-period Stones. Despite support slots with Mercury Rev, Oasis (on their first US tour) and Sonic Boom, the band's chaotic, occasionally violent live shows (often triggered by Gion's full blown rants) precluded any immediate major label link-up. Newcombe, Hollywood, Gion, Taylor, Jeff Davies (guitar), Peter Hayes (guitar) and Brad Artley (drums) recorded 1997's *Give It Back!*, which produced further classic tracks including 'Not If You Were The Last Dandy On Earth' (a nod to associates Dandy Warhols) and 'This Is Why You Love Me'. Newcombe also launched another label, The Committee To Keep Music Evil. After signing with TVT Records, the band reverted to full-blown psychedelic rock on June 1998's *Strung Out In Heaven*. Mixing new songs with reworkings of previously released material, the album's relatively focused production came as something of a shock to fans of their earlier recordings.

● ALBUMS: *Methodrone* (Bomp 1995)★★★, *Their Satanic Majesties 'Second Request* (Bomp 1996)★★★, *Take It From The Man!* (Bomp 1996)★★★★, *Thank God For Mental Illness* (Bomp 1996)★★★, *Give It Back!* (Bomp 1997)★★★, *Strung Out In Heaven* (TVT 1998)★★★.

● COMPILATIONS: *Space Girl And Other Favorites* (Tangible 1996)★★.

Brickman, Jim

b. Cleveland, Ohio, USA. Brickman is a pianist who has surprised many during his increasingly successful career, and the basis for any understanding of him is a recognition of the simplicity of his ideas and execution. His reinstatement of a classic pop sound is at odds with his background in classical music, but his studies of composition and performance were always compromised by his love of popular music while at the Cleveland Institute Of Music. As he recalls: 'That's what came naturally to me, pop songwriting.' He launched a career as a commercial jingle writer while still cloistered in the campus dormitory. After despatching demo tapes to various New York advertising agencies, Brickman won high-profile commissions from, among others, Jim Henson and Henson Associates, consequently writing a good deal of music for *The Muppets* and Henson's Children's Television Workshop. His jingles also accompanied television commercials for major American corporations such as 7-Up, Sony and McDonalds. He then founded his own production company after moving to Los Angeles. The Brickman Arrangement created music for clients including G.E., The Gap, Sprint, Kellogg's and Disney TV. A series of nominations and awards came in recognition of this work, including the Houston International Film Festival and London's International Advertising Awards. Another career change arrived in 1994 when Brickman signed with Windham Hill Records to release *No Words*. Featuring, as the title intimated, no lyrics, this proved a small obstacle to commercial success as consumers turned to the artist's unaffected pop tunes and powerful hooks, all provided via his solo, upright Yamaha piano skills. The 1995 follow-up, *By Heart*, continued to mine a similar love of 50s and 60s bubblegum pop, though this time a vocalist was used for the first time - albeit on a single track, 'By Heart'. Other cameos included the presence of a vibraphone and cello, but elsewhere there was a reluctance to clutter any idea or melody with undue sophistication: 'The world is such a noisy place that this is a refreshing change; the simplicity of the whole thing is attractive.' A good example of this was the success of the single, 'Rocket To The Moon', which became the first solo instrumental song ever to break the *Billboard* pop charts. In its wake Brickman took his Yamaha on tour throughout his native Midwest America, the Far East and Asia. His next album, *Picture This*, was quickly followed by a collection of seasonal favourites, *The Gift*. The duets album *Visions Of Love* featured collaborators Janis Ian, Peabo Bryson and Stephen Bishop. Now a fixture on the Adult Contemporary chart, Brickman enjoyed further success with 1999's *Destiny*.

● ALBUMS: *No Words* (Windham Hill 1994)★★★, *By Heart* (Windham Hill 1995)★★★, *Picture This* (Windham Hill 1996)★★★★, *The Gift* (Windham Hill 1997)★★★, *Visions Of Love* (Windham Hill 1998)★★★, *Destiny* (Windham Hill 1999)★★★★.

Brooke, Jonatha

b. Boston, Massachusetts, USA. Initially recording with the Story, singer-songwriter Jonatha Brooke has earned several comparisons with Rickie Lee Jones for her work in the 90s. Trained as a ballet dancer, she first played rock music as a 13-year-old bass player with a local rock band called Science Function, which included her biology teacher. However, her first experience of Joni Mitchell, whose unusual tunings and textures have become an abiding influence, changed her musical reference points. She became entranced by Rickie Lee Jones after interviewing her for the US magazine *Performing Songwriter*. The Story were effectively a duo of Brooke with associate Jennifer Kimball, a creative partnership that spanned 12 years. After two albums with the Story, Kimball departed, in the same week that the duo were dropped by Elektra Records despite sales of over 100,000 for *The Angel In The House* and a favourable critical reception. Brooke eventually found a sympathetic ear in Tommy LiPuma who had originally signed the Story to Elektra and recently established Blue Thumb Records. Brooke relegated the Story's name to that of support billing for 1996's *Plumb*, produced by her husband, the jazz pianist Alain Mallet. Among the songs were 'Where Were You?', a bitter and autobiographical indictment of the treatment of artists by record

companies. Certainly there were fewer of the metaphysical references to mermaids and angels observed on *The Angel In The House*, Brooke opting instead for narratives dealing frankly with loneliness and despair. The backing band featured long-standing the Story collaborators Michael Rivard (bass) and Duke Levine (guitar) as well as drummer Abe Laboriel. A wide-ranging collection, *Plumb* included such diverse selections as the Irish jig 'Charming' (with uilleann piper Jerry O'Sullivan) and the despondent 'The War' (a duet with Bruce Cockburn). Her real solo debut arrived the following year with *10c Wings*, a partially successful attempt to mine the fashionable singer-songwriter vein popularised by artists such as Sarah McLachlan and Meredith Brooks. The album was not successful, and Brooke subsequently severed her ties with MCA to form her own Bad Dog label. Her first release on Bad Dog was an excellent concert set, with the natural setting giving her powerful songs room to breathe.
● ALBUMS as Jonatha Brooke And The Story *Plumb* (Blue Thumb 1996)★★★, *10c Wings* (Refuge/MCA 1997)★★★, *Jonatha Brooke Live* (Bad Dog 1999)★★★.

Brooks And Dunn

This highly successful country duo comprises Kix Brooks (b. Leon Eric Brooks, 12 May 1955, Shreveport, Louisiana, USA) and Ronnie Gene Dunn (b. 1 June 1953, Coleman, Texas, USA). As an adolescent, Brooks lived close to Johnny Horton and sang with Horton's daughter. He moved to Nashville and found success as a songwriter, co-writing a US country number 1 by John Conlee ('I'm Only In It For The Love') in 1983, and then the Nitty Gritty Dirt Band's 'Modern Day Romance' and Highway 101's 'Who's Lonely Now'. Having limited success with 'There's A Telephone Ringing', he wanted to succeed as a solo performer but his Capitol Records debut album, *Kix Brooks*, in 1989, made little impression, all songs being written by Brooks with 11 other writers. Although Ronnie Dunn planned to be a Baptist minister, he could not reconcile it with his love of honky tonks, and eventually he was leading the house band at Duke's Country, a successful club in Tulsa. He had minor US country chart entries with 'It's Written All Over Your Face' and 'She Put The Sad In All His Songs'. After winning a talent contest in 1989, he moved to Nashville and Arista's vice-president, Tim DuBois, suggested that he should try to write some songs with Brooks. They came up with 'Brand New Man' and, as they sounded good together and became friends, they formed the duo Brooks And Dunn. Their high-energy, debut album sold three million copies and yielded four chart-topping country singles; one of them, the line-dancing 'Boot Scootin' Boogie', was also a US pop hit. The song also appears in a dance version on their second album and as Brooks says, 'We added a synthesiser and pumped this hillbilly record full of steroids.' 'Rock My World (Little Country Girl)', with its Rolling Stones-styled intro, boasted eight international versions and a video. Their stage act features a manic performance by Brooks, complete with duck-walks and wild leaps. Not surprisingly, they have won several Country Music Association Vocal Duo Of The Year awards and with their success, they have been able to design and model western shirts for Panhandle Slim. *Borderline* debuted at number 1 on the *Billboard* country chart in May 1996 and was followed by a number 1 single, 'My Maria'. They culminated the year with a CMA award for Entertainer

Of the Year and once more Duo Of The Year. Whether they will have the longevity of the Bellamy Brothers remains to be seen, but to date, they rock harder, write sharper novelty songs and have considerably more stage personality. They are the most popular male duo in country music since the heyday of the Everly Brothers. In 1997, they received a further CMA award for Best Vocal Duo. *If You See Her* peaked at number 11 on the *Billboard* Hot 200, and was followed by the equally successful *Tight Rope*. The latter featured some excellent production work by Byron Gallimore.
● ALBUMS: *Brand New Man* (Arista 1991)★★★★, *Hard Workin' Man* (Arista 1993)★★★★, *Waitin' On Sundown* (Arista 1994)★★★★, *Borderline* (Arista 1996)★★★★, *If You See Her* (Arista 1998)★★★, *Tight Rope* (Arista 1999)★★★.
Solo: Kix Brooks *Kix Brooks* (Capitol 1993)★★★.
● COMPILATIONS: *The Greatest Hits Collection* (Arista 1997)★★★★.
● VIDEOS: *That Ain't No Way To Go* (DNA 1994), *The Greatest Hits Video Collection* (BMG 1997).

Brooks, Garth

b. Troyal Garth Brooks, 7 February 1962, Yukon, Oklahoma, USA. Brooks' mother, country singer Colleen Carroll, appeared on the *Ozark Jubilee* and recorded for Capitol Records. Brooks won an athletic scholarship in Oklahoma and entertained in clubs at night. He preferred music and was soon playing full-time. While having a club residency, he learned over 350 songs. Working as a bouncer in Stillwater, he broke up a fight and hence met his future wife, Sandy. When he first married, he reminisced about his high school sweetheart and wondered if he had made a mistake. A few years later, he met her, realized that they had both changed, and wrote the song 'Unanswered Prayers'. Brooks signed with Capitol Records and was assigned to producer Allen Reynolds, known for his work with Don Williams. His first album, *Garth Brooks*, had an old-time, western swing and country feel and included a revival of a Jim Reeves success ('I Know One'), a western saga ('Cowboy Bill') and several new love songs ('The Dance', 'If Tomorrow Never Comes' and his own 'Not Counting You'). Brooks' second album, *No Fences*, was even better, including his concert-stopping 'Friends In Low Places', and a revival of the Fleetwoods' 'Mr. Blue', both written by Dwayne Blackwell. The album sold 10 million copies in the USA and Brooks has won numerous awards. *Ropin' The Wind* sold four million copies in its first month of release and topped both the US pop and country charts (nine million sales by mid-1993). His version of Billy Joel's 'Shameless' was a US country number 1, as were his recordings of 'The Thunder Rolls', 'Two Of A Kind' and 'Working On A Full House'. Brooks chooses his songs carefully but he has yet to find the right duet song for himself and his mother. He says, 'My mother has told me to take care of myself. In that way, I'll be around in 10 or 15 years and I can pay back the people who have invested time in me.' Brooks' survival as a commercial force seems in no doubt, but during 1992 rumours began to circulate that he was planning to quit the music business to concentrate on raising a family (his first daughter, named Taylor in honour of James Taylor, was born that spring). In the event, Brooks cancelled his touring engagements for the summer, but re-emerged before the end of the year with a Christmas record, *Beyond The Season*, and another album, *The Chase*. Within four months, that album had sold five million copies. Critics noted that Brooks was moving subtly away from the honky-tonk style of his debut towards a 70s-orientated soft rock sound. Brooks reached the UK pop chart in 1994 with 'The Red Strokes', one of the few US country singers to do so; this further reinforced the view that he was not just a US phenomenon. *Fresh Horses* was his first album to have simultaneous worldwide release, and a further international hit came with the sugar-drenched 'She's Every Woman'. In 1995, he was distracted by having his former managers suing each other. He took over his own business affairs with the help of his wife Sandy. Brooks has changed the whole perception of country music, making it fashionable. He is still ambitious and he is determined to initiate One World Flag when, one day of the year, the world flag would be flown in every country as a symbol of unity. Brooks was named Entertainer Of The Year at the 1997 Country Music Awards. At the end of the year he released *Sevens*, which predictably debuted at number 1 in the *Billboard* pop and country charts with pre-orders of more than five million units. *Double Live* also topped the charts in the first week of December, breaking the one million mark for first week sales. His worldwide album sales reached 81 million in 1998, confirming him as the all-time biggest-selling solo artist in America. Brooks shocked the country establishment in 1999 when he recorded an entire pop album under the pseudonym of Chris Gaines, a character in his forthcoming movie *The Lamb*. The attendant single, 'Lost In You', was a US Top 5 hit in September, but sales for the album were disappointing and a swift return to straightforward country songs was forecasted.

● ALBUMS: *Garth Brooks* (Liberty 1989)★★★★, *No Fences* (Liberty 1990)★★★★, *Ropin' The Wind* (Liberty 1991)★★★, *The Chase* (Liberty 1992)★★★★, *Beyond The Season* (Liberty 1992)★★, *In Pieces* (Liberty 1993)★★★★, *Fresh Horses* (Capitol Nashville 1995)★★★, *Sevens* (Capitol Nashville 1997)★★★, *Double Live* (Capitol 1998)★★★, *Garth Brooks In ... The Life Of Chris Gaines* (Capitol 1999)★★★, *Garth Brooks & The Magic Of Christmas* (Capitol 1999)★★★.

● COMPILATIONS: *The Hits* (Liberty 1994)★★★★, *The Limited Series* 6-CD box set (Capitol 1998)★★★.

● VIDEOS: *Garth Brooks* (Liberty 1991), *This Is Garth Brooks* (Liberty 1992), *The Video Collection Volume II* (Capitol 1996), *Garth Live From Central Park* (Orion Home Video 1998).

● FURTHER READING: *Garth Brooks: Platinum Cowboy*, Edward Morris. *One Of A Kind, Workin' On A Full House*, Rick Mitchell. *The Road Out Of Santa Fe*, Matt O'Meilia.

Brooks, Meredith

b. Oregon City, Oregon, USA. Brooks launched her solo career in the mid-90s after a gap of over eight years from her previous recording efforts. In 1989, she was signed to A&M Records as a member of the Graces, a band she co-founded with Gina Clambotti, later a member of Bruce Springsteen's touring group, and Charlotte Caffey, formerly of the Go-Go's. However, she soon became dissatisfied with life as part of that band. She took a break to marry, and thereafter concentrated on her own writing. She settled into running a restaurant alongside her husband, before meeting her future manager, Laurie Levy, in 1995. He encouraged her to become a full-time professional singer once again. She later explained that her long sabbatical was due to her disenchantment with the hold grunge had over the American music market. The material included on her excellent solo

debut, *Blurring The Edges*, was written alongside a number of collaborators, including close friend Shelley Peiken. Among Peiken's co-credits was 'Bitch', the first hit single to be taken from the album. It was also the only song to be produced by Geza X, the legendary Los Angeles punk producer (Dead Kennedys). The other tracks on the album were produced by David Ricketts (ex-David And David, and a veteran of sessions with Sheryl Crow and Toni Childs). Brooks herself played all the guitar parts and fits the bill perfectly alongside 90s female singer-songwriters such as Alanis Morissette and Sheryl Crow, but with inflections of Rickie Lee Jones also noticeable. Brooks' sophomore collection was introduced by a cover version of Melanie's 1970 hit, 'Lay Down (Candles In The Rain)'.

● ALBUMS: *Blurring The Edges* (Capitol 1997)★★★, *Deconstruction* (Capitol 1999)★★★★.

Brothers In Rhythm

London, UK-based producer Steve Anderson and Leeds, UK-based DJ Dave Seaman, who met through the DMC organization in 1988, established themselves as one of the UK house scene's most adventurous and popular remixing teams. They initially came to public prominence with startling revisions of yesteryear such as Heaven 17's 'Temptation' and Frankie Goes To Hollywood's 'Welcome To The Pleasuredome'. Other work included engagements with Sabrina Johnson ('Peace'), Pet Shop Boys ('We All Feel Better In The Dark', 'DJ Culture', 'Was It Worth It?', 'Seriously'), Kylie Minogue ('Finer Feelings'), Ce Ce Peniston ('We Got A Love Thang'), Lulu ('Independence') and Judy Cheeks ('Reach'). They also earned the honour of being the first British team to remix Michael Jackson ('Who Is It?' - and they would also work on a track for sister Janet Jackson). Their own work as Brothers In Rhythm included the singles 'Such A Good Feeling' (remixed by Sasha) and 'Peace And Harmony', though they left 4th & Broadway in 1992, delaying the release of a third, 'Forever And A Day'. They have also recorded under the alias Brothers Love Dub ('Ming's Incredible Disco Machine') and Creative Thieves ('Nasty Rhythm'). Seaman was also a leading light behind the DMC/Stress Records empire, including the development of the clubber's bible, *Mixmag*, and also signed a publishing contract with MCA.

Broudie, Ian

b. 4 August 1958, Liverpool, England. As well as piloting the successful and widely revered 90s pop band the Lightning Seeds, Broudie established himself as one of the UK's most talented pop producers. He formed his first band at Quarrybank Comprehensive in Liverpool. The O'Boogie Brothers also featured future Culture Club member Jon Moss on drums. He subsequently joined Big In Japan, Merseyside's primal punk band and artistic blood bank, which also included Bill Drummond (later of KLF), Budgie (later Siouxsie And The Banshees), Holly Johnson (later Frankie Goes To Hollywood) and vocalist Jayne Casey (later Pink Industry/Pink Military). When that band broke down after a final performance at celebrated Liverpool venue Eric's in August 1978, Broudie moved on to a new band, the Opium Eaters, with Pete Wylie, Budgie and Paul Rutherford (another future star of Frankie Goes To Hollywood). However, they never recorded. His next band was the

Original Mirrors, formed with Steve Allen (of Deaf School), who secured a contract with Mercury Records. Despite two albums, that band had collapsed by the beginning of the 80s, and with this string of failures behind him, Broudie decided a career in production might offer more security. The first record he had produced, Echo And The Bunnymen's 'Rescue', their first UK Top 20 single, had been completed while still a member of the Original Mirrors. In 1983, he formed another band with ex-Wild Swans singer Paul Simpson, adopting the name Care when they expanded to a quartet. Despite three well-received singles, the band never recorded an album, and Broudie returned to production in January 1986 for the Icicle Works' *If You Want To Defeat Your Enemy Sing His Song*. Rather than return to a group format, Broudie inaugurated the Lightning Seeds in 1989 to record their much-admired debut single, 'Pure'. It immediately entered the UK Top 20. Despite initial problems with record labels the Lightning Seeds have survived to become something of a British pop institution, enjoying considerable success with singles such as 'The Life Of Riley', 'Perfect' and 'Lucky You', the latter co-written with Terry Hall, with whom Broudie had formerly worked when he was a member of the Colour Field. By now he was an established producer, despite his claim that 'Even now, I can't operate things in a studio.' His clients have included the Fall, the Primitives, Frazier Chorus, Wah!, the Wedding Present, Sleeper and Dodgy. In 1996, Broudie composed England's anthem for soccer's European championship, 'Three Lions' (recorded with comedians David Baddiel and Frank Skinner), which reached number 1 in the UK chart. He repeated the feat with the revamped 'Three Lions 98' in June 1998, released to coincide with England's World Cup challenge.

Brown, Bobby

b. Robert Brown, 5 February 1969, Boston, Massachusetts, USA. A former member of New Edition, Brown emerged in the late 80s as the king of swingbeat, the fusion of hip-hop beats and soul vocals also referred to as 'new jack swing'. Like many of the genre's stars, Brown is not gifted with either huge ability or personality, yet he stamped his authority on the scene via a series of immaculately presented crossover singles. On his debut album he was joined by Larry Blackmon and John Luongo, but it was the follow-up set, and the seamless production technique of Teddy Riley and L.A. And Babyface, that pushed him high in the R&B and pop charts. Cuts such as the US number 1 single 'My Prerogative' were infectious, irresistible workouts, confirming Brown's presence as a commercial hot potato. Further US Top 5 singles included 'Roni', 'Every Little Step', 'On Our Own', and 'Humpin' Around', while a collaboration with Glenn Medeiros, 'She Ain't Worth It', topped the charts in summer 1990. Brown married Whitney Houston in July 1992, and made further tentative steps into acting (he had already shot a cameo part in *Ghostbusters II*). He had a UK Top 5 hit with 'Two Can Play That Game' in 1995, the same year he was arrested on a felony charge. In 1996, he was arrested on a drink-driving charge and made an out-of-court settlement over an assault charge, following which he began working again with the members of New Edition on the successful reunion album, *Home Again*. *Forever* was released in 1997 amid further stories of marital strife and bad behaviour.

● ALBUMS: *King Of Stage* (MCA 1986)★★, *Don't Be Cruel* (MCA 1988)★★★★, *Dance! ... Ya Know It!* (MCA 1989)★★★★, *Bobby* (MCA 1992)★★★, *Forever* (MCA 1997)★★★.

● VIDEOS: *His Prerogative* (MCA 1989).

● FILMS: *Gojira* aka *Godzilla* (1984), *Ghostbusters II* (1989), *Knights* (1993), *Nemseis 2: Nebula* (1995), *Nemesis III: Prey Harder* (1995), *Panther* (1995), *A Thin Line Between Love And Hate* (1996), *Pecker* (1998).

Brown, Foxy

b. Inga Marchand, 6 September 1979, Brooklyn, New York, USA. Marchand grew up with another future female rap star, Lil' Kim, in Park Slope, Brooklyn. Naming herself after the eponymous Pam Grier character in the cult blaxploitation movie, Brown's rapid rise to fame began when, at the age of 15, she won a talent contest in Brooklyn. She was invited by Trackmasterz, who were working on LL Cool J's 1995 set *Mr. Smith*, to add a rap to a remix of 'I Shot Ya'. The song proved to be a highly successful single, leading to further high profile guest appearances on tracks by Total ('No One Else'), Toni Braxton ('You're Makin' Me High') and Case ('Touch Me, Tease Me'). Her provocative rap on Jay-Z's 'Ain't No Nigga' ('Ain't no nigga like the one I got/sleeps around but he gives me a lot') established her highly sexual and ultra confident persona, which came as a breath of fresh air on the male dominated hip-hop scene. A major-label scramble for her signature ended when Def Jam Records signed her in March 1996. Production maestros Trackmasterz oversaw her debut set, *Ill Na Na*. Debuting at number 7 on the *Billboard* chart in December, the album has gone on to sell in excess of 1.5 million units. Almost overnight Brown had become a powerful female icon, revolutionizing hip-hop with her sexually explicit lyrics and provocative image. Her standing in hip-hop circles was indicated by guest appearances on the album by artists including BLACKstreet, Method Man and Jay-Z. She also appeared with Nas, AZ and Nature as part of rap supergroup the Firm, whose Mafia-inspired debut was released the following year. Now a bona fide rap superstar, Brown's *Chyna Doll* went straight in at number 1 on the *Billboard* album chart in February 1999, despite the failure of the single 'Hot Spot'. The album featured the expected high profile collaborations, including duets with Total ('I Can't'), DMX ('Dog & A Fox') and Jay-Z ('Bonnie And Clyde Part II'), and a hard hitting jam with Mia X and Gangsta Boom on 'BWA'. There was also a cover version of Salt-N-Pepa's 'Tramp', while the stand-out track 'My Life' hinted at vulnerability behind Brown's hard bitch persona.

● ALBUMS: *Ill Na Na* (Def Jam 1996)★★★★, *Chyna Doll* (Def Jam 1998)★★★★.

● FILMS: *Woo* (1998).

Brown, Ian

Formerly the lead vocalist with seminal indie-rock outfit the Stone Roses, few expected Brown (b. Ian George Brown, 20 February 1963, Ancoats, Greater Manchester, England) to launch a viable solo career following the bad-natured disintegration of the former band. Brown learned to play various instruments before beginning work on his self-produced and self-financed debut album at Chiswick Reach Studios in London. Using a primitive all-valve desk, the recording process took only three weeks. Brown was assisted by former Stone Roses members Aziz Ibrahim, Reni and Mani, with additional help from keyboard player Nigel Ippinson,

drummer Simon Moore and vocalist Denise Johnson. Brown signed a deal with Polydor Records on the understanding that the album would be released in its original unadorned, demo quality state. The label's faith in the artist was rewarded when 'My Star' debuted at UK number 5 in January 1998, and *Unfinished Monkey Business* entered the UK album chart at number 4 in February. Critical reaction was muted, however, with the album's rough charm offset by the absence of any truly strong material. Brown's resurrection suffered a setback when he was charged with a public order offence at Manchester airport, following an incident on a flight from Paris on 13 February. With a court case hanging over him, Brown released the follow-up singles 'Corpses' (number 14, April 1998) and 'Can't See Me' (number 21, June 1998). Brown was given a four-month custodial sentence following his conviction in October, but was released in December. He celebrated with a guest lead vocal on U.N.K.L.E.'s 'Be There', which reached the UK Top 10 in February 1999. He subsequently returned to the studio to record material for his second solo collection, *Golden Greats*.
● ALBUMS: *Unfinished Monkey Business* (Polydor 1998)★★, *Golden Greats* (Polydor 1999)★★★.

Brown, Tony

In 1974, Tony Brown replaced Glen D. Hardin as pianist in Elvis Presley's touring band and remained with him until his death. Brown moved into country music through being on the road with Emmylou Harris' Hot Band. He enjoyed further success with Rodney Crowell and Rosanne Cash, as part of support band Cherry Bombs, and subsequently produced Crowell's *Diamonds And Dirt*, which included five number 1 country singles. He had sustained success with Steve Wariner, producing several number 1 singles, and then with Vince Gill. By the late 90s Brown was one of the most popular producers in Nashville, enjoying success with Tracy Byrd, Reba McEntire, Mark Chesnutt, George Strait, Trisha Yearwood and Wynonna. As President of MCA/Nashville he has established the label as the most successful in the capital of country music.

Brownstone

Urban R&B trio Brownstone were formed in Los Angeles, California, USA, by Nicci (b. Nicole Gilbert, Detroit, Michigan, USA), Maxee (b. Charmayne Maxwell, Guyana) and Mimi (b. Monica Doby, New Orleans, Louisiana, USA). Signed after performing *a cappella* at their audition, the trio became the first act on the Epic-distributed MJJ Music label. Their debut album featured the Grammy-nominated Top 10 single 'If You Love Me', and led to a prestigious support slot on Boyz II Men's 1995 US tour. Despite a personnel change when Kina (b. Kina Cosper, Detroit, Michigan, USA) replaced Mimi in June 1995, their growing reputation led to further tours with Anita Baker, BLACKstreet and Patti Labelle. Recorded over the course of a busy year, *Still Climbing* featured the same successful blend of hip-hop grooves and vocal harmonies that characterized their platinum-selling debut. All three members were rumoured to be working on solo projects by the end of the 90s.
● ALBUMS: *From The Bottom Up* (MJJ/Epic 1995)★★★, *Still Climbing* (Epic 1997)★★★.

BT

b. Brian Transeau, Maryland, USA. Arguably the most accomplished and recognizable of the largely anonymous trance set, Transeau made a huge mid-90s impact with releases such as 'Loving You More' and 'Embracing The Sunshine' for Perfecto Records. As well as being staples of European dancefloors, they also reached the UK charts. Both songs were segued together in a 40-minute blockbuster by Sasha to form the centrepiece of BT's similarly successful debut album, *Ima*. Afterwards, his 'dream house' style became widely impersonated (but rarely equalled), to the evident frustration of the artist: 'So many people were ripping off things I was emotionally attached to without putting any of their own emotion into them. They were turning it into a formula and it was never intended to be like that. It was very emotional, altruistic, heartfelt music.' As a consequence he jettisoned an album's worth of material for a projected follow-up effort, and concentrated on remixing duties (including Grace's UK Top 20 hit, 'Not Over Yet', and Tori Amos' 'Blue Skies'). His own solo output suffered as a result. Laborious sessions for the 25-minute single 'Hand In Hand', which paired him with 'Loving You More' singer Vincent Covello, were highly stressful: 'I was going nuts trying to finish it,' he told *Music Week*. In the event he elected to go back to basics for the follow-up single, 'Flaming June'/'Orbitus Terranium', and his second album, *ESCM*. Again, this featured a bizarre array of sounds, ranging from the mating calls of tree frogs and wild turkeys to the vocals of Manchester folk singer Jan Johnston and Sufi vocalist T.H. Culhane. Transeau changed tack for October 1999's *Movement In Still Life*, which replaced the pounding trance with tough breakbeats.
● ALBUMS: *Ima* (Perfecto 1995)★★★, *ESCM* (Perfecto 1997)★★★★, *Movement In Still Life* (Pioneer 1999)★★★.

Buckcherry

This sleazy hard-rock outfit was formed in Los Angeles, California, USA in 1995 by Keith Nelson (guitar) and Joshua Todd (vocals), with Jonathan Brightman (bass) and Devon Glenn (drums) added to the line-up shortly afterwards. Fronted by the cocksure Todd, the band's blistering live show earned them a serious word-of-mouth reputation on the Los Angeles music scene. Bolstering the line-up with a second guitarist, Yogi, the band was signed to the newly-formed DreamWorks label, and set about recording their self-titled debut with established rock producer Terry Date and ex-Sex Pistols guitarist Steve Jones. Their avowed intention to rescue rock 'n' roll was thrillingly realised on the opening track 'Lit Up' (with its insinuating 'I love the cocaine' chorus), but the remainder of the album was a disappointing, over-hyped mess, lacking the sheer rock 'n' roll intensity of Guns N'Roses and Kiss.
● ALBUMS: *Buckcherry* (DreamWorks 1999)★★★.

Bucketheads

The creation of revered DJ and producer Kenny 'Dope' Gonzalez, the Bucketheads project arose out of a 'burst of inspiration' in 1994. From his home in Brooklyn, New York, USA, Gonzalez crafted the US and UK hit single 'The Bomb! (These Sounds Fall Into My Mind)'. Released on Henry Street/Big Beat Records in America and on Positiva Records in the UK, the single included an unlikely sample of

Chicago's 'Street Player'. The resultant album, *All In The Mind*, a collection of largely instrumental hip-hop and house tunes, confirmed the promise. It was a major departure from Gonzalez's established sound as half of the Masters At Work production team. As he told *Billboard* magazine in 1995, 'I was tired of everyone being on the same tip as we were. Everything out there sounded the same. I was bored.' The first single taken from it was 'Whew!', which established the foundation for the success of 'The Bomb!'. A third single, 'Got Myself Together', provided another worldwide club and chart hit.
● ALBUMS: *All In The Mind* (Henry Street/Positiva 1995)★★★★.

Buckley, Jeff

b. Jeffrey Scott Buckley, 1966, Orange County, California, USA, d. 29 May 1997, Memphis, Tennessee, USA. The son of respected singer-songwriter Tim Buckley, Jeff Buckley not unnaturally took exception to comparisons with his father, and cited his mother as a greater influence. Having studied at the Los Angeles Musicians' Institute, Jeff moved to New York, where he first garnered attention at a 1991 Tim Buckley tribute performing 'Once I Was'. He made numerous appearances at several of the city's clubs, including the Fez and Bang On, recording his debut mini-album at the Sin-é coffee-house. This tentative four-song set included two original compositions, alongside versions of Van Morrison's 'The Way Young Lovers Do' and Edith Piaf's 'Je N'En Connais Pas Le Fin'. Having secured a major contract with Sony Records, Buckley completed the critically acclaimed *Grace* with his regular band: Michael Tighe (guitar), Mick Grondhal (bass) and Matt Johnson (drums). An expressive singer with an astonishing range, Buckley soared and swept across a near-perfect collection, which included cover versions of Elkie Brooks' 'Lilac Wine' and Leonard Cohen's 'Hallelujah' alongside several breathtakingly original songs. His live appearances were acclaimed as revelatory, blending expressive readings of material from *Grace* with an array of interpretations ranging from Big Star ('Kanga Roo') to the MC5 ('Kick Out The Jams'). Buckley was a gifted, melodic composer whose awareness of contemporary guitar bands brought dynamism to the singer-songwriter form. An increasingly troubled man, he was about to resume working on aborted sessions for his second album when he drowned in a hazardous stretch of the Mississippi. Having entered the river fully clothed for a swim, Buckley was fatally pulled under by the wake from a passing tugboat. His final recordings were released as *Sketches (For My Sweetheart The Drunk)* in May 1998, comprising sessions recorded with Tom Verlaine and the basic four-track demos on which Buckley was working at the time of his death. The album charted in the UK Top 10, revealing an abiding interest in Buckley's music.
● ALBUMS: *Live At Sin-é* mini-album (Big Cat 1992)★★★, *Grace* (Sony 1994)★★★★, *Live From The Bataclan* mini-album (Columbia 1996)★★, *Sketches (For My Sweetheart The Drunk)* (Columbia 1998)★★★.

Buena Vista Social Club

The original Buena Vista Social Club album was one of three projects recorded during the two-week session organized by World Circuit Records at EGREM Studios, Havana, Cuba, in March 1996. The session also produced *Introducing Rubén González* and the Afro-Cuban All Stars' *A Toda Cuba Le Gusta*. The original concept for the Buena Vista Social Club was of a small guitar-based band, featuring Ry Cooder (who also acted as producer) playing alongside musicians from Mali and Cuba. However, this was abandoned after the two Malian musicians booked to play failed to arrive because of problems with their passports. The line-up for the session was finally comprised of musicians who had played on the Afro-Cuban All Stars album, including bolero vocalist Ibrahim Ferrer (b. 20 February 1927, San Luis, Cuba) and pianist Rubén González, plus others suggested by Cooder, such as veteran singers Compay Segundo (b. Maximo Francisco Repilado Munoz, 18 November 1907, Siboney, Cuba) and Omara Portuondo, as well as Eliades Ochoa of Cuarteto Patria. The songs chosen for the session were a collection of Cuban classics, both old and new. The resulting album was gentle and folky but also passionate, with a variety of sounds and styles including piano instrumentals, acoustic ballads, dance tunes and a bolero sung by former lovers Portuondo and Segundo. Cooder described the recording session as 'the greatest musical experience of my life' and he appeared happy to let the Cuban veterans take the spotlight, allowing his presence to be felt through his distinctive playing, as he had done three years earlier on Ali Farka Touré's *Talking Timbuktu*. The Buena Vista Social Club was released in June 1997, and was well received by the critics, featuring in many best world, Latin and folk album polls for that year. It also appeared in many national album charts around the world and went on to sell millions. The album was awarded a Grammy for Best Tropical Dance Abum Of 1997. Released two years later, *Buena Vista Social Club Presents Ibrahim Ferrer*, featured the venerable vocalist performing a varied programme of up-tempo dance tunes, swampy sounding Cuban–blues fusions and lush, string-laden boleros. Cooder again produced and played guitar. Other contributors to the first album, including Ruben Gonzalez, were again involved, alongside other well-known Cuban musicians. Ferrer promoted the album with tours of Europe and the USA. A documentary film, *Buena Vista Social Club*, was made in 1999 by German director Wim Wenders and was shown in cinemas and on television throughout the world.
● ALBUMS: *The Buena Vista Social Club* (World Circuit 1997)★★★★, *Buena Vista Social Club Presents Ibrahim Ferrer* (World Circuit 1999)★★★★.
● FILMS: *Buena Vista Social Club* (1999).

Buffalo Tom

This Boston, Massachusetts, USA-based melodic hardcore trio features Bill Janovitz (vocals/guitar), Tom Maginnis (drums) and Chris Colbourn (bass). They were formed in 1986 at Massachusetts University, taking their inspiration from bands such as Hüsker Dü and Soul Asylum. Their first album was simply called *Buffalo Tom* in the UK, and the producer was Dinosaur Jr's J. Mascis. His involvement led to similarities between the two bands being regularly overstated by critics (some nicknamed them Dinosaur Jr Jr). *Let Me Come Over*, the follow-up, this time licensed to Beggars Banquet Records in the UK, was released in 1992, by which time the band had established a healthy reputation among both critics and live audiences, touring with the Wedding Present, among others. Generally acknowledged as being of a superior hue to many members of the underground US rock movement, Buffalo Tom had yet to escape critical comparisons to inappropriate sources. *Big Red Letter Day* saw the band undertake a more polished, orchestrated approach to songwriting, which contrasted with the three-week sessions for 1995's *Sleepy Eyed*. The limited time afforded this album was explained by Maginnis' impending fatherhood, but if anything, the sense of urgency this engendered added to the band's song craft. In 1996, Janovitz released a country-styled solo debut with Joey Burns and John Convertino of Giant Sand. Buffalo Tom reconvened for *Smitten*, a more polished collection that lacked the charm of their earlier work.

● ALBUMS: *Sunflower Suit* (SST 1989)★★★, *Birdbrain* (Situation 2 1990)★★★, *Let Me Come Over* (Situation 2 1992)★★★★, *Big Red Letter Day* (Beggars Banquet 1993)★★★, *Sleepy Eyed* (Beggars Banquet 1995)★★★, *Smitten* (Beggars Banquet 1998)★★★.
Solo: Bill Janovitz *Lonesome Billy* (Beggars Banquet 1996)★★★.

Built To Spill

An alternative rock trio formed in Boise, Idaho, USA, Built To Spill developed a reputation for their energetic performances, strong songwriting and frenetic musicianship for a variety of independent labels before making the move to Warner Brothers Records in the mid-90s. Long-standing fans were divided about this development, though most were pleased that this talented band's records would now get the professional distribution and marketing that they deserved. There had been several other interested parties following the success of 1994's *There's Nothing Wrong With Love*, an accomplished collection that triggered a major-label bidding war. The band is essentially the creation of songwriter Doug (or Dug) Martsch (vocals/guitar), who had previously recorded several albums with Seattle's Treepeople, and has also recorded three eclectic albums as the Halo Benders with Calvin Johnson of Beat Happening. Martsch embarked on recording Built To Spill's major label debut with just a drummer. This effort was abandoned, as was a second attempt with Scott Plouf (drums, ex-Spinanes) and Brett Nelson (bass - a veteran of *There's Nothing Wrong With Love*). Both musicians subsequently become permanent members. However, the resultant tapes were damaged by heat in the producer's car, so Martsch was forced to tackle the songs for *Perfect From Now On* for a third time. Together with John McMahon (cello) and Robert Roth (mellotron), the finished album won rave reviews - with many surprised at the eclecticism it displayed, not least on the nine-minute 'Untrustable/Pt. 2 (About Someone Else)'. That song was chosen as a promotional release, divided into two parts on one 7-inch 'jukebox' single. Confident of the long-term success of Built To Spill, Warner Brothers Records re-released their back-catalogue. *Keep It Like A Secret* sacrificed some of the band's indie charm for pop accessiblity, but was still warmly received.

● ALBUMS: *Ultimate Alternative Wavers* (C/Z 1993)★★★, *There's Nothing Wrong With Love* (Up! 1994)★★★, *Perfect From Now On* (Warners 1997)★★★★, *Keep It Like A Secret* (Warners 1999)★★★.
● COMPILATIONS: *The Normal Years* (K 1996)★★★.

Burzum

Founded in 1991 by Norwegian Satanist Count Grishnackh (real name Varg Vikernes), Burzum became one of the leading lights in Scandinavia's black metal revival of the

early 90s. Largely a solo project, Grishnackh composes, sings and plays almost all of Burzum's material himself. The project first surfaced under the name of Uruk Hai in 1987. Significantly, the name was drawn from J.R.R. Tolkien's fantasy classic, *The Lord Of The Rings*, in which the Uruk Hai were a particularly brutal tribe of orcs (the subhuman villains of the book). Burzum was the orcish language, while Grishnackh was a treacherous orc who plays a small, but pivotal, role in the proceedings. Count Grishnackh used Tolkien's epic struggle between good and evil as a model for his own brand of Satanism, casting himself among the hordes of darkness. Grishnackh went on to collaborate with Euronymous, godfather of the Scandinavian black metal revival, playing with the latter's band Mayhem, releasing material on his Deathlike Silence Productions (DSP) label, and playing a leading part in the curious hate cult known as the Black Metal Circle. Meanwhile, Burzum recordings were receiving increasing acclaim on the heavy metal underground, with their tortured mix of overheated guitars, screamed vocals and strange, ambient keyboards. In the spring of 1993, Grishnackh, along with a number of other prominent members of the Black Metal Circle, was arrested for a series of church burnings. Several months later, Grishnackh was arrested for the brutal murder of Euronymous. He was subsequently convicted in 1994, but showed no remorse for his crime, instead relishing the consequent notoriety and publicity. Sentenced to 21 years (the maximum possible under Norwegian law), Grishnackh continues to record increasingly strange and twisted material in jail. Satanism and the works of Tolkien now take a back seat to the right-wing occultism and Viking paganism that are currently his chief obsessions, with many of his lyrics now sung in Old Norse. He managed to record 1997's *Daudi Baldrs* while in prison, using a keyboard and computer. *Hlidskjalf* followed in 1999.

● ALBUMS: *Burzum* (DSP 1992)★★, *Aske* mini-album (DSP 1993)★★★, *Det Som Engang Var* (Cymophane/Misanthropy 1993)★★, *Hvis Lyset Tar Oss* (Misanthropy 1994)★★★, *Filosofem* (Misanthropy 1996)★★, *Daudi Baldrs* (Misanthropy 1997)★★, *Hlidskjalf* (Misanthropy 1999)★★★.
● FURTHER READING: *Lords Of Chaos: The Bloody Rise Of The Satanic Metal Underground*, Michael Moynihan and Didrik Soderlind.

Bush

This contemporary rock band are a phenomenon: no UK act with such an indifferent reception in their homeland has experienced such success elsewhere. Formed in west London, England, their initial success in the USA was thanks to college radio, which picked up on tracks from their debut *Sixteen Stone*. By the summer of 1995 that record had become a million-seller, while highly promoted UK artists such as Blur and Oasis were still struggling to achieve one tenth of those sales. This was largely attributable to Bush's musical style - generic grunge sitting somewhere between Pearl Jam and Soundgarden. However, Bush had previously spent two years toiling around small London venues, despite being managed by Dave Dorrell, the man behind MARRS' UK number 1, 'Pump Up The Volume'. The songs on their debut were principally written by vocalist/guitarist Gavin Rossdale (b. Kilburn, London, England). Rossdale, a former student at Westminster school who had trials for Chelsea Football Club, had previously recorded two singles with his first band

Midnight, who also included in their ranks film director David Puttnam's son Sasha. After that band was dropped, he spent six months in California in 1991 - significantly, seeing Nirvana at Los Angeles' Roxy Club during this time. He formed Bush with Dave Parsons (b. 2 July 1962, Uxbridge, London, England; bass, ex-Transvision Vamp), Robin Goodridge (b. Crawley, Sussex, England; drums, ex-Beautiful People) and Nigel Pulsford (b. Newport, Gwent, Wales; guitar, ex-King Blank). The band made their US connection when disc jockey Gary Crowley passed one of their tapes to Rob Kahane, former manager of George Michael and in the process of setting up his own Trauma Records label. An earlier agreement with the Walt Disney-owned Hollywood Records in 1993 had sundered when Kahane's relations with the label soured. After gaining airplay on Los Angeles' KROQ station in late 1994, particularly for the single 'Everything Zen', interest in the band snowballed. The songs on *Sixteen Stone* dealt with issues as diverse as the bombing of a Covent Garden pub ('Bomb'), death ('Little Things'), religious cults ('Monkey') and sex ('Testosterone'). By 1996 this had resulted in three million sales of their debut, at which time they confirmed an intriguing choice of producer for the follow-up set - Steve Albini. The excellent *Razorblade Suitcase* entered the US album chart at number 1 at the end of 1996. Following in the wake was the UK, who finally recognized the band's existence by buying enough copies to put them in the album chart. A desultory remix album followed while the band set about recording material for their third studio set. *The Science Of Things* saw a marked drop in sales Stateside. Ironically, given their past history, the band seems to be now caught up in the general malaise afflicting UK acts attempting to sell records in America.

● ALBUMS: *Sixteen Stone* (Trauma/Interscope 1995)★★★★, *Razorblade Suitcase* (Trauma 1996)★★★★, *Deconstructed* remixes (Trauma 1997)★★★, *The Science Of Things* (Trauma 1999)★★★.
● VIDEOS: *Alleys And Motorways* (Universal/Interscope 1998).

Bushman

b. Dwight Duncan, 1973, Prospect Beach, Jamaica, West Indies. Duncan was raised in the Rastafarian faith in his early years, and he later attended drama school and sang in the local church choir where his idiosyncratic vocals were nurtured. He began work as a DJ under the name Junior Melody at the Black Star Line sound system in St. Thomas, and later hitch-hiked the 70 miles to Kingston where he met Wycliffe 'Steely' Johnson at the Arrows Dub Plate Studio. Duncan was invited to record at Studio 2000, performing 'Grow Your Natty', followed by 'Call The Hearse' over Steely And Clevie's popular 'Skettel' rhythm. Steely decided to release the single under the pseudonym of Bushman, and although initially Duncan felt this was a derogatory title, it was in fact an African term for 'medicine man'. 'Call The Hearse' was a success in Jamaica, and led to the equally popular 'Rude Boy Life', and the albums *Nyah Man Chant* and *Total Commitment*. Bushman's songs proclaim his spiritual beliefs: he maintains a strict ital diet, bathes in the hot water springs of his parish and takes to the hills with his bible.

● ALBUMS: *Nyah Man Chant* (Greensleeves 1997)★★★, *Total Commitment* (Greensleeves 1999)★★★★.

Bushwick Bill

b. Richard Shaw, 8 December 1966, Jamaica, West Indies. A founder-member of the notorious Geto Boys, from Texas, USA, Bushwick Bill aka Dr Wolfgang Von Bushwick began his solo career in 1992 with a highly successful solo album. He had lost his right eye in an accidental shooting in May 1991 (detailed in the track 'Ever Clear'), and some critics, appalled by his graphic descriptions of violence and sex, pointed out that he suffered from myopia both literally and figuratively. It was one of the first records, however, to predict the rise of the horror film-fixated raps ('horrorcore') subsequently taken up by New York's Wu-Tang Clan and others. *Phantom Of The Rapra*, despite the awful pun of its title, was a much more accomplished recording. This time west coast G-funk rhythms had replaced the samples of 70s funk, and Bushwick Bill's raps now boasted a clear-headed tone distinct from his debut. He reunited with his former sparring partners Scarface and Willie D. for the 1996 Geto Boys comeback set, *The Resurrection*, before returning to his solo career with *No Surrender ... No Retreat*.

● ALBUMS: *Little Big Man* (Rap-A-Lot 1992)★★★, *Phantom Of The Rapra* (Rap-A-Lot 1995)★★★, *No Surrender ... No Retreat* (Ichiban 1998)★★★.
● FILMS: *Who's The Man?* (1993), *Original Gangstas* (1996).

Busta Rhymes

b. Trevor Smith Jnr., 20 May 1972, Brooklyn, New York, USA. Rapper Busta Rhymes became the toast of the American hip-hop community with the release of his Elektra Records debut, *The Coming*, in 1996. Although offering nothing outstanding in its lyrics, album tracks such as 'Everything Remains Raw' and 'It's A Party' highlighted his compelling ragga-influenced delivery to good effect, and the catchy single 'Woo-Hah!! Got You All In Check' broke into the US Top 10. Rhymes had originally rapped as part of the highly praised Leaders Of The New School, with MC Charlie Brown, Dinco D and Milo In De Dance, releasing the acclaimed *A Future Without A Past* in 1991. He has also worked with a stellar cast of singers including Boyz II Men, Mary J. Blige, TLC and A Tribe Called Quest, and appeared in the movies *Who's The Man?* and *Higher Learning*. Attempts to promote *The Coming* in the UK ended in disaster. His planned performance at the Kentish Town Forum in May ended in calamity when delays in securing a work permit prevented him from appearing. Outraged fans caused an estimated £75,000 of damage after they rioted in protest. Rhymes released the ambitious US Top 5 album *When Disaster Strikes ...* in September 1997, exploring premillennial fears and the future of rap. The album included a powerful duet with Erykah Badu on 'One' and 'Turn It Up/Fire It Up', with a remix of the latter entering the US Top 10. The track also provided Rhymes with his highest UK chart placing the following April when it debuted at number 2. The same year he released *The Imperial* as part of the Flipmode Squad, a collaborative project with rappers Rampage, Lord Have Mercy, Spliff Star, Rah Digga and Baby Sham. Rhymes' fascination with film informed the same year's *Extinction Level Event: The Final World Front*, which took its title from the disaster movie *Deep Impact*. The frenetic 'Gimme Some More' reached number 5 in the UK singles chart in January 1999. Rhymes enjoyed further transatlantic success in April when the highly catchy 'What's It

Gonna Be?!', featuring Janet Jackson, climbed to US number 3 and UK number 6.

● ALBUMS: *The Coming* (Elektra 1996)★★, *When Disaster Strikes ...* (Elektra 1997)★★★, *Extinction Level Event: The Final World Front* (Elektra 1998)★★★.

● FILMS: *Who's The Man?* (1993), *Higher Learning* (1995), *Rhyme & Reason* (1997), *The Rugrats Movie* voice only (1998).

Butler, Bernard

b. 1970, Leyton, London, England. Guitarist Butler studied violin and piano before rising to fame with Suede as the perceived inheritor of Johnny Marr's mantle as the guitar player of the 90s. Indeed, he had first learnt the instrument by playing along to Smiths records. As a 13-year-old, Butler formed his first band, Slowdive (not the Creation Records outfit of the same name), with his brothers. It lasted only a short time, and by his mid-teens he was subsidizing his bedroom study of guitar with part-time work. After failing his first-year history exams at London's Queen Mary College, he joined Suede in 1989, answering an advertisement in the *New Musical Express*. Butler wrote all the band's music and provided the perfect antidote to Brett Anderson's mannered vocals and lyrics, until his acrimonious departure in June 1994. Lauded as a brilliant, original guitarist, the break from Anderson was seen in much the same light as Marr's from Morrissey, and like Marr, Butler immediately took on the role of itinerant guitarist. His first post-Suede employment came alongside former All About Eve singer Julianne Regan in France. After a period of recuperation, he began writing songs in the north London flat he shared with wife Elisa, framing one composition in particular, 'Yes', which was only fully realized when he made the acquaintance of flamboyant former Thieves singer David McAlmont. Butler played all the instruments beneath McAlmont's sweet soul vocal, surprising many critics in the process with his new direction. A second single, 'You Do', and a hastily assembled album, *McAlmont And Butler*, followed, before the partnership dissolved in yet more acrimony. Further collaborations with Bryan Ferry (a version of John Lennon's 'Whatever Gets You Through The Night'), old friend Edwyn Collins, Aimee Mann (two tracks on her 1995 set *I'm With Stupid*), Eddi Reader, Neneh Cherry and Tim Booth And Angelo Badalamenti were also released, while Butler set about recording his debut solo album for Creation. Premiered by the singles 'Stay' and 'People Move On', the album proved to be an elegant showcase for his Neil Young style of guitar rock, although the biggest surprise was hearing Butler's fragile voice singing his own songs. That element of surprise was sorely missing from the follow-up *Friends And Lovers*, a pedestrian collection of 70s styled rock songs.

● ALBUMS: *People Move On* (Creation 1998)★★★, *Friends And Lovers* (Creation 1999)★★★.

Buzzov.en

Revelling in their own musical and aesthetic ugliness, Buzzov.en formed from the ashes of Sewer Puppet in the early 90s. Based in North Carolina and featuring Kirk Fisher (vocals/guitar), Brian Hill (bass) and Ashley Williamson (drums), they played anywhere that would have them, until by 1991 they had raised the money for a studio recording of their first demo tape, *Buttrash*. One of the songs from that demo, 'Wound', was released as a single by a friend setting up his own label. However, the cassette also reached John Yates, founder of San Francisco label Allied Recordings. Yates brought the group into the studio to record the *Wound EP* (although it did not include the song of that name). On the back of this, and with east coast gigs where the music was largely distinguished by its savagery and volume, Buzzov.en embarked on building a cult audience. They completed their debut album in San Francisco with Billy Anderson (who had previously lent his production expertise to projects by Steel Pole Bathtub, Melvins and others). After experimenting with a second guitarist, the band made Buddy Apostolis a permanent fixture, and embarked on some 200 gigs inside a year. A show at 1993's CMJ Music Convention led to them signing to Roadrunner Records through Monte Conner, and the following year saw them back in the studio with Billy Anderson, recording their second 'studio' album in just nine days (the first had taken only three). Content to play anytime, anywhere, Buzzov.en, with their astonishing G.G. Allin-inspired stage displays, struggled to capture similar spontaneity and riotousness on record. By the time of 1998's *... At A Loss*, only Fisher remained from the original line-up.

● ALBUMS: *To A Frown* (Allied Recordings 1992)★★, *Sore* (Roadrunner 1994)★★★, *... At A Loss* (Off The Records 1998)★★★.

● COMPILATIONS: *Music For The Proletariat* (Very Small 1993)★★, *Vinyl Retentive* (Very Small 1993)★★.

Byrd, Tracy

b. 18 December 1966, Vidor, Texas, USA. Neo-traditionalist country singer Byrd paid $8 to sing Hank Williams' 'Your Cheatin' Heart' over a pre-recorded backing track in a shopping mall. The store manageress was so impressed by Byrd's voice that she booked him for a talent show. On that show he sang 'Weary Blues' and 'Folsom Prison Blues'. He began a residency with Mark Chestnutt, at a local club Cutters and when Chestnutt began to have some chart success, Byrd formed his own band and took over the residency. He signed with MCA Records in 1992 and had to wait a year before he fitted in with their release schedule. Byrd's first records were honky tonk in the George Strait mould, but he has gradually found his own voice, starting with a remake of Johnny Paycheck's 'Someone To Give My Love To' in 1993. His major breakthrough came with the number 1 country hit 'Holdin' Heaven'. He further established himself with 'Why Don't The Telephone Ring' the same year. *No Ordinary Man* consolidated the success of his debut, and a third collection *Love Lessons* was also well received. Further hit singles came with 'Watermelon Crawl' and 'Love Lessons', as Byrd attempted (alongside the likes of fellow Beaumont singer Clay Walker) to establish himself at the forefront of contemporary country. *Big Love* and *I'm From The Country* were two solid, reliable albums that nevertheless failed to hoist Byrd into the same league as Garth Brooks. Byrd crossed over to RCA Records for the following year's *It's About Time*, which diluted his traditional country twang with misguided forays into a more pop-orientated style.

● ALBUMS: *Tracy Byrd* (MCA 1993)★★★, *No Ordinary Man* (MCA 1994)★★★★, *Love Lessons* (MCA 1995)★★★, *Big Love* (MCA 1996)★★★, *I'm From The Country* (MCA 1998)★★★★, *It's About Time* (RCA 1999)★★★.

● COMPILATIONS: *Keepers: Greatest Hits* (MCA 1999)★★★★.

● VIDEOS: *Keeper Of The Stars* (MCA 1995).

C & C Music Factory

A production team comprising Robert Clivillés (b. New York, USA) and David Cole (b. Tennessee, USA, d. 1995), who first recorded as A Black Man And A Dominican with 'Do It Properly' on their own label in 1987. As C & C Music Factory they reached US number 1 and UK number 3 in 1990 with 'Gonna Make You Sweat (Everybody Dance Now)'. Although this was credited to C + C Music Factory featuring Freedom Williams (a rapper who also appeared on records by New Kids On The Block and Grace Jones), the duo were solely in charge of matters, hiring vocalists and musicians and programming the backbeat. Over the next two years guest singers included Zelma Davis (b. Liberia), whose contribution was lip-synched, with the vocal actually provided by Martha Wash of the Weather Girls, Q Unique and Deborah Cooper. Though they enjoyed six further UK Top 40 hits during 1991 and 1992, including a re-recording of U2's 'Pride (In The Name Of Love)', only 'Things That Make You Go Hmmm ...', again jointly credited with Williams, reached the Top 10. The latter also provided the duo with their third consecutive US Top 5 hit, following the number 3 hit 'Here We Go'. It was later widely played during a television advertising campaign. The duo also worked as remixers on songs by Seduction, Sandee and Lisa Lisa And Cult Jam, examples of which were contained on their 1992 album, credited under their own names. Their first remix had been Natalie Cole's 'Pink Cadillac', which, in drastically altered form, broke into the US and UK Top 5 in 1988. They released a final album in 1994, but the following year David Cole died of spinal meningitis.

● ALBUMS: *Gonna Make You Sweat* (Columbia 1991)★★★, as Clivillés And Cole *Greatest Remixes Vol. 1* (Columbia 1992)★★★★, *Anything Goes* (Columbia 1994)★★, *Sessions 3 - Clivillés & Cole* (MOS 1994)★★★.

C-Murder

b. New Orleans, Louisiana, USA. Gangsta rapper C-Murder is the younger brother of Master P, founder of US underground label No Limit Records. He first appeared as a member of Tru, alongside Master P and another brother Silkk The Shocker. The trio's albums, including 1995's *True* and 1997's *Tru 2 Da Game*, helped establish No Limit as a mainstream commercial force. C-Murder also cropped up on several other No Limit releases, including Master P's *Ghetto D* and the *I'm Bout It* movie soundtrack. He released his debut *Life Or Death* in 1998, which entered the *Billboard* album chart at number 3 in April. The album's success was virtually guaranteed following extensive promotion of the album on other No Limit product. With his rapping ability offsetting the predictable G-funk backing of the No Limit production crew,

Life Or Death established C-Murder alongside Silkk as arguably the label's most talented artist. His inferior sophomore set, *Bossalinie*, entered the US album chart at number 2 in March 1999.

● ALBUMS: *Life Or Death* (No Limit 1998)★★★★, *Bossalinie* (No Limit 1999)★★★.

● FILMS: *I'm Bout It* (1997), *Hot Boyz* (1999).

C., Melanie

b. Melanie Jayne Chisholm, 12 January 1974, Merseyside, England. Amid a flurry of solo Spice Girls activity during 1999, Mel C's reinvention as a rock singer attracted the most criticism. Routinely described as the most talented member of the Spice Girls, Chisholm had already enjoyed success outside the band in late 1998. Her highly catchy duet with Canadian rock star Bryan Adams, 'When You're Gone', spent 10 weeks in the UK Top 10, reaching a peak position of number 3 in December. With the Spice Girls having already announced a prolonged sabbatical, Chisholm relocated to Los Angeles, California to record her debut album with respected producer Rick Rubin, with further contributions from Marius De Vries and William Orbit. Adams, meanwhile, popped up as a guest vocalist on an album which, for all the punk bluster of 'Goin' Down' (a UK Top 5 single) and 'Ga Ga', was more effective when Chisholm toned it down on several ballads which were reminiscent of none other than the Spice Girls. She had already premiered material from the album at selective live dates during the summer, including an infamous appearance at the V99 festival in August, during which she was roundly jeered for attempting a cover version of the Sex Pistols 'Anarchy In The UK'.

● ALBUMS: *Northern Star* (Virgin 1999)★★.

Cajmere

b. Curtis Alan Jones, 26 April 1967, Chicago, Illinois, USA. The house music artist Cajmere, with vocalist Dajae (real name Karen), first broke through in 1993 with the club hits 'Brighter Days' and the ragtime-themed 'U Got Me Up'. Cajmere abandoned his degree course to pursue his musical ambitions, and, establishing himself among local house music producers, he soon cut his first tracks, including 'The Percolator'. Influenced by the UK's A Guy Called Gerald as much as by Chicago house music, he settled on a successful combination of diva-style vocals and 'breakdowns'. Before working with Dajae, he was best known for his collaboration with Lidell Townsell on 'Get With You', plus the *Underground Goodies* EP for Clubhouse. He also remixed 'Feel It' for Italians Workin' Happily. He runs Cajual Records, and its offshoot Relief, on which he aimed to develop new talent. He has recorded artists including Dajae, DJ Sneak, Gemini and Boo Williams, and 12-inch singles such as 'Preacherman', which owe an obvious debt to one of his idols, Lil' Louis.

● ALBUMS: *Future Sound Of Chicago - Cajmere & DJ Sneak* (MOS 1995)★★★, *Brighter Days* (Emotive 1996)★★★.

Cake

Sacramento, California, USA outfit founded in 1991 by John McCrea (vocals/guitar), a songwriter who had spent the previous decade playing in various bands. McCrea recruited Frank French (drums), Greg Brown (guitar), Vincent di Fiore (trumpet/vocals) and Sean McFessel (bass), although the latter was soon replaced by Gabriel Nelson. A one-off single in 1993 was followed by their self-produced debut, *Motorcade Of Generosity*, which was originally sold without any distribution backing. A deal with Capricorn Records followed, although French and Nelson were subsequently replaced by Todd Roper and Victor Damiani. Cake made their first impression on the charts in 1995 with the sarcastic 'Rock 'N' Roll Lifestyle', a witty 'view from the trenches of the music industry' taken from their debut that quickly became the band's signature song. Nevertheless, the single was only partially representative of their true songwriting canon, which combines the alternative rock nuances of the Butthole Surfers and Beck with classic country textures derived from the work of Hank Williams and George Jones. Alongside band originals on *Fashion Nugget*, their second, self-produced release, were cover versions of 'Sad Songs And Waltzes' (Willie Nelson) and 'I Will Survive' (Donna Summer). The lead-off single, 'The Distance' also attracted strong reviews and radio support. Further line-up changes saw Nelson returning in place of Damiani in mid-1997, and the departure of Brown in January 1998 during recording sessions for the band's third album. Released in September, *Prolonging The Magic* included the band's biggest hit to date, 'Never There'. Following the album's release the band added new guitarist Xan McCurdy to the line-up.

● ALBUMS: *Motorcade Of Generosity* (Capricorn 1995)★★★★, *Fashion Nugget* (Capricorn 1996)★★, *Prolonging The Magic* (Capricorn 1998)★★★.

Calderone, Victor

b. Brooklyn, New York, USA. Calderone's passion for dance music began in the mid-80s when he saw Jellybean spinning records at the Fun House in New York. Making tentative steps into the music industry, Calderone recorded as part of the techno duo Program 2, releasing a couple of singles on the influential Belgian label, R&S Records. An EP later appeared on the short-lived Vortex Records. In the mid-90s, Calderone adopted a more pronounced house style, and completed work on the club anthem 'Give It Up'. The track came to the attention of A&R staff at Eight Ball Records who began plugging the record in clubs. The track gained rapid exposure and topped several dance charts in early 1997. Calderone built on its success to establish his own DJing reputation on the New York gay circuit, while a follow-up single, 'Beat Me Harder', became another huge dance hit later in the year. Calderone also gained high exposure residencies at the Liquid Club in Miami, and the Roxy back in New York. In 1998, he was commissioned to remix Madonna's 'Frozen'. The track became a huge dance hit and led to subsequent work with the singer on tracks from her acclaimed *Ray Of Light*, and commissions from artists including Sting, Gloria Estefan and Garbage. Later in the year, Calderone collaborated with Peter Rauhofer (aka Club 69) on a remix of the Clivillés And Cole house classic, 'Do It Properly', featuring vocals by club diva Deborah Cooper. Calderone also signed a multi-album deal with Tommy Boy Records, releasing the remix collection *E = VC2* in October 1999

● COMPILATIONS: *E = VC2* (Tommy Boy 1999)★★★★.

Campbell, Kate

b. 31 October 1961, New Orleans, Mississippi, USA. Despite her origins in the Mississippi Delta, Campbell has crafted her reputation in the singer-songwriter field rather than the blues. Growing up in Sledge, Mississippi, her father was the pastor of the local Baptist Church. She too attended church regularly, but as she later confessed: 'I always enjoyed the singing part more than the preaching'. As a four-year-old she was given her first musical instrument, a ukulele, and two years later began piano lessons. While still in elementary school she took up the guitar and started composing her own songs. The family moved to Orlando, Florida, during her junior high school year, where she sang in a jazz ensemble. She subsequently attended Samford University in Birmingham, Alabama, studying music and history, before a master's degree from graduate school in Auburn. Her subject - Southern History - had already informed many of the songs she had written to this point. In 1988, she moved to Nashville, teaching history while continuing to develop her songwriting. She performed regularly at clubs and writer's nights until, in 1994, she signed a publishing contract with Fame and a recording contract with Nashville's Compass Records. Her debut album, *Songs From The Levee*, was released in 1996 as a culmination of her 'efforts to merge history, memories and music'. Featuring 10 originals, guest artists included Al Perkins, Dan Dugmore and Joey Miskulin, all renowned Nashville session musicians. It prompted Guy Clark to endorse her thus: 'One of the finest singer-songwriters to emerge from Nashville.' The follow-up repeated the winning formula, and included a duet with Clark on 'Bud's Sea-Mint Boat'. Emmylou Harris guested on 1998's *Visions Of Plenty*, another strong collection centred around Campbell's richly evocative songwriting. Her purple patch continued with the following year's *Rosaryville*.

● ALBUMS: *Songs From The Levee* (Compass 1996)★★★, *Moonpie Dreams* (Compass 1997)★★★, *Visions Of Plenty* (Compass 1998)★★★★, *Rosaryville* (Compass 1999)★★★★.

Campbell, Tevin

b. 12 November 1978, Waxahachie, Texas, USA. Discovered by Quincy Jones (or the flautist Bobbi Humphrey, according to some accounts), the singer Tevin Campbell first appeared in 1988 on the US television show *Wally & The Valentines*, which was followed by a part in Prince's movie *Graffiti Bridge*. He was still only 14 years old when he appeared on Quincy Jones' *Back On The Block* album, masterfully handling lead vocals on the track 'Tomorrow'. This earned him a contract with QWest Records, primarily through Jones' recommendation. His excellent 1991 debut collection, *T.E.V.I.N.*, included two major pop hits, 'Round And Round', written by Prince and featured on the *Graffiti Bridge* soundtrack, and 'Tell Me What You Want Me To Do'. As well as up-tempo dance numbers, it also included a series of ballads handled with maturity. The reaction to *I'm Ready* was slightly frostier, with several critics mentioning the limitations its urban R&B put on Campbell's expressive singing. He silenced the same critics with 1996's *Back To The World*, an expressive and mature outing that included the track 'I Need You', cut with Sean 'Puffy' Combs. A polished self-titled effort followed three years later, with a stellar list of contributors including Wyclef Jean, Faith Evans and Narada Michael Walden.

● ALBUMS: *T.E.V.I.N.* (QWest/Reprise 1991)★★★★, *I'm Ready* (QWest/Reprise 1993)★★★, *Back To The World* (QWest 1996)★★★, *Tevin Campbell* (QWest 1999)★★★.

Candlebox

Formed by Kevin Martin (vocals), Peter Klett (guitar), Bardi Martin (bass) and Scott Mercado (drums), this alternative rock band burst onto the US music scene in the mid-90s. They signed to Madonna's Maverick label and, buoyed by the media interest that accompanies the singer's every move, Candlebox soon found themselves a major success. Both 'Far Behind' and 'You' were hits in the singles chart and in 1995 sales of *Candlebox* reached three million copies in the USA. *Candlebox* was co-produced by Kelly Gray and revealed a band happy to explore territory somewhere between traditional pop-metal and Seattle-styled grunge. This was an assured debut and one that placed the band in the anticipated difficult second album category. *Lucy* was, unfortunately, a major disappointment to fans and critics. Ex-Pearl Jam drummer Dave Krusen replaced Mercado shortly before the recording of a back-to-basics third album, produced by Ron Nevison.
● ALBUMS: *Candlebox* (Maverick/Reprise 1994)★★★★, *Lucy* (Maverick/Reprise 1995)★★, *Happy Pills* (Maverick/Reprise 1998)★★★.

Candy Flip

UK house music duo Candy Flip consisted of Ric Peet (b. Richard Anderson-Peet, Merseyside, England) and Dizzy Dee (b. Daniel Mould, Stoke, Staffordshire, England). They originally joined the UK house outfit This Ain't Chicago, who released 'Ride The Rhythm' on the Club label. By the time of Candy Flip, they were dressed in psychedelic flares, boots and shirts that saw them earmarked as part of the 'Madchester' 60s revival. As a duo their first release was the minor club hit 'Love Is Life'. However, a cover version of the Beatles' 'Strawberry Fields Forever' earned them their first UK chart success, reaching number 3 in March 1990. Originally intended as a b-side to 'Can You Feel The Love', it was perfect fodder for the second summer of love generation. The follow-up, 'This Can Be Real', and its successors, failed to make the Top 50, and the duo split-up in 1992. Mould now works as a producer with his brother Kelvin, remixing tracks for Blueboy, Sister Sledge and Bentley Rhythm Ace, while Peet has engineered albums by the Charlatans, Six By Seven and the Wildhearts.
● ALBUMS: *Madstock ... The Continuing Adventures Of Bubblefish Car* (Debut 1991)★★.

Canibus

b. Germaine Williams, Jamaica, West Indies. Basing himself in New Jersey, this Jamaican born rapper also spent time in London and Georgia, where he studied computer information systems at Dekalb College. His hard-edged rapping skills made him an in-demand member of the underground mix-tape circuit, before coming to the attention of Fugees rapper Wyclef Jean. Williams contributed to Wyclef's 1997 solo debut, and made further appearances on the *Rhyme And Reason* soundtrack (with Heltah Skeltah on 'Uni-4-Orm'), and the Lost Boyz' *Love Peace And Nappiness*. His big break came about through a very public falling out with the veteran LL Cool J. The two rappers clashed over Canibus' contribution to the track '4,3,2,1' on LL's *Phenomenon*, with the result that LL included some less than complimentary lines about Canibus in the released product. The media coverage helped boost Canibus' into the public eye, leading to a

deal with Universal Records. The single 'Second Round KO', featuring an unlikely contribution from boxer Mike Tyson and a vitriolic reply to LL's tirade, broke into the US Top 30 in May 1998. Canibus' intense in-your-face delivery proved wearing over the course of a full-length album, but *Can-I-Bus'* musically diverse backing tracks, skilfully constructed by Wyclef and star producer Jerry Wonder, were a redeeming feature. The album was highly successful, debuting at US number 2 in September 1998. Canibus also collaborated with world music star Youssou N'Dour on 'How Come', included on the excellent soundtrack to Warren Beatty's *Bulworth*.
● ALBUMS: *Can-I-Bus* (Universal 1998)★★★.

Cannibal Corpse

This controversial death metal act was formed in Buffalo, New York, USA, by Chris Barnes (vocals), guitarists Bob Rusay and Jack Owen, Alex Webster (bass) and Paul Mazurkiewicz (drums). The band adopted an almost cartoon-like approach to their material, which stood out even from the extreme grotesqueries of the death scene, and have thrived on the controversy created by offensive song titles such as 'Meat Hook Sodomy', 'Necropedophile' and the infamous 'Entrails Ripped From A Virgin's Cunt'. The band's cover art has not been immune to criticism either, with some retailers refusing to stock both *Butchered At Birth* and *Tomb Of The Mutilated* until the gruesome cover paintings by Vincent Locke (of Dead World Comics) were replaced. Musically, the band have made steady progress from their *Eaten Back To Life* debut, refining a death metal assault to match the song titles, although Rob Barrett (ex-Malevolent Creation) replaced Rusay on *The Bleeding*. The band were also exposed to a major audience with their cameo appearance in the *Ace Ventura: Pet Detective* movie, where they were seen performing 'Hammer Smashed Face'. Barnes was allegedly sacked from the band in 1995, to be replaced on vocals by ex-Monstrosity singer George 'Corpsegrinder' Fisher. The first evidence of his contribution to the band came on 1996's *Vile*, which included familiar lyrical subject matter such as 'Devoured By Vermin' and 'Orgasm Through Torture'.
● ALBUMS: *Eaten Back To Life* (Metal Blade 1990)★★, *Butchered At Birth* (Metal Blade 1991)★★★★, *Tomb Of The Mutilated* (Metal Blade 1992)★★★, *Hammer Smashed Face* mini-album (Metal Blade 1993)★★★★, *The Bleeding* (Metal Blade 1994)★★, *Vile* (Metal Blade 1996)★★★, *Gallery Of Suicide* (Metal Blade 1998)★★★, *Bloodthirst* (Metal Blade 1999)★★★.

Cappella

Cappella scored a major and somewhat unexpected success in 1989 when their 'Heylom Halib' crashed into the UK Top 20. It was made by Gianfranco Bortolotti's Media Records empire, which soon became the dominant force on the Euro dance music scene. Although their founder continued to release a number of records under various umbrella names, he retained Cappella as his priority act. Their first chart entry had come the year before, when 'Bauhaus (Push The Beat)' was a minor hit. Bortolotti subsequently employed two Londoners, Rodney Bishop and Kelly Overett, as full-time members of the project. They continued to enjoy hits throughout the early 90s, including 'Be Master In One's Own House', 'House Of Energy Revenge', and the UK Top 30 hit

'Take Me Away', licensed to PWL in the UK. This featured the guest vocals of Loleatta Holloway - ironic, since Cappella's success instigated the Italo-house scene, the biggest commercial hit of which was Black Box's 'Ride On Time', on which Holloway's vocals were sampled. Cappella reached their commercial peak in 1993 and 1994, with hits including the typically immediate and anthemic 'U Got 2 Know', followed by the similarly styled but equally successful 'U Got 2 Let The Music', 'Move On Baby', and 'U & Me'. Featured vocalists on these records included Kelly Overett and Allison Jordan. Their unpretentious, hook-heavy synth pop subsequently fell from grace as the dance scene embraced more challenging styles.

● ALBUMS: *U Got 2 Know* (Internal/ZYX 1994)★★, *War In Heaven* (ZYX 1996)★★.

Capleton

b. Clifton Bailey, 1974, Kingston, Jamaica, West Indies. By 1994, Capleton's work for the African Star label had led to him being regarded as one of the most innovative cultural DJs of his generation. 'Number One (On The Good Look Chart)' on Jah Life first caught the attention of the dancehall audience in 1990 and was Capleton's debut hit. *Capleton Gold* was released in 1991 and compiled many of his recordings for various producers, including Philip 'Fatis' Burrell ('Bumbo Red'/'Bible Fi Dem'), King Jammy ('The Red'), Roof International ('Dem No Like Me'), Peterkins ('We No Lotion Man') and Black Scorpio ('Ghetto Youth'/'Somebody'). In the same year he sang on half an album for Gussie P ('Double Trouble'), combined with Johnny Osbourne on 'Special Guest' on Outernational, released several tracks for African Star and duetted on 'Young, Fresh And Green' with Bobby Zarro. He visited the UK with Pan Head in December amid controversy over a shooting at a London venue. He also recorded 'Dance Can't Done' for the Brixton-based label, Jungle Rock. On his return to Jamaica, Capleton began recording for Burrell's Exterminator label. 'Almshouse' (1992) was a rallying cry for unification through music and demonstrated that Capleton could address social and cultural topics with the same perceptiveness as his characteristic 'slackness'. In a successful year, he released an album for Burrell and had hits with 'F.C.T.', 'Matey A Dead', 'Make Hay' and 'Unno Hear'. In 1993, he maintained his profile with the singles 'Everybody Needs Somebody', 'Mankind' for Colin Fat, 'Good Love', 'Stampede' for Mad House, 'Cold Blooded Murderer' for Black Scorpio and the rabid 'Buggering' for African Star. He also recorded combinations with Brian And Tony Gold and Nadine Sutherland, and worked with Gussie Clarke. In the USA, a hip-hop mix of the smash hit 'Tour' prompted Def Jam Records to sign him for the remarkable *Prophecy*. The forthright *I-Testament* saw Capleton at the peak of his powers.

● ALBUMS: with Ninjaman, Tony Rebel *Real Rough* (1990)★★★, *We No Lotion Man* (Charm 1991)★★★, *Capleton Gold* (Charm 1991)★★★★, with General Levy *Double Trouble* (Gussie P. 1991)★★★, with Cutty Ranks, Reggie Stepper *Three The Hard Way* (Techniques 1991)★★★, *Almshouse* (Exterminator 1993)★★★, *Prophecy* (Def Jam/African Star 1995)★★★★, *I-Testament* (Def Jam/Mercury 1998)★★★★.

Cappadonna

b. Darryl Hill, New York, USA. Raised in New York's Staten Island district, Cappadonna became the tenth official member of the Wu-Tang Clan. Hill had known members of the crew since grade school, and began writing and performing himself from the age of 15 onwards. His first recorded appearance on a Wu-Tang Clan product was in 1995, adding a lewd rap to 'Ice Cream' on Raekwon's *Only Built 4 Cuban Linx* …. Later in the same year he was heard on 'Winter Warz', the opening track on the soundtrack to *Don't Be A Menace To South Central While You're Drinking Your Juice In The Hood*. His big break came in 1996 when he received third billing on Ghostface Killah's hugely successful *Ironman*. By the time *Wu-Tang Forever*, the Wu-Tang Clan's sophomore album, appeared the following year, Cappadonna was their chosen guest rapper. His eagerly anticipated debut *The Pillage* debuted at US number 3 in March 1998. Employing the usual production team of RZA, True Master and Goldfinghaz, the album featured cameo appearances from several Wu-Tang Clan rappers. The superb backing tracks featured some of the finest examples to date of RZA's pared down sound, with Cappadonna throwing out winning raps over the top on the title track and 'Dart Throwing'.

● ALBUMS: *The Pillage* (Razor Sharp/Epic 1998)★★★★.

Captain America

Formed in 1991, Captain America was one of several bands to emerge from the flourishing milieu centred on the Scottish town of Bellshill. Vocalist/guitarist Eugene Kelly and bass player James Seenan were former members of the Vaselines, while the original line-up also featured BMX Bandits guitarist Gordon Keen and Teenage Fanclub drummer Brendan O'Hare. The last-named was replaced by Andy Bollen soon after the quartet's inception. Captain America completed two 12-inch EPs, *Captain America* and *Flame On*, both of which revealed a penchant for distorted guitar work, but progress was halted when Marvel Comics, publishers of the *Captain America* title, threatened litigation. The C&A company also objected to the band's use of their trading logo on *Flame On*. Pressure on the band was increased when Kurt Cobain was widely pictured wearing a Captain America T-shirt, and having jettisoned Seenan and Bollen, Kelly and Keen re-emerged with a new rhythm section and a new name - Eugenius.

Cardigans

From Malmö in Sweden, where they are widely regarded as the country's 'top alternative rock band', the Cardigans comprise Bengt Lagerberg (drums), Peter Svensson (guitar), Lars Olof Johansson (keyboards), Nina Persson (vocals) and Magnus Sveningsson (bass). Their delicate, intricate melodies saw critics link their debut album, *Emmerdale*, with the introspective, acoustic tradition of early 80s UK bands including the Young Marble Giants and Everything But The Girl. Certainly it was difficult to detect the presence of any clues to Svensson and Sveningsson's previous work in Malmö heavy metal bands. However, 1995's *Life*, promoted on a UK support tour with Blur, did include a cover version of 'Sabbath Bloody Sabbath'. Further strong press, encouraged by radio play on BBC Radio 1 and daytime British television, prompted healthy sales in Sweden, the UK and

Japan, where the Cardigans enjoy immense popularity. On *First Band On The Moon* they abandoned pure pop simplicity and chose to experiment with shades of progressive rock and harder guitar. The strongest material, however, was the straightforward pop of memorable tracks such as 'Been It' and 'Never Recover'. The band enjoyed a huge UK summer hit in 1997 with the re-released 'Lovefool', featured on the soundtrack to *William Shakespeare's Romeo & Juliet*. 'My Favourite Game' was another highly addictive hit single, debuting at UK number 14 in October 1998 and providing a taster for *Gran Turismo*. 'Erase/Rewind' returned the band to the UK Top 10 in March 1999.

● ALBUMS: *Emmerdale* (Stockholm/Polydor 1994)★★★, *Life* (Stockholm/Polydor 1995)★★★, *First Band On The Moon* (Stockholm/Polydor 1996)★★★★, *Gran Turismo* (Stockholm/Polydor 1998)★★★★.

Carey, Mariah

b. 27 March 1970, Long Island, New York, USA. This rock diva enjoyed an unprecedented string of US chart-toppers that helped establish her as the most successful female solo artist of the 90s. Carey was the third child of an Irish-American mother, a former opera singer turned voice tutor, and a half-Venezuelan father. As a schoolgirl Carey began singing on R&B sessions in New York when she met keyboard player and songwriter Ben Margulies who became her songwriting partner and close friend. With Carey writing the melodies and most of the lyrics, and Margulies arranging the songs, they developed a simple blend of soul, gospel and pop that showed off Carey's amazing vocal range to the full. Carey struggled as a waitress until fortune smiled on her. While at a show business party, a friend of the singer thrust a demo cassette into the hands of Sony Music's US president Tommy Mottola. While driving home from the party Mottola played the cassette in the car and was so impressed that he immediately set out on a Prince Charming-like quest to find his Cinderella. Carey was duly signed and her debut single, 'Visions Of Love', was a smash hit. It became the first of five US number 1s. Managed by Randy Hoffman (whose roster also includes Hall And Oates) the success story proved swift and efficient in construction. In addition to providing four chart-topping singles ('Vision Of Love', 'Love Takes Time', 'Someday' and 'I Don't Wanna Cry'), her debut album stayed on top of the US album charts for 22 weeks, as she duly picked up 1991 Grammys for Best Female Vocalist and Best New Artist, an extraordinary start to a career. The title track of *Emotions* gave Carey a record fifth consecutive US number 1. Subsequent number 1 singles included a cover of the Jackson Five's 'I'll Be There' (from *MTV Unplugged*), 'Dreamlover' and 'Hero' (both from *Music Box*). Her only UK number 1 to date, however, came with a cover version of Badfinger's 'Without You' in February 1994. In 1993, she married Mottola (they subsequently divorced in 1997). Her seasonal *Merry Christmas* featured another hit single, 'All I Want For Christmas Is You'. Her 1995 release, *Daydream*, exceeded all expectations and notched up sales of over six million in the USA within three months of release. Some critics did question whether *Daydream* was a controlled exercise in vacuous formula writing, with little emotion or heart. Nevertheless, it produced two further huge-selling number 1 singles, 'Fantasy' and 'One Sweet Day', the latter a collaboration with Boyz II Men that topped the US charts for

a staggering 16 weeks. *Butterfly* featured Carey's most adventurous collection of songs to date, and inevitably repeated the success of her previous albums. 'My All' became Carey's thirteenth American number 1, placing her behind only Elvis Presley and the Beatles in the all-time US singles chart. 'When You Believe', a duet with fellow diva Whitney Houston taken from the animated DreamWorks movie *The Prince Of Egypt*, was a huge worldwide hit during 1998. Carey returned in October 1999 with yet another US chart-topper, 'Heartbreaker', featuring rapper Jay-Z. Her records have already sold over 110 million copies worldwide, and she is the biggest-selling female solo artist of the 90s.

● ALBUMS: *Mariah Carey* (Columbia 1990)★★★, *Emotions* (Columbia 1991)★★★, *MTV Unplugged* (Columbia 1992)★★★, *Music Box* (Columbia 1993)★★★, *Merry Christmas* (Columbia 1994)★★, *Daydream* (Columbia 1995)★★★, *Butterfly* (Columbia 1997)★★★, with Celine Dion, Gloria Estefan, Aretha Franklin, Shania Twain *Divas Live* (Epic 1998)★★, *Rainbow* (Columbia 1999)★★★.

● COMPILATIONS: *#1s* (Columbia 1998)★★★★.

● VIDEOS: *Mariah Carey* (Columbia Music Video 1994), *Fantasy: Live At Madison Square Garden* (Columbia Music Video 1996), *My All* (Columbia Music Video 1998), with Celine Dion, Gloria Estefan, Aretha Franklin, Shania Twain *Divas Live* (Sony Music Video 1998), *Around The World* (Sony Music Video 1999), *MTV Unplugged + 3* (Sony Music Video 1999), *#1s* (Sony Music Video 1999).

Carpenter, Mary-Chapin

b. 21 February 1958, Princeton, New Jersey, USA. Carpenter's father was an executive for *Life* magazine, and she spent part of her early life living in Japan. She grew up with a love of contemporary pop hits, although her mother's Woody Guthrie and Judy Collins records gave her some interest in country/folk music. She spent her time at home with her guitar, and her father encouraged her to perform at a talent night. At university, she achieved a degree in American Civilization. By 1986, she was a local star, winning five Washington Area Music Awards without having made a record, after which she signed to a major label in Nashville with guitarist/producer John Jennings. She had felt she should have a conventional job, but continued performing in bars, often having to sing current favourites; unsatisfied with this situation, she resolved to perform only in bars that would let her play original material. She had also recorded John Stewart's song 'Runaway Train' for her first album, but Columbia Records decided that it would be better suited to Rosanne Cash, who took it to the top of the US country charts. Since then, she has made steady progress up the commercial ladder, attracting cover versions of her songs by artists such as Tony Rice and Joan Baez. A notable songwriter, Carpenter has also recorded cover versions, including 'Downtown Train' by Tom Waits - more recently a hit for Rod Stewart - on *Hometown Girl*, and the stunning 'Quittin' Time', co-written by Robb Royer of Bread, from *State Of The Heart*. In 1991, she made the US country charts with a revival of Gene Vincent's light-hearted 'Right Now'. Her 1992 hit, the raunchy and self-mocking 'I Feel Lucky', preceded the release of another excellent album, *Come On, Come On*. Carpenter's complete acceptance by a country audience was sealed when she was voted the Country Music Association's Female Vocalist Of The Year that September. On this album, in addition to country rockers with chiming 12-string guitars ('The Hard Way' and 'Passionate Kisses'), there are beautiful folk ballads (the title track is magnificent). Two years later she was able to deliver more of the same recipe with another million-seller *Stones In The Road*. This time she answered 'Passionate Kisses' with 'Shut Up And Kiss Me' and complemented 'The Hard Way' with the equally thought-provoking 'House Of Cards'. Her lyrics continue to flow without any writer's block, but what is particularly interesting is how, together with the likes of Trisha Yearwood, Suzy Bogguss and Kathy Mattea, she has brought fresh impetus to an old and sometimes predictable genre. Her productivity is impressive, particularly as she suffers from depression. 'Early on, I thought I was just moody,' she told the *Daily Telegraph*, 'but I've learnt to accept it is a part of me.' This partially accounts for her subject matter: drinking, divorce and bad love affairs - but she can rock with the best of them, as demonstrated by the Grammy-winning 'Down At The Twist And Shout'. She has participated on tribute albums, notably with 'Wishing' on the Buddy Holly set *notfadeaway*, and a stunning performance of 'Grow Old With Me' on *A Tribute To John Lennon*. *A Place In The World* maintained her reputation in the country field, but also attracted a new audience as she crossed over into mainstream rock.

● ALBUMS: *Hometown Girl* (Columbia 1987)★★, *State Of The Heart* (Columbia 1989)★★★, *Shooting Straight In The Dark* (Columbia 1990)★★★, *Come On, Come On* (Columbia 1992)★★★★, *Stones In The Road* (Columbia 1994)★★★★, *A Place In The World* (Columbia 1996)★★★.

● COMPILATIONS: *Party Doll And Other Favorites* (Columbia 1999)★★★★.

● VIDEOS: *Shut Up And Kiss Me* (1994), *5* (1994), *My Record Company Made Me Do This!* (1995), *Jubilee: Live At The Wolf Trap* (Columbia Music Video 1995).

Carroll, Dina

b. Newmarket, Suffolk, England. Carroll's place of birth could actually be a contentious issue bearing in mind that it took place in the back of a taxi speeding towards Newmarket Hospital. The daughter of a US serviceman and British mother, Carroll spent a few years in Philadelphia, but was largely brought up in the UK. Her soulful voice brought her to the attention of Streetsounds, where she auditioned and was rewarded with session work. She released 'People All Around The World' on Jive Records in 1989 as Dina Carroll before reverting to Dina for a cover of 'Walk On By'. In 1991, she provided vocals for Quartz's 'It's Too Late' (UK number 8). Following their split, Carroll nearly abandoned the music business, but A&M Records signed her as a solo act, and in 1992 released the UK hit singles 'Ain't No Man' (number 16) and 'Special Kind Of Love' (number 16). Her debut album followed in 1993, with 'Don't Be A Stranger' (number 3) and 'The Perfect Year' (number 5) providing her with two breakthrough hits. After a three-year break she returned in 1996 with the UK number 3 single, 'Escaping', and follow-up album *Only Human*. 'One, Two, Three' debuted at UK number 16 in October 1998. 'Without Love' charted three places higher the following July.

● ALBUMS: *So Close* (A&M 1993)★★★, *Only Human* (Mercury 1996)★★★.

● VIDEOS: *So Close - The Videos* (1994).

Carson, Lori

b. USA. Carson is a singer-songwriter who once analogized her method of writing as 'capturing emotional memories'. Based in New York, USA, she served her apprenticeship on the live circuit before signing with Geffen Records in 1990. *Shelter* was produced by Hal Willner and featured an all-star cast of supporting musicians, but it failed to sell in a market as yet reluctant to take on board an intelligent female songwriter working in the modern rock idiom. She found more success as a long-term collaborator with Anton Fier in the Golden Palominos. Her vocal work on Golden Palominos tracks such as 'Gun', 'Little Suicides' and 'Pure' gave her a reputation as a singer with a distinct voice, capable of echoing and expanding on the intimacy of Fier's early 90s work. Her second solo album, and her first for Restless Records, followed in 1995. *Where It Goes* was produced by Fier and included 'You Won't Fall', which featured on the soundtrack to *Sleeping Beauty*. A third set, *Everything I Touch Runs Wild*, was co-produced by Carson herself, alongside Fier. It was distinguished by the inclusion of arguably Carson's most effective song to date, the aching 'Something's Got Me'. This was heavily promoted by the singer's record label, with Philip Steir (who remixed the Butthole Surfers' 'Pepper') and Fier contributing remixes to a 'bonus disc'. The attendant video was directed by Matthew Rolston (most famous for shooting the Salt-N-Pepa/En Vogue video for 'What A Man').

● ALBUMS: *Shelter* (Geffen 1990)★★★, *Where It Goes* (Restless 1995)★★★★, *Everything I Touch Runs Wild* (Restless 1997)★★★.

Carter USM

When the UK band Jamie Wednesday folded in the face of public apathy, they left two singles in their wake, 'Vote For Love' and 'We Three Kings Of Orient Aren't', on the Pink Records label. Prior to this, there had been several incarnations of the band, namely the Ballpoints, the End, Dead Clergy and Peter Pan's Playground. Then the south London pair of Jimbob (b. James Morrison, 22 November 1960) and Fruitbat (b. Leslie Carter, 12 December 1958) acquired a drum machine and took their name from a newspaper cutting, around July/August 1987, to create Carter The Unstoppable Sex Machine. The single 'Sheltered Life', on the independent label Big Cat, revealed a formula that had more in common with other irreverent samplers such as the KLF than the Pet Shop Boys or Erasure. The single made little impression, unlike Carter's next single, 'Sheriff Fatman' (1989), an exciting amalgam of a great riff, strong rhythm and strident lyrics about a maverick landlord. *101 Damnations* was an innovative melting pot of samples, ideas and tunes, shot through with a punk-inspired ethos. Lyrically, the duo used a mix-and-match approach, swapping punned words and phrases in a manner that soon became a trademark. 'Rubbish' (1990) followed 'Fatman' into the UK indie charts, and attracted considerable attention, helped by a cover of the Pet Shop Boys' 'Rent' on the b-side. Carter had moved to Rough Trade Records by the end of the year, releasing their fourth single, 'Anytime, Anyplace, Anywhere'. After the export-only *Handbuilt For Perverts* and a special Christmas giveaway single, 'Christmas Shopper's Paradise', came the controversial 'Bloodsports For All' in 1991. This document of bullying in the military received little airplay as it coincided with the start of the Gulf conflict, but *30 Something* topped the UK Independent chart and reached the national Top 10. Financial upheaval at Rough Trade and Carter's growing success led to a contract with Chrysalis Records, commencing with a chart-bound reissue of 'Sheriff Fatman' in June. In the meantime, the band visited the USA and toured Japan later in the year. Carter's Top 20 hit later in 1991, 'After The Watershed', motivated lawyers representing the Rolling Stones to demand substantial payment (allegedly 100% of all royalties) for an infringement of copyright in using a snippet of the Stones' 1967 hit, 'Ruby Tuesday'. Meanwhile, Carter's lighting engineer and MC, Jon 'Fat' Beast, had ingratiated himself within the band's entourage (prompting the legendary cries of 'You Fat Bastard' at gigs), though they would amicably part company in early 1992 when his fame became disproportionate to that of the band's. Carter's albums from here on displayed a gradually more sophisticated approach, though the cornerstone of their appeal remained their incisive lyrics and propulsive live shows. *Starry Eyed And Bollock Naked* was a collection of b-sides, and coincided with a return to the Top 20 with the single 'Glam Rock Cops'. The band recruited a full-time drummer, Wez, who had formerly played in the Byrds-inspired early 90s band Resque, and Carter played a historic gig in Zagreb, Croatia, the first band to play there since the start of the civil war. Early copies of 1995's *Worry Bomb*, their fourth consecutive Top 10 UK album, included a live recording of the concert. The extravagant haircuts and stage gear had also been toned down, in keeping with songs that now demanded more from the listener than had previously been the case. In 1996, the band left Chrysalis and joined the Cooking Vinyl Records label, expanding to a six-piece with the addition of new bass-player Salv (ex-S*M*A*S*H), guitarist Steve B. (brother of Wez) and keyboard player Simon Painter (replaced by Ben at the end of the year). The mini-album *A World Without Dave* was followed by their final recording, *I Blame The Government*, bringing to an end a most entertaining chapter in the annals of the UK's independent music scene.

● ALBUMS: *101 Damnations* (Big Cat 1990)★★★★, *30 Something* (Rough Trade 1991)★★★, *1992 - The Love Album* (Chrysalis 1992)★★★★, *Post Historic Monsters* (Chrysalis 1993)★★★★, *Starry Eyed And Bollock Naked* (Chrysalis 1994)★★★, *Worry Bomb* (Chrysalis 1995)★★★, *A World Without Dave* mini-album (Cooking Vinyl 1997)★★★, *I Blame The Government* (Cooking Vinyl 1997)★★★.

● COMPILATIONS: *Straw Donkey* (Chrysalis 1995)★★★.

● VIDEOS: *In Bed With Carter* (PMI 1991), *What Do You Think Of The Programme So Far?* (PMI 1992), *Straw Donkey: The Videos* (PMI 1995), *Flicking The V's-Live In Croatia* (1995).

Carter, Deana

b. 1964, Nashville, Tennessee, USA. Something of a late-comer to country music, Carter recorded her first album at the age of 29. The daughter of Nashville alumnus Fred Carter Jnr. (a guitarist who played with everyone from Elvis Presley to Simon And Garfunkel to Roy Orbison), she grafted pop influences onto the country singer-songwriter tradition, earning comparisons to the crossover appeal of Dolly Parton or Tammy Wynette. Songs such as 'Turn Those Wheels Around' and 'Angel Without A Prayer' caught the attention of Willie Nelson (another artist with whom Carter's father had played), and he invited her to perform at 1994's Farm Aid. Produced by Jimmy Bowen, her debut offered polished

pop and country songs in 'Are You Coming Home', 'Rita Valentine' and 'Graffiti Bridge'. The critical and commercial success of *Did I Shave Me Legs For This?* garnered her a Country Music Association Award in September 1997. Her song 'Why Don't You Stay', co-written with Mike Read, was one of the strongest songs featured in the movie *Hope Floats* in 1998. *Everything's Gonna Be Alright* fell short of expectations even though it made the higher reaches of the country album chart in the USA.

● ALBUMS: *Did I Shave Me Legs For This?* (Capitol 1996)★★★★, *Everything's Gonna Be Alright* (Capitol 1998)★★★.

Carter, Derrick

One of the biggest names in 90s Chicago house music, Carter was described by Richie Hawtin as 'America's last true underground DJ' in 1994. His debut single, 'Love Me Right', appeared way back in 1987, but it wasn't until the mid-90s resurgence of Chicago house that Carter began to attract the attention his reputation deserved. *The Sound Patrol* EP was released on the local Organico label, and was followed by a second EP, *The Music*, another slice of pure house. It included excellent cuts such as 'An Open Secret', which utilized Chaka Khan's 'Ain't Nobody' at its base. Carter continues to work in a 'DJ commune' near the downtown skyscraper precincts of Chicago, equipped with a built-in studio. He had started life as part of the experimental outfit Symbols And Instruments, who scored an underground techno success for Network Records. He was only 16 at the time, and went on to a scholarship at engineering college MIT. Following the EPs he embarked on a project for David Holmes' Exploding Plastic Inevitable label and founded the labels, Blue Cucaracha and Classic. He also began performing live with the Sound Patrol Orchestra. Carter's work can be heard on several mix albums released in the late 90s.

● COMPILATIONS: *Future Sound Of Chicago II - Derrick Carter* (MOS 1995)★★★, as Sound Patrol *As Long As It's Groovy* (Organico 1995)★★★, *Cosmic Disco* (DMC 1997)★★★, *Mixmag Presents* (Mixmag 1997)★★★, *Pagan Offering* (Pagan 1998)★★★.

Carter, Jon

(see Monkey Mafia)

Carthy, Eliza

b. 1975, Yorkshire, England. The daughter of Martin Carthy and Norma Waterson (the Watersons), Eliza Carthy could hardly escape the music of her parents. Her earliest memory is of falling asleep in the kitchen to the strains of a Watersons' practice session. As she grew older she was quickly inducted into the Watersons' ranks, but chose fiddle rather than learn from her master guitarist father - principally because he was too often absent to teach her. In 1989, she formed the Waterdaughters with her mother, aunt and cousin. In 1990 she met fiddle player Nancy Kerr (see Eliza Carthy And Nancy Kerr). They toured together extensively as a duo and recorded two acclaimed albums for Mrs Casey Records. The first of these included, alongside traditional material, Carthy's first self-composition, 'The Wrong Favour'. Between albums she teamed up with her parents to record one of the best-received English folk albums for several years, *Waterson:Carthy*, voted *Folk Roots'* Critic's Choice of 1994. Wide-ranging critical approval also greeted the February 1996 release of her debut solo album, *Heat, Light &*

Sound. A beautiful 12-song collection of traditional material fluidly arranged by Carthy herself, the lightness of touch demonstrated in both her vocals and fiddle playing confirmed her rising status within contemporary English folk song. *Eliza Carthy And The Kings Of Calicutt* and the double *Red Rice* were two more brilliant genre-bending albums that successfully redefined the boundaries of folk music.

● ALBUMS: *Hirutruku* (Emakbakia 1994)★★★, with Martin Carthy, Norma Waterson *Waterson Carthy* (Topic 1995)★★★★, *Heat, Light & Sound* (Topic 1996)★★★★, *Eliza Carthy And The Kings Of Calicutt* (Topic 1997)★★★★, *Red Rice* (Topic 1998)★★★★, with Martin Carthy, Norma Waterson *Broken Ground* (Topic 1999)★★★★.

Case

b. New York City, New York, USA. This rising star of swing-beat spent several years recording demos while holding down a day job for the local housing authority. He performed cameo roles on records by Al B. Sure!, Christopher Williams and Jodeci, among others, before launching his solo career proper in 1996. His self-titled debut album was composed of romantic R&B with hip-hop grooves, though the high sexual quotient normally associated with swingbeat was largely absent. Having grown up listening to Marvin Gaye, Donny Hathaway and Stevie Wonder, he confirmed to *Billboard* magazine that he focuses 'heavily on the melody of a song'. The album's attendant single, 'Touch Me, Tease Me', was written in collaboration with Mary J. Blige, and featured Foxy Brown on backing vocals. It was included on the soundtrack to *The Nutty Professor*, the multi-million-dollar-grossing Eddie Murphy movie. In a tribute to Case's hip-hop roots, the single featured a sample of Schoolly D's 'PSK', one of the first gangsta rap narratives. Blige also collaborated on the second single release, 'I Gotcha'. The singer returned in 1999 with another strong collection, *Personal Conversation*, which featured the US hit singles 'Faded Pictures' and 'Happily Ever After'.

● ALBUMS: *Case* (Def Jam 1996)★★★, *Personal Conversation* (Def Jam 1999)★★★.

Cassidy, Eva

b. 2 February 1963, Oxon Hill, Maryland, USA, d. 2 November 1996. Growing up in a musical family on the outskirts of Washington, DC, Cassidy sang as a small child and later learned to play the guitar. Her father, a teacher of children with learning disabilities and a part-time musician, formed a family band with Eva, her brother, Danny, on violin, and himself on bass. She became more involved with music and painting as a teenager. In 1986 she did the art work for a projected album by a band, Method Actor, led by a friend, Dave Lourim. She was asked to sing on the album and was heard by producer Chris Biondi who, impressed by her raw talent, encouraged her and introduced her to other musicians. Cassidy appeared on several albums as a backing singer. Meantime, Biondi was stockpiling tapes by Cassidy and in 1991, while recording Chuck Brown And The Soul Searchers, played examples for the band's leader. Brown was immediately taken with her sound, and in 1992 Brown and Cassidy recorded *The Other Side* (Liaison). Early the following year Brown and Cassidy began performing live, including an appearance at Washington's Blues Alley, and went on the road. Later in the year, following a medical check-up, Cassidy had outpatient surgery for a malignant

skin lesion. Early in 1994 she recorded for Blue Note Records and toured with Pieces Of A Dream, but, unlike the sessions with Brown, she found this musically unsatisfying. In January 1996, she appeared at Blues Alley again, a session that was recorded, but when summer came she was unwell. This time the check-up revealed advanced melanoma and she was told that she had three to five months to live. In September, a tribute concert was organized at which she sang, as did Brown. She died two months later. Cassidy's singing voice was a crystalline soprano, ideal for the ballads and folk songs she performed. But she also had tremendous power and when she turned to soul and gospel-flavoured material her voice resounded with emotional sincerity. Her repertoire drew from all these areas and from the more melodic aspects of contemporary pop. While she might be placed only on the edges of jazz her conviction and integrity would often ably carry her over the hazy boundary. The excellent interpretation of Sting's 'Fields Of Gold', on *Eva By Heart*, is breathtaking in clarity and delivery. Most of her recorded work displays a remarkable and unspoiled talent, and almost all of it has been released posthumously.

● ALBUMS: *Live At Blues Alley* (Blix Street 1996)★★★★, *Eva By Heart* (Blix Street 1997)★★★★.

● COMPILATIONS: *Songbird* (Blix Street 1998)★★★.

Cassius

Cassius comprises two 31-year-old Parisians, Boombass and Phillipe Zdar, who have also recorded as La Funk Mob on James Lavelle's Mo' Wax Records label. Zdar was one of France's most respected DJs, famous for his sets at 'Respect' in Paris as well as 'Basement Jaxx' and 'Scaramanga' in south London. Boombass grew up in Paris where his father was a successful record producer, so it was a natural step for him into the music business. By 1991, he had become a producer and was working on MC Solaar's first album. Zdar grew up in the Alps but met Boombass in 1988 after landing a job assisting Boombass' father. Sharing interests in hip-hop, American movies and fashion, they became friends and eventually a production team. They produced three highly successful albums for MC Solaar and developed the proto-trip-hop sound of La Funk Mob. In 1992, Zdar discovered house music and techno and, with Etienne De Crecy (the man behind the influential *Superdiscount*), made *Pansoul*, a landmark in the development of French house. Zdar persuaded Boombass to make a house record and the result – 'Foxy Lady' released under the name L'Homme Qui Valait Trois Millards ('The Six Million Dollar Man') was the first indication of the coming wave of funky French disco. It became a classic single, played by many UK DJs. *1999* was recorded in three weeks during the summer of 1998 and its influences include Daft Punk, DJ Sneak, Tuff Jam and Masters At Work. The infectious single 'Cassius 1999' was released in January 1999 and was an immediate critical and commercial success.

● ALBUMS: *1999* (Virgin 1999)★★★★.

Cast

With a line-up of John Power (vocals/guitar), Peter Wilkinson (bass), Keith O'Neill (drums) and Skin (b. Liam Tyson; guitar), much of the attention initially surrounding Liverpool, England-based rock band Cast, arose from Power's previous position as bass player in the La's. When it became apparent at the end of 1991 that the band's second album was never going to materialize, Powers 'left to get something new. I was just feeling uninspired. I left to do my own stuff, somewhere along the line you have to make a decision about what you want out of life.' An early version of Cast recorded demos for Go! Discs, before the present quartet took shape in 1993. The new line-up began their career as support to the Lightning Seeds, before signing to Polydor Records (largely through their reputation for working with Jimi Hendrix and the Who - evidently the 60s were still a big factor in the evolution of Power's musical style). O'Neill was a former solicitor's assistant, Wilkinson had played bass with Shack and Supercharge, while Tyson had played with Pyramid Dream. Cast made their debut in July 1995 with 'Finetime', a superb distillation of guitar pop that reached number 17 in the UK singles chart. Significantly, the choice of producer for the band's debut album was John Leckie. A upbeat Britpop album that fitted perfectly into the current musical climate, *All Change* was rewarded with a Top 10 placing in the UK album charts, and became the fastest-selling debut album ever released by Polydor. Subsequent singles 'Alright' (number 13), 'Sandstorm' (number 8) and 'Walkaway' (number 9) showed no sign of the band's success story waning. In a revealing interview conducted by Mark Beaumont in *New Musical Express*, John Power reflected on his recent binges and offered a thoughtful anti-drug message: 'I don't wanna get the wrong bus home to my head, and forever miss the stop'. The band reconvened in Rockfield studio in Wales to record their second album, while an interim single, 'Flying', kept them in the public eye by reaching number 4 in October 1996. Released in May 1997, *Mother Nature Calls* was previewed by the number 7 single, 'Free Me', but failed to prompt the same ripples of excitement that their debut had created, even though the quality of Power's songwriting was undiminished. However, 'Guiding Star' provided the band with their highest-charting single to date when it reached number 3 in June 1997. The anthemic 'Beat Mama' provided the band with yet another UK Top 10 single in May 1999, and was followed by the critically acclaimed *Magic Hour*.

● ALBUMS: *All Change* (Polydor 1995)★★★★, *Mother Nature Calls* (Polydor 1997)★★★, *Magic Hour* (Polydor 1999)★★★★.

Catatonia

Welsh band Catatonia made their breakthrough in the mid-90s with a series of energetic singles that combined attitude with highly melodic hooklines. Indeed, their first four releases each secured a Single Of The Week nomination from either the *New Musical Express* or *Melody Maker*. The band was originally formed in 1992 in Cardiff, Wales, when guitarist Mark Roberts met Cerys Matthews (b. 11 April 1969, Cardiff, South Wales) while she was busking acoustic Jefferson Airplane songs outside Debenhams' department store. With the addition of Paul Jones (who had played with Roberts in Y Criff), drummer Dafydd Ieuan (b. 1 March 1969, Bangor, North Wales) and keyboard player Clancy Pegg, the band recorded two EPs for the Welsh independent label Crai Records, September 1993's 'For Tinkerbell' and May 1994's 'Hooked'. In August 1994, they released a third single, 'Whale', on the Rough Trade Records' Singles Club. With a good deal of press interest the band relocated to London for the 'free drinks' A&R men were offering them. Their next

single, February 1995's 'Bleed', was released on the Nursery (Trident Music) label before the band was signed to Warner Brothers Records subsidiary Blanco y Negro by Geoff Travis (Rough Trade's founder). Ieuan and Pegg had left by this point, to join Super Furry Animals and Crac respectively. Owen Powell was drafted in as an additional guitarist while Aled Richards took over on drums. Their major label debut was December's limited edition 'Christmas 1995' single, which was quickly followed by January 1996's 'Sweet Catatonia'. In advance of their debut studio album Catatonia supported Marion on tour, while Nursery released a Japanese/European import collection of their singles to date, *The Sublime Magic Of ... (The Songs 1994 - 1995)*. Their UK Top 40 breakthrough came with 'You've Got A Lot To Answer For', paving the way for the following month's *Way Beyond Blue*, co-produced with Stephen Street. The real commercial breakthrough in the UK came in January 1998, when the topical and highly catchy 'Mulder And Scully' reached number 3. Another single from the album, 'Road Rage', debuted at number 5 in May, and *International Velvet* reached number 1 after 14 weeks on the album chart. Cerys Matthews also appeared as a guest vocalist on Space's UK number 4 single 'The Ballad Of Tom Jones'. The lush melodic ballad 'Dead From The Waist Down' debuted at UK number 7 in April 1999. *Equally Cursed And Blessed* entered the album chart at number 1 the same month.

● ALBUMS: *Way Beyond Blue* (Blanco y Negro 1996)★★★, *International Velvet* (Blanco y Negro 1997)★★★★, *Equally Cursed And Blessed* (Blanco y Negro 1999)★★★★.

● COMPILATIONS: *The Sublime Magic Of ... (The Songs 1994 - 1995)* (Nursery 1995)★★★, *The Crai EPs* (Crai 1999)★★★.

Cathedral

This excellent UK doom/grind band was formed by vocalist Lee Dorrian after his departure from Napalm Death, with his bass player friend Mark Griffiths, former Acid Reign guitarists Garry Jennings and Adam Lehan, and drummer Ben Mockrie. This line-up was in place for the release of a four-track demo, *In Memoriam*. Interestingly, this included a cover version of Pentagram's 'All Your Sins' - a band from which Cathedral would later draw members. Dorrian's vocals changed remarkably from his Napalm days to suit a style that drew heavily from early Black Sabbath and late 60s/early 70s underground rock. *Forest Of Equilibrium* was an impressive debut, with ex-Penance/Dream Death drummer Mike Smail standing in for the departed Mockrie. A permanent replacement was then found in Mark Ramsey Wharton (ex-Acid Reign) in time for the *Soul Sacrifice* EP, as Cathedral's live ability was amply demonstrated on the 'Gods Of Grind' UK tour with Carcass, Entombed and Confessor, and dates with Trouble and the Obsessed. A US tour with Brutal Truth, Napalm Death and Carcass followed, and although Griffiths departed, Cathedral signed a US contract with Columbia Records. *The Ethereal Mirror*, produced by Trouble, Danzig and Mick Jagger collaborator Dave Bianco, deservedly received a wealth of critical acclaim, and the band toured the UK with Sleep and Penance in tow before recording the *Statik Majik* EP with Cronos guitarist Mike Hickey guesting on bass. This included the 23-minute epic 'The Voyage Of The Homeless Sapien'. However, Lehan and Wharton left after a US tour with Mercyful Fate, and a new line-up with former Pentagram members Victor Griffin (drums) and Joe Hasselvander (guitar) was assembled for a Black Sabbath support tour. However, personality clashes led to Hasselvander's premature departure. Cathedral re-emerged as a quartet in late 1994 with Dorrian and Jennings joined by Scott Carlson (bass, ex-Repulsion) and Dave Hornyak (drums). *The Carnival Bizarre* was premiered on 8 August 1995 at a location appropriate to its title - the Clink, an ancient dungeon on the banks of the River Thames. It was produced by Kit Woolven (Thin Lizzy/UFO) at Parkgate Studios in Hastings, Sussex, and saw the core duo of Dorrian and Jennings joined by Leo Smee (bass) and Brian Dixon (drums). Subsequent albums, in particular 1999's *Caravan Beyond Redemption*, confirmed their reputation as purveyors of quality doom metal.

● ALBUMS: *Forest Of Equilibrium* (Earache 1991)★★, *The Ethereal Mirror* (Earache 1993)★★★★, *The Carnival Bizarre* (Earache 1995)★★★, *Hopkins (The Witchfinder General)* (Earache 1996)★★★, *Supernatural Birth Machine* (Earache 1996)★★★, *Caravan Beyond Redemption* (Earache 1999)★★★.

● COMPILATIONS: *In Memoriam* (Rise Above 1999)★★.

● VIDEOS: *Our God Has Landed (AD 1990-1999)* (Mosh 1999).

Catherine Wheel

After playing with various local bands, Rob Dickinson (b. 23 July 1965, Norwich, Norfolk, England; vocals) and Brian Futter (b. 7 December 1965, London, England; guitar) instigated the Catherine Wheel in the spring of 1990 by acquiring an eight-track tape machine and embarking on bedroom recording sessions. Joined by the rhythm section of Neil Sims (b. 4 October 1965, Norwich, Norfolk, England; drums) and David Hawes (b. 10 November 1965, Great Yarmouth, Norfolk, England; bass) for live shows, the band had an immediate impact which took them by surprise. Armed with a guitar-propelled sound that was sufficiently fashionable to attract attention without sacrificing creative depth, they released a debut EP, *She's My Friend*, on the Wilde Club label at the start of 1991. This hinted at a potential that warranted certain members of the band forsaking lucrative jobs in the local oil industry in order to concentrate on playing full-time. British tours with such names as Blur and the Charlatans gave the Catherine Wheel an even higher profile, resulting in a major contract with Fontana Records in the summer of the same year. Admirably, they never sought to exploit the family ties between singer Rob Dickinson and cousin Bruce, former Iron Maiden vocalist. Their debut album included the seven-minute 'Black Metallic', a US college radio hit. However, by the end of 1992 the press had turned on what it perceived to be the 'shoegazing' scene, and the Catherine Wheel were also targeted for volleys of abuse despite aural evidence to the contrary. *Chrome* was again produced by Gil Norton and featured cover artwork by Hipgnosis designer Storm Thorgesen (Pink Floyd's *Dark Side Of The Moon*, etc.), but the album failed to revive fortunes in the UK, though their international audience continued to grow. *Happy Days* included a duet with Tanya Donelly (Belly) on 'Judy Staring At The Sun', while the album's uncompromising, bitter aftertaste was summed up by one of its titles, 'Eat My Dust You Insensitive Fuck'. After concentrating on touring America, where they are far more popular than in their homeland, the band returned on a new label with 1997's *Adam And Eve*.

● ALBUMS: *Ferment* (Fontana 1992)★★★, *Chrome* (Fontana 1993)★★★, *Happy Days* (Fontana 1995)★★★, *Like Cats And Dogs* (Mercury 1996)★★★, *Adam And Eve* (Mercury 1997)★★★.

Cave, Nick

b. 22 September 1957, Warracknabeal, Australia. After the Birthday Party disbanded, the enigmatic vocalist Nick Cave retained his association with Berlin by teaming up with ex-Einsturzende Neubauten member Blixa Bargeld (b. 12 January 1959, Berlin, Germany; guitar), together with ex-Magazine personnel Barry Adamson (b. 1 June 1958, Moss Side, Manchester, England; bass/other instruments) and multi-instrumentalist Mick Harvey (b. 29 September 1958, Rochester, Australia), who became the Bad Seeds. The debut, *From Her To Eternity*, was accompanied by a startling rendition of Elvis Presley's 'In the Ghetto', and showed that Cave had lost none of his passion or ability to inject dramatic tension into his music. *The Firstborn Is Dead* followed a year later, promoted by the excellent 'Tupelo', but the Bad Seeds made their mark with *Kicking Against The Pricks* in the summer of 1986, bolstered by the UK Independent number 1, 'The Singer'. Cave had always drawn from a variety of sources, from Captain Beefheart to delta blues, and the Bad Seeds' material betrayed a claustrophobic, swamp-like aura. Although purely cover versions, *Kicking Against The Pricks* (which featured drummer Thomas Wylder) fully displayed his abilities as an original interpreter of other artists' material. The subsequent *Your Funeral, My Trial* emphasized the power of his self-penned compositions, with improved production giving his vocals added clarity. After a brief hiatus from recording, Cave returned with 'The Mercy Seat'. A taut, brooding example of Cave's ability to build a story, followed by the milder 'Oh Deanna', which still contained considerable menace in its lyric. Both elements were present on October 1988's *Tender Prey*, as well as a more melodious approach to both his song constructions and singing voice. 'The Ship Song', released in February 1990, continued Cave's exploration of the more traditional ballad, and was followed by another strong album, *The Good Son*, in April. This accentuated several themes previously explored, notably spirituality and mortality, aided by the introduction of strings. Cave's literary aspirations had already been given an outlet by Black Spring Press in 1989, who published his first novel, *And The Ass Saw The Angel*. He also appeared in the Wim Wenders' film Wings *Of Desire* (1987), following it with a powerful performance as a prison inmate in the Australian production *Ghosts Of The Civil Dead* (1989). Still prolific on the music side, Cave released the comparatively pedestrian *Henry's Dream* in 1992. It was followed by a live collection and contributions to the soundtrack of Wenders' *Faraway, So Close!* The brooding, self-obsessed *Let Love In* was recorded during an increasingly turbulent period in Cave's personal life, but was one of his finest releases. In 1995 Cave (with the Dirty Three) provided a live soundtrack to Carl Dreyer's 1928 silent classic *La Passion De Jeanne d'Arc*, while an unlikely musical coupling with Kylie Minogue on 'Where The Wild Roses Grow' proved to be a commercial success. This in turn spawned *Murder Ballads*, a dark concept album. In 1997 Cave released *The Boatman's Call*, arguably his best. Sounding deeply introspective yet never mundane on this offering, he came over like a cross between Tom Waits and a depressed Leonard Cohen.

● ALBUMS: *From Her To Eternity* (Mute 1984)★★★, *The Firstborn Is*

Dead (Mute 1985)★★★, *Kicking Against The Pricks* (Mute 1986)★★★, *Your Funeral, My Trial* (Mute 1986)★★★, *Tender Prey* (Mute 1988)★★★, with Mick Harvey, Blixa Bargeld *Ghosts Of The Civil Dead* film soundtrack (Mute 1989)★★★, *The Good Son* (Mute 1990)★★★★, *Henry's Dream* (Mute 1992)★★★, *Live Seeds* (Mute 1993)★★★, *Let Love In* (Mute 1994)★★★★, *Murder Ballads* (Mute/Reprise 1996)★★★★, with Harvey, Bargeld *To Have And To Hold* film soundtrack (Mute 1996)★★★, *The Boatman's Call* (Mute 1997)★★★★.
● COMPILATIONS: *The Best Of Nick Cave & The Bad Seeds* (Mute 1998)★★★★.
● VIDEOS: *Kings Of Independence* (Studio 1989), *The Road To God Knows Where* (BMG Video 1990), *Live At The Paradiso* (Mute 1992), *Ritual Habitual* (PolyGram Music Video 1996), *The Videos* (Mute 1998).
● FURTHER READING: *King Ink*, Nick Cave. *And The Ass Saw The Angel*, Nick Cave. *Fish In A Barrel: Nick Cave & The Bad Seeds On Tour*, Peter Milne. *Hellfire: Life According To Nick Cave*, Jeremy Dean. *Bad Seed: The Biography Of Nick Cave*, Ian Johnston. *Nick Cave: The Birthday Party And Other Epic Adventures*, Robert Brokenmouth. *King Ink II*, Nick Cave.

Chaka Demus And Pliers

The list of DJ/singer combinations in reggae is endless. None have been as commercially successful - and deservedly so - as Chaka Demus And Pliers. Chaka Demus (b. John Taylor, 1965, West Kingston, Jamaica, West Indies), the rapping half of the pairing, began his career chatting on a variety of sound systems, the most famous of these being Supreme and Jammy's, as Nicodemus Jnr. In 1985 a name change provoked a shift of fortunes, and Chaka, whose gruff but avuncular tones made him a stand-out in any DJ company, cut his first single, 'Increase Your Knowledge', soon afterwards. A string of 45s bearing his name arrived, 'One Scotch, One Bourbon, One Beer', an adaptation of the old Amos Milburn R&B chestnut, and '2 Foot Walk', among them. However, chiefly associated with Jammy's studio, Chaka's mild manner perhaps held him back in what was then the biggest recording stable in Jamaica. A move to Penthouse Studio for 'Chaka On The Move' (1987) improved matters, and it was here that Chaka first became friendly with Pliers, a singer who, like Chaka, had not yet made the fullest impact on reggae's landscape. Pliers (b. Everton Bonner, 1965, Kingston, Jamaica) first found fame cutting sides with Black Scorpio (Maurice Johnson). Influenced by his brother, Spanner Banner, and fellow tool/tunesmith Pinchers, Pliers cut sides for a variety of labels, among them Pickout, Pioneer Musik ('Murder We Wrote', a song to which he would later return), Jammys, Harry J. and Studio One. Successful though he was, Pliers always seemed to trail in the wake of more celebrated, if faddish, singers such as Wayne Wonder and Sanchez. While playing shows together in Miami in 1991, Chaka and Pliers decided to team up. 'Gal Wine' for Ossie Hibbert was their first 45 together, which led to a slew of reggae chart successes, 'Rough This Year', 'Love Up The Gal', 'Without Love', 'Winning Machine' and 'Worl' A Girls', among them. A collaboration with producers Sly Dunbar and Robbie Shakespeare created a new model of 'Murder She Wrote', which hit number 1 in the specialist charts worldwide. Having evidently developed a successful formula, they secured a contract with the Mango label, Island Records' reggae division, and, in 1993, hit the UK Top 10 with 'Tease Me', a fine, bright ragga-pop record. 'She Don't

Let Nobody', the follow-up, also broke into the pop Top 10, and a version of 'Twist & Shout', with extra vocal support from Jack Radics, became a UK number 1. All these titles were included on the *Tease Me* album. For a long time, it seemed that Chaka and Pliers would not make it as big as their peers - now those same rivals can only gape in amazement and envy.
● ALBUMS: *Gal Wine* (Greensleeves 1992)★★★, *Ruff This Year* (RAS 1992)★★★, *Chaka Demus And Pliers* (Charm 1992)★★★★, *Tease Me* (Mango/Island 1993)★★★★, *For Every Kinda People* (Island 1996)★★★★.
Solo: Chaka Demus *Rough & Rugged* (with Shabba Ranks) (Jammys 1988)★★★, *Everybody Loves The Chaka* (Black Scorpio 1988)★★, with Shabba Ranks *Best Baby Father* (John John/Blue Mountain 1989)★★★, *The Original Chaka* (Witty 1989)★★★. Pliers (with Pinchers) *Pinchers With Pliers* (Black Scorpio 1988)★★★.
● VIDEOS: *Chaka Demus And Pliers* (PolyGram Video 1994), *Tease Me* (Island Video 1994).

Channel Light Vessel

Self-analogized as a 'meeting of like minds' rather than a supergroup, the starting point for UK rock pop band Channel Light Vessel came in 1993 when Roger Eno was introduced to Kate St. John by a mutual friend. St. John had previously played oboe and saxophone for the Ravishing Beauties, Dream Academy and Van Morrison. Eno is best known for his solo work and television and film scores, which include *Mr Wroe's Virgins* (nominated for a BAFTA award) and a succession of advertisements for companies including Guinness. They began writing what would become *The Familiar* together, and met Be Bop Deluxe founder and solo artist Bill Nelson while searching for a producer. The trio toured Japan in 1994 where their set was opened by US instrumentalist Laraaji, who thereafter joined the band along with cellist Mayumi Tachibana. This collaboration led to the announcement of a second album, *Automatic*, a sumptuous interchange of musical ideas which caused *Billboard* magazine to note that it was 'a record so lovely and transporting it's painful to have it end.' However, thereafter each member returned to their solo commitments, which resulted in four solo or collaborative albums in 1995. Tachibana was unable to join the reconstituted band in 1996, where other musicians such as Ian Freese joined the core group. *Excellent Spirits* was recorded in the north of England and the album's contents were conversely more upbeat and rhythmic than had been the case with previous releases. Once again, reviews were overwhelmingly positive.
● ALBUMS: *The Familiar* (All Saints 1993)★★★, *Automatic* (All Saints 1995)★★★★, *Excellent Spirits* (All Saints 1996)★★★★.

Chapterhouse

Formed in Reading, England in 1987 by Andrew Sherriff (b. 5 May 1969, Wokingham, England; guitar/vocals), Stephen Patman (b. 8 November 1968, Windsor, Berkshire, England; guitar), Simon Rowe (b. 23 June 1969, Reading, Berkshire, England; guitar), Jon Curtis (bass) and Ashley Bates (b. 2 November 1971, Reading, Berkshire, England; drums), Chapterhouse took the unusual step of rehearsing and gigging for well over a year before recording even a demo tape. They were initially lumped in with the British acid rock scene of the time, a mistake hardly rectified by the band's early performances supporting Spacemen 3. Chapterhouse eventually escaped from one genre only to find themselves thrust among the infamous 'shoegazer' bands of 1991 (with Lush, Moose and Slowdive), so called because of their static live shows and insular, effects pedal-driven music. Bass player Jon Curtis left early on to study, being replaced by Russell Barrett (b. 7 November 1968, Vermont, USA), who also fronted his own garage band, the Bikinis. Chapterhouse eventually signed to the newly formed Dedicated Records label, releasing the *Freefall* EP and a series of lavishly acclaimed singles, including 'Pearl', which reached the UK Top 70 in March 1991. By the autumn of 1991, the band were aiming their sights on the US market, but they were to make little headway. Back home in Britain, too, the press were now reluctant to embrace them, with the 'shoegazing' scene becoming the target of the traditional backlash. Bates had already left the band after the release of *Whirlpool*, with his place taken by drum machines. Reviews for *Blood Music* were lukewarm at best, and the band themselves were reluctant to promote the album. They split-up shortly afterwards, with Rowe joining Mojave 3 and the other members becoming involved with various dance music projects.

● ALBUMS: *Whirlpool* (Dedicated 1991)★★★, *Blood Music* (Dedicated 1993)★★.

Charlatans

Of all the 'Madchester' bands to emerge in the late 80s, the Charlatans' rise was undoubtedly the swiftest. Tim Burgess (b. 30 May 1968, Salford, Manchester, England; lead vocals, ex-Electric Crayons), Martin Blunt (bass, ex-Makin' Time), Jon Baker (guitar), Jon Brookes (drums) and Rob Collins (b. 23 February 1963, Sedgeley, England, d. 22 July 1996; keyboards) fused 60s melodies, Hammond organ riffs and a generally loose feel that was instantly adopted by those taken with the Stone Roses and the Happy Mondays. The band's stage presentation was boosted by the recruitment of veteran Californian lighting director 'Captain Whizzo', who provided the psychedelic visuals. With all the optimism that accompanies a new decade, February 1990's 'Indian Rope', a 12-inch-only debut on their own Dead Dead Good Records, sold well enough to secure a contract with Beggars Banquet Records/Situation 2. That proved a stepping stone to 'The Only One I Know', a swirling, grooved pop song that borrowed from the Byrds and Booker T. And The MGs, and provided the perfect summer anthem. A UK number 9 hit in June, the single catapulted the Charlatans into the mainstream, and was consolidated by the follow-up, 'Then' (number 12, September), and the band's debut album. With the delightful compositions that made up the UK chart-topping *Some Friendly*, the band ended the year on a high note. The following year proved far quieter, although a fourth single and a further hit, 'Over Rising' (number 15, March), steered away from the previous organ-based approach. However, 1992 brought major problems. Bass player Martin Blunt suffered a nervous breakdown, guitarist Baker departed (to be replaced by Mark Collins), their follow-up album *Between 10th And 11th* disappointed and lead-off single 'Weirdo' stalled at number 19 in March. Most bizarre of all, keyboard player Rob Collins was jailed for being an accessory to an armed robbery at a Northwich off-licence. *Up To Our Hips*, recorded in Rob Collins' absence with Steve Hillage as producer, repaired some of the damage. Confident

songs such as 'Can't Get Out Of Bed' (number 24, February 1994) and 'Autograph', plus a strong fanbase, kept the Charlatans intact after the UK press had turned on them. Despite *Up To Our Hips*' good reviews, the Charlatans were still widely perceived to be yesterday's men. In spite of this perception, and a career dogged by misfortune and adverse criticism, their revival in both the singles and albums charts continued, with 'Just When You're Thinkin' Things Over' reaching number 12 in August 1995, and their fourth, self-titled album debuting at the top of the album charts. Tragedy struck in July 1996 when Collins was killed when his car overturned while returning from a local public house to the recording studio at Rockfield Studio in South Wales. Martin Duffy of Primal Scream was drafted in to help out as a temporary replacement (a band that has used the Hammond organ as a lead instrument must replicate the sound or drastically change direction). They played a major gig at Knebworth a month later, and climbed to number 3 in the UK charts in September with 'One To Another', before resuming work on their half-completed new album. However, just as tragedy spurred the Manic Street Preachers to produce their finest album (*Everything Must Go*), so too it inspired the Charlatans with the swirling, glorious *Tellin' Stories* in 1997. The *Melting Pot* compilation was the band's final album for Beggars Banquet. New keyboard player Tony Rogers debuted on *Us And Us Only*, their bold debut for Universal Records, which was premiered by the epic single 'Forever', a UK number 12 hit in October 1999.

● ALBUMS: *Some Friendly* (Situation 2 1990)★★★, *Between 10th And 11th* (Situation 2 1992)★★, *Up To Our Hips* (Beggars Banquet 1994)★★★, *Charlatans* (Beggars Banquet 1995)★★★, *Tellin' Stories* (Beggars Banquet 1997)★★★★, *Us And Us Only* (Universal 1999)★★★★.

● COMPILATIONS: *Melting Pot* (Beggars Banquet 1997)★★★★.

● FURTHER READING: *The Charlatans: The Authorised History*, Dominic Wills And Tom Sheehan.

Charles And Eddie

This soul duo consisting of Charles Pettigrew and Eddie Chacon met on a New York subway train. Apparently, Chacon was clutching a copy of Marvin Gaye's *Trouble Man*, and so the two of them struck up a conversation and later started performing together. Chacon had grown up in Oakland, California, where he was in a soul band, and later moved to Miami, Florida, where his recording career continued on projects with the Dust Brothers and Daddy-O. Daddy-O produced Chacon's two solo albums, both of which left him feeling frustrated and determined to return to the soul music he had known in his youth. Pettigrew, meanwhile, was raised in Philadelphia, and went on to study jazz vocals at the Berklee College Of Music in Boston, while also singing with the pop band Down Avenue. Charles and Eddie enjoyed a worldwide hit in 1992 with 'Would I Lie To You?', which was followed in early 1993 with 'NYC (Can You Believe This City)', based on the story of their meeting. Both tracks were on their debut *Duophonic*, which was produced by Josh Deutsch and consisted mainly of original material, notably Chacon's 'December 2', a tribute to his brother's death on that date. *Chocolate Milk* was a bland collection, and after its release the duo split-up to work on solo projects.

● ALBUMS: *Duophonic* (Stateside/Capitol 1992)★★★, *Chocolate Milk* (Capitol 1995)★★.

Cheeks, Judy

b. Florida, Miami, USA. Of mixed black American and Cherokee ancestry, Cheeks is the daughter of gospel singer Rev. Julius Cheeks, cited by James Brown, Otis Redding and others as a pivotal influence in the development of black music. She grew up in Miami where her godfather was Sam Cooke, who once plucked her from the front row of a 6,000 audience and sang the rest of the set to her while cradling her in his arms. Before her solo career began in earnest her voice had been employed by Tina Turner, Betty Wright, Leon Ware, Georgio Moroder and Harold Faltermeyer, and she has long been a close friend of Stevie Wonder. Indeed, her recording career stretches back to the mid-70s, when she recorded a debut album with Ike and Tina Turner. She subsequently moved to Europe and Ariola Records, her first record for whom, 'Mellow Lovin', was an international success. After she had traversed the language barrier, she became a major German star, appearing in several movies and hosting a television game show with a hamster called Willie. She came to England in 1987, though an album for Polydor Records was never released outside of mainland Europe. Her career lapsed until she finally began recording demos again in the 90s. There was interest from the PWL stable, but she eventually chose Positiva Records, a contract cemented by the release of 'So In Love', written by China Burton. Remixes from Frankie Foncett and Sasha added greatly to the cult status of this minor garage classic. The follow-up, 'Reach', capitalized on this and her tours of select dance venues, and this time employed the Brothers In Rhythm production team. She subsequently worked with Nigel Lowis (producer of Eternal and Dina Carroll) on tracks for her first Positiva album.

● ALBUMS: *Judy Cheeks* (United Artists 1973)★★, *Mellow Lovin'* (Salsoul 1978)★★, *No Outsiders* (Polydor 1988)★★★, *Respect* (Positiva 1996)★★★.

Chemical Brothers

Tom Rowlands (b. Henley-on-Thames, Oxfordshire, England) and Edward Simons (b. Dulwich, London, England) met while studying at Manchester University in the late 80s. Rowlands became a member of the Balearic group Ariel, which put out a number of releases on Deconstruction Records. At the same time the pair found a common interest in acid house, techno and hip-hop and began DJing at house parties, calling themselves the Dust Brothers after the west coast hip-hop producers. They subsequently played at a club called 'Naked Under Leather' and began writing their own material to use. One track, 'Song To The Siren', was picked up by Junior Boy's Own Records and released early in 1993. The pair were consequently invited to remix Lionrock's 'Packet Of Peace' and tracks by various other artists, including Leftfield/John Lydon, Republica and the Sandals. The next year the Dust Brothers released the EPs *14th Century Sky*, which became well-known for the track 'Chemical Beats', and *My Mercury Mouth*. Following the success of these records and the Sunday Social, a club that they ran in London in conjunction with Heavenly Records, they signed to Virgin Records in early 1995 as the Chemical Brothers, after the threat of legal action from the original Dust Brothers. Their first releases included the single 'Leave Home' and the album *Exit Planet Dust* on their own subsidiary, Freestyle Dust. As well as their trademark sound of guitars, heavy breakbeats and analogue noise, the album surprisingly included vocals from the Charlatans' Tim Burgess ('Life Is Sweet') and Beth Orton ('Alive: Alone'). During 1995 the duo promoted the album with successful performances at many rock and dance music festivals throughout the UK and Europe and also toured America alongside Orbital and Underworld. A live mix album appeared alongside remixes for Dave Clarke, the Manic Street Preachers and Method Man. In the autumn of 1996, the pair released 'Setting Sun', which featured lead vocals by Oasis' Noel Gallagher, and became their first number 1 single. The Chemical Brothers' huge popularity was confirmed with the release of their second album, *Dig Your Own Hole*, which also received critical acclaim, being nominated for Mercury and BRIT Awards in the UK, while the number 1 single 'Block Rockin' Beats' won a Grammy for Best Rock Instrumental. The Chemical Brothers' big beat music became the crossover success of the year, appealing to rock and dance fans in equal measure. Remix work for Spiritualized, Mercury Rev and the original Dust Brothers followed in 1998, as well as another mix album. They returned to the UK pop charts in June 1999 with the number 3 single, 'Hey Boy Hey Girl', and the chart-topping *Surrender*. The album featured guest vocal turns from New Order's Bernard Sumner, Primal Scream's Bobby Gillespie and Mazzy Star's Hope Sandoval.

● ALBUMS: *Exit Planet Dust* (Junior Boy's Own 1995)★★★★, *Dig Your Own Hole* (Freestyle Dust 1997)★★★★, *Surrender* (Freestyle Dust 1999)★★★★.

● COMPILATIONS: *Live At The Social: Volume One* (Heavenly 1996)★★★★, *Brothers Gonna Work It Out* (Freestyle Dust 1998)★★★.

Cherry Poppin' Daddies

This Eugene, Oregon, USA eight-piece were formed by vocalist and songwriter Steve Perry in 1989, after the one-time punk rocker had grown tired of the grunge sound overcoming north-western USA. The Cherry Poppin' Daddies certainly offered a departure from musical norms of the period. 'My mother had bought me *The Smithsonian Collection Of Classic Jazz*. I got it for my birthday early in life, and I listened to it all the time . . . around the late 80s I had the idea – what if I fused punk and swing? What would that sound like? 'Cos I didn't want to do what everybody else was doing.' He managed to recruit similar-minded musicians around him, but attracting an audience would take much more effort. They eventually rose to prominence during California's late 90s fascination with all things ska. In truth, the band's sound owed more to jive and swing than punk and rocksteady, but it was a heady brew, nevertheless, best sampled on the single 'Zoot Suit Riot'. A minor hit in 1998, it also served as the title track to the band's debut album for Mojo Records, which entered the *Billboard* album chart at number 17 in August. The song was inspired by the renowned 1943 incident when white servicemen entered Los Angeles' ghettos in mobs to attack Hispanics. Cherry Poppin' Daddies had released three independent albums between 1990 and 1995 on their own Space Age Bachelor Pad Records prior to this.

● ALBUMS: *Ferociously Stoned* (Space Age Bachelor Pad 1994)★★★, *Rapid City Muscle Car* (Space Age Bachelor Pad 1994)★★★, *Kids On The Street* (Space Age Bachelor Pad 1996)★★★, *Zoot Suit Riot* (Mojo/Universal 1998)★★★.

Cherry, Eagle-Eye

b. 7 May 1969, Stockholm, Sweden. Cherry is the son of legendary jazz trumpeter Don Cherry and the brother of Neneh Cherry. Born in Sweden, Eagle-Eye was so named because when he was born he looked at his father with one eye. Cherry moved to New York in 1984, and graduated to playing drums in several teenage bands. His early career, however, was directed towards acting. He attended the New York School of Performing Arts with future *Friends* star Jennifer Aniston, and appeared in off-Broadway theatre productions and several television pilots. A slot presenting the critically derided UK television show *Big World Café* followed a small part in *The Cosby Show*. Cherry relocated to Sweden with his actress girlfriend in 1996 following his father's death, and began concentrating on writing songs. His debut album was recorded in Stockholm and released on the local Diesel label. Two chart-topping Swedish singles were taken from the album, which went on to register platinum sales and won four Swedish Grammi Awards. *Desireless*' mixture of loose funky rhythms and highly catchy folk/pop melodies proved ideal for crossover success on the international market. 'Save Tonight' debuted at UK number 6 in June 1998, staying in the Top 10 for six weeks, while 'Falling In Love Again' reached number 8 in November 1998. *Desireless* debuted at number 3 in the UK album chart in August, and went platinum in several countries. 'Save Tonight' climbed to a peak position of number 5 in the US in January 1999.

● ALBUMS: *Desireless* (Diesel/Polydor/Work 1997)★★★.

Cherry, Neneh

b. Neneh Mariann Karlsson, 10 March 1964, Stockholm, Sweden. Cherry is the step-daughter of jazz trumpeter Don Cherry. She joined English post-punk band Rip, Rig And Panic in 1981 as a vocalist, later performing with several ex-members of that band as Float Up CP. In the mid-80s she also sang backing vocals for the Slits and The The ('Slow Train To Dawn', 1987). In 1989, Cherry recorded a series of dance tracks for Circa, including the international hit single 'Buffalo Stance' (which was featured on the soundtrack of the movie *Slaves Of New York*), 'Manchild' and 'Kisses On The Wind'. Her main co-writer was husband Cameron McVey. Her debut *Raw Like Sushi*'s eclectic blend of hip-hop rhythms and pop melodies earned Cherry excellent reviews and sizeable sales figures. In 1990, Cherry contributed to the AIDS-charity collection, *Red Hot And Blue*, singing Cole Porter's 'I've Got You Under My Skin', but was quiet again until the release of *Homebrew* in 1992. A noticeably mellower album, it featured production and writing collaborations with a pre-Portishead Geoff Barrow and cameo appearances by Gang Starr and Michael Stipe. Cherry reasserted herself as a commercial force in 1994 with the international hit single 'Seven Seconds', which saw her collaborating with African superstar Youssou N'Dour. In March 1995, in the company of Chrissie Hynde, Cher and Eric Clapton, she topped the UK charts with the charity single 'Love Can Build A Bridge'. Family commitments meant another lengthy recording hiatus before she released *Man* in 1996.

● ALBUMS: *Raw Like Sushi* (Circa 1989)★★★★, *Homebrew* (Virgin 1992)★★★, *Man* (Hut 1996)★★★.

● VIDEOS: *The Rise Of Neneh Cherry* (BMG Video 1989).

Chesney, Kenny

b. USA. A country singer-songwriter specializing in heartfelt ballads, Kenny Chesney has earned a reputation as a genial and hard-working traditional artist. In 1994, he made his debut for Capricorn Records with a self-titled collection that established him as a competent writer, though one lacking the unique qualities needed to make a bigger impression on the marketplace. Both *All I Need To Know* and *Me And You*, his two subsequent albums for BNA Records in the mid-90s, revealed steady progression, with the title track of the latter album performing well on country radio. He accompanied its release with a major nationwide tour in support of country rock veterans Alabama, and since then, his following has continued to build. George Jones and Tracy Lawrence joined Chesney on 'From Hillbilly Heaven To Honky Tonk Hell', the best track on 1997's *I Will Stand*.

● ALBUMS: *Kenny Chesney* (Capricorn 1994)★★, *All I Need To Know* (BNA 1995)★★★, *Me And You* (BNA 1996)★★★, *I Will Stand* (BNA 1997)★★★★, *Everywhere We Go* (BNA 1999)★★★.

Chesnutt, Mark

b. 6 September 1963, Beaumont, Texas, USA. His father, Bob Chesnutt, was a singer who, although failing to find success in Nashville in the mid-60s, was popular in Texas; however, he quit music in favour of the used-car business, because he wanted to be with his family. It is, therefore, not surprising to find that, with strong parental encouragement, Mark followed in his father's footsteps (Bob died in 1990, just before his son achieved the success that had eluded him in his career). Impressed by George Jones (who also grew up in Beaumont), Chesnutt learned to play guitar and drums, and as a 15-year-old was singing in Texas clubs. He later formed his own band and worked all over Texas. He first recorded for Axbar and other independent labels until, in 1990, his recording of 'Too Cold At Home' gained him a contract with MCA. Written by Bobby Harden, the song (which, apparently, George Jones had turned down) became a number 3 country chart hit. Chesnutt moved to Nashville and before the year was out, he gained his first number 1 with 'Brother Jukebox'. During the next three years, he charted regularly, enjoying further number 1s with 'I'll Think Of Something', 'It Sure Is Monday' and 'Almost Goodbye'. He recorded a duet, 'Talking To Hank', with George Jones, which appeared on his second album. Since his father's death, Chesnutt has become great friends with Jones and, on occasions, worked with his idol on tours. He appears on the video *George Jones - Live In Tennessee*. He was honoured with the Country Music Association's Horizon Award in 1993. In 1994, he added a further number 1 with 'I Just Wanted You To Know', and a Top 10 hit with 'She Dreams'. When the Decca Records label was re-formed, he was one of the biggest names to sign with it, and early in 1995 he proved his point with 'Goin' Through The Big D'. He has since released consistently strong albums for the label, *Thank God For Believers* reuniting him with Mark Wright, producer of his first four albums. *I Don't Want To Miss A Thing* featured a surprisingly credible cover version of the Aerosmith title track (written by Diane Warren), which topped the country charts and climbed to number 17 on the *Billboard* Hot 100 in February 1999.

● ALBUMS: *Too Cold At Home* (MCA 1990)★★, *Longnecks And Short Stories* (MCA 1992)★★★, *Almost Goodbye* (MCA 1993)★★★★, *What A Way To Live* (Decca 1994)★★★★, *Wings* (Decca 1995)★★★, *Thank*

God For Believers (Decca 1997)★★★, *I Don't Want To Miss A Thing* (Decca 1999)★★★★.
● COMPILATIONS: *Mark Chesnutt's Greatest Hits* (Decca 1996)★★★★.
● VIDEOS: *Almost Goodbye* (1993), *Gonna Get A Life* (1995).

Chesnutt, Vic

b. 1965, Athens, Georgia, USA. Chesnutt was playing keyboards in local band the La De Das when a 1983 car smash left him paraplegic. Switching to guitar, he evolved a curious but compelling style, writing aching stream-of-consciousness lullabies, suggestive of a super-distilled essence of Neil Young at his most despairing. Despite a heavy drinking schedule, he held down a residency at Athens' 40 Watt Club until R.E.M.'s Michael Stipe recognized his unique gifts and produced his ragged first album, *Little*, in one afternoon at a cost of $100. Stipe returned to spend three whole days on the second album, *West Of Rome*, while the Stipe-free third, *Drunk*, was recorded in 'a room with candles for that mood thang'. Chesnutt had perfected his *métier* over a weekly residency at the 40 Watt Club, honing his simple stories of 'bars and boozing', conducted in a musical fashion that encompassed both country and folk, while the lyrics had more in common with the attitudinal qualities of punk. Performing live from his wheelchair, he could mesmerize an audience even while forgetting his own lyrics. In 1993, director Peter Sillen completed the engrossing documentary feature *Speed Racer: Welcome To The World Of Vic Chesnutt*. By mid-1994, Chesnutt seemed to have developed a measure of stability and independence, his songs taking on more shape and coherence. His fourth album, *Is The Actor Happy?*, this time featured Stipe singing on 'Guilty By Association', Chesnutt attributing Stipe's influence as inspirational: 'I would never have made a record without him. I'm just too darned lazy.' On this album he was backed by the Scared Skiffle Band, who include his wife Tina as well as Jimmy Davidson and Alex McManus. His self-deprecating image and powerful songwriting would even see Chesnutt immortalized in a song, 'Vic', recorded by UK indie band Animals That Swim. In 1995, he also announced plans to write his first novel, and collaborated with Athens rock band Widespread Panic on the Brute project. In 1996, *Sweet Relief II: Gravity Of The Situation* was released. This tribute album featuring Chesnutt's songs demonstrated the high standing he holds with fellow artists. The glitterati included Smashing Pumpkins, R.E.M., Live, Madonna and Hootie And The Blowfish, and proceeds went to the Sweet Relief Musicians Fund. Chesnutt made his major label debut on Capitol Records with *About To Choke*, featuring a more accessible sound but with his usual uncompromising lyrics. On *The Salesman And Bernadette* Chesnutt was backed by Kurt Wagner's maverick big band Lambchop, marking a striking change from the acoustic simplicity of his previous albums.
● ALBUMS: *Little* (Texas Hotel 1990)★★★, *West Of Rome* (Texas Hotel 1992)★★★★, *Drunk* (Texas Hotel 1994)★★★★, *Is The Actor Happy?* (Texas Hotel 1995)★★★, with Widespread Panic *Brute: Nine High A Pallet* (Capricorn 1995)★★, *About To Choke* (Capitol 1996)★★★, *The Salesman And Bernadette* (Pinnacle 1998)★★★.
● COMPILATIONS: various artists *Sweet Relief II: Gravity Of The Situation: The Songs Of Vic Chesnutt* (Columbia 1996)★★.
● VIDEOS: *Speed Racer: Welcome To The World Of Vic Chesnutt* (1993).

Chicane

Chicane is the recording name used by Nick Bracegirdle. As Chicane, his reputation has been established on the strength of several lush, melodic singles, particularly 'Offshore', 'Sunstroke', 'Strong In Love' and 'Saltwater' on Alex Gold's Xtravaganza Recordings. As Disco Citizens, he has performed numerous remixes for high-profile artists such as BT, Everything But The Girl, B*Witched and Bryan Adams. Bracegirdle was initially inspired by electronic music when he heard Jean-Michel Jarre's 'Oxygene' at the age of 11 or 12. Already studying classical guitar and piano, he saved his money to buy some cheap analogue synthesisers. Meanwhile, he pursued a career in graphic design, even having his own design company at one point. It was 'Anthem' by N-Joi however, that really prompted Bracegirdle's change of career direction. He was excited by the track's melody and chord changes combined with a dancefloor-friendly bass and rhythm section. With a friend, he recorded and released a 'white label' single called 'Right Here, Right Now', sampling the same track by the Fatback Band that Fatboy Slim later used on his hit of the same name. The track provoked a great deal of A&R interest and they eventually signed to Deconstruction Records. As Disco Citizens, the duo saw the single reach number 40 in the UK in July 1995. Later, Bracegirdle established his own label, Modena, and released an EP that included 'Offshore'. The track was not only a huge dancefloor hit, especially in Ibiza, where its ambient, feel-good textures were entirely appropriate, but also crossed over into the UK Top 20 in December 1996. It has also been heavily used as incidental music on BBC television programmes such as *Grandstand*. Since then, Chicane has released several well-received and commercially successful singles and the debut album, *Far From The Maddening Crowd*. In May 1999, Bracegirdle teamed up with Maire Brennan of Clannad to re-record the vocals of the theme from *Harry's Game* (originally recorded in 1982) for a trance reworking of the track that became a massive club hit and entered the UK Top 20. The track's success consolidated Chicane's growing reputation for consistently good commercial dance music and kept the requests for remixes arriving at Bracegirdle's door.
● ALBUMS: *Far From The Maddening Crowd* (Xtravaganza 1998)★★★★.

Childs, Toni

b. Orange County, Los Angeles, California, USA. Childs endured a migratory youth that took her across many state borders within North America, as well as a spell of four years in London, England. There she signed a publishing contract with Island Records. Returning to Los Angeles, she worked with David Ricketts (of David And David), eventually collaborating on the soundtrack to 1986's *Echo Park*. Reflecting her diverse past, her debut, *Union*, was recorded in several locations, including London, Paris, Los Angeles and Africa and featured the music of Zimbabwe, as well as more conventional singer-songwriter touches. Reaching number 67 in the *Billboard* charts, it earned her a Grammy nomination for Best Female Rock Vocal and a support slot on tour with Bob Dylan. The best of the material, notably the single, 'Don't Walk Away', blended dense, dreamlike imagery with Childs' rugged alto delivery to sparkling effect. In the wake of this breakthrough, *House Of Hope* proved something of a commercial disappointment, though once again it boasted precise and passionate songwriting. For *The Woman's Boat* Childs moved to Peter Gabriel's Real World Studios. The music traced its heritage to the Indian subcontinent (where Childs had travelled widely during the break between albums), with guests including Robert Fripp and Kurt Wallinger (World Party) as well as Gabriel himself. Of its title and orientation Childs would say: 'Women have sat in a certain circle of society and had a certain demeanour, said very few words, not rocked the boat - and yet what has been hidden underneath has been this incredible amount of talent and specialness that is the female spirit.' Naturally such a statement could have been pure hokum, but critics were not lining up to argue with Childs' obvious sincerity channelled, as it was, through such a devastating voice.

● ALBUMS: *Union* (A&M 1988)★★★★, *House Of Hope* (A&M 1991)★★, *The Woman's Boat* (A&M 1994)★★.

● COMPILATIONS: *The Very Best Of Toni Childs* (A&M 1996)★★★★.

Chimes

UK soul/dance trio originating in Edinburgh, Scotland, in 1981, when they were initially put together by Mike Pedan (keyboards/bass) and the much-travelled James Locke (keyboards/drums). The pair had met when they were backing former Parliament keyboard player Bernie Worrell at a local club. Deciding to form their own group, they set about writing material and auditioning female singers, eventually choosing Pauline Henry in 1987. With the duo's desperation mounting, her successful audition was held over the telephone, after which she was flown up from London for sessions. After signing to CBS Records in 1988 they finally released their debut single a year later. '1-2-3' was produced by Jazzie B. (from Soul II Soul), a band to whom the Chimes were frequently compared. Their biggest UK breakthrough came in 1990 when they covered U2's 'I Still Haven't Found What I'm Looking For'. Apparently approved by Bono, the cover version was chosen when the band heard Henry singing it in the studio. Aided by an appearance on the mainstream television show *Wogan*, it eventually went Top 5 in both the UK and USA. The boys also contributed to old friend Paul Haig's solo album during 1990, and produced several other artists. Subsequent minor hits included 'True Love' and 'Love Comes To Mind', before Henry left for a solo career midway through sessions for a second album.

● ALBUMS: *The Chimes* (Columbia 1990)★★★.

China Black

China Black is the collective title given to Simon Fung (b. Hong Kong, China) and Errol Reid (b. Montego Bay, Jamaica, West Indies). Reid emigrated to the UK with his parents, settling in Birmingham. He began singing at an early age being influenced by soul artists including Luther Vandross, Freddie Jackson and Teddy Pendergrass. He entered and won numerous talent competitions, which led to him serving his musical apprenticeship on the sound system circuit. Reid recorded a number of solo outings that, having garnered airplay on local radio stations, led to him re-establishing his career in London. Fung was also living in London at the time and had graduated into production work, working with the Fredericks, Cornell McKoy and jazz guitarist Ronny Jordan. It was Jordan who introduced Fung and Reid in 1990, a meeting that led to the formation of China

Black. The duo first recorded in the soul style, including their celebrated opus 'Searching'. In 1992, the song was released as a lovers rock tune, which signalled the return of the Big One label to the reggae charts after an eight-year absence, with Longsy D co-producing. 'Searching' topped the reggae chart, maintaining a high profile for three months. In 1994, the ballad was licensed to Wildcard, which led to a crossover hit in the UK Top 10 when remixed by ex-Steel Pulse, Headline and Reggae Philharmonic Orchestra performer Mykaell S. Riley. The duo followed the hit with 'Stars' and, in 1995, 'Almost See You (Somewhere)', neither of which was able to repeat the success of their debut in spite of the latter's Steely And Clevie remix. Their fourth release, 'Don't Throw It All Away', proved a club anthem with remixes by Rokstone and the Beatmasters. The duo maintained a high profile on the performance circuit, including an appearance at the Anti Racist Alliance Festival playing to an audience in excess of 50,000. In 1997, the duo recorded a version of the spiritual 'Swing Low Sweet Chariot', to promote the Five Nations rugby tournament, accompanied by the England Rugby Squad.

● ALBUMS: *Born* (Wildcard 1994)★★★.

Chubb Rock

b. Richard Simpson, 28 May 1968, Jamaica, West Indies. The cousin of Hitman Howie Tee, with whom he collaborated at the beginning of his career, Simpson moved to New York at an early age. A rap colossus, his ample frame and smooth style has seen him compared with Barry White. He started his own band in New York, but after dropping out of medical college elected to set out on a solo career. The first results of this were a debut album that sank without trace. A remixed version of 'Caught Up' secured the public's interest, however, and introduced them to *And The Winner Is ...*, on which humour and reflections on urban violence sat side by side. By the dawn of the 90s interest in Rock had escalated to the point at which he was achieving regular *Billboard* hits with singles such as 'Treat 'Em Right', 'Ya Bad Chubbs' and 'Just The Two Of Us', but he fell from commercial grace following the release of *The One*. Rock remained quiet for several years, although in the interim his production team the Trackmasterz rose to prominence in hip-hop circles. *The Mind* was his 1997 comeback, but despite the rapper gaining critical respect for his endearing lyrical style the album's sound was too old school to make much of an impact.

● ALBUMS: with Howie Tee *Featuring Hitman Howie Tee* (Select 1988)★★★, with Tee *And The Winner Is ...* (Select 1989)★★★★, *Treat 'Em Right* mini-album (Select 1991)★★★, *The One* (Select 1991)★★★★, *I Gotta Get Mine Yo! - Book Of Rhymes* (Select 1992)★★★, *The Mind* (Select 1997)★★★.

Chuck D.

b. Carlton Douglas Ridenhour, 1 August 1960, Roosevelt, Long Island, New York City, USA. As the principal lyricist of Public Enemy, Chuck D. can lay claim to having written some of the highest-impact lines in the history of rock 'n' roll. However, as that group's vitality decreased, by the mid-90s a Chuck D. solo album seemed an obvious next step for the artist. *Autobiography Of Mistachuck* reinforced his credentials as rap music's most eloquent commentator. As he stressed on 'Free Big Willie': 'There once was a time we fought the power with a rhyme, Now the attitude goin' round, no use tryin'.' In fact, much of the album offered a critique on the rise of gangsta rap, its glamorization of violence and misogyny, and the rise of the car and clothes as consumer status symbols. One of the most effective tracks was 'But Can You Kill The Nigger In You?', a collaboration with Isaac Hayes that asked pertinent questions about the end result for those who invest in their own mythology rather than their own community. A further track, 'Horizontal Heroin', featured Professor Griff, the controversial former member of Public Enemy who left the group in 1989 after making allegedly anti-Semitic comments to the *Washington Times*. Media work and a book followed before Chuck D. rejoined the original line-up of Public Enemy to provide the soundtrack for Spike Lee's *He Got Game*. The singer subsequently crossed swords with Def Jam Records when he posted new Public Enemy material on the Internet, including the single 'Swindler's Lust', a blatant attack on the music industry. The group then signed up with an Internet record company, Atomic Pop, and became the first mainstream artists to release an album online.

● ALBUMS: *Autobiography Of Mistachuck* (Mercury 1996)★★★.
● FURTHER READING: *Fight The Power - Rap, Race And Reality*, Chuck D. with Yusuf Jah.
● FILMS: *Burn Hollywood Burn* (1997).

Chumbawamba

The multi-member Chumbawamba, whose line-up includes Harry Hamer, Alice Nutter, Boff, Mavis Dillon, Louise Mary Watts, Danbert Nobacon, Paul Greco and Dunstan Bruce, was originally an anarchist outfit formed in Leeds, England, out of a household situated in the shadow of Armley jail. In a similar manner to Crass, who were an obvious early influence, the band dynamic was powered by their communal life. First playing live in 1983, the band, whose regional origins are in Burnley and Bradford, alternated between instruments and theatricals on stage and record. Their first single, 'Revolution', was startling, opening with the sound of John Lennon's 'Imagine', before having it removed from the stereo and smashed. It was just as precise lyrically: 'The history books from every age, Have the same words written on every page, Always starting with revolution, Always ending with capitulation, Always silenced by the truncheon, or bought out with concessions, Always repetition...'. It was a powerful introduction, finishing at number 6 in disc jockey John Peel's 1985 Festive 50 radio poll. The follow-up, 'We Are The World', was banned from airplay due to its explicit support of direct action. *Pictures of Starving Children Sell Records* used polemic and agit-prop to subvert a common theme in the music industry at that time, denouncing the self-indulgence of Band Aid. Other targets included multinationals (the band had published a booklet on immoral activities titled *Dirty Fingers In Dirty Pies*), apartheid and imperialism. Their discourse was made all the more articulate by the surprising virtuosity of musics employed, from polka to ballad to thrash. Pouring red paint over the Clash on their comeback 'busking' tour in Leeds demonstrated their contempt for what they saw as false prophets, while the second album considered the role of government in oppression and the futility of the vote. *English Rebel Songs* acknowledged their place in the folk protest movement, and *Slap!* saw hope in the rebellious dance music that characterized the end of the 80s. By this time the band had somewhat abandoned

their previous austerity - now Danbert and Alice were all-singing, all-dancing compères to a live show that celebrated resistance and deviance rather than complaining about 'the system'. *Anarchy!*, somewhat ironically titled in view of new perceptions of the band, dismissed the blind-alley myopia of the punk set ('Give The Anarchist A Cigarette'), while still railing against intolerance ('Homophobia' gave a musical backdrop to a true story of a gay slaying in Bradford). Chumbawamba may no longer share the same living space, or even the same ideas, but they are as powerful and attractive a force in the underbelly of the British music scene as ever. They are humorous, politically correct and genuine - all the ingredients for a doomed cult band. However, this fate may have been reversed by the surprise success of 'Tubthumping', their ode to alcohol, which only narrowly missed reaching number 1 in the UK in 1997, and also made the US Top 10. The following album (on major record label EMI Records) was much slicker than past efforts, yet beneath the often lush melody lay a strong bite in the lyric; particularly noteworthy were 'The Good Ship Lifestyle', 'Drip Drip Drip' and 'Mary Mary'.

● ALBUMS: *Pictures Of Starving Children Sell Records* (Agit Prop 1986)★★★★, *Never Mind The Ballots, Here's The Rest Of Your Life* (Agit Prop 1987)★★★★, *English Rebel Songs 1381-1914* mini-album (Agit Prop 1989)★★★, *Slap!* (Agit Prop 1990)★★★, *Anarchy* (One Little Indian 1994)★★★, *Show business! Chumbawamba Live* (One Little Indian 1995)★★, *Swingin' With Raymond* (One Little Indian 1996)★★★, *Tubthumper* (EMI 1997)★★★★.
● COMPILATIONS: *First 2* (Agit Prop 1993)★★★★, *Uneasy Listening* (EMI 1999)★★★.

Cibo Matto

This highly original New York, USA-based band were formed by Japanese expatriates Miho Hatori (vocals) and Yuka Honda (keyboards). Honda had gone to New York in the mid-80s, playing with several experimental groups including Brooklyn Funk Essential. Hatori, who arrived in the USA in the early 90s, had originally sung in the Tokyo-based hip-hop band Kimidori. The two women came together in the short-lived punk outfit Leito Lychee, before branching out on their own. Their provocative live act, with the dynamic Hatori screeching, rapping or crooning in front of the stoical Honda, quickly attracted attention. They released a debut mini album on the Japanese label Error Records in 1995, which included two earlier independent 7-inch singles. A deal with Warner Brothers Records quickly followed, and their debut album, featuring additional production input from Mitchell Froom and Tchad Blake, appeared in early 1996. The songs on *Viva! La Woman* were inspired by the diversity of food (the band's name roughly translates as 'food crazy') available in New York, and included live favourites 'Beef Jerky' and 'Birthday Cake', alongside a unique cover version of Anthony Newley's 'The Candy Man'. The duo's eclectic musical stew of samples and hip-hop beats, meanwhile, drew favourable comparisons to the Beastie Boys. The duo also released an album, as Butter 08, with Russell Simins of the Jon Spencer Blues Explosion. Honda introduced her multi-instrumentalist boyfriend, Sean Lennon (b. 9 October 1975, New York, USA), on the band's 1997 *Super Relax* EP, which included various remixes of the track 'Sugar Water'. Lennon and Timo Ellis (b. 7 June 1970), originally enlisted for touring purposes, subsequently joined Hatori and Honda as full-time members. During recording sessions for the full-length follow-up, *Stereo Type A*, Duma Love (drums, percussion, vocals) became the fifth member of the band. Largely eschewing the whimsy of the debut album, the band earned further praise for their musical inventiveness. This was thanks, in no small part, to Honda's growing stature as a producer.

● ALBUMS: *Viva! La Woman* (Warners 1996)★★★, *Stereo Type A* (Warners 1998)★★★★.

CIV

Formed in New York City in 1995, CIV (pronounced 'sieve' - also the name of the band's singer and leader, Anthony Civocelli) are one of the new generation of hardcore outfits from the city. With a line-up completed by Sammy Siegle (drums), Charlie Garriga (guitar) and Arthur Smilios (bass), the band took that particular scene by storm with their 1995 debut album, *Set Your Goals*. Their stage performances were also eye-catching, the band favouring sharp suits rather than the army surplus more usually associated with the hardcore fraternity, while the accent on percussion saw them labelled by some as a hardcore version of Adam And The Ants. Each member had previously played with other local bands, most notably Gorilla Biscuits and Youth of Today. CIV were signed by Atlantic Records when A&R executive Mike Gitter saw their self-funded 'demo video' for 'Wait One Minute More'. This featured a chat show parody and was regularly aired by MTV. After signing to Atlantic the band consolidated their progress with support dates to L7, Sick Of It All and others. In 1996, they toured the UK for the first time and released another acclaimed single, 'Choices Made'. Smilios was replaced by Cache Tohnan in March 1998, prior to the release of *Thirteen Day Getaway*.

● ALBUMS: *Set Your Goals* (Lava/Atlantic 1995)★★★, *Thirteen Day Getaway* (Atlantic 1998)★★★.

Clan Alba

A folk supergroup, Clan Alba were formed in the UK in the mid-90s and featured veteran artists Dick Gaughan, Mary Macmaster, Brian MacNeill, Fred Morrison, Patsy Seddon, Davy Steele, Mike Travis and Dave Tulloch. While the instrumental line-up featured guitars, harps, pipes, fiddles and percussion, just as much interest was focused on how well the distinctive singing voices blended as part of Clan Alba's collective harmonies. The answer was based on the evidence of their self-titled 1996 debut album. A double compact disc spanning 87 minutes and a plethora of styles, the most effective moments included 'Bye Bye Big Blue', a lament for the closure of the Ravenscraig Steel Works, and Gaughan's evocative 'Childhood's End'.

● ALBUMS: *Clan Alba* (Clan Alba 1996)★★★.

Clarke, Dave

One of the UK's most accomplished techno producers, Dave Clarke has sustained a career spanning the 90s, displaying an instinct for creating classic tracks which have won him international acclaim. Starting out as a hip-hop DJ in the late eighties, Clarke honed his knowledge of mixing and knowledge of music, moving on to acid house, hardcore, and his own brand of up-front techno, which combined the elation and intensity of hardcore with the funk of hip-hop and house. Becoming affiliated in the mid-nineties with the top

record labels R&S Records, XL Records, Deconstruction Records, Reload and Bush, Clarke began to make a real impact on international dance music. His Aphrohead remixes of 1993 introduced the filtered house sound, diluted aspects of which are ubiquitous in today's club music. 'Red One', 'Red Two' and 'Red Three' were classic sounding Detroit-tinged workouts with a unique feel and displaying a mastery of drum programming. 'Red Three' broke into the UK Top 50 - a rare feat for a techno record. These were followed by 'Southside', a fantastically funky track which quoted from old-school Chicago soul, yet managed to sound completely unique. Clarke's blistering DJ sets received a great deal of attention, earning him a reputation as one of the fastest and most idiosyncratic DJs around. Being criticised in certain branches of the dance media for the seriousness of his attitude to music and his anti-drugs stance, Clarke has always shown himself to be indifferent to the whims of an arguably destructive culture, being invariably more interested in the music. His stylishly presented red sleeved album *Archive 1* reflected his dedication to musical perfection, containing all of the Red series, along with more brilliantly executed techno. Extending this eclectic approach, his *Electro Boogie* albums for Studio !K7 displayed another facet to his mixing technique, coinciding with electro DJ sets which demonstrated his ability to work a crowd. Recently he has established residencies at Liverpool's Bugged Out!, Belfast's Shine and has made regular appearances at the UK's Atomic Jam and Pure. He is also a resident at Belgium's world famous Fuse club and Barcelona's Nitsa, and his weekly schedule takes in clubs all over the world. Clarke has also been a much sought-after remixer, having added his inimitable touch to releases by, amongst others, Emperion, the Chemical Brothers, Christopher Just, Carl Cox and Leftfield. He also delivered a wonderful remix of Underworld's 'King Of Snake' for Junior Boy's Own. His latest album, a compilation of early releases and remixes, confirms his reputation as one of the most exciting techno producers on the planet.

● ALBUMS: *Electro Boogie* (Studio !K7 1996)★★★, *Electro Boogie, Vol.2: The Throw Down* (Studio !K7 1998)★★★.

● COMPILATIONS: *Fuse Presents Dave Clarke Music Man* (Fuse 1999)★★★★.

Cleopatra

Originating from Manchester, England's Moss Side district, this highly talented teenage trio comprised sisters Cleopatra Madonna (b. 30 April 1982), Zainam (b. 5 December 1980) and Yonah Higgins (b. 27 April 1984). The girls were brought up single-handedly by their mother Christine while she completed a degree course. They first appeared in local talent competitions around Manchester, before a home video of one of their performances was passed onto UK swingbeat singer Mark Morrison. Morrison in turn passed it on to his record company, WEA Records, and an impromptu *a cappella* rendition at Warner's London offices allegedly finalized the deal. The trio's exuberant blend of Motown Records-influenced pop and swingbeat was all the more impressive given that most of their material was written by middle sister Cleopatra (from whom the band derived their name). The trio supported Gabrielle and Louise on tour, and made a show-stopping appearance at the 1998 BRIT Awards, before releasing 'Cleopatra's Theme' ('fresh new talent's

here and we know'), which entered the UK charts at number 3 in February 1998. A lucrative US deal with Madonna's Maverick Records label followed in March 1998. The follow-up singles 'Life Ain't Easy' (number 4 in May) and a cover version of the Jackson Five's 'I Want You Back' (number 3 in August) established the trio as regulars in the UK Top 10, while 'Cleopatra's Theme' climbed to US number 26 in August. The debut album *Comin' Atcha!* entered the UK charts at a rather disappointing number 20 in June 1998, indicating the trio's forte as a singles act. 'A Touch Of Love' broke their run of hit singles when it failed to enter the Top 20 in March 1999. They have subsequently made forays into television with the cartoon show *Comin' Atcha* and *In The House With Cleopatra*.
● ALBUMS: *Comin' Atcha!* (WEA 1998)★★★.

Coal Chamber

Formed in Los Angeles, California, USA, in 1994, Coal Chamber are led by gruff vocalist Dez Fafara and operate in territory somewhere between the traditional hard riffing of Black Sabbath and the sensationalist techno rock of Marilyn Manson. Fafara met guitarist Miguel 'Meegs' Rascon through a classified ad, and they later added drummer Mike Cox and bass player Rayna Foss, the room-mate of Fafara's future wife. They signed to Roadrunner Records in 1995 after being recommended by Dino Cazares of Fear Factory, and received widespread exposure in the metal press as that label's hottest new property since Machine Head. Their debut attained further strong reviews, despite having been recorded under stressful conditions - on the day recording started, Fafara's wife left him. An already intimidating suite of songs was thus transformed into something of a personal exorcism. Having previously toured with Danzig, they also supported labelmates Machine Head on their 1997 UK tour. Their sophomore set, *Chamber Music*, was boosted by the inclusion of their highly popular cover version of Peter Gabriel's 'Shock The Monkey', featuring Ozzy Osbourne on vocals.
● ALBUMS: *Coal Chamber* (Roadrunner 1997)★★★, *Chamber Music* (Roadrunner 1999)★★★.

Codeine

US band Codeine comprises Steve Immerwahr (bass/vocals), John Engle (guitar), with Douglas Scharin and then Matthews McGuigan (ex-Coral) replacing Come guitarist Chris Brokaw as drummer. Signed to the Sub Pop Records label, Codeine play at a deliberate, slovenly, lo-fi pace: 'It's not a see how slow you can go thing, more a compositional tool. A lot of the songs are about having a very low amount of energy or being physically unable to move. So it's performing the songs in a way that's analogous to what they're about - moments of inertia.' *Barely Real* is, on first hearing, slightly soporific and listless, but it rewards repeated listening with its depth and emotional texture. Afterwards they moved to Louisville, Kentucky, to rehearse songs that would form *The White Birch*, which was eventually recorded in Chicago. Inspired by a painting by American artist Thomas Dewing, it prompted the German magazine *Howl* to describe Codeine as 'a group that uses tears instead of notes'.
● ALBUMS: *Barley Real* mini-album (Sub Pop 1993)★★, *The White Birch* (Sub Pop 1994)★★★.

Cohn, Marc

b. Cleveland, Ohio, USA. Singer songwriter and pianist Cohn used his husky voice and distinctive songs to great effect in the 90s when his debut album won the 1991 Grammy for Best New Artist. The album was a collection of melodic pop-rock songs with passionate lyrics drawn from the artist's own turbulent background. Cohn's mother died when he was two, and his father remarried when he was 12. Cohn senior worked seven days a week as a pharmacist but was always in debt. He is recalled as the slightly absurd figure in 'Silver Thunderbird', who maintains that car at the cost of all other material comforts. Although the song was dismissed by casual critics as an automobile tribute, in reality it was a song purely for his father and had taken Cohn 15 different versions to perfect. Having written songs from an early age he played his first solo acoustic sets around Cleveland coffee bars in his late teens. Afterwards he moved to New York, and embarked on demoing songs for various writers, including Jimmy Webb and Leiber And Stoller. He also became a prominent session keyboard player, including a stint on Tracy Chapman's second album, while also fronting his own 14-piece swing band, who played at Caroline Kennedy's wedding. One night in Arkansas he saw a sign marked 'Hollywood' - a former slave shack now converted into a honky-tonk and catfish eatery. There he met a 70-year-old black pianist and singer, Muriel, who played elegant versions of spirituals and R&B songs and with whom Cohn was soon in rapt conversation. He joined in an ad-libbed performance, and by the end of it the pair had brought the house down. The experience resulted in Cohn writing 'Walking In Memphis', a UK and US hit and the centrepiece of his debut album. Another cornerstone was 'True Companion', a popular lovers song which even became the soundtrack to a live marriage proposal on US television's *Johnny Carson Tonight* show. A second album arrived to a lesser fanfare but contained another strong batch of songs, including 'Rest For The Weary', a continuation of 'Silver Thunderbird'. After an extended hiatus Cohn returned in 1998 with *Burning The Daze*, another polished collection of adult contemporary pop which unfortunately lacked a stand-out track of the stature of 'Walking In Memphis'.
● ALBUMS: *Marc Cohn* (Atlantic 1991)★★★★, *The Rainy Season* (Atlantic 1993)★★★, *Burning The Daze* (East West 1998)★★★.

Coldcut

Since the mid-80s ex-art teacher Jonathon Moore and computer programmer Matt Black have been responsible for a number of important innovations in the dance music arena. Like DJ Steinski, they realized the creative potential of sampling records, television, Walt Disney sounds and other non-musical sources, and in 1987 made their first records, 'Say Kids What Time Is It?', 'Greedy Beat' and 'Bits And Pieces'; a sample of 'Say Kids …' was later used on MARRS' 'Pump Up The Volume'. With the acid house boom, Coldcut became a widely respected remix team, beginning with a mix of Eric B And Rakim's 'Paid In Full'. At the same time they were DJing on pirate radio stations, notably their *Solid Steel* show on Kiss, and at acid house parties such as Shoom. In 1988, with Yazz, Moore and Black (as the Plastic Population) produced groundbreaking pop that combined hip-hop and house styles on such tracks as 'Doctorin' The House' and 'The Only Way Is Up'. The following year they helped to launch the career of Lisa Stansfield with 'People Hold On', which was featured on their debut album, *What's That Noise?*. In 1990 they were voted producers of the year at the BPI awards, at which point it was conceivable that they would continue in a Stock, Aitken And Waterman mould, churning out more hits. However, their vision extended beyond the formulae of house and techno and, following difficulties with major labels, Moore and Black established Ninja Tune Records as a vehicle for their own experimentation. Coldcut released the album *Philosophy* for Arista Records in 1993 in order to fulfil contractual obligations, a number of singles including 'Autumn Leaves', and a number of tracks on Ninja Tune compilations. In 1997, 'Atomic Moog 2000' and 'More Bits And Pieces' heralded *Let Us Play*, the CD release of which contained an 'interactive toybox full of Coldcut games toys and videos', designed in collaboration with Hex. Like the DJ Food albums, *Let Us Play* explores the abstract hip-hop idea where funk beats underpin various textures, often based on dialogue, including poets, rappers and other pre-recorded segments, and other non-melodic sources. In the meantime, they developed the Ninja Tune concept and were involved in a range of projects linked with the label, including the DJ Food albums and various club nights. They have continued to broadcast on Kiss FM and to DJ worldwide. Like many of the most creative artists of the 90s, Moore and Black envisage a future that combines music with technology, where DJs may have any number of sources at their disposal, rather than two decks and a mixer.

● ALBUMS: *What's That Noise?* (Ahead Of Our Time 1989)★★★★, *Some Like It Cold* (Ahead Of Our Time 1990)★★★, *Philosophy* (Arista 1993)★★, *Let Us Play* (Ninja Tune 1997)★★★★.

● COMPILATIONS: *Let Us Replay!* (Ninja Tune 1999)★★★★.

● VIDEOS: *Let Us Play* (Ninja Tune 1998).

Cole, Paula

b. USA. Alternative pop-rock singer/songwriter Paula Cole launched her career with the spirited, persuasive *Harbinger* set for Imago Records in July 1994. Among several notable tracks was the high-impact single, 'I Am So Ordinary', which forcefully dealt with Cole's low self-esteem problems. However, its potential impact was scuppered when Imago lost its distribution deal with BMG - the same problem befalling fellow label artists Henry Rollins and Aimee Mann. Eventually she moved to a new contract with Warner Brothers Records, though the Imago imprint remained on future releases. *Harbinger* was re-released by Warners in July 1995, but the sales returns remained modest. Speaking of her first full effort for her new home, 1996's *This Fire*, Cole told the music press: 'I think this album is an emergence of self. *Harbinger* was written with an adolescent point of view. But now I don't have to be so gentle.' Much of the material was written while on the road, Cole touring as a member of Peter Gabriel's Secret World Live band, and appearing as support act to Melissa Etheridge, Sarah McLachlan and Counting Crows. Gabriel repaid the compliment by contributing backing vocals to the ballad, 'Hush Hush Hush', on *This Fire*. An obvious contrast to her earlier material, the pleading, vulnerable 'Where Have All The Cowboys Gone?' served as the album's first single. Providing her commercial breakthrough, the song climbed to number 8 on the *Billboard* Hot 100 in May 1997. 'I Don't Want To Wait' reached US number 11 the following January, buoyed by its inclusion in the popular television series *Dawson's Creek*. Her third album, *Amen*, was released in September 1999.

● ALBUMS: *Harbinger* (Imago 1994)★★★, *This Fire* (Imago/Warners 1996)★★★★, *Amen* (Warners 1999)★★★.

Collective Soul

Formed in Stockbridge, Georgia, USA, Collective Soul have earned their reputation with strong, hook-laden pop rock songs, the best example of which is 'Shine', which topped *Billboard*'s Rock Album Tracks poll in May 1994. The band's history up to then, however, had been a tortuous one spanning more than a decade. Ed Roland (vocals/guitar) grew up in a strict family, with access to music and radio denied by his parents. Despite this, he left Stockbridge to study guitar at Boston's Berklee College Of Music. When he ran out of money he returned to Stockbridge to work in a 24-track recording studio, where he taught himself production technique and formed the band Collective Soul. (The only surviving member of that version of the band is the drummer Shane Evans.) After years of rejection from major labels, Roland disbanded the band in 1992. A year later he was contacted after radio stations expressed interest in 'Shine'. This led to a contract with Atlantic Records and together with his brother Dean Roland (guitars), Ross Childress (lead guitar), Will Turpin (bass) and Evans, Collective Soul were reformed. Although the follow-up single 'Breathe' failed to replicate the success of 'Shine', the band's debut album (now on Atlantic) was repackaged to become a million-seller by the year's end. The quintet began 1995 with 'Gel', the first single from their second album. With strong rotation play from MTV, it was also featured on the soundtrack of the cult *Jerky Boys* movie. In March 1995, they embarked on a major tour supporting Van Halen. Since then their fanbase has not grown and their recent recordings, although commercially successful, have been somewhat disappointing.

● ALBUMS: *Hints, Allegations & Things Left Unsaid* (Atlantic 1993)★★★, *Collective Soul* (Atlantic 1995)★★★★, *Disciplined Breakdown* (Atlantic 1997)★★, *Dosage* (Atlantic 1999)★★.

Collins, Edwyn

b. 23 August 1959, Edinburgh, Scotland. Following the collapse of Orange Juice, a band acclaimed in the UK music press but who did not enjoy commercial success, Edwyn Collins launched a solo career that has had a similar pattern. Both the Orange Juice producer, Dennis Bovell, and their drummer, Zeke Manyika, were present on Collins' 1989 debut, *Hope And Despair*, which also featured Aztec Camera's Roddy Frame. The single 'Don't Shilly Shally' was produced by Robin Guthrie of the Cocteau Twins, who handled the lighting at early Orange Juice gigs. *Hellbent On Compromise* was a more intimate and atmospheric recording, with Collins stating his intention to present a 'cinematic' effect. Afterwards Collins produced records for A House, Vic Godard and Frank And Walters. His 1994 album, *Gorgeous George*, was produced on an old EMI/Neve mixing console. Filled with cantankerous phrases such as 'the truly detestable summer festival', Collins' writing proved to be sharper than on the morose *Hellbent On Compromise*, especially on tracks such as 'A Girl Like You' and 'Make Me Feel Again'. The former, released as a single, became the most successful instalment in his 15-year recording career when it entered the Top 10s in Australia, France and the UK. Three years later Collins returned with *I'm Not Following You*, an album whose title accurately reflected his fiercely independent position in the music industry.

● ALBUMS: *Hope And Despair* (Demon 1989)★★★, *Hellbent On Compromise* (Demon 1990)★★, *Gorgeous George* (Setanta 1994)★★★★, *I'm Not Following You* (Setanta 1997)★★★.

● VIDEOS: *Phantasmagoria* (Alternative Image 1992).

Collister, Christine

b. 28 December 1961, Douglas, Isle Of Man. Since breaking up with Clive Gregson, Collister has become a popular support solo artist in the UK. As her confidence grows as a performer in her own right, so her voice has continued to improve and gain strength. Her live performance of Rickie Lee Jones' 'Last Chance To Texaco', in particular, shows off her vocal range, although she has yet to find a regular songwriter of the calibre of Gregson. *The Dark Gift Of Time* features bold interpretations of Billie Holiday ('God Bless The Child'), Nick Drake ('Black Eyed Dog') and Tom Waits ('Dirt In The Ground').

● ALBUMS: *Live* (Fledg'ling 1994)★★★, *Blue Aconite* (Fledg'ling 1996)★★★★, *The Dark Gift Of Time* (Fledg'ling 1998)★★★★.

● COMPILATIONS: *Songbird* (Fledg'ling 1999)★★★★.

Color Me Badd

This US harmony and *a cappella* quartet, comprising Oklahoma college students, Bryan Abrams (b. 16 November 1969, USA), Mark Calderon (b. 27 September 1970, USA), Sam Watters (b. 23 July 1970, USA) and Kevin Thornton (b. 17 June 1969, USA), triumphed on both sides of the Atlantic in 1991 with the dubious sexual slant of their breakthrough single, 'I Wanna Sex You Up' (US number 2/UK number 1) It was while they were performing as a support band in Oklahoma that they were spotted by Robert Bell (of Kool And The Gang), who swept them off to New York. Originally arranged by Dr. Freeze, 'I Wanna Sex You Up' was featured in the soundtrack to the movie *New Jack City*. Their poppy R&B harmony shared similarities with the Pasadenas, though their unshaven, adolescent hoodlum image was doubtless more contrived. The US chart-topping follow-ups, 'I Adore Mi Amor' and 'All 4 Love', were typical radio-friendly pop workouts, though the vocal harmonics were rendered with aplomb. For their second album producer David Foster was recruited, alongside the barely complementary skills of DJ Pooh, more familiar from his work with Ice Cube. The gangsta rapper himself stopped by to direct the video for the title track, which was also the first single to be lifted from the album. The single failed to break into the US Top 20, and marked the start of a commercial decline for the quartet which weak albums such as *Now And Forever* and *Awakening* failed to remedy.

● ALBUMS: *C.M.B.* (Giant 1991)★★★★, *Time And Chance* (Giant 1993)★★★, *Now And Forever* (Giant 1996)★★, *Awakening* (Sony 1998)★★★.

Colvin, Shawn

b. South Dakota, USA. A singer-songwriter in the tradition of her teen idol Joni Mitchell. Backed by fellow guitarist and songwriting partner John Leventhal (later a collaborator with Marc Cohn), her debut pulled together arresting material with an understated approach that accentuated the confessional appeal of the songs. Colvin was raised in the small Midwest towns of Vermillion, South Dakota, and Carbondale, Illinois. Having first picked up a guitar aged 10, she joined a hard rock band at college, then the Dixie Diesels, a country swing band from Austin, Texas. After a brief sojourn playing solo acoustic in San Francisco, she relocated to New York in 1980 and began working her way up the local folk pecking order. She also appeared in off-Broadway productions such as *Pump Boys And Dinettes*, *Diamond Studs* and *Lie Of The Mind*. Her reflections on this transitory period of her life ('In each one of those places I made great friends - as far as I can remember') are indicative of the alcohol- and drug-induced self-destruction at which her later songwriting hints. When she stopped drinking in 1983, she came by her first big break. A live tape was repeatedly aired by a local station and those songs attracted the attention of Columbia Records. Having honed a body of work over a decade, she was well placed to capitalize and her debut was awarded a Grammy in 1989 for Best Folk Album. It was co-produced by Suzanne Vega's producer Steve Addaboo and Leventhal, and Vega herself guested, Colvin having contributed backing vocals to Vega's 'Luka' and toured widely supporting her. Relieved at her commercial acclaim, Colvin made the most of her fame by working with some of her idols - joining Richard Thompson on tour (and later marrying his road manager) and recording a second album with Mitchell's husband, Larry Klein, at Mitchell's home studio. Klein also joined her for selected touring dates, although many found the over-production worked against Colvin's songs on *Fat City*. After two strong collections it was disappointing that she returned in 1994 with an album of meek cover versions. Evidently with one eye on the MTV profile to which she so frequently alluded in interviews, this set was only interesting on those songs without significant previous exposure - such as her bass player Rowland Salley's 'Killing The Blues'. Elsewhere critics balked at unnecessary fillers, such as Sting's 'Every Little Thing She Does Is Magic'. The excellent *A Few Small Repairs* was more rock-orientated. After going through a divorce, Colvin had no shortage of philosophical emotions to turn into song.

● ALBUMS: *Steady On* (Columbia 1989)★★★★, *Fat City* (Columbia 1992)★★★, *Cover Girl* (Columbia 1994)★★, *Live '88* (Plump 1995)★, *A Few Small Repairs* (Columbia 1996)★★★★, *Holiday Songs And Lullabies* (Columbia 1998)★★★.

Combs, Sean 'Puffy'

b. 4 November 1970, Harlem, New York, USA. The most prosperous of a new breed of entrepreneurs in black music, Sean 'Puffy' Combs is a hugely successful hip-hop artist (under the name Puff Daddy) and noted producer for artists including TLC and Mary J. Blige. He also excels in business - the value of his Bad Boy empire was estimated at $170,000,000 during 1997. Although his sample-heavy sound has been criticised for taking hip-hop too far into the mainstream, its commercial appeal is unquestionable, and has made Combs one of the most powerful players in American music. Brought up in the contrasting New York districts of Harlem and Mount Vernon by a single mother, Combs was bright enough to secure a university place, before his musical instincts took over. He danced in a Fine Young Cannibals video, and found a job at Uptown Records, run by Motown Records boss Andre Harrell. By the age of 18 he had been made head of A&R for Uptown, and was involved in successful albums by Mary J. Blige, Father MC and Heavy D And The Boyz. Having been fired from Uptown, Combs worked as a remixer before launching his own company, Bad Boy Entertainment, in 1993. There, he quickly assembled a pool of talented R&B and hip-hop artists around him. Craig Mack's 1994 'Flava In Ya Ear' single earned Bad Boy their first platinum record, and the label enjoyed huge success thereafter, notably with the controversial rapper Notorious B.I.G., and R&B/hip-hop acts including Faith Evans and Total. Combs also produced other prominent artists including Mariah Carey, Boyz II Men and Aretha Franklin. His involvement in the east coast/west coast gangsta rap feud, which pitched Combs and Notorious B.I.G. against 2Pac and Marion 'Suge' Knight's Death Row Records, was an unpleasant distraction from his seemingly unstoppable assault on both the pop and R&B charts. The untimely death of Notorious B.I.G. delayed Comb's own solo album while he mourned his long-time friend. Released in summer 1997, the single 'Can't Nobody Hold Me Down' was US number one for almost eight weeks, and was followed by the international number 1 tribute single 'I'll Be Missing You', a rewrite of the Police's 'Every Breath You Take', with new lyrics dedicated to Notorious B.I.G. The long-awaited *No Way Out* was almost inevitably a multi-platinum number 1 album, which earned Combs a 1998 Grammy for Best Rap Album. 'I'll Be Missing You' also won the Grammy for Best Rap Performance. 'Come With Me', a collaboration with Jimmy Page based around the Led Zeppelin track 'Kashmir', was featured on the soundtrack to 1998's remake of *Godzilla*. Released as a single, it reached US number 4 in July and UK number 2 a month later. *Forever* was a less effective album, with Combs' pop nous ultimately swamped by the overcooked arrangements and gloating raps.

● ALBUMS: *No Way Out* (Bad Boy 1997)★★★, *Forever* (Bad Boy 1999)★★.

Come

Formed in 1991, this highly rated quartet centres on musicians already involved in New York's alternative music circuit. Singer/guitarist Thalia Zedek began her recording career with the Dangerous Birds and Uzi, before joining the influential Live Skull. Guitarist Chris Brokaw was formerly drummer in Codeine, while Sean O'Brien (bass) and Arthur Johnson (drums) were both ex-members of the Bar B Q Killers. Come made their debut in August 1991 with 'Car', a slow, menacing performance issued on the Sub Pop Records label. The equally atmospheric 'Fast Piss Blues' succeeded it, backed by a languid version of the Rolling Stones' 'I Got The Blues'. These served as the perfect introduction to *Eleven: Eleven*, rightly lauded as one of 1992's finest releases. The spirit of Patti Smith, Delta blues and the Stooges permeated this startling collection which highlighted Zedek's emotive voice and Brokow's dense guitarwork. A period of seclusion ensued, but Come re-emerged with 1994's powerful second collection, which included further high-calibre recordings in 'Finish Line' and 'Let's Get Lost'. Johnson and O'Brien left the group in 1995, and were replaced by Tara Jane O'Neil (bass) and Kevin Coutlas (drums), both ex-Rodan members. Subsequent albums have failed to scale the heights of their debut, but pay testament to Come's unrelenting musical vision.

● ALBUMS: *Eleven: Eleven* (Matador 1992)★★★★, *Don't Ask, Don't Tell*

(Matador 1994)★★★, *Near Life Experience* (Matador 1996)★★★, *Gently Down The Stream* (Matador 1998)★★★.

Common

b. Lonnie Rashied Lynn, Chicago, Illinois, USA. Originally recording under the expanded pseudonym Common Sense, Lynn is one of the more enlightened contemporary rappers, proffering a heady mix of verbiage and syncopated hip-hop rhythms. He made his debut in 1992 with *Can I Borrow A Dollar?*, a series of tracts on consumer identity with the occasional lapse into X-rated anatomical detail to make it a hit with the hardcore hip-hop audience. Conversely, the best song was 'Take It EZ', a laid-back statement of identity and individuality. By the advent of *Resurrection* in 1994, Lynn had abandoned some of the bloated misogyny of the debut, and the results were excellent. Fuelled by the soul and funk beats of his DJ No I.D., the album provided the rapper with a license to indulge his self-evident love of vocabulary and syntax (particularly affecting was his sketch of black economics - 'Chapter 13 (Rich Man vs. Poor Man)'). A follow-up set was then delayed as Lynn lost a court battle to retain the rights to his name Common Sense, eventually abbreviating it simply to Common. In the interim, he also completed classes in music theory, encouraging him to bring live instrumentation to the fore on his new recordings. *One Day It'll All Make Sense* also displayed further development in songwriting. Although it lacked the consistency of its predecessor, there were several stand-out cuts, notably the single 'Reminding Me (Of Sef)', which mourned the loss of a childhood friend.

● ALBUMS: as Common Sense *Can I Borrow A Dollar?* (Relativity 1992)★★★, as Common Sense *Resurrection* (Relativity 1994)★★★★, *One Day It'll All Make Sense* (Relativity/Epic 1997)★★★★.

Company Flow

Brooklyn, New York, USA-based crew comprising MCs El-P, Mr. Len and Bigg Jus, Company Flow are an integral part of the late-90s underground hip-hop scene. Alongside Jurassic 5, Black Star and Canibus, and in a direct reaction to gangsta rap and the Puff Daddy-dominated mainstream, they have re-established hip-hop's credibility and social agenda. The trio first appeared as far back as 1993, releasing their debut single 'Juvenile Techniques'. For subsequent releases they set-up their own label, Official Recordings, allowing them to retain complete control of the product. The *Funcrusher* EP and '8 Steps To Perfection' became underground hits, leading to a deal with Rawkus Records, the New York independent responsible for the scene-defining compilations *Soundbombing* and *Lyricist Lounge Volume 1*. Rawkus issued the double set *Funcrusher Plus*, which compiled the old hits and new material. Tracks such as first single 'Blind' and 'End To End Burners' established Company Flow as one of the underground's most talked about acts. They also record with the Juggaknots as the Indelible MCs, releasing 1998's incendiary 'Fire In Which You Burn' single. *Little Johnny From The Hospital*, the new Company Flow album, was released in July 1999.

● ALBUMS: *Funcrusher Plus* (Rawkus 1997)★★★★, *Little Johnny From The Hospital* (Rawkus 1999)★★★.

Compay Segundo

b. Maximo Francisco Repilado Munoz, 18 November 1907, Siboney, Cuba. He moved to Santiago (birthplace of 'son', Cuba's national musical style) at the age of seven, and by the age of 13 he was playing guitar and tres (Cuban variant of the guitar) in the bars of the city, as well as working as a barber and tobacco picker by day. At 15 he began to compose his own material and also started playing the clarinet, joining the Municipal Band Of Santiago as a clarinet player five years later. He invented his own musical instrument, a cross between a guitar and a tres, known as an 'aromonico' or 'trilina'. By 1934 Munoz had moved to Havana (having toured there as a member of Nico Saquito's Quinteto Cuban Stars), where he played with Cuarteto Hatey (1934-39) and Cunjunto Matamaros (1939-51). In 1942, he formed the duo Los Campadres ('The Friends') with Lorenzo Hierrezuelo. As Hierrezuelo was the lead vocalist he became known as Compay Primo ('first friend'), while Munoz sang bass harmonies and gained the nickname Compay Segundo ('second friend'). In 1950, Segundo formed his own group, Compay Segundo Y Sus Muchachos ('Compay Segundo And His Boys'), with whom he played until 1960, when he retired from music to work as a tobacconist. In 1977, he re-formed his group, with some personnel changes, and became a popular live attraction throughout Cuba. By the 90s Segundo and his band were also selling out concerts in France and Spain (Segundo's earthy sound has similarities to flamenco). They signed to East West Records and recorded *Yo Vengo Aqui* in November 1995. Featuring a selection of old favourites from the group's repertoire, the album was released in 1996 to general acclaim. Following his central role in the award-winning Buena Vista Social Club project, East West released the smooth-sounding *Lo Mejor De La Vida*, which featured guest appearances by Silvio Rodriguez and Omara Portuondo. The follow-up, *Calle Salud*, featured mainly self-composed boleros sung by Segundo in a languid, sensuous style.

● ALBUMS: *Yo Vengo Aqui* (East West 1996)★★★★, *Lo Mejor De La Vida* (East West 1998)★★★, *Calle Salud* (Gasa 1999)★★★.
● COMPILATIONS: *Cien Anos De Son* (WEA 1999)★★★★.

Confederate Railroad

Danny Shirley (b. Chattanooga, Tennessee, USA; lead vocals/guitar), Mark DuFresne (drums), Michael Lamb (guitar/vocals), Chris McDaniel (keyboards/vocals), Gates Nichols (steel guitar/vocals) and Wayne Secrest (bass). Drenched in the southern country rock of Charlie Daniels and Lynyrd Skynyrd, Danny Shirley formed a powerful country band, which, for a time, worked as David Allan Coe's touring band. In 1991, Shirley recorded a solo album for Atlantic Records and then persuaded the label to release it as a group effort under the name of Confederate Railroad. The CD listed both the band members and the musicians on the record, with Shirley's the only common name! Promoting the stars-and-bars flag, Confederate Railroad developed a politically incorrect stance with their praise of 'Trashy Women', a witty song by the underrated Chris Wall, and they even dressed as 'trashy women' for the video. The sentimental side to their macho posturings came through in 'Jesus And Mama'. Their theme song, 'I Am Just A Rebel', has been covered by Joy Lynn White and they showed sensitivity on 'Daddy Never Was The Cadillac Kind'. Confederate Railroad parodied their success in 'Elvis And

Andy', in a video going from polka to rap and including a narration by Craig Baguley, editor of the UK magazine *Country Music People*. Although touted as the bad boys of country music, in reality they are no more 'bad boys' than Alabama.

● ALBUMS: *Confederate Railroad* (Atlantic 1992)★★★★, *Notorious* (Atlantic 1994)★★★, *When And Where* (Atlantic 1995)★★★, *Keep On Rockin'* (Atlantic 1998)★★.
● COMPILATIONS: *Greatest Hits* (Atlantic 1996)★★★★.
● VIDEOS: *Elvis & Andy* (1994), *Notorious: The Video* (1994).

Connells

Formed in Raleigh, North Carolina, USA, rock sextet the Connells quietly began building a local fanbase following their 1984 inception. A steady stream of albums followed, each delivering a combination of strong musicianship with accomplished, if rarely inspired, songwriting. However, the band, which includes lead singer Doug MacMillan, lead guitarist George Huntley and Mike Connell, failed to secure mainstream interest, despite steady sales. In 1992, they brought a lawsuit in an unsuccessful attempt to leave their record label, TVT Records. By the time this was resolved the following year, the band had begun work on *Ring*. This proved to be their most successful album, particularly in Europe, where the single '74-75' hit the number 1 spot in Germany, Norway and Sweden, as well as Israel. The band set about building on this success with extensive tours in those regions, gathering new experiences which triggered both the title and the contents of the follow-up collection, *Weird Food & Devastation*. For this the band made a concerted effort to translate their overseas popularity into domestic sales - an ambition made more likely by the commercial success of similar artists such as the Gin Blossoms and Dishwalla. The most notable song was 'Friendly Time', an acidic put-down of music critics, written by Mike Connell. The band had also been busily engaged in extracurricular activities: Huntley released a solo album, *Brain Junk*, for TVT in 1996, while MacMillan played a tour manager in the independent movie, *Bandwagon*.

● ALBUMS: *Darker Days* (Black Park 1985)★★★, *Boylan Heights* (TVT 1987)★★★, *Fun & Games* (TVT 1989)★★★, *One Simple Word* (TVT 1990)★★★, *Ring* (TVT 1993)★★, *Weird Food & Devastation* (TVT 1996)★★★.

Connick, Harry, Jnr.

b. 11 September 1967, New Orleans, Louisiana, USA. As a pianist and singer, Connick is a young man with a sound that has been around for sometime, often being favourably compared to Frank Sinatra. Connick's studied influences take in many from the late 40s and 50s, encompassing bebop, 'cocktail' jazz and swing. Despite the critical acclaim afforded to his first two albums, it was not until he sung a group of standard songs on the soundtrack of the 1989 movie, *When Harry Met Sally*, that he came to national prominence. His work on the film earned him the Grammy Award for Male Jazz Vocal, and his clean cut, chisel-jawed good looks, plus a penchant for sharp suits, also made him a favourite with the ladies. He won another Grammy in 1990 for *We Are In Love*. Supported by Shannon Powell (drums) and Ben Wolfe (bass), Connick's Trio has earned sufficient plaudits from their jazz peers, endorsed by *Blue Light, Red Light* elevation to number 1 on the *Billboard* jazz chart. In 1990, he extended himself further

Consolidated

when he played the role of a crew member of a US B17 bomber aircraft in the World War II movie, *Memphis Belle*, and a year later co-starred with Jodie Foster in *Little Man Tate*. In 1992, he was arrested, and charged with having a 9mm pistol in his possession while passing through Kennedy Airport, New York. He spent a night in jail before agreeing to make a public service television commercial warning against breaking gun laws, in exchange for a promise to drop the charges if he stayed out of trouble for six months. After giving a splendid, 'old fashioned' rendering of the Oscar-nominated 'A Wink And A Smile' in the 1993 movie *Sleepless In Seattle*, Connick's 1994 album *She*, and his *Funk Tour* of the UK in the same year, came as somewhat of a surprise. It signalled a departure from the 'smooth crooning' and a move to down-home New Orleans funk - or as one of the many disillusioned fans who left before the end of each performance put it: 'We expected Frank Sinatra but we got Mötorhead instead.' He continues his acting career, and in 1998 made a credible leading man alongside Sandra Bullock in *Hope Floats*.

● ALBUMS: *Harry Connick Jnr.* (Columbia 1987)★★★, *20* (Columbia 1989)★★★, *When Harry Met Sally* film soundtrack (Columbia 1989)★★★★, *We Are In Love* (Columbia 1990)★★★, *Blue Light, Red Light* (Columbia 1991)★★★, as the Harry Connick Jnr. Trio *Lofty's Roach Souffle* (Columbia 1991)★★, *25* (Columbia 1992)★★★, *11* (Columbia 1993)★★★, *Forever For Now* (Columbia 1993)★★, *She* (Columbia 1994)★★★, *Star Turtle* (Columbia 1996)★★★, *To See You* (Columbia 1998)★★★, *Come By Me* (Columbia 1999)★★★.
● VIDEOS: *Singin' And Swingin'* (1990), *Swinging Out Live* (Sony Music Video 1992), *The New York Big Band Concert* (1993).
● FURTHER READING: *Wild About Harry: The Illustrated Biography*, Antonia Felix.
● FILMS: *Memphis Belle* (1990), *Little Man Tate* (1991), *Copycat* (1995), *Independence Day* (1996), *Action League Now!!* voice (1997), *Excess Baggage* (1997), *Hope Floats* (1998), *Wayward Son* (1999).

Consolidated

Highly political funk/rap/rock trio from San Francisco, USA, comprising Adam Sherburne (vocals, guitar; the son of an American Two Star General), Mark Pistel (sampler/technician) and Philip Steir (drums). Their approach to rock music reflects the anti-establishment, left field approach of Crass or Minor Threat; their 'mission' is to agitate, to provide more than a passive spectacle for an audience to consume. At the end of gigs the microphone is turned open to the audience, a format which has annoyed as well as intrigued paying customers (witness 'Play More Music', on which they are berated by audience members for not doing just that). As a background to their generally impressive arrangements, projected visuals comprise various images of totalitarianism, linking such themes as animal abuse to men's treatment of women. Acknowledging themselves as 'Typical Men' despite their political stance, they also co-operate with the polemic of female cohorts the Yeastie Girlz (Cammie, Kate and Wendy). They made a surprise move to a major label for 1994's *Business Of Punishment*, the wisdom of which was hinted at in the title of the delayed follow-up, *Dropped*. While Consolidated continue to tread a path on the right side of dogma, their status as artists of conscience serves as a reminder of the potential of music to inform and improve. Sherburne has also recorded solo as Childman.
● ALBUMS: *Consolidated* mini-album (Antler 1989)★★, *The Myth Of*

Rock (Nettwerk 1990)★★★, *Friendly Fa$cism* (Nettwerk 1991)★★, *Play More Music* (Nettwerk 1992)★★★, *Business Of Punishment* (London 1994)★★★, *Dropped* (Roadrunner 1997)★★★, *Tikkun* (Clearspot 1999)★★★.
Solo: Adam Sherburne as Childman: *Childman* (Nettwerk 1993)★★★.

Cook, Norman

b. 31 July 1963, England. This musical chameleon grew up in Surrey and began to DJ when he moved to Brighton to study for a degree. After playing bass guitar with the Housemartins, he had his first success as a solo artist with a remix of Erik B And Rakim's 'I Know You Got Soul' which reached number 13 in the charts in the late 80s. In the 90s, he formed Beats International, who achieved a UK number 1 in February 1990 with 'Dub Be Good To Me', and later Freak Power (with Ashley Slater), who reached number 2 in the UK charts in March 1995 after their 'Tune In, Turn On, Drop Out' single was featured in a Levis jeans commercial. Cook has achieved most success producing dance music under a number of different names, and in his roles as a club DJ and in-demand remixer. In 1994, he turned to house music as Pizzaman and had a number of Top 20 hits including 'Tripping On Sunshine' (Loaded Records). At the same time he began to write in a style that later became known as big beat, and to purvey this sound at the Big Beat Boutique (from which the movement took its name). Following the success of the club, he signed to Damian Harris' newly formed Skint Records as Fatboy Slim and released 'Santa Cruz' as his first single. He subsequently became big beat's best-known and most successful artist with a number of hit singles including 'Everybody Needs A 303', the album *Better Living Through Chemistry* and various remixes including Wildchild's 'Renegade Master' (Hi-Life) and Cornershop's number 1 single 'Brimful Of Asha' (Wiija). He has also recorded for Southern Fried Records as the Mighty Dub Katz, notably 'Its Just Another Groove' and 'Magic Carpet Ride'. In 1998, his success continued with a Fatboy Slim single 'Rockafeller Skank' and Freak Power single 'No Way', recorded with just Ashley Slater. In October, he was honoured with the UK's *Muzik* magazine's award for best producer. In January 1999, the Fatboy Slim single 'Praise You' topped the UK chart, while *You've Come A Long Way, Baby* consolidated its crossover appeal and enjoyed transatlantic success. In February, he won a BRIT Award for best producer, and in August married Radio 1 DJ and television presenter Zoe Ball. He also won three MTV Video Awards in September.
Cook's success lies in his ability to blend funky breakbeats with the most catchy melodies and riffs, and he has reached a wider audience than many DJs by combining elements of rock and dance music. 'Everybody Needs A 303' mixes a funky bass guitar riff with various analogue effects and 'Song For Lindy' features slide guitar, busy percussion, tubular bells and house-style piano, while 'Magic Carpet Ride' has a ska-edged feel with its guitar and horn hook. In this way he has coloured his music with a variety of styles and been broadminded enough to look further than the 'old-school' hip-hop and acid jazz clichés which pervade much of the scene. While he admits his music is simple, cheesy and obvious, describing himself as 'just a party fiend who nicks bits of other people's records', his light-hearted attitude and unashamedly amateurish approach, which also pervades

Skint, could prove more important in the long run than the sound itself.

Coolio

b. Artis Ivey, 1 August 1963, Compton, Los Angeles, California, USA. Boasting a long, though infrequently recorded, career in hip-hop, rapper Coolio's career finally took off after attending rehabilitation classes in an attempt to kick his cocaine habit. Coolio started making music again with WC And The MADD Circle, contributing to their 1991 release, *Ain't A Damn Thang Changed* (he would also perform on one track on their belated follow-up, 1995's *Curb Servin'*). He then joined the 40 Thevz, a hip-hop community made up of producers, rappers and dancers who would collaborate with him on all his recordings. Along with his friend DJ Bryan 'Wino' Dobbs, Coolio signed to Tommy Boy Records who released the single 'County Line' about his experiences on welfare assistance. 'Fantastic Voyage', based on Lakeside's 1980 hit, became a Top 5 single, and Coolio's profile was further enhanced by an autumn tour with R&B megastar R. Kelly. *It Takes A Thief* was a major seller, going platinum and establishing Coolio at the forefront of mid-90s hip-hop. 'Gangsta's Paradise', taken from his sophomore album of the same name, was a resigned lament performed with the gospel singer L.V. and a full choir that sampled Stevie Wonder's 'Pastime Paradise'. The single, featured in the movie *Dangerous Minds*, went to number 1 in the US and the UK. In the UK this was the first time anything approaching true 'street rap' had achieved such sales. As the music business magazine *Music Week* commented, 'in Britain for such a record to reach number one is quite sensational'. The song won a Grammy in 1996 for Best Rap Solo Performance. *My Soul*, which included the hit single 'C U When U Get There', was another downbeat collection that confirmed Coolio as one of hip-hop's most interesting artists. He subsequently set up his own Crowbar label and concentrated on an acting career.

● ALBUMS: *It Takes A Thief* (Tommy Boy 1994)★★★, *Gangsta's Paradise* (Tommy Boy 1995)★★★★, *My Soul* (Tommy Boy 1997)★★★.
● FILMS: *Phat Beach* (1996), *Dear God* (1996), *Burn Hollywood Burn* (1997), *Batman & Robin* (1997), *Tyrone* (1999), *Midnight Mass* (1999), *Judgement Day* (1999), *I Know What You Screamed Last Summer* (1999).

Cornelius

b. Keigo Oyamada, Japan. An eclectic Japanese artist with a style rooted in the use of samples and electronica, Cornelius also cites influences ranging from Burt Bacharach to Brian Wilson and contemporary indie/alternative rock bands. He first pursued a solo career in 1993 after serving several years in the cult Japanese rock band, Flipper's Guitar. Taking his stage name from Roddy McDowell's wizened scientist in *Planet Of The Apes*, he released three acclaimed collections on his own Japanese label, Trattoria. The best of his solo albums so far, *Fantasma*, was given a US release that year on Matador Records. The album was well received throughout the west, though UK critics were dismayed by live UK appearances where he abandoned the subtleties of his studio work in favour of a guitar-orientated rock sound.

● ALBUMS: *69/96* (Trattoria 1996)★★★, *96/69* (Trattoria 1996)★★★, *First Question Award* (Trattoria 1997)★★★, *Fantasma* (Trattoria/Matador 1997)★★★★, *FM Fantasma Mix* (Matador 1999)★★★.

Cornell, Chris

b. 20 July 1964, Seattle, Washington, USA. Cornell rose to prominence as a member of Soundgarden, one of the leading exponents, alongside Nirvana and Pearl Jam, of the Seattle grunge sound of the early 90s. Cornell set about recording his debut album with the help of Alain Johannes and Natasha Sneider of cult Los Angeles band, Eleven, following the break-up of Soundgarden in April 1997. *Euphoria Morning*, eventually released in September 1999, largely eschewed the muscular rock style of his former band, while building on the creative leaps made by them on their 1994 high water mark, *Superunknown*. The album earned glowing comparisons to the late Jeff Buckley, thanks in no part to the sweeping range of musical styles and Cornell's emotive lyrics, most evident on standout track 'Wave Goodbye' with its aching falsetto bridge. Cornell's lyrical preoccupation with death and loss, often a stumbling block for critics of Soundgarden, here found a more suitable outlet on tracks such as the acoustic 'Sweet Euphoria' and the 'Disappearing One'.

● ALBUMS: *Euphoria Morning* (Polydor 1999)★★★★.

Cornershop

This half-Asian, half-white indie band rose to prominence in the UK in 1993 by attacking some dubious statements made at that time by former idol Morrissey. The band, Ben Ayres (b. 30 April 1968, St John's, Newfoundland, Canada; guitar/vocals), Tjinder Singh (b. 8 February 1968, New Cross, Wolverhampton, England; guitar), Avtar Singh (b. 11 May 1965, Punjab, India; bass/vocals) and David Chambers (b. 1969, Lincoln, Lincolnshire, England; drums, ex-Dandelion Adventure), based themselves in Leicester, London and Preston. Signing to Wiiija Records they were invited to comment on Morrissey after his Finsbury Park glorification of skinhead culture and 'British' values. In the process, they became willing spokesmen for what seemed a significant debate, although it was just as well that their own musical abilities were not under the microscope. They had evolved out of the ashes of General Havoc in 1991, whose whole ethos was enshrined in the motto: 'Don't rehearse; hardly play; get media attention.' The debut single, 'In The Days Of Ford Cortina', while in many ways charming, was proto-punk amateurism at best. It also came in 'curry-coloured' vinyl, while other song titles included 'Kawasaki, Hotter Than Chapati', evidence that while Morrissey may have slipped into dubious waters, Cornershop looked unlikely to rival him in terms of irony. However, the band underlined their versatility by releasing a club-friendly 12-inch as their dance music alter-ego Clinton, while Tjinder Singh also produced an album by the Danish band Murmur. By 1995's *Woman's Gotta Have It* the style had been refined and remodelled, with less of a reliance on guitar chords and more on world music rhythms and instruments. David Byrne was so impressed he signed the band to a new five year contract with his Luka Bop label, distributed by Warner Brothers Records. Meanwhile, Brian Eno sampled the album's '6am Jullandar Shere' for his soundtrack to the War Child Fashion Show. The single (originally issued on Wiiija's 99p budget series) was also remixed by Richard Norris of the Grid for September 1995 release. Chambers and Avtar departed that year as the band struggled to win back support on their home market. It was against all expectations, then, that Ayres and Tjinder Singh produced one of 1997's best albums. *When I Was Born For The 7th Time* was an impressively diverse and exuberant blend of indie rock, hip-hop, reggae and dub, which included a cover of the Beatles' 'Norwegian Wood' sung entirely in Punjabi. Their dodgy musical days far behind them, Cornershop reaped the rewards this groovy album deserved when the extracted 'Brimful Of Asha' (featuring a Norman Cook remix) topped the UK charts in February 1998. Singh and Ayres released their debut album as Clinton, *Disco And The Halfway To Discontent*, in September 1999.

● ALBUMS: *Elvis Sex-Change* mini-album (Wiija 1993)★★, *Hold On It Hurts* (Wiiija 1994)★★★, *Woman's Gotta Have It* (Wiiija 1995)★★★, *When I Was Born For The 7th Time* (Beggars Banquet 1997)★★★★.

Corrosion Of Conformity

This mid-80s American hardcore crossover band, originally known as No Labels, was formed in Raleigh, North Carolina, USA, in 1982 by Reed Mullin (drums), Woody Weatherman (guitar) and Mike Dean (bass/vocals), and rose to become one of the biggest draws on the US underground scene with their stunning live shows. *Eye For An Eye*, with vocals supplied by Eric Eyke, separated them from the pack by mixing hardcore speed with Black Sabbath and Deep Purple-influenced power riffing. A more metallic crossover style became evident with *Animosity*, although the band lost neither their aggression nor their hardcore ideals. Following the blistering *Technocracy*, with Simon Bob (ex-Ugly Americans) on vocals, the size of the band's audience expanded with the rise of thrash, but record company problems and the loss of Simon Bob and Dean led to Corrosion Of Conformity's collapse. However, just when it seemed that *Six Songs With Mike Singing* would be their epitaph, Corrosion Of Conformity returned, with Mullin and Weatherman joined by Karl Agell (vocals, ex-School Of Violence), Pepper Keenan (guitar/vocals) and Phil Swisher (bass). Impressive tours with D.R.I. and Danzig helped to gain a new recording contract, and the acclaimed *Blind* saw the band adopt a slower, more melodic, but still fiercely heavy style. It also continued the hardcore lyrical stance of an increasingly politically active band, challenging social, political and ecological issues. Success with 'Vote With A Bullet' and electrifying live shows, including a UK tour supporting Soundgarden, re-established Corrosion Of Conformity as a force, but the departure of Agell and Swisher slowed the momentum once more. *Deliverance*, with Keenan taking lead vocals and Dean back in place, saw the band incorporate ever more diverse influences into their weighty sound, adding southern rock grooves and Thin Lizzy-style guitar harmonies for a varied album that was a departure from their hardcore musical roots. The hardcore image continued to fade as *Wiseblood* demonstrated an excellent grasp of 70s heavy rock.

● ALBUMS: *Eye For An Eye* (No Core 1984)★★★, *Animosity* (Combat 1985)★★★, *Technocracy* mini-album (Combat 1987)★★★, *Six Songs With Mike Singing* mini-album, 1985 recording (Caroline 1988)★★, *Blind* (Combat 1991)★★★, *Deliverance* (Sony 1994)★★★, *Wiseblood* (Sony 1996)★★★.

Corrs

One of Ireland's most successful pop exports of the 90s, family group the Corrs comprise Jim (b. 31 July 1964, Dundalk, Co. Louth, Eire; guitar/keyboards/backing vocals),

Sharon (b. 24 March 1970, Dundalk, Co. Louth, Eire; violin/vocals), Caroline (b. 17 March 1973, Dundalk, Co. Louth, Eire; drums/bodhrán/keyboards/vocals) and Andrea (b. 17 May 1974, Dundalk, Co. Louth, Eire; lead vocals/tin whistle). After gigging locally as a duo, Jim and Sharon Corr brought in their younger sisters Caroline and Andrea in order to audition for Alan Parker's 1991 movie *The Commitments*. Andrea secured the role of Jimmy Rabbitte's sister in the film and the others featured in bit parts. During filming, the sibling quartet were signed by manager John Hughes, after which they underwent a long apprenticeship honing their repertoire in an attempt to secure an international recording deal. A big break came when they were seen playing at a small gig at Whelen's, Dublin in 1994 by the US Ambassador to Ireland Jean Kennedy Smith. She invited them to play in Boston prior to America's hosting of the football World Cup. While in America they won an audience with Michael Jackson's producer David Foster and signed to Atlantic Records in collaboration with the Lava and 143 labels. Their 1995 debut, *Forgiven, Not Forgotten*, was a striking work, deftly combining traditional music with a strong pop sensibility. The traditional opener 'Erin Shore' featured some stunning violin from Sharon Corr, and segued into the title track, which remains one of their most accomplished compositions. In addition to many strong self-penned numbers such as 'Someday', 'Secret Life' and 'Runaway', the album included the raucous 'Toss The Feathers', their perennial concert finale. The album was a best seller in Eire and before long substantial sales were logged in Australia and continental Europe, with figures in excess of two million. Meanwhile, the group toured non-stop, securing a strong fanbase in America and Asia. Britain remained strangely resistant to their charms, and although the album subsequently charted none of their singles secured substantial airplay. By now the foursome's live appearances had won a devoted following while their model good looks ensured that they were frequently photographed in numerous magazines. Andrea Corr took time off to continue her acting career, appearing alongside Madonna in Alan Parker's 1996 film adaptation of *Evita* as Juan Peron's mistress. As a result of their arduous touring, the group decided to recruit several name writers to assist them in completing compositions for their next album. Among the supporting cast of composers was Glen Ballard, Oliver Leiber, Rick Nowells, Billy Steinberg and Carole Bayer Sager. The resultant *Talk On Corners*, although it contained some traditional elements, was a much more pop-orientated album with a broader appeal. It was a warm treat for an army of new fans who could enjoy the group's beautifully structured tunes as well as marvelling to the surprise finale - a reworking of Jimi Hendrix's 'Little Wing', in a collaboration with the Chieftains. Initially, the album followed the same sales pattern as its predecessor, with Britain again showing only limited interest. Two singles were issued, the sensual 'Only When I Sleep' and the witty 'I Never Loved You Anyway', but both failed to break through into the UK charts. Their persistence and determination finally paid off in 1998, firstly via a St Patrick's Day appearance at the Royal Albert Hall, which was broadcast later that evening on BBC Television. The show featured a guest appearance on drums by Mick Fleetwood, and it was revealed that the Corrs' next single would be a cover of Fleetwood Mac's 'Dreams', reworked by Todd Terry. When 'Dreams' hit the UK Top 10, the Corrs exploded in Britain and suddenly were everywhere, appearing regularly on prime time radio/television slots and earnestly promoting their album. By June 1998 the previously modest sales of *Talk On Corners* were transformed and the work rose to number 1, going on to become the biggest selling UK album of 1998. Renewed interest in the album prompted Atlantic to select two more singles from the work: a remix of the ballad 'What Can I Do' courtesy of Tin Tin Out, and a K Klass remix of the strident 'So Young'. Both reached the UK Top 10 confirming the Corrs' arrival as a strong singles act. The same year, Andrea Corr was featured as the singing voice of the heroine Kayley in Warner Brothers' first fully animated movie, *The Quest For Camelot*. A remix of 'Runaway' debuted at UK number 2 in February 1999. In April, their albums occupied the top two slots in the UK album charts. The *MTV Unplugged* collection featured five new tracks, including the single 'Radio'.

● ALBUMS: *Forgiven, Not Forgotten* (143/Lava 1995)★★★★, *Talk On Corners* (143/Lava 1997)★★★, *MTV Unplugged* (143/Lava 1999)★★★.
● VIDEOS: *Live At The Royal Albert Hall* (Warner Music Vision 1998), *The Corrs Unplugged* (Atlantic 1999).
● FURTHER READING: *The Corrs*, Jane Cornwell.

Corsten, Ferry

b. Netherlands. Corsten is a prolific Rotterdam-based trance DJ-producer whose successful single releases have appeared under a variety of monikers, including: System F, Moonman, Albion, Pulp Victim, Disco Droids, Veracocha and Gouryella. Corsten's productions were considered by some to epitomise the new commercial breed of trance and were labelled 'trance-by-numbers' by some critics. Purists felt that the tracks' bombastic use of dancefloor formulas such as dramatic breakdowns, surging synthesiser crescendos and epic string sounds were moving away from trance's original darker, subtler sound. He is one of a school of DJ/producers from continental Europe (notably Germany and Holland) including Paul Van Dyk, DJ Tiesto, DJ Jean, ATB, Taucher and Vincent De Moor who spearheaded the rise of a commercial form of trance in 1998 and 1999. Corsten's emotive and melodic style certainly captured the zeitgeist of 1999 and his tracks 'Out Of The Blue' (as System F), 'Carte Blanche' (as Veracocha) and 'Gouryella' (as Gouryella) were enormous club hits and also entered the UK's national Top 40, the latter reaching entering the UK charts at number 15, a considerable achievement for an instrumental trance record. Corsten's club and chart success as an artist and producer led him to become an in-demand remixer for both underground and high-profile artists including the Space Brothers, Binary Finary, William Orbit, Moby, Faithless and U2. He has been a full-time producer since 1991 and initially produced 'gabba' (phenomenally fast hardcore) before becoming more interested in house, techno and trance. His first release was 'Dancing Sparks' as A Jolly Good Fellow on Blue Records. Later in 1996, Corsten's 'Don't Be Afraid' as Moonman reached number 46 in the UK national singles chart and sold well in the rest of Europe, Australia and South Africa. His tracks as Moonman and Pulp Victim were released on the UK labels, Additive and Neo Records respectively. They caused a great deal of public interest through 'white label' plays by influential DJs such as Judge Jules, Seb Fontaine, Pete Tong and 'Tall' Paul Newman before

making their impression on the charts and as part of numerous club-based compilations. His track 'Air' as Albion was released on the UK's Platipus Records label and also featured on John Digweed's compilation *Global Underground 06 – Sydney* in 1998. Like many studio whizz-kids in dance music, Corsten is also an accomplished DJ and was commissioned to mix the first two volumes of the Ministry Of Sound's *Trance Nation* series. Perhaps unsurprisingly, several of his own productions featured on the albums. His distinctive tracks can also be heard on other 'superclub' compilations such as those for Cream and Gatecrasher. In late 1999, Corsten's name could be found as the remixer on Moby's 'Why Does My Heart Feel So Bad?', Faithless' 'Why Go', William Orbit's 'Adagio For Strings' (the classical music by Samuel Barber used in the movies *Platoon* and *The Elephant Man*) and U2's 'New Year's Day 2000'. In October 1999, he won the Producer Of The Year award at the UK's Ericsson *Muzik* Awards (dance music's 'Grammy') in London. In November, his single 'Walhalla' by Gouryella entered the national UK singles chart at number 27.

● COMPILATIONS: *Trance Nation* (MOS 1999)★★★, *Trance Nation 2* (MOS 1999)★★★★.

Cosmosis

This psychedelic trance outfit was originally formed in the mid-90s by the guitarist Bill Halsey and Jez Van Kampen. Their first release was 'Cannabanoid' for Transient Records in September 1995, after which they brought out a number of singles including 'Deus', 'Morphic Resonance', 'Gift Of The Gods' and 'Howling At The Moon'. At the same time they recorded together as Laughing Buddha for TIP Records and released 'Infinite Depth'/'Andromeda' in December 1995. The following year Cosmosis' debut album *Cosmology* (Transient) received an enthusiastic response. After the Laughing Buddha release 'Karma / Earth Medecine / Megamorphosis' (TIP 1997) the pair decided to pursue individual projects, with Halsey working as Cosmosis and Van Kampen as Laughing Buddha. The second Cosmosis album, *Synergy*, was released on Transient in March 1998 and in the spring Halsey took part in a tour of South Africa, Australia, Japan and the USA organized by Transient and Phantasm Records. Cosmosis' music is characterized by funky, multi-layered riffs and the most psychedelic, abstract noises and effects, which fade in and out and shoot around, lending a three-dimensional shape to the sound. As many psy-trance artists had moved towards a sparser sound that was less reliant on swirling effects and riffs, *Synergy* was not the most original trance album at the time of its release. However, the quality of production and arrangements combined with the sheer size of the tracks, overrides any bias one might have towards trends. Halsey sometimes employs guitar in his music, notably 'Down At The Crossroad', and recently he has been joined in live performances by the DJ Pied Piper or the guitarist Wei.

● ALBUMS: *Cosmology* (Transient 1996)★★★★, *Synergy* (Transient 1998)★★★★.

Counting Crows

Berkeley Hills, California-based folk rock band comprising Adam Duritz (vocals), David Bryson (guitar), Mat Malley (bass), Steve Bowman (drums), Charlie Gillingham (Hammond organ/keyboards) and Dan Vickrey (lead guitar/mandolin). Early reports suggested the influence of the singer-songwriter tradition, notably Van Morrison. Other comparisons were made with the Band. In interviews Duritz was keen to point out that they were more than a retro outfit, although he applauded the organic approach to musicianship that lay behind the Band and their ilk. This was reflected on their well-received debut, produced by T-Bone Burnett, which mixed traditional R&B elements with a raw, rocky delivery. The MTV rotation of 'Mr Jones' undoubtedly augmented sales, as did critical reaction, David Cavanagh noting in the *Independent* that: 'Its musical warmth makes it sound like a bunch of understated anthems in which, conceivably, millions could find solace'. By mid-1995 their remarkable debut had sold over 5 million copies in their homeland. The 'difficult' second album, *Recovering The Satellites*, debuted at number 1 in the *Billboard* album chart in 1996, although the band sounded strained in their attempt to recreate the impact of their debut. The stopgap live set, *Across A Wire: Live In New York*, reached the US Top 20 in July 1998. *This Desert Life* was a return to form, with the loose swagger of tracks such as 'Hanginaround' and 'Mrs Potter's Lullabye' attaining an effortless peak.

● ALBUMS: *August And Everything After* (Geffen 1993)★★★★, *Recovering The Satellites* (Geffen 1996)★★★, *Across A Wire: Live In New York City* (Geffen 1998)★★★, *This Desert Life* (Geffen 1999)★★★★.

Coverdale Page

Following Whitesnake's headline appearance at the 1990 Donington Festival, and the comparatively poor sales of *Slip Of The Tongue*, vocalist David Coverdale (b. 22 September 1951, Saltburn-By-The Sea, Cleveland, England) put his band on ice, and had all but retired. Former Led Zeppelin guitarist Jimmy Page (b. James Patrick Page, 9 January 1944, Heston, Middlesex, England) was, however, searching for a singer with whom to work, and Coverdale was suggested by his booking agent during a conversation with Page's manager. The pair met in New York in March 1991, and quickly gelled on personal and professional levels. Their first attempt at writing together produced an album track, 'Absolution Blues', and the duo began writing and recording their debut, enlisting the services of Heart drummer Denny Carmassi and bass players Jorge Casas and Ricky Phillips in the studio. The partnership was viewed rather cynically by sections of the music press as a corporate rock supergroup, and was subject to much speculation on all fronts - 'Legends' was rumoured as a possible band name for some time - before the appearance of the simply titled *Coverdale Page*. The album saw the duo rediscovering their blues-rock roots, and was widely regarded as the finest work produced by either for some time. Majestic ballads such as 'Take Me For A Little While' and the mellow 'Take A Look At Yourself' sat comfortably amid the thunderous hard rock of 'Shake My Tree', 'Waiting On You' and 'Pride And Joy', while the atmospheric delivery of 'Over Now' evoked the epic air of the Zeppelin classic, 'Kashmir'. The album reached the Top 5 on both sides of the Atlantic, and Carmassi' Bonhamesque performance ensured that his services were retained for the live band, along with bass player Guy Pratt and ex-Dave Lee Roth keyboard player Brett Tuggle. However, the band were unable to arrange a financially viable world tour, with promoters sceptical of their drawing power in a poor market for traditional heavy rock, and without that support, album sales dwindled. They played six shows in Japan in December 1993, successfully mixing Whitesnake and Zeppelin material with Coverdale Page originals, but these performances were the band's swansong. It seems unlikely that the main protagonists will work together again, especially in view of Page's reunification with Robert Plant.

● ALBUMS: *Coverdale Page* (EMI 1993)★★★.

Cox Family

Willard Cox, an oil field worker from Cotton Valley, Louisiana, USA, grew up listening to country, bluegrass and gospel music. He played the fiddle and sang with his brothers for pleasure. His wife Marie was a local country singer and their children, Evelyn (guitar), Lynn (bass), Sidney (banjo) and Suzanne (mandolin) inherited a love of the same music. Willard put together a demo tape in 1974 to obtain bookings. Soon they were performing far afield and Willard was able to give up his day job. In 1989, Alison Krauss heard one of their tapes and was captivated by their sound and by Sidney's songwriting. The title track of Krauss' *I've Got That Old Feeling* was written by Sidney, while Suzanne sang harmony on the album. Krauss produced their highly acclaimed albums for Rounder Records, and collaborated on 1994's Grammy-nominated *Who Holds Tomorrow* (indeed, Krauss' own vocal stylings are now very close to Suzanne Cox's). Since signing for Rounder, the Cox Family, in various combinations, have sung harmony for singers such as Randy Travis and Emmylou Harris. Both Krauss and Suzanne Cox were featured on Dolly Parton's live album *Heartsongs*. Alison Krauss has said of their singing: 'When you reach the Pearly Gates, they'll be playing the Cox Family.' The Cox Family benefited from Krauss' success by signing to a major label, with Krauss producing *Just When We're Thinking It's Over*. Further surprises were in store with the first single, the Del Shannon falsetto classic 'Runaway'.

● ALBUMS: *Quiet Storm* (Wilcox)★★★, *Everybody's Reaching Out For Someone* (Rounder 1993)★★★, with Krauss *I Know Who Holds Tomorrow* (Rounder 1994)★★★, *Beyond The City* (Rounder 1995)★★★★, *Just When We're Thinking It's Over* (Arista 1996)★★★★.

Cox, Carl

b. 29 July 1962, Oldham, Lancashire, England. Cox is one of the UK's best loved DJs, his reputation for playing up to 14 sets a week and being a permanent fixture on the circuit is well known. He became a full-time DJ in 1985. After serving an apprenticeship as host to a thousand private parties, he eventually graduated to weddings and finally clubs. He helped pioneer the house scene in Brighton in the late 80s, and was highly involved in the development of acid house. He played at the first night of the Shoom club as well as other famous clubs such as Spectrum and Land Of Oz. He was the first to introduce a 'third' deck into a set at the 1989 Sunrise show. Cox remains a great advocate of European techno and house, which forms the basis of most of his live sets. As his popularity grew, it became inevitable that he would release a record of his own. Following his 1991 hit single, 'I Want You (Forever)' (UK number 23), he attempted to woo the airwaves with 'Does It Feel Good To You'. His first 'mix' album arrived on the React Music label in 1995. Cox is also the managing director of Ultimate Music Management and MMR Productions. Cox continues to tour relentlessly all over the world, playing at major clubs and festivals. He has residencies at The End in London and at Twilo in New York City. In 1998, his single 'The Latin Theme' was praised by the critics and a club success, and his 'Essential Mix' on the UK's BBC Radio 1 won the Essential Mix Of The Year award at the *Muzik* (UK magazine) Dance Awards. *Phuture 2000* was released in June 1999, and Cox was voted number 2 in the UK's *DJ* magazine's Top 100 DJs in the world. His exhausting DJing schedule took in Asia, Malta, Ibiza, Amsterdam, Berlin (the Love Parade), Zurich and the UK (including Creamfields, T In The Park, and Glastonbury). A US tour was rounded off by two gigs on New Year's eve, at Home in Sydney and Honolulu in Hawaii.

● COMPILATIONS: *F.A.C.T. (Future Alliance Of Communication And Technology)* (React 1995)★★★, *At The End Of The Cliché* (World Wide Ultimatum 1996)★★★, *F.A.C.T. 2* (World Wide Ultimatum 1997)★★★, *Non-Stop* (ffrr/London 1998)★★★, *The Sound Of Ultimate B.A.S.E* (Moonshine 1998)★★★, *Essential Mix Summer Selection* (ffrr/London 1998)★★★, *Phuture 2000* (World Wide Ultimatum 1999)★★★★, *Non-Stop 2000* (ffrr 1999)★★★.

● FILMS: *Human Traffic* (1999).

Cox, Deborah

b. Toronto, Canada. R&B singer Cox was signed by Arista Records' famed president Clive Davis, previously responsible for discovering names such as Bruce Springsteen, Whitney Houston, Janis Joplin and TLC. Davis' reputation in the industry meant that he was able to unite Cox with some of American R&B's finest producers. Her debut album was recorded with the aid of Keith Thomas (Vanessa Williams, Amy Grant), Keith Crouch, Darryl Simmons and Dallas Austin. Cox had begun singing in her childhood and turned professional at the age of 12, playing small Toronto clubs before attending a performing arts school. She first met her songwriting partner Lascelles Stephens when she was 18, forging a productive creative relationship. A demo recorded together served to alert Davis to Cox's presence, and within months she had moved to Los Angeles and signed with Arista. Before the recording of her debut album was complete she had toured Canada with Celine Dion and performed at showcases in Europe and Asia. Her first single, 'Sentimental', was released in October 1995. The second single, 'Who Do U Love?', sold over half a million copies. As a self-proclaimed R&B diva, her material falls equally between up-tempo/swingbeat numbers and slickly produced ballads. While she is clearly a more able vocalist than many of her peers, sometimes that attribute is lost in her conservative choice of material. Her eagerly anticipated sophomore set, *One Wish*, helped to establish the singer as a recording star. Justifying the praise heaped on the album, the old school ballad 'Nobody's Supposed To Be Here' topped the R&B charts for a record-breaking 14 weeks, and climbed to number 2 on the Hot 100 in January 1999. She enjoyed another US Top 10 hit in October with 'We Can't Be Friends'.

● ALBUMS: *Deborah Cox* (Vaz/Arista 1995)★★★, *One Wish* (Arista 1998)★★★★.

Cracker

A rowdy update of the 70s Californian folk rock fraternity, Cracker are fronted by Redlands natives David Lowery (b. 10 October 1960, San Antonio, USA; formerly the founder of skewed rock architects Camper Van Beethoven) and fellow guitarist Johnny Hickman. Vocalist Lowery had been recording offbeat pop songs from the age of 16, issuing a number of tapes before joining covers bands. From there he graduated to original material with Box Of Laughs and Estonian Gauchos - who included Hickman. When Camper Van Beethoven imploded on tour in 1989, Lowery once again approached Hickman, who had been unable to join the latter band due to solo commitments and his work with ill-fated country band the Unforgiven. Immediately the duo picked up the Lynyrd Skynyrd mantle, also appropriated with less raucous abandon by the Counting Crows, with whom they would tour during 1994. Cracker had by this time already recorded its self-titled debut album for Virgin Records, who still had Lowery under contract following the dissolution of Camper Van Beethoven. The album, with guest help from veteran drummer Jim Keltner and bass player Benmont Tench (of Tom Petty And The Heartbreakers) melded influences as diverse as psychedelia, country rock and delta blues, forging a style that was at once ethnic yet universal - its wry centrepiece, 'Teen Angst' was the first to alert commentators to something a little special about their activities. *Cracker* would sell over 200,000 copies, a figure soon doubled by the follow-up collection, *Kerosene Hat*, which saw a more permanent rhythm aggregation in David Lowering and Bruce Hughes. Much of the 'buzz' concerned opening single 'Low', and its black-and-white video featuring Lowery boxing Sandra Bernhardt - the perfect backdrop to the song's moody, overpowering grunge guitar and lyrical paranoia. Now based in Richmond, Virginia, where Lowery co-owns a studio, some of Camper Van Beethoven's more dizzy excesses spilled over onto the album. These included a final listed track, the beautifully titled 'Hi-Desert Biker Meth Lab', which they never actually completed, instead inserting a 40-second sound collage. The CD release was then programmed with 99 tracks, most of which consisted of three seconds of silence. However, *Kerosene Hat* also worked on a more sober level. 'Nostalgia' offered salutations to the lonely Soviet cosmonaut who spent a year drifting (space being a recurring theme). Other fine moments included a cover version of the Grateful Dead's 'Loser', or the neo-Rolling Stones interlude, 'Take Me Down To The Infirmary'. *The Golden Age*'s move towards country rock indicated their future direction.

● ALBUMS: *Cracker* (Virgin 1992)★★★, *Kerosene Hat* (Virgin 1994)★★★, *The Golden Age* (Virgin 1996)★★, *Gentleman's Blues* (Virgin 1998)★★.

Cradle Of Filth

This outlandish band quickly became the most popular UK representatives of the Satanic black metal revival of the early 90s with the release of their formidable 1994 debut, *The Principal Of Evil Made Flesh*. Visually, Cradle Of Filth were evidently influenced by the Scandinavian bands who led the movement, such as Mayhem and Emperor. This influence included adopting the black and white make-up known as 'corpse-paint' and funereal garb, while incorporating displays of fire-breathing and drenching themselves in blood on stage. While the Scandinavian black metal bands have become increasingly interested in the occult, right-wing philosophies of Viking mythology, Cradle Of Filth have a more gothic, quasi-poetic musical outlook. This is evidenced in their darkly poignant lyrics, use of a cello player

and the haunting singing of Andrea Mayer (a German Satanist who has since married a member of Emperor). The core of Cradle Of Filth's sound, however, remains a blizzard of apocalyptic guitars and vocals. The group entered a tumultuous phase, with the loss of group members and several problems with management and their record label. They eventually regrouped in 1996 for *Vempire: Dark Faerytales In Phallustein*, by which time the group incorporated singer Dani Filth as well as Irish keyboard player Damien, guitarist Stuart and guitarist Jared. The new album was released on Cacophonous as a compromise solution to allow them to escape their contract and release a third studio album, *Dusk ... And Her Embrace*, on the Music For Nations label. Once again it explored at some length their fascination with vampire mythology and Victorian and Medieval romanticism. Jeff Acres (bass, ex-Brutality) joined the band in 1995 and Bryan Hipp (guitar) departed in early 1996. The band gained further notoriety by insulting socialite Tara Palmer Tomkinson at the 1998 *Kerrang!* music awards. The same year's *Cruelty And The Beast* featured a guest appearance from actress Ingrid Pitt on 'Bathory Aria'.
● ALBUMS: *The Principle Of Evil Made Flesh* (Cacophonous 1994)★★, *Vempire: Dark Faerytales In Phallustein* mini-album (Cacophonous 1996)★★★, *Dusk ... And Her Embrace* (Music For Nations 1996)★★, *Cruelty And The Beast* (Music For Nations 1998)★★★★.
● VIDEOS: *PanDaemonAeon* (Music For Nations 1999).

Craig, Carl

A prolific techno third columnist from Detroit, Michigan, Craig rose to prominence on Derrick May's Transmat Records imprint, releasing material under names like Psyche (famed for the pre-trance 'Crackdown' epic) and BFC (notably 'Static Friendly'). Originally he had been inspired by Kraftwerk and early Human League, but after supporting May as a component of Rhythim Is Rhythim his tastes broadened, taking a more ethno-centric view of his surroundings. Following recording sessions for 'Stringz Of Life '89' with May he set up his own label, Planet E, before a six-month sabbatical to England in 1990 (during which time Fragile released 'Galaxy'). Increasingly welcomed across two continents as a prime mover in the Detroit techno sound, Craig has issued a plethora of subsequent material. Most notable among these are his collaboration with Maurizio ('Mind') and his work as Paperclip People ('Remake Uno'), which were licensed from Planet E to the Ministry Of Sound's Open label in the UK. He signed his 69 moniker to R&S Records in 1994. That name had first been employed for the epic 1991 12-inch track 'Ladies And Gentleman', which latterly found favour as a Sound On Sound reissue with DJs like DJ Pierre, Andy Weatherall and Amsterdam's Dimitri. In the meantime the duo remixed 'Le Funk Mob' for Planet E, while Craig offered a new version of 'Throw' for Open. Craig has also performed remix work for prominent artists including the Orb, Yello and Tori Amos. He released his debut long-player (on Blanco y Negro) in 1995, but the follow-up *More Songs About Food And Revolutionary Art* offered more compelling evidence of Craig's superb melodic talent. Craig has subsequently recorded as Innerzone Orchestra.
● ALBUMS: *Landcruising* (Blanco y Negro 1995)★★★, *More Songs About Food And Revolutionary Art* (SSR/Planet 1997)★★★, as Innerzone Orchestra *Programmed* (Talkin' Loud 1999)★★★, *More Songs About Food* (Planet E 1999)★★★.

Cranberries

This band, emanating from Limerick, Eire, boasts the honeyed voice of frontperson Dolores O'Riordan (b. Dolores Mary Eileen O'Riordan, 6 September 1971, Ballybricken, Limerick, Eire). From a conservative, rural Catholic background, she had sung since the age of four in schools and churches. Her guitarist and main co-songwriter is Noel Hogan (b. 25 December 1971), and the line-up is completed by his brother, Mike (b. 29 April 1973; bass), and Feargal Lawler (b. 4 March 1971; drums). The male members had been involved as a band for some time but it had never amounted to much until they joined forces with O'Riordan. The band's original vocalist had given them their previous name - The Cranberry Saw Us. Their debut EP *Uncertain* was released in late 1991 on the Xeric label, whose owner, Pearse Gilmore, became their manager. With its circulation the buzz surrounding the band transferred to the UK, where Island Records underwent tough negotiations (not least due to Gilmore's self-interested protectionism) to tie up a six-album contract. However, *Uncertain* disappointed many journalists who had been given a preview of the far superior songs on the demo (which included 'Put Me Down', 'Dreams' and 'Linger'). Sessions for their debut album also produced rancour, with Gilmore attempting to act as producer, leading to the end of that relationship. The band contacted Rough Trade Records founder Geoff Travis, who had been interested in signing them but who instead took over management (with Jeanette Lee, a former member of Public Image Limited). The album was started from scratch at Windmill Studios, Dublin, with Stephen Street. *Everybody Else Is Doing It, So Why Can't We?* was finally issued in March 1993, following the release of 'Dreams' and 'Linger' as singles. By now much of the original impetus had dissipated, though a 1993 tour with Belly at least seemed to offer some exposure. It helped the band renew their confidence, and was followed by dates with Hothouse Flowers. However, it was American audiences who would first truly appreciate the band. On 10 June they began a six-week tour with The The and they were picked up by college radio. The USA proved to have none of the preconceptions associated with the capricious British press, and the band soon became a hot radio and concert ticket. In July 1994, O'Riordan married their tour manager, Don Burton, in a ceremony distinguished by her see-through bridal attire. The Americans kept buying the album in their droves, and it was also successful in the UK, reaching number 1 in the album chart in June 1994. *No Need To Argue* followed in October, and with its release the Cranberries were crowned as the new kings of AOR. Including the strong single 'Zombie' (despite its rather crude and untimely lyrics concerning the Northern Ireland struggle), the album caused the band to be welcomed anew by the UK media that had long since deserted them. The only doubt hanging over the band's future was the much-repeated opinion that O'Riordan was the star and that, ultimately, she did not need her compatriots. Fortunately this notion was in abeyance on *To The Faithful Departed*, as both chiming guitar and solid drums were very much in the picture. The instruments were solid as O'Riordan wafted in and out with more political diatribes and tortured love stories. This time, 'Bosnia' and the anti-drugs song 'Salvation' shared space with the perplexing 'I Just Shot John Lennon' and the wonderful doo-wop-styled 'When You're Gone', all contributing to another hit of considerable magnitude, although those undecided should digest John Mulvey's highly critical review in the *New Musical Express*, which offers a different appraisal and food for thought. After an extended hiatus, the band returned with 1999's *Bury The Hatchet*, which struggled to reassert their commercial and critical status.

● ALBUMS: *Everybody Else Is Doing It, So Why Can't We?* (Island 1993)★★★★, *No Need To Argue* (Island 1994)★★★★, *To The Faithful Departed* (Island 1996)★★★, *Sa Va Bella (For Lady Legends)* (Qwest/Warners 1997)★★★★, *Bury The Hatchet* (Island 1999)★★.

● CD-ROM: *Doors And Windows* (Philips 1995)★★.

● VIDEOS: *Live* (Island 1994).

● FURTHER READING: *The Cranberries*, Stuart Bailee.

Crash Test Dummies

When songwriter Brad Roberts (vocals/guitar) graduated from the University of Winnipeg, Canada, with an honours degree in English literature, he was still a dedicated student, planning to take a Ph.D. and become a professor. His chronic asthma and penchant for the lyrics of XTC's Andy Partridge did little to dispel his 'college geek' image. However, when the band he had started with friends in the mid-80s took off, his academic interests had to be suspended. Building on impromptu get-togethers as a group formed at an after-hours club in Winnipeg, the name Crash Test Dummies was eventually selected. When record company executives heard some of Roberts' demo tapes (which he had been using to try to secure the band festival gigs), the interest encouraged him to concentrate more fully on music. The band comprised Roberts, his younger brother Dan (bass), Benjamin Darvill (mandolin/harmonica) and Ellen Reid (piano/accordion/backing vocals). Their debut, *The Ghosts That Haunt Me*, rose to number 1 on the Canadian chart on the back of the hit single 'Superman's Song'. A blend of blues-based rock 'n' roll and folk pop, its best moments occurred when Robert's strange vocal amalgam of Scott Walker and Tom Waits combined with Darvill's harmonica. However, despite selling over a quarter of a million copies domestically, the rest of north America remained uninterested. This situation was radically amended with the release of *God Shuffled His Feet*, which introduced drummer Michel Dorge and was co-produced by Talking Heads' Jerry Harrison. Their breakthrough arrived with another distinctive single, 'Mmmm Mmmm Mmmm', with its stuttering title as the song's chorus. A catchy, radio-friendly novelty song, it was only partly representative of the band's more astute and perky pop compositions. Nevertheless, it rose to number 12 on the *Billboard* chart in March 1994. *God Shuffled His Feet* was a strong album, although occasionally its references to literature and schools of philosophy, such as Dada, cubism and Sartre, overbalanced some of the songs. *A Worm's Life* contained more wonderful lyrics about God and life but the songs they accompanied were indifferent, and the momentum gained by the second album was lost when this album, and the subsequent *Give Yourself A Hand*, failed to sell.

● ALBUMS: *The Ghosts That Haunt Me* (Arista 1991)★★, *God Shuffled His Feet* (RCA 1994)★★★★, *A Worm's Life* (Arista 1996)★★, *Give Yourself A Hand* (Arista 1999)★★★.

● VIDEOS: *Symptomology Of A Rock Band* (1994).

Craven, Beverley

b. 28 June 1963, Sri Lanka. Craven grew up in the Home Counties of England before leaving for London at 19. The following years were spent squatting, waitressing and auditioning for an endless cycle of bands. When she could not find the musicians she required she reverted back to the singer/songwriter format, wherein her childhood piano lessons and musical education via Kate Bush came to the fore. Four years of abject poverty eventually led to a deal with Epic Records, under a 'development' contract, who flew her to Los Angeles for a two-month club tour. After abortive and expensive sessions with Stewart Levine she hooked up with Cat Stevens producer Paul Samwell-Smith and members of Fairport Convention. The results of this work bore fruit with her debut, *Promise Me*, initially only successful in Europe, which eventually led to a number 3 placing in the UK charts. The title track reached the same position on the singles chart. She lifted the Best British Newcomer at the 1992 BRIT Awards before giving birth to a daughter in March 1992, and a year later embarked upon a UK concert tour. Her 1993 album release was produced by Samwell-Smith and although it briefly charted, the songs gave an indication that Craven's career was at a crossroads, and that her brand of solo pop belonged to her debut album. She returned after a hiatus of six years with the self-produced, self-written *Mixed Emotions*.

● ALBUMS: *Promise Me* (Columbia 1990)★★★, *Love Scenes* (Epic 1993)★★, *Mixed Emotions* (Epic 1999)★★★.

Cream (club)

In the UK, along with the Ministry Of Sound and Renaissance, Cream became part of the 'superclub' phenomenon of the 90s. It was started by James Barton, Stuart Davenport and Darren Hughes (who left the organisation in July 1997) at Liverpool's Nation club in October 1992, and originally attracted 400 people from the local area. From these humble beginnings, Cream is now a huge business empire, comprising record releases, festivals, merchandise and bars. Weekly, it attracts over 3,000 people from all over the country (and many foreign tourists) to see and hear the skills of some of the world's finest DJs. An often-quoted statistic is that in 1996, 70% of all students applying to the city's John Moore's University said it was their choice because it would allow them to attend Cream. Cream helped form the 'superclub' prototype with its commitment to a quality experience for the clubber: excellent standards of sound, lighting, music and notably, safety. It remains one of the few clubs to provide a free water tap at its bar, essential for those experiencing drug-induced dehydration, was one of the first to have a paramedic in attendance and to work with the local council and emergency services to improve safety standards. The appearance of Cream has also helped bring new commercial life to what was once a desolate part of Liverpool. In 1996, Cream won the UK's *Muzik* magazine's Club Of The Year and, most recently, was voted Mega Club Of The Year by the readers of *Mixmag*. Paul Oakenfold's weekly residency at the club (now commemorated on *Resident – 2 Years Of Oakenfold At Cream*) certainly helped raise its profile in the late 90s. His sets in the club's 'Courtyard' became synonymous with the progressive house and trance which have since become the predominant style of dance music. In January 1999, Seb Fontaine became the club's new resident DJ. The club's annual summer events in Ibiza also became renowned as being among the best clubbing in the world. In 1998, Cream undertook two major new ventures: it staged a US tour, taking some of its well-known DJs to several cities, and Creamfields, a huge outdoor festival which attracted 30,000 people and featured acts such as Run DMC, Primal Scream and the Chemical Brothers, and DJs such as Sasha and Oakenfold. Cream has plans to stage further Creamfields events both in the UK and abroad, as well as residencies and tours in countries such as Ireland, Spain, Greece, Brazil, Argentina, Portugal and the USA. Whether these ambitious plans succeed or fail, there can be no doubt that Cream remains a hugely influential part of the global dance music scene.

● COMPILATIONS: *Cream Live* (Deconstruction 1995)★★★★, *Cream Anthems* (Deconstruction 1997)★★★, *Cream Live 2* (Deconstruction 1997)★★★, *Cream Separates* 3-CD set (Deconstruction 1997)★★★, *Cream Anthems 97* (Deconstruction 1997)★★★, *Resident - 2 Years Of Oakenfold At Cream* (Virgin 1998)★★★★, *Cream Anthems* (Virgin 1998)★★★, *Cream Ibiza Arrivals* (Virgin 1999)★★★, *Cream Ibiza Departures* (Virgin 1999)★★★, *Cream Anthems 2000* (Virgin 2000)★★.

Creation Records

This UK independent record label was formed by Dick Green, Joe Foster (b. 9 August 1960, Bloomsbury, London, England) and music business entrepreneur/reformed British Rail clerk Alan McGee (b. 29 September 1960, Glasgow, Scotland), whose first venture was the dubious Laughing Apple. McGee was brought up in East Kilbride, Scotland. His childhood friends included the members of Creation's first 'name' signing, the Jesus And Mary Chain. McGee's first love was 60s music, particularly psychedelia, and he named his label after the UK cult band of the same name, exhibiting a fond regard for the energy and irreverence of punk. After a tentative step into the world of fanzines with *Communication Blur*, McGee moved to London in 1982. There he established the Living Room, a venue of no fixed abode. The first release on Creation, however, did little to justify his already bold claims. ''77 In '83' was the work of The Legend!, a fanzine editor as eccentric by reputation as McGee. The next 20 singles cultivated a strong identity, if not fervent sales. They came in wraparound plastic sleeves, with 1,000 pressings for each. The best of these saw the debut of the Pastels, which had charm to compensate for the nostalgic arrangements and impoverished production values it shared with its brethren. Other featured bands included the Revolving Paint Dream, Jasmine Minks and McGee's own Biff Bang Pow! There were, however, three milestone records that really signposted the arrival of the label. The first was the Loft's 'Why Does The Rain?', similar in feel to many Creation singles but with a much more focused and emotive delivery. The second was the Jesus And Mary Chain's 'Upside Down'. The latter crystallized the meeting of 60s songwriting with punk's brash shock value, inspiring massive interest in the band, the label, and the numerous imitators that sprung up around them. Finally, Primal Scream's 'Velocity Girl', although not their first record, was the one that brought them to the public's attention. Although the Loft would be short-lived, and the Jesus And Mary Chain would switch to the Warner Brothers Records-distributed Blanco y Negro label, Creation had earned its spurs with the public. Primal Scream would prove pivotal, the lucrative jewel in the Creation crown. Although the glut of success dried up with the arrival of diverse acts such as Nikki Sudden, Clive Langer and Baby Amphetamine, the House Of Love revived fortunes in 1987. They were another band who later left for a larger record company, but new mainstays arrived with music press favourites My Bloody Valentine and then Ride. The high recording costs incurred by the former led to yet another parting of the ways after 1991's *Loveless*. Although McGee sold part of the label to Sony Records to improve its financial position in the 90s, his inspired A&R track record continued. He was able to pick up the Boo Radleys following their split with Rough Trade Records, at a time when their career seemed doomed. The marriage between Creation and the band found first critical success with 1993's *Giant Steps*, then enormous chart and commercial acceptance with 1995's garlanded *Wake Up*. Even more contagious than the Liverpool band's 60s revisionism was the overnight success of Oasis - typically signed by McGee on a whim after seeing them support another Creation act, 18 Wheeler, at a Glasgow concert. Oasis' critical and commercial success between 1994 and 1997, despite looking as though they might implode on various occasions, established Creation as a key player in the UK music industry. McGee, meanwhile, continued to be as uniquely provocative as ever: 'No praise is high enough for Creation. What we are doing is wonderful'. In truth, Creation could arguably lay claim to being the most genuinely innovative of the UK independents. As one critic noted: '[McGee's] willingness to give free reign to bands who seem impossible commercial ventures has resulted in occasionally great artistic, and ironically fiscal, success.' Although the joint venture with Sony was renewed for five years in May 1996, the company experienced increasing difficulties in the late 90s. 3 Colours Red, Hurricane #1, Mishka and One Lady Owner all failed to sell. After a difficult period and no new product from Oasis, it was mooted that Creation was in trouble. The hyped relaunch of Kevin Rowland's career with *My Beauty* was a sales disaster. Two years earlier the label had experienced a similar failure with Nick Heyward. With all hopes pinned on future releases from Primal Scream and Oasis in the year 2000, the label was dealt a double bodyblow with the departure of McGee and Green in November 1999, followed by Oasis' announcement that their new album would be released through their own label.

● COMPILATIONS: *Creation Soup (Volumes 1-5)* (Creation 1991)★★★.

Credit To The Nation

Among the most commercially viable of the UK hip-hop outfits to appear in the early 90s, Credit To The Nation were formed by Matty Hanson (b. Wednesbury, West Midlands, England, aka MC Fusion), with his dancers, Tyrone and Kelvin (aka T-Swing and Mista-G). Credit To The Nation broke through in 1993 after several months of sponsorship by agit-prop anarchists Chumbawamba, with whom they recorded the joint single, 'Enough Is Enough'. They also shared a lyrical platform which attacked racism, sexism and homophobia. Hanson took time out to point out the flaws in the gangsta philosophies of artists such as Ice-T and Onyx, but received short shrift from hardcore hip-hop fans. 'Call It What You Want', which cheekily sampled the guitar motif used by Nirvana on 'Smells Like Teen Spirit', helped them find an audience in hip indie kids outside of the hardcore rap fraternity. There was a backlash to be observed: after threats to his life Hanson was eventually forced to move out of his home in Wednesbury. The band continued with the release of the singles 'Teenage Sensation', which broke into the UK Top 30 in March 1994, and 'Hear No Bullshit, See No Bullshit, Say No Bullshit' - often dedicated to the likes of East 17 and Kriss Kross on stage. Their debut album included pro-female tracks like 'The Lady Needs Respect', the anthemic 'Pump Your Fist', on which Tyrone enjoyed a rare chance to rap, and 'Rising Tide', influenced by the election of BNP councillor Derek Beacon. Among the samples were Benjamin Britten, Glenn Miller, the Sex Pistols and even the Coldstream Guard. The second album was delayed by external pressures, and following its release Hanson left One Little Indian Records. He signed to the German independent Laughing Horse in 1997, and recorded an album in Hamburg. The first fruits of this were heard on the August 1998 release 'Tacky Love Song', which sampled Radiohead's 'High And Dry'.

● ALBUMS: *Take Dis* (One Little Indian 1993)★★★, *Daddy Always Wanted Me To Grow A Pair Of Wings* (One Little Indian 1996)★★★.

Creed

Released in August 1998, Creed's debut album, *My Own Prison*, quickly made an impact on the US *Billboard* charts, after initially being released independently six months earlier. Singer-songwriter Scott Stapp put Creed's connection with his fanbase down to the Tallahassee, Florida, USA band's sense of personal honesty and integrity: 'However they may interpret our music, I think they're feeling the honesty and passion of it, and they know it's sincere.' Stapp had dropped out of Florida State University, where he was studying to be a lawyer, to pursue his musical interests. He became estranged from his religious parents, and most of the lyrics for Creed's debut were written while he slept in his car. Despite his parental troubles, *My Own Prison* contained an unmistakably spiritual edge. The other members of the band were Mark Tremonti (guitar/vocals), Brian Marshall (bass) and Scott Phillips (drums). Producer John Kurzweg worked on both versions of the album, with final mixing for the Wind-up reissue conducted by Soundgarden producer Ron Saint-Germain. The album reached a peak position of 22 on the US album chart. The follow-up, *Human Clay*, debuted at number 1 in October 1999, confirming the band as one of the most popular rock acts of the late 90s.

● ALBUMS: *My Own Prison* (Wind-up 1998)★★★, *Human Clay* (Wind-up 1999)★★★.

Crow, Sheryl

b. Sheryl Crow, 11 February 1962, Kennett, Missouri, USA. Sheryl Crow's asymmetric and abrasive songwriting is not the stuff for lazy listeners. She tackles difficult subjects head-on, wrapping the spare lyrics in angular melodies which stick in the mind. Raised in small town Missouri, Crow's father was a 'driven' lawyer who prosecuted the Ku Klux Klan for ballot-rigging, and defended civil rights in many cases. Both he and Crow's mother played in swing bands, she as vocalist, he as a trumpeter with his close friend Leo. After Leo's sudden death, Wendell put away his trumpet and did not play again until his daughter recorded the tribute song, 'We Do What We Can'. The Crow household also echoed to the sound of an ancient Magnavox record player,

belting out her parents' recordings of the Beatles, Bob Dylan, James Taylor and the Rolling Stones.

Crow arrived in Los Angeles from St Louis in 1986 with $10,000 savings, having broken up with her boyfriend, and determined to be a musician. A classical music degree from Missouri State University and singing with college band Kashmir provided the credentials, but with her savings gone Crow branched out into session work. She soon became one of the most respected and sought-after support artists in LA, working with Dylan, Eric Clapton, Stevie Wonder, Rod Stewart, George Harrison, Don Henley, John Hiatt, Joe Cocker and Sinead O'Connor. Bette Midler and Wynonna also recorded her songs. It had taken Crow over five years to achieve this status, pulling herself back from the brink of despair and over-indulgence at the end of the eighties. This crisis in her life was a consequence of her first big break, an 18-month stint hacking round the world as a backing vocalist on Michael Jackson's *Bad* tour. Three nights a week Jackson, all leather and buckles, stroked the thigh of Shirley (sic) Crow, all leather and lace, as they performed 'I Just Can't Stop Loving You'. However, Crow's vocal ability impressed enough rock luminaries that many doors were open to her when she eventually returned to LA. Unfortunately, all the doors led into rooms of Jackson-style pop, and Crow was sufficiently strong-willed to resist, even as the doors slammed shut, one after another, leaving her isolated and at rock-bottom. After some six month's of retreat (much of it spent in bed, lacking the will to get up) and a little help, she ventured back into the session world.

Her own recording career has an unusual history. Producer Bill Bottrell ran a Pasadena studio called Toad Hall, where Crow and various other musicians used to meet and play informally every week. They adopted *Tuesday Night Music Club* as a sobriquet, and the experience provided the impetus for her debut album. The inspiration was fortuitous and sorely-needed; she had already spent over $250,000 recording a previous debut, only to decide that it was far too polished and unrepresentative to be released. A&M Records had signed her at the behest of Sting's producer Hugh Padgham after she had done some session work for him. Padgham produced her first attempt, but although the relationship worked at a personal level, it failed to ignite the musical spark they sought. Fortunately, the record company thought enough of her talent that they agreed to stand by her and wait for the replacement. The resulting *Tuesday Night Music Club*, recorded with many of the musicians from the Toad Hall sessions, was something of a sleeper when first issued in 1993. The album took almost a year to make an impact, despite being plugged by a succession of marginally successful singles, including 'Run, Baby, Run' and 'Leaving Las Vegas' (US Top 50). Believing that the album was sliding irrevocably into the commercial shadow lands, Crow was about to begin recording its follow-up when A&M suggested releasing 'All I Wanna Do' on a 'what do we have to lose?' basis. The track subsequently became one of the major singles of 1994, reaching number 2 in the USA and number 4 in the UK, and pushing the album into multi-platinum status. 'All I Wanna Do' is a surprising hit. The subject matter relates to a couple of frustrated no-hopers, pouring time down the drain as they indulge in an 'early-morning beer buzz' and hoping in vain to 'have some fun/Before the sun goes down/Over Santa Monica Boulevard'. It was inspired by (previously) obscure poet Wyn Cooper, writing coincidentally about a bar near Crow's Santa Monica home. The idiosyncratic meter and conversational verse structure defy the imposition of an accessible melody. Instead, their memorable phrasing and imagery are contrasted with the catchy and ironically up-beat refrain, and it was this which tripped lightly from the lips of the record-buying public. The remaining tracks were as good as or better than the hit single. 'Strong Enough' dealt with the strains placed on relationships by PMS ('God, I feel like hell tonight ... / ... Are you strong enough to be my man?'). Her earlier experience of manoeuvring around rock's casting couches inspired 'What Can I Do For You' and 'The Na-Na Song'.

In November 1994, Crow duetted with Mick Jagger on 'Under My Thumb' as the Stones played to 65,000 in Miami. The same year she had been one of only two female acts to appear at Woodstock II, in front of 300,000. In 1995, she opened for the Eagles at their massive comeback concerts, as well as touring extensively both on her own account and with Joe Cocker. Finding time to record a follow-up to *Tuesday Night Music Club* proved difficult, but a new album was released at the end of 1996. Retaining just enough of the spontaneity, courage and flair of its predecessor, *Sheryl Crow* won a Grammy for Best Rock Album at the February 1997 awards. Success could become a habit for Crow if radio programmers could discipline themselves not to overplay hit singles such as 'If It Makes You Happy' and 'Everyday is A Winding Road', which has the unfortunate effect of trivializing her songs and making her voice grate on the ear. Both *The Globe Sessions* and 1999's live collection provide a welcome antidote to the AOR slickness of her second album.

● ALBUMS: *Tuesday Night Music Club* (A&M 1993)★★★★, *Sheryl Crow* (A&M 1996)★★★, *The Globe Sessions* (A&M 1998)★★★, *Live From Central Park* (A&M 1999)★★★.

Crowbar

This US quartet emerged in the early 90s as one of the leading lights of the New Orleans extreme metal scene, purveying a sound that blended Black Sabbath/St Vitus-styled heaviness with hardcore aggression. Kirk Windstein (vocals/guitar), Kevin Noonan (guitar), Todd Strange (bass) and Craig Nunenmacher (drums) made their debut with the dark and doom-laden *Obedience Thru Suffering*, after which Noonan was replaced by Matt Thomas, a former bandmate of Pantera frontman Phil Anselmo in Razor White. Anselmo, an old friend who collaborated with Windstein on side-projects such as Down and Both Legs Broken, helped to refine and improve the band's sound with his sympathetic production on *Crowbar*, which included a brutally heavy interpretation of Led Zeppelin's 'No Quarter', adapted stylishly to the Crowbar sound. The band were well received on tour with Paradise Lost in the UK and Pantera in the USA, and released the *Live +1 EP* (which was packaged with *Crowbar* in the UK) before returning to the studio with the stated intention of making *Crowbar* sound 'like Jethro Tull'. In 1995 Jimmy Bowers (ex-Eyehategod) was recruited as the drummer, although *Time Heals Nothing* was recorded by the original line-up. True to form and promise, it provided a thunderous blast of controlled aggression and dark melodicism.

● ALBUMS: *Obedience Thru Suffering* (Grindcore 1992)★★, *Crowbar* (Pavement 1993)★★★, *Time Heals Nothing* (Pavement 1995)★★★,

Broken Glass (Pavement 1996)★★★, *Odd Fellows Rest* (Mayhem 1998)★★★★.

Crowded House

After the break up of Split Enz in 1984, one of its major songwriters, Neil Finn (b. 27 May 1958, Te Awamutu, New Zealand; guitar), along with Split Enz drummer Paul Hester plus Craig Hooper (guitar) and Nick Seymour (bass) formed Crowded House in 1986, after originally calling themselves the Mullanes. Signed to Capitol Records the band resided in Los Angeles (where they were given their new name after their cramped living conditions), and worked with producer Mitchell Froom. With the band by now reduced to a trio with the departure of Hooper, Crowded House's debut album was released to little fanfare, but two singles lifted from it became enormously successful giving the band US chart hits with 'Don't Dream It's Over' (number 2) and 'Something So Strong' (number 7) in 1987. The album had one of the longest ascents up the charts ever noted, eventually peaking at number 12. A subdued reaction to the second album failed to consolidate the band's reputation in the singles chart despite reaching the US Top 40. Paul Young gave the band some welcome publicity in the UK by singing 'Don't Dream It's Over' at the Nelson Mandela concert at Wembley Stadium in June 1988. Neil's reconciliation with brother Tim Finn led to Crowded House strengthening the line-up when he joined in February 1991. The Finn brothers subsequently cracked the UK market with the Top 20 hit 'Fall At Your Feet' (1991) and the Top 10 with 'Weather With You' (1992). The much acclaimed album *Woodface* also reached the Top 10 in the UK. Crowded House's standing in their adopted home of Melbourne, Australia prompted the Melbourne Museum For Performing Arts to inaugurate a Crowded House exhibition containing assorted memorabilia. In November 1991, while the band were enjoying worldwide success, Tim Finn decided to leave the line-up and continue with his solo career. Both brothers were awarded the OBE in June 1993 for their contribution to New Zealand music. In June 1996, they announced their farewell, bowing out with an excellent compilation package featuring three new songs. Their emotional final performance was in Sydney on 24 November 1996. Neil Finn moved on to a solo career, releasing his debut album in June 1998.

● ALBUMS: *Crowded House* (Capitol 1986)★★★, *Temple Of Low Men* (Capitol 1988)★★★, *Woodface* (Capitol 1991)★★★★, *Together Alone* (Capitol 1993)★★★.

● COMPILATIONS: *Recurring Dreams* (Capitol 1996)★★★★★, *After Glow* (Capitol 1999)★★★.

● VIDEOS: *Farewell To The World: Live At The Sydney Opera House* (PolyGram Video 1997).

● FURTHER READING: *Private Universe: The Illustrated Biography*, Chris Twomey and Kerry Doole.

Crystal Method

Perhaps a crude simplification, Ken Jordan and Scott Kirkland - the Crystal Method – have been described as the USA's answer to the Chemical Brothers. They relocated from Las Vegas to Los Angeles in 1989 after working on vocal house tracks but having become increasingly interested in underground, non-vocal dance music. The Crystal Method's sound is a hybrid of 70s funk and disco samples (from artists such as Stevie Wonder and Isaac Hayes) and dense layers of percussion and synthesized loops. The distortion and treatment of these electronic sounds can, paradoxically, often make them sound like more traditional instruments. Their tracks have appeared on many trip-hop compilations and they have made numerous appearances at events and clubs in the USA and Europe. Like the Chemical Brothers, their music is at its best as accelerated breakbeats with funky basslines, startling crescendos and unexpected drops.

● ALBUMS: *Vegas* (Sony 1998)★★★.

Cubanismo

This all-star Cuban big band was formed in 1995 by Jesús Alemañy (b. 14 October 1962, Guanabacoa, Havana, Cuba; trumpet, ex-Sierra Maestra), initially for a recording session at Egrem studios in Havana with producer Joe Boyd. Also in the line-up were Alfredo Rodriquez, veteran percussionist Tata Gianes, trumpeters Louis Alemany and Louis Alemany Jnr. (Jesus' uncle and cousin, respectively) and various members of Irakere. *Jesús Alemañy's ¡Cubanismo!* (the word 'Cubanismo' translates as 'typical of Cuba') featured a selection of mostly instrumental tracks, based around classic Cuban dance rhythms, all performed with the raw energy and improvisational flair of the best Latin jazz. Critical response to the album was highly favourable and it featured in many world music polls for 1996, in the Best Of Latin category. The band subsequently toured and recorded a follow-up, *Malembe*. Released in 1997, it utilized the same formula of Cuban dance rhythms performed in a big-band Latin jazz style. *Reencarnación* introduced pianist Nachito Herrera, who replaced Alfredo Rodriquez, and was a more straight ahead Latin album, with less of a big band feel and more vocals (singer Rollo Martinez had also been added to the line-up). The band promoted it with an extensive tour of Europe and the USA, which included performances at the North Sea Jazz and Montreux International Jazz Festivals.

● ALBUMS: *Jesús Alemañy's ¡Cubanismo!* (Hannibal 1996)★★★★, *Malembe* (Hannibal 1997)★★★, *Reencarnación* (Hannibal 1998)★★★★.

Culture Beat

Euro-dance sensations created by Torsten Fenslau (d. November 1993, Darmstadt, Germany) in 1989 by putting together the more visual duo of Jay Supreme and Tania Evans. Fenslau had begun his career DJing at the Dorian Gray club at Frankfurt Airport, also working on Hessen State radio presenting the Club Night and Maxi-Mix shows. He subsequently moved into production, scoring a solo hit under the banner Out Of The Ordinary with 'Los Ninos Mix', although it did not find success outside of his native Germany. The same could hardly be said for Culture Beat, who quickly racked up huge overground dancefloor hits with 'No Deeper Meaning', 'Mr Vain', and 'Got To Get It'. In its wake Fenslau remixed for the Shamen ('Coming On Strong') and released a solo progressive trance single, 'Come Into My Heart', as Abfahrt, and was behind Cheery Lips' 'Das Erdbbermund'. 'Mr Vain' sold over two million copies and topped the UK charts, but sadly Fenslau didn't live long enough to see his endeavours bear fruit. He was involved in a car crash in November 1993, dying from internal injuries when he reached hospital. The Culture Beat members informed the press of their intention to carry on in his absence, scoring another UK Top 5 hit with 'Anything' in 1994. Alex Abraham became Fenslau's replacement as musical guru to Culture Beat, alongside long-term collaborators Peter Zweier and Nosie Katzman.

● ALBUMS: *Horizon* (Epic 1991)★★★, *Serenity* (Epic 1993)★★★.

Curve

A chart-topping indie act who never quite made the transition to commercial success despite an armoury of impressive songs. Their most prominent feature was the distinctive and opinionated voice of Toni Halliday, one of three children born to a liberal Roman Catholic mother and single parent. Her major collaborator and songwriting partner was Dean Garcia (guitar). The original precocious child, Halliday secured her first recording contract at the age of 14, moving to London where she floundered with pop duo the Uncles. She later met David A. Stewart in Sunderland and they remained friends; at this stage, Halliday met another member of Stewart's inner sanctum, Garcia, who had played on the Eurythmics albums *Touch* and *Be Yourself Tonight*. They joined forces in the equally pallid State Of Play, who were signed to Virgin Records and released two singles and an album, *Balancing The Scales*. After their acrimonious split, Halliday turned to session work (appearing on Robert Plant's *Now And Zen*) and released a ghastly solo album, 1989's *Hearts And Handshakes*, before reuniting with Garcia to sign to the Eurythmics' AnXious label as Curve. Halliday had taken a tape of the song 'Ten Little Girls' to Stewart, who was immediately impressed. The results were three EPs, *Blindfold*, *Frozen* and *Cherry* (collected on *Pubic Fruit*), which were well received by the UK indie rock press, and purchased in hefty quantities despite cynics citing Halliday as a stubborn careerist. The groundwork laid for a potentially rich recording career continued with the creation of their own studio and an expanded line-up including Debbie Smith and Alex Mitchell (guitars) and Monti (drums). However, although the critics remained somewhat in awe of the band's distant resonance, two albums and a series of singles (later efforts such as 'Blackerthreetracker') merged the Curve sound with industrial and techno elements) failed to build on the press profile. The band eventually sundered, amicably, in 1994. Halliday collaborated with cult dance music outfit Leftfield for 1995's 'Original' and worked with Curve producer/guitarist Andrew Moulder as Scylla, while Debbie Smith went on to join Echobelly. Garcia and Halliday regrouped in November 1997 with new members Rob Holliday (guitar) and Stephen Spring (drums) for live gigs and *Come Clean*. The album featured the excellent single 'Chinese Burn' (also used on a Sony Discman commercial), but showed little sign of any musical progress. Garcia later recorded as Headcase.

● ALBUMS: *Doppelgänger* (AnXious/Charisma 1992)★★★, *Cuckoo* (AnXious/Charisma 1993)★★★, *Come Clean* (Universal 1998)★★★.
Solo: Toni Halliday *Hearts And Handshakes* (WTG 1989)★★.

● COMPILATIONS: *Pubic Fruit* (AnXious/Charisma 1992)★★★★, *Radio Sessions* (AnXious 1993)★★★.

Cyclefly

This European metal outfit were formed in 1995 from the ashes of French band Seventeen. The multi-national trio, Christian Montagne (b. France; bass), Jean Michel Cavallo (b. France; drums), and Nono Presta (b. Italy; guitar), decamped to Ireland where they linked up with brothers

Ciaran (b. Aghada, County Cork, Eire; guitar) and Declan O'Shea (b. 18 May 1972, Aghada, County Cork, Eire; vocals). Declan's manic stage presence earned the band as much notice as their music, which fused the energy of US industrial rock with a keen melodic sensibility, earning comparisons to alternative rock legends Jane's Addiction and Smashing Pumpkins. Several showcase gigs in London confirmed their live ability, and led to a deal with Radioactive Records. Taking a break from their touring schedule, the band relocated to California to work on their debut album with the experienced producer Sylvia Massy. The moody, angst-ridden *Generation Sap* earned the band uniformly positive reviews when it was released in May 1999.

● ALBUMS: *Generation Sap* (Radioactive 1999)★★★.

Cypress Hill

Another of the new rap breed to extol the creative use of marijuana/hemp, this interracial trio from the Latin quarter of Los Angeles are champions of NORML (National Organisation To Reform Marijuana Laws), and perform tracks such as 'I Wanna Get High', 'Legalize It' and 'Insane In The Brain' which advocate marijuana as a cultural replacement for alcohol. However, the reason for their widespread success lies instead with their blend of full and funky R&B, tales of dope and guns adding the final sheen to the laid-back beats. The crew was formed by DJ Muggs (b. Lawrence Muggerud, 28 January 1968, Queens, New York, USA, of Italian descent), and vocalists B-Real (b. Louis Freese, 2 June 1970, Los Angeles, California, USA, of Mexican/Cuban descent) and Sen Dog (b. Senen Reyes, 20 November 1965, Cuba). Sen Dog had come to Los Angeles from his native Cuba at the age of 14. With his younger brother Mellow Man Ace, he had formed the prototype rap outfit, DVX, and claims to have invented the Spanglish 'lingo' style. The line-up also included former 7A3 members DJ Muggs and B-Real. When Mellow Man Ace left to start a solo career the remaining trio renamed themselves after a local street. Their self-titled 1991 debut was only available in the UK on import for some time, though in the US it created a lot of interest almost immediately, and eventually went platinum. Longstanding B-boys, touring for free and opening for Naughty By Nature, Cypress Hill represented rap's new wave. After the militancy and radicalism of Public Enemy and NWA, Cypress Hill were advocating escapism via blunts, and making it sound very attractive indeed, particularly to the all important white alternative rock audience. The second album, rather than pursuing a more commercial bent, was informed by dark events in their home city, specifically the Rodney King beating. *Black Sunday* debuted at Number 1 in the US R&B and Pop charts in 1993, and contained the Top 20 crossover hit 'Insane In The Brain'. The gun-touting 'Cock The Hammer' also turned up on the soundtrack to Arnold Schwarzenegger's mega-flop, *Last Action Hero*. Their reputation for violent lyrics (a method they justified as: 'not promoting, more explaining what goes on') was underscored when they appeared on the soundtrack for another movie, *Mad Dog And Glory*, in a scene which accompanies a drug killing. They also recorded tracks with Pearl Jam ('Real Thing') and Sonic Youth ('I Love You Mary Jane') for the movie *Judgement Night*. Their breakthrough in the UK came when they supported House Of Pain on dates through 1993, after which they achieved a

string of Top 20 singles. The latter crew, and several others including Ice Cube and the Beastie Boys, benefited from the services of DJ Muggs' in-demand production skills. Eric Bobo joined the crew in 1994 as a percussionist. Their third long-player, the dark, edgy *III: Temples Of Boom*, lost Cypress Hill their college audience but regained the respect of the hip-hop community. It was also a commercial success, debuting at US number 3. Sen Dog left in February 1996 to work with his punk/metal outfit SX-10 and was replaced by DJ Scandalous, who had already worked with the crew. A nine-track EP of rare remixes followed before the members concentrated on solo projects, with Muggs releasing *Muggs Presents ... The Soul Assassins Chapter 1* and B-Real working with the Psycho Realm. Cypress Hill, with Sen Dog back on board, made an impressive artistic comeback in 1998 with *Cypress Hill IV*, although the album failed to break into the US Top 10.

● ALBUMS: *Cypress Hill* (Ruffhouse/Columbia 1991)★★★★, *Black Sunday* (Ruffhouse/Columbia 1993)★★★, *III: Temples Of Boom* (Ruffhouse/Columbia 1995)★★★, *Unreleased & Revamped EP* mini-album (Ruffhouse/Columbia 1996)★★, *Cypress Hill IV* (Ruffhouse/Columbia 1998)★★★.

● COMPILATIONS: *Los Grandes Exitos En Espanol* (Sony 1999)★★★.

Cyrus, Billy Ray

b. 25 August 1961, Flatwoods, Kentucky, USA. Cyrus comes from a preaching family and made his singing debut in his father's gospel group. In 1983, he formed his own band, Sly Dog, but they lost their equipment in a fire in Los Angeles. He then worked as a car salesman, but he kept visiting Nashville in the hope of finding musical success. In 1992, he turned the Marcy Brothers' 'Don't Tell My Heart' into the simple but immensely catchy 'Achy Breaky Heart'. Although the Cyrus virus proved infectious, the song's rhythms were close to Don Williams' 'Tulsa Time'. The video, in which the muscular, ponytailed Cyrus was mobbed by adoring women, also introduced a country music dance - the Achy Breaky. The song topped both the US pop and country charts and was easily the most successful country single released in the UK during 1992. Another star, Travis Tritt, derided Cyrus for turning country music into 'an asswiggling contest'. Cyprus' album, *Some Gave All*, also topped the US pop and country charts, while he had a further transatlantic hit, 'Could've Been Me', and recorded a parody of 'Achy Breaky Heart' with the Chipmunks. *Storm In The Heartland*, featuring guest appearances from the Oak Ridge Boys and Danny Shirley of Confederate Railroad, and subsequent releases *Trail Of Tears* and *Shot Full Of Love* attempted to move Cyrus away from his lightweight image. Unfortunately with the proliferation of line-dancing clubs, it appears as though he will remain indelibly associated with the Achy Breaky. Whatever happens, his Mel Gibson looks and Chippendale body will always work to his advantage.

● ALBUMS: *Some Gave All* (Mercury 1992)★★★★, *It Won't Be The Last* (Mercury 1993)★★★, *Storm In The Heartland* (Mercury 1994)★★★, *Trail Of Tears* (Mercury 1996)★★, *Shot Full Of Love* (Mercury 1998)★★.

● COMPILATIONS: *The Best Of Billy Ray Cyrus Cover To Cover* (Mercury 1997)★★★.

● VIDEOS: *Billy Ray Cyrus* (1992), *Live* (1992), *Storm In the Heartland* (Mercury 1994), *One On One* (PolyGram Music Video 1994), *The Complete Video Collection* (PolyGram Music Video 1997).

D'Angelo

b. Michael Archer, 11 February 1974, Richmond Virginia, USA. R&B singer-songwriter and multi-instrumentalist D'Angelo was signed by EMI Records at the age of 18, whereupon he relocated to New York to develop his musical career. He quickly repaid EMI's investment, co-writing and co-producing the major US hit single 'U Will Know', sung by an all-star cast (including Jodeci, R. Kelly and Tevin Campbell), and credited to Black Men United. Influenced by Marvin Gaye and Curtis Mayfield, with a vernacular lifted from modern urban R&B, D'Angelo won the Harlem Apollo talent contest three times in succession before embarking on sessions for his debut album. This utilized antiquated equipment including a Wurlitzer and old effects boxes as well as modern technology in the form of drum machines and computers. Alongside Ben Harper, it saw D'Angelo celebrated as representing a return to the singer-songwriter tradition in black music following the dominance of hip-hop. Ironically, it emerged on dance/rap label Cooltempo Records in the UK. His concert appearances in support of the record, with strictly live instrumentation, also drew strong reviews and further mainstream press. D'Angelo subsequently contributed soundtrack work to the movies *Scream 2*, *Down In The Delta* and *Belly*, and duetted with Lauryn Hill on 'Nothing Even Matters' from her acclaimed *The Miseducation Of Lauryn Hill*. D'Angelo debuted at US number 1 in February 2000 with the long-awaited *Voodoo*, an occasionally inspired collection of songs crafted from endless studio jams.
● ALBUMS: *Brown Sugar* (EMI 1995)★★★★, *Live At The Jazz Cafe, London* (EMI 1998)★★★, *Voodoo* (EMI 2000)★★★.

D'Arby, Terence Trent

b. 15 March 1962, Manhattan, New York, USA. A soulful pop singer, D'Arby first became involved with the music business while posted as a soldier in Germany where he joined a local funk band, Touch, in 1983 (*Early Works*, a collection of his contributions to Touch, was released in 1989). Following his move to London he recorded a demo tape which was impressive enough for CBS Records to sign him. His first single, 1987's 'If You Let Me Stay', reached the UK Top 10 and *Introducing The Hardline According To Terence Trent D'Arby* was one of the most successful debut albums of recent years. In addition to reaching UK number 1 and US number 4, it spent over a year in the top half of the UK charts and sold several million copies worldwide. The album also generated two further UK hit singles, 'Wishing Well' (number 4) and 'Sign Your Name' (number 2). Both songs were also huge hits in America, with the former topping the pop charts in 1988. D'Arby's self-publicity was less well-received, and his clumsy criticism of his homeland and his posing naked on a cross

both backfired. This was followed by the commercial and artistic failure of 1989's *Neither Fish Nor Flesh* which spent barely a month in the UK charts (a commercial decline repeated in the USA). Although 1993's *Symphony Or Damn: Exploring The Tension Inside The Sweetness* was well-received, its more rock-orientated styles were still suspiciously viewed. The album helped to restore D'Arby as a commercial force in the UK, reaching number 4 and generating four Top 20 singles, 'Do You Love Me Like You Say?', 'Delicate' (with Des'ree), 'She Kissed Me' and 'Let Her Down Easy'. *Vibrator* finally arrived after a two-year wait, and continued the transition from smooth soul to a harder-edged sound. It was preceded by the Sam Cooke-influenced single 'Holding On To You', and 'Supermodel Sandwich', which achieved strong airplay because of its inclusion on the soundtrack of the much-publicized Robert Altman movie *Prêt-A-Porter*. The album featured a new recording line-up of Luke Goss (drums, ex-Bros), Branford Marsalis (saxophone), Patrice Rushen (piano) and Charlie Sepulveda (trumpet).
● ALBUMS: *Introducing The Hardline According To Terence Trent D'Arby* (Columbia 1987)★★★★, *Neither Fish Nor Flesh* (Columbia 1989)★★, *Symphony Or Damn: Exploring The Tension Inside The Sweetness* (Columbia 1993)★★★, *Vibrator* (Columbia 1995)★★★.
● VIDEOS: *Introducing The Hardline: Live* (CBS-Fox 1988).
● FURTHER READING: *Neither Fish Nor Flesh: Inspiration For An Album*, Paolo Hewitt.

D-Influence

A jazz funk quartet from London, England, D-Influence made an immediate impact with their debut white label release in 1990. 'I'm The One'/'The Classic' combined a hip-hop beat, programmed by the band's guitarist, Ned B (aka Ed Baden Powell), with the distinctive vocals of the then 18 year-old jazz singer Sarah Ann Webb. Steve Marston (multi-instrumentalist) and Kwame Kwaten (keyboards) are the other long-standing members. Previously the band had worked with artists such as Neneh Cherry, and came together through a mutual interest in club music and nightlife. As might have been predicted by descriptions of their music, they initially signed to the Acid Jazz Records stable, preceding a debut album for East West Records, but the record saw them suffer numerous comparisons to Soul II Soul and De La Soul. However, its sales of only 30,000 attested more to a lack of adequate promotion and radio play than talent, and it did earn the band the admiration of artists such as Prince, Michael Jackson and Mick Jagger, each of whom they would support later in their career. They also collaborated with Björk (on her *Later With Jools Holland* television appearance) and Seal (his second album). Their own second album in 1995, *Prayer 4 Unity*, included contributions from dub poet Linton Kwesi Johnson and Kenny Wellington, formerly horn player with Light Of The World. The album was well received, *Muzik* magazine citing it as a 'lovely mixture of British black music with the odd boogie tune thrown in to make sure you know where they're coming from.' *London* incorporated a wider range of influences from rap to gospel, held together by Webb's distinctive vocals.
● ALBUMS: *Good 4 We* (East West 1992)★★, *Prayer 4 Unity* (East West 1995)★★★, *London* (Echo 1997)★★★.

D:Ream

This London-based outfit crossed over from dance music clubs to daytime radio, and won themselves impressive chart placings in the process. D:Ream originally comprised Al Mackenzie (b. Alan Mackenzie, 31 October 1968, Edinburgh, Scotland) and Peter Cunnah (b. 30 August 1966, Derry, Northern Ireland; ex-Tie The Boy, Baby June). Their first outing came at the JFK Bar in Great Portland Street, London, in February 1992. Four months later Rhythm King Records released their debut 45, 'U R The Best Thing' (the Prince-like spellings would become a regular feature of their titles). Although they failed to score many credibility points amongst their dance music peers, they nevertheless became a sought-after remix team among mainstream pop artists (Deborah Harry, EMF, Duran Duran). Both 'U R The Best Thing' and, later, 'Things Can Only Get Better' were reissued in the wake of their higher profile and initial chart appearances. Their debut album, released in August 1993, was roundly rubbished by the press. Mackenzie too appeared less than happy with its new pop direction, and announced his decision to leave the band in October 1993 and return to DJ work. The revitalised 'Things Can Only Get Better' enjoyed a long stay at the top of the UK pop charts in early 1994, when there was some derision among the puritan dance community, with Pressure Of Speech lambasting the track for its potential to be 'the next Tory Conference song' (ironically, the song was used by the Labour Party in their triumphant 1997 election campaign). Shortly afterwards, a second remix of 'U R The Best Thing' reached UK number 4. Mackenzie, meanwhile, was embarking on a solo career as (among other things) Kitsch In Sync ('Jazz Ma Ass' for Global Grooves in 1994). The band's only other Top 10 hit came in summer 1995 when 'Shoot Me With Your Love' reached UK number 7.
● ALBUMS: *D:Ream On Vol. 1* (Rhythm King 1993)★★★, *World* (Magnet 1995)★★.
● COMPILATIONS: *The Best Of D:Ream* (Magnet 1997)★★★.

Da Brat

b. Shawntae Harris, Chicago, Illinois, USA. A forerunner of the new breed of female hip-hop artists Lil' Kim and Foxy Brown, the foul-mouthed Da Brat became the most successful female rapper of all time in 1994 with her platinum-selling debut *Funkdafied*. Harris' first musical experience was as a drummer in her church choir, but her big break came in 1992 when she won a local MC contest sponsored by *Yo MTV Raps*. The prize for winning was a meeting with the hugely successful teenage rap duo Kriss Kross. The duo introduced her to their producer/manager Jermaine Dupri, who promptly signed the rapper to his So So Def label. Dupri set about styling Da Brat as a female version of Snoop Doggy Dogg, underpinning her in-your-face rapping style with his trademark G-funk rhythms. Released in June 1994, *Funkdafied* shocked the male-dominated world of hip-hop when it debuted at number 1 on the *Billboard* rap chart and also broke into the Top 20 of the Hot 200. The title track, which was built around a sample of the Isley Brothers' 'Between The Sheets', was a million-seller which topped the rap singles chart for an incredible 11 weeks. Da Brat's success was all the more encouraging in that it was achieved without recourse to any of the blatant sexual exploitation that marked the careers of the female rappers who followed

in her wake. The follow-up, *Anuthatantrum*, was a partially successful response to critics who insisted she was just another of Dupri's pawns. It included the hit single 'Ghetto Love', featuring TLC's T-Boz. Although she returned to the studio to begin work on a third album, Da Brat has also been attempting to establish an acting career.
● ALBUMS: *Funkdafied* (So So Def 1994)★★★, *Anuthatantrum* (So So Def 1996)★★★.
● FILMS: *Kazaam* (1996), *Rhyme & Reason* (1997).

Da Bush Babees

A New York, USA-based hip-hop trio comprising Khaliyl (aka Mister Man), Lee Major (aka Babyface Kaos) and Light (aka Y-Tee). They had only been together for three months before signing to Warner Brothers Records and releasing their 1994 debut, *Ambushed*. This borrowed heavily from downtown reggae as well as the hip-hop tradition, reflecting the trio's West Indian upbringings. The trio were also keen to emphasise their positivity, writing a number of songs reacting angrily to the ghetto stereotypes propagated by gangsta rap. That theme continued on *Gravity*, the 1996 follow-up collection released under the shortened name of Bush Babees, which was produced by the trio alongside Posdnous (De La Soul), Sean J. Period, Ali Shaheed and Q-Tip (A Tribe Called Quest). Among the album's strongest tracks was 'The Love Song', a freestyle hip-hop tune harking back to the old school values of Grandmaster Flash and Melle Mel And The Furious 5.
● ALBUMS: *Ambushed* (Warners 1994)★★★, as Bush Babees *Gravity* (Warners 1996)★★★.

Da Lench Mob

Hardcore gangsta rappers and protégés of Ice Cube, signed to his Street Knowledge label, Da Lench Mob were originally employed as backing musicians on their benefactor's first three solo recordings, before eventually making their own debut on *Guerillas In Tha Mist*. The title, an obvious pun on the movie of similar name, was picked up by the trio from a police report issued after attending a Los Angeles domestic incident. Although Da Lench Mob share many lyrical concerns with Ice Cube, there is a distinct moral tone stressed in their distrust of drugs and dealers. Front person J-Dee numbers amongst the more articulate of rap's inner city spokesmen. He was joined by the backing duo of T-Bone (b. Terry Gray) and Shorty (b. Jerome Washington). However, after his arrest for attempted murder and subsequent imprisonment, J-Dee was dropped from the crew at the end of 1993. This was caused, according to press statements, because of contractual obligations with which Da Lench Mob were enforced to comply. His replacement was Maulkie, from ex-rap duo Yomo And Maulkie. Ironically, it was always Da Lench Mob's intention to recruit Maulkie, but contractual problems, once again, prevented this at the start of their career. His vocals were dubbed over their previously completed set, *Planet Of Da Apes*. However, T-Bone too would subsequently be charged with murder (he was acquitted the following year), and East West dropped the group in 1994.
● ALBUMS: *Guerillas In Tha Mist* (Street Knowledge/East West 1992)★★★★, *Planet Of Da Apes* (Street Knowledge/Priority 1994)★★★.

Daft Punk

Guy-Manuel de Homem Christo (b. 8 February 1974) met Thomas Bangalter (b. 3 January 1975) when they both attended school in Paris, France, in 1987. In 1992, heavily influenced by the Beach Boys, they recorded a song under the name Darling, which in turn found its way onto a compilation single issued on Stereolab's Duophonic label. A review in the UK's *Melody Maker* described their effort as 'a bunch of daft punk', which depressed the pair but unwittingly gave them a name for their next project. Increasingly influenced by the house sounds filtering across from the UK and the USA, they signed with the Scottish label Soma Records and, in 1994, released the single 'New Wave'. However, it was their 1995 offering, an insanely catchy slice of techno/funk, 'Da Funk', that really set the Daft Punk bandwagon rolling, especially when the Chemical Brothers spotted its floor-filling potential during their DJ sets. One important factor in the duo's sound is that they are not dance music purists; neither had been to a dance club until 1992 and their music is as influenced as much by Roxy Music and the Ramones as it is by house and techno pioneers such as Laurent Garnier. There is also a strong streak of old-style disco running through their work; Bangalter's father wrote hits for Ottawan and the Gibson Brothers, and 'Da Funk' is based around a riff from a vintage R303 bass machine. The re-release of 'Da Funk' by Virgin Records, and the subsequent *Homework*, broke Daft Punk to an overground audience that had for too many years seen French pop as synonymous with crooners such as Johnny Hallyday. Bangalter's alter ego, Stardust, was responsible for 'Music Sounds Better With You', one of the club anthems of 1998.

● ALBUMS: *Homework* (Virgin 1997)★★★★.

Daisy Chainsaw

Contrived but fun UK pop punk outfit whose sudden appearance brightened up the independent scene of the early 90sl. Led by fragile singer Katie Jane Garside, the band also comprised Richard Adams (bass), Vince Johnson (drums) and Crispin Gray (guitar). They debuted with the *LoveSickPleasure* EP, which spiralled into the UK Top 30, aided by the highly colourful video for lead track 'Love Your Money'. Radio 1 had picked up on the song's frenetic pace, and the indie media were similarly impressed by Garside's 'Victorian chimney sweep' image, barefoot with torn dresses and covered in dirt. Allegations of sexual and psychological abuse suggested by one interview were later vehemently denied, but there is little doubt that the band's presentation was disturbingly resonant of the child as victim. The success of the EP encouraged them to sign with larger independent One Little Indian Records, despite tantalizing offers from the majors. However, their record company must have quickly learned to regret their enthusiasm. Shortly after a hit-and-miss debut album produced by Ken Thomas (although there were strong tracks in 'Lonely Ugly Brutal World' and 'Use Me Use You'), Garside announced her departure. The band attempted to soldier on and finally re-emerged with 'You're Gruesome' for Fluffy Bunny Records in 1995. Gray and Garside later reunited in Queen Adreena.

● ALBUMS: *Eleventeen* (Wayward/One Little Indian 1992)★★★.

Damage

Led by the striking figure of singer Andrez, Damage was one of several British R&B outfits who attempted to capitalize on Mark Morrison's international breakthrough. The quintet was formed at school at the beginning of the 90s, when the members were all teenagers. They sent a demo tape of a version of a Jackson Five song to Jazz Summers of Big Life Records in early 1995. Although Summers was impressed by the quality of their singing and harmonies, he waited 18 months before issuing their first record. 'Anything', composed by US songwriter Terri Robinson and featuring Little Caesar (of Junior MAFIA), was released in July 1996. Although it only charted at a lowly number 62, the record received excellent reviews (including Single Of The Week in *Blues & Soul* magazine). Encouraged by the response, Big Life set about establishing the quintet's name with a series of showcases and public appearances. Thereafter, they made quick inroads into the charts. Their second single, 'Love II Love', reached number 12, while the follow-up, 'Forever', was a number 6 hit during the lucrative Christmas period. Damage also supported teen sensations Boyzone at their Wembley Stadium performance. Their self-titled debut album followed, along with two further UK Top 10 singles - 'Love Guaranteed' and a cover version of Eric Clapton's 'Wonderful Tonight', the latter reaching number 3.

● ALBUMS: *Damage* (Big Life 1997)★★★★.

Damn Yankees

Formed in 1989, the Damn Yankees were one of several supergroups, including Bad English, to emerge in the USA towards the end of the decade. Tommy Shaw (guitar/vocals, ex-Styx) had already been writing with the larger-than-life solo artist Ted Nugent (guitar)and they were soon joined by Jack Blades (bass/vocals, ex-Night Ranger) and Michael Cartellone, a previously unknown drummer. Warner Brothers beat Geffen Records in the race to sign the band, and their self-titled debut album was released in 1990. The music was hard-edged melodic rock, much heavier than the work of Styx and Night Ranger, with Shaw and Blades handling the bulk of the vocal duties, although Nugent contributed lead vocals to the outrageous 'Piledriver'. The album reached number 13 in the US *Billboard* charts with the help of a Top 5 single - the power ballad 'High Enough', which reached number 3 in September 1990. Damn Yankees, however, were not simply a record company creation. They could also produce sparkling live performances, gaining a glowing reputation for their shows. These included tantalizing snippets from the respective back catalogues of Styx, Night Ranger and Ted Nugent's solo work. The melodic influence of Shaw and Blades, combined with the melodramatic antics of Nugent, created a highly successful unit in terms of both critical acclaim and commercial success. A second album, *Don't Tread*, climbed to number 22 in August 1992, but the following year the band called it a day.

● ALBUMS: *Damn Yankees* (Warners 1990)★★★, *Don't Tread* (Warners 1992)★★★.

Dandy Warhols

This Portland, Oregon, USA quartet emerged when Peter Holmstrom (guitar) pressured friend Courtney Taylor (vocals/guitar/keyboards) into forming a band in mid-1993. The duo enlisted the aid of the equally inexperienced Eric

Hedford (keyboards/drums/vocals). Fourth member Zia McCabe (keyboards/bass/percussion) was asked to round out the line-up despite having never played an instrument before. Originally calling themselves Andy Warhol's Wet Dream, the band changed its name to the Dandy Warhols and soon made a name for itself on the Portland club scene. Tapping into the trippier side of psychedelic rock, the band's shows travelled the same astral plane as early Pink Floyd, Syd Barrett and Hawkwind. In 1995, the Dandy Warhols recorded *Dandys Rule OK* for Portland label Tim Kerr. Their moody debut was coached in lots of atmospherics and featured tributes to Lou Reed ('(Tony, This Song Is Called) Lou Weed') and Andy Warhol's quip on fame via an extended 16-minute jam ('It's A Fast-Driving Rave Up With The Dandy Warhols'). The band's live shows and impressive debut soon started a major-label bidding war which the cheeky quartet took advantage of by going out to dinner with as many A&R reps as possible. After signing with Capitol Records, the band released *The Dandy Warhols Come Down*. The album showed them delving into 'shoegazing' space-rock reminiscent of Spiritualized and My Bloody Valentine, particularly on songs such as 'Be-In' and 'Pete International Airport', and showing a knack for straightforward garage rock ('Cool As Kim Deal'). The biggest attention grabber was 'Not If You Were The Last Junkie On Earth', a song that ostensibly criticized heroin use but instead passed it off as being merely passé. A video was later made by famed photographer David LaChappelle. After touring as an opening act for Teenage Fanclub and Radiohead, the Dandy Warhols returned to the studio in early 1999.

● ALBUMS: *Dandys Rule OK* (Tim Kerr 1995)★★★, *The Dandy Warhols Come Down* (Tim Kerr/Capitol 1997)★★★★.

Danzig

US rock band Danzig are largely a vehicle for the lyrical and musical talents of Glenn Danzig (b. 23 June 1959, Lodi, New Jersey, USA). Using musicians from his previous bands, the Misfits and Samhain - guitarist John Christ (b. 19 February 1965, Baltimore, Maryland, USA) and bass player Eerie Von (b. 25 August 1964, Lodi, New Jersey, USA) - plus stylish hardcore veteran Chuck Biscuits on drums (ex-D.O.A.; Black Flag; Circle Jerks), he founded Danzig in 1987 and sold the concept to Rick Rubin's Def American label the following year. The resultant album realized all of the promise shown in Glenn's former projects, producing work with a soulful profundity at which he had previously only hinted. While satanically inclined, Danzig have managed to avoid most of the pitfalls that have plagued other bands who court a devilish image. Younger, more overtly aggressive acts such as Deicide and Slayer presented images dominated by rage and pain, whereas Danzig approached other aspects of the satanic in artfully composed songs, from the seductive to the quietly sinister. However, this subtlety tempered their appeal within the heavy metal fraternity, many of whom demanded a more direct or traditional approach, and Danzig remained a connoisseur's metal band. Their second release, *Lucifuge*, did little to alter this. None of the elements used were in themselves original - vocals in the style of 50s crooners, rich, black blues guitars, evocative heavy metal riffs - but it was the cunningly seamless way in which they were combined that generated Danzig's dark magic. A third long-playing release, *How The Gods Kill*, formed a bridge between the high melodrama of heavy metal and the alluring menace of gothic mood. *Black Aria* was a solo project for Glenn Danzig, and was something of a stylistic departure from his previous guitar-based material. It consisted of quasi-classical instrumentals, with one side dedicated to portraying the story of Lucifer's fall from grace. In late 1993 the mainstream rock crowd discovered Danzig through the runaway success of the video for 'Mother' on MTV. 'Mother' was, in fact, a track from their debut, but it took five years for this twisted classic to gain widespread recognition. *Danzig 4* followed and was met with critical accusations that it was a deliberately commercial outing for the band, designed to please their new audience. Indeed, the album contained little of the rousing anthemic rock that had peppered previous albums, but this fourth instalment was still distinctively Danzig (indeed, it echoed Samhain days). Glenn Danzig had long since demonstrated that he could yell up a storm with the Misfits, but this collection proved that he was at his most menacing and creative when he was at his quietest. During touring to support *Danzig 4*, Joey Castillo (b. 30 March 1966, Gardena, California, USA) replaced Biscuits. Danzig, a long-standing comic book fan, founded his own company, Verotix, in 1995, with the intention of publishing adult comics. A new line-up (Danzig, Castillo, ex-Prong guitarist/vocalist Tommy Victor, bass player Josh Lazie) recorded *Blackacidevil* in 1996. Both this album and the belated follow-up, *6.66 Satans Child*, met with limited commercial and critical interest.

● ALBUMS: *Danzig* (Def American/Geffen 1988)★★★, *Danzig II - Lucifuge* (Def American/Geffen 1990)★★★, *How The Gods Kill* (Def American 1992)★★★, *Thrall - Demonsweatlive* (Def American 1993)★★, *Black Aria* (Plan 9 1993)★★, *Danzig 4* (American 1994)★★★, *Blackacidevil* (Hollywood 1996)★★★, *6.66 Satans Child* (Evilive Records 1999)★★.

● VIDEOS: *Danzig* (PolyGram Music Video 1992).

Darey, Matt

b. 29 November 1968, Leicester, Leicestershire, England. Darey has become a successful remixer and producer of commercial house and trance. He also records under various names including Lost Tribe, Tekara and Mash Up. Darey has remixed some of the most influential and popular dance music tracks of the late 90s, including Agnelli And Nelson's 'El Niño', Binary Finary's '1998', Greece 2000's 'Three Drives', ATB's '9pm (Till I Come)' (a UK number 1) and Grace's 'Not Over'. He has also remixed tracks for high-profile pop artists such as Erasure, Kim Wilde and Mark Morrison. In the dance arena, he has worked with highly respected artists and producers such as 'Tall' Paul Newman, Westbam, Tin Tin Out, Mike Koglin, Ruff Driverz, Space Brothers, Brandon Block, Tilt and 'Red' Jerry (Dickens of Hooj Choons). Darey made his first track with a Student Loan during the final year of a degree in Marketing. The track secured an album deal with Warner Brothers Records but the album never materialised when Darey and a friend (Jamie White of PF Project) squandered their £80,000 advance. As LiKwan, he released 'I Need A Man'/'Point Zero' in 1995 on Deconstruction Records. The single was the 'Essential New Tune' on Pete Tong's influential BBC Radio 1 FM show and this exposure led to Darey's first remixing work. Darey remixed the 7-inch and 12-inch versions of 'Deeper' by Escrima (aka 'Tall' Paul Newman) and the track reached number 27 in the UK national charts. Since immersing himself in the clubbing scene in 1997, Darey started to make 'bangin'' house tracks and remixes, featuring drum rolls and breakdowns, which, he says, may be somewhat 'cheesy' but '. . . they make people happy. You can't be worried about what's cool.' The late 90s' vogue for trance and 'harder' forms of house music has certainly helped to popularise Darey's uplifting remixing and production style.

Das-EFX

Drayz (b. Andre Weston, 9 September 1970, New Jersey, USA) and Skoob (b. Willie Hines, 27 November 1970, Brooklyn, New York, USA; Skoob is 'books' spelled backwards) are two easy-natured rappers whose success story is of the genuine rags to riches variety. As college friends who had met during English classes, they entered a rap contest at a small Richmond, Virginia nightclub. Luckily for them Erick Sermon and Parrish Smith of EPMD were in attendance, and, despite not winning, they walked off with an instant record contract. The judgement shown by EPMD proved impeccable when Das-EFX's debut release, Dead Serious, charted strongly. Soon they were touring together, despite the fact that neither Drayz nor Skoob were old enough to legally enter the premises on some of the dates. As rap aficionados began to look once more to the old school and its freestyle vocals, Das-EFX were the perfect modern proponents, with their jagged, cutting rhymes and sweet wordplay. They developed a wonderful habit of making words up if they could not find something appropriate in the dictionary to shore up their rhymes: 'We're not too worried about really putting heavy messages in our records - we just try and make sure all the lyrics are super dope'. It was a style that was to be, in typical hip-hop fashion, quickly adopted and mimicked by a hundred other artists, and by the time of their follow-up some of its impact had been lost. Their debut self-production, 'Freak It', followed in 1993, and was the first release to see them drop their familiar tongue-flipping style, which detractors accused them of copying from UK rappers like the Demon Boyz. The advent of west coast gangsta funk saw the duo suffering a blow to their credibility, allied to criticisms that their style possessed only novelty value. Toughening up their stance, they silenced some of these detractors with 1998's streetwise Generation EFX.

● ALBUMS: Dead Serious (East West 1992)★★★, Straight Up Sewaside (East West 1993)★★★, Hold It Down (East West 1995)★★, Generation EFX (Elektra/Asylum 1998)★★★.

Davies, Richard

b. 1964, Sydney, Australia. Davies formed his first band, the Moles, at the University of New South Wales. The quartet recorded several EPs and an album (Untune The Sky) in the early 90s, released on their native Seaside label, before moving to New York to record four tracks for their American debut. 'What's The New Mary Jane' borrowed more than just a song title from the Beatles, the song's heavily produced orchestral pop revealing Davies' talent for recreating period psychedelia. The nine-track Instinct at times sounded like a lost Brian Wilson session, although tracks such as 'Did You See The Red Queen?' highlighted Davies' very personal skewed sensibility. Davies then teamed up with the classically trained Oregonian musician Eric Matthews in Cardinal, with the duo releasing one gloriously lush album in 1994.

Following Cardinal's split, Davies based himself in Saugerties, releasing his solo debut, There's Never Been A Crowd Like This, in 1996. Sparser and more musically restrained than his previous work, tracks such as 'Chips Rafferty' and 'Transcontinental' revealed a lyrical fascination with a mythical America reminiscent of Van Dyke Parks' work. Recorded with Ron Jones of the Flaming Lips, the follow-up Telegraph was another strong collection, with stand-out tracks including 'Cantina' and 'Main Street Electrical Parade', a beautiful, country-tinged lament to a closed attraction at Disneyland.

● ALBUMS: There's Never Been A Crowd Like This (Flydaddy 1996)★★★, Telegraph (Flydaddy 1998)★★★.

Days Of The New

A modern rock quartet from Louisville, Kentucky, USA that was signed up to the Outpost Records management team after just three shows, Days Of The New released their self-titled debut album in June 1997. Three of the band, Travis Meeks (singer/songwriter), Jesse Vest (bass) and Matt Taul (drums), grew up together in Charlestown, Indiana, and previously performed as the Metallica-influenced Dead Reckoning. For Days Of The New they added guitarist Todd Whitener. Their debut album was produced by Scott Litt, an R.E.M. veteran and the founder of Outpost Records. The first single to be released from the album, 'Touch, Peel And Stand', quickly hit the number 1 spot on Billboard's Mainstream Rock chart, and was featured heavily on MTV. They subsequently toured in support of the record with the stylistically sympathetic Veruca Salt, while Meeks' voice was frequently compared to that of Alice In Chains' Layne Staley. Meeks, having parted company with the others members of the band, wrote, recorded and produced the second Days Of The New album on his own. Eschewing the somewhat one-dimensional alternative rock thrash of the debut album, he experimented with lush orchestration, Eastern percussion and tape loops to create an impressively mature collection.

● ALBUMS: Days Of The New (Outpost 1997)★★★, Days Of The New II (Outpost 1999)★★★★.

DC Talk

This inter-racial trio have cultivated a large and diverse audience in the USA through their sophisticated and adept blend of pop, soul and hip-hop. Primarily orientated towards the gospel/Christian market, they have become one of that genre's most popular acts in the 90s. They originally comprised Michael Tait and Toby McKeehan, who formed the band while at college in Washington, DC. They were soon joined by Kevin Smith from Grand Rapids, Michigan. The name was alternatively stated to express either DC referring to the area of their origin or 'Decent Christian' talk. Using street poetry as their central mode of communication, their sophomore album was Nu Thang, a title that accurately reflected the Christian pop/hip-hop style of its contents. More declamatory was the follow-up, Free At Last, which included cover versions of 'Jesus Is Just Alright' and 'Lean On Me', alongside the trio's original compositions. It was still a fixture on Billboard's Contemporary Christian chart at the end of 1995, having sold over a million copies. In the three years before the trio entered the studio again each member concentrated on solo activities - Smith writing a poetry book,

McKeehan launching Gotee Records and Tait concentrating on songwriting. Released in December 1995, *Jesus Freak* took their Christian concerns into alternative pop/rock territory. Most impressive was the title track, an unashamed declaration of personal commitment set against dense guitar riffs. It saw them cited in *Billboard* as 'Christian music's most innovative and accomplished group'. Though the music was now as secular as it had ever been, the trio's gospel background was still much in evidence. With record sales of 85,000 copies in its first week of release, the album went on to sell over one million copies. It was followed by a powerful live album and 1998's *Supernatural*, on which the trio smoothed out their sound to great effect, debuting at number 4 on the *Billboard* 200 album chart in October.

● ALBUMS: *DC Talk* (Forefront 1988)★★★, *Nu Thang* (Forefront 1991)★★★, *Free At Last* (Forefront 1992)★★★, *Jesus Freak* (Forefront 1995)★★★, *Welcome To The Freak Show: Live In Concert* (Forefront 1997)★★★★, *Supernatural* (Forefront/Virgin 1998)★★★.
● VIDEOS: *Welcome To The Freak Show* (Forefront Video 1997), *DC Talk Video Collection* (Forefront 1998).

De La Soul

Hailing from Long Island, New York, USA, De La Soul was formed by Posdnous (b. Kelvin Mercer, 17 August 1969, Bronx, New York, USA), Trugoy the Dove (b. David Jude Joliceur, 21 September 1968, Brooklyn, New York, USA), and Pasemaster Mace (b. Vincent Lamont Mason Jnr., 24 March 1970, Brooklyn, New York, USA) who were contemporaries of Queen Latifah, Monie Love and A Tribe Called Quest. With the aforementioned crews they formed the Native Tongues Posse, who were at the forefront of the black renaissance of the early 90s. Less harsh than many of their fellow rappers, De La Soul's pleasantly lilting rhythms helped them chart their debut LP - one of the first such acts to cross into the album market. Produced by Stetsasonic's Prince Paul, it revealed an altogether delightful array of funky rhythms and comic touches, presenting an influential alternative to the macho aggression of gangsta rap. As well as hit singles like 'Me Myself And I', and 'The Magic Number', they also charted in conjunction with Queen Latifah on 'Mama Gave Birth To The Soul Children' and guested on the Jungle Brothers' 'Doing Our Own Dang'. Some of De La Soul's more esoteric samples ranged from Curiosity Killed The Cat to Steely Dan, though their mellow approach belied difficult subject matter. *De La Soul Is Dead*, however, saw them return to tougher rhythms and a less whimsical melodic approach. Evidently they had grown tired of the 'hippies of hip-hop' tag dreamt up by their press officer. With over 100 artists sampled, they sidestepped injunctions by gaining clearance from all concerned artists, having previously been sued by the Turtles for sampling 'You Showed Me' on the *3 Feet High And Rising* track 'Transmitting Live From Mars'. The painstaking procedure delayed the album for over a year. When it did emerge it was roundly denounced by critics, who were not taken by De La Soul's drastic gear change. However, infectious songs like 'Ring Ring Ring (Ha Ha Hey)' kept their profile high in the singles chart. *Buhloone Mindstate* saw them move back towards the stylings of their debut, and received better press, although by now the trio's fortunes had waned and the album quickly dropped off the charts. A similar fate befell 1996's *Stakes Is High*, which, despite returning to the tougher stylings of *De La Soul Is*

Dead, struggled against the commercial ascendancy of gangsta rap.

● ALBUMS: *3 Feet High And Rising* (Tommy Boy 1989)★★★, *De La Soul Is Dead* (Tommy Boy 1991)★★★, *Buhloone Mindstate* (Tommy Boy 1993)★★★, *Stakes Is High* (Tommy Boy 1996)★★★.
● VIDEOS: *3 Feet High And Rising* (Big Life 1989).

De Vit, Tony

b. 12 September 1957 Kidderminster, Englan, d. 2 July 1998, Birmingham, West Midlands, England. Tony De Vit's huge impact on the international dance music scene was not fully appreciated until his life was cut tragically short. In the UK's *DJ* magazine's 1998 poll of the Top 100 DJs, he was ranked fifth. De Vit became interested in US funk music in his teens, listening to George Clinton and his Parliament/Funkadelic brand of psychedelic disco and, at the age of 18, he persuaded a local pub to let him put on a club night. For years he worked as a stock controller and computer programmer, but his musical skills would put him to the fore of the UK club culture when it began to boom in the early 90s. He earned a reputation on the scene as a true professional, a worker, rather than one who enjoyed the limelight and glamour of the music business. Initially, De Vit was a popular DJ on the gay club scene, but the turning point came when he sent a tape of one of his sets to Laurence Malice, the promoter of Trade, then an underground gay night at Turnmills in Farringdon, London. Malice was very impressed and later commented that it was perfect for Trade. What Malice liked about the tape was the sound that De Vit would pioneer – pounding, dynamic, up-tempo house music that was uplifting rather than sombre in tone. It would later be termed 'nu-energy'. He would play marathon 12-hour sets and, as the club gradually became internationally famous, so did De Vit. He also developed a highly successful career as a producer and remixer, working on singles by Louise, East 17 and Michelle Gayle among many others, as well as running the Jump Wax and TdV labels. His DJing work took him all over the world. Tony De Vit was one of the first DJs to be popular with both gay and straight audiences. He was HIV-positive but appeared to be sustaining good health. When he collapsed early in 1998, it was blamed on his characteristically punishing workload and he took a month off. However, he fell ill while working in Miami, Florida after a bout of food poisoning. It was discovered that he was also suffering from bronchial pneumonia, aggravated by bone-marrow failure. He died at Hartland Hospital in Birmingham, England.

● COMPILATIONS: *Global Underground 001 - Tony De Vit Live In Tel Aviv* (Boxed 1996)★★★ *Global Underground 005 - Tony De Vit Live In Tokyo* (Boxed 1997)★★★★, *Trade* (Priority 1998)★★★★.

Dead Can Dance

Based in London, England, but tracing their origins to Australia, Dead Can Dance's long campaign in the music industry has rarely attracted attention outside of a devoted following. Whether this is a result of wilful obscurism or a disciplined artistic vision is a moot point, but the band have now left behind more than a decade's worth of, by turns, infuriating and blissful, *avant garde* pop. Their name had the unfortunate effect of nailing their colours to the gothic masthead, though in truth they were light years away from this genre. The band's debut collection was not as focused as later efforts, mingling their trademark male/female vocals with an unco-ordinated mesh of chants and drawling guitar. However, from packaging to production it fitted the 4AD Records aesthetic perfectly, and there were enough hints of the less prosaic gems to come to distinguish the band. Reduced to the core duo of Brendan Perry and Lisa Gerrard, *Spleen And Ideal* was an altogether more thrilling and cohesive record, with the discordant guitar barrage abandoned in favour of a considered array of instruments, including cello, trombones and timpani. The clean production also lent the improved material greater clarity, though what the songs actually concerned was, typically, something for listeners to decide for themselves. *Within The Realm Of A Dying Sun* gave further indication of their talent, though some critics balked at the idea of giving the two singers one side each of the record, making its tone uneven. It also revealed a debt to music from the Middle East, a process that was further explored by the less satisfying *The Serpent's Egg*. *Aion* took as its premise medieval or 'early music', using Gregorian chants, similar in many ways to the work of Bel Canto, and baroque stylistics, played with genuine folk instruments (including hurdy gurdy and bagpipes). *Into The Labyrinth* confirmed Perry's greater awareness of electronics and samplers, and while *Towards The Within* is a basic live album, it primarily contains a phenomenal live repertoire never before committed to vinyl. By 1995 Perry had begun work on his first solo album, while Gerrard's stunning vocal presence had seen her record in an orchestral context. The mother band's seventh studio album, *Spiritchaser*, arrived at a time when Dead Can Dance were becoming acknowledged influences on the UK dance music community (Black Grape and Future Sound Of London having both sampled their work). This time the band moved away from the Celtic influences that exerted themselves on *Into The Labyrinth*, towards sounds reminiscent of African and South American music. However, as Gerrard succinctly informed the press: 'It's gone past the point of being 'this' and 'that'. Music has come to a new age, where we're exposed to music from all over the world, from a much larger palate of colours.' For similar reasons, *Spiritchaser* served to validate the reason for Dead Can Dance's continuation into the 90s, the band having proved themselves to be among the most accurate cultural conductors in popular music, shifting emphasis effortlessly in keeping with the zeitgeist. Gerrard collaborated with Australian keyboard player Pieter Bourke on 1998's haunting *Duality*, and Perry released his solo debut a year later.

● ALBUMS: *Dead Can Dance* (4AD 1984)★★★★, *Spleen And Ideal* (4AD 1985)★★★, *Within The Realm Of A Dying Sun* (4AD 1987)★★★, *The Serpent's Egg* (4AD 1988)★★★, *Aion* (4AD 1990)★★★, *Into The Labyrinth* (4AD 1993)★★★, *Towards The Within* (4AD 1994)★★★★, *Spiritchaser* (4AD 1995)★★★★.
Solo: Lisa Gerrard and Pieter Bourke *Duality* (4AD 1998)★★★★. Brendan Perry *Eye Of The Hunter* (4AD 1999)★★★.
● VIDEOS: *Toward The Within* (Warners 1994).

Death In Vegas

Formerly called Dead Elvis, Death In Vegas occupy similar ground to Andy Weatherall's Sabres Of Paradise, in that their aggressive, rock-edged dancefloor sound owes a huge debt to the punk ethos of 1977. Led by DJ Richard Fearless (who took over at the Heavenly Jukebox when the Chemical Brothers residency ended) and producer Steve Hellier, the group announced itself with the release of a series of mesmerizing, bombastic singles, 'Opium Shuffle', 'Dirt', 'Rocco', 'GBH' and 'Rekkit'. All of these were included on their debut album, *Dead Elvis*, which was celebrated within both the mainstream and dance music communities for its intelligence, musical freshness and daring. Fearless contributed music to the soundtracks of *Lost In Space* and *The Acid House*, before returning with a new Death In Vegas album two years later. Featuring new partner Tim Holmes, *The Contino Sessions* was another fearsome blend of twisted lyrics and innovative backing tracks, with guest vocals from Iggy Pop ('Aisha') and Bobby Gillespie ('Soul Auctioneer'). 'Aisha' provided the duo with their first UK Top 10 hit in February 2000.

● ALBUMS: *Dead Elvis* (Concrete 1997)★★★★, *The Contino Sessions* (Concrete 1999)★★★★.

Death Row Records

For a short time in the mid-90s Death Row was rap's most successful record company. The label was formed in 1991 by Dr. Dre of NWA after he complained bitterly about restraint of trade and moneys owed by his previous employers, for whom he produced several million-sellers. Not content with cursing Ruthless Records' General Manager Jerry Heller, and being sued by Eazy-E, he finally managed to find a deal with Jimmy Iovine at Interscope. Iovine agreed to finance Dre's own label, Death Row. Former bodyguard and Vanilla Ice publicist Marion 'Suge' Knight, who had warned Dre about his NWA contract, was the new label's co-founder. Unfortunately, Knight revealed a similar propensity for trouble that had already marred Dre's career. He was charged with assault with a deadly weapon in late 1993, and allegedly attacked two rappers, Lynwood and George Stanley, with a gun in July 1992, at Dr. Dre's recording studio. The attack was witnessed by both Dre and Snoop Doggy Dogg, and concerned the use of an office telephone. The money Knight invested in Death Row was drawn from the publishing rights he partly owned for Vanilla Ice's hit album - a huge irony in the wake of the war of words between Vanilla and the west coast gangsta rappers a few years previously. Several months later Dr. Dre's *The Chronic* justified his decision to back the rapper by becoming a huge crossover success. The label also released the big-selling soundtrack to the basketball movie *Above The Rim*, ensuring that Death Row's first three albums all went multi-platinum. However, it was Snoop Doggy Dogg's phenomenally successful debut *Doggy Style* that really capped the label's multi-million status. Dogg had first come to prominence on Dre's *The Chronic*, but was already embroiled in a murder case that put his career on hold for a further two years. Other artists signed to the label include Dat Nigga Daz, Kurrupt, Lady Of Rage, Jewell and, infamously, hip-hop's brightest new star 2Pac. A series of incidents then escalated the much-hyped east coast/west coast feud between Death Row and Sean 'Puffy' Combs' Bad Boy label, indirectly leading to the gangland-related murders of 2Pac (September 1996) and the Notorious B.I.G. (March 1997). By 1997, the increasingly troubled label had received a series of bodyblows from which it seemed unlikely to recover. Dr. Dre left acrimoniously to form his own Aftermath label, Snoop Doggy Dogg filed a $10 million lawsuit against Death Row for alleged negligence and intentional misconduct, and Knight was sentenced to nine years imprisonment for parole violations. The label was also the subject of a federal investigation and was facing numerous lawsuits. Time Warner relinquished their involvement with Death Row's distributor Interscope, and MCA Entertainment's $200 million share deal was swiftly rescinded following Knight's incarceration.

● COMPILATIONS: various artists *Above The Rim* (Death Row 1994)★★★, various artists *Greatest Hits* (Death Row 1997)★★★★.

● FURTHER READING: *Have Gun Will Travel: The Spectacular Rise And Violent Fall Of Death Row Records*, Ronin Ro.

Deconstruction Records

During the 90s Deconstruction was responsible for bringing dance music into the mainstream. It was co-founded in 1987 by Keith Blackhurst and Mike Pickering (also a member of M People), who were later joined by Pete Hadfield, in order to release good house that was being overlooked by the major labels. They opened their account with Hot! House's 'Don't Come To Stay' in 1987 and achieved success with their three other records that year, T-COY's (Pickering and Richie Close) 'Carino', 'Nightrain' and 'Da Me Mas/I Like To Listen' which claimed to be the first British house tracks. Towards the end of 1987 they also released the country's first house compilation *North* although it mainly contained material by Pickering. While singles by Zuzan ('Girls Can Jack Too'), T-COY ('Nightclubbin'') and Hot!House in 1988 covered the same kind of territory, Black Box's 'Ride On Time' (1989), licensed from the Italian label Discomagic, introduced what became known as the Italian house sound, notable for its uplifting piano lines, and was a UK number 1 for six weeks. At the same time Deconstruction continued to foster such UK artists as Gina Foster, Annette and Dynasty Of Two. More success followed in 1990 with Guru Josh's 'Infinity' (for some the definitive rave track) and in 1991 with the compilations *Italia* and *Decoded And Danced Up*. Over the next few years they released material by Felix (notably 'Don't You Want Me'), Hyper Go-Go ('High'), N-Joi, M People, K Klass, the Grid, Kylie Minogue and the DJs Sasha, Justin Robertson (as Lionrock) and Danny Rampling (the Millionaire Hippies). In 1995, Deconstruction signed a deal to become part of the BMG company and also formed an alliance with the Liverpool club Cream to produce a number of compilations including *Cream Live* (1995), *Cream Anthems* (1995) and *Cream Live Vol. 2* (1996). They also signed Robert Miles, Republica, Dave Clarke and Beth Orton among others in an attempt to broaden their range. A period of slight uncertainty followed the disastrous sales of Kylie Minogue's 1997 album and subsequent dropping of the artist from the roster. Orton remained with the label even when Heavenly Records' contract with Deconstruction ended and EMI/Chrysalis became their parent company. Her albums *Trailer Park* and *Central Reservation* were well received and sold well and in 2000, Orton was nominated for a UK BRIT Award. Way Out West's 1997 debut was also praised by the music press and achieved respectable sales. Sasha, one of the label's longest-serving producers and remixers released his highly successful *Xpander* EP in 1999, preceding his debut album in 2000. The Deconstruction imprint, Concrete, released Death In Vegas' first two acclaimed albums, and the same act enjoyed their first UK Top 10 hit in February 2000 with 'Aisha'. The female vocalist Maria Nayler continues to release singles through Deconstruction, in conjunction with

dance music producers such as Sasha and Tilt. The label also struck a deal with the German label, Cosmo in 1999 to release various tracks by their trance and techno artists.

● COMPILATIONS: *Deconstruction Classics: A History Of Dance Music* (Deconstruction 1995)★★★★.

Deee-Lite

This multi-national trio shot into the UK and US Top 5 in August 1990 with the groundbreaking 'Groove Is In The Heart', blending 70s disco with house beats in an outrageously funky mix. The outfit was formed by Lady Miss Kier (b. Kier Kirby, Youngstown, Ohio, USA; vocals) and Super DJ Dmitry Brill (b. Kiev, Russia, his parents having defected from the East) after they met in a New York park in 1982. The pair, who later married, then added Korean-raised computer expert Jungle DJ Towa Towa (b. Towa Tei, Tokyo, Japan), who saw them perform in a nightclub in 1987 after moving to New York to study Graphic Design. His presence helped make them a truly cosmopolitan act (another early member, Booty, left the band prior to their major success). 'Groove Is In The Heart' featured additional guest artists Bootsy Collins and Q-Tip (A Tribe Called Quest), though the follow-up, 'Power Of Love', and subsequent efforts failed to replicate their debut's impact. *Infinity Within* saw a band toned down in sound as well as visual garb. It included tracks such as the half-minute 'Vote, Baby, Vote', which served as an antidote to the aesthetics of the 'Second Summer Of Love' to which 'Groove Is In The Heart' had proved so pivotal. By the advent of their third and final album Kirby and Brill had been joined by new member One-e, while Towa left to work on a far more enjoyable solo career. Kirby also earned herself a niche market in computer graphics, designing covers for Deee-Lite and others, as a parallel career.

● ALBUMS: *World Clique* (Elektra 1990)★★★★, *Infinity Within* (Elektra 1992)★★★, *Dew Drops In The Garden* (Elektra 1994)★★. Solo: Towa Tei *Future Listening!* (Elektra 1995)★★★, *Sound Museum* (Akashic 1996)★★★, *Sweet Robots Against The Machine* (Akashic 1997)★★★.

● COMPILATIONS: *Sampladelic Relics & Dancefloor Oddities* (Elektra 1996)★★★.

Deejay Punk-Roc

b. Brooklyn, New York City, USA. This hip-hop/big beat artist is the youngest of six children. He grew up listening to his father's wide-ranging musical tastes, including Barry White and the Isley Brothers. As a teenager, he DJed at 'block parties' and organised his own musical event at a local park. He was a teenage delinquent until he joined the US army at the age of 16 and was posted to Japan, Germany and England. He felt that the experience of the army gave him a sense of self-discipline and that the travel helped to broaden his mind. When he left the army in his early twenties, he returned to his musical interests and, collaborating with a friend who had some recording equipment, he made 'My Beatbox'. The track was picked up by Airdog Recordings and included on their compilation *Still Searchin'* in May 1997. His debut album, *ChickenEye* was released in the UK by Independiente in September 1998 and later by Epic Records in the USA. It received excellent reviews. The music takes from influences including funk, 50s lounge music and, of course, hip-hop and old school electro. It features sounds

such as police sirens, obscure samples of film and television dialogue and breakbeats. Naturally, Deejay Punk-Roc performs as a DJ and is a popular name on the UK's big beat scene, often playing at Fatboy Slim's club The Boutique (formerly The Big Beat Boutique) in Brighton, and in London. He has also supported the Prodigy on tour, and released a mix album in 1999.
● ALBUMS: *ChickenEye* (Independiente 1998)★★★.
● COMPILATIONS: *Anarchy In The USA* (Moonshine 1999)★★★.

Deep Blue Something

The core of Deep Blue Something is the Pipes brothers, Todd (bass/vocals) and Toby (guitar/vocals), from Denton, Texas, who were both attending the University of North Texas in 1992 when they formed Leper Messiah (a quotation from David Bowie's 'Ziggy Stardust') with Austin-born drummer John Kirtland and guitarist Clay Bergus, later replaced by Kirk Tatom. After a period juggling their academic studies with gigs around Denton and Dallas, the band, now renamed Deep Blue Something, hit the big time with the clever 'Breakfast At Tiffany's', a tale of lovers failing to resolve their differences. The single, with its layered acoustic guitars, was catchy enough to make the *Billboard* Top 10 (and was number 1 in the UK for a week). By this time Bergus had returned to replace Tatom. The band achieved some level of notoriety when Todd was fired from his teaching job at a Christian school when parents got wind of his hedonistic rock 'n' roll lifestyle. Despite this whiff of scandal, most of their material is a variety of country-tinged indie-lite, ever-so-slightly alternative guitar pop for people who find R.E.M. too challenging.
● ALBUMS: *11th Song* (Crystal Clear 1993)★★, *Home* (Rainmaker/Interscope 1994)★★★, *Byzantium* (Universal 1998)★★.

Deep Dish

A prolific US remixing, recording and producing outfit, Washington, DC-based Deep Dish comprises Iranian-born Ali 'Dubfire' Shirazinia and Sharam Taybei. They met in 1991, DJing at the same party. In 1992, they formed Deep Dish Records and set out to expand the boundaries of 'deep house'. They quickly established a distinctive sound, using collaborators such as BT (Brian Transeau) and John Selway. They have continued to DJ all over the world and have remained committed to their purist notions of what good house music should be. They began a subsidiary of Deep Dish Records, Yoshitoshi, in 1994, which has released several respected singles by Hani, Satori, and Alcatraz. They were signed to the major UK dance music label, Deconstruction Records, in December 1995. Their debut singles 'Stay Gold' and 'Stranded', released in October 1996 and 1997 respectively, were well received. Their mix of De'Lacy's 'Hideaway' was also very successful, and led to further remix work for the Pet Shop Boys, Michael Jackson, Janet Jackson, and the Shamen. Having already released several mix albums, the duo began work on their studio debut, *Junk Science*, which was released in July 1998. The UK's *Mixmag* commented: '12 years in and somebody's finally made a house album you'll want to listen to all the way through and play again and again . . . Washington's finest make the first truly great house album.' A reworking of 'Stay Gold', using the vocal talent of Everything But The Girl's Tracey Thorn, was a UK Top 10 hit in September 1998 and Deep Dish won

the UK's *Muzik* magazine's award for Best International DJ in October that year. The duo started a hip-hop label, Middle East Recordings, and acquired a Friday night residency at 'Move' at the Ministry Of Sound in London.
● ALBUMS: *Junk Science* (Deconstruction 1998)★★★★.
● COMPILATIONS: *DJs Take Control* (One 1996)★★★, *Cream Separates* (Deconstruction 1997)★★★, *Yoshiesque* (React 1999)★★★★.

Deep Forest

This ambient new age group are based in France. Their 'Sweet Lullaby' track was one of the most popular of its kind during 1993, with its rich, warm tones and ethnic instrumentation. It was based on the sampled voices of Pygmies drawn directly from the African rain forest. The duo in charge of proceedings were Eric Mouquet and film composer Michel Sanchez. Based in Paris and Lille, their collaboration was the result of Sanchez returning from Africa with boxes of records from all over that continent. However, most of the actual sounds used on the track were taken from record libraries. 'Sweet Lullaby' is the story of a young girl who tries to get her brother to stop crying by insisting that if he doesn't his parents will never come back. Remixes of the track were made by both Apollo 440 and Jam And Spoon. (Deep Forest in turn remixed Apollo 440's 1994 single, 'Liquid Cool'.) *Boheme* (which won a Grammy in February 1996 for the Best World Music Album) and *Comparsa* continued previous themes, visiting new areas of the world including Mongolia, Taiwan, India and Hungary.
● ALBUMS: *Deep Forest* (Columbia 1993)★★★★, *Boheme* (Columbia 1995)★★★★, *Comparsa* (Columbia 1997)★★★, *Made In Japan* (Columbia 1999)★★★.

Deftones

An intense, thoroughly contemporary hard rock band, the Deftones comprise Chino Moreno (vocals), Chi Cheng (bass), Stephen Carpenter (guitar) and Abe Cunningham (drums). They are based in Sacramento, California, USA, where they enjoyed the early sponsorship of local favourites Korn. With that band they also shared a fan community drawn from skateboarders. The members of the band actually met while skateboarding, and their first rehearsals together took place in 1989, where they jammed on rough versions of Danzig's 'Twist Of Cain'. With the line-up complete, they began playing low-key sets, gradually building support within their neighbourhood. The band eventually signed with Madonna's label, Maverick Records, and made their debut in 1995 with *Adrenaline*. They then toured with Kiss and Ozzy Osbourne, as sales of their debut increased to more than half a million. By now widely championed in both the US and UK metal press, the group began work on their second album, *Around The Fur*, which proved to be an equally solid collection highlighted by the radio favourite 'My Own Summer (Shove It)'.
● ALBUMS: *Adrenaline* (Maverick 1995)★★★, *Around The Fur* (Maverick/Warners 1997)★★★, *Live* mini-album (1999)★★.

Deicide

This controversial Satanic metal outfit was formed in 1987 in Florida, USA, as Amon, with the line-up of Glen Benton (bass/vocals), guitarists Eric and Brian Hoffman, and Steve Asheim (drums). The band became notorious owing to their conflict both with the Christian establishment in America, and with animal rights groups, because of Benton's outrageous statements concerning the mutilation of small animals. Repeated bomb threats from the Animal Militia during European tours culminated in an explosion at a Stockholm venue in 1992 during support band Gorefest's set. The fact that the outspoken Benton branded his own forehead with an inverted cross, created an air of evil charisma that *Deicide*'s workmanlike death metal struggled to match. Nevertheless, the publicity helped to establish them as a major death metal act. *Legion* saw considerable progression, with a more focused approach channelling Deicide's aggression into better musicianship and songs. The band subsequently released two raw Amon demos, 'Feasting The Beast' and 'Sacrificial', as *Amon: Feasting The Beast. Once Upon The Cross* provided the best evidence to date of the musical talent that lurked somewhere beneath Benton's ludicrous self-aggrandisement. Scott Burns' production added clarity to a once murky sound, propelled by the superbly efficient twin guitars of the Hoffman brothers. Deicide's ability to win converts from the mainstream must still be limited by songs such as 'When Satan Rules His World' and 'Kill The Christian'. In 1997, Benton retracted his claim that he would commit suicide upon reaching the age of 33, saying: 'The whole thing's ridiculous'. The band released their first live album the following year.

● ALBUMS: *Deicide* (Roadrunner 1990)★★, *Legion* (Roadrunner 1992)★★★, as Amon *Amon: Feasting The Beast* (Roadrunner 1993)★★, *Once Upon The Cross* (Roadrunner 1995)★★★, *Serpents Of The Light* (Roadrunner 1997)★★★, *When Satan Lives* (Roadrunner 1998)★★★.

Del Amitri

This Glaswegian semi-acoustic rock band emerged in the wake of the Postcard Records scene when they were formed by 16-year-old singer, pianist and bass player Justin Currie (b. 11 December 1964, Scotland) and his guitarist friend Iain Harvie (b. 19 May 1962, Scotland). They were joined for 'Sense Sickness', their debut on the No Strings independent label, by Bryan Tolland (guitar) and Paul Tyagi (drums). Numerous sessions for disc jockey John Peel and tours with everyone from the Fall to the Smiths ensured a cult following and a growing reputation for Currie's wry lyrics. Having taken second guitarist David Cummings and drummer Brian McDermott aboard, they came to the attention of Chrysalis Records who signed them to their own 'indie' label, Big Star. Del Amitri, meaning 'from the womb' in Greek, released their debut album in 1985 but fell foul of the label shortly afterwards. The band's career entered a restorative period during which they toured via a network of fans who organized and promoted events in individual regions. A tour of the USA led to Del Amitri being signed to A&M Records in 1987 and resuming their recording career. They hit the UK singles chart with 'Kiss This Thing Goodbye', 'Nothing Ever Happens', and 'Spit In The Rain'. The reissue of 'Kiss This Thing Goodbye' helped to break them in the USA, while domestically the plaintive protest ballad 'Nothing Ever Happens' won many supporters: 'And computer terminals report some gains, On the values of copper and tin, While American businessmen snap up Van Goghs, For the price of a hospital wing'. Though their singles success abated somewhat, this was tempered by the platinum success of 1992's *Change Everything*. Touring con-

tinued throughout that year while most of 1993 was spent at Haremere House in East Sussex, working on their fourth album. McDermott was also replaced by Ashley Soan. *Twisted* was produced by Al Clay (Frank Black, Pere Ubu) and further refined the band's familiar AOR formula, with the lyrics almost exclusively dealing with loneliness and the establishment and breakdown of relationships. Of their transition from indie wordsmiths to stadium rockers, Currie philosophically preferred to think that 'Del Amitri fans only hold ironic lighters aloft'. There were enough ironic electric 12-string soundalikes on the energetic and excellent 1997 album *Some Other Sucker's Parade*. The following year the band provided the Scottish soccer team with the typically wry 'Don't Come Home Too Soon' for their official World Cup song. It struggled to reach number 15 in June 1998. If you love the Byrds and Crazy Horse you will appreciate Del Amitri.

● ALBUMS: *Del Amitri* (Chrysalis 1985)★★★, *Waking Hours* (A&M 1989)★★★, *Change Everything* (A&M 1992)★★★★, *Twisted* (A&M 1995)★★★, *Some Other Sucker's Parade* (A&M 1997)★★★★.
● COMPILATIONS: *The Best Of Del Amitri: Hatful Of Rain* (A&M 1998)★★★★, *Lousy With Love: The B-Sides* (A&M 1998)★★★★.
● VIDEOS: *Let's Go Home* (VVL 1996), *The Best Of Del Amitri: Hatful Of Rain* (VVL 1998).

Del Tha Funky Homosapien

Formerly a part of his cousin, Ice Cube's backing band, Da Lench Mob, Del (b. Teren Delvon Jones, 12 August 1972, Oakland, California, USA) earned his first, glowing reviews for his debut solo set in 1992. Far from the hardcore streak of his more celebrated relation (though there are definite similarities in musical inclination), Del offered a more detached viewpoint, laced with humour. Like many of his West Coast rap colleagues, there was a scarcely disguised debt to the rhythms of P-Funk and George Clinton in his work, acknowledged in its title. However, this approach was abandoned for the follow-up, a much more dour, self-consciously worthy affair (this time without Cube on production) that completely lost the magic of his debut, and placed him at a definite crossroads in his career. However, if Del has faltered, then the achievements of his Hieroglyphics crew (Casual, Souls Of Mischief) have gone some way to compensating. Now working on the crew's own Imperium label, his 1998 set *Future Development* was made available only to users accessing the Hieroglyphics website.

● ALBUMS: *I Wish My Brother George Was Here* (Elektra 1992)★★★★, *No Need For Alarm* (Elektra 1994)★★★, *Future Development* (Hiero Imperium 1998)★★★.

Delgados

If any band can be identified as kick-starting the Glasgow lo-fi scene that spawned the likes of Bis and Urusei Yatsura it is the Delgados, both for their own music and for the label they set up, Chemikal Underground Records. In 1994/5, while the rest of the UK was concentrating on the chirpy hype of Britpop, Alun Woodward (vocals/guitar), Emma Pollock (vocals/guitar), Stewart Henderson (bass) and Paul Savage (drums), all graduates of Glasgow University, were mining a seam of guitar pop that owed more to Pavement than to the Kinks, with its blend of melodic guitar-fuzz and low-key, almost conversational, vocals. A series of one-off singles and compilations on various labels in Scotland,

England and Japan grabbed the attention of *Melody Maker* (which voted their debut, 'Monica Webster/Brand New Car', single of the week) and indie disc jockeys such as John Peel and Steve Lamacq, while a set at their home-town's T In The Park festival cemented their live reputation. Support slots for Elastica and Sebadoh followed. They ended 1996 with the striking 'Under Canvas Under Wraps' and their debut album figuring in many critics' polls. Although somewhat eclipsed by Chemikal Underground acts such as Arab Strap and Mogwai, the self-produced *Peloton* confirmed their staying power.

● ALBUMS: *Domestiques* (Chemikal Underground 1996)★★★★, *Peloton* (Chemikal Underground 1998)★★★.

● COMPILATIONS: *BBC Sessions* (Strange Fruit 1997)★★★.

Delicatessen

This subdued but evocative indie guitar quartet from Leicester, England, comprises vocalist Neil Carlill, Stuart Daymen (drums), Craig Brown (guitar, flute) and Will Foster (bass). As their name implies, cinema has played an equal role to that of music in influencing this band, who recall the experimentalism of Throbbing Gristle. Their early 1995 single, 'C F Kane', was a deliberation on Orson Welles' classic film, *Citizen Kane*. Early in their career the band had already recorded a soundtrack for a BBC television short film, *George And Ramona*. Their debut release was 'Inviting Both Sisters Out To Dinner', issued on Big Life Records' Starfish subsidiary in October 1994. Comparisons to Nick Cave and Marc Bolan ensued, with the band alternating between bountiful melody and more noisy guitar incisions. Certainly song titles such as 'Embalming The Dead Entertainer' suggested a band placed outside of standard indie concerns. With the subsequent demise of Britrock, 1998's excellent *There's No Confusing Some People* gained the band more favourable media coverage.

● ALBUMS: *Skin Touching Water* (Starfish 1995)★★★, *Hustle Into Bed* (Starfish 1996)★★★, *There's No Confusing Some People* (Viper 1998)★★★★.

DeMent, Iris

b. 5 January, 1961, Paragould, Arkansas, USA. A singer-songwriter based in Kansas City, via California, Nashville, and originally the rural regions of Arkansas, USA, DeMent made her initial impact in 1991. Her early influences included gospel, Loretta Lynn and Johnny Cash, but she was 25 years of age before she began to write her own songs, and 30 when her debut album was released. She grew up close to the Tennessee and Missouri borders, the youngest of 14 children in a farming family. Finances eventually forced the DeMents to settle first in Long Beach, Los Angeles, when she was three, and then Anaheim. Her mother's ambition had always been to sing at the *Grand Ole Opry* in Nashville (a fact later recalled in the song 'Mama's Opry' on her debut album) and the family had its own singing sessions. Indeed, one of her sisters, Faye DeMent, recorded two country/gospel albums. Iris moved to Nashville when she was 25 and embarked on writing her own songs for the first time. She subsisted by working as a secretary and waitress while trying to secure a recording contract. Eventually Philo Records signed her. Surrounded by accomplished players such as Al Perkins and Jerry Douglas, as well as friend and producer Jimmy Rooney, her debut album, *Infamous Angel*,

was an acclaimed, acoustically based country folk set, that mixed homespun reflection with charming, accessible lyrics. A good example of her approach was 'Let The Mystery Be', a highly spiritual song that was later recorded by 10,000 Maniacs on their MTV *Unplugged* appearance. The rave notices that accompanied the album resulted in a recording contract with Warner Brothers Records, and she was subsequently invited to appear on Nanci Griffith's *Other Voices, Other Rooms*. Her other hero, Emmylou Harris, had appeared on *Infamous Angel*. DeMent subsequently appeared at the Cambridge Folk Festival in 1993, though audiences were not entirely convinced of her ability to take what remain fundamentally intimate songs into a major live arena. Her first Warners album, *My Life*, introduced a much darker approach. One song, 'Easy's Getting Harder Every Day', is explained by DeMent herself thus: 'Nothing dramatic happens in that song - her husband turns over and goes to sleep after they make love, but she's not going to divorce him for that. It's not a tragedy.' It is exactly that ability to create nuance out of the everyday pain and triumph in life that continues to attract critics. *The Way I Should* included her controversial child abuse song 'Letter To Mom', but was criticised for being over-produced.

● ALBUMS: *Infamous Angel* (Philo 1992)★★★, *My Life* (Warners 1993)★★★★, *The Way I Should* (Warners 1996)★★★.

Denim

After leaving behind long-standing indie institution Felt at the end of the 80s, Lawrence Hayward (b. Birmingham, West Midlands, England) travelled to New York to consider his next move. He launched Denim in 1990 as a homage to the glam rock era. Their debut album included songs with titles such as 'The Osmonds' and 'I Saw Glitter On Your Face', as the band were propelled forward on a wave of 70s nostalgia (some critics considered Denim to offer the 'first serious manifesto' of the 'new glam rock generation'). *Back In Denim* included contributions from two ex-members of the Glitter Band, Gerry Shephard and Pete Phipps, as well as vocalist and synthesizer player Siobhan Brooks. *Denim On Ice* revealed a further shift of perspective. Though sessions for the album began in August 1993, Hayward struggled through a sustained period of depression caused by his split from a long-standing girlfriend and disagreements with studio technicians. As he stated clearly in one of the album's lyrics, 'It's been a long slow trawl/Thank god it's over/I nearly went off my rocker once or twice'. More amusing was a side swipe at Felt's former record company, Cherry Red Records: 'Talent show in a village hall/Look out here comes Cherry Red/They'll sign you up for 50 quid/You'll be making records in a shed'. Afterwards, Denim set out on a UK support tour with Pulp, a band whose longevity and persistence matched Hayward's own history. *Novelty Ice* collected together b-sides and unreleased material alongside throwaway new songs. A deal with EMI Records was scuppered when, in August 1998, the label cancelled the band's new single, 'Summer Smash', because the title was deemed offensive in the wake of Princess Diana's fatal car crash. Putting Denim on hold, Hayward adopted the Go-Kart Mozart moniker for 1999's *Instant Wig-Wam And Igloo Mixture*.

● ALBUMS: *Back In Denim* (Creation 1992)★★★, *Denim On Ice* (Echo 1996)★★★, *Novelty Ice* (Emidisc 1997)★.

Dennis, Cathy

b. 25 March 1969, Norwich, Norfolk, England. Dennis displayed early vocal poise and by the age of 13 she was singing in her father's Alan Dennis Band at Butlin's holiday resorts. Cathy started her career proper in the mid-80s singing in a covers band where she was spotted by Dancin' Danny D's manager, Simon Fuller, at the time looking for a female singer to work with the producer and remixer. She subsequently signed to Polydor Records and started writing her own songs and recording solo. She put this parallel career on hold to work with Danny D's D-Mob, between them achieving a chart hit with 'C'Mon Get My Love'. While other D-Mob tracks employed a variety of backing vocalists, Dennis was also featured on 'That's The Way Of The World'. By the end of 1989 she was able to resume her solo career with 'Just Another Dream' and her debut album. Her first significant success came in the US, with three Top 10 hits including 'Touch Me (All Night Long)', after which recognition in her native country followed. She was, in fact, the most successful UK singles artist in the US charts in 1991. *Into The Skyline* saw her team with Madonna's favoured producer, Shep Pettibone. She also reunited with Danny D for the 1993 D-Mob single, 'Why'. In 1995 she released the Japan-only single, 'Love's A Cradle', providing English lyrics to Japanese composer Ryo Aska's music (the track was later released on *One Voice - The Songs Of Chage And Aska*). The following year she released, *Am I The Kinda Girl?*

● ALBUMS: *Move To This* (Polydor 1991)★★★, *Into The Skyline* (Polydor 1992)★★★, *Am I The Kinda Girl?* (Polydor 1996)★★★.

Depth Charge

Depth Charge is the name under which the former DJ Jonathon Saul Kane releases his bizarre house singles, whose big beat rhythms prefigured the music of the Chemical Brothers, Propellerheads and Bentley Rhythm Ace. The most memorable of these was undoubtedly 'Goal', which sampled an excitable Brazilian football commentator holding the 'Gooooooaaaall' crow throughout its recording. Released at the height of World Cup 90 fever, it caught the imagination of the terraces after they had retired to the clubs of a Saturday evening. Other such releases included 'Depth Charge (Han Do Jin)' (sampling U-Boats from hoary old black and white movies), 'Bounty Killers' (cowboy movies) and 'Dead By Dawn (horror movies). All were released on the Vinyl Solution imprint, and Kane also records under other pseudonyms, including Octagon Man, Grimm Death, Spider and Alexander's Dark Band. Choosing to lay low and release limited edition singles and martial arts videos meant that Kane missed out on the late 90s big beat bonanza sparked by the success of Fatboy Slim. The two *Lust* albums released in 1999 repeated the weird and wonderful formula of his debut to great effect.

● ALBUMS: *Nine Deadly Venoms* (Vinyl Solution 1994)★★★★, *Lust* (DC 1999)★★★★, *Lust 2* (DC 1999)★★★.

● COMPILATIONS: *Electro Boogie: Shape Generator* (Studio !K7 1999)★★★.

Des'ree

b. London, England. Des'ree had a convent school upbringing in Norwood, London. She signed to Sony subsidiary Dusted Records in 1991 after being spotted by A&R scout Lincoln Elias, and her first two singles, 'Feel So High' and 'Mind Adventures', both charted. 'Mind Adventures' was helped enormously by her appearance on the UK's prime-time television programme, *Wogan*. Its spiritual edge was fuelled by her lengthy apprenticeship in gospel choirs. On the strength of this *Mind Adventures* broke into the UK Top 20. In 1993, she duetted with Terence Trent D'Arby on the UK Top 20 single, 'Delicate'. The first single from her second album, 'You Gotta Be', looked ready to repeat the success when it broke into the UK Top 20 in February 1994, but when it was not played on BBC Television's *Top Of The Pops* it fell straight out of the charts - a fate that also befell its successor. However, this was compensated for by an expanding international audience, with 'You Gotta Be' going Top 10 in the Australian charts. In America, her record company, 550 (an offshoot of Epic Records), promoted the single for no less than 32 weeks, an effort that paid off with a number 6 chart placing. Supporting Seal on tour helped her avoid the expected R&B bracket, and television appearances included *The Late Show With David Letterman* and *Tonight*. Afterwards, Des'ree toured with collaborator and co-writer Ashley Ingrams (ex-Imagination), and also wrote with the US hit songwriter/performer Brenda Russell. Her third album, *Supernatural*, was another well-crafted collection of catchy pop/soul songs featuring the international hit single 'Life'.

● ALBUMS: *Mind Adventures* (Dusted/Sony 1992)★★, *I Ain't Movin'* (Dusted/Sony 1994)★★★★, *Supernatural* (S2 1998)★★★.

Destiny's Child

Urban R&B quartet comprising Beyoncé Knowles (b. 4 September 1981, Houston, Texas, USA), LeToya Luckett (b. 11 March 1981, Houston, Texas, USA), LaTavia Roberson (b. 1 November 1981, Houston, Texas, USA) and Kelendria Rowland (b. 11 February 1981, Houston, Texas, USA). Knowles and Roberson first began singing together when they were only 10 years old. Rowland joined the duo in 1992, with Luckett completing the line-up the following year. The quartet adopted their biblically inspired name from a chapter in the Book Of Isaiah. Knowles' father became their manager and set about grooming the quartet for success. They gained a strong local following with their street cool image and impressive vocal harmonies, leading to opening slots for big name acts including Immature, SWV and Dru Hill. Signed to Columbia Records in 1997 their breakthrough came when the track 'Killing Time' appeared on *The Men In Black* soundtrack. Their self-titled debut, released in 1998, featured collaborations with leading R&B/hip-hop producers Timbaland, R. Kelly, Wyclef Jean and Missy 'Misdemeanor' Elliott. The funky 'No No No' reached both the US and UK Top 10, and was followed by further hits including 'With Me' and 'Get On The Bus', the latter taken from the *Why Do Fools Fall In Love?* soundtrack. *The Writing's On The Wall* was premiered by 'Bills, Bills, Bills', a track which echoed the men-bashing sentiments of TLC's massive summer hit 'No Scrubs', and even featured the same producer (Kevin She'kspere Briggs). The song provided the quartet with their first US chart-topper in July 1999, and also reached the UK Top 10. The album featured a greater creative input from the quartet, although they still relied on a heavyweight production crew including Rodney Jerkins, Missy Elliott, Chad Elliot, and Dwayne Wiggins of Tony! Toni! Toné!

● ALBUMS: *Destiny's Child* (Columbia 1998)★★★, *The Writing's On The Wall* (Columbia 1999)★★★.

dEUS

Formed in Antwerp, Belgium, in the early 90s, eclectic alternative rock band dEUS originally comprised Tom Barman (b. 1 January 1972; vocals, guitar), Stef Kamil Carlens (bass), Julle De Borgher (drums), Klaas Janzoons (violin) and Rudy Trouvé (b. 31 July 1967; guitar). Barman only really became interested in music in his late teens when he discovered the Velvet Underground and Violent Femmes. The first incarnation of dEUS, indeed, specialized in cover versions of those groups' material. Their earliest performances were at the Music Box in Antwerp, a regular haunt of actors, musicians and artists, from whom the band subsequently took much of its bohemian bent. At this time Barman had been joined by Carlens and the duo embarked on writing songs together. One of their first demos reached the finals of the domestic RockRally competition and afterwards they set out on an ill-fated tour. On their return to Antwerp they recruited De Borgher (previously their van driver), established painter Trouvé (the band's only 'real' musician) and Janzoons to cement the line-up. Sharing a mutual affection for the works of Captain Beefheart and Tom Waits, as well as jazz musicians including John Coltrane, the band set about writing a wide-ranging set of songs that zigzagged between a number of musical traditions. The first single to achieve widespread recognition was 'Suds And Soda', which was followed by the similarly bracing 'Via'. Signed to Island Records, the band embarked on work on their debut album, the well-received and stylistically diverse *Worst Case Scenario*. However, touring to promote it was delayed when De Borgher broke his ankle in Berlin. Instead, the band members concentrated on their array of solo and collaborative projects (Barman in General Electric, Carlens in Moondog Jr., and Carlens and Trouvé in Kiss My Jazz). In the interim, dEUS issued a mail-order-only album, titled *My Sister = My Clock*. Trouvé and Carlens subsequently departed, although both have continued to collaborate with the band. Danny Mommens (b. 20 April 1973; bass) and Craig Ward (guitar) were brought in as replacements. *In A Bar, Under The Sea* opened with what initially sounded like a reworking of the Velvet Underground's 'Murder Mystery'. Other tracks (such as 'Gimme The Heat') hinted at *Smiley Smile*-period Beach Boys, yet these influences failed to detract from the startling originality of dEUS' sound. The band returned in 1999 with *The Ideal Crash*, another superbly imaginative collection which suffered from poor promotion as Island was in the process of being swallowed up by the Universal group. Guitarist Tim Vanhamel, who had already toured with the band, replaced Ward early the following year.

● ALBUMS: *Worst Case Scenario* (Island 1994)★★★, *My Sister = My Clock* (Bang! 1995)★★★, *In A Bar, Under The Sea* (Island 1996)★★★★, *The Ideal Crash* (Island 1999)★★★★.

Diabaté, Toumani

b. 10 August 1965, Bamako, Mali. Descended from a long line of musicians, Diabaté's father Sidiki was responsible for introducing the kora (a 21-string cross between a lute and a harp) into Mali in the 50s. Toumani took up the kora from a young age and taught himself how to play. He developed a style of playing that, while being strongly rooted in the Malian tradition, was also open to a wide range of other influences (such as jazz and flamenco). He has subsequently sought out other musicians from around the world who are willing to experiment, even performing a concert in Amsterdam with a classical harpist. His 1989 debut *Kaira* made history as the first ever solo kora album to be released. Stark, haunting and full of breathtaking improvisational flourishes, it made him a star in his homeland and a sought-after performer internationally. In the same year, Songhai, a highly acclaimed collaboration between Diabaté and musicians from Spain and Britain, also released an album. Over the next six years Diabaté performed at festivals and concerts all over the globe, doing much to broaden the appeal of the music of Mali in general and the kora in particular. In 1995, he released *Djelika* (named after Diabaté's daughter), on which he led a group of musicians featuring Keletigui Diabaté (a veteran master of the xylophone-like balafon, and no relation to Toumani), and the ngoni (a miniature guitar-like stringed instrument) player Basekou Kouyate. The album features astonishing interplay between these three musicians, with support on some tracks from UK bass player Danny Thompson and Spanish-born flamenco jazz bass player Javier Colina, both of whom had previously played with Toumani in Songhai. *New Ancient Strings* featured Diabaté and fellow kora player Ballake Sissoko performing a series of magical duets. Thirty years previously Diabate and Sissoko's fathers had recorded *Ancient Strings*, the first album of purely instrumental kora music to be released to which *New Ancient Strings* is both a tribute and follow-up. The same year's *Kulanjan* was a wonderful collaboration with American roots music giant, Taj Mahal, featuring fellow musicians Sissoko, Baasekou Koyate (ngoni), Lassana Diabate (balafon), Dougouye Koulibaly (kamalengoni), Kasse Mady (vocals) and Ramatou Diakitc (vocals).

● ALBUMS: *Kaira* (Hannibal 1989)★★★★, *Djelika* (Hannibal 1995)★★★, with Ballake Sissoko *New Ancient Strings* (Hannibal 1999)★★★★, with Taj Mahal *Kulanjan* (Hannibal 1999)★★★★.

Diamond D

Not the white artist of the same name, who arrived on the scene much later but had copyrighted the name, Diamond D is one of rap music's top flight production experts from the USA, who, although he really broke through in the 90s, started out as DJ back in 1979, going on to join Jazzy Jay's team in the early 80s. He followed that with engagements for Master Rob (who also appeared in the *Wild Style* movie as one of the Romantic Fantastic Five) as a component of the Ultimate Force. They released one single on Strong City Records, 'I'm Not Playing', but it was not considered lyrically tough enough by prevailing hip hop standards. Diamond D pressed on, teaching himself rhyming to add to his deck skills, making a debut appearance on A Tribe Called Quest's 'Show Business'. Together with his Psychotic Neurotics posse Diamond D made his 'solo' debut with 'Best Kept Secret' on Chemistry/Mercury Records. It was an attempt to reinstate the principals of the old school Bronx pioneers in lyrical showdowns and couplets. The album that followed saw co-production assistance from DJ Mark The 45 King and Large Professor (Main Source), and remains a classic of its kind. However, it is as a producer that Diamond D remains best known, and his client list is growing. These include Showbiz And AG (often working in tandem with the former), Lord Finesse, Apache, the Geto Girlz, Chill Rob G, Pharcyde, Run DMC, KRS-One, Fugees and Brand Nubian. His most acclaimed work came with A Tribe Called Quest's *The Low-End Theory* (1991) and the Fugees' massive-selling *The Score* (1996). Several top rappers appeared on his second album, including Busta Rhymes and Pete Rock, another highly creative and enjoyable collection.

● ALBUMS: *Stunts, Blunts & Hip Hop* (Chemistry/Mercury 1992)★★★★, *Hatred, Passion & Infidelity* (Mercury 1997)★★★.

Diamond Rio

This highly successful 90s country band comprises Gene Johnson (b. 10 August 1949, Sugar Grove, Pennsylvania, USA; mandolin/fiddle), Jimmy Olander (b. 26 August 1961, Palos Verdes, California, USA; lead guitar/banjo), Brian Prout (b. 4 December 1955, Troy, New York, USA; drums), Marty Roe (b. 28 December 1960, Lebanon, Ohio, USA; lead vocals/guitar), Dan Truman (b. 29 August 1966, St. George, Utah, USA; keyboards) and Dana Williams (b. 22 May 1961, Dayton, Ohio, USA; bass). Lead singer Roe was named after Marty Robbins and was singing country songs from the age of three. Johnson had played with David Bromberg and J.D. Crowe And The New South, while Olander was a veteran of the Nitty Gritty Dirt Band. Williams is a nephew of the Osborne Brothers, making a great many interesting musical connections in Diamond Rio. They began playing as the Grizzly River Boys and by the time they were signed to Arista Records, they were the Tennessee River Boys. The band were told to change their name because it sounded too much like a gospel outfit. Two American truck manufacturers, Diamond T and Reo, merged as Diamond-Reo and with a little misspelling, Diamond Rio was born (so, incidentally, was REO Speedwagon). In 1991, Diamond Rio became the first band to top the US country charts with their debut single, the love ballad 'Meet In The Middle'. Their first album went platinum and yielded several more hit singles. They added a powerful rhythm section for their second album, an unusual move for country music. With singles such as 'Mirror Mirror', 'Mama, Don't Forget To Pray For Me', 'Sawmill Road' and 'In A Week Or Two', the band went from strength to strength. They developed their good humour with the catchy 'Norma Jean Riley' ('Fool, fool, nothing you can do/Never going to see her with the likes of you.') and 'Bubba Hyde'. With the addition of Lee Roy Parnell and Steve Wariner, they become Jed Zepplin for a new treatment of 'Workin' Man Blues' on the Merle Haggard tribute album, *Mama's Hungry Eyes*. They also performed 'Ten Feet Away' on a tribute album to Keith Whitley. Prout's wife, Nancy, is also a drummer, playing with Wild Rose, the all-female country band. In 1997, Diamond Rio won a Country Music Association Award for Vocal Group Of The Year, a deserved accolade as they blend state-of-the-art modern country rock with high harmonies and bluegrass instruments. They celebrated by releasing their finest album to date, *Unbelievable*, a near faultless collection.

● ALBUMS: *Diamond Rio* (Arista 1991)★★★, *Close To The Edge* (Arista 1992)★★★, *Love A Little Stronger* (Arista 1994)★★★, *IV* (Arista 1996)★★★, *Unbelievable* (Arista 1998)★★★★.

● COMPILATIONS: *Greatest Hits* (Arista 1997)★★★★, *Super Hits* (Arista 1999)★★★★.

● VIDEOS: *Bubba Hyde* (Arista 1994).

Dickinson, Bruce

b. Paul Bruce Dickinson, 7 August 1958, Worksop, Nottinghamshire, England. Dickinson left the heavy metal band Samson to join pioneering contemporaries Iron Maiden, replacing Paul Di'Anno in 1981. By the following year Dickinson had fully established himself within the line-up through his performances on the road and on 1982's UK number 1 album, *The Number Of The Beast*. Iron Maiden went on to become one of the most popular heavy metal bands in the world, with spectacular live shows and a run of hit singles and albums. At the start of the 90s, Dickinson began to branch out from the band. His aspirations to become a novelist were realized in his comic-novel, *The Adventures Of Lord Iffy Boatrace*, a substandard attempt in the style of Tom Sharpe. However, legions of Iron Maiden fans propelled the book into the bestseller lists. In the same year, Dickinson's solo album, *Tattooed Millionaire*, reached number 14 in the UK album charts, while the title track climbed to number 18 in April 1980. A cover version of Mott The Hoople's 'All The Young Dudes' also reached the UK Top 30. As well as being an accomplished light aeroplane pilot, Dickinson is a keen fencer, at one time having been ranked seventh in the men's foils for Great Britain, serving to reaffirm his reputation as metal's renaissance man. He finally left Iron Maiden in 1993, a year after releasing a second book, *The Missionary Position*. A second solo album for EMI Records followed a year later, sandwiched between his broadcasting duties as a presenter for BBC Radio 1. In 1996 he enlisted the legendary grunge and ex-Nirvana producer Jack Endino for *Bruce Dickinson's Skunkworks*. Dickinson then set up his own Air Raid label, for which he recorded 1998's *The Chemical Wedding*. In February 1999, it was announced that Dickinson had rejoined Iron Maiden.

● ALBUMS: *Tattooed Millionaire* (EMI 1990)★★★, *Balls To Picasso* (EMI 1994)★★★★, *Alive In Studio A* (EMI 1995)★★, *Bruce Dickinson's Skunkworks* (Raw Power 1996)★★★, *Accident Of Birth* (Raw Power 1997)★★★, *The Chemical Wedding* (Air Raid 1998)★★, *Scream For Me Brazil* (Air Raid 1999)★★.

● FURTHER READING: *The Adventures Of Lord Iffy Boatrace*, Bruce Dickinson. *The Missionary Position*, Bruce Dickinson.

Diffie, Joe

b. 28 December 1958, Tulsa, Oklahoma, USA. According to *Entertainment Weekly*, country singer Joe Diffie is a 'first rate interpreter of working class woes', while Tammy Wynette described him as all her favourite vocalists rolled into one. His career took off in the 90s by dint of his honest, earthy narratives and accomplished balladeering. He grew up listening to his father's collection of Lefty Frizzell, Johnny Cash and Merle Haggard discs, although he also loved the energy of rock 'n' roll after seeing live performances from ZZ Top and Boston. After several years working in an iron foundry in Duncan, Oklahoma, Diffie sparked a second career by playing locally with gospel, country and bluegrass groups. His break came when one of the many songs he wrote in this period, 'Love On The Rocks', was recorded by Hank Thompson. Another composition, 'Love's Hurtin' Game', was also considered by Randy Travis, and, although this later fell through, the ensuing press gave him enough impetus to relocate to Nashville. There he found work as a staff-writer with Forest Hills Music, for whom he provided material for Doug Stone and the Forester Sisters, while becoming a much demanded session singer. 'I had to keep working at developing my own style . . . I credit my friend Lonnie Wilson for the fact that I was able to find where I fit best. Lonnie had a little studio, and sometimes I'd sing demos all day, then work on my stuff half the night.' These recordings eventually reached Epic Records, resulting in his debut album, 1990's *A Thousand Winding Roads*. His arrival was confirmed by an astonishing chart feat - his first release, 'Home', simultaneously reached number 1 in the *Billboard*, *Radio & Records* and *Gavin Report* charts. Three additional number 1s followed; 'If You Want Me To', 'If The Devil Danced In Empty Pockets' and the first of his own compositions released as a single, 'New Way To Light Up An Old Flame'. The title of *Regular Joe* reflected his no-nonsense, unpretentious appeal, and it provided two more chart-toppers, 'Is It Cold In Here' and 'Ships That Don't Come In'. Although *Honky Tonk Attitude* also contained two sizeable hits in the title track and 'Prop Me Up (Beside The Jukebox)', it was 'John Deere Green' that truly took off, with many now citing Diffie as a modern-day George Jones, able to switch effortlessly from sentimental ballads to invigorating barn hops. Indeed, he earned a Country Music Association award for his 1993 collaboration with Jones, 'I Don't Need Your Rocking Chair', and a duet with Mary-Chapin Carpenter was nominated for a Grammy for Best Vocal Collaboration. *Third Rock From The Sun* surprisingly only saw one Diffie composition, 'The Cows Came Home' (written alongside Lee Bogan and Lonnie Wilson), on a set that reflected the improvement in Diffie's love life, but that also maintained his tradition for confessional material, such as 'That Road Not Taken', 'So Help Me Girl' and 'From Here On Out'. He joined the *Grand Ole Opry* in 1993. In the wake of the renewed Beatlemania in late 1995, Diffie enjoyed a number 1 hit in the spring of 1996 with the amusingly titled 'Bigger Than The Beatles'. 'This Is Your Brain' and 'Houston, We Have A Problem' from *Twice Upon A Time* were further examples of his quirky songwriting. His *Greatest Hits* collection featured the new single 'Texas Size Heartache'. *A Night To Remember* was a hard-hitting collection of straightforward country material that eschewed the novelty angle of his previous albums.

● ALBUMS: *A Thousand Winding Roads* (Epic 1990)★★★, *Regular Joe* (Epic 1991)★★★, *Honky Tonk Attitude* (Epic 1993)★★★★, *Third Rock From The Sun* (Epic 1994)★★★★, *Mr Christmas* (Epic 1995)★★, *Life's So Funny* (Epic 1995)★★★, *Twice Upon A Time* (Epic 1997)★★★, *A Night To Remember* (Epic 1999)★★★.

● COMPILATIONS: *Greatest Hits* (Epic 1998)★★★★.

DiFranco, Ani

b. 23 September 1970, Buffalo, New York, USA. Prolific 90s feminist singer-songwriter Ani (pronounced Ah-nee) DiFranco began performing at the age of nine, establishing her independence by living on her own from the age of 15 onwards. She released her initial recordings on her own Righteous Babe Records in 1990, quickly cultivating an identity through her visual appearance (piercings, dyed or shorn hair) that had little to do with precursors such as Joan Baez. After attending art school in her native Buffalo, DiFranco moved to New York City and the New School for Social Research. In the evenings she played sets at local bars, writing songs which soon identified her as a precocious talent. Literate, ebullient and a natural live performer, she quickly won converts drawn equally from folk and rock

audiences. Her debut album confirmed this promise, its lyrics informed by feminist theory but never subsumed by rhetoric or preciousness. As she told *Billboard* magazine in 1995: 'It's not like I have an agenda in my music. It's just that to me, the world is political. Politics is music - is life! That's the lens I look through.' Her versatile guitar playing, a facet often overlooked by critics, was displayed admirably on 1991's *Not So Soft*, which saw a continuation of the themes explored on her debut. For the subsequent *Imperfectly*, more complex musical arrangements were deemed necessary, with guest viola, trumpet and mandolin accompanists providing greater texture on a collection of songs discernibly more sombre and less optimistic than before. In 1993 DiFranco travelled to Santa Cruz, California, at the behest of producer Tracye Lawson, as audiences began to warm to her startling material and pugnacious delivery. In the same year *Puddle Dive* spent 10 weeks in the college charts. This new suite of songs featured several celebrated collaborators, including Mary Ramsey (from John And Mary) on violin, Rory McLeod on harmonica, Anne Rabson (from Saffire - The Uppity Blueswomen) on piano and the Uppity Blueswomen. DiFranco's focus had not shifted much, but herein she further refined her approach without compromising either the integrity or intensity of earlier compositions. The self-produced *Dilate* was a more rock-orientated album that at times came across as self-parodic. Her collaboration with folk legend Utah Phillips revealed DiFranco to be a sympathetic collaborator, providing backing to his offbeat lyrics. The same year's *Living In Clip* was a double live album. The following year's *Little Plastic Castle* featured DiFranco at her eclectic best on contrasting tracks such as 'Gravel' and 'Pulse'. In a prolific 1999, DiFranco released two new solo albums and another collaborative effort with Phillips.

● ALBUMS: *Ani DiFranco* (Righteous Babe 1990)★★★, *Not So Soft* (Righteous Babe 1991)★★★, *Imperfectly* (Righteous Babe 1992)★★★, *Puddle Dive* (Righteous Babe 1993)★★★★, *Not A Pretty Girl* (Righteous Babe 1995)★★★★, *Dilate* (Righteous Babe 1996)★★★, with Utah Phillips *The Past Didn't Go Anywhere* (Righteous Babe 1996)★★★, *More Joy, Less Shame* (Righteous Babe 1997)★★★, *Living In Clip* (Righteous Babe 1997)★★★★, *Little Plastic Castle* (Righteous Babe 1998)★★★★, *Up, Up, Up, Up, Up, Up* (Righteous Babe 1999)★★★★, with Phillips *Fellow Workers* (Righteous Babe 1999)★★★, *To The Teeth* (Righteous Babe 1999)★★★.

● COMPILATIONS: *Like I Said/Songs 1990-1991* (Righteous Babe 1994)★★★.

Digable Planets

US psychedelic jazz rappers who, along with Gang Starr, were hailed as the instigators of the genre. Contextually they are more accurately the legacy of De La Soul/P.M. Dawn's Daisy-age rap, as might be detected from their colourful pseudonyms; Doodle Bug (b. Craig Irving, Philadelphia, Pennsylvania, USA), Butterfly (b. Ishmael Butler, Brooklyn, New York, USA) and Ladybug (b. Mary Ann Vierra, Silver Springs, Maryland, USA). This conveyed their kooky, spaced-out philosophy, their names derived from an admiration for the community structures of ants and insects. Musically it was a delicious combination of wordplay and dreamy jazz backing utilising samples from artists as diverse as Art Blakey and Curtis Mayfield. The crew admitted that 'We use a lot of the colloquialisms that came out of jazz'.

However, there was an underlying political bent, as expressed on debut album cuts like 'La Femme Fetal', an attack on the Pro-Life lobby who firebomb abortion clinics. The trio then toured with live musicians in an attempt to recreate the jazzy atmosphere of the album. They returned to the recording studio to lay down tracks for *Blowout Comb*, a strong follow-up that sadly failed to match the success of *Reachin'*. Lacking a single track as catchy as the debut's hit single 'Rebirth Of Slick (Cool Like Dat)' partly explained the album's commercial failure.

● ALBUMS: *Reachin' (A New Refutation Of Time And Space)* (WEA 1993)★★★, *Blowout Comb* (Pendulum/EMI 1994)★★★★.

Digital Underground

This rap crew are among the genre's most faithful advocates of the style of funk created by the likes of Parliament and Funkadelic. The unit was formed in the mid-80s in Oakland, California by Shock-G (b. Gregory E. Jacobs, 25 August 1963, USA; keyboards, vocals) and Chopmaster J (samples, percussion). Other key members included DJ Fuze (b. David Elliot, 8 October 1970, Syracuse, New York, USA). Shock-G subsequently introduced his alter-ego, Eddie 'Humpty Hump' Humphrey, and Money B (b. Ron Brooks). According to Digital legends, back in 1987 Humphrey sustained severe burns in a freak kitchen accident. He was forced to continue his rapping career with the addition of a false nose. Instead of hiding the event surreptitiously, however, Humphrey chose a joke nose, leading to much merriment and a series of tribute records. Among these were 'the 'Humpty Dance' routine, wherein the protagonist extols his ability to still, despite such deformity, get his snout into the object of his desire's pants. Typically, there is a good-natured verve to the recording that militates against any possible offence. Their staple diet of P-Funk and Funkadelic samples is evident on most of their recordings, including a concept debut album. The subtext was the ruse of a mad scientist marketing a drug that caused the recipients to have wet dreams. Shock-G/Humpty Hump adopted the characters of two dealers, and despite the threadbare plot it actually managed to exceed its comic potential. Alongside the samples it also introduced live piano and musicians, which were also in evidence on the follow-up, *This Is An EP*. The latter included two tracks from the dreadful *Nothing But Trouble* movie in which Digital Underground appeared. However, *The Body-Hat Syndrome*, its name alluding to prophylactics, paid simply too many compliments to the P-Funk coalition, ending up sounding highly derivative. 2Pac, formerly a full-time member, joined for a few verses on 'Wussup Wit The Luv', complaining about drug dealers selling to children, a rare outbreak of moral responsibility. There were three new-comers for *The Body-Hat Syndrome*: DJ Jay Z, Clee and Saafir (aka the Saucy Nomad). In the grim world of hardcore rap Digital Underground offered a welcome release from corpses and curses. Money B and DJ Fuze also recorded two albums as Raw Fusion. Following their move from Tommy Boy Records the unit signed with a smaller label, Critique, and issued *Future Rhythm* after a three-year gap in 1996. Despite having been eclipsed commercially by a new generation of hip-hop crews, the vibrant *Who Got The Gravy?* proved Digital Underground still had the capability to create some memorable music.

● ALBUMS: *Sex Packets* (Tommy Boy 1990)★★★★, *Sons Of The P*

(Tommy Boy 1991)★★★, *The Body-Hat Syndrome* (Tommy Boy 1993)★★, *Future Rhythm* (Critique 1996)★★★, *Who Got The Gravy?* (Interscope 1998)★★★.
Solo: Saafir *Boxcar Sessions* (Qwest/Reprise 1994)★★.

Digital, Bobby

b. Robert Dixon, Kingston, Jamaica, West Indies. Dixon was given the name 'Digital' because he arrived at King Jammy's in 1985 at the same time that Steely And Clevie were experimenting with computerized rhythms. Owing to Jammy's tuition, he learned dub-cutting, continuing a heritage started by King Tubby. Before long, Digital took a key role in the studio and was instrumental in advancing the careers of artists such as Cocoa Tea, Shabba Ranks, Chaka Demus, Admiral Bailey, Sanchez and Pinchers. In 1988, he left to build his own studio and set up the Digital B label, and to form the Heatwave sound system. Shabba Ranks had hits with 'Wicked Inna Bed' and 'Gal Yuh Good' which led to 1990's *Just Reality*. 'Serious Time' was a collaboration between Digital, Ninjaman and Admiral Tibet and, by 1991, he had accumulated new talent such as Mad Cobra ('Tek Him'), Tony Rebel, Penny Irie and Shaka Shamba ('Reggae Fight'), alongside Gregory Isaacs, Johnny Osbourne and Cornell Campbell. His skilled production brought success that year with albums by Pinchers, Sanchez and Admiral Tibet, various 'version' sets and 'Substitute Lover' by Half Pint. Garnett Silk recorded his debut album and a number of hit singles at the studio in 1992, resulting in a major contract with Atlantic Records. Digital was by then producing material for the international market for artists such as Shabba Ranks, Buju Banton, Mad Cobra and Tiger. He had released an impressive amount of music by 1993, including albums by Glen Ricks and Leroy Smart, Gregory Isaacs, Cocoa Tea, Red Dragon, Sugar Minott, Josey Wales and Lieutenant Stitchie. Many younger artists, such as Terror Fabulous, Daddy Screw, Roundhead, Jigsy King and Saaba Tooth successfully used the new rhythms of 'Mad Dog' and 'Top Ten' created by Mafia And Fluxy, Sly And Robbie and Danny Browne. In 1994, Digital worked on creating rhythms that re-established Shabba Ranks with his dancehall audience. With his credibility as a ghetto youth and a roster of gifted artists Digital is likely to remain a highly respected and successful producer for many years. His productions include Shabba Ranks' *Just Reality*, Sanchez's *I Can't Wait*, Dirtsman's *Acid*, Admiral Tibet's *Separate Class*, Pinchers' *Hotter*, Leroy Smart's *Talk About Friend* and Garnett Silk's *It's Growing*.

● COMPILATIONS: *Wicked In Bed* (Blue Mountain 1989)★★★, *Gal Yuh Good* (Blue Mountain 1990)★★★, *Full House* (Digital B 1991)★★★, *Ripe Cherry* (Digital B 1991)★★, *Moving Away* (VP 1992)★★, *Top Ten* (VP 1993)★★★, *Mad Dog* (VP 1993)★★★, *Strictly Dancehall* (VP 1993)★★★, *Digital B Presents Kette Drum* (Digital B 1995)★★★.

Digitalis

One of the most exciting and original producers of psyche-delic music in the mid- to late 90s, Seb Taylor began playing the guitar in a death metal band at the age of 15, inspired by such groups as Ministry, Nine Inch Nails and 808 State. He started recording electronic music around 1994 and the next year had his first release, 'Repeater', as Digitalis on Roost Records, which was followed by two releases as Shakta, 'Lepton Head Pt. 2' (Celtic Records) and 'Amber Mantra'

(Psychic Deli). In 1996 he signed to Dragonfly Records as Shakta and released the single 'Cosmic Trigger'/'Spiritual Beings In Physical Bodies' to accompany his debut album, *Silicon Trip*, the following January. The album was well received on the trance scene and over the next year Taylor performed at parties in the UK and around the world. At the same time he continued to work as Digitalis and during 1997 released the single 'Rapid Eye'/'The Mind Gap' on 21-3 Productions, and contributed the tracks 'Double Helix' and 'Chaos By Design' (as CBD) to that label's *All Boundaries Are Illusion* compilation. In the same year he also produced the track '3rd State' for Matsuri Productions' *Let It Rip* and continued to work with these two labels in 1998. For Matsuri he recorded the *Soma Junkies* EP and the track 'Telepresence', which was released on *Forever Psychedelic*, while 21-3 included 'Not Human' and 'Waving Not Drowning' on their compilation *Elastic*. Taylor also records as Somaton for Phantasm Records and has released, *Future Memories*, and a single, 'Monogatari/Mutate And Survive'. He works in a slightly different area of the psychedelic techno sound under each pseudonym. *Silicon Trip* presents straightforward powerful, four-on-the-floor psychedelic trance characterized by excellent production, well-balanced arrangements and funky riffs. His work as Digitalis moves away from melodic-sounding, modal riffs to concentrate on abstract psychedelia and often rather metallic textures, combined with more varied rhythms that incorporate breakbeats and elements of drum 'n' bass. Taylor is distinguished from the majority of artists in the field of psychedelic music through his original choice of sounds, his arrangements and considerable production skills. He has also recorded material under the name Biotone, and has released material on Indica, Inspiral and Phantasm.
● ALBUMS: as Shakta *Silicon Trip* (Dragonfly 1997)★★★★, as Somaton *Future Memories* (Phantasm 1997)★★★, as Digitalis *The Third State* (Matsuri 1998)★★★★.

Digweed, John

b. Sussex, England. Now part of the jet-setting DJ elite, John Digweed has paid his dues by working from the bottom up. He is now an in-demand name at clubs and events throughout the world and, along with occasional partner, Sasha, is synonymous with intelligent, progressive house music. In the UK's *DJ* magazine's Top 100 of 1998, Digweed was voted number 7. Growing up in Hastings on England's south coast, Digweed's DJing ambitions began while he was still at school and he would spend evenings practising on two primitive turntables. Having left school, he secured a job at a hotel, playing for college parties. In 1987, he moved to London, unsuccessfully sending mix tapes to clubs. Digweed improvised by staging his own successful 'Bedrock' nights in Hastings. Eventually, in 1992, Renaissance liked what they heard and booked him. There, he worked hard, developing a slightly edgier sound than the 'handbag' house that was becoming popular at the time. The media called it 'epic house'. Since then, he has mixed many CD compilations, notably those for Renaissance, and has completed many remixes. The first Renaissance compilation album, mixed by Sasha and Digweed, was something of a dance music milestone, critically acclaimed and bringing new credibility (and new audiences) to house music. He has released his own material under the Bedrock banner,

notably 1995's 'For What You Dream Of', which was memorably used in the soundtrack of the movie *Trainspotting*. For two years, Digweed and Sasha have had a monthly residency at New York City's Twilo club and their *Northern Exposure* compilations and club events have been very successful. Digweed's recently-launched 'Bedrock' night at London's Heaven club has been extremely popular and has been host to DJing luminaries such as Paul Van Dyk and Nick Warren. The success of 'Bedrock', along with the *Northern Exposure* mix albums, have raised Digweed's media profile to new heights and his face is frequently seen on magazine covers. In early 1999, he recorded a second *Global Underground* compilation in Hong Kong for the Boxed label and completed remix work for Danny Tenaglia and Terminalhead. Later in the year, he was voted number 6 in the UK's *DJ* magazine's Top 100 DJs in the world, and enjoyed a huge club hit with 'Heaven Scent'.
● COMPILATIONS: with Sasha *Northern Exposure* (MOS 1996)★★★, with Sasha *Northern Exposure 2* (MOS 1997)★★★★, *Global Underground 006 – Sydney* (Boxed 1998)★★★★, *Global Underground 014 - Hong Kong* (Boxed 1999)★★★, *Bedrock* (Sony/INCredible 1999)★★★★.

Dimitri From Paris

b. October 1963, Istanbul, Turkey. Dimitri is a founding father of the recent wave of French house DJs, producers and artists, such as Etienne De Crecy, Cassius and Bob Sinclair, who take their influences from diverse sources such as 50s lounge music, 60s film scores, disco, hip-hop and New York house music. These styles are all blended into a kitsch, funky, mid-tempo sound that has had a broad appeal on the European club scene. Dimitri was born to hippie intellectual parents, whose travels took them to Paris. Growing up there, he was enchanted by disco at its peak and later, hip-hop and electro. He began mixing his collection of US import 12-inches on a pair of decks in his bedroom. Instead of the usual teenage activities, Dimitri spent hours honing his turntable skills and this led to a series of jobs at various European radio stations. At NRJ, in 1985, he presented *Megamix*, Europe's first house music radio programme. In the same year, he began producing and remixing, working on tracks by artists including Björk, Brand New Heavies, New Order, James Brown, Etienne Daho and Mory Kanté. At the time remixes were a rare phenomenon in France, and Dimitri's skills helped to pioneer the remix in France. During the early 90s Dimitri's mixing skills were used by famous fashion designers to accompany their models down the catwalk. In order to avoid copyright problems, Dimitri was asked to provide original music. The mixes were recorded onto tape and used in boutiques around the world. Eventually, Dimitri signed a deal with underground label, Yellow Productions, who released two EPs and a mini-LP. His long-playing debut, 1996's *Sacrebleu*, was voted Best Dance Album Of The Year by *Mixmag*. The album sold 50,000 copies worldwide before Dimitri was signed to East West Records, although his two mix albums have been released on independent labels. Idiosyncratic and uncompromising, Dimitri From Paris' witty eclecticism continues to win new fans.
● ALBUMS: *Sacrebleu* (Yellow 1996)★★★★.
● COMPILATIONS: *Monsieur Dimitri's De-Luxe House Of Funk* (Mixmag 1997)★★★, *ICU Session.: Three* (Max 1999)★★★★.

Dion, Celine

b. 30 March 1968, Charlemagne, Montreal, Quebec, Canada. The youngest of 14 children, Celine Dion was a vastly popular artist at home long before her success in the US and European charts as the 'new Whitney Houston or Mariah Carey'. Her parents and large family had a singing group and toured playing folk music, the influence of which was soon felt. It was Dion's mother who wrote the first song for her, which she recorded with her brother at the age of 12. Together with Mrs Dion, the two siblings were sent to the office of René Angélil, then a local rock manager, who took over the young star's guidance (later, in December 1994, he married Dion, despite a 26-year age gap). Following a series of albums addressed to her French Canadian audience she made her English language debut in 1990 with *Unison*, an impressive achievement as she had only learned English in 1989. Although this produced four hit singles her true international breakthrough arrived with the soundtrack of the Walt Disney movie, *Beauty And The Beast*. Her duet with Peabo Bryson on the title track went to number 1 in the US and earned an Academy Award for Best Song and a Grammy. Following a tribute collection comprising Dion's interpretations of the songs of Canadian writer Luc Lamondon, she concentrated on developing an international audience. 'Beauty And The Beast' formed the centrepiece of her second English language album, which also produced the hit singles 'Love Can Move Mountains', 'Water From The Moon', 'If You Asked Me To' and 'Did You Give Enough Love'. In its wake Dion became a veritable staple of awards ceremonies, making a second appearance at the Grammy's, becoming a personal favourite of *The Tonight Show*'s Jay Leno, and herself hosting Canada's Juno Awards where in 1993 she won the Female Vocalist Of The Year Award for the third time in succession. Before the release of a third English language set, Dion recorded 'When I Fall In Love', the theme tune to the hit movie *Sleepless In Seattle*. This was included on *The Colour Of My Love* alongside a cover of Jennifer Rush's AOR classic, 'The Power Of Love', also released as a single. It saw her work with songwriters including David Foster, Diane Warren, Phil Goldstone, Albert Hammond, Charlie Dore and Ric Wake. A similarly impressive cast of producers added Guy Roche, Aldo Nova and many others to a project seemingly without budget restrictions. Regardless, Epic Records' investment was repaid multi-fold by the astonishing singles success of 'Think Twice', which spent several weeks on top of the UK charts and also charted strongly in the US during 1995. The album, and its follow-up *Falling Into You*, simultaneously topped both UK and US charts in 1994 and 1996, and 'Because You Loved Me' became the best-selling adult contemporary single ever. Dion was chosen to sing (in front of billions of television viewers) at the opening of the 1996 Olympic Games in Atlanta, USA. In 1997, she released *Let's Talk About Love*, and achieved another huge worldwide hit with 'My Heart Will Go On' from the soundtrack of the blockbuster movie, *Titanic*. She also collaborated with the Bee Gees on 'Immortality', and R. Kelly on 'I'm Your Angel', both of which were predictably international hit singles.

● ALBUMS: *La Voix Du Bon Dieu* (Disques Super Etoiles 1981)★★, *Celine Dion Chante Noël* (Disques Super Etoiles 1981)★★, *Tellement J'ai D'amour* (Saisons 1982)★★, *Les Chemins De Ma Maison* (Saisons 1983)★★, *Du Soleil Au Coeur* (Pathe Marconi 1983)★★, *Chants Et Contes De Noël* (1983)★★, *Mélanie* (TBS 1984)★★, *Les Oiseaux Du Bonheur* (Pathe Marconi 1984)★★, *C'est Pour Toi* (TBS 1985)★★, *Celine Dion En Concert* (TBS 1985)★★, *Incognito* (Columbia 1987)★★, *Unison* (Epic 1990)★★, *Dion Chante Plamondon/Des Mots Qui Sonnent* (Epic 1991)★★★, *Celine Dion* (Epic 1992)★★★★, *The Colour Of My Love* (Epic 1993)★★★★, *Celine Dion À L'Olympia* (Columbia 1994)★★★, *D'Eux/The French Album* (Epic 1995)★★★, *Falling Into You* (Epic 1996)★★★, *Live À Paris* (Epic 1996)★★★, *Let's Talk About Love* (Epic 1997)★★★, *S'Il Suffisait D'Aimer* (Epic 1998)★★, with Mariah Carey, Gloria Estefan, Aretha Franklin, Shania Twain *Divas Live* (Epic 1998)★★, *These Are Special Times* (Epic 1998)★★.

● COMPILATIONS: *Les Plus Grands Succès De Celine Dion* (TBS 1984)★★★, *Les Chansons En Or* (TBS 1986)★★, *Vivre: The Best Of Celine Dion* (Carrere 1988)★★, *Les Premières Années* (Versailles 1993)★★, *Celine Dion Gold* (Versailles 1995)★★★, *Celine Dion Gold Volume 2* (Versailles 1995)★★★, *C'est Pour Vivre* (Eureka 1997)★★★, *All The Way ... A Decade Of Song* (Epic 1999)★★★.

● VIDEOS: *Unison* (1991), *The Colour Of My Love Concert* (Epic Music Video 1995), *Live À Paris* (1996), with Mariah Carey, Gloria Estefan, Aretha Franklin, Shania Twain *Divas Live* (Sony Music Video 1998), *Live In Memphis - The Concert* (Sony Music Video 1998).

● FURTHER READING: *Celine: The Authorized Biography*, Georges-Hébert Germain. *Celine Dion: The Complete Biography*, Lisa Peters with Della Druick.

● FILMS: *Quest For Camelot* voice only (1998), *Passionnément* (1999).

Disposable Heroes Of Hiphoprisy

A hugely innovative contemporary hip-hop crew formed by Rono Tse (percussion) and Michael Franti (vocals). Both residents of the Bay area of San Francisco, USA, the duo worked together for several years, most notably in *avant garde* industrial jazz band the Beatnigs. Following their inception as the Disposable Heroes they won significant allies amongst press and peers; support slots to Billy Bragg, U2, Public Enemy, Arrested Development and Nirvana demonstrating the range of their appeal. Their sound recalled some of the experimental edge of their former incarnation, while Franti's raps were arguably the most articulate and challenging of his generation. Typically he broke down his subject matter beyond the black/white rhetoric of much urban rap, and was willing to place his own inadequacies as a person at the forefront of his manifesto. When he called himself a 'Jerk' in the intensely personal 'Music And Politics', Franti took rap into a whole new dimension. Examples of his skilled deployment of words litter the band's debut album; 'Imagination is sucked out of children by a cathode-ray nipple, Television is the only wet-nurse, that would create a cripple' (from 'Television The Drug Of The Nation', which also bemoans the amount of violence visited upon an average American child through his television set). 'Language Of Violence' took to task rap's penchant for homophobia, forging a link between a wider circle of prejudice. Franti was more effective still when dealing with subjects on a personal level; 'I was adopted by parents who loved me; they were the same colour as the kids who called me nigger on the way home from school' (from 'Socio-Genetic Experiment'). One unfortunate consequence of Franti's eloquence was that the Disposable Heroes became the token rap band that it was 'safe for white liberals to like'. Otherwise there was precious little to fault in them. In 1993, they recorded an album with *Naked Lunch* author, William Burroughs. However, as the year closed they informed the press that the Disposable Heroes were no longer a going concern, with both parties going on to solo careers. The first result of which was Franti's 1994 album *Home*, as Spearhead, with producer Joe 'The Butcher' Nicolo. There were also liaisons with the Disposables' live guitarist Charlie Hunter, and a projected dub album with Adrian Sherwood. Rono, meanwhile, has worked with Oakland rappers Mystic Journeymen.

● ALBUMS: *Hypocrisy Is The Greatest Luxury* (4th & Broadway 1992)★★★★, with William Burroughs *Spare Ass Annie & Other Tales* (4th & Broadway 1993)★★★.

Divine Comedy

These days the Divine Comedy is just one man, Neil Hannon (b. 7 November 1970, Londonderry, Northern Ireland), the son of the Bishop of Clogher. Hannon originally formed the band in 1989 with John McCullagh (vocals) and drummer Kevin Traynor, and signed to Setanta Records (a spiritual home for wayward pop stars such as Frank And Walters and A House). The band's opening salvo was 1990's *Fanfare For The Comic Muse*. Filled with elegant, resourceful observations on the perversities of Irish and British life, this proved the most pop-orientated of Hannon's 90s work. Of his ensuing albums he would confess: 'I was very interested in the purity of three chords and all that but I was lured away by polyphonic harmony.' Following the album's release, McCullagh and Traynor elected to return to their studies with Hannon candidly pointing out that the decision was partially due to the band members 'realising Neil's an arrogant, egocentric bastard'. The prevailing influences on the ensuing *Liberation* and *Promenade* included Michael Nyman, European art and Scott Walker. Critics were full of praise for both albums, partly because of Hannon's ability to provide self-conscious but highly amusing interview copy. *Promenade* included 'The Booklovers', in which Hannon recounted the names of some 60 authors, leaving a gap for them to answer (many of the replying voices were provided by the Irish comedian Sean Hughes). Hannon also struck up a fruitful working partnership with Joby Talbot, who was named BBC Young Composer Of The Year in 1996. A breakthrough beyond critical success came in 1996 with the highly accessible, yet bleak, *Casanova*, which put Hannon in the UK Top 20 courtesy of the singles 'Something For The Weekend' (number 14) and 'The Frog Princess' (number 15). He returned a few months later with the wondrous minialbum *A Short Album About Love*, featuring seven heavily orchestrated new songs including another Top 20 single, 'Everbody Knows (Except You)'. Hannon also collaborated with composer Michael Nyman and recorded his final album for Setanta, *Fin De Siècle*, which provided him with his first Top 10 album placing in September 1998. The jaunty 'National Express' entered the UK charts at number 8 in January 1999. A re-recorded version of 'The Pop Singer's Fear Of The Pollen Count', a track originally featured on *Liberation*, was released to promote the bestselling compilation *A Secret History*.

● ALBUMS: *Fanfare For The Comic Muse* (Setanta 1990)★★, *Liberation* (Setanta 1993)★★★, *Promenade* (Setanta 1994)★★★★, *Casanova* (Setanta 1996)★★★★, *A Short Album About Love* mini-album (Setanta 1997)★★★★, *Fin De Siècle* (Setanta 1998)★★★★.

● COMPILATIONS: *A Secret History* (Setanta 1999)★★★★.

Dixie Chicks

This female trio's beguiling mixture of bluegrass, straight country and pop shook up the contemporary country scene in the late 90s. Raised in Texas, USA, sisters Martie Seidel (mandolin/fiddle) and Emily Erwin (banjo/dobro) were still only teenagers they toured throughout the USA with the bluegrass group Blue Night Express. Taking their name from the Little Feat song 'Dixie Chicken', the Dixie Chicks were founded in 1989 when the sisters, with Laura Lynch and Robin Lynn Macy (ex-Danger In The Air), began busking on street corners in Dallas. They performed at clubs and dance halls and released two bluegrass-orientated independent label albums and a Christmas single, before Macy left to form the Domestic Social Club with Sara Hickman and Patty Lege. The more contemporary sounding *Shouldn't A Told You That* was the last recording to feature Lynch, who was replaced by new lead vocalist Natalie Maines (daughter of steel guitarist Lloyd Maines) in 1995. The new look Dixie Chicks were considered the perfect flagship act for the 1997 relaunch of Monument Records . Released in January 1998, *Wide Open Spaces* quickly became the best-selling country album released by a group in that year, and eventually climbed to number 4 on the *Billboard* 200 album chart the following year. Its success was buoyed by the release of the singles 'I Can Love You Better' and 'There's Your Trouble' (a US country number 1). They also made a name for themselves in the press, Maines making statements opposing the legalization of marijuana on the *Politically Incorrect* television show. At September's CMA Awards they completed a fine year by winning the Vocal Group and Horizon trophies. At the following year's Grammy Awards, *Wide Open Spaces* was voted Best Country Album. The follow-up *Fly*, which introduced a more pop-orientated style, shot to the top of the US album chart in September 1999.

● ALBUMS: *Thank Heavens For Dale Evans* (Crystal Clear 1990)★★★, *Little Ol' Cowgirl* (Crystal Clear 1992)★★★, *Shouldn't A Told You That* (Crystal Clear 1993)★★★, *Wide Open Spaces* (Monument 1998)★★★★, *Fly* (Monument 1999)★★★.

DJ Food

As part of Coldcut's DJing angle on creating music, Jonathon Moore and Matt Black released a series of albums entitled *Jazz Brakes*, beginning in 1990 when they formed Ninja Tune Records, under the name DJ Food. Containing mainly funk and hip-hop instrumentals, often cut up with samples of bizarre dialogue, it was partly intended as material for mixing, remixing and producing. Volumes 4 and 5 (1993, 1994) were co-written with the producer PC (Patrick Carpenter) and developed the abstract hip-hop sound by incorporating shades of Latin, dub, techno, ambient, jungle and non-Western music. The two 12-inch records, *Refried Food*, in 1995, contained mixes by Autechre, Fila Brazilia and Ashley Beedle, among others, and were collected onto one album the following year. PC and Strictly (Kevin Foakes) became more involved on *A Recipe For Disaster* (1995), and later took over the reins, still with the assistance of Coldcut. DJ Food present live sets during which PC works with Strictly on four decks.

● ALBUMS: *Jazz Brakes Vols. 1 – 5* (Ninja Tune 1990–94)★★★★, *A Recipe For Disaster* (Ninja Tune 1995)★★★, *Refried Food* (Ninja Tune 1996)★★★.

DJ Hurricane

b. USA. The Beastie Boys' long-standing musical collaborator, DJ Hurricane finally made his solo debut in 1995, but boasted a much longer history in hip-hop. Before joining the Beastie Boys in 1986, Hurricane had been part of the Solo Sounds - the first ever rap group in Hollis, Queens, New York (even pre-dating Run DMC). While with the Beasties he was also a component of the entertaining Afros side-show. His debut solo album used more up-to-date moves, however, with the strong rhythmic influence being Cypress Hill (Sen Dog guested on one track, 'Feel The Blast'). Other guests included MC Breed ('What's Really Going On' and newcomer Tye Bud ('Comin' O-F-F'). The Beastie Boys themselves turned in a strong performance for the agenda-setting 'Four Fly Guys', while Beastie associate Mario Caldato Jnr. provided production. Hurricane returned in 1997 with the harder-hitting *Severe Damage*.

● ALBUMS: *The Hurra* (Wiiija 1995)★★★, *Severe Damage* (Wiiija 1997)★★★.

DJ Krush

b. Hideaki Ishii, Tokyo, Japan. DJ Krush is a leading figure on the Japanese hip-hop scene and one of Mo' Wax Records' most influential artists. As a result of seeing a Tokyo screening of the rap film *Wild Style*, he began DJing to accompany breakdancers and in 1987 formed the Krush Posse. Several releases in the early 90s passed with little recognition until he met James Lavelle, who signed Krush to Mo' Wax. His first release for that label was the track 'Kemuri', which appeared on a double a-side with DJ Shadow's 'Lost And Found' in September 1994. This was followed the next month by the eagerly awaited *Strictly Turntablized*. A collection of laid-back hip-hop beats with abstract jazz inflections, it received an enthusiastic response from both the public and the press. At the same time, Krush was also featured on Mo' Wax's *Headz* compilation (1994), helping to establish the label's unique sound. Since this time he has collaborated on a number of projects. The album *Meiso* featured a number of American rappers, including C.L. Smooth and Malika B (The Roots), and the stark texture of *Strictly Turntablized* was replaced by a more accessible, vocal-orientated sound. On *Milight* Krush worked with the Japanese singer Eri Ohno, Deborah Anderson and others, producing a set of contemplative and positive tracks quite unlike much 'gangsta rap' of the time. *Ki-Oku* was an interesting collaboration with Japanese trumpeter Toshinori Kondo and included a version of Bob Marley's 'Sun Is Shining'. Krush released *Holonic*, a mixed compilation of some of his previous work, in 1998.

● ALBUMS: *Krush* (Nipon 1994)★★★, *Strictly Turntablized* (Mo' Wax 1994)★★★★, *Meiso* (Mo' Wax 1995)★★★, *ColdKrushCuts* (Ninja Tune 1997)★★★, *Milight* (Mo' Wax 1997)★★★★, with Toshinori Kondo *Ki-Oku* (R&S 1998)★★★, *Kakusei* (Columbia 1999)★★★.

● COMPILATIONS: *Holonic* (Mo' Wax 1998)★★★.

DJ Rap

b. Charrissa Saverio, 1969, Singapore. DJ Rap is one of the UK's leading female DJs and certainly the most high-profile female drum 'n' bass DJ. Born to an Italian father and an Irish-Malaysian mother, Saverio was brought in many parts of the world and learned classical piano as a child. The family relocated to Southampton, England when she was a teenager, where she discovered pop music. After leaving school, she modelled for two years and travelled in Europe, before returning to the UK and joining a legal firm in London. Her friends took her to a rave and like many others, her life changed. After meeting budding producer Jeff B, they made a track 'Ambience – The Adored'. Written by Rap, it became a hit on the rave scene and elsewhere. Rap promoted the track by appearing on a few land-based pirate radio stations, including Rave FM, where she was taught to mix by Coolhand Flex, one of the original London 'junglists'. While at a hardcore night at London's Astoria, Rap was asked to fill in for the DJ Fabio when he did not appear for his set. She slowly began to establish her reputation and by 1993 had played at all the major raves in the UK, such as World Dance, Dreamscape, Lydd Airport and Rezerection. Rap continued to make her own productions and scored a dancefloor hit with 'Spiritual Aura' in 1993. Its success prompted Rap to start her own label, Proper Talent and a subsidiary in 1995, Low Key Recordings. She continues to DJ all over the world and is known for her eclectic taste and combination of gentle, ambient dreamscapes with tough breakbeats. She released her first album, *Intelligence* on Proper Talent. Though it proved her to be an able writer and vocalist, the album was not a significant commercial success. In 1997, she signed to the Higher Ground label, home of Grooverider and Leftfield. Her debut for them, *Learning Curve*, was released in April 1999. It demonstrated a range of styles, live instrumentation, drum 'n' bass, techno and trance, and elicited positive reviews.

● ALBUMS: *Intelligence* (Proper Talent 1996)★★, *Learning Curve* (Higher Ground 1999)★★★.

DJ Shadow

b. Josh Davis, Hayward, California, USA. Self-proclaimed 'vinyl-addict and beat-head' DJ Shadow was turned on to hip-hop by Grandmaster Flash's 'The Message' and later began compiling his own mix tapes. His first release on Mo' Wax Records, 'In Flux'/'Hindsight' (1993), was seen by some as a benchmark in instrumental hip-hop and helped to define that label's approach. His second Mo' Wax single, 'Lost And Found', was released together with DJ Krush's 'Kemuri' in 1994, and was followed by 'What Does Your Soul Look Like' the next year. Towards the end of 1996 he released his first album, *Endtroducing ...* , as well as the singles 'Midnight In A Perfect World' and 'Stem', which brought him to the mainstream consciousness through coverage in the national press. The album was widely acclaimed for the way in which Davis blends hip-hop grooves with elements of jazz, rock, ambient, techno and other styles to create a unique, coherent sound that never resorts to the formulae of these influences. As with some of the more melodic instrumental hip-hop, compared to the humorous abstract collages of artists such as DJ Food, much of the album seems deeply introspective and rather earnest, with its mournful cello, piano and organ melodies and sequences. This feeling is further emphasized by the raw production and the tendency towards slow tempos. In 1997 he released 'High Noon' and also DJed at the Verve's appearance at Wembley Arena in 1997, as a result of working with Richard Ashcroft on James Lavelle's U.N.K.L.E. project. Later that year, he released a set of his tracks performed by DJ Q-Bert (renowned for his technical mastery) entitled *Camel Bob Sled Race*. Davis has collaborated with other Mo' Wax artists, including Blackalicious and DJ Krush. Recording with old friends Blackalicious and Latyrx as Quannum, he released 1999's diversely entertaining *Spectrum*.

● ALBUMS: *Midnight In A Perfect World* (Mo Wax 1996)★★★, *Endtroducing . . .* (Mo Wax 1996)★★★★, with Q-Bert *Camel Bob Sled Race (Q-Bert Mega Mix)* mini-album (Mo Wax 1997)★★★, *Preemptive Strike* (Mo Wax 1998)★★.

DJ Sneak

b. 1 January 1969, Puerto Rico. Sneak is a highly respected member of Chicago's 'second generation' of house music producers. Arriving in Chicago in 1983, Sneak, who could not speak English, was drawn to instrumental music and graffiti art. He was later inspired by early pioneers such as DJ Pierre and Marshall Jefferson. Several of these inspirational figures had left for New York by the late 80s, just as Sneak was entering the music business. Nevertheless, Cajmere had begun to revive the city's classic house sound and established Cajual Records. DJ Sneak released a series of records on Cajual's sister-label, Relief Records, which promoted a slightly harder sound. He has also worked on productions for Strictly Rhythm Records, Henry Street, ZYX, 83 West and Feverpitch. Several of the Feverpitch recordings featured Armand Van Helden as co-producer and the partnership's strong Latin influences can be heard on them. Sneak has also remixed Sneaker Pimps and has worked with Roger Sanchez and Dave Clarke. His DJing skills are in demand all over the world and he is a regular visitor to Ibiza during the summer clubbing season. His 1996 track 'You Can't Hide From Your Bud' was something of a masterpiece, setting a blueprint for many subsequent 'filtered disco' tracks and preceding the wave of funky, disco-influenced house that would prove massively popular during the next few years – 'Music Sounds Better' by Stardust (Thomas Bangalter) being a prime example. Sneak remains committed to the original Chicago heritage of house music and feels that many current DJs and producers have lost touch with the music's roots. Sneak has a simple plan for when the 'underground' inevitably goes 'overground': 'I'll go deeper underground.'

● ALBUMS: *Blue Funk Files* (Ultra 1997)★★★.

● COMPILATIONS: *Kinky Trax Collection* (React Music 1996)★★★, *Buggin' Da Beats* (Moonshine Music 1997)★★★.

DJ Spooky

b. Paul Miller, Washington, DC, USA. An experimental DJ working in contemporary electronica, Spooky, aka That Subliminal Kid, is an energetic, as well as prolific, performer. His world view was partially shaped by his parents' involvement in the civil rights movement - his father was a lawyer for the Black Panthers and his mother a leading light in the Afro-Futurism fashion movement. He first became attuned to music when his father purchased a computer: 'The idea of sound becoming a way of creating text, or even code, really blew my mind.' As well as recording extensively, he exhibits his visual art, contributes articles to magazines such as the *Village Voice* and *Vibe*, and writes books (covering music theory, intellectual property, and, bizarrely, science fiction). He defended his billing as a modern renaissance man thus: 'We're in an aesthetic that is so linked to all these different world cultures, the music that I'm trying to create celebrates

that diversity. It's all in the mix.' As a continuation of this, his DJ sets routinely mix easy listening (Esquivel!), with reggae, drum 'n' bass and soul, a sonic collage reflected in his recorded work. *Songs Of A Dead Dreamer* included the club hit 'Galactic Funk', while the follow-up, 1998's *Riddim Warfare*, included intriguing collaborations with Dr. Octagon and Arto Lindsay. Spooky has also remixed tracks by Metallica, Spooky Ruben and Nick Cave, and wrote the soundtrack to the 1998 movie *Slam*. In 1999, Miller collaborated with avant garde electronic outfit the Freight Elevator Quartet on the stunning *'File Under Futurism'* project.

● ALBUMS: *Songs Of A Dead Dreamer* (Asphodel 1996)★★★★, *Necropolis: The Dialogic Project* remix album (Knitting Factory Works 1996)★★★, as Paul D. Miller *Viral Sonata* (Asphodel 1997)★★★, *Riddim Warfare* (Asphodel 1998)★★★★, as DJ Spooky vs The Freight Elevator Quartet *'File Under Futurism'* (Caipiranha 1999)★★★★.

DJ Vadim

Vadim was born in the Soviet Union but moved to London when he was three. After becoming interested in hip-hop, he began to DJ and in 1995 released his first EP, *Abstract Hallucinogenic Gases*, on his own Jazz Fudge label. Later that year he continued his abstract hip-hop experiments on the EP *Headz Ain't Ready*, after which he signed to Ninja Tune Records. His first release for Ninja was 'Non Lateral Hypothesis' in April 1996, and his debut album, *USSR Repertoire*, 'a crazy selection of minimal hip-hop, ansa machines, *musique concrete* and the old school', arrived towards the end of the year. His only release of 1997 was the EP *Conquest Of The Irrational*. While recording for Ninja Tune he has continued to develop 'audio research into minimal hip-hop' at Jazz Fudge, with a number of artists and collaborators such as Andre Gurov, Mark B, the Creators, Blade and the Bug. He also DJs around the world, with particular success in Japan, which prompted an album of remixes, *USSR Reconstrustion - Theories Explained* (1998), featuring work by the Prunes, Kid Koala, the Herbaliser and DJ Krush, among others.

● ALBUMS: *USSR Repertoire* (Ninja Tune 1997)★★★★, *USSR Reconstrustion - Theories Explained* (Ninja Tune 1998)★★★, *Life From The Other Side* (Ninja Tune 1999)★★★.

DMX

b. Earl Simmons, 18 December 1970, Baltimore, Maryland, USA. Simmons was raised from an early age by his aunt in New York City's Yonkers district. He took his name from the DMX digital sound machine, and developed a reputation as a DJ on the local projects. He won *Source* magazine's Unsigned Hype Award in January 1991, and released the promo single 'Born Loser' for Columbia Records the following year. He managed to escape from Columbia's punitive contract, but little was heard from him afterwards apart from a 1994 single, 'Make A Move'. He made a dramatic re-entry onto the hip-hop scene with a show stopping appearance on LL Cool J's '4,3,2,1'. Further cameos on Mase's '24 Hours To Live', the LOX's 'Money, Power & Respect' and the remix of Ice Cube's 'We Be Clubbin'' built up a highly marketable reputation. Newly signed to Ruff Ryders/Def Jam Records, DMX returned to recording with the powerful 'Get At Me Dog' single, a US Top 40 single built around a B.T. Express guitar sample. Marketed as a return to the chaotic, raw roots of street rap, he became hip-hop's latest sensation during 1998 when his debut album, *It's Dark And Hell Is Hot*, entered the US *Billboard* album chart at number 1. An impressive slice of east coast hardcore rap, the album centred around DMX's ferocious lyrical approach. The follow-up, *Flesh Of My Flesh, Blood Of My Blood*, stayed at number 1 in the US for three weeks during January 1999. The album included cameo appearances from the Lox, Jay-Z, Mary J. Blige ('Coming From') and Marilyn Manson ('The Omen'). After contributing to the Ruff Ryders' chart-topping *Ryde Or Die Vol. 1* set, DMX quickly laid down tracks for his new album. Despite being his third release in the space of two years, *... And Then There Was X* was another quality slice of hardcore rap and a welcome antidote to the bland hip-hop product still flooding the American market. The album followed its predecessors to the top of the US charts in December 1999.

● ALBUMS: *It's Dark And Hell Is Hot* (Def Jam 1998)★★★★, *Flesh Of My Flesh, Blood Of My Blood* (Def Jam 1998)★★★, *... And Then There Was X* (Def Jam 1999)★★★.

● FILMS: *Belly* (1998).

Dodgy

A pop trio based in north London, the roots of Dodgy can be traced to mid-80s Birmingham, where Nigel Clark (vocals/bass) joined local goth band Three Cheers For Tokyo, finding a musical ally in drummer Mathew Priest. Their shared tastes included The The's *Infected* and a revulsion for their guitarist's Flying V exhibitionism. The pair relocated to London instead and placed an advert in *Loot* that simply read: 'Wanted: Jimi Hendrix'. Andy Miller (guitar) rallied to the call, and the trio moved to Hounslow. They spent a year practising the three-part harmonies that would become their trademark. Taking the name Dodgy, the band played their first gig at the John Bull pub in Chiswick. Afterwards, the 'Dodgy Club' was inaugurated. By taking over a Kingston wine bar, the band created their own weekly hangout with DJs mixing up indie and dance cuts, with the band playing as the finale. Guests included Oasis, Shed Seven and even Ralph McTell. The band's first demo, featuring an early take on 'Lovebird', won BBC DJ Gary Crowley's 'Demo Clash' for several consecutive weeks, before A&M Records requested their signatures. *The Dodgy Album*, filled with buoyant 60s-styled pop tunes, nevertheless failed to sell, though The Dodgy Club was now being exported as far afield as Amsterdam and Scandinavia. 1994 was the band's breakthrough year, with *Homegrown* producing two memorable singles in 'Staying Out For The Summer' (a hit when reissued in 1995) and 'So Let Me Go Far'. Despite lacking any discernible image aside from that of three wide-eyed and unspoilt souls with a fondness for dressing down (matching red trousers apart) and big, eminently hummable songs, Dodgy were now welcome guests in both the charts and the pop press. *Free Peace Sweet* was a solid album containing some memorable songs. 'You've Gotta Look Up' (with shades of the Ad Libs' 'Boy From New York City') and 'Good Enough' (a UK number 4 single) were both outstanding, yet overall, it fell short of the greatness that many had expected. Paul Moody of the *New Musical Express* summed it up well: 'A fine pop album then, but not a great Dodgy album'. With rumours of personality clashes flying around, Clark left the band in June 1998. The trio's final single, 'Every Single Day', was released in September.

Miller and Priest returned in summer 1999 with new singer Dave Bassey and bass player Nick Abnett.

● ALBUMS: *The Dodgy Album* (A&M 1993)★★★★, *Homegrown* (A&M 1994)★★★, *Free Peace Sweet* (A&M 1996)★★★.

● COMPILATIONS: *Ace As & Killer Bs* (A&M 1998)★★★.

Dog, Tim

b. Timothy Blair, 1 January 1967, Bronx, New York, USA. A dropout from St John's University in Queens, Dog's 'Fuck Compton' single proved to be one of the most notorious releases in rap's chequered history. Yet this anti-NWA tirade (at one point he sings 'Shut up bitch/You can't sing' while simulating intercourse with Eazy-E's 'girlfriend') was an undeniably forceful manifesto, for all its wanton tribalism. Indeed, legend has it that it provoked death threats from members of the west coast rap community. Dog was also a guest member of Ultramagnetic MC's for a period, appearing on their 'Chorus Line' anthem. Dog's second album, *Do Or Die*, was a largely discredited offering, despite the presence of KRS-1 on 'I Get Wrecked'. Other tracks such as 'Silly Bitch' featured a refrain of 'Clean out the kitchen/And the bathroom sink', just in case listeners were unaware as to Dog's vision of women in the scheme of things. In 1994, Dog made a surprise signing to Phonogram Records' Talkin' Loud label, home to artists including Incognito and Galliano. The first result of this deal was the single, 'Bitch Wid A Perm', dedicated to fellow canine rapper Snoop Doggy Dogg.

● ALBUMS: *Penicillin On Wax* (Ruffhouse 1991)★★★, *Do Or Die* (Ruffhouse/Columbia 1993)★★★.

Doof

b. Nick Barber, 1968. With a background in punk, reggae, rock and Indian music, Taylor's first release, the EP *Disposable Hymn To The Infinite*, was on Novamute Records in 1991. He has since recorded for a number of the top trance labels, including the *Born Again* EP (Matsuri Productions 1995) and 'Double Dragons' (Dragonfly Records). In 1995 he released 'Let's Turn On' (a collaboration with Simon Posford aka Hallucinogen) on TIP Records, followed in 1996 by 'Angelina' and 'Destination Bom' (also on TIP), which all became favourites on the trance scene. Towards the end of that year, TIP released Doof's eagerly awaited debut album, *Let's Turn On*, one of the most coherent and enduring releases in the 'Goa' trance style. On tracks such as 'Mars Needs Women' and 'Destination Bom', Barber distilled the rip-roaring, four-on-the-floor/Indian mode style in careful, restrained arrangements, while presenting a more tranquil, chilled-out trance sound on 'Sunshrine' and 'Star Over Parvati'. At the same time, the album is characterized as a whole by his focused collection of sounds. In 1997, he contributed 'The Tower And The Star' to the TIP compilation *Infinite Excursions II*; the following year 'Wormhole' was released on TIP's *Beyond Colour*. He has also written tracks for the dub compilations *Dub Mashing Up Creation* and *Dubbed On Planet Skunk* for Dubmission Records. Barber frequently travels and performs around Europe and further afield. He has remixed for a number of artists including the Green Nuns Of The Revolution, Hallucinogen and the Infinity Project.

● ALBUMS: *Let's Turn On* (TIP 1996)★★★★.

Dope

This self-styled post-industrial USA metal outfit is named after the Dope brothers, Edsel (vocals/guitar) and Simon (keyboards). Though now based in New York, USA, the brothers were brought up in south Florida. Edsel Dope played drums in several local punk bands before travelling around America. Simon Dope studied chemistry at the University of Florida before relocating to New York. His brother joined him there in 1997, where their shared musical influences convinced them to form their own band. They signed up three musicians, Tripp Eisen (guitar), Acey Slade (bass) and Preston Nash (drums), who were all concurrently leading their own bands. The newly formed quintet played a handful of live dates before signing to Flip Records in October 1998. They recorded their provocatively titled debut album at Greene Street in Manhattan with producer John Travis (Kid Rock, Sugar Ray). Informed by the Dope brothers own experiences, the lyrics to tracks such as the openers 'Pig Society' and 'Debonaire' railed against America's hypocritical mainstream culture, over a furious soundtrack that demonstrated the enduring influence of Trent Reznor's industrial blueprint. Having already completed live dates with Orgy and Fear Factory, Dope landed a prime slot on a tour with Coal Chamber and Slipknot.
● ALBUMS: *Felons And Revolutionaries* (Flip/Epic 1999)★★★.

Down By Law

This Los Angeles, California, USA hardcore rock band were formed in the early 90s by veteran singer Dave Smalley, formerly of DYS, Dag Nasty and All. An ever changing list of compatriots, who by the mid-90s included Tampa Bay, Florida native Sam Williams (guitar, ex-Balance; Slap Of Reality), Angry John DiMambro (bass, ex-Clay Idols; Leonards) and Danny Westman (drums, ex-Florecene; Spindle), all boasted a similar level of achievement and experience. The band's debut album, featuring Smalley, Chris Bagarozzi (guitar), Ed Urlik (bass) and Dave Nazworthy (drums), illustrated their style and outlook - uncompromising rock 'n' roll delivered with pace and a high degree of musical dexterity. It saw them signed to the influential Epitaph Records label. Though subsequent albums revealed steadily more complex arrangements, Down By Law's work remains thoroughly consistent with the hardcore style. *All Scratched Up!* was introduced by the typically urgent 'Independence Day', the band demonstrating its commitment to vinyl purchasers by providing them with a full side of bonus tracks unavailable on the CD. However, the simplistic nature of too many of the songs argued against the possibility of Down By Law repeating the international success of labelmates such as Rancid or Offspring. They had returned to independent label status by the time of 1999's rousing *Fly The Flag*, which featured Smalley, Williams, Keith Davies (bass) and Milo Todesco (drums).
● ALBUMS: *Blue* (Epitaph 1992)★★★, *Punkrockacademyflightsong* (Epitaph 1994)★★★★, *All Scratched Up!* (Epitaph 1996)★★★, *Last Of The Sharpshooters* (Epitaph 1997)★★★, *Fly The Flag* (Go-Kart 1999)★★★★.

Downset

These fierce and confrontational metal-rappers (usually titled downset.), from the San Fernando Valley/Sylmar area of Los Angeles, originally formed under the name Social Justice in 1986. Immersed in the 90s US independent underground scene, Rey Anthony Oropeza (b. 2 June 1970; 'Messenger'), James Morris (b. 11 April 1974; bass) and Chris Lee (b. 27 January 1975; drums) were the founding members, later joined by guitarists Rogelio 'Roy' Lozano and Brian 'Ares' Schwager (b. 12 December 1973) as they slowly evolved into downset. Typically, the band began by recording and releasing a series of singles and cassettes on a variety of labels, with 'Angel'/'Ritual' (Theologian Records) and 'Our Suffocation' (Abstract Records) being among the best known. Having established a formidable fanbase, the band inevitably attracted major label interest. By early 1993 the band had to compromise their hardcore ethics in order to reach a wider audience; adopting their current name, they opted for Mercury Records. In autumn 1993, they entered Silver Cloud Studios with their friend, mentor and confidant Roy Z as their producer, with the intention of recording an EP. The resultant tracks were so intensely powerful and emotionally charged that they decided to record a full album. The self-titled result was one of the most brutally heavy and intelligent albums to emerge from the Los Angeles underground, with socially aware lyrics rapped in raging hip-hop style; their formative years in LA's violent and poverty-stricken neighbourhoods finally found full release. So impressive was their debut that they were invited to take part on a European tour with Biohazard and Dog Eat Dog, covering 42 shows in 15 countries. Unfortunately, the gruelling schedule proved too much; Lozano eventually left and the band recorded the 1996 follow-up *do we speak a dead language?* as a four-piece. Once again, the music was as uncompromising as the hip-hop, hardcore and graffiti art scenes that inspired it, mirroring their personal growth and cultivated from personal experience.
● ALBUMS: *downset.* (Mercury 1994)★★★★, *do we speak a dead language?* (Mercury 1996)★★★.

Dr. Alban

b. Alban Nwapa, Nigeria. Swedish-based dance music artist who rose to prominence with his curious potpourri of styles, christened 'jungle reggae hip-hop' by some commentators. Of all the artists to employ the title 'Doctor' in their names, Alban is one of the few to do so legitimately. He originally went to Stockholm, Sweden, to train as a dentist, and after qualifying, he started the Alphabet Club in the city, which eventually spawned a record and clothes shop of the same name. His attempts to 'toast' over the records he played at the venue attracted the attention of Swemix Records. The first result of his work with the studio was the 1990 single 'Hello Afrika', which immediately launched him in the national and international charts. With the anti-drug 'No Coke' and pro-unity 'U & Mi', Dr. Alban continued to cut himself a large slice of credibility in the European mainstream dance market. The musical style combined techno with club vocals and African rhythms. Among the most notable traits were the Nigerian percussive effects and dancehall chanting. In September 1992, he enjoyed a huge European hit with 'It's My Life', which reached number 2 in the UK pop chart. His unique Afro-Swedish patois earned praise from a variety of quarters, reinforcing the fact that rap had become a universal currency. The man behind the production on the big hits was Denniz Pop, who also produced Ace Of Base's number 1, 'All That She Wants'. Although he failed to reproduce the crossover success of 'It's My Life', Alban continued to enjoy club success throughout the decade. He also started his own Dr. label, whose first release was the 'Alrabaiye Take Me Up' single by Amadin.

● ALBUMS: *Hello Afrika The Album* (Swemix 1990)★★★, *One Love The Album* (Swemix 1992)★★★, *It's My Life The Album* (Logic/Arista 1993)★★★, *Look Who's Talking! The Album* (Logic/Arista 1995)★★★, *Born In Africa* (Dr. 1996)★★.

● COMPILATIONS: *The Very Best Of Dr. Alban 1990-1997* (Ariola 1997)★★★.

Dr. Didg

Graham Wiggins (b. 25 October 1962, New York City, New York, USA; didgeridoo, keyboards, percussion, melodica, samples), Ian Campbell (b. 4 April 1960, Ely, England; drums, percussion), Dave Motion (b. 6 July 1968, Legoa, Portugal; guitar). Formed in 1995 by Wiggins and Campbell (both previously members of Outback), the duo called themselves Dr. Didg, a nickname given to Wiggins while he was studying for his Physics PhD and learning to play the didgeridoo in the early 80s. With the addition of guitarist Mark Revell, they worked on developing a didgeridoo-based sound that combined African, Latin American, Eastern, rock, dance music and psychedelic influences and was built around improvisation and 'live sampling' (a process by which Wiggins created dense layers of sound by sampling and looping phrases he played on the didgeridoo). The trio quickly became popular amongst fans of world/dance, making regular appearances at festivals throughout Europe, including WOMAD and Glastonbury. During the recording of *Serotonality* (their second album, which featured live recordings and tracks developed from live samples), Motion replaced Mark Revell.

● ALBUMS: *Out Of The Woods* (Hannibal 1995)★★★, *Serotonality* (Hannibal 1998)★★★.

Dr. Dre

b. Andre Young, 18 February 1965, South Central, Los Angeles, USA. Widely regarded, by *Rolling Stone* magazine at least, as the chief architect of west coast gangsta rap, Dre's musical career began as a DJ at Los Angeles dance club, Eve After Dark. There he would splice up a mix of new records with soul classics like Martha And The Vandellas. The club had a back room with a small four-track studio where he, together with future-NWA member Yella and Lonzo WIlliams, would record demos. The first of these was 'Surgery', a basic electro track with a chorus of 'Calling Dr Dre to surgery'. These sessions, and nights at Eve After Dark, taught him the turntable techniques he would later bring to NWA, after forming the World Class Wreckin' Cru at the age of 17. Although other former members such as Ice Cube had laid the ground for rap's immersion into the mainstream, the success of Dre's 1992 solo debut, *The Chronic*, confirmed its commercial breakthrough. It also signalled a change in tack by modern gangsta rappers. The music now took its cue from the funk of George Clinton and Funkadelic, Dre freely admitting to the influence Clinton played on his life: 'Back in the 70s that's all people were doing: getting high, wearing Afros, bell-bottoms and listening to Parliament-Funkadelic. That's why I called my album *The Chronic* and based my music and the concepts like I did: because his shit was a big influence on my music. Very big'. To this end he created a

studio band for the sessions, which included the R&B talents of Tony Green (bass) and Ricky Rouse (guitar). While Dre's lyrics were just as forceful as those that had graced NWA, there was also a shift in subject matter. *The Chronic* referred heavily to the recreational use of marijuana, taking its name from a particularly virulent, and popular, brand. Together with the efforts of Cypress Hill, cannabis was now the drug of choice for the gangsta rapper, with crack cocaine much discussed but rarely endorsed. *The Chronic* would go on to spend eight months in the *Billboard* Top 10. At least as important was Dre's growing reputation as a producer. As well as producing an album for one of his many girlfriends, Michel'le, his work with Eazy-E, D.O.C., Above The Law and, most importantly, Snoop Doggy Dogg, broke new ground. Dogg had already rapped with Dre on the hit singles, 'Deep Cover' and 'Nuthin' But A 'G' Thang'. However, the *Doggystyle* opus would break box office records, bringing gangsta rap to the top of the album charts. Many sustained the belief that Dre was the driving force behind its success, the producer himself acknowledging: 'I can take a three year old and make a hit record with him'. At the same time he was dismissive of his own, pioneering efforts for NWA, particularly the epoch-making *Straight Outta Compton*: 'To this day I can't stand that album, I threw that thing together in six weeks so we could have something to sell out of the trunk'. During his involvement with the NWA posse he became the house producer for Eazy-E's Ruthless Records. Seven out of eight albums he produced for the label between 1983 and 1991 went platinum, but he broke from Ruthless over what he alleged was under-payment. Dre's on-record sneers at Eazy-E began shortly afterwards, including the single 'Dre Day', a put-down which Eazy-E would countermand for his reply, 'Muthaphukkin' Gs'.

Like many of rap's leading lights, Dre never strayed far from controversy, even after he bought into the comfort of a luxury home in San Fernando Valley. As if to reinstate himself as a 'true gangsta', Dre waged a war of attrition with authority. Television host Dee Barnes filed a multi-million dollar lawsuit against him for allegedly throwing her against the wall of a Hollywood nightclub in 1991. He was also convicted of breaking the jaw of a record producer (he was sentenced to house arrest and was fitted with a tracking device), and was detained by mounted police after a fracas in a New Orleans hotel lobby. Eazy-E sued him, while Dre complained bitterly about restraint of trade and moneys owed, cursed Ruthless' General Manager Jerry Heller, and finally managed to find a deal with Jimmy Iovine at Interscope Records, who let him set up his own label, Death Row Records, co-founded with the controversial Marion 'Suge' Knight, Vanilla Ice's ex-publicist. The success of *The Chronic* and *Doggystyle*, and the signing of rap's biggest new star 2Pac, briefly made Death Row one of America's most powerful labels. By 1996, however, its well documented problems culminated in Dre acrimoniously leaving to form his own Aftermath Records label. The label's first release was a various artists compilation, whose stand-out track was Dre's declamatory hit single 'Been There Done That', a kiss-off to gangsta rap and Death Row. In 1998, Dre was back in the news again as co-producer on his protégé Eminem's controversial breakthrough album, *The Slim Shady LP*. The following November he released his highly anticipated sophomore collection, *Dr. Dre 2001*. Featuring collaborations with

Eminem, Snoop Dogg, Mary J. Blige and Xzibit, the album was a highly effective reminder of Dre's pre-eminence in the world of gangsta rap.

● ALBUMS: *The Chronic* (Death Row 1992)★★★, *Dr. Dre 2001* (Aftermath 1999)★★★★.

● COMPILATIONS: *Concrete Roots* (Triple X 1994)★★, *Back 'N The Day* (Blue Dolphin 1996)★★, *First Round Knock Out* (Triple X 1996)★★★, *Dr. Dre Presents The Aftermath* (Aftermath 1996)★★★★.

● FILMS: *The Show* (1995), *Set It Off* (1996), *Rhyme & Reason* (1997), *Whiteboys* (1999).

Dr. Octagon

b. Keith Thornton, New York, USA. Formerly known as Kool Keith while a member of groundbreaking New York, US rap group the Ultramagnetic MC's, Thornton has also travelled under a variety of other pseudonyms - Poppa Large, the Reverend Tom, Sinister 6000, Big Willie Smith and Mr. Gerbik. In the mid-90s, and now based in Los Angeles, Thornton unveiled his latest project, Dr. Octagon. In principle a band, it was effectively just his latest solo musical outlet. However, after attracting favourable reviews for his live shows, he alarmed his backers (including record label DreamWorks) by failing to appear for performances in support of Beck and refusing to answer messages. This all fuelled a reputation for esoteric behaviour that had been with him since his time in the Ultramagnetic MC's. For example, he was said to have spent his entire five-figure advance from DreamWorks on pornography. However, he was indulged because of a precocious talent and, when he could be persuaded to marshal it, a prolific output. Between 1995 and 1996 he recorded tracks with Dan 'The Automator' Nakamura, DJ Q-Bert (of Invisibl Skratch Piklz), DJ Shadow and appeared on a track with the UK's Prodigy. The ensuing *Dr. Octagonecologyst* album was initially recorded for an independent label and featured a dazzling mixture of vibrant textures filled with Moog synthesizer, violin, flute, bass and even classical samples (including Pachelbel's Canon) that strove to redefine the hip-hop genre. However, the lyrics were a different matter, reflecting Thornton's obsession with pornography in lustful anatomical detail. As he told *Rolling Stone* magazine, 'I wrote that album in one day. I was like, "Fuck it. I'll write the sickest shit ever, just to bug out on it."' He followed this with *Sex Style*, released on his own Funky Ass label. In the meantime, Thornton was finding further time to waste on his favourite distraction by launching his own pornography magazine, *All Flavors*. Thornton adopted the Dr Dooom moniker for 1999's *First Come, First Served*.

● ALBUMS: *Dr. Octagonecologyst* (Bulk/DreamWorks 1996)★★★★, *Instrumentalyst: Octagon Beats* (DreamWorks 1996)★★★, *Sex Style* (Funky Ass 1997)★★★, as Dr Dooom *First Come, First Served* (Copasetik 1999)★★.

Dreadzone

This multi-faceted UK dub outfit is essentially a vehicle for Greg Roberts and Leo Williams (both ex-Big Audio Dynamite) who have been joined at various times by Dan Donovan, Tim and Chris Bran. Dreadzone's sound is particularly unique as at different times it mixes dub with elements of techno, trance, pop and folk music. Of the three albums *Second Light* captures their varied sound best, notably the folk-influenced melodies and bouncy grooves of 'Captain Dread' and 'Little Britain', and the trancey 'One

Way' and 'Zion Youth'. On 'A Canterbury Tale' they create a lush more ambient track, blending synthesized textures with acoustic sounds such as oboe, violin, piano and a female voice. Much of their work is flavoured with samples of dialogue from cult B-movies. However their real strength seems to lie in their singles and remixes where they venture into a variety of dance music styles to great effect without losing their identity – 'Life, Love And Unity' (1996) included excellent dub-techno, drum 'n' bass and straight-ahead techno-trance versions of the track. Perhaps their best work is on the *Maximum* EP (1995). The first track 'Fight The Power' which was written in opposition to the Criminal Justice Bill's legislation on parties blends the dub lines with drum 'n' bass tendencies, four-on-the-floor style techno, rock guitar and a sample from the Beastie Boys' 'Fight For Your Right To Party'. The energetic live drums on the final track 'Maximum' which was recorded for a John Peel session highlight the band's versatility further.

● ALBUMS: *360°* (Creation 1993)★★★, *Second Light* (Virgin 1995)★★★★, *Biological Radio* (Virgin 1997)★★.

Dream Warriors

A key part of the surprisingly active Canadian rap scene, West Indian duo King Lou (b. Louis Robinson, Jamaica, West Indies) and Capital Q (b. Frank Lennon Alert, Port Of Spain, Trinidad, West Indies - so named because his father was a John Lennon fan) had to go to the UK to secure a record contract with 4th & Broadway. Previously, they had released a single, 'Let Your Backbone Slide', on a New York independent. Their blend of hip-hop superstructure with jazz tempo arrived via arch lyrics, overflowing with obscure mystic imagery, from the pen of King Lou. The sound was big and loose, often punctuated by samples from television themes and psychedelic and African chants. They secured a hit almost immediately with 'Wash Your Face In My Sink', and the success continued with 'My Definition Of A Boombastic Jazz Style', derived from a Quincy Jones television theme tune. They also charted when they moved into reggae with 'Ludi' in 1991 (Ludi is a West Indian board game), and they worked with jazz legend Slim Gaillard shortly before his death the same year. The follow-up album attempted the same fusion of jazz and hip-hop, and also introduced some spoken word experiments. An extensive compilation set was released at the end of the decade, and offers a fine overview of the duo's often underappreciated work.

● ALBUMS: *And Now The Legacy Begins* (4th & Broadway 1991)★★★★, *Subliminal Simulation* (EMI Canada 1994)★★★.

● COMPILATIONS: *Anthology: A Decade Of Hits 1988-1998* (Beatfactory/Priority 1998)★★★★.

Dreams Come True

An oddball but appealing Japanese indie pop act, observed by some to be 'an oriental Parliament', Dreams Come True released their first English-language album in 1997 after a decade of popularity in their native country. Masato Nakamura (bass), Miwa Yoshida (vocals/lyrics) and Takahiro Nishikawa (keyboards) formed the band in 1988, releasing nine albums in the ensuing decade and amassing a sales tally of over 25 million units. *The Swinging Star* (1992) broke all Japanese sales records to become the best-selling album in the country's history. The band enjoys unprecedented popularity as a live act, and are regulars on Japanese television shows, domestic films and video game soundtracks. The band's music, built on Western influences ranging from classic soul to R&B, and from rock 'n' roll to disco and funk, became omnipresent in Japanese cultural life throughout the 90s. By 1998 they had moved from long-standing label Sony to Virgin Records, who were keen to promote the band to an international market, especially America. The move was hailed as the first time a major Japanese band had moved from a domestic imprint to an American-owned record label. The band confessed to frustration at Sony's insular marketing regime, although Dreams Come True had previously collaborated with American star Maurice White of Earth, Wind And Fire (for the single 'Wherever You Are') and appeared on 'Eternity', the theme for the US animation feature The Swan Princess. Following the disappointing reception received by other Japanese pop acts such as Toshi Kubota and Seiko Matsuda, Virgin were taking a gamble on their new act (who reportedly cost them $25 million to sign). They believed that Dreams Come True could follow the success of more left field or avant garde Asian artists such as Pizzicato Five, Buffalo Daughter and Cornelius.

● ALBUMS: Dreams Come True (Sony Japan 1989)★★★, Love Goes On (Sony Japan 1989)★★★, Wonder 3 (Sony Japan 1990)★★★, Million Kisses (Sony Japan 1991)★★★, The Swinging Star (Sony Japan 1992)★★★★, Magic (Sony Japan 1993)★★★, Delicious (Sony Japan 1995)★★, Love Unlimited (Sony Japan 1996)★★★, Sing Or Die (Virgin 1997)★★★.
Solo: Miwa Yoshida Beauty And Harmony (Sony Japan 1995)★★.

Droge, Pete

b. USA. Even if the world continues to ignore the talent of singer-songwriter Pete Droge he will always have one of rock 'n' roll's most outlandish song titles to his credit: 'If You Don't Love Me (I'll Kill Myself)'. The perfect summation of adolescent, unrequited love, it was housed on his 1994 debut album and was included on the soundtrack of the 1995 movie, Dumb And Dumber. The song was originally written in Droge's apartment in Portland, Oregon, in the summer of 1993. His mother was a music teacher and his father was a rock and folk fan, and Droge was taught to play the ukulele at the age of four. After mastering the guitar a few years later he hit the Seattle club circuit, having accumulated the songwriting influences of Bob Dylan and, more particularly, Tom Petty. However, the area was soon filled with the sound of grunge, and Droge formed his own roots band, Ramadillo, in direct opposition, although his friendship with Mike McCready of Pearl Jam was to prove valuable in gaining a deal with American Records. Droge stepped out alone with an album that stressed his songwriting strength, notably with the previously mentioned gem 'If You Don't Love Me (I'll Kill Myself)'. His second album featured his backing musicians the Sinners. Produced by Brendan O' Brien (Black Crowes), his debut for Epic Records subsidiary 57 Records, Spacey & Shakin', was a partially successful attempt to broaden Droge's roots-rock sound.

● ALBUMS: Necktie Second (Independent/American 1994)★★★, Find A Door (American 1996)★★, Spacey & Shakin' (57 1998)★★★.

Dru Hill

Urban R&B outfit Dru Hill took their name from the historic Druid Hill Park complex in Baltimore, USA, where all four members were raised. They began their rise to fame in the mid-90s, largely through the intervention of Island Records' Hiriam Hicks - formerly manager of Boyz II Men. He was looking for a group to record a song, 'Tell Me', for the soundtrack to the movie Eddie, to which Island held the rights. A tape of the quartet was passed to him by University Music president Haqq Islam. So impressed was Hicks after meeting the four men that, not only did he ask them to perform a version of 'Tell Me' on the spot, but he also signed them to a worldwide contract with Island. At that time the members - Jazz, Nokio, Woody and Sisqo (b. Mark Andrews), were all still in their teens. Nevertheless, their self-titled debut album sounded impressively mature. The smoky jazz and R&B tracks benefited enormously from the input of producers Keith Sweat, Stanley Brown and Darryl Simmons, though Nokio also co-wrote and produced much of the contents. While their syncopated vocals were one highlight, Sisqo and Jazz also contributed heavily as musicians, playing keyboards, bass and trumpet between them. By the late 90s the quartet had truly established themselves, with six consecutive American R&B Number 1 singles followed by the equally commercial follow-up Enter The Dru, which debuted at US number 2 on the Billboard 200 album chart in November 1998. The album ranged from the hard-edged urban R&B of 'How Deep Is Your Love' (US number 3/UK number 9) to the schmaltzy Babyface single 'These Are The Times' (US number 21/UK number 4). In 1999, they appeared on Will Smith's US chart-topping soundtrack hit, 'Wild Wild West', and set up their own Dru World Order production company. They also began work on separate solo projects, with Sisqo first out of the block on his Def Jam Records debut, Unleash The Dragon.

● ALBUMS: Dru Hill (Island 1996)★★★, Enter The Dru (Island 1998)★★★.

Drugstore

Led by Isabel Monterio (b. São Paulo, Brazil; vocals/bass), who relocated to England in 1990, Drugstore are a London three-piece specializing in dreamy but occasionally spiteful punk pop. They additionally comprise Daron Robinson (guitar) and Mike Chylinski (drums), Monterio meeting the latter, previously in a series of Los Angeles rock bands, after she had played bass in minor London groups. Drugstore came to nationwide prominence at the 1994 Phoenix Festival, at which Monterio took the stage in the national football strip of Brazil (this being only one of several unusual stage costumes adopted). This was enough to gain the attention of Go! Discs, who signed the band following the release of just one single ('Alive') on their own Honey label (just before Robinson had joined the band). Tours with Gene, Tindersticks, Jeff Buckley and Echobelly followed as did second single 'Modern Pleasures', before the advent of a debut album in 1995. With their vocalist proffering highly unusual lyrical matter with a delivery akin to Mazzy Star, there was delicious menace behind the seductive sound (sample lyric from Drugstore - 'I've still got the knife that I used to get rid of that guy' - from 'Nectarine'). A complementary single, 'Solitary Party Groover', earned numerous Single Of The Week awards as Drugstore's rise continued. The collapse of Go! Discs delayed their follow-up, but a duet with Thom Yorke of Radiohead on the excellent single 'El President' put the band firmly back in the spotlight. While not all of White Magic For Lovers was able to match the high standards set by the single, tracks such as 'Say Hello' and 'Mondo Cane' proved the band were capable of equally inspired moments.

● ALBUMS: *Drugstore* (Honey/Go! Discs 1995)★★★, *White Magic For Lovers* (Roadrunner 1998)★★★.

Drum Club

The Drum Club, named after a Sunderland nightspot that imported Balearic beat in 1983, and more recently Charlie Hall's own club night, comprised the duo of Lol Hammond (b. 7 January 1960, Stoke Newington, London, England) and Hall (b. 25 October 1959, Whitstable, Kent, England). The latter, self-effacing both on stage and off, and a former book reviewer for the *Catholic Herald*, was nevertheless perceived as the band's creative linchpin. Before the Drum Club he was already a well-known London club DJ, and had also played in rock/pop bands the Apaches and London Cowboys. Hammond, meanwhile, had been part of the many and varied line-ups of Spizz (Spizz Oil, Athletico Spizz, etc.). The Drum Club's first recording arrived via the Spiral Tribe label in March 1992. 'U Make Me Feel So Good' was an instant club classic, and was re-released a few months later on the Guerilla Records imprint. A follow-up, 'Alchemy', was similarly well-received. In the meantime the Drum Club were becoming a favoured remixing stable, a variety of musicians seeking out their talents. These included Jah Wobble's Invaders Of The Heart, Meat Beat Manifesto, Psychick Warriors Ov Gaia and would-be progressive indie outfits Curve and Chapterhouse. Most notable, however, was their work on Killing Joke's alternative dancefloor staple, 'Change'. In addition to their studio wizardry, the duo were also keen to 'play out', making their debut at the Ministry Of Sound, London, in October 1992. Steve Hillage and Emma Anderson (Lush) guested on their live dates. Anderson also contributed guitar to *Everything Is Now*, and recorded a 1993 single, 'Stray', with the Drum Club, under the name Never Never. It was Hall who came up with the idea of the MIDI circus (to rival rock's Lollapalooza touring phenomenon), which also featured Orbital, Aphex Twin, Underworld, etc. By the time of their debut album they had moved on to Big Life Records, signifying the very real commercial status open to their mesmeric, shimmering music. The venue, The Drum Club, closed its doors on 30 June 1994, with farewell appearances from Fabio Paris, Justin Robertson, Billy Nasty and others. The Drum Club themselves would finally disintegrate in the early months of 1996. Hammond had contacted Hall in advance of projected sessions in Ireland for a fourth studio album, explaining that his commitments to the Slab project with Nina Walsh of Sabrettes precluded him from taking part. Hall chose to concentrate on his MC Projects record label, whose releases include those by Phlex (his own pseudonym) and a remix of Consolidated's *This Is Fascism*. Hammond recorded albums with Roger Eno and Nina Walsh (as Slab) in 1999.

● ALBUMS: *Everything Is Now* (Butterfly 1993)★★★, *Drums Are Dangerous* (Butterfly 1994)★★★.

Duarte, Chris, Group

Formed in Austin, Texas, USA, the Chris Duarte Group are John Jordan (bass), Brannen Temple (drums) and band leader Chris Duarte (b. 16 February 1963, San Antonio, Texas, USA; guitar, vocals). The release of *Texas Sugar Strat Magik* brought immediate acclaim for the band's gritty, intense southern blues sound, with Duarte singled out for his technique. Indeed, in the 1995 *Guitar World* magazine Readers' Poll, he was voted fourth best blues guitarist behind the much more established and esteemed company of Eric Clapton, Buddy Guy and B.B. King. The group's debut was additionally voted fourth best blues album. Duarte has described the band's sound as 'blues based, but it has that loud aggressive edge that punk had. I liked Dead Kennedys, Sex Pistols, Dead Boys, anything that was hard.' The decision to employ producer Dennis Herring, the former Los Angeles session guitarist previously noted for his work with Camper Van Beethoven and Throwing Muses, was also interesting. Afterwards the album was promoted on US touring dates with Buddy Guy. *Tailspin Headwhack* built on the debut with a stronger blues edge.

● ALBUMS: *Texas Sugar Strat Magik* (Silvertone 1994)★★★, *Tailspin Headwhack* (Silvertone 1997)★★★★.

Dub War

A collision of ragga and punk, shot through with steely metallic guitar, Dub War emerged in 1994 as a high-octane, highly political extension of hard rock's new-found ability to merge innovative styles with the old. Formed in Newport, Wales, in 1993, the four-piece comprises Jeff Rose (guitar), Richie Glover (bass), Martin Ford (drums) and Benji (vocals), all of whom came from diverse musical backgrounds. Glover had played in several minor punk bands, while Benji's apprenticeship came in reggae dancehalls, and he had previously worked with Mad Professor. The band made its debut at the end of 1993 with a self-titled 12-inch EP that managed simultaneously to appear in three different *New Musical Express* charts - the 'Vibes', 'Turn Ons' and 'Hardcore' listings. Following a debut mini-album in 1994, they switched to Earache Records for the *Mental* EP, joining Pop Will Eat Itself and Manic Street Preachers on touring engagements. *Mental* featured remixes from Senser, Brand New Heavies and Jamiroquai, and was followed by a further EP, *Gorrit*. Their first full album came in February 1995 with *Pain*, by which time the band had established a strong live following to augment their press profile. Fans were rewarded by the uniformly excellent *Wrong Side Of Beautiful*, which was later re-released in a new limited edition version with a six-track CD of remixes, *Right Side Of Beautiful*. The album failed to provide the breakthrough the band deserved, however, and ultimately led to their demise two years later. Benji teamed up with Infectious Grooves bass player Rob Trujillo in Mass Mental.

● ALBUMS: *Dub Warning* mini-album (Words Of Warning 1994)★★★, *Pain* (Earache 1995)★★★, *Words Of Dubwarning* (Words Of Warning 1996)★★★, *Wrong Side Of Beautiful* (Earache 1996)★★★★.

● COMPILATIONS: *Step Ta Dis* (Earache 1998)★★★.

Dube, Lucky

b. Ermelo Dube, Eastern Transvaal, South Africa. The most successful African reggae artist of all time, Lucky Dube (pronounced Doobay) has taken his Peter Tosh-influenced music further than his hero himself managed. Guitarist-vocalist Dube formed his first group, a mbqanga combo entitled The Sky Way Band, while still at school. An interest in Rastafarianism complemented a musical predilection for reggae, although, as a member of the Love Brothers, his first album betrayed none of these influences. His first hit single, the 'Zulu soul' of 'Baxoleleni', arrived in 1983, from his debut solo set *Lengane Ngeyetha*. Several LPs later, he starred in a South African movie, *Getting Lucky*, and performed reggae tracks for its soundtrack. His first reggae album, *Rastas Never Die*, was banned in South Africa on account of its militancy, and Dupe diversified into rap for *Help My Krap*. In 1986, his new band, the Slaves, recorded 'Think About The Children', and their second album, *Slave*, sold 300,000 copies. In 1989, he toured France and the USA with the group and appeared in the movie *Voice In The Dark*. Two albums in that year, *Together As One* and *Prisoner*, sold heavily, the latter going double platinum in South Africa in only five days. In 1991, Dube became the first South African artist to play the Reggae Sunsplash festival in Jamaica, and again he issued two albums in one year, *Captured Live* (incidentally also the title of a Peter Tosh LP) and *House Of Exile*. Tours of Japan and Australia were also a success, and Dube additionally played WOMAD with Peter Gabriel. *Victims* again broke his own record for worldwide sales, shifting in excess of a million copies on various licensee imprints. Although Dube's style is probably too dated to achieve great success in Jamaica, he remains head and shoulders above his African reggae compatriots.

● ALBUMS: *Lengane Ngeyetha* (1983)★★★, *Rastas Never Die* (1985)★★★★, *Help My Krap* (1986)★★, *Slave* (Shanachie 1986)★★★, *Together As One* (1989)★★, *Prisoner* (Shanachie 1989)★★★★, *Captured Live* (Shanachie 1991)★★, *House Of Exile* (Shanachie 1991)★★★, *Victims* (Shanachie 1993)★★★, *Taxman* (Shanachie 1997)★★★, *The Way It Is* (Yazoo/Shanachie 1999)★★★.

● COMPILATIONS: *Serious Reggae Business* (Shanachie 1996)★★★★.

Dubstar

Dubstar were formed in 1994 when Steve Hillier (songwriting/programming) met Chris Wilkie (guitar) at a club in Newcastle where he was DJing. They auditioned for singers and eventually recruited student Sarah Blackwood (b. Halifax, Yorkshire, England) after she sang over two acoustic songs for them. They began to write and record songs together, keen to produce a sound that was authentically 'modern'. Their first demo tape, which secured a contract with Food Records, included a cover version of Billy Bragg's 'St Swithin's Day'. The band's debut album, *Disgraceful*, mixed club-orientated beats in addition to strong hooks and pop dynamics, earning several comparisons to Saint Etienne. Despite critical acclaim, it failed to produce a breakthrough, although it contained the Top 40 single 'Stars'. That changed with the UK Top 20 success of 'Not So Manic Now', which prompted a reissue of 'Stars' in early 1996. Their second album proper, *Goodbye*, contained more bittersweet songs and spawned two hit singles in 'Cathedral Park' and 'No More Talk'.

● ALBUMS: *Disgraceful* (Food 1995)★★★★, *Disgraceful Remixed* (Food 1996)★★★, *Goodbye* (Food 1997)★★★★.

Dulfer, Candy

b. 19 September 1969, Amsterdam, Netherlands. Saxophonist Dulfer was bought to prominence by Prince, who introduced her on the video mix of 'Party Man' with a cry of 'when I want sax, I call for Candy'. She was bought up in a family involved in the Dutch jazz scene. Her father, Hans Dulfer, a respected tenor saxophonist, exposed his

daughter to the playing of Sonny Rollins, Coleman Hawkins and Dexter Gordon. Candy's career evolved from playing with brass bands to performing on the jazz club circuit and later fronting her own band Funky Stuff, who were invited to support Madonna on part of her 1987 European tour. A similar support slot with Prince was abruptly cancelled, but the singer made amends by inviting Dulfer onstage during one of his shows. The resulting recording sessions with Prince, and in particular the aforementioned 'Party Man', led to session work with Eurythmics guitarist, David A. Stewart, who gave Dulfer a joint credit on 'Lily Was Here', a UK number 6 hit in 1990. Further credits have found her working with David Gilmour, Aretha Franklin and Van Morrison. Her 1990 debut album was nominated for a Grammy and certified gold. Her subsequent albums have been pleasant enough but have broken no new ground, their R&B leanings similar in content to David Sanborn's hardblowing work. However, she is regarded as one of Europe's leading young saxophonists.

● ALBUMS: *Saxuality* (RCA 1990)★★★, *Sax-a-Go-Go* (RCA 1991)★★★, *Big Girl* (RCA 1996)★★, *For The Love Of You* (N2K Encoded 1997)★★★.

● COMPILATIONS: *The Best Of Candy Dulfer* (N2K Encoded 1998)★★★.

Dupri, Jermaine

b. 23 September 1973, Atlanta, Georgia, USA. Dupri has established a reputation as one of the leading US producers of the 90s. He grew up in Atlanta where his father, Michael Mauldin, acted as road manager for local groups. His father's connections led to breakdancing slots for artists such as Diana Ross and Cameo. He also performed as the opening act at New York's Fresh Festival, on a bill featuring Whodini, Run DMC and Grandmaster Flash. Although he was barely in his teens, Dupri knew that he wanted to establish a career in record production. He gained early experience promoting and producing the anodyne female trio Silk Tymes Leather, who released one flop album, 1989's *It Ain't Where Ya From ... It's Where Ya At*, on Geffen Records. Shortly afterwards, Dupri established So So Def Recordings. The company's big break came about when Dupri saw Chris Kelly and Chris Smith performing in Greenbriar's shopping mall in Atlanta. He transformed the two 13-year-olds into Kriss Kross, enjoying massive success in 1991 with a US chart-topping single ('Jump') and album (*Totally Krossed Out*). Dupri has subsequently established the careers of gospel-rooted swingbeat quartet Xscape (*Hummin' Comin' At 'Cha, Off The Hook*), female rapper Da Brat (*Funkdafied*), Jagged Edge and Trina Broussard. So So Def's client list has grown rapidly, serving established artists such as Dru Hill (the hit remix of 'In My Bed'), TLC, Mariah Carey, Aretha Franklin, Lil' Kim, MC Lyte and Whodini among others. Dupri enjoyed his biggest commercial success since Kriss Kross' debut when he co-produced and contributed tracks to Usher's multi-platinum *My Way*, including the huge transatlantic hits 'You Make Me Wanna' and 'Nice & Slow'. During 1998, Dupri concentrated on establishing himself as a solo artist, releasing *The Party Continues* EP. The ambitious *Jermaine Dupri Presents Life In 1742: The Original Soundtrack* followed, with standout tracks including collaborations with Nas ('Turn It Out'), Slick Rick ('Fresh') and Jay-Z ('Money Ain't A Thang'). The stellar guest list also included appearances by Snoop Doggy Dogg,

DMX, Usher, Mariah Carey and Da Brat. The album debuted at US number 3 in August.
● ALBUMS: *Jermaine Dupri Presents Life In 1742: The Original Soundtrack* (Columbia 1998)★★★.

Dust Brothers

One of the pre-eminent remix/production teams of the 90s, the Dust Brothers comprise radio disc jockeys Mike Simpson and John King, who first came to prominence with Matt Dike of the Delicious Vinyl label. In addition to fostering the career of Delicious Vinyl's major acts (Tone Loc, Young MC, etc.), they also afforded Mellow Man Ace and the Beastie Boys (1989's groundbreaking *Paul's Boutique*), among others, their skills and expertise. The Beasties Boys album introduced their pioneering cut-and paste sampling technique, which in time saw them become among the most sought after producers/remixers in music. There was some confusion when a UK-based duo sought to use the same name for their recordings, but when Dike and his colleagues objected, the other group became the Chemical Brothers. The original Dust Brothers subsequently worked with acts as diverse as Technotronic, Shonen Knife, Hanson (1997's UK/US chart-topping single 'MMMBop'), Beck (1996's highly acclaimed *Odelay*) and the Rolling Stones (tracks on *Bridges To Babylon*). They set up their own label, Nickel Bag, in 1996. In 1999, they composed the soundtrack to the controversial Brad Pitt movie, *Fight Club*.
● ALBUMS: *Fight Club: Original Motion Picture Soundtrack* (BMG 1999)★★★.

Dust Junkys

Manchester, England's Dust Junkys initially faced both press and industry scepticism when it was revealed singer Nicholas Lockett was none other than MC Tunes - the much-derided white Mancunian rapper who had appeared on a series of records with 808 State in the late 80s/early 90s as well as releasing his own UK Top 20 solo album. However, Polydor Records looked beyond the cynicism and hostility, and liked what they saw in the five-piece, which also featured Steve Oliver Jones (bass), Mykey Wilson (drums), Sam Brox (guitar) and Ganiyu Pierre Gasper (DJ), in addition to Lockett. The Dust Junkys combine his pointed, sociological raps with sharp, furious blasts of rock music, Brox's guitar-playing winning particular praise from the cognoscenti (his father had played with Jimi Hendrix). Their first release was a white label three-track EP, featuring 'Fever', 'Got The Funk Up' and 'Nothing Personal' - the latter featuring a Lockett rap over a deconstructed version of Fleetwood Mac's 'Oh Well'. The band made its first public appearance at the In The City Festival in Dublin, Eire, at the end of 1996, quickly building a reputation as an intense and extremely loud live act. Their debut single, 'Living In The Pocket Of A Drug Queen', was released in August 1997. Further singles followed before they released the groove-heavy *Done And ... Dusted* in early 1998.
● ALBUMS: *Done And ... Dusted* (Polydor 1998)★★★.

Dylans

Formed in Sheffield, England, by Colin Gregory (bass, vocals), Andy Curtis (guitar) and Jim Rodger (guitar) in 1989, this trio recorded a rough demo that led to a contract with Beggars Banquet before they had ever appeared live.

With the addition of Garry Jones (drums) and Quentin Jennings (keyboards) they began touring, attracting comparisons with bands such as the Charlatans and the Stone Roses because of their 60s-styled jangly guitars and strong harmonies. The Dylans took the retro theme even further, however, displaying a fondness for wearing love beads around their necks and writing wide-eyed hippy lyrics. The debut single 'Godlike', released in early 1991, was widely praised and reached the UK indie Top 10, but shortly afterwards tensions in the band led to Curtis being replaced by Andy Cook. They continued to achieve indie hits with 'Lemon Afternoon' and the sublime 'Planet Love', before releasing a self-titled debut album in October. Though this also proved popular, their limited lyrical concerns were prone to become stale over the course of a whole album. After tours of the USA and Japan in 1992 the band began to fall apart, with Jones being replaced by guitarist Craig Scott, and Jennings by Ike Glover. The new line-up recorded two further singles and *Spirit Finger*, but by now their style of indie-pop was becoming increasingly dated, and with the album's lack of success the band folded.
● ALBUMS: *The Dylans* (Situation Two 1991)★★★, *Spirit Finger* (Situation Two 1993)★★.

E-40

b. Earl Stevens, San Francisco, California, USA. Considered a natural successor to Too $hort's reductionist thematic with his glorification of the 'player' hip-hop lifestyle, E-40 started his own independent label, Sick Wid It Records, in the Bay area of San Francisco in 1990. Working with his brothers and sisters as part of the Click, an underground sensation on the streets of Vallejo. E-40 released records with the Click, including 1993's *Down And Dirty* and 1995's *Game Related*, and as a solo artist. He enjoyed immediate success with records such as 'Captain Save-a-Ho', 'Sprinkle Me' and 'Ballin' Out Of Control', which all featured his trademark stop-start delivery and the inclusion of heavy regional slang such as 'scrilla' (money) and 'broccoli' (marijuana). By 1995, and *In A Major Way* (which included 'Sprinkle Me'), he had signed a major distribution deal with Jive Records. Having sold over half a million copies of this record, the subsequent *The Hall Of Game* set was given a major international push. With producers including Studio Tone, Ant Banks and Rick

Rock of the Cosmic Shop, the musical climate was more relaxed and smoother than had previously been the case. The first single from the album, 'Rapper's Ball', was a typical example, being an updated version of Too $hort's 1987 single, 'Playboy Short'. This new version featured Too $hort as well as Jodeci's K-Ci. Other highlights included 'On The One', featuring Digital Underground's Money B and Da Funk Mob's G-Note, and 'Things'll Never Change'. This reinterpreted Bruce Hornsby's 'That's The Way It Is' with a contribution from E-40's eight-year-old son, Li'l E. *The Element Of Surprise* debuted at number 13 on the *Billboard* Top 200 in August 1998. The rapper celebrated ten years in the business with the following year's semi-autobiographical *Charlie Hu$tle - The BluePrint Of A Self-Made Millionaire*.

● ALBUMS: *Federal* (Sick Wid It 1992)★★★, *The Mail Man* (Sick Wid It 1994)★★★, *In A Major Way* (Sick Wid It/Jive 1995)★★★★, *The Hall Of Game* (Sick Wid It/Jive 1996)★★★, *The Element Of Surprise* (Sick Wid It/Jive 1998)★★★★, *Charlie Hu$tle - The BluePrint Of A Self-Made Millionaire* (Sick Wid It/Jive 1999)★★★.

Earl Brutus

'Let's have none of that bollocks about great songwriters and their craft', declared singer Nicolas Sanderson. 'Let's have a trucker's beat and some big, bold sounds.' Sanderson, former keyboard player with World Of Twist, was describing as well as anyone can the sound of British cabaret situationists Earl Brutus. In 1996, the band, also including Jamie Fry (vocals, brother of ABC's Martin Fry), Rob Marche (guitar) and Gordon King (keyboards/drum machine), financed their first single, the Gary Glitter-tinged 'Life's Too Long', with donations to a sperm bank, and further band exploits seemed to pander to the UK music press' hunger for sordid stories of debauchery and drunkenness. However, the sound on the band's debut album was worth the hype. The rhythms and gruff vocals were offset by crunching glam rock guitars and bizarre synth doodles reminiscent of early 80s synth eccentrics such as the Passage and Landscape. Their live shows went beyond mere gigs, encompassing a Crimplene-clad dancer, neon light shows, radio samples, cheese-throwing and a revolving garage-forecourt sign reading 'PISS' on one side and 'OFF' on the other. Their closest neighbour in terms of attitude is probably the Creation, in that they combine primeval riffs with a sense of visual theatre, but Earl Brutus have an extra 30 years of pop tradition on which to draw. 'Great' songwriters may have looked on aghast, but any band with the iconoclastic chutzpah to announce 'I'm like James Brown/I like boys' must have something very special.

● ALBUMS: *Your Majesty ... We Are Here* (Deceptive 1996)★★★★, *Tonight, You Are The Special One* (Island Fruition 1998)★★★.

East 17

Tony Mortimer (b. 21 October 1970, England), Brian Harvey (b. 8 August 1974, England), John Hendy (b. 26 March 1971, England) and Terry Coldwell (b. 21 July 1974, England), the founding members of East 17, met while attending school in Walthamstow, London. Their name was taken from the London postal district from which they originate, and they even named their debut album after their home-town. Critics initially scoffed at their attempts to imitate hardcore Bronx rap crews. With former Bros svengali Tom Watkins as their manager, they cultivated an image of youthful arro-

gance and 'street style' in obvious opposition to the then prevalent UK teenage craze, Take That. Indeed, in early interviews they made a point of behaving badly, with incidents including pinching female journalists' bottoms and revelling in flatulence. Their debut single, 'House Of Love', became a major hit in August 1992, peaking at number 10 in the UK charts. The subsequent 'Gold' proved disappointing, but 'Deep' brought them to the Top 5. Both 'Slow It Down' and a lacklustre cover version of the Pet Shop Boys' 'West End Girls' also made the UK Top 20, accompanying the album *Walthamstow*. December 1993's 'It's Alright' was their bestselling single so far, reaching number 3 and staying in the UK charts for 14 weeks. Their first two 1994 singles, 'Around The World' and 'Steam', continued their commercial ascendancy. They finally hit the UK number 1 spot in December with 'Stay Another Day', a lush ballad with memorable harmonies and orchestration, which was 1994's Christmas number 1. During preparations for their 1995 tour Mortimer, who had recently been awarded an Ivor Novello Award for his songwriting, was rushed to hospital suffering from exhaustion. Harvey was sacked by the band in January 1997 after some ill-chosen comments about the drug Ecstasy. Fearing that his pro-drug statement could damage their reputation with a younger audience it appears that they were faced with no alternative. However, Mortimer himself left the band in 1997. Harvey subsequently returned, and plans to relaunch the group (now known as E-17) as an urban R&B trio met with initial success when 'Each Time' debuted at number 2 in the UK charts in November 1998. The commercial failure of follow-up singles and the attendant *Resurrection*, however, demonstrated just how vital Mortimer was to East 17.

● ALBUMS: *Walthamstow* (London 1993)★★★★, *Steam* (London 1994)★★★, *Stay Another Night* (London 1995)★★★, *Around The World - The Journey So Far* (London 1996)★★★, as E-17 *Resurrection* (Telstar 1998)★★.

● VIDEOS: *Up All Night* (PolyGram Music Video 1995), *Letting Of Steam: Live* (PolyGram Music Video 1995), *Greatest Hits* (PolyGram Music Video 1996).

● FURTHER READING: *East 17: Talk Back*, Carl Jenkins.

Eat Static

During the 80s, while they were performing with the Ozric Tentacles, Merv Peplar and Joie Hinton were inspired to start writing dance music after coming into contact with acts such as the Mutoid Waste Company at festivals and parties. They began by recording three weird acid house tracks with the engineer Steve Everitt and were soon performing live at Ozrics gigs. During the early 90s they developed their live shows at many of the legendary 'orbital' raves and free parties, as well as releasing three singles and a cassette album, *Prepare Your Spirit*, on their own Alien Records. In 1993, as a result of their connection with the Megadog parties, Eat Static signed to Planet Dog Records and released the *Lost In Time* EP, followed by the albums *Abduction* and *Implant*. These albums featured their unique brand of psychedelic electronic music which, while showing the influence of techno, trance, ambient and other dance styles, never simply regurgitated established formulae. They were as happy with straight four-on-the-floor beats (e.g., 'Prana' and 'Implant') as they were with more breakbeat-like grooves ('Abnormal Interference' and 'Dzhopa Dream'). Many of their titles were sci-fi and space-orientated, about which they commented: 'We can't take techno as seriously as some purists do so we've coated it in this sci-fi motif. And we're mad for all that anyway.' Over the next few years they performed live and released a number of EPs that pursued their eclectic sound, notably 'Dionysiac' (on the *Epsylon* EP), which combined an Eastern-influenced string melody with elements of dub and drum 'n' bass. 'Bony Incus' (1996) included collaborations with Andy Guthrie and a remix by Man With No Name, while 'Hybrid' (1997) featured remixes by Yum Yum and Dave Angel. Towards the end of 1997, Eat Static released the single 'Intercepter' and the album *Science Of The Gods*, which proved to be their most focused and adventurous work to date. While presenting a kind of psychedelic drum 'n' bass on such tracks as 'Interceptor', 'Dissection' and 'Bodystealers', Peplar and Hinton often vary the grooves and textures throughout a track, notably 'Science Of The Gods' and 'Kryll' (a collaboration with Tangerine Dream's Steve Joliffe), thereby structuring and developing their music in a manner unlike the variations-on-a-groove approach of much dance music. With their unique, eclectic sound, attention to detail and outrageous production skills, Eat Static have gained the respect of a number of different camps in an increasingly fickle and narrow-minded dance music community. Their broad-minded attitude predicted the trend towards mixing styles that developed in the late 90s.

● ALBUMS: *Abduction* (Planet Dog 1993)★★★, *Implant* (Planet Dog 1994)★★★, *Science Of The Gods* (Planet Dog 1997)★★★★.

● COMPILATIONS: *Decadence* (Mesmobeat 1999)★★★, *The Alien EPs* (Mesmobeat 1999)★★★.

Eazy-E

b. Eric Wright, 7 September 1963, Compton, California, USA, d. 26 March 1995, Los Angeles, California, USA. There are those critics who did not take well to Eazy-E's 'whine', but his debut kept up NWA's momentum by managing to offend just about every imaginable faction, right and left. Attending a fund-raising dinner for the Republican party and having lunch with police officer Tim Coon, one of the LAPD's finest charged with the beating of Rodney King, hardly helped to re-establish his hardcore credentials. His work as part of NWA, and as head of Ruthless Records (which he founded in 1985 allegedly with funds obtained from drug dealing) had already made him a household name. However, as a solo performer his raps lacked penetration, even if the musical backdrop was just as intense as that which distinguished NWA. His debut solo album contained a clean and dirty side. The first was accomplished with very little merit, cuts such as 'We Want Eazy' being self-centred and pointless. The 'street' side, however, offered something much more provocative and nasty. His ongoing bitter rivalry against former NWA member Dr. Dre provided much of his lyrical subject matter, including his 1994 single, 'Real Muhaphukkin' G's', which was essentially a rewrite of Dre's 'Dre Day'. Ruthless also released an EP, *It's On (Dr. Dre 187UM) Killa*, in the same year. Eazy-E subsequently moved on to production for artists including Tairrie B and Blood Of Abraham. Having been a pivotal figure of gangsta rap, he succumbed to AIDS and died through complications following a collapsed lung after having been hospitalized for some time. The material he had been working on prior to his death was released posthumously on *Str.8 Off Tha Streetz Of Muthaphukkin' Compton*.

● ALBUMS: *Eazy-Duz-It* (Ruthless/Priority 1988)★★★, *Str.8 Off Tha Streetz Of Muthaphukkin' Compton* (Ruthless 1995)★★★.

Echobelly

This UK indie pop band was formed by the Anglo-Asian singer Sonya Aurora Madan, along with Glenn Johansson (b. Sweden; guitar), Debbie Smith (guitar, ex-Curve), Andy Henderson (drums) and Alex Keyser (bass). Echobelly were put together when Madan met Johansson at a gig. After breaking the UK Top 40 with the momentous 'I Can't Imagine The World Without Me', the band became the darlings of the British music press. The original, rejected title of their debut album was taken from a Suffragette's reply when asked when women would obtain the vote: 'Today, Tomorrow, Sometime, Never', leading Madan to comment: 'I feel led by similar frustrations, politically and morally, encompassing feminism and gender. Things are made much more obvious coming from a coloured background.' This last point was made clear by her Union Jack T-shirt smeared with the legend: 'My Home Too'. However, she was also keen to point out that locating Echobelly solely in the world of gender and race politics dismissed their importance as a pop band. The band also began to win support in the USA by appearing at New York's New Music Seminar, leading to an American contract with Sony Records. *On* advanced the strengths of its predecessor, with notable songs including the hit single 'Great Things', and 'Pantyhose And Roses' about the UK Conservative MP Stephen Milligan, who died of asphyxiation during a sexual incident. Debbie Smith left the band in August 1997, and was replaced by new guitarist Julian Cooper. *Lustra* was a poorly received album that saw the band struggling to establish their musical direction, and also feel the effect of the commercial backlash against 'Britpop' bands.

● ALBUMS: *Everyone's Got One* (Rhythm King 1994)★★★, *On* (Rhythm King 1995)★★★★, *Lustra* (Epic 1997)★★.

Eels

Offering a novel twist on the post-grunge and lo-fi norms of American indie rock in the mid-90s, Eels hatched in the bohemian Echo Park area of Los Angeles in 1995. The band are the brainchild of the mysterious E (b. Mark Everett, Virginia, USA; vocals/guitar/keyboards), who had previously recorded two acclaimed solo albums for Polydor Records in the early 90s, and drummer Butch Norton. After finding bass player Tommy Walter at LA's Mint Club, the trio was produced by Michael Simpson, half of the Dust Brothers and an A&R man for DreamWorks Records. 'Novocaine For The Soul' was a big college/alternative hit in 1996, with a tension-and-release structure that seemed a throwback to the rock basics laid down by the Pixies and Nirvana, accentuated by characteristically indie themes of alienation and depression. Despite their apparently conventional power-trio line-up, the band's music evinces a fascination with sonic experimentation. Co-producer Simpson's dance music background and experience of sampling expanded *Beautiful Freak*'s overall sound with hip-hop rhythm loops, and all three band members brought unexpected textures to play: Norton's cannibalized drumkit includes a fire-alarm bell and part of a heating duct; Walter doubles on French horn; and

E is a devotee of the ghostly Theremin, the only instrument the musician does not touch. The follow-up, *Electro-Shock Blues*, was informed by several tragedies in E's personal life. The album's fascination with mortality found beautiful expression on compelling tracks such as 'Last Stop: This Town', 'Cancer For The Cure' and 'My Descent Into Madness'. The mellow *Daisies Of The Galaxy* featured the stand-out tracks 'Mr E's Beautiful Blues' and 'It's A Motherfucker'.

● ALBUMS: *Beautiful Freak* (DreamWorks 1996)★★★★, *Electro-Shock Blues* (DreamWorks 1998)★★★★, *Daisies Of The Galaxy* (DreamWorks 2000)★★★★.

Solo: E *A Man Called (E)* (Polydor 1992)★★★★, *Broken Toy Shop* (Polydor 1993)★★★.

Egg

The Egg were formed in the UK from a conglomeration of various Oxford-based dub-influenced dance music acts. Comprising Dave Gaydon (bass), Mark Revell (guitar) and twin brothers Maff Scott (drums) and Ned Scott (keyboards), they have developed a unique sound combining hip-hop, psychedelia, ambient and house, resulting in what has been described as a 'fluid trance groove'. In 1995, they recorded their debut EP, *The Shopping*, through the iconoclastic Bristol-based Cup Of Tea Records. The release was greeted with critical acclaim, which resulted in the initial pressing selling out within two weeks. They maintained a high profile with notable performances at the Glastonbury and Phoenix festivals. By 1996, they had secured a contract with Indochina Records who endorsed the 11-track opus *Albumen*, which was co-produced by Joe Gibb. They continued performing on the live circuit throughout Europe and the USA, where the band made an appearance at the prestigious South X South West Festival. Beyond the music was the Egg's visual presentation, wherein the band members dressed in white and performed as human cinema screens, with films and pictures being projected onto their outfits. In a review of their show, *Melody Maker* described the event as 'instant psychedelia meets Aunt Harriet's home movies'. The band achieved further notoriety when they performed a benefit gig for the people of the remote Scottish Isle Of Eigg on Glasgow's Renfrew Ferry, to help the residents to buy the island from an apathetic proprietor. Through to 1998 the band released the underground hit 'Bend', which featured a Steve Hillage sample, performed with Moby alongside Jah Wobble, made a triumphant appearance at the Third Post Apartheid Festival, and appeared in Todd Haynes' glam rock homage *Velvet Goldmine*. The band were also engrossed in studio work on a remix collection. A UK tour featuring their unique stage presentation was arranged to promote their 1998 follow-up, *Travelator*.

● ALBUMS: *Albumen* (Indochina 1996)★★★, *Get Some Mixes Together* (Indochina 1997)★★★★, *Travelator* (Indochina 1998)★★★.

Eggs

Influential US 'lo-fi' pop outfit the Eggs was formed in Richmond, Virginia, in 1990 by Andrew Beaujan (guitar/vocals) and Jonathon Rickman (guitar/vocals). Recruiting Dave Park (bass) and Marianne McGee (French horn) they recorded their debut album later that year for Teenbeat Records, the premier lo-fi label run by Mark Robinson (Grenadine, Tsunami, Air Miami). A succinct but

musically expansive record crossing boundaries between pop, funk and indie rock, *Bruiser*, recorded in New York on a budget of $600, was a triumph of individualism, comparable to early Syd Barrett. However, afterwards the band were handicapped by their inability to find a regular drummer and other personnel shifts (contributors at various times included Rob Christiansen of Grenadine on trombone and guitar). The band's irreverently eclectic but ultimately pop-orientated approach survived to prosper on 1994's misnamed *Teenbeat 96 Exploder*, however. This comprised 68 minutes of the band's idiosyncratic compositions recorded at American University in Washington. A delirious cocktail of pop cadences streamlined by the band's essentialist approach, it won them further fans throughout the alternative rock community (including disc jockey John Peel). Lacking the ambition to break out of their close circle of friends and admirers, the Eggs broke-up soon afterwards. Christiansen formed Viva Satellite!, releasing the bizarre concept album *Nishma* in 1996.

● ALBUMS: *Bruiser* (Teenbeat 1990)★★★★, *Teenbeat 96 Exploder* (Teenbeat 1994)★★★★.

● COMPILATIONS: *How Do You Like Your Lobster* (TeenBeat 1995)★★★.

Eiffel 65

Turin, Italy-based trio comprising singer Jeffrey Jey, Maurizio Lobina and Gabriele Ponte who rose to prominence in 1999 when (helped by extensive radio airplay) they scored an enormous hit in Europe with 'Blue (Da Ba Dee)'. The cloying, infectious single was a number 1 in 16 countries across Europe as well as in Canada and Australia. In the UK, it sold more than a million copies and remained at the top of the charts for three weeks. Perhaps best described as 'bubblegum-dance', the track featured nonsense lyrics, vocals filtered through a vocoder and an unusual video. It was also a Top 10 hit in the USA. The follow-up 'Move Your Body', was a number 1 single in their native Italy before becoming another Top 10 hit in the rest of Europe. The aptly-titled debut, *Europop*, released in February 2000, exhibited a range of dance styles but the disposability of their first hits would make it difficult to establish themselves as a credible act in dance music.

● ALBUMS: *Europop* (WEA/Eternal Records 2000)★★.

808 State

Manchester, England's finest acid music combo of the early 90s was founded by Martin Price (b. 26 March 1955, England), owner of the city's influential Eastern Bloc record shop, and Graham Massey (b. 4 August 1960, Manchester, Lancashire, England; ex-Biting Tongues), who had previously worked in a café opposite the shop. Together with Gerald Simpson, they began recording together as a loose electro/house collective, releasing *Newbuild* in 1988. Simpson subsequently left to form his own A Guy Called Gerald vehicle, and was replaced by Darren Partington (b. 1 November 1969, Manchester, Lancashire, England) and Andy Barker (b. 2 November 1969, Manchester, Lancashire, England), two young DJs working together as the Spin Masters who were regular visitors to Eastern Bloc, proffering a variety of tapes in the hope of securing a deal with Price's Creed label. *Quadrastate*, which included some input from Simpson, helped to establish the new line-up as premier exponents of UK dance music, with the attendant 'Pacific State' single becoming a massive underground hit which crossed over to the UK Top 10 at the end of 1989. A lucrative deal with ZTT Records proved to be a mixed blessing for the band, however, as they were lumped in with the pervading 'Madchester' indie/dance boom. Simpson, meanwhile, began launching a series of attacks in the press concerning unpaid royalties. *808:90*, the band's debut for ZTT, became an instant rave classic and established them as a commercial force. They also worked with Mancunian rapper MC Tunes on his debut *The North At Its Heights* and several singles, including June 1990's UK number 10 hit 'The Only Rhyme That Bites'. Further UK hits followed with 'Cubik/Olympic' (number 10, November 1990) and 'In Yer Face' (number 9, February 1991). *Ex:El* featured guest vocals from New Order's Bernard Sumner on 'Spanish Heart', and Sugarcubes vocalist Björk Gudmundsdóttir on 'Oops' (also a single) and 'Qmart'. In October 1991, Price declined to tour the USA with the band, electing to work on solo projects instead, including managing Rochdale rappers the Kaliphz, and his own musical project, Switzerland. He also established himself as a remixer, working with David Bowie, Shamen, Primal Scream and Soundgarden. 808 State persevered with another fine album, 1993's *Gorgeous*, which saw a new rash of collaborations. Featured this time were Ian McCulloch (Echo And The Bunnymen) adding vocals to 'Moses', and samples from the Jam's 'Start', UB40's 'One In Ten' and even *Star Wars*' Darth Vader. Massey occupied himself with co-writing Björk's 'Army Of Me' single and other material on her 1995 collection, *Post*, before 808 State regrouped for the following year's *Don Solaris*. Adopting a more experimental approach than their early 90s work, the album featured guest vocalists James Dean Bradfield (Manic Street Preachers) and Ragga. The *808:88:98* compilation included several new mixes.

● ALBUMS: *Newbuild* (Creed 1988)★★★, *Quadrastate* (Creed 1989)★★★★, *808:90* (ZTT 1989)★★★★, *Utd. State 90* US only (Tommy Boy 1990)★★★★, *Ex:El* (ZTT/Tommy Boy 1991)★★★, *Gorgeous* (ZTT/Tommy Boy 1993)★★★, *Don Solaris* (ZTT/Hypnotic 1996)★★★.

● COMPILATIONS: *Thermo Kings* (ZTT/WEA 1996)★★★, *808:88:98* (ZTT 1998)★★★★.

18 Wheeler

Formed in Scotland by Sean Jackson (guitar, vocals), Neil Halliday (drums), Alan Hake (bass) and Steven Haddow (guitar). The band released two singles, 'Nature Girl' and 'Suncrush', which bore the obvious influence of Glasgow's early 80s Postcard Records scene. They were followed in 1994 by 'Kum Back' and 'The Revealer'. On the debut album their familiar bubblegum pop was allied to rhythms drawn from folk, country and dub. Described in *The Guardian* newspaper as '1994's lost pop classic', this was not widespread opinion, as others saw the band as insubstantial and retrogressive. A more accomplished collection, *Formanka*, followed a year later, by which time the band's fortunes had been significantly outstripped by another Creation Records act, Oasis, who had once been third support to 18 Wheeler at a gig in Glasgow. *Year Zero* moved into crossover territory, further alienating their original fanbase.

● ALBUMS: *Twin Action* (Creation 1994)★★, *Formanka* (Creation 1995)★★★, *Year Zero* (Creation 1997)★★★.

Eitzel, Mark

b. 30 January 1959, Walnut Creek, San Francisco, California, USA. Widely acclaimed songwriter Mark Eitzel, formerly the leader of American Music Club, recorded his first solo studio album in 1996. *60 Watt Silver Lining* departed a little from Eitzel's established reputation as a despondent writer, offering instead his most optimistic suite of lyrics in a career that has received almost universal adoration. Released on Virgin Records, it featured long-standing American Music Club contributor Bruce Kaplan (pedal steel guitar/piano), drummer Simone White (of Disposable Heroes of Hiphoprisy and Spearhead fame) and renowned soundtrack composer Mark Isham on trumpet. Alongside a cover version of Carole King's 'There Is No Easy Way Down' were typically detailed narratives such as 'Some Bartenders Have The Gift Of Pardon' and 'Southend On Sea', a song documenting the time he spent in England during his youth. *West* was a startling departure with Eitzel sounding positively upbeat. The fuller sound was enriched by the participation of R.E.M.'s Peter Buck and the Screaming Trees' Barrett Martin. The follow-up was a largely acoustic affair, featuring material written before Eitzel's collaboration with Buck.

● ALBUMS: *Songs Of Love Live* (Demon 1992)★★★, *60 Watt Silver Lining* (Virgin 1996)★★, *West* (Warners 1997)★★★★, *Caught In A Trap And I Can't Back Out 'Cause I Love You Too Much Baby* (Matador 1998)★★★★.

● FURTHER READING: *Wish The World Away: Mark Eitzel And The American Music Club*, Sean Body.

Elastica

One of the most prominent bands on the UK independent scene during the 90s, Elastica's line-up coalesced around Justine Frischmann (b. Twickenham, London, England; vocals, guitar), Donna Matthews (bass), Justin Welch (drums) and Annie Holland (guitar). Frischmann is the daughter of a prominent architect (her father built London's Centre Point skyscraper), and she attended a private school in London. Some of Elastica's original notoriety sprang from the fact that Frischmann was in an early incarnation of Suede and was romantically linked with that band's singer, Brett Anderson, then Blur's Damon Albarn. Indeed, one of Elastica's songs, 'See That Animal' - the b-side to 'Connection' - was co-written with Anderson when both attended University College London. They lived together in a dilapidated north London house while Suede looked for a recording contract. She left in October 1991 just before they were signed by Nude Records. There was more to Elastica, however, than nepotism, as they demonstrated with a series of stunning singles after they formed as a result of Frischmann placing adverts in the British music press. Wearing punk and new wave influences as diverse as Adam And The Ants, Blondie and Bow Wow Wow on their sleeves, they nevertheless chose to avoid the New Wave Of The New Wave bandwagon, consolidating their appeal with a place on the bill of 1994's Reading Festival. 'Waking Up', practically a musical rewrite of the Stranglers' 'No More Heroes', was, nevertheless, as exciting a single as any to hit the UK charts in early 1995 (the song reached number 13). The song was included on the band's debut album. While the chord sequences could too often be linked directly to particular antecedents - the similarities between the two UK Top 20 singles, 'Line Up' and 'Connection', and *Chairs Missing*-era

Wire being the best of several examples (and one that resulted in a royalty settlement, as did 'Waking Up' with the Stranglers' publishers) - Frischmann's lyrics fitted the post-feminist 90s perfectly. Critics also leaped on veiled references to her past and present paramours: 'We were sitting there waiting and I told you my plan, You were far too busy writing lines that didn't scan'. Holland departed in 1996 to be replaced by Sheila Chipperfield, and Dave Bush (keyboards) became the fifth member. Further changes ensued in 1999, with Matthews leaving and Chipperfield making way for the returning Holland. The line-up was augmented by guitarist Paul Jones (ex-Linoleum) and keyboard player Mew. A six track EP of new material was released to mixed reviews at the end of the year. The band's long delayed second album, which by now had assumed almost mythical status, was due for release in February 2000

● ALBUMS: *Elastica* (Deceptive 1995)★★★★.

Electronic

This powerful UK duo comprises Johnny Marr (b. John Maher, 31 October 1963, Ardwick, Manchester, England) and Bernard Sumner (b. Bernard Dicken/Albrecht, 4 January 1956, Salford, Manchester, England), both formerly key members of very successful Manchester-based bands, the Smiths and New Order, respectively. Although they first worked together in 1983, Electronic was not formed until 1989. After a brief period as guitarist for Matt Johnson's The The and work with various well-known artists, such as David Byrne and the Pretenders, Electronic marked Marr's move into more commercial territory. His instinct for infectious, melodic pop guitar and Sumner's songwriting and programming ability proved to be an effective combination. Their first single, 'Getting Away With It', was released in 1989 on Manchester's highly respected Factory Records and featured the Pet Shop Boys' Neil Tennant as guest vocalist. This inspired move helped the record to number 12 in the UK chart. The individual track records of the three musicians immediately gave the band a high profile, arousing the interest of both the press and the public. This attention was intensified by the excitement surrounding the 'baggy' dance scene emerging from Manchester and the city's explosion of new musical talent, sparked by bands such as Happy Mondays and the Stone Roses. Electronic capitalized on the new credibility that dance music had acquired and were influenced by the fusions that were taking place, using 'electronic' dance rhythms and indie guitar pop. In July 1991, a self-titled debut album followed two more UK Top 20 singles, 'Get The Message' and 'Feel Every Beat'. The singles were witty and distinctive and were praised by the critics. Not surprisingly, the album was also very well received, reaching number 2 in the UK chart. After a short gap, 'Disappointed' consolidated their early promise by reaching number 6 in the UK in June 1992. Intelligent, original and fashionably marrying the sounds of the guitar and the computer, much was expected but did not arrive. *Raise The Pressure* blended Pet Shop Boys harmony and structure with the occasional hint of wah-wah pedal from Marr. Six of the tracks were co-written with Kraftwerk's Karl Bartos. Sumner and Marr returned in 1999 with the more guitar-orientated *Twisted Tenderness*.

● ALBUMS: *Electronic* (Parlophone 1991)★★★★, *Raise The Pressure* (Parlophone 1996)★★★, *Twisted Tenderness* (Parlophone 1999)★★★.

Elliott, Missy 'Misdemeanor'

b. 1972, Portsmouth, Virginia, USA. Hip-hop/R&B songwriter Missy 'Misdemeanor' Elliott has become one of the most esteemed composers in the New York 90s hip-hop firmament, providing material for artists including MC Lyte, Adina Howard and Jodeci, as well as working as an arranger, producer and talent scout. Elliott first performed as part of a neighbourhood singing group, Sista, who were signed up by DeVante from Jodeci in 1992. Elliott was already writing with her long-time collaborator, Tim Mosley aka Timbaland, and with Sista's career terminally stalled (DeVante would not release any of their recordings) she concentrated on songwriting and production. Her distinctive 'hee haw' rap on Gina Thompson's 'The Things You Do' brought her wider exposure, and several offers from record companies. Fiercely independent and ambitious, Elliott signed to Elektra Records as a solo artist on the understanding that they would subsidise her own label, Gold Mind Records. In 1997, she launched her solo career with the album *Supa Dupa Fly* and attendant single 'The Rain (Supa Dupa Fly)'. The well-connected Elliott was provided with immediate exposure for the song via rotation play of its Hype Williams-directed video on MTV. Co-produced with long-time collaborator Timbaland and producer DJ Magic, the album received excellent reviews, though Elliott was reluctant to commit herself fully to a career as a performer: 'I don't want to get caught up and be an artist always on the go, because once you do that, it's hard to get into the studio and do what I do.' The album also featured cameo appearances from Aaliyah and Busta Rhymes (Elliott has written songs for both). Despite her growing reputation and success, Elliott is still based in her home-town in Virginia. In September 1998 she collaborated with Mel B from the Spice Girls on the one-off single, 'I Want You Back', which debuted at number 1 in the UK chart. Further writing and remixing work for Whitney Houston and Janet Jackson followed, although Elliott found time in her busy schedule to release her excellent sophomore set, *Da Real World*, in July 1999.

● ALBUMS: *Supa Dupa Fly* (East West 1997)★★★, *Da Real World* (East West 1999)★★★★.

Embrace

Unrelated to the early 80s US hardcore band of the same name, this Embrace is a UK-based quartet of musicians who, although latecomers to the Britpop phenomenon, are arguably its most promising post-Oasis standard-bearers. Led by brothers Danny (vocals) and Richard McNamara (guitar), the group was founded in Huddersfield, Yorkshire, in the late 80s. Their debut single, 'All You Good Good People'/'My Weakness Is None Of Your Business', was released in a limited edition of 1,500 copies on the cult independent label Fierce Panda Records in late 1996. It brought rave reviews in the weekly music press and earned sporadic radio play. The result was a race among the major labels for the group's signatures, leading to a contract with the Virgin Records subsidiary Hut. The first result of this pact was the *Fireworks EP*, which charted at number 34 in May 1997. It built on the group's good press and confidence in interviews by mining influences as diverse as the articulate soul of Curtis Mayfield, as well as more conventional guitar rock sources. Danny McNamara explained his group's brash approach to the press: 'It's not arrogance, it's confidence. If you don't believe in yourself, in a contest with hundreds of others, you've already shot yourself in the foot.' As evidence of this, he pointed out that three years previously he had insisted on a hiatus in the group's activities because they 'weren't ready'. This may also have been influenced by the fact that a *Melody Maker* reviewer in 1993 described their appearance at the Heineken Music Festival as akin to 'U2's Live Aid performance minus the laughs.' Recent comparisons, partially inspired by the fact that the group are spearheaded by brothers, revolve around their similarities to Oasis. In keeping with this comparison, Embrace were formed when elder brother Danny took the reins of his younger brother's group, Gross Misconduct, a punk band who rehearsed in a shed at the bottom of the McNamaras' parents' garden. A new drummer, Mick Heaton, joined in 1990, with bass player Steve Firth finally completing the band's line-up in 1996. New demo tapes attracted the attention of manager Tony Perrin, who had previously handled the careers of Pulp, the Mission and All About Eve. The band's second EP for Hut, *One Big Family*, charted at number 21 and their debut single, 'All You Good Good People', reached number 8 when it was re-released in October 1997. The band's series of excellent releases continued with the emphatic but beautiful 'Come Back To What You Know', which debuted at number 6 in June 1998. Their debut album was released the same month. Despite entering the UK charts at number 1, the album was regarded by many as an anticlimax in view of the previous hype surrounding the band. A reissued 'My Weakness Is None Of Your Business' debuted at number 9 in September. The band returned in November 1999 with the *Hooligan* EP, a collection of roots-orientated material which indicated they had been listening closely to the work of UK media darlings, Gomez.

● ALBUMS: *The Good Will Out* (Hut 1998)★★★.

EMF

Formed in the Forest of Dean, Gloucestershire, England, in 1989, EMF consisted of James Atkin (b. 28 March 1969, Cinderford, Gloucestershire, England; vocals), Ian Dench (b. 7 August 1964, Cheltenham, Gloucestershire, England; guitar/keyboards), Derry Brownson (b. 10 November 1970, Gloucester, England; keyboards/samples), Zak Foley (b. 9 December 1970, Gloucester, England; bass), Mark Decloedt (b. 26 June 1969, Gloucester, England; drums), and Milf (DJ). All had previously been in local indie bands; Dench in Apple Mosaic, and Foley in the IUC's. The band claimed that EMF stood for Epsom Mad Funkers or, more controversially, and more attractive to the gutter press, Ecstasy Mother Fuckers. Parlophone Records countered that it stood for Every Mother's Favourites, which is hard to believe, given the band's notorious touring antics. Their record company signed them after just four gigs and without the advance warning of a demo. However, their opportunism was rewarded when the debut single 'Unbelievable' became a Top 5 UK hit. The follow-up, 'I Believe', was criticized in many quarters for being a straight rewrite, while many were also suggesting that the band had stolen Jesus Jones' pop/sample thunder. However, their ability to win over the teen-pop market was proved by debut album sales of over two million. Together with the aforementioned Jesus Jones, the band proved particularly successful in cracking the USA, where they were bracketed as part of a new 'British

Invasion'. The band ran into some trouble with Yoko Ono over 'Lies', where a sample of the voice of John Lennon's killer Mark Chapman reciting Lennon's lyric for 'Watching The Wheels' from his prison cell resulted in an out of court settlement of $15,000 and a retraction of the offending voice from subsequent pressings. Other samples proved less controversial, and included Radio 3 announcers and Kermit The Frog. *Stigma* disappointed, with sales less than one fifth of the debut, a fact blamed by chief songwriter Dench on an over-demanding schedule and tabloid controversy: 'It was a self-conscious record and deliberately anti-commercial. At least we got everything out of our system.' Their label encouraged the band to spend their time getting new material right, leading to a three-year gap between 1992's *Unexplained* EP and 1995's *Cha Cha Cha*. Band suggestions for producer included Jim Foetus and Butch Vig, but these were eventually rejected in favour of Johnny Dollar, who had previously worked with Youssou N'Dour and Neneh Cherry. Dollar, however, walked out of the sessions, and the resulting album failed to sell. The band did return to the charts when they teamed up with comedians Vic Reeves and Bob Mortimer on a cover of the Monkees' 'I'm A Believer', but having been dropped by Parlophone they decided to split up. Brownson and Atkin both went on to play with Bentley Rhythm Ace before forming LK and Cooler respectively. Foley toured with Carrie, Dench recorded with acoustic outfit Whistler, and Milf released singles as Jose Sanchez for Skint Records.

● ALBUMS: *Schubert Dip* (Parlophone 1991)★★★★, *Stigma* (Parlophone 1992)★★, *Cha Cha Cha* (Parlophone 1995)★★★.

Eminem

b. Marshall Mathers, Kansas City, USA. This white rapper burst onto the US charts in 1999 with a controversial take on the horrercore genre. Mathers endured an itinerant childhood, living with his mother in various states before eventually ending up in Detroit at the age of 12. He took up rapping in high school before dropping out in ninth grade, joining ad hoc groups Basement Productions and the New Jacks, and, later, the duo Soul Intent. The newly christened Eminem released a raw debut album in 1997 through independent label FBT. *Infinite* was poorly received, however, with Eminem earning unfavourable comparisons to leading rappers such as Nas and AZ. His determination to succeed was given a boost by a prominent feature in *Source*'s Unsigned Hype column, and he gained revenge on his former critics when he won the *Wake Up Show*'s Freestyle Performer Of The Year award, and finished runner-up in Los Angeles' annual Rap Olympics. The following year's *The Slim Shady EP* featured some vitriolic attacks on his detractors. The standout track, 'Just Don't Give A Fuck', became a highly popular underground hit, and led to guest appearances on MC Shabaam Sahddeq's 'Five Star Generals' single and Kid Rock's *Devil Without A Cause* set. As a result, Eminem was signed to Aftermath Records by label boss Dr. Dre, who adopted the young rapper as his protégé and acted as co-producer on Eminem's full-length debut. Dre's beats featured prominently on *The Slim Shady LP*, a provocative feast of violent, twisted lyrics, with a moral outlook partially redeemed by Eminem's claim to be only 'voicing' the thoughts of the Slim Shady character. Parody or no parody, lyrics to tracks such as '97 Bonnie And Clyde' (which contained lines about killing the mother of his child) and frequent verbal outbursts about his mother were held by many, outside even the usual Christian moral majority, to be deeply irresponsible. The album was buoyed by the commercial success of the singles 'My Name Is' and 'Guilty Conscience' (the former helped by a striking, MTV-friendly video), and climbed to number 2 on the US album chart in March 1999. Eminem subsequently made high profile appearances on Rawkus Records' *Soundbombing Volume 2* compilation and Missy 'Misdemeanor' Elliott's *Da Real World*. He was also in the news when his mother filed a lawsuit claiming that comments made by the rapper during interviews and on the *Slim Shady* album had caused, amongst other things, emotional distress, damage to her reputation and loss of self-esteem.

● ALBUMS: *Infinite* (FBT 1997)★★, *The Slim Shady LP* (Aftermath/Interscope 1999)★★★.

Emperor

Members of the bizarre Norwegian Satanic club known as the Black Metal Circle, led by Euronymous of Mayhem, Emperor form part of the black metal revival of the 90s. Musically, they whip up a cacophonous storm of blistering guitars and bellowed vocals, with aggressive, devilish themes and a few strange, quasi-classical flourishes. In 1993 they released a split CD with Scandinavian pagan heavy metal band Enslaved. In the same year the Black Metal Circle were linked with a series of church burnings in Norway and Samoth, Emperor's sinisterly flamboyant frontman, was arrested in connection with the crimes. He was later released; however, in addition to the arson, Emperor drummer Faust was convicted of the 1992 murder of a homosexual. Despite this, and the murder of fellow black metal Satanist Euronymous, Emperor continue to fly the Scandinavian black metal banner.

● ALBUMS: *Emperor* (Candlelight 1993)★★★, *In the Nightside Eclipse* (Candlelight 1994)★★★, *Anthems To The Welkin At Dusk* (Candlelight 1997)★★★, *IX Equilibrium* (Candlelight 1999)★★★.

En Vogue

Vocal R&B quartet comprising Dawn Robinson (b. Connecticut, USA), Terry Ellis (b. Texas, USA), Cindy Herron (b. San Francisco, California, USA) and Maxine Jones (b. Patterson, New Jersey, USA). They formed in Oakland, California, where they were auditioned by Denzil Foster and Thomas McElroy. The duo had worked together in both the Timex Social Club and Club Nouveau (who enjoyed big hits with 'Rumors' in 1986 and 'Lean On Me', a hip-hop version of Bill Withers' 70s classic, and a Grammy-winner, in 1987). Afterwards they decided to write and produce under their own steam: 'When Tommy and I bumped into each other in the early 80s, we had the same notion. Everyone was saying R&B was tired and worn out. The new era was hip-hop and rap. But we thought: why not combine the two eras? Put good songs - and the 70s were loaded with good songs - over the new grooves.' En Vogue were formed in October 1988 after the duo auditioned to establish their own 'girl group'. Of the four selected, only Cindy Herron had previous 'showbiz' experience, winning Miss San Francisco and Miss Black California pageants, and also working as an actress. The quartet remained primarily responsible for their own image and songs, but they were groomed for success by joining

M.C. Hammer's 1990 tour, and that of Freddie Jackson a year later. They went on to enjoy singles success with 'Hold On' and 'Lies' in 1990. The latter introduced female rapper Debbie T, and added a new, post-feminist outlook to traditional R&B concerns. Their second album, meanwhile, featured two Curtis Mayfield cover versions, and produced further hits in 'Free Your Mind' and 'Give It Up, Turn It Loose'. Heavily influenced by Chaka Khan, En Vogue, in turn, helped to start the 'new jill swing' movement, which threw up the equally successful SWV, Jade and TLC. They were approached by Roseanne Barr and her then-husband Tom Arnold to appear in their own sitcom. These distractions did not affect their singing or their commercial appeal into the mid-90s. Following a lengthy break from recording, during which Robinson left to pursue a solo career, they returned to a competitive market with the classy *EV3*.

● ALBUMS: *Born To Sing* (Atlantic 1990)★★★, *Remix To Sing* (Atlantic 1991)★★★, *Funky Divas* (East West 1992)★★★★, *Runaway Love* mini-album (East West 1993)★★★, *EV3* (East West 1997)★★★.

Solo: Terry Ellis *Southern Gal* (East West 1995)★★.

● COMPILATIONS: *Best Of En Vogue* (East West 1998)★★★★.

Energy Orchard

This pop rock sextet came from Belfast, Northern Ireland and were built around the nucleus of singer Bap Kennedy and guitarist Paul Toner. Snapped up by MCA in 1990 their first single was titled after their home-town, ironically after relocating to London. It dented the UK Top 70, paving the way for follow-ups 'Sailortown' and 'Lace Virginia'. After running the gauntlet of comparisons to U2 that face most rock bands from Ireland, the reaction of the mainstream UK press hardened. Bombast and over-production somewhat neutered their debut album and the band's subsequent releases ploughed a similar path. They disbanded in 1996, their final release being a credible live album. Kennedy later embarked on a solo career, releasing the Steve Earle-produced *Domestic Blues* in 1999.

● ALBUMS: *Energy Orchard* (MCA 1990)★★★, *Shinola* (MCA 1993)★★, *Painkiller* (Transatlantic 1995)★★★, *Orchardville* (Transatlantic 1996)★★★.

Enigma

Ambient pop sculptors Enigma are the brainchild of Michael Cretu (b. 18 May 1957, Bucharest, Romania), who enrolled in the Lyzeum No. 2, a college for gifted young musicians, as a pianist, in 1966. After completing his studies Cretu moved to the Academy Of Music in Frankfurt, where Professor Philipp Mohler began to take an interest in him. Having passed his final exams in 1978, Cretu immediately found work as a studio musician and arranger. By 1980 he had earned his first significant success as producer, and he released his solo debut, *Legionare*, three years later for Virgin Records. He was then the architect behind the 1985 number 1 European success of Moti Special as writer, producer and keyboard player. Afterwards he devoted many of his efforts to the rise of Sandra, including masterminding 'Maria Magdalena', a number 1 in over 30 countries, and several successful albums. Further gold record status arrived in 1987 for his production work with Mike Oldfield, and in France he helped revitalize the career of Sylvie Vartan by writing and producing 'C'est Fatale'. He married Sandra Lauer in 1988 before putting together his most commercially successful project, Enigma, two years later, stating that 'old rules and habits have to be rejected and dismissed so that something new can be created'. Enigma's Gregorian chants and dance music rhythms subsequently enchanted nearly all who heard them, with the meditative repetition giving it universal appeal. 'Sadeness Part 1' hit the UK number 1 spot in December 1990, leading Cretu, who had now turned his back on a prospective career as a concert pianist, to remark, 'I started writing hits the day I sold my piano.' Almost every movement of the accompanying *MCMXC AD* album, which also topped the charts and spent no less than 57 weeks on the UK list, was used in some form of television or movie production. Gold or platinum status was attained in 25 countries. With the phenomenal success of Enigma's debut, it was no surprise that the artist took a full three years to produce a follow-up. Film director Robert Evans invited Cretu to compose the title song to *Sliver*, resulting in the release of 'Age Of Loneliness (Carly's Song)', which also featured on the new album. Although it had pre-orders of 1.4 million units, *The Cross Of Changes*, which mined a wider range of influences than the debut, was hardly the expected blockbuster. The single 'Return To Innocence' reached number 9 in the UK charts in 1994, however, demonstrating the music's enduring appeal to the record-buying public. Subsequent albums have continued to mine Cretu's seamless fusion of new age, ambient and dance.

● ALBUMS: *MCMXC AD* (Virgin 1990)★★★★, *The Cross Of Changes* (Virgin 1993)★★★★, *Le Roi Est Mort, Vive Le Roi!* (Virgin 1996)★★★, *The Screen Behind The Mirror* (Virgin 2000)★★.

Entombed

This Swedish death metal band was formed in Stockholm in 1987 as Nihilist, releasing four acclaimed demos: *Drowned, Premature Autopsy, But Life Goes On* and *Only Shreds Remain*. After dissolving Nihilist, the band reunited a few days later as Entombed, with a line-up of Lars-Goran Petrov (vocals), Uffe Cederlund (guitar), Alex Hellid (lead guitar) and Nicke Andersson (drums). *Left Hand Path* adequately demonstrated the band's potential with an atmospheric and individual sound and live shows were equally impressive. Lars Rosenberg was added on bass and Petrov departed shortly after the debut. Devor Safstrom only lasted for one single ('Crawl') before Johnny Dordevic (ex-Carnage) took over, although Andersson performed the vocals on the well-reviewed *Clandestine*. After an extensive US tour with Morbid Angel, Dordevic was ousted in favour of the returning Petrov for the Gods Of Grind UK jaunt with Carcass, Cathedral and Confessor. The mini-album *Hollowman* was swiftly followed by the hugely impressive *Wolverine Blues* as Entombed continued to ignore death metal convention, establishing themselves as one of the genre's leading acts, and creating more accessible material by incorporating into the fierce death metal framework traditional rock song structures and a rhythmic groove. Entombed's popularity continued to increase as they toured Europe on a frighteningly intense bill with labelmates Napalm Death, while an EP, *Out Of Hand*, saw high-class cover versions of material by Kiss ('God Of Thunder') and Repulsion ('Blackbreath'). The group left Earache Records in the mid-90s, but their tenure at major label East West Records was brief, and they were dropped without releasing an album. Moving to independent label Music For Nations,

they sounded admirably unbowed on *To Ride, Shoot Straight And Speak The Truth!*, which featured new bass player Jörgen Sandström. Andersson left the band shortly afterwards to concentrate on his band the Hellacopters. He was replaced by Peter Stjärnwind, who made his first appearance on November 1998's *Same Difference*.

● ALBUMS: *Left Hand Path* (Earache 1990)★★★, *Clandestine* (Earache 1991)★★★, *Hollowman* mini-album (Earache 1993)★★, *Wolverine Blues* (Earache 1993)★★★★, *To Ride, Shoot Straight And Speak The Truth!* (Music For Nations 1997)★★★, *Monkey Puss (Live In London)* 1992 recording (Earache 1998)★★, *Same Difference* (Earache 1998)★★★.

● COMPILATIONS: *Entombed* (Earache 1997)★★★.

Enya

b. Eithne Ni Bhraonain, 17 May 1961, Gweedore, Co. Donegal, Eire. Enya, a classically trained pianist, was formerly a member of Clannad before embarking on a solo career that blossomed unexpectedly with her 1988 UK chart-topper, 'Orinoco Flow'. Daughter of noted Irish Showband leader Leo Brennan (Brennan is the non-Gaelic form of Bhraonain) who led the Slieve Foy Band, Enya was born into a highly musical family. Her mother was also a musician, and in 1976 some of her brothers, sisters and uncles formed the band Clannad (Gaelic for family). Enya joined the band on keyboards in 1979 and shared in some of their success as they recorded haunting themes for a variety of television programmes, giving them their first chart success. However, Enya, who has professed she has little time for conventional pop music, never quite fitted into the band and left amicably in 1982. A few years later she recorded the music for the BBC Television series *The Celts* which was subsequently released as her debut album in 1987. An endearing blend of ethereal singing (in Gaelic and English), the album was largely ignored, as was the accompanying single, 'I Want Tomorrow'. However, the following year, Enya released *Watermark* in much the same vein and had a surprise UK number 1 with the single 'Orinoco Flow'. Working with her long-time collaborators, Roma Ryan (her lyric writer) and Nicky Ryan (her producer), Enya followed the chart-topper with two smaller hits - 'Evening Falls' and 'Storms In Africa Part II'. She adopted a lower profile for the next couple of years except for an appearance with Sinead O'Connor. She returned in 1991 with *Shepherd Moons*, which by the mid-90s had reached world sales of 10 million copies. Her third collection, *The Memory Of Trees*, didn't alter the winning formula, but at some stage her warm, ambient music will begin to pale as listeners realize it is the same delicious cake with a different topping. The artist spent the remainder of the decade contributing soundtrack material to various projects.

● ALBUMS: *Enya* (BBC 1987)★★, *Watermark* (Warners 1988)★★★★, *Shepherd Moons* (Warners 1991)★★★, *The Memory Of Trees* (Warners 1995)★★★.

● COMPILATIONS: *Paint The Sky With Stars: The Best Of* (Warners 1997)★★★★, *A Box Of Dreams* box-set (Warners 1998)★★★.

Equation

This UK folk ensemble originally featured Kate Rusby (b. 1 December 1973, Barnsley, Yorkshire, England; fiddle, piano, guitar, vocals), Kathryn Roberts (clarinet, flute, saxophone, vocals), and the three Lakeman Brothers, Sean (guitar), Sam (keyboards) and Seth (violin). All of them were from musical families. Rusby and Roberts had appeared with numerous traditional and ceilidh bands, and had worked together previously as child dancers and on other collaborative projects. They released their first album as a duo in 1995. The Lakeman brothers also boasted a prodigious musical background, and formed their own group as teenagers, appearing on BBC Television's *Saturday Superstore*. For several years they proved popular attractions on the jazz and folk circuits throughout their native south-west England. The Equation were formed in the spring of 1995, when none was older than 21. Roberts, who had been awarded BBC Radio 2's Young Tradition Award, had sung vocals on the Lakeman Brothers' debut album, *3 Piece Suite*. She was then requested to put together a group of young musicians to play a Portuguese festival but the group, the Equation, stayed together afterwards. On their return to the UK they became so successful on the folk circuit that they had bookings until the end of 1997. They played the main stage at the 1995 Cambridge Folk Festival. The folk music press celebrated them as the scene's brightest new hopes for a young, traditional English folk band of the 90s. However, following the signing of a five-album deal with Warner Music, Rusby left the band. She was replaced by Cara Dillon (ex-Oige), but musical disagreements led to Dillon and Sam Lakeman also leaving. The remaining members opted to start from scratch, writing the new material that constituted the long-awaited debut *Hazy Daze*.

● ALBUMS: *Hazy Daze* (Blanco y Negro 1998)★★★.

Estefan, Gloria

b. Gloria Fajardo, 1 September 1957, Havana, Cuba. Estefan, the most popular Latin American singer of the 80s and 90s, originally rose to prominence in the 70s by joining soon-to-be husband Emilio Estefan in Miami Sound Machine. Educated at Catholic high school in Miami after moving there from Cuba at the age of two, she first learned to play guitar and sing during her leisure hours. She met the other members of the band when Emilio came to her high school to offer advice on music. Together they played at a friend's wedding, but Gloria initially refused to join the group permanently, preferring to concentrate on her psychology degree and career as an interpreter. She eventually relented, marrying Emilio in 1978, shortly afterwards collecting her BA degree from the University of Miami. Miami Sound Machine recorded a sequence of Spanish-language albums during the late 70s and early 80s, becoming massively successful not only in the USA and Europe but especially Latin America. By 1986 they had been named the Top Singles Act Of 1986 by *Billboard*. The group officially changed its name to Gloria Estefan And Miami Sound Machine the following year, and enjoyed further substantial hits with 'Rhythm Is Gonna Get You' and 'Anything For You' before Estefan launched her solo career in 1989 with *Cuts Both Ways*. Three singles taken from the album reached the US Top 10 - 'Get On Your Feet', 'Here We Are' and the number 1, 'I Don't Wanna Lose You'. However, early in 1990 her impetus was halted when she was involved in a serious accident in Syracuse, New York. Having just met with President George Bush to discuss participation in an anti-drugs campaign, the group's bus was struck from behind, resulting in a broken vertebra and surgery for Estefan. She returned in 1991 with new material, after reportedly being awarded £5 million for

loss of earnings caused by the accident. While songs on *Into The Light* dealt with her recovery and rejuvenation, she embarked on an eight-month world tour in March 1991. This was followed in January 1992 with a performance at the interval of Super Bowl XXVI between the Washington Redskins and Buffalo Bills. In the summer she and Emilio purchased Miami Beach's famed art deco Cardozo Hotel from Chris Blackwell for $5 million. Estefan's 1993 and 1995 albums, *Mi Tierra* and *Abriendo Puertas*, were Spanish-language efforts that distanced her somewhat from the American pop mainstream, but proved hugely popular in South America. *Destiny* was her first English-language collection for over five years (excepting the lacklustre pop covers collection, *Hold Me, Thrill Me, Kiss Me*). It featured 'Reach', the theme to the 1996 Olympic Games in Atlanta, an event at which Estefan sang during the closing ceremony. *Gloria!* marked a welcome return to the Latin sound of the Miami Sound Machine.

● ALBUMS: *Cuts Both Ways* (Epic 1989)★★★, *Exitos De Gloria Estefan* (Columbia 1990)★★★, *Into The Light* (Epic 1991)★★★★, *Mi Tierra* (Epic 1993)★★★, *Hold Me, Thrill Me, Kiss Me* (Epic 1994)★★, *Abriendo Puertas* (Epic 1995)★★★★, *Destiny* (Epic 1996)★★★, *Gloria!* (Epic 1998)★★★, with Mariah Carey, Celine Dion, Aretha Franklin, Shania Twain *Divas Live* (Epic 1998)★★.

● COMPILATIONS: *Greatest Hits* (Epic 1992)★★★★.

● VIDEOS: *Everlasting Gloria* (Sony Music Video 1995), *The Evolution Tour: Live In Miami* (Epic Music Video 1996), with Mariah Carey, Celine Dion, Aretha Franklin, Shania Twain *Divas Live* (Sony Music Video 1998), *Don't Stop!* (Sony Music Video 1999).

● FURTHER READING: *Gloria Estefan*, Grace Catalano.

● FILMS: *Music Of The Heart* (1999).

Eternal

This UK pop quartet originally comprised lead singer Easther Bennett plus sister Vernie Bennett, Louise Nurding and Kéllé Bryan. Nurding and Bryan both attended London's Italia Conti stage school, and the Bennett sisters sang in a Croydon Baptist church. It was through Nurding that they came to the attention of manager Dennis Ingoldsby (co-owner of management agency and record label 1st Avenue). Their first two singles, 'Stay' and 'Save Our Love', made an immediate impact on the UK charts and launched the group as one of the teen phenomena of 1993. However, much more strident and demanding of the listener was their third single, 'Just A Step From Heaven', the accompanying video for which depicted gangs of youths in urban wastelands, before switching to a woman giving a lecture on self-awareness. It was perhaps a little disappointing, then, to learn that Eternal's songs were not of their own creation, and written instead by backroom staff. Nevertheless, *Always And Forever* spawned no less than six Top 15 UK hit singles (another record). By the time Nurding left amicably in the summer of 1995 to forge a solo career (billed simply as Louise), Eternal had become Britain's most successful all-female group since Bananarama. *Power Of A Woman* became Ingoldsby's first serious attempt to break the group in America, writing material around a formula that drew obvious comparisons to modern R&B stars such as En Vogue. The title track was taken from the album as the group's first single as a trio, entering the UK Top 10 in October 1995 (joining Louise's first solo single). For the first time, too, roughly half the songs on the album were self-composed. The trio claimed their first UK number 1 in 1997 with 'I Wanna Be The Only One'. The following album, *Before The Rain*, confirmed the trio's soul credentials but suffered from a shortage of stand-out tracks. Bryan left the group in late 1998, and launched a solo career the following October with the UK Top 20 single 'Higher Than Heaven'. The Bennett sisters released the hard-hitting 'What'cha Gonna Do' the same month, which introduced the more pronounced swingbeat direction of their self-titled fourth album.

● ALBUMS: *Always And Forever* (First Avenue/EMI 1994)★★, *Power Of A Woman* (First Avenue/EMI 1995)★★★, *Before The Rain* (First Avenue/EMI 1997)★★, *Eternal* (EMI 1999)★★★.
● COMPILATIONS: *Greatest Hits* (EMI 1997)★★★.
● VIDEOS: *Always And Forever* (1994), *The Greatest Clips* (EMI 1997).

Etheridge, Melissa

b. 29 May 1961, Leavenworth, Kansas, USA. Etheridge was still only a teenager when she began playing piano and guitar in various covers bands around Kansas. After this grounding she had a more formal training at the Berklee College Of Music before playing the club circuit around Boston, Massachusetts. However, it was after she relocated to Los Angeles and was spotted performing by Island Records chief Chris Blackwell, that her career took off. Signed in 1986, her first break was writing the music for the movie *Weeds*. She had recruited one band to work with her but when this did not work out, she settled for a simple trio with Kevin McCormick on bass and Craig Kampf on drums. The first album was recorded live in the studio and spawned the single 'Bring Me Some Water'. A turntable hit, it took some time to pick up sales but ended up a Grammy nom-inee. Former Iggy Pop sideman Scott Thurston had made a guest appearance on the first album and he returned for the second, alongside artists including Waddy Weichtel, and Island Records cohort Bono (U2). Kampf did not play on the album as he had been replaced by Maurigio Fritz Lewak. In the early 90s the excellent *Never Enough* won a Grammy award. *Yes I Am* was a similar mix of up-tempo, 'love crazy' material, showing a lyrical side of Etheridge that tolerates no fools, yet maintained the romantic tradition. 'If I Wanted To' for example: 'If I wanted to I could run as fast as a train, be as sharp as a needle that's twisting your brain, If I wanted to I could turn mountains to sand, have political leaders in the palm of my hand'. She also announced herself as a lesbian by jumping onstage to kiss Elvira at the gay and lesbian Triangle Ball during the inaugural celebrations of President Clinton's victory. The Hugh Padgham-produced *Your Little Secret* was further confirmation of her writing talents. She was able to swing from rockers such as the title track to the beautiful 'Nowhere To Go' about a clandestine lesbian rela-tionship. She won the 1996 ASCAP songwriter of the year award, but took a lengthy break from the music business to concentrate on her domestic arrangements. She returned in 1999 with the intimate, but low-key *Breakdown*. Far more high profile was the media's obsessive interest in unearthing the biological father of her and partner Julie Cypher's two children. The sperm donor turned out to be David Crosby.

● ALBUMS: *Melissa Etheridge* (Island 1988)★★, *Brave And Crazy* (Island 1989)★★★, *Never Enough* (Island 1991)★★★★, *Yes I Am* (Island 1993)★★★, *Your Little Secret* (Island 1995)★★★, *Breakdown* (Island 1999)★★.
● FURTHER READING: *Our Little Secret*, Joyce Luck.

Evans, Faith

Married to hardcore rapper the Notorious B.I.G., urban R&B singer Faith Evans originally rose to prominence by singing background vocals and co-writing songs for Mary J. Blige, Color Me Badd and Tony Thompson. She broke through as a solo artist in the mid-90s with the release of her winning debut single, 'You Used To Love Me'. Mixing slightly lisped rap sections with soulful singing of her predominantly romantic concerns, her self-titled debut album followed expertly in the tradition of Blige, with a wide cast of pro-ducers and collaborators. Without ever demonstrating the originality to separate her from a host of 'new jill swing' peers, *Faith* was sufficiently contemporaneous and lavishly executed to arouse interest throughout the R&B community. It peaked at number 2 on the *Billboard* R&B album chart, and number 22 on the Top 200. Following Notorious B.I.G.'s murder in March 1997, Evans appeared on the international number 1 tribute single 'I'll Be Missing You' by Sean 'Puffy' Combs. Her own 'Love Like This' (US number 7/UK number 24) was built around a sample from Chic's 'Chic Cheer', and premiered the US Top 10 album *Keep The Faith*.

● ALBUMS: *Faith* (Bad Boy/Arista 1995)★★★, *Keep The Faith* (Bad Boy/Arista 1998)★★★★.

Eve

b. Eve Jihan Jeffers, 1979, Philadelphia, Pennsylvania, USA. The only female MC on the New York-based Ruff Ryders label, this bleach blonde self-styled 'pit bull in a skirt' emerged in the late 90s as a genuine rival to Foxy Brown and Lil' Kim. Jeffers first began rapping in a high school rap group under the name Gangsta. A spell as a go-go dancer fol-lowed before she changed her name to Eve Of Destruction and began creating a stir as a warm-up MC at local talent shows. Her first break came when Dr. Dre signed her to his Aftermath label, and helped produce her demo tape. One of the tracks on the demo, 'Eve Of Destruction', gained wide-spread exposure when it was featured on 1998's *Bulworth* soundtrack. Unfortunately, Eve's contract with Aftermath lapsed and she was left without a label. A chance meeting with the up-and-coming rapper DMX in Los Angeles resulted in her signing up with the fledgling Ruff Ryders label. 'What Ya Want', featured on the bestselling *Ryde Or Die Vol. 1* com-pilation, set out her stall, and guest appearances on the Roots' *Things Fall Apart* and BLACKstreet's 'Girlfriend/Boyfriend' helped raise her profile. Her debut album, which debuted at US number 1 in September 1999, featured beats by Ruff Ryders' in-house producer Swizz Beatz and guest appearances by label mates DMX and the LOX, as well as a cameo from Missy 'Misdemeanor' Elliott. The assertive declaration of independence, 'Gotta Man', made it clear that the star of the show was undoubtedly Eve.

● ALBUMS: *Ruff Ryders' First Lady* (Ruff Ryders/Interscope 1999)★★★★.

Eve6

Young US alternative rock band Eve6 were formed and sub-sequently signed by RCA Records while guitarist Jon Siebels and bass player Max Collins were still at high school. The line-up was completed by drummer Tony Fagenson, son of producer Don Was. The single 'Inside Out' announced their pop-punk style, compared by some critics to Green Day. Their subsequent self-titled debut album was promoted by extensive touring with Third Eye Blind, and within a few months of release had risen to number 33 on the *Billboard* Top 200. A second single, 'Leech', was written by Siebels and Collins about a problematic work relationship, and was typical of material dubbed by critics as 'superior brat rock'.

● ALBUMS: *Eve6* (RCA 1998)★★★.

Everclear

Comprising Art Alexakis (b. 12 April 1962, Los Angeles, California, USA; vocals, guitar), Craig Montoya (b. 14 September 1970; bass, vocals) and Greg Eklund (b. 18 April 1970), who replaced original drummer Scott Cuthbert in 1994. Everclear were formed in Portland, Oregon, in 1991. Alexakis had previously worked as a roadie for a succession of north-west punk bands. Indulging himself in copious quantities of drugs, he only decided to start his own group when a cocaine overdose temporarily stopped his heart. Early comparisons to Nirvana (exacerbated by the singer's blonde hair) went into overdrive when Kurt Cobain publicly stated his approval. They made their debut in 1994 with *World Of Noise*, which included the intriguing 'Sparkle' ('Fire pulls the spirit from the corporate whore/I'm embarrassed by the plaid you wear/If I were you I'd hide behind that stupid bleached blond hair'). Critics were left unsure as to whom the reference concerned, Alexakis or Cobain. It was followed by a mini-album, *White Trash Hell*, again on Fire Records, before a major recording contract with Capitol Records. They were signed by Gary Gersh, who had previously taken both Nirvana and Sonic Youth to Geffen Records. In 1995 they released their first album for the new label, the critically lauded and commercially successful *Sparkle And Fade*. They repeated this success two years later with the release of the infectious *So Much For The Afterglow*.

● ALBUMS: *World Of Noise* (Fire 1994)★★★, *White Trash Hell* mini-album (Fire 1995)★★★, *Sparkle And Fade* (Capitol 1995)★★★★, *So Much For The Afterglow* (Capitol 1997)★★★.

Everlast

b. Erik Schrody, USA. A former graffiti artist and protégé of Ice-T, US rapper Everlast was one of the few white members in the Rhyme Syndicate posse. Everything on his debut album was as might have been expected: hardcore visions of violence, extensive use of expletives, and puerile, anatomical descriptions of women. There was, at least, room for an anti-PMRC rap, and samples drawn from the diverse tangents of Sly And Robbie, Sly Stone and even Bananarama and the Knack. Everlast was introduced to hip-hop while at summer camp, a friend there teaching him both graffiti and elementary street rap. Everlast laid down a couple of tracks with the help of his friend's DJ partner, Bahal, and Ice-T liked what he heard. He released his first single as far back as 1988. Everlast toured the UK supporting Ice-T, but abandoned his solo career when he joined Irish American hip-hoppers House Of Pain, who enjoyed a US Top 10 smash in June 1992 with the addictive 'Jump Around'. He quit the music business in 1996, but returned to recording two years later with *Whitey Ford Sings The Blues*, an impressive slow-mo fusion of hip-hop beats and folk stylings that climbed to US number 9. In an eventful year, Everlast had already suffered a near fatal cardiac arrest and converted to Islam.

● ALBUMS: *Forever Everlasting* (Warners 1990)★★, *Whitey Ford Sings The Blues* (Tommy Boy 1998)★★★★.

Everything But The Girl

The duo of Tracey Thorn (b. 26 September 1962, Hertfordshire, England) and Ben Watt (b. 6 December 1962, Barnes, London, England) first came together when they were students at Hull University, their name coming from a local clothes shop. Thorn was also a member of the Marine Girls who issued two albums. They performed together in 1982 and released a gentle and simply produced version of Cole Porter's 'Night And Day'. Thorn made a solo acoustic mini-album in 1982, *A Distant Shore*, which was a strong seller in the UK independent charts. Watt released the critically acclaimed *North Marine Drive* the following year. They subsequently left Cherry Red Records and signed to the major-distributed Blanco y Negro label. In 1984, they made the national Top 30 with 'Each And Everyone', which preceded the superb *Eden*. This jazz-flavoured pop collection hallmarked the duo's understated but beautific compositional skills, displaying a great leap from the comparative naïveté of their previous offerings. Subsequent albums revealed a much more gradual growth in songwriting, though many of their older fans contend they have never surpassed that debut. Their biggest single breakthrough, meanwhile, came when a cover version of Danny Whitten's 'I Don't Want To Talk About It' reached UK number 3 in 1988. The attendant *Idlewild* enjoyed critical and commercial success. *The Language Of Life*, a collection more firmly fixated with jazz stylings, found further critical acclaim; one track, 'The Road', featured Stan Getz on saxophone. However, a more pop-orientated follow-up, *World-wide*, was released to mediocre reviews in 1991. Watt's increasingly busy DJing schedule and Thorn's vocal contributions to trip-hop pioneers Massive Attack's 1994 opus, *Protection*, demonstrated their increasing interest in the UK's dance music scene. This was reflected in the textures of *Amplified Heart*, which featured contributions from Danny Thompson, Dave Mattacks, Richard Thompson and arranger Harry Robinson. The album was recorded following Watt's recovery from a life-threatening illness (chronicled in the quirky *Patient: The History Of A Rare Illness*). Todd Terry's remix of the track 'Missing' provided their big breakthrough, becoming a huge club hit and reaching the UK and US Top 5. The duo's new approach was confirmed on *Walking Wounded*, their Virgin Records debut, which embellished their acoustic songs with drum 'n' bass and trip-hop rhythms to stunning effect. The title track and 'Wrong' both reached the UK Top 10. Watt's involvement in the club scene meant that the follow-up did not appear until 1999. *Temperamental* retained some of the low-key charm of *Walking Wounded*, although three years on the duo's work sounded less groundbreaking.

● ALBUMS: *Eden* (Blanco y Negro 1984)★★★★, *Love Not Money* (Blanco y Negro 1985)★★, *Baby The Stars Shine Bright* (Blanco y Negro 1986)★★, *Idlewild* (Blanco y Negro 1988)★★★★, *The Language Of Life* (Blanco y Negro 1990)★★★, *World-wide* (Blanco y Negro 1991)★★, *Amplified Heart* (Blanco y Negro 1994)★★★★, *Walking Wounded* (Virgin 1996)★★★★, *Temperamental* (Virgin 1999)★★★.

Solo: Tracey Thorn *A Distant Shore* mini-album (Cherry Red 1982)★★★. Ben Watt *North Marine Drive* (Cherry Red 1983)★★★.

● COMPILATIONS: *Home Movies: The Best Of Everything But The Girl* (Blanco y Negro 1993)★★★★, *The Best Of Everything But The Girl* (Blanco y Negro 1997)★★★★.

● FURTHER READING: *Patient: The History Of A Rare Illness*, Ben Watt.

Evora, Cesaria

b. c.1944, Mindelo, San Vincente, Cape Verde (an archipelago of islands 500 miles from Africa's west coast). Evora originates from the main port city of San Vincente, Mindelo, a base for the islands' intelligentsia and industrialists following the end of Portuguese rule in 1975. It is also home to a music named morna. Morna sounds akin to a sophisticated blend of Portuguese fado, jazz and Latin, with its name a derivation of the English word 'mourn'. Cesaria Evora is ubiquitously recognized as the pre-eminent force in the music, while her uncle, Xavier Francisco de Cruz, was the architect of many of its songs. However, recognition came late in life for the singer, who had sung since her teenage years for subsistence.

She eventually found fame at the turn of the 90s, with her success triggered by rave reviews in Parisian magazines (she is now partially based in the French capital). *Cosmopolitan* and *Elle*, as well as the nation's largest circulation music magazine, *Actuel*, which put her on their cover, all proclaimed her as a genuine star and original talent. Prestige dates at major French music celebrations such as the Musique Metisses (Angouleme) and Francophiles (La Rochelle) ensued. Aided by fellow Capverdian Paulino Vieira, her recordings pursue a reflective, highly melodic approach backed by acoustic instrumentation. Gentle piano, percussion, ukulele and guitar underpins the deep melancholy at the heart of morna, for which Evora's troubled life makes her the perfect cipher. The deep sadness of this music is known as 'sodade', or nostalgia without the sentiment, although a direct translation is difficult. Her emotional resonance has seen the press compare her to artists as diverse as Edith Piaf, Mahalia Jackson and Billie Holiday, the latter partially due to a similarity of lifestyle (she has been married and deserted three times - on the last occasion her husband left her to join a football team in Porto - and she drinks and smokes heavily). These experiences with men have left her deeply embittered, and family aside, she has sworn that no other man shall ever again sleep under her roof. She also insists on performing barefoot, as a symbolic salute to the poverty that afflicted (and continues to afflict) her fellow Capverdians.

Her first stroke of good fortune arrived in 1985 when, after years of singing in local bars for peanuts (literally) and beer, she was invited to travel to Europe as one of four singers chosen by the Women's Organisation of Cap Vert. She made a profound impression, and was soon invited to record and to tour America by an expatriate Capverdian singer known as Bana. With her reputation established, a series of albums were issued for Melodie Records, most with the aid of producer Jose Da Silva and her aforementioned arranger, Vieira. These scaled the top of the French charts. Her growing international success led to a major label deal with RCA Records, for whom she has recorded three popular albums, the most recent of which was 1999's outstanding *Café Atlantico*.

● ALBUMS: *Miss Perfumado* (Melodie 1992)★★★, *Mar Azul* (Melodie 1993)★★★, *Cesaria Evora* (Melodie 1995)★★★★, *Cesaria* (RCA 1996)★★★, *Cabo Verde* (BMG 1997)★★★, *Café Atlantico* (RCA Victor 1999)★★★★.

Extreme

This Boston quartet comprised Gary Cherone (b. 26 July 1961, Malden, Massachusetts, USA; vocals), Nuno Bettencourt (b. 20 September 1966, Azores, Portugal; guitar), Pat Badger (b. 22 July 1967, Boston, Massachusetts, USA; bass) and Paul Geary (b. 24 July 1961, Medford, Massachusetts, USA; drums). The origins of the band can be traced to local act the Dream, whose sole six-track EP in 1983 featured Cherone and Geary. As Extreme, the original line-up found themselves on television in 1985 via a video clip for 'Mutha (Don't Wanna Go To School Today)', as part of an MTV competition, but it was the arrival of Bettencourt in 1986 and Badger the following year that boosted their career. A recording contract with A&M Records was quickly secured and the band made their vinyl debut with 'Play With Me' for the soundtrack to *Bill And Ted's Excellent Adventure*. The inevitable self-titled debut album followed. Encompassing elements of pop, metal, funk and blues, their songwriting powers were still in their infancy at this stage and although competent, the album met with widespread critical indifference. *Pornograffitti* was a stunning second release, being an ambitious concept affair, subtitled 'A Funked Up Fairy Tale'. 'Get The Funk Out' reached number 19 in the UK charts in June 1991, but the band had already broken through in America in March when the simple acoustic ballad 'More Than Words' topped the charts. The song climbed to UK number 2 in July the same year. 'Hole Hearted' was their only other US success, reaching number 4 later that year, although they would continue to achieve Top 20 singles in the UK until 1995. The band's music was now characterized by Bettencourt's innovative guitar playing, intelligent lyrics and a diverse style that transcended a variety of musical genres. Their appearance at the Freddie Mercury memorial concert in May 1992, which interrupted sessions for *III Sides To Every Story*, gave them considerable exposure beyond the heavy metal fraternity. Prior to the band's appearance at the Donington Festival in the summer of 1994, Mike Mangini (ex-Annihilator) replaced Paul Geary on drums. After the disappointing critical and commercial reaction to 1995's *Waiting For The Punchline*, Bettencourt announced plans to release a solo album through Colorblind Records, the company he runs through A&M. The band formally broke up in October 1996, with Cherone moving on to become lead singer with Van Halen.

● ALBUMS: *Extreme* (A&M 1989)★★★, *Pornograffitti* (A&M 1990)★★★★, *III Sides To Every Story* (A&M 1992)★★★, *Waiting For The Punchline* (A&M 1995)★★.

● COMPILATIONS: *The Best Of Extreme* (A&M 1998)★★★.

Faith No More

Formed in San Francisco in 1980, Faith No More, titled after a greyhound on which the members had placed a bet, were among the first outfits to experiment with the fusion of funk, thrash and hardcore styles that effectively became a new musical subgenre. The band initially comprised Jim Martin (b. 21 July 1961, Oakland, California, USA; guitar, ex-Vicious Hatred), Roddy Böttum (b. 1 July 1963, Los Angeles, California, USA; keyboards), Bill Gould (b. 24 April 1963, Los Angeles, California, USA; bass), Mike Bordin (b. 27 November 1962, San Francisco, California, USA; drums) and Chuck Mosley (vocals). Böttum had attended the same school as Gould, while Bordin was recruited from his course in tribal rhythm at Berkeley University. Gould had met Mosley on the Los Angeles club circuit in 1980, while Martin had been recommended by Metallica's Cliff Burton. This line-up recorded a low-budget, self-titled debut on the independent Mordam label, followed by the groundbreaking *Introduce Yourself* on Slash, a subsidiary of Warner Brothers Records. It encompassed a variety of styles but exuded a rare warmth and energy, mainly through Mosley's melodramatic vocals, and was well received by the critics (not least for the signature tune 'We Care A Lot'). However, internal disputes led to the firing of Mosley on the eve of widespread press coverage and favourable live reviews, although it had been reported that the band underwent a period when every single member walked out at some point. Mosley went on to gig temporarily with Bad Brains, before putting together his own band, Cement. Against the odds, his replacement, Mike Patton (b. 27 January 1968, Eureka, California, USA), was even more flamboyant and actually more accomplished as a singer (it was also rumoured that Courtney Love of Hole auditioned/rehearsed with the group). *The Real Thing*, the album that followed Patton's recruitment, was a runaway success, with the single 'Epic' reaching number 9 on the *Billboard* chart in June 1990, and denting the UK Top 40. Their style was now both offbeat and unpredictable, yet retained enough melody to remain a commercial proposition. Despite the universal adulation, however, it transpired that offstage, there was still a great deal of acrimony between the band members. *Live At The Brixton Academy* was released as a stop-gap affair, while the band toured for nearly three years on the back of the worldwide success of their most recent studio album. After Patton temporarily defected back to his original, pre-Faith No More outfit, Mr. Bungle, the group finally returned with *Angel Dust*. A tougher, less accessible record, in keeping with the group's origins (despite a cover version of the Commodores' 'I'm Easy', which reached UK number 3 in January 1993), it made the US Top 10 and UK number 2 as their commercial ascent continued. However, in 1994, following a good deal of press speculation, the ever-volatile line-up of Faith No More switched again as Jim Martin was ousted in favour of Trey Spruance, who had formerly worked in Mr. Bungle. Martin went on to form The Behemoth. Böttum formed Imperial Teen as a side project in 1996. *Album Of The Year* received a mixed reaction, including one or two scathing reviews. The same year they collaborated with Sparks on a bizarre reworking of the latter's 'This Town Ain't Big Enough For The Both Of Us'. In April 1998, they announced that they were disbanding.

● ALBUMS: *Faith No More* (Mordam 1984)★★, *Introduce Yourself* (Slash 1987)★★★★, *The Real Thing* (Slash/Reprise 1989)★★★★, *Live At The Brixton Academy* (Slash/London 1991)★★★, *Angel Dust* (Slash/Reprise 1992)★★, *King For A Day ... Fool For A Lifetime* (Slash/Reprise 1995)★★★, *Album Of The Year* (Slash/Reprise 1997)★★.
● COMPILATIONS: *Who Cares A Lot?* (Slash/Reprise 1998)★★★.
● VIDEOS: *Live At Brixton* (London 1990), *Who Cares A Lot?: The Greatest Videos* (London 1998).
● FURTHER READING: *Faith No More: The Real Story*, Steffan Chirazi.

Faithless

This unusual dance music outfit is formed around the nucleus of Rollo, one of the prime movers in the UK house scene, and Sister Bliss, one of the most successful and respected female DJs. It is truly an eclectic collaboration, with both Sister Bliss and Rollo being innovative and highly-skilled programmers and producers. They are joined by rapper Maxi Jazz, singer/writer instrumentalist Jamie Catto (who is from a folk background), and guitarist Dave Randall. It is perhaps this unique blend of skills and styles and the band's relentless global touring that has enabled Faithless' gradual but assured rise to critical and commercial success. The band's debut single on Rollo's Cheeky Records, 'Salva Mea', can certainly be described as one of the decade's greatest and most influential house records. When it was first released in 1995, it made a fleeting appearance in the UK Top 30 in August before disappearing by the following week. Its grass-roots popularity on the UK's dancefloors was emphatically confirmed when it shot straight into the UK's Top 10 upon its re-release in December 1996. It went on to sell over one million copies worldwide and its exhilarating pizzicato string sound has spawned countless imitators who have also achieved chart success using the 'Faithless sound', one notable example being Sash!'s 'Encore Une Fois'. Their debut *Reverence* was, like the band itself, a slow-burning phenomenon, initially not selling well. On the back of subsequent Top 10 singles and a double album of remix material, however, the album has now been certified gold in 22 countries. *Reverence* was refreshingly difficult to categorize as its tracks ranged from brooding, dub-influenced ruminations on urban life and relationships, through rap, more traditional love songs ('Don't Leave') to storming dancefloor epics, such as 'Salva Mea' and 'Insomnia'. Maxi Jazz's melodic, semi-whispered raps always add an intelligent and provocative edge to the soaring electronic sweeps created by Rollo and Sister Bliss. Since its release, the band have been nominated for and won many awards, including a European Grammy for Best International Dance Band. Critical accolades have included Michael Stipe of R.E.M. naming *Reverence* as his favourite album of the year. The band's second album, *Sunday 8pm*, saw them developing the more ambient, meditative element of their work but big-name DJ remixes (Paul Van Dyk, Robbie Rivera) of the singles ensured their sustained popularity in the clubs. The first single from the album, the provocatively titled 'God Is A DJ', was a UK Top 10 hit in 1998. Something of an anomaly in dance music, Faithless strive for originality in their sounds, intelligence in their lyrics as well as seeking to become a respected live band in the fullest sense of the word. In October 1998, they won the UK's *Muzik* magazine's award for the Best Live Act. Awards, critical plaudits and commercial success all form unequivocal confirmation that integrity and hard work are paying off for Faithless.

● ALBUMS: *Reverence* (Cheeky 1996)★★★, *Sunday 8pm* (Cheeky 1998)★★★★, *Saturday 3am* remix album (Cheeky 1999)★★★.

Falkner, Jason

b. 2 June 1970, Texas, USA. Before making his solo debut as the multi-instrumentalist and singer behind 1996's *Jason Falkner Presents Another Unknown*, Falkner had released records with three other groups. As a teenager he had answered a magazine advert to become guitarist with the cult 60s revivalists the Three O'Clock, contributing to their 1988 *Vermillion* set for Prince's Paisley Park label. He subsequently joined Jellyfish for 1990's critically acclaimed *Bellybutton*. Then, as the result of impromptu jamming sessions, Falkner became a member of the Grays, alongside Dan McCarroll (drums), Buddy Judge (vocals/guitar) and Jon Brion (vocals/guitar). Formed by accident, the band quickly became the subject of a minor bidding war amongst record labels, but their sole album *Ro Sham Bo* proved a disappointment. Nevertheless, it did contain the Falkner composition and minor hit 'Very Best Years', which presaged the style and sweep of his solo work. After the release of his 1996 debut he commented: 'It's something I've always wanted to do. I would do demos playing all the instruments. The album is really just an extension of the 4-tracks.' Falkner also worked with Eric Matthews on his acclaimed debut before releasing 1999's *Can You Still Feel?*, another minor masterpiece. The record bursts with hooks and changes laced with imaginative arrangements. Every pop ingredient was used, and although highly derivative and Beatlesque, tracks such as 'Revelation', 'The Plan' and 'Eloquence' deliver the 60s experience with great panache.

● ALBUMS: *Jason Falkner Presents Another Unknown* (Elektra 1996)★★★★, *Can You Still Feel?* (Elektra 1999)★★★★.

Farley And Heller

Respected UK dance music producers and remixers, Terry Farley and Pete Heller initially found success at the forefront of the Balearic/acid house scene in the UK in the early 90s. Londoner Farley was a fan of Studio One reggae and ska before becoming involved with the London soul club scene during the 80s, DJing alongside a youthful Paul Oakenfold. Heller grew up on the south coast of England and began his musical career by DJing in a Brighton discotheque, playing disco, hip-hop and house. A visit to Danny Rampling's legendary south London club, Shoom, opened a new chapter in his life. After playing warm-up sets for Rampling, Heller and Andrew Weatherall formed the *Boy's Own* collective, running a fanzine, Boy's Own club nights and eventually a

record label – Junior Boy's Own. It was during this period that Farley and Heller met and began remixing. Farley had already remixed the Happy Mondays' 'Wrote For Luck' with Oakenfold, as well as other tracks by that band and several by Primal Scream. His credibility as a producer-remixer was also enhanced by his work on the Farm's cover version of the Monkees' 'Stepping Stone' and the subsequent 'Groovy Train'. The productions' funky dance-influenced sound lent the band kudos at the height of the Manchester-based 'baggy' scene and helped to make 'Groovy Train' a UK Top 10 hit. Farley and Heller's initial productions as a team with Hugo Nicholson were released as Bocca Juniors. Since then, their remixing skills have been used by many artists including Michael Jackson, Jamiroquai, Sunscreem, K-Klass, Simply Red, New Order, U2, Janet Jackson, Boy George, and the Pet Shop Boys. They have also produced for Kylie Minogue. Their own productions have appeared under the name Fire Island and have been hugely popular on the club scene. As Fire Island, they covered Machine's 1979 classic 'There But For The Grace Of God'. Their 1997 recording 'Ultra Flava' was a huge hit in European clubs and Ibiza and eventually became a UK Top 40 hit when the vocals of Ultra Naté were added. In 1999, Heller's track 'Big Love' was signed to Pete Tong's London Records and quickly became ubiquitous on European dancefloors (especially those in Ibiza) before entering the UK charts at number 12. Building on their reputation as excellent club DJs, they also mixed *Late Night Sessions* for the Ministry Of Sound. In 2000, Farley began producing a fanzine called *Faith*, which featured a mix of music, politics and satire and was given away in hip London clothes and record stores.

● COMPILATIONS: *Journeys By DJ Volume 12 – Mixed By Farley And Heller* (JDJ 1997)★★★, *Late Night Sessions III* (MOS 1999)★★★★.

Farm

If perseverance warrants its own unique award, the Farm could have expected the equivalent of the Nobel Prize for their incessant efforts. Formed in 1983 by former youth worker Peter Hooton (b. 28 September 1962, Liverpool, England; vocals), Steve Grimes (b. 4 June 1962, Liverpool, England; guitar), Phillip Strongman (bass) and Andy McVann (drums), the Farm were to become synonymous with so many cultural 'scenes' over the ensuing years that their music was rendered almost irrelevant. For much of the 80s the band flirted with politics, tagged 'The Soul Of Socialism', encouraged the 'Scally' fashions of their Liverpool home-town, and maintained strong soccer interests - primarily through singer Peter Hooton's fanzine *The End*, a precursor to the explosion of football fanzines at the end of the decade. By 1984, John Melvin, George Maher, Steve Levy and Anthony Evans had joined, bringing with them a brass section and adding a northern soul influence to the Farm's unfashionable pop sound. Two years on, the line-up changed again when McVann was killed in a police car chase. He was replaced by Roy Boulter (b. 2 July 1964, Liverpool, England) and the line-up was bolstered by Keith Mullen (b. Bootle, England; guitar) and new bass player Carl Hunter (b. 14 April 1965, Bootle, England). The horn section departed and Ben Leach (b. 2 May 1969, Liverpool, England; keyboards) completed a new six-piece collective that was destined to change the Farm's fortunes. After the synth-pop flop of their fourth independent release, 'Body And Soul', the

Farm started their own Produce label and had a fortuitous meeting with in-vogue dance music producer Terry Farley (of Farley And Heller). Consequently, a cover version of the Monkees' 'Stepping Stone' was augmented with fashionable club beats and samples and, come 1990, the Farm suddenly found themselves caught up in the Madchester 'baggy' boom. The anthemic 'Groovy Train' and 'All Together Now', (the latter incorporating a sample of the seventeenth-century composer Johann Pachelbel's 'Canon And Gigue'), swept the band into the Top 10 of the UK charts, to be followed in 1991 by their debut album, *Spartacus*, entering the UK charts at number 1. If these placings were not proof enough of the Farm's new-found fame, the next achievement certainly was: the band's football connection was sealed when toy manufacturers Subbuteo designed a unique team-kit, just for the band. Later they also had the great honour of playing, alongside frequent collaborator Pete Wylie, Ian McCulloch and Gerry Marsden, to 15,000 Liverpool soccer fans for the 'Last Night Of The Kop', before Liverpool FC's legendary terrace was demolished. However, as the UK media tired of the 'baggy' sound, so a decline in the Farm's fortunes set in. *Love See No Colour* was bland and, indeed, colourless. Few bands can have gone with such velocity from an album that entered the UK charts at number 1 to one that failed to break the Top 75. The blame lay in some outrageous squandering of the money earned through their debut album, and a total lack of direction in the songwriting. The band's new contract with Sony (which fostered their own End Product label) was over as quickly as it had started (although an ill-judged attempt in 1992 at the Human League's 'Don't You Want Me Baby' reached the Top 20). Help, surprisingly, came from the USA, where Seymour Stein of Sire Records saw some remaining commercial potential in the band. In 1994, they adopted a more orthodox guitar/bass/drums approach for their parting shot, *Hullabaloo*.

● ALBUMS: *Spartacus* (Produce 1991)★★★★, *Love See No Colour* (End Product 1992)★★, *Hullabaloo* (Sire 1994)★★★.
● COMPILATIONS: *The Best Of The Farm* (Castle 1998)★★★.
● VIDEOS: *Groovy Times* (Produce 1991).

Fastball

Based in Austin, Texas, USA, alternative rock trio Fastball comprises Miles Zuniga (vocals/guitar), Tony Scalzo (vocals/bass) and Joey Shuffield (drums). Previously Shuffield and Zuniga had been members of pop/rock band Big Car, who released one album, *Normal*, for Giant Records in 1992. However, that band disintegrated owing to record company problems, and the duo began playing with Scalzo through their mutual membership of Austin singer-songwriter Beaver Nelson's backing band. The trio originally adopted the name Magneto U.S.A., before changing their title to Fastball. A series of local gigs brought rave reviews in *The Austin Chronicle*, leading to Fastball dead-heating for the best pop band category at the 1995/6 Austin Music Awards. Enlisting the services of joint-manager Russel Carter (also in charge of Matthew Sweet and the Indigo Girls), they then signed a contract with Hollywood Records for the release of their debut album. *Make Your Mama Proud* was produced by Jerry Finn, who had previously worked with Rancid and Green Day, and faithfully recreated a stage show that matched energy with melodicism. In particular, the dual singing and writing roles of Zuniga and Scalzo drew initial comparisons with Fugazi, though in truth Fastball are a much more commercially orientated proposition. This was reinforced with 1998's exceptional *All The Pain Money Can Buy*. They had perfected the art of the snappy pop song, with every track bouncing along. Success came with 'The Way', a hypnotic track that created further interest when they reached the top of the alternative singles chart in the USA. The song also charted at number 21 in the UK in September.

● ALBUMS: *Make Your Mama Proud* (Hollywood 1996)★★★, *All The Pain Money Can Buy* (Hollywood 1998)★★★★.

Fat Joe

b. Joseph Cartagena, Bronx, New York, USA. As a youth coming of age in the harsh atmosphere of the South Bronx, Joey Cartagena was profoundly affected by the tapes of Zulu Nation hip-hop parties brought home by his older brother Angel. Shortly thereafter he was making his own local reputation as a graffiti artist (he still maintains strong ties with Bronx-based TATS crew) under the *nom de guerre* of Joey Crack, and as the nickname implies, he also made a reputation in the narcotics trade. He eventually parlayed these multiple sources of street credibility into a record deal with Relativity Records, releasing his debut *Represent* under the new-found persona of Fat Joe Da Gangsta, and promptly scored a *Billboard* number 1 rap single in 'Flow Joe'. The debut's combination of ruthless realism and sterling production, furnished mostly by fellow Bronx residents DITC crew, garnered considerable attention and numerous fans, although a certain inconsistency of lyrical content engendered rumours that Joe was not always writing his own rhymes. The 1995 follow-up *Jealous One's Envy* addressed these criticisms in no uncertain terms while largely maintaining the winning formula; a hustler's-eye view of reality backed by unassailable hardcore production (provided by DJ Premier among others). This period found Joe building alliances and broadening his appeal somewhat, appearing with LL Cool J on 'I Shot Ya' and with Raekwon on 'Firewater'. Similar power-moves resulted in the formation of his own Mystic imprint and a distribution-deal with Big Beat/Atlantic Records for the 1998 release of *Don Cartagena*. Although this latest incarnation of Fat Joe hardly abandoned the gangsta image, it did mark an increase in social consciousness purportedly inspired by a meeting with Nation Of Islam leader Louis Farrakhan, whose influence can be heard in the twin strains of cultural nationalism and conspiracy theory running through 'The Hidden Hand'. Living up to the mantle of 'don' assumed with that record, Joe began grooming a right hand man of comparable stature (Big Punisher), and placed himself at the helm of a group of younger artists (the Terror Squad). Like their mentor, both acts reached the upper tiers of the US charts with their respective debuts.

● ALBUMS: as Fat Joe Da Gangsta *Represent* (Relativity 1993)★★★★, *Jealous One's Envy* (Relativity 1995)★★★, *Don Cartagena* (Big Beat/Atlantic 1998)★★★.

Fatboy Slim

A man of many musical faces, Norman Cook's Fatboy Slim is arguably his most successful alter ego, and one which made big beat music (a combination of rock and dance music styles) a huge crossover success. Cook began recording in the big beat style at the Big Beat Boutique (from which the movement took its name). Signing to Damian Harris' Skint Records, Fatboy Slim's debut single was 'Santa Cruz', and was followed by further hit records including 'Everybody Needs A 303' and the debut album *Better Living Through Chemistry*. 'Going Out Of My Head', the March 1997 single featuring samples of the Who, gained Cook a place in the *Guinness Book Of Records* for achieving the most UK Top 40 hits under different names (seven). The irresistible 'The Rockafeller Skank' brightened up the UK singles chart the following year, reaching number 6 in June. 'Gangster Trippin' provided Cook with another hit single, reaching number 3 in October and paving the way for *You've Come A Long Way, Baby*. 'Praise You' provided Cook with his first UK number 1 single in January 1999, and in the process dragged the album to the top of the charts. 'Right Here Right Now' was another hit, debuting at number 2 in April. *You've Come A Long Way, Baby* also enjoyed crossover success in the USA, thanks to the prominent use of several tracks in movies including *She's All That* and *Cruel Intentions*, and advertisements for Adidas. Cook was honoured with three MTV Video Awards in September.

● ALBUMS: *Better Living Through Chemistry* (Skint 1996)★★★, *You've Come A Long Way, Baby* (Skint 1998)★★★★.

● COMPILATIONS: *On The Floor At The Boutique Mixed By Fatboy Slim* (Skint Brassic 1998)★★★, shared with Pete Tong, Paul Oakenfold *Essential Millennium* (ffrr 1999)★★★★.

Fatima Mansions

A category-defying band formed in August 1989 by Cork singer Cathal Coughlan, fresh from his stint with the more restrained Microdisney, with the inspiration for the new name coming from a decrepit Dublin housing estate. They were almost immediately ensconced in a London studio with Kitchenware Records to record their debut album. *Against Nature* was released in September 1989 to almost universal critical acclaim and a large degree of astonishment; 'staggering in its weight of ideas . . . never loses its capacity to suddenly stun you', stated the *New Musical Express*. Its abrasive lyrics might have been anticipated given Coughlan's pedigree, but the directness of the musical attack certainly was not. Andreas O'Gruama's guitar contributed richly to the final results, although the Fatima Mansions served primarily as a vehicle for its singer and songwriter. It was followed by 'Blues For Ceausescu', a fire and brimstone political tirade that held prophetic warnings of East European tragedy. Its operatic tilt enabled it to be at once hysterical, comic and sinister. Coughlan was now established in the press as a delicious anti-hero and mischief maker. *Bugs Fucking Bunny* was dropped as the title of the second album, in favour of the comparatively nondescript *Viva Dead Ponies*. This time Coughlan's lyrics were totally submerged in vitriolic observations on the absurdities of living in the UK. The title track, for instance, considered the case of Jesus being reincarnated as a Jewish shopkeeper. A particular vehemence, as ever, was reserved for British imperialism. It prompted the *Guardian* newspaper to describe Coughlan as 'the most underrated lyricist in pop today', while John Peel confirmed he could 'listen to Cathal Coughlan sing the phone book'. Further paranoia, bile and doses of his full-bodied vocal were poured in to the mini-album *Bertie's*

Brochures, in 1991. Notable among its eight tracks was a full-scale assassination of R.E.M.'s 'Shiny Happy People'. The title track this time referred to an Irish artist wrongly imprisoned for terrorism, coinciding with highly topical, real-life events. In 1992, Coughlan managed to alienate a Milan audience ostensibly there to see headliners U2, by attempting to insert a Virgin Mary shampoo holder into his anus whilst singing 'fuck the Pope, I want to fuck your traitor Pope'. After a sojourn in Newcastle Coughlan returned in 1994 with the release of *Lost In The Former West*, which again identified him as the sort of left-field maverick genius who makes the broad church of pop music infinitely more entertaining than it might otherwise be. The only thing holding him back are the minuscule sales figures that have been his curse since Microdisney days. Coughlan also recorded two self-indulgent albums under the banner of Bubonique (including contributions from Irish comedian Sean Hughes), before releasing his debut solo album in 1996.

● ALBUMS: *Against Nature* (Kitchenware 1989)★★★, *Viva Dead Ponies* (Kitchenware 1990)★★★★, *Bertie's Brochures* mini-album (Kitchenware 1991)★★★, *Valhalla Avenue* (Kitchenware 1992)★★★★, *Lost In The Former West* (Radioactive 1994)★★★. Solo: Cathal Coughlan as Bubonique *20 Golden Showers* (Kitchenware 1993)★★, as Bubonique *Trance Arse Volume 3* (Kitchenware 1995)★★, *The Grand Necropolitan* (Kitchenware 1996)★★★.

● COMPILATIONS: *Come Back My Children* (Kitchenware 1992)★★★.

● VIDEOS: *Y'Knaa* (1994).

Faze Action

Faze Action is the recording name of brothers Simon and Robin Lee (b. Amersham, Buckinghamshire, England). Signed to the influential London-based label, Nuphonic, their sound has disco as its foundation but also draws heavily on Latin, jazz, African music, funk and, notably, classical elements. Robin taught himself to play bass guitar when he was 15, and went on to study music at London's Goldsmith's College, specialising in Asian folk and classical composition. While Robin taught English in Japan, Simon worked in various London record shops, indulging his interest in early 80s New York disco. They collaborated on tracks, despite the geographical divide, by sending material via e-mail. Their first single for Nuphonic, 'Original Disco Motion', became a cult classic in the UK and was played by many influential DJs. The second single, 1996's 'In The Trees', was noteworthy for its funky, bass-driven groove and soaring cello melody. It became an instant dancefloor classic and appeared on several compilation albums. The track's success led to remix work for artists such as Yellow Sox, Diana Brown, D*Note and Saint Etienne among others. Faze Action's debut, *Plans And Designs* was highly acclaimed; its uncompromising progressiveness was compared to Talking Heads' art school funk and the electronic disco of François Kevorkian and bands such as D-Train and Dinosaur L. The album was distinctive for its use of classical instrumentation such as strings and timpani drums alongside disco and house rhythm sections. *Moving Cities* continued in such an eclectic vein but more obviously embraced Latin and African influences. Drummer Zeke Manyika (ex-Orange Juice; Style Council) contributed African chants and percussion to four tracks. Faze Action have developed a live dimension to their music, appearing as a six-piece band on BBC television and at numerous clubs and festivals including

Homelands and superclub Cream's Creamfields in 1998 and 1999. Like Groove Armada, Faze Action are sophisticated musicians: reverential to their disco heritage but unafraid to find inspiration in any interesting musical form.

● ALBUMS: *Plans And Designs* (Nuphonic 1997)★★★★, *Moving Cities* (Nuphonic/Warners 1999)★★★★.

Fear Factory

This Los Angeles, California-based band are one of the few truly innovative acts in death metal, mixing industrial-style electronic rhythms and samples with grinding guitars and harsh vocals to create their own brutal soundscape. Formed in late 1991 with the line-up of Burton C. Bell (vocals), Dino Cazares (guitar, who has an additional side project, Brujeria), Andrew Shives (bass) and Raymond Herrera (drums), the band rapidly made an impact with two tracks on the *LA Death Metal* compilation, produced by Faith No More bass player Bill Gould, and subsequently signed to Roadrunner Records. The Colin Richardson-produced *Soul Of A New Machine* established Fear Factory as a genuine death metal force, with a good collection of songs delivered with originality and ferocity. Meanwhile, the band set about developing their live show on their debut tour with Brutal Truth in Europe, followed by US dates with Sick Of It All and Biohazard. *Fear Is The Mind Killer*, a mini-album of remixes by Canadian industrialists Front Line Assembly, demonstrated further dimensions and possibilities available to the Factory sound by adding an industrial dance edge, bringing the band further acclaim. The band also found a permanent bass player with the addition of Belgian Christian Olde Wolbers. *Demanufacture* was produced by Colin Richardson, but the band were unhappy with the final mix and invited Rhys Fulbert (Front Line Assembly) and Greg Reely (Front Line Assembly, Skinny Puppy) to remix it to reflect the futuristic atmosphere they desired. The bonus tracks on one of the CD formats included a cover version of Agnostic Front's 'Your Mistake', with Madball's Freddy Cricien guesting on vocals. Press response ranked it alongside Therapy?'s *Infernal Love* and White Zombie's *Astro Creep 2000* as one of the definitive noise albums of 1995. In the meantime, singer Bell found work as the vocalist on Black Sabbath bass player Geezer Butler's GZR project. Following a remix album in 1997, the band returned in 1998 with the brutal metal noisefest *Obsolete*. They also gained extensive US radio play for one of their b-sides, a cover version of Gary Numan's 'Cars'.

● ALBUMS: *Soul Of A New Machine* (Roadrunner 1992)★★★, *Fear Is The Mind Killer* mini-album (Roadrunner 1993)★★★, *Demanufacture* (Roadrunner 1995)★★★★, *Remanufacture (Cloning Technology)* (Roadrunner 1997)★★★, *Obsolete* (Roadrunner 1998)★★★★.

Feeder

Highly fêted UK alternative rock band Feeder were formed in 1995 by sound engineer Grant Nicholas (b. Newport, Wales; guitar/vocals) and Jon Lee (b. Newport, Wales; drums), who had previously played together in Reel and Rain Dancer. They were joined by Taka Hirose (b. Nagoya, Japan; bass), and began playing under the name of Real. After signing to the Echo label later the same year, the trio changed their name to Feeder and played their first gig in Yeovil, Somerset on 25 May. The band released their debut *Two Colours* EP in November 1995, and built up a substantial live reputation as a support act for Terrorvision and Reef. An acclaimed six-track mini-album, *Swim*, followed in June 1996, but their early singles 'Stereo World' (October 1996), 'Tangerine' (February 1997), 'Cement' (April 1997, UK number 49) and 'Crash' (August 1997, UK number 41) made little progress in the charts. A new song, the dramatically charged 'High', gained heavy airplay on mainstream radio, and entered the UK charts at number 24 in October 1997, with the band finally looking like achieving the success their highly melodic guitar rock deserved. 'High' was included on a reformatted version of their debut long-player *Polythene*, originally released in May 1997. An excellent collection of post-grunge alternative rock, the album saw the band receiving further high praise from the music press. They returned in March 1999 with a new single, 'Day In Day Out', followed by the supercharged 'Insomnia' and *Yesterday Went Too Soon*.

● ALBUMS: *Swim* mini-album (Echo 1996)★★★, *Polythene* (Echo 1997)★★★★, *Yesterday Went Too Soon* (Echo 1999)★★★.

Felix

b. Essex, England. UK house artist and alleged former tax inspector Felix represented something of an enigma - never talking to the press or appearing in his videos. He even took the stage at the DMC awards sporting a lion suit. However, his anonymity was not helped by the massive success of singles like 'Don't You Want Me' and 'It Will Make Me Crazy', which sold nearly two million copies between them worldwide. Both predicted the rise of trance and hard house.

● ALBUMS: *#1* (Deconstruction 1993)★★★.

Felix Da Housecat

b. Felix Stallings, Chicago, Illinois, USA. The childhood friend of house legend DJ Pierre, Stallings' youth was spent experimenting with electronic musical equipment. He taught himself keyboards by the age of 14, and a year later stepped into a studio for the first time. An early tape had been passed on to the elder Pierre by a mutual playground acquaintance. Intrigued, he decided to record it properly, and from those sessions 'Phantasy Girl' emerged. Based on the original keyboard motif from the demo tape, it became one of house music's biggest early cult smashes. Felix went on to release a steady stream of dance music vinyl, establishing his name alongside that of Pierre, who remained his mentor. Unfortunately, as school ended so did his parents' tolerance of his extra-curricular pursuits, and he was ordered to attend college in Alabama. Three years later he returned to Chicago, taking up the house mantle once again. Numerous releases followed on all the major imprints: Strictly Rhythm Records, Guerilla Records ('Thee Dawn'), Nervous Records, D-Jax Up, Chicago Underground and Freetown. He also set up his own Radikal Fear Records imprint, which has released classic cuts by the likes of DJ Sneak, Armando, and Mike Dunn, and provided remixes for mainstream artists such as Diana Ross and Kylie Minogue. Under the title Thee Madkatt Courtship he also provided a long player for Deep Distraxion, while as Afrohead he proffered 'In The Garden', a classic cut, much revered by DJ's such as Darren Emerson. After a lengthy break from the dance scene, Stallings returned in 1999 under his Thee Madkatt Courtship moniker with *I Know Electrikboy*.

● ALBUMS: as Thee Madkatt Courtship *Alone In The Dark* (Deep

Distraxion 1995)★★★, *Metropolis Present Day? Thee Album* (Radikal Fear 1998)★★★, as Thee Madkatt Courtship III *I Know Electrikboy* (London 1999)★★★.
● COMPILATIONS: *Felix Da Housecat's Clashbakk Compilation Mix* (Livewire 1999)★★★★.

Field Mice

Formed in Surrey, England, in 1987 by principal songwriter Robert Wratten (b. 5 August 1966, Carshalton, Surrey, England; guitar/vocals) and Mark Dobson (b. 27 April 1965, Hartlepool, England; drums), the Field Mice linked up with Bristol-based Sarah Records for a series of records that unwittingly pigeonholed both band and label as exponents of whimsical, sensitive pop songs. With the label's initial independent idealism - which manifested itself in seven inch-only releases in the era of 12-inch singles and compact disc singles - merely adding fire to cynics' vitriol. The Field Mice established a small yet fanatical following that spread as far as Japan, by virtue of gently struck acoustic guitars and lyrics of the decidedly lovelorn variety. The line-up was expanded by the arrival of labelmate Harvey Williams (b. 31 December 1965, Cornwall, England; guitar), who had previously worked under the name Another Sunny Day. It was unfortunate that the prejudice of the music business ensured that the Field Mice remained condemned to the periphery even though the band were furthering their eclectic tastes by developing a penchant for danceable electronics ('Triangle') and experimental noise ('Humblebee'). This was in spite of contemporary crossover outfit Saint Etienne taking the Field Mice into the nation's clubs by covering the band's 'Let's Kiss And Make Up' single. In 1990, the trio became a quintet with the arrival of Michael Hiscock (b. 24 February 1966, Carshalton, Surrey, England; bass) and Annemari Davies (b. 9 February 1971, Oxfordshire, England; guitar/keyboards). Having previously only issued material on 7-inch and mini-albums (including the 10-inch *Snowball*), it was not until 1991 that the band released their first full albums. The first, *Coastal*, was a retrospective and *For Keeps*, a mature collection that promised much in the future. However, after the release of the acclaimed 'Missing The Moon', the Field Mice's frustrating reluctance to pursue a potentially rewarding higher profile, and a growing estrangement with their label, eventually led to the band dissolving in November 1991. Wratten resurfaced in the late-90s as part of the Trembling Blue Stars.
● ALBUMS: *Snowball* mini-album (Sarah 1989)★★★, *Skywriting* (Sarah 1990)★★★, *For Keeps* (Sarah 1991)★★★.
● COMPILATIONS: *Coastal* (Sarah 1991)★★★, *Where'd You Learn To Kiss That Way?* (Shinkansen 1998)★★★★.

Filter

Brian Liesegang (programming, guitar, keyboards, drums) and Richard Patrick (vocals, guitar, bass, programming, drums, ex-Nine Inch Nails) first hatched the idea of working together during a cross-country trek when they visited the Grand Canyon. Patrick had already been experimenting on an eight-track console in his parents' basement in Cleveland, Ohio, USA. Liesegang, meanwhile, had just finished a degree in philosophy and turned his hand to music himself, experimenting in his own small electronic studio, which was adjacent to that owned by Robert A. Moog (originator of the Moog synthesizer). Occupying his time by investigating the world of computers and their applications to music, he found what he describes as a 'perfect musical match' in Patrick. Both were interested in producing hard electronic music. The line-up of the band was completed for touring purposes by Geno Lenardo (guitar), Matt Walker (drums) and Frank Cavanaugh (bass). *Short Bus* was co-produced by Ben Gross (Jane's Addiction, Red Hot Chili Peppers), while the single 'Hey Man Nice Shot' became a staple of college radio. Walker left the band to join the Smashing Pumpkins in August 1996. Liesegang also abandoned the band in September 1997 to pursue a solo career. The same year, Patrick contributed '(Can't You) Trip Like I Do', a collaboration with the Crystal Method, to the soundtrack of the movie *Spawn*. The second Filter album, *Title Of Record*, eventually appeared two years later, featuring a backing band comprising Cavanaugh, Lenardo and drummer Steve Gillis.
● ALBUMS: *Short Bus* (Reprise/Warners 1995)★★★, *Title Of Record* (Reprise/Warners 1999)★★★.

Finn, Neil

b. 27 May 1958, Te Awamutu, New Zealand. Finn's reputation as one of New Zealand's leading songwriters was confirmed when he was awarded an OBE in 1993, in recognition of his work with Split Enz and Crowded House. Following the latter band's emotional farewell performance in Sydney on 24 November 1996, Finn set about recording his debut solo outing for Parlophone Records. The presence of producers Nigel Godrich (Radiohead, Beck, Natalie Imbruglia) and Marius De Vries (Björk, Madonna) added a richer atmosphere to Finn's tuneful pop melodies. Despite living in the UK and having to contribute his mixes by ISDN, Godrich added weight to the album's standout tracks, 'Sinner' and 'Twisty Bass'. De Fries joined Finn in New Zealand to add his peculiar variety of computer wizardry to the sessions. Guest musicians on the album included guitarist Jim Moginie (Midnight Oil), bass player Sebastian Steinberg (Soul Coughing) and producer Mitchell Froom, with Finn's son contributing drums to two tracks. The Crowded House soundalike, 'She Will Have Her Way', dented the UK charts at number 26 in June 1998. The album enjoyed more commercial success, entering the UK chart at number 5 the same month, but follow-up singles failed to break into the UK Top 30.
● ALBUMS: *Try Whistling This* (Parlophone 1998)★★★.

Firm

The Brooklyn, New York, USA-based rappers Nas, Foxy Brown, AZ and Cormega formed this hip-hop supergroup, although the latter was replaced by Nas associate Nature before the release of their self-titled 1997 debut. With three of the rap scene's biggest stars involved the project generated a huge amount of interest. Brown enjoyed huge success, but became an instant enemy of the moral majority, with the previous year's *Ill Na Na*. Nas was declared the future of the New York scene following the release of his *Illmatic* and *It Was Written* albums, while AZ scored a crossover hit single with 'Sugar Hill' from 1995's *Doe Or Die*. Their collaboration was delayed by various commitments, but the finished product, with production shared by Dr. Dre and the Trackmasterz, was finally released in October 1997. Although a host of other rappers including Pretty Boy, Wizard, Canibus, Noreaga and Half-A-Mil cropped up at various points, the album's celebration of the gangster lifestyle was very much the work of its co-creators. Inspired by the Mafia, the album celebrated the twin themes of violence and blatant carnality with a provocative zeal.

● ALBUMS: *The Firm* (Aftermath 1997)★★★.

Fish

b. Derek William Dick, 25 April 1958, Dalkeith, Edinburgh, Scotland. Fish acquired his nickname from a landlord who objected to the lengthy periods he spent in the bath. He sang for Nottingham band the Stone Dome before auditioning for progressive rockers Marillion by writing lyrics for their instrumental, 'The Web'. The band established a strong following through constant touring, before releasing their debut single 'Market Square Heroes'. Fish's bombastic vocals, markedly similar to Peter Gabriel, strengthened critics' arguments that Marillion were mere Genesis copyists. Despite this, Marillion went from strength to strength, with Fish structuring a series of elaborately linked concept albums that were still capable of yielding UK hit singles including 'Garden Party' and the melodic ballad 'Kayleigh', which reached number 2 in May 1985. His lyrics were strongly influenced in style and content by the work of Peter Hammill, former leader of progressive 70s band Van Der Graaf Generator, a debt he acknowledged by inviting Hammill to be special guest on Marillion's 1983 tour of Britain. After the success of 1987's *Clutching At Straws*, he began to disagree with the rest of the band about their musical direction and left in 1988 to embark on a solo career; he was replaced by Steve Hogarth. Fish's debut solo album utilized stylistically diverse elements such as folk tunes and brass arrangements, as shown on the UK number 25 single 'Big Wedge', but he also retained a mixture of hard rockers and ballads. In 1989, he worked with Hammill on his opera, *The Fall Of The House Of Usher*, but their voices clashed and Fish was replaced on the project by Andy Bell. A more successful collaboration was the single 'Shortcut To Somewhere', recorded with Genesis keyboard player Tony Banks in 1986. His 1993 release was a desultory album of cover versions, including the Kinks' 'Apeman' and the Moody Blues' 'Question'. Far more satisfying was his 1995 duet with Sam Brown on 'Just Good Friends', and 1997's *Sunsets On Empire* helped to further restore favour. After struggling for several years with his own Dick Bros label Fish signed to Roadrunner Records, celebrating with the typically bombastic *Raingods With Zippos*.

● ALBUMS: *Vigil In A Wilderness Of Mirrors* (EMI 1990)★★, *Internal Exile* (Polydor 1991)★★, *Songs From The Mirror* (Polydor 1993)★, *Sushi* (Dick Bros 1994)★★★, *Acoustic Session* (Dick Bros 1994)★★★, *Suits* (Dick Bros 1994)★★, *Sunsets On Empire* (Dick Bros 1997)★★★★, *Fortunes Of War* (Dick Bros 1998)★★★, *Raingods With Zippos* (Roadrunner 1999)★★★.

● COMPILATIONS: *Yin* (Dick Bros 1995)★★★, *Yan* (Dick Bros 1995)★★★, *Kettle Of Fish '88-'98* (Roadrunner 1998)★★★.

Fishbone

Funk metal hybrid from Los Angeles, USA who never managed to achieve the commercial success that their reputation deserved. Five of the seven band members met through the Los Angeles School Bussing Program, a scheme that encouraged black and white children to visit each other's schools. Although their recorded output is sparse given their

longevity, their hard political edge and high-octane rhythmic onslaught is every bit as deserving of mass attention as the Red Hot Chili Peppers or Living Colour. Their line-up boasts Chris 'Maverick Meat' Dowd (b. Christopher Gordon Dowd, 20 September 1965, Las Vegas, Nevada, USA; trombone, keyboards), 'Dirty' Walter Kibby (b. Walter Adam Kibby II, 13 November 1964, Columbus, Ohio, USA; trumpet, horn, vocals), 'Big' John Bigham (b. 3 March 1969, Lidsville, USA), Kendall Jones (b. Kendall Rey Jones, USA; guitar), Philip 'Fish' Fisher (b. 16 July 1967, El Camino, Los Angeles, California, USA; drums), John Fisher (b. John Norwood Fisher, 9 December 1965, El Camino, Los Angeles, California, USA; bass) and Angelo Moore (b. Angelo Christopher Moore, 5 November 1965, USA; lead vocals). Norwood was stabbed on stage early in their career when Fishbone played alongside hardcore bands such as the Dead Kennedys (the influence of Bad Brains is obvious in their output). After a debut mini-album, the production expertise of David Kahne saw them touch on a more conventional metal direction, before exposing their true talents for the first time on *Truth And Soul*. This was helped in no small part by the airplay success of a cover version of Curtis Mayfield's 'Freddie's Dead'. Subsequent recordings saw Fishbone branching out and working with rap artists such as the Jungle Brothers, although *The Reality Of My Own Surroundings* had more in common with the hard-spined funk of Sly Stone. 'Fight The Youth' and 'Sunless Saturday' demonstrated a serious angle with socio-political, anti-racist and anti-drug lyrics, in contrast to their lighter side on the humorous 'Naz-Tee May'en'. Fishbone's live shows continued to sell out without a hit to be seen, and Moore caused a minor sensation by ending a London show naked but for his saxophone. However, just as transatlantic commercial success beckoned with the *Give A Monkey* ... set, bizarre press stories began to circulate concerning the activities of Jones, who, at the instigation of his father, had left the flock to join a religious cult. The band, whom he had renounced, were accused of attempted kidnap in their attempts to retrieve him. Appearing on 1993's Lollapalooza tour failed to restore their diminishing reputation, as did a lacklustre new album in 1996, although they remained a popular live draw.

● ALBUMS: *Fishbone* mini-album (Columbia 1985)★★, *In Your Face* (Columbia 1986)★★, *Truth And Soul* (Columbia 1988)★★★★, *The Reality Of My Surroundings* (Columbia 1991)★★★, *Give A Monkey A Brain And He'll Swear He's The Centre Of The Universe* (Columbia 1993)★★★, *Chim Chim's Badass Revenge* (Rowdy 1996)★★★.

● COMPILATIONS: *Singles* (Sony Japan 1993)★★★, *Fishbone 101 - Nuttasaurusmeg Fossil Fuelin'* (Columbia/Legacy 1996)★★★.

Fisher, Cevin

b. 26 October 1963, East Orange, New Jersey, USA. Although he only made an impact in the late 90s with his club hits 'The Freaks Come Out', 'The Way We Used To', and '(You Got Me) Burning Up', Fisher has been involved with the music industry since leaving high school. He spent his formative years going to all-night parties in his native New Jersey run by Tony Humphries. He took to DJing and eventually picked up production work for Timmy Regisford at Motown Records. He was incorporated into Arthur Baker's production team at Shakedown Studios, where he worked on remixes for Chaka Khan ('Love You All My Lifetime') and Quincy Jones ('I'll Be Good To You') – both of which were number 1s on the *Billboard* dance chart. As house music developed, Fisher was instrumental in developing the sound, writing 'Hands On Love' and 'House Is A Feeling' for the New York-based independent label, Hardtrax. In 1996, he released 'The Way We Used To' and 'Check This Out' on the Maxi label which were dancefloor hits in the USA and UK, particularly at the Twilo and the Ministry Of Sound. His EPs *Shine The Light/New York, New York* and *I Want Music/Lead Me To The Mountain Top* were international club hits and played by influential DJs such as Frankie Knuckles, Terry Farley, Junior Vasquez and David Morales among others. It was 1998's 'The Freaks Come Out' that made Fisher's name in the UK, championed by BBC Radio 1 DJs Pete Tong and Danny Rampling, licensed by the Ministry Of Sound record label and featured on many mix compilation albums, including the Ministry's *Annual IV*. The same year Fisher provided vocals for Danny Tenaglia's *Tourism*, repaying a favour to the man who had first convinced him to record his own material. In January 1999, '(You Got Me) Burning Up', sampling Loleatta Holloway's 'Love Sensation' (the same track used by Black Box for their 1989 UK number 1 'Ride On Time'), received extensive radio airplay, notably from Radio 1's Dave Pearce and was yet another smash hit in the clubs. Fisher continues to DJ in Europe, Asia and the USA and holds a residency at the D! Club in Geneva, Switzerland.

Five

British quintet who enjoyed widespread success in the late 90s with their polished hip-hop inspired sound. Richard Neville (b. 23 August 1979, Birmingham, West Midlands, England), Scott Robinson (b. 22 November 1979, Basildon, Essex, England), Richard Abidin Breen (b. 29 June 1979, Enfield, Middlesex, England), Jason 'J' Brown (b. 13 June 1976, Aldershot, England) and Sean Conlon (b. 20 May 1981, Leeds, England) were hand-picked from 3,000 hopefuls at an audition set up by the creators of the Spice Girls. The five members all boasted stage and music backgrounds. Neville and Robinson were, respectively, graduates of the National Youth Theatre and the Sylvia Young Stage School. Breen had attended the distinguished Italia Conti Stage School and built up experience as a DJ. Brown also worked as a DJ, while Conlon was a previous winner of Yamaha's Young Composer Of The Year award. Following in the footsteps of the Spice Girls, the band lived together in Surrey (later featuring unflatteringly in the ITV documentary series *Neighbours From Hell*). Intensive promotional work boosted the band's profile and resulted in a string of Top 10 UK hits. The debut single 'Slam Dunk (Da Funk)' reached number 7 in December 1997, and was followed by 'When The Lights Go Out' (number 4, March 1998), 'Got The Feelin'' (number 3, June 1998), 'Everybody Get Up' (number 2, September 1998) and 'Until The Time Is Through' (number 2, November 1998). 'When The Lights Go Out' broke the band in the US, steadily climbing the *Billboard* chart before reaching a peak position of number 10 in August 1998. The follow-up, 'It's The Things You Do', failed to reach the American Top 50. The band's self-titled debut album was co-written and produced by Denniz Pop, Cutfather and Joe and Max Martin, and debuted at number one on the UK chart in June. It also broke into the US Top 30 the following year. They returned to the UK charts in July 1999 with the number 2 single, 'If

Ya Gettin' Down', and finally achieved the top slot in October with 'Keep On Movin''. The attendant *Invincible* was another mixed bag of surprisingly durable pop songs and weak ballads.

● ALBUMS: *Five* (RCA/Arista 1998)★★★, *Invincible* (RCA 1999)★★★.
● VIDEOS: *Five Inside* (BMG Video 1998).

Flaming Lips

Formed in Oklahoma City, Oklahoma, USA, the Flaming Lips won a deserved reputation in the 80s and 90s for their discordant, psychedelia-tinged garage rock, and have recorded a fine body of off-kilter and unpredictable work. They are led by lyricist, vocalist and guitarist Wayne Coyne (b. Wayne Ruby Coyne, 17 March 1965, Pittsburgh, Pennsylvania, USA), who started playing music during his high school days. Coyne was joined in the band by his brother, Mark Coyne, who is best remembered for his vocals on the debut album's 'My Own Planet'. Taking up the microphone following his brother's departure, Wayne Coyne fronted a line-up completed by Steven Drozd (b. Steven Gregory Drozd, 6 December 1969, Houston, Texas, USA; drums/vocals, replacing Richard English and Nathan Roberts), Ron Jones (b. Ronald Lee Jones, 26 November 1970, Angeles, Philippines; guitars/vocals) and Michael Ivins (b. Michael Lee Ivins, 17 March 1965, Omaha, Nebraska, USA; bass/vocals). John 'Dingus' Donahue, of Mercury Rev fame, was also a member during the sessions for *In A Priest Driven Ambulance*. In 1993, they played at the Reading Festival and toured with Porno For Pyros, Butthole Surfers and Stone Temple Pilots. They returned to Reading in 1994 to support the release of 'She Don't Use Jelly', which finally took off on MTV over the following year. This, combined with a storming appearance on the second stage at Lollapalooza, at last helped to build a substantial popular as well as critical following. A two-year break preceded the release of *Clouds Taste Metallic*, their seventh album, a typically confusing but arresting exercise in wide-eyed, skewed pop rock, akin to a restrained Pavement. Song titles such as 'Guy Who Got A Headache And Accidentally Saved The World' and 'Psychiatric Explorations Of The Fetus With Needles' continued the penchant for adolescent shock value. Guitarist Jones departed shortly after the album was released. Reduced to a trio, the band returned with *Zaireeka*, a defiantly uncommercial 'experiment in listener participation, using multiple sound sources', whereby four separate CDs needed to be played simultaneously to hear the final mix. *The Soft Bulletin* was a far more satisfying record, representing the perfect fusion of the band's experimental urges and pop instincts.

● ALBUMS: *The Flaming Lips* (Lovely Sorts Of Death 1985)★★★, *Hear It Is* (Pink Dust 1986)★★★, *Oh My Gawd!!! ...The Flaming Lips* (Restless 1987)★★★, *Telepathic Surgery* (Restless 1988)★★, *Live* cassette only (Lovely Sorts Of Death 1989)★★, *In A Priest Driven Ambulance* (Restless 1990)★★★, *Hit To Death In The Future Head* (Warners 1992)★★★, *Transmissions From The Satellite Heart* (Warners 1993)★★★, *Providing Needles For Your Balloons* (Warners 1995)★★, *Clouds Taste Metallic* (Warners 1995)★★★★, *Zaireeka* 4-CD set (Warners 1998)★★, *The Soft Bulletin* (Warners 1999)★★★★.
● COMPILATIONS: *A Collection Of Songs Representing An Enthusiasm For Recording ... By Amateurs ... Or The Accidental Career* (Restless 1998)★★★.

Flaming Stars

A raucous quintet formed in Camden, north London, England, in November 1994, the Flaming Stars took their name from an Elvis Presley movie. Initial media comparisons placed them within the doomed romantic tradition of Gallon Drunk or the Tindersticks - unsurprising, given vocalist/keyboard player Max Decharne's previous employment as Gallon Drunk's drummer. He had also been a member of the Earls Of Suave, from whom Paul Dempsey (bass), Johnny Johnson (guitar/harmonica) and Joe Whitney (drums) were also drawn. Johnson and Dempsey had previously also played with Thee Headcoats and the Stingrays. Mark Hosking was then drafted in to provide additional guitar as the Flaming Stars took shape in order to fulfil a support slot at short notice. They made their debut on London-based Vinyl Japan with the typically moribund *Hospital, Heaven Or Hell* EP in March 1995, a record distinguished by the presence of the impressive 'Kiss Tomorrow Goodbye' - which Decharne had earlier contributed as a solo composition to a Death Cigarettes compilation. The alcohol tribute 'The Face On The Bar Room Floor' was followed by another EP, *Money To Burn*. They also recorded a succession of sessions for John Peel, Mark Radcliffe and Mark Lamarr. The alcohol theme was continued on the band's 1996 debut album, succinctly titled *Songs From The Bar Room Floor*. Huck Whitney was then brought in to replace Johnny Johnson, adding extra fuel to the band's chaotic live performances. Their prolific single releases were collected on *Bring Me The Rest Of Alfredo Garcia*. 'New Hope For The Dead', released in October 1997, premiered the garage band classic, *Sell Your Soul To The Flaming Stars*. Extensive worldwide touring followed before the band set about recording their new album, *Pathway*.

● ALBUMS: *Songs From The Bar Room Floor* (Vinyl Japan 1996)★★★, *Sell Your Soul To The Flaming Stars* (Vinyl Japan 1998)★★★, *Pathway* (Vinyl Japan 1999)★★★.

● COMPILATIONS: *Bring Me The Rest Of Alfredo Garcia* (Vinyl Japan 1997)★★★.

Fleming, John 'OO'

b. John Fleming, 1969, Sunderland, England. Fleming is one of the UK's hardest working DJs, who has made a name for himself in both Europe and the USA for his driving trance and hard house sound. His distinctive moniker comes from the famous fictional spy in the books by Ian Fleming, whose code name was 007. Fleming was diagnosed with lung cancer in 1989 but battled to overcome it and to continue DJing. While convalescing in Florida, USA, he played at events such as 'Unity', 'Limelight Club' and 'Obsession' and gained a following in Florida, Texas, Georgia and Minneapolis. He quickly re-established himself upon his return to the UK and has played at all the major clubs, including Renaissance, Cream and Ministry Of Sound. He holds residencies at UK clubs, Trade, The Zap Club, Naughty But Nice, The Manor, Sunny Side Up, Freedom, Mirage, The Opera House and Ultra Vegas. His remixing credits include Mansun ('Tax Loss' and 'Wide Open Space'), Erasure, My Life Story, Junior Vasquez, N-Trance, Gloria Estefan and X-Cabs. Fleming describes his two styles of set as 'beefy, chunky, energetic, uplifting house' or 'funky, nu-energy techno' depending on the club and the crowd. He has mixed many compilations, including several Ibiza-themed albums

and *Reactivate 13* and *Reactivate 14* for React Music. He also mixed Virgin Records' *The Best Trance Anthems ... Ever!*, released in July 1999, which entered the UK's national compilation chart at number 7. Fleming regularly appears on the radio in the UK, including Danny Rampling's and Pete Tong's Radio 1 FM shows. He has released his own singles in 1999, including 'Come On Baby' with Russell Floorplay (Automatic Records), 'Alpha 5' and, as S2POR, 'Make Me Feel' on his own Joof Recordings. He also has another record label, Bond-Age Records.

● COMPILATIONS: *Q-Music* (Fifty-First Recordings 1997)★★★, *The Real Ibiza* (Telstar 1997)★★★, *Ibiza Anthems 1998* (Concept Recordings 1998)★★★, *Reacitvate 13* (React Music 1998)★★★★, *Licensed To Thrill* (Automatic 1999)★★★, *Sunny Side Up* (Passion Music 1999)★★★, *Reactivate 14* (React Music 1999)★★★, *The Best Trance Anthems ... Ever!* (Virgin 1999)★★★.

Flowered Up

As cultural phenomenons go, rarely has a band mirrored their social surroundings more graphically than Flowered Up from the UK. Formed on a north London housing estate in 1989, they were immediately championed by so many disparate causes (the working classes, the drug dealer, proud Southerners) that their rise to fame was virtually inevitable. Born out of the ecstasy boom that swept the musical underground at the turn of the 90s, Flowered Up's first gig at the close of 1989 was a shambolic affair that outraged as many onlookers as it excited. Within six months the line-up had settled down with Liam Maher (vocals), brother Joe (guitar), Andy Jackson (bass, later replaced by Mick Leander), Tim Dorney (keyboards), John Tuvey (drums), and a man called Barry Mooncult who had taken to dancing with the band onstage, wearing a giant flower. Signed to London-based indie label Heavenly Records, the release of their debut single, 'It's On', encouraged the UK weekly music papers to take the unusual step of putting a brand new band on its front pages, but all the accusations of hype were drowned out by Flowered Up revellers convinced that the band were London's answer to Manchester's Happy Mondays. They were not, nor were they another Clash or another Madness, mainly because although Flowered Up's flowing rock/funk grooves graced the Top 40 of all the UK charts, they failed to upset the commercial apple cart, in spite of all the attention. A move to London Records ended inimically when the label refused to release the 13-minute single 'Weekender' which, with its accompanying 20-minute film, was a perfect snapshot of rave culture. *A Life With Brian* appeared to show that the band, for all their Cockney quirkiness, could make an album that stood on its own two feet without fear of falling over. It would also provide the band with their tombstone, however, and they released one more single ('Better Life') before splitting up in 1993. Tim Dorney went on to work with Clive Langer and Republica, while Liam Maher returned to his bootleg stall in Camden Market and further musical projects.

● ALBUMS: *A Life With Brian* (Heavenly 1991)★★★.

Flowers, Mike, Pops

The debonair Mike Flowers caused a brief mid-90s sensation when he rode into the UK charts on the crest of the 'easy listening' revival with a cover version of Oasis' 'Wonderwall'. It remained in the charts for several weeks and was only narrowly kept off the Christmas 1995 number 1 spot by Michael Jackson. Dressed in a suit which time had forgotten and bedecked by the most outrageous blonde wig, Flowers' version of 'Wonderwall' caused more grins than grimaces, and sold nearly half a million copies. Even the song's writer, Noel Gallagher, was reportedly impressed by this, the cheekiest of cover versions (Oasis' 'Wonderwall' was still in the charts when it was released). It was followed by a version of Engelbert Humperdinck's 'Please Release Me' in 1996, and the band's debut album, *A Groovy Place*. Alongside the singles this included original material - though titles such as 'Crusty Girl' and 'Freebase' demonstrated that the Mike Flowers Pops' tongues were still firmly in their collective cheek.

● ALBUMS: *A Groovy Place* (London 1996)★★★.

Folk Implosion

A US alternative rock duo comprising Lou Barlow of Sebadoh and solo artist John Davis, Folk Implosion came to prominence in 1996 when 'Natural One', included on the soundtrack to the controversial movie *Kids*, became a major US hit. London Records, who issued the soundtrack, were keen to sign the band to a contract, but in the event, Barlow and Davis elected to release their new album on the tiny San Franciscan independent label Communion Records. Davis explained their choice to *Billboard* magazine: 'It will be really exciting to see where the limits are and to see if a real indie label can get played on the radio.' Barlow was also keen to emphasize that Folk Implosion was an act in its own right, with two songwriters, and not simply an extension of his activities with Sebadoh. The duo had already released a cassette only debut on the UK label Chocolate Monk, and *Take A Look Inside ...* on Communion long before 'Natural One' had become a hit. By the time the endearing *Dare To Be Suprised* was released in April 1997, Davis had resigned from his previous full-time occupation as a librarian. The album also coincided with the release of Davis' solo effort, *Blue Mountain*, for Shrimper Records. The duo's major label follow-up, *One Part Lullaby*, was a more cohesive and slickly produced collection of material lacking the lo-fi charm of their earlier work.

● ALBUMS: *Folk Implosion* cassette only (Chocolate Monk 1994)★★★, *Take A Look Inside ... The Folk Implosion* (Communion 1995)★★★, *Dare To Be Surprised* (Communion Records 1997)★★★★, *One Part Lullaby* (Interscope/Domino 1999)★★★.

Fontaine, Seb

b. London, England. Fontaine is one of the UK's leading house DJs, voted 10th in the UK's *DJ* magazine readers' poll of the Top 100 DJs In The World. Initially, Fontaine was interested in rare groove and hip-hop and would skip school in order to practise his mixing skills. While at Richmond College and Kingston Polytechnic in London, he would play warm up sets for DJs such as Norman Jay and Jeremy Healy (ex-Haysi Fantayzee) at clubs such as The Fridge, The Wag and Subterrania. His distinctive brand of funky hard house led to bookings at Deluxe in Nottingham and the seminal 'Back To Basics' night in Leeds. The DJ's style was also influenced by a visit to Ibiza in 1994. Fontaine established a higher profile running his own very successful night, 'Malibu Stacey' (the name of Barbie-type dolls in the US television cartoon show, *The Simpsons*) at London's Hanover Grand, which ran from November 1994 until July 1998. The club became renowned for its good-looking, well-dressed crowd (derided by some as 'Glam House') and thumping house, played by DJs such as Mark Moore (ex-S'Express), Boy George and Dave Seaman. He has DJed all over the world, including Brazil, the USA and in Hong Kong for the hand over party in 1997, and regularly plays at clubs during the summer clubbing season in Ibiza. In January 1999, he succeeded Paul Oakenfold in taking the prestigious position of resident DJ in the Annexe of Liverpool's Cream. He has also been a regular guest DJ at clubs such as Gatecrasher, Golden, Godskitchen and The Gallery, and with close friend and colleague, 'Tall' Paul Newman, he was presenting a radio show on London's Kiss 100. Fontaine has been producing and remixing tracks since 1990 and releases his own material under the moniker Itchy and Scratchy (another reference to *The Simpsons*). Fontaine set up his own label, Spot On Records in 1991 with Jules Vern (of Stretch And Vern), with whom he also records. He has also mixed 10 compilations, including those for the label Sound Dimension and the clubs Ministry Of Sound and Cream. In 1999, the DJ was signed by the Boxed label to mix three compilation albums under their *Global Underground* banner. The first launched their *Prototype* series and demonstrated Fontaine's growing fondness for well-produced, thumping house and melodic, crowd-pleasing trance.

● COMPILATIONS: *Cream Anthems* (Virgin 1998)★★★★, *Global Underground – Prototype* (Boxed 1999)★★★★, *Prototype 2* (Boxed 1999)★★★.

Foo Fighters

The Foo Fighters were formed at the end of 1994 by former Scream and Nirvana drummer Dave Grohl (b. 14 January 1969, Warren, Ohio, USA), now switched to guitar and vocals. There was some conjecture that the Nirvana bass player Krist Novoselic would join him in this venture, but Grohl eventually recruited Pat Smear (guitar, ex-Germs and a 'fourth' member of Nirvana during their later career), Nate Mendel (b. 2 December 1968, Seattle, Washington, USA; bass) and William Goldsmith (b. 4 July 1972, Seattle, Washington, USA; drums). The latter pair had previously played with Seattle band Sunny Day Real Estate. Their debut single, 'This Is A Call', was released on Roswell/Capitol Records in June 1995. The Foo Fighters' arrival initiated intense A&R activity, but Grohl opted for Capitol through the auspices of Gary Gersh, who had been Nirvana's A&R representative at Geffen Records. With media expectations weighing heavily on the project, analysis of the band's debut album focused on tracks such as 'I'll Stick Around', which some alleged was an attack on Cobain's widow, Courtney Love. Both the song's title and its lyrical refrain ('I don't owe you anything') seemed to pursue some form of personal exorcism, but it was hard to argue against the sheer impact of Grohl's new canon of songs. Detractors pointed at the similarity to Nirvana in the stop-start construction of several tracks, and Grohl's inability on occasion to match Cobain's evocation of mood. However, the simplicity of execution added greatly to the immediacy of the project. Grohl's original demos had simply been remixed rather than glossed over by a new production, and the result was, on the whole, enthralling. Goldsmith left the band during the recording of their second album and was replaced by Taylor Hawkins from Alanis Morissette's touring band. Although the critics were waiting to pounce on *The Colour And The Shape* it was another hard and tough album of blistering, paced songs, which were lightened by the band's great grasp of melody - songs such as 'Monkey Wrench' and 'My Poor Brain' burst into life in the middle eight. Smear left the band following the album's release, and was later replaced by Franz Stahl (ex-Scream). In 1998, Grohl recorded the soundtrack to Paul Schrader's *Touch*. Stahl left in June 1999, shortly before the release of yet another strong set *There Is Nothing Left To Lose*, the band's first album for RCA Records.

● ALBUMS: *Foo Fighters* (Roswell/Capitol 1995)★★★★, *The Colour And The Shape* (Roswell/Capitol 1997)★★★★, *There Is Nothing Left To Lose* (Roswell/RCA 1999)★★★★.

Fountains Of Wayne

The idiosyncratic pop duo Adam Schlesinger (b. New Jersey, USA) and Chris Collingwood (b. Pennsylvania, USA) first met on the roof of their college dorm in Williamstown, Massachusetts, in the mid-80s. The idea to collaborate came after Collingwood showed Schlesinger the chords to an R.E.M. song. They were members of a succession of college bands, including Wooly Mammoth, Are You My Mother? and the esoterically named Three Men When Stood Side By Side Have A Wingspan Of Over 12 Feet. However, when college ended Collingwood concentrated on writing one-act plays, while his partner took a number of temporary positions. They eventually reunited in Boston, but after signing a recording contract as the Wallflowers they abandoned their claim to that name (they actually sold the rights to the name to another Wallflowers, featuring Bob Dylan's son Jakob). The proposed record never appeared. Despite problems over freedom of contract that dogged them for three years, and their geographical separation (Collingwood was now living in New York), they continued to play the occasional gig under the name Pinwheel, then worked together as Ivy. By the time the pair finally found the time to record new songs together, Schlesinger had become co-owner of Scratchie Records with D'Arcy Wretzky and James Iha of Smashing Pumpkins. The result was a self-titled collection of 12 brittle songs that were occasionally arch about pop music history, but still affectionate towards it: 'When we came across some total cliché, we'd immediately leap right into it. If there was a bit of the melody that sounded like the Beach Boys or Cheap Trick, or a guitar riff that sounded like Blue Öyster Cult, we immediately put it in.' Little wonder the duo had adopted the mocking self-description 'The grunge Everly Brothers'. The first single to be extracted from the album, the irritatingly catchy 'Radiation Vibe', reached UK number 32. The band also achieved a flurry of publicity when their song 'That Thing You Do!' was included in the Tom Hanks movie of the same name, and led to them being nominated for an Oscar. By the time Fountains Of Wayne began their European tour of 1997 they had expanded their line-up to include Brian Young of the Posies on drums and former Belltower guitarist Jody Porter. *Utopia Parkway*, another collection of note perfect power pop classics, was released in 1999.

● ALBUMS: *Fountains Of Wayne* (Scratchie/Atlantic 1997)★★★★, *Utopia Parkway* (Atlantic 1999)★★★★.

4 Hero

A publicity shy London, England duo comprising Dego MacFarlane and Mark 'Mac' Clair, who first emerged at the height of the late 80s acid house explosion. Together they established Reinforced Records, which became the foremost UK outlet for hardcore techno (at that time often referred to as dark hardcore). Their releases for Reinforced included the devastating 'Mr Kirk's Nightmare', which provided a thematic bridge between hardcore and the embryonic jungle/breakbeat scene. Alongside Goldie, who joined Reinforced in the early 90s, 4 Hero became innovative members of a new aristocracy in the dance music community, though unlike Goldie, the duo eschewed publicity. As well as 4 Hero the duo released singles as Manix, Tom&Jerry (not the Simon And Garfunkel duo), Jacob (whose *Optical Stairway* EP was inspired by the writings of Nostradamus), Nu Era and MacFarlane's solo project, Tek 9. The debut 4 Hero album, *Parallel Universe*, was considered by many to be the first album to showcase the full potential of drum 'n' bass music. Its themes included science-fiction television programmes and science fact (with references to author Stephen Hawking). It was followed by an album credited to Tek 9 and remix and production work for Nicolette, DJ Krush and Courtney Pine. As 4 Hero, collaborations with Josh Wink and Juan Atkins preceded their second album, *Two Pages*, which was attacked in some quarters for its perceived pretension and its two hour length. A remix version of the album was released the following year.

● ALBUMS: *Parallel Universe* (Reinforced 1994)★★★★, *Two Pages* (Talkin' Loud 1998)★★★, *Two Pages Reinterpretations* remix album (Talkin' Loud 1999)★★★.

4 Non Blondes

San Francisco quartet who formed in 1989, making a slow rise through the traditional round of bar shows and club dates, going on to win a Best Unsigned Band award and then a prestigious support date to Primus. In 1993, their commercial arrival corresponded to that of fellow San Franciscans the Spin Doctors, achieving a surprise UK number 2 single ('What's Up') and a Top 10 debut album, *Bigger, Better, Faster, More!*, produced by Prince associate David Tickle. Selling half a million copies in the USA where it was originally released in 1992, it also topped charts in Germany and Sweden. The band comprised the strong visual and almost hectoring vocal presence of Linda Perry alongside Christa Hillhouse (bass), Roger Rocha (guitar) and Dawn Richardson (drums). Rocha, the grandson of abstract expressionist Clyfford Still and an art school veteran, stepped in to replace original incumbent Shanna Hall during sessions for the debut album. Richardson, a trained percussionist with a degree from California State University and several years' experience in jazz and salsa bands, replaced Wanda Day shortly before pre-production. Hillhouse and Perry began the band together, having to cancel their first ever rehearsal on 7 October 1989 when an earthquake hit the Bay Area. Hillhouse had first spotted Perry playing an acoustic set, and the latter's songs quickly became the dominant force within 4 Non Blondes, including 'Spaceman', the follow-up to 'What's Up'. However, suspicions were raised in the press that 4 Non Blondes represented a corporate chart raid, providing designer grunge for the post-Nirvana and Lemonheads (to whose label, Interscope/Atlantic Records, they signed) generation. Support slots to Prince and Neil Young did little to dispel these assumptions, and Perry broke up the band to pursue a solo career. However, there was an undeniable infectious simplicity to 'What's Up' that indelibly marked it as one of the records of 1993.

● ALBUMS: *Bigger, Better, Faster, More!* (Interscope 1993)★★★.

Fowlkes, Eddie 'Flashin''

b. 24 December 1962, Detroit, Michigan, USA. One of the less celebrated techno artists from the ever fertile Detroit region, Fowlkes began making mix tapes at the age of 14. His first booking as a DJ came in 1981 at a campus party. In the early 80s he built up his record collection and began to secure a reputation for both his live appearances at the Music Institute and his mix tapes. His nickname, 'Flashin', came from his early prowess as a scratch and mix DJ. Fowlkes was a friend of many of the Detroit giants, DJing alongside Derrick May and Juan Atkins in the early 80s. He recorded his debut, 1986's 'Goodbye Kiss', on Atkins' Metroplex imprint, and also released singles on the labels KMS Records, 430 West Records ('Inequality') and Play It Again Sam. His style, which blended in elements of deep house music and soul, was dubbed 'black technosoul' by Fowlkes himself. In the 90s, he began to build his recording profile, working with labels including Jump Street, React Music and Tresor Records. Among the best of these releases were 'Turn Me Out', produced by Graeme Park. Throughout the 90s he performed regularly at Detroit's The Alley club, and in 1991 relocated to Berlin to record *Serious Techno Vol. 1*, featuring his brand of tough but soulful techno. As he reasoned, 'most Euro techno has no feeling because the makers haven't got the history'. He also recorded for Infonet Records, Back To Basics, Peacefrog, as well as issuing a third album, *Black Technosoul*, for Tresor. During the late 90s he issued material on the City Boy, Dance Pool and Azuli labels.

● ALBUMS: *Serious Techno Vol. 1* (Tresor 1991)★★★★, *The Birth Of Technosoul* (Tresor/Pow Wow 1993)★★★★, *Deep Detroit Techno-Soul Volume 1* (Tresor/Pow Wow 1993)★★★, *Black Technosoul* (Tresor 1996)★★★.

Frank And Walters

This three-piece band from Cork, Ireland was named after two tramps who inhabited a nearby village. Comprising Paul Linehan (vocals/bass), Niall Linehan (guitar) and Ashley Keating (drums), they attracted immediate press attention through a debut EP on the homely Setanta label, the songwriting on which was highly unassuming in its parochial good humour. 'Michael', for instance, concerned the band's best friend who was the star of the town via his expensive car, until he crashed it and reverted to the use of a bicycle. Paul Linehan's tender lyrics emphasized the cathartic nature of this bodyblow in a manner heavily reminiscent of the slow passage of time and wisdom in rural Ireland. Two Single Of The Week awards later, 'Fashion Crisis Hits New York' proved another instant favourite: 'Fashion Crisis hits New York, I saw a blind man who was eating his fork, He said that's what you've got to do to be cool, you eat your cutlery instead of your food'. This was enough to ensure Go! Discs would step in to shepherd future releases, as the band took up residence at a YMCA in Wimbledon. A third EP, led off by the typically infectious 'Happy Busman', was piloted

by Edwyn Collins. However, the resulting debut album failed to fulfil critical expectations for journalists primed on the band's superior early material (which was largely rehashed to less immediate effect). 'This Is Not A Song' and a reissued 'Fashion Crisis Hits New York' offered chart hits via bigger promotion and production, with the reworked album track 'After All' narrowly failing to reach the UK Top 10. Afterwards, the band retreated to Cork in an attempt to recover from the 'too much too early' syndrome which, as some critics were already suggesting, had robbed them of their native charm. By the time the more earnest *The Grand Parade* was released, however, the fickle world of pop had moved on. An extended sojourn in the US inspired the lush, melancholic songs on 1999's *Beauty Becomes More Than Life*.

● ALBUMS: *Trains, Boats And Planes* (Go! Discs 1992)★★★, *The Grand Parade* (Go! Discs 1996)★★, *Beauty Becomes More Than Life* (Setanta 1999)★★★.

Franklin, Kirk, And The Family

b. Fort Worth, Texas, USA. A meteoric success story in gospel music, a genre more usually associated with the longevity of its artists, Kirk Franklin And The Family made a huge impact with their debut album. A fixture at the top of the US Contemporary Christian and Gospel charts, and the first platinum selling gospel album, it featured powerful performances from the 17-piece 'Family' of musicians and singers, many of whom were drawn from Franklin's home town of Fort Worth, Texas. Franklin was raised by his aunt as a strict Baptist, and he was leading the Mt. Rose Baptist Church choir by the time he was 11. Despite a troubled and rebellious teenage period, by his early twenties Franklin was writing material for gospel greats including Rev. Milton Biggham, Daryl Coley, Yolanda Adams and Rev. John P. Kee. The success his debut saw the Family booked to appear on syndicated USA television programme the *Arsenio Hall Show*, while contemporary artists as diverse as Ice Cube and R. Kelly paid public respect to their craft. Subsequent albums have established Franklin and his bands (God's Property and Nu Nation) as arguably contemporary gospel's biggest and most commercially successful star, and have featured guest appearances from artists including Kelly, Bono and Mary J. Blige. *The Nu Nation Project* debuted at number 7 on the *Billboard* 200 album chart in October 1998.

● ALBUMS: *Kirk Franklin And The Family* (Gospo Centric 1994)★★★, *Kirk Franklin & The Family Christmas* (Chordant 1995)★★★, *Whatcha Lookin' 4* (Gospo Centric 1995)★★★, *God's Property From Kirk Franklin's New Nation* (B-Rite/Interscope 1997)★★★★, *The Nu Nation Project* (Gospo Centric/Interscope 1998)★★★.

Freakwater

Formed in Louisville, Kentucky, USA, the original idea behind Freakwater arose from informal country jams improvised in a basement by Janet Beveridge Bean (also drummer for Eleventh Dream Day) and Catherine Irwin. When Bean moved to Chicago they kept their songwriting partnership alive by singing to each other over the telephone. Bean's stay in Chicago was beneficial, however, as it was here she met bass player Dave Gay. It was at this point the trio (augmented by guitar player Bob Egan and other musicians as necessary) began to record for the first time. Early critical comparisons to the Carter Family ensued, with the central duo's songwriting evoking a similar sense of innocence, albeit in a much more contemporaneous vein. As the *New Musical Express* wrote, 'Despite their straight-ahead approach to heartache folkisms and bourbon blues, Freakwater's gorgeous songs share the indie-led, country cliché-shaking agenda.' This view is confirmed by the fact that early in their career they released a cover version of Black Sabbath's 'War Pigs'. Their fourth recording, *Old Paint*, was again produced by Brad Wood and witnessed their expressive voices addressing familiar subjects such as love, regret and drinking. Cover versions included Woody Guthrie's 'Little Black Train' and Loudon Wainwright III's 'Out Of This World'. *Springtime* concentrated on original material, but the album's seamless flow was indicative of Bean and Irwin's ability to create new folk and country classics. *End Time*, featuring entirely self-composed material, fleshed out the band's sound with strings and percussion.

● ALBUMS: *Freakwater* (Amoeba 1989)★★★, *Dancing Underwater* (Amoeba 1991)★★★, *Feels Like The Third Time* (Thrill Jockey 1993)★★★★, *Old Paint* (Thrill Jockey 1995)★★★, *Springtime* (Thrill Jockey 1998)★★★★, *End Time* (Thrill Jockey 1999)★★★★.

Freeland, Adam

b. 7 August 1973, Welwyn Garden City, England. Like James Lavelle of Mo' Wax Records, Freeland rose to prominence as a dance music *wünderkind*, becoming a highly successful, DJ, remixer, club promoter and record label boss while still in his early twenties. In 1998, the UK's *DJ* magazine's reader's poll of the world's Top 100 DJs ranked him at number 34. Originally a deep house DJ, Freeland became known for seamlessly blending hip-hop and electro into his sets. He pioneered 'nu-school breaks' – breakbeats with an eclectic range of influences including techno, drum 'n' bass and world music. Although DJing on the London club scene from 1992, his first mix compilation, *Coastal Breaks*, was not released until 1996. A double CD comprising 32 tracks, it received high praise from the critics and raised Freeland's profile, enabling him to tour in the UK and the USA. He won the admiration of many respected UK DJs such as Carl Cox, Sasha, the Chemical Brothers and Andy Weatherall. He supported Cox on several dates of his F.A.C.T. 2 world tour. In 1997, he ran a successful night, 'Friction', in Soho, London with DJ friends, Rennie Pilgrem and Tayo. In that year, he also released a single with his friend Kevin Beber, 'Number 43 With Steamed Rice Please' under the name Tsunami One. The popularity of the track in the clubs led to remix work for the Orb, DeeJay Punk-Roc, Headrillaz and Orbital. Freeland began 1998 by touring Australia with DJ Krush, Pressure Drop and José Padilla. *Coastal Breaks 2* was released and was a critical and commercial success. With his determination to innovate and experiment, the master of 'nu-school breaks' is being tipped by many dance music journalists as the next DJ superstar.

● COMPILATIONS: *Coastal Breaks* (Avex 1996)★★★★, *Coastal Breaks 2* (React 1998)★★★★.

Freestylers

This hip-hop/rock crossover band comprises Matt Cantor, Aston Harvey and Andrew Galea and was formed in London in 1996. All three were involved in the UK's dance music scene in the late-80s. Harvey had written the 1990 breakbeat classic 'Don't Hold Back' as the Blapps! Posse and had worked with the Rebel MC and Definition Of Sound. The band's name came from their first sample – 'Don't Stop the Rock' – and they released their first single 'Drop The Boom (AK-48)' on their own label, Scratch City Records in 1996. Using the vocoder, the track was old school electro and became an underground club classic. In late 1996, they released *The Freestyle EP* and had a chart hit and *Top Of The Pops* television appearance with 'B-Boy Stance', featuring the vocalist Tenor Fly. Following this, they completed various remix projects, including those for Audioweb, Afrika Bambaataa and the Jungle Brothers. They also mixed the Ministry Of Sound's big beat compilation *FSUK 2* and played an 'Essential Mix' for the UK's BBC Radio 1. They also made live appearances on the European festival circuit, including the Glastonbury Festival. Their debut, *We Rock Hard* was released in 1998 to a positive critical reception. The same year the trio won the UK's *Muzik* magazine's award for Best Band.

● ALBUMS: *We Rock Hard* (Mammoth 1999)★★★.
● COMPILATIONS: *FSUK 2* (MOS 1998)★★★.

Freq Nasty

b. Darin McFadyen, 15 November 1969, Fiji. Raised in New Zealand, Freq Nasty is, despite his exotic origins, signed to the UK's influential independent Botchit & Scarper. The label is a purveyor of 'nu-school breaks' - experimental, abstract electro as practised by artists such as Adam Freeland, Soul Of Man, Tayo and Rennie Pilgrem. Indeed, his single 'Funky As...' was released on Freeland's label, Marine Parade. His tough, electronic rhythms are punctuated with obscure, kitsch samples of film dialogue and synthesised squelches and bleeps. Occasionally, he uses the vocal skills of rappers such as Phoebe One and the drum 'n' bass MC, Skibadee. His debut single for Botchit & Scarper, 'Boomin' Back Atcha', became popular with more underground DJs. His next single 'Underglass' also made an impact on dancefloors and in the music press and established his trademark sound of 'acid' sounds underpinned by fierce breakbeats and powerful bass. 'Freq-A-Zoid', his third single, was a surprise. Alluding to Kraftwerk, Daft Punk and Les Rythmes Digitales, it was an unusual slice of 'tech-funk' that proved to work equally well on techno, house and hip-hop dancefloors. Freq Nasty, and his studio partner Blim, have remixed Sousounde's 'Metisse' and Steve Reich's 'Desert Music'. McFadyen is also an in-demand DJ, playing all over the world and at the seminal Big Beat Boutique (Norman Cook's home club) at its venue, London's Scala. His debut *Freq's Geeks & Mutilations* received ecstatic praise from the UK music press, won over by the album's refreshing experimentation and undeniable funkiness.

● ALBUMS: *Freq's Geeks & Mutilations* (Botchit & Scarper 1999)★★★★.

Fresh, Freddy

b. Frederick Schmidt, New York City, USA. Fresh is a leading hip-hop/big beat producer, remixer and DJ who has released over 100 records since his first in 1988, encompassing other electronic styles such as house, trance and techno. Based in Minneapolis, Fresh has his own imprints, Butterbeat, Analog Records, Boriqua and Socket. He has DJed all over the world, working alongside Jeff Mills, Roy Davis Jnr., Frankie Bones and Fatboy Slim (with whom he is friends) and other Skint Records artists. Fatboy Slim sampled Fresh's voice from an answerphone message, saying: 'Fatboy Slim is fucking in heaven' and used it on his album *You've Come A Long Way, Baby*. Growing up, Fresh had jobs as a pizza delivery boy and etching trophy plates for his father before pursuing his interests in electro, hip-hop and electronic music. He discovered analogue sounds when his wife took him to the Bronx in 1984 and he became obsessed with the dance music street culture of the time and producers such as Shep Pettibone and François Kevorkian. Fresh began to collect mix tapes by DJs such as Jeff Mills and Frankie Bones and records by a range of diverse artists from Jonzun Crew, Newcleus to Bill Withers and Cat Stevens. His first studio experience was with the famous Boogie Down Productions, where he mixed a b-side. He then began to amass a sizeable collection of analogue synthesizers and other equipment and began experimenting with his own sounds. His fondness for analogue equipment is evident in the sound of his productions - lo-fi and mixed live. Fresh released his debut singles on Nu Groove Records before establishing his Analog label in 1992. In 1995, Fresh signed a contract with the German techno label, Harthouse, on which he has released his last two albums. He has released many acclaimed singles and has found his popularity growing with the resurgence of interest in old school hip-hop and electro, particularly in Europe and the UK, where he is a frequent visitor, playing DJ sets at major clubs and festivals, including the Glastonbury Festival and Creamfields. He has also DJed at the UK's Cream, Ministry Of Sound and at Norman Cook's Big Beat Boutique, the club that gave the musical style its name. Fresh has also broadcast many DJ mixes on UK regional and national radio, including an 'Essential Mix' on BBC Radio 1 FM. In 1999, Fresh released the singles 'Badder Badder Schwing' (which reached the UK Top 40) and 'What It Is'. *The Last True Family Man* received excellent reviews. Fresh also supported the Jungle Brothers on tour during summer 1999.

● ALBUMS: *Analog Space Funk* (Analog 1996)★★★, *Accidentally Classic* (Harthouse 1997)★★★, *The Last True Family Man* (Harthouse Eye Q 1999)★★★★.

Friday, Gavin

b. Fionan Hanvey, Dublin, Eire. Friday was founder of the Virgin Prunes and spent the late 80s and early 90s moving away from the discordant art expression that dominated the Prunes' turbulent but vivid career. Following their demise he took a break to concentrate on painting and open a cabaret nightclub (The Blue Jesus, a pun on Marlene Dietrich's 'Blue Angel' nightclub in the movie, *Touch Of Evil*), though he did also record a 12-inch single version of the Rolling Stones' 'You Can't Always Get What You Want' with friend Simon Carmody. The launch of a solo career proper was largely inspired through the efforts of his friend Agnes Bernelle, who years earlier had introduced him to the pre-war Germany of Edith Piaf, Jacques Brel, Bertolt Brecht and Kurt Weill. The Berlin vaudeville circuit of the 30s and 40s thus inspired both The Blue Jesus and *Each Man Kills The Thing He Loves*, produced by Hal Willner with skilled accompaniment from drummer Michael Blair, bass player Fernando Saunders and guitarist Marc Ribot. A densely crafted and moralistic take on the beauty and decadence of the period, measuring pathos with humour, it proved an instant critical success. *Adam 'N' Eve* was more playful, with

Friday parodying himself on the self-eulogizing 'King Of Trash', while elsewhere he was evidently still the maverick: 'It's egotistical and outrageous, but this record is the world according to me. It's saying no, no, no to everyone who just toes the line.' Tracks such as 'Fun And Entertainment' were delivered in an impenetrable, working-class Dublin accent. Later in the 90s he moved into film work, writing three tracks with Bono of U2 and long-time collaborator Maurice Roycroft (aka The Man Seezer) for the soundtrack to *In The Name Of The Father* and scoring Robert Altman's *Short Cuts*, though his attitude to this new art form was typically acidic: 'I generally dislike rock 'n' rollers getting involved in the music on a film. When you get to a very emotional part in the movie and you hear Phil Collins' voice you start getting the puke bag out.' *Shag Tobacco* was co-produced with Seezer and Tim Simenon of Bomb The Bass, and reflected some of the shifts in the mid-90s music scene. However, the cover version of Marc Bolan's 'The Slider' was one concession to an earlier period, while songs such as 'Dolls' and 'Little Black Dress' both alluded to Friday's camp cabaret fixations. Two more Australian film soundtracks followed, *The Passion Of Darkly Noon* and *Angel Baby*, before a radically altered, spoken-word version of *Shag Tobacco* was released early in 1996. The same year, Friday and Seezer's 'Angel' was featured on the soundtrack of *Romeo And Juliet*. In 1998, Friday and Seezer composed a full score for Jim Sheridan's *The Boxer*.

● ALBUMS: as Gavin Friday And The Man Seezer *Each Man Kills The Thing He Loves* (Island 1990)★★★, *Adam 'N' Eve* (Island 1992)★★, *Shag Tobacco* (Island 1995)★★★, *The Boxer* film soundtrack (MCA 1998)★★★.

Frisco Kid

b. Stephen Wray, Western Kingston, Jamaica, West Indies. Wray began to emulate leading DJs while still at school and was even given a chance on the microphone at smaller dances. While working in a garage in Kingston, a chance meeting with the owner of the Exodus Nuclear sound system led to his performing as the Paro Kid. He became the resident DJ for Exodus and subsequently went to King Jammy's studio to record some specials, changing his name to Frisco Kid. As his career developed, he recorded 'Dance Again' at Donovan Germain's Penthouse studio. Frisco Kid's career prospects looked promising as a result of this release, but after the initial fervour died down, no further recordings surfaced. He returned to recording specials for the sound and it was at Black Scorpio in 1993 that his recording career took an upward turn. Confusion over studio time led Frisco Kid and DJ Terror Fabulous back to Penthouse, where he recorded 'Big Speech'. His second break led to a number of hits, including 'Wakey News', 'Yuh And Yuh Man', 'Tribulation', 'Yuh A Boom', 'Step Up In Life' and 'Gal A Di Clothes'. His notoriety led to an appearance at the 1995 Reggae Sunsplash festival where he captivated the crowds with an exceptional performance. His success led to an alliance with Patrick Roberts, who enrolled Frisco Kid as part of the Shocking Vibes crew. The crew embarked on an international tour featuring Little Kirk, Silver Cat, Tanto Metro, Snagga Puss and Beenie Man; the tour represented the debut performances in Europe for Silver Cat and Frisco Kid. The shows received rave receptions from both the critics and audiences alike. In 1996 Frisco Kid joined Buju

Banton's label, the newly formed Cell Block 321. The enterprise was designed to promote new talent and Frisco Kid's career advanced with the release of the phenomenal 'Video Light'. His success continued with 'If Looks' and the multi-combination hit 'Matey Anthem', alongside Mega Banton, Spragga Benz, Mad Cobra, General Degree, Gringo and Johnny P. Many of his hits were featured on the excellent debut album, *Finally*.
● ALBUMS: *Finally* (VP 1999)★★★★.

Fu Manchu

Formed in Orange County, California, USA by Scott Hill (vocals/guitar), Ruben Romano (drums), Brad Davis (bass) and Eddie Glass (lead guitar). Their debut EP was released in 1990, establishing their headily psychedelic, groove-orientated approach. While many compared them to Kyuss, Fu Manchu preferred to make cryptic references to pharmaceuticals and produce cover images that tied them to older generations of rock bands. *In Search Of ...* , for example, featured a woman in flares preparing to start an illegal drag race, while the album's title derived from a lacklustre science-fiction programme of the 70s. Suitably, Hill has never spent much time perfecting his lyrics, instead using his voice as a fifth instrument to complement the band's dense, rhythmic passages. Glass and Romano both left in October 1996, later resurfacing in Nebula. They were replaced by Brant Bjork (ex-Kyuss) and Bob Balch, respectively. Fu Manchu's subsequent releases, 1997's *The Action Is Go* and 1999's *King Of The Road*, catapulted the band into the mainstream.
● ALBUMS: *No One Rides For Free* (Mammoth 1994)★★★, *Daredevil* (Mammoth 1995)★★, *In Search Of ...* (Mammoth 1996)★★, *The Action Is Go* (Mammoth 1998)★★★, *King Of The Road* (Mammoth 1999)★★★.
● COMPILATIONS: *Return To Earth 91 - 93* (Elastic 1998)★★.

Fugazi

The thinking person's modern hardcore band, and vocalist/guitarist Ian MacKaye's most permanent institution since his Minor Threat days. More so than Henry Rollins and, arguably, Jello Biafra, Fugazi have continued and expanded on the arguments of their antecedents. Door prices are kept down, mainstream press interviews are shunned, and they maintain a commitment to all-age shows that shames many bands. They have also been among the first to object publicly to the ridiculous macho ritual of slam-dancing: 'We're about challenging crowds, confronting ourselves and them with new ideas and if I was a teenager now, I would not be doing a dance that's been going on for ten years'. It is a shame that Fugazi's press seems to focus unerringly on MacKaye's Minor Threat connections, as the contribution from his co-lyricist Guy Picciotto (vocals/guitar, ex-Rites Of Spring) deserves to be ranked above that of supporting cast. His more abstract, less direct communiqués blend well with his partner's realism. The other members of the band are Brendan Canty (drums) and Joe Lally (bass), and together they have forged one of the most consistent and challenging discographies within the US underground. Although they have concentrated primarily on touring rather than studio efforts, each of their albums has gone on to sell more than 100,000 copies, produced entirely independently within their own Dischord Records framework. In a rare mainstream music press interview in 1995, MacKaye continued to decry those who would use the guise of punk rock to record for major corporations, commenting on the success of Green Day and Offspring by stating: 'They'll be forgotten, 'cos they're the fucking Ugly Kid Joe's of the 90s'. Fugazi's own record of the time, *Red Medicine*, proved just as abrasive and disciplined an exercise as usual. In 1999, the band were filmed by Jem Cohen for the documentary *Instrument*. The attendant soundtrack album featured several unreleased studio tracks and outtakes.
● ALBUMS: *Fugazi EP* (Dischord 1988)★★★, *Margin Walker EP* (Dischord 1989)★★★, *Repeater* (Dischord 1990)★★★★, *Steady Diet Of Nothing* (Dischord 1991)★★★, *In On The Killtaker* (Dischord 1993)★★★, *Red Medicine* (Dischord 1995)★★★, *End Hits* (Dischord 1998)★★★, *Instrument Soundtrack* (Dischord 1999)★★.
● COMPILATIONS: *13 Songs* first two EPs (Dischord 1988)★★★.
● VIDEOS: *Instrument* (Dischord 1999).

Fugees

New York, USA-based crew comprising Wyclef Jean (b. 17 October 1972, Haiti), his cousin Pras (b. Prakazrel Michel, 19 October 1972), and Lauryn Hill (b. 25 May 1975, South Orange, New Jersey, USA), who became the most successful crossover rap outfit of the 90s with 1996's best-selling *The Score*. Originally signed to Ruffhouse Records in 1992 as the Tranzlator Crew, their new name was a shortened version of Refugees (inspired by Wyclef and Pras' Haitian backgrounds). The Fugees' style combines dry, cushioning beats with clever, rhythmic wordplay. All three members rap over acoustic guitars, as well as more upbeat numbers informed by dub and reggae, both modes in which they excel. The sound was not exactly unfamiliar, and the title of their debut album, *Blunted On Reality*, seemed to suggest they were coming from a similar direction to Cypress Hill and Digable Planets. All three members professed to be non-users, however, indicating that the album title signified their belief that they did not need to smoke the weed to induce a state of heightened perception and relaxation. Similarly, the lyrical concerns on the album were somewhat different, as might be expected of a crew where the majority of members also attended university courses. Some of their targets included America's perception of Haitians as 'Boat People' (Pras stated his intention to return to Haiti, using profits from his music to help build schools and decent roads on the island) and their own mixed gender status. *The Score* was a magnificent follow-up, one of the musical highlights of 1996, and accessible enough to bring their soulful jazz-rap to a wider market. 'Ready Or Not' and reworkings of 'Killing Me Softly' (Roberta Flack) and 'No Woman No Cry' (Bob Marley) were all international hit singles, and the album achieved multi-platinum worldwide success. Hill's pregnancy meant the trio were largely inactive during 1997, with Wyclef Jean taking the time to release a solo album. In 1998, Pras and Hill also embarked on solo careers, with the latter's *The Miseducation Of Lauryn Hill* enjoying huge critical and commercial success.
● ALBUMS: as Fugees Tranzlator Crew *Blunted On Reality* (Ruffhouse/Columbia 1994)★★, *The Score* (Ruffhouse/Columbia 1996)★★★★, *Bootleg Versions* (Columbia 1996)★★★.
● VIDEOS: *The Score* (SMV 1996).
● FURTHER READING: *Fugees: The Unofficial Book*, Chris Roberts.

Fun Lovin' Criminals

This US hip-hop/alternative rock crossover outfit was formed in New York City in the early 90s by three pseudonymous former nightclub bouncers, Huey (vocals/guitar), Steve Borovini (drums/programming) and Fast (bass/keyboards/harmonica). Assimilating a variety of local music influences - predominantly hip-hop but also rock and blues - as well as cult cinema references, by 1994 they had begun releasing their first independent singles. With samples drawn from movies such as *Pulp Fiction* as well as records by obscure British gothic band Tones On Tail, and lyrical narratives describing New York's criminal underclass, they soon drew comparisons to the Beastie Boys, as well as other urban east coast hip-hop crews such as Lordz Of Brooklyn and Young Black Teenagers. In common with both those outfits, Fun Lovin' Criminals initially struggled to establish a singular identity outside of the Beastie Boys comparisons. The excellent *Come Find Yourself* and a string of single releases (including 'Fun Lovin' Criminal', 'Scooby Snacks' and 'King Of New York') did secure strong airplay, particularly in the UK where the album reached the Top 10. They also received a series of rave reviews for their concert appearances. *100% Colombian* downplayed the hip-hop rhythms in favour of a soulful vibe, characterised by the Barry White tribute single, 'Love Unlimited', which debuted at number 18 in August 1998. The album entered the UK charts at number 3 a month later, but failed to breakthrough in their homeland where they continue to be ignored. The following year's b-side compilation *Mimosa* collected together the band's lounge style cover versions of their own and other artist's material.

● ALBUMS: *Come Find Yourself* (EMI/Chrysalis 1996)★★★★, *100% Colombian* (Chrysalis 1998)★★★★.
● COMPILATIONS: *Mimosa* (EMI/Chrysalis 1999)★★★.

Fun-Da-Mental

An Asian 'world dance' band, the original Fun-Da-Mental formed in Bradford, Yorkshire, in August 1991, specifically to play the Notting Hill Carnival of that year. Though all of the initial four-piece were born in Pakistan or India, they had each grown up in Northern English cities. The initial line-up was Propa-Ghandi (b. Aki Nawaz; aka Haq Quereshi), DJ Obeyo, Bad-Sha Lallaman and Man Tharoo Goldfinger (b. Inder Matharu; also of Transglobal Underground). Their debut single was 'Janaam - The Message', which immediately brought them to the attention of the national music press, particularly the dance magazines. After a cassette-only release, they followed up with 'Gandhi's Revenge', before 'Sister India', initially recorded for a live John Peel Radio 1 session. On the back of such exposure they looked certain to be on the verge of a significant breakthrough - when they themselves broke in two in late 1993, during a video shoot in Pakistan. Industry conjecture suggested rows over royalty payments and allocations, as rappers Goldfinger and Bad-Sha Lallaman left to team up with DJ Obeyo, and attempted to take the name with them. Eventually they became Det-ri-Mental. Fun-Da-Mental carried on, now comprising Propa-Ghandi, Amir Ali (lyrics), Inder Matharu (percussion), Dave 'D' Watts (aka Impi-D; samples) and Count Dubulah (bass, guitar). Their first release following the departures was 'Countryman', in November 1993. Fun-Da-Mental's leader remained Propa-

Ghandi, formerly a member of gothic bands Southern Death Cult and Getting The Fear, and who is also responsible for Nation Records. They joined with Pop Will Eat Itself for the 'Ich Bin Ein Auslander' anti-racism tirade. Another controversial single followed in 1994, 'Dog Tribe', which began with a recorded answerphone message left at the offices of Youth Against Racism by a member of sinister far-right group, Combat 18. Fun-Da-Mental themselves have been targeted by the likes of the British National Party - who were forced to apologise after printing their picture in one of their magazines with the caption 'a gang of Asian thugs'. Fun-Da-Mental also became one of the first bands to visit the post-apartheid South Africa, which left a lasting impression on them, prior to the release of their debut album. This, the title adapted from Black Panther Bobby Seale, included remixes of 'Wrath Of The Black Man' and 'Countryman', guest appearances by Neil Sparkes of Transglobal Underground, poet Subi Shah and ex-Collapsed Lung singer Nihal. On subsequent albums the band have relentlessly pursued their political ideals, while their music has shown an increasing interest in traditional Asian styles. To this end, the band have toured with traditional qawwali singers and appeared at the 1997 *Tanz&FolkFest* in Rudolstadt. In 1999, they released the superbly titled remix set *Why America Will Go To Hell*. The album also included several new tracks.

● ALBUMS: *Seize The Time* (Beggars Banquet 1994)★★★★, *With Intent To Pervert The Cause Of Injustice!* (Nation 1995)★★★, *Erotic Terrorism* (Nation 1998)★★★.
● COMPILATIONS: *Why America Will Go To Hell* (Nation 1999)★★★★.

Funki Porcini

b. James Bradell, Oxfordshire, England. Bradell left England at the age of 19 and moved to California, later settling in Italy to run a multi-media business. While there he began recording for Ninja Tune Records as 9 Lazy 9, releasing two singles and the albums *Paradise Blown* and *Electric Lazyland* (both 1994) on which he combined hip-hop and funk breakbeats with jazz-influenced sounds. He later assumed the name Funki Porcini and returned to England, where he continued his association with Ninja Tune. His single 'Long Road/Poseathon' was released at the beginning of 1995 and was followed by the album *Hed Phone Sex* in May; the latter was described as 'a trip around a bedlam-addled musical sex asylum' and 'a lush voyeuristic fantasy'. 'Long Road' presents a chilled hip-hop groove, melodic dub bass, tinkling piano, sleazy saxophone, sampled voice and various other sounds, to create a lush, abstract texture. 'Big Pink Inflatable' (1995) and *Love, Pussycats & Carwrecks* (1996) pursued Funky Porcini's themes of sex, pornography and voyeurism. Tracks such as 'River Of Smack' move away from the hip-hop and drum 'n' bass rhythms of most of the album, creating a dark, psychedelic dirge, underpinned by double bass and shuffling percussion. Funki Porcini has subsequently balanced a busy remixing schedule with his own prolific output, which has included *The Ultimately Empty Million Pounds* and the *Zombie* EP.

● ALBUMS: *Hed Phone Sex* (Ninja Tune 1995)★★★, *Love Pussycats & Carwrecks* (Ninja Tune 1996)★★★★, *The Ultimately Empty Million Pounds* (Ninja Tune 1999)★★★★.

Funkmaster Flex

b. Aston Taylor, the Bronx, New York, USA. One of New York's most prominent hip-hop DJs thanks to his appearances on the Hot 97FM show, the number 1-rated rap outlet in Chicago and Los Angeles, where it is syndicated. Flex has also turned his skills to production and remix work for other artists, as well as making his own recordings. He started in hip-hop as a disc jockey for the band Deuces Wild, before securing his first radio slots for Chuck Chillout at Kiss FM in 1987. He went on to play the Manhattan club circuit until the end of the decade, having already served his apprenticeship on block parties in the early 80s. Together with his 'Flip Squad', which started as a partnership with Big Kap but expanded to include DJ Enuff, DJ Boodakhan, DJ Riz, Frankie Cutlass and Biz Markie, he has gone on to become a prominent remixer. His own recording career began with 'Dope On Plastic', for Bobby Konders' label Massive B. It was followed by 'Six Million Ways To Die' and 'C'Mon Baby' for Nervous Records' subsidiary Wreck Records. His debut mix set followed in 1995, comprising 'old school jams' as well as the artist's own creations. 'Every Day & Every Night', sung by R&B singer Yvette Michell, was released as a single. Flex subsequently broadcast in the UK as co-host of Tim Westwood's regular link-ups for the Radio 1 *Rap Show*. Further instalments of his mix series continued to successfully capture the atmosphere of the unofficial mix tapes sold widely on the streets of New York. His 1999 'debut' featured an astonishing role call of big name MCs past and present, including a live recording of the ill-fated 2Pac and the Notorious B.I.G. from 1993.

● ALBUMS: with Big Kap *The Tunnel* (Def Jam 1999)★★★★.

● COMPILATIONS: *The Mix Tape Volume 1: 60 Minutes Of Funk* (Loud/RCA 1995)★★★★, *The Mix Tape Volume II: 60 Minutes Of Funk* (Loud/RCA 1997)★★★, *The Mix Tape Volume III: 60 Minutes Of Funk, The Final Chapter* (Loud/RCA 1998)★★★★.

Future Sound Of London

Offered to dance music punters as the 'intelligent way out of blind-alley hardcore', Future Sound Of London emerged in the 90s, the brainchild of Gary Cobain (b. Bedford, England) and Brian Dougans. They met at college in Manchester in 1985, but Cobain soon left in order to set up his own studio under an Enterprise Allowance scheme. Both went on to earn their spurs in the Manchester house scene, Dougans completing a groundbreaking Top 10 hit (as Stakker) with 'Humanoid', after it had been adopted by the BBC as the theme tune to a 'youth' television programme. Their other projects together spawned Semi Real ('People Livin' Today'), Yage, Metropolis (the industrial *Metropolis* EP), Art Science Technology, Mental Cube (the ambient 'So This Is Love'), Candese, Intelligent Communication and Smart Systems. However, as Future Sound Of London they enjoyed a major crossover success with 'Papua New Guinea', an enticing, beautifully orchestrated piece. Both 'Papua New Guinea' and 'Metropolis' can be found on *Accelerator*, a seamless collection of rhythmic tracks. Under the name Amorphous Androgynous the pair recorded *Tales Of Ephidrina*, which used imaginative samples from sources as diverse as Peter Gabriel's soundtrack to *The Last Temptation Of Christ* and the alien's voice from *Predator*. Back under the FSOL banner, the duo released the excellent 'Cascade' in October 1993, a 30-minute workout taken from their second album, *Lifeforms*,

which combined breakbeats with rumbling bass and heavy atmospherics. Unfortunately, the album was, at times, disappointing. On several of the pieces, they had the potential to allow an interesting groove to develop into a full-blown track, as with the 'Cascade' single. However, they were all too willing to allow the vibe to deconstruct to basic, although well-produced, chill-out fodder. Having already expressed their desire to break into other media, throughout 1994 the Future Sound Of London experimented with live broadcasts from their own north London studio, via ISDN telephone links to various national and international radio stations, inviting listeners to view accompanying video graphics on their home computers. They released a collection of these tracks on an (originally limited release) album, simply titled *ISDN*. Taken from various live radio broadcasts and electronic café sessions, *ISDN* proved to be an engaging and involving departure from their previous full-length work. In 1996, they released *Dead Cities*, which offered fresh sounds, ranging from the furiously harsh 'Herd Killing', to the pure choral piece, 'Everyone In The World Is Doing Something Without Me'.

● ALBUMS: *Accelerator* (Jumpin' & Pumpin' 1992)★★★★, as Amorphous Androgynous *Tales Of Ephidrina* (Virgin/Astralwerks 1993)★★★★, *Lifeforms* (Virgin/Astralwerks 1994)★★★, *ISDN* (Virgin/Astralwerks 1994)★★★, *Dead Cities* (Virgin/Astralwerks 1996)★★★.

G Love And Special Sauce

Formed by Philadelphia native Garrett Dutton III, aka G Love, this trio consciously recall the pre-pop blues world alongside scat lyrics from the jazz tradition and hip-hop beats. G Love met his partners, Jeffrey Clemmens (drums) and Jimmy Prescott (bass) in Boston, Massachusetts, USA, in 1992, after failing to earn a decent living busking in his native city. The intent was simple but unusual, as Clemmens recalls: 'G Love writes great songs and each of us brings the spirit of the blues to the music.' They met while Prescott was running a jam session at the Tam O Shanter bar, playing their debut performance there on 18 February 1993. Their debut album was the first to be released on the newly reactivated OKeh Records label, and the first ever by a white act in the label's history. Though taking critics by surprise, it received almost universal praise for its uninhibited approach, using acoustic instruments to propel a unique, unreconstructed blues sound. For their second album the trio relocated to New Orleans from their Boston base, and their attempts to capture something of the 'soul' of the city resulted in another acclaimed release. The key lay in their approach, never so reverent that it was haunted by the city's musical ghosts, with Dutton choosing instead to write in raw, scratchy but undeniably attractive movements. After experimenting with different musicians on 1997's *Yeah It's That Easy*, Dutton returned to the trio format for *Philadelphonic*. The album was named after the term used by Dutton to encapsulate their eclectic sound, and featured hip-hop beats provided by producer T-Ray.

● ALBUMS: *G Love And Special Sauce* (OKeh 1994)★★★★, *Coast To Coast Motel* (OKeh 1995)★★★, *Yeah It's That Easy* (OKeh 1997)★★★, *Philadelphonic* (OKeh 1999)★★★★.

G., Gina

Having moved to Melbourne, Australia, in 1987, this female vocalist began work as a DJ in that city's dance clubs. Eventually, she joined the influential dance music outfit, Bass Culture. Signed to Mushroom Records, the group reached the Australian Top 40 with their first single in 1992, which was written and sung by Gina herself. Later she moved to the UK, where she became involved in several projects before recording 'Ooh Aah ... Just A Little Bit'. A trite, Euro-pop dance song, it was entered in the Great British Song Contest (a preliminary round preceding the Eurovision Song Contest), and progressed to the final four of the competition before becoming the official British entry. Written by Simon Tauber and Motiv8's Steve Rodway (previously responsible for remixing Pulp's 'Disco 2000' and 'Common People', as well as their own hits 'Searching For The Golden Eye' and 'Break The Chain'), it was released on Warner Brothers Records' dance subsidiary, Eternal, in March 1996 and raced to the top of the UK charts. It also became the first Eurovision song contest entry to be voted Single Of The Week by *Melody Maker*. Two more irritatingly catchy singles, 'I Belong To You' and 'Fresh!', made it into the UK Top 10 before the singer's brief moment in the spotlight was over.

● ALBUMS: *Fresh* (Eternal/WEA 1997)★★★.

G., Kenny

b. Kenneth Gorelick, 6 July 1956, Seattle, Washington, USA. Gorelick learned saxophone as a child and toured Europe in 1974 with the Franklin High School band. Two years later he played with Barry White's Love Unlimited Orchestra in Seattle before entering the University of Washington to study accounting. Gorelick first recorded with local funk band Cold, Bold & Together and also backed many leading artists on their Seattle shows. After graduation, he joined the Jeff Lorber Fusion, recording with the jazz-rock band for Arista Records, the label which in 1981 signed him to a solo contract. Produced by Preston Glass and Narada Michael Walden, *Duotones* was a major success and it included 'Songbird', a US Top 5 hit in 1987. Like much of his other work, it featured a flawless, melodic alto saxophone solo. By now, Kenny G. was in demand to play solos on albums by such singers as Whitney Houston, Natalie Cole and Aretha Franklin. Among the guest artists on *Silhouette* was Smokey Robinson who sang 'We've Saved The Best For Last'. Like its predecessor, the album sold over three million copies world-wide. Kenny G.'s extraordinary success continued into the 90s. In 1992, he collaborated with Michael Bolton's on the US Top 20 hit 'Missing You Now', and released the multi-platinum *Breathless*. He was also acknowledged as fellow musician President Clinton's favourite saxophonist. The crossover into pop is felt to be too strong by most jazz critics, as the type of music he plays is very structured and contrived. Popular music has at least given rise to the 'great crossover debate'. Arguments aside; Kenny G. is a phenomenon, he sells albums in rock group proportions and his popularity is consistent. His *Miracles: The Holiday Album* rocketed to the top of the US pop chart, re-igniting interest in *Breathless* which, by the mid-90s had sold over 11 million copies in the USA alone and had remained at the top of the *Billboard* jazz chart for well over 18 months. It was finally toppled in October 1996 after an incredible run. The rude interloper to this was *The Moment*, the new album from . . . Kenny G. He changed tack for the subsequent *Classics In The Key Of G*, a collection of jazz standards which still managed to sound like all his other recordings.

● ALBUMS: *Kenny G* (Arista 1982)★★, *G Force* (Arista 1983)★★★, with G Force *Gravity* (Arista 1985)★★★, *Duotones* (Arista 1986)★★★, *Silhouette* (Arista 1988)★★★, *Kenny G Live* (Arista 1989)★★, *Breathless* (Arista 1992)★★★★, *Miracles: The Holiday Album*. (Arista 1994)★★, *The Moment* (Arista 1996)★★★, *Classics In The Key Of G* (Arista 1999)★★★, *Faith: A Holiday Album* (Arista 1999)★★.

● COMPILATIONS: *Greatest Hits* (Arista 1997)★★★.

G., Warren

b. Warren Griffin III, 10 November 1970, Long Beach, California, USA. Half-brother to Dr. Dre, Griffin's parents relocated to Long Beach from Tennessee and Oklahoma before he was born. He was raised in a staunchly Christian tradition, and despite affiliations with gangsta rap, he maintained his allegiance to 'Jesus' at the top of his list of dedications on his debut album. It was Dre's World Class Wreckin' Cru which inspired him to follow a musical path. He first began rapping and producing while working at the local VIP record store. Later he helped form Dre's Dogg Pound collective, with Nate Dogg and his best friend, Snoop Doggy Dogg. The trio also worked together as part of the unrecorded 213. His role in the development of west coast rap was crucial - he is credited with having introduced Snoop Doggy Dogg to Dre (a meeting recalled in his debut album's 'Do You See'). Having subsequently produced a track for M.C. Breed ('Gotta Get Mine'), and appeared on both *The Chronic* and *Doggy Style*, he then wrote, produced and guested on Mista Grimm's 'Indo Smoke' and 2Pac's 'Definition Of A Thug'. 'Indo Smoke' appeared in the movie *Poetic Justice*, while 'Definition Of A Thug' was included on the soundtrack album, *Above The Rim*, which hit the number 1 spot on the US R&B album charts. Griffin's own debut as Warren G., 'Regulate', was the keynote to that album's success. Built around a sample of Michael McDonald's 'I Keep Forgettin' (Every Time You're Near)', which his father had played constantly when he was a child, it also became his first US Top 10 single - the first release on Chris Lighty's Violator imprint. *Regulate*, also the title of his debut album, immediately achieved triple-platinum status, and confirmed the accessibility of his approach. He also departed from rap norms with his employment of live musicians. Following a US tour with R. Kelly and Heavy D, he concentrated on producing the debut of his protégés, Da Twinz, who were part of the collective involved with *Regulate*. In 1996, he scored further international success with 'What's Love Got To Do With It', a hit single from the soundtrack to *Super Cop* which topped the German charts and reached UK number 2. His disappointing second album, *Take A Look Over Your Shoulder (Reality)*, was released as part of a new contract with Def Jam Records in 1997. The album incorporated cover versions of Bob Marley's 'I Shot The Sheriff' (a UK number 2 hit) and the Isley Brothers' 'Smokin' Me Out' (with a chorus sung by Ronald Isley). *I Want It All* featured a stellar cast list of guest MCs, including Snoop Dogg, Mack 10 and Kurupt.

● ALBUMS: *Regulate ... G Funk Era* (Violator/Def Jam 1994)★★★★, *Take A Look Over Your Shoulder (Reality)* (G Funk/Def Jam 1997)★★★, *I Want It All* (G Funk 1999)★★★.

● FILMS: *The Show* (1995), *The Wizard Of Oz* (1998), *Speedway Junky* (1999).

Gabrielle

b. Louise Gabrielle Bobb, 16 April 1970, London, England. The corporate record industry's new soul diva of the 90s, Gabrielle earned a high commercial profile via a series of perfectly realized, expertly pitched releases. Visually distinguished by a black eye patch, she made a dramatic entrance with her UK chart-topping debut single, 'Dreams', in summer 1993. The song also entered the US Top 30 later in the year. Equally accessible was the UK Top 10 follow-up, 'Going Nowhere'. The album that followed was produced by seven different producers, including the Boilerhouse (Andy Cox and David Steele of the Fine Young Cannibals) and Steve Jervier (famed for his work with Take That). She was fêted at various awards ceremonies, and became such a celebrity that she was invited to appear at the Armani fashion show in Milan. During the break between her albums she gave birth to a child. Ten of the tracks on the heavily anticipated *Gabrielle* were written by Andy Dean and Ben Wolff, and they shared the production with Foster And McElroy. The Motown Records pastiche 'Give Me A Little More Time' was a Top 5 UK hit in the spring of 1996. Further singles were less successful, before 'If You Ever', a collaboration with boy band East 17, reached number 2 in November. Her third collection, *Rise*, benefited from the production skills of Johnny Dollar (Massive Attack), and was premiered by the UK Top 10 single 'Sunshine'. The title track, built around a hypnotic sample from Bob Dylan's 'Knockin' On Heaven's Door', provided the singer with her second UK chart-topper in February 2000.

● ALBUMS: *Find Your Way* (Go! Beat 1994)★★★, *Gabrielle* (Go! Beat 1996)★★★, *Rise* (Go! Beat 1999)★★★.

Galliano

This sprawling UK outfit enjoyed a fruitful period in the spotlight at the height of acid-jazz's popularity in the late 80s and early 90s. The band was formed by new age rapper and jazz poet Rob Gallagher (aka Earl Zinger), who was originally inspired by a school visit to see Linton Kwesi Johnson, and subsequently retraced rap's origins to the Last Poets. When he left school Gallagher began broadcasting on pirate radio and made appearances on the underground poetry circuit. The most important of these dates was at Gilles Peterson's Babylon club in Charing Cross, London. There he enthusiastically partook of the resident rare groove/jazz sounds, and incorporated these as his musical backing. He released his first record, 'Frederick Lies Still', a tribute to Curtis Mayfield and Last Poets' Jalal Nuridin, with Peterson, but his first vinyl as Galliano was to be 'Welcome To The Story'. Galliano became an intrinsic component in the rise of Acid Jazz Records, building a fruitful relationship with producer Chris Bangs. When Peterson was headhunted by Phonogram Records to set up the similarly-inclined Talkin' Loud Records label, Galliano was his first signing. Although his solo work had thus far been successful, he elected to extend his live and studio performances by adding musicians and collaborators. Vocalist Constantine Weir (who had sung with S'Express', and managed the 70s funk club, The Shack) and percussionist Brother Spry (b. Crispin Robinson; formerly a professional skateboarder and an experienced session musician) became official members of Galliano, as well as occasional appearances from Jalal Nuridin. Aided by former Style Council member Mick Talbot, this line-up completed Galliano's 1991 debut. The excellent follow-up, *A Joyful Noise Unto The Creator*, featured the minor hit singles 'Skunk Funk' and 'Prince Of Peace'. Galliano extended their cult reputation by touring incessantly throughout the world, thrilling crowds with their inspirational live shows. By this point, the line-up boasted Gallagher, Talbot, Brother Spry, Valerie Étienne (vocals), Ernie McKone (bass), Crispin Taylor (drums), Mark Vandergucht (guitar), Brother Constantine (vocals), and Daddy Smith (vibe controller). The 1994 UK Top 20 single, 'Long Time Gone', based on the David Crosby song, was the band's first release in over two years. The subsequent album *The Plot Thickens* was acclaimed, despite mainstream critics who had only just noticed the band somewhat cumbersomely describing their sound as an acid jazz/funk/urban alternative. The album was to prove their commercial highpoint, however, as acid jazz's popularity waned and returned to the small clubs and cliqué status from whence it had risen. Following the release of a fourth album and a live set the various members have concentrated on solo projects.

● ALBUMS: *In Pursuit Of The 13th Note* (Talkin' Loud 1991)★★★, *A Joyful Noise Unto The Creator* (Talkin' Loud 1992)★★★★, *What Colour Our Flag* US only (Talkin' Loud/PolyGram 1994)★★★, *The Plot Thickens* (Talkin' Loud 1994)★★★★, *4* (Talkin' Loud 1996)★★★, *Live At The Liquid Rooms* (Talkin' Loud 1997)★★★.

Gallon Drunk

High-energy rock 'n' roll band who emerged as contenders for the vacant Birthday Party throne in the early 90s. The band's line-up was James Johnston (vocals, guitar, organ), Mike Delanian (bass) - both of whom were at school together, Max Decharne (drums, also keyboard player with the Earls Of Suave) and Joe Byfield (maracas), the latter having spent a brief period with My Bloody Valentine. Formed early in 1990 and based in north London, original drummer Nick Combe was soon jettisoned. They quickly garnered plaudits from the music press, the *New Musical Express* describing them as 'a synthesis of quite disparate elements, from Memphis soul slew to primal rockabilly'. Others noted a similarity to the more raucous Birthday Party/Nick Cave recordings. After releasing singles on their manager's own Massive label, they moved on to Clawfist where their debut album was released in 1992. Given their high press profile, this proved to be a little lacklustre, with strong songs smothered by a flat production. *From The Heart Of Town* was much closer to the mark, with Johnston's lyrics given a strong empathy by the band's voodoo rhythms and dry musicianship (including the contribution of new Gallon Drunk horn player Terry Edwards). Johnston's vignettes included some startling depictions of the grubbier elements of life in the capital, populated by characters of the grim majesty of 'Jake On The Make' and the tramp in 'Arlington Road'. Johnston played with the Bad Seeds, and then collaborated with Edwards on *Dora Saurez*, a spoken word album with crime writer Derek Raymond. The band returned in 1996 with new members Ian Watson (guitar/trumpet), Andy Dewar (percussion) and Ian White (drums), proving to be as raucous and menacing as ever. Despite Johnston's subsequent claim that the band was finished, and that he was embarking on a solo career under the name JJ Stone, they returned in October 1999 with a new EP, *Blood Is Red*.

● ALBUMS: *You, The Night And The Music* (Clawfist 1992)★★, *From The Heart Of Town* (Clawfist 1993)★★★, *In The Long Still Night* (City Slang 1996)★★★, *Fire Music* (City Slang 1996)★★★.

● COMPILATIONS: *Tonite ... The Singles Bar* (Clawfist 1991)★★.

Gang Starr

Arguably hip-hop's most literate, challenging act on both musical and lyrical fronts, Gang Starr comprises Guru Keith E (b. Keith Elam, 18 July 1966, Roxbury, Massachusetts, USA; vocals/lyrics) and DJ Premier (b. Chris Martin, 3 May 1969, Brooklyn, New York, USA; music). Guru (Gifted Unlimited Rhymes Universal) was born the son of a Boston municipal and superior court judge, but moved to Brooklyn following graduation with a degree in business administration from Atlanta's Morehouse College. He had previously worked as a counsellor in a maximum detention home in Boston, an experience which would inform many of his lyrics. Gang Starr was in existence before DJ Premier joined, originally also consisting of fellow rapper Damo D-Ski and DJ Wanna Be Down. Their early labours are recalled on cuts like 'The Lesson' and ' Bust A Move', both of which were produced by DJ Mark The 45 King. However, they were at that time still Boston-based, and in the end opted to pursue more geographically convenient projects. Premier, meanwhile, had relocated to Texas to attend college, but left demos of his work with various labels before his departure. In Texas, he put together the Inner City Posse, who finally saw their demo get some attention. Premier was offered a deal with Wild Pitch Records, but only on the condition he lost his original rapper. The label put him in touch with Guru instead, who had chanced upon one of Premier's demo tapes in their offices, and a marriage made in hip-hop heaven was born. However, Premier had to return to college in Texas, and so the duo's liaison took place largely over the phone, and by sending each other tapes. The fruits of their labour were unveiled on 1989's debut album, *No More Mr. Nice Guy*, completed in 10 days while Premier was on vacation. 'Manifest', taken from the album, picked up airplay on *Yo! MTV Raps*, and caught the attention of film director Spike Lee. In the process of completing his new movie, *Mo Better Blues*, Lee was greatly impressed by album track 'Jazz Thing', and asked his musical director, Branford Marsalis, to track Gang Starr down. Marsalis urged the duo to cut a recording of Lotis Eli's poem about the history of jazz to a hip-hop rhythm, for inclusion on the movie's soundtrack.

The song they eventually came up with would see release as 'Jazz Thing'. Not only one of rap's most crucial moments, 'Jazz Thing' also gave Gang Starr a manifesto for their subsequent career. Credited with popularising jazz-rap, they took the form to its logical conclusion with *Step In The Arena*, before retreating to hardcore pastures for *Daily Operation*.

Both Guru and Premier have striven to be seen as individuals outside of the Gang Starr hallmark. A joint collaboration with the Dream Warriors on 'I've Lost My Ignorance' aside, each has increased their profile with solo projects. Premier has produced widely for KRS-One, Fu-Schnickens, Big Daddy Kane and Heavy D among many others, while Guru set up the winning Jazzmatazz situation. The latter comprised his distinctive rap style with the best of modern freeform jazz. An interesting departure considering that Premier has always used samples rather than live instruments, though since *Daily Operation* he has been forced to credit and clear them. Though such forays encouraged speculation that Gang Starr were about to split, the duo belied the critics with a storming return on *Hard To Earn*. Back to their freestyle, flowing best, it was the second outing for the posse of rappers that Guru had formed into the Gang Starr Foundation: Jeru The Damaja, Big Shug (who was a collaborator with Guru in his early days in Boston), Little Dap and Felachi The Nutcracker. After a prolonged absence they returned to the scene in 1998 with the inventive *Moment Of Truth*. The following year's compilation, *Full Clip: A Decade Of Gang Starr*, provided a comprehensive overview of a most consistently excellent team.

● ALBUMS: *No More Mr. Nice Guy* (Wild Pitch 1989)★★★, *Step In The Arena* (Chrysalis 1990)★★★★, *Daily Operation* (Chrysalis 1992)★★, *Hard To Earn* (Chrysalis 1994)★★★, *Moment Of Truth* (Cooltempo 1998)★★★.

● COMPILATIONS: *Full Clip: A Decade Of Gang Starr* (Noo Trybe/Virgin 1999)★★★★.

Garbage

This US band, founded in 1994, was immediately heralded in the press as a producers' supergroup. In addition to several other notable bands (Smashing Pumpkins, U2), Butch Vig had previously produced Nirvana's influential *Nevermind*. He formed Garbage with the help of his long-standing remixing partners Steve Marker and Duke Erikson, with whom he had been involved in the bands Spooner and Firetown. To this core trio was added singer Shirley Manson (b. Edinburgh, Scotland), recruited after the members saw her fronting her former unit, Angel Fish, on a video shown on MTV (she had previously sung with the unheralded Goodbye Mr Mackenzie). Garbage's debut single, 'Vow', issued in a metal sleeve, was widely acclaimed, as was the follow-up, 'Subhuman'. Both borrowed from various traditions, notably punk, glam rock and art rock, with Vig commenting: 'We want to use all these different elements like techno, punk and noise, ambient, jazz and rock, and mix them all up around a pop song.' This eclecticism was further explored on their self-titled debut album, a dark collection of songs with the main emotions being fear, lust and envy. Symptomatic of these concerns was 'Only Happy When It Rains', which also reached the charts when issued as a single. Further chart success came with a remix of 'Milk' (featuring Tricky as guest vocalist) and 'Stupid Girl'. The band's unexpected global success (especially in America) delayed the recording of their follow-up as they committed themselves to a relentless touring schedule. When *Version 2.0* finally appeared the band gained further praise for their compelling blend of slick electronic pop featuring Manson's emotive vocals. The album topped the UK charts in May 1998. The following year the band was commissioned to write the theme tune to the new James Bond movie, *The World Is Not Enough*.

● ALBUMS: *Garbage* (Mushroom 1995)★★★★, *Version 2.0* (Mushroom 1998)★★★.

● VIDEOS: *Garbage Video* (Mushroom 1996), *Garbage* (Geffen Video 1996).

Garnier, Laurent

b. 1 February 1966, Boulogne sur Seine, near Paris, France. Influential European DJ figurehead Garnier enjoyed a previous life as a restaurant manager, then footman at the French Embassy (where he claims to have served UK dignitaries like the Queen, Princess Diana and Margaret Thatcher). Regarded as France's finest techno DJ, Garnier, who started behind the decks at Manchester, England's Haçienda in October 1987, insists that his musical spectrum is much wider. Although he has been a powerful advocate of all things Detroit for some time, he has also had a hand in the establishment of the European hard trance movement. A typical evening will see him mixing standbys from Rhythim Is Rhythim (Derrick May) and Joe Smooth ('Promised Land') against classic Salsoul and disco records (typically Donna Summer's 'I Feel Love'), in addition to the hottest new underground sounds. His reputation is built on a punishing schedule, performing five nights a week at up to four different countries within Europe. He also runs a club in Paris called Wake Up, whose free-ranging music policy was reflected on the 'Wake Up' remix of Moby's 'Hymn'. The latter was just one such remixing project, which has brought him to the forefront of dance music. So too his label, FNAC, which, together with Eric Morand (his PR) pioneered French dance music. It has been superseded by a new imprint, F-Communications. However, before they bowed out of their involvement with FNAC, they put together a compilation, *La Collection*, which was extraordinarily well-received by dance critics and pundits. Many of the acts featured followed Garnier and Morand to their new label. Garnier has released several challenging long-players, while his singles output includes the club favourites 'Acid Eiffel' and 'Crispy Bacon'. Ironically, he is most associated with the novelty item 'Flat Beat' by Mr Oizo. The single, a UK chart-topper in March 1999, gained cult status when it was used as a soundtrack to a series of Levis television advertisements. Garnier has recently begun to experiment with a live show that eschews samplers and sequencers in favour of real musicians and dancers.

● ALBUMS: *Shot In The Dark* (F Communications 1994)★★★★, *Laboratoire Mix* (F Communications 1995)★★★, *Raw Works* (F Communications 1996)★★★, *30* (F Communications 1997)★★★, *Unreasonable Behaviour* (F Communications 2000)★★★★.

Gastr Del Sol

The creation of David Grubbs (guitar/piano/vocals), a former member of the Louisville, Kentucky, USA-based hardcore outfit Squirrel Bait. When that influential band

split-up in 1987, Grubbs formed Bastro and recorded three albums for Homestead Records that gradually moved away from the noise-rock squall of Squirrel Bait towards *avant garde* experimentalism, although he continued to satisfy his rock instincts as guitarist for Bitch Magnet. Grubbs first used the Gastr Del Sol moniker for 1991's *The Serpentine Similar* EP, recorded with bass player Bundy K. Brown and drummer John McEntire from Bastro. Eschewing conventional rock melody altogether, the EP's exploratory tone set the tone for future Gastr Del Sol releases. The '20 Songs Less' single introduced an important new member to the line-up, guitarist/composer/tape manipulator and *avant garde* hero, Jim O'Rourke. Brown left before the esoteric *Crookt, Crackt, Or Fly*, recorded like all subsequent Gastr Del Sol releases, by Grubbs and O'Rourke and a loose collective of guest musicians. Their EPs and albums focused on the interplay of Grubbs and O'Rourke's acoustic guitars, reminiscent at times of the plangent tones of John Fahey, although there was the occasional rock workout in a nod to Grubbs' hardcore past. O'Rourke's subtle tape work and Grubbs' impressionistic lyrics were vital elements in the creation of unconventional tonal patterns. Moving further away from the mainstream, 1995's *The Harp Factory On Lake Street* EP, released on the Table Of The Elements label, comprised a single extended piece of music for a small orchestra. Grubbs released his abstract solo work, *Banana Cabbage Potato Lettuce Onion Orange*, on the same label. *Upgrade & Afterlife* saw Grubbs and O'Rourke making a few concessions to the mainstream in terms of melody and structure, and emerging with their most accessible and likeable album. O'Rourke left in July 1997, although he featured alongside fellow electronic genius Markus Popp on *Camoufleur*, a deceptively complex release that radiated a Zen-like aura of calming restraint. With Gastr Del Sol seemingly laid to rest, Grubbs has subsequently concentrated on solo work and his continued involvement with the Red Crayola. *The Thicket* and *The Coxcomb* were engaging albums that saw Grubbs in, for him at least, almost conventional singer-songwriter mode.

● ALBUMS: *The Serpentine Similar* (TeenBeat 1993)★★★, *Crookt, Crackt, Or Fly* (Drag City 1994)★★★, *Upgrade & Afterlife* (Drag City 1996)★★★★, *Camoufleur* (Drag City 1998)★★★.
Solo: David Grubbs *Banana Cabbage Potato Lettuce Onion Orange* (Table Of The Elements 1997)★★★, *The Thicket* (Drag City 1998)★★★, *The Coxcomb* (Rectangle 1999)★★★★.

Gatecrasher

In only a few years, Gatecrasher has become one of the most important, popular and influential clubs on the UK and European dance music scene. It is famous for its outrageously flamboyant and notoriously 'up for it' crowds and the uncompromisingly 'full on' trance sound of its music. Gatecrasher can now certainly be ranked alongside Cream, Renaissance and the Ministry Of Sound as being one of the world's most successful and trend-setting clubs. It was started by UK DJ Scott Bond with partner, Simon Raine and, after a number of informal parties began its life at Sheffield's the Arches in 1994. Gatecrasher moved in 1997 to the Republic, a former iron and steel works which was converted to a nightclub venue by architect Charles Baker. The club purchased the Republic in 1998 and, later that year, undertook a major refurbishment and improvement of sound, lighting and facilities. Gatecrasher's groundbreaking musical policy is the result of experimenting with less well-known DJ talent, which it 'imports' from continental Europe and elsewhere. Germany's Paul Van Dyk first found popularity in the UK by being invited to play at the club and the same can be said for fellow German, DJ Taucher, Dutchman DJ Tiesto and Israel's Jez and Choopie. The approach that the club seems to take is if the quality and style of the music fit the unique Gatecrasher atmosphere, then whether or not it is played by a big name DJ is of no consequence. Other innovations are the five and six-hour sets now being played by DJs such as Sasha and Paul Van Dyk, an information point within the club and a travel service from other UK cities. The club has also released several very successful compilations through the Sony dance subsidiary, INCredible. In 1998, the club won the UK's *Muzik* magazine's Club Of The Year award and *Mixmag*'s Crowd Of The Year. The club's millennium gig featured over 15 hours worth of classic tracks played by some of the finest names in contemporary dance music, including the Chemical Brothers, Paul Oakenfold, Sasha, Judge Jules, Paul Van Dyk, 'Tall' Paul Newman, Sonique, Scott Bond and Matt Hardwick

● COMPILATIONS: *Gatecrasher – Gold* (Sony/INCredible 1998)★★★★, *Gatecrasher – Red* (Sony/INCredible 1999)★★★★, *Gatecrasher - Wet* (Sony/INCredible 1999)★★★★, *Disco-Tech* (Sony/INCredible 1999)★★★★.

Gay Dad

The brainchild of a music journalist, this UK band arrived on the back of a wave of hype generated by a music press desperate to promote them as the new saviours of indie music. After floating around the fringes of the music scene for several years, Gay Dad eventually became a reality in 1997, with a line-up comprising Cliff Jones (guitar/vocals), James Risebero (keyboards), Nigel Hoyle (bass) and Nicholas 'Baz' Crowe (drummer). Jones was a marginally successful journalist who had been published in magazines including *The Face* and *Mojo*. Hoyle was a medical student, Crowe worked in publishing, and Risebero was a trained architect. The quartet recorded demos at Raezor Studios, including a song called 'To Earth With Love'. Although originally intended to win the band some live dates, the demo soon attracted keen record company interest. The band signed to London Records in December 1997 after an A&R scramble. Adding guitarist Charley Stone they embarked on a low-key tour with Superstar in early 1998. Afterwards, the band began recording sessions at The Dairy studio in Brixton with producers/engineers Gary Langan (ex-Art Of Noise) and Chris Hughes (ex-Adam And The Ants). A re-recorded 'To Earth With Love' was released on the back of tremendous press hype, with the band's name and their logo (road sign posters depicting a white man against a blue background) skilfully exploiting the zeitgeist. The single debuted at UK number 10 in January 1999, but poor live shows initiated the predictable critical backlash. The follow-up single 'Joy' stalled outside the Top 20 in May, while *Leisurenoise* entered the charts at number 14. The album was a surprisingly effective pastiche of 70s musical styles, from the driving glam rock of their debut single to the power pop of 'Pathfinder' and 'Different Kind Of Blue'.

● ALBUMS: *Leisurenoise* (London 1999)★★★.

Gayle, Michelle

b. London, England. Immediately recognizable to fans of pop culture through her role as Hattie Tavernier in BBC Television soap opera *EastEnders*, Gayle's crossover to the music charts in the mid-90s was one of the most viable amid a slew of sorry cash-ins: 'I wasn't even going to do *EastEnders*. I was going to turn it down because I just wanted to focus on music. I was in a band, Amorphous, at the time and basically agreed to play Hattie to help make some money to pay for demos and equipment for the group.' She had started writing songs at the age of 13, following advice from her music teacher, by which time she had already appeared in another BBC Television programme, *Grange Hill*. Certainly, her attempts to convince the press that her real calling had always been music were backed up by a voice with impressive range and control, best demonstrated on the UK hit singles 'Looking Up' (number 11) and 'Sweetness' (number 4). Taken under the wing of Dennis Ingoldsby, he helped to procure a series of suitable musical compositions for her chart forays, over which Gayle would customize lyrics. Although the selection of material on her debut was certainly limited, the best of it was undoubtedly first-class pop soul. Its reward was gold status in the UK charts, as Gayle became a major star via widespread UK touring in support of Eternal. She enjoyed further UK hit singles in 1995 with 'Freedom' (number 16), 'Happy Just To Be With You' (number 11). Her second album was premiered by the excellent 'Do You Know', which reached UK number 6 in February 1997. The title track was also a Top 20 hit.

● ALBUMS: *Michelle Gayle* (RCA 1994)★★★, *Sensational* (RCA 1997)★★★.

Gene

Foppish aesthetes Gene formed in the summer of 1993, quickly melding a waspish chemistry from the base components of Steve Mason (b. England; guitar), Martin Rossiter (b. England; vocals), Kevin Miles (b. England; bass) and Matt James (b. England; drums). Mason and James were formerly together in Spin. Writing songs together and honing their live profile, their influences were culled from Paul Weller, the Small Faces and, most obviously, the Smiths. Their debut release, the double a-side 'For The Dead'/'Child's Body', released on the fledgling Costermonger label in May 1994, set out a distinct musical agenda. Single Of The Week and Month awards followed from *New Musical Express* and *Select* magazines, with the limited 1,994 pressing selling out within two days after it was play-listed by BBC Radio 1. A strong reaction was also gained as support to Pulp at London's Forum, where Rossiter's stage presence illuminated Gene's performance. August brought a second single, this time promoted as a 'triple a-side', featuring 'Be My Light, Be My Guide', 'This Is Not My Crime' and 'I Can't Help Myself'. Gaining pole position in the UK independent poll, and reaching number 54 in the UK charts proper, the band set out on their first headlining UK tour. Following further positive press, the band signed with Polydor Records. A third single, 'Sleep Well Tonight', followed an appearance at the Reading Festival, also playing mainland Europe for the first time with Elastica and Oasis. *Select*'s description of the single, 'ace crooning and rock and roll iridescence', came closest to cornering Gene's appeal. It saw them break the Top 40, as they featured highly in various end of year polls for brightest UK newcomers. The release of 'Haunted By You' in February 1995 prefigured a debut album proper, produced by Phil Vinall. With less direct, even nebulous material sandwiching the energy of the singles, there was much for critics to reflect on. Eschewing the self-consciously fey approach of Suede, the uncouth voyeurism of Pulp or the 'new lad' abrasiveness of Oasis, Rossiter's songs were dominated instead by a wholly unromantic cast of characters inhabiting a down-at-heel, broken world with little hope of redemption. *To See The Lights* collected together b-sides and live recordings, acting as a stop-gap for the accomplished *Drawn To The Deep End*, released in early 1997, with the band displaying a greater musical diversity to back-up Rossiter's lyrical dramas. *Revelations* was another occasionally inspired collection, although critics bemoaned the fact that the band still seemed unable to successfully translate their excellent live sound onto record. The band was released from its Polydor contract at the end of the year.

● ALBUMS: *Olympian* (Costermonger 1995)★★★★, *To See The Lights* (Costermonger 1996)★★★, *Drawn To The Deep End* (Polydor 1997)★★★, *Revelations* (Polydor 1999)★★★.

Geneva

Formed in Aberdeen, Scotland, in 1993, Geneva comprise former *Sunday Post* journalist Andrew Montgomery (vocals), former marine biologist Steven Dora (guitar) and ex-students Douglas Caskie (drums), Keith Graham (bass) and Stuart Evans (guitar). It was several years into the band's existence before the members decided to take their music seriously. Once they did, however, the rewards were instantaneous. They signed a recording contract with Nude Records in December 1995, after their progress had been noted in London. They then came to the attention of the UK press through support tours with labelmates Suede. Montgomery's highly affecting vocals, by turns vulnerable and stoic, became the subject of heightened media interest, and critical comparisons to Tim Buckley. A series of singles followed, bringing the band to the periphery of the British charts. *Further*, released early in 1997, was cited by many reviewers as one of the best British debut albums of the 90s. Andrew Mueller in *The Independent* was just one of those impressed by its marriage of Scottish pop craft and expressionistic songwriting: 'They are . . . fluent in the peculiarly haunting dialect of Scottish pop, that strange and lovely language of luxurious, exuberant, redemptive melancholy that characterises acts as disparate as Aztec Camera, the Associates, Teenage Fanclub, Jesus And Mary Chain and the Blue Nile.' The last-named band provides the most opportune reference point, the Blue Nile sharing Geneva's devotion to aural aesthetics and texture. The band enlisted the heavyweight help of producer Howie B for the eagerly anticipated follow-up, *Weather Underground*.

● ALBUMS: *Further* (Nude 1997)★★★★, *Weather Underground* (Nude 2000)★★★.

Genius

b. Gary Grice, New York, USA. The Genius (aka GZA) is one of the many talents who comprise the Wu-Tang Clan, the chess-playing, martial arts hip-hop crew whose members include Raekwon, Method Man, Ol' Dirty Bastard and RZA, among others. The roots of the Wu-Tang Clan lay in All In

Together Now, formed by Genius with his cousins RZA and Ol' Dirty Bastard. Like the majority of his compatriots he is a native of New York's Staten Island district. In common with RZA, the Genius had already recorded as a solo artist for Cold Chillin' Records before becoming part of the collective. However, when the Clan as a whole signed with BMG Records, provision for each member to work solo was enshrined in the contract, and the Genius used the opportunity to link with his third record company, Geffen Records. The Genius' *Liquid Swords* closely mirrored the sound of the Wu-Tang Clan, built around a musical backing of stripped down beats, with samples culled from martial arts movies and movie dialogue. This came as little surprise given that RZA, the production mastermind behind both the collective Wu-Tang Clan and several associated solo releases, was again involved in *Liquid Swords*. Lyrically, Genius continued to concentrate on down at heel scenarios concerning blue collar crime and drug smuggling, epitomised by the chilling true story tale of 'Killah Hills 10304'. Following the Wu-Tang Clan's disappointing sophomore collection, 1997's *Wu-Tang Forever*, Genius began work on *Beneath The Surface*. Released in June 1999, album tracks such as 'Publicity' and 'Victim' served as a timely reminder of Genius' striking lyrical talent.

● ALBUMS: *Words From The Genius* (Cold Chillin' 1991)★★★, *Liquid Swords* (Geffen 1995)★★★★, *Beneath The Surface* (MCA 1999)★★★.

Geraldine Fibbers

Carla Bozulich and her band, the Geraldine Fibbers, have frequently been cited as natural inheritors of X's crown, through their animation of the disillusionment and moral abandonment that is present-day Los Angeles. However, where X hinted at discordant country rock as the appropriate metaphor for the death of the old west, Geraldine Fibbers embrace this medium with less reservation. Prior to forming the band, which comprises William Tutton (bass), Kevin Fitzgerald (drums) and Nels Cline (guitar), who replaced Daniel Keenan in 1996 (violin player Jessy Greene also left the band in 1997), Bozulich had been the centrepiece of controversial industrial punk outfit Ethyl Meatplow. Geraldine Fibbers' debut album, *Lost Somewhere Between The Earth And My Home*, continued the theme of punk isolationism but combined it with a musical platform featuring double bass, fiddle and drums. This blend of country roots proved an excellent platform for Bozulich's feisty lyrics, especially on the more self-conscious material such as 'Dragon Lady' and 'The French Song'. The follow-up *Butch* received strong reviews, focusing again on Bozulich's twisted vision. The album also contained a brave cover version of Can's 'Yoo Do Right'.

● ALBUMS: *Lost Somewhere Between The Earth And My Home* (Virgin 1996)★★★, *Butch* (Virgin 1997)★★★★.

● COMPILATIONS: *What Part Of "Get Thee Gone" Don't You Understand?* (Sympathy For The Record Industry 1997)★★★.

Germano, Lisa

This Indiana, USA native folk-rocker and multi-instrumentalist first started playing piano aged seven, alongside her six other siblings, each of whom were forced to play an instrument until they were 18. Afterwards, she went on to become violinist with John Mellencamp and Bob Seger, also working as a session musician for Billy Joel, Simple Minds and Iggy Pop. Her 1991 debut album arrived on her own label, Major

Bill, but suffered from inadequate production and distribution. Her second album was released by Capitol Records, and on it she added feedback, samples and tape loops to the diet of guitar and violin. It was presented in a radically different form to UK audiences by 4AD Records, whose Ivo Watts Russell also remixed a five-track mini-album sampler, *Inconsiderate Bitch*, in January 1994. This was Germano at her most effective, with stunning arrangements of her multi-instrumental skills, including effects-driven guitar, synthesizer, piano, violin and mandolin. *Geek The Girl*, as Germano wrote in her sleeve notes, was 'the story of a girl who is confused about how to be sexual and cool in the world'. Harrowing and committed, songs such as '... A Psychopath' revealed artistic positioning somewhere between PJ Harvey and Tori Amos, though Germano has yet to reap a similar level of commercial reward. An excellent remix of 'Love Sick' by the Underdog was released in late 1997. Germano also collaborated with Giant Sand on their OP8 project *Slush* the same year, before completing work on her next solo album, *Slide*.

● ALBUMS: *On The Way Down From The Moon Palace* (Major Bill 1991)★★★, *Happiness* (Capitol/4AD 1993)★★★★, *Inconsiderate Bitch* mini-album (4AD 1994)★★★, *Geek The Girl* (4AD 1994)★★★★, *Excerpts From A Love Circus* (4AD 1996)★★★★, with OP8 *Slush* (V2 1997)★★, *Slide* (4AD 1998)★★★.

Geto Boys

Houston, Texas, USA-based gangsta rappers, led by the notorious Bushwick Bill (b. Richard Shaw, Jamaica, West Indies), Scarface (b. Brad Jordan, Houston, Texas, USA) and Willie D. (b. Willie Dennis, Houston, Texas, USA), alongside DJ Ready Red (b. Collins Lyaseth). The latter had left the crew by early 1991. In fact the Geto Boys had originally started with a completely different line-up in 1988, featuring Slim Jukebox, DJ Reddy Red and Prince Johnny C, with Bushwick a dancer. When Johnny C and Jukebox quit (Jukebox was subsequently jailed for murder) former Rap-A-Lot Records solo artists Scarface and Willie D. were added by the record company. It was this line-up which made the headlines. In 1990, Geffen Records refused to distribute *Grip It! On That Other Level*, following the controversy over some of its lyrics (which included allusions to necrophilia). The crew returned to Rap-A-Lot, but shortly afterwards Bushwick Bill forced his girlfriend to shoot him after threatening their baby (he lost an eye). Their next album was bedecked with a picture of him being pushed through a hospital by his two pals after the incident. A fair introduction into the world of the Geto Boys, characterised by thoroughly nasty, sensationalist tales, which made their work difficult to evaluate objectively. Some of the most vile sequences of words ever used in popular music appeared on their albums, glorying in rape, mutilation and violence. Though at first appearance a cocktail of pure hatred, hidden beneath their more self-serving statements were tiny vignettes filled with persuasive detail - 'Life In The Fast Lane' on their debut, and 'Mind Playing Tricks On Me' on the follow-up being the best examples. Certainly though, the defence of 'reporting from the front-line' would seem to be more honourable in their case than many others, bearing in mind Bushwick Bill's aforementioned partial blinding, and the alarmingly high gun profile of the deep south. The crew went on to concentrate more on their solo careers, following internal friction

(Bushwick and Willie D. at several points refusing to appear on stage at the same time), and Willie D. was replaced by Big Mike on *Till Death Us Do Part*. Bushwick, Willie D. and Scarface were reunited for 1996's *The Resurrection*. In a further upheaval, Bushwick Bill was replaced by DMG on the follow-up, *Da Good, Da Bad & Da Ugly*.

● ALBUMS: as the Ghetto Boys *Grip It! On That Other Level* (Rap-A-Lot 1990)★★★, *We Can't Be Stopped* (Rap-A-Lot 1991)★★★, *Till Death Us Do Part* (Rap-A-Lot 1993)★★, *The Resurrection* (Virgin 1996)★★★, *Da Good, Da Bad & Da Ugly* (Rap-A-Lot 1998)★★.

● COMPILATIONS: *Uncut Dope: Geto Boys Best* (Rap-A-Lot 1992)★★★.

Ghostface Killah

b. Dennis Coles, 9 May 1970, USA. Raised in the Staten Island district of New York, Ghostface Killah was an original member of the Wu-Tang Clan crew. On early appearances his face was hidden behind a stocking mask, although no explanation was ever given for his anonymity. Ghostface Killah's voice was the first to be heard on their acclaimed 1993 debut, *Enter The Wu-Tang (36 Chambers)*. Minus the mask, he made his mark in Wu-Tang Clan lore with a major contribution to Raekwon's hard hitting *Only Built 4 Cuban Linx ...*, adopting the Tony Starks moniker on the album cover. Further appearances on the *Sunset Park* and *Don't Be A Menace To South Central While You're Drinking Your Juice In The Hood* soundtracks, prefigured the release of his debut album in November 1996. *Ironman* was the first release on producer RZA's Razor Sharp Records imprint. Featuring major contributions from new Wu-Tang Clan rapper Cappadonna and Raekwon (the three appeared on the album cover together), *Ironman* was one of the Wu-Tang family's most acclaimed releases. Featuring a more soul-orientated production than other Wu-Tang releases, the album included the highly successful duet with Mary J. Blige on 'All That I Got Is You'. *Ironman* proved to be the most commercially successful Wu-Tang Clan product until the release of the following year's *Wu-Tang Forever*, debuting at number 2 on the *Billboard* album chart. Further work with various members of the Wu-Tang Clan preceded the release of his eagerly anticipated sophomore collection.

● ALBUMS: *Ironman* (Razor Sharp/Epic 1996)★★★★, *Supreme Clientele* (Razor Sharp/Epic 2000)★★★★.

Giant Sand

Formed by singer-songwriter Howe Gelb (vocals, guitar, bass, keyboards) in his home-town of Tucson, Arizona, USA, in 1980 with Rainer Ptacek (guitar) and Billy Sed (drums). The line-up recorded a four-track EP as Giant Sandworms on a local label before departing for New York, where Sed's drug escapades forced a return to Arizona. They were joined by David Seger (bass) for a further EP, before he left to join Naked Prey. His replacement was Scott Gerber. Shortly afterwards the band's name was changed to Giant Sand (the original name had unintentional connotations with the wildlife in the science fiction novel *Dune*), with Gelb firing all personnel except Gerber in the process. Ptacek, though, reappeared in Gelb's countrified alter ego group, the Band Of Blacky Ranchette. Tom Larkins, who played concurrently with Naked Prey, joined as drummer, and together they recorded 1985's *Valley Of Rain* with guest pianist Chris Cavacas from Green On Red. Gelb's girlfriend Paula Brown joined on bass and guitar, and together they had their first child. After recording *Ballad Of A Thin Line Man* Gerber left to join the Sidewinders, eventually moving on to Los Cruzos with former Sandworms' drummer Sed. A variety of personnel have populated more recent recordings, including Neil Harry (pedal steel guitar), John Convertino (drums), and Mark Walton (bass, ex-Dream Syndicate). The band's early stark sound (often described as 'desert rock', and a noted influence on the alternative country movement) has evolved into a crisp mix of swing, country, rock, and beatnik lyricism. It remains tempered, as ever, by Gelb's evocative, arid imagery. The band teamed up with Lisa Germano in 1997 for the strangely evocative *Slush*, recording under the name OP8. Convertino and Joey Burns also collaborate together as Calexico, releasing the highly acclaimed *Spoke* and *The Black Light*. Gelb put Giant Sand on hold to work on his second solo album, 1999's *Hisser*.

● ALBUMS: *Valley Of Rain* (Enigma 1985)★★★, *Ballad Of A Thin Line Man* (Zippo 1986)★★★, *Storm* (What Goes On 1988)★★★, *The Love Songs LP* (Homestead 1988)★★★, *Long Stem Rant* (Homestead 1989)★★★, *Swerve* (Amazing Black Sand 1990)★★★, *Ramp* (Amazing Black Sand 1992)★★★, *Center Of The Universe* (Restless 1992)★★★, *Purge And Slouch* (Restless 1993)★★★, *Stromausfall* (Return To Sender 1993)★★★, *Glum* (Imago 1994)★★★, *Backyard Barbeque Broadcast* (Koch 1995)★★★, as OP8 *Slush* (V2 1997)★★★.
Solo: Howe Gelb *Dreaded Brown Recluse* (Amazing Black Sand 1991)★★★, *Hisser* (V2 1999)★★★.
● COMPILATIONS: *Giant Songs: The Best Of Giant Sand* (Demon 1989)★★★, *Giant Sandwich* (Homestead 1989)★★★, *Giant Songs Two: The Best Of Giant Sand Volume 2* (Demon 1995)★★★.

Gigolo Aunts

Formed in 1986 in Boston, Massachusetts, USA, the Gigolo Aunts originally comprised Dave Gibbs (vocals/rhythm guitar), brothers Phil (lead guitar) and Steve Hurley (bass), and Paul Brouwer (drums), who had played together since 1981, initially as a band entitled Sniper. This name was soon jettisoned for Marauder, then Rosetta Stone (since they did not know a band of the same name already existed). When they finally became the Gigolo Aunts (from a Syd Barrett song), there was little immediate fanfare, despite a developing ability to write inviting guitar pop songs in the tradition of Big Star. In fact the band remained practically unknown until Gibbs journeyed to the UK in 1992 to play guest guitar with Velvet Crush, where he met Creation Records' boss Alan McGee and swapped anecdotes with the similarly inclined Teenage Fanclub. The resultant *Flippin' Out* was a marvellous summary of progress so far, with top notch playing and execution. It led to Gibbs and Phil Hurley being invited to join the re-formed Big Star, an offer they had to decline due to European touring commitments. They signed to Fire Records in the UK shortly thereafter. Their live reputation grew on the back of a formidable array of cover versions amassed over their 14 years together (ranging from Duran Duran's 'Rio' to Foreigner's 'Hot Blooded' and the Vapors' 'Turning Japanese'). Having once opened for a Beastie Boys covers band, there was little left to faze them. A six-track EP, *Full On Bloom*, followed, and included a cover version of the BMX Bandits' 'Serious Drugs'. In 1995, the band's composition 'Where I Find My Heaven', taken from their debut album, appeared on the soundtrack to the hit movie *Dumb And Dumber* and also as the theme to BBC Television sitcom *Game On*. The same year saw a tour-weary

Brouwer replaced on drums by Fred Eltringham. Phil Hurley was later replaced by new guitarist Jon Skibic. The band returned in 1999 on Adam Duritz's new label with *Minor Chords And Major Themes*.
● ALBUMS: *Flippin' Out* (Fire 1993)★★★, *Flippin' Out/Full - On Bloom* re-issue (Fire 1995)★★★, *Where I Find My Heaven* (Nectar 1997)★★★, *Minor Chords And Major Themes* (E Pluribus Unum 1999)★★★.

Gin Blossoms

'A big slice of American cheese' was how the singer of this American country rock band once described their sound. Favoured sons of MTV, they had earlier attracted a fierce local following after formation in Tempe, Arizona, USA, in 1987. Their line-up comprised Robin Wilson (vocals, acoustic guitar), Jesse Valenzuela (guitar, mandolin), Phillip Rhodes (drums), Bill Leen (bass) and Doug Hopkins (guitar). The musical backdrop and Wilson's vocals brought critical comparisons to R.E.M. and the Byrds. Comparisons which found fruition on the major hit single, 'Hey Jealousy', and accompanying album, *New Miserable Experience*, which had sold 4 million copies in the USA by June 1996. However, soon after tragedy struck the band. After struggling for years against depression and alcoholism, chief songwriter Hopkins' behaviour had became so unstable that it was necessary to eject him from the band. His departure came in April 1992, soon after recording sessions for the album were completed. A bitter wrangle ensued, with the band reportedly forcing him to sign over half his publishing royalties in return for a one-off payment of $15,000 owed to him. As 'Hey Jealousy' and 'Found Out About You', two excellent songs he had written for the Gin Blossoms, became major hits, his personal problems increased. On 3 December 1993 he left a detox unit in Phoenix, Arizona, and shot himself. Hopkins had been replaced in the band by Scott Johnson, but of more concern was how the Gin Blossoms would replace him as a songwriter. Although both Wilson and Valenzuela had written songs on the band's debut, critics were in no doubt as to who the author of the more compelling tracks was. Marshall Crenshaw was recruited as co-writer on "Til I Hear It From You', the hit single from the predictably weaker *Congratulations I'm Sorry*. The band eventually split-up in 1998, with Wilson going on to form the Gas Giants.
● ALBUMS: *New Miserable Experience* (A&M 1993)★★★★, *Congratulations I'm Sorry* (A&M 1996)★★★.

Ginuwine

b. Elgin Lumpkin, Washington, DC, USA. Talented R&B performer Ginuwine began his musical apprenticeship at the age of 12, performing at parties and (illegally) at bars with his friends in the neighbourhood outfit, Finesse Five. From this he progressed to a solo act, which was initially built around impersonations of his childhood idol, Michael Jackson. Working on his education at the same time, he graduated from Princes Georges Community College with a paralegal degree. He met rookie producer Timbaland in New York, and the two recorded the unusual, synthesizer-infused R&B effort 'The Pony' together. The song attracted strong interest, and at the age of 21 Ginuwine chose to sign with the New York-based Sony subsidiary 550 Records. He enjoyed immediate success with the release of 'Pony' which reached number 1 on *Billboard*'s R&B chart, and number 6 on the Hot

100 chart. As a result his debut album, written and recorded with Timbaland, was assured of mainstream media attention, and reached number 45 on the album chart. To promote the set, Ginuwine set out on a national tour supporting Aaliyah, Dru Hill, Mary J. Blige and Bone Thugs-N-Harmony. A string of crossover hit singles followed, including 'Tell Me Do U Wanna', 'I'll Do Anything/I'm Sorry' and 'Only When U R Lonely'. On the strength of his work with the singer, Timbaland went on to become one of the main forces in late 90s R&B. Ginuwine made his acting debut in November 1998, appearing in the CBS series *Martial Law*. Another standout Timbaland track, March 1999's 'What's So Different' (which reached UK number 10), provided him with his strongest single to date. The US Top 10 album *100% Ginuwine* was another showcase for his classy vocal skills and Timbaland's inventive production, featuring the huge radio hit 'So Anxious'.

● ALBUMS: *Ginuwine: The Bachelor* (550/Sony 1997)★★★★, *100% Ginuwine* (550/Sony 1999)★★★★.

Glamma Kid

b. Iyael Constable, 14 March 1978, Hackney, London, England. Constable began his quest for stardom in his formative years by imitating Michael Jackson's dance steps and emulating his singing style. He attended acting classes at the Anna Shears Drama School where he secured a role on the television series *Corners*. In addition to pursuing his quest to be an all-round entertainer, he joined the Air Training Corps and in two years climbed to the rank of corporal. In 1989, he entered a talent competition and was pipped at the winning post by a DJ; this influenced his subsequent change of direction. In the next competition, he switched from dancing to performing as a DJ and came away with first prize. His success led to the formation of his own Glamma Guard sound system, playing in local blues and house parties in and around London. The system disbanded in 1994 with the members branching out in different musical directions. In the autumn of 1994, Constable, performing as Glamma Kid, met up with Mafia And Fluxy who both managed his career and produced his debut, 'Fashion Magazine'. The song led to a number of sessions and Glamma Kid became regarded as the UK's answer to Bounty Killer. He provided the DJ lyrics to a number of hits including 'Moschino', 'Girls Terminus', 'Nation Of Girls' and the anti-cocaine anthem, 'Outertain'. He was also notable for comments regarding the unhealthy obsession of some musicians with the gangster image, leading to the release of 'Eastwood Clint', where he warned against guns: 'Bwoy you could a bad like a Eastwood Clint - but you tink bad man gun fire flint'. He was also in demand for recording in a combination style, notably alongside Sylvia Tella, Peter Hunningale, Nerious Joseph and Robbie Valentine. In January 1997, he joined forces with Mafia And Fluxy, Hunningale and Joseph as part of the reggae supergroup Passion, for 'Share Your Love', which crossed over into the lower end of the UK pop chart. Glamma Kid was offered and accepted the role of supporting act to his Jamaican counterpart Bounty Killer on his 1997 UK tour, and continued working on his debut album. He enjoyed huge crossover success in 1999 with two UK Top 10 hits; 'Taboo', a collaboration with R&B singer Shola Ama, and 'Why'.

Goats

This Philadelphia, USA rap trio comprised Oa Tiekato, Madd and Swayzack. From early in their career they made a conscious decision to play live (without DAT, often rapping freestyle) whenever possible, and earned immediate notoriety by playing at a celebration of Columbus' discovery of America - educating their audience about the degradation native Americans consequently suffered. They were snapped up by Columbia Records' subsidiary Ruffhouse Records on the basis of their first, four-track demo. Their 1993 debut was a joy, with alter-egos Chickenlittle and his kid brother Hangerhead acting as tour guides through the strange world of 90s America. Their political targets included Dan Quayle, while 'Drive By Bumper Cars' parodied hardcore rap. Their puns were incisive, sometimes almost funny: ('Hey Mr Columbus! You took all my money/No I didn't kid, I discovered it'). Singles such as 'Do The Digs Dug?' again returned to the rights of the oppressed, singling out the imprisoned community leader Leonard Peltier as 'Our Mandela'. However, their UK appearances in 1993 without founder member Tiekato fuelled rumours of a split, which were confirmed on the advent of their less-politicised second album, on which Swayzack took the lead.

● ALBUMS: *Tricks Of The Shade* (Ruffhouse/Columbia 1993)★★★★, *No Goats, No Glory* (Ruffhouse/Columbia 1994)★★★.

Godflesh

The Godflesh partnership was inaugurated by Justin Broadrick (guitar/vocals) and G. Christian Green (bass) in 1988, when the former left the venerated (by UK radio presenter John Peel, at least) hardcore industrial trio, Head Of David. Green had formerly served time in industrialists Fall Of Because, and Godflesh were completed by the addition of a drum machine. A self-titled EP was released on the Swordfish label before moving to the more permanent home of Earache Records. By the advent of their debut album, the band had expanded temporarily to include guitarist Paul Neville (also ex-Fall Of Because). With strong critical reaction, they toured with Loop and as part of the Earache Grindcrusher USA package, alongside Napalm Death. Broadrick had actually appeared with the latter as guitarist on side one of the legendary *Scum* album. In 1991, there were three limited edition 12-inches (including one for the Sub Pop Records empire), which were eventually collected together as the *Slavestate* mini-album. With Neville opting to concentrate on his own project, Cabel Regime, Robert Hampson of Loop stepped in for additional guitar duties on the band's excellently reviewed *Pure*. He would choose to stay at home, however, as the duo embarked on a promotional European tour. In 1993, Broadrick branched out by providing guitar tracks for labelmates Scorn (on their *Vae Solis* debut), and he also produced a 'biomechanical' remix of Pantera's 'Walk'. This 'biomechanical' method is described by Green as involving: 'stripping them (the tracks) down and reconstructing them from scratch with different drum patterns, different vocal lines etc.' Meanwhile, Godflesh's first own-name project in nearly two years, the *Merciless* EP, resurrected an eight-year-old Fall Of Because song. October 1994 saw the introduction of a major new work, *Selfless*, a stunningly direct and brutal album from a band whose quality threshold has hardly wavered since their inception. *Songs Of Love And Hate* was challenging and provocative and one of their finest albums. Drummer Mantia left to join Primus in August 1996. Although Broadrick's involvement in side-projects Final and Techno Animal meant fans had to wait three years before the release of the new Godflesh album, *Us And Them*. The album's seamless fusion of metal and electronics received great acclaim - just reward for Broadrick and Green's pioneering work in the field.

● ALBUMS: *Godflesh* mini-album (Swordfish 1988)★★★, *Streetcleaner* (Earache 1989)★★★, *Slavestate* mini-album (Earache 1990)★★★, *Pure* (Earache 1992)★★★, *Selfless* (Earache 1994)★★★, *Songs Of Love And Hate* (Earache 1996)★★★, *Love And Hate In Dub* remix album (Earache 1997)★★★, *Us And Them* (Earache 1999)★★★★.

Godsmack

This US heavy rock band revolves around the diminutive figure of Sully Erna, a self-confessed witch from Boston, Massachusetts, USA. Erna had played drums with local Boston band Strip Mind, before taking a yearlong break from music. He formed Godsmack (named after an Alice In Chains song) in 1995 with Robbie Merrill (bass), Tommy Stewart (drums) and Lee Richards (guitar). The latter pair only lasted a few months, and were replaced by Tony Rombolo (guitar) and Joe Darko (drums). The new line-up, with Erna playing drums, recorded a self-titled album in 1996 on a budget of $2500 and sold it through local retail chain Newbury Comics. Local radio station WAAF picked up the track 'Keep Away' for heavy rotation, and the band also came to the attention of ex-Extreme drummer Paul Geary who signed them to his management company PGE. The album's stand-out track, 'Whatever', became a big local hit, and, with their fortunes rising, original drummer Stewart rejoined the band in mid-1997. The new line-up signed a deal with Republic Records in July 1998. The heavily remixed album (also released under the title *All Wound Up*) became a surprise hit, selling over a million copies in America, helped immeasurably by the band's appearance at the US Ozzfest and their subsequent support slot on Black Sabbath's reunion tour. Reaction to the album was mixed, with some critics accusing the band of straying too close to the sound of Alice In Chains and Metallica to be considered truly original.

● ALBUMS: *Godsmack* aka *All Wound Up* (Republic/Universal 1997)★★★.

Gold, Brian And Tony

During a trip to Jamaica, Anthony Anderson (b. 1968, Birmingham, West Midlands, England) entered a variety of talent shows on the island, frequently appearing on the same bill as Brian Thompson (b. 1967, Kingston, Jamaica, West Indies), and they eventually formed an illustrious partnership. They decided to perform together as Brian And Tony Gold and with the demise of vocal groups were in the fortunate position of being regarded as *the* unrivalled vocal duo in Jamaica. They embarked on recording sessions for King Jammy, Mickey Bennett, Donovan Germain, Philip 'Fatis' Burrell and Dave 'Rude Boy' Kelly. Although the duo were primarily considered to be session singers, they released the occasional hit, including the haunting, anti-apartheid 'Can You', in 1992. The song showcased their distinctive style, which inspired Sly And Robbie to enrol the singers to perform with DJ Red Dragon on 'Compliments On Your Kiss'. The relaxed rhythm and smooth singing, com-

bined with the laid-back DJ, was destined to cross over. The formula proved successful and the single reached number 2 in the UK pop chart in 1994. Following their commercial success, the duo returned to Jamaica where they recorded a series of notable songs including 'If Loving Was A Crime' with Buju Banton, who later released the favoured 'Searching For The Light' on his own Cell Block 321 label. The duo continue to release sporadic hits, including 'Girls Can't Do', 'All I Want', 'Free At Last', 'Ram Dance', 'Bulls Eye', and the popular combination hits 'Private Property' (with Shabba Ranks), 'Saturday Night At The Movies' (with Lady Saw), 'S.L.A.' (with Junior Tucker) and 'You Give Me Your Love' (with Shaggy).

● ALBUMS: *Green Light* (Pow Wow 1993)★★, *Bulls Eye* (VP 1995)★★★.

Gold, Graham

b. 5 July 1954, Ealing, London, England. Gold, who has been a DJ for over 25 years, has a reputation as one of the hardest working DJs in the UK. He broadcasts on Fridays and Mondays on London's Kiss 100 FM, DJs all over the world, promotes his own club nights and runs his own label, Good:As with business partner Giles Sawney. In the UK's *DJ* magazine readers' poll of the Top 100 DJs In The World, he was voted number 22. Gold is managed by Judge Jules' management company, Serious Artist Management. Originally, Gold was a soul DJ and played at the popular Caister Soul Weekends in the UK before presenting various radio shows, including one on London's Capital Radio. During the 80s, he broadcast on several pirate radio stations and wrote for the UK magazine, *Blues And Soul*. His musical style is now more orientated towards trance and energetic, uplifting house. He has played at most of the major clubs and events in the south of England and has been a resident at 'Peach' at the Camden Palace for more than five years. He has also DJed in the antipodes, South Africa, Tel Aviv, Canada, USA and the Balearic Islands, visiting Ibiza several times during the summer clubbing season. He has mixed many dance music compilations and had two mix albums in the UK Top 10 simultaneously in 1997 - *Kiss Mix 97* and *Club Cuts Volume 2*. He has remixed the work of artists such as Jez And Choopie, 666, Berri, Spirito, Ambrosia, Happy Nation, 2HD (aka Ferry Corsten) and Carl Cox. Always a crowd-pleasing DJ, Gold is also well liked within the music industry.

● COMPILATIONS: *DJs In The Box* (Urban Collective 1995)★★★, *Kiss Mix* (PolyGram TV 1996)★★★, *Worth Its Weight In Gold* (Bullion 1997)★★★, *Club Cuts Volume 2* (Telstar TV 1997)★★★, *Kiss Mix 97* (PolyGram TV 1997)★★★, *Club Connect* (Future Sound & Vision 1998)★★★, *Kiss Mix 98* (PolyGram TV)★★★, *Graham Gold: Delicious* (Logic/BMG 1999)★★★★.

Golden Smog

A side project for members of Soul Asylum, the Jayhawks, Run Westy Run, Wilco and the Honeydogs, the real names of those involved in the indie band Golden Smog were kept a closely guarded secret on the release of their debut album in 1996. However, the pseudonyms David Spear, Michael Macklyn, Raymond Virginia, Scott Summitt, Jarret Decatur-Lane and Leonardson Saratoga were deliberate clues - each including the actual middle name and part of the address of those involved. The songwriting credits, however, betrayed at least some of those involved - Kraig Johnson (Run Westy

Run), Gary Louris and Marc Perlman (Jayhawks), Jeff Tweedy (Wilco) and Dan Murphy (Soul Asylum). The band first appeared in 1992 with the release of an EP, *On Golden Pond*, which featured Chris Mars of the Replacements on drums (he was subsequently replaced by Noah Levy of the Honeydogs). Golden Smog's debut album was recorded in the autumn of 1994, the first occasion on which the band's various other activities allowed it. Recorded in just five days, *Down By The Old Mainstream* captured the band ethic: 'Once every six months we would learn a bunch of covers and play. It would be sloppy and fun. Then one day, we looked at what we had and said, "This is a really good band . . . Let's do it"'. Keen to dismiss accusations of Golden Smog being a 'joke' band, Rykodisc Records released a pre-emptive single, 'Redheaded Stepchild', prior to the album's release in January 1996. It was followed by a tour in February and March. Jody Stephens (drums, ex-Big Star) appeared on the follow-up, *Weird Tales*.

● ALBUMS: *Down By The Old Mainstream* (Rykodisc 1996)★★★, *Weird Tales* (Rykodisc 1998)★★★★.

Goldie

b. Clifford Price, Wolverhampton, England. A distinctive visual as well as aural presence, graffiti artist, hardcore and jungle innovator Goldie is distinguished by the gold-inlaid front teeth from which many assume he takes his name. In fact, Goldie is an abbreviation of 'Goldilocks', a nickname he earned from his gold-dreadlocked hip-hop days. Though he jealously guards his true identity, his origins can be fixed in Wolverhampton, England, though he currently spends much of his time at clubs in London. In his youth he travelled to Miami and New York but returned to subsidise his musical activities as a (somewhat unsuccessful) mugger. Possibly his most famous graffiti illustration was his 'Change The World' mural at Queens Park Rangers' Loftus Road football ground in London. Later his paintings, which had once been the main source of his criminal record, were sold for over £3,000 each. His early musical experiences were most notably conducted as part of the Metalheads collective (later Metalheadz) on hardcore imprint Reinforced Records. He had previously recorded a white label EP under the name Ajaz Project and then 'Killer Muffin' as a solo artist. The Metalheads' *Angel* EP was a major breakthrough for 'intelligent hardcore', and when offshoots of hardcore (an extreme hybrid of techno) mixed with reggae and evolved into jungle in 1993/4, Goldie found himself at the centre of the new movement. However, he had little time for General Levy, and other artists he saw as 'bandwagon jumpers'. His own 'Inner City Life' single maximised the possibilities of the drum 'n' bass sound of jungle, using them as a framework for melodious vocals and other musical innovations. Similarly, the sounds contained on *Timeless*, the first jungle album released on a major label and to find mainstream approval, eschewed any notion of observing dance music convention. He admitted to influences as diverse as the Stranglers (notably Jean Jacques Burnel's bass), 10cc and hip-hop behind this multi-layered recording. His compatriots in the project were Moving Shadow Records' boss Rob Playford, jungle artist Dillinja, keyboard player Justina Curtis, singers Diane Charlemagne and Lorna Harris, plus jazz musicians Cleveland Watkiss and Steve Williamson. This array of talent ensured a multi-dimensional sound, underpinned by break-

beats and rolling cycles of rhythm. The press had finally found a figurehead for the previously anonymous jungle movement, a role Goldie subsequently lived up to in sometimes reckless style. The uneven *Saturnz Return* was, for all its failings, jungle's most ambitious album to date, and boasted guest appearances from David Bowie, KRS-One, Noel Gallagher, Dillinja, Charlemagne and Virus Records' co-owner Optical (Matt Quinn).

● ALBUMS: *Goldie Presents Metalheadz: Timeless* (London 1995)★★★★, with Rob Playford *The Shadow* (Moving Shadow 1997)★★★, *Saturnz Return* (London 1998)★★★.

● COMPILATIONS: *Platinum Breakz* (Metalheadz/London 1996)★★★★.

● VIDEOS: *Talkin' Headz: The Metalheadz Documentary* (Manga Video 1998).

● FILMS: *The World Is Not Enough* (1999), *Everybody Loves Sunshine* (1999).

Gomez

This acclaimed 90s UK rock band was originally formed by four school friends from Southport, Ian Ball (guitar, harmonica, vocals), Tom Gray (guitar, keyboards, vocals), Olly Peacock (drums, percussion) and Paul Blackburn (bass). Ball and Peacock's musical background included a period spent on the local metal circuit in heavy rock band Severed. Ball met Ben Ottewell (b. Matlock Bath, Derbyshire, England) while studying at Sheffield University, inviting the fledgling vocalist to join the band. Briefly known as Gomez, Kill, Kill The Vortex, the band began recording four-track demo tapes in a Southport garage. They attracted immediate interest when tapes from these sessions were posted to record labels, triggering an A&R scramble for their signatures. With Stephen Fellows (ex-Comsat Angels) in position as their manager, the band signed to Virgin Records subsidiary Hut. They toured with Embrace in late 1997 and spent time in a 16-track studio polishing off their raw demos. Their debut single, '78 Stone Wobble', was released in March 1998, and was followed a month later by *Bring It On*. Acclaimed by critics on both sides of the Atlantic, the album drew comparisons to a diverse range of American artists including Tim Buckley, Tom Waits, Al Green, Marvin Gaye and Jimi Hendrix. Ottewell's raw, bluesy vocals added a further touch of authenticity to the band's stylized fusion of various forms of American roots music, with the songs often struggling to rise above their influences and establish an identity of their own. One of the stand-out tracks, 'Get Myself Arrested', was released as a single in May 1998. *Bring It On* won the UK's Mercury Music Prize in September 1998, boosting sales past gold and pushing the album to a UK chart high of number 11. The following month the band completed a US tour opening for Eagle-Eye Cherry, and continued working on recording sessions for their new album. A new single, 'Bring It On' (not featured on their debut), was released in June 1999. *Liquid Skin* was a mature, unselfconscious collection from a band under pressure to produce a worthy follow-up to their acclaimed debut.

● ALBUMS: *Bring It On* (Hut 1998)★★★★, *Liquid Skin* (Hut 1999)★★★.

Gonzalez, Kenny 'Dope'
(see Bucketheads; Masters At Work)

Goo Goo Dolls

This US rock trio, formed in Buffalo, New York, in 1986, comprises bass player and vocalist Robby Takac, guitarist and vocalist Johnny Rzeznik and drummer George Tutuska. The band's first two albums were compared to Cheap Trick and the Replacements. They started doing unlikely cover versions on *Jed*, when the professional crooner Lance Diamond sang guest vocals on a cover version of Creedence Clearwater Revival's 'Down On The Corner'. He also sang on a version of Prince's 'I Could Never Take The Place Of Your Man' on *Hold Me Up*. Both albums featured unpretentious pop punk songwriting, and the band was now being celebrated by a growing number of fans in the media. Their commercial breakthrough came with 1995's hit single 'Name' and *A Boy Named Goo*, which was produced by Pere Ubu, Hüsker Dü and Sugar accomplice Lou Giordano. Their career showed signs of stalling in 1997 following litigation with their record company Warner Brothers Records and the departure of Tutuska. They were saved by the song 'Iris', which became a huge radio hit after featuring on the soundtrack of the Nicolas Cage movie, *City Of Angels*. Having built up a strong following on the back of that single, the new album *Dizzy Up The Girl* climbed to number 15 on the *Billboard* 200 album chart in October 1998. 'Slide' hit the US Top 10 the following January.

● ALBUMS: *Goo Goo Dolls* (Mercenary/Celluloid 1987)★★, *Jed* (Death/Enigma 1989)★★, *Hold Me Up* (Metal Blade/Warners 1990)★★★, *Superstar Car Wash* (Metal Blade/Warners 1993)★★★, *A Boy Named Goo* (Metal Blade/Warners 1995)★★★★, *Dizzy Up The Girl* (Warners 1998)★★★.

Goofy

b. Chad Simpson, 1 June 1974, Kingston, Jamaica, West Indies. Simpson grew up within the reggae industry and drew help as well as inspiration in his burgeoning career from artists including Big Youth, Yellowman, Beenie Man, Bounty Killer and General Degree. In 1996, he recorded the chart-topping 'Fudgie', that also featured Lady Saw and Hawkeye on the 12-inch disco mix. A hit in Jamaica and the US, it led to a series of singles including 'Don't Talk', 'How You Bless' and 'Dog Bark'. Goofy's association with Danny Brownie's Main Street Crew led to him recording in combination with Red Rat, initially on 'Big Man Little Yute' for Studio 2000, which topped the reggae charts worldwide. The duo followed their success with 'Cruise'. The Main Street Crew made their UK debut at the 1997 Notting Hill Carnival in London, featuring the trio of Red Rat, Goofy and Hawkeye. Scheduled to appear on both the Radio 1 and Kiss FM stages, the trio's arrival caused a crushing surge towards the stage, an incident grossly exaggerated in the national press. Goofy continued to produce hits, including 'Brush Yu Teeth' and 'Bad Man Fearless'. Several of his hit singles were included on his debut album.

● ALBUMS: *I Don't Give A Damn!!* (Main Street 1999)★★★.

Gorky's Zygotic Mynci

One of the most idiosyncratic bands to emerge from the Welsh indie scene of the mid-90s, Gorky's Zygotic Mynci followed Super Furry Animals in getting Welsh language music onto mainstream radio. The band were formed in Camarthen by school friends Euros Childs (vocals/keyboards), Richard James (bass) and John Lawrence (guitar), later joined by Euros Rowlands (drums) and Megan Childs (violin). After recording demo tapes in their bedrooms (later released on the *Patio* CD), the band were signed to the Gwynedd-based independent label Ankst, and released a 10-inch single, 'Patio', in 1992. Commenting on the songs written in their native language, Euros Childs later stated: 'we used to sing mainly in Welsh just because we didn't really expect to be heard outside Wales'. Touring gave a curious press an opportunity to review the band, whose quasi-medieval music was matched by their retro-hippy garb, leading to inevitable comparisons with the Incredible String Band. Their debut album *Tatay* contained predominantly Welsh language songs, but it was the cover version of Robert Wyatt's 'O Caroline', and a track called 'Kevin Ayers', that revealed the source of the band's love of experimental whimsy. The catchy single 'Miss Trudy' gained them more critical praise and a wider audience, while 1995's *Bwyd Time* proved to be a more accessible record than the debut. Now touring as headliners in their own right, it was no surprise when the band secured a major recording contract with Fontana Records. *Barafundle* was released in 1997 to unanimous critical praise, a beautiful and haunting blend of psychedelic pop music and quirky, original lyrics. The ever-productive Gorky's then released the non-album single 'Young Girls And Happy Endings'. *Gorky 5* was a less accessible, harder-edged album, juxtaposing the Velvet Underground-inspired single 'Sweet Johnny' with the melodic beauty of 'Tidal Wave' and 'Only The Sea Makes Sense'. The band was dropped by Fontana shortly afterwards, and founder member Lawrence left the following June. Typically unfazed the remaining quartet bounced back with the excellent *Spanish Dance Troupe*.

● ALBUMS: *Tatay* (Ankst 1994)★★★, *Patio* mini-album (Ankst 1995)★★★, *Bwyd Time* (Ankst 1995)★★★, *Barafundle* (Fontana 1997)★★★★, *Gorky 5* (Fontana 1998)★★★, *Spanish Dance Troupe* (Mantra 1999)★★★★.

Grand Puba

b. Maxwell Dixon, New Rochelle, New York, USA. A founder member of Brand Nubian, and before that Masters Of Ceremony, Puba left the former following their acclaimed 1990 set, *One For All*. He kicked off his solo career with a track, 'Fat Rat', on the *Strictly Business* soundtrack. When his debut album was unveiled, the smooth reggae backing was subjugated by Puba's by now familiar lyrical subject matter. Born the son of a 5% Nation Islamic father, Puba's raps reinstated that doctrine just as forcefully as he had done with Brand Nubian, but it was generally a more playful set. It included a guest appearance from Mary J. Blige. He later appeared on Fat Joe's *Represent* album, performing on 'Watch The Sound'. His second solo outing was a less forceful set. Puba rejoined Brand Nubian for 1998's *Foundation*.

● ALBUMS: *Reel To Reel* (Elektra 1992)★★★, *2000* (Elektra 1995)★★★.

Grand, Otis

b. Fred Bishti, 14 February 1950, Beirut, Lebanon. Grand has spent most of his life in the USA, although he lived in France for a few years. He began playing guitar at the age of 13,

citing his influences as B.B. King, T-Bone Walker, Otis Rush and Johnny Otis, and he has played with many San Francisco Bay area blues artists. Otis Grand And The Dance Kings created a sensation when they burst onto the British blues scene in the late 80s, enhanced on the first album (a W.C. Handy award nomination) by the presence of Joe Louis Walker. The second album includes guests Jimmy Nelson, Pee Wee Ellis, and Walker again. A great live attraction, Grand was voted UK Blues Guitarist Of The Year in 1990 and still appears in annual polls throughout the 90s due to his constant touring schedule. In the late 90s he was residing in Croydon, gateway to the blues!
● ALBUMS: *Always Hot* (Special Delivery 1988)★★★, *He Knows The Blues* (Volt 1991)★★★, with Philip Walker *Big Blues From Texas* (1992)★★★, with Joe Houston *The Return Of Honk* (JSP 1994)★★, *Nothing Else Matters* (Sequel 1994)★★★, *Perfume And Grime* (Sequel 1996)★★★, with Debbie Davies, Anson Funderburgh *Grand Union* (Blueside 1998)★★★.
● COMPILATIONS: *The Blues Sessions 1990-1994* (JSP 1997)★★★★.

Grandaddy

Based in songwriter Jason Lytle's hometown of Modesto, California, USA, Grandaddy's lo-fi slacker rock insidiously worked its way into the heart of the alternative music press during the late 90s. Lytle was a former skateboarder whose employment record boasted a spell in a hazardous waste treatment plant. Around 1992, he formed Grandaddy with Kevin Garcia (bass) and Aaron Burtch (drums). The band spent several uneventful years putting together demo tapes recorded in Lytle's home studio, and playing bars and coffee shops in Modesto. Jim Fairchild (guitar) and Tim Dryden (keyboards) swelled the band's ranks for 1995's seven track cassette debut, *A Pretty Mess By This One Band*. A haphazard mix of lo-fi and college rock, the band only managed to rise above the sum of their influences on the standout track 'Taster'. The record attracted enough attention, however, for the band to be able to record a full-length album. *Under The Western Freeway* was another home-produced recording. Fleshing out their lo-fi production with some odd sound effects, songs such as the single 'Summer Here Kids' and 'A.M. 180' built around simple but winning melodies, at odds with Lytle's relentlessly downbeat lyrics.
● ALBUMS: *A Pretty Mess By This One Band* mini-album (Will 1995)★★, *Under The Western Freeway* (Will 1997)★★★★.
● COMPILATIONS: *The Broken Down Comforter Collection* (Big Cat 1999)★★★.

Graney, Dave, And The Coral Snakes

b. Mount Gambier, near Melbourne, Australia. Dave Graney first worked as a professional musician in the late 70s with Adelaide, Australia band the Sputniks. With Graney disguising himself under the pseudonym Dave Munroe, the band recorded one single, 'Second Chance', but they were best known for mingling cover versions of material by Wire and Wilson Pickett in a chaotic, drunken live set. In the 80s, he joined the Moodists - an acclaimed psychedelic rock/pop band who recorded one album for Creation Records with his involvement. He subsequently became a labelmate of the pre-success Pulp and Teenage Fanclub by signing to Fire Records and releasing material with his own band. That outfit was alternatively named Dave Graney With The Coral Snakes (for the debut *At His Stone Beach* EP) and Dave

Graney With The White Buffaloes (for the frontier-fixated 1989 album *My Life On The Plains*). However, despite critical approbation the sales response was subdued, and in the early 90s Graney returned to Australia and set up his own label, ID Records. Following the issue of *The Lure Of The Tropics*, Graney then began work on *Night Of The Wolverine* with a reshuffled Coral Snakes - his wife Clare Moore on drums, Robin Casinader on organ/piano, Gordy Blair on bass and Rod Hayward on guitar. Having always been a critical favourite, the results were seized upon by the Australian media as evidence of the return of a great songwriter. As the Australian listings magazine, *Time Off*, commented: 'It was almost a relief when Dave Graney arrived. All of a sudden, Australia had a new icon of musical sophistication, an artist to match the McCombs (the Triffids) and McLennans (the Go-Betweens) of the land. He'd always promised to do so, but it wasn't until this year's wonderful *Night Of The Wolverine* that it became a reality.' The contents of the album, which also received a five star review in *Rolling Stone*, swelled with the usual Graney touchstones, including cinema, adolescent yearning and loss, and self-deprecating humour. *The Soft 'N' Sexy Sound* was a strong follow-up, although by now Graney's music was moving noticeably towards the mainstream. Following one more album Graney disbanded the Coral Snakes in 1997. His new outfit, the Dave Graney Show, released their self-titled debut in 1998.
● ALBUMS: with the White Buffaloes *My Life On The Plains* (Fire 1989)★★★, *I Was The Hunter And I Was The Prey* (1991)★★★, *The Lure Of The Tropics* (ID 1991)★★★, *Night Of The Wolverine* (ID 1993)★★★★, *You Wanna Be There But You Don't Wanna Travel* (ID 1994)★★★, *The Soft 'N' Sexy Sound* (This Way Up 1995)★★★, *The Devil Drives* (Mercury 1997)★★★, with the Dave Graney Show *The Dave Graney Show* (Festival 1998)★★★.
● COMPILATIONS: *The Baddest* (Universal 1999)★★★★.
● FURTHER READING: *It Is Written Baby*, Dave Graney.

Grant Lee Buffalo

This Los Angeles, USA-based band was formed by Grant Lee Phillips (b. 1 September 1963, Stockton, California, USA; vocals/12-string guitar), Paul Kimble (b. 24 September 1960, Freeport, Illinois, USA; bass/keyboards) and Joey Peters (b. 9 April 1965, New York, USA; drums). Phillips grew up in California the son of a minister and the grandson of a southern gospel singer grandmother, before enrolling in film school. Grant Lee Buffalo began to evolve in 1989 when Phillips joined Peters and Kimble in Shiva Burlesque, but despite attracting critical acclaim they soon realized that the band's impetus was stalling. The trio became the only ones arriving for rehearsals, and sacked the other two members to concentrate on a new band. Mouth Of Rasputin, Rex Mundi, Soft Wolf Tread and Machine Elves were all rejected as names, choosing Grant Lee Buffalo after their singer's Christian names, and the image of a buffalo to symbolize all 'that had gone wrong in this country' (it had previously been employed by Phillips for a set of solo country standards he had sung before his former band King Of The World came onstage). Their influences were 'the music of America from the 30s to the 60s that's based on story-telling and improvisation, blues, jazz or country'. By the autumn of 1991 the band had recorded 11 songs in Kimble's home studio, a tape of which was passed to Bob Mould, who released 'Fuzzy' as a 7-inch on his Singles Only Label (SOL). A month later they had earned a contract with Slash Records, primarily because the band felt an affinity with several other acts on the label (X, Los Lobos, Violent Femmes). A debut album was recorded in two weeks in San Francisco, with Kimble again producing. The songs attacked modern America's complacency and pursuit of material wealth, harking back to a golden age of American optimism. Phillips' acute observation and lyrical poignancy, which earned comparisons to Neil Young and Mike Scott (Waterboys), was steeped in a grainy, cinematic sweep that saw the set lauded by Michael Stipe of R.E.M. as '1993's finest album, hands down'. 'America Snoring', released as a single in both the USA and UK, symbolized the faithless, faceless climate of the USA so despised by the author, and was written as a response to the Los Angeles riots. A companion piece, 'Stars N' Stripes', was Phillips' evocative homage to Elvis Presley's Vegas period, and offered another passionate chapter in his thematic dissection of modern Americana. *Mighty Joe Moon* proved more restrained, with its anger at the vulgarity of characters and situations tempered by greater texture and guile. The keynote spirituality implicit in earlier recordings was maintained by 'Rock Of Ages', one of the few dramatic gestures on offer. The band progressed further with the more vocally orientated *Copperopolis*, which broke away from the traditional rock band format by introducing pedal steel guitar (Greg Leisz), bass clarinet (Ralph Carney) and violin (Bob Fergo). Kimble left the band prior to the release of their final album *Jubilee*, which featured guest appearances from Michael Stipe, Robyn Hitchcock and Eels frontman, E.

● ALBUMS: *Fuzzy* (Slash 1993)★★★★, *Mighty Joe Moon* (Slash 1994)★★★★, *Copperopolis* (Slash 1996)★★★, *Jubilee* (Slash 1998)★★★.

Gravediggaz

A 90s New York, USA hip-hop 'supergroup', the Gravediggaz feature ex-Stetsasonic personnel Prince Paul (b. Paul Huston, USA) and Fruitkwan, renamed the Undertaker and the Gatekeeper respectively, plus Poetic the Grym Reaper and RZA the Rzarector. Poetic was formerly a member of the Grimm Brothers, while RZA was the production genius behind Staten Island's Wu-Tang Clan. Prince Paul started the group after his Doo Dew label collapsed, needing a new venture to express his frustration. He had originally contacted his fellow band members with the intention of putting together a compilation album. The outfit's debut single was 'Diary Of A Madman', which premiered their gothic/horror style, and utilised loops donated by producer RNS (famed for his work on Shyheim's debut set). They toured in the USA with the Wu-Tang Clan, while Prince Paul went back to production work for Soul II Soul (having already recorded *3 Feet High And Rising* with them) and Living Colour. Further work such as the *Nowhere To Run, Nowhere To Hide* EP and the *6 Feet Deep* set embossed a growing reputation for their horrorcore hip-hop. By 1995, they were also considered by many to be the nearest US approximation of the UK's trip-hop scene. This impression was cemented by a collaboration with Tricky on *The Hell* EP, which entered the UK Top 40. The Wu-Tang production crew of True Master and Goldfinghaz worked on *The Pick, The Sickle And The Shovel*, leaving RZA free to concentrate on his rhymes.

● ALBUMS: *6 Feet Deep* (Gee Street 1994)★★, *The Pick, The Sickle And The Shovel* (Gee Street 1997)★★★★.

Gray, David

b. Manchester, England but raised in the Welsh fishing village of Solva. Gray first aspired to being a rock performer after watching 2-Tone bands on television. He formed a punkish outfit at school, cranking out rock classics at double speed, then began writing songs when he was 17. Polydor Records A&R man Rob Holden heard a demo while recuperating from a motor-cycle crash and was sufficiently convinced to quit his job and become Gray's manager. Pegged as a 'crop-headed Welsh troubadour' with 'a chip on both shoulders', Gray's songs are in fact as sensitive as they are angry, and the manic energy communicated with his acoustic guitar thrash set him apart from the folkies. A number of tours as support to singer-songwriters (Maria McKee, Kirsty MacColl, Shawn Colvin) brought him early exposure in America, and a one-off support with Joan Baez led to her praising 'the best lyrics since the young Bob Dylan'. Although acknowledging a debt to Dylan, Gray tempers the spirit of folksy protest with a 90s street-level sensibility. This attitude has brought comparisons with Mark Eitzel of American Music Club, but has also consigned Gray to the same perennial cult status as Eitzel. *White Ladder*, featured songs recorded for the film *This Year's Love*.

● ALBUMS: *A Century Ends* (Hut 1993)★★★, *Flesh* (Hut 1994)★★★, *Sell, Sell, Sell* (EMI 1996)★★★, *White Ladder* (IHT 1999)★★★.

Gray, Macy

b. Natalie McIntyre, Canton, Ohio, USA. Downplaying the hype surrounding her as the saviour of soul music, Gray often repeated the story about how she was afraid to speak as a child because other kids would tease her about her voice. That voice, an amazing hybrid of Billie Holiday and Tina Turner refreshingly free from the modern clichés of the R&B diva and the rap gangstress, entranced critics and music fans alike when her debut album was released in autumn 1999. Gray, who received several years formal piano training, was raised on a classic soul diet of Stevie Wonder and Aretha Franklin, but was also drawn to hip-hop in the early 80s. She later moved to Los Angeles to enrol in a screen-writing programme at the USC Film School. Here she was cajoled into singing on demo sessions, and began creating a stir at live appearances fronting a covers band. She set up her own after hours club, the We Ours, in Hollywood, where an open mic policy allowed her to demo her own material in front of friends. Gray signed to Epic Records in April 1998, and set about recording an album with producer Andrew Slater. The cast of musicians included her songwriting partners Darryl Swann and Jeremy Ruzumna, Arik Marshall (guitar, ex-Red Hot Chili Peppers), and session musicians Blackbird McKnight (guitar, ex-Funkadelic) and Lenny Castro (percussion, ex-Tower Of Power). *Macy Gray On How Life Is* proved to be a melodic fusion of classic soul, urban R&B and hip-hop beats rounded off by Gray's earthy rasp. Stand-out tracks included the excellent singles 'Do Something' and 'I Try', and the dramatic 'Sex-o-matic Venus Freak' and 'Caligula'. The album was particularly well received in the UK; glowing reviews and word-of-mouth approval helping it climb steadily up the charts (eventually reaching number 6 in October). 'I Try' also stayed in the lower reaches of the Top 10 for several weeks. Gray's incredible voice sets her apart from many of her contemporaries.

● ALBUMS: *Macy Gray On How Life Is* (Epic 1999)★★★★.

Green Day

With alternative rock music going overground in the early 90s, few acts were better positioned to exploit the commercial possibilities than Green Day - Billie Joe Armstrong (b. 17 February 1972, California, USA; vocals/guitar), Mike Dirnt (b. 4 May 1972, California, USA; bass/vocals) and Tre Cool (b. Frank Edwin Wright III, 9 December 1972, Germany; drums/vocals). Armstrong and Dirnt had been playing together since the age of 11 in the refinery town of Rodeo, California, performing in various garage bands. Tre Cool had been in a band called The Lookouts who broke up in 1990, but their final EP, *IV*, featured Billie Joe Armstrong playing guitar and singing backing vocals on three tracks. Armstrong and Dirnt had already formed Sweet Children with ex-Isocracy drummer John Kiffmeyer. Their debut release came on Livermore's Lookout Records in 1989, the *1000 Hours* EP. However, two weeks before release the band informed Livermore that they had changed their name to Green Day, inspired by their fondness for marijuana and by the fact that another local band, Sweet Baby Jesus, had just changed their name to Sweet Baby and signed with Slash/Warner Brothers Records. Their debut album, *39/Smooth*, recorded in a single day, comprised 10 pop punk tracks. Two limited edition EPs followed, one for Lookout, the second for Chicago label Skene Records. Kiffmeyer booked their first national tour, but afterwards left the band to concentrate on college (his only subsequent musical activity came in the Ne'er Do Wells). Cool was asked to fill in, and immediately wrote the comedic 'Dominated Love Song' for *Kerplunk!*, where the 60s pop quotient was reduced in favour of a synthesis of 70s British punk bands the Jam and Stiff Little Fingers. It sold over 50,000 records through word of mouth and underground media support. Afterwards they decided to take the plunge and move to a major label, signing to Warner Brothers subsidiary Reprise Records, despite bigger offers from elsewhere. A&R man Rob Cavallo was also recruited as producer for their third album. *Dookie* gradually stalked the charts, going on to sell over nine million copies in the USA. Their arduous touring schedule was the chief reason for their rise, and was topped off by appearances on the 1994 Lollapalooza package and the revived Woodstock event. The other main factor was the estimable quality of their songwriting. As Dirnt said: 'We just figured out a formula and Billie Joe writes real good songs, that's all.' With *Dookie* being so successful, it came as no surprise when the band were nominated in no less than four Grammy categories. In 1995, it was confirmed that they had sold over 10 million albums worldwide, a stunning achievement for a band who have remained faithful to a basic punk pop framework. *Insomniac* and *Nimrod* confirmed their popularity, with the band's fans seemingly unfazed by the weakness of the songs compared to the material on *Dookie*.

● ALBUMS: *39/Smooth* (Lookout 1990)★★★, *Kerplunk!* (Lookout 1992)★★★, *Dookie* (Reprise 1994)★★★★, *Insomniac* (Reprise 1995)★★, *Nimrod* (WEA 1997)★★★.
● COMPILATIONS: *1,039/Smoothed Out Slappy Hours* (Lookout 1991)★★.

Green Velvet

b. Curtis Alan Jones, 26 April 1967, Chicago, Illinois, USA. Whereas Cajmere is the name associated with his house productions, Green Velvet is Jones' green-haired techno incarnation. Jones became interested in club culture while studying a degree in chemical engineering at the University Of Illinois. After graduating in 1991, he pursued his musical interests as both a DJ and producer. Establishing his own label, Cajual/Relief, he released his own infectious, humorous singles such as 'Preacherman', 'Answering Machine', 'The Stalker' and 'Flash' (released in the UK on the Open label) as well as those by DJ Sneak, Glenn Underground, Paul Johnson, Gemini, Tim Harper and Boo Williams. His debut as Green Velvet, *Constant Chaos* demonstrated Jones' fondness for both house and techno and drew inspiration from both the sinister disco of Grace Jones and the eccentricity of P-Funk. *The Nineties* compiled the best of his singles.

● ALBUMS: *Constant Chaos* (Music Man 1999)★★★.
● COMPILATIONS: *The Nineties* (Music Man 1999)★★★.

Gregson, Clive

b. 4 January 1955, Ashton-Under-Lyne, Manchester, England. This highly respected singer/songwriter started his career as a member of Any Trouble before he embarked on an acclaimed partnership with Christine Collister. They announced a parting of the ways after seven years of performing and recording together. Gregson then performed with Richard Thompson and worked as a record producer. Throughout this time he continued to write and record subtly powerful songs, as highlighted on *Welcome To The Workhouse*, with the pathos of Thompson and the humour of Billy Bragg. Gregson has also worked and toured with Boo Hewerdine, Eddi Reader and Plainsong. Gregson continues to release credible solo albums and like Thompson, is hugely talented, totally underrated and likely to remain a cult item only for those lucky enough to be aware of his fine catalogue of songs.

● ALBUMS: *Strange Persuasions* (Demon 1985)★★★, *Welcome To The Workhouse* (Special Delivery 1990)★★★★, *Carousel Of Noise* (Gregsongs 1994)★★★, *People & Places* (Compass/Demon 1995)★★★, *I Love This Town* (Compass 1996)★★★, *Clive Gregson* (Demon 1996)★★★, *Happy Hour* (Fellside 1999)★★★.

Grid

This innovative UK dance music outfit comprised Dave Ball (b. 3 May 1959, Blackpool, Lancashire, England) and Richard Norris (b. 23 June 1965, London, England). Ball's name was familiar to many through his work as part of another highly successful pair, Soft Cell. Having split from Marc Almond, Ball would work with Psychic TV and Jack The Tab before linking with Norris, a former music journalist and veteran of several outfits including the Fruitbats, Innocent Vicars, East Of Eden and Mr Suit. Like many of techno's new breed, the Grid did not limit themselves to their own releases, clocking up an impressive array of remixes for other artists. These included several major names, Brian Eno, Happy Mondays, Pet Shop Boys, the Art Of Noise and Ball's old friends, Soft Cell. Even Vic Reeves ('Abide With Me') came in for the Grid treatment. Their own recording career attracted plenty of praise in both the mainstream and specialist dance music press, who even tolerated the band playing live behind screens. However, since their debut, 'On The Grid', in June 1989, their CV was chequered by short tenures with record labels. Following four singles and an album for East West, the duo joined Rhythm King Records for a one-off single ('Timothy Leary Meets The Grid'), before departing for Virgin Records. Their eclectic *456* set for the latter included collaborations with Robert Fripp, Yello and Sun Ra. Singles like 'Crystal Clear', however, revealed a return to the stripped down, meaner techno sound. They split for Deconstruction Records in late 1993, their debut single for the label being 'Texas Cowboys'. However, it was the following year's 'Swamp Thing' that provided the real fanfare, predicting the hoedown sound that was creeping in to house with its use of banjos, and catapulting them into the UK Top 5. The duo, dismayed by record company pressure for a follow-up hit, called it a day shortly afterwards. Both men moved into soundtrack, writing and remixing work, and Norris set up his own Areeba label.

● ALBUMS: *Electric Head* (East West 1990)★★★, *456* (Virgin 1992)★★★, *Evolver* (Deconstruction 1994)★★★, *Music For Dancing* remixed singles (Deconstruction 1995)★★.

Groop Dogdrill

Founded in Doncaster, Yorkshire, England, Groop Dogdrill comprise drummer Hug Kelly, singer/guitarist Pete Spiby and bass player Damo Fowkes. In addition there is a fourth member, roadie Boz, who also writes the band's lyrics. That line-up gives some indication of the lack of convention inherent in the band, made explicit on their ferocious debut album, 1998's *Half Nelson*. Not averse to advising music journalists to 'pull some fanny', Groop Dogdrill quickly gained a reputation as natural successors to the Wildhearts as rock's resident hard-boiled nutcases (at one London support gig to Reef, Fowkes responded to a thrown bottle from the audience by pulling out a flick-knife). The following year's 'Angel Wings' single hinted at a more restrained approach.

● ALBUMS: *Half Nelson* (Mantra 1998)★★★.

Groove Armada

This UK duo comprises Tom Findlay (b. Cambridge, England; bass, trumpet, keyboards, sampler) and Andy Cato (b. Yorkshire, England; trombone, keyboards, bass guitar). Cato, a 6 feet 8 inches tall Yorkshireman, grew up playing in a colliery brass band and listening to disco music, such as that by Earth, Wind And Fire. He also won the UK's Young Jazz Musician Of The Year award. He was introduced to house music by his cousin, Digs, a member of the cult house collective DIY. He took up a DJing residency at the 'Spectrum' night in Cambridge before relocating to London to establish the label, Skinnymalinky. Findlay grew up in Cambridge, listening to rare funk records before moving to Manchester, promoting club nights, DJing and playing in some of the city's best funk bands. He then moved to London, where he continued to DJ and promoted a night with Cato, 'Captain Sensual At The Helm Of The Groove Armada' before they decided to record their own music under a shortened version of the name. Their music is an unusual blend of influences, spanning house, big beat, Balearic, disco and funk. It combines traditional instrumentation and influences with house rhythms and technology, and features samples of jazz as well as those from diverse artists such as the Chi-Lites, Platters and A Tribe Called Quest. Cato and Findlay record all their material at a countryside retreat in Cumbria, northern England. Their first album *Northern Star* was released on the London-based independent label, Tummy Touch in January 1998. The well-

received single 'At The River', built around a Patti Page vocal sample, was also released on the label. *Northern Star* was named Best New Artist Album by the UK's *Muzik* magazine. The duo was signed to Pepper Records for *Vertigo*. Like its predecessor the album was highly praised across the music press. A single from the album, 'If Everybody Looked The Same' was released in April 1999 and received much national UK radio airplay. A re-released 'At The River' entered the Top 20 three months later. Stylish, chilled-out and making all the right musical references, Groove Armada seem to have captured the zeitgeist of late-90s dance music.

● ALBUMS: *Northern Star* (Tummy Touch 1998)★★★★, *Vertigo* (Pepper 1999)★★★★.

Grooverider

b. Raymond Bingham, 16 April 1967, Dulwich, London, England. Best-known for his DJ partnership with Fabio, Grooverider's work has seen him proclaimed by at least one UK magazine as 'the Godfather' of contemporary dance music. A major contributor to both the hardcore and jungle phenomenons (frequent collaborator Goldie rates him as a pivotal influence), Grooverider has been active as a DJ at house parties since the mid-80s. He was particularly associated (alongside Fabio) with the outdoor rave movement of the late 80s when he was one of the few recognisable champions of a music which matched huge popularity with barely concealed hostility from the mainstream press. The base element of his music has always been exclusive dub plates, from whose breakbeats he fashioned what subsequently became known as drum 'n' bass music. His partnership with Fabio started in the early 80s when both were invited to DJ on a pirate radio station called Phase One. The show's creator was sufficiently impressed to invite the duo to host a new club he was opening in Brixton, south London. His recording career began much later, with tracks such as 'Sinister' and 'Dreams Of Heaven'. However, rather than ride his current boom in popularity, Grooverider has remained almost exclusively a performance DJ, earning his reputation by playing sets at venues throughout the country, and also appearing regularly on the Kiss FM radio station and at Goldie's Metalheadz Sunday Sessions at the Blue Note club in London. He also launched his own label, Prototype Records, in the early 90s, working with a new wave of break-beat artists such as Photek, Ed Rush, Origin Unknown, Boymerang, Dillinja and Lemon D, and recording the hugely influential tracks 'Dreams Of Heaven' and 'Deep Inside' under his alter ego, Codename John. The two hour drum 'n' bass marathon *Mysteries Of Funk*, finally appeared in 1998.

● ALBUMS: *Mysteries Of Funk* (Higher Ground 1998)★★★.
● COMPILATIONS: *Grooverider Presents: The Prototype Years* (Prototype/Higher Ground 1997)★★★★.

Guided By Voices

From Dayton, Ohio, USA, Guided By Voices took several years to find favour with America's alternative rock audience. Although consistently prolific, in truth, their obscurity had much to do with some unfulfilling early material that hardly predicted the comparative artistic grandeur of later albums such as *Bee Thousand* and *Crying Your Knife Away*. Led by part-time teacher Robert Pollard and Tobin Sprout, the band made its debut with the risible *Forever Since Breakfast* EP in 1986, which could have been categorized as progressive rock were it not for a lack of technical ability. The band's first four albums similarly failed to provide conclusive evidence of a defined songwriting ability. The real improvement began with 1992's *Propeller*, which saw them steer closer to a clean pop sound and suppress some of the irritating, ponderous excesses of earlier albums. Lyrically, too, Pollard was now communicating with more simplicity and conviction, with 'Exit Flagger' becoming their first bona fide 'classic song'. The accompanying *The Grand Hour* EP also featured 'Shocker In Gloomtown', which was later reinterpreted by Guided By Voices fans the Breeders. *Vampire On Titus* finally brought the band out of obscurity, with late-arriving fans of Sebadoh and Pavement sensing common ground with what became known as the 'lo-fi' movement (a sound demanding a simplicity of execution and emotional authenticity). Two 7-inch singles, 'Static Airplane Jive' and 'Fast Japanese Spin Cycle', then preceded *Bee Thousand*. On this recording they simultaneously managed to sound like a US garage band, the 1965 Beatles, early Velvet Underground and Captain Beefheart *circa Trout Mask Replica*; yet at no time did they sound anything less than highly original. The verdict on *Bee Thousand* was supported by a new maturity in Pollard's songwriting which swapped introspection for more erudite, prosaic character sketches. *Crying Your Knife Away*, a double live album, then the career-spanning *Box* compilation, built on their new-found popularity, as former music journalist Jim Greer joined the band as its new bass player. *Under The Bushes, Under The Stars*, a 24-track collection of minimal pop songs, pushed the band away from its lo-fi four-track origins, building on the success enjoyed by a spate of 7-inch singles including 'Motor Away' and 'My Valuable Hunting Knife'. Pollard and Sprout's overactive imaginations resulted in a glut of solo product in the mid-to-late 90s. *Mag Earwhig!* was released following debate about the band's future, with the two principle songwriters, Pollard and Sprout, falling out. The album featured Pollard and several new musicians, but proved to be as worthy as anything previously released under the Guided By Voices name. *Do The Collapse*, the band's first record for TVT Records, did away with the lo-fi ethic as producer Ric Ocasek opted for a commercial radio-friendly sound.

● ALBUMS: *Devil Between My Toes* (E 1987)★★, *Sandbox* (Halo 1987)★★, *Self Inflicted Aerial Nostalgia* (Halo 1989)★★, *Some Place The Fly Got Smashed* (Rocket Number 9 1990)★★★, *Propeller* (Rockathon 1992)★★★, *Vampire On Titus* (Scat 1993)★★★, *Bee Thousand* (Scat/Matador 1994)★★★★, *Crying Your Knife Away* (Lo-Fi 1994)★★★, *Alien Lanes* (Matador 1995)★★★, *Under The Bushes, Under The Stars* (Scat/Matador 1996)★★★, *Mag Earwhig!* (Matador 1997)★★★★, *Do The Collapse* (TVT 1999)★★★.
Solo: Robert Pollard *Not In My Airforce* (Matador 1996)★★★, *Waved Out* (Recordhead/Rockathon 1999)★★★, *Kid Marine* (Recordhead/Rockathon 1999)★★★. Tobin Sprout *Carnival Boy* (Matador 1996)★★★, *Sunfish Holy Breakfast* (Matador 1996)★★★, *Moonflower Plastic (Welcome To My Wigwam)* (Matador 1997)★★, *Let's Welcome The Circus People* (Recordhead 1999)★★★.
● COMPILATIONS: *Box* (Scat/Matador 1995)★★★★.

Guru Josh

b. Paul Walden, England. Noted for his goatee beard, flailing live performances and three word songs, Guru Josh nevertheless helped kick-start the Deconstruction Records success story. He had originally run a club night in Putney entitled the Happy House, and sang in a rock band, Joshua Cries Wolf. At least 'Infinity' (a UK Top 5 hit) was propelled by a great saxophone sequence, and 'Whose Law (Is It Anyway?)' also had its fans. The title might have given the impression that this was some sort of rave 'mission statement', but in fact the 'lyrics' made absolutely no sense whatsoever. If Guru Josh was, as *Smash Hits* magazine declared, 'spokesman for the warehouse generation', he was an embarrassingly inarticulate role model. Singles like the earlier asinine 'Time For The Guru' caught him at his 'peak', but when critics spotted a cover of 'Louie Louie' on his debut album the game was definitely up.
● ALBUMS: *Infinity* (Deconstruction 1990)★★★.

Gus Gus

Gus Gus is probably the most acclaimed and successful band to emerge from Reykjavik, Iceland since the Sugarcubes. Like their fellow national, Björk, they have developed a sound that is all their own: innovative and challenging, yet accessible and even 'dancefloor-friendly'. The band is a creative collective of nine members, ranging in ages from 19 to over 30 and spanning a wide spectrum of backgrounds and interests, including two film makers, a computer programmer, a photographer, a DJ, an actor, a political campaigner and a film producer. The band comprises Steph, Daniel Agust, Biggi Thorarinsson, Magnus Jonsson, Herr Legowitz, Hafdis Huld, Stefan Arni, Siggi Kjartansson and Baldur Stefansson. They assembled almost accidentally when Siggi Kjartansson and Stefan Arni sought a cast for a short film they were making. When shooting was postponed, songwriters Daniel and Siggi suggested they make an album. *Polydistortion* was recorded in 11 hectic days and was released in Iceland in late 1995. A copy found its way to the UK's independent label, 4AD Records, home of the Pixies and the Cocteau Twins. Liking what they heard, 4AD signed the band and *Polydistortion* was released in the UK in Spring 1997, receiving widespread critical acclaim. In 1997, they toured Europe and the USA, supporting bands such as Lamb and Cornershop. Alfred and Biggi remixed Depeche Mode's 'Only When I Lose Myself' in 1998. Gus Gus has also established its own fashion and record label, Elf 19, to release material by various Icelandic acts. *This Is Normal* displayed an eclectic range of influences, taking in several styles including hip-hop, funk, electro, techno and house. Their sound has an ethereal quality, combined with funky bass and drum sounds and intelligent use of technology. Despite their experimental tendencies and often unusual lyrical themes ('Ladyshave' explores a sexual fetish), dance music is integral to their sound and influences such as Carl Craig (who remixed the single 'Polyesterday'), Masters At Work, Sly Stone and Prince can be heard. The band have gained plaudits from such respected names as Madonna, Beck, the Beastie Boys, Nellee Hooper, David Byrne and the DJ, Sasha, who remixed their track 'Purple' with the Light in 1998.
● ALBUMS: *Polydistortion* (4AD 1997)★★★★, *This Is Normal* (4AD 1999)★★★.

Guster

Reminiscent of They Might Be Giants both in their music style, a bizarre folk/pop hybrid, and their loyal grassroots support, this US trio, originally known as Gus, formed in 1992. The members, Adam Gardner (vocals/guitar), Brian

Rosenworcel (percussion) and Ryan Miller (vocals/guitar), met while studying at Tufts University in Boston. The unusual line-up, incorporating two acoustic guitars and Rosenworcel's bongos, attracted a dedicated live following in the Boston area. They collaborated with local independent producer Mike Denneen on April 1994's *Parachute*, which was released by Aware Records. The surprising commercial success of this album and the follow-up, *Goldfly*, owed much to the dedication of their fans, who traded live tapes on the Internet and some of whom worked as unpaid reps for the band. Guster received a further boost when they were named Best Live Act at the Boston Music Awards in 1997. They then signed a major-label deal with Hybrid/Sire Records, who re-released a re-mixed *Goldfly* in 1997. As a thank you to their reps the band also recorded a five-track CD, *The Pasty Tapes*, solely for their pleasure. Guster's proper major-label debut, *Lost And Gone Forever*, was released in September 1999. Producer Steve Lillywhite smoothed out some of the band's rough edges and fleshed out their sound with brass and woodwind, while managing to retain their left-field charm and melodic wit.

● ALBUMS: *Parachute* (Aware 1995)★★★, *Goldfly* (Aware/Hybrid 1996)★★★, *Lost And Gone Forever* (Hybrid 1999)★★★★.

Guthrie, Andy

b. 20 January 1965, Camberwell, London. During the 90s Guthrie was involved with some of the most interesting and enduring dance music of the time. At school he learned classical music and later played rock, funk, reggae, bhangra and other styles in a number of bands. He began writing his own tunes on a sequencer and four-track recorder at home and subsequently did some work programming for Island Records. During the late 80s Guthrie became interested in dance music and in 1989 co-founded Banco De Gaia with Toby Marks. He worked on the first Planet Dog Records release, the 1993 EP *Desert Wind*, and subsequently on the albums *Maya* and *Last Train To Lhasa* after which he began to concentrate on his own work. He had formed Medicine Drum with Chris Dekker around 1993 and was producing such bands as Children Of The Bong and Senser. As 100th Monkey he made his solo debut with 'Spiritus' on Matsuri Productions in 1995. The following year, with Jaki Kenley (of 21-3 Productions), Guthrie put together the charity compilation *Earthtrance* for Positiva Records for which he contributed the track 'Invocation' (with Medicine Drum) and a remix of Banco De Gaia's 'Kincajou' (with Si Wild). At the same time he worked with Eat Static (*Bony Incus* EP) and with Tsuyoshi Suzuki for the Prana album *Geomantik*. He has continued to record with Medicine Drum and Prana and in 1997 released his first EP (*Skwirm/Skweel*) for 21-3 Productions, as Funkopath. With Medicine Drum Guthrie draws on 'world music' sources, while Funkopath and Prana have a purer psychedelic trance sound with a funky edge. Unlike much dance music which revolves around repetition and established formulas, his work is often characterized by varied textures and grooves, and the most detailed, original production. Other work includes remixes for Bentley Rhythm Ace and Digitalis, and collaborations with Mark Allen, Manmademan, Tristan and Process. As well as writing and producing, he teaches music technology and DJs dub and trip-hop sets as 100th Monkey.

Hall, Lynden David

b. London, England. One of the most promising UK soul artists of recent years, Hall is comparable to American singers such as D'Angelo, Eric Benét and Rahsaan Patterson for his championing of the singer-songwriter tradition in modern urban soul. Signed to Cooltempo Records, Hall's 'Do I Qualify', with its compelling blend of classic and modern soul styles, was a stand-out track on the label's *Nu Classic Soul* compilation. His debut album, *Medicine 4 My Pain*, featured four tracks recorded at Sony Studios in New York with producer Bob Power, whose impeccable nu-soul credits included Erykah Badu, the Roots and D'Angelo. The precociously talented Hall wrote, produced and played guitars, bass, keyboards and drums on all 11 tracks, paying homage to soul giants Al Green and Curtis Mayfield while still sounding utterly contemporary. The album's highlight, 'Sexy Cinderella', was the first track to be lifted as a single, although like subsequent releases it struggled to establish Hall as a commercial force. Re-released in November 1998, however, the song finally broke Hall into the UK Top 20, debuting at number 17.

● ALBUMS: *Medicine 4 My Pain* (Cooltempo/EMI 1998)★★★★.

Hall, Terry

b. 19 March 1959, Coventry, England. Former vocalist with the Specials, Fun Boy Three, Colour Field, Terry, Blair And Anoushka and Vegas (with Dave Stewart), Hall finally released his debut solo album after 15 years in the music industry in 1994. It was preceded by the promotional 45, 'Forever J', and an appearance at the Phoenix Festival - backed by Craig Gannon (ex-Smiths), Les Pattinson (Echo And The Bunnymen) and Chris Sharrock (ex-World Party), amongst others. The single was co-written with Gannon, while its long playing companion contained credits for XTC's Andy Partridge, Nick Heyward and Ian Broudie, who also helped produce. Hall had already worked with Broudie on the second Lightning Seeds album, 1992's *Sense*, co-writing three songs including the title track, a minor UK hit. He also co-wrote 'Lucky You' on the second Lightning Seeds album, *Jollification*, a reissued version of which broke into the UK Top 20 in 1995. The same year's *Rainbows* EP featured Tricky (on a new version of the Specials 'Ghost Town') and Damon Albarn of Blur (who co-wrote 'Chasing A Rainbow'). The following year, Hall appeared on the *War Child* charity album and collaborated with Tricky on his *Nearly God* project. Despite featuring Hall's cover version of Todd Rundgren's 'I Saw The Light', *Laugh*, on the new South Sea Bubble label, was a compellingly downbeat record informed by the break-up of his marriage that earned the singer high praise from the music press. The following year

Hall duetted with Sinead O'Connor on a version of Dana's 'All Kinds Of Everything' for an album of Eurovision covers.
● ALBUMS: *Home* (Anxious 1994)★★★, *Laugh* (South Sea Bubble Company 1997)★★★★.

Halliwell, Geri

b. 6 August 1972, Watford, Hertfordshire, England, although her date of birth has been the subject of some conjecture. Halliwell's time as part of the Spice Girls, the pop phenomenon of the late 90s, has effectively set her up for life. Before joining the band her varied CV included stints as a topless model and, bizarrely, a Turkish game show host. As a member of the Spice Girls, Halliwell enjoyed huge transatlantic success with songs such as 'Wannabe', '2 Become 1' and 'Spice Up Your Life', and was viewed by many in the media as the band's *de facto* leader. Although featured on the band's August 1998 UK chart-topping single, 'Viva Forever', Halliwell had actually left the band in May amid press rumours of disputes and personality clashes with the other members. In a remarkable volte-face, Halliwell shed the provocative outfits she had become famous for wearing in the Spice Girls in favour of a demure new image. Shortly afterwards she became a UN ambassador, responsible for promoting breast cancer awareness. EMI Records won the chase for Halliwell's signature in October 1998, and she set about recording her debut album with an exceptional team of session musicians and writers. In a bold move, Halliwell released the Shirley Bassey-styled ballad 'Look At Me' as her debut single in May 1999. Despite the song's obvious vocal limitations, it still managed to debut at UK number 2, although for many observers this was viewed as outright failure for an ex-Spice Girl. *Schiz-ophonic* proved to be a ragbag of musical influences, ranging from the token attempts at Latin ('Mi Chico Latino') and Eastern pop ('Let Me Love You'), to the more straightforward pop of 'Lift Me Up' and 'Bag It Up'. The album debuted at UK number 4 in June, which was also viewed by many as a disappointing return. Halliwell had the last laugh, however, by going on to enjoy two consecutive UK chart-toppers with 'Mi Chico Latino' and 'Lift Me Up', the latter winning a highly publicised 'battle of the singles' with her former bandmate Emma Bunton's dull cover version of Edie Brickell's 'What I Am'. She also published her autobiography, *If Only*.
● ALBUMS: *Schiz-ophonic* (EMI 1999)★★★.
● FURTHER READING: *If Only*, Geri Halliwell.

Handsome Family

Chicago, USA-based musician Brett Sparks originally formed the Handsome Family with his wife Rennie and friend Mike Werner. The Sparks' unique acoustic folk music is commonly lumped with the 'No Depression' alternative country scene, a style commonly associated with bands such as Uncle Tupelo, Whiskeytown and Son Volt. Their compelling blend of the plaintive country moans of Hank Williams and Southside Chicago blues, however, creates a bizarre rustic hybrid that has far more in common with the pre-war stylings of the Carter Family. Rennie's lyrics deftly incorporate cultural references that reveal an acute awareness of the modern mindset. Their scratchy 1994 debut sneaked in the dirty rock 'n' roll of 'Claire Said' amongst the funereal folk laments. *Milk And Scissors* was a more coherent follow-up, with an expanded lyrical range evident on the fables

'Emily Shore 1819-1839' and 'Amelia Earhart vs. The Dancing Bear'. Jeff Tweedy of Wilco helped out with guitar and harmony vocals on 1998's *Through The Trees*, the Sparks' best set to date. The unlikely instrumental pairing of drum machine and autoharp added to the brooding atmosphere conjured up by tracks such as 'Last Night I Went Out Walking', 'Weightless Again' and the bizarre tall-tale 'The Giant Of Illinois'.
● ALBUMS: *Odessa* (Carrot Top 1994)★★★, *Milk And Scissors* (Carrot Top 1996)★★★★, *Through The Trees* (Carrot Top 1998)★★★★, *In The Air* (Carrot Top 2000)★★★.
● COMPILATIONS: *Down In The Valley* (Loose 1999)★★★★.

Hanson

This precocious group of American teenagers shot to the top of the UK and US charts in the summer of 1997, with an energetic blend of Jackson Five-styled harmonies and crafted pop/soul melodies. The Hanson brothers, Isaac (b. Clarke Isaac Hanson, 17 November 1980, Tulsa, Oklahoma, USA; guitar/piano/vocals), Taylor (b. Jordan Taylor Hanson, 14 March 1983, Tulsa, Oklahoma, USA; keyboards/vocals) and Zac (b. Zachary Walker Hanson, 22 October 1985, Tulsa, Oklahoma, USA; drums/vocals), formed part of a wave of remarkably talented young performers, including Ben Kweller and country star LeAnn Rimes, emerging from America. Raised in Tulsa by music-loving parents, the Hansons also lived for short periods in Trinidad, Ecuador and Venezuela as a result of their father's work. Brought up musically on *Time/Life* compilations of classic 50s and 60s music, they began writing and performing publicly as a band in 1992 when Zac was six years old, including a performance at the May Fest Arts Festival in Tulsa. Two self-distributed CDs followed, along with extensive live performances that honed their instrumental abilities. Playing at the South by Southwest Music Convention for unsigned bands, they linked up with manager Chris Sabec, who finally landed them a contract with Mercury Records after they had been dismissed as hard to market by several other companies. Their debut single, the self-penned 'MMMBop', entered the US singles chart at number 16 before climbing to number 1, and also topped the UK charts. *Middle Of Nowhere* followed, recorded over a period of five months with 'name' producers Steve Lironi (Black Grape, Space) and the Dust Brothers (Beck), and featured four of their own songs alongside collaborations with established songwriters, including Barry Mann and Cynthia Weill. An exuberant blend of traditional pop and soul the album became one of the year's biggest sellers, aided by their hip and MTV-friendly 'slacker' image. Further transatlantic hit singles followed with 'Where's The Love', 'I Will Come To You', and 'Thinking Of You'. The brothers have continued to tour extensively, although their recorded output has been limited to a desultory seasonal album, a live set and a compilation of their early material.
● ALBUMS: *Middle Of Nowhere* (Mercury 1997)★★★★, *Snowed In For Christmas* (Mercury 1997)★, *Live From Albertane* (Mercury 1998)★★★.
● COMPILATIONS: *3 Car Garage: The Indie Recordings '95-'96* (Mercury 1998)★★★.
● VIDEOS: *Hanson: Tulsa, Tokyo And The Middle Of Nowhere* (PolyGram Music Video 1997), *Hanson Tour '98: Road To Albertane* (Polygram Video 1998).

Happy Mondays

Few debut records could lay claim to have had the impact (or length of title) of the Happy Mondays' *Squirrel And G-Man Twenty Four Hour Party People Plastic Face Carnt Smile (White Out)*. The sextet's raw brand of urban folk, with Shaun Ryder's accented, drawled vocals, was almost universally acclaimed. John Cale, formerly of the Velvet Underground, produced and gave the record a fresh, live feel. The original line-up remained unchanged (apart from the addition of backing singer Rowetta) from the band's formation in Manchester, England, early in the 80s. Joining singer Ryder (b. 23 August 1962) was his brother, Paul Ryder (b. 24 April 1964; bass), Mark Day (b. 29 December 1961; guitar), Gary Whelan (b. 12 February 1966; drums), Paul Davis (b. 7 March 1966; keyboards) and Mark Berry aka Bez (percussion), the latter widely noted for his manic onstage antics. Martin Hannett, famous for his work with a number of Manchester bands including Joy Division, produced the follow-up *Bummed*, which layered their music with diverse but strong dance rhythms. The following year's Paul Oakenfold remix of 'Wrote For Luck' (re-titled 'WFL') crystallised the band's emergent sound. The subsequent *Madchester Rave On* EP, which featured the club favourite 'Hallelujah', broke into the UK Top 20 and gave a name to the new Manchester scene led by the Happy Mondays and the Stone Roses. In 1990, the band covered John Kongos' 'He's Gonna Step On You Again' (retitled 'Step On') and reached the UK Top 10. Their manic third album *Pills 'N' Thrills And Bellyaches* went to number 1 in the UK and established the band as a major pop force. The album also coincided with support and re-promotion of 60s singer Donovan, who appeared alongside them on the front covers of the music press. They even recorded a tribute song, 'Donovan', which paraphrased the lyrics of the singer's 60s hit, 'Sunshine Superman'. Strong support from Factory Records and an unusually consistent output meant Happy Mondays quickly rose to the status of favourite sons, of the readership of the *New Musical Express* and *Melody Maker*, and they were achieving sales to match. However, the band's successes were tempered with a fair share of unpleasant publicity which came to a head when Ryder announced he was a heroin addict and was undergoing detoxification treatment. A highly publicized strife-torn recording session in the Caribbean, with producers Tina Weymouth and Chris Frantz (of Talking Heads), resulted in ... *Yes Please!*. However, its impact was dulled by a decline in press interest, at least outside of Ryder's drug habits. Fittingly, the band's eventual collapse could not be tied to a specific date, with various members breaking off at various points throughout 1993. The band's focal points, Ryder and Bez, eventually re-emerged in 1995 as part of a new coalition, Black Grape, after Ryder had contributed vocals to 'Can You Fly Like You Mean It' by fellow Mancunians Intastella. Following the break-up of Black Grape, Ryder re-formed the Happy Mondays for several live dates and a new recording of Thin Lizzy's 'The Boys Are Back In Town'. The 1999 line-up comprised Ryder, Paul Ryder, Bez, Gary Whelan and new member Nuts.

● ALBUMS: *Squirrel And G-Man Twenty Four Hour Party People Plastic Face Carnt Smile (White Out)* (Factory 1987)★★★, *Bummed* (Factory 1988)★★★★, *Pills 'N' Thrills And Bellyaches* (Factory 1990)★★★★, *Live* (Factory 1991)★★, ... *Yes Please!* (Factory 1992)★★, *The Peel Sessions* (Strange Fruit 1996)★★.

● COMPILATIONS: *Loads - The Best Of* (London 1995)★★★, *Loads More* limited edition (London 1995)★★, *Greatest Hits* (London 1999)★★★.

● FURTHER READING: *Shaun Ryder: Happy Mondays, Black Grape And Other Traumas*, Mick Middles. *High Life 'N' Low Down Dirty: The Thrills And Spills Of Shaun Ryder*, Lisa Verrico. *Freaky Dancin'*, Bez.

Hardfloor

Oliver Bandzio and Ramon Zenker from Germany form this Dusseldorf-based acid house revivalist outfit. Typically, Bandzio's life was changed by 1988's flourishing acid scene. Unlike many, however, he was determined to recreate the excitement of those heady days, and spent no less than three years attempting to track down his own Roland 303, responsible for much of the sound of that period. After having finally traced one he made the acquaintance of studio wizard Zenkler, and together they debuted with 'Hardtrance Acperience', on Sven Vath's Harthouse label late in 1992. Some critics questioned whether the track contained the longest snare roll ever committed to vinyl, while its stylings were inextricably those of the summer of 1988 (it became arguably the most important post-acid house acid house record ever). The follow-up 12-inch sampled hunting horns, hence its name 'Into The Nature', on which production was orchestrated by 303 guru Richie Hawtin. Following the genre-splicing success of 'Hardtrance Acperience', Hardfloor were the toast of the mid-90s when many major artists looked to them to inject their Acperience remix magic, and bring their releases up to date with post Acperience acid/techno music. Their remix work has included Sourmash's 'Pilgrimage To Paradise', More Kanté's 'Yeke Yeke', New Order's 'Blue Monday', Human League's 'Filling Up With Heaven', Depeche Mode's 'Its No Good', and Robert Armani's 'Circus Bells'. Hardfloor sustained justifiable criticism, however, for becoming formulaic and selling out, though their albums never reflected this. More recently, they have collaborated with 303 techno originators Phuture 303 on the 'Hardfloor Will Survive' track, both as an attempt to reclaim credibility and to explore authentic old-school acid sounds.

● ALBUMS: *Funalogue* mini-album (Harthouse 1994)★★★★, *Home Run* (Harthouse 1996)★★★, *All Targets Down* (Harthouse 1998)★★★.

Harper, Ben

b. 28 October 1969, California, USA. Acoustic folk-rocker Harper hails from the arid Inland Emire region, 50 miles east of Los Angeles. His family was musical; his grandfather played lute, his grandmother the guitar, his father drums and his mother combined guitar with vocals. It led to him soaking up a variety of influences in his youth, from Son House and Skip James to Bob Marley and Bob Dylan. He was six years old when he began strumming a guitar for the first time, performing in front of a live audience by the age of 12. His acoustic guitar style was tutored by the great folk and blues artists and often accomplished on his distinctive 'Weissenborn' instrument, a hollow-neck lap slide guitar built by Herman Weissenborn during the mid-20s. In 1992, Harper played with Taj Mahal, a great influence on him, and also performed alongside bluesman Brownie McGhee. He made his debut for Virgin Records in early 1994, earning good reviews, including one from the *L.A. Times* who said: 'They don't make records like this anymore . . . the appeal of his folk-blues melodies is immediate, the depth of his emotions rewarding and the promise of his talent note-worthy.' Most impressive was the urban lament of 'Like A King', which made direct reference to both Martin Luther and Rodney King in its exploration of the ongoing black struggle. Afterwards Harper worked with actor Morgan Freeman on a children's movie *Follow The Drinking Gourd*, a biopic of Harriet Tubman. He contributed the music to Freeman's narration. Harper's second album, *Fight For Your Mind*, continued to explore lyrical themes of freedom and the restraint of self-expression, though tracks such as 'By My Side' confirmed his ability to write songs from within a deeply personalised emotional spectrum. Both *The Will To Live* and *Burn To Shine* opted for a harder edged sound, framing Harper's superb songs in some new and unusual settings.

● ALBUMS: *Welcome To The Cruel World* (Virgin 1994)★★★, *Fight For Your Mind* (Virgin 1995)★★★, *The Will To Live* (Virgin 1997)★★★★, *The Will To Live - Bonus Live EP Edition* (Virgin 1998)★★★, *Burn To Shine* (Virgin 1999)★★★.

Harper, Nick

b. 22 June 1965, London, England and raised in Wiltshire. Son of the legendary UK singer-songwriter Roy Harper, Nick Harper made his recording debut on his father's *Whatever Happened To Jugula?* in 1985. His own powerful 1995 debut album naturally compared him (favourably) to his irascible father. Harper junior however has already equalled his father's formidable talent as a guitarist and judging by his live performances and songs contained on the debut recording, he is a talent waiting to be recognised. One of the most impressive tracks is 'Crazy Boy', a song about his father, showing the parent as the wild and irresponsible one. On other tracks a beautiful guitar style reminiscent of new age guitarists Alex De Grassi and Michael Hedges is notable. Harper continues the family tradition of radically addressing political issues with the scathing 'Mr Grey' and 'Thanks For The Miracle'. The former alludes to UK prime Minister John Major and the latter to Thatcherism of the 80s. *Smithereens* followed in 1998.

● ALBUMS: *Seed* (Sangraal 1995)★★★★, *Smithereens* (Quixotic 1998)★★★.

Harris, Corey

b. 21 February 1969, Denver, Colorado, USA. One of the new breed of young, acoustic country bluesmen currently reinventing the Delta Blues, Harris is a talented multi-instrumentalist who draws inspiration from a wide range of musical influences. After gaining a degree in anthropology, he visited Cameroon several times in the early 90s, studying the local patois Pidgin before returning to America to teach for a year in Louisiana. While he was teaching, Harris began performing on the streets of New Orleans (playing guitar, trumpet and kazoo), and he has stated in interviews how his experience as a street musician 'helped [me] to project, and [know] what songs to play to get people's attention.' Like fellow modern-day bluesmen Alvin Youngblood Hart and Eric Bibb, Harris only covers old blues songs that are still relevant, and the songs on his albums draw more lyrical inspiration from rap than from the blues. Musically he blends acoustic blues with African rhythms (including playing the jun-jun, a drum indigenous to West Africa), building upon the influence of country blues legend Taj Mahal. Harris'

musical eclecticism found richest expression on his third album, 1999's *Greens From The Garden*.

● ALBUMS: *Between Midnight And Day* (Alligator 1995)★★★, *Fish Ain't Bitin'* (Alligator 1997)★★★★, *Greens From The Garden* (Alligator 1999)★★★★.

Hart, Alvin Youngblood

b. 2 March 1963, Oakland, California, USA. Born and raised in Oakland, modern-day country bluesman Hart draws inspiration from his ancestral home in Carrollton, Mississippi (the run-down shacks pictured on *Big Mama's Door* are actually the homes of his grandmother and great-grandfather). Although he briefly played in high school rock bands, Hart was naturally drawn to the blues and tried to break into the local scene in Los Angeles. Dismayed with the commercialization of the blues, he decided to become a solely acoustic player in the mid-80s. Although he gave up playing for a period and worked at a variety of day jobs, Hart returned to music and quickly established himself as a distinctive and passionate acoustic blues player. A support slot for Taj Mahal in February 1995 brought Hart's name to a wider audience, and his debut release for the Sony-licensed OKeh Records label was a vital collection of songs by artists as diverse as Lead Belly ('Gallows Pole'), Charlie Patton ('Pony Blues') and 'Blind' Willie McTell ('Hillbilly Willie's Blues'). Still living in Mississippi where he runs a guitar repair shop with his wife, Hart is now signed to Hannibal following a disagreement with Sony over the promotion of his album. His reputation as a live performer was further enhanced by US support slots for Buddy Guy, Los Lobos and Richard Thompson.

● ALBUMS: *Big Mama's Door* (OKeh 1996)★★★★, *Territory* (Hannibal 1998)★★★.

Hawkes, Chesney

b. 22 September 1971. The son of former Tremeloes writer and vocalist Chip Hawkes. Chesney shot to prominence in 1991 with the UK chart-topper 'The One And Only', his first single, written for him by Nik Kershaw. The follow-up, 'I'm A Man Not A Boy', invited an obvious retort from incredulous critics. Chrysalis Records attempted to cash in on the success of 'The One And Only' by re-releasing *Buddy's Song* and crediting it solely to Hawkes. The attendant movie, which co-starred Roger Daltrey as Hawkes' father, dealt with the legend of Buddy Holly. Following the release of 1993's *Get The Picture* Hawkes concentrated on acting, although he still plays with the London-based Ebb.

● ALBUMS: *Buddy's Song* film soundtrack (Chrysalis 1991)★★, *Get The Picture* (Chrysalis 1993)★★.

Hawkins, Sophie B.

b. Sophie Ballantine Hawkins, Manhattan, New York, USA. Born of liberal, wealthy East Manhattan parents (her father a lawyer, her mother British writer Joan Winthrop), Hawkins' family background also boasted an aunt, Linda, who had been masseuse to Paul Simon. By the time she moved with Aunt Linda to the arty environs of West Greenwich, she had already began to develop her musical talent, taking drum lessons at an East Harlem jazz school from the age of nine. Her teens were spent studying New York percussionist Gordy Ryan (she also shared a room with him at the age of 14). By her late teens Hawkins and Ryan also shared a stage together, touring a show around New York State. In the meantime she had started to write her own material, and by the age of 20 had enough to approach prospective record companies. Between bar-tending stints she spent two months rehearsing with Bryan Ferry (who eventually sacked her before taking her on tour), then met Marc Cohn while she was waitressing. Through him she earned jingle contracts for advertisements including ones for Nestlé's Sweet Dreams, working in producer Ralph Shuckett's studio, and using his contacts to arrange meetings with record companies. Columbia Records were quick to bite following interest from both Sire Records and Arista Records, seeing in her a marketable songwriting ability which secured her a multi-album deal. She introduced herself with the smouldering worldwide summer 1992 success of 'Damn, I Wish I Was Your Lover'. The accompanying debut album, *Tongues And Tails*, invoked a similar sense of wilfulness and sexuality. Among the supporting cast were percussionist Omar Hakim (ex-Weather Report), though all the other arrangements were conducted by Hawkins. It signposted Hawkins as a 'star in the making' in many critical polls. However, further singles success did not follow, and Hawkins concentrated instead on crafting a clutch of 20 songs in her home studio. These demos were then fleshed out with Steve Lipson in London and, whittled down, formed the foundation for *Whaler*. The title was inspired by a youth spent in the whaling town of Sagg Harbour. It produced a hit single in 'Right Beside You', which came as no small comfort to an artist who had been expecting to be dropped in the run up to her second album (label executives were reportedly annoyed at nude pictures of Hawkins which appeared in *Interview* magazine, mainly, though, because she was not wearing make-up and did not look 'glamorous enough'). After an extended hiatus Hawkins returned in 1999 with *Timbre*, an assured and mature collection of adult contemporary pop.

● ALBUMS: *Tongues And Tails* (Columbia 1992)★★★, *Whaler* (Columbia 1994)★★, *Timbre* (Columbia 1999)★★★.

Hawtin, Richie

b. Windsor, Ontario, Canada. Just over the border from Detroit, Hawtin grew up under the influence of Detroit techno stars, Juan Atkins, Derrick May and Kevin Saunderson. A DJ since 1987 and a recording artist since 1990, Hawtin is perhaps better known for operations under two separate guises, F.U.S.E. and Plastikman. His first releases as a solo artist came as F.U.S.E. on his own label, Plus 8 Records, an acronym for Future Underground Subsonic Experiments. F.U.S.E. kicked off with the still fresh-sounding 'Approach And Identify', quickly gaining further popularity and respect with the 1991 release 'F.U.', which launched Plus 8's harder offshoot, Probe Records. These early releases were usually limited to between 500 and 800 copies, thereby ensuring that they were quickly circulated and collected by DJs. F.U.S.E. encompassed Hawtin's more disparate solo projects, with sounds ranging from the harsher early releases to beautifully blissed-out 'home-listening' music (the atmospheric 'Train Trac' was even likened to 'having sex in a bubble in space with someone you trust'). This range of styles was perhaps best captured on the album *Dimension Intrusion*, part of Warp Records' highly collectable Artificial Intelligence series. As Plastikman, Hawtin debuted with the 'Spastik' 12-inch, an unreservedly harsh and abrasive cut, followed by the album *Sheet One*, on his own Plus 8 label. The tail-end of 1993 saw the release of 'Krakpot' on Novamute Records, another intense house workout. The Plastikman title allows Hawtin to indulge his love of the 'acid' sound of the 303: 'a lot of the 303 tracks got very noisy and un-funky and against what I believed it was all about . . . that's why I came back with Plastikman. To me it reflects what the 303 was designed to do. It's a beautiful machine . . . "sexy"'. Hawtin achieved major acclaim with the Concept series, 12 releases over 12 months of minimally packaged, almost dublike techno, reminiscent of much of the work of Maurizio. Hawtin has continued releasing records and pursuing his busy DJing schedule, in addition to hosting his Hard, Harder And Hardest warehouse parties in Detroit. *Decks, EFX & 909* was the first long-player to be released under his real name.

● ALBUMS: as Plastikman *Sheet One* (Plus 8 1993)★★★, as Plastikman *Recycled Plastik* (Plus 8/Novamute 1994)★★★, as Plastikman *Mixmag Live Volume 20* (Mixmag Live 1995)★★★, as Plastikman *Consumed* (Mute 1998)★★★, as Plastikman *Artifakts (BC)* (Novamute 1998)★★★, as Richie Hawtin *Decks, EFX & 909* (Novamute 1999)★★★.

Hazeldine

Albuquerque, New Mexico, USA-based quartet built around the songwriting talents of Shawn Barton (guitar/vocals) and Tonya Lamm (guitar/vocals). Barton grew up in Florida, studying at the University of Florida under the influential southern novelist Harry Crews. Lamm was brought up in North Carolina, before moving to Athens, Georgia. Here she played in an electric folk band with guitarist and long-time friend Jeffrey Richards and bass player Jeff Mangum, the guiding force behind Neutral Milk Hotel. Barton, Lamm and Richards came together in Albuquerque in late 1994. Barton originally played drums, before swapping with Richards to join Lamm up front as co-vocalist. The addition of classically trained percussionist Anne Tkach on bass completed the line-up, taking their name from a local avenue. The quartet released their debut single 'Tarmac' (b/w 'Apothecary') the following year on Los Angeles independent label Cherry Smash Records. Their debut *How Bees Fly* was recorded in the basement of a pool hall on Route 66 in Albuquerque, gaining a Europe-only release through Glitterhouse Records in mid-1997. A compelling blend of bluegrass, folk and rock influences, the album contained both sides of the debut single plus cover versions of Grant Lee Buffalo's 'Fuzzy' and Eric's Trip's 'Allergic To Love'. The album was enthusiastically received by the European press, and led to an international deal with Polydor Records. The band recorded their second album in Los Angeles in early 1998 with renowned producer Jim Scott (Whiskeytown, Tom Petty), reworking versions of four songs from the debut. Barton and Lamm's evocative songwriting dwelt on the experience of growing up in smalltown America, finding particularly harrowing expression on the title track and 'Daddy'. Viewed by most critics as part of the 'No Depression' movement of neo-country rock acts, the standard of the songwriting on *Digging You Up* established Barton and Lamm as two of the alternative scene's leading songwriters. After finishing *Digging You Up*, they quickly recorded the limited edition covers album *Orphans* with instrumental contributions from Silos' frontman Walter Salas-Humara. Covering a diverse range of material, including tracks by Thin Lizzy, Genesis, Radiohead, Gram Parsons and Sparklehorse, the album was released through Glitterhouse in Europe and E Squared in America.

● ALBUMS: *How Bees Fly* (Glitterhouse 1997)★★★, *Orphans* (Glitterhouse/E Squared 1998)★★★, *Digging You Up* (Polydor 1998)★★★★.

Healey, Jeff

b. 25 March 1966, Toronto, Ontario, Canada. Blind since developing eye cancer at the age of 12 months, Healey is a white blues-rock guitarist and singer who plays in an unusual, instinctive lap-held style. He received his first guitar at the age of three and has been a proficient multi-instrumentalist since childhood. At 15, he formed Blue Direction and gigged regularly in the Toronto area. In 1985, Healey was invited to play alongside Texas bluesman Albert Collins who, much impressed, in turn introduced him to Stevie Ray Vaughan. The Jeff Healey Band - Joe Rockman (b. 1 January 1957, Toronto, Canada; bass/vocals) and Tom Stephen (b. 2 February 1955, St. John, New Brunswick, Canada; drums) - was formed the same year and began playing across Canada. They released singles on their own Forte label - and produced accompanying videos - before signing to Arista Records in 1988. *See the Light* was released in 1989 and came wrapped in a sash bearing tributes from guitar giants such as Vaughan and B.B. King. It sold nearly two million copies; a world tour followed later in the year. The 1989 movie *Roadhouse*, starring Patrick Swayze and Ben Gazzara, featured Healey in an acting/singing role as a blind blues guitarist. *Hell To Pay* tended more towards hard rock and featured Mark Knopfler, George Harrison, Jeff Lynne and Bobby Whitlock in addition to Healey's regular band. It went on to sell over two million copies worldwide. *Feel This* was a strong and energetic rock/blues album, and the back-to-his-roots *Cover To Cover* was a collection of favourite songs by some of Healey's mentors. He wanted this record to be fun and to recall the times when he made little money from his music.

● ALBUMS: *See The Light* (Arista 1989)★★★★, *Hell To Pay* (Arista 1990)★★, *Feel This* (Arista 1992)★★★, *Cover To Cover* (Arista 1995)★★★.

● COMPILATIONS: *The Very Best Of* (Camden 1998)★★★, *The Master Hits* (Arista 1999)★★★.

● FILMS: *Roadhouse* (1989).

Heavenly Records

Record label set up in 1990 by Jeff Barrett when old friend and music journalist Bob Stanley contacted him regarding a new track, 'Only Love Can Break Your Heart', he had written for his band Saint Etienne. The 'Heavenly' name came from Barrett's riposte that the decade that produced the original song was 'horrible'. The Heavenly label was promptly set up in response, although the first release was Sly And Lovechild's 'The World According To', in May 1990. Barrett had already garnered extensive experience in the UK independent scene, as a former Creation Records employee, gig promoter and public relations representative for Happy Mondays, Primal Scream and several other Factory Records/Creation acts. After Saint Etienne earned their own niche, Flowered Up became a hugely hyped but, perversely,

undervalued musical force, whom Barrett met when 'buying drugs off them'. The Manic Street Preachers' 'Motown Junk' and 'You Love Us' then premiered one of the UK's most important bands. The Manic Street Preachers made an amicable switch to Columbia Records shortly thereafter, amid a barrage of press speculation - Heavenly's artists rarely struggled to fill column inches. The Manic Street Preachers rewarded Barrett's faith in them with a royalty on their debut album, and partly as a consequence of this, Heavenly linked themselves with the Japanese corporation Sony. Despite considerable record company support, country rock act the Rockingbirds failed to take off, while the label again demonstrated its eclecticism by unveiling Latin dance music group Espiritu. In 1992, they released a special Right Said Fred cover version EP featuring the Rockingbirds, Saint Etienne and Flowered Up, which boosted both the bands' and the label's profile. From 1995 to April 1999, Heavenly worked as part of the Deconstruction Records set-up, following which they signed a joint venture deal with EMI/Chrysalis.

The company also branched out into other media by publishing a book, Kevin Pearce's *Something Beginning With O*. Barrett also collaborated with the Dust Brothers (soon to change their name to the Chemical Brothers) and Robin Turner on the groundbreaking Heavenly Social club nights. In August 1994, the first Sunday Social took place in the basement of the Albany pub on Great Portland Street, London, with Tom Rowlands and Ed Simons of the Chemical Brothers manning the decks. The club attracted an egalitarian mix of musicians and ordinary punters, and its musical ethos of 'anything goes' provided the blueprint for clubs such as Big Beat Boutique, It's On and the Big Kahuna Burger, and the Skint Records and Wall Of Sound labels. The club moved to Turnmills in February 1996, and changed its name to Heavenly Jukebox when the Chemical Brothers finally ended their residency. Richard Fearless and Jon Carter took over on the decks, and continued to refine the club's big beat sound. The Heavenly Jukebox was finally laid to rest on February 21 1999, with attention shifting to the team's new Metal Box club in Soho.

Heavy D And The Boyz

Self-proclaimed 'overweight lover of rap from money earnin' Mount Vernon', Heavy D (b. Dwight Myers, 24 May 1967, Jamaica, West Indies) fronted a mainstream rap outfit which has been considered the genre's equivalent of Luther Vandross. Though the vast majority of his material represents rap's familiar call to procreation, Heavy D's rhymes are imbued with warmth rather than breast-beating machismo. Similarly, though he makes much of his muchness (titles like 'Mr. Big Stuff' are frequent), there is more to Heavy D than novelty. His debut album, produced by Teddy Riley, comprised funk alongside hints of the swingbeat sound the producer was in the process of creating. Riley was also in tow for the follow-up, though this time he was in the company of fellow rap production legend Marley Marl, among others. Q-Tip (A Tribe Called Quest), Big Daddy Kane and Pete Rock and C.L. Smooth all featured on 'Don't Curse', a posse cut from *Peaceful Journey*. The album also included a tribute to former band member T-Roy (b. Troy Dixon, d. 15 July 1990). The other 'Boyz' comprised G. Whiz (b. Glen Parrish) and DJ Eddie F (b. Edward Ferrell). Success continued unabated when 'Now That We've Found Love' became a UK number 2 in July 1991, profiling a fresh, Jamaican DJ influenced style. He also made a high profile guest appearance on Michael Jackson's 'Jam' single and sister Janet's 'Alright With Me'. Strangely, despite this success MCA did not see fit to offer *Blue Funk*, which saw Heavy return to hardcore territory with guest production from Pete Rock and DJ Premier, an immediate UK release. His 1994 set *Nuttin' But Love* saw him reunite with rap's top rank of producers, including old hands Marl, Riley and Rock, alongside Erick Sermon, Trackmasterz and Troy Williams. It was another superb package, making Heavy D one of rap's heavyweights in more than the literal sense. He confirmed his longevity when *Waterbed Hev* enjoyed both critical and commercial acclaim, entering the US Top 10 in spring 1997. *Heavy* featured another solid collection of laidback grooves, delivered, as usual, with panache and skill.

● ALBUMS: *Living Large* (Uptown 1987)★★★, *Big Tyme* (Uptown 1989)★★★★, *Peaceful Journey* (Uptown 1991)★★★, *Blue Funk* (Uptown 1992)★★★, *Nuttin' But Love* (Uptown 1994)★★★★, *Waterbed Hev* (Uptown 1997)★★★, *Heavy* (Universal 1999)★★★.

Henry, Joe

b. Charlotte, North Carolina, USA. As a child Henry moved to the Midwest through his father's peripatetic job with car manufacturers Chevrolet. Most of his youth was spent in and around Detroit, where he met and married wife Melanie Ciccone (the sister of Madonna). They moved to Brooklyn, New York, in 1985, then Los Angeles in 1990 when Ciccone was offered a job with Brian Eno's Opal Records. Henry had recorded his first album in 1986 live in the studio, a methodology repeated on all his releases until 1996's *Trampoline*. In keeping with his Johnny Cash influences, his subsequent albums for A&M Records offered bleak narratives, relayed in detached, emotionally drained tones. In 1992, he moved to independent label Mammoth for *Short Man's Room*. That and 1993's *Kindness Of The World* continued to explore moribund themes in a quasi-country style - the title track of the latter album concerning a young boy climbing a high tree to get nearer to his maker. The same album featured backing from the Jayhawks. Literate and engaging, such songs earned him a strong media profile outside of the more obvious Madonna connections, though he felt a little constrained by the country singer-songwriter mantle he had earned himself. *Trampoline* thus brokered a major transition to electric instrumentation and more expressionistic songwriting. As well as hip-hop beats and jarring guitar effects, this featured Helmet guitarist Page Hamilton on several tracks, notably the album's stand-out song, 'Ohio Air Show Plane Crash', and was recorded in collaboration with producer Patrick McCarthy. In the same year Henry also collaborated with his famous sister-in-law for the first time, Madonna providing backing vocals to his interpretation of Vic Chesnutt's 'Guilty By Association', which was included on the soundtrack to the movie *Sweet Relief II: Gravity Of The Situation*. Henry returned to independent label status for 1999's *Fuse*.

● ALBUMS: *Talk Of Heaven* (Profile 1986)★★★, *Murder Of Crows* (A&M 1989)★★★, *Shuffletown* (A&M 1990)★★, *Short Man's Room* (Mammoth 1992)★★★, *Kindness Of The World* (Mammoth 1993)★★★, *Trampoline* (Atlantic/Mammoth 1996)★★★★, *Fuse* (Edel/Mammoth 1999)★★★.

Hersh, Kristin

b. Atlanta, Georgia, USA. Hersh initially enjoyed acclaim as the lead singer of Throwing Muses, one of alternative US rock music's most influential and enduring bands. She elected to pursue a simultaneous solo career after the parent band nearly dissolved in 1992. With her step-sister and bandmate Tanya Donelly setting out to form the commercially successful Belly, Hersh kept the name Throwing Muses but also began to write songs destined for self-accompaniment. She had already explored some disconcerting mental and psychological imagery on previous Muses albums, not least the loss of custody of her son Dylan (she now has a younger son, Ryder, five years Dylan's junior). It had resulted in Hersh relocating to her son's hometown of Newport, Rhode Island, where she herself grew up, sheltered from a stormy adolescence by her X and Violent Femmes records. Though her own parents were free-thinking liberals, she was equally influenced by her Baptist grandparents. She moved to Newport from Atlanta when she was six years old, and her father taught courses in Zen Buddhism and American Indian mythology. Her parents divorced at the age of 11, but this offered an unexpected boon: the father of her best friend, Tanya Donelly, marrying her mother. It was Hersh who was primarily behind the formation of Throwing Muses with Donelly, allowing her an outlet for the songs she had been writing from childhood. Some of these made extremely uncomfortable listening, and with the Muses' rise she found her new-found celebrity difficult to handle. By the advent of her solo career Hersh had partially conquered her psychological battle with the aid of lithium, and by the mid-90s she felt able to continue without any recourse to pharmaceuticals. Some of this turbulence was captured in the fibre of *Hips And Makers*, but so was a great deal more, the artist herself describing it as 'a real life record. It's personal, literally so; full of skin and coffee, shoes and sweat and babies and sex and food and stores - just stupid stuff that's a really big deal.' Michael Stipe of R.E.M. guested on backing vocals for promotional single 'Your Ghost', though elsewhere just Hersh's voice, guitar and intermittent cello carried the songs, produced by Lenny Kaye (Patti Smith). By now she had become wary of being characterized as the mad woman with a guitar, and the collection reflected her resentment with female creativity being so unobjectively linked with mental instability. After returning to the Throwing Muses format with palpable enthusiasm for *University* in 1995, she also revealed news of a first film project, *Guess What's Coming To Dinner*, written with husband and manager Billy O'Connell. Electing to leave Throwing Muses in 1997, Hersh released *Strange Angels*, a more confident and accessible collection. Out of left field Hersh released the mail order only *Murder, Misery And Then Goodnight*, an album of traditional Appalachian folk songs. *Sky Motel*, her most mainstream recording to date, was released the following year.

● ALBUMS: *Hips And Makers* (Warners/4AD 1994)★★★, *Strange Angels* (4AD 1998)★★★, *Murder, Misery And Then Goodnight* (4AD 1998)★★★, *Sky Motel* (4AD 1999)★★★.

Hewerdine, Boo

b. London, England. Singer-songwriter Hewerdine is a proud resident of Cambridge, England, where he moved with his parents aged 12 and which he likes because 'nothing ever happens here. You can get on with things.' However, at age

18 he returned to London to live in his late grandmother's house in Edgware, London, which set about a downward personal spiral. He suffered from agoraphobia and was (unjustly) accused of theft and fired from his job at a record shop. However, he found a friend with similar experiences and together they began to explore music as an outlet for their traumas. He returned to Cambridge to form Placebo Thing, then the marginally more successful the Great Divide. The latter released two singles for Enigma Records after being recommended to the label by Mike Scott of the Waterboys. These attracted a fair degree of attention within the UK's minor press, but more mainstream media support was not forthcoming. In January 1985, Hewerdine once again returned to Cambridge to work in a record shop, and set up a third band, the Bible. Working with jazz drummer Tony Shepherd he wrote an album of songs, *Walking The Ghost Back Home*, released through Norwich independent Backs Records in 1986. Two singles drawn from the set, 'Gracelands' and 'Mahalia', achieved slight success, with the album also earning extensive critical support. With the band having expanded to a quartet the Bible signed with Chrysalis Records and just missed the UK Top 40 with a re-recorded 'Gracelands' and 'Honey Be Good'. After the disappointing commercial performance of 1988's *Eureka*, Hewerdine grew unhappy about the band's direction: 'I thought we were turning into an ordinary group.' He began playing his first solo gigs as a result, while the rest of the Bible became Liberty Horses. Hewerdine then made the acquaintance of American 'new country' artist Darden Smith. Together they spent four days writing songs that later formed the collaborative *Evidence* album (they would also work together on Smith's solo album). Hewerdine's own solo debut came as a result of sessions spent recording nearly 30 songs at Church Studio in north London in 1990. These songs were whittled down and augmented with the help of co-producer Rob Peters (formerly of Birmingham's Dangerous Girls) to produce *Ignorance*. The lyrics addressed the period during the late 70s when the artist was slowly falling apart in north London, but escaped the morbidity that might have been triggered by those events with some bright, uplifting instrumentation. With support slots to Tori Amos and another widely applauded single, 'History', the album did just enough commercially to sustain Hewerdine's status. He also wrote songs for Eddi Reader (notably 'Patience of Angels') and Clive Gregson and did production work with Laurie Freelove. *Baptist Hospital* failed to match the anticipation, the results being somewhat lacklustre. Hewerdine subsequently worked on the soundtrack to *Fever Pitch*, before enlisting veteran producer John Wood to help with 1999's understated *Thanksgiving*.

● ALBUMS: with Darden Smith *Evidence* (Ensign 1989)★★★, *Ignorance* (Ensign 1992)★★★, *Baptist Hospital* (Blanco y Negro 1996)★★, *Thanksgiving* (Black Burst 1999)★★★.

Hex

Hex started as the multi-media side of Ninja Tune Records, firstly with Rob Pepperell in charge and later Stuart Warren Hall. Working closely with Jonathon Moore and Matt Black (aka Coldcut), Hex has created a number of projects aimed at developing the role of the DJ and evolved into a 'multi-armed posse manipulating multiple sound and vision sources'. Some of their software applications are based around sampling and remixing ideas, while two installations, 'Synopticon' (TRADEMARK) at the Barbican and 'Generator' (TRADEMARK) at the Glasgow Gallery of Modern Art, allowed visitors to create and mix sounds and visuals simultaneously. As a live attraction Hex has become an exciting VJ team working at Ninja Tune's club nights, Stealth and Kungfusion. Attempting to expand the established formats Hex created a scratch video *Natural Rhythm* to accompany Coldcut's 'Atomic Moog' (1998). It was the first in a trilogy of collaboration that also included 'More Bits And Pieces' and 'Timber' (as Hexstatic). They also contributed a number of games, creative tools and videos to Coldcut's album *Let Us Play*. By 1998, Hex were signed to Ninja Tune as an artist, no longer just the multi-media arm of the label.

High Llamas

London, England's High Llamas are the 90s vehicle of former Microdisney co-founder Sean O'Hagan (b. Eire). After that band sundered in 1987, O'Hagan spent three years incubating the High Llamas' debut album, released on Demon Records in 1990. Though a low-profile release, it received several encouraging reviews, not least from long-standing Microdisney fans within the press. Afterwards O'Hagan divided his time between the High Llamas and several side projects. He appeared on three albums by Stereolab (and one by that band's spin-off project Turn On), and also remixed the Boo Radleys' 'Find The Answer Within'. A second High Llamas album, *Gideon Gaye*, was produced on a budget of just £4,000, and released on the small Brighton independent label Target Records. Again, the critical response was encouraging, the resulting comparisons to Brian Wilson and the Beach Boys enticing Sony Records to offer O'Hagan a contract. *Gideon Gaye* was subsequently re-released via the band's own Alpaca Park label, with its international release handled by Sony/Epic Records. A single take from it, 'Checking In, Checking Out', proved especially popular in Germany, becoming an unexpected chart hit. The follow-up *Hawaii* was an extraordinary album in so far as it sounded closer to what Brian Wilson was trying to achieve in 1966/67 than anything the Beach Boys subsequently released. Although a reincarnation of the Beach Boys' *Friends*, *Smiley Smile*, *Sunflower* and *Pet Sounds* combined, the album sounds surprisingly fresh. *Cold And Bouncy* and the following year's remix collection, *Lollo Rosso*, saw O'Hagan eschewing the Beach Boys comparisons for his equal fascination with electronica. This process was repeated on the ensuing *Snowbug*, which employed Stereolab's Laetitia Sadier and Mary Hansen on vocals and the production skills of Chicago post-rock gurus John McEntire and Jim O'Rourke.

● ALBUMS: as Sean O'Hagan *High Llamas* (Demon 1990)★★★, *Apricots* mini-album (Plastic 1992)★★, *Santa Barbara* (Vogue/Mute 1994)★★★, *Gideon Gaye* (Target 1994)★★★★, *Hawaii* (Alpaca Park 1996)★★★★, *Cold And Bouncy* (Alpaca Park 1997)★★★, *Lollo Rosso* remix album (V2 1998)★★★, *Snowbug* (V2 1999)★★★.

Hill, Faith

b. Audrey Faith Perry, 21 September, 1967, Jackson, Mississippi, USA. Raised in the small town of Star, Mississippi, USA, the 90s country singer Faith Hill was singing at family gatherings from the age of three. She was influenced by Reba McEntire and formed her first band when she was 17 years old, performing at local rodeos. She moved to Nashville in 1989 and her first job was selling T-shirts at the Country Music Fan Fair. Attempts to make a name for herself in Nashville were fruitless, and Hill eventually accepted a secretarial job with a music publisher. Legend has it that the publisher/singer Gary Morris urged her to leave the job and take up singing as a career. She befriended songwriter Gary Burr, who produced her demo tape, and suitably impressed Warner Brothers Records. Hill subsequently recorded several of Burr's songs, including 'I Would Be Stronger Than That', 'Just Around The Eyes' and 'Just About Now'. Her first album was produced by then flame Scott Hendricks, who had previously had some success with Brooks And Dunn and Restless Heart. Her sparkling debut US country single, the rocking 'Wild One', topped the country charts and she followed it with a version of Janis Joplin's 'Piece Of My Heart', another cheerful country-rocker. *Take Me As I Am* was successful, but surgery on her vocal cords delayed the making of *It Matters To Me*. This included a song about wife-beating, 'A Man's Home Is His Castle', a duet with Shelby Lynne, 'Keep Walkin' On', and a song written for her by Alan Jackson, 'I Can't Do That Anymore'. Her regular band features Trey Grey (drums), Steve Hornbeak (keyboards), Tom Rutledge (guitar/fiddle), Anthony Joyner (bass), Lou Toomey (lead guitar), Karen Staley (guitar/vocals) and is masterminded by dobro and steel guitarist Gary Carter. Much of Hill's popularity has been fuelled by having one of the best touring bands in the business. 'It Matters To Me' was a further US country chart topper in 1996. In 1997, she recorded with her husband Tim McGraw, resulting in the number 1 hit and Country Music Association Award-winning 'It's Your Love'. The following year's *Faith* broke into the US Top 10. 'This Kiss' climbed steadily to a peak position of 7 on the *Billboard* Hot 100 in October, and also provided Hill with her debut entry on the UK singles chart. *Breathe* followed in the footsteps of the previous album in terms of enormous success, although it was not such a strong album in terms of quality.

● ALBUMS: *Take Me As I Am* (Warners 1993)★★★, *It Matters To Me* (Warners 1995)★★★★, *Faith* US title, *Love Will Always Win* UK title (Warners 1998)★★★★, *Breathe* (Warners 1999)★★★.

● VIDEOS: *Piece Of My Heart* (Deaton Flanigen 1994).

Hill, Lauryn

b. 25 May 1975, South Orange, New Jersey, USA. The multi-talented Hill originally balanced an acting career, which included a cameo in the Whoopi Goldberg vehicle *Sister Act 2: Back In The Habit*, with her degree course and membership of the Fugees. The trio, comprising Hill and rappers Pras and Wyclef Jean, shot to hip-hop super stardom when their sophomore set *The Score* became a huge international success in 1996. Hill began work on her self-produced debut after giving birth to a son by Rohan Marley, and writing for Aretha Franklin's 1998 comeback set *A Rose Is Not A Rose*. She also directed videos for Franklin and Common through her production company, Zion Films. *The Miseducation Of Lauryn Hill* was released in September 1998, and went straight in at number 1 on the *Billboard* Top 200 album chart. In the process, Hill became the first female solo artist to sell more than 400,000 units in the first week of release. The album stayed at the top for three weeks before being knocked off by Marilyn Manson's *Mechanical Animals*, but

returned to the top a week later. It also proved to be a worldwide bestseller, debuting at number 2 in the UK album chart in October. Although it featured some stellar guest appearances from artists including Mary J. Blige (on 'I Used To Love Him') and D'Angelo ('Nothing Even Matters'), the album was dominated by Hill's singular presence. The lead-off singles, 'Doo Wop (That Thing)' (US number 1/UK number 3) and 'Ex-Factor' (US number 22/UK number 4), showcased her winning blend of soulful vocals and hip-hop rhythms, while on 'Forgive Them Father' she explored a roots reggae direction. Hill set a new record for a female artist at the 1999 Grammies, walking away with five awards (Best New Artist, Album Of The Year, Best Female R&B Vocal Performance, Best R&B Song, Best R&B Album).

● ALBUMS: *The Miseducation Of Lauryn Hill* (Columbia 1998)★★★★.

● FILMS: *King Of The Hill* (1993), *Sister Act 2: Back In The Habit* (1993), *Rhyme & Reason* (1997), *Hav Plenty* (1997), *Restaraunt* (1998).

Hole

This US hardcore guitar band is fronted by the effervescent Courtney Love (b. 9 July 1965, San Francisco, California, USA; vocals/guitar). An ex-stripper and actress, who had minor roles in Alex Cox's *Sid And Nancy* and *Straight To Hell*, she was born to hippie parents (Grateful Dead associate Hank Harrison and Oregon therapist Linda Carroll) and even attended the Woodstock Festival as a small child. She spent the rest of her childhood years at boarding schools in England and New Zealand, where her parents had bought a sheep farm, before travelling around the world in her teens. She spent some time in San Francisco, founding the ill-fated Sugar Baby Doll (with L7's Jennifer Finch and Kat Bjelland), and also participated in a formative line-up of Bjelland's Babes In Toyland. In Los Angeles, Love appeared for a while as vocalist with Faith No More in an incarnation that only reached the rehearsal stage. Still in LA, she formed Hole with Caroline Rue (drums), Jill Emery (bass) and Eric Erlandson (b. 9 January 1963, Los Angeles, California, USA; guitar), following encouragement from Sonic Youth's Kim Gordon. The band quickly produced a trio of fine singles; 'Retard Girl', 'Dicknail', and 'Teenage Whore', which were pointed and unsettling dirges, set in a grimly sexual lyrical environment. Favourable UK press coverage, in particular from the *Melody Maker*'s Everett True, helped make Hole one of the most promising new bands of 1991. Equally impressive was a debut album, produced by Don Fleming and Kim Gordon (Sonic Youth), followed by massive exposure supporting Mudhoney throughout Europe. It was on this jaunt that Love achieved further notoriety by being the first woman musician to 'trash' her guitar on stage in the UK. In March 1992, Love married Nirvana singer/guitarist Kurt Cobain. That same month bass player Emery departed from the line-up, with Rue following shortly afterwards. Love's domestic travails continued to dominate coverage of her musical project, with Cobain's death on the eve of the release of *Live Through This* practically obliterating that album's impact. This served to do the much-maligned Love a genuine disservice, as the album contained another startling collection of songs, written with intellect as well as invective. It included 'I Think That I Would Die', co-written with old friend and sparring partner Kat Bjelland, as well as a cover version of the Young Marble Giants' 'Credit In The Straight World'. Replacements for Emery and Rue had been found in Kristen Pfaff (bass) and Patty Schemel (b. 24 April 1967, Seattle, Washington, USA; drums), though tragedy again followed Love when Pfaff was found dead from a heroin overdose in her bathtub shortly after the album's release, and just two months after Cobain's death. She was replaced by Melissa Auf der Maur (b. 17 March 1972, Montreal, Canada) for Hole's 1994 tour, which extended into the following year with stays in Australasia and Europe. These dates again saw Love dominate headlines with violent and/or inflammatory stage behaviour. In 1997, she moved back into acting with a starring role in *The People Vs Larry Flynt*. *My Body The Hand Grenade* was a compilation of rare and unreleased material from the band's early days, compiled by Erlandson that served as a stopgap for the eagerly awaited *Celebrity Skin*. Lacking the raw abrasiveness of *Live Through This*, the album was ultimately a disappointingly mainstream work, although maybe this was not surprising considering Love's new 'media friendly' image. Auf der Maur left the band the following year to join the Smashing Pumpkins.

● ALBUMS: *Pretty On The Inside* (City Slang 1991)★★★, *Live Through This* (Geffen 1994)★★★★, *Celebrity Skin* (Geffen 1998)★★★.

● COMPILATIONS: *My Body The Hand Grenade* (City Slang 1997)★★★.

● FURTHER READING: *Courtney Love*, Nick Wise. *Queen Of Noise: A Most Unauthorised Biography*, Melissa Rossi. *Look Through This*, Susan Wilson. *Courtney Love: The Real Story*, Poppy Z. Brite.

● FILMS: *The People Vs Larry Flynt* (1997), *Kurt & Courtney* (1998).

Holmes, David

b. Belfast, Northern Ireland. This leading house mixer, DJ and recording artist is a former member of the Disco Evangelists. After the latter band's successes for Positiva Records ('De Niro', 'A New Dawn'), he recorded his first solo effort, 'Johnny Favourite', for Warp Records. An enormously popular DJ, Holmes also found time to collaborate with former Dub Federation musicians Andy Ellison and Pete Latham as one third of the Scubadevils. The latter two met him while performing at the Sugarsweet nightclub. Together they recorded 'Celestial Symphony' for the *Trance Europe Express* compilation, which was also remixed for a Novamute Records 12-inch release. This was backed by Holmes solo on 'Ministry' (credited to Death Before Disco). He has also recorded as the Well Charged Latinos ('Latin Prayer') and 4 Boy 1 Girl Action ('Hawaiian Death Stomp'). Holmes' remixing projects have included commissions for the Sandals ('We Wanna Live'), Robotman ('Do Da Doo'), Fortran 5 ('Persian Blues', 'Time To Dream'), Freaky Realistic ('Koochie Ryder'), Secret Knowledge ('Sugar Daddy'), Abfahrt ('Come Into My Life'), Bahia Black ('Capitao Do Asfolto') and Sabres Of Paradise ('Smokebelch'). He was also partially behind Sugarsweet Records, the Belfast dance music label, run with Ian McCready and Jim McDonald. As Holmes explained at the time: 'It's more of a front to feed our obsession with music, to put out what we like, when we like.' Releases on the label included the Arabic house excursions of Wah Wah Warrior (essentially Ian McCready), plus Holmes' Death Before Disco. However, when it was clear that Sugarsweet was not going to take off it was replaced by the Exploding Plastic Inevitable imprint. In 1994, Holmes signed with Sabres Of Paradise as a solo artist, but when that label's Andy Weatherall decided to

rethink his strategy, he found a new home at Go! Discs. His debut album emerged in 1995, with Sarah Cracknell (Saint Etienne) contributing to the quasi-James Bond theme, 'Gone', while elsewhere Holmes luxuriated in the possibilities of the long playing format by incorporating cinematic elements, Celtic flavours and ambient guitar (provided by Steve Hillage). The superb follow-up *Let's Get Killed* expanded on the debut's sound, and provided enough of a breakthrough for Holmes to place two singles, 'Don't Die Just Yet' and 'My Mate Paul', in the UK Top 40. In 1998, Holmes composed his first full-length movie score for Steven Soderbergh's highly acclaimed *Out Of Sight*.

● ALBUMS: *This Film's Crap, Let's Slash The Seats* (Go! Discs 1995)★★★, *Let's Get Killed* (Go! Beat 1997)★★★★, *Stop Arresting Artists* (Go! Beat 1998)★★★, *Essential Mix* (ffrr 1998)★★★★, *Out Of Sight OS* film soundtrack (Jersey/MCA 1998)★★★.

Honeyz

This UK-based female swingbeat trio was formed by Heavenli Abdi (b. 10 November 1974, London, England), Naima Belkhiati (b. 4 December 1973, Avignon, France), and Célena Cherry (b. 26 April 1977, London, England). After being discovered by the influential First Avenue management team, the trio was snapped up by Mercury Records in summer 1997. They entered the studio with producer Steve Levine to record material for their debut album, *Wonder No. 8*. This slick and rather soulless collection of MOR swingbeat, released in November 1998, was promoted by the UK Top 10 singles 'Finally Found' (number 4), and 'End Of The Line' (number 5), but failed to make much of an impression on the album chart. By the start of 1999, Abdi had left to spend more time with her boyfriend, the ex-actor turned pop singer Matthew Marsden. She was replaced by Mariama Goodman (b. 25 December 1977, London, England; ex-Solid Harmonie). The new line-up enjoyed further UK hits with 'Love Of A Lifetime' (number 9) and 'Never Let You Down' (number 7). Mercury also released a new version of *Wonder No. 8*.

● ALBUMS: *Wonder No. 8* (Mercury 1998)★★★.

Hooj Choons

Born in early 1990, amid the creative chaos of the acid house years, a decade later, London-based Hooj Choons remains one of the more 'up-front' (commercial), independent UK house labels, whose *esprit de corps* seems to rise from its continuing skill in spotting a breaking tune. Established by Jerry Dickens (Red Jerry for producing and remixing purposes) as the original Balearic sound reached its peak (soon to be replaced by the altogether moodier 'progressive house'), the label has ridden the crest of various dance music waves and, by making sure it remained abreast of prevailing trends, has survived the scene's stormier seas. Throughout its history, there have been many notable releases: from the Balearic exuberance of Rio Rhythm Band's 'Carnival Da Casa', 1992's acclaimed classics, Felix's 'Don't You Want Me' (which made the UK Top 10) and Hyper Go-Go's 'High', the early Trade sound of Dis-Cuss' (DJ Malcolm Duffy, Jonathan Blanks and DJ Kenny Clarke) 'Pissed Apache', to the prototype 'euro' excesses of JX's 'Son Of A Gun'. In more recent years, the label has had huge success with trance-house crossover classics such as Energy 52's 'Café Del Mar' and Greece 2000's 'Three Drives On Vinyl'.

The former is regarded by some as one of the best house tracks ever released and it certainly epitomises the often misused terms 'uplifting', 'epic' and 'anthemic' with its huge string sweeps, dramatic breakdown and pizzicato crescendos. Another sometimes overlooked success was Lustral's 'Everytime' in 1997, the Nalin And Kane remix of which was a dancefloor hit and was featured on several compilations. Subsidiary labels Prolekult and Airtight have allowed Dickens to indulge his techno and deep house inclinations but Hooj remains the cornerstone of his unassuming but thriving mini-empire. Late 90s signings included the trance 'supergroup' Tilt and Salt Tank.

● COMPILATIONS: *Some Of These Were Hooj Volumes 1-3* (Hooj Choons 1994)★★, *Deeper Shades* (Hooj Choons 1997)★★★, *Deeper Shades Of Hooj: Volume Two* (Hooj Choons 1998)★★★★, *Deeper Shades: Volume Three* (Hooj Choons 1999)★★★★.

Hooper, Nellee

b. Bristol, Avon, England. The most successful individual member of the Wild Bunch, the ultra-hip sound system from Bristol that emerged in the late 80s and led to the formation of Massive Attack. Initially, Hooper DJed with members of Massive Attack at clubs in Bristol, playing a mixture of funk and hip-hop, before departing to work with the highly successful Soul II Soul, contributing to the writing and producing of the seminal *Club Classics Vol. 1* in 1989. Indeed, it is as a remixer and producer that Hooper has had most success, his services having been sought by Sinead O'Connor, Björk, Janet Jackson, All Saints, Smashing Pumpkins, U2 and Madonna among many high-profile artists. His productions are distinctive for their use of subtly funky rhythms, unusual sounds and moody instrumentation. More recently, he has worked on the soundtrack material for Baz Luhrmann's *Romeo And Juliet*. He has also worked with the award-winning composer Craig Armstrong, and inaugurated his own label, Meanwhile..., in conjunction with Virgin Records.

Hootie And The Blowfish

This hugely successful South Carolina, USA quartet was formed at the turn of the 90s. They are led by Darius Rucker (Hootie), whose soulful vocals add sparkle to an otherwise fairly formulaic rock sound. The quartet is completed by Mark Bryan (guitar, ex-Missing In Action), Dean Felber (bass) and Jim 'Soni' Sonefield (drums). Sonefield stated in *Rolling Stone*, 'Everyone says we're one black guy in an all-white band, but that's not true - we're actually three white guys in an all-black band'. Bryan and Rucker played together in a soft rock duo as the Wolf Brothers. Following an aborted contract with J.R.S. Records they put out a self-financed EP, which contained 'Hold My Hand'. They sold it at gigs and after a short time it had sold over 50,000 copies. Their spectacularly successful debut, 1994's *Cracked Rear View*, was a slow burner on the US charts, climbing into the Top 10 after over seven months on the chart. Rucker was a strong live performer on their vast 1994 tour (of more than 300 dates), presiding over a clutch of songs about emotional isolation and yearning. Part of the 'buzz' surrounding the band followed US television talk show host David Letterman's pronouncement that Hootie And The Blowfish were 'my favourite new band'. *Cracked Rear View* took its title from a John Hiatt lyric and was produced by R.E.M./John

Mellencamp associate Don Gehman. It documented the band's career, and included the single 'Hold My Hand', one of several numbers to address ecological concerns and human frailty, which featured guest vocals from David Crosby. The album became one of the most successful rock debuts of all time, sales in its homeland having already surpassed 15 million (by February 1997). Strong sales over the rest of the world indicated that theirs would be the most 'difficult second album' in rock history. At the 1995 Grammy Awards, however, they picked up two statuettes, for Best New Artist and Best Pop Performance By A Group. It was inevitable that the follow-up proved to be anti-climatic. Having performed songs from *Fairweather Johnson* onstage they were now familiar to their loyal fans. Even though it debuted in the US at number 1, by the band's previous standards the album was seen as something of a flop; by anybody else's it was a massive success. *Musical Chairs* failed to reach the top of the US charts, debuting at number 4 in October 1998, although the fall off in sales has not harmed their popularity as a live act.

● ALBUMS: *Cracked Rear View* (East West 1994)★★★★, *Fairweather Johnson* (Atlantic 1996)★★, *Musical Chairs* (Atlantic 1998)★★★.

● VIDEOS: *Summer Camp With Trucks* (Warners 1995), *A Series Of Short Trips* (Atlantic Video 1996).

House Of Pain

Hardcore Irish American hip-hoppers whose origins can be traced to Taft High School in Los Angeles (former students of which include Ice Cube). The outfit comprised lead rapper Everlast (b. Erik Schrody, USA), his co-lyricist Danny Boy (b. Daniel O'Connor, USA), and DJ Lethal (b. Leor DiMant, Latvia). Everlast was originally signed to Warner Brothers Records, and was often to be seen 'hanging' with Ice-T and his Rhyme Syndicate at that time. With House Of Pain he reached US number 3 in summer 1992 with the addictive 'Jump Around', a good example of the street poetry hybrid which they branded 'Fine malt lyricism'. 'Jump Around' seemed to offer the pinnacle in House Of Pain's career, however. Their debut album, recorded with DJ Muggs of Cypress Hill, gloried in self-styled Gaelic dressing. 'Shamrocks And Shenanigans (Boom Shalock Lock Boom)', an ode to their spurious links with the Emerald Isle, contained a novelty sample of David Bowie's 'Fame'. Elsewhere the album's grooves were populated with familiar, dumb macho lines. No strangers to controversy, House Of Pain were involved in two near riots on their 1993 tour with Rage Against The Machine. Once in Baltimore when they refused to take the stage, and again when a member of the band's road crew was assaulted by security staff at a Manchester Academy gig. This was only a matter of days after the rapper had been arrested at JFK Airport in New York for illegal possession of a handgun. Such incidents led to his being subject to a tracking device and house arrest for three months in 1994. The press were also starting to ask awkward questions about Sinn Fein tattoos. Everlast also ventured into the film world, appearing in both the US rap vehicle *Who's The Man* (alongside Public Enemy, Heavy D), and the Dennis Leary movie, *Judgement Day*, where, unsurprisingly, he played a gangster. House Of Pain also opened a pizza restaurant, in partnership with Mickey Rourke (House Of Pizza). *Same As It Ever Was*, despite the title, proved to be a much more impressive outing, with Everlast unleashing his frustration with his 'imprisonment' and the media in tracks like 'Back From The Dead'. The rapper quit the music business in 1996 following the break-up of House Of Pain. He returned to recording in 1998 with the surprise US bestseller, *Whitey Ford Sings The Blues*. DJ Lethal joined the hugely popular alternative rock band, Limp Bizkit.

● ALBUMS: *House Of Pain* (Tommy Boy 1992)★★★, *Same As It Ever Was* (Tommy Boy 1994)★★★★, *Truth Crushed To Earth Shall Rise Again* (Tommy Boy 1996)★★★.

Houston, Whitney

b. 9 August 1963, Newark, New Jersey, USA. This pop and soul singer followed the traditions of her mother Cissy and cousin Dionne Warwick by beginning her vocal career in gospel. There was much diversity in her early performances, however. These included engagements as backing singer with established acts, such as Chaka Khan, as well as lead vocals on the Michael Zager Band's single 'Life's A Party'. She also appeared as a model in various magazines and as an actress in television shows such as *Give Me A Break*. By 1983, she had entered a worldwide contract with Arista Records, and the following year had her first commercial success when 'Hold Me', a duet with Teddy Pendergrass, crept into the US Top 50. However, the rest of that year was taken up with the recording of a debut album. Clive Davis, the head of Arista, who had taken a strong personal interest in the vocalist, insisted on selecting the best songwriters and producers in search of the definitive debut album. *Whitney Houston* was finally released in March 1984, from which time it would begin its slow stalking of the album charts, topping them early the next year. Its steady climb was encouraged by the success of the singles 'You Give Good Love' and 'Saving All My Love For You', which hit numbers 3 and 1, respectively. The latter single also saw her on top of the charts in the UK and much of the rest of the world. The disco-influenced 'How Will I Know' and the more soul-flavoured 'Greatest Love Of All', both topped the US charts in rapid succession. Her domination was acknowledged by a series of prestigious awards, notably a Grammy for 'Saving All My Love For You' and an Emmy for Outstanding Individual Performance In A Variety Program On US TV. 'I Wanna Dance With Somebody (Who Loves Me)', released in 1987, topped the charts on both sides of the Atlantic, paving the way for *Whitney* to become the first album by a female artist to debut at number 1 on the US album chart, a feat it also achieved in the UK. The album included a version of 'I Know Him So Well', sang as a duet with her mother Cissy, and the ballad 'Didn't We Almost Have It All' which became her fifth successive US number 1 shortly afterwards. However, even this was surpassed when 'So Emotional' and 'Where Do Broken Hearts Go' continued the sequence, breaking a record previously shared by the Beatles and the Bee Gees. In 1988, she made a controversial appearance at Nelson Mandela's 70th Birthday Party, where other acts accused her of behaving like a prima donna. By September, 'Love Will Save The Day' had finally broken the winning sequence in the USA where it could only manage number 9. Another series of awards followed, including Pop Female Vocal and Soul/R&B Female Vocal categories in the American Music Awards, while rumours abounded of film offers alongside Robert De Niro and Eddie Murphy. Her recording of the title track to the 1988 Olympics tribute, *One*

Moment In Time, restored her to US Top 5 prominence and topped the UK singles chart. The follow-up 'I'm Your Baby Tonight' put her back on top of the US singles chart. Despite the relatively modest success of the album of the same name (number 3 in the US charts), 'All The Man That I Need' compensated by becoming her ninth number 1. She became permanently enshrined in the hearts of the American public, however, when she took the microphone to perform 'The Star Spangled Banner' at Super Bowl XXV in Miami. The public response ensured that the version emerged as a single shortly afterwards. She also performed the song at Houston as she welcomed back US troops returning from the Gulf War. Such open displays of patriotism have not endeared her to all. Her remarkably rich voice also caused some debate, with some critics claiming that her masterful vocal technique is not equalled by her emotional commitment to her music. In July 1992, Houston married singer Bobby Brown. The same year she made a credible acting debut in the movie *The Bodyguard*. Four songs recorded by her were lifted from the phenomenally successful soundtrack album - cover versions of Dolly Parton's powerful 'I Will Always Love You', which topped the US chart for 14 weeks and the UK charts for nine, and Chaka Khan's 'I'm Every Woman', and 'I Have Nothing' and 'Run To You'. Houston spent most of the 90s concentrating on her acting career, but made a surprise return to the studio for 1998's *My Love Is Your Love*. Enlisting the songwriting help of Missy 'Misdemeanor' Elliott, Diane Warren and Wyclef Jean, the album was a confident attempt by Houston to reclaim ground lost to the new diva superstars Mariah Carey and Celine Dion. 'When You Believe', a duet with Carey taken from the animated DreamWorks movie *The Prince Of Egypt*, was a transatlantic hit. With the album selling poorly, however, Houston's fortunes were revived by the US number 2 single, 'Heartbreak Hotel', and the atypical and hard-hitting 'It's Not Right But It's Okay', a US/UK Top 5 hit single.

● ALBUMS: *Whitney Houston* (Arista 1985)★★★★, *Whitney* (Arista 1987)★★★★, *I'm Your Baby Tonight* (Arista 1990)★★★, various artists *The Bodyguard* film soundtrack (Arista 1992)★★★, *The Preacher's Wife* film soundtrack (Arista 1996)★★, *My Love Is Your Love* (Arista 1998)★★★.

● FILMS: *The Bodyguard* (1992), *The Preacher's Wife* (1996).

Howard, Adina

b. Grand Rapids, Michigan, USA. With her 1995 debut, *Do You Wanna Ride?*, assertive soul singer Adina Howard managed to achieve commercial success as well as raising eyebrows with her volatile cocktail of sexually potent imagery and effusive R&B. The mainstream success of the attendant single, 'Freak Like Me', helped pave the way for other upfront female R&B singers, including Foxy Brown and Lil' Kim. Peaking at number 7 in the *Billboard* R&B charts, the debut album's sales profile of over half a million copies was encouraging. The follow-up, 1997's *Welcome To Fantasy Island*, opted for sensuality over sexuality. Howard was also more closely involved in the creative process, writing four of the songs and co-producing two others. However, the promotional single, '(Freak) And U Know It', at least maintained some of the titular traditions of the previous album.

● ALBUMS: *Do You Wanna Ride?* (Mecca Don/Elektra 1995)★★★, *Welcome To Fantasy Island* (Mecca Don/Elektra 1997)★★★.

Hunter, James

b. 1962. As a youngster in Essex, England, Hunter was interested in 50s rock 'n' roll, leading to a later appreciation of Chicago blues, particularly the music of Little Walter. He received his first electric guitar in 1977 when he was around 15 years of age, while his first band, the DMFs, played at Colchester Labour Club in 1983. He initially recorded with a rockabilly band for a compilation issued by Lost Moment Records in 1984. Two years later he moved to London, and began performing as Howling Wilf. With his band the Vee-Jays he quickly established himself as one of the mainstays of the capital's blues scene, and was touted as one of England's best young blues singers. In 1989, he disbanded the Vee-Jays and took his music in more of an R&B direction, assembling a band including Jonathan Lee (drums), Dave Lagnado (double bass), Nick Lunt (baritone saxophone) and Damian Hand (tenor saxophone). His biggest break came when he was invited to play guitar with Van Morrison's Rhythm And Blues Revue, and he featured prominently on the Morrison albums *A Night In San Francisco* and *Days Like This*. Hunter has also worked with a diverse group of artists, including Solomon Burke, Mary Love and Captain Sensible, and briefly appeared in the West End musical *Buddy*. His debut album featured a winning mix of Hunter originals and choice cover versions, including duets with Van Morrison ('Turn On Your Lovelight', 'Ain't Nothing You Can Do') and Doris Troy 'Hear Me Calling'). Central to the album's success were Hunter's vocals, with his powerful and expressive voice. The follow-up, *Kickin' It Around*, was produced live in the studio by Boz Boorer.

● ALBUMS: *Believe What I Say* (Ace 1996)★★★★, *Kickin' It Around* (Ruf 1999)★★★.

Hurricane #1

After the acrimonious ending to his former band Ride, Andy Bell underwent a period of soul-searching that saw him performing occasional solo shows and writing new material at his wife Idha's parents' home in Sweden. With the support of Alan McGee at Creation Records, Bell announced a new band, Hurricane #1, at the start of 1997. His new singer, Glaswegian ex-boxer Alex Lowe, was joined by Gareth Farmer (drums) and Will Pepper (bass, ex-Thee Hypnotics). Having laid down the material for their debut within three weeks of forming, the band quickly developed a reputation as an aggressive and truculent outfit, somewhat at odds with Bell's former reputation. However, the release of the singles 'Just Another Illusion' and 'Step Into My World' showed them in a better light, with Bell's melodic touch and Lowe's bluesy voice establishing themselves as the band's strong points. Their self-titled debut album, produced by Kula Shaker associate Steve Harris, suffered from a lack of variety, earning them mixed reviews in the music press. The title track to their second album gained widespread airplay when it was used in a television advertisement for *The Sun* newspaper. The stand-out track, 'Long Way Down', sounded very reminiscent of Bell's former band. The album was overlooked owing to a glut of similar material on the shelves from newer and more media-friendly faces, and the band's fate was confirmed in November when Bell was announced as the replacement for Paul McGuigan in Oasis.

● ALBUMS: *Hurricane #1* (Creation 1997)★★★, *Only The Strongest Will Survive* (Creation 1999)★★★.

Hyper Go-Go

Never regarded as strikingly original, Hyper Go-Go were nevertheless one of the most commercially prominent UK house acts, a fact confirmed when their early singles, including 'High' (number 30, August 1992) and 'Never Let Go' (number 45, July 1993), both crossed over into the UK charts. The team, James Diplock and Alex Ball, had been working together since they left school in the mid-80s. They worked from their own studio, a converted warehouse in the middle of a disused airfield, in the heart of the Essex countryside. 'High' was originally released on Hooj Choons before being picked up by Deconstruction Records. For 'Never Let Go', a typical storming piano house tune, they switched to the Positiva Records label on a more permanent footing. 'Raise', which reached UK number 36 in February 1994, used the familiar 'Raise Your Hands' vocal line as its core, with guest vocals from Brian Chambers. Other contributors have included Sally Anne Marsh of Hysterix, and Adeva (April 1996's 'Do Watcha Do'). Bell and Diplock also formed one half of the techno sideline Electroset (whose 'How Does It Feel?' was their 'rave thing') and experimental electronic outfit Compufonic. The latter released 'Ecstacy 0376' for Ocean Records in 1992, before signing to Mute Records for whom they debuted with the *Make It Move* EP.

Ibiza

One of the Balearic islands, approximately 90 kilometres east of mainland Spain, Ibiza has been a retreat for artists, writers, bohemians and hippies since the mid-70s. The Spanish holiday boom of the 60s helped to make it an affordable holiday destination for the British and other Europeans. In the 80s, the huge clubs of San Antonio began to boom, owing to a number of experimental Spanish DJs, an affluent and hedonistic holidaying elite and the island's liberal acceptance of alcoholic and narcotic excess. The Balearic sound was a blend of sophisticated UK and US pop with funky US house sounds, all with an ethereal 'spaced out' feel. Famously, it was the likes of Paul Oakenfold, Danny Rampling and Nicky Holloway who visited the island in 1987 and tried to recreate the magic formula in London when they returned. Since then, clubs such as Ku, Pacha, Space, and Amnesia have attracted an increasingly large number of foreign visitors, predominantly from the UK. Many Ibiza-themed compilations (including *'Avin' It In Ibiza* and the *Café Del Mar* series) have been released and a thriving tourist industry has grown around the bright lights of San Antonio. The Spanish inhabitants of the rest of the island remain largely oblivious. Several UK-based superclubs, such as Ministry Of Sound, Cream, Renaissance, Gatecrasher, Trade, Godskitchen and Manumission have summer residencies at clubs on the island. Most of the UK and USA's top DJs visit several times during the summer season. Some UK holiday companies now run tailor-made Ibizan holidays for clubbers. In 1998, the UK's BBC Radio 1 sent a number of its DJs there to broadcast live shows at the peak of the season. Purists feel that the special atmosphere of the island in the late 80s and early 90s has been spoiled by the huge numbers of visitors in the summer and the mindless 'lager-lout' contingent that has come from the UK. Nevertheless, most of the UK's dance music scene and thousands of committed clubbers spend part of the summer there every year.

● FURTHER READING: *Ibiza: Inspired Images From The Island Of Dance*, Ben Turner (ed.).

Ice Cube

b. O'Shea Jackson, 15 June 1969, Crenshaw, South Central Los Angeles, California, USA. Controversial hardcore rapper who formerly worked with the equally inflammatory NWA. Following a relatively stable background, with both his mother and father working at UCLA, Cube entered the homeboy lifestyle: 'One day I was sitting in class with a friend called Kiddo and we had some time on our hands, so he said let's write a rap'. At the age of 16 he penned his first important rap, 'Boyz 'N The Hood', which was later recorded by Eazy-E. He subsequently spent time with CIA, an embryonic rap outfit produced by Dr. Dre. As guest lyricist, he brought NWA '8 Ball' and 'Dopeman', which would comprise their opening salvo. After studying architectural draughtsmanship in Phoenix, Arizona, he returned to the NWA fold in time for 1989's groundbreaking *Straight Outta Compton*. He would leave NWA at the tail-end of the year, amid thinly veiled attacks on their Jewish manager Jerry Heller. His debut *AmeriKKKa's Most Wanted*, recorded with Public Enemy producers the Bomb Squad, drew immediate mainstream attention. The album's controversial lyrical platform included homophobia and the glamorization of violence, although his work was attacked primarily for its overt sexism, raps about kicking a pregnant girlfriend ('You Can't Fade Me') notwithstanding. Conversely, Ice Cube overlooked a production empire (Street Knowledge) run for him by a woman, and he also fostered the career of female rapper Yo Yo (who appeared defending her gender on *AmeriKKKa's Most Wanted*'s 'It's A Man's World'). The politicization of his solo work should also be noted; in his NWA days he had once written, 'Life ain't nothing but bitches and money', but his words since then have incorporated numerous references to black ideology that add up to something approaching a manifesto. His defence against critical discomfort with his rhymes, 'I put a mirror to black America', has been hijacked by many other, less worthy cases. Following the mini-album *Kill At Will*, he released another highly controversial set, *Death Certificate*, which included outrageous tracks such as the Heller-baiting 'No Vaseline' and 'Black Korea'. Nevertheless, the album was a huge commercial success, reaching US number 2 at the end of 1991. To Ice Cube's credit, he went on to produce two excellent sets, the chart-topping *The Predator* (including the single 'It Was A Good Day', which gave him a massive profile via MTV) and *Lethal Injection*. The latter, in particular, boasted a much more discursive approach to the problems of the ghetto, including reflections on the Los Angeles riots and the Rodney King beating. Perhaps it was marred by the blunt sexism of tracks such as 'Cave Bitch', but it was certainly an advance which demonstrated the influence of his recent conversion to the Nation Of Islam. Musically it was typified by a stirring cover version of 'One Nation Under A Groove', retitled 'Bop Gun (One Nation)', with a lead vocal by the song's writer, George Clinton. Having completed four million-selling albums, his career had also attracted the attention of those outside the hip-hop fraternity. Like Ice-T, Cube was targeted on right wing assassination lists discovered by the police in 1993.

Following the release of *Lethal Injection*, which experimented with the G-funk stylings of Dr. Dre's hugely successful *The Chronic*, Ice Cube elected to concentrate on his commercial interests. Street Knowledge had already provided Da Lench Mob and Kam with successful albums on which Cube acted as executive producer, and he set up a second subsidiary, titled after his posse, Lench Mob. He also consolidated his movie career by moving into writing and production. Cube had already starred in John Singleton's 1991 hit movie, titled after his first rap, *Boyz N The Hood*, and later appeared in the same director's *Higher Learning*. The 1992 movie *Trespass*, retitled after the LA Riots deemed original moniker *Looters* unsavoury, saw him team up with Ice-T once more. His several screenplays included the 1995 comedy *Friday*. The soundtrack to his 1998 directorial debut, *The Players Club*, was a Top 10 success in the USA. The movie itself, set in a strip club, was one of the year's surprise successes, having grossed $20 million at the box office only six weeks after its April release.

In 1996, Cube returned to recording with Westside Connection, a hip-hop supergroup he formed with rappers Mack 10 and WC. The violent gangsta rap musings on *Bow Down* may have alienated some critics, but the album helped revive Cube's commercial fortunes, breaking into the US Top 5 shortly after its release. Two years later he released his first solo set in over five years, *War & Peace, Vol. 1 (The War Disc)*, a failed attempt to recapture the intensity and shock value of his earlier albums.

● ALBUMS: *AmeriKKKa's Most Wanted* (Priority 1990)★★★★, *Kill At Will* mini-album (Priority 1990)★★★, *Death Certificate* (Priority 1991)★★★, *The Predator* (Lench Mob/Priority 1992)★★★, *Lethal Injection* (Lench Mob/Priority 1993)★★★, *War & Peace, Vol. 1 (The War Disc)* (Priority 1998)★★.

● COMPILATIONS: *Bootlegs & B-Sides* (Lench Mob/Priority 1994)★★, *Featuring ... Ice Cube* (Priority 1997)★★★.

● FILMS: *Boyz N The Hood* (1991), *Trespass* (1992), *CB4* (1993), *The Glass Shield* (1994), *Higher Learning* (1995), *Friday* (1995), *Dangerous Ground* (1997), *Anaconda* (1997), *The Players Club* (1998), *I Got The Hook Up* (1998), *Thicker Than Water* (1999), *Three Kings* (1999).

Ice-T

b. Tracy Marrow, 16 February 1958, Newark, New Jersey, USA. One of the most outspoken rappers on the west coast, Ice-T boasts (sometimes literally) a violent past in which he was shot twice - once whilst involved in an armed robbery.

His name, fittingly, is taken from black exploitation author Iceberg Slim, and he is backed on record by Afrika Islam and DJ Aladdin's hardcore hip-hop. His first record was actually 'The Coldest Rapper' in 1983, which was improvised over a Jimmy Jam And Terry Lewis rhythm, and made him the first Los Angeles hip-hop artist. Unfortunately, he was subsequently held under contract by mogul Willie Strong for several years. Disillusioned, he made his money from petty and not so petty crime, and also appeared in the breakdance movie *Breakin'*, which included his 'Reckless' cut on the soundtrack. He followed it with the faddish 'Killers' single. The breakthrough, however, came with 'Ya Don't Know', which was widely credited with being the first west coast hip-hop artefact (although the honour was undoubtedly Ice-T's, the real beneficiary should have been the obscure 'The Coldest Rapper' cut). Four LPs in just three years created something of a stir in the USA, based as they were largely on his experiences as a gang member in Los Angeles. In 1989, he reached the lower end of the UK charts with 'High Rollers', but did better the following year teaming up with Curtis Mayfield on a remake of 'Superfly'. He married Darlene, the model who normally appeared semi-clad on his record sleeves, and admitted to owning a pit bull terrier affectionately titled Felony. For a time, too, he delighted in inviting journalists to his luxury Beverly Hills home to show them his personal armoury of semi-automatic weapons. Success also enabled him to start his own record company, Rhyme Syndicate. His vision of the black man as sophisticated and articulate (being hard as nails is, of course, *de rigueur*) ranks him among the most potent forces in contemporary black culture. His refusal to engage in a white liberal agenda (he was the first rap artist to have warning stickers placed on his album sleeves) has irritated many, but helped to establish him as an authentic spokesperson for dispossessed black youth.

Ice-T's debut, *Rhyme Pays*, features an Uzi emblazoned on the cover, an image which has served as a particularly effective mission statement: hardcore raps on street violence and survival being the order of the day. By the time of its follow-up, there was demonstrably greater imagination displayed in terms of backing music. Like many of his west coast brethren, Ice-T had rediscovered funk. Notable tracks included 'Girls L.G.B.N.A.F., which the PMRC later discovered stood for 'Let's Get Butt Naked And Fuck'. Their reaction to this (arguably among the least offensive statements on Ice-T's records) was so overheated that the debate heavily informed his follow-up set. However, his crowning glory to date is *OG* (an acronym for Original Gangster that has passed into rap's lexicon) which ranks alongside the best work of Ice Cube, Public Enemy or NWA in terms of sustained intensity, yet managed to maintain a little more finesse than his previous work. In 1991, with appealing irony, he starred as a cop in the movie *New Jack City*. He had earlier contributed the title track to the LA gangster movie *Colors*. He also appeared with former NWA and solo artist Ice Cube in the Walter Hill movie *Looters* (renamed *Trespassers* due to its release at the same time as the LA riots), as well as *Surviving The Game* and the cult comic hero movie, *Tank Girl*. His other soundtrack credits include *Dick Tracy*. Ice-T's hobbies include his own thrash metal outfit, Body Count, who released an album in 1992 and stirred up immeasurable controversy via one of its cuts, 'Cop Killer' (detailed under

Body Count entry). Little wonder that he was targeted on right-wing assassination lists discovered by the police in 1993. His album from that year, *Home Invasion*, saw him take on the mantle of agent provocateur in the young white male's home, a theme reinforced in its cover and title - Ice-T was a threat in your neighbourhood, with another manifesto of spiteful intent ('I'm takin' your kids' brains, You ain't getting them back, I'm gonna fill 'em with hard drugs, big guns, bitches, hoes and death'). Then he went and spoiled all the good work by writing a book, the *Ice-T Opinion*, which was so full of dumb ideas that it largely discredited such achievements. On 22 March 1994 he introduced Channel 4's *Without Walls*, a documentary on the rise of the blaxploitation movies. His own recording career in the late 90s was side-tracked by his movie commitments, although he managed to find the time to record 1999's poorly received *7th Deadly Sin*. His own life would make an excellent documentary subject, although, as he notes in *Home Invasion*'s 'Ice Muthafuckin' T', 'Every fucking thing I write, Is going to be analysed by somebody white'.

● ALBUMS: *Rhyme Pays* (Sire 1987)★★★, *Power* (Sire 1988)★★, *The Iceberg/Freedom Of Speech . . . Just Watch What You Say* (Sire 1989)★★★, *OG (Original Gangster)* (Syndicate/Sire 1991)★★★★, *Home Invasion* (Priority 1993)★★★, *Born Dead* (Priority 1994)★★★, *7th Deadly Sin* (Roadrunner 1999)★★.
● VIDEOS: *OG: The Original Gangster Video* (1991).
● FURTHER READING: *The Ice Opinion*, Ice-T and Heidi Seigmund.
● FILMS: *Breakin'* (1984), *Rappin'* (1985), *Listen Up: The Lives Of Quincy Jones* (1990), *New Jack City* (1991), *Ricochet* (1991), *Trespass* (1992), *Who's The Man* (1993), *CB4* (1993), *Surviving The Game* (1994), *The Legend Of Dolemite* (1994), *Mr Payback: An Interactive Movie* (1995), *Tank Girl* (1995), *Johnny Mnemonic* (1995), *Mean Guns* (1997), *Below Utopia* (1997), *Rhyme & Reason* (1997), *The Deli* (1997), *Crazy Six* (1998), *Stealth Fighter* (1999).

Iglesias, Enrique

b. Spain. The son of global superstar Julio Iglesias, Enrique recorded his self-titled debut album of Latin-influenced pop in 1995. The album's release catapulted him to superstar status in the Spanish-speaking music world. Assured of media exposure of similar intensity to the elder Iglesias, certain sections of the media also implied a rivalry between father and progeny. Certainly Enrique's statement to Spain's top-selling daily newspaper, *El Pais*, 'When I have children, I'll leave work to one side for a while - something my father never did', helped to fuel the conjecture. Although his love songs and ballads, such as 'Experiencia Religiosa' and 'No Llores Por Mi', placed him in the same stylistic area as his father, Enrique claims to have been influenced as much by rock acts such as Journey, Foreigner and Roxy Music, having spent much of his youth growing up in Miami, Florida. His follow-up collection, *Vivir*, won a Grammy Award, and by 1997 the two albums were credited with global sales in excess of eight million. By that time he had also achieved a sequence of seven chart-topping singles on *Billboard*'s Latin Top 50 chart. Iglesias was even more successful in 1999, the commercial breakthrough year for Latin music, with 'Bailamos' topping the *Billboard* Hot 100 in September and breaking into the UK Top 5.
● ALBUMS: *Enrique Iglesias* (Fonovisa 1995)★★★, *Vivir* (Fonovisa 1997)★★★★, *Cosas Del Amor* (Fonovisa 1998)★★★, *Bailamos* (Fonovisa 1999)★★★.

Imbruglia, Natalie

b. 4 February 1975, Sydney, Australia. One of 1998's surprise pop successes, Imbruglia's first brush with stardom came when she played Beth in the popular Australian soap opera *Neighbours*. She had originally started out as a singer, turning to acting later. Imbruglia spent two years on *Neighbours*, but after leaving struggled to find work in Australia. A move to England in 1996 offered little in the way of career progress, but she began turning her thoughts and experiences into songs. In 1997 she gained a contract with RCA Records in London, helped by her perceived affinity with the chart-topping 'feminine angst rock' of Alanis Morissette and Meredith Brooks. Recorded in London with Phil Thornalley (ex-Cure) and Nigel Godrich (Radiohead), in Los Angeles with Mark Goldenberg (Eels), and in New York with Mark Plati (David Bowie, Deee-Lite), *Left Of The Middle* sold strongly on the back of the success of her debut single, 'Torn', a massive hit throughout Europe, and the number one airplay hit in America for over 10 weeks. The album reached number 10 on the US album chart, although Imbruglia subsequently ran into controversy over the songwriting credits for 'Torn'. Subsequent UK hit singles, 'Big Mistake' (number 2), 'Wishing I Was There' (number 19) and 'Smoke' (number 5) repeated the highly melodic indie-rock formula of her debut. The following autumn, Imbruglia contributed 'Identify', co-written by Billy Corgan and Mike Garson, to the soundtrack of the movie *Stigmata*.
● ALBUMS: *Left Of The Middle* (RCA 1997)★★★.

Immature

Starting out as MCA Records' answer to the teenage R&B boy band boom, US trio Immature have belied both these inauspicious beginnings and their own choice of moniker by prospering as a commercial act in the 90s. Comprising lead singer Marques 'Batman' Houston, Jerome 'Romeo' Jones and Kelton 'LDB' Kessee, they became regulars on the pages of the American teen press from their inception in the late 80s. Following a 1992 debut for Virgin Records, they moved to MCA and enjoyed encouraging commercial success in 1994 with 'Never Lie', a number 5 hit on *Billboard*'s R&B chart. The attendant album, *We Got It*, peaked at number 14 in the equivalent album chart, and sold close to half a million copies. Their 1997 release, *The Journey*, was their most ambitious to date, and paired them with R&B songwriting/production veterans Keith Sweat, Rodney Jerkins and Marc Gordon of LeVert. The up-tempo, party-orientated atmosphere was further embossed by the presence of rappers Bizzy Bones (Bone Thugs-N-Harmony) and Daz (Tha Dogg Pound). In the same year the trio also recorded a pilot for their own television show, entitled *Keepin' It Real*. To mark their passage into adulthood, the trio changed their name to IMx for September 1999's 'Stay The Night'.
● ALBUMS: *On Our Worst Behavior* (Virgin 1992)★★, *Playtyme Is Over* (MCA 1994)★★★, *We Got It* (MCA 1995)★★★, *The Journey* (MCA 1997)★★★.

Incognito

Among the most prolific and popular of the 90s UK jazz funk generation, Incognito's origins can be traced back to the previous decade's Britfunk movement. The mainstay of the band is Jean Paul 'Bluey' Maunick, a veteran of Light Of The World. His original co-conspirator in Incognito was Paul 'Tubs' Williams, plus a loose collection of friends and associates including Ganiyu 'Gee' Bello, Ray Carless, Jef Dunn, Vin Gordon and Peter Hinds. Incognito made their debut when a demo single, 'Parisienne Girl', received such strong club and radio support that it was made an official release, peaking at number 73 in the UK charts in 1980. However, this early incarnation of the band was a brief one, and yielded just a single album for Ensign Records. Williams joined The Team, a funk group assembled by Bello, also working with Maunick on his Warriors side project. However, at the prompting of Gilles Peterson of Talkin' Loud Records, Incognito reconvened in the 90s with Maunick again at the helm. This time, a variety of guest singers were included in the package. 'Always There' (1991) featured the vocals of Jocelyn Brown, and was also remixed by David Morales (though Maunick was none too happy with the experiment). It reached number 6 in the UK charts. Maysa Leak, who had begun by guesting on their 1991 single 'Crazy For You', left the band amicably in June 1994. She was previously best known for her contribution to Stock, Aitken And Waterman's hit single 'Roadblock'. The highly-rated *Positivity* sold over 350,000 copies in the USA, a market where Maunick was also beginning to enjoy success as a producer (Chaka Khan, George Benson). For 1995's fifth album the new vocal recruits were Joy Malcolm (ex-Young Disciples) and Pamela Anderson (a relative of Carleen and Jhelisa Anderson). This time the sound veered from jazz funk to include Philly soul-styled orchestral arrangements and more luxuriant vocal interplay.
● ALBUMS: *Jazz Funk* (Ensign 1981)★★, *Inside Life* (Talkin' Loud 1991)★★★, *Tribes Vibes And Scribes* (Talkin' Loud 1992)★★★, *Positivity* (Talkin' Loud 1993)★★★★, *100° And Rising* (Talkin' Loud 1995)★★★★, *Beneath The Surface* (Talkin' Loud 1996)★★★, *Remixed* (Talkin' Loud 1996)★★★, *No Time Like The Future* (Talkin' Loud 1999)★★★, *Future Remixed* (Talkin' Loud 2000)★★★.

Infinity Project

Raja Ram (b. Ron Rothfield), who had trained as a jazz flautist in the 50s and played in the band Quintessence in the 60s, began making music with Graham Wood as the Infinity Project in 1989. Over the next few years they experimented with a kind of abstract techno gradually forming a sound that became known as the psychedelic or 'Goa' trance, often in collaboration with Simon Posford (Hallucinogen), Nick Barber (Doof) and Martin Freeland (Man With No Name). After producing material on DATs and white labels, in 1992 they started to release their music via the labels Fabulous ('Freedom In The Flesh'), Spiritzone ('Telepathy/Binary Neuronaut') and Dragonfly Records ('Bizarro', 'Time And Space', 'Super Booster' and 'Feeling Very Wierd'). In 1994, with Ian St. Paul they formed TIP Records and launched the label with 'Stimuli/Uforica'. At the same time they worked on projects with Posford and others, including the *Mystery Of The Yeti* album (TIP 1996) and various releases as Total Eclipse. After an ambient album *Mystical Experiences* (1995) for Blue Room Released, they released 'Alien Airport/Hyperspaced' on TIP followed by the album *Feeling Wierd* which was mostly made up of their previous releases. In the spirit of the Goa scene. *Feeling Wierd* was steeped in psychedelic hippie/sci-fi imagery. While tracks such as 'Telepathy', 'Stimuli' and the Doof remix of 'Hyperspaced' successfully blend the rigid four-on-the-floor rhythms, modal riffs, mysterious dialogue and abstract electronic phasing and filter sweeps that characterize the early psy-trance sound, 'Noises From The Darkness' and the early track 'Freedom From The Flesh' (written 1992) sound rather limp in comparison. In 1997, the group released the single 'Overwind/Incandescence' and contributed 'Mindboggler' to the TIP compilation *3D*. Wood also began recording as Excess Head for TIP's subsidiary 10 Kilo while Ram continued to work with Posford. By 1998 the Infinity Project had split-up to concentrate on individual projects.

● ALBUMS: *Mystical Experiences* (Blue Room 1995)★★★, *Feeling Wierd* (TIP 1995)★★★.

Inner City

This dance music outfit are built around the prolific genius of Kevin Saunderson (b. 9 May 1964, Brooklyn, New York, USA; programming), and the vocals of Paris Grey (b. Shanna Jackson, 5 November 1965, Glencove, Illinois, USA). Saunderson, who is also widely revered for his remix and recorded work under the title Reese Project, is the son of a member of the Marvelettes. He studied telecommunications at university, firing an interest in technology that would quickly become obvious in his musical leanings. Saunderson is the creative powerhouse of Inner City, writing all the songs and playing all the instruments, although Grey was responsible for writing her own melodies. Their first single together, 1988's 'Big Fun', was lying around unissued in Saunderson's home base of Detroit until a friend discovered it while looking for tracks for a compilation album. The record-buying public homed in on the strength of the tune (arguably one of dance music's all-time top five anthems), and with its follow-up, 'Good Life', Inner City had discovered a commercial career, with their debut album going on to worldwide sales of six million and both singles breaking into the UK Top 10. Further singles have included 'Ain't Nobody Better', 'That Man (He's All Mine)' and 'Pennies From Heaven'. Other notable singles included 'Back Together Again', a stylish 1993 cover version of Roberta Flack and Donny Hathaway's standard. Saunderson runs his own label, KMS Records, through Network Records, whose Neil Rushton is his manager. This led to Network also picking up the Inner City name when Virgin Records allowed the group to run out of contract in the 90s. A remix of 'Good Life' entered the UK charts at number 10 in January 1999.

● ALBUMS: *Paradise* (UK) *Big Fun* (US) (Ten 1989)★★★★, *Paradise Remixed* (Ten 1990)★★★, *Fire* (Ten 1990)★★, *Praise* (Ten 1992)★★.

● VIDEOS: *Paradise Live* (1990).

Insane Clown Posse

Formed in Detroit, Michigan, USA. Insane Clown Posse's highly shocking rap/metal fusion and spectacular live performances had, by the time they were signed to a major label in 1997, earned them both public notoriety and commercial success. Violent J. (b. Joseph Bruce) and Shaggy 2 Dope (b. Joey Ulster) originally performed as the Inner City Posse in the late 80s, releasing the hardcore gangsta rap *Dog Beats* in 1991. Following the underground success of this album, Bruce and Ulster changed their name to Insane Clown Posse and underwent a startling change of image, adopting Kiss-style clown make-up and rapping about the apocalypse. The duo released several albums on their own Psychopathic Records imprint (each claiming to contain a

further revelation from the final judgement), and gained a sizeable underground following in the Midwest without the backing of any radio play. They also roused the public ire of several local politicians and moral and religious campaigners, who reacted with shock to the foul-mouthed lyrics, open fires, chainsaws and barely contained violence of the duo's live shows. Jive Records signed the duo and released *The Riddle Box* in 1995, but the album failed to sell. [Walt] Disney's Hollywood Records signed the band a year later and poured nearly a million dollars into *The Great Milenko*, Insane Clown Posse's 1997 major label debut recorded with guest artists including Slash and Alice Cooper. The label recalled the album only six hours after it was released, however, with the duo's obscene lyrics placing Disney under further pressure from powerful Christian groups. Island Records bought out the Hollywood contract, and re-released the album later in the year with Insane Clown Posse still a permanent fixture in the media pages. *The Amazing Jeckel Brothers*, debuted at US number 4 in June 1999.

● ALBUMS: *Carnival Of Carnage* (Psychopathic 1992)★★★, *The Ringmaster* (Psychopathic 1994)★★, *The Riddle Box* (Battery 1995)★★, *The Great Milenko* (Hollywood 1997)★★★, *The Amazing Jeckel Brothers* (Island 1999)★★★.

● COMPILATIONS: *Forgotten Freshness* (PSY 1995)★★, *Forgotten Freshness Volumes 1 & 2* (Island 1998)★★★.

● VIDEOS: *Shockumentary* (PolyGram Music Video 1998).

Intelligent Hoodlum

b. Percy Chapman, New York, USA. Chapman grew up on the same street as Marley Marl, whom he pestered every day to try and get a record out, after having picked up the rap bug from his cousin Kadiya. Finally Marl acquiesced, and Chapman had his first record released, 'Coke Is It'. It was later retitled 'Tragedy', after his own sorry tale. He was only 14, but instead of further releases he pursued a life of crime to support his crack habit. Inevitably, in 1988, he found himself in Riker's Island prison on a one- to three-year sentence. However, the prison term gave him the chance to cool off, and he spent his time reading avidly. Having got through black-consciousness standards by Malcolm X and Elijah Muhammed, he was paroled just as Public Enemy arrived on the scene. Chuck D.'s bleak messages struck a chord with Chapman, and although he returned to the drug trade to support himself, he also attended college to learn more about his new heroes, Marcus Garvey and Malcolm X. Eventually he met up with Marley Marl again, by now a major hip-hop talent, who invited him to perform some more raps. The eventual results were the improvised 'Party Pack' and 'Vitally Tragic'. The Intelligent Hoodlum moniker indicated a path for the future, renouncing his illegal activities but acknowledging the necessary part his criminal past had played in his development. The intelligent prefix inferred his desire to learn, and use his new-found wisdom for the benefit of himself and others. This attitude was clearly demonstrated on his debut album by the ferocious protest of 'Black And Proud' and 'Arrest The President'. A second collection provided further bleak reportage of ghetto life. Now a practising Muslim, and affiliated to the Nation of Islam, Hoodlum also set up his own organization, MAAPS - Movement Against The American Power Structure.

● ALBUMS: *The Intelligent Hoodlum* (A&M 1990)★★★★, *Tragedy: Saga Of A Hoodlum* (A&M 1993)★★★★.

Invisibl Skratch Piklz

A crew of battle DJs comprising MixMaster Mike (b. Michael Schwartz, 4 April 1970, Daly City, California, USA), QBert (b. Richard Quitevis, 7 October 1969, San Francisco, California, USA), Shortkut (b. Jonathan Cruz, 15 October 1975, San Francisco, California, USA), D-Styles (b. Dave Cuasito, 6 July 1972, Philippines) and Yogafrog (b. Ritchie Desuasido, 26 September 1974, Philippines). This most prominent of turntablist outfits emerged in the early 80s from a network of mobile DJ crews, which in the San Francisco bay area was dominated by Filipino youth. In Daly City MixMaster Mike was affiliated with the Hi-Tech crew, and DJ Apollo with Unlimited Sounds, while nearby QBert was collaborating with Live Style Productions. Apollo and MixMaster Mike soon crossed paths and in 1985 as TWS (Together With Style), they pioneered the idea of a 'scratch ensemble' with their two-man 'Peter Piper' routine. In 1989, they linked up with QBert and by 1992 the trio took the DMC world championship as west coast representatives of New York's Rocksteady Crew. These three, along with Shortkut DJ Disk (b. Lou Quintanilla), constituted the core of the original Invisibl Skratch Piklz, although they have also played together under the names Shadow Of The Prophet, FM20, Dirt-Style Productions and the Tern Tabel Dragunz. Once incorporated as a crew, they completely dominated the battle circuit, winning the DMC finals so consistently that they were officially barred from competition, in the process taking the idea of turntable instrumentalism to its full potential. Both in the individual development of new techniques and with their orchestrated routines as a scratch 'band', they defined the emergent practice of turntablism. Apollo and Disk ultimatcly left the crew, Apollo going on to tour with Souls Of Mischief, contributing to their 1995 *No Man's Land* set, and recording with Branford Marsalis' acid jazz project Buckshot LeFonque (where he replaced DJ Premier). In the wake of these departures, the crew gained several new members, including D-Styles, who maintained dual affiliation with the Los Angeles-based Beat Junkies, and Yogafrog The ISP's output includes several compilation appearances (notably 'Invasion Of The Octopus People' on Bill Laswell's *Altered Beats*) and 1997's *The Invisibl Skratch Piklz Vs. The Klams Uv Deth* EP on the Asphodel label. They also released several instalments of *The Shiggar Fraggar Show* mixtape series, originally recorded for pirate radio jock Billy Jam's show on Radio Free Berkeley. QBert and MixMaster Mike both stayed active with the crew while making their respective names as solo artists. The former appeared on Dr. Octagon's notorious *Dr. Octagonecolygyst* release before going on to work on his own Wave Twisters (which, true to the cartoonish Invisibl Skratch Piklz ethos, was designed to accompany an animated feature of the same name). Mix Master Mike, meanwhile, made his presence felt in 1998 on the Beastie Boys' *Hello Nasty* and his own solo effort, *Anti-Theft Device*. Various configurations of Piklz have also been involved in the production of 'break' records, specially designed for battle DJs, instructional video-tapes and, perhaps most importantly, the Vestax line of DJ mixers, including an ISP signature model.

● ALBUMS: *The Shiggar Fraggar Show* (Hip-Hop Slam 1998)★★★.

Isaak, Chris

b. 26 June 1956, Stockton, California, USA. Isaak is a crooner in the Roy Orbison mould who had been active on the music scene a long time before he broke through in the late 80s. The son of a forklift truck driver, Isaak spent time participating in an exchange programme at university which led him to study in Japan. He also worked as a tour guide for a film studio and held teenage boxing ambitions, ultimately leading to his distinctive flattened nose. After graduating with a degree in English and Communication Arts, he put together his first band, Silvertone. This rockabilly outfit, comprising James Calvin Wilsey (guitar), Rowland Salley (bass) and Kenney Dale Johnson (drums), remained with Isaak as his permanent backing band. After acquiring a contract with Warner Brothers Records in 1985, Isaak and the band moved through three years and two albums with little success, apart from 'Blue Hotel' which was a hit in France. The debut *Silvertone* was raw and diverse, with country blues mingling with conventional folk ballads. The self-titled follow-up saw him hone his style to sophisticated R&B. Throughout he was backed by the excellent moody guitar of Wilsey, whose mimicry of 50s styles is impeccable. After working with David Lynch on the movie *Wild At Heart*, he finally had a major hit in December 1990 with 'Wicked Game' (US number 6/UK number 10), while a re-released 'Blue Hotel' also charted at UK number 17 in February 1991. Another superb single, April 1993's 'Can't Do A Thing (To Stop Me)', failed to recreate the success of his earlier hits. In a music scene frequently dominated by synthesized, frantic pop, his simple approach has proved refreshing: 'I just respond to music where the singer and melody are right up in the mix, whereas in most modern stuff the drum is usually the loudest thing'. This viewpoint makes Isaak strangely out of time. His music is too well-recorded to be regarded as a recreation of the Sun Records sound, yet the influences are too apparent to make him wholly contemporary. His acting career has ploughed a parallel path to his singing career with cameo roles in *Married To The Mob* and *Silence Of The Lambs*, and a headlining role in *Little Buddha*.

● ALBUMS: *Silvertone* (Warners 1985)★★, *Chris Isaak* (Warners 1987)★★★, *Heart Shaped World* reissued as *Wicked Game* (Reprise 1989)★★★, *San Francisco Days* (Reprise 1993)★★★, *Forever Blue* (Reprise 1995)★★, *Baja Sessions* (Reprise 1996)★★, *Speak Of The Devil* (Reprise 1998)★★.

● VIDEOS: *Wicked Game* (Warner Music Video 1991).

● FILMS: *Let's Get Lost* (1988), *Married To The Mob* (1988), *The Silence Of The Lambs* (1991), *Twin Peaks: Fire Walk With Me* (1992), *Little Buddha* (1993), *That Thing You Do!* (1996), *Grace Of My Heart* (1996), *Blue Ridge Fall* (1999).

Ivy

Comprising Dominique Durand (b. France), her husband Andy Chase and Adam Schlesinger, this offbeat US pop band's profile rose in the 90s as a consequence of Schlesinger's other musical project, Fountains Of Wayne. Schlesinger is also the joint founder of Scratchie Records with James Iha and D'Arcy Wretzky of Smashing Pumpkins. Ivy's sound proved to be slightly divorced from the lo-fi pop of Fountains Of Wayne; Durand's breathy vocals, in particular, added a touch of grandiloquence to a musical backing compared to artists including Stereolab and the Cardigans. The band's debut album, released prior to the success of

Schlesinger's extracurricular activities, received strong reviews but disappointing sales. Their second effort, *Apartment Life*, was completed in a piecemeal fashion due to his increased workload and touring commitments with Fountains Of Wayne. The better songs on *Apartment Life* included 'This Is The Day' and 'Baker', both featuring a prominent horn section. Chris Collingwood and Jody Porter of Fountains Of Wayne also contributed to the album, as did drummer Stanley Demeski (ex-Luna). The producers were Kolderie And Slade. Durand also returned the compliment by singing backing vocals on Fountains Of Wayne's debut set. For touring purposes, Ivy were joined in late 1997 by Brian Young, also of the Posies and, inevitably, Fountains Of Wayne. The following year they contributed 'This Is The Day' to the soundtrack of the Farrelly brothers' movie *There's Something About Mary*.

● ALBUMS: *Realistic* (Seed/Atlantic 1995)★★★, *Apartment Life* (Atlantic 1997)★★★.

Jack

Anthony Reynolds formed Jack at the age of 19 with fellow Cardiff, Wales native Matthew Scott (guitar), the two drawing on a shared love of the bleak humour of Nick Cave and the drink-raddled prose of Charles Bukowski. By March 1995 the rest of the band was in place, with Richard Adderley (guitar), Patrick Pulzer (drums), Colin Williams (bass) and George Wright (keyboards) on board in time for their debut London gig, after which they were immediately snapped up by Too Pure Records. Their first release, the limited edition 'Kid Stardust', was single of the week in *Melody Maker*; this was followed by *Pioneer Soundtracks*, the bohemian ambience of which was accentuated by the work of ex-Scott Walker producer Peter Walsh and the string arrangements of seventh member, cellist Audrey Morse. The album was released at a point when the *cabaret noir* sound of Cave (almost parodied in 'I Didn't Mean It, Marie'), Walker, Jacques Brel and the Tindersticks was flavour of the month. Reynolds, however, took their black-clad moodiness to a new extreme: 'I don't believe in happiness,' he declared, 'do you?' He expressed the darkness more fully in Jacques, described as Jack's 'older, slightly eccentric brother', a spin-off collaboration with fellow Brel-obsessive Momus that resulted in 1997's *How To Make Love Volume 1*. The parent band's vision was fully realised on 1998's *The Jazz Age*, a lush

romantic masterpiece that reached a sublime peak on the epic ballad 'Nico's Children'.

● ALBUMS: *Pioneer Soundtracks* (Too Pure 1996)★★★, *The Jazz Age* (Too Pure 1998)★★★★.

Jackson, Alan

b. 17 October 1958, Newman, Georgia, USA. Jackson, the son of a motor mechanic, had a love of gospel music through church and his family. His roots can be heard in 'Home' (written for Mother's Day), 'Chattahoochee' and his tribute to Hank Williams, 'Midnight In Montgomery'. He has also revived several songs from his youth including Eddie Cochran's 'Summertime Blues' and a joint composition from Roger Miller and George Jones, 'Tall Tall Trees'. Jackson worked in various trades before moving to Nashville in 1986, with his wife Denise, to try and succeed as a country performer. Through a chance meeting with Glen Campbell, he gained an audition with his publishing company, and became the first artist to be signed to Arista Records' Nashville division. He wrote most of his debut album, *Here In The Real World*, which remained on the US country album chart for over a year. 'Blue Blooded Woman' was an immediate success, and four more singles from the album topped the US country charts - 'Here In The Real World', 'Wanted', 'Chasin' That Neon Rainbow' and 'I'd Love You All Over Again'. In 1991, Jackson joined the *Grand Ole Opry*. *Don't Rock The Jukebox* confirmed that his initial success was no fluke, spawning five number 1 singles - 'Don't Rock The Jukebox', 'Someday', 'Midnight In Montgomery', 'Dallas' and 'Love's Got A Hold On You'. He also wrote songs with Randy Travis, including the latter's number 1 single 'Forever Together', and his own number 1 hit 'She's Got The Rhythm And I Got The Blues'. The album on which the latter featured, *A Lot About Livin' (And A Little 'Bout Lovin)*, was a multi-platinum success which included the number 1 hits 'Tonight I Climbed The Wall', 'Chattahoochee' and 'Who Says You Can't Have It All'. *Honky Tonk Christmas* included Alison Krauss, the Chipmunks and a duet with the late Keith Whitley. *Who I Am* included four more country number 1s, 'Summertime Blues', 'Livin' On Love', 'Gone Country' and 'I Don't Even Know Your Name'. 'Gone Country' wittily parodied people who turned to country music when it became fashionable: 'I heard down there, it's changed, you see/They're not as backward as they used to be.' Jackson contributed to tribute albums for the Eagles and Merle Haggard and displayed his traditional side by recording a duet of 'A Good Year For The Roses' with its originator, George Jones. He also wrote 'Job Description' to explain to his daughters, Mattie Denise and Alexandra Jane, why he was rarely home. Jackson has won a succession of industry awards, establishing himself as a top ranking country star, not too far behind Garth Brooks. His 1998 set, *High Mileage*, debuted at number 4 on the *Billboard* 200 album chart in September. The UK magazine *Country Music People* said of him, 'He's uncontroversial, stands for the flag, Mom and apple pie, looks like he washes every day and sings for middle America.' He stands for simple truths in straightforward, well-crafted songs and he says, 'I don't dance, I don't swing from ropes, I just stand there.'

● ALBUMS: *Here In The Real World* (Arista 1990)★★★, *Don't Rock The Jukebox* (Arista 1991)★★★★, *A Lot About Livin' (And A Little 'Bout Lovin)* (Arista 1992)★★★★, *Honky Tonk Christmas* (Arista 1993)★★,

Who I Am (Arista 1994)★★★, *Everything I Love* (Arista 1996)★★★★, *High Mileage* (Arista 1998)★★★, *Under The Influence* (Arista 1999)★★★.

● COMPILATIONS: *The Greatest Hits Collection* (Arista 1995)★★★★.

● VIDEOS: *Here In The Reel World* (1990), *Livin', Lovin', And Rockin' That Jukebox* (1994), *Who Says You Can't Have It All* (DNA 1994), *The Greatest Video Hits Collection* (6 West Home Video 1995).

Jackson, Janet

b. Janet Damita Jackson, 16 May 1966, Gary, Indiana, USA. Jackson was the youngest of the nine children in the family that produced the Jackson Five (including Michael Jackson, Jermaine Jackson and LaToya Jackson). When she was four years old, the family moved to the Los Angeles area; three years later she made her performing debut in Las Vegas with her brothers. At the age of nine, she joined them on a tele-vision special. She was cast in the US television programmes *Good Times* from 1977-79 and *Diff'rent Strokes* from 1981-82. She signed to A&M Records in 1982 and recorded her self-titled debut album, followed by *Dream Street* in 1984. Both albums sold only moderately. Jackson's breakthrough came in 1986 with *Control*, which reached number 1 and produced an astonishing five US Top 10 singles (including the chart-topping 'When I Think Of You') and three UK Top 10 singles. The album was ultimately certified quadruple platinum for sales of over four million copies in the USA. Jackson fol-lowed up in 1989 with *Janet Jackson's Rhythm Nation 1814*, another quadruple platinum album, which yielded the US chart-topping singles 'Miss You Much', 'Escapade', 'Black Cat', and 'Love Will Never Do (Without You)'. Jackson under-took her first concert tour in 1990. By the end of the year she had scooped eight *Billboard* awards, including Top R&B Albums and Singles Artist, Best Pop and R&B Album Award for *Rhythm Nation*, and Top Hot 100 Singles Artist. The suc-cess of the *Rhythm Nation* album continued into 1991 when, in January, Jackson became the first artist in history to have culled from one album seven Top 5 singles in the *Billboard* chart. Jackson's commercial peak continued into the 90s with the unprecedented performance of her Virgin Records' debut *Janet*, which entered the US album chart at number 1, beating brother Michael's sales record by selling 350,000 copies in its first week. Further US chart-topping singles included 'That's The Way Love Goes' (number 1 for eight weeks) and 'Again', which were also UK bestsellers. The compilation album *Design Of A Decade* was another huge seller, and followed her collaboration with brother Michael on 'Scream'. Performing as simply Janet, Jackson released her first studio set in four years, *The Velvet Rope*, a deeply personal album that dealt frankly with her much publicised emotional breakdown. The album entered the charts at number 1 in America, while the single 'Together Again' topped the Hot 100 in January 1998. A collaboration with BLACKstreet, 'I Get Lonely', was a US number 3 hit in May. Both tracks also reached the UK Top 5.

● ALBUMS: *Janet Jackson* (A&M 1982)★★, *Dream Street* (A&M 1984)★★★, *Control* (A&M 1986)★★★★, *Control: The Remixes* (A&M 1987)★★★, *Janet Jackson's Rhythm Nation 1814* (A&M 1989)★★★★, *Janet* (Virgin 1993)★★★★, *Janet Remixed* (Virgin 1993)★★★, *The Velvet Rope* (Virgin 1997)★★★.

● COMPILATIONS: *Design Of A Decade 1986/1996* (A&M 1995)★★★★.

● VIDEOS: *Janet* (Virgin 1994), *Design Of A Decade 86-96* (VVL 1995).

● FURTHER READING: *Out Of The Madness (The Strictly Unauthorised Biography Of ...)*, Andrew Bart and J Randy Taraborrelli (eds.).

● FILMS: *Poetic Justice* (1993).

Jam And Spoon

Duo credited by some as the originators of the trance style of dance music. Based in Frankfurt, Germany, the faces behind the team are producer Jam El Mar and DJ Mark Spoon. Their groundbreaking work on a 1992 remix of Alex Lee's 'Age Of Love' was the first track to set the ball rolling, followed in quick succession by work with Moby ('Go'), Cosmic Baby and Frankie Goes To Hollywood ('Relax'). The latter was a difficult but rewarding project, as it had been this band and the production work of Trevor Horn in general which had originally inspired Jam El Mar into music. Another key reference point are the soundtrack recordings of Tangerine Dream. Only one single under their own name, 'Stella', preceded the release of their debut double album. This time they had moved away from the fast, pumping backbeat and acid house tones which had flavoured their remixes, opting instead for a much more commercial slant. A sleevenote written for R&S Records label boss Renaat wryly declares: 'I hope this is not too commercial for your uncommercial label'. Perhaps not, but it did see them crossover into the pop charts proper. Other 45s like 'Follow Me' were considered to be bona fide trance classics. After signing a major label contract with Epic Records and hooking up with female vocalist Plavka, the duo enjoyed a string of UK hits, including a Top 10 placing for the club anthem, 'Right In The Night (Fall In Love With Music)'. After issuing an album under the Tokyo Ghetto Pussy alias, the duo returned in 1997 with their second long-player, *Kaleidoscope*, another impressive slice of progressive trance.

● ALBUMS: *Tripomatic Fairytales 2001* (R&S/Epic 1993)★★★★, *Kaleidoscope* (Sony 1997)★★★.

James

Championed initially by Morrissey of the Smiths, James signed with their hometown record label, Manchester's Factory Records, in 1983. Their early singles, 'What's The World?' and 'Hymn From A Village', and the EPs *JimOne* and *James II*, were acclaimed for their unusual mixture of folk and new wave textures. The original line-up was Timothy Booth (b. 4 February 1960; vocals), James Glennie (b. 10 October 1963; bass), Larry Gott (guitar) and Gavan Whelan (drums). They signed to Sire Records in 1985 and began an unsettled three-year relationship with the company. *Stutter* was a collection of strange but striking songs, followed two years later by *Strip Mine*, which had a stronger melodic edge. *One Man Clapping*, a live set recorded in Bath, England, marked a return to independent status with Rough Trade Records. Dave Baynton-Power replaced Whelan and soon afterwards the band was augmented by Saul Davies (guitar/violin), Mark Hunter (keyboards) and Andy Diagram (trumpet). Fontana Records, with its policy of signing England's leading independent bands, re-released 'Come Home' and 'Sit Down', the latter single reaching number 2 in the UK charts. *Gold Mother* was more accessible than previous albums; the band writing in a more direct lyrical style, though there were still echoes of earlier eccen-tricities. The title track was a paean to mothers and the extreme physical pain they underwent during childbirth, and drew from Booth's personal exposure to the birth of his own child. Although their recording career stretched back further than their contemporaries, they became part of an upsurge in talent from Manchester during the late 80s and early 90s, and the media attention on the city made the transition from independent to major league status that much easier. *Seven* saw the band digress further away from the immediacy of 'Sit Down', which up to that point was their most enduring and popular song. Instead, the emphasis was on atmosphere and multi-layered, unconventional song structures. The upshot of this was a fall-off in commercial viability, although the band maintained a loyal fanbase. *Laid*, meanwhile, was a title presumably inspired by Booth's return from a life of celibacy, and its hit single of the same title was the first to make an impression in the USA. The other contents were described as 'paranoid love songs, ecstatic laments and perverse lullabies' by *Select* magazine's reviewer. The heavily experimental *Wah Wah* was seen by some critics as an attempt to steal U2's *Zooropa* thunder. It was recorded with Brian Eno during sessions for *Laid*, for release as an 'alternative' album. The move into ambient electronics had, however, been signposted by the 1993 Sabres Of Paradise remix of 'Jam J'. Tim Booth recorded an album with American composer Angelo Badalamenti as Booth And The Bad Angel before, in 1997, the band broke a three-year silence with the well-received *Whiplash* and the hit single 'She's A Star'. The recordings featured new guitarist Adrian Oxaal, who replaced founder member Gott. A remix of 'Sit Down' reached UK number 7 in November 1998 on the back of the commercial success of their compilation album. The excellent *Millionaires* benefited from the creative input of Hunter and Davies and the production wiles of Brian Eno, employed by the band for the first time since *Laid*.

● ALBUMS: *Stutter* (Sire 1986)★★★★, *Strip Mine* (Sire 1988)★★★, *One Man Clapping* (Rough Trade 1989)★★★, *Gold Mother* (Fontana 1990)★★★★, *Seven* (Fontana 1992)★★★★, *Laid* (Fontana 1993)★★★, *Wah Wah* (Fontana 1994)★★, *Whiplash* (Fontana 1997)★★★, *Millionaires* (Fontana 1999)★★★★.

● COMPILATIONS: *James: The Best Of* (Fontana 1998)★★★★.

● VIDEOS: *Come Home Live* (PolyGram Music Video 1991), *Seven - The Live Video* (PolyGram Music Video 1992).

Jamiroquai

Jason 'Jay' Kay's UK funk band Jamiroquai (named after the Iroquois tribe whose pantheism inspired him) made a rapid impact - they were signed to Sony Records for an eight-album contract on the strength of just one single for Acid Jazz Records - 'When You Gonna Learn?'. Kay (b. London, England) was brought up in Ealing by his jazz-singer mother, Karen Kay. Inspired by Sly Stone, Gil Scott-Heron and Roy Ayers, he integrated those influences into a 90s pop format that also combined 'new age' mysticism and the growing urban funk movement, which took its name from the Acid Jazz label. However, as a former breakdancer, he had already recorded in a hip-hop style, releasing a single with a sampler and drum machine for Morgan Khan's Streetsounds label in 1986. His first major label single, 'Too Young To Die', immediately broke into the UK Top 10 in 1993, while the debut album entered the chart at number 1. However, a press backlash soon followed, not helped by Kay's naïve statements about the environment after he had blown his

advance on petrol-guzzling cars. Despite the healthy sales, his case was not helped by a less than spectacular debut album, which came with an order form for his own brand clothing (seven per cent of profits going to Greenpeace), although there were strong compositions such as 'If I Like It, I Do It'. The second album was a considerable improvement, with the previous emphasis on his media relations now switched to his music. Songs such as 'Kids', 'Return' and 'Morning Glory' gave his obvious vocal talents better service, adding ghetto hip-hop rhythms to the previous acid jazz and funk backdrops. *Travelling Without Moving* confirmed Jamiroquai as a highly commercial act, selling over seven million copies worldwide, and winning four trophies at the 1997 MTV Awards. Following a string of UK hit singles including 'Virtual Insanity', 'Cosmic Girl' and 'Alright', the band achieved their first UK chart-topper when 'Deeper Underground', taken from the soundtrack of the movie *Godzilla*, topped the charts in August 1998. Kay's long-serving bass player, Stuart Zender, left during the recording of the following year's *Synkronized*.

● ALBUMS: *Emergency On Planet Earth* (Sony 1993)★★★, *The Return Of The Space Cowboy* (Sony 1994)★★★★, *Travelling Without Moving* (Sony 1996)★★★★, *Synkronized* (Sony 1999)★★★★.

Jars Of Clay

Jars Of Clay rose to sudden prominence in May 1995 when their self-titled album became the first debut by a contemporary Christian act to achieve platinum status. The band was formed in 1993 by two friends from Greenville College in Illinois, USA - Dan Haseltine (b. 12 January 1973, Rochester, New York, USA; vocals) and Charlie Lowell (b. 21 October 1973, Rochester, New York, USA; keyboards). With the addition of Stephen Mason (b. 8 July 1975, Decatur, Illinois, USA; guitar), Matt Bronleewe (guitar) and Scott Savage (touring drummer), they began playing the campus circuit. They won a competition for unsigned bands sponsored by the Gospel Music Association, and, with Matt Odmark (b. 25 January 1974, Rochester, New York, USA) replacing Bronleewe, signed a contract with Brentwood Music's Essential label. Buoyed by the success of the debut album's first single, 'Flood', Jars Of Clay became fixtures on MTV and played a series of support slots to Sting among 300 tour dates completed in 1996. Their second album, *Much Afraid*, was titled after one of the characters in Hannah Hurnard's book *Hind's Feet On High Places* - a Christian allegory in which each of the characters plays a human emotion. The album, which was even more successful than their debut, was completed in London and Nashville and was produced by Stephen Lipson (a former collaborator of Sting, Whitney Houston and Simple Minds). Their third album, *If I Left The Zoo*, was a challenging and dark-hued alt rock classic.

● ALBUMS: *Jars Of Clay* (Essential/Silvertone 1995)★★★, *Much Afraid* (Essential/Silvertone 1997)★★★, *If I Left The Zoo* (Essential/Silvertone 1999)★★★★.

Jay, Norman

b. London, England. Perhaps hyperbolically described as a clubland 'legend', Jay is certainly a hugely popular and highly respected figure in dance music. As a DJ, his style encompasses many forms of black music, including soul, funk, disco, hip-hop and garage. Perhaps his enduring popularity (the UK's *Muzik* magazine called him a 'man of the people') lies in this rare democratic approach to his playlist. Another factor is his foresight and innovation: Jay was listening to early Chicago house records and staging warehouse parties three years before the UK's acid house explosion of 1988. He is also the 'DJ's DJ', with many contemporary superstar DJ's citing him as an early influence.

Jay was born in the early 60s to West Indian parents. He had DJing ambitions even at the tender age of eight and first 'played out' at his cousin's 10th birthday party. As he matured, he was inspired by the American R&B of the late 60s, especially the sound of Sly And The Family Stone, Aretha Franklin and James Brown. By the late 70s, he had become an almost obsessive collector of US black music, collecting Motown Records, Stax Records, Atlantic Records, Salsoul and jazz recordings. He witnessed the disco phenomenon first-hand while visiting family in New York. One of his relatives was a successful Brooklyn DJ and Jay stayed for several months, visiting the seminal Paradise Garage and forming friendships with Larry Levan, Timmy Regisford, Tee Scott and then later, David Morales, Tony Humphries and Little Louie Vega before they had been heard of in the UK. Jay was inspired to take up DJing more seriously and began to build the Good Times sound system with his brother to play at the Notting Hill Carnival. With his reputation and audiences growing steadily, he and Gordon Mac started a pirate radio station, Kiss FM (named after its US predecessor) in 1985. Jay's reputation and influence attracted many talented DJs to the station, several of whom have since become household names: Jonathon More and Matt Black (Coldcut), Jazzie B. (Soul II Soul), Dr. Bob Jones, Danny Rampling, Trevor Nelson, Gilles Peterson and his partner and protégé, the ubiquitous Judge Jules. Jay and Jules were the originators of the rare groove scene, staging warehouse parties as Shake And Fingerpop and Family Funktion respectively, and playing a mixture of classics and early house records. The arrival of acid house brought dance music to a much larger audience and by 1990, Kiss FM had received a license to broadcast legally. Jay also established the UK's first garage-style club, High On Hope, playing host to US talent such as Tony Humphries, Marshall Jefferson, Blaze, Ten City and Adeva. PolyGram Records sought the skills of Jay and Gilles Peterson to launch their new subsidiary, Talkin' Loud Records, whose early signings included Omar, Bryan Powell, the Young Disciples, Galliano and Incognito. Jay has played all over the world and is often hired for celebrity parties, fashion shows and film premieres and has won numerous awards. *The Face* magazine once described him as a 'clubland institution'.

Jay-Z

b. Shawn Carter, New York, USA. Raised in Brooklyn, Carter was a school friend of the Notorious B.I.G. He first started releasing records in the late 80s, part-financing his music by hustling. In 1990, he appeared on records by his close friend Jaz ('The Originators') and Original Flavor ('Can I Get Open'), and later scored an underground hit single with 1995's 'In My Lifetime'. Drawing on Jaz's dealings with mercenary labels, Jay-Z set-up his own Roc-A-Fella imprint in 1996 with entrepreneur Damon Dash and Kareem 'Biggs' Burke. His debut set, *Reasonable Doubt*, went on to achieve gold sales and produced the US number 50 pop single 'Ain't

No Nigga'/'Dead Presidents', featuring future rap star Foxy Brown. The album, which reached US number 23 in July, attracted fans with a mixture of hard-hitting street lyrics and rhymes, epitomized by the collaboration with Notorious B.I.G. on 'Brooklyn's Finest'. The follow-up *In My Lifetime, Vol. 1* was released in the aftermath of Notorious B.I.G.'s murder, and debuted at US number 3 in November 1997. Featuring guest appearances from Puff Daddy, Lil' Kim, Too Short, BLACKstreet and DJ Premier, this sombre and intensely personal album included the stand-out tracks 'You Must Love Me' and 'Where I'm From'. Although in demand as a guest artist, Jay-Z found the time to write, produce, and direct the semi-autobiographical short *Streets Is Watching*. The gold-selling soundtrack introduced several of Roc-A-Fella's rising stars, including Memphis Bleek, Rell and Diamonds In The Rough, and featured the hit single 'It's Alright'. Jay-Z then became a major star with the hit singles, 'Can I Get A ... ' and 'Hard Knock Life (Ghetto Anthem)', the latter built around a line from the musical *Annie*. One of the more bizarre samples to be used on a hip-hop track, the single nevertheless became an international hit (UK number 2, December 1998/US number 15, March 1999). The album of the same name featured hotshot producer Timbaland, in addition to the usual team of Ski and DJ Premier. Guest rappers included DMX, Foxy Brown and Too Short, on a package that diluted Jay-Z's hard-hitting lyrical edge in an attempt to corner the crossover market. *Vol. 2 ... Hard Knock Life* easily succeeded in its aim, staying at US number 1 for five weeks before finally being deposed by Alanis Morissette's new album. Despite a hectic schedule as a guest producer/writer and rapper, Jay-Z still found the time to enter the studio and record tracks for his new album. Released in December 1999, *Vol. 3 ... Life And Times Of S. Carter* confirmed his status as one of hip-hop's most popular artists when it topped the album charts the following month.

● ALBUMS: *Reasonable Doubt* (Roc-A-Fella 1996)★★★, *In My Lifetime, Vol. 1 ...* (Roc-A-Fella/Def Jam 1997)★★★★, *Vol. 2 ... Hard Knock Life* (Roc-A-Fella/Def Jam 1998)★★★, *Vol. 3 ... Life And Times Of S. Carter* (Roc-A-Fella/Def Jam 1999)★★★★.

Jayhawks

Def American Records producer George Drakoulias discovered the country/rock/R&B-influenced Jayhawks after they had made two low-key records. Legend has it that he phoned Dave Ayers of Twin/Tone Records and, on overhearing a collection of the band's demos during the conversation, signed them up. The band, who come from Minneapolis, Minnesota, USA, boasted a core line-up of Mark Olson (vocals/guitar) and Gary Louris (vocals/guitar), joined by Ken Callahan (bass), and subsequently Karen Grotberg (keyboards) and Marc Perlman, who replaced Callahan. Together since 1985, until their induction to Rick Rubin's eclectic label they had only sold approximately 10,000 records. Songs such as 'Waiting For The Sun' saw them compared to the Black Crowes (another Drakoulias discovery), combining rugged country imagery with harsh, rough hewn bar blues. Their second album, *The Blue Earth*, threw up another name; that of Neil Young. For their own part they cited the Flying Burrito Brothers and Charlie and Ira Louvin of the Louvin Brothers as their greatest influences. They also record widely as session musicians, including work for acts such as Soul Asylum, Counting Crows and Maria McKee.

The band's rapid turnover of drummers continued on *Tomorrow The Green Grass*, with Don Heffington on hand in the studio and Tim O'Regan available for touring duties. Songs on this set included 'Miss Williams' Guitar', a tribute to Mark Olson's wife, Victoria Williams, and the exquisite single, 'Blue'. It saw them still playing simple, direct music, a traditional but never stultifying sound. Olson left the band in 1996, leaving the main songwriting duties to be completed by Louris. The superlative *Sound of Lies* was a deep and often sad album with many of the songs relating to the break up of Louris' marriage. Similarities between Richard Thompson's 'The Calvary Cross' and 'Stick In The Mud' were purely coincidental, while 'Big Star' was one of their best songs in years.

● ALBUMS: *The Jayhawks* (Bunkhouse 1986)★★★, *The Blue Earth* (Twin/Tone 1989)★★★, *Hollywood Town Hall* (Def American 1992)★★★, *Tomorrow The Green Grass* (American 1995)★★★★, *Sound Of Lies* (American 1997)★★★★.

Jazzie B.

b. Beresford Romeo, 26 January 1963, London, England. The larger-than-life svengali Jazzie B. began his musical apprenticeship on the London sound system circuit before fronting the enormous international success of Soul II Soul. As such, Jazzie B. is widely credited with having pioneered a renaissance in British soul and dance music in the late 80s - certainly his band were the first of their generation to make a serious impact on the US R&B charts. By the advent of Soul II Soul's fifth album, Jazzie B. had signed a new contract with Island Records' subsidiary 4th & Broadway, following six successful years with Virgin Records. Island also provided a home for his record label, production and publishing company, Soul II Soul Records, and an artist roster including Yorker, Backroom, the Funki Dreds and EFUA. Although his publishing agreement with EMI Publishing for the Jazzie B. Music, Soul II Soul and Mad Music catalogues also expired in 1996, his music remained omnipresent in the UK media, including advertisements for Renault and Levis. Indeed, his only significant setback has been the clothes stores opened in the late 80s under the Soul II Soul banner, which have since closed. Jazzie B. continued to occupy himself by running his studio complex in Camden, north London.

Jazzmatazz

A early 90s collaboration between seasoned jazz exponents and Guru (b. Keith Elam, 18 July 1966, Roxbury, Massachusetts, USA) of Gang Starr. Some of the names involved included N'Dea Davenport (Brand New Heavies), Carleen Anderson, Courtney Pine, Branford Marsalis, Roy Ayers, Donald Byrd, Lonnie Liston Smith and French rapper MC Solaar. An inventive combination, highlighted by a single, 'No Time To Play', featuring the vocals of D.C. Lee (Style Council), which in turn helped relaunch the latter's career. The Jazzmatazz project's roots were undoubtedly laid in Gang Starr's 'Jazz Thing', a collaboration with Marsalis which Spike Lee has used to theme his movie, *Mo' Better Blues*. A second volume, featuring a duet with Chaka Khan and production work by the Solsonics, was released in 1995.

● ALBUMS: *Jazzmatazz Volume 1: An Experimental Fusion Of Hip-Hop And Jazz* (Chrysalis 1993)★★★★, *Jazzmatazz Volume II: The New Reality* (Chrysalis 1995)★★★.

Jean, Wyclef

b. 17 October 1972, Haiti. Despite the Fugees becoming the biggest rap crossover success of the 90s, lead rapper Wyclef Jean still found time to release a solo album in 1997. Long regarded as the production mastermind behind the Fugees' intoxicating blend of rap, soul and Haitian music, Wyclef Jean is also active as a remixer and producer to the R&B and dance music communities, enjoying particular success with the US number 1 single 'No No No' by Destiny's Child. Guests on his debut solo effort included Lauryn Hill and Pras (his fellow Fugees), the Neville Brothers, the I-Threes, the New York Philharmonic Orchestra and Cuban superstar Celia Cruz. Tracks such as 'Sang Fezi' and 'Jaspora' exploited his own musical ancestry while adding modern production methods to produce an intoxicating and seamlessly rhythmic collection. The album was promoted by the release of 'We Trying To Stay Alive', a more contemporary-sounding effort that sampled the refrain from the Bee Gees' 'Stayin' Alive', and 'Gone Till November', a UK number 3 single in May 1998. Wyclef enjoyed further UK Top 5 success in November with a remix of Queen's 'Another One Bites The Dust'. In October 1999, he teamed up with U2's Bono to record 'New Day', the official song for the Net Aid charity concert.

● ALBUMS: *Wyclef Jean Presents The Carnival Featuring The Refugee Allstars* (Columbia 1997)★★★.

● FILMS: *Rhyme & Reason* (1997).

Jefferson, Marshall

One of the legends of USA acid house music, Jefferson claims to have invented the familiar 'squelch' of the Roland TR 303 (a claim hotly countered by DJ Pierre). Jefferson's reputation rests more squarely on records such as Reggie Hall's 'Music', Richard Rogers' mighty 'Can't Stop Loving You', and Ce Ce Rogers' epic 'Someday'. Afterwards he moved on to helm production for Ten City, but was criticised at the time of their arrival for what some critics observed to be a fixation with nostalgia in the latter's soulful house grooves. Jefferson preferred the description deep house, and was quick to proclaim the death knell for acid. Nevertheless, Ten City hit with singles like 'Devotion', 'That's The Way Love Is' and 'Right Back To You', with Byron Stingily's distinctive vocals providing an excellent outlet for Jefferson's studio craft. He has also worked with Tyrrel Corporation and Kym Mazelle ('I'm A Lover') amongst many others, and recorded as Jungle Wonz ('Time Marches On') and Truth ('Open Your Eyes'). In 1994, Jefferson recorded only the second track under his own name, 'I Found You', for Centrestage Records, as well as continuing to produce artists of the calibre of Tom Jones, System 7 and Keith Thompson.

Jellyfish

This US band from San Francisco broke into the 90s by brilliantly repackaging the most gaudy elements of 60s and 70s pop with irresistible kitsch appeal. The band's dress sense was particularly colourful, one critic observing that it could have been drawn from the wardrobes of colour-blind charity shop consumers. The group was composed of Andy Sturmer (b. Pleasanton, San Francisco, California, USA; drums, vocals), Jason Falkner (guitar), along with brothers Chris Manning (b. Pleasanton, San Francisco, California, USA; bass) and Roger Manning (b. Pleasanton, San Francisco,

California, USA; keyboards). Members of the band were previously in Beatnik Beach, a short-lived funk pop outfit on Atlantic Records. Their debut single, 'The King Is Half Undressed', was a classy slice of retro-pop. Allied to their childlike dress sense, the formula guaranteed immediate television exposure. An album followed shortly after, which was assured and close to outright Beatles pastiche with strange overtones of Earth Opera. It was produced by Albhy Galuten, his first job since *Saturday Night Fever*. However, subsequent highly commercial singles, 'Baby's Coming Back', 'I Wanna Stay Home' and 'Now She Knows She's Wrong', failed to build on a strong chart platform. Jellyfish were more than happy to be able to play with at least two of their heroes, Ringo Starr and Brian Wilson, following introductions from Don Was. *Bellybutton* remains one of the more exciting debuts of the 90s and was followed in 1993 by the similarly crafted *Spilt Milk*. More complex arrangements and sometimes breathtaking harmonies showed definite influences of 10cc, Queen and Badfinger. The line-up in 1993 included Eric Dover (guitar), who replaced Falkner, and Tim Smith (bass), who took over from Chris Manning. The band collapsed shortly afterwards. Falkner formed the Greys, who lasted for only one album, before working with Eric Matthews and releasing an excellent solo album. Manning and Dover formed Imperial Drag in 1996.

● ALBUMS: *Bellybutton* (Virgin 1991)★★★★, *Spilt Milk* (Virgin 1993)★★★★.

Jennings, Will

b. 27 June 1944, Kilgore, East Texas, USA. Jennings moved to Tyler when he was 12 and at that time took up the trombone as he had become fascinated with traditional jazz. He is one of the leading lyric writers of the 80s and 90s, best known for his work with the Crusaders, B.B. King, Jimmy Buffett and Steve Winwood. As a teenager Jennings played guitar in rock bands, the most notable was Blue Mountain Marriage. He then became a literature teacher at the University of Wisconsin, Eau Claire. He moved to Nashville in 1971 and co-wrote four songs with Troy Seals for Dobie Gray's *Drift Away*. During the 70s he composed further material for country artists but had his first pop success co-writing with Richard Kerr. Together they composed 'Somewhere In The Night' for Barry Manilow and 'I Know I'll Never Love This Way Again' and 'No Night So Long' for Dionne Warwick. Next, Jennings forged a partnership with Joe Sample of the Crusaders to create the big hits 'Street Life' and 'One Day I'll Fly Away', recorded by Randy Crawford. He continued to write with Sample and B.B. King used their songs for three albums, *Midnight Believer*, *Take It Home* and *There's Always One More Time*. One of his biggest selling pop-soul ballads, however, was 'Didn't We Almost Have It All', co-written with Michael Masser for Whitney Houston. Jennings' most fruitful long-lasting collaboration has been with Winwood, whom he met in 1981 following an introduction by Chris Blackwell. Their first success together was the US hit 'While You See A Chance', from *Arc Of A Diver*. Jennings co-composed a number of tracks from that album. He subsequently wrote the lyrics for many tracks on all further Winwood solo albums, including the hymn-like 'There's A River', 'Talking Back To The Night', 'And I Go', 'Back In The High Life', 'I Will Be Here', 'Valerie' and the US hit singles, 'Higher Love' (1986) and 'Roll With It' (1988). He met country star Jimmy

Buffett in 1982 and wrote two albums with him *Riddle In The Sand* and *Last Mango In Paris*. The anthem of the movie *An Officer And A Gentleman* 'Up Where We Belong' was written with Buffy Saint-Marie and was a worldwide hit for Joe Cocker and Jennifer Warnes and is Jenning's most lucrative copyright. He received a BMI Award with Eric Clapton for 'Tears In Heaven' in 1996. He also struck up a friendship and musical partnership with Roy Orbison, writing a number of songs including 'Wild Hearts Run Out Of Time' from the Nic Roeg movie *Insignificance*. Hits and Academy and BAFTA Awards continued into the 90s as Jennings was commissioned to write songs for movies and established artists. In 1998, he co-wrote (with James Horner) Celine Dion's chart-topping 'My Heart Will Go On', the theme tune to the phenomenally successful *Titanic*. His success is now self-perpetuating and he is one of the most sought-after writers of the past two decades. Jennings is humble about working with talented musicians like Winwood and Sample and yet he paints their music with colourful romantic lyrics. In 1996, he collaborated with Winwood again and spent time working in Ireland with Paul Brady. Jennings states 'a great piece of (popular) music is so important, it deserves the very best I can write to it'. All this is maintained with a down-to-earth attitude, painful modesty, a love of flat caps, British poetry and literature.

Jesus Jones

Blending the driving force of punk guitar with liberal use of samples and dance music rhythms, Jesus Jones made an audacious debut with the single 'Info-Freako'. The song was voted into the Top 10 year-end charts of all the UK music papers. Singer and songwriter Mike Edwards (b. 22 June 1964, London, England) was joined in the line-up by Gen (b. Simon Matthews, 23 April 1964, Devizes, Wiltshire, England; drums), Al Jaworski (b. 31 January 1966, Plymouth, Devon, England; bass), Jerry De Borg (b. 30 October 1963, London, England; guitar) and Barry D (b. Iain Richard Foxwell Baker, 29 September 1965, Carshalton, Surrey, England; keyboards). The band was formed in London, early in 1988, and was signed soon afterwards by Food Records. *Liquidizer* was an energetic debut that provided further UK hits with 'Never Enough' and 'Bring It On Down'. *Doubt*, produced mainly by Edwards, saw the band inject a stronger commercial element. After six weeks at the top of the US alternative chart it entered the *Billboard* chart and in the UK it reached number 1. In the summer of 1991 the band, who had always kept up a busy live schedule, became part of a nucleus of young UK bands enjoying hits in the USA. 'Right Here, Right Now' and 'Real, Real, Real' both broke into the US Top 5, and along with EMF, who many claim were stylistically indebted to Jesus Jones, they found their abrasive pop suddenly highly popular within the USA's generally conservative market. Further domestic success followed with 'International Bright Young Thing' (number 7) and 'The Devil You Know' (number 10), before a fall-off in their popularity highlighted by the poor chart returns afforded *Perverse*. A four-year gap preceded the poorly received *Already*, with the album offering little of interest to attract new fans.

● ALBUMS: *Liquidizer* (Food 1989)★★★, *Doubt* (Food/SBK 1991)★★★, *Perverse* (Food/SBK 1993)★★, *Already* (Food 1997)★★.

● VIDEOS: *Big In Alaska* (PMI 1991).

Jesus Lizard

Formed in 1989, the Jesus Lizard originally comprised David Yow (vocals), David Sims (bass) - both formerly of the Austin, Texas act Scratch Acid - and Duane Denison (guitar), with the help of a drum machine. *Pure*, their abbreviated debut, maintained the uncompromising style of their former incarnation with its ponderous basslines, growled vocals and crashing guitar. The set was produced by Steve Albini (ex-Big Black), with whom Sims had worked in the controversially named Rapeman. Albini engineered and co-produced *Head*, on which the Jesus Lizard were joined by drummer Mac McNeilly. The band's sound remained as powerful and compulsive as ever, although some critics detected an artistic impasse. Jesus Lizard would join Nirvana on a joint single that broke the UK charts, but *Down* saw the band maintain a ferocity that deemed them very much a secular concern. They planned to expand their fanbase by signing to Capitol Records in 1995, but both *Shot* and *Blue* showed little sign of compromise. The band's strength is as an exciting live act, with frontman Yow as a formidable singer and showman.

● ALBUMS: *Pure* mini-album (Touch & Go 1989)★★★, *Head* (Touch & Go 1990)★★★, *Goat* (Touch & Go 1991)★★★, *Liar* (Touch & Go 1992)★★★, *Show* (Collision Arts/Giant 1994)★★★, *Down* (Touch & Go 1994)★★★, *Shot* (Capitol 1996)★★★, *Blue* (Capitol 1998)★★★.

Jewel

b. Jewel Kilcher, 23 May 1974, Payson, Utah, USA. Singer-songwriter Jewel was raised in Homer, Alaska, but left her home at the age of 16 to study opera in Michigan, Illinois. She then joined her mother in her Volkswagen van mobile home in San Diego, California. At that time Jewel first began to sing professionally at the Innerchange coffee shop, an establishment serving the local surfing community. These concerts quickly attracted a strong local following, and inevitably drew the attendance of several major label A&R staff. There were also early indications of her sense of humour - notably a popular on-stage imitation of Dolores O'Riordan of the Cranberries. Warner Brothers Records won her signature, leading to the release of her February 1995 debut album, *Pieces Of You*. A low-key release, Jewel promoted it with a tour of west coast coffee houses and the release of the album's strongest track, 'Who Will Save Your Soul', as a single. Her first major exposure followed in May with an appearance on the syndicated *Late Night With Conan O'Brien* television show. She subsequently made frequent appearances in the tabloid gossip columns through her on-off relationship with actor Sean Penn (formerly Madonna's husband). Penn, keen to launch himself as a director, later directed the video to Jewel's second single release, 'You Were Meant For Me', which became one of the most successful singles in US chart history. As the album's sales profile began to increase, Jewel was offered the lead in a TNT benefit production of *The Wizard Of Oz*. However, a tour with former Bauhaus singer Peter Murphy was less well-received ('I wanted to kill myself after every show', she later told *Rolling Stone* magazine). She also performed one show in Detroit where the assembled audience were convinced they were there to see the similarly-named Death Row Records rapper, Jewell. Despite this, further television exposure on programmes such as *The Tonight Show With Jay Leno* and *Entertainment Tonight* ensured that *Pieces Of You* eventually achieved gold status. She also signed a $2 million dollar pub-

lishing deal with Harper Collins. Her book of poetry, *A Night Without Armor*, sold over two million copies in America alone. *Spirit*, her eagerly awaited follow-up album, was recorded with veteran producer and Madonna collaborator Patrick Leonard. The album debuted at US number 3 in December 1998, and included the Top 10 single 'Hands'. The following year the singer made her acting debut in Ang Lee's acclaimed civil war drama, *Ride With The Devil*. She also released the seasonal *Joy*.

● ALBUMS: *Pieces Of You* (Atlantic 1995)★★★★, *Spirit* (Atlantic 1998)★★★, *Joy: A Holiday Collection* (Atlantic 1999)★★★.
● FURTHER READING: *A Night Without Armor*, Jewel. *Scrapbook*, Jewel.
● FILMS: *Ride With The Devil* (1999).

Jive Bunny And The Mastermixers

A throwback to the medley craze of the early 80s, with a similarly repetitive disco beat cushioning the samples, Jive Bunny were single handedly responsible for making recent generations believe that rock and pop classics of yesteryear are only 10 seconds long. A UK production/mixing group comprising John Pickles and disc jockey Ian Morgan, they became UK chart-toppers with their first three singles 'Swing The Mood', 'That's What I Like', and 'Let's Party' during 1989. The idea was conceived by Pickles, previously the owner of an electrical shop. The concept for 'Swing The Mood' had originally come from an ex-miner living in Norway called Les Hemstock. John's son Andy Pickles also helped out. They also appeared on 'It Takes Two Baby', by DJs Liz Kershaw and Bruno Brookes in December 1989. Subsequent hits scored progressively lower chart placings, doubtless to the relief of many. 'That Sounds Good To Me' (number 4), 'Can Can You Party' (number 8), 'Let's Swing Again' (number 19) and 'The Crazy Party Mixes' (number 13) completed their run of Top 20 chart entries. They have subsequently disappeared up their own bobtails, although Pickles became highly successful as head of Music Factory, which controls a number of dance music labels such as Trax, Defcon and Energize.

● ALBUMS: *Jive Bunny - The Album* (Telstar 1989)★★★, *It's Party Time* (Telstar 1990)★★, *Christmas Party* (Crimson 1998)★★, *Hop Around The Clock* (Global 1998)★★.
● COMPILATIONS: *The Best Of ...* (Music Collection 1995)★★★.

Jodeci

Among the more eloquent practitioners of 'new jack swing' or swingbeat, Jodeci enjoyed huge success in the USA during the 90s. The band was formed by two pairs of brothers: Joel 'JoJo' (b. 10 June 1971, Charlotte, North Carolina, USA) and Cedric 'K-Ci' Hailey (b. 2 September 1969, Charlotte, North Carolina, USA), and 'Mr' Dalvin and Donald 'DeVante Swing' DeGrate Jnr. The latter was responsible for most of their writing and production. Jodeci began their musical career by harmonizing in their local Tiny Grove, North Carolina church services. They signed to prominent swingbeat stable Uptown Records in 1991, and the initial results were impressive. Their silky, soulful vocals were stretched over sparse hip-hop beats to produce a debut album that was at once tough and elegant. It sold two million copies and earned Jodeci numerous accolades. 'Come & Talk To Me' reached number 11 on the US charts in 1992. *Diary Of A Mad Band*, much in the vein of their debut, also went multi-platinum, and earned them an appearance on MTV's *Unplugged* showcase - a rare recognition afforded a band working in their territory. 'Lately', a live recording from the show, was a number 1 R&B single and reached number 4 on the pop charts in summer 1993. For 1995's third album the band slightly altered their musical backdrop, adopting the G-funk beats made prevalent by Dr. Dre and his various acolytes. However, this softer, more resonant sound was once again subordinate to their dynamic sense of harmony. K-Ci And JoJo were featured on 2Pac's US number 1 single 'How Do U Want It' in June 1996, before breaking away on their own as a successful chart act.

● ALBUMS: *Forever My Lady* (Uptown/MCA 1991)★★★, *Diary Of A Mad Band* (Uptown/MCA 1993)★★★, *The Show, The After Party, The Hotel* (Uptown/MCA 1995)★★★.

Joey Negro

b. David Lee, Essex, England. A highly prolific remixer, producer and artist, and champion of the garage/disco revival, Lee is often labelled by the UK media as England's answer to Masters At Work. Lee can trace his heritage back to M-D-Emm in the late 80s. He is a fanatical record collector who, during the 90s, worked extensively with DJ Andrew 'Doc' Livingstone, latterly as the Hedboys. Lee's career began in the late 80s at the Republic Records label, where he was taught the art of remixing by a friend. Together with Mark Ryder, he produced a number of cuts for the same label, using production team names ranging from Quest For Excellence to Masters Of The Universe. However, he ran into trouble when he created the persona Kid Valdez of Mystique. Under that name they mixed the club hit 'Forver Together' as Raven Maize. The track was licensed to an American label, but when the single was topped the dance charts journalist tried to hunt down Mr. Maize. He was of course totally fictional, the figure on the cover having been scanned in and adapted from an old rap record. Lee also licensed tracks to Republic, including several house classics, and compiled the Garage Sound Of New York/Chicago series. From this point on Lee picked up the Negro moniker, his most well-known and successful, and began to establish an identity as a talented disco remixer. His own material reflects the tastes of his record collection: a penchant for US labels like Prelude and West End, 70s funk, jazz fusion and disco. Joey Negro's 1993 debut included a version of the Gibson Brothers' 'Oooh What A Life', featuring Gwen Guthrie. The album was released on Virgin Records, to whom Negro was briefly affiliated. He has subsequently issued material on his own Z Records imprint. Club hits such as 'Can't Get High Without You' (featuring Taka Boom on vocals) and 'Universe Of Love' helped spearhead the disco/house revival, alongside a plethora of material under aliases such as Doug Willis, Z-Factor, Foreal People, Sunburst Band, Mistura, Agora, the Hedboys, Raw Essence and Swingtime Dee. As well as enjoying commercial success with some of these incarnations, Lee is also an in-demand remixer, working with artists such as Take That ('Relight My Fire'), M People, Pet Shop Boys, Lisa Stansfield, Brand New Heavies, Blaze and Crystal Waters among others.

● ALBUMS: *Universe Of Love* (Virgin 1993)★★★.
● COMPILATIONS: *Joey Negro: Can't Get High Without You* (Azuli 1999)★★★★.

Johnston, Freedy

b. Kansas, USA. Johnston, a critically acclaimed singer and songwriter whose music defies easy categorization, made his debut for Bar/None Records in 1990 with the Chris Butler-produced *The Trouble Tree*. An accomplished record, highlighted by the artist's succinct lyrics and able characterization of his subjects, it received positive reviews throughout the US underground. *Can You Fly* was better still. The opening line: 'Well I sold the dirt to feed the band', was clearly autobiographical, the singer having pawned his family farm to raise money for the studio recording. The results of this investment were impressive, Johnston raising the standard of his still emotive songwriting to produce a succession of neat, charming pop songs. It won him significant praise and a major label recording contract with Elektra Records. *This Perfect World* was produced by Butch Vig and, while lacking some of the irreverent exuberance of *Can You Fly*, again won critical plaudits. *Never Home* and *Blue Days Black Nights* further consolidated Johnston's reputation as one of the most original singer-songwriters of the 90s. His thought provoking and often oblique lyrics are balanced by his high, innocent sounding voice.

● ALBUMS: *The Trouble Tree* (Restless/Bar/None 1990)★★★, *Can You Fly* (Bar/None 1992)★★★★, *This Perfect World* (Elektra 1994)★★★, *Never Home* (Elektra 1997)★★★★, *Blue Days Black Nights* (Elektra 1999)★★★.

Joi

Long before the fashion for Asian-influenced dance music took off in the mid- to late 90s, Farook and Haroon Shamsher (d. 8 July 1999) were fusing the sounds of traditional Bengali music with hip-hop and contemporary dance styles. In the mid-80s, they were part of a youth movement in east London called Joi Bangla, which aimed to promote various aspects of Bengali culture. Wishing to concentrate on the music side, the brothers formed a sound system with the same name and began playing around local community centres. At the same time they wrote their own material and in 1988 recorded a promo, 'Taj Ma House' (BPM Records), which coincided with the acid house movement. As they continued to write, they produced DATs that they played out on the sound system, with additional live percussion and samples, in the same way as dub plates. In 1992, they released 'Desert Storm' on Rhythm King Records as Joi, which was also the name of a club night they hosted the following year that ran weekly at London's Bass Clef. Over the next few years they continued to play their own material, and tracks recorded by like-minded artists, as the Joi sound system at various clubs and parties, including Bar Rumba, the Big Chill, Megatripolis, Ministry Of Sound and Return To The Source. They developed a live act and performed at such events as Tribal Gathering, Whirl-Y-Gig and WOMAD, as well as others around Europe. In October 1996, the *Bangladesh* EP was released on Nation Records to raise awareness of disastrous Western interference in that country's affairs. 'High Times' and 'Nargin' are typical of their unique, melodic sound, which blends Asian and Middle Eastern sounds with various styles of dance music without adhering to any one in particular. In 1998, they contributed a remix of Nusrat Fateh Ali Khan's 'Sweet Pain' to the tribute album *Star Rise*, and signed to Real World Records, releasing their debut album at the end of the year.

They also contributed tracks to a large number of compilations, notably 'Goddess' on Sony's *Eastern Uprising* (1997), 'India' on Zip Dog's *Global Explorer* (1997) and 'Shanti' on Law And Auder's *Further East* (1998). Their highly influential sound system helped promote their fusion ethic regardless of trends within the music industry. Over the years the duo worked with various other artists and DJs, including Asian Dub Foundation, Athletico, Mixmaster Morris, Plaid and Spring Heel Jack. Tragically, Haroon Shamsher died of a heart attack in July 1999.

● ALBUMS: *One And One Is One* (Real World 1998)★★★★.

Jonathan Fire*eater

The members of Jonathan Fire*eater - Stewart Lupton (b. 1975, Washington DC, USA; vocals), Walter Martin (b. Washington DC, USA; organ), Paul Maroon (b. Washington DC, USA; guitar), Matt Barrick (b. Washington DC, USA; drums) and Tom Frank (b. Washington, DC, USA; bass) - began playing together as a punk outfit. In 1995 they transplanted to a one-bedroom apartment in New York City in the hope that the city's atmosphere would be more receptive to their fusion of garage-rock sounds with smart suits and bohemian overtones. Within a year the quintet was playing to thousand-strong houses and comparisons with everyone from Smokey Robinson to Nick Cave were flying around. A succession of independently released singles, dominated by Lupton's intensity and Martin's atmospheric keyboard lines, attracted major label interest and they were among the first signings to DreamWorks Records in the USA. There was initial suspicion in the UK, where post-Goth 'suit' bands were ten a penny, but the band's live set and debut releases soon won over the critics.

● ALBUMS: *Tremble Under Boom Lights* mini-album (Deceptive 1997)★★★, *Wolf Songs For Lambs* (Deceptive 1997)★★★.

Jordan, Montell

b. Los Angeles, California, USA. Montell Jordan made a huge impact in both the US and UK charts in 1995 with the runaway success of his Def Jam Records' single 'This Is How We Do It'. Utilising a sample from Slick Rick, this celebration of life in South Central, Los Angeles, struck a chord with both hip-hop fans and modern R&B audiences. Within weeks of release it entered the US R&B Top 10 and then the pop charts, preceding a debut album of the same title. This included several B.B. King samples and a guest rap from Coolio on the excellent 'Payback'. The lyrics also diverged somewhat from typical Californian swing subjects - 'Daddy's Home' addressing the importance of black fatherhood in the ghettos. He attributes his development in an otherwise hostile environment to the rare presence of both a father and mother as he grew up. Rather than running with the gangs in the 'South Central 'hood', Jordan attended both church and school regularly, eventually graduating from Pepperdine University in Malibu with a degree in Organisational Communication. However, his growing interest in music eventually diverted him from a projected career in law. Jordan has built on the success of *This Is How We Do It* with a series of stylish urban R&B collections. The title track to *Let's Ride*, featuring No Limit Records stars Master P and Silkk The Shocker, reached US number 6 in April 1998. The follow-up, 'I Can Do That', climbed to number 14 in September. Jordan returned to the charts in

November 1999, with his new collection *Get It On ... Tonite*.

● ALBUMS: *This Is How We Do It* (Def Jam 1995)★★★, *More* (Def Jam 1996)★★, *Let's Ride* (Def Jam 1998)★★★, *Get It On ... Tonite* (Def Soul 1999)★★★.

Joseph, Martyn

b. July 1960, Cardiff, Wales. Joseph's first abiding passion was golf and it was only when he realised a professional career was not on the cards that he started paying serious attention to the songs he had been writing since the age of 12. He began to build up a loyal following with his sensitive, often spiritual brand of folky AOR, selling 30,000 copies of his self-financed debut, mostly at gigs. Epic Records saw the commercial potential and signed him in 1992. It was an unfashionable move, which Joseph compounded with rather superior sniping about the commercial pop (such as Mr. Blobby) which sold better than his own 'grown-up' music, although he did enjoy an unexpected UK Top 40 single that year with 'Dolphins Make Me Cry'. Joseph was well-received on support slots with artists such as Celine Dion, Joan Armatrading and Chris De Burgh, but, unable to make a real commercial breakthrough, he was dropped by his record company in 1996. Undeterred, Joseph played a number of Christian concerts, including the Greenbelt Festival and then had the last laugh when *Full Colour Black And White* started getting the commercial acclaim that his Epic material had missed. By the end of the decade he had reactivated his own label, the first release on which was *Far From Silent*.

● ALBUMS: *An Aching And A Longing* (Shark 1989)★★★, *Being There* (Epic 1992)★★★, *Martyn Joseph* (Epic 1995), *Full Colour Black And White* (Riff 1996)★★★, *Tangled Souls* (Grapevine 1998)★★★, *Far From Silent* (Pipe 1999)★★★.

Judge Jules

b. Julius O'Rearden, 26 October 1965, London, England. Jules has become one of the UK's leading remixers and is among the DJing jet-set. In the UK's *DJ* magazine's Top 100 DJ's of 1998, he was voted number 3, after Paul Oakenfold and Carl Cox. He was given the Judge prefix by Norman Jay during the mid-80s' house/rare groove scene, at which time he was studying law at the London School Of Economics. He proved exceedingly useful when police raided parties, confusing officers in legal jargon while his friends extinguished their herbal cigarettes. Together with Jay (nicknamed Shake And Finger Pop, while Jules was Family Funktion) they performed at about 30 warehouse parties between 1984 and 1987. He earned a living from buying up rare house records on trips to America and bringing them back to England to sell at exorbitant prices. As house turned to acid house, he remained a prominent figure in the rave scene, playing at many of the larger events like Evolution, Sunrise and World Dance, after which he earned his first remixing credits. The clients included Soft House Company, Fat Men, Big Audio Dynamite and, bizarrely, the Stranglers. In 1991, he re-aquainted himself with an old school-friend, Rollo. They set up a studio together, and learned to produce and engineer properly, an aspect they'd previously bluffed their way through. A studio was slowly established in the basement of his house, before he teamed up with ex-reggae drummer Michael Skins. By remixing a devastating version of M People's 'Excited' in 1992 the team was established, with guesting musicians such as guitarist Miles Kayne adding to the musical melting pot. Having set up Tomahawk Records, Jules has gone on record his own work. These have included Datman (licensed to ffrr Records), the All Stars ('Wanna Get Funky', which sampled Andrew Lloyd Webber's *Jesus Christ Superstar*) and 290 North ('Footsteps'), as well as guest appearances from ex-KLF singer Maxine Hardy (Icon's 'I Can Make You Feel So Good') and ex-O'Jays singer Ronnie Canada ('Heading For Self-Destruction'). Other remixes have included T-Empo's handbag house classic 'Saturday Night, Sunday Morning' , Melanie Williams ('Everyday Thing'), B.T. Express ('Express'), Jeanie Tracy ('Is This Love'), Our Tribe ('Love Come Home'), plus the big money-spinners Doop ('Doop') and Reel 2 Real ('I Like To Move It'). He can practically write his own cheque for remixing engagements now, of which he is offered at least 10 a week. Jules has since become a head A&R man for Manifesto Records and one of the world's most in-demand DJs. He also records two radio shows a week for Radio 1. Jules won the 1999 Best British DJ accolade at the 1999 *Muzik* magazine's awards, and was voted number 4 in the UK's *DJ* magazine's Top 100 DJs in the world.

● COMPILATIONS: with Pete Tong *Dance Nation 3* (MOS 1997)★★★★, *Classics* (MOS 1997)★★★★, with Tong *Clubbers Guide* (MOS 1998)★★★, with Tong *Ibiza Annual* (MOS 1998)★★★, with Tall Paul *The Ibiza Annual* (MOS 1999)★★★, *Clubber's Guide To Ibiza* (MOS 1999)★★★, with Tall Paul *The Annual - Millennium Edition* (MOS 1999)★★★, *Clubber's Guide To 2000 - Judge Jules* (MOS 2000)★★★★.

Junior Boy's Own Records

This label was founded in 1992 by Steven Hall and Terry Farley (who records with Pete Heller and Gary Wilkinson as Fire Island) from the ashes of Boy's Own Records, which they had formed in 1990 with Andrew Weatherall. Junior Boy's Own became one of the most important independent dance music labels of the 90s, with strong releases from the Ballistic Brothers, Black Science Orchestra, the Dust Brothers (who later became the Chemical Brothers), Underworld, X-Press 2 and others. Among their first singles were Fire Island's 'In Your Bones' and 'Fire Island', Black Science Orchestra's 'Where Were You', Known Chic's 'Dance' and Outrage's 'That Piano Track'. During the same period Underworld released two early singles, 'Big Mouth' and 'Dirty', as Lemon Interupt. In 1993, the label signed the Dust Brothers on the strength of their track 'Song To The Siren', which, with its reliance on prominent hip-hop beats, helped to kick off the movement that became known as big beat. After more singles from Fire Island ('There But For The Grace Of God'), Roach Motel ('Movin' On', 'Transatlantic'), Underworld ('Spikee'/'Dogman Go Woof', 'Dark And Long') and X-Press 2 ('Rock 2 House'/'Hip Housin''), Junior Boy's Own achieved widespread success in 1994 with their first album release, Underworld's *Dubnobasswithmyheadman*. Their compilation *Junior Boy's Own Collection* was followed by the Ballistic Brothers' *London Hooligan School*, Underworld's *Second Toughest In The Infants* and Black Science Orchestra's *Walter's Room*. At the same time they have continued to release a number of hit singles, notably Underworld's 'Born Slippy', Fire Island's 'If I Should Need A Friend' and the Farley And Heller Project's 'Ultra Flava'. In 1998, the label changed their name to JBO (encompassing Underworld and Sycamore) when they signed a deal with Virgin Records' dance subsidiary V2. With their roots in the

Balearic movement, Junior Boy's Own has always had an array of sounds: such artists as the Dust Brothers, Underworld and, more recently, Sycamore have blended a broad range of influences in their music to make what could sometimes only be loosely described as dance music.

Jurassic 5

One of the hip-hop underground's leading lights, this six-piece crew was formed in 1993 at the Los Angeles, California venue Good Life. Rappers Chali 2na, Akil, Zaakir, Mark 7even, and turntable maestros DJ Nu-Mark and DJ Cut Chemist (b. Lucas McFadden) came together from two separate crews, the Rebels And Rhythm and Unity Committee. They debuted for TVT Records in 1995 with the 'Unified Rebelution' single. Their position at the head of the late 90s new wave of underground rap, alongside artists including Company Flow, Black Star and Dr. Octagon, was confirmed when the *Jurassic 5* EP was released in December 1997. The nine tracks were concise and razor sharp in comparison to the bloated epics being released by the rap mainstream, and the EP was immediately hailed as one of the decade's most important hip-hop releases. The tracks harked back to the old school attitude of New York's Native Tongues Posse, the seminal late 80s coalition of artists including De La Soul, the Jungle Brothers and A Tribe Called Quest who reaffirmed rap's social agenda. This was evident on the manifesto-defining 'Concrete Schoolyard' ('Let's take it back to the concrete streets/Original beats from real live MCs'), which even provided the troupe with a surprise UK Top 40 single when it reached number 35 in November 1998. The other stand-out track, 'Jayou', was built around a hypnotic flute loop from Bob Marley's 'Get Up, Stand Up'. Cut Chemist and Chali 2na also record with the Latin funk/hip-hop crew Ozomatli, while Chemist collaborated with Shortkut from Invisibl Skratch Piklz on 1998's jaw dropping *Live At Future Primitive Sound Session*.

● ALBUMS: *Jurassic 5* (Rumble/Pan 1997)★★★★.

Juvenile

b. Terius Gray. This highly talented New Orleans, Louisiana, USA-based rapper earned his name from a youth spent on the streets. He originally made his mark on the southern underground scene in the early 90s as part of the trio 3Grand, before signing a short-term solo deal with Warlock Records, who released 1995's *Being Myself*. His big break came when he signed to the pioneering New Orleans underground label, Cash Money Records. Cash Money, like the city's other leading label, Master P's No Limit Records, was responsible for establishing southern rap as a viable alternative to the east coast/west coast domination of the late 90s hip-hop scene. Juvenile's sophomore set, 1996's *Soljah Rags*, was one of the albums responsible for Cash Money's success, selling over 200,000 copies without any mainstream exposure and helping to alert major labels to southern hip-hop. The in-house production team's seamless G-funk beats provided the perfect backdrop for Juvenile to demonstrate his peerless technical ability and mastery of various styles. The following year he teamed up with label mates B.G., Lil Wayne and Young Turk as the Hot Boy$ on the highly popular *Get It How U Live!!* In 1998, he released his third set, *400 Degreez*, an album which eventually reaped the benefits of Cash Money's lucrative distribution deal with Universal

Records, climbing steadily to a peak position of US number 9 the following September. The album, which featured Mannie Fresh's usual high production standards and guest appearances from the Hot Boy$ and the Big Tymer$, was also helped by the radio success of the tracks 'Ghetto Children' and 'Ha'. Juvenile's early albums were reissued in 1999, while *400 Degreez* was joined in the US Top 10 by the sophomore Hot Boy$ collection, *Guerrilla Warfare*.

● ALBUMS: *Being Myself* (Warlock 1995)★★★, *Soljah Rags* (Cash Money 1996)★★★★, *400 Degreez* (Cash Money/Universal 1998)★★★★.

K-Ci And JoJo

Cedric Hailey (b. 2 September 1969, Charlotte, North Carolina, USA) and Joel Hailey (b. 10 June 1971, Charlotte, North Carolina, USA). The Hailey brothers were founder members of Jodeci, the sexually provocative swingbeat outfit who enjoyed several US chart hits during the mid-90s, including 'Come & Talk To Me', 'Lately' and 'Cry For You'. The duo featured prominently on 2Pac's number 1 single 'How Do U Want It' in June 1996, before breaking away from Jodeci with the release of their debut single, 'How Could You'. *Love Always*, released in June 1997, was a strong collection of modern R&B songs, which showcased the brothers' superb voices and lyrical nous. The album, which reached the US Top 10 and went multi-platinum, included April 1998's chart-topping single 'All My Life'. The duo repeated the debut album's winning formula on 1999's *It's Real*, mixing sultry ballads that dealt with highly emotional subject matter such as infidelity ('Fee Fie Foe Fum') and betrayal ('Makin' Me Say Goodbye'), with sexually charged dance numbers such as 'I Wanna Make Love To You'. The album went platinum within two weeks of release, and the single 'Tell Me It's Real' reached US number 2 in August.

● ALBUMS: *Love Always* (MCA 1997)★★★, *It's Real* (MCA 1999)★★★.

Kamoze, Ini

b. Cecil Campbell, 9 October 1957, Port Maria, St. Mary, Jamaica, West Indies. Although he enjoyed huge crossover success in the mid-90s, Kamoze was already a veteran on the reggae scene. His debut single 'World Affairs' was released in 1981. On the strength of this track and other singles he soon

became known as the Voice Of Jamaica. His reputation brought him to the attention of the Taxi Gang, led by Sly Dunbar and Robbie Shakespeare. In 1983, the duo produced *Ini Kamoze*, released through Island Records, which earned him international acclaim, but at the same time his local success faltered, as message music was becoming less popular in the dancehall. At the 1984 Jamaican Sunsplash, however, Kamoze appeared in the line-up on dancehall night, giving an impressive performance to an audience in the grip of DJ mania. The release of *Statement* followed in the same year, including the track 'Call The Police', which was included on the soundtrack of *Good To Go*. His debut performance in the UK was at the 1985 Reggae Sunsplash, as part of Sly And Robbie's showcase, which also featured Gregory Isaacs and Sugar Minott. His performance was greeted with enthusiasm and the tour was equally successful in Europe. *Pirate* did not enjoy the success of its predecessors, despite the inclusion of some notable tracks, including 'Betty Brown's Mother', 'Gunshot', a warning about the dangers of firearms, and 'Queen Of My House'. In the same year Kamoze toured with Yellowman, Half Pint and the Taxi Gang, including a show at the Town & Country Club that was recorded and released as *The Taxi Connection Live In London*. A condensed showcase of the tour was featured on the UK television music show *The Tube*. In 1987, Kamoze left the Taxi Gang and Island and began working with the One Two Crew, with whom he shared production duties on *Shocking Out*. He won new fans with his single 'Stress', featured on the one rhythm album *Selekta Showcase*, released on his own Selekta label. His work remained popular in reggae charts, and the compilation set *16 Vibes Of Ini Kamoze* enjoyed strong sales. The popular 'Stalag' rhythm found the singer winning dancehall approval with the hit 'Another Sound'. In the winter of 1994, he topped the US pop charts with 'Here Comes The Hotstepper', owing to its inclusion on the soundtrack of Robert Altman's *Prêt A Porter*. The song, which was originally recorded with Philip 'Fatis' Burrell for the *Stir It Up* compilation on Epic Records, was also a UK Top 5 hit in January 1995. The success of the single led to a contract with Elektra Records, for whom he released the hip-hop influenced *Lyrical Gangsta*. Subsequent singles for Burrell marked a welcome return to the dancehall style.

● ALBUMS: *Ini Kamoze* (Island 1983)★★★, *Statement* (Island 1984)★★★, *Pirate* (Island 1986)★★★, *Shocking Out* (Greensleeves 1987)★★★★, various artists *Selekta Showcase* (Selekta 1989)★★★★, *Lyrical Gangsta* (East West 1995)★★★.

● COMPILATIONS: *16 Vibes Of Ini Kamoze* (Sonic Sounds 1992)★★★, *Here Comes The Hotstepper* (Sony 1995)★★★★.

Kane And Abel

The half-Puerto Rican twin brothers, David (Kane) and Daniel Garcia (Abel), were born in the Bronx, New York, USA. Their parents died in a car accident shortly after they were born, after which the brothers relocated to New Orleans to live with their grandparents. They began rapping together as Double Vision, releasing the low-key *Keep Your Eyes Open* on Ionic Records in 1994. The brothers subsequently met up with female rapper Mia X, who introduced them to local hip-hop entrepreneur Master P. Signing a deal with his fledgling No Limit Records, the brothers released 1996's *The 7 Sins* under their new moniker, Kane And Abel. The album, as with all No Limit releases, featured production work by in-house engineers Mo B. Dick and KLC and guest appearances from labelmates including Master P and Mia X. One of the tracks, 'Gangstafied', was the first song they played to Master P at their demo sessions. The US Top 5 album *Am I My Brothers Keeper* followed in July 1998, and helped establish the brothers as among the leading artists in the No Limit stable. It was also one of the better products to emerge from the New Orleans gangsta rap scene, tempering the hardcore flow with some subtle lyrical and melodic turns. The Garcias left No Limit after the release of the album to set up their own Most Wanted imprint. *Rise To Power* was released in September 1999 by Elektra Records.

● ALBUMS: *The 7 Sins* (No Limit 1996)★★★, *Am I My Brothers Keeper* (No Limit 1998)★★★★, *Rise To Power* (Elektra 1999)★★★.

Kaplansky, Lucy

b. 2 February 1960, Chicago, Illinois, USA. Kaplansky's father was a professor of mathematics as well as an accomplished pianist, which gave his young daughter an equal grounding in academia and music. She became involved in the Chicago folk scene, and then moved up to New York in 1978 to catch the current folk revival. Kaplansky worked with another young singer, Shawn Colvin, but when the duo were offered a recording contract Kaplansky elected to study psychology. After gaining her doctorate, Kaplansky worked at St. Luke's Hospital in Manhattan with the mentally ill and homeless. She still found the time to appear on albums by Colvin (1989's *Steady On*), Nanci Griffith (1987's *Lone Star State Of Mind* and 1988's *Little Love Affairs*) and John Gorka, and worked with Suzanne Vega on the soundtrack to *Pretty In Pink*. Colvin returned the favour by producing Kaplansky's debut album, *The Tide*, which eventually appeared in 1994, although it had been recorded while she was still at graduate school. The burgeoning acclaim which greeted the album and the accomplished follow-up *Flesh And Bone* meant that, in January 1997, the singer had to relinquish her hospital job. She has developed into a fine singer-songwriter with folk and country roots, who still has a good line in cover versions, including the Police's 'Secret Journey' and Richard Thompson's 'When I Get To The Border' and 'Don't Renege On Our Love'. Kaplansky has also collaborated, on 1999's *Cry Cry Cry*, with fellow US singer-songwriters Dar Williams and Richard Shindell. Her third solo album featured only one cover version, Steve Earle's 'Somewhere Out There', alongside nine original songs composed by Kaplansky and her husband Rick Litvin.

● ALBUMS: *The Tide* (Red House 1994)★★★★, *Flesh And Bone* (Red House 1996)★★★★, with Richard Shindell, Dar Williams *Cry Cry Cry* (Razor & Tie 1999)★★★, *Ten Year Night* (Red House 1999)★★★★.

Kavana

b. Anthony Kavanagh, 4 November 1977, Manchester, England. A pop protégé developed by well-known entrepreneur Nigel Martin-Smith, who originally pieced together Take That, Kavana made his debut for Martin-Smith's Virgin Records-affiliated Nemesis label in 1996. His debut single, 'Crazy Chance', was written by former Take That member Howard Donald, though his second release and all bar one track of his subsequent debut album were self-penned. The smooth soul pop of 'Where Are You' provided typical boy-pop fare, with a quotient of street hipness lent by the production work of Joey Negro on the b-side, 'For The Very First

Time'. The a-side was produced by Phil Green, previously a collaborator with Carleen Anderson and the Brand New Heavies, who also worked on Kavana's album debut. Throughout 1996 Kavana built his profile by appearing on a number of British youth television shows and touring with Boyzone, and achieved UK Top 10 success the following year with a slick cover version of Shalamar's 'I Can Make You Feel Good' and 'MFEO'. He was voted Best Male Singer at 1997's *Smash Hits* Poll Winners' Party, before jetting off to Italy to record his second album with producers Absolute. 'Special Kind Of Something' debuted at number 13 in September 1998, but the Philly soul-styled 'Funky Love' stalled at number 32 in December.

● ALBUMS: *K* (Nemesis 1996)★★★, *Instinct* (Virgin 1999)★★.

Keb' Mo'

b. Kevin Moore, 3 October 1951, Los Angeles, California, USA. Although he was born on the west coast of America, Moore's parents came from Texas and Louisiana, instilling in him an appreciation of blues and gospel. At 21, his band were hired to back violinist Papa John Creach. Three years later, Moore was employed by Almo Music as contractor and arranger of the company's demo sessions. In 1980, he made an album for Chocolate City, a subsidiary of Casablanca Records, just before the label's collapse. He met veteran band leader Monk Higgins in 1983, joining the saxophonist's Whodunit Band on guitar and playing a residency at Marla's Memory Lane. In 1990, he was contacted by the Los Angeles Theater Center to play a blues guitarist in a play called *Rabbit Foot*, and he continued this line of work by becoming understudy to Chick Streetman in *Spunk*, adapted from the writings of Zora Neale Hurston. The nickname for his blues persona was given to him by drummer Quentin Dennard when Moore sat in with his jazz band. Dennard also backed him on his OKeh Records debut *Keb' Mo'*, an album that tempered its blues bias (reworkings of Robert Johnson's 'Come On In My Kitchen' and 'Kind Hearted Woman') with elements of folk and soul music. Keb' Mo' is adept at both electric and acoustic guitar styles, with a tasteful approach to the use of slide. These skills stood him in good stead when he portrayed Robert Johnson in *Can't You Hear The Wind Howl?*, a documentary-drama narrated by Danny Glover and including interviews with musicians and acquaintances who knew or were influenced by Johnson. *Just Like You* featured even more varied material, from the beautiful, feel-good pop/soul of 'More Than One Way Home' to the raw acoustic blues of 'Momma, Where's My Daddy', and some singer-songwriter material featuring Bonnie Raitt and Jackson Browne ('Just Like You'). Although it could be criticised for smoothing out any remaining rough edges, *Slow Down* was another highly impressive collection of contemporary blues material. Keb' Mo' is an exciting new talent with a voice that can melt hearts and make the listener shiver.

● ALBUMS: *Rainmaker* (Chocolate City 1981)★★, *Keb' Mo'* (OKeh 1994)★★★, *Just Like You* (OKeh 1996)★★★★, *Slow Down* (Epic 1998)★★★★.

Keith, Toby

b. 8 July 1961, Elk Town, Clinton, Oklahoma, USA. This highly popular honky tonk country artist grew up on an Oklahoma farm listening to his father's favourite, Bob Wills, and finding his own hero in Merle Haggard. He tested broncs and bulls for a rodeo during his summers in high school. Oil was found in Elk Town and Keith worked as a roughneck and then an operational manager. This experience inspired 'Boomtown', of which he says, 'The wells ran dry. The rich people got rich by saving their money. The fools who spent it were broke.' Keith formed the Easy Money Band, originally playing Alabama hits but then widening the repertoire as they accumulated new and better equipment. Keith recorded for independent labels before being signed to PolyGram Records by Harold Shedd, who produced his 1993 debut, *Toby Keith*. It included a tribute to the film stars of yesteryear, 'Should've Been A Cowboy', a number 1 country record that also became the anthem of the Dallas Cowboys football team. The album included further hits with 'Wish I Didn't Know Now', 'He Ain't Worth Missing' and 'A Little Less Talk And A Lot More Action'. *Billboard* named him the Top New Country Artist of 1993. The country chart-topper 'Who's That Man', included on his sophomore collection *Boomtown*, started as a joke: 'You know the old one that goes, "What do you get if you play country music backwards? Answer: your wife back, your dog back, your house back and your car back." I was kicking that idea round as a fun song when I hit upon the line, "Who's that man running my life?" It dawned on me that it would work better as a serious song.' In 1995, he released a sentimental seasonal album, *Christmas To Christmas*, which featured songs from the cream of Nashville's songwriters. The following year he had a major country hit with 'Does That Blue Moon Ever Shine On You' and released the bestselling *Blue Moon*. The following year's *Dream Walkin'*, produced by James Stroud, featured the hit single 'We Were In Love'. Keith subsequently followed Stroud to the DreamWorks label, contributing to *The Prince Of Egypt - Nashville* collection and releasing *How Do You Like Me Now?!*

● ALBUMS: *Toby Keith* (PolyGram 1993)★★★, *Boomtown* (PolyGram 1994)★★★, *Christmas To Christmas* (PolyGram 1995)★★, *Blue Moon* (A&M 1996)★★★★, *Dream Walkin'* (Mercury 1997)★★★★, *How Do You Like Me Now?!* (DreamWorks 1999)★★★.

● COMPILATIONS: *Greatest Hits Volume 1* (PolyGram 1998)★★★★.

● VIDEOS: *Video Collection* (PolyGram Music Video 1994).

Kelly, R.

b. Robert Kelly, Chicago, Illinois, USA. Urban R&B singer-songwriter and producer who first made an impact in 1991 with his band Public Announcement, and has since become one of America's most successful solo artists. Kelly grew up in the housing projects of Chicago's South Side, but channelled his energies away from fast money-making schemes and into long-term musicianship. He had a natural flair for most instruments, eventually becoming, more by accident than design, a useful busking act. It earned him a living, until constant police disruptions forced him to reconsider his employment. He put together the R&B outfit MGM, and went on to win a national talent contest on the *Big Break* television show, hosted by Natalie Cole. Unfortunately, that outfit's energy dissipated, and his next major break came when manager Barry Hankerson spotted him while auditioning for a play at the Regal Theatre in Chicago. He soon had Kelly acting as musical co-ordinator/producer for a slew of acts, including Gladys Knight, David Peaston, Aaliyah and the Hi-Five (who had a number 1 single, 'Quality Time', with Kelly at the controls). His diversity was confirmed with his

work with the Winans gospel family, notably a duet with Ronald Winans on 'That Extra Mile'. However, all this would be surpassed by the success of his second album, *12 Play*, which stayed on top of the R&B charts for nine weeks. Two bestselling singles were included on the set, 'Sex Me (Parts I & II)' and 'Bump 'N Grind' (US number 1/UK number 8). As if from nowhere, despite a long apprenticeship, Kelly seemed to have acquired the Midas touch. His third album eschewed the blatant sexuality of *12 Play*, attributed in part to his friendship with gospel singer Kirk Franklin (Kelly later confirmed that he had found God). The same year he wrote and produced the Grammy-nominated 'You Are Not Alone' for Michael Jackson. He also signed a contract to play with the Atlantic City Seagulls of the United States Basketball League (the sport is the other great love of his life). The Grammy Award-winning 'I Believe I Can Fly' became another massive international hit when it was featured as the theme for the 1997 movie *Space Jam*. The increasingly prolific Kelly, whose writing and production credits also include work for Whitney Houston and Boyz II Men, then released the sprawling double album *R*, which debuted at number 2 on the *Billboard* album chart in November 1998. The album was an ambitious and diverse set featuring contributions from Celine Dion (the US number 1 single 'I'm Your Angel'), Nas and Foxy Brown. The moving ballad 'If I Could Turn Back The Hands Of Time' later became a bestselling UK Top 5 hit.

● ALBUMS: with Public Announcement *Born Into The 90's* (Jive 1992)★★★, *12 Play* (Jive 1993)★★★★, *R. Kelly* (Jive 1995)★★★, *R* (Jive 1998)★★★★.

● VIDEOS: *12 Play-The Hit Videos Vol. 1* (Jive 1994), *Top Secret Down Low Videos* (6 West 1996)

Kenickie

One of a number of UK 'lo-fi' indie bands, Kenickie, named after a character in *Grease*, formed in August 1994 after Lauren Le Laverne (vocals), Marie Du Santiago (guitar) and Emmy-Kate Montrose (bass) left their convent school in Tyne And Wear, England. Drafting in Lauren's brother, Johnny Le Laverne, nicknamed X, as their drummer, they established the band as a means of staying in touch while they pursued courses in further education. By the mid-90s their demo tapes were receiving airplay from John Peel, leading to the release of their debut single, 'Cat Suit', on Slampt Records in April 1995. Their second release, the *Skillex* EP, followed on Fierce Panda Records. By 1996, they had been signed to Emidisc, the new major-backed label launched by Bob Stanley and Pete Wiggs of Saint Etienne with EMI Records A&R director, Tris Penna. The first single to result from the new contract was 'Punka', but the band showed a commendable indifference to music industry manners, turning down a cover feature for *Melody Maker* before its release because of fear of 'over-exposure'. *Kenickie At The Club* was a confident and punchy debut containing short, sharp, power-pop songs. An over ambitious follow-up attempted to broaden the band's musical base, but bypassed some of the charm of their debut in the process. The band announced they were splitting-up in October 1998. Montrose and Du Santiago subsequently formed Rosita.

● ALBUMS: *Kenickie At The Club* (EMI 1997)★★★, *Get In* (EMI 1998)★★★, *The John Peel Sessions* (Strange Fruit 1999)★★★.

Kennedy, Brian

b. 12 October 1966, Belfast, Northern Ireland. Having grown up in the notorious Falls Road district of Belfast where he played in his brother's band, singer-songwriter Kennedy relocated to London in 1985. Now hugely popular in his home country and beginning to make a serious impact throughout the rest of Europe, Kennedy originally launched his career in 1990 with a critically acclaimed solo album that topped the Irish charts. Kennedy then collaborated with ex-Fairground Attraction songwriter Mark Nevin as Sweetmouth, releasing one unsuccessful album. After being released from his contract, Kennedy flew to New Orleans and began travelling around the USA, employing his unusual, somewhat feminine vocals at bar-singing sessions. On his return, he became a regular associate and duettist with Van Morrison. This led to a recording contract, ironically with the same record label, RCA Records, which had dropped him a few years previously. As well as its Irish success, *A Better Man* also broke into the UK Top 20. Kennedy subsequently appeared with Ray Charles and Tina Turner, toured extensively, and worked with Eddi Reader. He also fine tuned the material for his new album, which was premiered by the single 'These Days', a duet with Ronan Keating of Boyzone.

● ALBUMS: *The Great War Of Words* (RCA 1990)★★★★, as Sweetmouth *Goodbye To Songtown* (RCA 1991)★★★, *A Better Man* (BMG 1996)★★★★, *Now That I Know What I Want* (BMG 1999)★★★.

Kennedys

A husband and wife team of Maura (b. Maura Boudreau, Syracuse, New York, USA) and Pete Kennedy (b. Washington, D.C., USA), the Kennedys play jangly folk-pop shot through with the influences of the Byrds and Beatles. The couple's first date came at Buddy Holly's grave in Lubbock, Texas, while their first gig was held in Liverpool as part of Nanci Griffith's Blue Moon Orchestra. Working in tandem, they discovered a shared love for American roots rock 'n' roll and British pop and folk rock. The Kennedys made a strong impression in 1995 with the release of their Green Linnet Records debut, *River Of Fallen Stars*. Pete Kennedy's exquisite Rickenbacker guitar tones gelled easily with his partner's sweet voice and her own rhythmic guitar playing. The album was largely written in Ireland while the duo toured as part of Nanci Griffith's band. Pete Kennedy had also formerly worked with Mary-Chapin Carpenter and before that with Kate Wolf, while his numerous solo albums have achieved massive local success in Washington, including the award of Artist Of The Year in 1992. Maura had formerly been a member of the Austin country group, the Delta Rays. *River Of Fallen Stars* drew excellent reviews - *Goldmine* magazine recommended the record as a 'nearly flawless amalgamation of the sort of ringing Byrdsy guitars and gorgeous floating harmonies that make a pure pop fan swoon'. For the follow-up collection, the duo envisaged a more 'straightforward record, a live band, with different musical personalities bouncing off each other'. *Life Is Large* succeeded in this goal with the help of a star-studded cast, including Roger McGuinn, Steve Earle, Nils Logfren, Charlie Sexton, John Gorka, the Dixie Hummingbirds, Peter Holsapple (formerly of the dB's) and Susan Cowsill. Despite this impressive cast, reviewers were not as sympathetic to the duo's efforts as had previously been the case, the UK's Q

magazine noting that the record 'never really gets into orbit and the cast of thousands can't add the weight of their experience'.

● ALBUMS: *River Of Fallen Stars* (Green Linnet/Redbird 1995)★★★★, *Life Is Large* (Green Linnet 1996)★★★, *Angel Fire* (Philo/Rounder 1998)★★★.

Kershaw, Sammy

b 24 February 1958, Kaplan, Louisiana, USA. This singer-songwriter is related to Doug Kershaw, which goes some way to explaining the strong Cajun feel to his work. Kershaw started playing country clubs when he was 12 years old, working with local musician J.B. Perry. During his eight years with Perry, they opened for George Jones and Ray Charles (years later he would duet with Jones on 'Never Bit A Bullet Like This'). He joined a local band, Blackwater, but after a few years, decided to leave the industry and help design shops for the Wal-Mart Corporation. Some of his early tracks were released in the USA in 1993 on a MTE album, *Sammy Kershaw*, that was designed to look like his current product. He was encouraged back into music by a contract with Mercury Records in 1990. Kershaw had his first country hit with 'Cadillac Style' and ended up as spokesman for their 1992 sales campaign. He courted controversy when he recorded 'National Working Women's Holiday' but he is well able to deal with hecklers, having once been a stand-up comic. He topped the US country charts with 'She Don't Know She's Beautiful' in 1993. He has been married three times and says, 'I'm a ballad-singing fool and I've lived all those songs at one time or another.' Following a greatest hits compilation, Kershaw released the disappointing *Politics, Religion And Her*, but bounced back with *Labor Of Love*.

● ALBUMS: *Don't Go Near The Water* (Mercury 1991)★★★, *Haunted Heart* (Mercury 1993)★★★, *Sammy Kershaw* (MTE 1993)★★, *Feelin' Good Train* (Mercury 1994)★★★, *Christmas Time's A Comin'* (Mercury 1994)★★, *Politics, Religion And Her* (Mercury 1996)★★, *Labor Of Love* (Mercury 1997)★★★, *Maybe Not Tonight* (Mercury 1999)★★★.

● COMPILATIONS: *The Hits Chapter 1* (Mercury 1995)★★★.

● VIDEOS: *The Hit Video Collection* (1994).

Ketchum, Hal

b. Hal Michael Ketchum, 9 April 1953, Greenwich, New York, USA. Ketchum credits his early influences as Buck Owens, Merle Haggard and Marty Robbins, but he was equally inspired by the novels of John Steinbeck. His early musical career included playing drums for an R&B band and guitar in a blues outfit. He then began to establish himself as a singer and songwriter, appearing at the Kerrville Folk Festival. In 1987, he recorded his self-produced, first album as Hal Michael Ketchum, which was initially only released in cassette form. In 1989, it was reissued on CD by the German Sawdust label. In 1991, Ketchum joined Curb Records where, with his grey hair, he could hardly be marketed as a new country act. *Past The Point Of Rescue*, however, produced the US country chart hits 'Small Town Saturday Night', 'Past The Point Of Rescue' and 'Somebody's Love'. His producer, Allen Reynolds, wrote the Vogues' 1965 US hit 'Five O'Clock World', and Ketchum worked up a new version of the song. *Sure Love* was a confident second album, including tributes to his working-class roots in 'Mama Knows The Highway' and 'Daddy's Oldsmobile'. He made a cameo appearance in the movie *Maverick* singing 'Amazing Grace', and became a member of the *Grand Ole Opry* in 1994. Ketchum tours with his band, the Alibis, and is touted by many to develop into a major country star. He says, 'I have a two hundred song catalogue which is, by Nashville standards, not a lot.' Ketchum also paints and writes children's stories, should his two-hundred song catalogue prove insufficient. *Hal Yes* was produced by Stephen Bruton and proved to be one of his finest albums.

● ALBUMS: *Threadbare Alibi* (Watermelon 1989)★★★, *Past The Point Of Rescue* (Curb 1991)★★★, *Sure Love* (Curb 1992)★★★, *Every Little Word* (Curb/Hit 1994)★★★, *Hal Yes* (Curb/Hit 1997)★★★★, *I Saw The Light* (Curb 1998)★★★, *Awaiting Redemption* (Curb 1999)★★★★.
● COMPILATIONS: *Hal Ketchum The Hits* (Curb 1996)★★★★.
● FILMS: *Maverick* (1994).

Khan, Nusrat Fateh Ali

b. 12 July 1948, Lyallpur (later renamed Faisalabad), Pakistan, d. 16 August 1997. One of the most popular singers to emerge from the Indian subcontinent, Khan predominantly sang qawwali, the music of devotional Sufism, but incorporated other forms including Khyal (traditional classical) to produce a unique style that appealed to followers of all religions. He performed with the Party, a group of highly trained Pakistani musicians which included several family members. In 1971, Nusrat took over from his father (Ustad Fateh Ali Khan) as leader of the Party after experiencing recurring dreams that he was singing at the famous Muslim shrine of Hazratja Khawaja Moid-Ud-Din Christie in Ajmer, India. This dream became reality eight years later. Through the 70s and 80s Khan's music began to become increasingly synonymous with India and Pakistan's vibrant film industry. Such was his popularity with the stars of the movies that in 1979 he was invited to sing at the wedding of Rishi, son of actor/director Raj Kapoor, in front of the most prominent members of the Bombay film industry. Peter Gabriel's admiration of Khan's singing led to him working with WOMAD on projects including a compilation album, many festival appearances and releases on the Virgin/Real World Records label, recorded in England. The first of these, *Shahen-Shah* was named after his Pakistani nickname, Shahen-Shah-e-Qawwali (The Brightest Star In Qawwali). For *Mustt Mustt*, Khan worked with experimental composer Michael Brook in an attempt to give his sound a Western orientation. On all but two tracks, traditional songs were replaced by classical vocal exercises which were edited around Western rhythms. Brook said of the project 'everyone was excited, although it wasn't painless - it worked'. A remix of the title track by Massive Attack led to a surprise UK club hit. Khan returned to his roots with *Shahbaaz*, four traditional qawwali songs all praising the Devine Beloved. Successive albums for Real World continued to see cross-experimentation between qawwali and Western influences, though none were as integrationist as *Mustt Mustt*. Despite this, the vibrancy of the artist's deeply spiritual performances, on record and stage, militated against the suspicion that he had forgotten his roots. His sudden death robbed the world of one of its finest voices.

● ALBUMS: *Shahen-Shah* (Real World 1989)★★, *Mustt Mustt* (Real World 1990)★★★★, *En Concert A Paris, Volumes 1 & 2* (Ocoro 1990)★★★, *En Concert A Paris, Volumes 3-5* (Ocoro 1990)★★★, *Shahbaaz* (Real World 1991)★★★, with Jan Garbarek *Ragas & Sagas* (ECM 1992)★★★, *Revelation* (Real World 1993)★★, *The Last Prophet* (Real World 1994)★★★, *Night Song* (Real World 1995)★★★, with Jaed Akhtar *Sangam* (EMI India 1997)★★★, with Michael Brook *Star Rise* (Real World 1997)★★★★.

Kid Capri

b. David Anthony Love, Bronx, New York, USA. Immersed in the burgeoning hip-hop culture of 70s uptown New York, Capri began seriously developing his skills as a DJ at the tender age of eight. He soon graduated to block parties and by 1976 landed a club gig at a venue called the Diplomat. By the time he began a residency at the legendary disco Studio 54, he was beginning to make his presence known on the wider music scene by taping his sets and selling them on 145th St. with his partner Starchild. Although underground tapes of hip-hop parties and live shows had been circulating around New York as long as there had been hip-hop events to record, Capri was largely responsible for elevating the mixtape to an art form in its own right, in the process realizing its potential as a powerful promotional tool. Starting with tapes of his live sets, then 'pause-tapes' that were essentially bootleg compilations of rare records, he was soon producing multi-tracked affairs that displayed the full creative potential of the DJ as editor and re-mixer. These efforts culminated in 1991's *The Tape*, a groundbreaking LP-as-mixtape released by Warner Brothers Records four years before Funkmaster Flex's *The Mixtape Volume 1*, as well as remix and production work for the likes of Heavy D, Grand Puba, Big L, and KRS-One. Throughout the next several years he maintained his profile as a celebrity DJ, beginning an eight-year stint as the DJ-in-residence for Russell Simmons' Def Comedy Jam and appearing in the 1993 movie *Who's The Man*. A long-standing connection with members of the Trackmasterz production crew lead to a prominent spot on the 1997 Puff Daddy And The Family world tour. This successful collaboration prompted Capri to switch from Warner Brothers to the Trackmasterz' label Columbia Records, for whom he put together his first proper album *Soundtrack To The Streets*, that featured a cross-section of rising stars (Jay-Z, Big Pun, Nas) and old school peers like Slick Rick and KRS-One.

● ALBUMS: *The Tape* (Cold Chillin'/Warners 1991)★★★, *Soundtrack To The Streets* (Columbia 1998)★★★★.

Kid Rock

b. Bob Ritchie, Romeo, Michigan, USA. Although his name has often been linked to the inner-city Detroit rap scene, Ritchie grew up in the overwhelmingly white suburb of Romeo, only venturing into the city proper as a teenager to attend rap concerts and talent shows. His early musical environment was a paradoxical mix of Midwest rock such as Bob Seger and the hip-hop and electro sounds accompanying the first national craze for breakdancing. After witnessing a DJ battle between Davy D and AJ Scratch on the Fresh Fest tour, young Ritchie was inspired to try his hand at DJing, ruining his mother's phonograph in the process. His continued efforts as a rapper and DJ led to basement parties and criminal mischief in the black neighbourhoods of nearby Mt. Clemens. It was at this stage that he adopted the name Kid Rock, although it is not entirely clear whether he earned the name from his prowess as a DJ, or from an apprenticeship in the retail side of the local freebase cocaine business. In either case his local talent show appearances and demo tapes eventually landed him a gig opening for Boogie Down Productions, and a $100,000 record deal with their new label Jive Records. The resultant debut *Grits Sandwiches For Breakfast* featured production work from BDP extended-family members D-Square and D-Nice, as well as Too $hort, and a local engineer named Mike E. Clark (who went on to unleash the Insane Clown Posse on an unsuspecting world). Aiming for a stylistic niche somewhere between the Beastie Boys and 2 Live Crew, the pro-cunnilingus single 'Yo-Da-Lin In The Valley' generated little chart success but made history nonetheless by earning the college radio station of SUNY Cortland (WSUC) a fine of $23,750; the largest ever levelled at a non-commercial radio station for the broadcast of obscene material. Continuing his association with the emergent gangsta-rap genre, Kid Rock supported Ice Cube and Too $hort on tour, trailing the tour bus in a Grand Marquis with his turntables in the trunk. After the tour he relocated to Brooklyn, New York and began work on the first of two poorly received releases for Continuum Records, *The Polyfuze Method* and the cassette-only *Fire It Up* EP. He then turned his efforts to running his own independent Top Dog imprint from the basement of his Michigan home, releasing and distributing *Early Mornin' Stoned Pimp*. This was a foray into a west coast G-Funk sound, albeit filtered through his ever-present rock influences and incorporating the work of Black Crowes keyboard player Ed Harsch and Sub Pop Records vocalist Thornetta Davis. The relative success of his self-distributed work on Top Dog prompted a distribution-deal with Atlantic Records for his next effort. On *Devil Without A Cause*, timing and major-label promotional muscle finally combined to deliver his confident fusion of a bewildering range of rap, country and hard-rock influences to a wider audience, causing the album to climb into the *Billboard* Top 5 in the process.

● ALBUMS: *Grits Sandwiches For Breakfast* (Jive 1990)★★, *The Polyfuze Method* (Continuum 1993)★★★, *Fire It Up* mini-album (Continuum 1995)★, *Early Mornin' Stoned Pimp* (Top Dog 1996)★★★, *Devil Without A Cause* (Lava/Atlantic 1998)★★★★.

Kidjo, Angelique

b. Ouidah, Benin, West Africa. Angelique Kidjo's family background provided her with both the impetus and platform to launch her singing career. Her mother, the director of Benin's first professional theatre/dance company, travelled widely to research different dances and rhythms for the company's ballets. Kidjo was part of the company from the age of six, and progressed from dancing to learning French *variété* songs, gradually adding material from the Beatles and Miriam Makeba. The local music most popular in Ouidah was based on the gobahon rhythm, a percussion effect achieved by slapping different parts of the body in a steady pulse similar to that of reggae. Traditional singers, who rooted their storytelling in an anecdotal, blues-based style, also influenced Kidjo's technique. Although the market for her marriage of cool jazz and soul has long since extended beyond her native continent, there is plenty in her work that militates against Western values. The title track of *Mogozo*, for example, attacks the lack of community in France, which she discovered on her arrival in Paris in 1983. At that time she spent two fruitless years studying classical voice technique, before enrolling at the CIMS jazz school. There she discovered old masters such as Billie Holiday,

Sarah Vaughan and Duke Ellington, who were much more to her taste. Playing with jazz groups around Paris, she eventually teamed up with Dutch pianist Jasper Van't Hof and his group, Pili-Pili. After six albums and five years as vocalist and co-songwriter, Kidjo decided it was time to move on, and her solo album was signed up by Island Records subsidiary Mango. Despite lyrics delivered predominantly in her native tongue, Fon, a language not well appointed to a traditional harmonic approach to singing, there was a universality to the melodies and rhythms of *Parakou*. Produced by Miami Sound Machine's Joe Galdo, *Logozo* saw her dabbling in other African dialects such as Yoruba (on 'Eledjire'). The album acknowledged the position of artists like herself as emissaries from the third world, with songs such as 'We We' attacking the continuing torture and denial of human rights. She is married to French musician Jean Hebrail, who guested on *Logozo* alongside other African stars, Manu Dibango and Ray Lema. *Ayé* (which means 'life') was produced by Fine Young Cannibals associate David Z and Will Mowat (Soul II Soul). Recorded at the Paisley Park studio complex, it comprised a selection of new compositions about love, and maintained its political edge on tracks such as 'Houngbati' and 'Azan Nan Kpé'. *Fifa* and *Oremi* were her most contemporary-sounding albums to date, although on both Kidjo's soulful vocals were forced to struggle against bland production.

● ALBUMS: *Pretty* (1980)★★, *Parakou* (Mango 1992)★★★, *Logozo* (Mango 1993)★★★, *Ayé* (Mango 1994)★★★★, *Fifa* (Mango 1996)★★★, *Oremi* (Mango 1998)★★★.

● VIDEOS: *Angelique Kidjo, The Video* (1994).

Killah Priest

b. Walter Reed, New York, USA. Born in Brooklyn and raised in Bedford-Stuyvesant and Brownsville, Reed was inspired by neighbourhood rappers such as future Wu-Tang Clan member GZA and Onyx's Suavé. Despite building up a formidable reputation of his own, Reed embarked on an educational sabbatical during which he immersed himself in an intensive study of religious history. As Killah Priest he recorded as part of the Sunz Of Man collective with fellow rappers Prodigal Sunn, 60 Second Assassin and Hell Razah, and appeared on several Wu-Tang Clan releases. Cameos on albums by the Gravediggaz and Ol' Dirty Bastard, and the 1996 AIDS charity album *America Is Dying Slowly*, were overshadowed by his contribution to GZA's excellent *Liquid Swords*. His association with GZA led to a recording contract with Geffen Records. Released in early 1998, his debut set *Heavy Mental* featured production from Wu-Tang associates True Master and 4th Disciple, and vocal contributions from GZA, Inspectah Deck and Ol' Dirty Bastard. The album's inventive sampling resulted in a more refreshing approach to the usual Wu-Tang Clan sound. This musical diversity proved an apt backdrop to Killah Priest's surreal lyrics, which mixed Old Testament imagery with conventional hip-hop fury on cuts such as 'B.I.B.L.E.' and the title track. On the back of a positive critical response, *Heavy Mental* debuted at number 24 on the *Billboard* album chart in March.

● ALBUMS: *Heavy Mental* (Geffen 1998)★★★★.

Killarmy

New York, USA-based rap crew comprising Killa Sin, Shogun Assasson, 9th Prince (aka North Star/Madman), Beretta 9, Islord (aka Thief Of Bagdad) and Dom Pachino (aka PR Terrorist). Affiliated with Staten Island's Wu-Tang Clan, Killarmy have managed to forge their own distinctive and unique identity. In keeping with their title, the crew's use of samples draws on war movies and military dialogue. They released 1996's debut single, 'Camouflage Ninjas', through Wu-Tang/Priority. 'Wu-Renegades' followed in 1997. Both singles were featured on their debut *Silent Weapons For Quiet Wars*, which was released in August. With beats supplied by up-and-coming producer 4th Disciple, the album was a solid if uninspiring addition to the Wu-Tang Clan stable. It debuted at a respectable number 34 on the *Billboard* album chart. The follow-up *Dirty Weaponry* was completed barely a year later, but demonstrated a more confident approach that helped to distinguish the album from other Wu-Tang releases. 4th Disciple provided fluid and smooth beats over which the six MCs laid down accomplished and lyrical raps on standout tracks such as 'Galactics' and 'Allah Sees Everything'. Unusually for a Wu-Tang Clan product no guest artists were featured. One of the highlights of the hip-hop year, *Dirty Weaponry* deserved to fare better on the charts than its peak position of 40.

● ALBUMS: *Silent Weapons For Quiet Wars* (Wu-Tang/Priority 1997)★★★, *Dirty Weaponry* (Wu-Tang/Priority 1998)★★★★.

Kirk, Richard H.

Founding member of pioneering electronic outfit Cabaret Voltaire whose releases under a variety of guises in the 90s have seen him increasingly accommodated by the dance music generation. Kirk released his first solo set in 1981, following it with the double album, *Time High Fiction* two years later. His taste for dance music was previewed by the release of Cabaret Voltaire's 'James Brown', before further solo work in 1986 with *Black Jesus Voice*, a mini-album, and *Ugly Spirit*. This was followed a year later by a collaborative project, *Hoodoo Talk*, with the Box's Peter Hope. Further expansions in Cabaret Voltaire's dance sound were refined by the 1989 single 'Hypnotised', which reflected their visit to the house music capital, Chicago. A year later Kirk released 'Testone', an excellent example of UK techno, under the guise of Sweet Exorcist. It launched what became known as the 'bleep' sound, which was widely imitated and dominated clubs for almost a year. A second hugely popular 12-inch arrived with 'Clonk'. Following the dissolution of Cabaret Voltaire in 1994, Kirk has continued to release challenging dance-orientated material under a variety of guises, including Electronic Eye, Sandoz, Xon, Citrus, and Richard H. Kirk. Still based in Sheffield, he looks to be one of the true survivors of the late 70s industrial scene centred in that town.

● ALBUMS: *Disposable Half Truths* (Rough Trade 1981)★★★, *Time High Fiction* (Rough Trade 1983)★★★★, *Black Jesus Voice* (Rough Trade 1986)★★, *Ugly Spirit* mini-album (Rough Trade 1986)★★★, with Peter Hope *Hoodoo Talk* (Native 1987)★★, as Sweet Exorcist *Clonk's Coming* (Warp 1991)★★★, as Sandoz *Digital Lifeforms* (Touch 1993)★★★, *Virtual State* (Warp 1994)★★★, *The Number Of Magic* (Warp 1995)★★★, *Darkness At Noon* (Touch 1999)★★★★, as Electronic Eye *Neurometrik* (Alphaphone 2000)★★★.

Klezmatics

Lorin Sklamberg (b. 6 March 1956, Los Angeles, California, USA; vocals, accordion, keyboards), Frank London (b. 29 March 1958, New York City, USA; trumpet, cornet, keyboards, vocals), Alicia Svigals (b. 8 January 1963, New York City, New York, USA; violin, vocals), Paul Morrissett (b. 19 October 1956, Indianapolis, Indiana, USA; bass, vocals), David Licht (b. 13 September 1954, Detroit, Michigan, USA; drums) and Matt Darriau (b. 21 February 1960, Colorado Springs, Colorado, USA; clarinet, saxophone, flute). Formed by London (who had previously played with David Byrne and the Art Ensemble Of Chicago, among many others), in New York in 1986, the Klezmatics set out to play the traditional Klezmer music of the Jewish communities of Eastern and Central Europe. However, the band instinctively added their own contemporary influences, (rock, funk, *avant garde* jazz), creating an old world/new world fusion of hard-edged, modern Yiddish dance music. In 1988, they played at the anti-Fascist Heimatklinge festival in Berlin. Performing a set of tunes traditional to both the Yiddish and German cultures. These songs subsequently formed the basis of the Klezmatics' debut, *Shvaygn = Toyt* (Silence = Death), released the following year. Subsequent releases *Rhythm And Jews* (1992) and *Jews With Horns* (1995) featured their mix of fast-paced, mournful ballads, improvised experimentation and overtly political sentiments. They have toured extensively throughout the world and have collaborated with a number of other artists, including Allen Ginsberg, the Master Musicians Of Joujouka, John Zorn and classical violinist Itzhak Perlman (whom they backed on two award-winning albums and a number of well-received tour dates). The Klezmatics have also produced the music for various films, dance productions and plays, including 'The Third Seder' (their own 'multimedia Passover production') and playwright Tony Kushner's 'A Dybbuk: Between Two Worlds', the score of which subsequently made up half of *Possessed*, their fourth release and the first to feature predominantly contemporary material. Their most recent collection, 1998's *The Well*, featured the Klezmatics backing Israeli singer/songwriter Chava Alberstein on a collection of Yiddish poems put to music.

● ALBUMS: *Shvaygn = Toyt* (Piranha 1989)★★★, *Rhythm And Jews* (Piranha 1992)★★★★, *Jews With Horns* (Piranha 1995)★★★★, *Possessed* (Piranha 1997)★★★, with Chava Alberstein *The Well* (Xenophile 1998)★★★★.

KLF

Since 1987 the KLF have operated under a series of guises, only gradually revealing their true nature to the public at large. Their principal spokesman is Bill Drummond (b. William Butterworth, 29 April 1953, South Africa), who had already enjoyed a chequered music industry career. As co-founder of the influential Zoo label in the late 70s, he introduced and later managed Echo And The Bunnymen and the Teardrop Explodes. Later he joined forces with Jimmy Cauty, an artist of various persuasions and a member of Brilliant in the mid-80s. Their first project was undertaken under the title JAMS (Justified Ancients Of Mu Mu - a title lifted from Robert Shea and Robert Anton Wilson's conspiracy novels dealing with the *Illuminati*). An early version of 'All You Need Is Love' caused little reaction compared to the provocatively titled LP that followed - *1987 (What The*

Fuck Is Going On?) Released under the KLF moniker (standing for Kopyright Liberation Front), it liberally disposed of the works of the Beatles, Led Zeppelin *et al* with the careless abandon the duo had picked up from the heyday of punk. One of the disfigured supergroups, Abba, promptly took action to ensure the offending article was withdrawn. In the wake of the emerging house scene the next move was to compromise the theme tune to well-loved British television show *Dr Who*, adding a strong disco beat and Gary Glitter yelps to secure an instant UK number 1 with 'Doctorin' The Tardis'. Working under the title Timelords, this one-off coup was achieved with such simplicity that its originators took the step of writing a book; *How To Have A Number One The Easy Way*. After the throwaway send-up of Australian pop, 'Kylie Said To Jason', and Disco 2000's 'Uptight', the duo branched out into ambient music. Cauty, alongside Alex Paterson, played a significant part in creating arguably the leading exponents of the genre, the Orb, while as the KLF they released *Chill Out*, an ambient house recording that is now recognised as a classic. Back in the pop charts the duo enjoyed worldwide success with their Stadium House Trilogy. The first instalment, 'What Time Is Love (Live At Trancentral)', reached the UK Top 5 in autumn 1990. The duo reached their commercial peak at the start of 1991 when the soulful house of '3 AM Eternal' topped the UK charts and broke into the US Top 5. The final instalment, 'Last Train To Transcentral', reached UK number 2 and the attendant *The White Room* was also a bestseller. Further releases followed from the myriad of names employed by the duo (JAMS - 'Down Town', 'Its Grim Up North'; Space - *Space*), but perhaps the most startling was the KLF's 'Justified And Ancient', featuring the unmistakable voice of country legend Tammy Wynette. The song revealed the KLF at the peak of their creative powers, selling millions of records worldwide while effectively taking the mickey. They were voted the Top British Group by the BPI. Instead of lapping up the acclaim, the KLF, typically, rejected the comfort of a music biz career, and deliberately imploded at the ceremony. There they performed an 'upbeat' version of '3AM Eternal', backed by breakneck-speed punk band Extreme Noise Terror, amid press speculation that they would be bathing the ceremony's assembled masses with pig's blood. They contented themselves instead with (allegedly) dumping the carcass of a dead sheep in the foyer of the hotel staging the post-ceremony party, and Drummond mock machine-gunning the assembled dignitaries. They then announced that the proud tradition of musical anarchy they had brought to a nation was at a close: the KLF were no more. Althought a remix of 'America: What Time Is Love?' subsequently became another huge hit, their only new recording in 1992 came with a version of 'Whatever Will Be, Will Be (Que Sera, Sera)' (naturally renamed 'K Sera Sera', and recorded with the Soviet Army Chorale), which, they insisted, would only see the light of day on the advent of world peace. The KLF returned to their rightful throne, that of England's foremost musical pranksters, with a stinging art terrorist racket staged under the K Foundation banner. In late 1993, a series of advertisements began to appear in the quality press concerning the Turner Prize art awards. While that body was responsible for granting £20,000 to a piece of non-mainstream art, the K Foundation (a new vehicle for Messrs Drummond and Cauty) promised double that for the worst piece of art displayed. The Turner short list was identical to that of the KLF's. More bizarre still, exactly £1,000,000 was withdrawn from the National Westminster bank (the biggest cash withdrawal in the institution's history), nailed to a board, and paraded in front of a select gathering of press and art luminaries. The money was eventually returned to their bank accounts (although members of the press pocketed a substantial portion), while the £40,000 was awarded to one Rachel Whiteread, who also won the 'proper' prize. The K Foundation later cemented its notoriety by burning the aforementioned one million pounds, an event captured on home video. Since that time, Drummond and Cauty have made several pseudonymous returns to the singles charts, including the 1996 tribute to footballer Eric Cantona, 'Ooh! Aah! Cantona', as 1300 Drums Featuring The Unjustified Ancients Of Mu, and in 1997 as 2K for the charmingly titled 'Fuck The Millennium'. Urban guerrillas specializing in highly original shock tactics, the KLF offer the prospect of a brighter decade should their various disguises continue to prosper.

● ALBUMS: *Towards The Trance* (KLF Communications 1988)★★★★, *The What Time Is Love Story* (KLF Communications 1989)★★★, *The White Room* (KLF Communications/Arista 1990)★★★, *Chill Out* (KLF Communications/Wax Trax! 1990)★★★★.

● VIDEOS: *Stadium House* (PMI 1991).

● FURTHER READING: *Justified And Ancient: The Unfolding Story Of The KLF*, Pete Robinson. *Bad Wisdom*, Mark Manning and Bill Drummond.

KMFDM

Nihilistic industrial band originally formed in Hamburg, Germany, but who later enjoyed cult success in the USA. The band's name is an acronym of 'Kein Mehrheit Für Die Mitleid', a piece of German wordplay translating as 'No Pity For The Majority'. The band was formed in February 1984 by electronics expert Sascha Konietzko and painter and multimedia performer Udo Sturm to play at an exhibition of young European artists in Paris. Back in Hamburg, Konietzko teamed up with En Esch (vocals/drums) and Englishman Raymond Watts to play experimental electronic music, characterised by mechanistic beats and sampled vocals. The cassette-only release *Opium* spread their reputation on the German underground scene. It was followed by the more widely available *What Do You Know, Deutschland?*, which collected material recorded between 1983 and 1986. The band was then introduced to the UK's Skysaw Records label, leading to the release of the 'Kickin' Ass' single and a meeting with graphic artist Brute! (b. Aidan Hughes), who was subsequently employed to design the band's striking album covers. In the USA, the band was licensed to Chicago's Wax Trax Records, where their martial dance rhythms and dense imagery provided a perfect European counterpoint to the output of US labelmates Ministry, Revolting Cocks, and My Life With The Thrill Kill Kult. Their first releases for Wax Trax were *Don't Blow Your Top* and *UAIOE*. The band's angst-ridden lyrics ('If I had a shotgun, I'd blow myself to hell') allied to Brute!'s album covers saw them pick up a cult following in the USA, where both Konietzko and Esch, the only remaining original members, based themselves from the early 90s. Now signed directly to Wax Trax, they also began to adopt a more guitar-orientated approach while still retaining an experimental edge. *Naïve* was deleted following a lawsuit over the band's use of a sample of Carl Orff's 'O Fortuna', although the songs were later remixed and released as *Naïve: Hell To Go*. Konietzko also collaborated with Buzz McCoy in the house-orientated side project, Excessive Force. *Angst*, released in 1993, perfected the band's aggressive fusion of pounding electro rhythms and screeching guitars. Following the album's release Esch released an electro-pop album and moved to New Orleans. Konietzko, who relocated to Seattle, collaborated with former member Raymond Watts, who had been recording under the name Pig, on the *Sin Sex & Salvation* EP. The band returned, with Watts in tow, for 1995's dark, impenetrable *Nihil*. Further albums followed before Konietzko and Esch broke up the band in January 1999. They were catapulted into the national headlines in April, however, when their final recording, *Adios*, was released at the same time as Dylan Klebold and Eric Harris were murdering 15 of their classmates at Colombine High School in Denver, Colorado. One of the boys was wearing a cap with the KMFDM logo and, it was subsequently revealed, quoted the band's lyrics on his personal website. The band went to great lengths to express their remorse for the victims. Konietzko subsequently formed MDFMK with latter-day KMFDM member Tim Skold. Esch announced he was also working on solo projects.

● ALBUMS: *Don't Blow Your Top* (Wax Trax 1988)★★★, *UAIOE* (Wax Trax 1989)★★★, *Naïve* (Wax Trax 1992)★★★, *Money* (Wax Trax 1992)★★★, *Angst* (Wax Trax 1993)★★★★, *Naïve: Hell To Go* (Wax Trax 1994)★★★, *Nihil* (Wax Trax 1995)★★★, *Xtort* (Wax Trax 1996)★★★, *Symbols* (Wax Trax 1997)★★★, *Adios* (Wax Trax 1999)★★★.
Solo: En Esch *Cheesy* (TVT 1993)★★★.

● COMPILATIONS: *What Do You Know, Deutschland?* (Z/Skysaw 1986)★★★, *Retro* (Wax Trax 1998)★★★★, *Agogo* (TVT 1998)★★★.

Knight, Beverley

b. Beverley Ann Smith, Wolverhampton, England. Knight grew up singing in church, but by the time she was in her late teens had progressed to performing in clubs in and around her hometown. Aided by her producer cousin Don E she signed to the independent Dome Records in 1994. The following year's debut single, 'Flavour Of The Old School', was a hot slice of UK swingbeat co-written with production team 2B3. The song became a big club hit and also scraped into the national Top 50 in April. Follow-up singles 'Down For The One' and 'Moving On Up (On The Right Side)' were lesser hits, but a re-released 'Flava' peaked at number 33 in March 1996, buoyed by the critical acclaim heaped on her debut album *The B-Funk*. Disagreements with her label over musical direction briefly interrupted Knight's career, before she landed a major label deal with Parlophone Records in February 1997. She enlisted producers 2B3, Don E and Carl McIntosh (ex-Loose Ends) for the recording of *Prodigal Sista*, which on release was hailed as one of the greatest UK soul albums of the 90s. The album featured several UK Top 40 hits, including 'Made It Back', 'Rewind (Find A Way)' and the peerless 'Greatest Day', which climbed to number 14 in July 1999. Standing out amidst a wealth of inferior swingbeat acts, Knight's gospel-influenced old school soul was deservedly rewarded with two MOBO awards for best R&B artist and best album.

● ALBUMS: *The B-Funk* (Dome 1995)★★★, *Prodigal Sista* (Parlophone 1998)★★★★.

Knight, Marion 'Suge'

(see Death Row Records)

Knuckles, Frankie

b. New York, USA. Knuckles is often credited with 'creating' house music while a Chicago DJ at venues like the Warehouse and Powerplant. As a child he was inspired by his sister's jazz records, and took up the double bass. He attended the Dwyer School Of Art in the Bronx and F.I.T. in Manhattan to study textile design. However, he was soon lured into DJing at $50 a night at the Better Days emporium. Eventually Larry Levan of the Paradise Garage asked him to work at the Continental Baths club, and he was subsequently invited to travel to Chicago for the opening of the Warehouse. At the time he played mainly Philadelphia soul and R&B, bringing back hot records from New York for his shows. According to Knuckles, the term 'house' had not yet been coined. 'One day I was driving in the South Side and passed a club that had a sign outside that read 'We Play House Music'. I asked them what it meant and he told me that they played the same music as I did'. Into the 90s, he was still to be found orchestrating the dancefloor until 10 am at New York's Sound Factory on a Saturday night. The Powerplant, which he set up after the Warehouse, lasted for three years before outbreaks of violence and the criminal fraternity appeared on the fringes. Knuckles moved into production and recording work with DJ International, recording 'Tears' with the help of Robert Owens and also producing 'Baby Wants To Ride' for Jamie Principle on Trax Records. He had first started to remix records for his own DJing purposes, and later would go on to become an in-demand remixer for everyone from Chaka Khan to the Pet Shop Boys and Kenny Thomas following his unofficial peerage by dance music cognoscenti. He even remixed Nu Colours version of his own classic, 'Tears'. He also recorded as a solo artist for Ten/Virgin Records. Knuckles became the partner of David Morales in Def-Mix Productions, one of the most high profile remix and production teams ever. Morales was present on Knuckles' 1991 album, along with frequent co-conspirators Satoshi Tomiie, Ed Kupper (who wrote the hit single, 'The Whistle Song') and Danny Madden. Brave attempts to tackle ballads proved misguided, although back in the familiar territory of house Knuckles can usually be relied upon to at least pull muster, and at best pull the foundations down. His collaboration with Adeva on *Welcome To The Real World* enhanced and spread his reputation.

● ALBUMS: *Frankie Knuckles Presents: The Album* (Westside 1990)★★★★, *Beyond The Mix* (Ten 1991)★★★, *Welcome To The Real World* (Virgin America 1995)★★★.

● COMPILATIONS: *Sessions 6 - Frankie Knuckles* (MOS 1995)★★★.

Kojak

Kojak is a funky French house outfit, comprising techno DJ Gregorie Galian, soul singer Jayhem Racon and DJ Vas from hip-hop act, Mauvais Graine. Their blend of funk, disco, house and electro has seen them compared to fellow French 'filtered disco' acts such as Cassius, Daft Punk, Air and Etienne De Crecy. Their debut, *Crime In The City*, received much critical acclaim when it was released in the UK in September 1999. The album was an infectious blend of funky basslines, house and techno beats and 70s film and television soundtrack-inspired grooves. Kojak built a strong following in France and the UK through their live appearances. Their fusion of various 70s and 90s dance music genres is reminiscent of the new wave of acts such as Basement Jaxx and Groove Armada that are making soulful, inventive yet dancefloor-friendly music.

● ALBUMS: *Crime In The City* (Polydor/Pro-Zak Trax 1999)★★★★.

Korn

Hardcore rock band Korn formed in the early 90s in Bakersfield, California, USA, and toured widely, playing over 200 shows before releasing their self-titled debut album for East West Records in 1994. Subsequently based in Huntington Beach in California, the quintet, comprising Jonathan Davis (vocals), Reggie Fieldy Arvizu (bass), James Munky Shaffer (guitar), Brian Welch (guitar/vocals) and David Silveria (drums), released their first single, 'Blind', which was widely shown on late-night MTV shows. The album gave them their commercial breakthrough and saw them cited in *Billboard* magazine as 'the first debut hardcore rock act to top the Heatseekers chart and one of the first to crack the upper half of the *Billboard* 200 in the last two years.' Much of this success arose from the reputation garnered by their live work, which was bolstered by tours alongside House Of Pain, Biohazard, 311, Sick Of It All, Danzig, Marilyn Manson and Megadeth. A second single, 'Shoots And Ladders', featured Davis playing the bagpipes. The Ross Robinson-produced *Life Is Peachy* was another ferocious set, although further breakthrough success was limited by the explicit lyrics liberally laced throughout. In late 1997, Korn established their own label, Elementree. They also made the news by serving a cease-and-desist order to the assistant principal of a Michigan high school, who had suspended a student for wearing a T-shirt featuring the band's name. The eagerly anticipated *Follow The Leader* was recorded with help from Guns N'Roses collaborator, Steve Thompson. The album was a commercial and critical success, debuting at US number 1 in September 1998. Highlights included 'It's On' and first single 'Got The Life'. Their *Family Values* touring show also established itself as one of the most successful live ventures of the 90s. The band's prominence on the hugely popular US nu metal scene, alongside acts such as Limp Bizkit, Fear Factory and Slipknot, was confirmed by the chart-topping success of 1999's *Issues*.

● ALBUMS: *Korn* (Immortal 1995)★★★★, *Life Is Peachy* (Epic 1996)★★★, *Follow The Leader* (Epic 1998)★★★★, *Issues* (Epic 1999)★★★★.

● VIDEOS: *Who Then Now?* (SMV 1997).

Krauss, Alison

b. 23 July 1971, Champaign, Illinois, USA. Krauss is unique in the new crop of female country singers to emerge in the 90s in that she leans strongly towards more traditional forms of country music, especially bluegrass. She began learning classical music on violin at the age of five and won her first fiddle contest at the age of eight when she took the honours in the Western Longbow competition. In 1983, at the age of 12, she met singer-songwriter John Pennell, who introduced her to old bluegrass cassettes. By the end of the same year she had been awarded the Most Promising Fiddle Player (Mid West) accolade by the Society For The Preservation of Bluegrass Music. Pennell encouraged her to join his group Silver Rail when she was 14 years old. After two years with

them she spent a year playing in Indiana group Classified Grass, with whom she recorded the demo tape that successfully attracted the attention of Rounder Records' head, Ken Irwin. Krauss then returned to Pennell's group, who had changed their name to Union Station, replacing the fiddler Andrea Zonn. In 1987, she recorded *Too Late To Cry* with them; it included the fiddle classic 'Dusty Miller', alongside six originals by Pennell. The album also included noted acoustic musicians such as Sam Bush and Jerry Douglas. Union Station again joined her for the Grammy-nominated follow-up album, which included a duet of 'Wild Bill Jones' with her lead guitarist, Jeff White. Inspired by Ricky Skaggs, who had brought bluegrass back into contemporary country music's mainstream, she worked hard to achieve similar acclaim. Though *I've Got That Old Feeling* was subsequently awarded a Grammy as best bluegrass recording of 1990, she insisted on maintaining her links with Union Station and remained with the independent Rounder label despite offers from several major labels. Her popularity was furthered in 1993 as opening act on a major Garth Brooks tour. Her video for 'Steel Rails' topped the CMT video chart and she made a successful debut in London in 1994. She has recorded albums of gospel songs with the Cox Family from Louisiana and her harmony vocals and fiddle playing can be heard to good advantage on Dolly Parton's *Eagle When She Flies* and *Heartsongs* and Michelle Shocked's *Arkansas Traveller*. She contributed 'When You Say Nothing At All' with Union Station to the tribute album to Keith Whitley and also performed 'Teach Your Children' with Crosby, Stills And Nash on *Red Hot + Country*. She subsequently became the youngest member of the *Grand Old Opry*. On inducting her, Bill Monroe opined, 'Alison Krauss is a fine singer and she really knows how to play bluegrass music like it should be played.' In 1995, she received five nominations at the annual Country Music Association awards, though one had to be withdrawn when the organizers realized that the platinum-selling compilation *Now That I've Found You* did not meet the criteria for Album Of The Year, which requires 60% new material. She did, however, win all other sections for which she was nominated, including Female Vocalist, Horizon Award, Single Of The Year (for 'When You Say Nothing At All') and Vocal Event (her collaboration with Shenandoah). *So Long So Wrong*, her first new album with Union Station in five years, proved to be another outstanding collection of songs that justified all the accolades.

● ALBUMS: with Union Station *Too Late To Cry* (Rounder 1987)★★★, with Union Station *Two Highways* (Rounder 1989)★★★, with Union Station *I've Got That Old Feeling* (Rounder 1990)★★★, with Union Station *Every Time You Say Goodbye* (Rounder 1992)★★★★, with the Cox Family *Everybody's Reaching Out For Someone* (Rounder 1993)★★★, with the Cox Family *I Know Who Holds Tomorrow* (Rounder 1994)★★★, with the Cox Family *Beyond The City* (Rounder 1995)★★★, with Union Station *So Long So Wrong* (Rounder 1997)★★★★, *Forget About It* (Rounder 1999)★★★★.

● COMPILATIONS: *Now That I've Found You: A Collection* (Rounder 1995)★★★★.

Kravitz, Lenny

b. 26 May 1964, New York, USA. Kravitz's family ties - his Jewish father was a top television producer; his Bahamian mother an actress - suggested a future in showbusiness. As a teenager he attended the Beverly Hills High School where his contemporaries included Slash, later of Guns N'Roses, and Maria McKee of Lone Justice. Kravitz's interest in music flourished in 1987 with the completion of the first of several demos which concluded with an early version of *Let Love Rule*. These recordings engendered a contract with Virgin America, but the company was initially wary of Kravitz's insistence that the finished product should only feature 'real' instruments - guitar, bass, keyboards and drums - rather than digital and computerized passages. Although denigrated in some quarters as merely retrogressive, notably in its indebtedness to Jimi Hendrix, *Let Love Rule* proved highly popular. Kravitz then gained greater success when Madonna recorded 'Justify My Love', a new, rap-influenced composition quite unlike his previous work. In 1991, the artist continued his unconventional path by writing a new arrangement to John Lennon's 'Give Peace A Chance' as a comment on the impending Gulf War. The resultant recording, credited to the Peace Choir, featured several con-temporaries, including Yoko Ono and Sean Lennon. The latter also appeared on *Mama Said*, wherein Kravitz's flirta-tion with 60s and early 70s rock was even more apparent. The set spawned the US Top 5/UK Top 20 hit 'It Ain't Over 'Til It's Over', a kiss-off to his soon to be ex-wife, actress Lisa Bonet. The prolific Kravitz then wrote an entire album for French chanteuse Vanessa Paradis, and collaborated with artists as diverse as Curtis Mayfield, Aerosmith and Mick Jagger. The hard rocking title track of the follow-up *Are You Gonna Go My Way?* was another worldwide success, breaking into the UK Top 5. *Circus* featured a stripped-down version of his trademark sound, displaying his talent as a writer of more contemporary sounding material rather than the 60s pastiches of his earlier albums. The belated follow-up, *5*, saw Kravitz embracing digital recording and attempting a more relaxed fusion of soul and hip-hop styles. The singer topped the UK charts in February 1999 with 'Fly Away', thanks to extensive media exposure as the sound-track to a Peugeot car advertisement.

● ALBUMS: *Let Love Rule* (Virgin 1989)★★★, *Mama Said* (Virgin 1991)★★★★, *Are You Gonna Go My Way?* (Virgin 1993)★★, *Circus* (Virgin 1995)★★★, *5* (Virgin 1998)★★★.
● VIDEOS: *Alive From Planet Earth* (1994)★★★.

Kriss Kross

Two youths from Atlanta, Georgia, USA, who topped the *Billboard* Hot 100 singles chart for eight weeks with 'Jump', a song anchored by the bassline to the Jackson Five's 'I Want You Back'. Chris 'Mack Daddy' Kelly (b. 1 May 1978, USA) and Chris 'Daddy Mack' Smith (b. 10 January 1979, USA) were both just 13 years old when they scored with 'Jump', the fastest-selling single the US had seen for 15 years. In the process they instigated a batch of 'kiddie rap' clones. They were discovered in 1991 by writer/producer Jermaine Dupri, himself only 19, when he was shopping for shoes in Atlanta. Influenced by the likes of Run DMC and Eric B And Rakim, their visual character was enhanced by their deter-mination to wear all their clothes backwards. Strangely enough, considering their natural teen appeal, they were signed up to the genuinely hardcore New York label Ruffhouse, home of Tim Dog and others. The US chart-topper *Totally Krossed Out* sold over four million copies and spawned another US Top 20 hit, 'Warm It Up'. Both singles were also successful in the UK, reaching number 2 and

number 16 respectively. The follow-up, *Da Bomb*, attempted to crossover to the hardcore audience with limited success. Despite charting with the smooth 'Tonight's Tha Night' at the end of 1995, the duo's new recording *Young, Ri¢h & Dangerou$* stalled. Their debut album's success and critical acclaim now seemed like a distant memory.

● ALBUMS: *Totally Krossed Out* (Ruffhouse/Columbia 1992)★★★★, *Da Bomb* (Ruffhouse/Columbia 1993)★★★, *Young, Ri¢h & Dangerou$* (Ruffhouse/Columbia 1996)★★.

KRS-One

b. Lawrence Krsna Parker, 20 August 1965, New York, USA. The kingpin of Boogie Down Productions and a genuine hip-hop pioneer, KRS-One's standing is reflected not only in terms of his music, but also his lecture tours of the US, appearing at Yale, Harvard, and countless other institutions to the dismay of some members of those establishments. His list of achievements is hardly limited to this, however. He has been given the keys to Kansas City, Philadelphia and Compton, California, was nominated for the NACA 1992 Harry Chapman Humanitarian Award, and holds the Reebok Humanitarian Award and three Ampex Golden Reel Awards. He inaugurated the Stop The Violence Movement, and recorded 'Self-Destruction', which raised over $600,000 for the National Urban League, and the human awareness single, 'Heal Yourself'. He has collaborated with R.E.M. (rap-ping on *Out Of Time*'s 'Radio Song', Michael Stipe returning the favour by assisting on the HEAL project), Sly And Robbie, Shelly Thunder, Shabba Ranks, Ziggy Marley, Billy Bragg, the Neville Brothers, Kool Moe Dee, Chuck D. and Tim Dog, among many others, and taken part in several important benefit shows (including ones for Nelson Mandela, Earth Day), as well as attending rallies with Jesse Jackson. Following the death of his erstwhile partner, Scott LaRock (whose violent exit in 1987 played a significant role in KRS-One's anti-violence tracts), he has been joined on studio recordings by DJ Premier and Kid Capri. His post-BDP work combines hints of ragga with strong, bass-driven funk and beatbox samples. KRS-One remains one of the philosophically more enlightened rappers: in particular fighting against the use of the terms 'ho' and 'bitch' when discussing women. However, he remains as arrogant as they come: 'I'm not a rapper. I am rap. I am the embodiment of what a lot of MCs are trying to be and do. I'm not doing hip-hop, I am hip-hop'. His first album to be released outside of the Boogie Down Productions banner was *Return Of The Boom Bap*, though many references to his past remained. 'KRS-One Attacks', for instance, looped part of the *Criminal Minded* title track, and 'P Is Still Free' updated his 1986 anti-crack opus, 'P Is Free'. The early 90s also saw some words and actions that would seem to contradict earlier state-ments, notably his physical attack on Prince Be of P.M. Dawn. 'The way I stop the violence is with a baseball bat and beat the shit out of you . . . If negativity comes with a .22, positivity comes with a .45. If negativity comes with .45, pos-itivity comes with an Uzi: The light has got to be stronger than darkness'. An adequate rebuttal, but apparently all P.M. Dawn had done to diss KRS-One was to suggest in a copy of *Details* magazine that: 'KRS-One wants to be a teacher, but a teacher of what?'. In retaliation, KRS-One and his posse invaded the stage during the following night's P.M. Dawn gig at the Sound Factory Club in New York, throwing Prince Be offstage and commandeering the microphone for his own set. The whole event was filmed live by *Yo! MTV Raps*. Though he later apologised publicly, in private KRS-One was telling the world that he was tired of MCs and hip-hop crews disrespecting him. That he felt it necessary so piously to protect it is the only real blemish on his reputation.

● ALBUMS: various artists *HEAL: Civilization Versus Technology* (Elektra 1991)★★★, *Return Of The Boom Bap* (Jive 1993)★★★★, *KRS-One* (Jive 1995)★★★, *I Got Next* (Jive 1997)★★.

Kruder And Dorfmeister

This respected acid jazz/trip-hop production, remix and recording team comprises Peter Kruder (b. Vienna, Austria) and Richard Dorfmeister (b. Vienna, Austria). Their remix credits include work for William Orbit, United Future Organization, Bomb The Bass, Bone Thugs-N-Harmony, Lamb, Depeche Mode, Roni Size and in March 1999, Madonna's single 'Nothing Really Matters'. They have released several DJ mix albums and an EP of their own work. The latter, *G-Stoned* (named after their label, G-Stone) attracted some notoriety for its witty parody of the cover of Simon And Garfunkel's *Bookends*. The duo received support from UK DJs such as Gilles Peterson and Wall Of Sound's Mark Jones. They take a unique approach to their remixes, each session lasting weeks and involving a complete reconstruction of the track. The 'K&D' sound is bass-heavy, tinged with jazz, dub and hip-hop and experimental in approach. They have been known to use bossa nova and waltz rhythms to embellish their tracks.

● ALBUMS: *G-Stoned EP* (Studio !K7 1996)★★★.
● COMPILATIONS: *Conversions: A K&D Selection* (Shadow 1996)★★★, *DJ Kicks* (Studio !K7 1996)★★★★, *The Kruder & Dorfmeister Sessions* (Studio !K7 1998)★★★★.

Krust

b. England. Krust is an experienced DJ and producer on the UK's drum 'n' bass scene. He first released material as part of the Fresh 4, which included a member of Roni Size's Reprazent, Suv. They had a UK number 10 hit in October 1989 with 'Wishing On A Star'. His involvement with the emergent rave scene led to an interest in the blending of breakbeats that became known as jungle. With Roni Size, he formed Full Cycle Records in 1993 but his early releases appeared on V Recordings. Undoubtedly, his most successful work has been as part of Reprazent with Size but his own singles such as 'Maintain' and 'Warhead' have been club hits. In 1999, he completed remix work for Björk and his first solo album.

● ALBUMS: *Coded Language* (Talkin' Loud 1999)★★★★.

Kula Shaker

This UK retro-rock band (named after an Indian emperor) formed originally as the Kays then the Lovely Lads in 1994. Despite regular live work, that band was abandoned when the singer left. Ex-Objects Of Desire members Crispian Mills (b. 18 January 1963, England; vocals), Paul Winter-Hart (b. Somerset, England; drums) and Alonza Bevan (bass) then regrouped under a new name with Jay Darlington (keyboards), and embarked on a support tour with Reef that resulted in a contract with Columbia Records. Columbia were evidently impressed by Kula Shaker's commitment to recreating the 'authenticity' of 60s bands the Beatles and

Small Faces. Their debut single, 'Grateful When You're Dead' (a reference to the recent death of Jerry Garcia), immediately entered the UK Top 40 as critics feverishly scrambled to interview them. Mills, the son of 60s actress Hayley Mills and grandson of venerated actor Sir John Mills, did his best not to disappoint them: 'By the end of the century we're gonna be the biggest band in the world, and to celebrate we'll play a gig at the Pyramids on the last day of 1999. That's where we're headed.' Further singles proved no fluke. 'Tattva' and 'Hey Dude' were sparkling slices of intelligent guitar pop, with its heart in the sounds of the late 60s. Their debut album entered the UK chart at number 1. The band crowned an extraordinary first year by winning a BRIT Award in February 1997 and released a frenetic cover version of Joe South's 'Hush', previously a hit for Deep Purple. Mills' reputation was subsequently tarnished by some ill-advised remarks about the Nazi swastika, provoking a hostile reaction from the music press. Mills subsequently retired from public view, embarking on a spiritual quest to India. The band returned in May 1998 with the UK Top 5 single, 'Sound Of Drums'. *Peasants Pigs & Astronauts* followed in March 1999, but failed to match the success of its predecessor, debuting at number 9 on the UK album chart. Mills left the band in September to concentrate on solo work.

● ALBUMS: *K* (Columbia 1996)★★★★, *Peasants Pigs & Astronauts* (Columbia 1999)★★★.
● FURTHER READING: *Kula Shaker*, Nigel Cross.

L.A. And Babyface

US songwriters and producers who became the Chinn And Chapman of black pop music in the early 90s thanks to the huge success of the Atlanta, Georgia-based LaFace Records label. Sharing a knack for knowing what was palatable both on radio and in clubland, L.A. Reid (b. Antonio Reid, USA) and Babyface (b. Kenneth Edmonds, 10 April 1959, Indianapolis, Indiana, USA) first played together in the mid-80s in the Cincinnati, Ohio-based R&B outfit, the Deele. L.A. And Babyface began their glittering production career with the Whispers' 'Rock Steady' and Pebbles' instant smash, 'Girlfriend', in 1988. Reid later married the San Franciscan diva, while Babyface boasts kinship with Kevon and Melvin Edmonds of After 7. L.A. And Babyface's output featured hard, fast rhythms, and an up-tempo approach enhanced by the strong melodic abilities of their chosen vocalists. These included such prestigious names as Bobby Brown, TLC, Paula Abdul, Boyz II Men, Whitney Houston, Toni Braxton and the Jacksons. Babyface also released a succession of increasingly successful lovers rock albums, and his partnership with Reid has subsequently faded into the background.

L7

Guitarist/vocalists Donita Sparks (b. 8 April 1963, Chicago, Illinois, USA) and Suzi Gardner (b. 1 August 1960, Sacramento, California, USA) formed L7 in 1985, linking with Jennifer Finch (b. 5 August 1966, Los Angeles, California, USA; bass/vocals, ex-Sugar Baby Doll) and trying several drummers, finally finding Demetra 'Dee' Plakas (b. 9 November 1960, Chicago, Illinois, USA) after domestic touring to promote L7, supporting Bad Religion (drummer on their debut album was Roy Koutsky). The band's raw punk-metal caught the interest of Sub Pop Records, who released Smell The Magic, a raucous, grunge-flavoured blast that further enhanced the band's growing underground reputation. Bricks Are Heavy brought major success, with the surprisingly poppy 'Pretend We're Dead' becoming a major hit on both sides of the Atlantic. Subsequently, the band became darlings of the music press with their multicoloured hair and shock-tactic humour - at 1992's Reading Festival, Sparks retaliated against missile throwers by removing her tampon on stage and throwing it into the crowd, and later dropped her shorts during a live television performance on The Word - but the band's serious side led them to form Rock For Choice, a pro-abortion women's rights organization that has gathered supporters from Pearl Jam to Corrosion Of Conformity for fund-raising concerts. L7 went on to appear as a band named Camel Lips in a John Waters movie, Serial Mom, before Hungry For Stink picked up where Bricks Are Heavy left off, blending serious and humorous lyrics against a still-thunderous musical backdrop. Jennifer Finch departed in the summer of 1996 to form Lyme and then Other Star People. Her replacement was Gail Greenwood (b. 3 October 1960, USA) from Belly, who joined following the release of 1997's The Beauty Process: Triple Platinum. The Beauty Process, a tour film directed by Krist Novoselic, was shot in late 1998. Greenwood left the band shortly afterwards. The remaining members returned to their indie roots for the following year's Slap-Happy, released on their own Wax Tadpole label and distributed by Bongload Records.
● ALBUMS: L7 (Epitaph 1988)★★★, Smell The Magic mini-album (Sup Pop 1990)★★★, Bricks Are Heavy (Slash/Reprise 1992)★★★★, Hungry For Stink (Slash/Reprise 1994)★★★, The Beauty Process: Triple Platinum (Slash/Reprise 1997)★★★, Live Omaha To Osaka (Man's Ruin 1998)★★, Slap-Happy (Wax Tadpole/Bongload 1999)★★★.

La's

The La's were originally formed by artist/musician Mike Badger (b. 18 March 1962) in 1984 in Liverpool, Merseyside, England, but his departure in 1986 left a line-up comprising songwriter Lee Mavers (b. 2 August 1962, Huyton, Liverpool, England; guitar/vocals), John Power (b. 14 September 1967; bass), Paul Hemmings (guitar) and John Timson (drums). Early demo tapes resulted in their signing with Go! Discs in 1987. After a well-received debut single, 'Way Out', which hallmarked the band's effortless, 60s-inspired pop, they took a year out before issuing the wonderfully melodic 'There

She Goes'. When this too eluded the charts, the La's, far from disillusioned, returned to the studio for two years to perfect tracks for their debut album. The line-up also changed, with Lee's brother Neil (b. 8 July 1971, Huyton, Liverpool, England) taking up drums and ex-Marshmellow Overcoats guitarist Cammy (b. Peter James Camell, 30 June 1967, Huyton, Liverpool, England) joining the line-up. In the meantime, 'There She Goes' became a massive underground favourite, prompting a reissue two years on (after another single, 'Timeless Melody'). In late 1990, it reached the UK Top 20. The La's followed that same month, an invigorating and highly musical collection of tunes that matched, and some would argue outstripped, the Stone Roses' more garlanded debut. Its comparative lack of impact could be put down to Mavers' truculence in the press, verbally abusing Go! Discs for insisting on releasing the record and disowning its contents: 'That's the worst LP I've ever heard by anyone.' Comparisons with the best of the 60s, notably the Byrds and Beach Boys, stemmed from the band's obsession with real instruments, creating a rootsy, authentic air. After 'Feelin'' was drawn from the album, the La's set about recording tracks for a new work and spent much of summer 1991 touring America and Japan. Little was then heard of the band for the next four years, which took few acquainted with Mavers' studio perfectionism by surprise. The delays proved too much for Power, however, who departed to set up the highly successful Cast (Mavers has subsequently expressed his extreme dislike for the band). Back in the notoriously insular La's camp, rumours continued to circulate of madness and drug addiction. A collaboration with Edgar Summertyme of the Stairs was vaunted, but no public assignments were forthcoming. Mavers finally performed a solo acoustic set in 1995, in support of Paul Weller, which went so badly awry that he had the plug pulled on him. In April, he spoke to the New Musical Express about a 'second' La's album. Sessions were undertaken in the west London studio owned by Rat Scabies of the Damned, with Mavers playing all the instruments. Predictably, no material from the sessions has ever been released.
● ALBUMS: The La's (Go! Discs 1990)★★★★.
● COMPILATIONS: Lost La's 1984-1986: Breakloose (Viper 1999)★★★.

Labradford

Formed by Carter Brown (keyboards) and Mark Nelson (guitar/vocals), Richmond, Virginia, USA-based Labradford have established themselves as vital innovators in the influential post-rock music scene. The duo made an immediate impact with their 1993 debut, Prazision LP. Informed by Brown's studies into early and medieval music, it offered listeners an entirely new take on conventional music semantics, in keeping with their stated intention to 'move beyond pop'. Many critics were enraptured by the band's ability to balance improvised ambient, almost ecclesiastical textures with more accessible passages. The claustrophobic nature of several songs, 'Accelerating On A Smoother Road' in particular, recalled the dense atmospherics of Joy Division. Bass player Robert Donne was added to the line-up for A Stable Reference, which featured a spacey sound reminiscent of the work of fellow pioneers, Flying Saucer Attack. Subsequent albums, recorded with an extended line-up, have become successively more experimental and minimal, with Mi Media Naranja reducing song titles down to bare initials ('S',

'G', 'WR', etc.). The sonic landscapes on *E Luxo So*, meanwhile, were created without the use of any vocals. Nelson also records as Pan-American, releasing a self-titled debut in 1998.

● ALBUMS: *Prazision LP* (Kranky 1993)★★★★, *A Stable Reference* (Kranky/Flying Nun 1995)★★★★, *Labradford* (Kranky/Blast First 1996)★★★, *Mi Media Naranja* (Kranky/Blast First 1997)★★★★, *E Luxo So* (Kranky/Blast First 1999)★★★.

Lady Of Rage

b. Robin Allen, Farmville, Virginia, USA. Coming to prominence via her engaging support/crowd-warmer spot on tours with Snoop Doggy Dogg and mentor Dr. Dre, the Lady Of Rage also part-times as hairdresser to the stars of the Dogg Pound. She was living in New York when Dre called her at her job at Chung King Studios, where she was the receptionist. He had heard her guesting on the L.A. Posse's 1991 set, *They Come In All Colors*, by which time she had also performed with Chubb Rock and Branford Marsalis. She did not believe it was Dre until he sent her an air ticket in the post, but Rage has remained in Los Angeles since she arrived there in 1990. Part of the Dogg Pound alongside luminaries like Snoop Doggy Dogg, and signed to Dre's Death Row Records, her debut release was 1994's ruffhouse 'Afro Puffs' cut, which also featured on the soundtrack to *Above The Rim*. Further soundtrack work and guest appearances on albums by other Death Row artists followed before she finally released her debut, *Necessary Roughness*, in June 1997. The Top 40 album, which included guest appearances from several of her labelmates, confirmed her mic skills and saw her hailed as the First Lady of Death Row.

● ALBUMS: *Necessary Roughness* (Death Row/Interscope 1997)★★★★.

● FILMS: *Ride* (1998).

Lady Saw

b. Marion Hall, St. Mary's, Jamaica, West Indies. Lady Saw began chatting on the microphone at the age of 15. Being located some distance from the recording studios, she served an apprenticeship on local sound systems before appearing on vinyl. Inspired by the popularity of the slackness style, she performed lewd songs, which earned her a reputation as an X-rated DJ. Her earliest tunes, 'Stab Out The Meat' and 'Just Anuddah Day', reinforced her bad girl image which she eloquently defended on the controversial television documentary *Yardies*. In 1994, her shows were banned in certain Jamaican parishes, to which she responded with 'Freedom Of Speech'. She complained that many male performers had performed slack lyrics without having to endure the censorship to which she was exposed. Her grievance faltered when she performed 'Peanut Punch Mek Man Shit Up Gal Bed' on her video *The Legend Returns* with Lady G, Shamara, Michelle and Lo Lo. In spite of the controversies, she maintained a high musical profile with the hits 'Me Naw Lock Mi Mouth', 'Lonely Without You' and the popular 'Good Wuk'. Other releases followed, including the celebratory 'Glory Be To God' and 'Ask God For A Miracle'. She enjoyed her biggest hit in 1995 with 'Hardcore', while with King Jammy's son John John, her rendition of 'Welding Torch' left little doubt as to the subject matter. The controversy surrounding the AIDS virus resulted in Buju Banton's recording of 'Don't Be Silly (Put A Rubber On Your Willy)'. The tune and a television report inspired Lady Saw to advise girls of the dangers of unprotected sex with her recording of 'Condom'. By the autumn of 1995, the continued drive towards conscientious lyrics found Lady Saw being drawn into the roots and culture style, though her audiences demanded to see the more notorious raunchy performances. In 1996, she enjoyed hits with 'Give Me A Reason' and 'Husband A Mine'. The same year, *Give Me The Reason* was released and included 'Condom' and 'Saturday Night At The Movies' in combination with Brian And Tony Gold. *Passion* featured collaborations with Shaggy and Beenie Man, but was eclipsed by the ensuing *99 Ways* which confirmed Lady Saw's position as the First Lady of Dancehall.

● ALBUMS: *Bare As You Dare* (Diamond Rush 1994)★★★★, *Give Me The Reason* (VP 1996)★★★, *Passion* (VP 1997)★★★, *99 Ways* (VP 1999)★★★★.

● COMPILATIONS: *The Collection* (Diamond Rush 1997)★★★★, *Raw: The Best Of Lady Saw* (VP 1998)★★★★.

● FILMS: *Dancehall Queen* (1997).

Lambchop

Led by singer and guitarist Kurt Wagner, Lambchop are a large, Nashville, Tennessee-based ensemble whose instrumentation is highly unique within the popular music tradition. Wagner's world-weary vocals (which in an earlier age would have delineated him as a 'crooner') are backed by a sprawling jugband orchestra featuring clarinet, lap steel guitar, saxophone, trombone, organ, cello and 'open-end wrenches'. While the band appear immaculately dressed in suits for their live appearances, Wagner's urbane, often seedy narratives offer a highly contrary proposition, describing such delights as suicide and romantic allure on their highly praised alternative country debut, *I Hope You're Sitting Down*. For 1996's *How I Quit Smoking*, Lambchop employed the services of arranger John Mock, previously best known for his work with Kathy Mattea, to embellish the lush orchestral backdrop. This was aided by the presence of a string quartet. The results were excellent, allowing Wagner to indulge himself in the sort of grandiose country melodramas not heard since the heyday of Jim Reeves. *Thriller* included three tracks composed by another maverick US songwriter, FM Cornog aka East River Pipe, while 1998's *What Another Man Spills* featured an unlikely cover version of Curtis Mayfield's 'Give Me Your Love'. The band also backed Vic Chesnutt's on the same year's *The Salesman And Bernadette*. Wagner collaborated with singer-songwriter Josh Rouse on the excellent *Chester* EP before returning to the Lambchop set-up for February 2000's *Nixon*.

● ALBUMS: *I Hope You're Sitting Down/Jack's Tulips* (Merge 1994)★★★, *How I Quit Smoking* (Merge 1996)★★★★, *Thriller* (Merge/City Slang 1996)★★★★, *What Another Man Spills* (Merge/City Slang 1998)★★★, *Nixon* (Merge/City Slang 2000)★★★.

Lang, Jonny

b. Johnny Langseth, 29 January 1981, Fargo, North Dakota, USA. Blues guitarist/singer Jonny Lang was signed to A&M Records as a child prodigy before his sixteenth birthday - having only received his first guitar at the age of 13. By this time he had already earned a strong regional reputation as an interpreter of the blues, eventually moving from Fargo to Minneapolis to become leader of Kid Jonny Lang And The Big Bang. That band's independently released *Smokin'* album underscored Lang's growing reputation, selling an impressive 25,000 copies without the aid of national distribution. By the time A&M stepped in for his signature, he had also played alongside such blues greats as Luther Allison, Lonnie Brooks and Buddy Guy. *Lie To Me*, produced by David Z (Janet Jackson, Collective Soul, Fine Young Cannibals), was an impressive major label debut. Although more mainstream in its combination of blues and soul textures than the raw *Smokin'*, it confirmed Lang as a guitarist of impressive range and astonishing maturity. It included songs written by David Z, Lang's keyboard player, Bruce McCabe, Dennis Morgan and Lang himself, alongside cover versions of material by Sonny Boy Williamson ('Good Morning Little Schoolgirl') and Ike Turner ('Matchbox'). *Wander This World* broadened the musical range even further, emphasising Lang's mastery of rock and soul styles. The album broke into the US Top 30 in November 1998.

● ALBUMS: *Smokin'* (Own Label 1996)★★, *Lie To Me* (A&M 1997)★★★★, *Wander This World* (A&M 1998)★★★.

lang, k.d.

b. Kathryn Dawn Lang, 2 November 1961, Consort, Alberta, Canada. She prefers the lower case appearance of her name because 'it's generic and unlike Cherry Bomb, it's a name, not a sexuality'. This farmer's daughter had become a skilled pianist and guitarist by adolescence and, on leaving school, scratched a living in the performing arts, classical and *avant garde* music, before choosing to sing country - a genre that she had once despised as the corniest in pop. She forsook much of its rhinestoned tackiness for a leaner, more abandoned approach on her independent debut, *A Truly Western Experience*. She was known for her slightly skewered sensibility and a tough backing combo, originally comprising Gordon Matthews (guitar), Ben Mink (violin, mandolin), Mike Creber (piano), John Dymond (bass) and Michel Pouliot (drums). She named them the Reclines - a genuflexion towards Patsy Cline. Overseen by Dave Edmunds, her major label debut *Angel With A Lariat* was favoured by influential rock journals such as *Rolling Stone* (who voted lang Female Vocalist of the Year), but many country radio stations refused to play it, prejudiced as they were by lang's spiky haircut, vegetarian stance and ambiguous sexuality (she would only go public on the latter subject in a June 1992 interview with *Advocate* magazine). Nevertheless, she charted via 'Crying', a duet with Roy Orbison for 1987's *Hiding Out* comedy movie soundtrack. The following year, she gained a breakthrough with the lush *Shadowland*, which was rendered agreeable to country consumers through a Nashville production by Owen Bradley and the presence of the Jordanaires, Brenda Lee, Loretta Lynn, Kitty Wells. Tracks such as the tear-jerking 'I Wish I Didn't Love You So' and Chris Isaak's 'Western Stars' exemplified what lang described as 'torch and twang' - an expression incorporated into the title of her next collection. Mostly self-composed with Mink, it set the seal on the grudging acceptance of her by bigots and, more to the point, confirmed her as a behemoth of country's New Tradition. In 1992, lang became newsworthy and featured in dozens of magazines in Europe and the USA, who finally picked up on her considerable talent when the acclaimed *Ingénue* (credited to lang alone) was released. This excellent release was, however, far removed from country, C&W or new country; it was a sen-

sual and deep collection that enjoyed great crossover success on both sides of the Atlantic, and even generated a Grammy award-winning hit single, 'Constant Craving'. The same year showed lang to possess a promising acting ability with the general release of her movie debut in the low budget *Salmonberries*. In 1993, she provided the soundtrack to Gus Van Sant's adaptation of Tom Robbins' *Even Cowgirls Get The Blues*. Since *Ingénue*, her commercial profile has waned, although she has continued to produce interesting albums. The covers album *Drag* included a highly original interpretation of Steve Miller's 'The Joker', but the singer has kept a low profile since its release.

● ALBUMS: *A Truly Western Experience* (Bumstead 1984)★★, *Angel With A Lariat* (Sire 1987)★★★, *Shadowland* (Sire 1988)★★★, *Absolute Torch And Twang* (Sire 1989)★★★, *Ingénue* (Sire/Warners 1992)★★★★, *Even Cowgirls Get The Blues* film soundtrack (Sire/Warners 1993)★★, *All You Can Eat* (Warners 1995)★★★, *Drag* (Warners 1997)★★★.

● VIDEOS: *Harvest Of Seven Years* (Warner Music Video 1992), *Live In Sydney* (Warner Music Video 1998).

● FURTHER READING: *Carrying The Torch*, William Robertson. *k.d. lang, In Her Own Words*, David Bennahum. *All You Get Is Me*, Victoria Starr. *An Illustrated Biography*, David Bennahum. *k.d. lang*, Rose Collis.

● FILMS: *Salmonberries* (1991), *Teresa's Tattoo* (1994), *Eye Of The Beholder* (1999).

Larkin, Patty

b. Iowa, USA. Expert guitarist and singer-songwriter Patty Larkin has described her style as 'folk music meets the beat generation meets rock 'n' roll.' In the meantime, critics have described her acoustic, electric and slide guitar technique and presentation as 'comparable to the best of Bonnie Raitt'. Raised in Milwaukee, Wisconsin, Larkin studied classical piano for four years before she took up slide guitar as her primary instrument during her seventh grade. Her first songs were written a year later. She enrolled at Berklee College Of Music in the 70s after first attending the University Of Oregon and studying jazz guitar privately. Her time at Berklee saw her researching composition skills and music theory and history, also playing mandolin and guitar in a Celtic band that busked on the streets of Cambridge, Massachusetts. It was during this time that she developed her distinctive playing style, a highly percussive and melodic framework derived from her education in Irish folk tunes by John Martyn and jazz by various local musicians. In the early 80s, Larkin formed a rock band as rhythm and lead guitarist, before electing to embark on her own solo career, influenced by Ry Cooder and Richard Thompson. Regularly playing about 150 shows a year, Larkin made her album debut in 1985 with *Step Into The Light*, which included fine compositions such as the feisty 'If I Were Made Of Metal'. Though well received, the subsequent *I'm Fine* collection was the more enduring. After a lively recording of her potent stage show (*Live In The Square*), she moved over to High Street Records. *Tango* added more studio polish, and included guest appearances by fellow High Street/Windham Hill Records associates Darol Anger and John Gorka. By this time she was well into her record run of nine Boston Music Awards (she lives in Cape Cod, Massachusetts), and she had also gained the Distinguished Alumnae Award from Berklee College. *Angels Running* was another highly acclaimed release, placing Larkin in the Top 10 of the AAA (Adult

Album Alternative) charts. The startling *Strangers World* united her with multi-instrumentalist producer John Leventhal (a veteran of work with Shawn Colvin, Marc Cohn and Rosanne Cash), and was described by the artist as a 'song cycle'. Certainly it evaded the dichotomy of old, where Larkin would often craft either instrumentals or comedic pieces. Larkin produced herself for the first time on the acclaimed follow-up, *Perishable Fruit*, an unusual record which eschewed any conventional form of percussion. Larkin marked the end of the millennium with the release of the live set *À Gogo*, her debut album for new label Vanguard Records.
● ALBUMS: *Step Into The Light* (Philo 1985)★★★, *I'm Fine* (Philo 1987)★★★★, *Live In The Square* (Philo 1990)★★★, *Tango* (High Street 1991)★★★, *Angels Running* (High Street 1993)★★★★, *Strangers World* (High Street 1995)★★★, *Perishable Fruit* (High Street 1997)★★★, *À Gogo* (Road Narrows/Vanguard 1999)★★★.

Lattimore, Kenny
b. Washington, DC, USA. Lattimore first entered the music industry at the age of 14 when he joined the R&B vocal group Maniquin, who recorded briefly for Epic Records in the 80s. When that band broke up, Lattimore remained in the industry as a songwriter for artists including Glenn Jones and Jon Lucien. As a solo artist, Lattimore and new label Columbia Records were keen to project a more mature, sophisticated image, though one still rooted in a traditional R&B style. The reward was two minor hit singles, 'Never Too Busy' and 'For You', and substantial sales for his solo debut, which marked him out as a strong male R&B voice, sympathetic towards but stylistically opposed to the hold hip-hop had taken on the genre. As he told the press: 'I have an appreciation for hip-hop and what it's about, but that's not the life I live. I grew up listening to Earth, Wind And Fire albums, and that's what I know.' He also stressed his wish to address the negative portrayal of African-American males in the media, and the music industry in particular. Columbia's marketing of Lattimore was certainly targeted at the mainstream, with support slots for R&B/soul traditionalists such as Chaka Khan and Barry White. Following the release of his acclaimed sophomore collection, *From The Soul Of Man*, Lattimore signed a new deal with Arista Records.
● ALBUMS: *Kenny Lattimore* (Columbia 1996)★★★, *From The Soul Of Man* (Columbia 1998)★★★★.

Lauderdale, Jim
b. 11 April 1957, Statesville, North Carolina, USA. Lauderdale's father was a minister and his mother a music teacher and choir director. He played drums in the school band and after graduation decided to become a solo performer in New York. He impressed record producer Pete Anderson while in the Los Angeles production of *Pump Boys And Dinettes* and was recorded for the compilation *A Town South Of Bakersfield, Volume 2*. Lauderdale then sang backing vocals for various artists including Carlene Carter and Dwight Yoakam, and had his songs recorded by Vince Gill and George Strait. *Planet Of Love*, his impressive 1991 debut, was co-produced by Rodney Crowell and John Leventhal and included Marc Cohn and Shawn Colvin among the musicians. Lauderdale wrote all the songs, performing them in a variety of styles ranging from western swing to Jerry Lee Lewis. Subsequent releases met with favourable reviews,

although Lauderdale enjoyed more success placing songs with artists including Kelly Willis, Crowell and Carter. *Persimmons*, his finest set to date, was sprinkled with classy country rock and ballads and featured a formidable list of helpers - Emmylou Harris, Dan Dugmore (guitar), Al Perkins (guitar), Pat Buchanan (guitar) and Larry Knechtel (piano). *Whisper*, his debut for BNA Records, was a more country-orientated album which featured a selection of Nashville's finest songwriters, including Harlan Howard, Melba Montgomery and Buddy Miller. The follow-up, *Onward Through It All*, was a well-crafted but occasionally over slick collection. In contrast, the same year's *I Feel Like Singing Today* was a defiantly uncommercial bluegrass album recorded with veteran Ralph Stanley.
● ALBUMS: *Planet Of Love* (Reprise 1991)★★★★, *Pretty Close To The Truth* (Atlantic 1993)★★★, *Every Second Counts* (Atlantic 1995)★★★, *Persimmons* (Upstart 1996)★★★★, *Whisper* (BNA 1998)★★★, *Onward Through It All* (RCA 1999)★★★, with Ralph Stanley *I Feel Like Singing Today* (Rebel 1999)★★★★.

Lavelle, James
(see Mo' Wax Records; U.N.K.L.E.)

Lawrence, Tracy
b. 27 January 1968, Atlanta, Texas, USA. Lawrence was raised in Foreman, Arkansas, and sang in the church choir. He started working in honky tonks when he was 17 years old and moved to Nashville in 1990. He recorded his first album and the future looked bright until, on May 31 1991, he and his girlfriend were accosted by four thugs in a hotel parking lot. He suffered gunshot wounds and his album was put on hold for five months while he recovered. *Sticks And Stones* sold over 500,000 copies and he had country hits with 'Today's Lonely Fool', 'Runnin' Behind' and 'Somebody Paints The Wall'. In 1993, he had a hat trick of number 1s, 'Alibis', 'Can't Break It To My Heart' and 'My Second Home' (the video for which is a who's who of New Country music). The following year Lawrence released *I See It Now*, one of the best collections of new honky-tonk recorded in the 90s. In 1996, he reached number 1 again with 'Time Marches On', although the album of the same name and the follow-up *The Coast Is Clear* were lesser collections. His road band is called Little Elvis, even though, with his string of country chart-toppers, the most likely crown he could steal would be Garth Brooks' and not Presley's.
● ALBUMS: *Sticks And Stones* (Atlantic 1991)★★★, *Alibis* (Atlantic 1993)★★★, *I See It Now* (Atlantic 1994)★★★★, *Tracy Lawrence Live* (Atlantic 1995)★★, *Time Marches On* (Atlantic 1996)★★★, *The Coast Is Clear* (Atlantic 1997)★★★, *Lessons Learned* (Atlantic 2000)★★★.
● COMPILATIONS: *The Best Of Tracy Lawrence* (Atlantic 1998)★★★★.
● VIDEOS: *I See It Now* (A*Vision 1994), *In The Round* (Warner Vision 1996).

Leftfield
Progressive house act who originally comprised just Neil Barnes, formerly of Elephant Stampede and, bizarrely, the London School Of Samba. He released a solo track, 'Not Forgotten', on Outer Rhythm Records, before Leftfield were expanded to a duo with the addition of former A Man Called Adam and Brand New Heavies contributor Paul Daley. Barnes first met him through a poetry group who wanted

live backing. However, as 'Not Forgotten', a deeply resonant song, broke big, disputes with Outer Rhythm followed. Unable to record due to contractual restraints, they embarked instead on a career as remixers to the stars. This first batch included React 2 Rhythm, Ultra Naté and Inner City. They were profligate in order to keep the Leftfield name prominent in the absence of their own brand material. Later remixes for David Bowie, Renegade Soundwave and Yothu Yindi would follow, but by now the duo had already established their Hard Hands imprint. This debuted with the reggae-tinted 'Release The Pressure' (featuring Earl Sixteen), then the more trance-based 'Song Of Life', which gave them a minor chart success in 1992. They subsequently teamed up with John Lydon (Sex Pistols/PiL) for what Q magazine described as the unofficial single of 1993, 'Open Up'. Remixed in turn by Andy Weatherall and the Dust Brothers, it was an enormous cross-party success - especially for Barnes, whose primary musical influence had always been PiL. It might have risen higher in the charts had it not been pulled from ITV's *The Chart Show* at the last minute because of the line 'Burn Hollywood, burn' embedded in its fade, as parts of Los Angeles were by coincidence affected by fire. Gaining favour with a mainstream audience, 1995's ground-breaking *Leftism* paved the way for the later crossover success of the Chemical Brothers and the Prodigy. Daley and Barnes, who had already produced a soundtrack for 1994's *Shallow Grave*, gained further exposure through their contribution ('A Final Hit') to the cult UK movie, *Trainspotting*. They also recorded as Herbal Infusion ('The Hunter (The Returns)'), alongside Zoom Records boss Dave Wesson. They spent three years recording and re-recording the follow-up, *Rhythm And Stealth*, which debuted at number 1 in the UK album chart in October 1999. Stand-out track 'Africa Shox' featured guest vocals by electro pioneer Afrika Bambaataa.

● ALBUMS: *Leftism* (Hard Hands/Columbia 1995)★★★★★, *Rhythm And Stealth* (Hard Hands/Higher Ground 1999)★★★★.

Lemonheads

From their origins in the sweaty back-street punk clubs of the Boston hardcore scene, the Lemonheads and their photogenic singer/guitarist Evan Dando (b. Evan Griffith Dando, 4 March 1967, Boston, Massachusetts, USA) came full circle to feature on the cover of teen-pop magazines such as *Smash Hits*. The band first formed as the Whelps in 1985, with Jesse Peretz on bass and Dando and Ben Deily sharing guitar and drum duties. Enthused by DJ Curtis W. Casella's radio show, they pestered him into releasing their debut EP, *Laughing All The Way To The Cleaners*, in a pressing of 1,000 copies, on his newly activated Taang! label. It featured a cover version of Proud Scum's 'I Am A Rabbit', an obscure New Zealand punk disc often aired by the DJ. By January 1987, Dando had recruited the band's first regular drummer, Doug Trachten, but he stayed permanent only for their debut album, *Hate Your Friends*, allegedly pressed in over 70 different versions by Taang! with an eye on the collector's market. This was a more balanced effort than the follow-up, which this time boasted the services of Blake Babies member John Strohm. *Creator* (reissued in 1996 with extra tracks) revealed Dando's frustration at marrying commercial punk-pop with a darker lyrical perspective, evident in the cover version of Charles Manson's 'Your Home Is Where You're Happy' (the first of several references to the

60s figurehead). The band split shortly afterwards, following a disastrous Cambridge, Massachusetts gig, where Dando insisted on playing sections of Guns N'Roses' 'Sweet Child O' Mine' during every guitar solo. However, the offer of a European tour encouraged him to reunite the band, this time with himself as drummer, adding second guitarist Coorey Loog Brennan (ex-Italian band Superfetazione; Bullet Lavolta). After *Lick* was issued in 1989, Deily, Dando's long-time associate and co-writer, decided to leave to continue his studies. He would subsequently assemble his own band, Pods. However, for the second time Dando dissolved the Lemonheads, immediately following their acclaimed major label debut, *Lovey*. Peretz moved to New York to pursue his interests in photography and film, while new recruit David Ryan (b. 20 October 1964, Fort Wayne, Indiana, USA) vacated the drum-stool. The new line-up featured Ben Daughtry (bass; ex-Squirrel Bait) and Byron Hoagland (drums). However, the new rhythm section was deemed untenable because Daughtry 'had a beard', so Peretz and Ryan (both Harvard graduates) returned to the fold. The band, for some time hovering on the verge of a commercial breakthrough, finally achieved it by embarking on a series of cover versions; 'Luka' (Suzanne Vega) and 'Different Drum' (Michael Nesmith) were both *Melody Maker* singles of the week. There were also two cover versions on their *Patience And Prudence* EP, the old 50s chestnut 'Gonna Get Along Without You Now', plus a humorous reading of New Kids On The Block's 'Step By Step' - wherein Dando imitated each of the five vocal parts. Other choices included Gram Parsons, hardcore legends the Misfits, and even a track from the musical *Hair*. However, the cover version that made them cover stars proper was an affectionate reading of Simon And Garfunkel's 'Mrs Robinson'. By 1992, Nic Dalton (b. 6 June 1966, Canberra, Australia; ex-Hummingbirds, and several other less famous Antipodean bands) had stepped in on bass to help out with touring commitments, his place eventually becoming permanent. Dando had met him while he was in Australia, where he discovered Tom Morgan (ex-Sneeze, who had also included Dalton in their ranks), who would co-write several songs for 1992's *It's A Shame About Ray* set. Dando's 'girlfriend' Juliana Hatfield (bass, ex-Blake Babies) also helped out at various points, notably on 'Bit Part'. She was the subject of 'It's About Time' on the follow-up, *Come On Feel The Lemonheads*, on which she also sang backing vocals. Other guests included Belinda Carlisle. The success of *It's A Shame About Ray* offered a double-edged sword: the more pressure increased on Dando to write another hit album, the more he turned to hard drugs. Sessions were delayed as he took time out to repair a badly damaged voice, allegedly caused through smoking crack cocaine. That *Come On Feel The Lemonheads* emerged at the tail-end of 1993 was surprise enough, but to hear Dando's songwriting continue in its purple patch was even more gratifying. *Car Button Cloth*, recorded with a completely new line-up of the band, came in the wake of Dando's further attempts to clean himself up. It was generally well received and contained some of his most mellow (some would say broody) songs to date. The band was subsequently dropped by Atlantic Records, although the label issued a greatest hits album in 1998.

● ALBUMS: *Hate Your Friends* (Taang! 1987)★★, *Creator* (Taang! 1988)★★, *Lick* (Taang! 1989)★★★, *Lovey* (Atlantic 1990)★★, *Favorite Spanish Dishes* mini-album (Atlantic 1990)★★, *It's A Shame About Ray*

(Atlantic 1992)★★★★, *Come On Feel The Lemonheads* (Atlantic 1993)★★★★, *Car Button Cloth* (Atlantic 1996)★★★.
● COMPILATIONS: *Create Your Friends* (Taang! 1989)★★, *The Best Of The Atlantic Years* (Atlantic 1998)★★★.
● VIDEOS: *Two Weeks In Australia* (Atlantic 1993).
● FURTHER READING: *The Illustrated Story*, Everett True. *The Lemonheads*, Mick St. Michael.

Lennox, Annie

b. 25 December 1954, Aberdeen, Scotland. Following the amicable dissolution of the Eurythmics in 1991, the component parts of that band have gone on to widely varying degrees of success. Both of Lennox's first two solo albums reached number 1 in the UK charts, the second of which doing so while fellow Dave Stewart was underachieving with *Greetings From The Gutter*, which failed to break the UK Top 75. In fairness to Stewart, this may have more to do with the public's perceptions of the artists than any measure of their individual talents; Lennox was always the visual focus of their records, while her vocal presence defined their musical charm. She had already enjoyed a US Top 10/UK Top 30 solo hit in 1988, duetting with soul legend Al Green on 'Put A Little Love In Your Heart', taken from the soundtrack of *Scrooged*. In 1990, after winning her fourth Best British Female Artist award at the BRITS ceremony, Lennox returned backstage to tell reporters that she intended to take a two-year sabbatical, and to concentrate on her family life. She worked with computer expert Marius de Vries on songs she had recorded as rough demos, a process happily interrupted by the birth of Lennox's first child, Lola, in December 1990. Her debut solo album was produced with Steve Lipson (Simple Minds) at her home and at Mayfair Studios in London, with co-writing collaborations with Blue Nile and Jeff Lynne. *Diva* was released in February 1992 and its number 1 status confirmed that Lennox was still the subject of considerable affection among the British public. The album included the UK Top 10 hit singles 'Why' and 'Walking On Broken Glass' (which also reached the US Top 20). In February 1993, Lennox reached UK number 3 with 'Little Bird'/'Love Song For A Vampire', featured on the soundtrack of *Bram Stoker's Dracula*. 1995's *Medusa* offered a wide-ranging selection of cover versions, mainly of songs which had previously been aired by a male vocalist. The classics included 'A Whiter Shade Of Pale' and 'Take Me To The River', though others were drawn from less familiar sources, including the Lover Speaks' 'No More 'I Love You's' (a UK number 2 hit), the Clash's 'Train In Vain' and Blue Nile's 'Downtown Lights'. Aided by Anne Dudley's string arrangements, harmonica, tabla and accordion, it allowed the artist to escape the rigours of lyric writing which had proved such a strain on the previous album. Further delay in hearing new material was created by the release of the limited edition live album *Live In Central Park*. In 1998, Lennox teamed up with Stewart for select live dates which were successful enough for the duo to re-form the Eurythmics and record a new album, *Peace*.
● ALBUMS: *Diva* (RCA 1992)★★★★, *Medusa* (RCA 1995)★★★, *Live In Central Park* (Arista 1996)★★★.
● VIDEOS: *In The Park* (BMG 1996).
● FURTHER READING: *Annie Lennox*, Lucy O'Brien.
● FILMS: *Revolution* (1985), *Brand New Day* (1987), *Naissance d'un Golem* (1991), *Edward II* (1991).

Les Nubians

Born in Bordeaux, France, but raised for several years in Chad, sisters, Hélène and Célia Faussart, put a very modern spin on European black music in the late 90s. Their skilful cross genre fusion of the smooth hip-hop sounds of Arrested Development and De La Soul, the club-based soul music of Soul II Soul and Des'ree, and traditional African roots music, became a notable US success in 1999. The sisters' French father and Cameroonian mother encouraged them to sing from an early age, and their time in Africa exposed the girls to a wide spectrum of music. Inspired by a meeting with jazz singer Abbey Lincoln, they began to establish themselves on the French music scene. Their debut album was recorded in England and France with a stellar list of European session musicians, with beats provided by DJ Mounir Belkhir. Prior to the album's release in September 1998 the sisters were featured on the *Jazz A Saint Germain* compilation. *Princesses Nubiennes* included the pro-African tracks 'Makeda' and 'Bebela', while 'Sugar Cane', the only English language track on the album, was a forthright examination of black history. The album also featured 'Tabou', a highly commercial rewrite of Sade's 1985 hit single, 'The Sweetest Taboo'.
● ALBUMS: *Princesses Nubiennes* (Omtown/Virgin 1998)★★★★.

Les Rythmes Digitales

b. Paris, France. Les Rythmes Digitales is Jacques Lu Cont, born in France while his British born parents were on holiday. His mother and father were both concert pianists and Jacques was not allowed to listen to pop music until he was 14. His interest in making electronic music started in an unusual setting, namely the day centre of a mental institution to which he was admitted at the age of 15. Part of his group therapy sessions involved musical recreation and Lu Cont started using a keyboard: 'I was like the kid who wanted all the chocolate. As soon as I heard a bit of electronic music, I kept wanting more.' He recorded many experimental tapes and sent one to the independent label, Wall Of Sound, who subsequently signed him. His debut *Libération* was a melange of Chicago house, disco, slap bass and 80s synthesizer hooks. Lu Cont's sense of fun was more pronounced on the follow-up, *Darkdancer*, which featured some ridiculously catchy electro-pop tunes and guest appearances from 80s throwbacks Nik Kershaw and Shannon. Lu Cont's live performances have seen him wearing a red cape, glowing devil's horns and performing a cover version of Robert Palmer's 'Addicted To Love'. Les Rythmes Digitales has supported Bentley Rhythm Ace and Cornershop on tour, and remixed tracks for Cornershop and Pavement.
● ALBUMS: *Libération* (Wall Of Sound 1996)★★★, *Darkdancer* (Wall Of Sound/Astralwerks 1999)★★★★.

Let Loose

One of a gamut of 'boy bands' to dominate the UK charts in the mid-90s, Let Loose formed in 1987 when Richie Wermerling (vocals/keyboards) recruited Rob Jeffery (guitar) and Lee Murray (drums) via an advertisement in *Melody Maker*. However, their early efforts were rather different to the clean-cut incarnation of Let Loose which would grace the charts of the mid-90s. As Jeffrey told the press 'In the early days of Let Loose we always used to wear black, and the music was a lot more bikery, more metally. We didn't dance on stage - it wasn't dance music - we'd stand there and perform real music with guitars.' They toured widely, and, gradually changing style, signed a Virgin Records deal at the end of the 80s. However, they were one of several artists displaced when the company sold out to EMI Records. Mercury Records were keen to offer them a new contract and enjoyed minor chart returns in 1993 and 1994 when both 'Crazy For You' and 'Seventeen' peaked at number 44 in the UK charts. When 'Crazy For You' was re-released and re-promoted it spent 10 weeks in the UK Top 10, peaking at number 2 and earning a gold disc. When 'Seventeen' was also reissued and became another major hit it gave the band total sales of 700,000 singles in 1994, though their debut album's chart placing was a more modest number 20. The band started 1995 with 'One Night Stand', another accessible slice of boy band pop without offering anything too distinctive. They enjoyed further UK Top 10 hits with 'Best In Me' (1995) and 'Make It With You' (1996), but subsequently faded from view.

● ALBUMS: *Let Loose* (Mercury 1994)★★, *Rollercoaster* (Mercury 1996)★★★.

Levellers

The Levellers' affinity with the neo-hippie/new-age travellers initially seemed likely to prevent them from achieving mass appeal, but the success of their records and their huge following continues to surprise the cynics, of which there are many. A five-piece unit from Brighton, Sussex, England, the Levellers combine folk instrumentation with rock and punk ethics: 'We draw on some Celtic influences because it's a powerful source, but we're a very English band - this country does have roots worth using.' They took their name, and much of their ideology, from the Puritans active at the time of the English Civil War between 1647 and 1649, whose agenda advocated republicanism, a written constitution and abolition of the monarchy. Their original line-up featured songwriter Mark Chadwick (lead vocals, guitar, banjo), Jonathan Sevink (fiddle), Alan Miles (vocals, guitars, mandolin, harmonica), Jeremy Cunningham (bass, bouzouki) and Charlie Heather (drums). Sevink's violin, like many of their instruments, was typically unconventional and ecologically sound, 'recycled' from three different broken violin bodies. Chadwick, meanwhile, used a guitar that had an old record player arm acting as pick-ups, as well as an amplifier acquired from the Revillos. The *Carry Me* EP was released on Brighton's Hag Records in May 1989, after label boss Phil Nelson had taken over their management. They signed to French label Musidisc Records in 1989, and Waterboys producer Phil Tennant recorded their debut album. When their guitarist left during a tour of Belgium in April 1990, they recruited Simon Friend, a singer-songwriter and guitarist from the north of England, and set off on a typically extensive UK tour. Distribution problems with their debut led to a new contract with China Records, with whom they made a breakthrough into the national charts with the minor 1991 hits 'One Way' and 'Far From Home'. Their second album, *Levelling The Land*, reached the UK Top 20. A mixture of English and Celtic folk with powerful guitar-driven rock, it was acclaimed throughout Europe where the band toured before performing sell-out domestic concerts. May 1992 saw the *Fifteen Years* EP enter the UK chart at number 11, confirming that their widespread popularity had not been diminished by their almost total absence from the main-

stream press. Signed to Elektra Records in the USA, the Levellers made their initial impact touring small venues there before returning to the UK to stage three Christmas Freakshows, which combined music and circus acts at the Brighton Centre and Birmingham NEC. They also continued to play benefits for the environmental and social causes that remain the subject of many of their songs. In 1993, they again toured Europe, released a compilation of singles and live tracks, *See Nothing, Hear Nothing, Do Something*, and recorded songs for a new album at Peter Gabriel's Real World studios. In the summer of that year, 'Belaruse' reached number 12 in the UK charts, a position matched by follow-up single 'This Garden'. The accompanying self-titled album also rose to number 2 in the UK charts, and followed the familiar formula of rousing, agit-prop folk rock. In truth, the band themselves were disappointed with the lack of progress *The Levellers* demonstrated, and it would be a full two years before the next studio album. It sold well, however, and their popularity, particularly in live appearances, made them regulars in the underground music press, wherein they took to criticizing The Men They Couldn't Hang and New Model Army, who, paradoxically, appeared to be their biggest influences. By 1994, the band had purchased their own disused factory, the Metway, a base for various activities including the running of a fan club and pressure groups as well as an integral studio complex. The first album to be constructed in these surrounds, *Zeitgeist*, was recorded over a leisurely nine-month period which gave the songs, notably the UK hit singles 'Hope Street' (number 12) and 'Fantasy' (number 16), time to develop and breathe. The album debuted at number 2 in the UK charts, before climbing to the top spot a week later. The wry Christmas single, 'Just The One', reached number 12 and stayed in the Top 40 for six weeks. A double live album reached number 13 in the following year's charts, and the band's new-found appeal was confirmed in 1997 with the success of new single 'What A Beautiful Day' (number 13) and *Mouth To Mouth*. They announced the world's first Carbon Neutral Tour in 1998, pledging to plant trees to offset the damage caused by their transport vehicles.

● ALBUMS: *A Weapon Called The Word* (Musidisc 1990)★★★, *Levelling The Land* (China 1991)★★★, *The Levellers* (China 1993)★★★★, *Zeitgeist* (China 1995)★★★, *Best Live: Headlights, White Lines, Black Tar Rivers* (China 1996)★★, *Mouth To Mouth* (China 1997)★★★.

● COMPILATIONS: *See Nothing, Hear Nothing, Do Something* (China 1993)★★★, *One Way Of Life: Best Of The Levellers* (China 1998)★★★★.

● VIDEOS: *The Great Video Swindle (Live At Glasgow Barrowlands)* (1992), *Best Live: Headlights, White Lines, Black Tar Rivers* (Warner Home Video 1996).

● FURTHER READING: *Dance Before The Storm: The Official Story Of The Levellers*, George Berger.

Leven, Jackie

b. 1950, Fife, Scotland. Former Doll By Doll singer Jackie Leven saw that band fall apart in 1983, without any of the commercial recognition to match the warmth with which UK critics greeted them. If he thought that signalled the zenith of his misery, he was wrong. Shortly after releasing two solo singles he was attacked in a London street, receiving several broken ribs and a badly damaged larynx.

Unable to sing, his doctor prescribed anabolic steroids which only exacerbated matters. Down on his luck and utterly despondent about his prospects, Leven turned to heroin as a prop. Eventually, together with his partner Carol, he devised a new, holistic approach to his problems, which proved so successful that their new doctor urged them to spread news of the system. Together they set up the C.O.R.E. (Courage to stop, Order in life, Release from addiction, Entry into new life) charity. This organization has since become highly successful in treating those with substance abuse problems. Another effect of this rebirth was to reawaken Leven's interest in music. Concrete Bulletproof Invisible was a short-lived band put together with two former bandmates and ex-Sex Pistols bass player Glen Matlock. However, when he came to record again, it was as a solo artist (Leven had actually recorded an acid rock album in the early 70s which was originally released only in Spain under the pseudonymn John St. Field). The *Songs From The Argyll Cycle* EP was a Scotland-only release on Cooking Vinyl Records, comprising five tracks Leven had written while relaxing in his beloved West Scotland (shortly after his partner had left him). It was followed almost immediately by a second collection, *The Mystery Of Love Is Greater Than The Mystery Of Death*, completed with American poet Robert Bly and featuring readings from Mike Scott of the Waterboys. Leven had read Bly's work (Bly is the nominal head of the US 'men's movement') while at school, and his interest was reawakened by hearing recent tapes. Leven has gone on to become the UK representative/organizer of the men's movement, appearing on Gloria Hunniford's television show and other outlets in that capacity, making him a media personality on a par with another Scots refugee from the punk wars, Richard Jobson. *Forbidden Songs Of The Dying West* mined the same rich vein of Celtic soul, and served to emphasize what a powerful and distinctive voice Leven possesses. Following the CD reissue of *The Argyll Cycle* he released 1997's *Fairytales For Hardmen* which, aptly, had a harder-edged sound than the previous records. *Night Lilies* reunited Leven with ex-Doll By Doll partner Joe Shaw, and was a desperately bleak but ultimately moving collection of songs. Several limited edition live albums have also been released through the *Haunted Valley* fanzine and website.

● ALBUMS: *Control* Spain only (MCA 1975)★★★, *The Mystery Of Love Is Greater Than The Mystery Of Death* (Cooking Vinyl 1994)★★★★, *Forbidden Songs Of The Dying West* (Cooking Vinyl 1995)★★★★, *The Argyll Cycle: Volume One* (Cooking Vinyl 1996)★★★, *Fairytales For Hardmen* (Cooking Vinyl 1997)★★★, *For Peace Comes Dropping Slow* limited edition (Haunted Valley 1997)★★★, *Night Lilies* (Cooking Vinyl/Thirsty Ear 1998)★★★★, *Man Bleeds In Glasgow* limited edition (Haunted Valley 1998)★★★, *The Wanderer* limited edition (Haunted Valley 1999)★★★, *Defending Ancient Springs* (Cooking Vinyl 2000)★★★★.

LeVert, Gerald

b. 13 July 1966, Cleveland, Ohio, USA. The son of O'Jays founder Eddie LeVert. Bridging the gap between traditional and contemporary R&B, Gerald LeVert has a fine vocal technique first heard in 1985 with the release of the debut album by LeVert. By the time 1988's *Just Coolin'* had become a major US success, Gerald had already taken time off from the parent group to produce a number of artists with Marc Gordon, including Stephanie Mills, James Ingram, Miki Howard, the O'Jays and Troop. He also wrote 'Whatever It Takes' for Anita Baker's platinum-selling 1990 set, *Compositions*. The same year, LeVert's *Rope-A-Dope* went gold. As head of Atlantic Records' Trevel Productions, Gerald also worked with new vocal groups Rude Boy and Men At Large. All these endeavours preceded the announcement of his solo career in 1991. The timing had been carefully planned, and paid rewards when 'School Me', 'Can You Handle It', 'Baby Hold On To Me' (featuring his father) and the title track of the parent album *Private Line* achieved major success. The songs, written in conjunction with new partner Tony Nicholas, established him as a major force in contemporary R&B, with an equal emphasis on up-tempo dance numbers and balladeering. Afterwards, Gerald returned to work with LeVert (the band), and their fifth album, 1992's *For Real Tho'*, earned another gold disc. Further production work with Barry White, Little Joe (lead singer of Rude Boy), Drama and Men At Large interrupted preparations for a second solo set, which finally followed in 1994. *Groove On* was envisaged by the artist as 'a 90s version of a 60s soul show, with a band, a whole horn section, the works'. Once more working with Nicholas, this time the ballads included 'I'd Give Anything' (produced by the Grammy award-winning David Foster), which became the album's first hit single, and the 'issue' song 'How Many Times', which dealt with a woman suffering physical and emotional abuse. The reconstruction of a traditional soul dynamic was enshrined by the presence of his father as co-producer on 'Same Time, Same Place', while 'Can't Help Myself' was originally written for the Forest Whitaker movie *Strapped*. In 1995, he enjoyed further international success with 'Answering Service', confirming Gerald as one of the leading lights of modern soul and vocal R&B. The same year also produced a well-received collection of duets performed with his father (as Gerald And Eddie LeVert), titled *Father And Son*. In 1997, Gerald teamed-up with Keith Sweat and Johnny Gill for the 'soul supergroup' album, *Levert Sweat Gill*. His new solo album, *Love & Consequences*, which debuted at US number 17 in August 1998, featured the Top 20 singles, 'Thinkin' Bout It' and 'Taking Everything'.

● ALBUMS: *Private Line* (Atlantic 1991)★★★★, *Groove On* (Atlantic 1994)★★★, as Levert Sweat Gill *Levert Sweat Gill* (East West 1997)★★, *Love & Consequences* (East West 1998)★★★★, *G* (Elektra 2000)★★★.

Levitation

This indie combo featured several experienced UK musicians, and was formed by Terry Bickers (vocals/guitar) and Dave Francolini (drums, ex-Something Pretty Beautiful) after an altercation between the former and his ex-band leader, Guy Chadwick of the House Of Love, in 1989. Levitation's line-up was completed by Christian Hayes (guitar, ex-Cardiacs), Robert White (keyboards), Johnny T (violin), and Laurence O'Keefe (bass, ex-Jazz Butcher). Their pedigree was enough to see them shoot to prominence in the UK press, and two EPs, *Coppelia* and *After Ever* (without Johnny T), revealed a band with no lack of enthusiasm or ideas. They were ousted from an early Transvision Vamp support at the Brixton Academy officially because there was not enough room on stage for their equipment. Another story suggests that singer Wendy James was concerned that Levitation's growing live reputation might overshadow her own band. Bickers certainly enjoyed a reputation for being something of an eccentric, but initially seemed to have found a happier home for his obvious talents. Levitation's debut *Need For Not* featured John McGeoch of PiL guesting on guitar, and the critical response was strong. However, Bickers found himself moving on once more in 1993 following the band's debut single for Chrysalis Records ('Even When Your Eyes Are Open'), making the following announcement live on stage at the Tufnell Park Dome in London: 'Oh dear. We've completely lost it, haven't we?'. While Levitation attempted to soldier on in his absence, Bickers disappeared to write songs, using the name Cradle to cover these exploits, though this was no band as such. The new Levitation album, re-recorded with the help of various friends in a 'collective' set up (including new vocalist Steven Ludwin), was only released in Australia. The band split-up in September 1994. Bickers contributed guitar to Oedipussy's debut album, and produced Vex's 1997 debut, *Frontiers And New Technologies*. Shortly afterwards, he reunited with O'Keefe and Francolini in Dark Star.

● ALBUMS: *Coterie* mini-album (Capitol/Ultimate 1991)★★★★, *Need For Not* (Rough Trade/Capitol 1992)★★★, *Meanwhile Gardens* Australia only (Festival 1994)★★.

Lewis, C.J.

b. Stephen Lewis, London, England. Lewis shadowed the sound systems around London with his childhood friend Philip 'Leo' Pottinger, and soon established himself as a respected DJ. Pottinger himself began a recording career as a singer-songwriter and on his reworking of Frankie Lymon And The Teenagers' 'Why Do Fools Fall In Love', he introduced Lewis to a wider audience. The single had considerable exposure through ffrr Records. In 1990, Lewis appeared on a number of releases, notably in combination with Janet Lee Davis for a version of Keith And Enid's 'Worried Over You', while with Pottinger he recorded a version of the Sugar Minott hit, 'Good Thing Going'. In 1993, the duo recorded the reggae chart-topper 'Hypnotic Love', which was number 1 for seven weeks. This success resulted in Lewis signing with Black Market/MCA, with Pottinger as co-producer. The arrangement led to crossover success when 'Sweets For My Sweet' peaked at number 3 in the UK Top 10. He followed the hit with a Top 10 cover version of Stevie Wonder's 'Everything Is Alright (Uptight)', Earth, Wind And Fire's 'Best Of My Love' and an original composition, 'Dollars', utilizing Prince Buster's 'Ten Commandments' rhythm. In 1994, he toured Europe, Asia and the Far East and began working on his second album for the label. He continued to play the live circuit on a 28-day tour of the UK, resulting in an award for Best P.A. Of The Year In Britain. His popularity in Japan resulted in his second album selling 150,000 copies in one day, increasing to 250,000 in the first two weeks of its release. In September 1995, he played seven sell-out dates in the Far East, and had a UK Top 40 summer hit with 'R To The A'. By the beginning of 1996, he had returned to the UK to promote the release of 'Can't Take It (Street Life)'. The release of 'Phat Ting' went some way towards soothing the disaffected hardcore reggae fans, who had become somewhat disillusioned by Lewis' crossover success.

● ALBUMS: *Dollars* (Black Market 1994)★★, *Rough And Smooth* (Black Market 1995)★★.

● COMPILATIONS: *Young, Gifted & Black: The Early Years* (e2 1998)★★.

Lewis, Donna

b. Cardiff, Wales. Despite her initial inability to secure a UK recording contract, Lewis' career was galvanized meteorically when her debut single, 'I Love You Always Forever', climbed to number 2 on the *Billboard* charts in 1996. The singer-songwriter was commendably relaxed about this turn of events, that reaction a testament to the fact that she had been involved in making music from the age of 14. At that time, influenced by jazz, Motown Records and Rickie Lee Jones, she began writing her first songs. She then attended the Welsh College of Music and Drama, before spending four years playing in European piano bars as a cabaret singer. When she returned to the UK she took a residency at the Belfry Hotel in Birmingham, at which time she began sending out her first demo tapes to record companies. By a strange set of coincidences, one such tape was passed to Jennifer Stark of Atlantic Records by Jerry Marreta, the drummer with Peter Gabriel. Atlantic paired her with Kevin Killen, who had previously worked with U2, Kate Bush and Elvis Costello. She was marketed in similar terms to Enya, whose 'ethereal' singing technique is close to her own, but the success of 'I Love You Always Forever' (which also reached UK number 5) took everybody by surprise, not least UK record label executives who had passed on her demo tapes. The self-produced *Blue Planet* contained an equal quota of radio-friendly pop songs, maintaining Lewis' high standards.

● ALBUMS: *Now In A Minute* (East West 1996)★★★★, *Blue Planet* (Atlantic 1998)★★★.

LFO

Among the most unrelenting and popular exponents of hard techno, LFO's output on Warp Records represents everything an outsider might fear of the music: harsh, crashing, thumping 'bleep' music. When forced to play their debut single 'LFO' on Radio 1, Steve Wright described it as the worst record in the world. Gez Varley and Mark Bell are the mainstays, though extra keyboard players Simon Hartley and Richie Brook were drafted in for occasional live outings. The pair met at college in Leeds, where they discovered mutual interests in music and technology as well as partying in the city's clubs, where Nightmares On Wax worked. The duo gave the DJs a demo of a track they had recorded on a Casio SKI keyboard called 'LFO' which proved a success in the Leeds clubland. Among the audience were the fledgling Warp team who decided to release 'LFO' and were rewarded when it became a Top 20 hit in the summer of 1990. Along with NOW and the Forgemasters, LFO helped pioneer the sound that became known as 'bleep'. Almost a year later the single 'We Are Back' heralded their first album, *Frequencies*, and 'What Is House' followed in early 1992. Their next album, *Advance*, did not arrive until the beginning of 1996 with only 'Tied Up' in November 1994 in between. However, during this time the duo had remixed and collaborated with a number of other artists notably Kraftwerk (for their *Elektrik Music* recordings), Afrika Bambaataa, the Yellow Magic Orchestra and the Art Of Noise. Bell also teamed up with Simon Hartley of Wild Planet, releasing the EP *I'm For Real* under the name Feedback. Since *Advance* LFO have concentrated on individual projects, with Bell retaining the name and a contract with Warp. In 1997, he was involved in the production of Björk's album *Homogenic* and later toured

with the singer around Europe. He also remixed tracks by Radiohead, Gus Gus and Sabres Of Paradise among others.
● ALBUMS: *Frequencies* (Warp 1991)★★★★, *Advance* (Warp 1996)★★★.

Lighthouse Family

UK pop band the Lighthouse Family comprises the Newcastle-based duo of Tunde Baiyewu, a vocalist of Nigerian descent, and songwriter and musician Paul Tucker. They met while working at nightclub bars in the north-east of England, at which time Tucker was also recording his own compositions at home in his spare time. They formed a partnership in early 1993 after being introduced by a local soul DJ. After hearing a tape of the band's 'Ocean Drive' played down the phone, Polydor Records A&R director Colin Barlow recognized their potential, particularly in the mainstream album market, and signed them to a long-term development contract. Influenced by artists such as Bob Marley, Stevie Wonder and Marvin Gaye, the duo made their debut in May 1995 with 'Lifted', which entered the lower reaches of the UK chart. This, like their debut album, was produced by Mike Pedan, formerly of UK soul band the Chimes and producer for Shara Nelson and Darryl Hall. 'Ocean Drive', also the title of the debut album, was placed on the soundtrack to the Richard E. Grant movie *Jack And Sarah* before being released as their second single, reaching number 34 in October. Determined not to see a good song die, 'Lifted' was reissued in early 1996 and this time caught the mood of the public by reaching number 4. 'Ocean Drive' was also reissued, and reached number 11. 'Goodbye Heartbreak' (number 14) and 'Loving Every Minute' (number 20) completed the duo's impressive run of hit singles from *Ocean Drive*, although detractors took great satisfaction in attacking their brand of 'soul-lite' pop. The 1997 follow-up, *Postcards From Heaven*, confirmed Lighthouse Family's status as one of Britain's most successful new bands. The album featured the UK Top 10 singles 'Raincloud', 'High' and 'Lost In Space'.
● ALBUMS: *Ocean Drive* (Wild Card/Polydor 1995)★★★★, *Postcards From Heaven* (Wild Card/Polydor 1997)★★★.

Lightning Seeds

Contrary to the multiples suggested by the moniker, Lightning Seeds is the brainchild of one man, Ian Broudie (b. 4 August 1958, Liverpool, England), who had gouged a significant niche in the Merseyside music scene during the 80s. Originally a member of Big In Japan - a forerunner of the likes of Echo And The Bunnymen and Teardrop Explodes, not to mention a breeding ground for future Frankie Goes To Hollywood singer Holly Johnson and drummer Budgie, who was later to join Siouxsie And The Banshees - Broudie eventually ended up playing in the Original Mirrors and developed an appetite for production work. His efforts on the first two Echo And The Bunnymen albums acted as a springboard from which he was catapulted into the studio with numerous acts, including the Fall, Wah!, Icicle Works and Frazier Chorus. On the creative front, Broudie collaborated with Wild Swans singer Paul Simpson under the name Care, releasing three immaculate singles and preparing the blueprint for his own pop-obsessed project. Thus, Lightning Seeds was born as an opportunity for Broudie to expand his own songwriting ideas. The project had an immediate impact when his first single, 'Pure', fuelled everyone's interest by virtue of being a deliberately low-key release, and went on to reach number 16 in the UK chart in summer 1989. *Cloudcuckooland* followed, encapsulating Broudie's notion of the perfect, sweet pop song, whereupon he put his producer's hat back on to work with contemporary bands such as Northside, the Primitives, Frank And Walters, Alison Moyet and Sleeper, among many others. He continued his work under the Lightning Seeds moniker in 1992 with *Sense*, another collection of bittersweet pop confectionery, but he would have to wait until 1994's *Jollification* for a further commercial breakthrough. The album contained the glorious UK Top 20 hit singles, 'Change', 'Lucky You' and 'Perfect'. This time Broudie put together a full touring band, playing live for the first time since the Original Mirrors folded. The assembled line-up; Martin Campbell (bass, ex-Rain), Chris Sharrock (drums, ex-Icicle Works) and Paul Hemmings (guitar, ex-La's) drew on his Liverpool connections, but Broudie remained very much the nucleus. In 1996, Broudie composed England's anthem for soccer's European championships, 'Three Lions' (recorded with comedians David Baddiel and Frank Skinner), which reached number 1 in the UK chart. Later in the year his songwriting reached a creative peak with the gloriously melodic *Dizzy Heights*, which included three further Top 20 singles, 'Ready Or Not', 'What If ...!', and 'Sugar Coated Iceberg', and the Top 10 hit 'You Showed Me'. The compilation set *Like You Do* included two new tracks. 'Three Lions 98', released to coincide with England's World Cup challenge, topped the UK charts in June 1998. Broudie attempted to modernise the band's sound on *Tilt*, although the closest point of reference was arguably New Order.
● ALBUMS: *Cloudcuckooland* (Epic 1990)★★★, *Sense* (Epic 1992)★★★, *Jollification* (Epic 1994)★★★★, *Dizzy Heights* (Epic 1996)★★★★, *Tilt* (Epic 1999)★★★.
● COMPILATIONS: *Pure Lightning Seeds* (Virgin 1996)★★★, *Like You Do* (Epic 1997)★★★★.
● VIDEOS: *Like You Do - The Greatest Hits* (SMV 1997).

Lil' Kim

b. Kimberly Jones, 11 July 1975, Brooklyn, New York, USA. Having survived some time on the streets as a teenager, Lil' Kim was aided by Biggie Smalls (the Notorious B.I.G.) who helped her team up with the New York rap collective Junior MAFIA. A strong response to her contributions to their 1995 debut single, 'Player's Anthem', and the ensuing *Conspiracy*, earned her comparisons with MC Lyte for her adept microphone skills. She then worked on albums by artists including Skin Deep and Total, before launching her own career in 1996 with *Hard Core*. This sexually explicit hardcore rap album came as something of a shock in the male-dominated world of hip-hop, but an aggressive marketing campaign and strong reviews helped it reach number 11 in the *Billboard* charts. The album featured an array of star producers, including Puff Daddy, with whom Lil' Kim duetted on the number 1 rap single 'No Time'. Like many hip-hop artists she also established an acting career, appearing in 1999's hit comedy, *She's All That*.
● ALBUMS: *Hard Core* (Undeas/Big Beat 1996)★★★.
● FILMS: *She's All That* (1999).

Lil' Troy

b. Troy Birklett, South Park, Houston, Texas, USA. This southern rapper's entrepreneurial spirit - he runs his own Short Stop Records label - earned comparisons to Master P in its implicit challenge to the east coast/west coast domination of hip-hop. Birklett played saxophone and guitar in a high school band, but moved into hip-hop with producer Bruce 'Grim' Rhodes in the late 80s. The duo worked with DJ Akshun, who would shortly rename himself Scarface and join Houston's Geto Boys. An abortive deal with Payday Records followed, before Troy decided to set up his own label, Short Stop Records, recording and promoting local rap talent. Troy took the microphone on only four tracks on his debut, *Sittin' Fat Down South*, enlisting some of Houston's leading rappers as MCs. These included Scarface (on 'Another Head Put To Rest') and his Geto Boys partner Willie D. (on 'Where's The Love'), Big Ced, 2-Low and Nattie. The album, redistributed by Universal Records, rose to number 20 in the *Billboard* charts in autumn 1999 on the back of the hit single 'Wanna Be A Baller', an infectious slice of classic old school hip-hop.

● ALBUMS: *Sittin' Fat Down South* (Short Stop/Universal 1999)★★★★.

Lilith Fair

Founded by Canadian singer-songwriter Sarah McLachlan in 1997, the Lilith Fair concert tour proved to be one of the year's major surprises. Naming the all-female travelling festival after Adam's first wife (in Hebrew folklore), McLachlan's aim was to raise the profile of female musicians within an industry that has traditionally remained male-dominated. Based around a rotating roster of 61 artists and bands, the tour boasted a veritable who's who of women's music in the 90s, including Jewel, Sheryl Crow, Shawn Colvin, Fiona Apple, Paula Cole, Meredith Brooks, Abra Moore, Suzanne Vega, Victoria Williams, Lisa Loeb, Tracy Bonham, Joan Osborne, Cassandra Wilson, Emmylou Harris, Dar Williams, Susanna Hoffs, the Indigo Girls and McLachlan herself. Reflecting the increasingly dominant chart positions in America of female artists, the tour proved to be an astounding success, becoming the summer's highest grossing tour ($16.7m) at a time when other package tours were struggling to survive. Sponsorship of the tour eschewed the blatant consumerism of rival packages such as Ozzy Osbourne's Ozzfest, with the emphasis placed on the sponsor's charitable impulses. A double CD compiling highlights of the 1997 tour was released in mid-1998, generating increased interest in that year's tour. Playing at 57 sold-out venues, the tour added Erykah Badu, Missy 'Misdemeanor' Elliott, Bonnie Raitt, Neneh Cherry, Liz Phair, Meshell Ndegéocello, Heather Nova, Natalie Merchant and Sinead O'Connor to the bill. The following year's tour, which McLachlan announced was the final one, included Mya, Luscious Jackson, Beth Orton, Sixpence None The Richer, and comedienne Sandra Bernhard.

● COMPILATIONS: *Lilith Fair: A Celebration Of Women In Music* (Arista 1998)★★★, *Lilith Fair: A Celebration Of Women In Music, Volume 2* (Arista 1999)★★★, *Lilith Fair: A Celebration Of Women In Music, Volume 3* (Arista 1999)★★★★.

Lilys

The constantly changing line-ups of this US east coast band revolve around their one permanent member, maverick Texan songwriter Kurt Heasley. Over 25 musicians have passed through the band's ranks, with regulars including Mike Hammel, Michael Deming, Harold Evans, Aaron Sperske and Dave Frank. Heasley's musical heritage included a grandfather who played guitar in the Dixieland era. He also spent a brief period working with Dave Grohl, later of Nirvana, in Tower Records in New York City. After playing in a local band with friends, Heasley spent time travelling during the late 80s. He picked up a guitar again in 1991, and set about realizing his blueprint for a one-man band that would use a network of musicians and producers. The newly christened Lilys released their debut 'February 14th' single on the independent Slumberland label in 1991. Heasley recorded the band's 1992 debut *In The Presence Of Nothing* in Washington, DC, with members of Velocity Girl and Suddenly, Tammy!. The album was a rather insipid recreation of the 'shoegazing' sound pioneered by England's My Bloody Valentine, with tracks such as 'There's No Such Thing As Black Orchids' and 'The Way Snowflakes Fall' failing to add anything original to the genre. Heasley returned two years later with the *A Brief History Of Amazing Letdowns* EP, which demonstrated a shift towards more straightforward guitar pop. Calvin Klein lifted one of the tracks, 'Ginger', for an American television advertisement. The minimal dream pop of 1995's *Eccsame The Photon Band*, recorded with Harold Evans, saw Heasley perform another *volte-face*. The band also released a one-off single for Sub Pop Records, 'Which Studies The Past?'. After relocating to Boston, Heasley reverted to writing snappy 60s British Invasion-influenced pop songs on *Better Can't Make Your Life Better*. The album gained valuable exposure in Europe when Levis used 'A Nanny In Manhattan' as the soundtrack to one of their UK television advertisements during January 1998. Released as a single, the song reached UK number 16 the following month. A superior remastered version was later issued, with two new tracks replacing 'The Sammael Sea' from the original release. The six-track EP *Services For The Soon To Be Departed* followed in 1997, but Heasley sounded less at ease reproducing the late 60s psychedelic sounds of the Beach Boys and the Grateful Dead. 'The 3 Way', released in April 1999, was another glorious reproduction of the mid-60s sounds of the Kinks, the Small Faces and the Zombies.

● ALBUMS: *In The Presence Of Nothing* (Slumberland/SpinART 1992)★★, *Eccsame The Photon Band* (SpinART 1995)★★★, *Better Can't Make Your Life Better* (Ché/Sire 1996)★★★★, 'The 3 Way' (Sire 1999)★★★.

Limp Bizkit

Led by self-confessed 'freak' Fred Durst (b. North Carolina, USA), the son of a policeman, hard rock/hip-hop fusion band Limp Bizkit were formed in 1994 in Jacksonville, Florida. Completed by guitarist Wes Borland (b. Richmond, Virginia, USA), bass player Sam Rivers (b. Jacksonville, Florida, USA) and drummer John Otto (b. Jacksonville, Florida, USA), the band were further augmented in 1996 by the services of DJ Lethal (b. Leor DiMant, Latvia) when his former employers House Of Pain ran aground. The connection was made originally when Limp Bizkit supported House Of Pain on their final tour. On his move from hip-hop to an (admittedly eclectic) rock sound, he commented: '80% of the drums in rap come from old rock records. People who talk shit about me being white and doing hip-hop better check who the fuck they're sampling!' The band made its debut with *Three Dollar Bill, Y'all$* in 1997, a record that went on to notch up sales in excess of 1.5 million as it was adopted by a new generation of MTV rock fans. The band's striking live shows, complete with breakdancers and garish backdrops, also earned them high-profile slots on the Ozzfest, Warped and Family Values tours. Durst continued to court celebrity and self-publicity, making guest appearances on albums by Korn and Soulfly during this period. He also became an A&R executive for his record label, Flip, fellow Jacksonville band Cold being his first signing. Limp Bizkit returned in July 1999 with *Significant Other*, with production work by DJ Premier and a guest rap from Method Man affirming the band's hip-hop credentials. The album debuted at number 1 on the US album chart, confirming the band as one of the leading alternative acts in America.

● ALBUMS: *Three Dollar Bill, Y'all$* (Flip/Interscope 1997)★★★, *Significant Other* (Flip/Interscope 1999)★★★★.

Lindsay, Arto

b. 28 May 1953, Brazil. Musician and writer Arto Lindsay has a distinguished track record on the fringes of rock history. Founder and leader of the New York 'no wave' band DNA, he was venerated by cognoscenti as, alternatively, high priest of the musical intelligentsia or 'the sultan of skronk'. One other famous description of Lindsay analogized his musical stature as that of 'James Brown trapped in Don Knotts' body'. He was born in Brazil the son of a missionary, only returning to take up American citizenship in order to attend college in the 70s. After DNA's dissolution he became half of the critically championed Ambitious Lovers with keyboardist Peter Scherer. Over the course of three albums he worked with artists of the stature of Vernon Reid and John Zorn in addition to regular partner Scherer. His first solo record was put together as a response to an approach by Ryûichi Sakamoto. *The Subtle Body* was initially conceived of as a bossa nova record, but in typical Lindsay fashion, a single genre proved too limiting for his oeuvre. As well as English language songs, Portuguese language numbers such as 'Este Seu Olhar' were in evidence, as they had been on previous Ambitious Lovers albums. Guests included Marc Ribot, Bill Frisell, Brian Eno and Amedeo Pace of Blonde Redhead. The album, which once again attracted glowing reviews, was released outside of Japan on the cult independent label Bar/None Records. Following its release, Lindsay moved on to work on a series of bold experimental albums that successfully fused such disparate styles as avant rock, drum 'n' bass and samba. He also produced albums by Brazilian artists Marisa Monte and Caetano Veloso.

● ALBUMS: *The Subtle Body* aka *O Corpo Sutil* (Güt 1995)★★★★, *Mundo Civilzado* (Bar/None 1996)★★★, *Hyper Civilzado* remix album (Gramavision 1997)★★★, *Noon Chill* (Bar/None 1998)★★★★, *Prize* (Righteous Babe/Rykodisc 1999)★★★.

Lionrock

Lionrock is one of the many vehicles used by Manchester disc jockey/remixer/artist Justin Robertson. Robertson had risen to prominence in 1990 by launching the Spice club session, a meeting place for like-minds such as the Chemical

Brothers (at that time the Dust Brothers). Alongside Andy Weatherall, Robertson subsequently became among the most prominent of a new wave of DJs, with his sets at Manchester's Most Excellent club making him well-known within the dance music community. This impression was confirmed by remixing credits for Björk, New Order, the Shamen, Sugarcubes, Inspiral Carpets, Stereo MC's, Erasure and many others. Lionrock, a name synonymous with uplifting house music and originally featuring keyboard player Mark Stagg, was formed in 1992 for the release of a self-titled 12-inch single on Robertson's own MERC Records. The following year's 'Packet Of Peace' included a rap from MC Buzz B and saw the band transfer to Deconstruction Records. It entered the UK charts and became a staple of house clubs throughout the UK. 'Carnival', which sampled from the MC5, again secured several Single Of The Week awards, from both dance magazines and more mainstream publications. 'Tripwire' was released in 1994. Robertson described the contents of Lionrock's 1996 debut album as 'Coxsone Dodd meets Ennio Morricone', a statement which indicated that earlier experiments with reggae and dub were continuing. MC Buzz B again guested, with samples of dialogue taken from old Sherlock Holmes films. Lionrock's line-up now included Roger Lyons (keyboards/electronics), Paddy Steer (bass), Mandy Wigby (keyboards) and Buzz B on vocals, as the album was promoted with a full-scale national tour. Release of the follow-up was delayed, allowing Robertson the opportunity to record new tracks and rework the album, which was finally released in early 1998. *City Delirious* eschewed the guitar riffing of the debut to return to Robertson's dance roots on tracks such as 'Push Button Cocktail' and 'Best Foot Forward'. Robertson parted company with Deconstruction shortly afterwards, releasing new material under the pseudonym Gentleman Thief.

● ALBUMS: *An Instinct For Detection* (Deconstruction 1996)★★★★, *City Delirious* (Deconstruction 1998)★★★★.

Live

Alternative rock band from York, Pennsylvania, USA comprising Ed Kowalczyk (vocals), Patrick Dahlheimer (bass), Chad Taylor (guitar) and Chad Gracey (drums). The band was formed as First Aid in the mid-80s by blue-collar friends Taylor, Gracey and Dahlheimer, changing their name to Public Affection with the addition of Kowalczyk. The self-financed *The Death Of A Dictionary* was released in 1989, but a change of name and a reworking of their sound was necessary before they were signed to Radioactive Records. Their dynamic of fraught pop that occasionally expands into full-blown rock mode, complete with lyrics that strike an idealistic tone, was evident on the largely ignored *Mental Jewelry*, where spiritual overtones were also present. No less intense was 1994's *Throwing Copper*, produced, like their debut, by Jerry Harrison. By this point Kowalczyk's lyrics had developed in a less literal direction: 'I'm more into letting my subconscious write, I want to let go completely, without becoming addicted to anything - which is a danger'. Another danger was a track such as 'Shit Towne', which addressed the populace of hometown York, and did little to ingratiate the band to their old community. The band's unexpected success continued into 1996 when *Throwing Copper* was certified as selling six million copies in the USA alone. Jay Healy was hired to produce *Secret Samadhi*, an altogether bleaker-sounding record, which nevertheless attained double platinum status. Harrison returned to co-produce 1999's *The Distance To Here*, which largely eschewed the experimental approach of its predecessor.

● ALBUMS: *Mental Jewelry* (Radioactive 1991)★★, *Throwing Copper* (Radioactive 1994)★★★★, *Secret Samadhi* (Radioactive 1997)★★★, *The Distance To Here* (Radioactive 1999)★★★★.

Lo' Jo

Denis Pean (b. 18 May 1961, Ponts-de-Ce, France; vocals, keyboards, flute, melodica), Yamina Nid El Mourid (b. 14 October 1969, Angers, France; vocals, saxophone, tambourine), Nadia Nid El Mourid (b. 15 March 1967, Angers, France; vocals), Richard Bourreau (b. 12 December 1964, Cholet, France; violin, kora), Nico Gallard (b. 29 January 1966, Angers, France; drums, percussion, keyboards), Nico Kham Meslien (b. 3 March 1972, Angers, France; bass, vocals). Formed in the tiny French village of Brissac-Quince in the Loire Valley in 1982 by Pean and Bourreau as a vehicle for learning and exploring different styles of music, Lo' Jo went through countless line-up changes and developed their sound throughout the 80s. Run along communal lines, by the end of the decade they were working with the Jo Bithume Street Theatre Company, providing the music for mime, circus, magic and theatre productions and touring throughout France, Germany and Belgium. Having worked with the Theatre Company for four years they moved on to work with other media, including acrobats, mime artists and their local film collective. They also gave straight musical performances. By the time they recorded their 1997 debut *Mojo Radio*, which was not released until a year later owing to record company problems, they had developed into a close-knit community known as Triban De Lo' Jo. The album featured the Arabic vocals of the Nid El Mourid sisters (whose family are from North Africa), which offset Pean's Tom Waits-style growl. Musically the band displayed an array of influences ranging from reggae to French gypsy music, Indian to punk. Lo' Jo stirred interest outside of France, where critics hailed their multi-cultural style and uncompromising stance as a natural progression from earlier French rebels Les Negresses Vertes. In 1998, the band made well received appearances at WOMAD Festivals in England and the USA.

● ALBUMS: *Mojo Radio* (Emma Productions/Night And Day 1998)★★★.

Lô, Cheikh

b. 12 September 1955, Bobo Dioulassa, Burkina Faso. The son of Senegalese parents, Lô became interested in music, especially Congolese rumba and the Cuban 'son' style from which it derived, at an early age. He frequently played truant from school in order to practice on a borrowed guitar and drum-kit. He made his professional debut in 1976, playing percussion with a local band called Orchestra Volta Jazz. Lô then moved to Senegal where he played drums with Ouza, and in 1984, he became drummer and vocalist with the house band of the Hotel Savana. The following year he moved to Paris, where he spent three years working as a session musician; he played on a wide variety of recording sessions, including work with Papa Wemba. On his return to Senegal in 1987, Lô tried to rejoin the Hotel Savana band, only to be turned away because of the flowing dreadlocks he

now sported. He decided to concentrate on developing his own material and in 1990 'Doxandem', his debut cassette for the Senegalese market, was released. It became a big local hit and a follow-up was recorded, but owing to business complications, it was never released. In 1995, he gave a demo tape of his material to Youssou N'Dour, who was impressed by Lô's warm voice, spiritual lyrics and multicultural sound, and he offered to produce an album with him. The recording session took place at N'Dour's Xippi Studio in Dakar in August of that year and featured Lo with support from N'Dour, along with members of his Super Etoile band. Released in Senegal in early 1996, *Né La Thaiss* was a collection of strong, haunting melodies with light, predominantly acoustic, backing. Reflecting Lô's varied musical influences, the album incorporated elements of reggae, salsa, jazz and rumba, while retaining a firm base of Senegal's 'mbalax' sound. A huge success in Senegal (one track was even used by the Senegalese government as part of a campaign to clean up the streets), *Né La Thaiss* was released internationally in November 1996 and was immediately hailed as a major world music recording. Lô toured internationally with N'Dour's Jololi Review at the time of the album's release and subsequently with his own band. N'Dour was on board again for the follow-up, *Bambay Gueej*.

● ALBUMS: *Né La Thaiss* (World Circuit 1996)★★★★, *Bambay Gueej* (World Circuit 1999)★★★.

Lo-Fidelity Allstars

Formed in 1996, the Lo-Fidelity Allstars combine indie and dance music influences in a manner reminiscent of the late 80s' 'Madchester' or 'baggy' scene. From Brighton, Sussex, England, the quintet released their debut single, 'Kool Roc Bass', for local record label Skint Records in 1997. The band, who all employ impenetrable surnames, are led by songwriter Phil 'The Albino Priest' Ward. Originally from Leeds, he formed the band while working at Tower Records in London's Piccadilly Circus. He originally intended the Lo-Fidelity All Stars to be an instrumental-only band, until meeting with vocalist Dave 'The Wrekked Train' Randall and keyboard player Matt 'Sheriff Jon Stone', whose alcohol-fuelled ramblings neatly complemented their loose, funky sound. The band, who also include bass player Andy 'A One Man Crowd Called Gentilee' Dickson and drummer Johnny 'The Slammer' Machin, achieved further exposure with a series of 1997 support slots to 18 Wheeler, a remix of Cast's 'History' and two further singles, 'Disco Machine Gun' and 'Vision Incision'. Their swaggering debut album, which entered the UK charts at number 15 in June, was widely touted as one of 1998's key releases. Randall quit the band in December, followed, in February, by Stone. Later in the year the band released the mix set, *On The Floor At The Boutique 2*, and recruited new keyboard player, Dale 'Pele' Malloney.

● ALBUMS: *How To Operate With A Blown Mind* (Skint 1998)★★★★.
● COMPILATIONS: *On The Floor At The Boutique 2* (Brassic 1999)★★★.

Loeb, Lisa

b. Lisa Anne Loeb, 11 March 1968, Bethesda, Maryland, USA. Singer-songwriter Loeb grew up in Dallas and attended Brown University, where she played in a band with her friend Liz Mitchell and Duncan Sheik. Relocating to New York she recorded a demo tape and toured incessantly with her band Nine Stories, comprising Tim Bright (guitar), Jonathan Feinberg (drums) and Joe Quigley (bass). She sprang to fame in 1994 when her friend, actor Ethan Hawke, persuaded the producers of the movie *Reality Bites* to use her song 'Stay (I Missed You)' as its theme. The result was a US number 1 despite Loeb not yet having a recording contract. That situation was quickly rectified with the intervention of Geffen Records, who are alleged to have offered over $1 million for her signature. Some of the furore then died down while Loeb set about crafting her debut album, the first evidence of which arrived with the release of the US Top 20 single 'Do You Sleep?' in September 1995. The accompanying album was co-produced with long-standing colleague Juan Patiño and Nine Stories. The songs were drawn from over 10 years worth of writing, notably the very early composition 'Garden Of Delights'. In press interviews of the time she was keen to salute rock influences as diverse as Jimi Hendrix, Led Zeppelin and Fugazi, rather than the acoustic singer-songwriters with whom she has been most readily identified in the press. Tracks such as 'Alone' and 'It's Over' bore this out, though even the quieter selections were imbued with sarcasm and Loeb's confrontational instincts. Her sophomore set featured Quigley and new musicians Mark Spencer (guitar) and Ronny Crawford (drums). Introduced by the minor hit 'I Do', *Firecracker* was a confident and mature collection that proved less popular than her debut.

● ALBUMS: *Tails* (Geffen 1995)★★★, *Firecracker* (Geffen 1997)★★★.
● FILMS: *Tabloid* (1987), *Black Circle Boys* (1997), *The Rugrats Movie* voice only (1998), *Serial Killing 4 Dummys* (1999), *House On Haunted Hill* (1999).

Lohan, Sinéad

b. Cork, Eire. One of the most commercially successful artists based in Ireland in the mid-90s, singer-songwriter Sinéad Lohan made a huge impact with the release of her debut album. Initially released on the small independent label Dara Records, *Who Do You Think I Am*, which featured Mary Black collaborator and former Moving Hearts member Declan Sinnot as producer and principal musician, received rave reviews from publications stretching across several musical genres. It was re-packaged and re-released by Grapevine Records in the summer of 1995 and quickly achieved double platinum status in Ireland. The album's contents revealed a maturity in stark contrast to the fact that most of the songs it contained were written when Lohan was a teenager. She had risen to prominence initially by featuring on the Irish album, *A Woman's Heart 2*, alongside Mary Black, Mary Coughlan and Sinead O'Connor. It was through this project that she came to the attention of Sinott, a fellow Cork native. Lohan had originally come to music via her parents, who were both active in the local music community, though she loved the Jam and Madness more than ethnic Irish music, and these influences continue to inform her own songwriting. Following a major Irish hit single in 1996 with a cover version of Bob Dylan's 'To Ramona', Lohan debuted internationally in 1998 with the beautiful *No Mermaid*, aided by the crystal clear production work of Malcolm Burn.

● ALBUMS: *Who Do You Think I Am* (Dara/Grapevine 1995)★★★, *No Mermaid* (Grapevine/Interscope 1998)★★★★.

Lollapalooza

From its inception in 1990, the first modern 'travelling festival', a rolling convoy of packaged bands, became something of a cultural phenomenon on a par with the rise of MTV. The original idea came from Perry Farrell, the singer with Jane's Addiction (who co-headlined the first Lollapalooza) and Porno For Pyros. Inspired by the atmosphere of the UK's Glastonbury Festival, Farrell hoped to replicate that event's cosmopolitan, philanthropic nature with a roster of varied bands as well as various other activities and sideshows, including environmental and political stalls, world arts and body-piercing. The first line-up reflected Farrell's desire to provide a broad range of alternative rock music and featured the Butthole Surfers, Ice-T, Nine Inch Nails, Living Colour, Henry Rollins (the Rollins Band) and Siouxsie And The Banshees each taking turns to headline and support. It was an immediate success at a time when most US rock promoters were struggling to fill auditoriums. The following year's line-up included Pearl Jam, Ice Cube, Ministry and the Red Hot Chili Peppers, with an expansion of non-musical events. Another major success, the festival nevertheless suffered a decline in 1993 when Farrell, more concerned with launching Porno For Pyros, was less instrumental in picking the lacklustre line-up. He returned to direct 1994's Lollapalooza (alongside former Jane's Addiction manager and festival organiser Ted Gardner), however, promising to restore the festival's original intention of offering 'something special, excellent or exceptional'. However, Nirvana were forced to cancel (shortly before Kurt Cobain's suicide in April), leaving many of the participants with the hangover of filling the void he had left behind in alternative music. L7, Japan's Boredoms, A Tribe Called Quest, the Breeders, the Verve, Nick Cave, the Beastie Boys and George Clinton were all on the extended bill, though this time Smashing Pumpkins were awarded a 'headlining' role. While some, including Cave, complained of the 'fast food' nature of the event, Lollapalooza undoubtedly went at least some way towards satisfying Farrell's original vision. The festival struggled to attract big names in later years, however, and was wound up in 1998.

Lonestar

This US country rock band signed to RCA Records in the 90s after establishing their reputation through a touring schedule that regularly encompassed over 200 performances a year. Comprising Richie McDonald (b. 6 February 1962, Lubbock, Texas, USA; vocals/guitar), John Rich (b. 7 January 1974, Amarillo, Texas, USA; vocals/bass), Michael Britt (b. 15 June 1966, Fort Worth, Texas, USA; guitar), Keech Rainwater (b. 24 January 1963, Plano, Texas, USA; drums) and Dean Sams (b. 3 August 1966, Garland, Texas, USA; keyboards), the band formed in Nashville, Tennessee, though all the members are natives of Texas. They made their debut in January 1995 when BNA Records released the *Lonestar Live* EP, recorded at Nashville's renowned Wildhorse Saloon. The band's superb harmonies and deep-rooted affection for the country tradition soon won supporters, and the highly successful singles 'Tequila Talkin'' and 'No News', made them a hot property in contemporary country circles. When the latter release made number 1 on the *Billboard* Hot Country Singles & Tracks chart, it built interest for the release of the band's self-titled debut in 1995. This was promoted by a typically rigorous touring schedule, which had given Lonestar much of their fanbase in the first place. As a result the band were invited to perform at the annual ACM telecast, where five years previously, McDonald had heard a Miller Lite beer jingle he had sung air during the commercial break. Rich had left for a solo career by the time 'Come Cryin' To Me' and 'Everything's Changed' provided the band with two more country chart-toppers. Both singles were taken from 1997's *Crazy Nights*, the slick but enjoyable follow-up. The excellent *Lonely Grill* plumped for the middle ground between the straightforward country of their debut and the pop stylings of *Crazy Nights*.

● ALBUMS: *Lonestar* (BNA 1995)★★★, *Crazy Nights* (BNA 1997)★★★, *Lonely Grill* (BNA 1999)★★★★.

Longpigs

Comprising Crispin Hunt (b. London, England; vocals, guitar), Richard Hawley (guitar), Simon Stafford (bass) and Dee Boyle (drums), Longpigs formed in Sheffield, Yorkshire, England, in 1993. Their extended gravitation towards the mainstream since that time was hindered by a series of corrupt band managers and soured recording contracts, but by 1996 the Longpigs were standing on the threshold of a national breakthrough. Chief songwriter and lyricist Hunt moved to Bradford from his native London at the age of 10. After a dalliance with the Catholic church and dropping out of his university philosophy studies, he moved to Amsterdam as the first stage in his plan to busk around Europe. He soon returned, and by that time had written enough material to furnish the Longpigs' debut album. It was his explicit intention to return to the rock 'n' roll grandeur of artists such as Lou Reed, Iggy Pop and the Beatles. He recruited former Cabaret Voltaire drummer Boyle, Stafford and Hawley, the band making its performance debut at local venue The Owl. An album was recorded with Gil Norton but it was then that the band had its first setback. The label in question closed its UK offices and demanded a £500,000 'release-fee'. Eventually Longpigs were free to sign a new contract with U2's Mother Records and re-recorded their debut album. Tours with Echobelly, Supergrass and Radiohead followed, while the extracted single, 'Far', reached the UK Top 40 in February 1996. 'On And On' became another success, this time reaching the UK Top 20, before *The Sun Is Often Out* was finally released. Songs such as 'She Said' (an unlikely meeting point between the Beatles and Nirvana, and another chart hit), 'Lost Myself' and 'Sally Dances' confirmed the promise of the earlier singles, while the Longpigs' breakthrough was celebrated by a partisan media keen to present Hunt as a major new songwriting talent. Boyle left before the recording of the follow-up *Mobile Home*, which mixed trip-hop beats into the band's indie rock formula.

● ALBUMS: *The Sun Is Often Out* (Mother 1996)★★★, *Mobile Home* (Mother 1999)★★★.

Loop Guru

The eclectic listening tastes of spokesman Jamuud (Dave Muddyman) has informed the career of world/dance fusionists Loop Guru. Together with Salman Gita (Sam Dodson) he forms the core of the band, aided by up to 10 guest musicians for various events (who include former Pigbag drummer Chip Carpenter and percussionist Mad Jim). The duo have been involved in music since 1980 when they were early members of the Megadog enclave, meeting through mutual friend Alex Kasiek (Transglobal Underground). It was at this time that Jamuud: '. . . stopped listening to Western music altogether. I found that the wealth of sound and mood in Asian and African music was vastly more alive than its Western counterparts.' Offering their listeners 'total enlightenment through music', Loop Guru have perfected a package of chants, laments, tablas, Eastern religion and ethnic samples. Following their 1992 debut single 'Mrabet'/'The Shrine', the band released 'Paradigm Shuffle', which included at its core Martin Luther King's 'I Have A Dream' speech. The following year's *Sus-San-Tics* EP featured the guest vocals of Iranian Sussan Deyhim. A debut album also appeared on the Nation Records label, its title, *Duniya*, translating from Urdu as 'The World'. The album's fusion of found sounds and trance beats proved highly popular in chill-out rooms on the club circuit. Part of the working methodology evolved from Brian Eno's 'Choice Cards' ethos, wherein different instructions on musical structure are carried out via the turn of a set of cards. The band subsequently signed a deal with the North-South label, which gave them the freedom to release experimental work alongside more conventional offerings. The former included the hour long single 'The Third Chamber', and the ongoing ambient project, *Catalogue Of Desires*, which was edited and repackaged in 1999 as *The Fountains Of Paradise*. Their self-styled 'pop' records, *Amrita* and *Loop Bites Dog*, continued to enjoy success on the UK independent charts.

● ALBUMS: *Duniya (The Intrinsic Passion Of Mysterious Joy)* (Nation 1994)★★★★, *Amrita (All These And The Japanese Soup Warriors)* (North-South/World Domination 1995)★★★★, *Catalogue Of Desires, Vol. 3* (North-South/Hypnotic 1996)★★★, *Moksha (Peel To Reveal)* (Strange Fruit 1996)★★★, *Loop Bites Dog* (North-South/World Domination 1997)★★★, *The Fountains Of Paradise* (North-South/Hypnotic 1999)★★★.

● COMPILATIONS: *In A World Of Their Own* 4-CD box set (North-South/Cleopatra 1999)★★★.

Lopez, Jennifer

b. 24 July 1970, Bronx, New York, USA. Of Puerto Rican descent, Lopez enjoyed great success as an actress before emerging in the late 90s as one of the new wave of Latin pop stars, alongside leading male singers Ricky Martin and Enrique Iglesias. As a child Lopez appeared in musical theatre, before making her film debut as a 16 year old in the movie *My Little Girl*. Her break into television came in 1990 when she won a dance contest to become a Fly Girl on the Fox television comedy series *In Living Color*. Further television work ensued, including appearances in the series *Second Chances* and *Hotel Malibu* (credited on both as Melinda Lopez), the short-lived *South Central* and a television movie *Nurses On The Line: The Crash Of Flight 7* (1993). She made her first major big screen appearance opposite Wesley Snipes and Woody Harrelson in 1995's *Money Train*, before working with director Gregory Nava on *My Family, Mi Familia*. Her experience on the latter led indirectly to the high-profile role of murdered Tejano star Selena Quintanilla in the 1997 biopic *Selena*. Now considered a major player in Hollywood, Lopez's acclaimed appearance opposite George Clooney in 1998's *Out Of Sight* made her the highest paid Latin actress in history. However, it was her role in *Selena*

that led to the revival of her music career. Major label backing, heavyweight producers of the calibre of Emilio Estefan, Rodney Jerkins and Sean 'Puffy' Combs, and the attendant crossover success of Martin and Iglesias, made 1999's *On The 6* one of the summer's most hotly anticipated releases. The album, named after the train line the young Lopez used to take into the city, was a predictable commercial success. The first single 'If You Had My Love' (produced by Jerkins), topped the US charts for five weeks. The follow-up, 'Waiting For Tonight', was also a strong seller. The album's other tracks, most of which were co-written by executive producer Corey Rooney, included 'Feelin' So Good' (featuring cameos from rappers Fat Joe and Big Punisher), a duet with Marc Anthony on 'No Me Ames' and the Trackmasterz-produced 'Should Have Never'. Lopez has remained in the media spotlight through her romantic dalliance with Combs.
● ALBUMS: *On The 6* (Work/Epic 1999)★★★.
● FILMS: *My Little Girl* (1986), *My Family, Mi Familia* (1995), *Money Train* (1995), *Jack* (1996), *Blood And Wine* (1997), *Selena* (1997), *Anaconda* (1997), *U Turn* (1997), *Out Of Sight* (1998), *Antz* voice only (1998), *Thieves* (1999).

Los Del Rio

By the time long-standing musical partners Rafael Ruíz and Antonio Romero Monge took over the top of *Billboard*'s Hot 100 chart for fourteen weeks in the summer of 1996, they had recorded over 30 albums of traditional Spanish music since their formation in Seville in the mid-60s. The song which produced their breakthrough was 'Macarena', which they originally released on the independent label Zafiro Records in 1994. After gaining popularity on Latin radio stations and appearing on a number of Spanish compilations it was transferred to BMG Latin who commissioned a Bayside Boys remix for national distribution. Of the song, Monge commented: '[it] is a revelation of happiness, and that happiness is captured in the rhythm of the song. It puts the world in agreement to dance and celebrate.' It was included on the duo's major label breakthrough *Macarena Non Stop*, and was recorded in several languages for release in different international markets. It also served to launch the 'Macarena dance craze', culminating in a packed-house festival at the Dodger Stadium in Los Angeles. The song proved to be a durable international hit, including a UK number 2 slot in 1996.
● ALBUMS: *A Mi Me Gusta* (Zafiro/BMG Latin 1994)★★★, *Calentito* (RCA 1995)★★★, *Macarena Non Stop* (BMG Latin 1996)★★★★, *Baila* (RCA 1999)★★★.

Lotion

With a line-up comprising Tony Zajkowski (vocals/guitar), Bill Ferguson (bass), Rob Youngberg (drums) and Jim Ferguson (guitar), New York, USA guitar band Lotion displayed initial musical similarities to both R.E.M. and, particularly, the Stone Roses. With Lotion licensed to the UK indie label Big Cat Records from SpinART Records in the USA, their sound was more Anglophile than their typically noise-obsessed New York peers. This helped them escape accusations of being just another American guitar band, a fate that befell many other imported records of the period. The band released two singles ('Head' and 'Tear') on Kokopop before recording their SpinART debut *Full Isaac*, which received

substantial attention in Britain during 1994, particularly in the small press, and preceded an appearance at that year's Reading Festival stage. The band consolidated their European reputation with touring commitments throughout 1995, leading to the release of a second album in September. This featured sleeve notes penned by reclusive author Thomas Pynchon, and a full, mature guitar sound tied to Zajkowski's world-weary lyrics. Once again, the reviews were strong, with Lotion becoming the latest in a long tradition of Americans to use Europe in general and the UK in particular to attempt to launch their careers in the face of domestic apathy. By 1997's excellent *The Telephone Album* the band must have been wondering what they had to do to sell records.
● ALBUMS: *Full Isaac* (spinART/Big Cat 1994)★★★, *Nobody's Cool* (spinART/Big Cat 1995)★★★★, *The Telephone Album* (spinART 1997)★★★.

Louise

b. Louise Nurding, 4 November 1974, Croydon, Surrey, UK. After two successful years with Eternal, Nurding (now billed simply as Louise) took the risky step of embarking on a solo career when Eternal were at their chart-topping peak. Remaining at EMI Records, the gamble paid off when her debut single 'Light Of My Life' reached number 8 in the UK in October 1995. Although 'In Walked Love' stalled at number 17, her next three singles, 'Naked' (number 5), 'Undivided Love' (number 5) and 'One Kiss From Heaven' (number 9), all reached the UK Top 10 during 1996. On the back of widespread media coverage, her debut album *Naked* went on to sell over 400,000 units. Belying the perceived image of the beautiful but vacuous glamour girl voted 'sexiest woman in the world', Louise contributed to the writing and production of her follow-up album, *Woman In Me*, recorded with producers Steve Levine (Culture Club), Simon Climie (Climie Fisher) and Nigel Lowis (Eternal). Buoyed by the success of the album's first two singles, 'Arms Around The World' and a cover version of the Average White Band's 'Let's Go Round Again', Louise set off on her first UK solo tour. She kept in the spotlight by marrying her soccer player boyfriend Jamie Redknapp, shortly before the World Cup began in June 1998.
● ALBUMS: *Naked* (EMI 1996)★★★, *Woman In Me* (EMI 1997)★★★.

Love, Monie

b. Simone Johnson, 2 July 1970, Battersea, London, England. Monie Love is a female rapper who has lived in New York since 1989, and is one of the few English hip-hop artists to achieve recognition in America. Her first recordings were with childhood friend MC Mell 'O', Sparki and DJ Pogo, under the banner Jus Bad Productions. Formed in 1987, the crew released a solitary single, 'Freestyle'. Love started recording solo with DJ Pogo in 1988, releasing 12-inch singles on obscure underground labels which were eventually spotted by DJ Tim Westwood, who asked them to do a single for his Justice label. There were several delays in releasing it, so instead they approached Cooltempo Records with 'I Can Do This', which became a UK Top 40 hit in early 1989. Love has since worked with many other rap outfits including the Jungle Brothers, who she met at a London gig in September 1988. They subsequently introduced her to the Native Tongues Posse, while Afrika Baby Bambaataa would produce her debut album and she acted as their European road manager. Love had another UK Top 20 hit with 'Grandpa's Party', a tribute to the original Afrika Bambaataa. She also collaborated with Andy Cox and David Steele of the Fine Young Cannibals on the summer 1990 single 'Monie In The Middle', and with True Image on the UK number 12 cover version of the Spinners' 'It's A Shame (My Sister)'. The latter also broke into the US Top 30. Tracks on her debut album like 'RU Single' and the Queen Latifah collaboration 'Ladies First', were intelligent attacks on the expectations and stereotypes of black women. Despite maturity beyond her years, she recognised that this phase of her career was still an apprenticeship; 'To me, rap is a school. The heads are split between Public Enemy and KRS-1's Boogie Down Productions. The students are me, Jungle Brothers, De La Soul . . . but the best thing about it is that the classroom is open to all'. In 1991, she teamed up with Adeva on the UK Top 20 single 'Ring My Bell', as well as working with Queen Latifah and Almond Joy on the Bold Soul Sisters feminist project. Two years later she branched out into acting, appearing in Forest Whitaker's television movie, *Strapped*, and Ted Demme's 'hip-hop whodunnit', *Who's The Man?* Released the same year, *In A Word Or 2* was another challenging and articulate set that was also informed by Love's recent experience of motherhood. The album included the UK Top 20 single 'Born 2 B.R.E.E.D.', co-written and co-produced by Prince.

● ALBUMS: *Down To Earth* (Cooltempo/Warners 1990)★★★★, *In A Word Or 2* (Cooltempo/Warners 1993)★★★.

● FILMS: *Who's The Man?* (1993).

LOX

Comprising childhood friends Shawn 'Sheek' Jacobs, Jayson Phillips and David Styles, the LOX (Living Off Experience) grew up together in the Yonkers district of New York, USA. Rapping from an early age, they adopted the LOX name in their late teens. The trio came to the attention of Mary J. Blige, who passed a demo tape onto Bad Boy Records boss Sean 'Puffy' Combs. Combs hired the trio as staff writers, leading to several high profile writing and performing credits with artists such as Mariah Carey ('Honey'), Mary J. Blige ('Can't Get You Off My Mind'), Notorious B.I.G. ('Last Day') and Puff Daddy (Combs' recording moniker). The LOX's big breakthrough came when their Notorious B.I.G. tribute song, 'We'll Always Love Big Poppa', was used as the b-side to Puff Daddy's international hit single 'I'll Be Missing You'. Their stylish and highly melodic debut album entered the *Billboard* album chart at number 3 in January 1998. They also enjoyed two US Top 30 singles with 'If You Think I'm Jiggy' and the album's title track. The latter, which featured the vocal talents of Lil' Kim and DMX, peaked at number 17 in May. The trio subsequently teamed up with the Ruff Ryders crew on April 1999's chart-topping *Ryde Or Die Vol. 1* compilation. Their sophomore collection, *We Are The Streets*, debuted at US number 5 in February 2000.

● ALBUMS: *Money, Power & Respect* (Bad Boy 1998)★★★★, *We Are The Streets* (Ruff Ryders 2000)★★★.

LTJ Bukem

b. Daniel Williamson, Croydon, Surrey, England. Bukem has played a significant part in the development of drum 'n' bass during the 90s. He grew up around Harlesden, London and

then Watford where he learned the piano and listened to the Jam, the Police and the 2-Tone bands. He later became interested in rare groove, soul, funk and jazz and in the mid-80s began DJing with the Sunshine sound system; he subsequently became interested in dance music and made his DJing breakthrough in 1990 when he played at Raindance in Essex. His first release was 'Logical Progression' on Vinyl Mania in 1991 which was followed by 'Demon's Theme', 'Bang The Drums' (featuring Tayla) (both 1991), 'Return To Atlantis' (1992) and 'Music' (1993), on his own label Good Looking Records. 'Demon's Theme' introduced the strings and mellow ambience which characterizes much of Bukem's work and was one of the first records to feature the sound that became known as drum 'n' bass. Rather than sampling old breakbeats like many jungle and hardcore artists of the time, Bukem preferred to create his own rhythm tracks in this style thereby creating a more varied beat for his recordings. In 1993, with Fabio and MC Conrad he brought his sound to a wider audience with the launch of the club Speed at the Mars Bar in central London, which featured such DJs as Adam F., Alex Reece, Deep Blue, Goldie and lead to widespread media coverage of this new English cultural phenomenon. His success continued with a remix of Jodeci's 'Feenin'' (1995) and the development, along with business partner Tony Fordham, of Good Looking and associated labels, Looking Good and Earth. He has since presented his touring club Logical Progression, featuring an array of talent including Peshay, Photek, Blame, Tayla and Nookie, and the *Earth* compilations. In 1997, Bukem contributed a version of 'Thunderball' to David Arnold's album of *James Bond*-theme remakes, *Shaken And Stirred*. He was also featured on the BBC2 documentary *DJ*, alongside the larger than life Fordham. The following year Bukem inaugurated the *Progression Sessions* series.

● COMPILATIONS: *Mixmag Live!* (Mixmag 1996)★★★, *LTJ Bukem Presents Logical Progression* (Good Looking 1996)★★★★, *Promised Land Volume 1* (Mutant Sound 1996)★★★, *LTJ Bukem Presents Earth Volume One* (Good Looking 1996)★★★, *Intense Presents Logical Progression Level 2* (Good Looking 1997)★★★, *LTJ Bukem Presents Earth Volume Two* (Earth 1997)★★★, *Progression Sessions, Vol. 1* (Good Looking 1998)★★★, *Progression Sessions, Vol. 2* (Good Looking 1998)★★★, *Intense Presents Logical Progression Level 3* (Good Looking 1998)★★★, *LTJ Bukem Presents Earth Volume Three* (Earth 1998)★★★, *Progression Sessions, Vol. 3* (Good Looking 1999)★★★, *Progression Sessions, Vol. 4* (Good Looking 1999)★★★.

Luna

Singer/guitarist Dean Wareham (b. New Zealand), a graduate of Harvard University, left his previous band, Galaxie 500, in 1991. Luna effectively became his solo venture, with contributions from former members of the Feelies (drummer Stanley Demeski) and the Chills (bass player Justin Harwood), with guitarist Sean Eden joining after the release of their debut album. *Lunapark* (credited to Luna [2]) revisited Wareham's famously brittle songwriting, but added more rhythmic propulsion to the material, particularly on 'Slide'. The same track also headed Luna's 1993 EP, which included several cover versions alluding to Wareham's more obvious influences (notably a version of the Steve Wynn's 'That's What You Always Say'). *Bewitched* was a comparative disappointment, with the inappropriate production reducing Wareham's power as a natural lyricist. Produced by

Wareham with Pat McCarthy and Mario Salvati, *Penthouse* pushed the band towards more mainstream approval with songs such as 'Double Feature' and '23 Minutes In Brussels'. In 1996, Luna contributed a version of Donovan's 'Season Of The Witch' to the soundtrack of a new movie about Andy Warhol, *I Shot Andy Warhol*. The dark and hypnotic *Pup Tent* was well-received, but was dwarfed by the twisted, majestic pop of 1999's *The Days Of Our Nights*.

● ALBUMS: as Luna [2] *Lunapark* (Elektra 1992)★★★, *Bewitched* (Elektra 1994)★★, *Penthouse* (Elektra 1995)★★★, *Pup Tent* (Elektra/Beggars Banquet 1997)★★★, *The Days Of Our Nights* (Jericho/Beggars Banquet 1999)★★★★.

Luniz

From Oakland, California, USA, Yukmouth and Numskull began rapping together as junior high students in their hometown. They originally sung with B.W.P. (Brothers With Potential), a six-strong crew who eventually fell apart to leave only Yukmouth and Numskull. The duo renamed themselves Luni Tunz and got their first taste of recording in 1992 on Dru Down's *Explicit Game* set. A contract with Noo Trybe followed before the duo burst onto the hip-hop scene in 1995 with their debut, *Operation Stackola*. The album, which featured guest appearances from Dru Down, Shock-G of Digital Underground, Richie Rich, plus production work by DJ Fuse, N.O. Joe, Gino Blackwell, E-A-Ski and Tone Capone, was based around a heady mix of east and west coast styles. It reached number 1 in the US *Billboard* charts soon after release, taking many commentators, even within the hip-hop community, by surprise. The secret of their success lay in the duo's slick, empathetic performance, a theory endorsed by Yukmouth: 'Sometimes Numskull will just be freestyling, and I'll damned know exactly what he's about to say next. We're like two halves of a whole.' They also found success with the international hit single, 'I Got 5 On It', which was built around a sample of Club Noveau's 'Why You Treat Me So Bad'. The follow-up *Lunitik Muzik* was a sprawling and entertaining album featuring guest appearances from Redman, E-40 and Too Short among others. The downbeat 'Y Do Thugz Die', which commented on the murders of 2Pac and Notorious B.I.G., was arguably the best track.

● ALBUMS: *Operation Stackola* (Noo Trybe 1995)★★★, *Lunitik Muzik* (Noo Trybe/C-Note 1997)★★★★.

Luscious Jackson

The New York, USA-based band Luscious Jackson enjoyed almost universal press acclaim in the 90s with their spacious, bass-driven hip-hop/rock crossover. Their sound sampled New York life first-hand, with breakbeats married to traffic noise and overheard conversation, coupled with a slouching bass and guitar that managed to effect a Brooklyn drawl of its own. They were actually most heavily influenced by UK bands such as Delta 5, the Slits and Gang Of Four. Thus inspired, Jill Cunniff (vocals/bass), Gabrielle Glaser (vocals/guitar) and Kate Schellenbach (drums) used to forge ID to get into Manhattan's Lower East Side's punk clubs, as a result of which Schellenbach was recruited as drummer by the Beastie Boys, in their original hardcore guise. Having worked on their first two EP releases, *Polly Wog Stew* and *Cooky Puss*, she later drummed with Hippies With Guns before rejoining her old friends. However, the

trio then went off to separate art schools (Cunniff and Glaser also formed a punk band, Jaws, in San Francisco, and Cunniff edited the fanzines *Decline of Art* and *The Golfing Experience*). They returned to New York in 1991, and Cunniff and Glaser began to write short sketches, songs and rhymes together, recruiting Cunniff's art school friend, the classically trained musician Vivian Trimble, to add keyboards for their first shows. With a guitar and beatbox as their musical foundation, they added primal but amusing sampling on their first demo tape. Old friend Mike D heard it and was impressed enough to release it, virtually unchanged, as the band's 1992 debut mini-album on the Beastie Boys' Grand Royal label. Many were impressed by their erudite wit, displayed both in the songs themselves and in the choice of samples. *Natural Ingredients* was more reserved musically, but was just as barbed lyrically, concentrating on nostalgia, romance and relationships: 'A lot of the lyrics on this record are about coming to terms with womanhood and the search for the identity and confusion that women tend to experience in adolescence or in long-term relationships' - not that the band made it sound as prosaic as that, with their clever use of irresistible harmonies and low-slung bass on the fine track 'Energy Sucker' and promotional single 'Deep Shag'. The Daniel Lanois-produced third album tempered the band's aggression with more relaxed grooves, and featured backing vocals from Emmylou Harris on 'Soothe Yourself'. The prolific Cunniff and Trimble also recorded an album as Kostars, but the latter left the main band before the release of 1999's *Electric Honey*.

● ALBUMS: *In Search Of Manny* mini-album (Grand Royal 1992)★★★, *Natural Ingredients* (Grand Royal 1994)★★★, *Fever In, Fever Out* (Grand Royal 1997)★★★★, *Electric Honey* (Grand Royal 1999)★★★.

Lush

Though they made their live debut at the Camden Falcon on 6 March 1988, little was heard of London-based Lush's serene pop qualities and full-bodied guitar sound until their mini-album *Scar* was issued in October 1989 on 4AD Records. It was a critically acclaimed debut, and red-haired Miki Berenyi (b. 18 March 1967, St Stephen's, London, England; vocals/guitar), Emma Anderson (b. 10 June 1964, Raynes Park, London, England; guitar/backing vocals), Steve Rippon (bass) and Christopher Acland (b. 7 September 1966, Lancaster, Lancashire, England, d. 17 October 1996; drums) found themselves topping the independent charts. Previously Anderson, a former DHSS clerical assistant, had been bass player for the Rover Girls, Berenyi had played with I-Goat, Fuhrer Five and the Lillies, while Acland had been a member of Infection, Panik, A Touch of Hysteria, Poison In The Machine and others. Tours with the Darling Buds and Loop followed Lush's initial breakthrough, plus an appearance on BBC2's *Snub TV* and a John Peel radio session. The EP *Mad Love*, issued in February 1990, was less raw but soared to new heights with the help of producer Robin Guthrie from the Cocteau Twins. Lush's consistent coverage in the music press, not least for their perpetual appearances at pre/post-gig parties, made them one of the leading UK independent bands of the year; one that was taken up with tours in the UK and Europe and an appearance at the Glastonbury Festival. Another EP, *Sweetness And Light*, offered a further move towards a commercial pop sound and only narrowly missed the national charts. The three EPs were compiled, originally for the US market, on *Gala*. Much of 1991 was spent recording the long-awaited full debut album, during which time they also issued an EP, *Black Spring* (which included a cover version of Dennis Wilson's 'Fallin' In Love'). When *Spooky* was finally released, many were disappointed, some insisting that Guthrie's production had swamped the band's sound. Nevertheless, the album reached the national Top 10 and number 1 in the UK independent chart. During the winter of 1991 the line-up changed when bass player Steve Rippon left amicably, to be replaced by Phil King (b. 29 April 1960, Chiswick, London, England). The critical reception that awaited 1994's second album, *Split*, was fervent, with its cool guitar textures winning over many who had doubted their staying power. Berenyi and Anderson, dismissed in some quarters as 'two pissheads from London', had dispelled not only that notion, but also that of them being a 'typically glacial post-punk 4AD band', with a stunningly evocative collection of pop songs. Although *Lovelife* failed to a certain degree in putting Lush in the premier league of pop bands (as was touted) it did contain the engaging 'Single Girl', an effortless classic pop song, and '500', a paean to the tiny Fiat car. Anderson stated to the *New Musical Express*: 'I was sick of writing about bloody men, so I wrote about being in love with a car. They're more reliable than men'. Acland took his own life in October 1996, and the band split-up the following year. Berenyi was reported to be writing solo material, King joined the Jesus And Mary Chain and Anderson formed Sing Sing.

● ALBUMS: *Spooky* (4AD 1992)★★, *Split* (4AD 1994)★★★, *Lovelife* (4AD 1996)★★★.

● COMPILATIONS: *Gala* (4AD 1990)★★★.

Lynch Mob

Following Dokken's acrimonious split in 1988, guitarist George Lynch and drummer Mick Brown recruited bass player Anthony Esposito and tempted vocalist Oni Logan away from the embryonic Cold Sweat to complete Lynch Mob. *Wicked Sensation* was a decent hard rock debut, carried by Lynch's considerable ability, but youthful vocalist Logan's inexperience began to show through on the road. The band felt particularly uncomfortable when comparing Logan with Geoff Tate during a European tour with Queensrÿche, where the highlight of the set tended to be a rendition of 'Mr Scary', Lynch's Dokken-era instrumental guitar workout. Logan was replaced by another relative unknown, Robert Mason, when touring was complete. *Lynch Mob* incorporated more R&B influences, moving further from the Dokken sound, and this suited Mason's bluesy tones, while the band paid tribute to their influences with a cover version of Queen's 'Tie Your Mother Down'. However, neither album really took off, and Lynch split the band, opting to go solo. Brown rejoined Don Dokken in 1994, as did Lynch later in the year. The latter resurrected Lynch Mob with a new line-up for 1999's *Smoke This*.

● ALBUMS: *Wicked Sensation* (Elektra 1990)★★★, *Lynch Mob* (Elektra 1992)★★★★, *Smoke This* (Koch 1999)★★★.

Lynne, Shelby

b. Shelby Lynn Moore, 22 October 1968, Quantico, Virginia, USA. The exceptionally talented Lynne was raised in Jackson, Alabama, and her life reads like a soap opera: there were long arguments with her father who had her jailed on a trumped-up charge, and later, she saw her father shoot her mother dead and then commit suicide. When she appeared on the *Nashville Now* talent show at the age of 18, it was evident that she was a very good singer with a rather unusual, deep voice. Billy Sherrill offered to produce her records and her 1989 debut included the standards 'I Love You So Much It Hurts Me' and 'I'm Confessin''. Her first single, 'If I Could Bottle This Up', was with another of Sherrill's artists, George Jones. Lynne proved to be a very determined country performer who does not kowtow to the media by turning on smiles for the photographers, but this reputation made it difficult to obtain a record contract after parting with Epic Records. *Temptation* was a radical album, employing a full horn section, and sounded closer to Harry Connick Jnr. than country music - the video for 'Feelin' Kind Of Lonely Tonight' indicated her wish to tour with an orchestra, and for the first time Lynne contributed her own material. *Restless* marked something of a return to traditional country, although there were still jazz and R&B overtones. Despite her talent she has yet to win over US radio stations, however, a problem highlighted by the fact that the excellent *I Am Shelby Lynne*, recorded with Bill Bottrell, was primarily targeted at the European market.

● ALBUMS: *Sunrise* (Epic 1989)★★★, *Tough All Over* (Epic 1990)★★★★, *Soft Talk* (Epic 1991)★★★, *Temptation* (Morgan Creek 1993)★★★, *Restless* (Magnatone 1995)★★★, *I Am Shelby Lynne* (Mercury 1999)★★★★.

M People

The key component of M People is Mike Pickering (b. March 1958, Manchester, England; keyboards/programming), a former DJ at the Factory Records' owned Haçienda club in Manchester. His activities there once encouraged *The Face* magazine to proclaim him as 'England's most revered DJ'. After school, Pickering worked in a fish factory and engineering warehouse, becoming a big fan of northern soul. He played saxophone and sang for mid-80s indie/dance forerunners Quando Quango, and had various connections with New Order, including sharing a flat with their manager, Rob Gretton. He also had the distinction of booking the Smiths for their first Manchester gig, and signing both James and the Happy Mondays in his role as Factory's A&R representative. After leaving Factory he became a junior director at Deconstruction Records, to whom he brought Black Box and Guru Josh, the label's two most important early successes. He also provided Deconstruction with *North - The Sound Of The Dance Underground*, cited by many as the first UK house music compilation, though in truth it was Pickering and his band T-Coy behind seven of the eight songs. He is also the founder member and songwriter for M People - the M standing for his first name - who also record for Deconstruction. The band was formed by ex-Hot! House vocalist Heather Small (b. 20 January 1965, London, England) and Paul Heard (b. 5 October 1960, Hammersmith, London, England; keyboards/programming), formerly of Orange Juice and Working Week. They achieved major success with the club hit 'How Can I Love You More?' at the end of 1991. These singles promoted a first album which took its name from Pickering's early musical leanings, *Northern Soul*. The breakthrough year for M People was 1993, as they enjoyed a string of UK Top 10 hits with a reissued 'How Can I Love You More?', 'One Night In Heaven', 'Moving On Up' (later used as a campaign tune by the UK's Labour Party), and a cover version of Dennis Edwards' 'Don't Look Any Further'. The album which contained the hits, *Elegant Slumming* (the title was taken from a Tom Wolfe book), featured vocal support from Nu Colours. It won them the Best British Dance Act at the BRIT Awards, and the 1994 Mercury Music Prize for best UK act in any category, much to the chagrin of hotly tipped pretenders Blur. Meanwhile, their highly polished, commercial sound (omnipresent on car stereos and commercial radio) was being cited as the perfect example of 'handbag house', a term the band themselves despised. *Bizarre Fruit* and the attendant Top 10 singles 'Sight For Sore Eyes', 'Open Your Heart' and 'Search For The Hero', were greeted with mild disappointment. The band, by now a quartet with the permanent addition of their touring percussionist Shovell (ex-Natural Life), embarked on a tour of the world's stadia to ecstatic receptions. Their love affair with the critics had cooled, the media taking special pleasure in poking fun at Small's choice of boyfriend - rugby league player Shaun Edwards. *Bizarre Fruit II* merely compiled several remixes and edits as a prelude to a new album, though an ill-advised cover version of the Small Faces' 'Itchycoo Park' managed to irritate the critics further. *Fresco* proved to be another smooth slab of easy-listening soul, with the single 'Just For You' the stand-out track.

● ALBUMS: *Northern Soul* (Deconstruction 1992)★★★, *Elegant Slumming* (Deconstruction 1993)★★★★, *Bizarre Fruit* (Deconstruction 1994)★★★, *Bizarre Fruit II* (Deconstruction 1995)★★, *Fresco* (BMG 1997)★★, *Testify* US only (Epic 1999)★★★.
● COMPILATIONS: *The Best Of M People* (BMG 1998)★★★.
● VIDEOS: *Elegant TV* (BMG Video 1994), *Come Again* (BMG Video 1995), *One Night In Heaven* (Game Entertainment 1998).

MacGowan, Shane, And The Popes

There are doubtless those in the music industry, particularly some vulture-like members of the press, who never expected Shane MacGowan (b. 25 December 1957, Kent, England) to survive, never mind record again, after he left the Pogues in September 1991. He reappeared the following December duetting with Nick Cave on a seasonal cover version of Louis Armstrong's 'What A Wonderful World'. Following a promotional single, 'That Woman's Got Me Drinking' ('she must have been employed by the brewing industry', as one wag in the press noted), MacGowan unveiled his new band, the Popes, and the debut solo album, *The Snake*, in October 1994. The Popes included Paul 'Mad Dog' McGuinness (guitar), Berni France (bass), Tom 'McAnimal' McManamon (banjo) and Danny Heatley (drums). Unsurprisingly, given MacGowan's collaborative track record, there was also an array of guest musicians in attendance, including members of the Dubliners, Jem Finer and Spider Stacy from the Pogues, and the actor Johnny Depp, who directed and starred in the video for 'That Woman's Got Me Drinking', also contributing some elementary guitar on the track. *The Snake* was co-produced with Dave Jordan in London and Ireland, and featured a typically impressive range of musical styles, running from the raucous cowpunk of 'A Mexican Funeral In Paris', which could have graced any Pogues album, to more reflective and traditional songs such as 'Donegal Express'. The album was reissued the following year with additional tracks, including the Sinead O'Connor duet, 'Haunted', which broke into the UK Top 30. This feat was repeated the following year by his solo version of the evergreen 'My Way' thanks to its prominent use in a Nike commercial. The Popes line-up subsequently changed when France was replaced by Bob Dowling. MacGowan, meanwhile, continued to confound critics who had already signed his death warrant with 1997's *The Crock Of Gold*, with the track 'St. John Of Gods', in particular, providing further evidence of his undiminished songwriting abilities. MacGowan has since been released by ZTT Records, leaving one of the UK's finest songwriters of recent times without a recording contract.

● ALBUMS: *The Snake* (ZTT 1994)★★★, *The Snake* extended reissue (ZTT/Warners 1995)★★★, *The Crock Of Gold* (ZTT 1997)★★★.
● FURTHER READING: *The Pogues: The Lost Decade*, Ann Scanlon. *Poguetry: The Lyrics Of Shane MacGowan*, John Hewitt and Steve Pyke (illustrators). *Shane MacGowan: Last Of The Celtic Soul Rebels*, Ian O'Doherty.

Mack 10

b. D. Rolison, 9 August 1971, Inglewood, California, USA. This protégé of Ice Cube spent his early years involved in the seedier side of Los Angeles street life, but got his big break when he came to the attention of Ice Cube and signed a deal with Priority Records. He enjoyed instant success with his self-titled 1995 debut. Featuring the minor hit single 'Foe Life', the album was a vivid depiction of gangsta life that verged on the self-parodic at times. The track 'Westside Slaughterhouse' featured Mack 10 alongside Ice Cube and W.C., an early outing for the self-styled hip-hop supergroup Westside Connection. The trio's US Top 5 debut *Bow Down* was followed by Mack 10's sophomore set, *Based On A True Story*, which also went gold. The rapper also enjoyed two radio hits with his contributions to the soundtracks of *The Substitute* ('Hoo-Bangin'') and *Rhyme & Reason* ('Nothing But The Cavi Hit', recorded with Tha Dogg Pound). He also set-up his own Mack One-O Productions and Hoo-Bangin' Records enterprises. *The Recipe* provided further proof of the popularity of his extreme style.

● ALBUMS: *Mack 10* (Priority 1995)★★★, *Based On A True Story* (Priority 1996)★★★, *The Recipe* (Priority 1998)★★★.
● FILMS: *Rhyme & Reason* (1997).

Mackintosh, C.J.

b. Christopher John Mackintosh, 29 December 1962, Paris, France. One of the UK's most widely revered DJs and remixers of the early 90s, and a man for whom major record companies would, at times, regularly indulge their A&R budgets. Chris 'C.J.' Mackintosh's standard approach, that of radio-friendly, lush garage arrangements, proved too MOR for many of the nation's more underground clubbers, but his technique has become the epitome of taste in the mainstream, with clients including Whitney Houston, Lisa Stansfield and Janet Jackson. Inspired by his DJ brother, he began by playing funk and rap. His first club booking was at 'Flim Flam' in New Cross with Jonathan Moore of Coldcut. He went on to win the 1987 finals of the DMC mixing championships. After this initial success he provided hip-hop megamixes for labels such as Champion Records and joined the Nasty Rox Inc. production team. His first venture into remixing proved even more rewarding. Together with Dave Dorrell of the Nasty Rox, he mixed MARRS' 'Pump Up The Volume', one of dance music's seminal moments and a huge transatlantic crossover hit. Mackintosh returned to his daytime job, that of club DJ, and was one of the first of the UK's name DJs to play in the USA. He also became a regular at one of the first dance superclubs, the Ministry Of Sound in London, although he resigned from his residency in 1996. A list of his credits could fill a small book, but some of the most important include Inner City ('Good Life'), Dina Carroll ('Ain't No Man'), P.M. Dawn ('Reality Used To Be A Friend Of Mine'), A Tribe Called Quest ('Bonita Applebum'), De La Soul ('Ring, Ring, Ring'), Digital Underground ('Packet Man'), Simple Minds ('Sign Of The Times'), Gang Starr ('Take A Rest'), Whitney Houston ('Queen Of The Night') and Luther Vandross and Janet Jackson ('The Best Things In Life Are Free').
● COMPILATIONS: *Sessions 4 - C.J. Mackintosh* (MOS 1994)★★★.

MacMaster, Natalie

b. Inverness County, Nova Scotia, Canada. Fiddler Natalie MacMaster gives credit for her emergence in the 90s to the Cape Breton Fiddler's Association, started in the early 70s after a documentary, *The Vanishing Cape Breton Fiddler*, was screened. It led to a revival in this most dynamic of musical cultures, and MacMaster is just one of several young musicians to be inspired by the new climate. After growing up in a musical family she made her debut in traditional square dances and variety concerts. As is traditional with Cape Breton music, her playing is intrinsically linked to dancing and gaiety. 'The rhythms you use for the feet are the same as you use for the fiddle, the same with the piano. It's all tied in, the language (Gaelic), the dancing, the piano, the fiddle . . . everything matches,' says MacMaster. Indeed, she only began to learn the fiddle after becoming a proficient dancer. She took informal lessons for three years, learning the individual Cape Breton approach to the violin, which includes a distinctive bowing technique, and repetitive structures known as 'cuts' (triplets). She began to play outside Nova Scotia at the age of 12, touring the festival circuit throughout America and Canada. Her first record was issued in 1989, at the age of 16. It was followed two years later by *Road To The Isle*, which garnered several East Coast Music Awards, including Instrumental Artist Of The Year and the Roots/Traditional category. Her now regular pianist, Tracey

Dare, joined her in time for *Fit As A Fiddle*, and they also toured internationally as a trio with the assistance of guitar player Dave MacIsaac. MacMaster and Dare (who released *The Crooked Lake* in 1995) also perform with a full Cape Breton band with drums, bass and Gaelic singing. *No Boundaries* was a flawed attempt to breakthrough to a wider audience. Far more satisfying were the back to basics *My Roots Are Showing* and *In My Hands*, the latter including MacMaster's first ever vocal performance on the title track.
● ALBUMS: *Four On The Floor* cassette only (1989)★★★, *Road To The Isle* cassette only (1991)★★★★, *Fit As A Fiddle* (Warner Music Canada 1994)★★★, *No Boundaries* (Warner Music Canada 1996)★★★, *My Roots Are Showing* (Greentrax 1998)★★★★, *In My Hands* (Greentrax 1999)★★★.
● COMPILATIONS: *A Compilation* (Greentrax 1997)★★★.
● VIDEOS: *Fiddle Lesson With Natalie MacMaster* (Greentrax 1997)★★★.

Mad Cobra

b. 31 March 1968, Ewart Everton Brown, Kingston, Jamaica, West Indies. Brown began his career earnestly following his musical roots - his uncle was an engineer at Bob Marley's Tuff Gong studios. While still at school, Brown chanted on sound systems including the Mighty Ruler and Stereo One. After gaining his qualifications, he pursued a career in the music business. He recorded with a number of producers including Bobby Digital, King Jammy and Donovan Germain. In 1991, Brown recorded 'Tek Him', riding a version of Eric Donaldson's 20-year old Jamaican Music Festival winner, 'Cherry Oh Baby'. The song has since become an anthem and a myriad of versions to the rhythm surfaced, including a remake by Donaldson himself. The hits continued, including 'OPP' (Other Peoples Property), with Conroy Smith, 'Body Basics', 'Be Patient', 'Yush' and 'Gundelero'. His success led to a number of compilations, including *Cobra Gold*, which featured a variety of tracks from a number of producers, and *Ex-Clusive* produced by Clive Kennedy. By 1993, following the success of Shabba Ranks, the major labels took an interest in Jamaican performers and Sony signed Brown, who subsequently became known as Mad Cobra. With production credits to Clifton 'Specialist' Dillon and Sly Dunbar, the release of 'Flex' earned him international fame by breaking into the US pop charts. The success of the tune was eclipsed when the rhythm was used for Buju Banton's infamous 'Boom Bye Bye', although Mad Cobra's earlier homophobic song, 'Crucifixion', had been ignored by the media. In Jamaica, he recorded 'Fat And Buff' for Jammys and, inspired by the revival of conscious lyrics, 'Selassie I Rules' in 1994. Throughout 1995 his prolific output continued with notable hits such as 'Poor Mans Shoes', 'Live Good', 'Hell Swell', 'Send Them Come' and 'Dun Wife'. He was also the featured DJ on Bunny Rugs' remake of his Third World hit, 'Now That We've Found Love'. At the 1995 Sting concert, promoted by Isaiah Lang, Mad Cobra faced Ninjaman in a clash of the DJs. Unfortunately, on this Boxing Day event Mad Cobra had to accept defeat, but a rematch was scheduled in Montego Bay on New Year's Eve. The clash never took place and the two embraced, with Ninjaman announcing, 'Cobra ah mi bwoy, we come outa de same camp'.
● ALBUMS: *Ex-Clusive* (Charm 1991)★★★, *Bad Boy Talk* (Penthouse 1991)★★★, *Merciless Bad Boy* (Sinbad 1992)★★★, *Your Wish* (Esoldun

1992)★★★, *Spotlight* (Top Rank 1992)★★★, *Hard To Wet Easy To Dry* (Columbia 1993)★★★, *Venom* (Greensleeves 1994)★★★★, *Step Aside* (VP 1994)★★★, *Meets Lt Stitchie And Beenie Man* (VP 1995)★★★★, *Exclusive Decision* (VP 1996)★★★★, *Milkman* (EMI America 1996)★★★.

● COMPILATIONS: *Cobra Gold* (Charm 1991)★★★, *Goldmine* (VP 1993)★★★, *Shoot To Kill* (VP 1993)★★★, *Mad Cobra* (Sonic 1994)★★★, *Sexperience* (Critique 1996)★★★.

Madder Rose

Spuriously lauded on their arrival in 1993 as the new Velvet Underground, Manhattan, New York, USA-based Madder Rose was formed by Billy Coté (b. New Jersey, USA; guitar), Mary Lorson (vocals), Matt Verta-Ray (bass) and Johnny Kick (b. Chicago; drums, ex-Speedball). The initial ripples were caused by singles such as 'Swim', a yearning, slow-burning torch song reminiscent of Lou Reed's craft. However, they could hardly be described as anyone's 'new young thing', with all of the members aged over 30 at this early stage in their career. Each boasted an interesting, mainly non-musical background. Lorson was an ex-busker and film student, while both Verta-Ray and Kick worked at the Andy Warhol silk-screen factory and met the great man several times (a fact that helped to encourage the Velvet Underground comparisons). Coté had additionally spent much of the 80s working in No/New Wave bands Hammerdoll and Coté Coté, while struggling to overcome his heroin addiction. Cover versions of PiL's 'Rise' and the Cars' 'My Best Friend's Girl' on stage further revealed Madder Rose's diversity, while their debut album was heralded as one of the best releases of the year. Released on Atlantic Records' independently distributed subsidiary Seed, production was overseen by Kevin Salem of Dumptruck. *Panic On* was co-produced with veteran engineer Mark Freegard and saw Lorson emerge as a songwriting force to rival Coté on some of the album's best numbers, including the appealing 'Foolish Ways'. Verta-Ray subsequently left to concentrate on his own project, Speedball Baby, and was replaced by Chris Giammalvo (ex-Eve's Plumb). *Tragic Magic* was recorded in 1997, but was denied a UK release by Atlantic. The album eventually reappeared on the band's new label, Cooking Vinyl Records, with two new songs added. The band continued their undeserved dive into artistic obscurity with 1999's *Hello June Fool*, an album which eschewed the experimental touches of *Tragic Magic* and placed more emphasis on Lorson's haunting voice.

● ALBUMS: *Bring It Down* (Seed 1993)★★★★, *Panic On* (Seed/Atlantic 1994)★★★, *Tragic Magic* (Atlantic 1997)★★★, *Tragic Magic* reissue (Cooking Vinyl 1999)★★★, *Hello June Fool* (Thirsty Ear/Cooking Vinyl 1999)★★★.

Madonna

b. Madonna Louise Ciccone, 16 August 1958, Bay City, Michigan, USA. An icon for female pop stars thanks to her proven ability to artistically reinvent herself while still retaining complete control of her career, Madonna is also one of the most commercially successful artists in the history of popular music. The young Ciccone excelled at dance and drama at high school and during brief periods at colleges in Michigan and North Carolina. In 1977, she went to New York, studying with noted choreographer Alvin Ailey and taking modelling jobs. Two years later, Madonna moved to France to join a show featuring disco singer Patrick Hernandez. There she met Dan Gilroy and, back in New York, the pair formed club band the Breakfast Club. Madonna played drums and sang with the band before setting up Emmy in 1980 with Detroit-born drummer and former boyfriend, Steve Bray. Together, Madonna and Bray created club tracks which led to a recording deal with Sire Records. With leading New York disc jockey Mark Kamins producing, she recorded 'Everybody', a US club hit in 1982. Madonna broke out from the disco scene into mainstream pop with 'Holiday', written and produced by Jellybean. It reached the US Top 20 in late 1983 and was a Top 10 hit across Europe the following year. By now, her tough, raunchy persona was coming across to international audiences and the attitude was underlined by the choice of Tom Kelly and Billy Steinberg's catchy 'Like A Virgin' as a 1984 single. The track provided the singer with the first of her subsequent 11 US number 1s. The follow-up, 'Material Girl', included a promotional video which introduced one of Madonna's most characteristic visual styles, the mimicking of Marilyn Monroe's 'blonde bombshell' image. By the time of her appearance at 1985's Live Aid concert and her high-profile wedding to actor Sean Penn on 16 August the same year, Madonna had become an internationally recognized superstar, known to millions of tabloid newspaper readers without any interest in her music. Among the fans of her work were a growing number of 'wannabees', teenage girls who aped her independent and don't-care stance.

From 1985-87, Madonna turned out a stream of irresistibly catchy transatlantic Top 5 singles. 'Crazy For You', her second US chart-topper, was co-written by ex-Carpenters collaborator John Bettis, while she co-wrote her first UK number 1, 'Into The Groove', with Steve Bray. These were followed by 'Dress You Up', 'Live To Tell', and the transatlantic chart-topper, 'Papa Don't Preach'. 'True Blue', 'Open Your Heart' and 'La Isla Bonita' were further successes taken from 1986's *True Blue*. Like an increasing number of her songs, 'Who's That Girl' (her second transatlantic number 1) and 'Causing A Commotion' were tied-in to a movie - in this instance, a poorly received comedy in which she starred with Sir John Mills. Madonna's film career had begun with a minor role in the b-movie *A Certain Sacrifice* before she starred in the acclaimed *Desperately Seeking Susan*. The following year she appeared with husband Penn in her first real failure, *Shanghai Surprise*. She separated from Penn in 1988, the same year she appeared on Broadway in David Mamet's play *Speed The Plow*. Back on the music scene, the singer continued to attract controversy when, in 1989, the video for 'Like A Prayer' (her third transatlantic chart-topper), with its links between religion and eroticism, was condemned by the Vatican and caused Pepsi-Cola to cancel a sponsorship deal with the star. The resulting publicity helped the album of the same title - co-produced with new collaborator Patrick Leonard - to become a global bestseller. In 1990, her career reached a new peak of publicity and commercial success. She starred with Warren Beatty in the blockbuster movie *Dick Tracy*, while the extravagant costumes and choreography of the Blond Ambition world tour were the apotheosis of Madonna's uninhibited melange of sexuality, song, dance and religiosity. The tour was commemorated by the following year's documentary movie, *Truth Or Dare*. Among her hits of the early 90s were the transatlantic number 1 'Vogue', devoted to a short-lived dance craze, 'Hanky Panky', 'Justify My Love' (co-written with Lenny Kravitz), 'Rescue Me', and 'This Used To Be My Playground' (from the soundtrack of *A League Of Their Own*). Madonna's reputation as a strong businesswoman, in control of each aspect of her career, was confirmed in 1992 when she signed a multi-million dollar deal with the Time-Warner conglomerate, parent company of Sire. This guaranteed the release of albums, films and books created by her own Maverick production company. The publication of her graphic and erotic book *Sex* put her back on top of the charts, though this time it was in the bestselling book lists. The book was an unprecedented success, selling out within hours and needing an immediate reprint. The attendant *Erotica* marked a slight creative downturn, and was her first album since her debut not to generate a US number 1 single. She returned to form on *Bedtime Stories*, on which she teamed up with Soul II Soul producer Nellee Hooper, who wrote the title track in conjunction with Björk. 'Take A Bow' returned the singer to the top of the US singles chart, while the rest of the album boasted songs that combined, by her own description, pop, R&B, hip-hop and Madonna. The 1995 compilation of her slower material, *Something To Remember*, featured the excellent new song, 'You'll See'. In 1996, her need to shock had mellowed considerably with a credible movie portrayal of Eva Peron in Alan Parker's *Evita*. Later that year she became 'with child' on 14 October with the birth of Lourdes Maria Ciccone Leon. She returned to music with March 1998's *Ray Of Light*, one of her finest recordings to date. Collaborating with producer William Orbit, Madonna positively revelled in a new-found musical freedom. Her voice had also matured into a rich and expressive instrument. The album generated several transatlantic hit singles, including 'Frozen' (a UK chart-topper), 'Ray Of Light', 'Drowned World (Substitute For Love)', 'The Power Of Good-bye', and 'Nothing Really Matters'. 'Beautiful Stranger', taken from the soundtrack to the Mike Myers' movie *Austin Powers: The Spy Who Shagged Me*, reached number 2 in the UK charts in June 1999. Another soundtrack, for the movie *The Next Best Thing*, co-written and co-produced by Madonna and Orbit, was released on the singer's Maverick label. It featured her new single, a reworking of Don McLean's classic 'American Pie'.

● ALBUMS: *Madonna* (Sire 1983)★★★, *Like A Virgin* (Sire 1984)★★★, *True Blue* (Sire 1986)★★★★, *Who's That Girl* film soundtrack (Sire 1987)★★, *You Can Dance* remix album (Sire 1987)★★★, *Like A Prayer* (Sire 1989)★★★★, *I'm Breathless* (Sire 1990)★★★, *Erotica* (Maverick 1992)★★★, *Bedtime Stories* (Maverick 1994)★★★★, *Evita* film soundtrack (Warners 1996)★★★, *Ray Of Light* (Maverick/Warners 1998)★★★★.

● COMPILATIONS: *The Immaculate Collection* (Sire 1990)★★★★★, *Best Of The Rest Volume 2* (Sire 1993)★★★, *Something To Remember* (Maverick 1995)★★★★.

● VIDEOS: *The Virgin Tour* (Warner Music Video 1986), *Ciao Italia - Live From Italy* (Sire 1988), *Immaculate Collection* (Warner Music Video 1990), *Justify My Love* (Warner Music Video 1991), *The Real Story* (Wienerworld Video 1991), *Madonna Video EP* (Warner Music Video 1991), *In Bed With Madonna* (Video Collection 1991), *Madonna: The Unauthorised Biography* (MIA Video 1994), *Ray Of Light* (Warner Home Video 1998), *The Video Collection 93:99* (Warner Vision 1999).

● FURTHER READING: *Madonna: Her Story*, Michael McKenzie. *Madonna: The New Illustrated Biography*, Debbi Voller. *Madonna: In*

Her Own Words, Mick St Michael. *Madonna: The Biography*, Robert Matthew-Walker. *Madonna*, Marie Cahill. *Madonna: The Style Book*, Debbi Voller. *Like A Virgin: Madonna Revealed*, Douglas Thompson. *Sex*, Madonna. *Madonna Unauthorized*, Christopher Anderson. *I Dream Of Madonna: Women's Dreams Of The Goddess Of Pop*, Kay Turner (compiler). *The I Hate Madonna Handbook*, Ilene Rosenzweig. *Madonna: The Girlie Show*, Glenn O'Brien. *Deconstructing Madonna*, Fran Lloyd. *Live!*, no author listed. *The Madonna Scrapbook*, Lee Randall.

● FILMS: *A Certain Sacrifice* (1979), *Desperately Seeking Susan* (1985), *Vision Quest* (1985), *Shangai Surprise* (1986), *Who's That Girl?* (1987), *Bloodhounds Of Broadway* (1989), *Dick Tracy* (1990), *Madonna: Blond Ambition World Tour '90* (1990), *Madonna: Truth Or Dare* (1991), *A League Of Their Own* (1992), *Shadows And Fog* (1992), *Body Of Evidence* (1993), *Dangerous Game* (1993), *Blue In The Face* (1995), *Four Rooms* (1995), *Girl 6* (1996), *Evita* (1996), *The Next Best Thing* (2000).

Mafia And Fluxy

Initially inspired by Sly And Robbie, brothers Mafia (b. Leroy Heywood, 1962, London, England; bass) and Fluxy (b. David Heywood, 1963, London, England; drums) are the UK's foremost rhythm section. They have pursued careers as solo artists and as part of the Instigators. Early encouragement came via Uncle Wizard's sound system and then Fatman, who released the Instigators' 1977 debut, 'Let's Make Love'. By 1985, they had enjoyed several hits and gained valuable experience backing touring Jamaican acts, quickly coming to terms with the new digital technology. In 1987, they visited Jamaica, building rhythm tracks for Bunny Lee, Blacker Dread, King Jammy and Exterminator. That year they started their own self-titled label, producing Cinderella, Billy Melody, Sugar Minott and, later, Private Collection ('Dreamer'). Their debut album, 1990's *Dancehall Connection Volume 1*, featured such diverse talents as General Trees, King Kong and General Levy. The same year, Mafia And Fluxy returned to Jamaica, providing many notable hits for Black Scorpio, Jammys, Gussie Clarke, Mikey Bennett, Mr Doo and Roy Francis. In the UK, they backed Maxi Priest and Lloyd Brown, and were voted Producers Of The Year, the Instigators winning the Best Reggae Band Award. On their own label, tracks by Tiger ('Winery'), Gregory Isaacs, Johnny Osbourne, Sugar Black, Cornell Campbell, Sanchez ('Whip Appeal') and Sugar Minott were released at regular intervals. In 1992, Mafia issued his debut album, *Finders Keepers*, while hits by Cobra ('Off Guard'), Dirtsman, Poison Chang ('Do Me A Favour'), Sweetie Irie, Red Dragon, Cutty Ranks ('Armed And Dangerous'), Tenor Fly and Chaka Demus And Pliers ('Wining Machine') witnessed no shortage of success throughout 1992/3. Back in Jamaica, Mafia And Fluxy laid down further tracks for Bobby Digital, Penthouse and Stone Love, with whom they won a Jamaican award for Best Juggling [mixing] Record. By 1994, they were remixing artists such as Boy George, Barrington Levy and the Rhythm Kings, Mega Banton's 'First Position' was a number 1 hit and they had become one of the most in-demand rhythm sections in reggae music, even occasionally pairing with Sly (Mafia) and Steely (Fluxy).

● ALBUMS: various artists *Dancehall Collection Volume 1* (Mafia & Fluxy 1990)★★★, *Mafia And Fluxy Revival Hits Volumes 1-3* (Mafia & Fluxy 90s)★★★.

Solo: Mafia *Finders Keepers* (Mafia & Fluxy 1992)★★★★.

Magnetic Fields

The creation of Stephen Merritt, a singer-songwriter, keyboard and guitar player based in New York, USA, Magnetic Fields have established a strong reputation in the US underground without ever achieving that success internationally, though Merritt remains a darling of critics worldwide. As a writer he is, if not unique, certainly unusual. The details of his dealings with others and himself are rarely embellished with anything other than minimalist notation, provided by long-term collaborators Sam Davol (cello/flute) and Claudia Gonson (percussion). The simplicity of style gives genuine weight to the impact of his observations on tracks such as 'Lovers From The Moon', 'Smoke Signals' and 'Falling In Love With The Wolfboy' from his first two albums. Both featured Susan Anway as singer, Merritt declaring little faith in his own vocal abilities. *Holiday* continued in this style but covered Merritt's experiences in various American locations. The travelogue approach was then transplanted to *The Charm Of The Highway Strip*, with the music now rooted in a blunt country tradition. Afterwards he embarked on new horizons under the name the 6ths - initially recording an album featuring 14 separate vocal contributions from artists drawn from the American underground (including Luna, Superchunk, Sebadoh). He has since recorded with Chris Ewen (ex-Figures On A Beach) as the Future Bible Heroes, but released 1996's surprisingly upbeat and optimistic *Get Lost* under the Magnetic Fields name. Merritt returned in September 1999 with the hugely ambitious and largely successful three-disc collection *69 Love Songs*, a witty, erudite and eclectic musical exploration of the vagaries of modern romance.
● ALBUMS: *Distant Plastic Trees* (Red Flame 1990)★★★, *The Wayward Bus* (PoPuP 1992)★★★★, *Holiday* (Feels Good All Over 1994)★★★, *The Charm Of The Highway Strip* (Merge 1994)★★★, *Get Lost* (Merge/Setanta 1995)★★★, *69 Love Songs, Pt. 1* (Merge 1999)★★★★, *69 Love Songs, Pt. 2* (Merge 1999)★★★, *69 Love Songs, Pt. 3* (Merge 1999)★★★.
● COMPILATIONS: *The Wayward Bus/Distant Plastic Trees* (Merge 1994)★★★.

Make-Up

Comprising Ian Svenonius (vocals), James Canty (guitar, organ, vocals), Michelle Mae (bass, vocals, ex-Frumpies) and Steve Gamboa (drums), Washington DC, USA alternative rock band Make-Up formed from the ashes of the highly regarded local hardcore outfit Nation Of Ulysses, and the short-lived follow-up Cupid Car Club. All three male members of Make-Up had been in the controversial, highly politicized Nation Of Ulysses, and many of their political aspirations were carried over to the new band - albeit with a more vaudevillian twist, delivered in a frantic wail by self-styled 'preacher' Svenonius. Their debut album, *Destination: Love Live! At Cold Rice*, was recorded 'live' at a DC venue and featured '16 items, 13 of which are songs'. The other three 'items' were pieces of oratory grandly introducing the band's membership - recalling the highly-charged melodrama of their stage shows. This was captured on the following year's genuine live set, *After Dark*, which was recorded in London. Subsequent albums evoked comparisons to James Brown, Jon Spencer Blues Explosion and Rocket From The Crypt - the latter band having originally been heavily influenced by Nation Of Ulysses. The compilation, *I Want Some*, was an exhaustive trawl through the band's singles discography.
● ALBUMS: *Destination: Love Live! At Cold Rice* (Dischord 1996)★★★, *After Dark* (Dischord 1997)★★★, *Sound Verite* (K 1997)★★★, *In Mass Mind* (Dischord 1998)★★★, *Save Yourself* (K 1999)★★★.
● COMPILATIONS: *I Want Some* (K 1999)★★★.

Manic Street Preachers

In their rise from cult punk revivalists to stadium conquering rockers, this Welsh band have enjoyed a love-hate relationship with the music press, opening with a bizarre encounter in 1991. The catalyst was Richey Edwards, who cut the words '4 Real' into his forearm to the amazement of *New Musical Express* critic Steve Lamacq, when he dared to call into question the band's authenticity. They were formed in Blackwood, Gwent, Wales by James Dean Bradfield (b. 21 February 1969; vocals/guitar), Richey James Edwards (b. 22 December 1966; rhythm guitar), Nicky Wire (b. Nick Jones, 20 January 1969; bass) and Sean Moore (b. 30 July 1970; drums). Their calculated insults at a wide variety of targets, particularly their peers, had already won them infamy following the release of their 1990 debut on the Damaged Goods label, the *New Art Riot EP* (a previous single, 'Suicide Alley', featuring original rhythm guitarist Flicker, had been a limited pressing distributed at gigs and to journalists only). The Public Enemy-sampling 'Motown Junk' and 'You Love Us' were issued on the fashionable Heavenly Records label, before the band signed a major-label deal with Sony in May 1991. Their personal manifesto was explicit: rock bands should cut down the previous generation, release one explosive album, then disappear. Although the music press pointed out the obvious contradictions and naïveté of this credo, the band polarized opinion to a degree that far outweighed their early musical proficiency. The singles, 'Stay Beautiful' and 'Love's Sweet Exile' (backed by the superior 'Repeat' - 'Repeat after me, fuck Queen and Country') were inconclusive, but the reissued version of 'You Love Us', with its taut, vicious refrain, revealed a band beginning to approach in power what they had always had in vision. Their 1992 debut album, too, was an injection of bile that proved perversely refreshing in a year of industry contraction and self-congratulation. Unfortunately, it never quite achieved its intention to outsell Guns N'Roses' *Appetite For Destruction*, nor did the band split immediately afterwards as stated. The polished, less caustic approach of *Gold Against The Soul* saw the band hitting a brick wall in expectation and execution, though as always, there were moments of sublime lyricism (notably the singles 'Roses In The Hospital' and 'Life Becoming A Landslide'). *The Holy Bible* returned the band to the bleak world view of yesteryear, notably on the haunting '4st 7lb', written by an anorexic Richey Edwards before a nervous breakdown that saw him temporarily admitted to a mental facility. Other subject matter was drawn from prostitution, the holocaust and the penal system. Never easy listening at the best of times (despite the ability to write genuinely affecting songs such as 'Motorcycle Emptiness'), the band had produced enough inspired moments to justify their protracted early claims. However, all that seemed somehow irrelevant following Edwards' disappearance on 1 February 1995, with several parties expressing concern as to his well-being. Early in 1996, the band announced plans for their first album in Edwards' absence. The result was *Everything Must Go*;

although highly commercial it was an outstanding record. Played with power and sung with passion, the songs ripped out of the speakers with a confidence and self-assured manner that was remarkable given the band's recent tragic upheaval. They culminated their finest year by winning three BRIT Awards, for Best Live Act, Best Single (the UK number 2 hit 'A Design For Life') and Best Album. In September 1998, the band achieved their first UK number 1 single with 'If You Tolerate This Your Children Will Be Next', inspired by the Spanish civil war. The attendant *This Is My Truth Tell Me Yours* went straight in at the top of the UK album charts, although it was not released until the following year in the US. Underlying their popularity, the band played a sold-out concert in Cardiff on New Year's Eve. A month later they topped the UK charts with the limited edition *Masses Against The Classes* EP, an abrasive response to critics who had accused the band of selling out.

● ALBUMS: *Generation Terrorists* (Columbia 1992)★★★★, *Gold Against The Soul* (Columbia 1993)★★★, *The Holy Bible* (Columbia 1994)★★★, *Everything Must Go* (Epic 1996)★★★★★, *This Is My Truth Tell Me Yours* (Epic 1998)★★★★.

● VIDEOS: *Everything Live* (Sony Music Video 1997).

● FURTHER READING: *Design For Living*, Paula Shutkever. *Manic Street Preachers, Sweet Venom*, Martin Clarke. *Everything (A Book About Manic Street Preachers)*, Simon Price.

Manifesto Records

Since 1994, the Manifesto label has released a stream of commercial and successful singles without losing credibility among the highly discerning dance music fraternity. Its origins lie with Eddie Gordon, a UK dance industry figurehead, who enlisted the services of Luke Neville and Judge Jules, a former stockbroker and law graduate, respectively. Together, they engineered the rise of a label that is known for its proactive A&R and its consistent quality (Gordon subsequently moved on to found Neo Records with Trevor Porter). Almost uniquely for the dance music industry, the label's artists are signed for album projects, from which spin-off singles are released. Avoiding the approach of signing single tracks, Manifesto manages to keep other labels from signing its artists for one-single deals. On its roster are such respected names as Byron Stingly, Todd Terry, the Space Brothers, Karen Ramirez and José Padilla. The label won the UK's *Music Week* magazine's award for Dance Label Of The Year in 1996 and 1997. The fact that two of the label's A&R men are high-profile working DJs allows it to 'road test' new material on the nation's dancefloors. Judge Jules comments: 'I really don't think I could do A&R properly if I didn't play out . . . playing in clubs is the ultimate litmus test for quality. Too many industry execs listen to records in the air-conditioned comfort of their oak-panelled offices. If they tried dancing to it they might have a better idea of whether it works or not . . .'. Manifesto's UK Top 10 successes include Karen Ramirez ('Looking For Love'), David Morales ('The Need In U') Byron Stingly ('Get Up Everybody') and Josh Wink ('Higher State Of Consciousness') and Yomanda's 'Synths And Strings'.

Mann, Aimee

b. 9 August 1960, Boston, Massachusetts, USA. Having begun performing with the punk-inspired Young Snakes, Aimee Mann achieved recognition as the lead vocalist of the criti-

cally acclaimed 'Til Tuesday. Frustrated with the industry trying to push a more mainstream approach - and suggesting that writers outside the band should contribute material - Mann left for a solo career in 1990. Released in 1993, *Whatever* was a remarkable set, drawing rave reviews and the generous plaudits of Elvis Costello, with whom she had previously collaborated on the 'Til Tuesday track, 'The Other End (Of The Telescope)'. A literate and skilled composer, Mann attacked the corporate music business on 'I've Had It' and detailed estrangement and heartbreak on 'I Should've Known' and 'I Know There's A Word' (allegedly concerning her former relationship with Jules Shear). Former Byrds guitarist Roger McGuinn was persuaded to contribute distinctive 12-string backing on a set reviving pop's traditions of melody and chorus, while placing them in an unquestionably contemporary context. Imago Records fell apart after *Whatever* appeared, and after a lengthy battle with the label Mann signed to Geffen Records. *I'm With Stupid* still appeared to carry emotional baggage from the Shear relationship, although musically the album was a more mellow and relaxed affair. In 1998, Mann married songwriter Michael Penn, made a walk-on appearance in the Coen brothers' *The Big Lebowski*, and completed the recording of her new album. When Geffen was swallowed up by Interscope, Mann started being pressurised by her new bosses to make the album more commercial. She escaped the corporate clutches of the new Universal empire by buying back the rights to her album and gaining a release from her contract. In 1999, she released the limited edition *Bachelor No. 2* EP. Several of her new songs also featured heavily on the soundtrack to Paul Thomas Anderson's *Magnolia*.

● ALBUMS: *Whatever* (Imago 1993)★★★★, *I'm With Stupid* (Geffen 1995)★★★, *Magnolia* film soundtrack (Reprise 1999)★★★.

● FILMS: *The Big Lebowski* (1998).

Mansun

One of the most hotly touted UK indie bands of the mid-90s, Mansun confirmed the validity of their good press when their 1996 single, 'Stripper Vicar', written about a cross-dressing vicar, entered the UK Top 20. The band, originally known as Grey Lantern and A Man Called Sun, was formed in the northern city of Chester in summer 1995 by Paul Draper (b. 26 September 1972, Liverpool, Merseyside, England; guitar/vocals), Dominic Chad (b. 5 June 1973, Cheltenham, Gloucestershire, England; guitar), and Stove King (b. 8 January 1974, Ellesmere Port, Cheshire, England; bass). Two limited edition singles were released in late 1995 on their own Sci Fi Hi Fi label before the band signed to Parlophone Records in the UK and Epic in the US. A number of other major labels were said to be interested in the band, but proved unable to meet their demands for a record label to underwrite their 200-gig schedule for 1996. They also demanded from Parlophone the freedom to continue releasing EPs and the right to self-produce their debut album. By this time the trio had been augmented by Andie Rathbone (b. 8 September 1971, Chester, Cheshire, England; drums). They cultivated a supportive relationship with UK music papers *New Musical Express* and *Melody Maker* through a series of acclaimed EPs, and mainstream success soon followed when the *Stripper Vicar* and *Wide Open Space* EPs broke into the UK Top 20. By the advent of their number

1 debut *Attack Of The Grey Lantern* early in 1997, the band had become regulars on BBC Television's *Top Of The Pops*. The only outside influence on *Attack Of The Grey Lantern* came with slight remixing by Cliff Norrell and Mike 'Spike' Stent. The album, proffering a clash of musical styles ranging from 70s pop to classic rock, was clearly influenced by Radiohead, with Draper's songwriting the outstanding feature. In September 1997, the band released an EP of new material, *Closed For Business*, and continued with their seemingly endless touring schedule. The following July's *Legacy* EP was the band's most successful release to date, debuting at number 7 in the UK singles chart. *Six* was an outrageously ambitious, maverick rock album, which, if not always entirely successful, served to distance Mansun from other run of the mill indie bands.

● ALBUMS: *Attack Of The Grey Lantern* (Parlophone/Epic 1997)★★★★, *Six* (Parlophone/Epic 1998)★★★.
● FURTHER READING: *Tax-Loss Lovers From Chester*, Mick Middles.

Marcy Playground

The creation of singer John Wozniak, this US alternative rock outfit was signed by EMI Records in the mid-90s on the strength of Wozniak's demo album *From The Marcy Playground*, recorded under the name Zog Bogbean. Shortly after the release of Marcy Playground's self-titled debut album, EMI America closed its offices and Wozniak was forced to move to a new home at Capitol Records. Luckily, a single culled from the debut, 'Sex And Candy', was beginning to pick up radio and press attention, eventually reaching number 1 on *Billboard*'s Modern Rock Tracks chart and number 8 on the Hot 100 singles chart. Capitol repressed the debut album under its own imprint. However, Wozniak was keen that the single's success should not distract listeners from the other material on the album and considered leaving it off. Other stand-out tracks on the record included 'Poppies', which dealt with the opium wars, and 'Saint Joe On The School Bus', an endearing tale about school misfits. Other contributors to the project included drummer Dan Rieser, bass player Dylan Keefe and cellist Jen Handler, though Marcy Playground remains very much Wozniak's creation. *Shapeshifter*, released in November 1999, was a more impressive album which unfortunately lacked a stand-out track of the quality of 'Sex And Candy'.

● ALBUMS: *Marcy Playground* (EMI 1997)★★★, *Shapeshifter* (Capitol 1999)★★★.

Marilyn Manson

Controversial by design rather than accident, Florida, USA-based band Marilyn Manson were formed in 1989 with the express intention of 'exploring the limits of censorship'. The original line-up consisted of Manson (b. Brian Warner, 5 January 1969, Canton, Ohio, USA; vocals/tape loops), Daisy Berkowitz (guitar), Olivia Newton-Bundy (bass) and Zsa Zsa Speck (keyboards), later joined by Sara Lee Lucas (drums) - all the band members assuming forenames of female icons and surnames of famous murderers. Bundy and Speck were replaced at the end of 1989 by Gidget Gein and Madonna Wayne Gacy (b. Steve Bier), respectively. In keeping with their controversial image, they were the first band to be signed to Trent Reznor (Nine Inch Nails) and John A. Malm Jnr.'s Nothing label. Support slots with artists such as Suicidal Tendencies, Meat Beat Manifesto, Murphy's Law

and the Genitorturers brought them considerable local recognition, in the form of the 1993 'Slammy' Awards (taking the Song Of The Year nomination for 'Dope Hat') and sundry other baubles (not least, short-heading Gloria Estefan for the Best Local Musician category in *South Florida* magazine). In December 1993, bass player Gein was replaced by Twiggy Ramirez (b. Jeordie Francis White, 20 June 1971, Florida, USA). Reznor acted as guest musician and executive producer on the band's 1994 debut album, with half of the tracks mixed at the house of the infamous Tate murders by the Manson family (where Nine Inch Nails also recorded). In March 1995, Lucas was replaced on drums by Ginger Fish (b. Kenny Wilson). Berkowitz also departed in June 1996 (he later sued the band for unpaid royalties and breach of contract) and was replaced by Zim Zum (b. Mike Nastasi). *Antichrist Superstar* included the American hit single 'The Beautiful People', and reached number 3 on the *Billboard* album charts. By 1998, they had become one of the biggest bands in the USA, assuming virtual cult status, a position aided as much by their notoriety and propensity for upsetting US right-wing and Christian groups as by their music. *Mechanical Animals* was a huge American chart-topper that also placed the band in the UK Top 10 for the first time. During the recording of the album, Zim Zum left and was replaced by Johnnie 5. Manson was forced to morally defend himself when, in April 1999, two fans, Dylan Klebold and Eric Harris, murdered 15 of their classmates at Colombine High School in Denver, Colorado. The band were forced to abort their nationwide tour, although fans were rewarded with the release of a live album.

● ALBUMS: *Portrait Of An American Family* (Nothing/Interscope 1994)★★, *Smells Like Children* (Nothing/Interscope 1995)★★, *Antichrist Superstar* (Nothing/Interscope 1996)★★★★, *Remix And Repent* (Nothing/Interscope 1998)★★★, *Mechanical Animals* (Nothing/Interscope 1998)★★★, *The Last Tour On Earth* (Nothing/Interscope 1999)★★★.
● VIDEOS: *Dead To The World* (Nothing/Interscope 1998).
● FURTHER READING: *The Long Hard Road Out Of Hell*, Marilyn Manson with Neil Strauss. *Marilyn Manson - A Biography*, Kurt B. Reighley.

Marion

Macclesfield, Cheshire, England-based indie band formed in 1993 by Jaime Harding (vocals), Anthony Grantham (guitar), Phil Cunningham (guitar), Murad Mousa (drums), and Julian Philips (bass), although the latter was soon replaced by Nick Gilbert. The quintet created an immediate stir in 1994 with the release of two independent singles, 'Violent Men' (on Rough Trade Records) and 'The Only Way'. This brace of fierce, anthemic songs, together with the fact that they were represented by ex-Smiths manager Joe Moss, helped ensure a frenzied A&R chase in the summer of that year, which was eventually concluded at the In The City seminar in September when they were signed by London Records. However, there was a degree of longevity to Marion's pursuits that might not have been suggested by their average age of 20 - Harding, Cunningham and Grantham had been in youthful bands together for nine years before this current incarnation. Their new label sent them to work with Stephen Street, provoking further Smiths comparisons, which were hardly deflated by the news that Morrissey had attended two of their early gigs (he subsequently invited them to support him on UK dates). Their single 'Sleep' was subsequently used in a Citröen advertisement, and was followed by the debut album, which was not entirely successful in capturing the band's live sound. Following Harding's recovery from a sustained period of drug abuse, the band recorded their delayed second album, *The Program*, with Johnny Marr on production duties. Beset by problems with their record company the band split-up in May 1999.

● ALBUMS: *This World And Body* (London 1996)★★★, *The Program* (London 1998)★★.

Marky Mark

The younger brother of New Kids On The Block's Donnie Wahlberg, Mark Wahlberg (b. 5 June 1971, Boston, Massachusetts, USA) was once proclaimed as the 'thinking rapper's Madonna' upon his entrance into the music industry in the early 90s. Also employed as an underwear model for Calvin Klein, Marky Mark's two albums did little to dispel his image as a clothes horse for white rap, even though all of his Funky Bunch (who included DJ Terry Yancey and five mixed gender dancers) were black. Mark enjoyed almost instant success when 'Good Vibrations', featuring a sample of Loleatta Holloway's disco hit 'Love Sensation', topped the US charts in July 1991 and broke into the UK Top 20. It was followed by the Top 10 single 'Wildside', a revision of Lou Reed's urban mantra, 'Walk On The Wild Side'. The attendant debut album, *Music For The People*, achieved platinum sales in 1991. He was subsequently widely attacked in the UK by gay activists for what they described as a conspiratorial silence during Shabba Ranks' homophobic outbursts on the Channel 4 series, *The Word*. His second album failed to provide significant sales and like New Kids On The Block, Marky Mark's association with the *Billboard* charts had ended by the mid-90s. After appearing in 1994's *Renaissance Man*, alongside Danny DeVito and Wesley Snipes, Wahlberg established a new career as a talented actor. He received excellent reviews for his starring role in Paul Thomas Anderson's acclaimed *Boogie Nights*, a 1997 homage to the 70s porn industry.

● ALBUMS: *Music For The People* (Interscope 1991)★★★, *You Gotta Believe* (Interscope 1992)★★★.

● FILMS: *Renaissance Man* (1994), *The Basketball Diaries* (1995), *Fear* (1996), *Traveller* (1997), *Boogie Nights* (1997), *The Big Hit* (1998), *The Corruptor* (1999), *Three Kings* (1999).

Martika

b. Marta Marrera, 18 May 1969, California, USA. This pop singer grew up in California, her parents having fled Cuba shortly after the revolution. Her first experience in show-business came early, with an appearance as a dancer in John Huston's 1982 movie *Annie*. From 1984-86 she played the role of Gloria in the television series *Kids Incorporated*. She enjoyed almost immediate success with her music career when her debut single, December 1988's 'More Than You Know', broke into the US Top 20. Her second single, 'Toy Soldiers', topped the US chart for two weeks in the summer of 1989, and also reached the UK Top 5. A cover version of Carole King's 'I Feel The Earth Move' reached UK number 7, but stalled at US number 25. An appearance in the television series *Wiseguy* as jazz singer Dahlia Mendez followed. Although 'Love ... Thy Will Be Done', her first single from

1991's sophomore album, was cited by one journalist as being 'sub-Tiffany', it was popular enough to put the singer back in the US and UK Top 10. Her profile was also bolstered by consistent rumours of romances with pop stars (Nuno Bettencourt, Prince). She co-wrote the UK Top 20 hit single 'Martika's Kitchen' with Prince, who also helped out with several tracks on the album. Although her popularity lingered for a while in England, the singer subsequently faded from view as she took a break from music. She returned to recording with 'The Happy Song' for the *Welcome To The Conga Club* collection, and began work on a new album in the late 90s.

● ALBUMS: *Martika* (Columbia 1989)★★★, *Martika's Kitchen* (Columbia 1991)★★, *The 12 Inch Mixes* (Columbia 1993)★★.

● COMPILATIONS: *The Best Of Martika* (Columbia 1997)★★★.

● FILMS: *Annie* (1982).

Martin, Ricky

b. Enrique Martin Morales, 24 December 1971, San Juan, Puerto Rico. Formerly a member of the perennially youthful boy band, Menudo, Ricky Martin has established himself as one of the leading Latin pop stars of the 90s. By the end of the decade he had also enjoyed crossover success on the back of the chart-topping English language single, 'Livin' La Vida Loca'. Martin first began acting and singing in grade school, and when he was 10 gained an audition with Latin teen-idols Menudo. Martin eventually joined Menudo in 1984, and continued to record and tour with them until the late 80s (to ensure the band's youthful image, members were required to leave when they reached the age of 16). Martin spent a short period in New York before moving to Mexico, where he gained a regular slot in the Mexican soap opera *Alcanzar Una Estrella II*. His recording career also took off when his self-titled debut and *Me Amaras* achieved gold status in several countries. Martin moved to Los Angeles in 1994, and broke into the North American television market playing singing bartender Miguel Morez in the long-running soap opera *General Hospital*. His third Spanish-language album, 1995's *A Medio Vivir* (produced by fellow Menudo veteran Robi Rosa), broadened his fanbase by introducing rock stylings into the Latin mix, and generated the international hit single, 'Maria'. Martin also performed 'No Importa La Distancia' for the Spanish language version of Walt Disney's *Hercules*, and landed the role of Marius in the Broadway production of *Les Misérables*. *Vuelve* was released in February 1998, and debuted at number 1 on the *Billboard* Latin chart. The title track topped the Latin singles chart for four weeks, while 'La Copa De La Vida', the official song of the soccer World Cup, was also highly successful when released as a single, reaching number 1 in several countries. Martin won the 1999 Grammy Award for Best Latin Pop Performance, and his sensational performance at February's ceremony caused a dramatic surge in sales of *Vuelve*. All of a sudden Martin's media-friendly face was everywhere, and he was hyped as the leading figure in a new wave of Latin pop stars including Jennifer Lopez, Enrique Iglesias, Chris Perez and Luis Miguel. Exploiting the hype to the full Martin released the lively 'Livin' La Vida Loca', which reached number 1 in the US Hot 100 in May 1999, and stayed at the top for five weeks. In the process, it became Columbia Records' biggest-selling number 1 single of all time. His self-titled English language debut, produced by Rosa and

Desmond Child, entered the US album chart at number 1 at the end of the month, although it was soon knocked off the top by the Backstreet Boys' *Millennium*. In July, 'Livin' La Vida Loca' entered the UK singles chart at number 1. Martin's crucial follow-up single, 'She's All I Ever Had', climbed to US number 2 in September.
● ALBUMS: *Ricky Martin* (Sony Discos 1991)★★, *Me Amaras* (Sony Discos 1993)★★, *A Medio Vivir* (Sony Discos 1995)★★★, *Vuelve* (Sony Discos 1998)★★★, *Ricky Martin* (C2/Columbia 1999)★★★.
● VIDEOS: *The Ricky Martin Video Collection* (SMV 1999).

Mase

b. Mason Betha, USA. By the time rapper Ma$e (as his name is normally written) launched his solo career, he was already an A-list celebrity among hip-hop fans by dint of appearances on gold and platinum singles by Puff Daddy ('Can't Nobody Hold Me Down'), Brian McKnight ('You Should Hold Me'), 112 ('Only You') and Notorious B.I.G. ('Mo Money Mo Problems'). He had also performed live at the MTV Video Music Awards alongside Sting and Puff Daddy in consort with the latter's extended musical family (the Bad Boy posse). Ma$e's solo debut, *Harlem World*, eventually emerged in 1998 via a contract with Arista Records. The US number 1 album was produced by Deric Angelettie, Stevie J., Ron Lawrence and Carlos Thompson and others, collectively known as the Hitmen. Among the guests were Jermaine Dupri, Busta Rhymes, Lil' Kim, Lil' Caesar, Black Rob and Puff Daddy. The highlights included 'Feel So Good', a typically jocular effort married to a sample of Kool And The Gang's 'Hollywood Swinging', and 'I Need To Be', an attempt to write from a female perspective. 'Feel So Good' was used as the first single, climbing to number 5 on the *Billboard* Hot 100 in January, and was also included on the soundtrack to the movie *Money Talks*. To support it, Ma$e set out on a major world tour in tandem with his mentor, Puff Daddy. The two men also enjoyed a US number 8 hit single in September with 'Lookin' At Me'. Two further transatlantic hit singles followed with the Brandy duet 'Top Of The World' and 'Take Me There', a collaboration with BLACKstreet, Mya and Blinky Blink taken from the *Rugrats* movie soundtrack. *The Movement* showcased a new generation of east coast talent, with Mase assuming the Puff Daddy mentor role. A sophomore effort was accompanied by reports that the rapper had decided to retire from the music business and concentrate on religious work.
● ALBUMS: *Harlem World* (Arista 1998)★★★, Ma$e Presents Harlem World *The Movement* (All Out/Columbia 1999)★★★, *Double Up* (Puff Daddy 1999)★★★.

Massive Attack

This loose UK collective, comprising rapper 3D (b. Robert Del Naja), Daddy G (b. Grant Marshall) and Mushroom (b. Andrew Vowles, Knowle West, Bristol, England), emerged from Bristol's experimental music scene. The trio spent several years working on various mobile sound systems, as well as releasing records as part of the Wild Bunch ('Fucking Me Up', 'Tearing Down The Avenue'). Nellee Hooper, a former member of the Wild Bunch, left to work with Soul II Soul and subsequently became one of the leading producers and remixers of the 90s. Another original member, Milo Johnson, began work in Japan. Liaisons with Neneh Cherry eventually led to a meeting with Cameron McVey, who pro-

duced Massive Attack's 1991 debut. The resultant *Blue Lines* boasted three hit singles; 'Daydreaming', 'Unfinished Sympathy' (which featured an orchestral score) and 'Safe From Harm'. The blend of rap, deep reggae and soul was provocative and rich in texture, and featured singing from Cherry and Shara Nelson. An outstanding achievement, it had taken eight months to create, 'with breaks for Christmas and the World Cup'. 'Unfinished Sympathy' was particularly well received. *Melody Maker* magazine ranked it as the best single of 1991, and it remains a perennial club favourite. One minor hiccup occurred when they were forced, somewhat hysterically, to change their name during the Gulf War in order to maintain airplay. It was duly shortened to Massive. Their philosophy singled them out as dance music's new sophisticates: 'We don't ever make direct dance music. You've got to be able to listen and then dance.' That status was confirmed when U2 asked them to remix their single 'Mysterious Ways'. Despite *Blue Lines* being widely acclaimed, the band disappeared shortly afterwards. Shara Nelson pursued a solo career, with Massive Attack put on hold until the mid-90s. Another early contributor, Tricky, launched himself to considerable fanfare. A second album finally arrived in 1994, with former collaborator Nellee Hooper returning as producer. The featured singers this time included Tricky, Nigerian-born Nicolette, Everything But The Girl's Tracey Thorn and Horace Andy (who had also contributed to the debut) on a selection of tracks that sadly failed to recapture the magic of *Blue Lines*. Many critics suggested that others had now run so far with the baton handed them by the collective that the instigators themselves were yet to catch up. Apart from a dub remix of *Protection* recorded with the Mad Professor, little was heard from Massive Attack until 'Risingson' was released in autumn 1997. The single's menacing atmosphere was a taster for the downbeat grooves of *Mezzanine*, which was released to widespread critical acclaim in April 1998, and also became their first UK chart-topper. Guest vocalists included Andy, newcomer Sara Jay, and Elizabeth Fraser of the Cocteau Twins, the latter featuring on the wondrous 'Teardrop', which deservedly broke into the UK Top 10 in May 1998, aided by a stunning video. Rumours of personality clashes were confirmed when Mushroom left to pursue solo interests the following year.
● ALBUMS: *Blue Lines* (Wild Bunch/EMI 1991)★★★★★, *Protection* (EMI 1994)★★★, as Massive Attack Vs the Mad Professor *No Protection* (Circa 1995)★★★, *Mezzanine* (Virgin 1998)★★★★.
● COMPILATIONS: *The Singles Box* 11-CD box set (Virgin 1998)★★★★.

Master P

b. Percy Miller, 29 April 1970, New Orleans, Louisiana, USA. As the founder of the highly successful underground hip-hop label No Limit Records, Master P is the mastermind behind one of the biggest commercial sensations of the late 90s. With mainstream labels disassociating themselves from the gangsta rap genre, Master P and his crew of MCs have tapped a rich vein with a remarkable glut of gangsta-related product. Miller grew up in New Orleans, a city with a violent underbelly but far removed from the urban centres that would become associated with rap music, New York and Los Angeles. He spent time in California as a teenager, and eventually moved to that state to study business in Oakland.

Left a substantial sum of money by his grandfather in the late 80s, he invested it in a music store in Richmond, California, No Limit, before starting the label of the same name in 1990. Noting a gap in the market for hardcore rap records with street beats, Master P and his production team Beats By The Pound began churning out records characterised by their use of lifted hooklines and rather clichéd G-funk backing. Cheaply produced and recorded, and with no backing from mainstream radio or television, Master P and his team exploited the rap market to such an extent that the label soon became an underground sensation. Scoring an underground hit with his solo debut, 1994's *Ghetto's Tryin' To Kill Me!*, Master P shocked a music business used to records that followed a proven formula to commercial success. He formed Tru with his brothers C-Murder and Silkk The Shocker, providing the label with its mainstream breakthrough when their debut album entered the R&B Top 30. Further Master P albums, *99 Ways To Die*, *Ice Cream Man* (US number 26, May 1996) and *Ghetto D* (US number 1, September 1997), established the highly successful No Limit practice of using an album to promote its roster of rappers and advertise future releases. With Silkk The Shocker and C-Murder releasing breakthrough albums, and a support cast including Mia X, Mystikal and Young Bleed, No Limit was by now firmly established as one of hip-hop's most popular labels. Master P's self-produced and self-financed autobiographical movie *I'm Bout It*, was another showcase for No Limit's gangsta rap and G-funk fixations. Denied a cinema release the movie went straight to video, while the soundtrack entered the US album chart at number 4 in June 1997. Another movie, *I Got The Hook-Up* appeared in summer 1998 at the same time as the chart-topping Master P album, *MP Da Last Don*. The same year No Limit released the new Snoop Doggy Dogg album, *Da Game Is To Be Sold, Not To Be Told*, under the rapper's new moniker Snoop Dogg. In February 1999, Silkk The Shocker's *Made Man* topped the *Billboard* album chart. The indefatigable Master P's other interests include a clothing line, a sports management agency, and personal forays into basketball and pro-wrestling.

● ALBUMS: *Ghetto's Tryin' To Kill Me!* (No Limit 1994)★★★, *99 Ways To Die* (No Limit 1995)★★★, *Ice Cream Man* (No Limit 1996)★★★, *Ghetto D* (No Limit 1997)★★★, *MP Da Last Don* (No Limit 1998)★★★, *Only God Can Judge Me* (No Limit 1999)★★★.

● COMPILATIONS: *Master P Presents ... West Coast Bad Boyz Vol. 1* (No Limit 90s)★★★, *Master P Presents ... West Coast Bad Boyz II* (No Limit 1997)★★★, *No Limit Soldiers Compilation: We Can't Be Stopped* (No Limit 1998)★★★.

● VIDEOS: *Master P Presents No Limit Records Video Compilation Vol. 1* (Ventura 1999).

● FILMS: *Rhyme & Reason* (1997), *No Tomorrow* (1998), *I Got The Hook-Up* (1998), *Takedown* (1999), *Lock Down* (1999), *Hot Boyz* (1999), *Foolish* (1999).

Masters At Work

This highly successful remix/production team was formed by Little Louie Vega and Kenny 'Dope' Gonzalez. The duo marked the inception of their partnership by releasing 'Ride On The Rhythm' in 1991. On the back of that and their well established personal reputations (appearances as extras in Spaghetti Westerns notwithstanding), they subsequently undertook a vast array of remix projects that have estab-

lished them as the leading lights of the US house/garage scene. These began with Saint Etienne ('Only Love Can Break Your Heart'), Debbie Gibson, Melissa Morgan, BG The Prince Of Rap ('Take Control Of The Party'), Deee-Lite ('Bittersweet Loving'), plus legendary Latin musician Tito Puente's 'Ran Kan Kan'. In turn Puente contributed to Vega's 1991 album with singer Marc Anthony. They also recorded, in their own right, material like 'Can't Stop The Rhythm' (with Jocelyn Brown) for US label Cutting Records. After releasing their debut album they were inundated with remix work for major label artists including Michael Jackson, Brand New Heavies, Donna Summer, Madonna, George Benson, Lisa Stansfield, and Soul II Soul. Widely regarded as the cream of their profession, not everybody was clamouring for their wares - Jamiroquai's 'Emergency On Planet Earth' remix was rumoured to be hated by the artist concerned. His was a rare dissenting voice, however. The duo also launched their own MAW Records label, and went on to dominate the US dance charts in the mid-90s with the highly successful side projects the Bucketheads and NuYorican Soul, enjoying huge club hits with tracks such as 'The Nervous Track', 'Love And Happiness', 'When You Touch Me', and 'The Bomb (These Sounds Fall Into My Mind)'.

● ALBUMS: *The Album* (Cutting 1991)★★★.

● COMPILATIONS: *Sessions 5 - Masters At Work* (MOS 1995)★★★, *Masterworks: The Essential KenLou House Mixes* (Harmless 1998)★★★★.

Matchbox 20

US alternative rock band comprising Rob Thomas (b. 14 February 1971, Germany; vocals), Kyle Cook (b. 29 August 1975, Indiana, USA; guitar), Adam Gaynor (b. 26 November 1964; guitar), Brian Yale (b. 24 October 1968, USA; bass), and Paul Doucette (b. 22 August 1972, Pittsburgh, Pennsylvania, USA; drums). Thomas, Doucette and Yale formed Tabitha's Secret in 1995, but quickly left that band to join forces with Cook and Gaynor. The new quintet's extensive touring schedule, aided by several demo tapes recorded for producer Matt Serletic, brought them to the attention of Lava, a subsidiary of Atlantic Records. The band's debut was given a boost when, on the day it was released, Lava was brought under the major label's auspices. Given greater promotion and access to Atlantic's marketing departments, *Yourself Or Someone Like You* quickly gained a tenacious foothold in the *Billboard* Hot 100, eventually peaking at number 5. The promotional single, 'Long Day', also proved a minor hit on America's modern rock radio formats. The follow-up, 'Push', was an even bigger radio hit, although Thomas was forced to hastily explain the rationale behind lyrics relating to emotional and physical abuse. The band continued to tour heavily on the US club circuit, helping push the album to its exalted position on the Hot 200. Thomas enjoyed even greater success as the featured vocalist on Santana's US chart-topper 'Smooth', *the* surprise hit single of 1999.

● ALBUMS: *Yourself Or Someone Like You* (Lava/Atlantic 1996)★★★.

Matthews, Dave, Band

Matthews moved from his native South Africa to New York when he was just two years old. When his father died he moved back to Johannesburg with his mother, where he finished high school. He finally settled back in Charlottesville, Virginia, and assembled his self-titled, multiracial band in

1990. Matthews (guitar/vocals), Leroi Moore (reeds/saxophone), Boyd Tinsley (violin), Steffan Lessard (bass), and Carter Beauford (drums) forged a vibrant, individual sound from their wide instrumental range, with the eclectic mix significantly complementing Matthews' own expanded world view. Together they built a formidable reputation on the back of a punishing touring schedule, which helped their self-produced and financed debut, *Remember Two Things*, sell over 150,000 copies. In its wake the band were afforded the luxury of picking from the majors. Eventually choosing RCA Records (who offered the most malleable contract), their major label debut, *Under The Table And Dreaming*, produced by Steve Lillywhite, entered the *Billboard* charts in 1994 at number 34. Because of the record's continued success, the band were faced with the problem of having new material written to perform at gigs and yet having an album that was still selling strongly. They wisely issued *Crash*, to satisfy demand for a new product and it immediately went to number 2 in the US chart, confirming their arrival as one of the most successful rock acts of the 90s. *Before These Crowded Streets* debuted at US number 1, deposing the *Titanic* soundtrack album in the process, but showed little sign of any creative progress, indicating that the band may have become victims of their own astonishing success. Their popularity was confirmed when *Live At Luther College*, a 1996 recording by Matthews and collaborator Tim Reynolds, debuted at number 2 in February 1999.

● ALBUMS: *Remember Two Things* (Bama Rags 1993)★★★, *Under The Table And Dreaming* (RCA 1994)★★★★, *Crash* (RCA 1996)★★★★, *Live At Red Rocks 8.15.95* (RCA 1997)★★, *Before These Crowded Streets* (RCA 1998)★★★, with Tim Reynolds *Live At Luther College* (Bama Rags/RCA 1999)★★★, *Listener Supported* (RCA 1999)★★★.

Matthews, Eric

b. 12 January 1969, Compton, California, USA. Trumpeter, composer, vocalist and a student of classical music at college in San Francisco, Matthews collaborated with Australian Richard Davics as Cardinal, releasing an acclaimed self-titled album in 1995. Matthews subsequently delivered an outstanding solo album that demonstrated the influence of artists such as the Beach Boys and the Beatles, with the trumpet intro of his debut single 'Fanfare' sounding uncannily similar to the latter's 'Penny Lane'. Matthews' breathy vocals more specifically owed a debt to former Zombies vocalist, Colin Blunstone. *It's Heavy In Here* subsequently appeared on many rock critics' best of the year lists. The follow-up album came with a free 7-inch single, the sublime 'My Morning Parade', and was another collection of beautifully arranged orchestral pop songs that earned Matthews further comparisons to Brian Wilson's *Pet Sounds*-era work with the Beach Boys.

● ALBUMS: *It's Heavy In Here* (Sub Pop 1995)★★★★, *The Lateness Of The Hour* (Sub Pop 1997)★★★.

Mavericks

This country-rock band was formed in Miami, Florida, USA, a region better known for its dance and rock music than any fondness for country. Lead singer and songwriter Raul Malo (b. 7 August 1965, Miami, Florida, USA; vocals/guitar) was born of Cuban descent. His parents' record collection was full of American roots music and rockabilly, and led to his discovery of Johnny Cash, Elvis Presley and Bill Haley. He

also grew particularly fond of the dramatic intensity of the ballads sung by Roy Orbison and Patsy Cline. However, nobody at his school shared his taste, until he came across Robert Reynolds (b. 30 April 1962, Kansas City, Missouri, USA; bass). Reynolds was also a fan of older bands, and had previously been unable to find anyone to share his fascination with old country records. His best friend was Paul Deakin (b. 2 September 1959, Miami, Florida, USA; drums), who had played with local progressive rock bands for several years. They played the Florida rock circuit, having realized that the few country venues wanted covers bands only. They used the opportunity to set about building a set of strong original songs, steering away from too close an approximation of their heroes because, as Reynolds conceded, 'it's one thing to touch the nerve of older styles, it's another to let yourself be engulfed by them'. The band independently released a 13-song album in 1990. This eventually reached the ears of the Nashville record companies, and MCA Records flew them to the country music capital for a showcase. Legend has it that the company decided to make their offer before the end of the band's soundcheck. Their debut for MCA, *From Hell To Paradise*, featured their new lead guitarist David Lee Holt and was a minor success. It was with 1994's *What A Crying Shame* that they made their breakthrough (the same year that Reynolds married country star Trisha Yearwood). The album steadily racked up sales, eventually going platinum in spring 1995. The album was produced by Don Cook (who had also worked with Mark Collie and Brooks And Dunn) and included cover versions such as Bruce Springsteen's 'All That Heaven Will Allow' and Jesse Winchester's 'O What A Thrill' (a Top 20 hit when released as a single), alongside the title track and 'There Goes My Heart' (both of which were also Top 40 country hits). The band replaced Holt with Nick Kane (b. 21 August 1954, Jerusalem, Georgia, USA) shortly after the album's release. In 1995, they won a CMA award and released the excellent *Music For All Occasions*, another bestselling and critically acclaimed album. They received a further CMA award in 1996. The band's bold genre-hopping was in further evidence on 1998's *Trampoline*, with a four-piece horn section bolstering the songs. They also gained a surprise crossover UK hit with the catchy single 'Dance The Night Away', which spent several weeks in the Top 20 before peaking at number 4 in May. The album also broke into the UK Top 10.

● ALBUMS: *The Mavericks* (Y&T 1990)★★★, *From Hell To Paradise* (MCA 1992)★★★, *What A Crying Shame* (MCA 1994)★★★★, *Music For All Occasions* (MCA 1995)★★★★, *Trampoline* (MCA 1998)★★★★. Solo: Nick Kane *Songs In The Key Of E* (Demon 1999)★★★.

● COMPILATIONS: *The Best Of The Mavericks* (Mercury 1999)★★★.

● VIDEOS: *Live At The Royal Albert Hall* (VVL 1999).

Maxwell

b. 23 May 1973, Brooklyn, New York, USA. Of mixed West Indian and Puerto Rican parentage, soul singer Maxwell (his middle name) had to suffer the ignominy of his record company sitting on his debut album for a year, ignoring his traditional soul style in favour of the hip-hop-influenced singers dominating the R&B charts. Finally released in April 1996, *Maxwell's Urban Hang Suite* was a concept album about monogamy that eschewed male braggadocio to explore old-fashioned, romantic love. Featuring a collaboration with

Leon Ware, co-writer of Marvin Gaye's *I Want You*, the album proved to be an unexpected critical and commercial success. Maxwell was voted Best R&B Artist by *Rolling Stone* magazine, and *Urban Hang Suite* was nominated for a Grammy. At the 11th Annual Soul Train Awards in March 1997, Maxwell won both Best Male R&B/Soul Album and Single (for 'Ascension'), and Best R&B/Soul or Rap New Artist. The same month, *Urban Hang Suite* went platinum. Maxwell collaborated with guitarist Stuart Matthewman again for the 1998 follow-up, *Embrya*, slowing the pace down to create a wonderfully sensual and dreamlike record. The album debuted at US number 3 in July. The following year Maxwell enjoyed a huge US hit single with 'Fortunate', taken from the soundtrack of *Life*.

● ALBUMS: *Maxwell's Urban Hang Suite* (Columbia 1996)★★★★, *Embrya* (Columbia 1998)★★★★.

May, Brian

b. 19 July 1947, Twickenham, Middlesex, England. Best known as the guitarist in rock band Queen, May has also enjoyed notable solo success. In the summer of 1983, he teamed up with Eddie Van Halen (guitar), REO Speedwagon's Alan Gratzer (drums), Fred Mandel (keybords) and Phil Chen (bass) for a supergroup session, which was released under the title Star Fleet Project. He subsequently produced the spoof heavy metal group Bad News, as well as the recording of 'Anyone Can Fall In Love' by his actress partner Anita Dobson. He also worked with Steve Hackett, completed a solo album and, in 1991, wrote and recorded the score for a production of Shakespeare's *Macbeth*. Following a commission for an advertisement by the Ford Motor Company in 1991, May released a further single, 'Driven By You', which became a UK Top 10 hit in December 1991. He was also one of the prime movers behind the Freddie Mercury AIDS Benefit in 1992, following the death of Queen's flamboyant lead singer the previous November. May enjoyed his biggest UK solo hit in September 1992 with the number 5 single, 'Too Much Love Will Kill You'. A belated follow-up album, *Another World*, featured Cozy Powell on drums but, like its predecessor, was a largely anonymous collection of MOR-orientated material.

● ALBUMS: *Star Fleet Project* (EMI 1983)★★, *Back To The Light* (Parlophone 1992)★★, *Live At The Brixton Academy* (Parlophone 1994)★★★, *Another World* (Parlophone 1998)★★.

● VIDEOS: *Star Licks* (Star Licks Master Series 1986), *Live At The Brixton Academy* (Parlophone 1994).

● FURTHER READING *Queen & I: The Brian May Story*, Laura Jackson.

May, Derrick

b. USA. If one name crops up again and again in discussions of techno, it is that of Derrick 'Mayday' May. Alongside Juan Atkins, Carl Craig and Kevin Saunderson, May is regarded as one of the kings of the Detroit sound. Inspired by Yello and Kraftwerk, he began to make electronic music with Atkins and Saunderson while studying with them at Belleville High, Detroit. Recording either as Mayday or Rhythim Is Rhythim (occasionally in conjunction with Carl Craig) and generally on his own Transmat Records label, he went on to carve out a new vein in dance music that synthesized the advances of the electro movement with the more challenging end of the house movement - a music that defined 'techno'. Early cuts

such as 'Nude Photo' and 'The Dance', both on Transmat, were inspirational to many. However, it was the release of 'Strings Of Life' in 1987, which, with its wide appeal to the house music fans of the late 80s, simultaneously brought May his deserved acclaim and Detroit techno to European club-goers. However, May has never proved prolific in his recordings. After the success of 'Strings Of Life' he largely fled the dance scene, aside from a remix of Yello's 'The Race'. Rhythim Is Rhythim did not follow-up 'Strings Of Life' until 1990, when 'The Beginning' was released. May went on to cut three disappointing tracks on System 7's debut album, before Network released *Innovator: Soundtrack For The Tenth Planet* in 1991, a six-track EP that comprised some of May's definitive moments to date. In the same year, May was responsible for what Carl Craig has called the finest remix ever, Sueño Latino's 'Sueño Latino', itself a reworking of Manuel Goettschring's epic 'E2-M4'. It was followed in 1992 by *Relics*, a double album of Transmat's finest moments, heavily featuring Rhythim Is Rhythim, which coincided with a re-release of 'Strings Of Life' on the Belgium label Buzz, this time in a drumless version reminiscent of May's 'Sueño Latino' remix. More recently, Transmat has been revived following its signing to Sony. This has resulted in the long-awaited release of Rhythim Is Rhythim's 1991 recordings, 'Kao-tic Harmony' and 'Icon', and the Japanese (and subsequent American) release of a comprehensive Derrick May retrospective, *Innovator*, which contains all May's work for the Transmat label including remixes and tracks released for the first time.

● COMPILATIONS: *Relics: A Transmat Compilation* (Buzz 1992)★★★★, *Mayday Mix - Derrick May* (MOS 1997)★★★, *Innovator* (10th Planet 1998)★★★★.

Mazzy Star

Highly regarded US duo featuring the soothing timbre of singer Hope Sandoval's textured voice and guitarist David Roback. The partners had begun working together on a projected album as Opal (under which name Roback had formerly operated). Previously, he had been a member of Paisley Underground legends the Rain Parade, and recorded the *Rainy Day* album with vocalists Susanna Hoffs (the Bangles) and Kendra Smith. He met Sandoval while she was part of female duo Going Home. Enjoying a profitable working relationship, Roback and Sandoval adopted the name Mazzy Star for their sessions together, which eventually resulted in a critically lauded debut album. They released a comeback album on Capitol Records in 1993 after an absence that was mourned by many rock critics. Various musicians were employed, but the core of the project remained Roback and Sandoval (who would also contribute to the Jesus And Mary Chain's 'Sometimes Always' single). Contrary to expectations established by its forerunner, the resultant album included a cover version of the Stooges' 'We Will Fall'. Elsewhere, however, Roback's stinging lyrical poignancy and effortless song construction continued to hold sway. *Among My Swan* was a lo-fi excursion with Sandoval and Roback's latest songs sounding like a cross between the Cowboy Junkies and Neil Young.

● ALBUMS: *She Hangs Brightly* (Rough Trade 1990)★★★, *So Tonight That I Might See* (Capitol 1993)★★★, *Among My Swan* (Capitol 1996)★★★.

M.C. Hammer

b. Stanley Kirk Burrell, 30 March 1963, Oakland, California, USA. Immensely popular rap artist who synthesized the street sounds of black cultural alienation, or his interpretation thereof, to great commercial gain. After failing in professional baseball and attending a college course in communications, Hammer (named after his likeness to Oakland A's big hitter Henry 'Hammerin' Hank' Aaron) joined the US Navy for three years. Indeed, his first forays into music were financed by baseball players Mike Davis and Dwayne Murphy, allowing him to form Bustin' Records and release the solo single, 'Ring 'Em'. He had previously been part of religious rap group the Holy Ghost Boys. Together with a backing band consisting of two DJs and singers Tabatha King, Djuana Johnican and Phyllis Charles, he cut a 1987 debut set, *Feel My Power*. A minor hit, it did enough to bring Hammer to the attention of Capitol Records. After contracts were completed, the album was reissued under the title *Let's Get It Started*. Such success was overshadowed, however, by that of the follow-up, 1990's *Please Hammer Don't Hurt 'Em*. Following massive exposure due to sponsorship deals with British Knights footwear and Pepsi-Cola, the album began a residency at the top of the US charts for a record-breaking 21-week run. The US/UK Top 5 single, 'U Can't Touch This', embodied his appeal, with near constant rotation on pop channel MTV, and dance routines that were the equal of Michael Jackson. The single sampled Rick James' 'Super Freak', creating a precedent for follow-ups 'Have You Seen Her' (the Chi-Lites) and 'Pray' (Prince's 'When Doves Cry'), the latter achieving his highest chart position when it reached US number 2. While an on-going duel with white rapper Vanilla Ice raged, critics pointed out the plagiarism that underpinned both artists' most successful work. Unperturbed, Hammer was being praised as a suitable role model for black youth (not least by himself), and was honoured by M.C. Hammer Days in Los Angeles and Fremont. 'Here Comes The Hammer' became an unexpected failure by stalling at number 54 in the US charts, despite its appearance on the soundtrack to *Rocky V*. A multitude of awards, including Grammys, Bammys and International Album Of The Year at the Juno awards in Canada, reflected the global success of the album and the M.C. Hammer name - at this point in his career, his exposure to US audiences included the television adventures of cartoon hero 'Hammerman', and a Mattel Hammer doll with attached ghetto blaster. The follow-up, *Too Legit To Quit*, was released under the name Hammer. The sleeve notes to the album expanded on his desire for black youth to rid themselves of drugs and resurrect their Christian morality through self-education. Despite a soundtrack hit with 'Addams Groove', heavily promoted in *The Addams Family* movie, Hammer's fortunes declined. In 1992, *The San Francisco Examiner* reported that Hammer faced financial ruin after poor attendances for his *Too Legit To Quit* tour, promoting an album that had seen him tracing a more R&B-based groove. Though Hammer denied there was any truth in such stories, it was obvious a re-think was needed. By 1994, there was a huge image switch, from harem pants and leather catsuits to dark glasses and a goatee beard. The resultant album pulled in producers G-Bomb from Grand Jury Records, the Hines brothers from Detroit, Teddy Riley and members of the Dogg Pound, and specifically went after the Oakland G-funk sound of artists such as Too $hort. Hammer as a gangsta rapper? As Simon Price of the *Melody Maker* bluntly pointed out: 'Please Hammer, don't hurt me. My sides are killing me'. Hammer reverted to using the M.C. prefix for 1995's *Inside Out*.

● ALBUMS: *Feel My Power* (Bustin' 1987)★★★, *Let's Get It Started* (Capitol 1988)★★★, *Please Hammer Don't Hurt 'Em* (Capitol 1990)★★★, as Hammer *Too Legit To Quit* (Capitol 1991)★★, as Hammer *The Funky Headhunter* (RCA 1994)★★, *Inside Out* (Giant 1995)★★.

● COMPILATIONS: *Greatest Hits* (Capitol 1996)★★★★, *Back To Back Hits* (CEMA 1998)★★★.

● FURTHER READING: *M.C. Hammer: U Can't Touch This*, Bruce Dessau.

MC Lyte

b. Lana Moorer, 11 October 1970, Queens, New York, USA, but raised in Brooklyn. The daughter of First Priority boss Nat Robinson, and sister to the Audio Two brothers, Lyte began her career in fine style with the 45 'I Cram To Understand U (Sam)', released when she was still a teenager. The story told of personal deceit in a relationship, the narrator unable to compete for her boyfriend's attentions with his new mistress - crack. It was delivered with such force that it still has few peers in terms of adult, hardcore female rap. Lyte has gone on to underscore her patent scouring wit, often referring to the out of control egos of her male counterparts, with synthesizer and funk beats coalescing beneath. Her 1988 debut album additionally sampled Ray Charles, Helen Reddy and the Four Seasons. Her songs are populated by fully realised characters, though its an unfortunate truism that they often wind up dead (via AIDS, lung cancer, violence or drugs). Despite the contributions of Grand Puba to *Eyes On This*, there was a lack of lyrical progression which limited its appeal. *Ain't No Other* included attacks on fellow rappers Roxanne Shanté ('Steady F. King') and an answer record to Apache's 'Gangsta Bitch' ('Ruffneck', which would go gold when released on single). Rap legend KRS-1 introduced the tracks in a pseudo ragga-style. Like Queen Latifah and others before her, Lyte founded her own management company, Dupe The Moon Productions, which also handles Isis and Brooklyn rappers Born In Hell. After an extended hiatus, Lyte returned in 1996 with the US Top 10 hit single 'Keep On, Keepin' On', a collaboration with Xscape taken from the soundtrack of *Sunset Park*. The Diana Ross-sampling hit single 'Cold Rock A Party' was fairly unreflective of the more mature style evident on *Bad As I Wanna Be* and its attendant remix album, *Badder Than B-fore*. In 1998, Lyte celebrated a remarkable 10 years on the rap scene with *Seven & Seven*.

● ALBUMS: *Lyte As A Rock* (First Priority 1988)★★★, *Eyes On This* (First Priority 1989)★★★, *Act Like You Know* (First Priority 1991)★★★, *Ain't No Other* (First Priority 1993)★★★, *Bad As I Wanna Be* (East West 1996)★★★★, *Badder Than B-fore* remix album (East West 1997)★★★, *Seven & Seven* (Elektra 1998)★★★.

MC Solaar

b. Dakar, Senegal. Raised in Cairo and Paris, MC Solaar is the most prominent of the new breed of French rappers. His debut album (translating as Who Sows The Wind Will Reap The Beat) gave him four Top 10 French singles, the album itself moving over 200,000 copies. It brought him to the attention of the UK's Talkin' Loud Records imprint. They, like many others, were impressed by his free-flowing, relaxed style, and its easy musical backdrop, formulated by his DJ/producer Jimmy Jay. Gang Starr were so taken with the album that after a single hearing they asked if they could remix the title track. Solaar also took part in many collaborative projects for the Talkin' Loud stable (United Future Organization, Urban Species) and the Guru of Gang Starr-orchestrated Jazzamatazz project. His own material most often concerns sad stories about malcontents in the stream of French life. The wordplay and nuances do not translate easily, but the musicality of the French language does. As well as rappers like Big Daddy Kane, Solaar draws his inspiration from the French literary tradition of Baudelaire and Jaques Prevert.

● ALBUMS: *Qui Seme Le Vent Recolte Le Tempo* (Talkin' Loud 1993)★★, *Prose Combat* (Talkin' Loud 1994)★★, *Paradisiaque* (Mercury 1997)★★★, *Le Tour De La Question* (East West 1999)★★.

McAlmont And Butler

One of the most intriguing and unexpected collaborations of the mid-90s, this London, England-based duo paired former Suede guitarist Bernard Butler (b. 1970, Leyton, London, England) with ex-Thieves' singer David McAlmont. They were immediately successful in 1995 with 'Yes' (UK number 8) and 'You Do' (UK number 17), polished songs on which Butler's guitar accompanied McAlmont's sweet vocals. Although statements in the press continually stressed that the collaboration was only a temporary one, so successful were the singles that an album was eventually compiled. This comprised all the songs they had worked on together, including a cover version of the soul classic 'You'll Lose A Good Thing' (Barbara Lynn). Both members immersed themselves in other projects soon after the album's release, and with both going on to solo careers a second collaboration seems unlikely.

● ALBUMS: *The Sound Of McAlmont And Butler* (Hut 1995)★★★.

McAlmont, David

McAlmont's first exposure to the music industry came as half of the hotly tipped but underachieving London duo Thieves, who split up before the planned release of their debut album in 1994 (the album was released under the name of McAlmont). McAlmont, who possesses a three-and-a-half-octave vocal range, has gone on to further critical acclaim in his solo career, including supporting Morrissey on live dates. Through a mutual producer friend, McAlmont subsequently teamed up with ex-Suede guitarist Bernard Butler to form McAlmont And Butler. The relationship was never intended to be permanent, but two singles, 'Yes' and 'You Do', enjoyed UK chart success in 1995, and an album was also released. Following the dissolution of the partnership, McAlmont filled his diary as a guest vocalist, including a dramatic cover version of 'Diamonds Are Forever' for David Arnold's James Bond project. The stylish and exuberant *A Little Communication*, released in 1998, failed to reap the commercial reward it deserved.

● ALBUMS: *A Little Communication* (Hut 1998)★★★★.

McBride, Martina

b. Martina Mariea Schiff, 29 July 1966, Sharon, Kansas, USA. One of the leaders in contemporary country music, McBride has also won converts within more puritanical country fac-

tions for the respect she affords the roots of the music. She and her husband sold T-shirts at Garth Brooks concerts before McBride graduated to becoming his opening act. *The Time Has Come*, her 1992 debut album, impressed many with its cultured treatment of traditional material such as 'Cheap Whiskey' and 'That's Me'. Her breakthrough came as the result of two singles in 1993, 'My Baby Loves Me The Way That I Am' and the much removed 'Independence Day', which gave her considerable momentum on country radio. The latter single's accompanying video also won the CMA's Video Of The Year category in 1993. This time the subject matter was far from traditional, depicting an abused wife who takes justice into her own hands. Sales of her second album, *The Way That I Am*, climbed to the half million mark as a result of this exposure. She won the CMA Video Of The Year award in 1994 for 'Independence Day'. In 1995, RCA Records launched a major campaign to back her third album, *Wild Angels*, with numerous television appearances (including the CMT Showcase Artist Of The Month) and special retail promotion via the K-mart chain. Preceded by the single 'Safe In The Arms Of Love', *Wild Angels* was produced by McBride alongside Paul Worley and Ed Seay. Its composition relied heavily on the melancholy and sadness of her earlier releases, with her compassionate, third-person songs reflecting sympathetically on relationships with a series of characters. 'Safe In The Arms Of Love' was a country hit although for many, her revival of Delbert McClinton's 'Two More Bottles Of Wine' was a stronger track. Other songs, such as 'Born To Give My Love To You' which addressed the birth of her daughter Delaney, were more optimistic (her baby daughter gurgles on the number 1 hit 'Wild Angels'). In addition to the release of the album and extensive touring commitments she joined Reba McEntire, Trisha Yearwood and Linda Davis on a new version of the Michael McDonald/Patti LaBelle hit, 'On My Own'. The opening track on 1997's *Evolution*, 'I'm Little But I'm Loud', featured the recorded talents of a seven year old McBride, but overall the album strayed too close to slick MOR to match *Wild Angels*. *Emotion* contained a number of excellent compositions that saw McBride moving further away from country towards the crossover audience targeted by LeAnn Rimes and Shania Twain.

● ALBUMS: *The Time Has Come* (RCA 1992)★★★, *The Way That I Am* (RCA 1993)★★★★, *Wild Angels* (RCA 1995)★★★★, *Evolution* (RCA 1997)★★★, *White Christmas* (RCA 1998)★★, with Sara Evans, Mindy McCready, Lorrie Morgan *Girls' Night Out* (BNA 1999)★★★, *Emotion* (RCA 1999)★★★★.

● VIDEOS: *Independence Day* (1994).

McCready, Mindy

b. Malinda Gayle McCready, 30 November 1975, Fort Meyers, Florida, USA. McCready is one of the brightest new voices in country music, updating the traditional values of the genre for a new generation of listeners. Born and raised in southern Florida, she moved to Nashville when she was 18. Meeting up with producer David Malloy, she spent almost a year performing and preparing her demo tape, before signing with RLG Records. Released in April 1996, her debut *Ten Thousand Angels* was an assertive and confident collection that revealed McCready as an icon of female independence and self-reliance. The album gained strong reviews and by 1997 had gone platinum. The follow-up, *If I*

Don't Stay The Night, was released in November 1997 to further acclaim and widespread commercial acceptance. Though McCready does not write any of her own material, she covers songs such as 'What If I Do' and 'This Is Me' that deal frankly with relationships and sexual dilemmas. Her rising status was confirmed by support slots for George Strait, Alan Jackson and Tim McGraw. On 1999's disappointing *I'm Not So Tough*, McCready seemed to have put more of an effort into the photographic poses on the album sleeve and the detailed liner notes. In the latter, she managed to thank the entire planet and repeated the dedication 'I love you' an impressive 36 times. In this wave of saccharine benevolence the music was buried.

● ALBUMS: *Ten Thousand Angels* (BNA 1996)★★★, *If I Don't Stay The Night* (BNA 1997)★★★★, with Sara Evans, Martina McBride, Lorrie Morgan *Girls' Night Out* (BNA 1999)★★★, *I'm Not So Tough* (BNA 1999)★★.

McCutcheon, Martine

b. 14 May 1976, England. Actress McCutcheon endeared herself to the UK public as the feisty Tiffany Mitchell in the long-running television soap opera, *EastEnders*. One of a glut of television actors and actresses to attempt a pop career in the late 90s, McCutcheon rose above the wannabes thanks to a strong voice and her record company's shrewd targeting of the MOR market. McCutcheon first appeared in the public eye at the tender age of six weeks on a Labour Party billboard. Further modelling work followed before she attended the famous Italia Conti Academy stage school. The role of 'tart with a heart' Tiffany in *EastEnders* established McCutcheon as one of the UK's best-loved media personalities, and her dramatic exit from the series in December 1998 attracted record audiences. McCutcheon launched her singing career in the same year as fellow soap stars Adam Rickitt and Matthew Marsden, but her torch singer image was a marked contrast to the dance/pop-orientated approach of the ex-*Coronation Street* actors. The British public warmed to McCutcheon the singer as readily as they had to Tiffany the barmaid, with the dramatic ballad 'Perfect Moment' topping the charts for two weeks in April. The up-tempo R&B track 'I've Got You', written by her producer Tony Moran, was less successful in September, stalling at number 6. Her debut album, *You Me & Us*, was released the same month. Featuring material co-written with UK songwriters Ben And Jason and Moran, the album received good reviews and a UK Top 5 placing. 'Love Me'/'Talking In Your Sleep', a double a-side comprising cover versions of the Yvonne Elliman and Crystal Gayle songs, was the official Children In Need fund-raising single for 1999.

● ALBUMS: *You Me & Us* (Innocent 1999)★★★.
● VIDEOS: *View Me & Us* (Innocent 1999).

McEntire, Reba

b. Reba Nell McEntire, 28 March 1955, Chockie, Oklahoma, USA. One of four children, McEntire's family owned a 7,000-acre ranch and participated in rodeos, a background which later inspired the song 'Daddy'. She sang with her sister Susie and brother Pake McEntire as the Singing McEntires, and in 1972, they recorded for the small Boss label. In 1974, she was asked to sing 'The Star-Spangled Banner' at the National Rodeo Finals in Oklahoma City. Honky-tonk singer Red Steagall heard her, which led to a recording contract

with Mercury Records. Her first single, 'I Don't Want To Be A One Night Stand', made the US country charts in 1976, the year in which she married rodeo rider Charlie Battles. It was followed by several minor successes, including a revival of 'Sweet Dreams' and two duets with Jacky Ward ('Three Sheets To The Wind' and 'That Makes Two Of Us'). She made the US country Top 10 with '(You Lift Me) Up To Heaven', the Top 5 with 'Today All Over Again', and in 1982, number 1 with 'Can't Even Get The Blues'. She had another chart-topper in 1983 with 'You're The First Time I've Thought About Leaving'. She then left Mercury for MCA Records, although the label was to release an album of out-takes, *Reba Nell McEntire*, in 1986. Her string of country hits continued with 'Just A Little Love', 'He Broke Your Memory Last Night', 'Have I Got A New Deal For You', and the number 1 hits 'How Blue' and 'Somebody Should Leave'. Her best-known single, and the title track of a bestselling album, was 'Whoever's In New England'. McEntire's own battles with Battles ended in their divorce in 1987, and she married her band leader, Narvel Blackstock, in 1989. Several of her successes, although not written for her ('I Know How He Feels' and 'New Fool At An Old Game'), have overtones from her own life. She has won numerous country music awards, but her 1988 album *Reba*, although very successful, irritated very traditionalists who questioned her revival of a pop hit, 'Sunday Kind Of Love', and her version of Otis Redding's 'Respect'. McEntire was adamant: 'I can sing any kind of song, but whatever I sing, it'll come out country.' In 1990, she appeared, killing graboids with an elephant gun, in the well-reviewed horror movie *Tremors*. On 16 March 1991, tragedy struck when Chris Austin, Kirk Cappello, Joey Cigainero, Paula Kaye Evans, Terry Jackson, Michael Thomas, Tony Saputo - seven of the nine members of McEntire's band - died in a plane crash shortly after taking off from San Diego. The following year, McEntire herself was involved in a forced landing at Nashville airport, evoking memories of the earlier tragedy. She dedicated her next album, *For My Broken Heart*, to her friends and colleagues. It proved to be one of her most successful projects, and the title track was a major hit single. She tried to come to terms with the previous tragedy in 'If I Had Only Known', but the whole song selection evoked memories of it. Despite its melancholia, the album became one of her biggest hits. Having committed her feelings to record, McEntire then had a massive success via the dramatic video for the 'cheating' song, 'Does He Love You', which she sang with Linda Davis. She also began to establish herself as a film actress, playing alongside Kenny Rogers in *The Gambler Returns: The Luck Of The Draw*, Burt Reynolds in the 1993 television movie *The Man From Left Field*, and Bruce Willis in *North*. In 1995, she looked to her roots for an album of her favourite songs, *Starting Over*, including 'Talking In Your Sleep' and 'By The Time I Get To Phoenix'. For 'On My Own', she was joined by Linda Davis, Martina McBride and Trisha Yearwood. The follow-up, *What If It's You*, featured the excellent singles 'The Fear Of Being Alone' and 'I'd Rather Ride Around With You'.

● ALBUMS: *Reba McEntire* (Mercury 1977)★★, *Out Of A Dream* (Mercury 1979)★★★, *Feel The Fire* (Mercury 1980)★★★, *Heart To Heart* (Mercury 1981)★★★, *Unlimited* (Mercury 1982)★★★, *Behind The Scene* (Mercury 1983)★★★, *Just A Little Love* (MCA 1984)★★★, *Have I Got A Deal For You* (MCA 1985)★★★, *My Kind Of Country* (MCA 1986)★★★, *Whoever's In New England* (MCA 1986)★★★, *Reba*

Nell McEntire (MCA 1986)★★★, *What Am I Gonna Do About You* (MCA 1986)★★★, *The Last One To Know* (MCA 1987)★★★, *So So So Long* (MCA 1988)★★★, *Merry Christmas To You* (MCA 1988)★★★, *Reba* (MCA 1988)★★★, *Sweet Sixteen* (MCA 1989)★★★, *Live* (MCA 1989)★★★, *Rumour Has It* (MCA 1990)★★★, *For My Broken Heart* (MCA 1991)★★★, *It's Your Call* (MCA 1992)★★★★, *Read My Mind* (MCA 1994)★★★★, *Starting Over* (MCA 1995)★★★★, *What If It's You* (MCA 1996)★★★, *If You See Him* (MCA 1998)★★★, *So Good Together* (MCA 1999)★★★, *Secret Of Giving: A Christmas Collection* (MCA 1999)★★.

● COMPILATIONS: *The Best Of Reba McEntire* (Mercury 1985)★★★★, *The Very Best Of Reba McEntire* (Country Store 1987)★★★, *Greatest Hits* (MCA 1987)★★★★, *Greatest Hits Volume 2* (MCA 1993)★★★★, *Moments & Memories: The Best Of Reba McEntire* (Universal 1998)★★★★.

● VIDEOS: *Reba In Concert* (1992), *For My Broken Heart* (1993), *Greatest Hits* (MCA 1994), *Why Haven't I Heard From You* (Picture Vision 1994), *Reba Live* (MCA 1995), *And Still* (MCA 1995), *Reba Celebrating 20 Years* (MCA 1996), *The Video Collection* (MCA Video 1999).

● FURTHER READING: *Reba: Country Music's Queen*, Don Cusic. *Reba - My Story*, Reba McEntire with Tom Carter. *Comfort From A Country Quilt*, Reba McEntire.

● FILMS: *Tremors* (1990), *The Gambler Returns: The Luck Of The Draw* (1991), *North* (1994), *The Little Rascals* (1994).

McGraw, Tim

b. 1 May 1967, Delhi, Louisiana, USA. This highly popular country singer was raised in Start, Louisiana, and is the son of Frank Edwin 'Tug' McGraw, a noted left-handed relief pitcher for the New York Mets and Philadelphia Phillies, who retired in 1984 after a 19-year major league baseball career. Tim began his musical career singing in local clubs and also worked as a demo singer. He was signed to Curb Records in 1990 but did not achieve his first chart entry until 1992 with 'Welcome To The Club'. In 1993, he had two further minor hits with 'Memory Lane' and 'Two Steppin' Mind', all three of these songs taken from his debut album. He appeared on the Honky Tonk Attitude tour with Joe Diffie. McGraw's career took off with the release, early in 1994, of the single 'Indian Outlaw'. The song, written by John D. Loudermilk, caused considerable controversy in the USA, where some claimed that it degraded the accepted image of the American Indian. Controversy always helps sales, and the recording, with its war dance, rhythmic drum beat, quickly gave McGraw his first country number 1 record and broke into the pop Top 20. The song naturally appeared on his second album, from which he also gained further chart success with the recording of 'Down On The Farm' and the title track. The album, *Not A Moment Too Soon*, entered the *Billboard* country chart at number 1. The album sales topped four million and it remained in the Top 5 for over a year. The following album, *All I Want*, also amassed huge sales and McGraw topped the country singles chart with 'I Like It, I Love It' and just missed with 'Can't Be Really Gone'. Many see him as the successor to Garth Brooks, and although his records are not quite as distinctive, he does seem determined to remain a country artist (whatever that means today) with titles such as 'Don't Mention Memphis', 'Give It To Me Strait', 'It Doesn't Get Any Countrier Than This' and his 1996 US country number 1 'She Never Lets It Go To her Heart'. His run of success continued with *Everywhere*

reaching number 2 on the *Billboard* 200 album chart in 1997, and a CMA Award for Vocal Event Of The Year on 'It's Your Love' (with his wife Faith Hill). McGraw broke into the US pop Top 10 in May 1999 with 'Please Remember Me', and topped the album charts with *A Place In The Sun*.

● ALBUMS: *Tim McGraw* (Curb 1993)★★★, *Not A Moment Too Soon* (Curb 1994)★★★★, *All I Want* (Curb/Hit 1995)★★★★, *Everywhere* (Curb 1997)★★★★, *A Place In The Sun* (Curb 1999)★★★.

● VIDEOS: *Indian Outlaw* (Curb 1994), *Refried Dreams* (Curb 1995), *An Hour With Tim* (Curb 1995), *It's Your Love* (Curb 1997).

McKee, Maria

b. Maria Louise McKee, 17 August 1964, Los Angeles, California, USA. Before her solo career McKee was the singer with Lone Justice, a band formed by her half-brother, Bryan Maclean, the former Love guitarist and vocalist. Both Lone Justice albums, 1985's *Lone Justice* and 1987's *Shelter*, were critically acclaimed. After the break-up of the band McKee took time to compose herself, and her debut solo album provided a good platform for her powerful voice and distinctive register (similar to a more cultured Janis Joplin) with more pop-orientated hooks. Predominantly concerned with romance and heartbreak, it was boosted commercially by 1990's unrepresentative UK number 1 single, 'Show Me Heaven', taken from the soundtrack to the Tom Cruise movie, *Days Of Thunder*. Touring extensively in support of the album, McKee eventually decided to move to Ireland. This period also saw McKee collaborate with a variety of Irish musicians, including Gavin Friday, at a series of gigs for the Dublin AIDS Alliance. She also recorded the UK club hit 'Sweetest Child', with the help of noted producer Youth. She eventually returned to Los Angeles in 1992 to begin work on a follow-up set. This time she recruited producer George Drakoulias, veteran of successful albums by Black Crowes and the Jayhawks. *You Gotta Sin To Get Saved* reunited three-quarters of the original line-up of Lone Justice: Marvin Etzioni (bass), Don Heffington (drums) and Bruce Brody (keyboards), alongside Gary Louris and Mark Olson (guitar/vocals) of the Jayhawks. Bob Fisher provided guitar on live dates, with McKee seemingly much more comfortable with the return to rootsy material. Three years later she released her most representative work to date, *Life Is Sweet*.

● ALBUMS: *Maria McKee* (Geffen 1989)★★★, *You Gotta Sin To Get Saved* (Geffen 1993)★★★, *Life Is Sweet* (Geffen 1996)★★★★.

McKnight, Brian

b. 5 June 1969, Buffalo, New York, USA. The younger brother of Claude V. McKnight of *a cappella* gospel outfit Take 6, R&B singer Brian McKnight began his musical career in and around Buffalo, performing self-written material with his own band. Attracting the attention of Mercury Records, he recorded a self-titled debut set which reached the Top 20 of the US R&B album chart, although its sales returns were modest. 'Love Is', a duet with Vanessa Williams taken from the television series *Beverly Hills, 90210*, crossed over to the pop charts, reaching number 3 in May 1993. Another single, 'One Last Cry', climbed to number 13 later in the year. His second effort, *I Remember You*, sold more than half a million copies and included five Top 20 R&B singles. With his reputation and image established, Mercury decided to pull out all the stops for his third album, the immaculately produced

Anytime. Involved in its creation were star names such as Sean 'Puffy' Combs (production), Ma$e (rapping) and Mary J. Blige and Diane Warren (songwriting). The first single to be taken from the album, the US number 17 hit 'You Should Be Mine (Don't Waste Your Time)', featured Ma$e, in an attempt to convert sections of the hip-hop audience to McKnight's work and expand his growing fanbase. However, the single was hardly representative of the mature R&B and romantic balladry that comprised much of the album's contents, which is where McKnight's true talent lies. *Anytime* was rewarded with a US Top 20 chart placing. McKnight switched to Motown Records for the Christmas album, *Bethlehem*. The highly succesful *Back At One* followed.

● ALBUMS: *Brian McKnight* (Mercury 1992)★★, *I Remember You* (Mercury 1995)★★★★, *Anytime* (Mercury 1997)★★★★, *Bethlehem* (Motown 1998)★★★, *Back At One* (Motown 1999)★★★.

McLachlan, Sarah

b. 28 January 1968, Bedford, Halifax, Nova Scotia, Canada. Singer-songwriter Sarah McLachlan has featured on the Canadian folk scene since she was a 20-year-old, and through a series of well-received albums and tours has blossomed into a well-rounded folk-rock artist and a confident live performer. Her third album, 1994's *Fumbling Towards Ecstasy*, was produced by Daniel Lanois' protégé Pierre Marchand and was inspired partly by a disturbing trip the singer undertook with the World Vision charity to Cambodia and Thailand. The album blended her pastoral and reflective songwriting with a high-tech production that gave her sound a sophisticated edginess. In 1997, McLachlan inaugurated the Lilith Fair touring festival, a hugely successful showcase for female artists. 'Adia', taken from her US number 2 album *Surfacing*, proved to be an enduring radio hit, eventually climbing to number 3 on the singles chart in August 1998. As on all her releases her earthy voice is the perfect vehicle for songs about the deeper, darker aspects of the human condition.

● ALBUMS: *Touch* (Arista 1988)★★★, *Solace* (Arista 1992)★★★, *Fumbling Towards Ecstasy* (Arista 1994)★★★★, *The Freedom Sessions* (Nettwerk/Arista 1995)★★, *Surfacing* (Arista 1997)★★★★, *Mirrorball* (Arista 1999)★★★.

McNabb, Ian

b. 3 November 1960, Liverpool, Merseyside, England. Former Icicle Works guitarist, singer and songwriter Ian McNabb never earned the commercial rewards he deserved first time round with his highly individual, underrated band. The Liverpool outfit's back-catalogue reputedly continues to sell better since their demise than it ever did while active, but more pertinent compensation for McNabb has arrived in a highly acclaimed solo career. Though he has steered closer to the mainstream since the Icicle Works dissolved, he remains essentially the same prolific and acute songwriting commentator that many critics adored in the previous decade. His debut album, *Truth And Beauty*, was recorded on a small budget (allegedly via a loan secured by the artist's own mortgage) in Oldham, Lancashire. Andrew Lauder of This Way Up Records was the only one to express any interest, and the record was eventually released early in 1993. It housed one notable single, 'If Love Was Like Guitars'. His breakthrough album, *Head Like A Rock*, was afforded a much grander platform. It was recorded over three weeks in

Los Angeles, California, with expert help from Meters' drummer Joseph Modeliste, pedal steel guitar player Greg Leisz (of k.d. lang fame), plus Hutch Hutchings (rhythm guitar), Ralph Molina (drums) and Billy Talbot (bass) of Crazy Horse, Neil Young's erstwhile backing band. Amazingly, nobody had ever asked Crazy Horse to play on anybody else's record before, but they were happy to oblige, despite the almost 20-year age gap. The album, with sonic similarities to Neil Young that proved inescapable, earned rave critical reviews, ensuring a Mercury Prize nomination for a man whose career looked unlikely to be sustainable just a few months previously. *Merseybeast* continued the run of excellent quality pop with lyrical maturity and hair-raising melody, but sadly this album did not build on the critical success of *Head Like A Rock*. McNabb decamped to South Wales for the follow-up, an engaging acoustic set recorded with the help of Anthony Thistlewaite and Danny Thompson.

● ALBUMS: *Truth And Beauty* (This Way Up 1993)★★★★, *Head Like A Rock* (This Way Up 1994)★★★★, *Merseybeast* (This Way Up 1996)★★★, *A Party Political Broadcast On Behalf Of The Emotional Party* (Fairfield 1998)★★★.

Meat Beat Manifesto

Their name a grotesque reference to masturbation, London, England's Meat Beat Manifesto are a post-industrial dance music outfit comprising multi-instrumentalist/vocalist Jack Dangers and programmer Jonny Stephens, aided by non-musical contributors Marcus Adams (dancer and choreographer) and Craig Morrison (stage and costume design). Taking their theme as the modern information/consumer society, the band combines samples drawn from television and commercials with hip-hop beats and dub grooves to create mesmerizing aural soundscapes. They began releasing a series of 12-inch singles (still their best medium) in the late 80s, which were later anthologized on *Storm The Studio*. Herein the 'cut-up' techniques pioneered in literature by William Burroughs were transposed to diverse musical cultures, a process confirmed by the fact that the title *Storm The Studio* was adapted from a statement made by Burroughs' character Uranian Willy in *The Soft Machine*. Enigmatically, none of the songs were given individual titles. The tapes for a debut album proper had been lost during a fire at their London studio, thus *Armed Audio Warfare* again comprised largely dated material. Their first studio album proper, *99%*, was less visceral and more attuned to the burgeoning house movement, though their lyrics were no less challenging. That was especially true of 1992's *Satyricon*, on which such subjects as consumerism ('That Shirt') and animal rights ('Untold Stories') were addressed without the band's sound becoming too didactic. In the 90s, Dangers also became a celebrated remixer, working with artists including Consolidated, the Shamen, David Byrne and MC 900ft Jesus. After a four-year gap Meat Beat Manifesto returned in 1996 with a striking single, 'Transmission', and the sprawlingly eclectic *Subliminal Sandwich*.

● ALBUMS: *Storm The Studio* (Wax Trax! 1989)★★★, *Armed Audio Warfare* (Wax Trax! 1990)★★★, *99%* (Play It Again Sam/Mute 1990)★★★, *Satyricon* (Play It Again Sam/Mute 1992)★★★, *Subliminal Sandwich* (Play It Again Sam/Mute 1996)★★★, *Actual Sounds + Voices* (Play It Again Sam 1998)★★.

Mega City Four

Thrash pop outfit from Surrey, England, influenced by early punks such as Stiff Little Fingers and the Buzzcocks, stabilizing their output with a sustained melodicism and growing lyrical awareness. They started out in 1982 as Capricorn, who played a few gigs and recorded demos (including one 15-track affair entitled *The Good News Tape*). However, in 1986 original drummer Martin left, leaving the remaining members to undergo a rethink. A replacement, Chris Jones (ex-Exit East, Moose Kaboose), joined Wiz (b. Darren Brown; vocals/guitar), his brother Danny Brown (rhythm guitar/backing vocals) and Gerry Bryant (bass). On 1 January 1987, Mega City Four had their first practice. They took their name from the home base of *Judge Dredd*, the popular comic book enforcer. A demo appeared in March, and after nationwide gigs a self-financed single, 'Miles Apart', was recorded in the autumn. Although it took six months to surface, reviews were impressive and disc jockey John Peel added his patronage. In the wake of its success it was reissued by Vinyl Solution subsidiary Decoy Records. 'Distant Relatives' followed in November 1988, announcing Wiz's lyrical preoccupation with relationships, and was awarded Single Of The Week status by Steve Lamacq in *New Musical Express*. Another single, 'Less Than Senseless', arrived during a relentless 300-gig touring schedule throughout 1989. These experiences would result in the title of their debut album, *Tranzophobia* - a term invoked to convey the horror of touring for extended periods out of the back of a transit van. Though at the time it perfectly described the earnest, hard-working nature of the band, it later became an albatross around their necks when they found themselves unable to escape the lack of sophistication it implied. Despite this, Mega City Four, alongside peers and friends the Senseless Things, helped revitalize a flagging UK live scene with wholly committed performances. Sadly, *Who Cares Wins* saw many of the band's newly acquired critical following renounce their previous advocacy, on a set neutered by flat production. Frustrated by budget restrictions, the band elected to move to Big Life Records for future recordings. 'Words That Say' and the *Stop* EP, the latter a UK Top 40 success in early 1992, prefaced the band's long-playing debut for their new home. *Sebastapol Road* was titled after the band's Farnborough rehearsal studio and comprised a succinct, energized collection of three-minute pop songs, with more highly evolved lyrical themes than had previously been the case. A live album, less perfunctory than efforts by bands without Mega City Four's onstage fluency, preceded 1993's *Magic Bullets*. With increasingly introverted songwriting from Wiz - though his words were as direct and antiglamour as ever - this was another fine, considered set, its quality emphasized by the promotional single, 'Iron Sky'. However, the band's fans had also moved on, to new favourites such as Carter USM, and sales proved disappointing. They signed to Fire Records in 1995, but *Soulscraper* was largely ignored on release.

● ALBUMS: *Tranzophobia* (Decoy 1989)★★★, *Who Cares Wins* (Decoy 1990)★★, *Sebastapol Road* (Big Life/Caroline 1991)★★★★, *Inspiringly Titled (The Live Album)* (Big Life 1992)★★★, *Magic Bullets* (Big Life 1993)★★★, *Soulscraper* (Fire 1995)★★★.

● COMPILATIONS: *Terribly Sorry Bob* (Decoy 1991)★★★.

● FURTHER READING: *Mega City Four: Tall Stories And Creepy Crawlies*, Martin Roach.

Megadeth

This thrash metal quartet was founded in San Francisco, California, USA, by guitarist Dave Mustaine (b. 13 September 1961, La Mesa, California, USA) after leaving Metallica in 1983 (he co-wrote four songs on the latter's debut album, though he did not actually appear on it). Recruiting bass player Dave Ellefson (b. 12 November 1964, Jackson, Minnesota, USA), Slayer guitarist Kerry King and drummer Lee Rash, Mustaine formed Megadeth. King and Rash were quickly replaced by Chris Poland and Gar Samuelson, and Mustaine negotiated a contract with the independent Combat Records label. Working on a tight budget, Megadeth produced *Killing Is My Business ... And Business Is Good!* in 1985. This was a ferocious blast of high-energy thrash metal, weakened by a thin production. Nevertheless, Capitol Records, realizing the band's potential, immediately signed them, even though Mustaine was beginning to acquire a reputation for his outspoken and provocative manner. *Peace Sells ... But Who's Buying?* was a marked improvement over their debut, both technically and musically. It was characterized by incessant, heavy-duty riffing, bursts of screaming guitar and lyrics that reflected Mustaine's outspoken perception of contemporary social and political issues. In 1986, Mustaine fired Poland and Samuelson (who then formed Fatal Opera), bringing in Jeff Young and Chuck Behler as replacements before the recording of *So Far, So Good ... So What!* This built on their aggressive and vitriolic style, and included a cover version of 'Anarchy In The UK', with the Sex Pistols' guitarist Steve Jones making a guest appearance. Following two years of heroin-related problems, and the enforced departure of Young and Behler, Mustaine reappeared in 1990 with guitar virtuoso Marty Friedman (b. 8 December 1962, Washington, DC, USA) and drummer Nick Menza. *Rust In Peace* was released to widespread critical acclaim, combining an anti-nuclear message with the explosive guitar pyrotechnics of Friedman. *Countdown To Extinction*, meanwhile, was a bruising encounter that entertained more melody in the execution of its theme - that of impending ecological disaster. It included the UK Top 20 hit singles, 'Skin O' My Teeth' and 'Symphony Of Destruction'. Reports of Mustaine's drug problems again overshadowed sessions for their sixth album, *Youthanasia*, recorded in Phoenix, Arizona, where three-quarters of the band now lived. It was produced by Max Norman (who co-produced *Countdown To Extinction* and mixed *Rust In Peace*), and featured the brilliant UK hit single 'Train Of Consequences'. Following the release of *Cryptic Writings* drummer Nick Menza left the band due to 'health problems'; he was replaced by Jimmy Degrasso. A 'clean' Mustaine steered the band in an even more melodic direction on 1999's *Risk*. Along with Slayer, Metallica and Anthrax, Megadeth remain at the forefront of the thrash metal genre, despite the vulnerability of their central creative force.

● ALBUMS: *Killing Is My Business ... And Business Is Good!* (Combat/Megaforce 1985)★★, *Peace Sells ... But Who's Buying?* (Capitol 1986)★★★, *So Far, So Good ... So What!* (Capitol 1988)★★★, *Rust In Peace* (Capitol 1990)★★★★, *Countdown To Extinction* (Capitol 1992)★★★, *Youthanasia* (Capitol 1994)★★★, *Cryptic Writings* (Capitol 1997)★★★, *Risk* (Capitol 1999)★★★.

● COMPILATIONS: *Hidden Treasures* (Capitol 1995)★★★.

● VIDEOS: *Rusted Pieces* (EMI 1991), *Exposure Of A Dream* (PMI 1993), *Evolver: The Making Of Youthanasia* (Capitol 1995).

Mekon

b. John Gosling, England. Mekon is the pseudonym used by Gosling whose first musical forays were with *avant garde* experimentalists Psychic TV. Via hip-hop and acid house, Gosling became involved with William Orbit's Bassomatic, and gave their 1990 UK Top 10 hit 'Fascinating Rhythm' a remix as Sugar J. With a singer, Cleo Torres and a guitarist, Matthew Ashman, Gosling formed the eclectic Agent Provocateur. Continuing to make his own instrumental hip-hop as Mekon, Gosling released 'Phatty's Lunchbox' which attracted the attention of Wall Of Sound's Mark Jones who signed Gosling for his second release. 'Mekon's Revenge' featured the voice of 'Mad' Frankie Fraser, a notorious 60s gangster from London's East End, who worked for the Kray Twins' rivals, the Richardsons. Gosling had met Fraser at a bus stop and the result was the single, a brooding piece of hip-hop with Fraser's voice edited and looped over the music. Mekon's debut set, *Welcome To Tackletown*, took its name from a long piece of graffiti in Hoxton Square, London, and was released in 1997. It featured Agent Provocateur's Daniel Peppe, Chris Blackman, Jah Norris and rude boy Evil B, as well as old school gangsta rapper Schoolly D, a hero of the big beat and trip-hop fraternity.
● ALBUMS: *Welcome To Tackletown* (Wall Of Sound 1997)★★★, *Mekon Plays 4 U* (Phat Sam 1999)★★★.

Melvins

The late Kurt Cobain of Nirvana described the US rock band the Melvins as his favourite group. Unsurprising, perhaps, as they are the only other band of note to originate from his hometown of Aberdeen in the USA (though they have since relocated to San Francisco), and he did once roadie for them. Drummer Dale Crover also played with Nirvana for a spell, while Cobain guested on and co-produced 1993's major label debut, *Houdini*, for the band. The other members of the Melvins, formed in 1984, were King Buzzo aka Buzz Osborne (vocals/guitar) and Lori Black (bass). Matt Lukin (Mudhoney) was also an early floating member. Reputed to be more influenced by the heavy rock angle than many who have fallen under the generic title grunge, the Melvins are big fans of Black Sabbath and even released three solo albums in a tribute to the Kiss strategy of similar pretensions. A cover version of Flipper's 'Way Of The World' and 'Sacrifice' sat alongside Alice Cooper's 'Ballad Of Dwight Fry' on 1992's *Melvins*, which featured new bass player Joe Preston (who had joined in time to release one of the three solo sets). *Stoner Witch*, their second album for Atlantic Records following *Houdini*, saw Crover and Osborne joined by bass player Mark Deutrom, who had previously produced the band's first two albums. This time, they were working with Garth Richardson of Red Hot Chili Peppers and L7 fame. Two albums with Atlantic failed to break the band into the mainstream and they moved to a subsidiary for *Stag*. It was felt that a smaller label would be more supportive to the band, rather than being lost in the wave of releases from a large label. They retreated further away from the mainstream in the late 90s with two further albums on the independent Amphetamine Reptile label. *The Maggot* appeared on the band's newly-formed Ipecac label.
● ALBUMS: *Gluey Porch Treatments* (Alchemy 1987)★★★, *Ozma* (Boner 1989)★★, *Bullhead* (Boner 1990)★★, *10 Songs* (C/Z/ 1991)★★, *Melvins* aka *Lysol* (Boner/Tupelo 1992)★★★, *Houdini* (Atlantic 1993)★★★, as Snivlem *Prick* (Amphetamine Reptile 1994)★, *Stoner Witch* (Atlantic 1994)★★★, *Live* (X-mas 1996)★★, *Stag* (Mammoth/Atlantic 1996)★★★, *Honky* (Amphetamine Reptile 1997)★★, *Live At The F*cker Club: Australia* (Amphetamine Reptile 1998)★★, *The Maggot* (Ipecac 1999)★★★.
● COMPILATIONS: *Singles 1-12* (Amphetamine Reptile 1997)★★★.

Menswear

The rise of Menswear (actually spelt Menswe@r) was one of 1995's biggest UK media events. They appeared on the BBC Television chart show *Top Of The Pops* performing 'I'll Manage Somehow' before they had even released a single. When 'Daydreamer', the first song they had written together, was released as a single, it peaked at number 14 in the UK charts. The band was founded by Johnny Dean (b. John Hutchinson Dean, 12 December 1971, Salisbury, England; vocals), Chris Gentry (b. 23 February 1977, Southend, England; guitar) and Stuart Black (b. Stuart Lee Black, 1 April 1974, Walthamstow, London, England; bass). The line-up was completed with the addition of Matt Everett (b. Matthew Stephen Everett, 13 August 1972, Birmingham, England; drums) and Simon White (b. Simon Ian White, 1 July 1977, Moseley, Birmingham, England; guitar). Original drummer Todd Parmenter had been replaced in late 1994, the band having formed officially on 13 October 1994. Their debut gig five days later was reportedly 'filled with A&R men'. Much of the initial attention stemmed from the fact that their career was steered by local London celebrities Howard Gough (former manager of Lush) of Laurel Records and their manager Adrian. 'Daydreamer' was accused by some of plagiarizing Wire, while *Nuisance* possessed a few reasonable tunes, but nothing approaching the songwriting required to justify their early claims or the initial press interest. They finally managed to break into the UK Top 10 in March 1996 with the single 'Being Brave'. Everett left the band in July to join Montrose Avenue, and was replaced by their percussion roadie Tud.
● ALBUMS: *Nuisance* (Laurel 1995)★★★.

Merchant, Natalie

b. 26 October 1963, Jamestown, New York, USA. Having originally sung in a church choir, Merchant joined the highly regarded 10,000 Maniacs in 1981 while studying at Jamestown Community College in New York. She would eventually leave that band over a decade later in 1992, three years before she made her solo bow. Merchant self-evidently relished the control afforded her by this enterprise, writing all the lyrics and music for her debut album, *Tigerlily*, which she also produced. She had made her intentions to leave known to her former band as early as 1990, but only jumped ship after their label, Elektra Records, offered her a solo contract. When she took it up they promptly dropped 10,000 Maniacs. Her reflections on her time in the band were revisited on *Tigerlily*'s 'I May Know The Word', which amplified some of the frustration she felt in the later stages of their career (though the break-up was generally amicable). However, she still felt the need to recruit a core backing band, with Jennifer Turner (lead guitar), Peter Yanowitz (drums) and Barry Maguire (bass/guitar) as her accomplices. The most obvious change from her 10,000 Maniacs days signalled by *Tigerlily* was the vocal emphasis. Always a distinctive, affecting singer, her vocals were now mixed much higher and were less prone to smothering by her former band's multi-layered musicianship. The album was also a commercial success, reaching the US Top 20 in July 1995, and established her as one of the leading female pop artists of the 90s. The ambitious follow-up, *Ophelia*, was a semi-successful attempt by Merchant to broaden her musical and lyrical horizons. The album was another commercial success, however, reaching the US Top 10 in June 1998. An enjoyable live album was released the following year.

● ALBUMS: *Tigerlily* (Elektra 1995)★★★★, *Ophelia* (Elektra 1998)★★★, *Live In Concert New York City June 13, 1999* (Elektra 1999)★★★.

Mercury Rev

A six-piece band from Buffalo, New York State, USA, Mercury Rev burst onto the music scene in 1991 to unanimous critical acclaim for their enterprising mix of Pink Floyd and Dinosaur Jr dynamics. However, the sounds produced by Jonathan Donahue (vocals/guitar, ex-Flaming Lips), David Fridmann (bass), Jimmy Chambers (drums), Sean 'Grasshopper' Mackowiak (guitar), Suzanne Thorpe (flute) and David Baker (vocals/guitar) were difficult to classify. Their album, *Yerself Is Steam*, although practically ignored in their native country, created the sort of snowballing press acclaim in the UK that has rarely been accorded a debut. The *Melody Maker*'s comment: 'Universally acclaimed by UK critics as the draughtsmen behind the first, and so far only, great rock long player of 1991', was among the more conservative of the plaudits, and with only a handful of gigs under their belt they were to be seen filling support slots for artists such as My Bloody Valentine and, incredibly, Bob Dylan. The music press saw them as the next step forward from the previous wave of influential US guitar bands such as the Pixies, Sonic Youth and Dinosaur Jr. However, the ability to capitalize on this flying start rested, rather precariously, on their ability to remain together as a collective unit. A variety of stories filtered through concerning their self-destructive, almost psychotic behaviour. Already banned from one airline due to Donahue trying to remove Mackowiak's eye with a spoon, another minor crisis concerned Fridmann's disposal of the band's entire advance for their 'Carwash Hair' single on a holiday for his mother in Bermuda, without telling anyone. However, even by Mercury Rev's standards David Baker offered an unsettled musical visage, often simply stepping off the stage during performances to fetch a drink, and enriching the surreal nature of their songs with lines like: 'Tonight I'll dig tunnels to your nightmare room' in 'Downs Are Feminine Balloons'. This was drawn from *Boces*, another complex journey through multitudinous musical motifs and styles, producing a sonic anomaly drawing on the traditions of left-field art rockers such as Wire, Pere Ubu and Suicide. Baker was eventually deselected when his behaviour became intolerable in February 1994, leaving him to concentrate on his solo project, Shady. Reduced to a quintet, *See You On The Other Side* provided no other evidence of a reduction in the band's talents, revealing instead a more focused, though no less exciting or adventurous, sound. Growing disillusionment, brought on by the lack of record company support for their experimental music, saw the band's original members reduced to a core of Mackowiak and Donahue by

the time they signed to V2 Records in June 1997. Mackowiak had used the spare time to retire to a monastery and then record a solo album, *The Orbit Of Eternal Grace*, featuring new Mercury Rev members Jason and Justin Russo. The band returned with the acclaimed *Deserter's Song* in 1998. Engineered by Fridmann, the album also featured contributions from Levon Helm and Garth Hudson of the Band.

● ALBUMS: *Yerself Is Steam* (Rough Trade/Mint Films 1991)★★★, *Boces* (Columbia/Beggars Banquet 1993)★★, *See You On The Other Side* (Work/Beggars Banquet 1995)★★★, *Deserter's Song* (V2 1998)★★★★.

Messina, Jo Dee

b. New England, USA. Singer-songwriter Jo Dee Messina began her career as a teenager playing in local country bands around New England. By the age of 19 she had decamped to Nashville, where she struggled on the local talent show circuit. Eventually producer James Stroud at Curb Records took a chance on her. She finally announced herself with the US country hit 'Heads Carolina, Tails California' in 1996, and seemed set fair for a successful career with the release of her self-titled debut album (produced by Tim McGraw and Byron Gallimore). However, while attempting to write a follow-up she underwent severe financial problems, and had to hand back the keys of the tour bus she had leased. By December 1997 her house was on the market owing to touring debts. However, 1998 proved a better year. 'Bye Bye' performed well on country radio before she triumphed once again with 'I'm Alright' in August, which spent two weeks atop *Billboard*'s Hot Country Singles & Tracks chart. The single's success enabled her to pay off some of her debts and take her home back off the market. An album of the same title followed, once again produced in collaboration with McGraw and Gallimore.

● ALBUMS: *Jo Dee Messina* (Curb 1996)★★★, *I'm Alright* (Curb 1998)★★★★.

Metalheadz

Metalheadz rose to prominence in the early 90s as home to jungle's first global superstar - Goldie. He makes up the nucleus of Metalheadz in collaboration with Fabio and Grooverider, two DJs who made their name on the hardcore rave scene of the early 90s, and Ronnie Randall, the more elusive fourth member. Together they have fashioned Metalheadz into an all-conquering drum 'n' bass collective. Their *Angel* EP was one of the first records to invoke the intelligent techno description in the mid-90s, before 'jungle' or 'junglist' had been coined to describe their employment of dub plates and frenetic breakbeats. While that effort was Goldie's own work, other releases under the Metalheadz banner come from disparate sources, such as 'Here Come The Drums' (by extended family member Doc Scott) and 'Predator' (by Photek collaborator Peshay). With Goldie's brief relationship with Björk dominating the headlines, Metalheadz adopted the Blue Note club in London's Hoxton Square as their new residency in 1995. This has subsequently become jungle's first home, with a fleet of celebrities including Tricky, Malcolm McLaren, recent drum 'n' bass acolyte David Bowie and former members of Duran Duran among those who have attended. The team has expanded to include female DJs Kemistry And Storm (who were responsible for first introducing Goldie to hardcore) and MC Cleveland Watkiss in addition to the core quartet. As well as the club, there is also a Metalheadz label, run on a day-to-day basis by Kemistry And Storm.

● VIDEOS: *Talkin' Headz: The Metalheadz Documentary* (Manga Video 1998).

Metallica

The most consistently innovative metal band of the late 80s and 90s was formed in 1981 in California, USA, by Lars Ulrich (b. 26 December 1963, Copenhagen, Denmark; drums) and James Alan Hetfield (b. 3 August 1963, USA; guitar/vocals) after each separately advertised for fellow musicians in the classified section of American publication *The Recycler*. They recorded their first demo, *No Life Til' Leather*, with Lloyd Grand (guitar), who was replaced in January 1982 by David Mustaine (b. 13 September 1961, La Mesa, California, USA), whose relationship with Ulrich and Hetfield proved unsatisfactory. Jef Warner (guitar) and Ron McGovney (bass) each had a brief tenure with the band. At the end of 1982 Clifford Lee Burton (b. 10 February 1962, USA, d. 27 September 1986; bass, ex-Trauma) joined the band, playing his first live performance on 5 March 1983. Mustaine departed to form Megadeth and was replaced by Kirk Hammett (b. 18 November 1962, San Francisco, California, USA; guitar). Hammett, who came to the attention of Ulrich and Hetfield while playing with rock band Exodus, played his first concert with Metallica on 16 April 1983. The Ulrich, Hetfield, Burton and Hammett combination endured until disaster struck the band in the small hours of 27 September 1986, when Metallica's tour bus overturned in Sweden, killing Cliff Burton. During those four years, the band put thrash metal on the map with the aggression and exuberance of their debut, *Kill 'Em All*, the album sleeve of which bore the legend 'Bang that head that doesn't bang'. This served as a template for a whole new breed of metal, though the originators themselves were quick to dispense with their own rule book. Touring with New Wave Of British Heavy Metal bands Raven and Venom followed, while Music For Nations signed them for European distribution. Although *Ride The Lightning* was not without distinction, notably on 'For Whom The Bell Tolls', it was 1986's *Master Of Puppets* that offered further evidence of Metallica's appetite for the epic. Their first album for Elektra Records in the USA (who had also re-released its predecessor), this was a taut, multi-faceted collection that both raged and lamented with equal conviction. After the death of Burton, the band elected to continue, the remaining three members recruiting Jason Newsted (b. 4 March 1963; bass) of Flotsam And Jetsam. Newsted played his first concert with the band on 8 November 1986. The original partnership of Ulrich and Hetfield, however, remained responsible for Metallica's lyrics and musical direction. The new line-up's first recording together was *The $5.98 EP - Garage Days Re-Revisited* - a collection of cover versions including material from Budgie, Diamond Head, Killing Joke and the Misfits, which also served as a neat summation of the band's influences to date. Sessions for ... *And Justice For All* initially began with Guns N'Roses producer Mike Clink at the helm, before the band opted to return to Johnny Zazula, a relationship they had begun in *Ride The Lightning*. A long and densely constructed effort, this 1988 opus included an appropriately singular spectacular moment in 'One' (a US

Top 40/UK Top 20 single), while elsewhere the barrage of riffs somewhat obscured the usual Metallica artistry. The songs on 1991's US/UK chart-topper *Metallica* continued to deal with large themes - justice and retribution, insanity, war, religion and relationships. Compared to *Kill 'Em All* nearly a decade previously, however, the band had grown from iconoclastic chaos to thoughtful harmony, hallmarked by sudden and unexpected changes of mood and tempo. The MTV-friendly 'Enter Sandman' broke the band on a stadium level and entered the US Top 20. The single also reached the UK Top 10, as did another album track, 'Nothing Else Matters'. Constant touring in the wake of the album ensued, along with a regular itinerary of awards ceremonies. There could surely be no more deserving recipients, Metallica having dragged mainstream metal, not so much kicking and screaming as whining and complaining, into a bright new dawn when artistic redundancy seemed inevitable. *Metallica* was certified as having sold nine million copies in the USA by June 1996, and one month later *Load* entered the US charts at number 1. The album marked a change in image for the band, who began to court the alternative rock audience. The following year's *ReLoad* collected together more tracks recorded at the *Load* sessions, and featured 60s icon Marianne Faithfull on the first single to be released from the album, 'The Memory Remains'. *Garage Inc.* collected assorted cover versions, and broke the band's run of US number 1 albums when it debuted at number 2 in December 1998. The following year's *S&M*, recorded live with the San Francisco Symphony Orchestra, evoked the worst excesses of heavy rock icons Deep Purple.

● ALBUMS: *Kill 'Em All* (Megaforce 1983)★★★, *Ride The Lightning* (Megaforce 1984)★★, *Master Of Puppets* (Elektra 1986)★★★★, ... *And Justice For All* (Elektra 1988)★★★, *Metallica* (Elektra 1991)★★★★, *Live Shit: Binge & Purge* 3-CD/video set (Elektra 1993)★★★★, *Load* (Mercury 1996)★★★★, *ReLoad* (Vertigo 1997)★★★, *Garage Inc.* (Vertigo 1998)★★★, *S&M* (Vertigo 1999)★★.

● VIDEOS: *Cliff 'Em All* (Channel 5 1988), *2 Of One* (Channel 5 1989), *A Year And A Half In The Life Of Metallica* (PolyGram Music Video 1992), *Metal Up Your Ass: The Interview Sessions* (Startalk 1996), *Cunning Stunts* (PolyGram Music Video 1998).

● FURTHER READING: *A Visual Documentary*, Mark Putterford. *In Their Own Words*, Mark Putterford. *Metallica Unbound*, K.J. Doughton. *Metallica's Lars Ulrich: An Up-Close Look At The Playing Style Of ...*, Dino Fauci. *Metallica Unbound*, K.J. Doughton. *Metallica Live!*, Mark Putterford. *Metallica: The Frayed Ends Of Metal*, Chris Crocker. *The Making Of: Metallica's Metallica*, Mick Wall and Malcolm Dome. *From Silver To Black*, Ross Halfin.

Method Man

b. Clifford Smith, 1 April 1971, Staten Island, New York, USA. Smith rose to acclaim as one of the leading members of Staten Island's hip-hop collective, Wu-Tang Clan. Adopting the Method Man moniker, his smoky, flowing vocals were a prominent feature of 1993's landmark debut *Enter The Wu-Tang (36 Chambers)*. His own *Tical* set, released the following year, was the first in a glut of Wu-Tang Clan solo product. Produced by associate RZA, the album's drug-infused atmosphere was perfectly complemented by Method Man's laid-back delivery. The album debuted at US number 4 in December, while the single 'Bring The Pain' broke into the national Top 50 the same month. The following year Method Man was involved in two highly successful collaborations.

His Grammy-winning duet with Mary J. Blige on 'I'll Be There For You'/'You're All I Need To Get By' was a US number 3 hit in June, and was followed by the 'How High' single with Redman, which reached number 13 in September. Following further work with the Wu-Tang Clan, and a screen appearance in Hype Williams' *Belly*, Method Man released his sophomore effort, *Tical 2000: Judgement Day*. The highly inventive production work provided a perfect backdrop for Method Man's fluid delivery, hitting a peak on the millennium inspired title track. Odd cameos from Donald Trump and Janet Jackson featured alongside the usual Wu-Tang guest slots. Debuting at US number 2 in December, *Tical 2000: Judgement Day* was kept off the top of the charts by the new Garth Brooks album. The rapper then joined forces with Redman to record the following year's *Blackout!*

● ALBUMS: *Tical* (Def Jam 1994)★★★, *Tical 2000: Judgement Day* (Def Jam 1998)★★★, with Redman *Blackout!* (Def Jam 1999)★★★.
● FILMS: *The Show* (1995), *The Great White Hype* (1996), *Rhyme & Reason* (1997), *One Eight Seven* (1997), *Cop Land* (1997), *Belly* (1998), *P.I.G.S.* (1999), *Black And White* (1999).

Mia X

b. New Orleans, Louisiana, USA. The first female rapper to sign to Master P's highly successful No Limit Records. Like most of her fellow labelmates, Mia X was born in New Orleans. She moved to Queens as a teenager, however, gaining her first recording experience with New York Incorporated. She moved back to Louisiana where she became involved with Master P and his rapidly expanding No Limit empire. Her 1995 debut *Good Girl Gone Bad* appeared through Priority Records, but she made her real breakthrough with *Unlady Like*, which debuted at US number 21 in July 1997. By now Mia X was deliberately aping the provocative sexuality of female rappers such as Foxy Brown and Lil' Kim, but without the originality and musical nous of the former. The follow-up *Mama Drama* broke her into the US Top 10 when it debuted at number 7 in November 1998.

● ALBUMS: *Good Girl Gone Bad* (Priority 1995)★★★, *Unlady Like* (No Limit 1997)★★★, *Mama Drama* (No Limit 1998)★★★.
● FILMS: *I Got The Hook-Up* (1998).

Michael, George

b. Georgios (Yorgos) Kyriacos Panayiotou, 25 June 1963, Finchley, London, England. Michael first served his pop apprenticeship in the million-selling duo Wham!, the most commercially successful, teen-orientated band of the 80s. His solo career was foreshadowed in 1984's UK chart-topper 'Careless Whisper', a song about a promiscuous two-timer with the oddly attractive line: 'Guilty feet have got no rhythm'. By the time Wham! split in 1986, Michael was left with the unenviable task of reinventing himself as a solo artist. The balladeering 'Careless Whisper' had indicated a possible direction, but the initial problem was one of image. As a pin-up pop idol, Michael had allowed himself to become a paste-board figure, best remembered for glorifying a hedonistic lifestyle and shoving shuttlecocks down his shorts in concert. The rapid transition from dole queue reject to Club Tropicana playboy had left a nasty taste in the mouths of many music critics. Breaking the Wham! icon was the great challenge of Michael's solo career, and his finest and most

decisive move was to take a sabbatical before recording an album, to allow time to put his old image to rest. In the meantime, he cut 1986's UK chart-topper 'A Different Corner', a song stylistically similar to 'Careless Whisper' and clearly designed to show off his talent as a serious singer-songwriter. Enlivening his alternate image as a blue-eyed soul singer, he teamed up with Aretha Franklin the same year for the uplifting 'I Knew You Were Waiting (For Me)', a transatlantic chart-topper. Michael's re-emergence came in 1988, resplendent in leather and shades and his customary designer stubble. A pilot single, 'I Want Your Sex' was banned by daytime radio stations and broke his string of number 1s in the UK. The transatlantic chart-topper *Faith* followed, and was not only well-received but sold in excess of 10 million copies. The album spawned four US number 1 singles, with the title track, 'Father Figure', 'One More Try' and 'Monkey' all reaching the top. Equally adept at soul workouts and ballads, and regarded by some as one of the best new pop songwriters of his era, Michael seemed set for a long career. In 1990, he released his second album, *Listen Without Prejudice, Vol. 1*, a varied work which predictably sold millions and topped the UK album chart. The first single from the album, 'Praying For Time' reached number 1 in the USA. In the UK, however, the comeback single was surprisingly only a Top 10 hit. Still dissatisfied with his media image, Michael announced that he would cease conducting interviews in future and concentrate on pursuing his career as a serious songwriter and musician. A duet with Elton John on 'Don't Let The Sun Go Down On Me' revived his UK chart fortunes, reaching number 1 in December 1991, and also topping the US charts. In 1992, the *Sunday Times* announced his arrival as one of the richest men in the UK. Although Michael, with some help from Queen and Lisa Stansfield, topped the UK charts with the *Five Live* EP in summer 1993, a court clash with his record label Sony dominated his activities in the following two years. The case, which was eventually estimated to have cost him $7 million, saw Michael arguing that his contract rendered him a 'pop slave' and demanding to be released from it. Mr Justice Jonathan Parker ruled in Sony's favour and Michael stated he would appeal, and also insisted that he would never again record for the label. In July 1995, it looked likely that Michael had managed to free himself from Sony - but only at the cost of $40 million. The buy-out was financed by David Geffen's new media empire, DreamWorks, and Virgin Records, who were also reputed to have paid him an advance of £30 million for two albums. The first was *Older*, one of the decade's slickest productions. Although it became a huge success there was no great depth to the songs underneath the immaculate production. The album yielded two UK chart-toppers, 'Jesus To A Child' and 'Fastlove'. Michael announced the formation of his own record label Aegean Records, in February 1997. On April 7 1998, he was arrested for 'lewd behaviour' in a toilet cubicle at the Will Rogers Memorial Park in Beverly Hills, California. Michael later confirmed his long-rumoured homosexuality and was sentenced to perform community service. He bounced back with an excellent single, 'Outside', which entered the UK charts at number 2 in October 1998. The *Ladies & Gentlemen* compilation was a bestseller, topping the UK chart for 8 weeks. His duet with Mary J. Blige on a cover version of Stevie Wonder's 'As' broke into the UK Top 5 in March 1999. At the end of the year Michael released *Songs*

From The Last Century, a motley selection of cover versions that drew a bemused response from most critics.

● ALBUMS: *Faith* (Epic 1987)★★★★, *Listen Without Prejudice, Vol. 1* (Epic 1990)★★★, *Older* (Virgin 1996)★★★, *Songs From The Last Century* (Aegean/Virgin 1999)★★.

● COMPILATIONS: *Ladies & Gentlemen: The Best Of George Michael* (Epic 1998)★★★★.

● CD-ROM: *Older/Upper* (Aegean/Virgin 1998)★★★.

● VIDEOS: *Faith* (CMV Enterprises 1988), *George Michael* (CMV Enterprises 1990), *The Video Selection* (SMV 1998).

● FURTHER READING: *Wham! (Confidential) The Death Of A Supergroup*, Johnny Rogan. *George Michael: The Making Of A Super Star*, Bruce Dessau. *Bare*, George Michael with Tony Parsons. *In His Own Words*, Nigel Goodall. *Older: The Unauthorised Biography Of George Michael*, Nicholas and Tim Wapshott.

Mighty Mighty Bosstones

Formed in Boston, Massachusetts, USA, during the mid-80s, by Nate Albert (guitar), Joe Gittleman (bass) and Ben Carr (vocals). They were joined by Dicky Barrett (vocals) and Tim 'Johnny Vegas' Burton (saxophone) completing the line-up of the original Bosstones. After a laconic lacuna during the Reagan years the band returned as the Mighty Mighty Bosstones, having enrolled Joe Sirois (drums), Dennis Brockenborough (trombone) and Kevin Leanear (saxophone). The change of name was justified by Barrett who claimed that 'any band can just be mighty'. The musicians built a solid foundation in the USA through their fusion of ska and punk, with influences from soul and funk as well as thrash and heavy metal. They played across America to packed venues consisting of various US youth cult followers, skinheads, punks, metal heads and college students. In 1992, they were recognized at the Boston Music Awards where they received accolades for Best Single, Best Album and Best Rock Band. Their early recordings surfaced through the independent Taang! label, including an EP featuring cover versions of hits by Aerosmith, Metallica and Van Halen. Their increasing notoriety led to interest from the major labels with Mercury Records signing the band. The first release was an EP featuring 'Someday I Suppose', 'Lights Out', 'Police Beat' and a cover version of the Wailers' 'Simmer Down'. In 1992, the band began working on their debut album for Mercury with producer Tony Platt who, apart from his rock productions, had worked with Bob Marley in the early 70s. In 1993, Mercury promoted the Bosstones in the UK, releasing 'Ska-Core The Devil And More' and *Don't Know How To Party*. The band's success led to media interest in the USA which resulted in a cameo appearance in the movie *Clueless*, a ska version of Kiss' 'Detroit Rock City' - featured on the tribute compilation *Kiss My Ass* - and imaginative merchandising. By 1997, the band's high profile was elevated in America by an exhaustive promotional campaign and the release of the excellent *Let's Face It*. The following year they enjoyed a UK Top 20 hit with 'The Impression That I Get'.

● ALBUMS: *Devils Night Out* (Taang! 1990)★★★, *More Noise And Other Disturbances* (Taang! 1991)★★★, *Don't Know How To Party* (Mercury 1993)★★★★, *Question The Answers* (Mercury 1994)★★★, *Let's Face It* (Mercury 1997)★★★★, *Devil's Night Out* (Roadrunner 1998)★★★, *Live From The Middle East* (Big Rig/Mercury 1998)★★★★.

● VIDEOS: *Video Stew* (PolyGram Video 1997).

Miguel, Luis

b. Luis Miguel Gallegos, 19 April 1970, Puerto Rico. Undoubtedly the most successful Latin star of the 90s, singer Luis Miguel has won four Grammys and sold over 36 million records worldwide. Born in Puerto Rico, but raised in Spain and Mexico, Miguel is the son of Italian actress Marcela Basteri and Spanish singer Luisito Rey, himself a Latin star in the 60s. The young Miguel was spotted performing at a birthday party in Veracruz by a Mexican record executive, and was promptly given a record deal. Within a year, under the direction of his father, he had recorded *1+1=2 Enamorados* and *Directo Al Corazón*, and was on the way to becoming one of Mexico's biggest teen stars. He made his film debut in 1984 in the risible *Ya Nunca Más*, although the soundtrack collection became his first gold-selling record. Miguel won his first Grammy in 1985 for his Spanish language duet with UK singer Sheena Easton on 'Me Gustas Tal Como Eres' ('I Like You Just The Way You Are'). He signed a long-term contract with WEA Latina in 1987, and in the process wrestled control of his career away from his father. Developing a more sophisticated image modelled on singers such as Julio Iglesias and Frank Sinatra, Miguel began singing less pop-orientated material, and in the process achieved a multitude of gold and platinum selling singles and albums on the Latin American charts. This approach reaped rich international rewards on 1991's *Romance*, a collection of Latin boleros that was also Miguel's first co-production. The album became the first ever gold-selling Spanish language album in the USA. He subsequently appeared on the Barcelona Olympics soundtrack album in 1992, and made his debut at the crooner's Mecca, Las Vegas. He also duetted with Sinatra on 'Come Fly With Me', featured on the singer's 1993 all-star collection, *Duets*. In 1995, Miguel recorded 'Suena' for the soundtrack of Walt Disney's *Hunchback Of Notre Dame*. Two further collections of boleros, 1994's *Segundo Romance* and 1997's *Romances*, were a huge success in mainland America. In September 1996, Miguel received the ultimate accolade, a star on Hollywood's Walk of Fame.

● ALBUMS: *1+1=2 Enamorados* (Odeon-EMI 1982)★★, *Directo Al Corazón* (Odeon-EMI Capitol México 1982)★★, *Decídete* (Odeon-EMI Capitol México 1983)★★, *Ya Nunca Más* soundtrack (Odeon-EMI Capitol México 1984)★★, *Palabre De Honor* (Odeon-EMI Capitol México 1984)★★★, *Fiebre De Amor* soundtrack (Odeon-EMI Capitol México 1985)★★, *Luis Miguel Canta In Italiano* (EMI Capitol México 1985)★★, *Tambien Es Rock* (EMI Capitol México 1987)★★★, *Soy Como Quiero Ser* (WEA Latina 1987)★★★, *Busca Una Mujer* (WEA Latina 1988)★★★, *20 Años* (WEA Latina 1990)★★★, *Romance* (WEA Latina 1991)★★★★, *Aries* (WEA Latina 1993)★★★, *Segundo Romance* (WEA Latina 1994)★★★, *El Concierto* (WEA Latina 1995)★★★, *Nada Es Igual* (WEA Latina 1996)★★★, *Romances* (WEA Latina 1997)★★★, *Amarte Es Un Placer* (WEA Latina 1999)★★★★.

● COMPILATIONS: *Ritmo/Disco* (EMI Capitol México 1984)★★★, *14 Grandes Éxitos* (Capitol 1989)★★, *América & En Vivo* (WEA Latina 1992)★★★, *Directo Al Corazón* (Capitol/EMI Latin 1992)★★, *El Idolo De Mexico* (Capitol/EMI Latin 1992)★★★, *Collezione Privata* (Capitol/EMI Latin 1993)★★, *El Mejor De Los Mejores Vol. 1* (EMI Latin 1994)★★★★, *Romántico Desde Siempre* (Capitol/EMI Latin 1994)★★★, *Sentimental* (WEA Latina 1994)★★★, *El Mejor De Los Mejores Vol. 2* (EMI Latin 1995)★★★, *Romántico Desde Siempre II* (Capitol/EMI Latin 1997)★★★, *Mis Momentos* (EMI 1997)★★★, *Todos Los Romances* (WEA Latina 1998)★★★, *40 Temas* 4-CD set (WEA Latin

1998)★★★, *Legend: Luis Miguel* (EMI 1998)★★★, *Luis Miguel Colección Aniversario* (EMI 1999)★★★★.

● VIDEOS: *Luis Miguel En Vivo, Un Año De Conciertos* (Televisa 1989), *Luis Miguel 20 Años* (Warner Music 1991), *El Concierto* (Warner Music 1995), *Luis Miguel: Los Videos* (Warner Music 1997), *Luis Miguel En Concierto* (Mariachi Films 1998).

● FILMS: *Ya Nunca Más* (1984), *Fiebre De Amor* (1985).

Mike And The Mechanics

Mike Rutherford (b. 2 October 1950, Guildford, Surrey, England; bass) formed the Mechanics in 1985, during a pause in the career of Genesis while vocalist Phil Collins was engrossed in his solo career. The line-up comprised Paul Carrack (b. 22 April 1951, Sheffield, Yorkshire, England; vocals/keyboards, ex-Ace), Paul Young (vocals, ex-Sad Cafe), Peter Van Hooke and Adrian Lee. Van Hooke was already an accomplished session musician, having played or toured with many singers, from Van Morrison to Rod Argent. The band's first UK Top 30 hit came with 'Silent Running (On Dangerous Ground)' in 1986, which was used as the theme to the movie *On Dangerous Ground*. They enjoyed greater success in the USA where the single reached number 6, and its follow-up, 'All I Need Is A Miracle', climbed one place higher. In early 1989, the band reached US number 1 and UK number 2 with the Rutherford/B.A. Robertson-penned 'The Living Years', an emotive song expressing Rutherford's regret at the lack of communication he had with his father while he was alive. The attendant album reached number 2 on the UK charts and number 13 in America. With the exception of the UK number 13 single 'Word Of Mouth', further chart success eluded the band. Quality singles such as the highly emotive 'A Time And Place', and 'Everybody Gets A Second Chance', failed to make the UK Top 50, a sobering thought for future songwriters with high hopes of chart success. *Beggar On A Beach Of Gold* was preceded by the lively UK Top 20 single 'Over My Shoulder'; unfortunately this proved to be the album's only ingot. The title track was written by B.A. Robertson and was a top 40 hit in the UK in 1995. Pedestrian cover versions of the Miracles' 'You Really Got A Hold On Me' and Stevie Wonder's 'I Believe (When I Fall In Love Again It Will be Forever)' added nothing and the album, although competent, did not break any new ground. The band continues to be as fluid as its members' careers allow, with a new album appearing in July 1999.

● ALBUMS: *Mike + The Mechanics* (WEA 1985)★★, *Living Years* (WEA 1988)★★★★, *Word Of Mouth* (Virgin 1991)★★★, *Beggar On A Beach Of Gold* (Virgin 1995)★★, *Mike And The Mechanics* (Virgin 1999)★★★.

● COMPILATIONS: *Hits* (Virgin 1996)★★★.

● VIDEOS: *Hits* (Warner Music Vision 1996).

Mikey General

b. Michael Taylor, 9 October 1963, London, England. Taylor spent his formative years commuting between London and Jamaica. Inspired by the established singers on the island, including Dennis Brown and Barrington Levy, he embarked on his own singing career. His vocal range was initially in the high tenor dancehall-style favoured by Pinchers, Sanchez and Pliers. He began his recording career during the mid-80s in the UK, recording with Studio One producer Jackie Mittoo. The recordings surfaced on Mikey's own MGR label through Omega, and other notable recordings followed, including 'Kuff N Dem', 'A Sound Gonna Die Tonight', and the allegorical 'Cowboy Life'. In combination, he found success with Richie Davis ('Back To Life' and 'Suzy Wong'), while he joined Skipper Ranking for the anti-cocaine anthem, 'Don't Nose It Up'. He accepted a starring role in the television play *We The Raggamuffin*, for which he also provided the theme tune. In 1992, Mikey returned to Jamaica, where he met Luciano during a recording session - the association led to his becoming part of the Firehouse Crew alongside DJ Sizzla and saxophonist Dean Fraser. In 1997, the Firehouse Crew shared top billing with Buju Banton and Bunny Wailer at the Essential Roots Day festival, and by this time, Mikey's recording career was enjoying a renaissance. Philip 'Fatis' Burrell produced his Firehouse debut, *Stronger Rastaman*, while his combination with Sizzla, 'Babylon A Listen/Unseen Blessings', became a dancehall anthem.

● ALBUMS: with Andrew Paul *Sound Bwoy Burial* (1989)★★★, *Sinners* (Charm 1995)★★, *Stronger Rastaman* (VP 1996)★★★.

Miles, Robert

b. Roberto Concina, 1969, Fluerier, Switzerland. Miles, aka Roberto Milani, was born to Italian parents and later moved to Italy. As a child he learned the piano and began DJing when he was 13. Four years later he took his first job at a local club, around the same time as he set up a pirate radio station. After a few years he was playing at various clubs throughout northern Italy and by the time he was 22 he had become one of the most successful broadcasters in the region on account of his show on Radio Supernetwork. He subsequently invested in a studio to concentrate on writing his own material, while continuing to DJ at clubs and parties. After a number of minor successes in Italy he achieved widespread success with his single 'Children' (1996), which was initially signed to Platypus Records in the UK from the Italian independent DBX, before being picked up by Deconstruction Records. Inspired by the sounds he had heard while DJing in Goa, Ibiza, Bali and other such places, while aiming to create a contrast to the hard techno which was popular in Italy at the same time, 'Children' created a rather sickening ethereal atmosphere, blending a basic trance sound with live instruments including strings, guitar and its famous piano hook. With its commercial melodic sound it was extremely successful, particularly in Europe and the UK (number 2) and brought Miles' name into the mainstream. The Top 10 follow-ups 'Fable' and 'One & One' (featuring Maria Nayler), and debut album *Dreamland*, were equally popular and lead to Miles winning various industry awards, including the BRITS' Best International Newcomer and the World Music's Highest-Selling Male Newcomer. In 1997, he released the single 'Freedom' (featuring Kathy Sledge) and a second album *23AM* which extended his sound to incorporate breakbeats and elements of drum 'n' bass as well as vocalists and jazz musicians. In the same year he mixed one side of the compilation *London* for the 'superclub' Renaissance. He has remained a popular DJ throughout Europe.

● ALBUMS: *Dreamland* (Deconstruction 1996)★★★, *Dreamland II remixes* (Deconstruction 1996)★★★, *23AM* (Deconstruction 1997)★★★.

Ministry

'The difference between Ministry and other bands is that we sold out before we even started.' Alain Jourgensen (b. 8 October 1958, Havana, Cuba) began producing music under the Ministry name in the early 80s in Chicago, but was unhappy with the Euro-pop direction in which his record company pushed him for *With Sympathy*, later describing it as 'that first abortion of an album'. Ministry took on a more acceptable shape for Jourgensen after *'Twitch'*, with the addition to Jourgensen's guitar, vocals and keyboards of Paul Barker (b. Palo Alto, California, USA) on bass and keyboards, and drummer Bill Rieflin. The band evolved their own brand of guitar-based industrial metal, considering *The Land Of Rape And Honey* to be their true debut, and employed a variety of guest musicians for both live and studio work, with regular contributions from ex-Rigor Mortis guitarist Mike Scaccia and ex-Finitribe vocalist Chris Connelly. Despite Jourgensen's dislike of touring, Ministry developed a stunning live show, with a backdrop of disturbing visual images to accompany the intense musical barrage, and the sinister figure of Jourgensen taking centre stage behind a bone-encrusted microphone stand. *In Case You Didn't Feel Like Showing Up (Live)* displayed the metamorphosis of the songs as the band extended themselves in concert. At this stage, Jourgensen and Barker were working on numerous other studio projects in a variety of styles, including Lard with Jello Biafra, but Ministry remained one of two main acts. The other, the outrageous Revolting Cocks, served as a more blatantly humorous outlet for the pair's creative talents, in contrast to the dark anger and socio-political themes of Ministry. As alternative culture became more acceptable to the mainstream, Ministry achieved major success with *Psalm 69* (subtitled *The Way To Succeed And The Way To Suck Eggs*), helped by the popularity on MTV of 'Jesus Built My Hotrod', featuring a guest vocal and lyric from Butthole Surfers' frontman Gibby Haynes. The band were a huge draw on the 1992 Lollapalooza tour, playing second on the bill, and their debut European tour later that year was also a resounding success. In 1994, Rieflin was replaced by former Didjits drummer Rey Washam. Jourgensen was arrested on a drugs charge in August 1995. *Filth Pig* contained, in true Ministry fashion, a distorted and raucous version of Bob Dylan's beautiful love song, 'Lay Lady Lay'. Retreating from the public eye for another lengthy lay-off, Jourgensen and Barker returned in 1999 with *Dark Side Of The Spoon*, which reasserted their credentials as leading industrial noise terrorists.

● ALBUMS: *With Sympathy* aka *Work For Love* (Arista 1983)★★, *'Twitch'* (Sire 1986)★★★, *The Land Of Rape And Honey* (Sire 1988)★★★, *The Mind Is A Terrible Thing To Taste* (Sire 1989)★★★, *In Case You Didn't Feel Like Showing Up (Live)* mini-album (Sire 1990)★★★, *Psalm 69* (Sire/Warners 1992)★★★, *Filth Pig* (Warners 1996)★★★, *Dark Side Of The Spoon* (Warners 1999)★★★★.
Solo: Paul Barker as Lead Into Gold *Age Of Reason* (Wax Trax! 1992)★★.
● COMPILATIONS: *Twelve Inch Singles 1981-1984* (Wax Trax! 1987)★★★.

Ministry Of Sound

One of the first and most successful of the 'superclubs' in the UK and certainly one of the most famous club names and logos in the world. The club rose to prominence after opening its doors in September 1991, a business venture of James Palumbo, the son of the UK's Lord Palumbo. Situated in a former warehouse in the decidedly unglamorous area of Elephant And Castle, in south London, the club quickly established itself as *the* hip place for London's cool young things to go at the weekend. It also set the blueprint for the new breed of 90s clubs such as Cream, Renaissance and Gatecrasher that put the emphasis on quality sound, lighting and 'big name' DJs. The club became renowned for its exceptional sound system in its dark, cavernous room known as The Box. Now an obvious progression for any large, successful club, 'the Ministry' (as it is called affectionately by UK clubbers) was the first to release a compilation album in 1993. Mixed by famous US DJ, Tony Humphries, it sold well in the UK's dance music outlets, selling 35,000 copies. The Ministry *Sessions* series was extremely successful during the early 90s, featuring both US and UK high-profile DJs such as David Morales, Junior Vasquez, Clivillés And Cole (C & C Music Factory) and Paul Oakenfold. Oakenfold also headlined a touring version of the club in 1994, when it visited various venues throughout the UK. In the same year, the club attracted publicity when it famously projected its logo - a parody of the Houses Of Commons' portcullis logo - onto the House itself to celebrate its second birthday. Since then, the club has gone from strength to strength, playing host to nearly all of world's most famous DJs, including Masters At Work, David Morales, Roger Sanchez, Erick Morillo, Frankie Knuckles, Sasha, John Digweed, Tony De Vit, Paul Van Dyk, Carl Cox and many others. The Ministry empire has included a very successful record label for both singles and its own compilations, a line of merchandise, a short-lived Covent Garden, London shop, and a club and lifestyle magazine, *Ministry*, started in December 1997. It has an annual residency in Ibiza at the club, Pacha. The mainstays of the club's recorded output are its *Dance Nation* and *The Annual* series, mixed by DJs such as Judge Jules, Pete Tong, Boy George, 'Tall' Paul Newman and Brandon Block. As its name suggests, *The Annual* is released at the end of the year, a retrospective compilation of the biggest tracks on the dancefloor. The club's musical policy has focused mainly on garage and funky, vocal house over the years but its *Northern Exposure* releases, featuring Sasha and John Digweed and its *Trance Nation* double-CD in May 1999 (mixed by Dutch trance superstar, Ferry Corsten) have shown an inclination towards the harder trance sound of the UK's clubs in the late 90s.

● COMPILATIONS: *Sessions - Tony Humphries* (MOS 1993)★★★, *Sessions 2 - Paul Oakenfold* (MOS 1994)★★★, *Future Sound Of New York - Junior Vasquez* (MOS 1994)★★★, *Sessions 3 - Clivillés & Cole* (MOS 1994)★★★, *A Day In The Life - Todd Terry* (MOS 1994)★★★, *Sessions 4 - C.J. Mackintosh* (MOS 1994)★★★, *Sessions 5 - Masters At Work* (MOS 1995)★★★, *Future Sound Of Chicago - Cajmere & DJ Sneak* (MOS 1995)★★★, *Late Night Sessions 1 - DJ Harvey* (MOS 1995)★★★, *Future Sound Of Chicago II - Derrick Carter* (MOS 1995)★★★, *The Annual - Pete Tong & Boy George* (MOS 1995)★★★, *Sessions 6 - Frankie Knuckles* (MOS 1995)★★★, *One Half Of A Whole Decade* (MOS 1996)★★★, *Northern Exposure - Sasha & John Digweed* (MOS 1996)★★★, *Dance Nation 2 - Pete Tong & Boy George* (MOS 1996)★★★, *The Annual II - Pete Tong & Boy George* (MOS 1996)★★★★, *Sessions 7 - David Morales* (MOS 1997)★★★, *Dance Nation 3 - Pete Tong & Judge Jules* (MOS 1997)★★★★, *Classics - Judge Jules* (MOS 1997)★★★★, *Mayday Mix - Derrick May* (MOS 1997)★★★, *Dance Nation 4 - Pete Tong & Boy George*

(MOS 1997)★★★, *Sessions 8 - Todd Terry* (MOS 1997)★★★, *Late Night Sessions II - X-Press 2* (MOS 1997)★★★, *Northern Exposure 2 - Sasha & John Digweed* (MOS 1997)★★★★, *FSUK - Derek Dahlarge* (MOS 1997)★★★, *The Annual III* (MOS 1997)★★★, *Sessions 9 - Erick Morillo* (MOS 1998)★★★, *Dance Nation 5 - Pete Tong & Boy George* (MOS 1998)★★★, *FSUK 2 - The Freestylers* (MOS 1998)★★★, *Clubbers Guide - Judge Jules & Pete Tong* (MOS 1998)★★★, *Ibiza Annual - Judge Jules & Pete Tong* (MOS 1998)★★★, *FSUK 3* (MOS 1998)★★★, *The Annual IV - Pete Tong & Boy George* (MOS 1998)★★★★, *Clubbers Guide To 1999* (MOS 1999)★★★, *Trance Nation - Ferry Corsten* (MOS 1999)★★★, *Dance Nation 6 - 'Tall' Paul Newman & Brandon Block* (MOS 1999)★★★★, *Trance Nation 2 - Ferry Corsten* (MOS 1999)★★★★, *The Ibiza Annual - Judge Jules & Tall Paul* (MOS 1999)★★★, *Clubber's Guide To Ibiza - Judge Jules* (MOS 1999)★★★, *FSUK 4 - Cut La Roc* (MOS 1999)★★★, *Ten Years Of Strictly Rhythm* (MOS 1999)★★★★, *Clubber's Guide To Trance - ATB* (MOS 1999)★★★, *The Annual - Millennium Edition - Judge Jules & Tall Paul* (MOS 1999)★★★, *Late Night Sessions III - Farley & Heller* (MOS 1999)★★★★, *Clubber's Guide To 2000 - Judge Jules* (MOS 2000)★★★★, *Rewind - The Sound Of UK Garage - The Artful Dodger* (MOS 2000)★★★.

Mo' Wax Records

This label was formed by James Lavelle (b. Oxford, England) in 1992 and helped to develop the abstract hip-hop sound. As a child Lavelle heard jazz at home and later developed an interest in hip-hop through artists such as Grandmaster Flash and Doug E. Fresh. He began DJing when he was 14 and while working in specialist jazz and dance music shops in London developed his broad tastes in music. In 1992, he formed Mo' Wax Records, with the aid of £1,000 from his boss at Honest Jon's record shop, to 'bring together all the different types of music that I've grown up with'. The first release was 'Promise' from the New York jazz outfit Repercussions, followed in 1993 by tracks from Raw Stylus, Palmskin Productions and DJ Takemura. However, it was DJ Shadow's 'In Flux/Hindsight' that really established the Mo' Wax approach, helping to introduce hip-hop to the techno community and vice versa. In 1994, Mo' Wax pursued this idea with releases from DJ Krush, Attica Blues and Lavelle's own project, U.N.K.L.E. La Funk Mob's 'Tribulations Extra Sensorielles' included remixes by Richie Hawtin and Carl Craig, while the excellent compilation *Headz*, as well as containing material from Mo' Wax artists, featured Howie B. and Autechre, further highlighting the label's aim to unite artists and sounds from supposedly disparate backgrounds. After turning down offers from London Records and other major labels, in 1996 Lavelle signed a distribution deal with A&M Records. The two *Headz II* compilations released in the same year included tracks from the Beastie Boys, Black Dog Productions, Photek, Alex Reece, Roni Size, the Jungle Brothers and Massive Attack. Other artists who have released material on the label include Air, Deborah Anderson, Innerzone Orchestra (Carl Craig), Major Force, Money Mark, Dr. Octagon, Andrea Parker and Sukia. Following A&M's absorption into the giant Seagram corporation in 1998, Lavelle set up a joint venture with Beggars Banquet Records and XL Records.

Mobb Deep

This rap duo, comprising Havoc (b. Queensbridge, New York, USA) and Prodigy (b. Queensbridge, New York, USA), made a colossal impact in 1995 with their hardcore hip-hop

single 'Shook Ones Part II'. Compared in the music press to the experience of hearing Schoolly D for the first time, it saw the New York-based rap team propelled to the top of the *Billboard* charts and national fame. It accompanied the release of their second album, *The Infamous*, which offered a succession of bleak inner-city narratives such as 'Survival Of The Fittest' and the Q-Tip-produced 'Drink Away The Pain'. Mobb Deep had first received attention in 1991 when US rap magazine *The Source* praised them in its 'Unsigned Hype' column. Both partners were just 16 years old, but their first demo possessed obvious maturity and skill, boosted by their experience of watching MC Shan and Roxanne Shanté rapping in local parks. They met in 1988, Havoc having been tutored by his rapping cousin MC Tragedy. By 1992, they had secured a recording contract with Island Records' subsidiary 4th And Broadway, recruiting Large Professor and DJ Premier to help with the production of their somewhat listless debut album. Despite the initial momentum, however, the deal fell apart amid squabbles with an unethical manager. The duo regrouped in time for *The Infamous*, which was much-improved in terms of both production and lyrics. 'Survival Of The Fittest' was promoted by a 'paintball' competition in Long Island, with competing teams including members of the Wu-Tang Clan and Loud Records' staff. Ensuing releases have continued to earn the duo both critical praise and commercial reward, with 1999's *Murda Muzik* particularly successful.

● ALBUMS: *Mobb Deep* (4th And Broadway 1993)★★★, *The Infamous* (Loud/RCA 1995)★★★★, *Hell On Earth* (Loud/RCA 1996)★★★, *Murda Muzik* (Loud 1999)★★★.

Moby

b. Richard Melville Hall, 11 September 1965, New York, USA. A New York DJ, recording artist, Christian, vegan and Philosophy graduate. Moby is so nicknamed because of the fact that he can trace his ancestry to the author of the famous whaling tale. This is by no means the only interesting aspect of his idiosyncratic artistic life. He refuses to travel anywhere by car because of the environmental considerations, and generally displays little of the public anonymity that is the creed of the underground DJ. In 1991, he took the *Twin Peaks* theme, under the guise of 'Go', into the UK Top 10. Although that appealed to the more perverse natures of both mainstream and club audiences, the release of 'I Feel It'/'Thousand' in 1993 was yet more bizarre. The latter track was classified by *The Guinness Book Of Records* as the fastest single ever, climaxing at 1,015 bpm. It was typical of Moby's playful, irreverent attitude to his work. In his youth he was a member of hardcore punk outfit the Vatican Commandos, and even substituted as singer for Flipper while their vocalist was in prison. He has brought these rock 'n' roll inclinations to bear on the world of dance music: at the 1992 *DMC/Mixmag* Awards ceremony he trashed his keyboards at the end of his set. His introduction to dance music began in the mid-80s: 'I was drawn to it, I started reading about it, started hanging out in clubs. For me house music was the synthesis of the punk era.' He collected cheap, second hand recording equipment, basing himself in an old factory/converted prison in New York's Little Italy district. The albums issued by New York dance label Instinct collect the artist's early work. *Ambient* comprised unissued cuts from 1988-91, composed of barely audible atmospheric interludes. Moby signed to leading independent Mute Records in 1993, and the following year released 'Hymn', a transcendental religious techno odyssey, distinguished by a 35-minute ambient mix and a Laurent Garner remix. The track was included on his eclectic major label debut, *Everything Is Wrong*. His own remix catalogue includes Brian Eno, LFO ('Tan Ta Ra'), Pet Shop Boys, Erasure ('Chorus'), Orbital ('Speed Freak'), Depeche Mode and even Michael Jackson. He moved away from his dance base in 1996 with the thrash rock of *Animal Rights*, and in turn sounded more like Johnny Rotten. His 'James Bond Theme' debuted at UK number 8 in November 1997. The attendant *I Like To Score* was an uneasy experiment in soundtrack work. Another change of style was apparent on 1999's *Play*, a superb album on which several tracks were based around sampled field recordings made by folklorist Alan Lomax in the earlier part of the century.

● ALBUMS: *Moby* (Instinct 1992)★★★, *Early Underground* (Instinct 1993)★★★, *Ambient* (Instinct 1993)★★, *Everything Is Wrong* (Mute/Elektra 1995)★★★★, *Everything Is Wrong (DJ Mix Album)* (Mute 1996)★★★, *Animal Rights* (Mute 1996)★★★★, *I Like To Score* (Mute 1997)★★★, *Play* (Mute 1999)★★★★.
● COMPILATIONS: *The Story So Far* (Equator 1993)★★★, *Rare: The Collected B-Sides* (Instinct 1996)★★★.

Mock Turtles

With their promising UK hit single 'Can You Dig It?', the Mock Turtles followed a line of success stories that had emanated from Manchester, England, between 1989 and 1991. Like many of their contemporaries, the band had been playing the independent circuit for several years before realizing their potential. The band's linchpin was singer, guitarist and songwriter Martin Coogan, who had previously fronted Judge Happiness, won a Salford University talent contest and subsequently issued a single, 'Hey Judge', on the Mynah label in 1985. As the Mock Turtles, Coogan was joined by Steve Green (bass), Krzysztof Korab (keyboards) and Steve Cowen (drums), and their recordings surfaced on several of the Imaginary label's popular tribute compilations (covering Syd Barrett's 'No Good Trying', Captain Beefheart's 'Big-Eyed Beans From Venus', the Kinks' 'Big Sky', the Byrds' 'Why' and the Velvet Underground's 'Pale Blue Eyes'), illustrating their eclectic tastes. Meanwhile, the band's first 12-inch EP, *Pomona*, was issued in 1987, and although it owed an obvious debt to early David Bowie and veered towards the overblown, the confidence of musicians, string arrangements and songwriting was obvious. Guitarist Martin Glyn Murray joined the band in time for 'The Wicker Man' (inspired by the film of the same name), followed by 'And Then She Smiles'. From pure folk to powerful songs verging on the pompous, the Mock Turtles conveyed a distinctive feel within their music. However, it was their next single, 1990's 'Lay Me Down', that hinted at bigger things, sporting a sparse yet infectious shuffling backbeat. Hot on its heels came a well-received debut album, *Turtle Soup*, in June, which fared well on the independent chart, as did the band's collaboration with one of Coogan's long-time influences, Bill Nelson, for 'Take Your Time' (the b-side of their next single, 'Magic Boomerang'). This was enough to lure Siren Records, and for their first major label single, the band chose to rework the b-side of 'Lay Me Down', 'Can You Dig It?'. The single was an instant Top 20 hit in 1991, with BBC

Television's *Top Of The Pops* appearances to match, and in its wake came another reissue of sorts, 'And Then She Smiles'. This failed to build on the success of 'Can You Dig It?', and the Mock Turtles' highly commercial *Two Sides* suffered from a low profile, despite its abundance of musical muscle and carefully crafted songs. In the meantime, Imaginary compiled most of their early single tracks on *87-90*, for those newcomers who had missed them first time around. However, the Mock Turtles' rapid progress soon transmuted into an equally swift decline. The band dissolved when Coogan formed a new band, Ugli, with Korab and Green after Murray left to pursue an acting career. Coogan (brother of English comic Steve Coogan) wrote songs for the latter's pseudonymous Latin crooner Tony Ferrino.

● ALBUMS: *Turtle Soup* (Imaginary 1990)★★★, *Two Sides* (Two Sides 1991)★★★★.
● COMPILATIONS: *87-90* (Imaginary 1991)★★★.

Mogwai

Glasgow lo-fi post-rockers, described as the 'best band of the 21st century' by Pavement's Stephen Malkmus, whose studied art-rock boldly attempts to emulate the sound of legendary US alternative rockers Slint and Sonic Youth. Formed by Stuart Braithwaite (guitar/occasional vocals) and Dominic Aitchison (bass) in 1995, they were soon joined by second guitarist John Cummings and drummer Martin Bulloch. Their debut single 'Tuner/Lower' appeared in March 1996 on their own Rock Action label. Other early singles, including 'Summer' and 'New Paths To Helicon' (collected on the Jet Set release), were released on various independent labels. They received high praise from a music press anxious for an antidote to the Oasis-dominated guitar-rock scene, although they left many listeners bemused by a 'difficult' live broadcast on BBC Radio 1 that ended with 10 minutes of white noise. After signing to Glasgow-based independent label Chemikal Underground, and with former Teenage Fanclub drummer Brendan O'Hare as a temporary member, the band released their 1997 debut. *Young Team* confirmed their brash claims to greatness. The gradually rising guitar crescendo of tracks such as 'Yes I Am A Long Way From Home' and 'Like Herod', merged seamlessly with the delicate 'With Portfolio' and the rare vocal track (courtesy of Arab Strap's Aidan Moffat) on 'R U Still In 2 It', establishing the album as one of the year's most important releases. The remix collection *Kicking A Dead Pig* featured contributions from Alec Empire, Kid Loco and Arab Strap. Their follow-up album, *Come On Die Young*, was recorded in America with Mercury Rev producer David Fridmann.

● ALBUMS: *Young Team* (Chemikal Underground 1997)★★★★, *Kicking A Dead Pig* remixes (Eye-Q 1998)★★★, *Come On Die Young* (Chemikal Underground 1999)★★★★.
● COMPILATIONS: *Ten Rapid* (Rock Action/Jetset 1997)★★★.

Moloko

UK-based Moloko is a curious duo of singer Roisin Murphy (b. Dublin, Ireland) and multi-instrumentalist Mark Brydon (b. Sheffield, England). Embracing a sense of kitsch drama reminiscent of Deee-Lite and mid-period Human League, their debut album was actually recorded in a studio adjacent to the latter band's regular base in Sheffield. By this time they had already recorded two singles, 'Where Is The What If The What Is The Why' and 'Fe Fi Fo Fun For Me', which both impressed with their cultured electro-pop textures and weird lyrical narratives. Entirely self-composed and produced, other delights on their debut album rejoiced in titles such as 'Killer Bunnies'. *Do You Like My Tight Sweater?* included some entertaining artwork and the very bizarre 'Cheeky Monkey'. Both partners had previous diverse experiences in the music industry; Murphy with the strangely named performance art group And Turquoise Car Crash, The, and Brydon with acid jazz act Cloud 9. An acclaimed second album followed, before the duo enjoyed a surprise UK Top 5 hit single in August 1999 with the highly catchy club favourite, 'Sing It Back'.

● ALBUMS: *Do You Like My Tight Sweater?* (Echo 1995)★★★★, *I Am Not A Doctor* (Echo 1998)★★★.

Momus

b. Nicholas Currie, Paisley, Scotland. After living in Canada for a spell as a teenager, Currie returned to the UK and, during the mid-80s, began recording on the independent circuit. His primary influence was Jacques Brel, whose earthy sexuality soon infiltrated Momus' work. An EP, *Beast With No Backs*, on El Records, garnered minor critical attention, as did the album *Circus Maximus*. Momus promised a follow-up, *The Poison Boyfriend*, but that title was abandoned after he signed with Alan McGee's Creation Records. Finally, in 1988, Momus returned with *Tender Pervert*, a lacerating document of sexual and emotional psychoanalysis. His strength was his strong narrative line, particularly on songs such as 'Love On Ice' and 'Bishonen'. The following year, he issued *Don't Stop The Night*, which featured a more electronic, dance-orientated approach in keeping with current fashion. One song, 'Righthand Heart', was a less effective reworking of an essentially acoustic song on the previous album. His 1991 album, *Hippopotamomus*, was less well received and was greeted with a zero out of 10 rating in the *New Musical Express* as a result of its moral perversity. The artist no doubt appreciated the irony. The early 90s saw Currie build on his audience within the gay community (parts of which admired his openness), contributing one track, 'Cocksucking Lesbian Man', to Derek Jarman's *Blue*. *Philosophy Of Momus* continued Curry's forays into the netherworld of twisted sexuality, utilizing a third-person mechanism as a defence against accusations of amorality. *Slender Sherbet* in 1996 was an intriguing re-recording of *Tender Pervert*. In 1997, Currie collaborated with the like-minded Anthony Reynolds of Jack. Calling themselves Jacques, they released the self-indulgent *How To Make Love Volume 1*. Currie also collaborated with French singer Leila France on *Orgonon*, a bizarre album dedicated to psychoanalyst Wilhelm Reich. *Ping Pong* was 1997's new Momus album, featuring the usual provocative material. A track recorded for the following year's *Little Red Songbook* resulted in a costly lawsuit issued by electronic composer Wendy Carlos. In response, Currie offered to write a song for anyone who donated $1,000 towards his legal costs. He ended up writing 30 'musical portraits', which featured on the self-released *Stars Forever*, a sprawling epic which also included karaoke renditions of Momus songs by his fans, and a lengthy explanation from Currie about the making of the record.

● ALBUMS: *Circus Maximus* (El 1986)★★★, *The Poison Boyfriend* (Creation 1987)★★★, *Tender Pervert* (Creation 1988)★★★, *Don't Stop The Night* (Creation 1989)★★, *Hippopotamomus* (Creation 1991)★★,

Voyager (Creation 1992)★★★, *The Ultracomformist* (Creation 1992)★★★, *Timelord* (Creation 1993)★★★, *The Philosophy Of Momus* (Cherry Red 1995)★★★, *Slender Sherbet* (Cherry Red 1996)★★★, *Twenty Vodka Jellies* (Cherry Red 1996)★★★, *Ping Pong* (Satyricon 1997)★★★, *Little Red Songbook* (Cherry Red 1998)★★★, *Stars Forever* (Analog Baroque 1999)★★★.

● COMPILATIONS: *Monsters Of Love - Singles 1985-90* (Creation 1990)★★★★.

● FURTHER READING: *Lust Of A Moron: The Lyrics Of Momus*, Momus.

Monaco

To many, the starkly undulating basslines of Peter Hook (b. 13 February 1956, Manchester, England) were what gave New Order its propulsion during their peak years in the late 80s and early 90s. However, when that band broke up (or at least lost its work ethic on a permanent basis), Hook's initial attempts to form his own outfit were sniped at by critics. With the subsequent success of Monaco, Hook can now afford to be candid about the folly that was Revenge. Their 1991 EP, *Gun World Porn*, featured the guitar work of David Potts, formerly tape operator at Hook's studio. Potts duly became the second member of Monaco, which Hook launched in 1996, to more favourable critical reviews and much stronger sales. Rather than attempting to nullify Hook's lineage, as Revenge had done with over-complex synthesizer work, the first Monaco single, the UK Top 20 hit 'What Do You Want From Me', was driven by his distinctive bass work. Just as distinctive was Potts' singing voice. The attendant album, *Music For Pleasure*, also proved popular with critics, although the return of New Order in 1998 will presumably force Hook to put Monaco on hold for the foreseeable future.

● ALBUMS: *Music For Pleasure* (Polydor 1997)★★★★.

Money Mark

b. Mark Ramos Nishita, USA. Money Mark first rose to prominence as keyboard player in the Beastie Boys' powerful stage show of the late 80s and early 90s. However, from his base in Los Angeles, California, he maintained a desire to write and perform his own material. Rather than use the Beastie Boys' own imprint, Grand Royal Records, Nishita was recruited by England's Mo' Wax Records, whose proprietor, James Lavelle, travelled to California to persuade him to sign. His debut album was recorded with Lavelle's help, and followed the Mo' Wax house-style of mellow, deep hip-hop with jazz flourishes, over which Nishita added keyboard motifs and laconic narratives. He repeated the process on 1996's *Third Version EP*, but broadened the range for the follow-up album. *Push The Button* took in hip-hop, dub, funk, soul, art-rock and pop-styles and shaped them into an endlessly inventive and dazzling 18-track epic.

● ALBUMS: *Mark's Keyboard Repair* (Mo' Wax 1995)★★★★, *Third Version EP* (Mo' Wax 1996)★★★, *Push The Button* (Mo' Wax 1998)★★★★.

Monica

b. Monica Arnold, 24 October 1980, Atlanta, Georgia, USA. Alongside Brandy, Monica is the most successful of the new breed of urban R&B female vocalists. She grew up in the College Park suburb of Atlanta, and was immersed in gospel music from an early age. Her mother was a church singer, and by the age of 10 Monica was the youngest member of a travelling 12-piece choir called Charles Thompson And The Majestics. She also began performing at the Atlanta talent showcases held at Center Stage Auditorium, singing a cover version of Whitney Houston's 'The Greatest Love Of All'. The 12-year old singer was discovered at one of these showcases by Rowdy Records executive Dallas Austin, who had previously worked with big-name artists such as TLC, Grace Jones and Madonna. Label boss Clive Davis signed her up to Arista Records, and Austin and his production team oversaw her first recordings. Her first single, 'Don't Take It Personal (Just One Of Dem Days)', topped the *Billboard* R&B chart in June 1995, and climbed to the number 2 slot on the national chart a month later. The follow-up, 'Before You Walk Out Of My Life', was another R&B chart-topper and reached number 7 on the Hot 100 in December. With a full-time tutor as part of her entourage, Monica embarked on promotional tours in support of her debut album, featuring on bills with artists such as TLC, Keith Sweat and Bone Thugs-N-Harmony. *Miss Thang* broke into the Top 40 in August 1995, and had soon followed her debut singles in achieving platinum sales. Further hit singles followed with 'Why I Love You So Much'/'Ain't Nobody' (number 9 in July 1996), and the Diane Warren-penned 'For You I Will' (number 4 in April 1997), taken from the best-selling *Lost In Space* soundtrack. Her second album, which debuted at US number 8 in August, was produced and co-written by Austin and Rodney Jerkins, with contributions from hot writer/producers Jermaine Dupri and Darryl Simmons. Monica became the youngest artist ever to have a US number 1 (aged 14) when her sparky duet with Brandy, 'The Boy Is Mine', topped the charts. The song eventually spent 13 weeks at the top of the *Billboard* Hot 100, in the process becoming the all-time number one female duet in US chart history. The song was also a huge international hit. 'The First Night', written by Dupri, topped the US charts in October and reached number 6 in the UK. 'Angel Of Mine', a cover version of Eternal's 1997 UK hit, became Monica's third US chart-topper in February 1999.

● ALBUMS: *Miss Thang* (Arista 1995)★★★, *The Boy Is Mine* (Arista 1998)★★★★.

Monkey Mafia

b. Jon Carter, London, England. Monkey Mafia is the recording name used by DJ Carter, a regular on the big beat scene. Although it is a term Carter resents, the big beat sound, which became massively popular in the late 90s, was spearheaded not only by him but by acts such as the Chemical Brothers, Fatboy Slim, Bentley Rhythm Ace, the Propellerheads and the Skint Records label. He was a member of various mediocre pub-rock and cover bands while studying philosophy in Southampton. His influences reach beyond the usual reference points of Kraftwerk, Public Enemy, Schoolly D and obscure electro and hip-hop, encompassing 60s rock, soul, dub, dancehall and reggae. His sound, both DJing and recorded, is a dynamic soundclash of ragga, funk, menacing dub and stuttering guitar-based grooves. Carter moved back to London in 1993 and began learning engineering and production skills in the studios of hardcore and jungle labels such as Trouble On Vinyl and No U-Turn. In 1995, he also recorded a number of tracks for the Wall Of Sound label under the name Artery, including 'The

Dollar'. Carter signed to Heavenly Records (a subsidiary of Deconstruction Records) later that year. His debut single for the label, 'Blow The Whole Joint Up' was an immediate hit with the booming 'acid-hop' scene in the UK. Along with Richard Fearless, he became resident DJ at Heavenly's hugely popular anything-goes night, the Sunday Social at the Albany, London, and its reincarnation, the Heavenly Jukebox at Turnmills. Carter mixed the second compilation based on the club's sound, *Live At The Social*. In 1996, Carter toured with the Prodigy as well as fulfilling numerous DJing commitments. He also remixed tracks for the Prodigy, Kula Shaker, Saint Etienne and Supergrass. In early 1997, Monkey Mafia released 'Work Mi Body', featuring vocal samples from 'Queen Of The Dancehall', Petra. In May 1997, the EP *15 Steps*, led by 'Lion In The Hall', was released to critical acclaim. Carter assembled a band to present a live experience, comprising Daniel Peppe (bass), Tom Symmons (drums), Douge Rouben (vocals/MC) and First Rate (scratch technician). In late 1997, they supported Mercury Prize-winners, Roni Size and Reprazent on a sold-out tour. The following May, they released a cover version of Creedence Clearwater Revival's 'Long As I Can See The Light'. Three years in the making, *Shoot The Boss* appeared in May 1998 to a very positive critical reception. The following October Carter released 'Women Beat Their Men' under the Junior Cartier moniker.

● ALBUMS: *Shoot The Boss* (Heavenly 1998)★★★★.

Monster Magnet

This space-rock revivalist band was formed in New Jersey, USA in 1989 by David Wyndorf (vocals/guitar, ex-Shrapnel), with John McBain (guitar), Joe Calandra (bass) and Jon Kleinman (drums). After a couple of self-released tapes and a rather self-indulgent debut album, Monster Magnet suddenly found broad press and public support with *Spine Of God*, despite the back cover disclaimer that 'It's a satanic drug thing . . . you wouldn't understand'. The sound and songs drew on Wyndorf's obsession with late 60s psychedelia, music and culture, producing a hypnotic set that blended *Space Ritual*-era Hawkwind-style with an MC5/Black Sabbath guitar barrage and a liberal sprinkling of drug references, all played with a 90s venom. The band were quick to capitalize, touring almost non-stop around Europe and the USA, and, following a US tour with Soundgarden, they lost McBain but gained a contract with A&M Records, who were happy to give the band creative freedom. The resultant *Superjudge*, with new guitarist Ed Mundell, was, if anything, more intense, and saw Monster Magnet pay tribute to Hawkwind with an affectionate blast through 'Brainstorm'. Their live shows remained an experience in themselves, with lighting engineer Tim Cronin's astral projection backdrop proving to be an essential component as the band whipped up a frenzy on stage, touring Europe with Paw and the USA with Raging Slab in 1994. *Dopes To Infinity* and *Powertrip* honed their space rock sound to perfection and established them as arguably the leaders of the genre.

● ALBUMS: *Monster Magnet* (Glitterhouse 1990)★★★, *Spine Of God* (Primo Scree 1992)★★★, *25...........tab* (Caroline 1993)★★, *Superjudge* (A&M 1993), *Dopes To Infinity* (A&M 1995)★★★, *Powertrip* (A&M 1998)★★★★.

● CD-ROM: *I Talk To Planets* (A&M 1995)★★★.

Montgomery, John Michael

b. 20 January 1965, Danville, Kentucky, USA. Montgomery arrived on the country music scene in 1993 with a debut album, *Life's A Dance*, that became the only million-seller on the country charts by a new artist that year. Its title track was a number 4 hit single, and was followed by his first country chart-topper, 'I Love The Way You Love Me'. The follow-up, *Kickin' It Up*, hit the top spot on both the US Country and Adult Contemporary charts, and produced four more successful singles, the chart-topping 'I Swear', 'Be My Baby Tonight' and 'If You Got Love', and the number 4 single 'Rope The Moon'. At this point Montgomery was one of the hottest artists in country music, appealing to lovers of both Garth Brooks and Lynyrd Skynyrd. He remained unchanged by his success, however, refusing to leave his Lexington home to go to Nashville. His musical talent had been initially encouraged by his father, who performed in a local country band and taught his son his first chords. Montgomery joined the family band as guitarist, before taking lead vocals when his parents divorced. Afterwards, he made a frugal living on the local honky tonk scene as a solo artist playing what he referred to as 'working man's country'. Eventually, Atlantic Records signed him, although it was Montgomery himself rather than the record company who rejected his own material for inclusion on his debut. There were problems during the recording, typified in an anecdote regarding a late-night call to the head of Atlantic that resulted in a change of producer. Atlantic's faith in their artist was subsequently rewarded by Montgomery's swift rise, even though some questioned his political correctness with songs such as 'Sold'. *What I Do The Best*, though a slightly disappointing set, showed no signs of his commercial appeal waning. It later transpired that Montgomery had throat surgery during this time. He was almost back to full health for *Leave A Mark*, which, like 1999's *Home To You*, saw Montgomery heading in an increasingly MOR direction.

● ALBUMS: *Life's A Dance* (Atlantic 1992)★★★, *Kickin' It Up* (Atlantic 1994)★★★★, *John Michael Montgomery* (Atlantic 1995)★★★★, *What I Do The Best* (Atlantic 1996)★★★, *Leave A Mark* (Atlantic 1998)★★, *Home To You* (Atlantic 1999)★★.

● COMPILATIONS: *Greatest Hits* (Atlantic 1997)★★★★.

● VIDEOS: *I Swear* (Atlantic 1993), *Kickin' It Up* (Atlantic 1994).

Morales, David

b. 21 August 1961, Brooklyn, New York, USA. Born of Puerto Rican parents, Morales is one of the USA's premier remixers. His style, melodic house with a strong disco influence, belies his personal physique and presence, that of a pencil-bearded, tattooed body-builder. Married with a son, he works out for two hours every day, although he also employs a bodyguard for his regular evening shows (he was shot in his youth). As a young man he attended both the Loft and Paradise Garage, before being invited to play at the latter through Judy Weinstein's For The Record organisation. His other stomping grounds included all the major New York clubs, including the Ozone Layer, Inferno and Better Days. The Morales' style has graced literally hundreds of records, his first remix being Insync's 'Sometimes Love'. He possibly works best in tandem with a strong garage vocalist (Alison Limerick, Ce Ce Penniston, Yazz, Jocelyn Brown). A good selection of his greatest work might be permutated from the following: Robert Owens' 'I'll Be Your Friend', Clive Griffin's 'I'll Be Waiting', Black Sheep's 'Strobelite Honey', the Pet Shop Boys' 'So Hard', Thompson Twins' 'The Saint' or Limerick's 'Where Love Lives', but the list of major stars who he has completed work for includes Madonna, U2, Björk, Mariah Carey, Michael Jackson and Janet Jackson. Many other remixes have been completed with long-standing friend Frankie Knuckles (as Def-Mix), who he also met through For The Record (Weinstein going on to manage both artists). His productivity is made possible by the fact that he is happy to churn out up to two remixes a week under his own auspices. His live sets, however, are often less glossy than the productions he is best known for: 'When I DJ I'm not as pretty as a lot of the records I make'. His debut album included guest appearances from Sly Dunbar and Ce Ce Rogers, and generated the club hit 'In De Ghetto'. As David Morales presents The Face, he enjoyed a UK Top 10 hit with 'Needin' U' in August 1998. He continues to DJ around the world but is particularly popular in the UK and his native New York City.

● ALBUMS: with the Bad Yard Club *The Program* (Mercury 1993)★★★.

● COMPILATIONS: *Sessions 7 - David Morales* (MOS 1997)★★★.

Morcheeba

Morcheeba, popularly known as the 'trigger hippie' UK trip-hop combo, comprises Paul Godfrey, Ross Godfrey and Skye Edwards. The Godfrey brothers began working from their home-town of Hythe, Kent, around the early 90s, drawing on a number of influences including 30s blues and 90s hip-hop. This fusion resulted in a complex sound that is difficult to categorize. Their quest for acclaim led the brothers to relocate to Clapham, London, where they continued recording, meeting Edwards at a party in Greenwich, London. The trio discovered a mutual affinity for songwriting, marijuana and soundtracks, and Edwards was enlisted to add her debonair vocals to their recording sessions. In the winter of 1995 they released their debut, 'Trigger Hippie', a huge underground hit. The success of the single led to the release of *Who Can You Trust*, which was selected by *DJ* magazine as one of the top 100 dub albums. The band were as astonished as the hardcore reggae fraternity, although the album did display clear traits of dub, notably on the title track. In 1996, the band released a remix of the album track 'The Music That We Hear', and also the crossover hit 'Tape Loop'. The latter led to a triumphant US tour, collaborations with David Byrne and major critical acclaim. In 1997, the band played the Phoenix Festival and A Day At The Races, followed by the release of 'Shoulder Holster'. The single included a mix by DJ Swamp with added vocals from Spikey T. The band embarked on the promotional circuit with television appearances and an acclaimed tour supported by Zion Train. Edwards also performed alongside Burning Spear *et al* on the UK chart-topping cover version of Lou Reed's 'Perfect Day', released in 1997 to promote BBC Radio and Television. In the spring of 1998, the band released their eagerly anticipated follow-up, *Big Calm*. Among the mellifluous melodies was the reggae-styled 'Friction', featuring the horn section from Zion Train.

● ALBUMS: *Who Can You Trust* (Indochina 1996)★★★, *Big Calm* (Indochina 1998)★★★★.

● COMPILATIONS: *Who Can You Trust/Beats And B Sides* (Indochina 1997)★★★.

Morgan, Lorrie

b. Loretta Lynn Morgan, 27 June 1959, Nashville, Tennessee, USA. The youngest daughter of country crooner and *Grand Ole Opry* star George Morgan, she followed in her father's footsteps. She naturally began singing with her father and made her own *Grand Ole Opry* debut at the age of 13 at the old Ryman Auditorium, where her rendition of 'Paper Roses' gained her a standing ovation. After her father's death in 1975, she worked as a backing singing with George Jones' roadshow and for a time was married to Ron Gaddis, who played steel guitar in Jones' band. In 1979, she scored her first minor chart successes with 'Two People In Love' and 'Tell Me I'm Only Dreaming', and charted with a duet recording made earlier with her late father, 'I'm Completely Satisfied With You'. The same year, she had a daughter but her marriage ended and, tiring of life on the road, she retired. In 1984, the lure of the music enticed her back. She became a member of the *Grand Ole Opry* and relaunched her career. She met and married singer Keith Whitley in 1986 but the marriage ended when Whitley's heavy drinking finally took his life in May 1989 (she later recorded a tribute to Whitley, 'If You Came Back From Heaven', which appeared on 1994's *War Paint*). In 1988, she joined RCA Records and had a Top 20 hit with 'Trainwreck Of Emotion', but it was a number 9 weepy, 'Dear Me', entering the charts just a few weeks before Whitley's death, that finally established her as a major star. In 1990, she achieved her first number 1 with 'Five Minutes' and from that point onwards, she registered a regular stream of hit recordings. They included 'Til A Tear Becomes A Rose' (a duet made with Whitley), 'Except For Monday' and 'A Picture Of Me Without You' (a brave and very successful cover version of a 1972 George Jones hit) on RCA. A change of label to BNA in 1992 immediately produced a number 2 hit with 'Watch Me', and a further number 1 with 'What Part Of No'. By now Morgan had proved herself equally at home with up-tempo numbers or with ballads, such as her brilliant recording of 'Something In Red', which peaked at number 14. She attempted something different in 1993, when she recorded a Christmas album that had the New World Philharmonic Orchestra providing the music, and vocal duets with Tammy Wynette, Andy Williams and Johnny Mathis (the music was recorded in London and the vocals added in Nashville, Branson or Los Angeles). In 1993, she gained a Top 10 hit with 'Half Enough' and a minor placement for her version of 'Crying Time', which came from the movie *The Beverly Hillbillies*. In 1995, the release of *Greatest Hits* led to further chart successes. 'I Didn't Know My Own Strength' gave her another number 1 and soon afterwards, 'Back In Your Arms Again', a Fred Knobloch/Paul Davis song, with a catchy chorus, peaked at number 4. Her stunning version of 'Standing Tall', a Larry Butler/Ben Peters song that Billie Jo Spears had taken to number 15 in 1980, followed. A video of her singing the number, actually filmed on the stage of the old Ryman Auditorium home of the *Grand Ole Opry*, gained her recording major exposure on CMT and represented her best vocal performance since 'Something In Red'. Morgan married Jon Randall on 16 November 1996. There seems little doubt that Morgan's chart success will continue, unless she is lost to country music in favour of the bright lights and highly paid circuits of venues such as Las Vegas.

● ALBUMS: *Leave The Light On* (RCA 1989)★★★, *Something In Red* (RCA 1991)★★★, *Watch Me* (BNA 1992)★★★★, *Merry Christmas From London* (BNA 1993)★★, *War Paint* (BNA 1994)★★★, *Greater Need* (BNA 1996)★★★, *Shakin' Things Up* (BNA 1997)★★★, *Secret Love* (BNA 1998)★★★, *My Heart* (BNA 1999)★★★, with Sara Evans, Martina McBride, Mindy McCready *Girls' Night Out* (BNA 1999)★★★.

● COMPILATIONS: *Greatest Hits* (BNA 1995)★★★★, *The Essential Lorrie Morgan* (BNA 1998)★★★★.

● VIDEOS: *War Paint: Video Hits* (BMG 1994), *I Didn't Know My Own Strength* (BNA 1995).

● FURTHER READING: *Forever Yours Faithfully: My Love Story*, Lorrie Morgan with George Vecsey. *Lorrie Morgan*, Ace Collins.

Morillo, Erick

b. USA. 'More' Morillo started DJing at the age of 11, playing sets in his local New Jersey that matched ragga with techno (a precursor to the sound of Reel 2 Real). As a student at New York's Centre For The Media Arts, he started collecting studio equipment, and became a self-taught maestro. He graduated to recording his own material by sampling Jamaican toasters on to DAT. One night a man came forward from the crowd to enquire as to the source of a particular sampled voice. It transpired that the questioner, known as General, was the owner of said larynx. Together they went on to record 'The Funky Buddha' and *Move It* for RCA Records. Influenced by old school Chicago house like Todd Terry and Kenny 'Dope' Gonzalez, Morillo has gone on to build his own studio, Double Platinum, where Little Louie Vega's *Hardrive* EP and Barbara Tucker's 'Deep Deep Inside' were recorded. He tried to get work at Nervous Records but was continually turned down by A&R head Gladys Pizarro. On the day he tried Strictly Rhythm Records instead Pizarro had just been installed in their offices, and this time she relented. Morillo went on to become of the leading lights of the Strictly Rhythm empire, for whom he released over 25 records, under nearly as many pseudonyms, within 1993 alone (His first release on the label having been Reel 2 Real's debut). His productions have included Deep Soul's 'Rhythm', RAW's 'Unbe', Smooth Touch's 'Come And Take A Trip' and Club Ultimate's 'Carnival 93'. He was also represented by albums in 1994 by Deep Soul and Reel 2 Real (whose 'I Like To Move It' and 'Go On Move' were both massive worldwide hits), and recorded his own *More* EP. Mix albums for Strictly Rhythm and the Ministry Of Sound followed. Part of the secret of Morillo's success may lie in his refusal to simply sample current rhythms and beats, preferring instead to write his own drum patterns and arrangements. He is nicknamed 'More' owing to everybody connected being astonished at the number of different mixes he would put on to each of his releases.

● COMPILATIONS: *Live & 'More'* (Strictly Rhythm 1996)★★★, *Sessions 9 - Erick Morillo* (MOS 1997)★★★.

Morissette, Alanis

b. Nadine Morissette, 1 June 1974, Ottawa, Ontario, Canada. Morissette enjoyed considerable critical and public acclaim in her native Canada before that success began to translate to international audiences in the mid-90s. An accomplished singer, dancer and pianist, she began writing her own material at the age of nine. She then achieved her first domestic hit single at the age of 10 ('Faith Stay With Me'). The single led to a publishing deal four years later, but she now dismisses her first two albums where she was pushed very strongly in a pop rock direction. Worldwide recognition followed her move to Madonna's Maverick Records in 1994, by which time she was based in Los Angeles with musical collaborator Glen Ballard (previously co-writer of Michael Jackson's 'Man In The Mirror'). A tape was passed to Maverick by the mixer Jimmy Boyelle. Her third album, *Jagged Little Pill*, was composed almost entirely of those unadulterated demo tracks. It earned rave reviews across America for her confrontational poise and loaded lyrics, reaching number 1 on the *Billboard* album chart. It included an appearance by friends the Red Hot Chili Peppers on 'You Oughta Know', which featured her most quoted lyric: 'Is she perverted like me?/Would she go down on you in a theater?' As Morissette surmised: 'I have a difficult time socially, emotionally and musically because I like to communicate on an overwhelmingly intense level. To get it all out, I write as an overt, aggressive woman.' Just about every music industry award was won by Morissette in 1995 in what was an extraordinary year. In the USA alone, by August 1998, *Jagged Little Pill* was certified as achieving 16 million sales, and world sales had topped 28 million. After disappearing from the music scene for a period, during which she travelled in India, Morissette returned with the inelegantly named *Supposed Former Infatuation Junkie*. Overlong, verbose and with an irritating line in American faux-spirituality, the album nevertheless contained several strong tracks, including the worldwide hit single 'Thank U', and debuted at number 1 on the *Billboard* album chart in November 1998. The following year, Morissette made her acting debut in Kevin Smith's controversial *Dogma*, playing a female God, and released the low-key *MTV Unplugged* in November.

● ALBUMS: *Alanis* (MCA Canada 1990)★★, *Now Is The Time* (MCA Canada 1992)★★, *Jagged Little Pill* (Maverick/Reprise 1995)★★★★, *Supposed Former Infatuation Junkie* (Maverick 1998)★★★, *MTV Unplugged* (Maverick 1999)★★★.

● FURTHER READING: *Alanis Morissette: Death Of Cinderella*, Stuart Coles. *Ironic - Alanis Morissette: The True Story*, Barry Grills.

● FILMS: *Dogma* (1999).

Morphine

Purveyors of quite startling, low-end alternative rock/jazz, US trio Morphine were one of the few bands in the field not to employ guitars. The bass of vocalist Mark Sandman (b. 24 September 1952, d. 3 July 1999, Palestrina, Italy) was a rudimentary affair, comprising two strings usually tuned to the same note, enabling him to produce a sound that doubled as a heavily distorted guitar and ordinary bass. The band was inaugurated by Sandman and Dana Colley (baritone saxophone) after the break-up of the former's Treat Her Right (who recorded three albums between 1986 and 1991). The line-up was completed by Jerome Deupree (drums), who was subsequently replaced by former Treat Her Right drummer Billy Conway. After playing a few tentative gigs the trio released their debut album, which, probably because no one had heard anything quite like it before, won many admirers. Their local community honoured them when they picked up Indie Debut Album Of The Year at the Boston Music Awards. On the back of the attention they were receiving they secured a contract with Rykodisc Records. The band's music continued to be more influenced by literature, notably Jim Thompson, than musical peers. They

came of age with *Yes* in 1995. The album's stand-out track, 'Honey White', was a blistering romp with the baritone sax sounding hauntingly like a 50s R&B band. The follow-up, *Like Swimming*, was gentle, surreal and lyrically fascinating. The same year's *B-Sides And Otherwise* compilation was culled from the band's singles releases. Addictive, offbeat and totally original, Morphine had completed a new album for the DreamWorks label when Sandman collapsed on stage at a concert outside Rome and died shortly afterwards. *The Night* was issued posthumously in February 2000.

● ALBUMS: *Good* (Accurate/Distortion 1992)★★★, *Cure For Pain* (Rykodisc 1993)★★★, *Yes* (Rykodisc 1995)★★★★, *Like Swimming* (Rykodisc 1997)★★★★, *The Night* (DreamWorks 2000)★★★★.

● COMPILATIONS: *B-Sides And Otherwise* (Rykodisc 1997)★★★★.

Morrison, Mark

b. Leicester, England. Although the swingbeat or urban R&B sound of R. Kelly, SWV, TLC and others had made a huge impression among British record buyers, until the breakthrough of Mark Morrison in 1995 the UK had failed to provide a credible domestic alternative. Morrison had grown up in Leicester and Palm Beach, Florida, USA, and was thus better disposed to adopt the style than most. His debut single, 1995's 'Crazy', saw him announce himself as the 'UK King of Swing', and brought immediate chart success. His irresistible March 1996 single 'Return Of The Mack' was highly derivative of his American peers in style, language and content, but gave him a UK chart-topper. A re-released 'Crazy' also broke into the UK Top 10. It was followed by an album of the same title which was co-produced with Phil Chill and featured three further UK Top 10 singles, 'Trippin'', 'Horny', and 'Moan & Groan'. Morrison was found guilty of threatening behaviour with a gun and was sentenced to three months' imprisonment in May 1997. In March 1998, a catalogue of further misdemeanours culminated in a 12-month jail sentence. He returned to the UK charts in September 1999 with 'Best Friend', a duet with Irish singer Connor Reeves.

● ALBUMS: *Return Of The Mack* (WEA 1996)★★★.

Morrissey

b. Steven Patrick Morrissey, 22 May 1959, Davyhulme, Manchester, England. Morrissey began his career with the vague intention of succeeding as a music journalist. Unemployed in Manchester during the late 70s, he frequently wrote letters to the music press and was eventually taken on by *Record Mirror* as a freelance local reviewer. During this period, he also ran a New York Dolls fan club and wrote a booklet about them. Another small illustrated volume, *James Dean Is Not Dead*, briefly catalogued the career of another Morrissey obsession. Two other projects, on girl groups and minor film stars, failed to reach the printed page. In the meantime, Morrissey was attempting unsuccessfully to progress as a performer. He had played a couple of gigs with local band the Nosebleeds and failed a record company audition with a relaunched version of Slaughter And The Dogs. In 1982, he was approached by Wythenshawe guitarist Johnny Maher (later Marr) with the idea of forming a songwriting team. They soon developed into the Smiths, the most important and critically acclaimed UK band of the 80s. Morrissey's arch lyrics, powerful persona and general news worthiness made him a pop figure whose articulacy was unmatched by any of his contemporaries. By the late summer of 1987, the Smiths had disbanded, leaving Morrissey to pursue a solo career. Early the following year he issued his first post-Smiths single, 'Suedehead', with Vini Reilly (Durutti Column) filling the guitarist's spot. The track was irresistibly commercial and reached the UK Top 5. The subsequent *Viva Hate* hit number 1 in the UK album charts soon after, indicating a long and successful future with EMI Records. A further UK Top 10 single with the John Betjeman-influenced 'Everyday Is Like Sunday' reiterated that point. In spite of his successes, Morrissey was initially keen on promoting a Smiths reunion but the closest this reached was the equivalent of a farewell concert in the unlikely setting of Wolverhampton Civic Hall. On 22 December 1988, Morrissey performed alongside former Smiths Andy Rourke, Mike Joyce and Craig Gannon for a 1,700 capacity audience, many of whom had queued for days in order to gain admittance to the venue. The following year brought several problems. Although he continued to release strong singles such as 'The Last Of The Famous International Playboys' and 'Interesting Drug', both reviews and chart placings were slightly less successful than expected. By the time of 'Ouija Board, Ouija Board', Morrissey suffered the most disappointing reviews of his career and, despite its charm, the single only reached number 18. Financial wrangles and management changes, which had characterized the Smiths' career, were repeated by Morrissey the soloist. A projected album, *Bona Drag*, was delayed and eventually cancelled, although the title served for a formidable hits and b-side compilation. In the meantime, Morrissey concentrated on the singles market, issuing some fascinating product, most notably the macabre 'November Spawned A Monster' and controversial 'Piccadilly Palare'. In March 1991, Morrissey issued the long-awaited *Kill Uncle*, a light yet not unappealing work, produced by Clive Langer and Alan Winstanley. By this time, the artist had not toured since the heyday of the Smiths, and there were some critics who wondered whether he would ever perform again. That question was answered in the summer and winter of 1991 when the singer embarked on a world tour, backed by a rockabilly band, whose raw energy and enthusiasm brought a new dimension to his recently understated studio work. The fruits of this collaboration were revealed on *Your Arsenal*, a neat fusion of 50s rockabilly influences and 70s glam rock. The presence of former David Bowie acolyte Mick Ronson as producer added to its impetus. During 1992 Morrissey again hit the headlines when he issued a bitter attack on author Johnny Rogan. Prior to the publication of a book on the Smiths, which he had yet to read, Morrissey decreed: 'Personally, I hope Johnny Rogan ends his days very soon in an M3 pile-up.' The much-publicized and long-running dispute merely served to focus attention on the book and heighten appreciation of his Smiths work. *Beethoven Was Deaf*, a live album that disappeared after only two weeks in the charts, was a dismal failure. However, Morrissey was now beginning to cultivate a following in the USA substantially beyond the cult devotees who had followed the Smiths in that country. This offered welcome succour at a time when UK critics were predicting his imminent downfall. Then came the Madstock disaster - a live appearance in support of a re-formed Madness that saw Morrissey bedecked in a Union

Jack - which, when combined with song titles such as 'Bengali In Platforms' and 'The National Front Disco', saw a huge debate rage in the media over the artist's interpretation of 'Englishness'. *Vauxhall And I*, a chilling treatise of pained reflection proved Morrissey's most outstanding release to date, reaching number 1 in the UK. With the more sedate production of Steve Lillywhite, this was the closest the artist had come to matching his lyricism with the right material components since the Smiths. Indeed, as *Select* magazine decreed: 'If he keeps making albums like this, you won't want the Smiths back'. However, it was to be his last album with EMI/HMV Records, apart from the much-criticized compilation *The World Of Morrissey*. Meanwhile, a collaboration with Siouxsie on the single 'Interlude', fell outside the UK Top 20. Morrissey next moved to BMG Records as they chose to revive another old label, this time RCA-Victor for 1995's *Southpaw Grammar*. This set opened with 'The Teachers Are Afraid Of The Pupils', an arresting 11-minute update to the Smiths' 'The Headmaster Ritual', which placed the secondary school teacher in the role of victim. Critics were not overly impressed and the album disappeared from the play lists and people's minds after a few weeks. Morrissey made the headlines in 1997 with the long-standing court case over Mike Joyce's claim on royalties. The judge ruled against Morrissey and Marr. This must have been his absolute nadir; even his tracker-dog biographer Rogan was able to confront him at the courtrooms. Ploughing on, Morrissey released the delayed *Maladjusted* for new label Island Records, although he was forced to omit a track that allegedly attacked Joyce and Rourke.

● ALBUMS: *Viva Hate* (HMV/Sire 1988)★★★★, *Kill Uncle* (HMV/Sire 1991)★★, *Your Arsenal* (HMV/Sire 1992)★★★★, *Beethoven Was Deaf* (HMV 1993)★★, *Vauxhall And I* (Parlophone/Sire 1994)★★★★, *Southpaw Grammar* (RCA Victor/Reprise 1995)★★★, *Maladjusted* (Island 1997)★★★.
● COMPILATIONS: *Bona Drag* (HMV/Sire 1990)★★★★, *The World Of Morrissey* (Parlophone/EMI 1995)★★, *Suedehead - The Best Of* (EMI 1997)★★★.
● VIDEOS: *Hulmerist* (PMI/EMI 1990), *Live In Dallas* (Warner Music Video 1992), *Introducing Morrissey* (Warner Music Video 1996).
● FURTHER READING: *Morrissey In His Own Words*, John Robertson. *Morrissey Shot*, Linder Sterling. *Morrissey & Marr: The Severed Alliance*, Johnny Rogan. *Peepholism: Into The Art Of Morrissey*, Jo Slee. *Landscapes Of The Mind*, David Bret.

Mos Def
(see Black Star)

Mother Love Bone
This short-lived, Seattle-based quintet comprised Andrew Wood (vocals, ex-Malfunkshun), Greg Gilmore (drums), and three members of recently demised grunge pioneers Green River, Bruce Fairweather (guitar), Stone Gossard (guitar), and Jeff Ament (bass). Drawing influences from the Stooges, MC5 and the Velvet Underground, Mother Love Bone specialized in heavy-duty garage rock laced with drug-fuelled psychotic overtones. Signing to Polydor Records, they debuted with 1989's *Shine* EP, released on the Stardog imprint. Their promising career was curtailed abruptly by the untimely overdose death of vocalist Andrew Wood in March, shortly before the release of the excellent *Apple*. Gossard and Ament went on to enjoy further success with

Temple Of The Dog and, to a much greater extent, Pearl Jam. The album and EP were later reissued on the *Mother Love Bone* compilation.

● ALBUMS: *Apple* (Polydor 1990)★★★★.
● COMPILATIONS: *Mother Love Bone* (Polydor 1992)★★★.

Mouse On Mars

This highly innovative Düsseldorf-based duo, comprising Jan St. Werner and Andi Toma, emerged in the mid-90s as the figureheads of a new wave of German electronic music. The pair met (allegedly) at a death metal concert in 1993, and began recording obscure soundtrack material together as Mouse On Mars. They hooked up with UK label Too Pure for the release of 1994's debut EP *Frosch*, an astonishing multi-layered recording that drew on krautrock, dub, techno and ambient to create a unique new sound. The duo's full-length debut, *Vulvaland*, was released to widespread acclaim, although the sound continued to baffle critics attempting to categorise their music. In a similar way to the UK's Seefeel, they use standard rock instruments to create lush, textured soundscapes that bear little resemblance to conventional rock music. The follow-up, *Iaora Tahiti*, was even better, a wildly adventurous exploration of the possibilities of stereo sound (note the duo's proud proclamation that 'this record does not sound in mono'). In 1997, the duo released *Autoditacker*, which introduced elements of drum 'n' bass into the mix, and the vinyl-only *Instrumentals*. The latter was issued on their own Sonig label and featured their contributions to a pair of tribute albums to the philosopher Gilles Deleuze originally issued on the Sub Rosa label. The following year's *Glam* featured tracks originally recorded in 1993 for an abortive film project starring Tony Danza. An album of new recordings, *Niun Niggung*, followed shortly afterwards. The duo are regular contributors to Volume's experimental *Trance Europe Express* series, and Werner also records with Markus Popp of Oval as Microstoria.

● ALBUMS: *Vulvaland* (Too Pure/American 1994)★★★★, *Iaora Tahiti* (Too Pure/American 1995)★★★★, *Autoditacker* (Thrill Jockey 1997)★★★★, *Instrumentals* (Sonig 1997)★★★★, *Glam* (Sonig 1998)★★★, *Niun Niggung* (Our Choice/Sonig 1999)★★★.

Moxy Fr9vous

A cappella Toronto, Canada-based band Moxy Fr9vous initially made their name opening for artists such as Bob Dylan and Bryan Adams. The members had, allegedly, previously met on a school trip to a pig-calling contest. They did not win, but shared instead the prize for Most Promising Pig-Caller. Hence Mike Ford (guitar/percussion), Murray Foster (bass/guitar), Jean Ghomeshi (drums) and David Matheson (guitar/bass/accordion) formed a band, taken after the pigs' names; Moxy and Fruvous. They subsequently began to write and rehearse together at high school. However, one pair broke off to write three full-length musicals, while the others started a pop/funk combo called Tall New Buildings. They quartet regrouped while attending university in 1990 and began busking on the streets of Toronto. Their eclectic tastes saw them draw on rap, soca, folk and theatrical traditions. The single unifying factor was the band's distinctive four-part vocal harmonies. The irreverent and occasionally incisive lyrics offered an additional attraction, as on the single 'Stuck In The '90s', a grim take on counter-culture and the politics of protest. A self-released cassette was followed

by 1993's *Bargainville*, whose songs were conducted with the type of alternating restraint and fervour which recalled the passionate melodicism of the Proclaimers. Others preferred to compare the quartet to another Canadian band, the Barenaked Ladies. While that band went on to enjoy international success, Moxy Fr9vous had returned to independent status by the time of 1999's *Thornhill*.

● ALBUMS: *Bargainville* (WEA/Atlantic 1993)★★★, *Wood* (WEA 1995)★★, *Thornhill* (Bottom Line 1999)★★★.

Mr. Oizo

b. Quentin Dupieux, France. The artist's moniker Mr. Oizo was obscured by that of a puppet, Flat Eric, an orange anthropomorph that featured in UK television commercials for Levis jeans, dancing to Dupieux's track 'Flat Beat'. The adverts, the puppet and the track became simultaneously popular and 'Flat Beat' was extensively play-listed on UK national radio, ultimately reaching number 1 in March 1999. The puppet's appearance in the accompanying video confirmed Flat Eric's place in the popular consciousness as the creator of the track, rather than Dupieux/Mr. Oizo. Dupieux had already released two EPs on Laurent Garnier's F Communications label, but the success of 'Flat Beat' raised his profile enormously before the release of his debut *Analog Worms Attack* in October 1999. Dupieux claims Herbie Hancock and Miles Davis as major influences, and he adopts a similarly experimental and abstract approach to his style of dance music, which has been described as 'dirty house' - stripped-down, using quirky and distorted sounds and 'acid' basslines - a style reminiscent of Garnier.

● ALBUMS: *Analog Worms Attack* (F Communications 1999)★★★.

Mr. Vegas

b. Clifford Smith, 1975, St. Andrew, Jamaica, West Indies. Smith spent his adolescence nurturing his soccer skills, and his tackling proficiency led to the nickname of Vegas, a reference to the twisting skills of the go-go dancers at the local Las Vegas Club. Smith began his musical career in 1986 when he visited a recording studio in Kingston. His recording career was put on hold until he completed his education, and by the time he was 21 he was singing his interpretation of Roberta Flack's 'Killing Me Softly With His Song' at Freddie McGregor's Big Ship Studio. The DJ/producer Don Yute brought him into the studio to work on the song, and the session led to a further collaboration for a version of Az Yet's 'Last Night'. At this point Yute suggested the addition to his name of 'Mr.', to give the artist and his sound more authority. Up until 1997, Vegas was primarily a reggae singer, although his career changed course when he broke his jaw, which was subsequently wired up for several weeks. Undeterred, he persevered with his singing career and returned to the recording studio. The wired jaw resulted in a new and unique singing-cum-DJ style. This characteristic sound impressed the up-and-coming producer Jeremy Harding, who enrolled Vegas to perform 'Nike Air' over the 'Playground' rhythm (Harding had already taken the rhythm into the UK Top 10 in February 1998 with Beenie Man's 'Who Am I (Zim Zimmer)'). Following on from the runaway success of 'Nike Air', Vegas went on to enjoy a run of hits in Jamaica, New York, Miami and London. In 1998, his releases included 'Jump Around' and 'Everywhere I Go' for Richie Stephens' 'Latest News' on Steely And Clevie's Bagpipe

rhythm, 'Sweet Pineapple' for Colin Fat Eyes, and the irrepressible 'Heads High' for Danny Brownie. The success of the single led to national radio exposure and the exceptional 'Kill 'Em With It' remix. Further hits followed, including the double a-side with Italee, 'Got To Be Me', 'Hand In The Air', 'Big Things A Gwaan', 'Hit Him Back' and 'Are Yu Sure'.
● ALBUMS: *Heads High* (Greensleeves 1998)★★★★.

Mudhoney

Mudhoney, forged from a host of hobbyist bands, can lay claim to the accolade 'godfathers of grunge' more legitimately than most. The band comprises Mark Arm (b. 21 February 1962, California, USA; vocals), Steve Turner (b. 28 March 1965, Houston, USA; guitar), Matt Lukin (b. 16 August 1964, Aberdeen, Washington, USA; bass) and Dan Peters (b. 18 August 1967, Seattle, Washington, USA; drums). Arm and Turner were both ex-Green River, the band that also gave birth to Pearl Jam, and the less serious Thrown-Ups. Lukin was ex-Melvins, and Peters ex-Bundles Of Hiss. Mudhoney were the band that first took the sound of Sub Pop Records to wider shores. In August 1988, they released 'Touch Me I'm Sick' single, one of the defining moments in the evolution of 'grunge', followed shortly by their debut mini-album. Early support included the admiration of Sonic Youth who covered their first a-side, while Mudhoney thrashed through Sonic Youth staple 'Halloween' on the flip-side of a split single. The first album was greeted as a comparative disappointment by many, though there were obvious stand-out tracks ('When Tomorrow Hits'). The EP *Boiled Beef And Rotting Teeth* contained a cover version of the Dicks' 'Hate The Police', demonstrating a good grasp of their 'hardcore' heritage. They had previously demonstrated an ability to choose a sprightly cover tune when Spacemen 3's 'Revolution' had appeared on the b-side to 'This Gift'. The band also hold artists such as Celibate Rifles and Billy Childish in high esteem. Members of the former have helped in production of the band, while on trips to England they have invited the latter to join as support. It was their patronage that led to Childish's Thee Headcoats releasing material through Sub Pop. *Every Good Boy Deserves Fudge* was a departure, with Hammond organ intruding into the band's accomplished rock formula. It demonstrated their increasing awareness of the possibilities of their own songwriting. The band members all have middle-class backgrounds, and while Arm is an English graduate, Turner has qualifications in anthropology. After much speculation, Mudhoney became the final big players in the Sub Pop empire to go major when they moved to Warner Brothers Records, though many argue that none of their efforts thus far have managed to reproduce the glory of 'Touch Me I'm Sick' or other highlights of their independent days. *My Brother The Cow*, however, revealed a band nearly back to its best. Released after extensive worldwide touring with Pearl Jam, highlights included 'Into Your Schtick', which reflected on the passing of one-time friend Kurt Cobain. Jack Endino's production, meanwhile, added lustre and managed effectively to capture the band's always compelling live sound. Mark Arm also plays with the trashy Australian garage rock band Bloodloss, who released their major label debut, *Live My Way*, in 1995. He returned to Mudhoney for their 1998 release, *Tomorrow Hit Today*.
● ALBUMS: *Superfuzz Bigmuff* mini-album (Sub Pop 1988)★★★,

Mudhoney (Sub Pop 1989)★★, *Every Good Boy Deserves Fudge* (Sub Pop 1991)★★★, *Piece Of Cake* (Reprise 1993)★★★, *Five Dollar Bob's Mock Cooter Stew* mini-album (Reprise 1993)★★, *My Brother The Cow* (Reprise 1995)★★★, *Tomorrow Hit Today* (Reprise 1998)★★★.
● COMPILATIONS. *Superfuzz Bigmuff Plus Early Singles* (Sub Pop 1991)★★★.
● VIDEOS: *Absolutely Live* (Pinnacle 1991), *No. 1 Video In America This Week* (Warner Music Video 1995).

Mullins, Shawn

b. USA. A literate, considered songwriter in the traditions of Tom Petty, Atlanta, Georgia resident Mullins made his commercial breakthrough in 1998 with 'Lullaby', the lead single from that year's *Soul's Core* collection. The high visibility of 'Lullaby' on modern rock stations subsequently pushed the album into the *Billboard* Top 100 chart, providing something of a jolt to the taciturn Mullins in the process (the song eventually reached both the US and UK Top 10). Previously he had released a cluster of albums on his own SM Records (later SMG), playing an average of 200 shows a year to a dedicated but tiny following. He had released his first self-titled album on cassette in 1989 while still a serving member of the US airborne infantry. Mullins merely shrugged off the new-found notoriety 'Lullaby' brought him: 'There are certain rules at modern rock [formats], and I broke a few with this song. There's not a big, heavy guitar presence. I'm singing in key for the most part, and I guess it's a little soft.' One of Mullins' most notable mannerisms on his records since 1995 has been the inclusion of spoken word passages (particularly on the live discs, *Jeff's Last Dance Vols. 1* and 2). Although partially inspired by Gil Scott-Heron and Kris Kristofferson, Mullins found these prosaic moments were a good way to win the attention of fickle audiences, and thereafter incorporated them into his studio recordings.
● ALBUMS: *Shawn Mullins* cassette only (SM 1989)★★★, *Better Days* (SM 1992)★★★, *Big Blue Sky* (SM 1994)★★, with Matthew Kahler *Jeff's Last Dance Vol. 1* (SMG 1995)★★★, *Eggshells* (SMG 1996)★★★, *Soul's Core* (SMG/Columbia 1998)★★★★, with Kahler *Jeff's Last Dance Vol. 2* (SMG 1999)★★★.

Murphy, David Lee

b. Herrin, Illinois, USA. Although it took Murphy more than 10 years to secure a major label recording contract with MCA Records, he quickly regained ground with the success of his debut album, *Out With A Bang*, which topped *Billboard*'s Heatseekers chart in 1995. Murphy had first been spotted by MCA Nashville president Tony Brown while leading his country band, Blue Tick Hounds, in 1985. However, a full decade passed before Brown offered Murphy a contract, though the artist conceded that his former band was 'too edgy for country radio at the time or, at least, too edgy to get a deal'. In the intervening period Murphy worked as a professional songwriter, writing 'Red Roses Won't Work Now' for Reba McEntire and 'High Weeds And Rust' for Doug Stone. A version of that song was also included on *Out With A Bang*, alongside other original material such as the singles 'Fish Ain't Bitin'' and 'Just Once', which featured on the soundtrack to *8 Seconds*. 'Every Time I Get Around You' was the hit single that previewed *Gettin' Out The Good Stuff*, but album sales have failed to live up to the success of his debut.
● ALBUMS: *Out With A Bang* (MCA 1994)★★★★, *Gettin' Out The Good Stuff* (MCA 1996)★★★, *We Can't All Be Angels* (MCA 1997)★★★.

Muse

This UK trio, not to be confused with the Florida-based US band of the same name, grew up in the sleepy small-town backwater of Teignmouth, Devon. School friends Matthew Bellamy (guitar/vocals), Chris Wolstenhome (bass) and Dominic Howard (drums) first formed a band as teenagers, struggling on the local pub circuit as Gothic Plague, Fixed Penalty and Rocket Baby Dolls. They eventually settled on Muse, a name far more in sync with a rapidly developing style clearly influenced by Radiohead and Nirvana. A well-received appearance at 1998's In The City showcase failed to land the trio a record deal. Two independent releases on Dangerous Records, the four-track *Muse* (May 1998) and six-track *Muscle Museum* (January 1999), garnered strong praise for the band's grandiose art rock-style. In the meantime, an appearance at CMJ in New York led to a high profile deal with Madonna's Maverick Records. Shortly afterwards, the band were snapped up by Mushroom Records in the UK. A strong set at 1999's Glastonbury Festival failed to push their debut single 'Uno' higher than number 73 in the UK charts, but the band were consoled by positive reviews for their John Leckie-produced, *Showbiz*. The explosive atmosphere of tracks such as 'Sunburn', 'Cave' and 'Sober' stood out on a record that failed to rise above the sum of its influences.

● ALBUMS: *Showbiz* (Mushroom/Maverick 1999)★★★.

Mutton Birds

Comprising Alan Gregg (bass), Ross Burge (guitar), Don McGlashan (vocals/guitar) and David Long (drums), New Zealand's Mutton Birds were formed when vocalist McGlashan pieced together the band from colleagues with whom he had worked in various local Auckland groups. One of his many previous outfits, Blam Blam Blam, had supported Split Enz in their early days, and the connection with the Finn brothers would later serve them well. In-between those early bands and Mutton Birds he had also worked extensively in film and theatre. The band released its debut album in 1992, building on McGlashan's 60s influences of the Beatles, Kinks, Byrds and early Pink Floyd. Its pastoral, understated pop motif encouraged comparisons with R.E.M. and won them two 1993 New Zealand Music Industry Awards for Best Group and Best Album. The subsequent *Salty* again saw Crowded House's Neil Finn co-produce. Drawn from it, 'Anchor Me' secured a major domestic songwriting award as well as enthusiastic local press. Its success led to an international contract with Virgin Records, who issued a compilation of the best of both albums titled *Nature*, and prompted a move to England to pursue their career on the back of a superb new collection, *Envy Of Angels*. McGlashan remained philosophical about the merits of New Zealand's domestic music scene: 'You'll never get rich being a musician in New Zealand, so there's no incentive to follow fashion. As a result, you form a band and you play the music you care most about, with no commercial pressure to do anything else.' Unable to capitalise on their critical standing, the band were subsequently dropped by Virgin. Undeterred, they reappeared on their own label with another glorious collection of thoughtful and melodic pop songs.

● ALBUMS: *The Mutton Birds* (1992)★★★, *Salty* (1993)★★★, *Envy Of Angels* (Virgin 1997)★★★★, *Rain, Steam & Speed* (Shhhhh! 1999)★★★★.

● COMPILATIONS: *Nature* (Virgin 1995)★★★.

µ-Ziq

Based in south London, England, µ-Ziq is effectively studio musician Mike Paradinas, although he has also worked in tandem with Francis Naughton. Both were students when they first met the Aphex Twin, Richard James, who invited them to join his new Rephlex Records imprint. Unlike the aforementioned ambient guru, neither were technocrats, preferring an organic, untutored approach to the creation of cerebral dance music. Their debut double album was recorded using only synthesizers, a beatbox, and a four-track mixer. Within a few months of studio time µ-Ziq claimed to have over 300 completed tracks sitting on the shelf, an output that threatened to eclipse even their mentor's notorious profligacy. By 1995's *In Pine Effect*, the first result of a new distribution deal for Paradinas' own Planet µ label within the Virgin Records empire, he was effectively a solo artist. He had also found time to record as Gary Moscheles And The Badass Motherfunkers (in a jazz funk vein) and Jake Slazenger (for the underground dance label Clear Records). *Lunatic Harness* and *Royal Astronomy*, enjoyed a cult following in America when they were released through the Astralwerks label.

● ALBUMS: *Tango N' Vectif* (Rephlex 1994)★★★, *In Pine Effect* (Planet µ/Virgin 1995)★★, *Lunatic Harness* (Virgin/Astralwerks 1997)★★★, *Royal Astronomy* (Virgin/Astralwerks 1999)★★★.

● COMPILATIONS: *Brace Yourself* (Astralwerks 1998)★★★.

My Life Story

My Life Story is effectively just one man, the multi-talented but idiosyncratic 'pop composer' Jake Shillingford (b. Southend-on-Sea, Essex, England). Formed at the turn of the 90s, Shillingford used the band to develop a songwriting style in keeping with the ambitious soundtrack work of John Barry. However, his 'assumed Cockney' delivery saw My Life Story compared to Blur at the height of the Britpop movement. Before he launched the band, Shillingford had run an 'indie' club in London at the end of the 80s. Various members were involved with the My Life Story project, which at times could run to 12 members, though Shillingford's main collaborator is non-performer Aaron Cahill. Though critically acclaimed, their 1995 debut album, *Mornington Crescent*, failed to provide a breakthrough, and Shillingford found himself on the hunt for a new recording contract. Eventually he moved to Parlophone Records, achieving an immediate breakthrough when his debut for the label, '12 Reasons Why I Love Her', became a UK Top 40 chart hit in late 1996. Plans for a second album were announced, while Shillingford kept himself busy arranging songs written by Marc Almond for P.J. Proby's comeback album. *The Golden Mile* was a suitably lush and glamorous affair, but poor sales meant that the band were subsequently dropped by Parlophone. Shillingford slimmed down the line-up to a quartet for the subsequent *Joined Up Talking*.

● ALBUMS: *Mornington Crescent* (1995)★★★, *The Golden Mile* (Parlophone 1997)★★★, *Joined Up Talking* (It 2000)★★★.

Mya

b. Mya Harrison, Washington, DC, USA. Growing up in suburban Maryland, Harrison took up tap-dancing and ballet as a child. She appeared with the TWA (Tappers With Attitude) troupe, and went to New York to study with choreographer Savion Glover (best known for the Broadway hit *Bring In 'Da*

Noise, Bring In 'Da Funk) in a residency with the Dance Theater Of Harlem. By the mid-90s, Mya had started to concentrate on her other great love, music. Her father was a professional R&B musician, and recorded demo tapes of his daughter singing. He played one tape to Haqq Islam of University Music, who made the unprecedented move of coming to the family home to hear the 16-year old prodigy sing. Signed to Interscope Records, Mya spent the next two years recording her debut album in New York, Philadelphia and Atlanta with notable contributors including label mates Dru Hill, Missy 'Misdemeanor' Elliott, Babyface, Darryl Pearson and Diane Warren. Released in April 1998, *Mya* was a mature urban R&B collection built around the singer's assured vocals and reflective lyrics. 'It's All About Me' featured Sisqo of Dru Hill, and climbed to US number 6 in May. Mya maintained her high profile with appearances on Pras' hit single 'Ghetto Supastar (That Is What You Are)', taken from the soundtrack to the Warren Beatty movie *Bulworth*. In September, her album climbed to a US chart peak of 29, and 'Movin' On', featuring No Limit Records' star Silkk The Shocker, reached number 34 on the Hot 100 singles chart. 'Take Me There', a collaboration with BLACKstreet, Ma$e and Blinky Blink taken from the *Rugrats* soundtrack, reached number 14 in January 1999. The subsequent Babyface/Diane Warren collaboration, 'My First Night With You', surprisingly failed to break into the US Top 50.

● ALBUMS: *Mya* (Interscope 1998)★★★★.

Myers, Billie

b. 14 June 1971, Coventry, England. This big voiced singer-songwriter enjoyed transatlantic success in 1998 with 'Kiss The Rain', one of the best AOR songs of the decade. Myers, whose mother is English and father Jamaican, trained as a nurse before relocating to London to work for an insurance company. She was spotted dancing at a club by producer Peter Harris, who was impressed enough to ask her if she sang as well as she danced. A publishing deal eventually led to a recording contract with Universal Records. Myers recorded her debut album in Miami, Florida with leading soft rock songwriter Desmond Child, and it was in America that 'Kiss The Rain', co-written with Eric Bazilian (ex-Hooters), first took off. The single proved highly popular on adult rock radio and had climbed to number 15 on the national charts by February 1998. The UK cottoned on two months later with the song debuting at number 4 on the singles chart. *Growing, Pains*, originally released in November the previous year, was an impressive collection of adult rock songs, with Myers' voice moving seamlessly from acoustic tenderness to full-blown angst rock *à la* Alanis Morissette. Subsequent singles 'Tell Me' (complete with risqué video) and 'You Send Me Flying' failed to repeat the success of 'Kiss The Rain', despite Myers high-profile appearance on the Lilith Fair tour.

● ALBUMS: *Growing, Pains* (Universal 1997)★★★.

Myles, Alannah

Toronto-based vocalist Myles spent much of her early career unsuccessfully shopping for a recording contract in her native Canada, but when she and writing partner Christopher Ward changed tack, targeting an American deal with a David Tyson-produced demo and a video for 'Just One Kiss', they met with almost instant success. Tyson produced

1989's *Alannah Myles*, an excellent commercial hard-rock debut on which the vocalist turned her deep, soulful voice to a variety of material, from gentle acoustic guitar-based ballads to raunchy rock 'n' roll. After the years of struggle, the debut ironically took off rapidly in Canada, with 'Love Is' helping Myles to achieve major status in just three months, but the slow, steamy raunch of 'Black Velvet' brought much wider success. She suddenly found herself topping the US singles chart and hitting number 2 in the UK as 'Black Velvet' became a worldwide hit. *Alannah Myles* went on to become the most successful debut in Canadian music history, selling more than five million copies globally. Myles subsequently proved that she was no mere studio songbird, taking her band out on the road. Her most recent albums, *Alannah* and *Arrival*, have failed to find favour beyond her loyal cult following.

● ALBUMS: *Alannah Myles* (Atlantic 1989)★★★★, *Rockinghorse* (Atlantic 1992)★★★, *Alannah* (Atlantic 1995)★★, *Arrival* (El Dorado 1997)★★★.

● COMPILATIONS: *The Very Best Of Alannah Myles* (Ark 1998)★★★.

'N Sync

Like their boy band predecessors, the Backstreet Boys, teenage vocal group 'N Sync were formed in Orlando, Florida, USA. Singers JC Chasez (b. Joshua Scott Chasez, 8 August 1976, Washington, DC, USA) and Justin Timberlake (b. 31 January 1981, Memphis, Tennessee, USA) had previously appeared on the [Walt] Disney Channel's *Mickey Mouse Club*, a training ground for other future teenage pop stars Britney Spears and Christina Aguilera. They met up again when working on separate solo projects in Nashville with the same vocal coaches. Returning to Orlando, Timberlake joined Chris Kirkpatrick (17 October 1971, Pittsburgh, Pennsylvania, USA) and Joey Fatone (b. 28 January 1977, New York City, New York, USA). With the addition of Chasez and James Lance Bass (b. 4 May 1979, Clinton, Mississippi, USA), and managed by former New Kids On The Block manager Johnny Wright, 'N Sync was formed in 1995. Enlisting several hot pop producers, including Kristian Lundin (Backstreet Boys), and Denniz Pop and Max Martin (Robyn, Ace Of Base), the team recorded a collection of lightweight pop/dance tracks designed to appeal to a teenage audience. Their debut album was originally released through BMG

Ariola Munich, and the band became an instant success in Europe on the strength of the bestselling singles 'I Want You Back' and 'Tearin' Up My Heart'. A tour of American roller rinks introduced them to the US audience, as a result of which 'I Want You Back' climbed to a high of 13 on the *Billboard* Hot 100 in May 1998. Their album gained a US release in spring 1998, and eventually climbed to number 2 in October. The band opened for Janet Jackson and performed their first television concert on the Disney Channel in August. *Home For Christmas* was released to cash in on the seasonal market. An insipid mix of new material and standards, the album still debuted at number 7 on the US album chart in November. In the UK, *'N Sync* entered the album chart at number 2 in January 1999, while 'I Want You Back' debuted at number 5 in February. Their new single, '(God Must Have Spent) A Little More Time On You', climbed to US number 8 in February 1999, while 'Music Of My Heart', a soundtrack single recorded with Gloria Estefan, debuted at number 2 in October.

● ALBUMS: *'N Sync* (BMG/RCA 1998)★★★, *Home For Christmas* (RCA 1998)★★.

● VIDEOS: *The Ultimate 'N Sync Party!* (MVP Home Entertainment 1999).

Nail, Jimmy

b. James Bradford, 16 March 1954, Newcastle-upon-Tyne, Tyne & Wear, England. Never the most natural pop star, the actor Jimmy Nail's efforts in front of a microphone have nevertheless brought him huge UK success. As the son of the boxer and Huddersfield Town footballer, Jimmy Bradford, Nail worked hard on misspending his youth. He was expelled from school and later jailed for football violence. After prison, though, he mended his alcoholic ways and began singing in pubs and clubs. He fronted the band King Crabs, before embarking on his own songwriting. After a few small acting parts, he received his break when he got the part of the loveable philistine 'Oz' in the widely acclaimed ITV television series, *Auf Wiedersehen, Pet!* Subsequent acting roles have played upon a gritty, rough-edged demeanour. His musical career took off when his cover version of Rose Royce's 'Love Don't Live Here Anymore' reached number 3 in the UK chart in 1985. However the follow-up single 'That's The Way Love Is' and his debut album flopped, and so he concentrated on his acting career, especially the detective series *Spender*, which ran for the next seven years. This drama, which Nail co-wrote with Ian La Frenais, had a musical background. When Nail returned to music it was with 1992's UK number 1 single 'Ain't No Doubt'. However, its follow-up, 'Laura', failed to breach the Top 50. Nail pressed on with a new television series, *Crocodile Shoes*, which followed the career of a down-at-heel pub-rocker on his way to Nashville and stardom. The album that accompanied it became the biggest-selling UK release of 1994, and featured guest writer Prefab Sprout's Paddy McAloon. The title track reached number 4 in the UK singles chart, while 'Cowboy Dreams' (whose *Top Of The Pops* BBC television transmission featured an appearance by fellow Newcastle native Sting) made the Top 20 early the following year. *Big River* featured Nail's cover version of a 60s beat group chestnut with the Merseybeats' 'I Think Of You'. The title track provided Nail with another Top 20 single at the end of the year. In 1996, Nail appeared alongside

Madonna in Alan Parker's adaptation of *Evita* and starred in *Crocodile Shoes II*. One of the songs featured in the new series, 'Country Boy', provided him with a UK Top 30 hit single. Two years later Nail appeared in Dick Clement and Ian La Frenais' warm-hearted comedy *Still Crazy*, which followed the exploits of a re-formed 70s rock band. His new album *Tadpoles In A Jar* was released the following year.

● ALBUMS: *Take It Or Leave It* (Virgin 1986)★★, *Growing Up In Public* (East West 1992)★★★★, *Crocodile Shoes* (East West 1994)★★★★, *Big River* (East West 1995)★★, *Crocodile Shoes II* (East West 1996)★★, *Tadpoles In A Jar* (East West 1999)★★★.

● COMPILATIONS: *The Nail File: The Best Of Jimmy Nail* (East West 1997)★★★.

● VIDEOS: *Somewhere In Time, Somewhere On Tour* (Warner Music Vision 1995), *The Nail File: The Best Of Jimmy Nail Video Collection* (Warner Music Vision 1998).

● FURTHER READING: *Spender: The Novel*, Jimmy Nail. *Crocodile Shoes: From The North East To The Wild West*, Jimmy Nail. *Crocodile Shoes II: From Tennessee To Tyneside*, Jimmy Nail. *Nailed: The Biography Of Jimmy Nail*, Geraint Jones.

● FILMS: *Morons From Outer Space* (1985), *Howling II* (1985), *Just Ask For Diamond's* (1988), *Dream Demon* (1988), *Crusoe* (1988), *Evita* (1996), *Still Crazy* (1998).

Nalin And Kane

Although this German production and remixing team, comprising Andry Nalin (b. 14 May 1969, Germany) and Harry Cane (b. Ralf Beck, 21 November 1966, Germany) have not had a prolific release schedule, their remixes and recordings have been extremely successful across Europe in both the clubs and the charts. Their international breakthrough came with the infectious Ibiza anthem, 'Beachball', in late 1996 and they have since had success with remixes of Energy 52's 'Cafe Del Mar' and fellow German, Da Hool's 'Meet Her At The Love Paradc'. Both tracks were given new leases of life after the remixing touch of the duo and were hugely successful dance music singles. Their mix of 'Meet Her At The Love Parade' became one of 1998's clubbing anthems, notably in Ibiza, and was featured on many mix compilation albums. Their remix of Lustral's (aka Space Brothers) 'Everytime' was also a club hit and was featured on mix compilation albums. They first began working together in 1993 as Nalin Inc. and released their first 12-inch single, 'Planet Orange' in 1994. They began their own label, Superfly Records in 1995, releasing the singles 'The K-People' and 'Backfire' before the turning point came with 'Beachball'. Artists whose work they have remixed include DJ Quicksilver, Kylie Minogue, Jam And Spoon, BBE and Sven Vath. Andry Nalin also has a thriving career as a DJ and has played in the USA and in Europe at Berlin's famous 'Love Parade' and major clubs such as Renaissance, Cream, Dorian Grey (Frankfurt, Germany), Ministry Of Sound and Pacha and Space in Ibiza. They continued to remix in 1997 and released 'Talking About' and 'Open Your Eyes'. A remix of 'Beachball' broke into the UK Top 20 the following year. In late 1999, they released their debut *Krystal Palace*.

● ALBUMS: *Krystal Palace* (Superfly 1999)★★★.

Nas

b. Nasir Jones, 14 September 1973, Long Island, New York, USA. From the tough Queensbridge housing projects which brought the world Marley Marl, MC Shan and Intelligent

Hoodlum, Nas made his name as a highly skilled rapper with the double whammy of 1994's *Illmatic* and 1996's *It Was Written*, albums whose music was crafted with a degree of subtlety and forethought often absent from the genre. Jones was heavily influenced by his jazz-playing father, and started rapping at the age of nine, graduating to a crew entitled the Devastatin' Seven in the mid-80s. He met Main Source producer Large Professor in 1989, in the course of recording his first demo tape. The producer introduced him to the crew, leading to his debut on Main Source's 1991 collection *Breaking Atoms*, guesting on the cut 'Live At The Barbeque', where he was part of a skilled chorus line, alongside Large Professor and Akinyele. Though he was widely applauded for his contribution he failed to build on the impact, drifting through life and becoming disillusioned by the death of his best friend Will, and the shooting of his brother. He may well have stayed on the outside of the hip-hop game had not MC Serch (Nas had guested on his 'Back To The Grill') hired him to provide a solo track for the soundtrack to 1992's *Zebrahead*. 'Half Time', again recorded with the Large Professor, was the result. A debut album followed, with contributions from the cream of New York's producers: DJ Premier (Gang Starr), Pete Rock and Q-Tip (A Tribe Called Quest). A hefty unit for which Columbia Records were happy to pay the bill, judging Nas to be their priority rap act for 1994. Nas, who had by now dropped his 'Nasty' prefix, honed a rapping style that was at once flamboyant, but with a lyrical armoury that far surpassed the expected humdrum 'bitches and ho's' routines. Serch, now A&R head of Wild Pitch Records, once declared Nas: 'Pound for pound, note for note, word for word, the best MC I ever heard in my life'. There was now evidence to suggest he may have been correct. Commercial success followed when Nas' sophomore collection, *It Was Written*, debuted at number 1 on the *Billboard* album chart in July 1996. In 1997, he collaborated with Foxy Brown, AZ and Dr. Dre on the 'supergroup' project, the Firm. Although it demonstrated signs of a creative impasse, *I Am ...* , which revealed the new Nas Escobar alias, showed no sign of his commercial popularity having diminished when it debuted at US number 1 in April 1999. His quality control standards dipped alarmingly on the half-baked follow-up *Nastradamus*, released the same November.

● ALBUMS: *Illmatic* (Columbia 1994)★★★★, *It Was Written* (Columbia 1996)★★★, *I Am ...* (Columbia 1999)★★★, *Nastradamus* (Columbia 1999)★★.

● FILMS: *Rhyme & Reason* (1997), *Belly* (1998), *In Too Deep* (1999).

Naughty By Nature

The New Jersey, USA-based trio of MC Treach (b. Anthony Criss, 27 December 1970, East Orange, New Jersey, USA), Vinnie (b. Vincent Brown, 17 September 1970, East Orange, New Jersey, USA) and DJ Kay Gee (b. Keir Gist, 15 September 1969, East Orange, New Jersey, USA) are a rap troupe utilizing the funkier rather than darker aspects of gangsta hip-hop. Heavily influenced by the patronage of Queen Latifah, the language was blue but not always in the overtly sexual sense. 'Ghetto Bastard', for example, was a master stroke, pickled in the atmosphere of the street and exact in its execution of ghetto vernacular. Unlike many other hardcore outfits, Naughty By Nature were not afraid of injecting a touch of soul into the mix (once more, *à la* Queen Latifah), which makes the best of their work all the more

endearing. They gave Tommy Boy Records their biggest ever hit with the 12-inch 'O.P.P.', the largest-grossing authentic rap single in the USA in 1990, selling over a million copies ('O.P.P.' stands for 'Other People's Pussy', though that did not prevent several generations enthusiastically singing along to 'I'm down with O.P.P.', making the record an American equivalent to the Shamen's notorious 'Ebeneezer Goode'). A second album upped the sleaze factor with some lyrics, but still maintained the crew's best traditions elsewhere. The single lifted from *19NaughtyIII*, 'Hip Hop Hooray', became another US Top 10 hit, helped in no small part by a Spike Lee-filmed video. Treach himself was to be found in Houston acting in the movie *Jason's Lyric*, though he had appeared previously in the widely ridiculed *The Meteor Man*. He has written his own film treatments, in-between bungee jumping sessions in Daytona with future wife Pepa of Salt-N-Pepa. He also launched the Naughty Gear clothing line. Kay Gee, meanwhile, earned a production deal with Motown Records, initial fruit from which was characterized by Zhané's debut album and hit single, 'Hey Mr DJ'. *Poverty's Paradise* was a mature and coherent set that earned the trio critical plaudits and serious respect from fellow hip-hop artists. A subsequent recording hiatus was broken in 1999 by the trio's debut set for Arista Records, which featured the raucous Top 10 collaboration with Zhané, 'Jamboree'.

● ALBUMS: *Naughty By Nature* (Tommy Boy 1991)★★★, *19NaughtyIII* (Tommy Boy 1993)★★★★, *Poverty's Paradise* (Tommy Boy 1995)★★★★, *Nineteen Naughty Nine: Nature's Fury* (Arista 1999)★★★.

Ndegéocello, Meshell

b. 29 August 1969, Berlin, West Germany. Introduced by her PR machine as a female equivalent to Prince, Ndegéocello has embarked on a solo career that embraces both the hip-hop and R&B markets. Like Prince, she is a multi-instrumentalist, and writes, produces and plays on all her songs. Her name is Swahili, meaning 'free like a bird'. After a nomadic life as the child of a US forces man, her first love was art rather than the jazz skills of her father and brother. Much of her youth was spent in Washington's 'go-go' scene, where at one point she was actually shot at while on stage with Little Bennie and the Masters, at the Cherry Atlantic Skating Rink. Her interest in music blossomed when her brother started playing guitar in a local band; when the bass player left his instrument lying around after rehearsal, Ndegéocello was a quick convert. At the age of 19, she left for New York 'with my baby and my bass'. There she joined Living Colour's Black Rock Coalition, and recorded sessions for artists of the calibre of Caron Wheeler and Steve Coleman. She was the musical director for Arrested Development's *Saturday Night Live* appearance, though her own demos attracted little response. Madonna subsequently stepped in, inviting her to become one of the first artists signed to her Maverick empire. A palpable maturity was revealed on her 1993 debut, with a combination of acid jazz and R&B rhythms backing her beat poetry and sexually ambiguous stance. She gained a breakthrough hit with 'If That's Your Boyfriend (He Wasn't Last Night)', a provocative post-feminist statement. Despite the sexual overtones of her packaging, she was not averse to strong political statements, with material such as 'Step Into The Projects' retaining a strong cutting edge, and lines such as 'The white man shall forever sleep with one eye open' (from 'Shoot'n Up And

Gett'n High') suggesting overtones of Public Enemy. The album was produced by Bob Power, alongside guests including DJ Premier and Geri Allen. Although she attracted some criticism for espousing the corporate rebellion angle, her connections with Maverick hardly passing unobserved, there was substance and fire in the best of her work. In 1994, she had a US Top 3 hit with 'Wild Night' a duet with John Mellencamp. Her sophomore album, *Peace Beyond Passion*, was a less effective attempt at 70s-style retro-funk. A more effective change in style was apparent on 1999's *Bitter*, with the stripped down sound complementing Ndegéocello's highly introspective lyrics.

● ALBUMS: *Plantation Lullabies* (Maverick/Sire 1993)★★★★, *Peace Beyond Passion* (Maverick 1996)★★★, *Bitter* (Maverick 1999)★★★.

Nectarine No.9

Formed in Edinburgh, Scotland, in 1993, Nectarine No.9 revolves around guitarist and vocalist Davey Henderson, an ex-member of both the Fire Engines and Win. Alan Horne, founder of Postcard Records, took great interest in both bands and Henderson's newest venture was one of his first signings on reactivating the label. *The Nectarine No.9* reinstated Henderson's love of abrasive pop and quirky rhythms, inhabiting a musical world that was part-T. Rex and part-Fall. However, it lacked the focus of Henderson's previous work and critical reaction was muted. *Guitar Thieves*, which collected various BBC Radio 1 sessions, included versions of Captain Beefheart's 'Frownland' and the Velvet Underground's 'Inside Of Your Heart', as well as an original song, 'Pull My Daisy', the title of which was drawn from a movie featuring Allen Ginsberg and Jack Kerouac. In 1997, the band backed former Clash associate Jock Scott on his spoken-word release, *My Personal Culloden*. The Creeping Bent compilation was an effective reminder of Henderson's enduring presence on the margins of the UK music scene.

● ALBUMS: *The Nectarine No.9* (Postcard 1993)★★, *Guitar Thieves* (Nightracks/Postcard 1994)★★★, *Saint Jack* (Postcard 1995)★★★.

● COMPILATIONS: *It's Just The Way Things Are Joe, It's Just The Way Things Are* (Creeping Bent 1999)★★★.

Ned's Atomic Dustbin

Formed in Stourbrige, West Midlands, England in 1988 by local characters Jonn Penney (b. 17 September 1968, Quarry Bank, West Midlands, England; lead vocals), Rat (b. Garath Pring, 8 November 1970, Sedgley, West Midlands, England; guitar), Matt Cheslin (b. 28 November 1970, Quarry Bank, West Midlands, England; bass), Alex Griffin (b. 29 August 1971, Kingswinford, West Midlands, England; bass) and Dan Warton (b. 28 July 1972, Sedgley, West Midlands, England; drums). After dubious gothic beginnings, Ned's Atomic Dustbin began to find their feet in 1989 with the establishment of their own Furtive Records label and a series of tour supports, notably with regional contemporaries the Wonderstuff. Notable for having two bass players, uniformly crimped hair and an unequivocally daft name (taken from BBC Radio's *The Goon Show*), the band's urgent, aggressive sub-hardcore sound still managed to offset any gimmicky connotations, turning a potential freak show into a challenging pop act. Armed with a multitude of original merchandising ideas - within three years the band produced 86 different T-shirt designs - their 'Kill Your Television' single (on the Chapter 22 label) entered the UK Top 60 and resulted

in a major contract with Sony Music. With the financial wherewithal to back their imagination, Ned's Atomic Dustbin soon translated their ideas into a phenomenal commercial success, peaking when *God Fodder* entered the UK charts at number four in 1991. The rest of the year was filled by hectic touring commitments, with America followed by Japan, a prestigious spot at the British Reading Festival, a UK Top 20 hit with 'Happy', back to America (with Jesus Jones) and then a British tour which resulted in singer Penney collapsing from exhaustion on the last night. *Are You Normal?*, with production by Nirvana-collaborator Andy Wallace, was a disappointing album despite featuring another UK Top 20 hit, 'Not Sleeping Around'. Following a lengthy period out of the spotlight, the band returned with their best album to date, *Brainbloodvolume*, but its lack of success in a vastly changed music scene led to their demise in August 1995.

● ALBUMS: *God Fodder* (Columbia 1991)★★★, *Are You Normal?* (Chaos/Columbia 1992)★★, *Brainbloodvolume* (Work/Furtive 1995)★★★.

● COMPILATIONS: *Bite* (Chapter 22 1991)★★★, *0.522* (Sony 1994)★★.

● VIDEOS: *Nothing Is Cool* (Sony Music Video 1991), *Lunatic Magnets* (Sony/Furtive 1992).

Nelson, Shara

b. London, England. Nelson, formerly vocalist for Massive Attack on their groundbreaking *Blue Lines*, began her solo career in July 1993 with the UK Top 20 hit 'Down That Road'. The single was released on Cooltempo Records after Nelson had returned to London from Bristol. Both Paul Oakenfold and Steve Osbourne were involved in remixing the single, which marketed her as the 'new Aretha Franklin'. She readily admitted to her Motown Records influences, and the arrangements on her debut album were sumptuous affairs, with heaped strings and gushing choruses. However, she did not desert her dance/hip-hop roots entirely, with co-writing credits for Prince Be of P.M. Dawn ('Down That Road'), Adrian Sherwood (the title track) and Saint Etienne ('One Goodbye In Ten') offering a good balance. The latter track was the second single to be taken from the album. *What Silence Knows*' commercial performance was something of a breakthrough for British R&B, and it was among the nominations for 1994's Mercury Music Prize and two categories in the BRIT Awards. In 1995, *Friendly Fire* firmly established her as an international soul artist, a fact at least partly attributable to Nelson's ability to write lyrics of much greater depth than is generally associated with the genre. The production assistance of Tim Simenon (Bomb The Bass) and Mike Pedan (ex-Chimes) and musicianship of Skip McDonald, Pressure Drop, Ashley Beadle and the ubiquitous Jah Wobble also contributed greatly to an exemplary collection of cool, resonant soul songs that sadly failed to find an audience. In 1998, Nelson was born again as a house diva, featuring on Presence's minor hit single, 'Sense Of Danger'.

● ALBUMS: *What Silence Knows* (Cooltempo/Chrysalis 1993)★★★, *Friendly Fire* (Cooltempo 1995)★★★★.

Neutral Milk Hotel

The creation of singer-songwriter Jeff Magnum, Neutral Milk Hotel forms part of the loose knit Elephant 6 Recording Company collective of psych pop bands based in Athens,

Georgia, USA. Magnum grew up in Ruston, Louisiana with fellow 60s enthusiasts Will Cullen Hart, Bill Doss and Robert Schneider, playing in various bands including Maggot and Cranberry Life Cycle. In 1990, Magnum relocated to Athens with Doss and Hart where they formed the Synthetic Flying Machine, which in turn evolved into the Olivia Tremor Control. Magnum appeared on that band's debut *California Demise* EP before moving to Seattle, where he recorded 'Everything Is'/'Snow Song Pt. One' and *The Amazing Phantom Third Channel* EP for Cher Doll Records. Magnum continued to perform live and record with other members of the Elephant 6 Recording Company before relocating to Denver to record his debut album with the aid of Schneider, now the leader of Apples In Stereo. *On Avery Island*'s folk-style melodies and lo-fi production provided the perfect accompaniment for Magnum's strident vocals and esoteric lyrics. Schneider also helped out on *In The Aeroplane Over The Sea*, which again eschewed the sunshine psych pop harmonies of Magnum's Elephant 6 colleagues for a more personal exploration of the possibilities of four-track recording.
● ALBUMS: *On Avery Island* (Merge/Fire 1996)★★★, *In The Aeroplane Over The Sea* (Merge/Blue Rose 1998)★★★★.

Nevins, Jason
b. New York City, New York, USA. A top New York producer/remixer of the 90s, whose first involvement with music was at his college radio station at Arizona State University, where his sets were primarily composed of techno material. He went on to release product as Plastick Project, Crazee Tunes, the Experience and Jason Nevins Movement. 'The Viper Rooms', licensed to Loaded Records, a UK record label in Brighton, Sussex, England, was typical of his output, being completely unabashed in its use of samples. He has since recorded for Nervous Records, Logic Records, Strictly Rhythm Records and Tribal, and recorded a full-length CD in 1995. He has also remixed Ann Consuelo for Champion Records. His 1998 remix of Run DMC's 'It's Like That', credited to Run DMC vs Jason Nevins, was an unexpected international hit, although Nevins only received a one-off payment of $5000 for his pains. It was followed by further remixes of classic 80s tracks such as 'It's Tricky' (Run DMC), 'Mickey' (Tony Basil), and 'Der Kommissar' (Falco).

New Bomb Turks
A loud but melodious US alternative punk band, New Bomb Turks' manifesto was to rid their genre of its more dour concerns, re-establishing the sheer adrenaline rush and hedonism of the music. They met while studying at Ohio State University, where each of the members - Eric Davidson (vocals), Jim Weber (guitar), Matt Reber (bass) and Bill Randt (drums) - read English. They first worked together as disc jockeys on campus radio station WSOR, gradually pulling together as a band and making their debut through a series of limited-issue 7-inch singles on the Datapanik label. It was with their 1992 debut album, however, that their arrival was recognized, with *Maximum Rock 'n' Roll* magazine calling it the 'album of the year, maybe of the last five years'. In its wake, New Bomb Turks sagged under the expectations of such hysterical praise, taking their time before preparing a follow-up set, then blasting through the recording sessions to produce *Information Highway Revisited* in just 60 hours. It was a recording that retained their spontaneity and estab-

lished them as qualitative peers of Green Day and the Offspring, even if its sales profile was dwarfed by the success of those bands. *Pissing Out The Poison* reminded fans of their early days, being a double album comprising singles for labels including Sympathy For The Record Industry, eMpTy, Get Hip, Demo Derby, Bag Of Hammers and Damaged Goods, plus cover versions of material by the New York Dolls and Hawkwind. The subsequent *Scared Straight* and *At Rope's End* retained all of the band's sleazy punk charm but were promoted to a wider audience thanks to a new deal with Epitaph Records.
● ALBUMS: *!!Destroy-Oh-Boy!!* (Crypt 1992)★★★, *Drunk On Cock* mini-album (Engine 1993)★★★★, *Information Highway Revisited* (Crypt 1994)★★★, *Scared Straight* (Epitaph 1996)★★★★, *At Rope's End* (Epitaph 1998)★★★.
● COMPILATIONS: *Pissing Out The Poison* (Crypt 1995)★★★, *The Big Combo: More Singles And Other Swill 1994-98* (Drop Kick 1999)★★★.

New Fast Automatic Daffodils
Manchester, England-based indie band (often referred to as the New FADS) whose arrival in 1989 coincided with their city's descent into rave culture and an upswing in the fortunes of 'baggy' bands such as the Stone Roses and Happy Mondays. From their debut at the Manchester Polytechnic Poetry Society in 1988, they were described in one quarter as resembling 'a team of sex psychologists at a mass orgy'. The band, Andy Spearpoint (vocals), Justin Crawford (bass), Dolan Hewison (guitar), Perry Saunders (drums) and Icarus Wilson-Wright (percussion), signed to Belgian label Play It Again Sam in 1989. Among their early singles, 'Big' and the caustic but wry *Music Is Shit* EP gained most prominence. 'Get Better' was remixed by Joy Division producer Martin Hannett, before a second album, *Body Exit Mind*, was recorded with Craig Leon producing. Their literate exposition of post-punk pop won them many friends in the media, though record sales failed to translate into chart placings outside the 'independent' sector. By the time of 1994's *Love It All* they had begun to lose this critical support, but by all accounts the band remained unperturbed by this fickleness. Crawford subsequently worked on his Only Child side-project while the band took a break from the music scene.
● ALBUMS: *Pigeonhole* (Play It Again Sam/Mute 1990)★★★, *The Peel Sessions* (Strange Fruit/Dutch East India Trading 1991)★★, *Body Exit Mind* (Mute/Elektra 1992)★★★, *Love It All* (Play It Again Sam 1994)★★★.
● VIDEOS: *Wake Up And Make Love Before 8:30 In The Morning* (1993).

New Radicals
Originally formed as a loose collective of musicians, the driving force behind New Radicals was multi-instrumentalist Gregg Alexander (b. 1972, Gross Point, Michigan, USA). His earliest exposure to music included being taught the chords to the Who's 'My Generation' and then rearranging them to create his own songs. Always a rebel, Alexander was soon sneaking into Detroit's house and punk clubs and listening to R&B. At the age of 15, he bought a four-track tape recorder and began distributing home-made demos at school. By the time he was 17, Alexander was living in California and had released his 1989 debut *Michigan Rain* under his own name. Three years later, he released the equally obscure follow-up *Intoxifornication*. Alexander continued a lifestyle of wanderlust that found him criss-crossing America 12 times and

living in London, all the while clubbing extensively and experiencing a life of drugs and debauchery. After settling in New York City and busking in Central Park and Tompkins Square Park, Alexander started to assemble a band of musicians that he had met through his travels, including television actress Danielle Brisebois. The New Radicals was the result and, in October 1998, they released *Maybe You've Been Brainwashed Too*. An uplifting combination of sweeping melodies, aggressive harmonies and large dollops of stream-of-consciousness soul, the album was a vehicle for Alexander to rail against the corporate driven mindset of popular culture à la Chumbawamba minus the left-wing politics. Using a voice that veered between World Party's Karl Wallinger's husky rasp and Smashing Pumpkins' Billy Corgan's nasal whine, Alexander and New Radicals played with an exuberance reminiscent of Style Council's breezier moments ('Mother We Just Can't Get Enough') and the blue-eyed soul side of Todd Rundgren ('In Need Of A Miracle'). Based on the success of the first single, the unremittingly uplifting 'You Get What You Give', New Radicals' debut album went gold in the USA. By the spring of 1999, the band's incessant touring had exhausted Alexander, who started cancelling dates including a UK tour. On 12 July 1999, Alexander announced that he was disbanding the New Radicals in order to pursue a songwriting and producing career. He planned to work with a number of artists including former bandmate Brisebois.

● ALBUMS: *Maybe You've Been Brainwashed Too* (MCA 1998)★★★★. Solo: Gregg Alexander *Michigan Rain* aka *Save Me From Myself* (A&M 1989)★★, *Intoxifornication* (Epic 1992)★★★.

Newman, 'Tall' Paul

b. 5 May 1971, London, England. Unlike Fat Tony, at 6 feet 6 inches, Paul Newman is certainly a DJ who fully deserves his moniker. His DJing career began at the age of 16 in 1987 when he was allowed behind the decks at his father's club, Turnmills in Farringdon, London. By 1990, his considerable skill was self-evident and he became resident at the ground-breaking gay night, Trade. Newman released his first recording, 'Love Rush', as a white label for Trade. Christened 'Tall' Paul by Hooj Choons' Red Jerry, they recorded 'Rock Da House' together. Re-released in 1997 on VC Recordings, the track reached number 11 in the UK singles chart. His increasingly high profile as an in-demand club DJ has led to remix work for artists including New Order, Stone Roses, East 17, Erasure, Human League, Marc Almond, Wildchild, Dario G., Duran Duran, Nalin And Kane, Blondie and Bizarre Inc. Newman has mixed many compilation albums, including those for the label Fantazia, Cream (*Anthems* with Seb Fontaine) and the Ministry Of Sound (*Dance Nation Six* with Brandon Block). He tours as a DJ in countries such as the USA and Japan but still makes regular appearances at UK clubs such as The Gallery, Gatecrasher, Godskitchen, Progress, Sundissential, Cream, and The Sanctuary. His DJing style is versatile: he can move from the more obviously 'up-front' vocal house, through hard house, to trance-inflected material. He has also had success with his own singles, especially as Camisra, with 'Let Me Show You', a massive club hit that entered the national UK charts at number 5, and 'Feel The Beat'. Newman remains highly popular as a DJ but his entrepreneurial skills have led to the building of his own studio and the establishing of a record label, Duty

Free Recordings. The single releases on the label, including those by Robbie Rivera and Radical Playaz, have been well received by the critics. Newman also hosts a show on UK radio station Kiss 100 FM with Fontaine. His achievements were officially recognized in 1998 when he won the Ericsson *Muzik* Dance Award for Best UK DJ.

● COMPILATIONS: with Seb Fontaine *Cream Anthems* (Virgin 1998)★★★★, with Brandon Block *Dance Nation 6* (MOS 1999)★★★★, with Judge Jules *The Ibiza Annual* (MOS 1999)★★★, with Judge Jules *The Annual - Millennium Edition* (MOS 1999)★★★.

Next

Minneapolis, Minnesota, USA-based hip-hop/R&B fusioneers Next were formed in 1992 by brothers T-Low (b. Terrance Brown, 7 June 1974, USA) and Tweety (b. Raphael Brown, 28 January 1976, USA) alongside friend R.L. (b. Robert Lavelle Huggar, 2 April 1977, USA). T-Low's godmother Ann Nesby took the outfit in hand, training and managing them during their first years. They secured their first breakthrough in 1994 when a home-town show was watched by Prof. T and Lance of Low Key? They brought the group to Jimmy Jam And Terry Lewis' Flyte Tyme Studio in Minneapolis. The resulting demo tape caught the attention of Kay Gee (Naughty By Nature), who saw Next as the perfect act to spearhead his new Arista Records-financed label, Divine Mill. The completed album featured collaborations with Naughty By Nature and Adina Howard, among others. A degree of critical carping ensued over the innuendo-saturated lyrics on display. Despite this, the trio saw the first single to be taken from the album, 'Butta Love', become a million-seller, peaking at number 16 in December 1997. The trio subsequently appeared on television shows including *Soul Train*, *Ricki Lake* and *Vibe* as their popularity soared. The follow-up, 'Too Close', topped the *Billboard* Hot 100 in April 1998 as they joined Mary J. Blige and Usher on tour and gained rave reviews for their polished live performances (particularly their dancing talents). 'I Still Love You' climbed to US number 14 in October.

● ALBUMS: *Rated Next* (Divine Mill/Arista 1998)★★★.

Nicolette

b. Nicolette Suwoton, Glasgow, Scotland. Raised in Nigeria, France, Switzerland and Wales, Nicolette joined her first band, Calliope, in Cardiff, but originally rose to prominence as singer on the sample-based house hits of Shut Up And Dance in the early 90s. Their first female signing, her approach to singing was more blues-based and less shrill than many of the garage divas. She also wrote her own songs, demonstrating a keen talent on singles such as 'Wicked Mathematics'. Other collaborations with the Shut Up And Dance duo, such as 'I Woke Up' and 'Dove Song', are regarded by many as forerunners of the jungle and drum 'n' bass sound. Later she toured with Massive Attack, featuring on 1994's *Protection*, before signing a solo deal with Talkin' Loud Records. Her second album featured more political material such as the single 'No Government'. She was aided by some of the cream of the UK production teams, including 4 Hero and Plaid. In 1997, she released *DJ-Kicks!*, a compilation of her favourite club tracks mixed together by Plaid.

● ALBUMS: *Now Is Early* (Shut Up And Dance 1992)★★★, *Let No-One Live Rent Free In Your Head* (Talkin' Loud 1996)★★★.

● COMPILATIONS: various artists *DJ-Kicks!* (Studio !K7 1997)★★★.

Nightcrawlers

The Nightcrawlers are a cover organization for the activities of house producer John Reid (b. Glasgow, Scotland). As he summarizes it, 'I see us as a collective of people and I'm the mouthpiece and the driving force behind it.' The Nightcrawlers' first single was 'Living Inside A Dream', but that failed to ignite significant interest. Much more successful was the subsequent effort, 'Push The Feeling On'. This became a major club success but had to be released three times before becoming a pop hit. Originally issued in 1993, it reached the UK Top 30 in October 1994 and number 3 the following March. Previously Reid had been involved in several successful musical projects. After being dropped from his original contract with Island Records, Reid had been contacted by producer/writer Ian Levine and asked whether he would be prepared to write songs for him. The results included 'Whenever You Need Someone' for Bad Boys Inc., his first major hit, and material for Eternal, Gemini and Optimystic. The Nightcrawlers' follow-ups to 'Push The Feeling On', including 'Surrender Your Love', 'Don't Let The Feeling Go', 'Let's Push It' and 'Keep On Pushing Our Love' (featuring Alysha Warren), repeated the formula with steadily diminishing returns, although they were all big club hits.

● ALBUMS: *Let's Push It* (Final Vinyl 1995)★★★, *The 12 Inch Remixes* (Arista 1996)★★★.

Nightmares On Wax

Based in Leeds, England, Nightmares On Wax began as a duo of George Evelyn (DJ EASE) and Kevin Harper. In the early 80s, Evelyn spent time breakdancing with the Soul City Rockers, alongside future members of Unique 3, and as Nightmares On Wax he began DJing with Harper at parties and then clubs in the mid-80s. At they same time they recorded three tracks, 'Let It Roll', 'Stating A Fact' and 'Dextrous', which they consequently sent out as a demo to various record companies in the UK and New York. Having been turned down, they released 'Let It Roll' on their own Positive Records which went on to sell 2,000 copies. In the meantime, they had met Steve Beckett who asked them to join Warp Records, who made 'Dextrous' their second release in 1989. Together with the work of acts such as LFO, Unique 3 and the Forgemasters, this track and 'Aftermath' (a UK Top 40 hit in 1990) helped to create the sound known as bleep. 'Aftermath' was unique in that its rhythms, although built on a solid four-on-the-floor foundation, sound like an embryonic drum 'n' bass track. Their next release, 'A Case Of Funk' (1991), was a successful club hit. According to many, their debut *A Word Of Science* created a blueprint for the trip-hop movement of the 90s as it merged funk and hip-hop rhythms with stark electronics, but at the time of its release it seemed to confuse those who had eagerly consumed their straight dance music singles. Subsequent releases, including 'Set Me Free' and 'Happiness', continued to gain critical applause. In 1992, Harper left to concentrate on his career as a DJ. Evelyn spent several years collecting samples, recording demos and co-running the club Headz in Leeds and released a few jazzy house tracks on the Warp subsidiary Nucleus. He eventually made his comeback as Nightmares On Wax in 1995 with the album *Smoker's Delight*, on which he worked with a guitarist, bass player, keyboard-player, rapper and singer. This low-tempoed abstract hip-hop album took in a broad range of influences, including funk, soul, jazz and dub, and even touched on country music. The following year Evelyn released 'Still Smokin'' and in 1997 remixed Omar's 'Sayin' Nothin''. He returned to the studio for 1999's *Carboot Soul*, another highly enjoyable and eclectic collection of warped electronica.

● ALBUMS: *A Word Of Science* (Warp 1991)★★★★, *Smoker's Delight* (Warp 1995)★★★★, *Carboot Soul* (Warp 1999)★★★.

Nine Inch Nails

Trent Reznor (b. 17 May 1965, Mercer, Pennsylvania, USA), the multi-instrumentalist, vocalist, and creative force behind Nine Inch Nails, trained as a classical pianist during his small-town Pennsylvania childhood, but his discovery of rock and early industrial bands, despite his dislike of the 'industrial' tag, changed his musical direction completely. Following a period working in a Cleveland recording studio and playing in local bands, Reznor began recording as Nine Inch Nails in 1988. The dark, atmospheric *Pretty Hate Machine*, written, played and co-produced by Reznor, was largely synthesizer-based, but the material was transformed onstage by a ferocious wall of guitars, and show-stealing Lollapalooza performances in 1991. Coupled with a major US radio hit with 'Head Like A Hole', it brought platinum status. Inspired by the live band, Reznor added an abrasive guitar barrage to the Nine Inch Nails sound for the *Broken* EP (a subsequent remix set was titled *Fixed*), which hit the US Top 10, winning a Grammy for 'Wish'. 'Happiness In Slavery', however, courted controversy with an almost universally banned video, where performance artist Bob Flanagan gave himself up to be torn apart as slave to a machine, acting out the theme of control common to Reznor's lyrics. Reznor also filmed an unreleased full-length *Broken* video, which he said 'makes *Happiness In Slavery* look like a Disney movie'. By this time, Reznor had relocated to Los Angeles, building a studio in a rented house at 10050 Cielo Drive, which he later discovered was the scene of the Tate murders by the Manson family (much to his disgust, due to eternal interview questions thereafter about the contribution of the house's atmosphere to *The Downward Spiral*). Occupying the middle ground between the styles of previous releases, *The Downward Spiral*'s multi-layered blend of synthesizer textures and guitar fury provided a fascinating soundscape for Reznor's exploration of human degradation through sex, drugs, violence, depression and suicide, closing with personal emotional pain on 'Hurt': 'I hurt myself today, To see if I still feel, I focus on the pain, The only thing that's real'. *The Downward Spiral* made its US debut at number 2, and a return to live work with Robin Finck (guitar), Danny Lohneer (bass/guitar), James Woolley (keyboards) and Reznor's long-time friend and drummer Chris Vrenna drew floods of praise, with Nine Inch Nails being one of the most talked-about acts at the Woodstock anniversary show. The first non-Nine Inch Nails releases on Reznor's Nothing label appeared in 1994 (beginning with Marilyn Manson), and the band also found time to construct an acclaimed soundtrack for Oliver Stone's movie *Natural Born Killers*. Reznor also relocated to New Orleans. During 1996, Reznor worked with film director David Lynch on the music score for *Lost Highway*, and produced Manson's *Antichrist Superstar*. In 1998, he acted as executive producer on ex-Judas Priest singer Rob Halford's Two project. He returned to his own music in autumn 1999 with the acclaimed 2-CD set, *The Fragile*, which debuted at US number 1.

● ALBUMS: *Pretty Hate Machine* (TVT 1989)★★★, *Broken* mini-album (Nothing 1992)★★, *Fixed* mini-album (Nothing 1992)★★, *The Downward Spiral* (Nothing 1994)★★★★, *Further Down The Spiral* remix mini-album (Island 1995)★★★, *The Fragile* (Nothing/Island 1999)★★★★.

● VIDEOS: *Closure* (Interscope Video 1997).

● FURTHER READING: *Nine Inch Nails*, Martin Huxley.

911

One of the most popular of the post-Take That boy bands, this UK trio comprises Jimmy Constable (b. 21 September 1973, Liverpool, England), Simon 'Spike' Dawbarn (b. 15 August 1974, Manchester, England) and Lee Brennan (b. 27 September 1975, Carlisle, England). Constable and Dawbarn first met as dancers on the late-night television show *The Hitman And Her*. With the addition of Brennan they formed 911 in 1995, and steadily built up a loyal fanbase in the north of England. The trio's initial releases came out on independent label Ginga Recordings, founded by their manager and A&R man Steve Gilmour, in partnership with Frank Shapiro. Their debut single, a cover version of the old Shalamar hit 'Night To Remember', sold 9,000 copies and reached number 38 on the national singles chart in April 1996. The follow-up single, 'Love Sensation', also sold strongly, reaching number 21 in July 1996. By the time 'Don't Make Me Wait' broke into the Top 10, the trio had signed with Virgin Records. A string of hit singles, 'The Day We Find Love' (number 4), 'Bodyshaking' (number 3) and 'The Journey' (number 3), quickly established the trio as one of the most successful of the new wave of boy bands. Their debut album was released in February 1997, reaching number 13 on the UK chart, but was overshadowed by their phenomenal success in the Far East. In Malaysia, *The Journey* topped the album chart for 20 weeks. 'Party People ... Friday Night', the first single from the band's second album, reached number 5 in October 1997. 'All I Want Is You' (number 4, March 1998) and 'How Do You Want Me To Love You?' (number 2, July 1998) continued the band's run of Top 10 hits. *Moving On* debuted at number 10 in the UK album chart in July 1998, and featured a highly commercial production courtesy of several top pop producers, including Jon Douglas (George Michael, All Saints) and Chris Porter (Gary Barlow). A cover version of the Tavares' 'More Than A Woman' reached number 2 in October 1998. The following January they went one better, when their version of Dr. Hook's 'A Little Bit More' topped the charts. *There It Is*, an album of cover versions including Rick Astley's 'Never Gonna Give You Up', Heatwave's 'Boogie Nights' and Style Council's 'You're The Best Thing', debuted at number 8 in January 1999. 'Private Number' continued their run of hit singles when it reached number 3 in May. 'Wonderland', taken from the 'best of' compilation, was a rare failure when it fell outside the Top 10 in October.

● ALBUMS: *The Journey* (Virgin 1997)★★★, *Moving On* (Virgin 1998)★★★, *There It Is* (Virgin 1999)★★.

● COMPILATIONS: *The Greatest Hits And A Little Bit More* (Virgin 1999)★★★.

● VIDEOS: *The Journey So Far ...* (Virgin 1997).

98°

An Ohio-based soul outfit featuring brothers Drew (b. 8 August 1976, Cincinnati, Ohio, USA) and Nick Lachey (b. 9 November 1973, Harlan, Kentucky, USA), as well as Jeff Timmons (b. 30 April 1973, Canton, Ohio, USA) and Justin Jeffre (b. 25 February 1973, Mount Clemens, Michigan, USA), 98° are four white men attempting to bridge the R&B/pop divide in a similar manner to the Backstreet Boys or stablemates Boyz II Men. They were discovered backstage by manager Paris D'Jon at a Boyz II Men performance, while attempting to hawk their demo tape. Their debut album featured the US Top 20 hit single 'Invisible Man', which achieved gold status. The follow-up collection, *98 ° And Rising*, was a superior collection of up-tempo dance numbers and soulful R&B ballads, with just enough character to distinguish the quartet in an overcrowded market. Among the producers were Pras of the Fugees and the Trackmasterz. Although 'Because Of You' and 'The Hardest Thing' were both US Top 10 hits, the keynote songs on the album were 'True To Your Heart', a collaboration with Stevie Wonder featured in the Walt Disney movie *Mulan*, and 'Fly With Me', which used extensive samples from Abba's 'Dancing Queen'. A pleasant if unremarkable Christmas album followed in October 1999.

● ALBUMS: *98°* (Motown 1997)★★★, *98° And Rising* (Motown 1998)★★★, *This Christmas* (Motown 1999)★★★.

● VIDEOS: *Heat It Up* (Universal 1999).

Nirvana

Formed in Aberdeen, Washington, USA, in 1988, the Nirvana that the MTV generation came to love comprised Kurt Cobain (b. Kurt Donald Cobain, 20 February 1967, Hoquiam, Washington, USA, d. 5 April 1994, Seattle, Washington, USA; guitar/vocals), Krist Novoselic (b. 16 May 1965, Croatia, Yugoslavia; bass) and Dave Grohl (b. 14 January 1969, Warren, Ohio, USA; drums). Grohl was 'something like our sixth drummer', explained Cobain, and had been recruited from east coast band Dain Bramage, having previously played with Scream, who recorded for Minor Threat's influential Dischord Records label. Their original drummer was Chad Channing; at one point Dinosaur Jr's J. Mascis had been touted as a permanent fixture, along with Dan Peters from Mudhoney. Having been signed by the Seattle-based Sub Pop Records, the trio completed their debut single, 'Love Buzz'/'Big Cheese', the former a song written and first recorded by 70s Dutch act Shocking Blue. Second guitarist Jason Everman was then added prior to *Bleach*, which cost a meagre $600 to record. Though he was pictured on the cover, he played no part in the actual recording (going on to join Mindfunk, via Soundgarden and Skunk). The set confirmed Nirvana's ability to match heavy riffs with melody and it quickly attracted a cult following. However, Channing left the band following a European tour, and as a likely replacement proved hard to find, Dan Peters from labelmates Mudhoney stepped in on a temporary basis. He was featured on the single 'Sliver', Nirvana's sole 1990 release. New drummer David Grohl reaffirmed a sense of stability. The revamped trio secured a prestigious contract with Geffen Records, whose faith was rewarded with *Nevermind*, which broke the band worldwide. This was a startling collection of songs that transcended structural boundaries, notably the distinctive slow verse/fast chorus format, and almost single-handedly brought the 'grunge' subculture overground. It topped the US charts early in 1992, eclipsing much-vaunted competition from Michael Jackson and Dire Straits and topped many Album Of The Year polls. The opening track, 'Smells Like Teen Spirit', reached the US and UK Top 10, further confirmation that Nirvana now combined critical and popular acclaim. In February 1992, the romance of Cobain and Courtney Love of Hole was sealed when the couple married (Love giving birth to a daughter, Frances Bean). It was already obvious, however, that Cobain was struggling with his new role as 'spokesman for a generation'. The first big story to break concerned an article in *Vanity Fayre* that alleged Love had taken heroin while pregnant; this saw the state intercede on the child's behalf by not allowing the Cobains alone with the child during its first month. Press interviews ruminated on the difficulties experienced in recording a follow-up album, and also revealed Cobain's use of a variety of drugs in order to stem the pain arising from a stomach complaint. The recording of *In Utero*, produced by Big Black/Rapeman alumnus Steve Albini, was not without difficulties. Rumours circulated concerning confrontations with both Albini and record company Geffen over the 'lo-fi' production. When the record was finally released, the effect was not as immediate as *Nevermind*, although Cobain's songwriting remained inspired on 'Penny Royal Tea', 'All Apologies' and the evocative 'Rape Me'. His descent into self-destruction accelerated in 1994, however, as he went into a coma during dates in Italy (it was later confirmed that this had all the markings of a failed suicide attempt), before returning to Seattle to shoot himself on 5 April 1994. The wake conducted in the press was matched by public demonstrations of affection and loss, which included suspected copycat suicides. The release of *MTV Unplugged In New York* offered some small comfort for Cobain's fans, with the singer's understated, aching delivery on a variety of cover versions and Nirvana standards enduring as one of the most emotive sights and sounds of the 90s. Grohl formed the excellent Foo Fighters, alongside ex-Germs guitarist Pat Smear (who had added second guitar to previous touring engagements and the band's *MTV Unplugged* appearance), following press rumours that Grohl would be working with Pearl Jam (much to Courtney Love's chagrin) or Tom Petty. Novoselic formed Sweet 75 early in 1997.

● ALBUMS: *Bleach* (Sub Pop 1989)★★★, *Nevermind* (Geffen 1991)★★★★★, *In Utero* (Geffen 1993)★★★★, *MTV Unplugged In New York* (Geffen 1994)★★★★.

● COMPILATIONS: *Incesticide* (Geffen 1992)★★★, *Singles* (Geffen 1995)★★★★, *From The Muddy Banks Of The Wishkah* (Geffen 1996)★★★★.

● VIDEOS: *Live! Tonight! Sold Out!!* (Geffen 1994), *Teen Spirit: The Tribute To Kurt Cobain* (Labyrinth 1996).

● FURTHER READING: *Route 666: On The Road To Nirvana*, Gina Arnold. *Nirvana And The Sound Of Seattle*, Brad Morrell. *Come As You Are*, Michael Azerrad. *Nirvana: An Illustrated Biography*, Suzi Black. *Nirvana: Tribute*, Suzi Black. *Never Fade Away*, Dave Thompson. *Kurt Cobain*, Christopher Sandford. *Teen Spirit: The Stories Behind Every Nirvana Song*, Chuck Crisafulli. *Nirvana: Nevermind*, Susan Wilson. *Who Killed Kurt Cobain?*, Ian Halperin and Max Wallace. *The Nirvana Companion*, John Rocco. *The Cobain Dossier*, Martin Clarke and Paul Woods (ed.).

● FILMS: *Kurt & Courtney* (1998).

No Doubt

This Orange County, California, USA-based outfit, comprising Gwen Stefani (b. 3 October 1969, Fullerton, California, USA; vocals), Tom Dumont (b. 11 January 1968, Los Angeles, California, USA; guitar), Tony Kanal (b. 27 August 1970, London, England; bass) and Adrian Young (b. 26 August 1969, Long Beach, California, USA; drums), took America by storm in 1996 following the release of their third album, *Tragic Kingdom*. Formed in December 1986 by Stefani's keyboard playing brother Eric, the band's original singer John Spence took his own life a year later. Kanal was part of the line-up by this point - Dumont joined in spring 1988 and Young a year later. The band signed a deal with Interscope Records in 1991. Their self-titled debut, released at the height of grunge's popularity, sold poorly and Eric Stefani left the band two years later to work as an animator. In 1995, the band self-released the excellent *The Beacon Street Collection*, featuring material recorded over the previous two years, while continuing to work on their second major label album. *Tragic Kingdom* was released in October, but sales only began to pick up when the single 'Just A Girl' broke into the Top 30 on the back of constant radio play. The band ended 1996 at a peak with their album spending nine weeks at the top of the US album chart, and the power ballad 'Don't Speak' all over the radio. As Gwen Stefani, very much the band's focal point, confirmed to the press, their mid-90s success had taken everyone by surprise: 'I can't believe it's happened to our loser band.' Others thought the reason had more to do with the 'fun punk' of Green Day, Presidents Of The United States Of America and Rancid, which had lifted the gloom of grunge and established an audience for less 'cerebral' or 'angst-ridden' rock music. In February 1997, the 'difficult' UK market was breached in spectacular style. During a promotional visit to the UK the band were rewarded with the news that 'Don't Speak' had entered the UK chart at number 1. A reissued 'Just A Girl' reached number 3 a few months later. Although a new album is not due until spring 2000, the highly photogenic and media friendly Stefani continues to keep the band's name in the spotlight.

● ALBUMS: *No Doubt* (Interscope 1992)★★★, *The Beacon Street Collection* (Beacon Street 1995)★★★★, *Tragic Kingdom* (Interscope 1995)★★★★.

● VIDEOS: *Live In The Tragic Kingdom* (Interscope 1997).

No Limit Records

(see Master P)

Noise Addict

Formed by the precociously talented Ben Lee, the aptly named Australian trio Noise Addict invoked immediate comparisons with their adolescent contemporaries Silverchair. Lee first came to the attention of both Thurston Moore of Sonic Youth and Mike D. of the Beastie Boys with his home-recorded single, 'I Wish I Was Him', a charming lo-fi tribute to Evan Dando of the Lemonheads. Mike D.'s Grand Royal label released the band's American debut, the *Young & Jaded* EP, which included the original version of 'I Wish I Was Him' alongside four new Lee originals and a cover version of Jonathan Richman's 'Back In Your Life'. The ramshackle *Def EP10* appeared on Moore's Ecstatic Peace! label, while *Noise Addict Vs Silverchair* was a reissue of the band's debut EP, *The*

Taste In My Eyes. The band expanded to a four-piece line-up for their debut album, *Meet The Real You*, which provided further evidence of Lee's talent, although there was little discernible improvement in the band's instrumental abilities. Lee then concentrated on a solo career. His 1995 debut, *Grandpaw Would*, was stronger (and better produced) than anything he had recorded with Noise Addict, with stand-out tracks including 'Away With The Pixies' and 'Trying To Sneeze'. In contrast, *Something To Remember Me By* and *Breathing Tornados* were flawed acoustic sets that saw Lee (still only in his late teens) attempting to broaden his songwriting, with mixed results.

● ALBUMS: *The Taste In My Eyes EP* reissued as *Noise Addict Vs Silverchair* (Fellaheen 1994)★★, *Young & Jaded EP* (Grand Royal 1994)★★★, *Def EP10* (Ecstatic Peace! 1994)★★, *Meet The Real You* (Fellaheen 1995)★★★.

Solo: Ben Lee *Grandpaw Would* (Fellaheen/Grand Royal 1995)★★★, *Something To Remember Me By* (Grand Royal 1996)★★★, *Breathing Tornados* (Grand Royal 1999)★★★.

Noreaga

b. Victor Santiago, Bronx, New York, USA. This hardcore rapper first began making waves as part of the Queens-based duo Capone-n-Noreaga (CNN) with Kiam 'Capone' Holley. The two men, who had both endured troubled upbringings in the New York projects, first met on kitchen duty at Collins Correctional Facility. When they were released they began rapping together and attempted to break into the music business. Their distinctive gangsta approach soon came to the attention of Martin Moore of Penalty Records, who signed the duo in 1996. The hardcore classic *The War Report* was released the following year, gaining strong reviews and sales of nearly half-a-million, but shortly before its release Holley was sent back to prison for parole violation. Santiago embarked on solo work while Holley served his three-year sentence. *N.O.R.E.* (Niggas On The Run Eating) featured production work by such noted names as L.E.S., Trackmasterz and the Neptunes, and guest appearances from rappers Nas, Busta Rhymes and Foxy Brown. The album, which reached US number 3 in August 1998, attracted praise for its hardcore authenticity and Noreaga's distinctive, stuttering rapping style, featuring his trademark 'What, What' signature. Stand-out tracks included the 'street' anthem 'Jump Off' and the Top 40 single 'SuperThug'. Noreaga adopted another pseudonym for his sophomore set, *Melvin Flynt – Da Hustler*, which debuted at US number 9 in September 1999. Featuring production work by the Neptunes and Swizz Beatz among others, and guest appearances from Missy 'Misdemeanor' Elliott and Juvenile, the album adopted a more thoughtful approach than the out-and-out gangsta rap of his debut album. 'Sometimes', a touching tribute to his recently deceased father, demonstrated Noreaga's lyrical talent. Shortly after the album's release, Noreaga began working with Capone on a new CNN album.

● ALBUMS: *N.O.R.E.* (Penalty/Tommy Boy 1998)★★★, *Melvin Flynt – Da Hustler* (Penalty/Tommy Boy 1999)★★★★.

Notorious B.I.G.

b. Christopher Wallace, 21 May 1972, New York, USA, d. 9 March 1997, Los Angeles, California, USA. A large, imposing figure in contemporary rap before his murder in 1997, Wallace grew up in the tough district of Bedford-Stuyvesant,

in Brooklyn, New York. He soon graduated to a life modelled on the activities of those around him, selling drugs and acting as a teenage lookout. He first rapped, under the name Biggie Smalls, as part of the neighbourhood group the Old Gold Brothers. He also experimented with his own demo recordings, a copy of which was eventually passed to Mister Cee, Big Daddy Kane's DJ. Cee passed the demo on to *The Source*, America's bestselling rap periodical, which gave it a glowing review in its 'Unsigned Hype' column. This attracted the attention of Sean 'Puffy' Combs of Bad Boy Entertainment, who signed Wallace. Having now adopted the stage name Notorious B.I.G., Wallace made his recording debut in 1993 backing Mary J. Blige on 'Real Love'. He also made a guest appearance on Supercat's 'Dolly My Baby'. His first solo effort was 'Party And Bullshit', included on the soundtrack to the movie *Who's The Man*. His debut album followed in 1994. *Ready To Die* became a major hit thanks to the inclusion of singles such as 'Juicy', 'One More Chance' and 'Big Poppa', the latter a US Top 10 hit which was voted *Billboard*'s rap single of the year. He scooped a number of end-of-year awards in *The Source*, as the album achieved platinum sales. He went to the UK to support R. Kelly at Wembley Stadium in London, and also guested on Michael Jackson's *HIStory - Past, Present And Future Book 1*. However, despite his elevation to such exalted company, Notorious B.I.G. never left the ghetto behind. He formed M.A.F.I.A. with some of his former hustler colleagues, releasing an album, *Conspiracy*, in 1995. He was also involved in sundry episodes involving violence, such as a fracas with a promoter in New Jersey and his attempt to take a baseball bat to autograph hunters (for which he received a 100 hours' community service sentence). He was also involved in a running feud with rapper 2Pac, who was convinced of B.I.G.'s involvement in a 1994 robbery in which he was injured. Their disagreement soon festered into a bitter feud between the east and west coast American rap scenes. When 2Pac was murdered, B.I.G.'s non-attendance at a rap peace summit in Harlem was widely criticized. Instead he began work on a second album, entitled, prophetically, *Life After Death*. Its cover featured the rapper standing next to a hearse with the number plate B.I.G. He never lived to see its official release. He was gunned down after leaving a party in California in March 1997. Subsequent conjecture indicated that his murder may have been in retaliation for 2Pac's killing. Issued three weeks later, *Life After Death* went straight to the top of the US charts. Two years later the Notorious B.I.G. was back in the charts with *Born Again*, a motley collection of unreleased material.

● ALBUMS: *Ready To Die* (Bad Boy/Arista 1994)★★★, *Life After Death* (Bad Boy/Arista 1997)★★★★, *Born Again* (Bad Boy/Arista 1999)★★★.

● VIDEOS: *Notorious B.I.G.: Bigger Than Life* (IMC/Scimitar 1998).

Nova, Heather

b. Heather Frith, 6 July 1968, Bermuda. This singer-songwriter's early childhood was spent on her family's yacht, sailing around the Caribbean (her brother is the reggae singer, Mishka). Frith's early interest in music intensified when, aged 19, she moved to Providence to study painting and film at the Rhode Island School of Design. She did not join in with the local rock scene but wrote music for her own films. Inspired by Patti Smith and Lou Reed, she soon started writing songs and recording demos, before moving to England and basing herself in south London. She made further demos and, in 1990, recorded the low-key mini-album *These Walls* for the British Academy Of Songwriters. Released under her birth name, this rare EP was later reissued as *The First Recordings*. Nova then met ex-Killing Joke guitar player Youth, who released the limited-edition *Glow Stars* on his own Butterfly label. Support slots for the Cranberries and Bob Mould followed as Nova's talent began to gain a wider audience. The raw live album, *Blow*, was recorded at the Mean Fiddler, London in early 1993 and released in October on the Big Cat Records label. In 1994, Nova collaborated with Youth on her first full studio album, *Oyster*, which included 'Island', a controversial track about domestic abuse, and the radio hit 'Walk This World'. Protracted recording sessions meant that her major label follow-up, *Siren*, was not released until 1998. Although the impact of Nova's songs was slightly dampened by the glossy production, the album proved popular enough to become her bestselling release to date.

● ALBUMS: *Glow Stars* (Butterfly 1993)★★★, *Blow* (Big Life 1993)★★★, *Oyster* (Big Life 1994)★★★★, *Siren* (V2 1998)★★★.
● COMPILATIONS: *The First Recordings* 1990 recordings (Big Cat)★★★.

Number One Cup

This Chicago, Illinois, USA-based band were formed by Michael Lenzi (guitar/vocals), Pat O'Connell (drums/vocals) and Seth Cohen (guitar/vocals) in 1993. Though unable to find a permanent bass player, the band prospered with their blend of college pop/rock, which brought several comparisons with Pavement. Much of the attraction lay in Cohen's lyrics and the band's relaxed, irreverent presentation of them. In common with other 'lo-fi' acts such as Pavement and Sebadoh, Number One Cup were not driven by ambition as much as the desire to please themselves musically. After some minor singles on the Sweet Pea label, the band signed to Flydaddy Records and recorded its debut album, *Possum Trot Plan*. Taken from it, 'Divebomb' secured extensive mainstream and alternative radio play. Following the bizarrely titled EP 'Kim Chee Is Cabbage', the band released their follow-up album, which was felt by many critics to be too derivative to qualify as a success. The engagingly melodic *People People Why Are We Fighting?* won a lot of the detractors back the following year.

● ALBUMS: *Possum Trot Plan* (Flydaddy 1995)★★★, *Wrecked By Lions* (Flydaddy 1997)★★, *People People Why Are We Fighting?* (Flydaddy 1998)★★★.

Nyman, Michael

b. 23 March 1944, London, England. A composer, pianist, orchestra leader, and author, Nyman studied at the London Academy of Music (of which he is a Fellow) and at King's College, London. He subsequently worked as a music critic before founding the Campiello Band (later renamed the Michael Nyman Band) in 1977. To the public at large, he is probably best known for his music to Jane Campion's award-winning 1993 movie *The Piano*, and for several 'propulsively pounding' scores he composed for the idiosyncratic director and screenwriter, Peter Greenaway. Most notable among these are *The Draughtsman's Contract* (1982), *A Zed & Two Noughts* (1985), *Drowning By Numbers* (1988), *The Cook, The* *Thief, His Wife & Her Lover* (1989), and *Prospero's Books* (1991). The two men parted after Nyman discovered that his original score for *Prospero's Books* had been overlaid with what he called 'awful phoney electronic music'. Nyman's film music is just a part of a prolific and extremely varied output that has consisted of several operas (including *The Man Who Mistook His Wife For A Hat*), string quartets, a saxophone concerto ('Where The Bee Dances'), the libretto for Harrison Birtwhistle's dramatic pastoral, *Down By The Greenwoodside*, other classical works, and numerous commissions. He also collaborated on the Channel 4 film, *The Final Score*, in which he paid tribute to the game of football, and in particular to his own favourite club, Queens Park Rangers. Nyman's score for *The Piano* received the Australian Film Institute Award for Best Original Music, was nominated for a Golden Globe Award, and won the first-ever Chicago Film Critics Award for Best Musical Score. Although the movie was nominated for eight Oscars, Nyman's brilliant score was ignored. In 1995, London's South Bank Centre presented a celebratory festival, Nyman On The South Bank, which opened with an all-night showing of a number of films associated with him. It continued with performances by his various ensembles, which 'showed off the grandeur of Nyman's orchestral writing, the amplified power of the Michael Nyman Big Band, and the intimate delights of his chamber music'. Among the works performed at the festival were premieres of 'The Upside-Down Violin', with the Orquesta Andalusi de Tetuan from Morocco, Nyman's score for *Carrington*, as well as his 'Harpsichord Concerto' with Elisabeth Chojnacka, and 'Six Celan Songs', sung by Hilary Summers. His work in the late 90s has included highly acclaimed scores for *Gattaca* (1998) and *Wonderland* (1999), and a collaboration with Blur singer Damon Albarn for the soundtrack to *Ravenous*. His music, which effortlessly spans the pop/classical divide, has attracted great attention from concert-goers and critics alike, making him a unique figure in UK contemporary music.

● ALBUMS: *Decay Music* (Obscure 1978)★★★, *Michael Nyman* (Sheet 1982)★★★★, *The Kiss And Other Movements* (Editions EG 1987)★★★, *And They Do/Zoo Caprices* (TER 1988)★★★, *Time Will Pronounce* (Argo/Decca 1993)★★★, *The Piano* film soundtrack (Virgin 1993)★★★★, *Michael Nyman Live* (Virgin 1995)★★★, *Carrington* film soundtrack (Argo 1995)★★★, *AET (After Extra Time)* (Virgin 1996)★★★, *Harpsicord, Bassoon And Horn Concertos* (EMI Classics 1997)★★, *Gattaca* film soundtrack (Virgin 1998)★★★, *The Suit & The Photograph* (EMI 1998)★★★, *Wonderland* film soundtrack (Venture 1999)★★★, with Damon Albarn *Ravenous - Music From The Motion Picture* film soundtrack (EMI 1999)★★★, *Music For David King's Book The Commissar Vanishes* (Venture 1999)★★★, *The End Of The Affair* film soundtrack (Venture 2000)★★★.
● COMPILATIONS: *Michael Nyman: Box Set* (Venture 1989)★★★★, *The Essential Michael Nyman* (Argo/Decca 1992)★★★★.
● FURTHER READING: *Experimental Music: Cage And Beyond*, Michael Nyman.

O'Connor, Sinead

b. 8 December 1966, Dublin, Eire. This Irish singer has combined her highly distinctive vocal range with striking post-feminist imagery to great commercial effect on both sides of the Atlantic. O'Connor is now established as one of the most potent left-field forces in popular music. She endured a turbulent youth and diagnoses of 'behavioural problems', which included shoplifting and being expelled from school. O'Connor signed her first record deal with Ensign Records in 1985. Her previous experience was limited to sessions with Dublin pop band Ton Ton Macoute. Nigel Grainge, the label's co-manager, allowed her a full year to develop her knowledge of music and the industry by helping around the office, before the sessions for her debut album began. Through connections on the Dublin music scene, O'Connor provided the vocals to U2 guitarist The Edge's soundtrack for *The Captive*. The track 'Heroine' was released by Virgin Records and stirred some interest when aired on BBC Television's *The Old Grey Whistle Test* in 1986. O'Connor's debut solo single, the disappointing 'Troy', emerged in late 1987, failing to capitalize on column inches seemingly generated only by the singer's shaven head. Early 1988 saw 'Mandinka' reach the UK Top 20, and proved a more suitable showcase for O'Connor's banshee-like attack. Although two subsequent singles failed to chart, *The Lion And The Cobra* sold well on the strength of 'Mandinka', and her media profile was bolstered by a series of highly opinionated interviews. There was lull in her solo output during 1989 as she worked on a variety of collaborative projects. She also appeared in her first acting role as a 15-year-old Catholic schoolgirl in *Hush-A-Bye Baby*, a project developed by the Derry Film Workshop. It explored the moral dilemmas forced upon unmarried pregnant women in the province, and motherhood as a theme would become central in her work thereafter. To promote her second solo album, O'Connor chose the Prince-written 'Nothing Compares 2 U', originally recorded by Family for the Paisley Park label. A remarkable ballad that demonstrated the strength and vulnerability which are pivotal elements in the singer's delivery, it transfixed audiences worldwide and topped the UK and US singles chart. The second album, *I Do Not Want What I Haven't Got*, was also a transatlantic number 1. Her 1990 tour of the USA prompted the first stirrings of a backlash. At the Garden State Arts Centre in New Jersey she refused to go on stage after 'The Star Spangled Banner' was played. It was her protest at the censorship which was sweeping the USA, but this fact was obscured under a wave of nationalistic vitriol from Frank Sinatra among others. It emerged in interviews that the artist was as troubled privately as her public persona may have suggested. Although the mother of a son, Jake, a series of miscarriages had been emotionally draining, catalogued in the tender singles 'Three Babies' and 'My Special Child'. Her third album, 1992's *Am I Not Your Girl?*, was a surprising collection of standards and torch songs which received mixed reviews. Further controversy ensued later in the year when O'Connor tore up a photograph of the Pope on US television. Her appearance at the Bob Dylan celebration concert shortly afterwards was highly charged as she defied numerous hecklers by staring them out, before being led from the stage by a reassuring Kris Kristofferson. In 1993, she appeared as a guest on Willie Nelson's *Across The Borderline*, duetting as a substitute Kate Bush on Peter Gabriel's 'Don't Give Up'. The following year's *Universal Mother* found only marginal success compared to her previous efforts, leading to the suspicion that perhaps her sermonizing had begun to cloud the music. In 1997, she once again turned her hand to acting, ironically, as an Irish Virgin Mary in Neil Jordan's *The Butcher Boy*, and released the low-key *Gospel Oak* EP. In April 1999, she was ordained as a Catholic priest in an unofficial ceremony in Lourdes, France. The new Mother Bernadette Marie was immediately denounced by the Vatican.

● ALBUMS: *The Lion And The Cobra* (Ensign/Chrysalis 1987)★★★, *I Do Not Want What I Haven't Got* (Ensign/Chrysalis 1990)★★★★, *Am I Not Your Girl?* (Ensign/Chrysalis 1992)★★★, *Universal Mother* (Ensign/Chrysalis 1994)★★.

● COMPILATIONS: *So Far ... The Best Of Sinead O'Connor* (Chrysalis 1997)★★★.

● VIDEOS: *The Value Of Ignorance* (PolyGram Music Video 1989), *The Year Of The Horse* (PolyGram Music Video 1991).

● FURTHER READING: *Sinead O'Connor: So Different*, Dermott Hayes. *Sinead: Her Life And Music*, Jimmy Guterman.

● FILMS: *Hush-A-Bye-Baby* (1990), *Wuthering Heights* (1992), *The Butcher Boy* (1997).

O'Donnell, Daniel

b. 12 December 1961, Kincasslagh, County Donegal, Eire. O'Donnell is without doubt the biggest-selling act in history in the musical genre known as 'Country 'n' Irish'. His success can be attributed to the fact that he is a clean-cut and gimmick-free vocalist with leanings towards sentimental MOR material. In musical terms, what O'Donnell records is unadventurous, yet his immense popularity makes it clear that his output has been brilliantly targeted. O'Donnell first emerged in the UK in 1985, although by this point he was already popular in Ireland. His first attempts at singing came when he worked as a backing vocalist in the band that backed his sister, folk/country singer Margo, during the early 80s, and his popularity among the female audiences quickly increased. After a handful of early recordings (later released after he came to fame as 'The Boy From Donegal'), he signed to Michael Clerkin's Ritz Records, an Irish label based in London, and *Two Sides Of Daniel O'Donnell* was released in 1985. It was promoted by the first in a continuing series of nationwide UK tours that attracted capacity audiences (largely composed of fans of artists such as the late Jim Reeves - O'Donnell usually features in his stage show a medley of songs connected with Reeves). In 1986, came a second O'Donnell release, *I Need You*, which the following March became his first album to reach the UK country charts. That year's album *Don't Forget To Remember* (featuring a cover version of the hit by the Bee Gees as its title track) was O'Donnell's first to enter the UK country chart at number 1, a feat he repeated with his five subsequent original albums, although the next one to be released in chronological terms, *The Boy From Donegal*, consisted mainly of material recorded in 1984 before he signed to Ritz, and was released in the UK by Prism Leisure. In 1988, Ritz licensed O'Donnell's next release, *From The Heart*, to Telstar Records, a television marketing company, and as well as entering the UK country chart at number 1, the album also reached the UK pop album chart in the autumn of that year, while a video, *Daniel O'Donnell Live In Concert*, was released. The following year brought *Thoughts Of Home*, an album and video that were both heavily advertised on television by Telstar - the album made the Top 40 of the pop chart and the video became O'Donnell's first to reach the UK Music Video chart; once again, all his subsequent video releases have featured in the latter chart, which the original *Live In Concert* also entered in the wake of *Thoughts From Home*. By 1990, O'Donnell was back with an album, *Favourites*, and a companion video, *TV Show Favourites*, which was composed of material filmed for a hugely successful Irish television series. However, of far greater interest in 1990 was the news that he was making an album in Nashville with noted producer Allen Reynolds (who had enjoyed major success with Don Williams, Crystal Gayle, Kathy Mattea and latterly, Garth Brooks). Released in late 1990, *The Last Waltz* was somewhat closer to genuine country music than its predecessors, and once again entered the UK country album charts at the top and charted strongly in the UK pop equivalent.

During 1991, it was decided that nearly all of O'Donnell's album catalogue was MOR rather than country, and at a stroke, the UK country album chart - in which O'Donnell usually occupied the majority of the Top 10 places - hardly featured his albums at all. This produced an avalanche of complaints (including one from a nun) and public demonstrations urging that the decision be reversed and his albums be reinstated in the country list, which eventually occurred in late 1991. Another release, *The Very Best Of Daniel O'Donnell*, a compilation composed partly of previously released items along with some newly recorded material, continued O'Donnell's remarkable success story. His imported albums have sold prodigiously in areas with populations of Irish extraction, and several concert appearances, including one at New York's Carnegie Hall in 1991, have been commercial triumphs. During the 90s he has attempted to conquer the gospel market, although both *Songs Of Inspiration* and *I Believe* proved to be lacklustre collections. In April 1998, O'Donnell finally broached the UK Top 10 with the charity single 'Give A Little Love', achieving the biggest hit of his career. 'The Magic Is There' and 'The Way Dreams Are' came close to repeating the success, debuting at number 16 and 18 respectively.

● ALBUMS: *Two Sides Of Daniel O'Donnell* (Ritz 1985)★★★, *I Need You* (Ritz 1986)★★★, *Don't Forget To Remember* (Ritz 1987)★★★, *The Boy From Donegal* 1984 recording (Ritz 1987)★★★, *From The Heart* (Telstar 1988)★★★, *Thoughts Of Home* (Telstar 1989)★★★, *Favourites* (Ritz 1990)★★★, *The Last Waltz* (Ritz 1990)★★★, *Follow Your Dream* (Ritz 1992)★★★, *A Date With Daniel Live* (Ritz 1993)★★★, *Especially For You* (Ritz 1994)★★★, *Christmas With Daniel* (Ritz 1994)★★, with Mary Duff *Timeless* (Ritz 1996)★★★, *Songs Of Inspiration* (Ritz 1996)★★, *I Believe* (Ritz 1997)★★★, *Love Songs* (Ritz 1998)★★★.
● COMPILATIONS: *The Very Best Of Daniel O'Donnell* (Ritz 1991)★★★, *The Classic Collection* (Ritz 1995)★★★, *Irish Collection* (Ritz 1996)★★★, *Greatest Hits* (Ritz 1999)★★★.
● VIDEOS: *Live In Concert* (Ritz 1988), *Thoughts Of Home* (Telstar Video 1989), *TV Show Favourites* (Ritz 1990), *An Evening With Daniel O'Donnell* (Ritz 1990), *Follow Your Dream* (Ritz 1992), *And Friends Live* (Ritz 1993), *Just For You* (Ritz 1994), *Christmas With Daniel O'Donnell* (Ritz 1996), *The Gospel Show: Live From The Point* (Ritz 1998), *Give A Little Love* (Ritz 1998).
● FURTHER READING: *Danny Boy: A Life Of Daniel O'Donnell*, Andrew Vaughan.

O'Neal, Shaquille

b. 6 March 1972, Newark, New Jersey, USA. O'Neal shot to fame as the star of the previously obscure Orlando Magic basketball team ('Rookie Of The Year' in 1992). After the media picked up on his demonstrative play, notably his cult slam-dunk action, he emerged as a major multi-media star of the early 90s - so much so that a contract with Jive Records was just around the corner. His generally sport-related raps such as '(I Know I Got) Skillz' and 'Shoot Pass Slam' kept the cash-tills rattling, the latter song being the soundtrack to the Reebok commercials of which he was the high-profile star. He did possess some history in the hip-hop idiom, having previously been a breakdancer in Newark until his size made the activity impossible. Later he moved to Germany where his stepfather, Sgt. Philip Harrison, took a post. He relocated to San Francisco to attend high school, playing for 68-1, who won the state championship. From there he was picked up by Louisiana State University coach Dale Brown, from where he joined Orlando. Basketball and music are by no means his only interests. In 1994, he appeared in the movie *Blue Chips* with Nick Nolte, and worked as executive producer on 1996's *Kazaam* and 1997's *Steel*. Incredibly, he had also penned his own autobiography, at the age of 21. His recording career has recovered from the critical mauling given to his long-playing debut, which featured over-familiar Gap Band breakbeats funnelled through guests including Erick Sermon (EPMD), Def Jef, Ali Shaheed (A Tribe Called Quest) and Fu-Schnickens. Subsequent albums continued to attract guest appearances from leading hip-hop artists, while demonstrating a marked improvement in O'Neal's own rapping skills. *You Can't Stop The Reign* appeared on O'Neal's T.W.I.M. (The World Is Mine) label through Interscope in 1996, the same year he joined the Los Angeles Lakers as a free agent. By the time of 1998's aptly-titled *Respect*, O'Neal was starting to gain that much desired commodity from previously hostile music critics.

● ALBUMS: *Shaq Diesel* (Jive 1993)★★, *Shaq Fu - Da Return* (Jive 1994)★★★, *You Can't Stop The Reign* (Interscope 1996)★★★, *Respect* (A&M 1998)★★★.
● COMPILATIONS: *The Best Of Shaquille O'Neal* (Jive 1996)★★★.
● FILMS: *CB4* (1993), *Blue Chips* (1994), *Special Effects: Anything Can Happen* (1996), *Kazaam* (1996), *Good Burger* (1997), *Steel* (1997), *He Got Game* (1998).

O'Rourke, Jim

This Chicago, Illinois, USA-based guitarist, composer and producer is a leading figure on the American *avant garde* scene. O'Rourke has been exploring the boundaries of the jazz, rock, ambient and classical fields since the late 80s, and his prolific work rate as solo artist, collaborator, producer and engineer is only hinted at in his discography. A precociously talented guitarist from a young age, O'Rourke first began recording his own tapes while a student at DePaul University. These home demos brought him to the attention of several *avant garde* musicians with whom he subsequently collaborated, including Derek Bailey, Henry Kaiser and Eddie Prévost. O'Rourke's prolific solo output at the beginning of the 90s focused on his exploratory guitar work and use of tape manipulation and found sounds, creating atmospheric *musique concrète* pieces that reached a reductionistic peak on the barely audible 'Cede', one of two tracks comprising 1995's *Terminal Pharmacy*. In addition to his solo work, the tireless O'Rourke has appeared as a member of several experimental outfits, including Illusion Of Safety, Brise-Glace, Red Crayola, Gastr Del Sol, Organum and Fennoberg; composed for acts as diverse as the Kronos Quartet, the ROVA Saxophone Quartet and Faust; and remixed material for Main, This Heat, Tortoise, Labradford and Oval among others. In the late 90s, after severing his ties with Gastr Del Sol, O'Rourke flirted with conventionality on *Bad Timing* and *Eureka*, two highly accessible and critically praised albums.

● ALBUMS: *Some Kind Of Pagan* cassette only (Sound Of Pig 1989)★★★, *Remove The Need* cassette only (Complacency 1989)★★★, *It Takes Time To Do Nothing* cassette only (Audiofile 1990)★★★, *Secure On The Loose Rim* cassette only (Sound Of Pig 1991)★★★, *The Ground Below Above Our Heads* (Entenpfuhl 1991)★★★, *Tamper* (Extreme 1991)★★★, with Henry Kaiser *Tomorrow Knows Where You Live* (Les Disques Victo 1992)★★★★, with Kazuyuki K. Null *Neuro Eco* cassette only (Nux Organisation 1992)★★★, *Disengage* (Staaltape 1992)★★★, *Scend* (Divided 1992)★★★★, with Null *New Kind Of Water* (Charnel House 1993)★★★, with Kaiser, Mari Kimura, John Oswald *Acoustics* (Les Disques Victo 1994)★★★, with Eddie Prévost *Third Straight Day Made Public* (Complacency 1994)★★★, *Rules Of Reduction EP3* (Metamkine 1994)★★★, *Use* cassette only (Soleilmoon 1994)★★, with Günter Müller *Slow Motion* (Sw. For 4 Ears 1995)★★★, *Terminal Pharmacy* (Tzadik 1995)★★★, *Happy Days* (Revenant 1997)★★★, *Bad Timing* (Drag City 1997)★★★★, *Eureka* (Drag City 1999)★★★★.

Oakenfold, Paul

b. 30 August 1963, England. Oakenfold was active in club promotions from the early 80s and became one of the most successful DJs and remixers of the 90s. Having trained as a chef, he decided instead to pursue a career in music after he had been introduced to the decks by his friend Trevor Fung in 1981. He later moved to New York City where he worked for a number of record companies and regularly visited the Paradise Garage. When he returned to the UK, he worked for Champion Records, promoting Jazzy Jeff and Salt-N-Pepa among others, and later Profile Records and Def Jam Records. He also DJed at the Project Club in Streatham, London, and wrote a hip-hop column in *Blues And Soul* magazine under the name Wotupski. In 1987, along with Danny Rampling and a few others, he visited Fung and Ian St. Paul (who later helped to set up TIP Records) in Ibiza where he went to clubs such as Amnesia, which were playing a mixture of Chicago house, pop and indie - known as Balearic. On his return, Oakenfold recreated the Balearic feeling at a few after-hours parties at the Project Club and towards the end of the year, with St. Paul, he organized a similar club at the Sanctuary in London's West End called Future - it became Spectrum when it moved to Heaven in 1988. Spectrum, along with Rampling's Shoom, helped to establish the under-

ground acid house movement. Later, Oakenfold played at a number of the huge Sunrise and Biology raves, opened shows for the Stone Roses and the Happy Mondays and later toured the world as a support act for U2. In 1989, he set up the label Perfecto Records and remixed the Happy Mondays' 'Wrote For Luck' with his musical collaborator Steve Osborne. The pair have subsequently remixed for a variety of artists including Arrested Development, Massive Attack, M People, New Order, the Shamen, Simply Red, the Stone Roses and U2, and have recorded under a number of names including Grace, Virus, the Perfecto Allstarz and Wild Colour. Oakenfold has compiled a number of compilation albums for the Ministry Of Sound and, in 1994 was employed by East West Records as an A&R consultant. The label also became the parent company to Oakenfold's Perfecto imprint, after his association with BMG. In 1998, Oakenfold parted company with East West and his next mix album was released through Virgin Records. During the late 90s, he helped to popularize the trance sound and has become one of the best-known DJs in the world, graduating from house towards a melodic, commercial style of trance, particularly through his residency at the UK's Cream - which is commemorated on *Resident - Two Years Of Oakenfold At Cream*. In 1999, Oakenfold found his name in *The Guinness Book Of Records* as The World's Most Successful Club DJ, although the book's estimate of his annual earnings at £250,000 was laughably short of the mark. He was also voted number 1 in the UK's *DJ* magazine's Top 100 DJs in the world, and became Director of Music at home, London's new superclub.

● COMPILATIONS: *Sessions 2 - Paul Oakenfold* (MOS 1994)★★★, *Perfection - A Perfecto Compilation* (Perfecto 1995)★★★, *Resident - Two Years Of Oakenfold At Cream* (Virgin 1999)★★★★, shared with Pete Tong, Fatboy Slim *Essential Millennium* (ffrr 1999)★★★★.

Oasis

From Manchester, England, Oasis became overnight sensations in 1994 on the back of sublime singles and exponentially increasing press interest. Widely regarded in the press as natural successors to the Happy Mondays, Oasis proffered a similar working-class, roughneck chic. The band's creative axis is the Gallagher brothers, Liam John (b. 21 September 1972, Longsight, Cheshire, England; vocals) and Noel Thomas (b. 29 May 1967, Longsight, Cheshire, England; guitar/vocals). They were brought up by Irish Roman Catholic parents in the south Manchester suburb of Burnage. While his younger brother was still in school, Noel, whose C&W DJ father had purchased a guitar for him at age 11, discovered punk, and like many of his peers happily engaged in truancy, burglary and glue-sniffing. After six months' probation for robbing a corner shop he began to take the instrument seriously at the age of 13, later finding his role model in Johnny Marr of the Smiths. Liam was not weaned on music until 1989 when his elder brother took him to see the Inspiral Carpets. Afterwards, Noel befriended that band's Clint Boon, subsequently becoming a guitar technician and travelling the world with them. When he telephoned home in 1991 he was informed by his mother that Liam had joined a band. Paul 'Bonehead' Arthurs (b. 23 June 1965, Manchester, England; guitar), Tony McCarroll (drums) and Paul 'Guigsy' McGuigan (b. 9 May 1971, Manchester, England) had been playing together as Rain (not the

Liverpool band of similar moniker) before meeting with Liam, who became their singer, as they changed their name to Oasis. When Noel returned to watch them play at Manchester's Boardwalk in 1992, he recognized their promise, but insisted that they install him as lead guitarist and only perform his songs if he were to help them. Noel continued as roadie to the Inspiral Carpets to help purchase equipment, as the band set about establishing a local reputation. The incident that led to them being signed to Creation Records quickly passed into rock mythology. In May 1993, they drove to Glasgow with fellow denizens of the Boardwalk rehearsal studios, Sister Lovers, to support 18 Wheeler at King Tut's Wah Wah Club. Strong-arming their way onto the bill, they played five songs early in the evening, but these were enough to hypnotize Creation boss Alan McGee who offered them a contract there and then. However, they did not sign until several months later, during which time a copy of the band's demo had been passed to Johnny Marr, who became an early convert to the cause and put the band in touch with Electronic's management company, Ignition. With news spreading of the band's rise it seemed likely that they would join any number of labels apart from Creation, with U2's Mother label rumoured to guarantee double any other offer. However, loyalty to the kindred spirits at Creation won through by October 1993, and two months later the label issued the band's 'debut', a one-sided 12-inch promo of 'Columbia' taken straight from the original demo. BBC Radio 1 immediately play listed it (an almost unheralded event for such a 'non-release'). The following year began with a torrent of press, much of it focusing on the band's errant behaviour. Punch-ups and the ingestion of large quantities of drink and drugs led to gig cancellations, while frequent, often violent, bickering between the Gallagher brothers lent the band a sense of danger and mischief. 'Supersonic' reached the UK Top 40 in May. 'Shakermaker', owing an obvious debt to the New Seekers' 'I'd Like To Teach The World To Sing (In Perfect Harmony)', duly made number 11 two months later. High-profile dates at the Glastonbury Festival and New York's New Music Seminar ensued, along with more stories of on-the-road indulgence. The Beatles-redolent 'Live Forever', with a sleeve featuring a photo of the house where John Lennon grew up, reached the Top 10 in October, all of which ensured that the expectation for a debut album was now phenomenal. After scrapping the original tapes recorded at Monmouth's Monnow Studios, the songs had been completed with Mark Coyle and Anjali Dutt, with subsequent mixing by Electronic producer Owen Morris, at a total cost of £75,000. In September 1994, Definitely Maybe entered the UK charts at number 1, and, backed by a live version of the Beatles' 'I Am The Walrus', 'Cigarettes And Alcohol', a stage favourite, became the band's biggest UK singles success to date, when it reached number 7 in October. In December, they released the non-album 'Whatever' (not quite the Christmas number 1), a lush pop song with full orchestration that sounded astonishingly accomplished for a band whose recording career stretched over only eight months. Their assault on America began in January 1995, and with a few gigs and word-of-mouth reports, they were soon hovering around the US Top 50. In mid-1995, it was announced that drummer McCarroll had amicably left the band and Alan White (b. 26 May 1972, London, England) sessioned on

their second album. The eagerly anticipated (What's The Story) Morning Glory? was a rich and assured record. Gallagher's Beatlesque melodies were spectacular, from the acoustic simplicity of 'Wonderwall' to the raucous and dense harmonies of 'Don't Look Back In Anger' and 'Morning Glory'. Further gems included 'Roll With It' and 'Some Might Say', the latter having already provided the band with their first UK chart-topping single during the summer. 'Roll With It' and 'Wonderwall' were also UK number 2 hit singles, while 'Don't Look Back In Anger' became their second chart-topper the following March. Nobody could dispute that (What's The Story) Morning Glory? was one of the finest albums of the pop era, and it went on to become one of the bestselling albums of the 90s by a UK act. Oasis were suddenly receiving the media attention that was previously bestowed on Liverpool's fab four. With the massive attention and success in the charts the volatile relationship of the two brothers came under public scrutiny. Their sex lives, drug habits and fist fights were all examined and dissected, their uncompromising behaviour and laddish attitudes increasingly both entertaining and irritating. Rumours of the band splitting came to a head on their ninth attempt to break America in September 1996. Following one of their many fights, Noel returned to the UK with the band in tow the following day. The rest of the US tour was cancelled and the press statement that followed reported that although touring was unlikely the band would stay together. Nevertheless, awards continued to flow throughout a remarkable year, highlighting the fact that few modern rock bands have created such a body of high-quality work in such a short time, and no other (except the Beatles) has become a such a massive media success. The band's greatly anticipated third album was introduced to the world by the UK chart-topping single, 'D'You Know What I Mean?'. The title of Be Here Now was inspired by John Lennon's response to a question regarding the transient state of rock 'n' roll. This philosophy was applied to the album: not since the release of Sgt. Pepper's Lonely Hearts Club Band in 1967 had there been such anticipation for a new record. Queues formed outside record shops on the day of release as 800,000 copies were sold in the UK within 24 hours. The music was much denser than in the past, with guitars overlaid on many tracks and Liam's vocals turned up to 11. Although still relying on the Beatles for inspiration, there were some outstanding songs, with no weak fillers. 'Stand By Me' will stand as one of Noel Gallagher's finest songs and the epic 'Hey Jude'-styled 'All Around The World' quickly became a live encore favourite. The 'difficult' third album mountain had been successfully climbed. There were further problems for the Gallagher brothers, however, when Liam was arrested in Australia for allegedly assaulting a fan, although the charges were later dropped. A compilation of the band's most popular b-sides, including live favourites 'Acquiesce' and 'Stay Young', was released in 1998. The following March, former drummer McCarroll, who had been pursuing a claim for loss of earnings and royalties, settled with the band out of court for an estimated £550,000. A turbulent year came to an end when both Arthurs and McGuigan left the band in August. Arthurs replacement was Gem (ex-Heavy Stereo) while McGuigan's place was taken by ex-Ride and Hurricane #1 leader Andy Bell. The band dealt a seemingly fatal body blow to the ailing Creation label at the start of 2000 by announcing that they would release their fourth album, *Standing On The Shoulder Of Giants*, through their own Big Brother label. The album was premiered by February's chart-topping single, 'Go Let It Out'.

● ALBUMS: *Definitely Maybe* (Creation/Epic 1994)★★★★, *(What's The Story) Morning Glory?* (Creation/Epic 1995)★★★★★, *Be Here Now* (Creation/Epic 1997)★★★★, *Standing On The Shoulder Of Giants* (Big Brother 2000)★★★.

● COMPILATIONS: *The Masterplan* (Creation/Epic 1998)★★★.

● VIDEOS: *Live By The Sea* (PMI 1995), ... *There And Then* (SMV 1996).

● FURTHER READING: *Oasis: How Does It Feel*, Jemma Wheeler. *Oasis: The Illustrated Story*, Paul Lester. *The World On The Street: The Unsanctioned Story Of Oasis*, Eugene Masterson. *Oasis Definitely*, Tim Abbot. *Oasis*, Mick St. Michael. *Oasis '96*, Pat Gilbert. *Oasis: What's The Story*, Ian Robertson. *Oasis: Round Their Way*, Mick Middles. *Brothers: From Childhood To Oasis: The Real Story*, Paul Gallagher and Terry Christian. *Oasis: The Story*, Paul Mathur. *Getting High: The Adventures Of Oasis*, Paolo Hewitt. *Don't Look Back In Anger: Growing Up With Oasis*, Chris Hutton and Richard Kurt. *Forever The People: Six Months On The Road With Oasis*, Paolo Hewitt.

Ocean Colour Scene

This Birmingham, England-based band survived several lean years in the early 90s to triumph in the Britpop era with a string of hugely popular retro-rock hit singles. Formed from the ashes of several local bands, Simon Fowler (b. 25 May 1965; vocals), Steve Cradock (guitar), Damon Minchella (bass) and Oscar Harrison (drums) peddled a rather indistinctive and generic indie guitar sound from 1989 onwards, heavily inspired by the breakthrough of the Stone Roses. Managed by Cradock's former policeman father Chris, the band recorded their debut single, 'Sway', for the Birmingham independent label Phffft in September 1990. Phonogram Records subsequently recruited Ocean Colour Scene for its Fontana Records roster at a total cost of over £1 million. Rolling Stones producer Jimmy Miller agreed to work on their debut album, sessions for which began in the summer of 1991. However, Phonogram were unimpressed with the Miller recordings, installing Hugo Nicholson (Primal Scream) in his stead. He too was replaced by Tim Palmer, as the debut album, with backing vocals from Alison Moyet, finally emerged in May 1992. As Fowler later conceded: 'It hasn't really got much personality. We did like it at the time, but a year later we were very different.' The momentum had been lost and Phonogram's excessive investment in the band seemed ill-fated. Moreover, when they returned from a tour of the USA at the end of 1992 they were unable to convince their label that their songs were strong enough for a follow-up set. The process dragged on for several months until Ocean Colour Scene walked out on the contract (using lawyer Michael Thomas to extricate themselves from massive debts). Deprived of a product to promote, they found touring opportunities hard to secure and struggled to continue. However, by the mid-90s Ocean Colour Scene had been endorsed by Noel Gallagher of Oasis, with whom they toured. Two members of the band, Steve Cradock and later Minchella, also worked in Paul Weller's backing band. Like Gallagher, Weller would make public his affection for the band, describing them as 'English 90s R&B'. Their 1996 single, 'The Riverboat Song', was heavily promoted on radio by disc jockeys such as Chris Evans, and became a UK Top

20 chart hit after the band had secured a new contract with MCA Records. An accompanying album, *Moseley Shoals*, named after the region of Birmingham in which the band formed, followed in April, and spawned UK Top 10 hits with 'You've Got It Bad', 'The Day We Caught The Train' and 'The Circle'. *Marchin' Already* was released in October 1997 to almost universal critical disapproval; the *Select* reviewer, Andrew Male, condemned it as 'a grab-bag of influences with nothing at the centre'. Nevertheless, the band's popularity was confirmed when the album topped the UK charts and the singles 'Hundred Mile High City', 'Travellers Tune' and 'Better Day' all reached the Top 10. The album also included vocal contributions from soul legend P.P. Arnold, who featured on the excellent single 'It's A Beautiful Thing'. The band returned in September 1999 with the underwhelming new single 'Profit In Peace', and *One From The Modern*. Cradock enjoyed solo success when he collaborated with Liam Gallagher on the Jam tribute single, 'Carnation', a UK Top 10 hit at the end of the year.

● ALBUMS: *Ocean Colour Scene* (Fontana 1992)★★, *Moseley Shoals* (MCA 1996)★★★★, *Marchin' Already* (MCA 1997)★★★, *One From The Modern* (Island 1999)★★★.

● COMPILATIONS: *B-Sides, Seasides & Freerides* (MCA 1997)★★.

● VIDEOS: *Travellers Tunes/Live At Stirling Castle August 1998* (Universal 1999).

Offspring

Although they achieved commercial fortune in the mid-90s, the Offspring had been a staple of the southern Californian punk community since 1984. Bryan 'Dexter' Holland (b. 29 December 1965; vocals/guitar) and Greg Kriesel (b. 20 January 1965, Glendale, California, USA; bass) announced their intention to form a band at a party where they heard TSOL's *Change Today* for the first time. Kriesel then joined Manic Subsidal, with former Clowns Of Death guitarist Holland, plus Doug Thompson (vocals) and Jim Benton (drums). When Thompson was forced out, Holland took over vocals, while Benton was replaced by Clowns Of Death drummer James Lilja. A third Clowns Of Death member, Kevin 'Noodles' Wasserman (b. 4 February 1963, Los Angeles, California, USA; guitar), joined later. Manic Subsidal was renamed the Offspring in 1985. Shows supporting artists such as Econo Christ and Isocraces followed, at an average of one performance every two months. Their debut single, 'I'll Be Waiting', was released on their own Black Records. However, by 1987 Lilja was losing interest in the band, and was replaced for a Las Vegas show by Ron Welty (b. 1 February 1971, Long Beach, California, USA; ex-FQX - Fuck Quality X-Rays). He joined them permanently in July 1987, ironically during an Offspring show supported by FQX, whom he had now abandoned. A demo was recorded in 1988 and touted around punk labels, but Offspring were initially forced to gain recognition by advertising in the classifieds of underground magazines *Flipside* and *Maximum Rock 'n' Roll*. These songs were lifted and placed on compilation cassettes and albums, spreading the band's name in the process. By March 1989 they were ready to record their debut studio album, recruiting Dead Kennedys, TSOL and Iggy Pop veteran Thom Wilson. Via a contract with Nemesis Records the world was at last able to hear the Offspring's unique cross-matching of hardcore with Middle Eastern guitar from chief songwriter Holland. A six-week national tour followed, though Noodles was stabbed during their Hollywood anti-nuclear benefit. The *Baghdad* EP bore witness to the band's progression, with a less self-consciously punk musical dialogue, and the notable absence of some of the cluttered tempo changes of their debut. It was their last record for Nemesis, however, and by 1992 they were in Brett Gurewitz's West Beach Studio working on a new project for Epitaph Records (Gurewitz had initially rejected the band, as had practically every other underground label in the USA, only to change his mind on hearing a new demo tape). *Ignition*'s more relaxed pace, dropped in favour of bigger, memorable choruses, opened up Holland's lyrics to closer scrutiny. There was evident craftsmanship in songs such as 'Take It Like A Man' and 'No Hero', which concerned suicide. This reflected the sophistication of the music, with Holland's Arabic guitar breaks contrasting with Noodles' forceful blues licks. Its release coincided with individual academic success, with Kriesel finishing his finance degree, Welty his electronics degree and Holland taking his masters (he went on to complete his doctorate in molecular biology). In June, they toured Europe for the first time with labelmates No FX, preceding a two-week domestic stint with the Lunachicks on which Noodles was temporarily replaced by his friend, Rob Barton, who also helped out on the following tour with Pennywise. The band's third album, *Smash*, was completed in February 1994 with Thom Wilson again producing. Ever more adventurous, this time Offspring combined punk with ska and hard rock, with a cover version of the Didjits' 'Killboy Powerhead' as a concession to their roots. 'What Happened To You' eloquently addressed the subject of hard drugs (to which so many of their So-Cal hardcore compatriots had fallen victim), while 'Something To Believe In' and 'Self-Esteem' were more detached and introspective than before. By the end of 1994 the album had achieved platinum status as the result of extensive touring with labelmates Rancid and Dutch hardcore band Guttermouth, and the crossover success of MTV favourite 'Come Out And Play (Keep 'Em Separated)'. By 1995, *Smash* was accredited with quadruple platinum sales, and their recording of the Damned's 'Smash It Up', for the soundtrack of *Batman Forever*, was another major success. Much of 1995 was spent in dispute with their record company, with the band eventually signing to Columbia Records in 1996. *Ixnay On The Hombre* was well received in February 1997, but their big break came with the single 'Pretty Fly (For A White Guy)', which was a huge international hit (topping the UK charts in January 1999) that helped boost sales of the attendant *Americana*. Warming to their new-found success, the band debuted at UK number 2 with the follow-up single, 'Why Don't You Get A Job?'. *Americana*, meanwhile, narrowly failed to top their domestic album chart.

● ALBUMS: *Offspring* (Nemesis 1989)★★, *Ignition* (Epitaph 1992)★★★, *Smash* (Epitaph 1994)★★★, *Ixnay On The Hombre* (Columbia 1997)★★★★, *Americana* (Columbia 1998)★★★.

Ol' Dirty Bastard

b. Russell Jones, 15 November 1968, Brooklyn, New York, USA. Rapper Ol' Dirty Bastard was a founder member of Staten Island's highly influential Wu-Tang Clan crew. His first solo album, however, was disappointingly formulaic. The album was interesting only on those tracks ('Brooklyn Zoo', 'Cuttin' Headz' and 'Snakes') which featured the

familiar beats of the Wu-Tang Clan's producer, RZA. Other guests from the Wu-Tang Clan included Method Man and U-God. At the time of the album's release, Ol' Dirty Bastard was pursued by police into an apartment. It was not a burglary, he claimed, but an attempt to escape from an assassin. A week later the same assailant shot him twice in the back. He has continued to work with the Wu-Tang Clan and affiliated releases, but also figured prominently on Pras' 1998 international hit single, 'Ghetto Supastar (That Is What You Are)'. His career has been punctuated by constant arrests, however, although he found the time to lay down tracks for September 1999's entertaining sophomore set, *N***a Please*.

● ALBUMS: *Return To The 36 Chambers: The Dirty Version* (Elektra 1995)★★★, *N***a Please* (Elektra 1999)★★★.

Old 97's

Texas, USA-based band who initially formed part of a second wave of grittier, grass-roots country rockers inspired by the breakthrough of bands such as Uncle Tupelo and Green On Red, although they are compared to the Replacements and Clash as much as the former artists. the Old 97's. Singer-songwriter Rhett Miller first started playing with bass player Murry Hammond and guitarist Ken Bethea in small clubs in Dallas. Adding drummer Philip Peeples, the band released a cassette only EP in 1993, and their full length debut the following year. Chicago independent Bloodshot Records released the band's second set, *Wreck Your Life*, which attempted to capture the intensity of their live shows. The band's 1997 major label debut for Elektra Records, *Too Far To Care*, highlighted Miller's affecting songwriting, ranging in tone from traditional country ('W. Tex. Teardrops') to stylish roots rock ('Time Bomb'). One of the best songs was 'Four Leaf Clover', a duet with punk legend Exene Cervenka (formerly of X, now of Auntie Christ - whose debut album featured Miller on backing vocals). Production was by ex-Orbit musician Wally Gagel, previously best known for his work with Sebadoh. Among the band's other high-profile fans was Waylon Jennings, who praised them in a newspaper interview for the *Austin Chronicle*. *Fight Songs* was a strong follow-up that featured the pop-orientated radio favourites 'Murder (Or A Heart Attack)' and '19'.

● ALBUMS: *Hitchhike To Rhome* (Big Iron 1994)★★★, *Wreck Your Life* (Bloodshot 1995)★★★, *Too Far To Care* (Elektra 1997)★★★★, *Fight Songs* (Elektra 1999)★★★.

Oldham, Will

(see Palace Brothers)

Olive

A studio-bound project inaugurated in 1995 by Tim Kellet, Robin Taylor-Firth and singer Ruth-Ann Boyle. Kellet had formerly been a member of the horn group, Rebop, while at music college in Manchester, England. He subsequently joined Vini Reilly's Durutti Column, before 10 years spent as a sideman for Simply Red. He finally left that band after their hugely successful *Stars* tour, retreating to a purpose-built home studio he had financed in Derbyshire. The first result of his self-employment was a successful co-production venture with the Lighthouse Family. Taylor-Firth had previously worked in the Sheffield area with underground legends Nightmares On Wax, playing and co-writing their 1995 album. Via a mutual friend he made the acquaintance of

Kellet, and the two agreed to work together on a collaborative project. The final piece of the jigsaw was completed by Boyle, a Sunderland native who had sung with many underground bands in that city and contributed a sample of her voice to Vini Reilly's 1996 project. Kellet discovered her by accident, playing a keyboard sample while in Reilly's company, and enquiring as to the origin of the voice. One hastily convened meeting later, Boyle had become the third and final member. They made their debut in 1996 with the single 'You're Not Alone'. The music was eerily similar to the trip-hop stylings of Portishead, but Boyle's haunting vibrato helped give the track some character. A reissue of the track finally gave the trio their UK breakthrough, topping the singles chart in May 1997. The failure of the follow-up singles 'Outlaw' and 'Miracle' to match the success of 'You're Not Alone' prompted the band's record label to unceremoniously drop them, however, and they were reduced to a duo when Taylor-Firth left shortly afterwards. Boyle and Kellett subsequently signed a new deal with Maverick Records and set about recording new material.

● ALBUMS: *Extra Virgin* (BMG/RCA 1997)★★★.

Olivia Tremor Control

Based in Athens, Georgia, USA, this 90s psych pop outfit form part of the loose knit Elephant 6 Recording Company collective with bands such as Jeff Magnum's Neutral Milk Hotel, Robert Schneider's Apples In Stereo, Elf Power and the Gerbils. Will Cullen Hart (guitar/vocals) and Bill Doss (guitar/vocals) grew up in Ruston, Louisiana with fellow 60s enthusiasts Schneider and Magnum, playing and recording music together in bands such as Maggot and Cranberry Life Cycle. Hart, Doss and Magnum moved to Athens in 1990, where they formed Synthetic Flying Machine, which in turn evolved into the Olivia Tremor Control. This early line-up recorded the *California Demise* EP in 1995 before Magnum relocated to Seattle and then Denver to concentrate on Neutral Milk Hotel, although he continued to make guest appearances with the band. John Fernandes (bass) and Eric Harris (drums) were in place for the band's debut album, which, as its title suggested, was loosely based around the concept of an imaginary movie. Flitting dizzyingly between melodic 60s sunshine pop songs and surreal sound collages, *Music From The Unrealized Film Script "Dusk At Cubist Castle"* was heralded upon arrival as a high point of 90s psychedelia. It was originally released with a bonus CD of ambient instrumentals, an avenue more fully explored by the band on their subsequent collaboration with the Black Swan Network. Keyboard player Peter Erchick was added to the line-up for 1999's *Black Foliage: Animation Music*, another sprawling, experimental collection which, on 'Hideaway' and 'Hilltop Procession', attained moments of genuine psych-pop nirvana.

● ALBUMS: *Music From The Unrealized Film Script "Dusk At Cubist Castle"* (Flydaddy/Blue Rose 1996)★★★★, *Black Foliage: Animation Music* (V2 1999)★★★.

Omar

b. Omar Lye Fook, 1969, Canterbury, Kent, England. Omar was born the son of a Chinese Jamaican father and an Indian Jamaican mother. A former principle percussionist of the Kent Youth Orchestra, he later graduated from the Guildhall School of Music in London. His debut singles were 'Mr Postman' and 'You And Me' (featuring backing vocals from Caron Wheeler), before his debut album was released, via Harlesden's Black Music Association's Kongo Dance label, on a slender budget. Nevertheless, it reached the Top 60. In its wake, Omar's name suddenly began to crop up everywhere, be it as a singer, writer or producer. Following a high-profile Hammersmith Odeon concert in December 1990, Gilles Peterson of Talkin' Loud Records persuaded financial backers Phonogram to open their wallets. The debut album was slightly remixed and re-released, the title track having already earned its stripes as a club favourite and a UK Top 20 breakthough. Although by definition a soul artist, Omar's use of reggae, ragga and particularly hip-hop endeared him to a wide cross-section of the dance music community. RCA Records won the scramble to sign Omar after departing from Talkin' Loud in January 1993. Since then, he has continued to collaborate with a number of premier R&B artists - songwriter Lamont Dozier, keyboard player David Frank (famed for his contribution to Chaka Khan's 'I Feel For You'), bass player Derek Bramble (ex-Heatwave), Leon Ware (arranger for Marvin Gaye) and no less than Stevie Wonder himself, who contacted Omar after hearing his 'Music' cut.

● ALBUMS: *There's Nothing Like This* (Kongo Dance 1990)★★★, *Music* (Talkin' Loud 1992)★★★, *For Pleasure* (RCA 1994)★★★, *This Is Not A Love Song* (RCA 1997)★★★.

One Dove

Glasgow, Scotland-based trio, who caught the nation's imagination in 1993 with their mellow musical depths. The members were Ian Carmichael (b. 1 June 1960, Glasgow, Scotland), Jim McKinven (b. David James McKinven, Glasgow, Scotland) and former chemical engineering student Dot Allison (b. Dorothy Elliot Allison, 17 August 1969, Edinburgh, Scotland). McKinven had been in an early incarnation of the Bluebells (rehearsal only), but was best known for his stint in Altered Images. Carmichael owned Toad Hall Studios, engineering or producing for many Glaswegian acts. The trio made their first public appearance at the Rock Garden, Queens Street, Glasgow, in August 1991. The fact that Andy Weatherall got involved attracted some initial attention, but there was more to One Dove than merely another of his side projects. They had already broken into the rave scene's elite with the single 'Fallen', prior to their collaboration. It was released on Soma Records, before the band had changed their name from their original selection, Dove. However, litigation followed from representatives of Supertramp (the band had, inadvertently, used a sample from an Italian house record which in turn had sampled the prog-rockers). They met Weatherall in Rimini, Italy in 1991. After he agreed to work with them there was some discussion in the press that One Dove's debut album would signal another landmark episode, *à la* Primal Scream's *Screamadelica*, but this was perhaps over-optimistic. It was at least a solid, musically enthralling collection conveying One Dove's biggest influence: King Tubby and Jamaican dub music. They disbanded in 1996, with Allison going on to sign a deal with Heavenly Records. She released her acclaimed solo debut, *Afterglow*, in autumn 1999.

● ALBUMS: *Morning Dove White* (ffrr 1993)★★★.

112

From Sean 'Puffy' Combs' Bad Boy stable, 112 comprise Q Parker, Slim Seandrick, Daron Jones and Michael Keith. To media-watchers, it quickly became obvious that this Atlanta, Georgia, USA-based vocal quartet were being marketed as individual talents who could also perform collectively, based 'on the model of New Edition. However, they made their bow just as the Notorious B.I.G. and Ma$e broke through commercially. Not surprisingly, their 1996 self-titled debut was somewhat overlooked as a result, though it still managed sales of close to a million copies. It also produced the major hit singles, 'Only You' and 'Come See Me'. Afterwards they were awarded a Grammy, alongside Combs and Faith Evans, for their contribution to 'I'll Be Missing You', a tribute to the Notorious B.I.G and a worldwide number 1 in autumn 1997. The quartet then refined their formula, offering a second album concentrating on love and romance rather than the hustler-related lyrics of their debut. They also lifted their tempos, in an effort to become less reliant on ballads. The resulting album, *Room 112*, was described by label boss Combs as 'one of the best R&B albums I've ever been involved in.' Among the other high profile writers employed by 112 was Diane Warren. Additional production was provided by Dallas Austin, with guest artists including Ma$e (on the US Top 20 single 'Love Me') and Lil' Kim.

● ALBUMS: *112* (Bad Boy 1996)★★★, *Room 112* (Bad Boy 1998)★★★.

Onyx

Hardcore gangsta rappers from Queens, New York, USA, Onyx are led by Sticky Fingaz (b. Kirk Jones), with the rest of the crew initially comprising Fredro Starr, Big D.S. and DJ Suavé Sonny Caesar. Their intense, gun-fixated image quickly became a popular receptacle for ill-conceived teenage fantasies in both the USA and UK. They originally recorded a solitary single for Profile Records, 1990's 'Ah, And We Do It Like This', before switching to Columbia Records. Boasting titles such as 'Blac Vagina Finda', a visual image of bald heads and bad attitudes, their debut album was co-produced by Jam Master Jay (Run DMC). It sold in huge quantities, arguably because the music itself, on tracks such as 'Throw Ya Gunz' and the US number 3 hit single 'Slam', was undeniably exciting as well as forceful. Living up to the crew's gangsta image, Fingaz found himself in trouble for allegedly assaulting a passenger on a United Airlines flight to New York from Chicago's O'Hare airport. Meanwhile, Fredro Starr appeared in Forest Whitaker's movie, *Strapped* in 1993, and (with Sticky) in Spike Lee's *Clockers*. By the advent of 1995's *All We Got Iz Us*, recorded by the remaining trio of Starr (aka Never), Sticky Fingaz and Caesar (aka Sonee Seeza) for Def Jam Records, their ultra-violent image had been usurped by the arrival of Staten Island's Wu-Tang Clan, but Onyx still offered ample evidence of their ability to hammer home their message in tracks such as '2 Wrongs' ('Two wrongs don't make a right, But it sure do make us even'). Sticky Fingaz and Starr have continued to build their acting careers, with the latter appearing alongside R&B singer Brandy in the hugely successful television series *Moesha*. The trio returned in 1998 with *Shut 'Em Down*, which proved to be a more successful attempt at recapturing the energy and attitude of their debut.

● ALBUMS: *Bacdafucup* (Ral/Columbia 1993)★★★, *All We Got Iz Us* (Ral/Def Jam 1995)★★, *Shut 'Em Down* (Def Jam 1998)★★★.

Orb

The Orb revolves around one man, Dr Alex Paterson (b. Duncan Robert Alex Paterson, hence the appropriation of the Dr title), whose specialist field is the creation of ambient house music. A former Killing Joke roadie, member of Bloodsport, and A&R man at EG Records, he formed the original Orb in 1988 with Jimmy Cauty of Brilliant fame (for whom he had also roadied). The name was taken from a line in Woody Allen's *Sleeper*. The band first appeared on WAU! Mr Modo's showcase set *Eternity Project One* (released via Gee Street Records), with the unrepresentative 'Tripping On Sunshine'. However, their first release proper came with 1989's *Kiss* EP, again on WAU! Mr Modo (which had been set up by Paterson with Orb manager Adam Morris). It was completely overshadowed by the success of the band's subsequent release, 'A Huge Ever-Growing Pulsating Brain Which Rules From The Centre Of The Ultraworld'. It was an extraordinary marriage of progressive rock trippiness and ambience, founded on a centre point sample of Minnie Riperton's 'Loving You' (at least on initial copies, later being voiced by a soundalike due to clearance worries). The band signed with Big Life Records, but Cauty departed in April 1990. He had wished to take Paterson and the Orb on board in his new KLF Communications set-up. There was no little acrimony at the time and Cauty re-recorded an album that was to have been the Orb's debut, deleting Paterson's contributions, and naming it *Space* (also the artist title). In the event the ethereal 'Little Fluffy Clouds', with co-writer Youth, was the next Orb release, though that too ran into difficulties when the sample of Rickie Lee Jones attracted the artist's displeasure. Paterson did at least meet future co-conspirator Thrash (b. Kristian Weston) during these sessions, who joined in late 1991 from a punk/metal background, hence his name (though he had also been a member of Fortran 5). Their debut album (and the remix set of similar title) was based on a journey to dimensions beyond known levels of consciousness, according to the participants. It sleepwalked to the top of the UK independent charts, and led to a plunge of remixes for other artists (including Front 242 and Primal Scream). The album was fully in tune with, and in many ways anticipative of, the blissed-out rave subculture of the early 90s, mingled with dashes of early 70s progressive rock (Pink Floyd were an obvious reference point). There was also an LP's worth of the band's recordings for John Peel's Radio 1 show. This included a 20-minute version of 'Huge Ever-Growing ... ', which prompted fellow disc jockey Andy Kershaw to ring the BBC to complain, mockingly, about the return of hippie indulgence on a gross scale polluting the nation's airwaves. Their popularity was confirmed when the excellent follow-up, *U.F.Orb*, soared to the top of the UK charts in 1992, and the 39 minute single 'Blue Room' reached the Top 10. The Orb signed to Island Records in 1993 following a departure from Big Life that took seven months (and eventually the high court) to settle. The contract with Island allowed Paterson to continue to work on collaborative projects through their own label InterModo, outside of the Orb name. Other projects included a remix album for Yellow Magic Orchestra, though a previous request by Jean-Michel Jarre for them to do the same for his *Oxygene* opus was declined. They also took the opportunity to play live at unlikely venues such as the Danish island of Trekroner, and generally appeared to be making a hugely enjoyable time of their unlikely celebrity, Paterson even being made honorary president of Strathclyde University's Student Union. Their first studio set for Island, *Pomme Fritz*, saw Paterson recording with German technoist Thomas Fehlmann and steering the Orb's sound away from ambient house. The album also witnessed the first signs of a critical backlash, and following its release Weston left the Orb to concentrate on his own solo work. Fehlmann adopted a more prominent role in the Orb set-up on 1995's *Orbus Terrarum*. The album's rhythmic pulse drew mixed reactions from critics, who were more impressed by the follow-up *Orblivion*'s return to the ambient house style of their earlier work.

● ALBUMS: *The Orb's Adventures Beyond The Ultraworld* (Big Life/Mercury 1991)★★★★, *Peel Sessions* (Strange Fruit 1991)★★★★, *Aubrey Mixes: The Ultraworld Excursions* (Big Life/Caroline 1992)★★★, *U.F.Orb* (Big Life/Mercury 1992)★★★★, *Live 93* (InterModo/Island 1993)★★, *Pomme Fritz* (InterModo/Island 1994)★★★, *Orbus Terrarum* (Island 1995)★★★, *Orblivion* (Island 1997)★★★.

● COMPILATIONS: *Peel Sessions 92-95* (Strange Fruit 1996)★★★, *U.F. Off: The Best Of The Orb* (Island 1998)★★★★.

● VIDEOS: *The Orb's Adventures Beyond The Ultraworld - Patterns And Textures* (Big Life 1992), *U.F. Off - The Best Of The Orb* (Island/Vision Video 1998).

Orbit, William

b. William Wainwright, England. Although he has been recording under various guises since 1983, it is only recently that William Orbit has become a household name because of his Emmy-award winning, internationally acclaimed production and writing work on Madonna's 1998 *Ray Of Light*. It was Orbit's work that gave the album its distinctive ethereal atmosphere and its breakbeats and drum 'n' bass-influenced sound. He also won Q magazine's 1999 Best Producer award for his production of Blur's *13*. Although this work has raised his profile enormously, Orbit has an impressive track record of remixing and production work. He has worked on tracks by a diverse and prestigious range of artists including: Sting, Belinda Carlisle, OMD, Julian Lennon, Les Negresses Vertes, Human League, Gary Numan, Prince, Shakespears Sister, Malcom Mclaren, Erasure, S'Express, Propaganda, Cure, Seal, Shamen, Kraftwerk, Scritti Politti, Peter Gabriel, Christians and All Saints. Orbit's renowned studio virtuosity took root as a teenager when he would splice tape recordings to make sound collages. In his early twenties he formed Torch Song with Laurie Mayer, Grant Gilbert and Rico Conning, who released *Wish Thing*, *Ecstasy*, *Exhibit A* and *Toward The Unknown* between 1984 and 1995. For his solo debut, 1987's *Orbit*, he continued to work with Mayer as his co-writer and brought in Peta Nikolich as vocalist. The album included unusual cover versions of the Psychedelic Furs' 'Love My Way' and Jackie Mittoo's 'Feel Like Jumping'. 'Fire And Mercy' became a club hit. Currently perceived as a hip dance music producer, Orbit is unsurprisingly keen to play down his production of novelty records during the 80s: Harry Enfield's 'Loadsamoney – Doin' Up The House' (a UK Top 5 hit in 1988) and his 1986 production of Stan Ridgway's 'Camouflage'. As Bassomatic, Orbit enjoyed his first UK Top 10 single in 1990 with the club anthem 'Fascinating Rhythm' – the follow-up to 'In The Realm Of The Senses'. The attendant *Set The Controls For The Heart Of The Bass* (the title alluded to Pink Floyd's 'Set The Controls For The Heart Of

The Sun') showed Orbit indulging his interest in funky, intelligent house and also demonstrated his skill with percussion and electronics. Alongside his work as Bassomatic, Orbit had been recording ambient soundscape albums, beginning with 1987's *Strange Cargo*. It was this and the subsequent two Strange Cargo albums, alongside those by the KLF, Orb, Aphex Twin and Future Sound Of London that gave rise to the term 'ambient house'. In 1992 and 1993, Orbit worked with Beth Orton as Spill and recorded *Superpinkymandy* but this was released only in Japan under Orton's name. In 1992, Orbit remixed Madonna's 'Justify My Love' which brought him to the attention of Rob Dickins, chairman of Warner Music at that time. Together they set up N-Gram Recordings in 1995 with the support of Discovery Records in the USA (Orbit's previous own label, Guerrilla Records had folded in 1984.) The first release on N-Gram was a single by cellist Caroline Lavelle, whom Orbit had discovered when she played on Massive Attack's 'Home And Way'. Orbit also released the second in his Strange Cargo series and worked with the Torch Song members once more. In 1995, as the Electric Chamber, Orbit released an album of reinterpreted modern classical pieces, *Pieces In A Modern Style* on N-Gram. It was quickly withdrawn when it was discovered that the estates of two of the composers had not given permission for him to record the works. The album, that included pieces by Ravel, Vivaldi, Beethoven and Satie, was effectively re-released in January 2000 by WEA Records with several new tracks and recordings. The album entered the UK album charts at number 2, somewhat assisted by the publicity gained for his work with Madonna and the single, 'Adagio For Strings' – which entered the charts at number 4 in December 1999. The track was a recording of a mournful piece by Samuel Barber, famously used in the movie *Platoon*. The single release featured a remix by the Dutch trance DJ, Ferry Corsten and it was this version that received extensive radio airplay and undoubtedly boosted the single's chart position and its popularity in European clubs. Earlier in 1999, Madonna's single, 'Beautiful Stranger', produced by Orbit, was a Top 10 hit in Europe and the US and featured on the soundtrack of the movie *Austin Powers: The Spy Who Shagged Me*. The single received a nomination for a Grammy Award (for Best Soundtrack and Song) and a Golden Globe. Orbit also produced All Saints' 'Pure Shores', which was featured on the soundtrack of the Leonardo DiCaprio movie, *The Beach*. The single was unmistakably a William Orbit production: using filtered and distorted sounds, ambient washes and electronic percussion. Another soundtrack, for the movie *The Next Best Thing*, co-written and co-produced by Madonna and Orbit, was released on the singer's Maverick label. It featured her new single, a cover version of Don McLean's 'American Pie'.

● ALBUMS: *Orbit* (IRS 1987)★★★★, *Strange Cargo* (IRS 1987)★★★★, *Strange Cargo II* (IRS 1990)★★★, *Strange Cargo 3* (IRS 1993)★★★, *Strange Cargo – Hinterland* (N-Gram 1995)★★★, *Pieces In A Modern Style* (N-Gram 1995)★★, *Pieces In A Modern Style* (WEA 2000)★★★.

● COMPILATIONS: *Strange Cargos* (IRS 1996)★★★★.

Orbital

This UK techno outfit have done much to deliver the possibilities of improvisation to live electronic music. Unlike many other techno acts their stage performances do not depend on DAT or backing tapes. They also use more varied samples than is the norm, including sources as diverse as the Butthole Surfers on 'Satan' and Crass on 'Choice'. Comprising brothers Paul Hartnoll (b. 19 May 1968, Dartford, Kent, England) and Phillip Hartnoll (b. 9 January 1964, Dartford, Kent, England), the Orbital name was first suggested by their friend Chris Daly of the Tufty Club. With several 'M25' rave parties happening so close to their homes in Dunton Green, they named themselves after the London's 'orbital' motor way, which encircles the capital and became known as the 'Magic Roundabout' to ravers at the time. Before the band began its active life in 1987, Paul had played with an outfit by the name of Noddy And The Satellites as well as doing labouring odd jobs, while his brother had been a bricklayer and barman. They made their live debut in the summer of 1989 at the Grasshopper, Westerham, Kent, joining the ffrr Records imprint shortly afterwards. They opened their account for the label with the UK Top 20 single 'Chime' in March 1990 (the track had already been released the previous December in a limited pressing on the Oh Zone imprint), setting a pattern for a sequence of dramatic, one-word titles ('Omen', 'Satan', 'Mutations', 'Radiccio'). Their remixing chores included work on releases by artists as diverse as the Shamen, Queen Latifah, Meat Beat Manifesto and EMF. Their first two albums, both untitled, were subsequently referred to as the 'Green Album' and the 'Brown Album'. Both showcased their ability to sustain a musical dynamic over a full-length album, a rare ability within their field, which saw them bracketed alongside artists such as Underworld and the Orb. In 1994, they appeared as headliners at the Glastonbury Festival and contributed to the *Shopping* soundtrack. The appearance at Glastonbury was a significant success, proving to sceptics that dance music could be exciting to watch live. An enduring image was that of the Hartnolls, shrouded in darkness, with only the twin torches attached to their temples like car headlights piercing the gloom. They also released *Snivilisation*, a largely instrumental political concept album which was successful on both a musical and thematic level and broke into the UK Top 5. Meanwhile, their live work earned them an award for Best Live Show at the *New Musical Express* BRAT Awards as they made a triumphant return to Glastonbury in 1995. In the same year, they completed a remix of Madonna's 'Bedtime Stories' and donated the track 'Adnan' to the *Help* album project for the War Child charity to aid Bosnian refugees. If previous albums had always hinted at a cinematic bent, 1996's 'The Box' was a fully fledged film soundtrack - comprising four distinct movements with vocal versions by lyricist Grant Fulton and Alison Goldfrapp. The film itself was Orbital's own exploration of science-fiction adventurism, ironically filmed in the highly terrestrial environs of Milton Keynes. It was followed by the release of Orbital's fourth studio album. The exquisitely dense rhythms on the six tracks that comprised *In Sides* emphasized the duo's critically acclaimed accommodation of the experimental with the accessible. It included tracks such as 'The Girl With The Sun In Her Head', recorded using solar power as a reaffirmation of their environmental standing. Having first experimented with the use of film soundtracks on *Snivilisation*, they reworked the theme of *The Saint* for the movie remake of the cult 60s television programme. Despite starring Val Kilmer, the movie was not a great critical or commercial success but the single

gave Orbital a UK number 3 hit. They also appeared at the UK festivals Tribal Gathering, Phoenix and in the USA on the Lollapalooza tour. They returned in April 1999 with *The Middle Of Nowhere*, which marked a return to a more 'danceable' sound.

● ALBUMS: *Untitled 1* (Internal/ffrr 1991)★★★, *Untitled 2* (Internal/ffrr 1993)★★★★, *Peel Session* (Internal/ffrr 1994)★★★, *Snivilisation* (Internal/ffrr 1994)★★★★, *In Sides* (London/ffrr 1996)★★★★, with Michael Kamen *Event Horizon* film soundtrack (London 1997)★★, *The Middle Of Nowhere* (London/PolyGram 1999)★★★★.

Orgy

This Southern California-based sleaze rock outfit rose to prominence in the USA as the first signings to Korn's Elementree label, and have done much to rejuvenate the industrial metal scene pioneered by forefathers Ministry and Nine Inch Nails. The five members, who came together in 1997, were all veterans of the Los Angeles metal circuit. Ryan Shuck (guitar) had played with Korn vocalist Jonathan Davis in Sex Art, Bobby Hewitt (b. Bobby Fernandez; drums) played with the Electric Love Hogs, Paige Haley (bass) was a member of various under performing LA bands, while Amir Derakh (guitar synthesizer) had recorded two albums with bog standard 80s metal act Rough Cutt. In the mid-90s, Derakh teamed up with Jay Gordon (vocals) to produce Coal Chamber's debut album. The band's creative spark was captured on *Candyass*, which was produced by Josh Abraham and recorded in a secluded cabin near Lake Tahoe on the Nevada border. The album demonstrated the band's sonic frisson – a relentless, abrasive rhythmic attack processed by computer and complemented by contrasting melodic hooks. Their first self-composed single, 'Stitches', was not successful, but their cover version of New Order's 'Blue Monday', became a highly popular US radio hit. The band's liberal use of make-up, meanwhile, drew comparisons to both Marilyn Manson and the New Romantic bands of the early 80s. Buoyed by the success of 'Blue Monday' and the band's appearance on Korn's Family Values tour, *Candyass* quickly achieved platinum status in America.

● ALBUMS: *Candyass* (Elementree/Reprise 1998)★★★★.

Orton, Beth

b. December 1970, Norwich, Norfolk, England. Beth Orton pulled off the unlikely task of making folk-influenced music hip among mid-90s clubbers. Her early musical heroes were artists such as Neil Young, Rickie Lee Jones and Joni Mitchell, but by her teens she was more interested in an acting career than in being a singer. However, when William Orbit recruited her to record some spoken text for his *Strange Cargo* project, the moderately drunk Orton sang instead. Bizarrely, shortly afterwards she went totally blind for five days, for reasons still unexplained. After she regained her sight she made further guest appearances with Orbit, recording the extremely rare *Superpinkymandy* for the Japanese market. She then worked with Red Snapper and the Chemical Brothers, singing the sublime 'Alive: Alone' on the latter's highly acclaimed 1995 debut, *Exit Planet Dust*. She recorded some demos with members of Primal Scream, which came to the attention of Heavenly Records boss Jeff Barrett and the *Winnebago* project was born. Orton's songs were definitely influenced by her 70s singer-songwriter idols but with the assistance of musicians such as Red Snapper's Ali Friend and Sandals drummer Will Blanchard, as well as remixes by dance music maestro Andy Weatherall, the songs maintained a sort of trip-folk momentum. The album, renamed *Trailer Park* after threats of legal action from the makers of the camper van, was rivalled only by Portishead's *Dummy* as a prime choice chill-out album for broad-minded, beautiful people. Finally, British folk/dance meant something other than fat men in white trousers hitting each other with bladders. In 1997, Orton appeared on the Chemical Brothers' massively successful *Dig Your Own Hole* singing the chill-out classic, 'Where Do I Begin?'. The *Best Bit* EP, released the same December, featured Orton duetting with her musical hero Terry Callier on a cover version of Fred Neil's 'Dolphins'. Callier appeared on Orton's eagerly anticipated follow-up, *Central Reservation*, an album which replicated the ramshackle charm of her debut.

● ALBUMS: *Superpinkymandy* (Toshiba/EMI 1993)★★★, *Trailer Park* (Heavenly 1996)★★★★, *Central Reservation* (Heavenly 1999)★★★★.

Osborne, Joan

b. 8 July 1962, Anchorage, Kentucky, USA. The rock singer Osborne began her singing career one evening at the Abilene blues bar in New York, USA. Prompted by several drinks, she took the stage at 3 am as a dare and sang Billie Holiday's 'God Bless The Child'. The resident pianist at the club encouraged her to attend the bar's regular open-microphone nights. Although a reluctant performer at first, she soon learned to enjoy these opportunities, building a solid reputation in the New York area. The live album *Soul Show* was released on her own Womanly Hips Records in 1991 and an EP, *Blue Million Miles*, followed in 1993. Later that year she became the first signing to Blue Gorilla, a new label set up by Rick Chertoff, senior vice-president of PolyGram Records. However, before the deal was completed, Chertoff invited Osborne to take part in writing workshops in Katonah, New York, alongside a variety of musicians. It was here that the band who appeared on her major label debut formed. *Relish* featured Rob Hyman (keyboards), Eric Bazilian (guitar, ex-Hooters), Charlie Quintana (drums; also of Cracker) and Rainy Orteca (bass). Bazilian wrote the infectious US Top 5 single 'One Of Us'. Osborne's own songwriting was helped by a workshop given by Doc Pomus, explaining the rootsy nature of much of her work which owes more to blues and R&B than to 90s rock music. The album also included two songs, 'Help Me' and 'Crazy Baby', originally included on *Soul Show*. Following the success of 'One Of Us', *Relish* received strong reviews from *Rolling Stone*, the *New York Times* and the *New Yorker*, the latter describing Osborne as 'one of the most distinct voices in rock'. Two television appearances on the *Late Show With David Letterman*, and national tours, during which she invited pro-life organizations to put their case to her audience, increased her profile throughout 1995. In 1996, 'One Of Us' found its way to the UK and was a Top 10 hit. Osborne does not deserve the same fate. While recording the follow-up to *Relish*, Osborne toured with Lilith Fair and, in 1999, contributed 'Baby Love' to the *For Love Of The Game* soundtrack.

● ALBUMS: *Soul Show* (Womanly Hips 1991)★★, *Relish* (Blue Gorilla/Mercury 1995)★★★★.

● COMPILATIONS: *Early Recordings* (Mercury 1996)★★.

Other Two

The most purely dance music-orientated project of the three major New Order spin-offs, the Other Two features arguably the least attention-seeking members of the Manchester quartet: Stephen Morris (b. 28 October 1957, Macclesfield, Cheshire, England) and Gillian Gilbert (b. 27 January 1961, Manchester, England). Recording at their own studio in rural Macclesfield, they debuted on the charts with the Factory Records single 'Tasty Fish' in 1991. The follow-up, 'Selfish', came out two years later on London Records, and featured fashionable remixes by both Moby and Farley And Heller. The Other Two also tampered with the work of other artists, as well as earning several credits for television and soundtrack motifs. Their two albums to date have been melodic if somewhat faceless electronic pop collections.

● ALBUMS: *The Other Two & You* (London/Qwest 1993)★★★, *Super Highways* (London 1999)★★★.

Our Lady Peace

Comprising Raine Maida (b. Michael Raine Maida; vocals), Mike Turner (guitar), Chris Eacrett (bass) and Jeremy Taggart (drums), Our Lady Peace were formed in Toronto, Canada, in 1992. The band took their unusual name from a 1943 poem by American poet Mark Van Doren. The unusual, eclectic nature of the band's music is as much a result of their varied experiences as their musical influences. Maida was a former criminology student at the University of Toronto, while English graduate Turner grew up in Bradford, England during the punk explosion. Eacrett was studying marketing at Ryerson University in Toronto when he made initial contact with founding members Maida and Turner, who then recruited 17 year old drummer Taggart. After meeting local producer Arnold Lanni they set about recording their first demos, which immediately attracted the attention of Sony Music Canada. The band's debut album, *Naveed*, took its title from 'the ancient Middle Eastern name for bearer of good news', and featured the popular radio hit 'Starseed'. The songwriting, which was undertaken before their stage debut, evolved out of a communal musical approach, with Maida supplying lyrics. Duncan Coutts replaced Eacrett shortly after the release of the album. *Clumsy* was a strong follow-up, showcasing a more mature songwriting approach which was rewarded with worldwide sales of over two million. A remixed version of 'Starseed' was featured on the following year's *Armageddon* soundtrack. The band's third album, *Happiness ... Is Not A Fish That You Can Catch*, was recorded with Lanni at Toronto's Arnyard Studios.

● ALBUMS: *Naveed* (Sony Canada/Relativity 1994)★★★, *Clumsy* (Sony 1997)★★★, *Happiness ... Is Not A Fish That You Can Catch* (Sony 1999)★★★.

Outhere Brothers

This rap duo from Chicago, Illinois, USA featured singer and lyricist Malik and producer Hula. Malik previously wrote the lyrics to Jazzy Jeff And The Fresh Prince's worldwide hit, 'Boom Boom Shake The Room'. He had also been a member of another crew, Lidell Townsell And M.T.F., who had a US Top 30 hit with 'Nu Nu'. He agreed to work with Hula through a mutual Jazzy Jeff connection. Hula produced the rapper/DJ team's Grammy award-winning platinum single, 'Summertime'. They were originally joined by two other members, who promptly disappeared on their first trip to Europe. As the Outhere Brothers they enjoyed considerable success first with 'Pass The Toilet Paper' then two UK number 1 singles, 'Don't Stop (Wiggle Wiggle)' and 'Boom Boom Boom'. The latter stayed at the top of the charts for several weeks in 1995, and featured a memorable video of the two Chicago Bulls fans playing basketball. Both singles were big sellers in Europe, despite a near absence of mainstream radio play due to their risqué lyrical contents. In April 1995, the duo were investigated by New Scotland Yard following a justified complaint from a Bradford mother that the album, purchased by her 10-year-old daughter, was obscene, especially deliberately provocative titles such as 'I'll Lick Your Pussy' and 'Fuk U In The Ass'. At the same time further complaints were received about the lyrics of a bonus track on their irritating number 1 hit, 'Don't Stop (Wiggle Wiggle)'. Two further singles, 'La La La Hey Hey' and 'If You Wanna Party', appeared in the UK Top 10 before 1995 ended. The duo continued to enjoy club hits with tracks such as 'Lad De Da De Da De (We Like To Party)' and 'Ae-Ah' but the repetitive nature of their work indicated a short commercial life, with thousands of parents doubtless breathing a sigh of relief.

● ALBUMS: *1 Polish 2 Biscuits And A Fish Sandwich* (Eternal/Aureus 1995)★★, *The Party Album* (Eternal/Aureus 1995)★★, *The Other Side* (Eternal/Aureus 1996)★★.

Outkast

This rap duo comprises 'Dre' (b. Andre Benjamin, 27 May 1975, Georgia, USA) and 'Big Boi' (b. Antoine Patton, 1 February 1975, Savannah, Georgia, USA), who first met while studying at Atlanta's Tri-City high school. The duo signed a contract with L.A. And Babyface's LaFace imprint prior to graduation, and immediately broke big with 'Player's Ball', produced by TLC backroom gang Organized Noise. The track, which topped the *Billboard* rap chart for over six weeks in 1994, featured on the duo's platinum selling debut, *Southernplayalisticadillacmuzik*. Comprising tales of the streets of their local East Point and Decateur neighbourhoods, the album helped establish the south as a new force in hip-hop. 'Elevators (Me & You)' became a major rap chart success in July 1996 and broke into the US Top 20, while the attendant *ATLiens* debuted at number 2 on the *Billboard* 200 album chart. The musically diverse and mystically inclined *Aquemini* repeated the success of its predecessor, debuting at US number 2 in October 1998.

● ALBUMS: *Southerplayalisticadillacmuzik* (LaFace 1994)★★★★, *ATLiens* (LaFace 1996)★★★, *Aquemini* (LaFace 1998)★★★.

Ovans, Tom

b. Boston, Massachusetts, USA. After leaving high school, folk-singer, songwriter and harmonica player Ovans headed to the west coast and then New York. Living on friends' floors and in cheap hotel rooms, he was initially disillusioned by the fact that the Village coffee house scene that birthed his hero Bob Dylan was dying on its feet. It was only when he moved to Nashville that he secured a recording contract, resulting in the release of *Industrial Days* in 1991. It prompted one reviewer to state that '. . . sometimes only a cliché will do, so - with apologies to all concerned - maybe Tom Ovans is the new Bob Dylan.' Often backed by his wife, singer/songwriter Lou Ann Bardash, Ovans' bleak portraits

of his homeland have found greater favour in Europe where he has attracted praise for his fiercely independent stance and his refusal to kowtow to any passing musical trends. His sparse blues/folk instrumentation and rasping voice create a unique ambience of their own, exemplified by tracks such as 'Killing Me' and 'Real Television' from the superb *Dead South*. The Demon Records compilation *Nuclear Sky* offers a useful introduction to the three albums he recorded before *Dead South*. His most recent work, 1999's *The Beat Trade*, was released on the UK independent label Floating World.

● ALBUMS: *Industrial Days* (Nebula Sound 1991)★★★★, *Unreal City* (Nebula Sound 1993)★★★, *Tales From The Underground* (Nebula Sound 1995)★★★, *Dead South* (Demon 1997)★★★★, *The Beat Trade* (Floating World 1999)★★★.

● COMPILATIONS: *Nuclear Sky* (Demon 1996)★★★★.

Owen, Mark

b. Mark Anthony Owen, 27 January 1972, Oldham, Lancashire, England. Widely regarded as 'the pretty one' in Take That, the diminutive Mark Owen was the third member of the highly successful boy band to launch a solo career in 1996, following Gary Barlow and Robbie Williams. Although his debut single, the UK number 3 single 'Child', was evidently intended to offer a bridge between Take That fans and a new audience, his debut solo album, *The Green Man*, was far more experimental in nature than anything issued by his former compatriots. Though it retained pop elements, there was a committed attempt to take the songwriting and production away from the 'teenybopper' constituency of old. Among the surprises was Owen's choice of collaborators. The producers involved were John Leckie (Radiohead, Fall) and Craig Leon (Blondie). The musicians included Dave Gregory (ex-XTC) and Clem Burke (ex-Blondie). Owen later confessed to not really knowing who Leckie was, but to admiring the depth of atmosphere created on Radiohead's *The Bends*. The songwriting was predominantly Owen's, despite the fact that he had only contributed two b-sides to Take That's extensive career. All the tracks, apart from 'Child', were solo efforts, which he had previously demoed at his Lancashire home with his father playing the guitar. The melodic but lightweight 'Clementine' was his only other chart success when it reached number 3 in February 1997. Owen was dropped by RCA Records in 1999 after they rejected his new material.

● ALBUMS: *Green Man* (RCA 1996)★★★.

P., Alex

b. Alex Petridis, England. Alex P. has been DJing professionally since 1988, thrilling clubbers all over the world with his
unpretentious form of hard house. Along with Brandon
Block he is from the old school of UK house DJs – hard-
working, hedonistic and completely absorbed by the music
and atmosphere of the club scene. He made his name during
the early days of acid house at events such as Sunrise, Back
To The Future and Energy. He was also a part of the original
Ibiza dance scene that took hold on the island in the early
90s, holding residencies at Amnesia, Ku and the Space
Garden in 1990. He remains devoted to Ibiza, playing there
every summer. Since those early days, he has played at
every major house club in the UK: the Ministry Of Sound,
Clockwork Orange, Up Yer Ronson, Gatecrasher, Passion,
Colours and The Gallery. He has mixed many compilation
albums and remixed many singles. His own releases include
'Predator' by Airtight and 'Forever' by Alex. He is known as
Peezee on the weekly UK radio show he presents on Kiss 100
FM with Brandon Block, which regularly attracts a large
audience. A populist, crowd-pleasing DJ but nevertheless a
hard-working and inventive one, Alex P. is assured a place in
the hearts and minds of the international house audience.

Padilla, José

b. 1956, Spain. Padilla's name is synonymous with Ibiza's
famous beach-side bar, the Café Del Mar, where he was the
resident DJ for more than 15 years. Although no longer
there, he remains an Ibizan institution playing at various
venues on the island every summer and all over Europe
during the rest of the year. Not an archetypal superstar DJ
(he was voted number 100 in *DJ* magazine's Top 100 of the
world's DJs), he is an unsung hero to many and certainly the
original chill out DJ. His sets at the Café Del Mar, which, like
the bar itself, used the sunset as their focal point, have
become part of clubbers' folklore. Padilla crafted the quintessential sunrise soundtrack, providing the perfect antidote
to the ferocious 'four-to-the-floor' (slang for the traditional
time signature of house) energy of the island's other clubs.
His style ranges freely through classic funk, ethereal house,
contemporary ambient music, soundtracks and artists as
diverse as Art Of Noise, Dusty Springfield and Vangelis. In
this sense, he has remained true to the Balearic tradition of
dance music: the old and new juxtaposed and orchestrated
into a fluid, blissful, subtly funky groove. Padilla moved to
Ibiza in the mid-70s to escape the city life, and began to DJ
at the Café Del Mar. The bar's clientele pestered him for
tapes of the unusually serene music he played. Eventually,
this led to the recording of the *Café Del Mar* compilation
series that was originally released on the React Music label

in the UK. Arguably, the albums have and continue to
inspire numerous inferior Ibiza/chill out compilations. In
addition to producing several of his own singles and an
album of original material, *Souvenir*, Padilla has also moved
into scoring film soundtracks.
● ALBUMS: *Souvenir* (Manifesto 1997)★★★.
● COMPILATIONS: *Café Del Mar - Volumen Uno* (React Music
1994)★★★★, *Café Del Mar - Volumen Dos* (React Music 1995)★★★,
Café Del Mar - Volumen Tres (React Music 1996)★★★★, *Café Del Mar
- Volumen Quatro* (React Music 1997)★★★, *Café Del Mar - Volumen
Cinco* (Manifesto 1998)★★★, *Café Del Mar - Volumen Seis* (Manifesto
1999)★★★.

Palace Brothers

The creation of Will Oldham (b. Louisville, Kentucky, USA),
who also releases music as Palace Songs, Palace Music,
Palace and Bonnie 'Prince' Billy. Alongside Bill Callahan of
Smog, Oldham is a pioneer of the lo-fi movement in
American independent music, garnering critical acclaim for
his astute, eloquent lyrics and assured songs documenting
anxiety and emotional repression. Oldham originally
worked as an actor, starring in John Sayles' low-budget 1987
movie *Matewan*, and also appearing in the television movie
Everybody's Baby: The Rescue Of Jessica McClure. After con-
tributing to work by the Sundowners and Box Of Chocolates,
Oldham signed to influential Chicago label Drag City
Records. Adopting the Palace Brothers moniker, he recorded
the wryly titled *There Is No One What Will Take Care Of You*.
The album featured guitarist Brian McMahan and drummer
Britt Walford, veterans of Kentucky bands Squirrel Bait and
Slint (Oldham took the picture on the cover of Slint's 1990
alternative rock classic, *Spiderland*). Combining diverse
influences including gospel, Appalachian mountain folk and
country, Oldham's words continually disorientated the listener, taking an obvious pride in confounding expectations
via his convoluted narratives. Several singles followed under
the Palace and Palace Songs monikers, before the release of
his self-titled second album, which was subsequently reissued as *Days In The Wake*. This album was recorded solo
with acoustic guitar, making his dense compositions more
direct and immediate. He returned to the band format for
Palace Songs' subsequent *Hope* EP, which featured Sean
O'Hagan (High Llamas) and Liam Hayes (who subsequently
formed Plush). *Arise Therefore* was credited simply to Palace
and saw Oldham experiment with bleak drum machine
rhythms, a typically disorientating challenge to his public
perception given the strutting country rock of his previous
collection, *Viva Last Blues* (as Palace Music). It was also
another lyrical journey further down the spiral of depression, highlighting his mordant, piercing lyricism. Gavin
Martin writing in the UK's *New Musical Express* noted that
'Oldham makes Leonard Cohen seem like a contestant on
(television show) *The Shane Ritchie Experience*'. Following the
release of the rarities collection *Lost Blues And Other Songs*,
Oldham concentrated on releasing new material under his
own name. The subject matter on *Joya* proved to be as wilfully perverse as the Palace albums, though the musical settings were his most conventional to date. Typically, Oldham
followed his most accessible record with the dark, fore-
boding lo-fi masterpiece *I See A Darkness*, recorded under
yet another pseudonym, Bonnie 'Prince' Billy.
● ALBUMS: *There Is No One What Will Take Care Of You* (Drag City

1993)★★★★, *Palace* aka *Days In The Wake* (Drag City/Domino 1993)★★★, as Palace Music *Viva Last Blues* (Drag City/Domino 1995)★★★, as Palace *Arise Therefore* (Drag City/Domino 1996)★★★, as Will Oldham *Joya* (Drag City/Domino 1997)★★★, as Bonnie 'Prince' Billy *I See A Darkness* (Palace/Domino 1998)★★★★.
● COMPILATIONS: as Palace Music *Lost Blues And Other Songs* (Drag City/Domino 1997)★★★, *Guarapero/Lost Blues 2* (Palace 2000)★★★.
● FILMS: *Matewan* (1987), *Thousand Pieces Of Gold* (1990), *Radiation* (1998).

Pale Saints

Indie band formed in Leeds, Yorkshire, England, in 1989 by Ian Masters (b. 4 January 1964, Potters Bar, Hertfordshire, England; bass/vocals), Chris Cooper (b. 17 November 1966, Portsmouth, England; drums) and Graeme Naysmith (b. 9 February 1967, Edinburgh, Scotland; guitar), in response to an advertisement in a music paper. Aided by occasional guitarist Ashley Horner, who eventually concentrated on his other band, Edsel Auctioneer, on a full-time basis, the Pale Saints spent a year playing local venues and perfecting an idiosyncratic array of material that relied heavily on textures and effects rather than traditional arrangements or blatantly commercial choruses. That was not to say that they were unattractive - their first ever London gig in the spring of 1989 brought them a recording contract with 4AD Records. They were signed at the same time as Lush, a band who mined a similar sonic vein but who ultimately enjoyed greater commercial success. The Pale Saints' debut EP, *Barging Into The Presence Of God*, and the subsequent *The Comforts Of Madness*, earned the band much critical appreciation and a UK Top 40 placing for the album. Canadian emigrate Meriel Barham (b. 15 October 1964, Yorkshire, England) joined as a permanent guitarist and vocalist soon after. The band continued their decidedly obtuse - if not downright perverse - path into the new decade with tours of Europe and Japan and an elegant cover version of Nancy Sinatra's 'Kinky Love', which reached number 72 in the UK charts. The subsequent *In Ribbons* housed a non-charting single in 'Throwing Back The Apple', while Hugh Jones' crisp production gave new impetus to the band's familiar grandeur. Masters departed in 1993, and went on to record two albums as Spoonfed Hybrid with Chris Trout (ex-A.C. Temple) and work with His Name Is Alive auteur Warren Defever. He was replaced by Colleen Browne (ex-Heart Throbs), leaving Barham in charge of lyric writing and vocals on the disappointing *Slow Buildings*. The band split-up in 1996, with Browne going on to play with Rialto and then the Warm Jets.
● ALBUMS: *The Comforts Of Madness* (4AD 1990)★★★, *In Ribbons* (4AD 1992)★★★★, *Slow Buildings* (4AD 1994)★★★.

Pantera

This Texas, USA-based heavy metal quartet was formed in 1981, and initially comprised Terry Glaze (guitar/vocals), Darrell Abbott (b. 20 August 1966, Dallas, Texas, USA; guitar), Vincent Abbott (b. 11 March 1964, Dallas, Texas, USA; drums) and Rex Rocker (b. Rex Brown, 27 July 1964, Graham, Texas, USA; bass). Drawing musical inspiration from Kiss, Aerosmith and Deep Purple, they debuted with 1983's *Metal Magic*. This well-received set led to prestigious support slots to Dokken, Stryper and Quiet Riot. *Projects In The Jungle* indicated that the band were evolving quickly and

starting to build a sound of their own. The Kiss nuances had disappeared and they sounded, at times, similar to early Def Leppard, with cuts such as 'Heavy Metal Rules' and 'Out For Blood' leading the charge. The membership altered their names at this juncture, with Glaze becoming Terence Lee, Darrell Abbott switching to Diamond (later Dimebag) Darrell and brother Vince emerging as Vinnie Paul. Phil Anselmo (b. 30 June 1968, New Orleans, Louisiana, USA) was the new lead vocalist on 1988's *Power Metal*, which saw the band beginning to make the conversion to the heavy thrash sound that would become their trademark. (The band have subsequently attempted to sweep any sign of their early career under the carpet). Diamond Darrell turned down the offer to join Megadeth at this point, in order to concentrate on new Pantera material. The decision proved crucial, as a return to form was made with 1990's *Cowboys From Hell*, their debut for Atco Records. This was an inspired collection of infectious hard rock, played with unabashed fervour, with Anselmo, who would later set up his own side-project Down, growing as a creative and visual force. *Vulgar Display Of Power*, meanwhile, belied half of its title by invoking a sense of genuine songwriting prowess to augment the bone-crushing arrangements of live favourites such as 'Fucking Hostile'. Establishing a fierce reputation, it surprised few of the band's supporters when *Far Beyond Driven* was a huge transatlantic success in 1994. Rock music had found powerful new ambassadors in their brutally honest and savagely executed thrash metal. The key word here is 'loud', as both *The Great Southern Trendkill* and *Official Live: 101 Proof* demonstrate without a doubt. Their influence on the new wave of alternative metal bands that emerged in the late 90s, such as Korn and Fear Factory, should also be noted.
● ALBUMS: *Metal Magic* (Metal Magic 1983)★★★, *Projects In The Jungle* (Metal Magic 1984)★★★, *I Am The Night* (Metal Magic 1985)★★★, *Power Metal* (Metal Magic 1988)★★, *Cowboys From Hell* (Atco 1990)★★★★, *Vulgar Display Of Power* (Atco 1992)★★★★, *Far Beyond Driven* (East West 1994)★★★★, *Driven Downunder Tour '94 Souvenir Collection* (East West 1995)★★, *The Great Southern Trendkill* (East West 1996)★★★, *Official Live: 101 Proof* (East West 1997)★★.
● VIDEOS: *Vulgar Video* (A*Vision 1993), *3 - Watch It Go* (East West 1998).

Paradise Lost

This Halifax, Yorkshire, England-based death metal quintet was formed in 1988, deriving their name from John Milton's epic poem. The band originally comprised Nick Holmes (b. 7 January 1970, Halifax, Yorkshire, England), Gregor Mackintosh (b. 20 June 1970, Halifax, Yorkshire, England; guitar), Aaron Aedy (b. 19 December 1969, Bridlington, Yorkshire, England; guitar), Stephen Edmondson (b. 30 December 1969, Bradford, Yorkshire, England; bass) and Matthew Archer (b. 14 July 1970, Leicester, Yorkshire, England; drums), and were signed to the independent Peaceville label on the strength of two impressive demos. They debuted in 1990 with *Lost Paradise*, which was heavily influenced by Napalm Death, Obituary and Death. It featured indecipherable grunting from Holmes, over a barrage of metallic white noise. *Gothic* saw a major innovation in the 'grindcore' genre, with female vocals, keyboards and guitar lines that, for once, were not lost in the mix. Importantly, the tempo had also eased: 'We started to play more slowly because all the others were playing as fast as possible.' Many, notably Asphyx and Autopsy, followed suit. With indications in the early 90s of the metal subgenres becoming accepted within the mainstream, it came as no surprise when Paradise Lost found a wider audience with *Shades Of God*, their first effort for Music For Nations. Recorded with producer Simon Efemey, and with artwork from cult cartoonist Dave McKean, this release was heralded in the press as a 'coming of age'. Sell-out shows in Europe followed, before the band returned to Longhome studios in the UK, with Efemey once again in attendance. The *As I Die* EP gained a strong foothold on MTV, and gained approval from peers including Metallica. If previous offerings had seen the band's fanbase expand, September 1993's *Icon* brought about an explosion of interest and acclaim usually reserved for the US gods of death metal. Reactions to the band's live shows in the USA with Sepultura were equally strong. However, before sessions for a fifth album could begin, Archer amicably departed, to be replaced by Lee Morris, who joined in time for the release of 1995's excellent *Draconian Times*. By this time the band's popularity was such that several promotional concerts had to be performed under the alias the Painless. Following the release of the disappointing, experimental *One Second*, the band signed to EMI Records and reaffirmed their metal credentials with 1999's *Host*.

● ALBUMS: *Lost Paradise* (Peaceville 1990)★★★, *Gothic* (Peaceville 1991)★★★, *Shades Of God* (Music For Nations 1992)★★★, *Icon* (Music For Nations 1993)★★★★, *Draconian Times* (Music For Nations 1995)★★★★, *One Second* (Music For Nations 1997)★★, *Host* (EMI 1999)★★★.

● COMPILATIONS: *The Singles Collection* 5-CD box set (Music For Nations 1997)★★★★, *Reflection* (Music For Nations 1998)★★★.

● VIDEOS: *Harmony Breaks* (Music For Nations 1994), *One Second Live* (Paradise Lost 1999).

Parker, Andrea

b. Kent, England. This experimental, London-based techno DJ and producer is signed to Mo' Wax Records. She contributed to experimental electronica releases by Inky Blacknuss (with Alex Knight) and Two Sandwiches Short Of A Lunchbox (with David Morley) and provided vocals on Koh Toa's single, 'Sundown' before being signed to Mo' Wax. Her first single for the label was 'Melodius Thunk' – the title punning on the name of the jazz musician, Thelonious Monk - which was an electro workout popular with both UK and US DJs. 'Rocking Chair', the second single, was an emotional ballad featuring string arrangements by Will Malone, who had worked on horror movie soundtracks and Massive Attack's classic 'Unfinished Sympathy'. Parker began as a DJ at London techno clubs such as Lost and the renowned Megatripolis but grew up in Yalding, Kent, listening to artists such as This Mortal Coil and the Cowboy Junkies. Her 1999 album, *Kiss My Arp*, was recorded with her long-time studio partner, David Morley, in rural Bavaria, Germany. The Arp in the title refers to one of Morley's antiquated ARP keyboards. Parker is also an enthusiast of other classic synthesisers such as Moogs and Fairlights. Influenced by artists including the Art Of Noise, she enjoys using 'found sounds' that are sampled and manipulated using studio equipment. These might even include the sound of her own sneezes, or that of her car tyres running over 'cats' eyes' lighting devices in the road. The result of this potpourri of interests is inno-

vative electronic music that also shows a love of the art of songwriting. Parker continues to work as a DJ and occasionally remixes for other artists, such as Depeche Mode.

● ALBUMS: *Kiss My Arp* (Mo' Wax 1999)★★★.

Patterson, Rahsaan

b. 11 January 1974, New York, USA. Progressive urban R&B vocalist Rahsaan Patterson attracted strong reviews upon the release of his self-titled 1997 debut album. A collection of ballads combining strong melodic and rhythmic elements, critics were impressed both by his sonorous voice and the maturity of the songwriting, earning the singer comparisons to artists such as Maxwell and Eric Bénet. Born in New York but resident in Los Angeles, the ambitious, engaging young artist was keen to state that his lyrics reflected the life he saw around him in urban California. Although *Rahsaan Patterson* was his first recording, the artist could already boast of considerable experience in the entertainment industry. As a child, he was a featured performer on *Kids Incorporated*, a televised variety series, and also appeared in various commercials. While recording demo material in Los Angeles he made his name as an in-demand backing vocalist, and also co-wrote two hit singles - 'Back To The World', written with Keith Crouch for Tevin Campbell, and 'Baby', written with Les Pierce for Brandy. Patterson's guest vocals for Pierce's own band, Colour Club, helped bring him to the attention of MCA Records. Pierce and Crouch both reappeared on Patterson's 1997 debut, alongside Jamey Jaz, Ira Schick and Dinky Bingham. The follow-up, *Love In Stereo*, was another superb collection of heartfelt contemporary soul.

● ALBUMS: *Rahsaan Patterson* (MCA 1997)★★★★, *Love In Stereo* (MCA 1999)★★★★.

Pavement

Darlings of the 90s US independent scene, Pavement were formed in 1989 in Stockton, California, USA, by college dropouts Steve Malkmus (vocals/guitar) and Scott 'Spiral Stairs' Kannberg (guitar). Later they extended to a five-piece by adding Gary Young (percussion), a venerable live attraction who was as likely to perform handstands on stage as any musical duties, plus Bob Nastanovich (drums) and Mark Ibold (bass). However, as three of the band were located on the east coast (New York), rehearsals were initially limited to perhaps once a year, and recording sessions and tours proved equally sporadic, resulting in songs that were 'meant to sound like Chrome or the Clean, but ended up sounding like the Fall and Swell Maps.' Their debut release was 1989's *Slay Tracks (1933-1969)*, the first in a series of EPs for the Drag City label that charmed the critics, culminating in the highly influential *Perfect Sound Forever*. The band's eclectic stew of musical styles was heard to great effect on their debut long-player, *Slanted And Enchanted*, with Malkmus' dry, free-ranging lyrics also attracting praise for their acute observational scope. Young left the band in 1993 (replaced by Steve West) when his stage behaviour became unbearable, but neither this, nor the insistence of UK critics that the band were a pale imitation of the Fall, hindered their rise to the top of the US alternative scene. *Wowee Zowee!* offered a more angular, less instantly accessible formula, with many of the tracks opting for outright experimentalism. Malkmus defended it thus: 'It's still a warm and open record if people are willing to join us'. By the time of 1997's *Brighten The Corners*, they were being primarily identified as an important influence on Blur's new lo-fi direction, which somewhat detracted from Malkmus' ability to write a song as engagingly melodic as 'Shady Lane'. *Terror Twilight* benefited from Nigel Godrich's production and earned the band an unlikely UK Top 20 placing, which was somewhat apt considering Malkmus' continuing obsession with all things English.

● ALBUMS: *Perfect Sound Forever* mini-album (Drag City 1991)★★★, *Slanted And Enchanted* (Matador 1992)★★★★, *Crooked Rain, Crooked Rain* (Matador 1994)★★★★, *Wowee Zowee!* (Matador 1995)★★, *Brighten The Corners* (Matador 1997)★★★, *Terror Twilight* (Matador 1999)★★★★.

● COMPILATIONS: *Westing (By Musket And Sextant)* (Drag City 1993)★★★.

Pearl Jam

This revisionist (or, depending on your viewpoint, visionary) rock quintet was formed in Seattle, USA, by Jeff Ament (b. 10 March 1963, Big Sandy, Montana, USA; bass) and Stone Gossard (b. 20 July 1965, Seattle, Washington, USA; rhythm guitar). Gossard had played with Steve Turner in the Ducky Boys, the latter going on to perform with Ament in Green River. Gossard became a member when Mark Arm (like Turner, later to join Mudhoney) switched from guitar to vocals. Gossard and Ament, however, elected to continue working together when Green River washed up, and moved on to Mother Love Bone, fronted by local 'celebrity' Andrew Wood. However, that ill-fated band collapsed when, four weeks after the release of their 1990 debut, *Apple*, Wood was found dead from a heroin overdose. Both Gossard and Ament subsequently participated in Seattle's tribute to Wood, Temple Of The Dog, alongside Chris Cornell of Soundgarden, who instigated the project, Soundgarden drummer Matt Cameron, plus Gossard's school friend Mike McCready (b. 5 April 1966, Pensacola, Florida, USA; guitar). Ex-Bad Radio vocalist Eddie Vedder (b. Edward Louis Severson II, 23 December 1964, Evanston, Illinois, USA), who had come to Seattle after being passed a tape of demos recorded by Ament, Gossard and McCready by Red Hot Chili Peppers drummer Jack Irons, helped out on vocals. Both Vedder and McCready subsequently hooked up with Ament and Gossard to become Pearl Jam, with the addition of drummer Dave Krusen (the band had also dabbled with the name Mookie Blaylock). They signed to Epic Records in 1991, debuting the following year with the powerful *Ten*, by which time Krusen had left the band (he was eventually replaced by Dave Abbruzzese). A bold diorama, it saw the band successfully incorporate elements of their native traditions (Soundgarden, Mother Love Bone, Nirvana) with older influences such as the Doors, Velvet Underground, the Stooges and the MC5. The self-produced recording (together with Rick Parashar) showed great maturity for a debut, particularly in the full-blooded songwriting, never better demonstrated than on the highly melodic singles 'Alive' and 'Jeremy'. Dynamic live performances and a subtle commercial edge to their material catapulted them from obscurity to virtual superstars overnight, as the Seattle scene debate raged and Kurt Cobain accused them of 'jumping the alternative bandwagon'. In the USA, *Ten* was still in the Top 20 a year and a half after its release. The touring commitments that followed brought Vedder to the

verge of nervous collapse. He struggled back to health in time for Pearl Jam's cameo as Matt Dillon's 'band', Citizen Dick, in the 1992 movie *Singles*, and appearances on *MTV Unplugged* and the Lollapalooza II tour. The following year, Vedder fronted a reunited Doors on their induction into the Rock And Roll Hall Of Fame in Los Angeles at the Century Plaza hotel, performing versions of 'Roadhouse Blues', 'Break On Through' and 'Light My Fire'. They also collaborated with Canadian rock singer Neil Young on his 1993 summer tour. Gossard, meanwhile, involved himself with the acclaimed Brad project. Pearl Jam's eagerly awaited follow-up *Vs* was announced in October 1993, close on the heels of Nirvana's latest offering. While reviews were mixed, the advance orders placed the album on top of the US charts. The band also reaffirmed their commitment to their fans by protesting against the Ticketmaster booking agency over inflated ticket prices. The US chart-topper *Vitalogy* seemed overtly concerned with re-establishing their grassroots credibility, a strong clue to which arrived in the fact that the album was available for a week on vinyl before a CD or cassette release (a theme revisited on 'Spin The Black Circle'). There were also numerous references, some oblique, others more immediate, to the death of Nirvana's Kurt Cobain. Ironically, 1994 also saw Abbruzzese dispensed with, amid unfounded rumours that former Nirvana drummer Dave Grohl would be invited into the ranks. Jack Irons (ex-Red Hot Chili Peppers) subsequently became the band's drummer. In 1995, McCready released an album with his Mad Season side-project and joined his band mates on Neil Young's *Mirror Ball*, although Pearl Jam's name was not allowed to appear on the album's front cover. *No Code* was a strong collection that eschewed the band's normal sound in favour of an experimental, semi-acoustic approach. Hailed as a return to their roots, the hard rocking *Yield* was not a great commercial success despite reaching number 2 on the US album chart, with the effects of the band's long-term feud with Ticketmaster cutting into their fanbase. Irons was replaced later in the year by Matt Cameron, who featured on the concert album *Live On Two Legs*. The band bounced back in summer 1999, reaching 2 in the US singles chart with their cover version of Wayne Cochran's 'Last Kiss'.

● ALBUMS: *Ten* (Epic 1991)★★★, *Vs.* (Epic 1993)★★★, *Vitalogy* (Epic 1994)★★★★, *No Code* (Epic 1996)★★★★, *Yield* (Epic 1998)★★★, *Live: On Two Legs* (Epic 1998)★★★.

● VIDEOS: *Single Video Theory* (SMV 1998).

● FURTHER READING: *Pearl Jam: The Illustrated Biography*, Brad Morrell. *Pearl Jam Live!*, Joey Lorenzo (compiler). *The Illustrated Story*, Allan Jones. *Pearl Jam & Eddie Vedder: None Too Fragile*, Martin Clarke. *Five Against One: The Pearl Jam Story*, Kim Neely.

Peniston, Ce Ce

b. Cecelia Peniston, 6 September 1969, Dayton, Ohio, USA. After moving to Phoenix, Arizona, Peniston started acting at school. She went on to appear in numerous talent contests and also won the beauty pageants Miss Black Arizona and Miss Galaxy. She worked as a backing singer for the Overweight Pooch, and while still at college wrote 'Finally', which would become her first solo single. The music that backed the song bore more than a passing resemblance to the Ce Ce Rogers underground hit, 'Someday'. Fresh out of college, and with only the faintest hopes of a music career, 'Finally' broke her into the US Top 10 in late 1991 on the back of a speculative demo. She also sung backing vocals on Kym Sims' US Top 40 hit, 'Too Blind To See It'. A singer and dancer slightly reminiscent of late 70s soul, most of Peniston's compositions are piano-based with strong similarities to Aretha Franklin and Whitney Houston. Her modelling career was put on the back burner as 'We Got A Love Thang' reached US number 20 early in 1992, before the release of a somewhat disjointed debut album, which featured a third US Top 20 hit, 'Keep On Walkin''. All three songs also broke into the UK Top 10, with a reissued 'Finally' climbing all the way to number 2. Her second album, which featured the UK Top 20 hit 'I'm In The Mood', included contributions from house gurus David Morales and Steve 'Silk' Hurley, but was generally more urban R&B-focused. After recording the gospel set *Good News In Hard Times* as the Sisters Of Glory, with Thelma Houston, Phoebe Snow, Lois Walden and Albertina Walker, Peniston continued her move towards a swingbeat-style with 1996's commercially unsuccessful *Movin' On*. She subsequently left A&M Records, since which she has recorded the club hit 'Nobody Else' for Hurley's Silk Entertainment label and appeared in the Broadway production of *The Wiz*.

● ALBUMS: *Finally* (A&M 1992)★★★, *Thought 'Ya Knew* (A&M 1994)★★★, *Movin' On* (A&M 1996)★★★.

● COMPILATIONS: *The Best Of Ce Ce Peniston* (A&M 1998)★★★★, *Essential* (Spectrum 1999)★★★★.

Peshay

b. Paul Pesce, London, England. Anglo-Italian Peshay, now one of the UK's foremost drum 'n' bass pioneers, grew up listening to a wide range of musical styles, owing, in part, to his mother, who was a classical singer. He was inspired by hip-hop and electro as well as jazz and funk and accumulated an enviable record collection, which led him into DJing. He got his first break at one of the 'Genesis' raves and soon left his job in the printing industry to pursue his musical calling. In 1991, the sound of hardcore was emerging and Peshay released an EP with Bizzy B, *The 2 Dope*, which became a raver's favourite. In 1992, Peshay worked with LTJ Bukem, releasing '19.5' and 'Piano Tune'/'Vocal Tune' on the Good Looking Records label in 1993. In the same year, Peshay worked with drum 'n' bass guru, Goldie on his *ProtUgU* EP for Reinforced Records. When Goldie established his Metalheadz label, Peshay was one of the first artists on the roster and released 'Psychosis'/'Reprazant'. Just as drum 'n' bass was finding mainstream acceptance and audiences in 1994, Peshay was struck with a debilitating illness that left him bed-ridden until his triumphant return, DJing at London's Blue Note club in 1996, alongside Doc Scott and Goldie. Since then, he has DJed throughout the world and released a critically acclaimed album, *Miles From Home*. Heavily influenced by modern jazz, the album was compared to Reprazent's *New Forms* as a milestone in the development of drum 'n' bass.

● ALBUMS: *Miles From Home* (Blue/Island 1999)★★★★.

Pet Shop Boys

Formed in 1981, this highly inventive UK pop duo features Neil Tennant (b. 10 July 1954, North Shields, Northumberland, England; vocals) and Chris Lowe (b. 4 October 1959, Blackpool, Lancashire, England; keyboards). Lowe had previously played in cabaret act, One Under The Eight, while Tennant was employed as a journalist on the UK pop magazine *Smash Hits*. After writing and recording demos, they came under the wing of New York dance music producer Bobby 'O' Orlando. In the summer of 1984, they issued the Orlando-produced 'West End Girls', which passed unnoticed. After being dropped from Epic Records, they were picked up by Parlophone Records the following year. A second single 'Opportunities (Let's Make Lots Of Money)' also failed but a re-recording of 'West End Girls', produced by Stephen Hague, began selling in late 1985. In January 1986, this hypnotic single topped the charts in the UK and repeated the feat later in the USA. The duo's debut *Please*, 'Love Comes Quickly', a re-mixed version of 'Opportunities (Let's Make Lots Of Money)' and 'Suburbia' consolidated their position in the UK during 1986. The following year, the duo returned to number 1 with the Cat Stevens' influenced 'It's A Sin'. By this time, they were critically fêted as one of the more interesting bands of their time, with an engaging love of pop irony, camp imagery and arch wordplay. The quality of their melodies was also evident in the successful collaboration with Dusty Springfield, 'What Have I Done To Deserve This?' which reached number 2 in both the UK and the USA. By the end of the year the duo were back at the top in their home country with a cover version of the Elvis Presley hit, 'Always On My Mind', also a US Top 5 single. After releasing the well-received *Actually*, the duo appeared in the documentary film, *It Couldn't Happen Here*, which co-starred *Carry On* actress, Barbara Windsor. The film was given the cold shoulder by reviewers and was seen as a mild hiccup in the duo's fortunes. A fourth UK number 1 with 'Heart' was followed by a production and songwriting credit on Eighth Wonder's hit single, 'I'm Not Scared'. *Introspective* spawned further UK Top 10 hits in 'Domino Dancing', 'Left To My Own Devices', and 'It's Alright'. Having previously eschewed live tours (they had hitherto performed one-off concerts only), the Pet Shop Boys made their debut in Japan and the Far East, before finally reaching the UK. In typical manner, the show's concept took them as far away from the traditional pop concert as possible and incorporated the use of actors, dancers and film. A surprise collaboration in 1989 with Liza Minnelli gave her a UK Top 10 hit with 'Losing My Mind'. The duo's own inventive wit was again in evidence on the UK Top 5 hit 'So Hard', the laconic 'Being Boring' (a rare failure that only reached number 20), and an odd fusion of U2's 'Where The Streets Have No Name' and Frankie Valli's 'Can't Take My Eyes Off You'. The attendant *Behaviour* was a downbeat, slightly disappointing album. In 1991, the duo issued one of the best compilations of the era, *Discography*. Despite Tennant's continued involvement with Johnny Marr and Bernard Sumner in Electronic, the duo insisted that the Pet Shop Boys were only taking a short break. The UK Top 10 hit 'Can You Forgive Her' was a fine trailer to 1993's *Very*, a superb collection that tinkered with the duo's sound to incorporate contemporary dance music sounds. Later in the year they enjoyed a UK number 2 hit with a bold cover version of the Village People's gay anthem, 'Go West'. *Alternative* was an excellent double CD of b-sides which fully demonstrated their pioneering sound in 'leftfield dance pop'. *Bilingual* experimented with Latin rhythms, and featured two further UK Top 10 singles, 'Before' and 'Se A Vide E (That's The Way Life Is)'. The duo's long-awaited new album, *Nightlife*, was premiered by the single 'I Don't Know What

You Want But I Can't Give It Any More'. Despite a rare lapse of taste on the camp 'New York City Boy', the album highlighted their remarkable creativity on tracks such as 'Happiness Is An Option' and the bittersweet single 'You Only Tell Me You Love Me When You're Drunk', which put them back in the UK Top 10 in January 2000.

● ALBUMS: *Please* (Parlophone 1986)★★★★, *Disco* (Parlophone 1986)★★★, *Actually* (Parlophone 1987)★★★★, *Introspective* (Parlophone 1988)★★★, *Behaviour* (Parlophone 1990)★★★, *Very* (Parlophone 1993)★★★★, *Disco 2* (Parlophone 1994)★★, *Bilingual* (Parlophone 1996)★★★, *Bilingual Remixed* (Parlophone 1997)★★★, *Nightlife* (Parlophone 1999)★★★★.

● COMPILATIONS: *Discography: The Complete Singles Collection* (Parlophone 1991)★★★★★, *Alternative* (Parlophone 1995)★★★, *Essential Pet Shop Boys* (EMI 1998)★★★.

● VIDEOS: *Highlights: Pet Shop Boys On Tour* (PMI 1990), *Videography: The Singles Collection On Video* (PMI 1991), *Performance* (PMI 1992), *Projections* (PMI 1993), *Various* (PMI 1994), *Discovery: Live In Rio* (PMI 1995), *Somewhere: Pet Shop Boys In Concert* (Game Entertainment 1997).

● FURTHER READING: *Pet Shop Boys, Literally*, Chris Heath. *Pet Shop Boys: Introspective*, Michael Crowton. *Pet Shop Boys Versus America*, Chris Heath and Pennie Smith.

Peterson, Gilles

b. 1964, Caen, Normandy, France. Peterson is a respected figure on the UK's less commercial dance music scene, staying successful and influential throughout many phases of its development. He has remained committed to truly eclectic forms of dance music that draw their influences from a broad palette, including Latin, jazz, funk, Caribbean and African styles. He is also known for bringing jazz into dance, particularly through his label, Acid Jazz Records, whose name became applied to a whole genre of funky, brass-inflected dance music in the early 90s, notably by artists such as the Brand New Heavies and Jamiroquai. Peterson grew up in south London, speaking French to his French/Swiss parents and quickly developing an interest in jazz. He broadcast his own pirate radio station from his parent's garden shed while still a teenager. He first played a DJ set at the age of 18 at Camden's Electric Ballroom before progressing to his own club nights at the Wag in Soho, London and 'The Sunday Afternoon Session' at Dingwalls in Camden, where his sets embraced jazz, soul, funk and rap. He has broadcast on pirate and legitimate radio stations, including the UK's Kiss 100 FM, Jazz FM, Radio 1 FM and various Internet 'radio stations'. With the backing of Phonogram and the help of Norman Jay, he set up Talkin' Loud Records in 1990. The label has had considerable success with artists such as Galliano, Young Disciples, Urban Species and especially with Roni Size, whose debut, *New Forms* won a UK Mercury Prize in 1997. In the late 90s, Peterson compiled a mix album, *The Desert Island Mix*, with Norman Jay and ran London clubs including 'The Way It Is' with James Lavelle of Mo' Wax Records and 'Far East' at the Blue Note. He also released *The INCredible Sound Of Gilles Peterson*, an eclectic blend of funk, jazz, Latin and soul united by his search for the perfect groove.

● COMPILATIONS: *The INCredible Sound Of Gilles Peterson* (Sony/INCredible 1999)★★★★.

Phair, Liz

b. 17 April 1967, New Haven, Connecticut, USA. Phair was brought up in a wealthy suburb of Chicago, Illinois, by her adoptive father (a physician) and mother (an art teacher). It was a perfectly happy childhood, during which she befriended the actress Julia Roberts (a friendship later recounted in the song 'Chopsticks'). Her first love was art, but at Oberlin College in Ohio she became involved in the local music scene, which included bands such as Codeine, Bitch Magnet, Seam and Come. Phair also began writing songs, and became friends with Chris Brokaw, the guitarist with Come, and after college they both moved to San Francisco and began playing together. When Brokaw moved back east, Phair sent him tapes of her music, which generally consisted of 14 new songs each. Brokaw recognized her talent and alerted others. Although Phair herself was not as confident in the quality of these still-evolving songs, she did agree to sign with Matador Records in the summer of 1992. Entering the studio with her drummer and co-producer Brad Wood, Phair announced her intention to make a 'female *Exile On Main Street*'. Ignoring traditional song structures, her approach allowed the low-key production to empower her confessional and occasionally abusive lyrics. With fellow musicians Casey Rice (guitar) and LeRoy Bach (bass) complementing her own playing (like her UK peer, PJ Harvey, critical attention is often concentrated on her voice at the expense of her distinctive guitar playing), Phair produced an album that was both widely acclaimed and enjoyed commercial success. *Exile In Guyville* (the title was a dig at Chicago's male-dominated underground scene) was a sprawling and powerful double album that inspired a new generation of bluntly articulate female singer-songwriters. Phair's only flaw became apparent during live shows, when her stage fright was increased by the presence of famous guests such as Winona Ryder and Rosanna Arquette. This was, perhaps, not to be expected from a woman with the confidence to write the overtly sexual 'Flower' ('Every time I see your face, I get all wet between my legs'). It was not simply the brash sexuality of her debut that was discarded for her second album, but also her desire to be part of the 'Guyville' set. As she explained in interviews, there was no reason to resent her exclusion now that she had proved herself and moved on. *Whip-Smart* was a more polished set, lacking some of her previous eccentricities. It was still, however, a genuinely exciting and turbulent album, welcomed once again by critics and fans alike. The same reception was not given to *Juvenilia*, a stop-gap collection of her early recordings which had originally been released on her own Girly Sound tapes. With motherhood preoccupying her Phair remained quiet for nearly five years, although she did appear on Sarah McLachlan's Lilith Fair touring show. *Whitechocolatespaceegg* adopted a more subtle approach, eschewing the abrasiveness of her earlier recordings.

● ALBUMS: *Exile In Guyville* (Matador 1993)★★★★, *Whip-Smart* (Matador 1994)★★★★, *Juvenilia* (Matador 1995)★★, *Whitechocolatespaceegg* (Matador 1999)★★★.

Pharcyde

Spaced-out rappers comprising Imaini Wilcox, Booty Brown (b. Romye Robinson), Slimkid (b. Tre Hardson) and Fatlip (b. Derrick Stewart). Based in Los Angeles, California, USA, their goofy, fast talking style defied the early 90s rash of gangsta vinyl from that area with a dogma-deflating blend of cool, loopy rhythms and cultural lyrics. Hardson, Robinson and Wilcox originally worked as dancers and choreographers, appearing on the television series *In Living Color*. They formed Pharcyde in 1990 with rapper Stewart, and cut a demo tape with producer J-Swift. The resulting battle for their signatures was won by the Delicious Vinyl label. The group contributed one of the most effective cuts, 'Soul Flower', to the Brand New Heavies' *Heavy Rhyme Experience: Vol. 1*, before releasing their excellent debut. A multi-layered comic masterpiece, *Bizarre Ride II The Pharcyde*'s appeal was epitomised by the single 'Ya Mama', a series of ridiculous and escalating insults (also referred to as 'Snaps' or 'Playing The Dozens') traded between the vocalists that was reminiscent at times of A Tribe Called Quest and Dream Warriors. However, the crew's observations remained genuinely funny, housed in swinging, almost harmonised rap couplets, jazz breaks and quirky narratives: 'We're all jigaboos - might as well take the money' was a half-stinging, half self-mocking assertion. The single, 'Passin' Me By', even contained a definition of old school stylings. The group then holed up in their new LabCabin home base to work on their sophomore collection. Appearances on the *Street Fighter* soundtrack and *Stolen Moments: Red Hot + Cool* compilation followed, before *Labcabincalifornia* was released late in 1995. The album reflected the crew's new found maturity, with the debut's charming idiosyncrasies ironed out in favour of smooth, jazzy beats, and a sober adult slant to the lyrical matter. Fatlip subsequently left the group to concentrate on a solo career. The remaining members released 1999's *Testing The Waters* EP on their own label.

● ALBUMS: *Bizarre Ride II The Pharcyde* (Delicious Vinyl 1992)★★★★, *Labcabincalifornia* (Delicious Vinyl 1995)★★★.

Phats And Small

Phats and Small comprises two experienced DJs from Brighton, England, Jason Phatts and Russell Small, and the vocals of B.I.G. Ben, a former member of 'boy band' Benz, who had UK Top 40 hits in 1996 and supported Take That on their last tour of the UK. Phats And Small achieved a huge UK number 2 hit with 'Turn Around' in early 1999. The track featured a sample from Tony Lee's 'Reach Up' and was the 'Essential New Tune' on Pete Tong's influential BBC Radio 1 FM programme when it was released in promotional format in December 1998. It was given a full release by the Telstar dance imprint, Multiply Records in March 1999 and quickly entered the UK national charts after substantial radio and club exposure. 'Turn Around' was also remixed by fellow Brighton resident, Norman Cook. The single covered similar territory to Stardust's huge 1998 hit 'Music Sounds Better With You', utilising a filtered disco sample and an infectious vocal coupled with funky house bass 'n' drums, a formula that, by the late 90s, was proving increasingly successful in chart-orientated dance music. Both Phatts and Small worked as DJs at Brighton's famous Zap Club in the early 90s. Phatts started to produce his own music in 1992, using various pseudonyms and working with more established names such as Martin Tyrell, Chris Day and Cathy Brown. He set up a label, Afro Cuts, releasing disco house tracks before carrying out remix work and then collaborating with Small. The follow-up to 'Turn Around', 'Feel Good' was released in August 1999 and followed the blueprint of its predecessor.

The single featured a remix by Rhythm Masters and received extensive UK radio airplay before entering the national UK charts at number 7. The singles' infectious, good-time vibe was revisited ad nauseam on November's *Now Phats What I Small Music*.

● ALBUMS: *Now Phats What I Small Music* (Multiply 1999)★★★.

Phish

Comprising Trey Anastasio (vocals/guitar), Page McConnell (keyboards/vocals), Mike Gordon (bass/vocals) and Jon Fishman (drums/vocals), Phish were founded in 1983 at the University of Vermont in New England, USA. Anastasio had posted flyers around the campus looking for like-minded musicians. Fishman, Gordon and original second guitarist Jeff Holdsworth responded, but the band only really took shape in 1985 after the recruitment of McConnell and Holdsworth's departure. A regular venue was found at Burlington's Nectar's, before Phish expanded their activities to tours of venues and halls nationwide. The band's avowedly eclectic music - drawing from jazz, funk, bluegrass, country, punk and pop - introduced them to a large cult audience throughout America, a following that has increased in size ever since. Their 1988 own label debut, *Junta*, captured their free-flowing improvisations, while 1990's *Lawn Boy* (on the Rough Trade Records' subsidiary, Absolute A Go Go) featured improved production and a relatively structured approach to their cross-genre experiments. Their debut for Elektra Records, *A Picture Of Nectar*, saw several critics draw comparisons with the Grateful Dead - as much for their self-reliance and relationship with their fans as any musical similarity. *Rift*, released in 1993, was just as enjoyable, though a little more restrained than its predecessor. By 1994 and *(Hoist)*, Phish had become both a major live attraction and important figures in the mainstream of American music. *(Hoist)* duly doubled the sales achieved by *Rift*, and included two highly successful radio singles, 'Down With Disease' and 'Sample In A Jar'. By this time membership of their fan newsletter had grown to over 80,000, while their Internet service, phish.net, was one of the most active throughout the USA. Just as importantly, the band's live reputation had not diminished. In 1994, they achieved a Top 50 placing in *Pollstar*'s Top 50 grossing acts of the year poll - a testament to the 100 plus shows they had played to an estimated 600,000 fans. One of the highlights was their 30 December appearance at New York's Madison Square Garden which sold out in less than four hours. Their Halloween show in Glens Falls, New York, saw the band perform the Beatles' *White Album* in its entirety between their own sets. The result of these activities was the 1995 issue of a live double album, *A Live One*, which captured the band in its natural environment - judging by the efficiency of their touring and merchandising they plan to be around for the long haul. *Billy Breathes* was assured and relaxed (their *Workingman's Dead*, it was noted). In further keeping with their Dead connection, Ben & Jerry the ice cream moguls introduced a Phish Food flavour to go along with their Cherry Garcia brand. The 1998 studio set, *The Story Of The Ghost*, featured the major radio hit 'Birds Of A Feather', and debuted at number 8 on the *Billboard* 200 album chart in November. The ultimate treat for Phish fans, the six-CD live set *Hampton Comes Alive*, was released the following year. Anastasio also records with an 11-piece fusion ensemble called Surrender To The Air, featuring alto saxophonist Marshall Allen and trumpeter Michael Ray from the Sun Ra Arkestra, and guitarist Marc Ribot.

● ALBUMS: *Junta* (Own Label 1988)★★, *Lawn Boy* (Absolute A Go Go 1990)★★★, *A Picture Of Nectar* (Elektra 1992)★★★, *Rift* (Elektra 1993)★★★, *(Hoist)* (Elektra 1994)★★★, *A Live One* (Elektra 1995)★★★★, *Billy Breathes* (Elektra 1996)★★★★, *Slip Stitch And Pass* (Elektra 1997)★★, *The Story Of The Ghost* (Elektra 1998)★★★, *Hampton Comes Alive* 6-CD set (Elektra 1999)★★★.

● COMPILATIONS: *Stash* (Elektra 1996)★★★.

● FURTHER READING: *The Phishing Manual: A Compendium To The Music Of Phish*, Dean Budnick. *Go Phish*, Dave Thompson.

Photek

b. Rupert Parkes, Ipswich, Suffolk, England. Parkes became interested in hip-hop while at school and later developed a taste for jazz and funk and learnt to play the saxophone. In 1989, he was turned onto dance music, in particular the Detroit techno sound of such artists as Derrick May, after a visit to the hardcore night 'Telepathy' in north-east London. After moving to Ipswich in the early 90s, Parkes began working at a record shop owned by Rob Solomon with whom he also began to record original material. An early result was the 1992 jazz-inflected hardcore track 'Sensation', recorded as Origination, which was picked up by Ray Keith a friend of Solomon's who was involved with Soho's Black Market Records and was influential in the rave scene at the time. The following year Parkes and Solomon released 'Make You Do Right/Out Of This World' under the same name and as Studio Pressure recorded 'Jump Mk2' for Certificate 18 Records. In 1994, Parkes launched Photek Records and with it a series of singles 'Photek 1-6' which began towards the end of that year. By this point he was established as an important name in the underground drum 'n' bass scene and was receiving the support of such DJs as Kemistry, Peshay, Storm and LTJ Bukem. Parkes recorded a number of tracks for Bukem's labels as Aquarius over the next few years, including 'Drift To The Centre/Waveforms' (Looking Good 1995) and 'Dolphin Tune/Aquatic' (Good Looking 1996). With his growing popularity he attracted attention from a wider audience and consequently was invited to remix artists such as Attica Blues, Therapy?, Dr. Octagon and later Björk; at the same time the major labels became interested and in 1995 Photek signed to Virgin Records' subsidiary Science Records (his work is released by Astralwerks in America). His first release was 1996's *The Hidden Camera* EP, followed, in 1997, by 'Ni-Ten-Ichi-Ryu' and *Modus Operandi*. In 1998, a new track 'Yendi' accompanied the release of the album's title track as a single. As he was emerging, Parkes' subtle style led the media to inadequately proclaim him as the leader of a new 'intelligent' drum 'n' bass sound, after the raw energy of early jungle. By the time of his work on Science he had distilled his approach into a unique personalized style quite unlike anything else around. Despite its variety and diverse influences *Modus Operandi* is coherent throughout as, with his thrifty instrumentation, the attention is mostly focused on Parkes' incredibly detailed drum programming. Many tracks such as 'The Hidden Camera' and 'KJZ' have a jazz feel, employing cyclic double bass and impressionistic chordal effects, as Parkes' taut drum sounds fidget underneath. At the same time other tracks such as 'Aleph 1' and 'Minotaur' illustrate the techno influence in their choice of sounds while 'Smoke Rings' and 'The Fifth Column' are virtually all drums accompanied by abstract associative sounds. The following year's *Form & Function* collected together early singles and various remixes alongside two new tracks. With his economical, static approach and a high level of abstraction, Parkes has summed up the direction of arguably the most creative dance music of the 90s in the most eloquent form.

● ALBUMS: *Modus Operandi* (Science/Astralwerks 1997)★★★★.

● COMPILATIONS: *Form & Function* (Science/Astralwerks 1998)★★★.

Pigeonhed

This Seattle, Washington, USA-based project managed to develop a new, industrial spin on the grunge sound at a time when most observers were beginning to dismiss it. Both the full-time band members have an impressive pedigree in the Seattle-inspired scene, Shawn Smith (vocals) being an ongoing member of Brad (with Pearl Jam's Stone Gossard) and Satchel, and Steve Fisk (samples) having worked with Nirvana, Soundgarden and Screaming Trees. The sonic possibilities of Fisk's tape manipulation allowed the band to stand out from their more puritanically guitar-orientated colleagues, deploying influences as diverse as techno, gospel and P-Funk among the usual noisy dynamics. Their second album, which eventually appeared in 1997, amounted to a gathering of the post-Cobain clans, including contributions from Matt Chamberlain (Pearl Jam), Kim Thayil (Soundgarden) and Jerry Cantrell (Alice In Chains). The same year's remix set featured contributions from Red Snapper and Lo-Fidelity Allstars among others.

● ALBUMS: *Pigeonhed* (Sub Pop 1993)★★★, *The Full Sentence* (Sub Pop 1997)★★★, *Flashbulb Emergency Overflow Cavalcade Of Remixes* (Sub Pop 1997)★★★.

Pitchshifter

Nottingham, England-based quartet founded in 1989, and originally comprising Jonathan 'JS' Clayden (vocals), Jonathan 'JA' Carter (guitar/programming), Stuart Toolin (guitar) and Mark 'MD' Clayden (bass). Formerly known as Scurf, in early 1991 they signed to Peaceville Records and launched their career with the release of *Industrial*. Among those impressed with the band's visceral guitar assault (at that time featuring no drummer) was disc jockey John Peel, who invited them to perform three tracks on his show in May 1991. Moving over to Earache Records, they recorded their debut for the label in January 1992, with *Submit*. By this time Toolin had departed and the band had recruited percussionist, 'D' Walters. For its full-length follow-up the band increased the ratio of technology, though its application remained intense. The lyrics built on the themes of oppression and social injustice, while the use of samplers and sequencers offered an extra aural dimension. Touring with Treponem Pal, Consolidated, Neurosis and Biohazard ensued, and this musical melting pot produced the germ of an idea within the band. The resultant *The Remix Wars* saw the band revisiting their back catalogue, and allowing access to other sympathetic hands, including Therapy?, Biohazard and rappers Gunshot. *Infotainment?* ferociously merged the band's hardcore roots with contemporary drum 'n' bass rhythms, although the band remained true to their political ideals by including free samples at the end of the CD and encouraging their fans to steal them. Ex-Prodigy guitarist Jim Davies joined prior to the recording of 1998's *www.pitchshifter.com*, their Geffen Records debut.

● ALBUMS: *Industrial* (Peaceville 1991)★★★★, *Submit* mini-album (Earache 1992)★★★, *Desensitized* (Earache 1993)★★★, *The Remix Wars* (Earache 1994)★★★★, *Infotainment?* (Earache 1996)★★★, *www.pitchshifter.com* (Geffen 1998)★★★.

● VIDEOS: *Deconstruction* (Earache 1992).

Pixies

This highly influential alternative rock band was formed in Boston, Massachusetts, USA, by room-mates Charles Thompson IV aka Black Francis (b. Long Beach, California, USA; vocals/guitar) and Joey Santiago (guitar). A newspaper advertisement, requiring applicants for a 'Hüsker Dü/Peter, Paul And Mary band', solicited bass player Kim Deal (b. 10 June 1961, Dayton, Ohio, USA) who in turn introduced drummer David Lovering. Originally known as Pixies In Panoply, the quartet secured a recording contract on the UK independent label 4AD Records on the strength of a series of superior demo tapes. Their debut release, 1987's *Come On Pilgrim*, introduced the band's abrasive, powerful sound and Francis' oblique lyrics. *Surfer Rosa*, produced by Big Black's Steve Albini, exaggerated the savage fury of its predecessor and the set was acclaimed Album Of The Year in much of the UK rock press. A new partnership with producer Gil Norton resulted in the superlative *Doolittle*, which emphasized the quartet's grasp of melody, yet retained their drive. This thrilling collection scaled the UK Top 10, aided and abetted by the band's most enduring single, 'Monkey Gone To Heaven'. The Pixies were now a highly popular attraction and their exciting live performances enhanced a growing reputation, establishing clear stage favourites in 'Debaser', 'Cactus', 'Wave Of Mutilation' and 'Bone Machine'. *Bossanova*, which reached number 3 on the UK album chart, showed an undiminished fire with a blend of pure pop ('Allison') and sheer ferocity ('Rock Music'). It also featured the UK Top 30 single, 'Velouria'. The band found themselves the darlings of the rock press and were once again widely regarded for recording one of the top albums of the year. Kim Deal, meanwhile, attracted glowing reviews for her off-shoot project, the Breeders. *Trompe Le Monde* was, if anything, an even harsher collection than those that had preceded it, prompting some critics to describe it as the 'Pixies' heavy metal album'. Following the renamed Frank Black's departure for a solo career in early 1993 the band effectively folded, but their reputation continues to outshine any of the membership's concurrent or subsequent projects. Released in 1997, the excellent CD compilation *Death To The Pixies* confirmed the band's enduring influence.

● ALBUMS: *Come On Pilgrim* (4AD 1987)★★★, *Surfer Rosa* (4AD 1988)★★★★, *Doolittle* (4AD/Elektra 1989)★★★★, *Bossanova* (4AD/Elektra 1990)★★★, *Trompe Le Monde* (4AD/Elektra 1991)★★★.

● COMPILATIONS: *Death To The Pixies 1987-1991* (4AD 1997)★★★★, *Pixies At The BBC* (4AD/Elektra 1998)★★★.

Pizzicato Five

Pizzicato Five are a union of fashion models and satirists from Japan, started in 1984 by Keitaro Takanami and Yasuharu Konishi (b. 3 February 1959, Japan), two college students obsessed with the Monkees. Konishi was born on the day Buddy Holly, Richie Valens and the Big Bopper died

in an air crash, and this fact led to an enduring interest in all aspects of rock 'n' roll. Fellow members included Ryo Kamomiya and singer Mamiko Sasaki. Their first single, 1985's 'Audrey Hepburn Complex', demonstrated their fascination with retro-chic. As had been the case with another Japanese band to earn notoriety in the West, Shonen Knife, Pizzicato Five released a number of domestic albums (some 17 before 1995) and singles before making inroads in the USA and UK markets. Line-up changes included the departure of Kamomiya and Sasaki and the hiring of short-lived vocalist Takao Tajima in 1988. Former Planet Pop vocalist Maki Nomiya joined in 1990. Their performance at New York's New Music Seminar was viewed by future manager Trit Macmillan, who negotiated the band's deal with the Atlantic Records-affiliated subsidiary, Matador Records. Takanami departed shortly before the release of their debut *Five By Five* EP, reducing the band to the core duo of Konishi and Nomiya. Entertaining singles such as 'Magic Carpet Ride' underscored the band's natural charm. A compilation album of the band's hits to date, titled *Made In USA*, followed, shortly after an appearance on UK television programme *The Word*. A second album compiled from previous Japanese material, *The Sound Of Music By Pizzicato Five*, was promoted by the release of 'Happy Sad', which featured on the soundtrack to *Unzipped*, the acclaimed documentary about fashion designer Isaac Mizrahi. The album drew from a broad array of musical influences (Sergio Mendes, Burt Bacharach, Steve Miller, etc.), an approach which has seen the band regularly compared with fellow eclectics such as Saint Etienne and Deee-Lite. *Happy End Of The World* was their first American release to comprise all-new material.

● ALBUMS: *Couples* (CBS/Sony 1987)★★★, *Pizzicatomania* (Teichiku 1987)★★, *Bellisima!* (CBS/Sony 1988)★★★, *On (By) Her Majesty's Request* (CBS/Sony 1989)★★★, *Soft Landing On The Moon* (CBS/Sony 1990)★★★, *This Year's Girl* (Columbia/Seven Gods 1991)★★★, *Sweet Pizzicato Five* (Columbia/Triad 1992)★★★★, *Pizzicato Free Soul* (Columbia/Triad 1992)★★★, *Instant Replay* (Columbia/Triad 1993)★★★, *Bossa Nova 2001* (Columbia/Triad 1993)★★★, *Souvenir 2001* (Columbia/Triad 1993)★★★, *Expo 2001* remixes (Columbia/Triad 1993)★★, *Free Soul 2001* remixes (Columbia/Triad 1993)★★, *Overdose* (Columbia/Triad 1994)★★★, *Romantique 96* (Columbia/Triad 1995)★★★, *Antiques 96* (Columbia/Triad 1995)★★★, *Combinaison Spaciale* (Columbia/Matador 1996)★★★, *Sister Freedom Tapes* (Columbia/Matador 1996)★★★, *Happy End Of The World* (Matador 1997)★★★, *Happy End Of You* remixes (Matador 1998)★★★, *The International Playboy & Playgirl Record* (Matador 1998)★★★.

● COMPILATIONS: *Made In USA* (Matador 1994)★★★★, *Big Hits And Jet Lags (1991-1995)* (Columbia/Triad 1995)★★★, *The Sound Of Music By Pizzicato Five* (Matador 1995)★★★★, *Non-Standard Years '85-'86* (NonStandard 1996)★★★, *Great White Wonder: Rare Masters 1990-1996* (Columbia/Triad 1996)★★★.

PJ And Duncan

UK duo Declan 'Dec' Donnelly and Anthony 'Ant' McPartlin took their stage billing from the mouthy but loveable characters they played in the children's television series, *Byker Grove*. Both had been a part of the band featured in the series, Grove Matrix, whose 'Tonight I'm Free', credited to PJ And Duncan, made number 62 in the UK charts in late 1993. Afterwards they launched their own career as a fresh-faced but anarchic duo with 'Why Me' and 'Let's Get Ready To

Rhumble', the latter becoming a UK Top 10 hit in the summer of 1994. Its success saw them secure the *Smash Hits* Best New Act Of 1994 award. A succession of UK Top 20 hit singles followed, including 'If I Give You My Number', 'Eternal Love' (a major hit throughout Asia), 'Our Radio Rocks', 'Stuck On U', 'U Krazy Katz' and 'Perfect'. *Psyche* had sold over half a million copies by April 1995, by which time the duo were also presenting their own television series, *The Ant & Dec Show*. The series drew favourable comparisons with the Monkees, and the pair even recorded a cover version of 'Stepping Stone' with a video directed by Mickey Dolenz. In the summer of 1996, they ditched the PJ and Duncan names and began, under the new moniker Ant And Dec, to make a concerted effort to woo the indie/alternative market, co-presenting the prestigious *Evening Session* radio show and declaring a fondness for the Jam, Happy Mondays and Manic Street Preachers. This shift was highlighted by a slightly more sophisticated edge to their music, with the Top 10 hit 'Better Watch Out' showing definite Blur influences. Three more Top 20 hits followed, 'When I Fall In Love', 'Shout' and 'Falling'. They also defected to Channel 4 television for the 'more grown-up' *Ant & Dec - Unzipped* show, courting the mildest of controversies by describing the hugely popular singing actors Robson And Jerome as 'turds'. Recently, they have returned to the UK's television screens with the shows *SM:TV Live*, *cd:uk* and *Friends Like These*.

● ALBUMS: *Psyche* (XSrhythm 1994)★★★, *Top Katz* (Telstar 1995)★★, as Ant And Dec *The Cult Of Ant & Dec* (Telstar 1997)★★★.

● VIDEOS: *Out On The Tiles - Live* (Telstar 1996).

PJ Harvey

b. 9 October 1969, Yeovil, Somerset, England. Polly Jean Harvey was the daughter of hippie parents who exposed her to art rock artists such as Captain Beefheart and folk singer-songwriters like Bob Dylan at an early age. After growing up on their farm in Dorset and playing saxophone with an eight-piece instrumental group, she wrote her first songs as part of the Polekats, a folk trio who toured local pubs, in which she was only just old enough to drink. Afterwards, she attended an art foundation course before joining Somerset-based band Automatic Dlamini for two and a half years (from whom would come several future collaborators). Over this period she contributed saxophone, guitar and vocals, and toured Europe twice, also appearing on the chorus of local band Grape's 'Baby In A Plastic Bag' single, and singing backing vocals on Bristol-based Family Cat's 'Colour Me Grey'. Bored with playing other people's material, she moved to London, ostensibly to attend a course in sculpture (her other love), and elected to work with bass player Ian Olliver and drummer and backing vocalist Rob Ellis (b. 13 February 1962, Bristol, Avon, England), both fellow Automatic Dlamini travellers. Together they played live for the first time in April 1991, using the name PJ Harvey. Independent label Too Pure Records, home of Th' Faith Healers and Stereolab, were so convinced by these nebulous performances that they mortgaged their home to finance the debut single 'Dress'. Olliver left to be replaced by Stephen Vaughan (b. 22 June 1962, Wolverhampton, West Midlands, England) on 'five-string fretless bass', after the record's release. Together with the impressive 'Sheela-Na-Gig' and her 1992 debut *Dry*, it was enough to bring her to the attention not only of Island Records but also the mainstream

press. Subverting the traditions of the female singer-songwriter with outbreaks of fire-and-brimstone guitar, Harvey possessed the sort of voice which, while not cultured in the traditional sense, offered a highly emotive cudgel. Allied to lyrics that laid naked her own relationships and feelings, her revisionary attitude to feminism was demonstrated by the *New Musical Express* cover on which she appeared topless, with her back to the photographer. An evocative and disturbing songwriter, most considered that she would leave too bitter an aftertaste for a mass audience, a truism that was partially dispelled by support slots to U2, but hardly by the choice of producer for *Rid Of Me*, Big Black/Rapeman controversialist Steve Albini. A vicious stew of rural blues, with Harvey's voice and guitar sounding almost animalized by the production, its title track centrepiece offered one of the most fearsome declarations ('You're not rid of me') ever articulated in rock music. Obsessive, haranguing imagery accompanied by stunning, committed musical performances (especially the distinctive drumming of Ellis), this was an album of such vehemence that its follow-up, by necessity, was forced to lower the extremity threshold. In the interim, PJ Harvey (now officially a solo artist) made a memorable appearance at the 1994 BRIT Awards, duetting with Björk on a remarkable cover version of the Rolling Stones' 'Satisfaction'. For *To Bring You My Love*, Harvey abandoned some of the psychosis, replacing it with a haunting, sinister ambience. With U2 producer Flood working in tandem with namesake Mick Harvey (of the Bad Seeds), Harvey left behind some of the less pleasant subject matter of yore (bodily dysfunction, revenge). The new approach was typified by the video to promotional single 'Down By The Water', evocative of Ophelia-like madness and sacrifice. Her band now consisted of guitarist John Parrish (another former colleague from Automatic Dlamini), Jean-Marc Butty (b. France; drums), Nick Bagnall (keyboards, bass), Joe Gore (b. San Francisco, California, USA; guitar, ex-Tom Waits' band) and Pere Ubu's Eric Feldman (b. San Francisco, California, USA; keyboards) - all musicians Harvey had met on previous travels. It was obvious, however, that she was still having problems with her public perception: 'If I hadn't been tarred with the angst-ridden old bitch cow image, it'd be something else. Now it's, oh, she's gone back to the farm'. Harvey has also appeared on acclaimed albums by Nick Cave and Tricky, and in 1996 collaborated with Parish on the theatrical *Dance Hall At Louse Point*. That album's oblique musical reference points informed 1998's *Is This Desire?*, a starkly beautiful work that proved to be Harvey's most compelling album to date.

● ALBUMS: *Dry* (Too Pure 1992)★★★★, *Demonstration* 'demo' album given away with initial copies of *Dry* (Too Pure 1992)★★★, *Rid Of Me* (Island 1993)★★★★, *4-Track Demos* (Island 1993)★★, *To Bring You My Love* (Island 1995)★★★★, *B-Sides* (Island 1995)★★, with John Parrish *Dance Hall At Louse Point* (Island 1996)★★★, *Is This Desire?* (Island 1998)★★★★.

● VIDEOS: *Reeling* (PolyGram Music Video 1994).

● FILMS: *The Book Of Life* (1998).

Placebo

A cosmopolitan trio comprising Brian Molko (b. 10 December 1972; vocals/guitar), Stefan Olsdal (b. 31 March 1974, Gothenburg, Sweden; bass) and Robert Schultzberg (b. Switzerland; drums), the seeds of Placebo were sown when

Molko met Olsdal at school in Luxembourg when both were eight years old. When they chanced upon each other again in 1994 at London's South Kensington tube station, they decided to mark the occasion of their reacquaintance by forming a band. Molko had spent the intervening years at drama college but now decided to pursue music full-time. The duo's music slowly evolved from art-rock to an offbeat punk/new wave base, a transition that was aided considerably by the recruitment of drummer Schultzberg. He had formerly played in a Swedish-based band with Olsdal, and had come to London to study percussion. They made their debut at the end of 1995 with a single, 'Bruise Pristine', for the independent record label Fierce Panda Records. The reaction this caused ensured a major label bidding war for their services. A second single, 'Come Home', released on Deceptive Records in February 1996 followed, while the band considered their options. They performed at David Bowie's 50th birthday party in 1997. Their self-titled debut album was well received, but the band's profile was subsequently heightened by the success of the UK number 4 hit 'Nancy Boy' and media interest in Molko's androgynous image. English drummer Steve Hewitt (ex-Liverpool Breed) replaced Schultzberg before recording began on the band's second album. The anthemic 'Pure Morning' (UK number 4) and 'You Don't Care About Us' (UK number 5) introduced *Without You I'm Nothing*, on which Molko's songwriting achieved a more assured, reflective tone. The band members also made cameo appearances in Todd Haynes' glam rock tribute movie, *Velvet Goldmine*. The band continued their occasional partnership with Bowie in 1999, performing an exciting live version of T. Rex's '20th Century Boy' at February's BRIT Awards, and in the summer recording a new version of 'Without You I'm Nothing'.

● ALBUMS: *Placebo* (Hut 1996)★★★, *Without You I'm Nothing* (Hut 1998)★★★★.

Plaid

Experimental UK-based techno outfit comprising Andy Turner and Ed Handley, who are signed to influential label Warp Records. Turner and Handley discovered electronic music while at school, where they had access to a Moog synthesizer in their music class, and listened to artists such as Ultravox, Human League and Howard Jones. They discovered dance music via raves such as 'Sunrise', 'Biology', 'Energy' and 'Raindance' in the early 90s and became more interested in the more *avant garde* fringes of the scene. Forming Black Dog Productions with Ken Downie they released several acclaimed singles and albums, and also recorded various EPs under pseudonyms such as Balil, Atypic, Repeat and Tyra. Following 1995's *Spanners*, Turner and Handley parted company with Black Dog Productions to concentrate on their side project, Plaid. They subsequently released the EP *Angry Dolphin/Android*, and supported Björk and Orbital. Their two long-players, *Not For Threes* and *Rest Proof Clockwork*, have been well-received by most of the dance music press, proving that there is still room for challenging electronica in the increasingly commercial domain of dance music.

● ALBUMS: *Not For Threes* (Warp/Nothing 1997)★★★, *Rest Proof Clockwork* (Warp/Nothing 1999)★★★★.

Plastikman
(see Hawtin, Richie)

P.M. Dawn

This hip-hop act, who enjoyed huge crossover success in the early 90s, was formed by brothers Prince Be (b. Attrell Cordes, 15 May 1970) and DJ Minute Mix (b. Jarrett Cordes, 17 July 1971). Hailing from Jersey City, New Jersey (their step-father was a member of Kool And The Gang), their backgrounds were shrouded in tragedy. Their real father died of pneumonia when they were children, and their brother Duncan drowned when he was two years old. They came from a highly musical family - 10 of their aunts and uncles were rappers and DJs in the genre's early days in the 70s, when Prince Be started rapping as a youngster at family parties. They were equally influenced by 60s pop and duly incorporated harmonies in their work - hence the later tag, Daisy Age Soul. They cut demos in 1989, including their first song, 'Check The Logic', at a Long Island studio. After signing to Gee Street Records, they took the name P.M. Dawn, indicating 'the transition from dark to light'. A debut single, 'Ode To A Forgetful Mind', was released in January 1991. Its follow-up, 'A Watcher's Point Of View', broke into the UK Top 40, introducing their melodic hip-hop to a larger audience. They were turned away by representatives of the Beatles in their attempts to sample 'Let It Be', but enjoyed more success in negotiations with Spandau Ballet, who allowed them to build the song 'Set Adrift On Memory Bliss' out of 'True'. P.M. Dawn went as far as to promote the release with an old 'new romantic' picture of Hadley and co, confirming their mischievous humour. The single hit number 3 in the UK charts, but was even more successful in their native country, where it topped the Hot 100. *Of The Heart, Of The Soul And Of The Cross: The Utopian Experience* emerged in September 1991 to rave reviews, with the group, now heralded as one of the most concise, creative forces in rap, losing the De La Soul comparisons that had previously plagued them. All seemed to be running smoothly for P.M. Dawn in 1991, until an unfortunate experience at the end of the year. While Prince Be took part in the live filming of a gig at New York's The Sound Factory, Boogie Down Productions main man KRS-1 became angered at what he considered disrespectful remarks made by Prince Be during a *Details* magazine interview, and forcefully evicted him from the stage, smashing a record on Minute Mix's turntable in the process. In 1992, the duo achieved two minor UK hits, 'Reality Used To Be A Friend Of Mine' and 'I'd Die Without You', which featured on the soundtrack to the Eddie Murphy movie, *Boomerang*. With Prince Be also appearing in a Nike trainers' commercial, the latter single climbed to US number 3. Following the release of 'Looking Through Patient Eyes', a US Top 10/UK Top 20 single which heavily sampled George Michael's 'Father Figure', P.M. Dawn released a long-awaited second album in April 1993. While writing tracks for *The Bliss*, Prince Be had Boy George in mind, and the former Culture Club singer duetted on 'More Than Likely', which also became a single. 'Fly Me To The Moon', meanwhile, sampled U2's 'The Fly'. However, critics still considered it to be a lesser album than their stunning debut. Minute Mix, meanwhile, had changed his name to J.C. The Eternal, and Prince Be had become The Nocturnal. P.M. Dawn also contributed to the AIDS benefit *Red Hot And Dance*, as well as remixing for Simply Red and appearing at several benefit shows, including Earth Day and LIFEbeat's CounterAid. Their subsequent releases have failed to match the commercial ascendancy of their earlier work. *Jesus Wept* was a disappointing collection that wallowed in bland R&B stylings. Their 1998 comeback, *Dearest Christian ...*, favoured a similar style, and was informed by Prince Be's experience of new fatherhood.

● ALBUMS: *Of The Heart, Of The Soul And Of The Cross: The Utopian Experience* (Gee Street 1991)★★★, *The Bliss Album? (Vibrations Of Love And Anger And The Ponderance Of Life And Existence)* (Gee Street 1993)★★★, *Jesus Wept* (Gee Street 1995)★★, *Dearest Christian, I'm So Very Sorry For Bringing You Here. Love, Dad* (Gee Street 1998)★★★.

Poozies

Originally formed by two members of Sileás, Patsy Seddon (b. 12 January 1961, Edinburgh, Scotland) and Mary Macmaster (b. 22 November 1955, Glasgow, Scotland; harps), Sally Barker (b. 19 September 1959, Barrow upon Soar, Leicestershire, England; guitar) and Karen Tweed (accordion), the Poozies are a UK-based quartet broadly operating within the traditional music format. They made their debut in 1993 with *Chantoozies*, an album demonstrating their considerable musical dexterity and sumptuously rendered harmonies, with vocals shared between each member. Among the best songs on the album were 'We Built Fires', a co-composition between Barker and Jim Woodland, Pete Morton's 'Another Train' and Martin Ansell's 'Honesty'. Cover versions included the Carter Family's 'Foggy Mountain Top', though some of the originals, notably the Macmaster/Barker co-composition, 'Crazy Raven', were just as strong. *Dansoozies* was another acclaimed collection, but following its release Barker announced she was departing to concentrate on her solo career. She was replaced by multi-instrumentalist Kate Rusby (b. 1 December 1973, Barnsley, Yorkshire, England), who had formerly worked with Kathryn Roberts and the Equation. Rusby introduced a softer touch to the band's sound on the *Come Raise Your Head* EP and *Infinite Blue*, but subsequently left to concentrate on her increasingly successful solo career.

● ALBUMS: *Chantoozies* (Hypertension 1993)★★★★, *Dansoozies* (Hypertension 1995)★★★, *Infinite Blue* (Pure 1998)★★★★.

Popinjays

Formed in London in 1988 by songwriters Wendy Robinson (b. 6 April 1964, Huddersfield, Yorkshire, England; vocals), Polly Hancock (b. 16 July 1964, Berkshire, England; guitar/vocals) and a drum machine, the Popinjays evolved out of the influential Timebox Club at the Bull & Gate pub in Kentish Town, north London (the duo later ran their own Pop Club at the same venue). Dana Baldinger (b. 26 December 1963, California, USA; bass) joined in 1989 as the offer of a combination of sweets, comics and biscuits won the band a recording contract with One Little Indian Records. Badlinger departed after one single, to be replaced by fellow countrywoman Anne Rogers (b. 17 October 1962, New York, USA) a move that was followed by a flood of critical recommendations for their 1990 debut, *Bang Up To Date With The Popinjays*, on which the band strove to perfect the ultimate pop formula. Ever conscious of the importance of fun in music, their promo video for the 'Vote Elvis' single featured much Monkees-style running around with special

guest Cathal Coughlan from the Fatima Mansions. Seamus Feeney (b. 19 November 1964, Middlesex, England) caused the drum machine to be sacked at the close of the year, just as the Popinjays were beginning to garner appreciative attention from America. *Flying Down To Mono Valley* did little to embellish their reputation, and it was left to their 1994 album to produce a significant stylistic departure. *Tales From The Urban Prairie* saw forays into country rock and singer-songwriter melancholia, an affecting performance but one that left their traditional fanbase in some degree of confusion.

● ALBUMS: *Bang Up To Date With The Popinjays* (One Little Indian 1990)★★★★, *Flying Down To Mono Valley* (One Little Indian 1992)★★★, *Tales From The Urban Prairie* (One Little Indian 1994)★★★.

Porcupine Tree

Steve Wilson (b. 3 November 1967, Kingston-Upon-Thames, England; guitar/vocals/programming), Colin Edwin (b. 2 July 1970, Melbourne, Australia; bass), Richard Barbieri (b. 30 November 1957, London, England; keyboards, cx-Japan), and Chris Maitland (b. 13 May 1964, Cambridge, England; drums) have been widely ascribed with bringing progressive rock back into vogue in the 90s. Wilson is the guiding light behind Porcupine Tree, which allows him to indulge his interests in ambient dance music and left-field, psychedelic rock. He began recording solo material in the late 80s, which was collected on the cassette-only releases *Tarquin's Seaweed Farm* (1989), *Love Death And Mussolini* (1990) and *The Nostalgia Factory* (1990) (later compiled by Delerium Records as *On The Sunday Of Life*). The epic *Voyage 34* EP, comprising one 30-minute track split into two phases, followed in 1992, before Wilson recruited a full complement of band members. Critics reviewing their material, particularly the *Moonloop* EP in 1994 and *The Sky Moves Sideways* album the following year, immediately pigeonholed them as a contemporary Pink Floyd. *Signify* did indeed have shades of David Gilmour, but ultimately, even with the Yes, Barclay James Harvest and Supertramp comparisons, Porcupine Tree sound only like themselves. On that album they demonstrated their originality, great harmonies and inter-galactic travel potential. Tracks such as 'Waiting Phase One' and 'Waiting Phase Two' hypnotically rumble and build to glorious peaks. *Stupid Dream* honed their art even further, and led many to wonder what major success would have befallen them if they had been around in 1971; mass acclaim and *Melody Maker* front covers would have been guaranteed. Swirling mellotrons and synthesizers abounded, laced with acoustic fills and biting electric solos. The album contained some stellar moments, notably on 'Even Less' with its gigantic lush chords, the furious wah-wah hook in 'This Is No Rehearsal', and the beautiful phased harmonies of 'Baby Dream In Cellophane' and 'Stranger By The Minute'. Hugely enjoyable and accessible 90s progressive rock.

● ALBUMS: *On The Sunday Of Life* (Delerium 1991)★★★, *Up The Downstair* (Delerium 1993)★★★, *Yellow Hedgerow Dreamscape* limited edition (Magic Gnome 1994)★★★, *The Sky Moves Sideways* (Delerium 1995)★★★, *Staircase Infinities* mini-album (Blueprint 1995)★★★, *Signify* (Delerium 1996)★★★★, *Coma Divine* (Delerium 1997)★★★, *Stupid Dream* (K-Scope/Snapper 1999)★★★★.

Porno For Pyros

This theatrical rock act was formed by Jane's Addiction frontman Perry Farrell (b. Perry Bernstein, 29 March 1959, Queens, New York, USA) in 1992, following the demise of his previous act. Enlisting former bandmate Stephen Perkins (b. 13 September 1967, Los Angeles, California, USA; drums), and new recruits Martyn LeNoble (b. 14 April 1969, Vlaardingen, Netherlands; bass), and Peter DiStefano (b. 10 July 1965, Los Angeles, California, USA; guitar), Farrell began developing his new band's direction during their low-key live debut on the Lollapalooza II second stage. With Farrell's creative input and Perkins' rhythmic talents, similarities between Porno For Pyros and Jane's Addiction's recorded output were inevitable, but the subtle shift in musical direction became more obvious in the live setting. Porno For Pyros' shows were closer in character to a carnival, with Farrell as ringmaster, than a traditional rock show, with the band augmented not only by Matt Hyde's keyboards but also by a cast of dancers and performance artists, from the ballerina pirouetting to 'Orgasm', to the sharp contrast of the fire-breathing stripper who appeared during 'Porno For Pyros'. The band subsequently headlined at the 1993 UK Reading Festival in spectacular fashion, and appeared at the Woodstock Anniversary show in 1994. Farrell had become a real star and great media fodder by the time their breakthrough album, *Good God's Urge*, was issued. DiStefano was diagnosed as having cancer in October 1996, and the band cancelled all work while he underwent chemotherapy. In 1997, Farrell announced the resurrection of Jane's Addiction for live dates, and not long afterwards it was reported that Porno For Pyros had disbanded.

● ALBUMS: *Porno For Pyros* (Warners 1993)★★★, *Good God's Urge* (Warners 1996)★★★.

● FURTHER READING: *Perry Farrell: Saga Of A Hypster*, Dave Thompson.

Portishead

Portishead were named after the sleepy port on the southwest coast of England where Geoff Barrow (b. Weston-Super-Mare, Avon, England) spent his teens. His intentions in forming the band were simple: 'I just wanted to make interesting music, proper songs with a proper life span and a decent place in people's record collections.' Barrow started out as a tape operator, working in a minor capacity with Massive Attack and Neneh Cherry, and also wrote songs for Cherry ('Somedays' was included on her 1992 collection, *Homebrew*). With the aid of an Enterprise Allowance grant he recruited jazz guitarist and musical director Adrian Utley, drummer/programmer Dave MacDonald and vocalist Beth Gibbons (b. Keynsham, Bristol, Avon, England), whom he encountered on a job creation scheme while she was singing Janis Joplin cover versions in a pub. Together they recorded a soundtrack and film, *To Kill A Dead Man*, with themselves as actors because 'we couldn't find anyone else to do the parts'. At this point they came to the attention of A&R man Ferdy Unger-Hamilton at the Go! Discs subsidiary, Go! Beat, who encouraged Barrow to remix Gabrielle's 'Dreams'. He was sufficiently impressed with the results to sign the band immediately, despite several other interested parties. The singles 'Numb' and 'Sour Times' emerged to good press reaction, although the debut album slipped in and out of the charts with little fanfare. There was some problem with mar-

keting the band - both Barrow and Gibbons were reluctant to do interviews, and had no initial interest in playing live. Instead the press campaign saw painted mannequin dummies distributed in strategic locations throughout London, ensuring press coverage outside of the expected media. Word of mouth continued to push the band's profile and, with virtually no radio support, their third single, 'Glory Box', entered the UK charts at number 13 in January 1995. Aided by a distinctive, gender-swapping video (visuals are central to the band's approach), its arrival came on the back of several Album Of The Year awards for *Dummy* from magazines as diverse as *Mixmag*, *ID*, *The Face* and *Melody Maker*. Mixing torch songs with blues, jazz and hip-hop, their sound became known as 'trip-hop'. The interest also translated to America, where the album sold over 150,000 copies without the band even setting foot there. They were then awarded the Mercury Music Prize for best album of 1995. Following their success, the band were invited to contribute to several soundtracks, including two low-budget art movies and *Tank Girl*. The long-awaited follow-up to *Dummy* was severely delayed when Barrow, a self-confessed perfectionist, reached a creative impasse that almost destroyed the band. His perseverance paid off, however, when *Portishead* was released in September 1997 to excellent critical reviews. Although first single 'All Mine' had suggested some variation to the Portishead sound, the album covered essentially the same ground as their debut, albeit in an impressively stylish manner. A perfunctory live album followed in 1998.

● ALBUMS: *Dummy* (Go! Beat 1994)★★★★, *Portishead* (Go! Beat 1997)★★★, *P Live In NYC* (Go! Beat 1998)★★★.

● VIDEOS: *PNYC* (Go! Beat 1998).

Posies

Formed in Seattle, Washington, USA, the Posies played powerfully melodic music that paid tribute to Merseybeat and the harmonies of the Hollies. Growing up in Bellingham, 90 miles north of Seattle, John Auer (vocals/guitar) and Ken Stringfellow (vocals/guitar) were both in bands in their early teens, and even joined their high school choir. Stringfellow married Kim Warnick of the Fastbacks, and mixed and produced for various Seattle/Sub Pop Records bands. He also guested for Mudhoney. However, the Posies were influenced as much by Hüsker Dü as by the songwriting prowess of XTC, Elvis Costello and Squeeze, and both members were part of the original 'industrial-noise' Sky Cries Mary. The duo's debut was recorded (originally on their own label as a cassette, later on PopLlama Products) in 1988 and introduced their penchant for sanguine, everyday lyrical topics. Entitled *Failure*, its title marked them out as singularly lacking in ambition, a trait that later became enshrined in the 'slacker' ethos. However, they signed to Geffen Records, and enlisted a rhythm section (Dave Fox and Mike Musburger) and brought in John Leckie to produce their major label debut. A varied, multi-textured album, it was reminiscent of the UK's Stone Roses, whom Leckie also produced. The Posies' third album, *Frosting On The Beater*, a reference to masturbation, was produced by Don Fleming, and attracted wide acclaim, finishing in the higher reaches of many end of year critical polls. The band supported Teenage Fanclub and their heroes Big Star on European tours, and Auer and Stringfellow both took part in the re-formation of the latter band. Having lost their major label deal, the Posies

released one final album, *Success*, before disbanding. Stringfellow's low-key solo debut appeared at the same time.
● ALBUMS: *Failure* (23/PopLlama 1988)★★★, *Dear 23* (DGC 1990)★★★★, *Frosting On The Beater* (DGC 1993)★★★★, *Amazing Disgrace* (DGC 1996)★★★, *Success* (PopLlama 1998)★★★.
Solo: Ken Stringfellow *This Sounds Like Goodbye* (Hidden Agenda 1997)★★★.

Pras

b. Prakazrel Michel, 1972. Like fellow members Lauryn Hill and Wyclef Jean, Pras has forged a successful solo career away from hip-hop stars the Fugees. Pras first recorded with fellow student Hill and cousin Wyclef Jean as the Tranzlator Crew. Following a name change and a moderately successful debut album, 1994's *Blunted On Reality*, the trio went on to enjoy huge crossover success with 1996's *The Score*. The Fugees were put on hold in the late 90s with each member working on solo projects. Pras enjoyed instant success, achieving an international hit single with 'Ghetto Supastar (That Is What You Are)'. Based around a sample of the Kenny Rogers/Dolly Parton hit 'Islands In The Stream', and featuring the vocals of Mya and Wu-Tang Clan member Ol' Dirty Bastard, the song benefited from its inclusion on the soundtrack to the Warren Beatty movie *Bulworth*. It eventually spent eight weeks in the UK Top 5, peaking at number 2 in July 1998, and reached US number 15 a month later. 'Blue Angels' was another UK Top 10 hit, reaching number 6 in November. Co-produced by Jerry Duplessis, *Ghetto Supastar* debuted outside the US Top 50, dwarfed by the phenomenal chart-topping success of Hill's Grammy-award winning *The Miseducation Of Lauryn Hill*. From a musical point of view, when compared with the audacity and verve of Hill's album, Pras' mainstream-orientated grooves sounded hackneyed and unimaginative.
● ALBUMS: *Ghetto Supastar* (Ruffhouse/Columbia 1998)★★★.

Presence

Presence is a UK-based deep house outfit based around Charles Webster (b. Matlock, Derbyshire, England). Webster secured his first recording contract at the age of 19 and released experimental electro under the name the Mile High Club. Later, he released house tracks using pseudonyms such as Furry Phreaks, Symetrix, Low Rise, Love From San Francisco and Sine. As Presence, he released the single 'Sense Of Danger' in November 1998 and the accompanying *All Systems Gone* in January 1999. Both the single and the album received ecstatic reviews from all areas of the music press: the UK's *DJ* magazine awarded the album 11 out of 10. Webster had used the vocals of Sara Jay and Shara Nelson, who had previously contributed their smoky, soulful vocals to some of Massive Attack's work. Webster professed an unusual range of influences, from Rickie Lee Jones and Natalie Merchant to Kraftwerk, and the sounds of Motown Records and Factory Records. The album was a down-tempo, at times melancholic, set of lush, well-crafted tracks, probably more suited to home-listening than the dancefloor. Rightly, it was praised for its musical intelligence and inventiveness.
● ALBUMS: *All Systems Gone* (Pagan 1999)★★★★.

Presidents Of The United States Of America

Formed in Seattle, Washington, USA, this alternative rock band broke into the US and UK charts in 1995 with their no-nonsense riff-laden music. Chris Ballew (vocals/basitar (two-string bass)) told *Billboard* that 'Ever since I was a kid, I'd make up songs about pigs, monkeys, and chickens with my brother. In years of writing songs, when I couldn't think of lyrics I went back to the monkey thing. I resisted it for a while, because I always wanted to write 'regular' songs. Then I got together with Mark Sandman from Morphine, and it loosened the floodgates for me. I decided not to censor myself anymore, and I let all the animal imagery come flying out.' He worked with Sandman in the ad hoc Supergroup, and also toured as part of Beck's backing band. In 1994, he recruited Dave Dederer (guitbass (three-string guitar)) and ex-Love Battery drummer Jason Finn and formed the Presidents Of The United States Of America. The band offered a refreshing break from conventional American 'angst-pop', with songs such as 'Kitty' describing the mood swings of Ballew's cat and 'Peaches', which was about peaches. After the independent release of 1995's self-titled debut, the band was signed to Columbia Records, who reissued the album with six of the tracks remixed. Columbia promoted the band heavily, including setting up an 'alternative' tour of venues such as hot-dog stands and polka clubs. At the same time MTV gave rotation play to the album's first single, 'Lump'. By the end of the year the band had ventured to Europe and repeated the US chart success of 'Lump' and 'Peaches' (a UK Top 10 single). Their debut album eventually sold over two million copies. They capitalized on this commercial momentum with a second album in 1996, but their brand of jokey alternative rock was by now beginning to wear thin. They officially broke up at the end of 1997, with a collection of rarities and unreleased material appearing shortly afterwards.
● ALBUMS: *The Presidents Of The United States Of America* (PopLlama 1995)★★★★, *The Presidents Of The United States Of America* remixed version of debut (Columbia 1995)★★★★, *II* (Columbia 1996)★★★.
● COMPILATIONS: *Pure Frosting* (Columbia 1998)★★.

Primal Scream

The line-up that achieved so much success in 1991 comprised Bobby Gillespie (b. 22 June 1962, Glasgow, Scotland; vocals), Andrew Innes (guitar), Robert Young (guitar), Henry Olsen (bass), Philip 'Toby' Tomanov (drums), Martin Duffy (organ, ex-Felt) and backing vocalist Denise Johnson (b. 31 August 1966, Manchester, Lancashire, England), but Primal Scream had been a fluctuating affair since the early 80s. Gillespie was the centrifugal force throughout, recording several low-key tracks with guitarist Jim Beattie while still serving as stand-up drummer in the nascent Jesus And Mary Chain. The line-up of Gillespie, Beattie, Young (their bass player at this point), Tom McGurk (drums) and Martin St. John (percussion) released 'All Fall Down' on Creation Records in May 1985. Further line-up changes ensued before the band achieved notoriety via the *New Musical Express*' alternative C86 cassette compilation, which featured a former b-side, 'Velocity Girl', an 80-second romp through the richer pastures of 60s guitar pop. Guitarist Innes was brought in to play on 1987's poorly received *Sonic Flower Groove*, a collection of melodic pop songs which was released on the short-lived Elevation label. Beattie left in 1988 as the band began to veer towards rock territory, releasing a self-titled album and revealing a penchant for leather trousers, wild guitars and idol-worshipping. The latter characteristic, at least, was to be a significant feature in their subsequent form, as Gillespie, encouraged by Innes, developed an interest in the burgeoning dance music scene. Come the start of the 90s, Primal Scream had been reinvented, with the aid of name remixers such as Andy Weatherall, into a groove machine. The 'Loaded' single was the first proof of the band's transformation, stealing from rock's heritage (Robert Johnson's 'Terraplane Blues') and cult biker movies (Peter Fonda's *Wild Angels*) yet invading Britain's dancefloors to become a Top 20 hit in the UK charts in April 1990, and inspiring a legion of other indie/dance crossovers. Their iconoclastic ideals persisted, no more so than on the road, where Primal Scream's hedonistic indulgences were well publicized. The following year's *Screamadelica* emphasized the band's cultural diversities and reaped rich critical acclaim and massive sales. It was followed by the *Dixie-Narco* EP, recorded in Memphis, which reached number 11 in the UK charts in early 1992. In September the same year, *Screamadelica* won the inaugural Mercury Music Prize. The band, beset by further personnel change, relocated to America to work on the follow-up. This finally emerged in March 1994, produced by veteran Atlantic Records soul man Tom Dowd, and revealing a stylistic debt to the Rolling Stones rather than the dance scene. Dowd was assisted by contributions from George Clinton and Black Crowes producer George Drakoulias. Though the critical reception was frosty, Gillespie had once again reinvented himself and his band, and was able to enjoy his first UK Top 10 single when 'Rocks' reached number 7. In November 1996, following months of speculation after the announcement that the Stone Roses were no more, bass player Gary 'Mani' Mounfield confirmed that he had joined the band. The new line-up recorded *Vanishing Point*, a timely return to the rhythms of *Screamadelica*; less like the Rolling Stones, more like Primal Scream, but with a far darker edge than the blissed out sentiments of the earlier album. 'Kowalski', named after the central character in Richard Sarafian's cult road movie which gave the album its name, shot into the UK Top 10. Drummer Paul Mulreany left the band in August 1997 after weeks of speculation about their future. He was later replaced by Darrin Mooney. The band also enlisted Adrian Sherwood to record *Echodek*, a dub version of *Vanishing Point*. In January 1999, the band contributed 'Insect Royalty' to the film adaptation of Irvine Welsh's *The Acid House*, while Gillespie worked on tracks by the Chemical Brothers and Death In Vegas. The band's new single, 'Swastika Eyes (War Pigs)', was released in November. The track served as a fitting introduction to the dark-hued eclecticism of *Xtrmntr*, an angry, uncommercial album that served as a welcome antidote to the increasingly bland products of the UK's music industry.

● ALBUMS: *Sonic Flower Groove* (Elevation 1987)★★, *Primal Scream* (Creation 1989)★★★, *Screamadelica* (Creation 1991)★★★★★, *Give Out But Don't Give Up* (Creation 1994)★★★, *Vanishing Point* (Creation 1997)★★★★, *Echodek* remixes (Creation 1997)★★★, *Xtrmntr* (Creation 2000)★★★★.

● FURTHER READING: *Higher Than The Sun*, Grant Fleming.

Primus

The vast majority of reviewers can generally agree on one word to describe Primus - weird. Formed in San Francisco, California, USA in 1984 by Les Claypool (bass, ex-Blind Illusion), seven drummers passed through before Tim 'Herb' Alexander settled in, with Larry Lalonde (guitar, ex-Blind Illusion, Possessed), replacing original guitarist Todd Huth shortly before the band recorded their debut. Musically, they are highly talented and original, mixing funk, punk, thrash, metal and rock in their own intense manner, once described by Claypool as 'psychedelic polka'. Claypool and Alexander produce quirky, sometimes hypnotic rhythms, accentuating each other's playing, while former Joe Satriani pupil Lalonde creates and colours within the framework, although his playing owes more to Frank Zappa than to that of his old teacher. Claypool's vocals lean towards cartoonish narrative, with lyrics of a suitably abstract and humorous nature, drawing from both life and his film and literary influences. A common theme to all their albums is marine life, reflecting the band's passion for sea-fishing (they have played with fish-shaped covers on their vocal microphones). Their 1989 debut, *Suck On This*, was a self-financed live set successfully released on their own Prawn Song label, and much of the material was to feature on *Frizzle Fry*, an independent studio release that won them a Bay Area Music Award and, helped by touring with Faith No More, Jane's Addiction, 24-7 Spyz and Living Colour, a major recording contract with Interscope Records. *Sailing The Seas Of Cheese* further raised their profile, with their reworking of 'Tommy The Cat' from the debut (with a Tom Waits guest vocal) featuring in hit movie *Bill And Ted's Bogus Journey*. A lengthy world tour in support of Rush was then followed by stadium dates with U2. Any doubts as to the band being a sufficient draw for the closing (effectively headlining) slot on the 1993 Lollapalooza tour were dispelled when *Pork Soda* debuted in the US charts at number 7, producing a hit in 'My Name Is Mud'. Claypool would also hook up with Huth and drummer Jay Lane to form side-project Sausage, recording *Riddles Are Abound Tonight* in 1994. The erratic *Tales From The Punch Bowl* included the novelty hit 'Wynona's Big Brown Beaver'. Claypool released a solo album in 1996, the same year Alexander left the band (he was replaced by ex-Godflesh drummer Brian Mantia). In 1997, Primus reaffirmed their slacker credibility by performing the theme music to cult US cartoon series *South Park*. On *Rhinoplasty* the band wildly misinterpreted a wide range of material by artists including Metallica, Peter Gabriel and the Police, before returning to original material on 1999's *Antipop*.

● ALBUMS: *Suck On This* (Prawn Song 1989)★★, *Frizzle Fry* (Caroline 1990)★★★, *Sailing The Seas Of Cheese* (Interscope 1991)★★★, *Pork Soda* (Interscope 1993)★★★★, *Tales From The Punchbowl* (Interscope 1995)★★★, *The Brown Album* (Interscope 1997)★★★, *Rhinoplasty* (Interscope 1998)★★, *Antipop* (Interscope 1999)★★★.

Solo: Les Claypool And The Holy Mackerel *Highball With The Devil* (Prawn Song/Interscope 1996)★★.

● VIDEOS: *Videoplasty* (Interscope Video 1998).

Pro-Pain

This New York hardcore outfit was assembled by the former Crumbsuckers rhythm section of Gary Meskill (bass/vocals) and Dan Richardson (drums) after the demise of their old band. Tom Klimchuck provided the guitars on *Foul Taste Of*

Freedom, a full-blooded and aggressive hardcore blast given a brutally heavy sound by producer Alex Perialas, and matched by typically challenging lyrics, an approach that drew Pantera and Biohazard comparisons. It also impressed Roadrunner Records sufficiently to gain the band a contract. However, Klimchuck departed shortly after the release to be replaced by Nick St Dennis, with a second guitarist in Mike Hollman (ex-Possessed) added later. He was in turn replaced by Rob Moschetti. Pro-Pain ran into problems over the original cover for *The Truth Hurts*, which depicted a stitched-up female torso after an autopsy, while the inner artwork featured a series of disturbing police photographs of street crime victims from the early 90s. Despite the fact that the cover was from an art exhibit in a prominent Indiana gallery and that the police photos were public domain, the cover was obscured by a large sticker in the USA, while it was replaced entirely in the UK, with the original available by mail order. The music had acquired a new groove from the band's touring experience, while Meskill's lyrics remained true to his roots, with the social decay in his Long Island home a favourite subject.

● ALBUMS: *Foul Taste Of Freedom* (Energy 1992)★★★, *The Truth Hurts* (Roadrunner 1994)★★★, *Contents Under Pressure* (Edel 1996)★★, *Pro-Pain* (High Gain/Active 1997)★★★, *Act Of God* (High Gain 1999)★★★.

● COMPILATIONS: *The Best Of Pro-Pain* (High Again 1998)★★★.

Prodigy

This Braintree, Essex, England-based outfit, comprising Liam Howlett, Keith Flint, Leeroy Thornhill and MC Maxim Reality, shot to fame in the mid-90s as one of the first dance music acts to achieve the same level of success and media coverage as rock bands. During the 80s Howlett was a break-dancer and DJ with the hip-hop crew Cut To Kill, but, inspired by the sounds of such artists as Meat Beat Manifesto and Joey Beltram, he began to write his own hard, edgy dance music. The Prodigy signed to XL Records in 1990 and, in February the following year, released their first EP, *What Evil Lurks*, which proved highly popular on the underground rave scene. Their next record, 'Charly', which used samples of the famous public information road safety advertisement, was equally popular on the underground scene. On its commercial release, however, it climbed to number 3 on the UK charts, bringing the Prodigy to the attention of a wider audience. Its success spawned a number of similar 'toytown' techno releases from other outfits, including tracks based on *The Magic Roundabout* and *Sesame Street*. The crew had already made a name for themselves performing at parties around the country, but differed from many anonymous dance acts by presenting a frenetic live show, with Flint and Thornhill dancing and Maxim on vocals. Their mainstream success continued with a series of Top 20 hits, including the *Everybody In the Place* EP, 'Fire', 'Out Of Space' and 'Wind It Up', which were included on their debut album, released in 1992. *The Prodigy Experience* was a frantic blend of hard fidgeting breakbeats, rumbling basslines, rigid, angular melodic ideas and fragments of vocals, interspersed with the occasional breakdown. Howlett mostly employed harsh, metallic, edgy synth sounds, which were frequently offset by pianos and trivial sounds, serving to relieve the tense industrial feeling. Their next single, 'One Love' (which had been released earlier that year as an anonymous white label enti-

tled 'Earthbound'), hinted at a change of direction in 1993, confirmed a year later by the Top 5 single 'No Good (Start the Dance)' and the album *Music For The Jilted Generation*, which entered the UK album chart at number 1. Two more singles, 'Voodoo People' and 'Poison', continued their commercial success. While they retained some elements of the hardcore sound (notably the breakbeats), musical mastermind Howlett had broadened their sound with 'radio-friendly' vocals ('No Good (Start The Dance)'), heavy rock guitar ('Their Law' and 'Voodoo People'), environmental sounds ('Break & Enter' and 'Speedway'), flute ('Poison' and '3 Kilos'), and live drums. At the same time he dropped the angular, hardcore-style melodies and created an individual sound more influenced by techno-style repetition and abstraction, but still distinctively Prodigy. Their reputation as a live act was further enhanced in the summer of 1995 by successful performances at Glastonbury and various other festivals, an area traditionally dominated by rock. Over the next 12 months they continued to tour around Europe, Australia and America. In March 1996, they achieved their first UK number 1 single with 'Firestarter'. Combining clattering breakbeats, dirty sub-bass and whining guitar with Flint's punk-influenced vocals, the single appealed to a wide audience and brought the Prodigy to the attention of the rock press. In performances on that year's festival circuit, the line-up was augmented by guitarist Gizz Butt. Towards the end of the year, 'Breathe' became their second UK number 1 single and confirmed their popularity with a mainstream audience both at home and abroad. In June 1997, *Fat Of The Land* entered the UK album chart at number 1. As with *Music For The Jilted Generation*, the album continued to explore new combinations of sound. By now they had completely abandoned the hardcore touches and, if anything, *Fat Of The Land* moved towards a punk and thrash-style, blending techno and breakbeat sounds with guitar, live drums and vocals to create a distinctive, futuristic hybrid of rock and dance. They invoked media outrage with the release of the controversial 'Smack My Bitch Up' and its 'pornographic' promotional video. This did not stop them winning Best Dance Act at the 1998 BRIT Awards. The following year Howlett released an acclaimed mix album under the Prodigy name.

● ALBUMS: *The Prodigy Experience* (XL 1992)★★★, *Music For The Jilted Generation* (XL 1994)★★★★, *Fat Of The Land* (XL 1997)★★★★, *Prodigy Present The Dirtchamber Sessions Volume One* (XL 1999)★★★★.

● VIDEOS: *Electronic Punks* (XL Recordings 1995), *Evolution* (Visual 1997).

● FURTHER READING: *Electronic Punks: The Official Story*, Martin Roach. *Prodigy: Exit The Underground*, Lisa Verrico. *Prodigy: The Fat Of The Land*, no author listed. *Adventures With The Voodoo Crew*, Martin James. *Prodigy - An Illustrated Biography*, Stuart Coles.

Propellerheads

Alex Gifford played piano for Van Morrison, saxophone for the Stranglers and was a member of the Grid before he met Will White when the latter was drumming for Junkwaffle at a gig in Bath. In 1996, Wall Of Sound released their first recording, the *Dive* EP, which later that year was given worldwide coverage as the theme to an Adidas advert. In late 1996, the Propellerheads brought the big beat sound to the Top 100 with 'Take California' and early the next year,

'Spybreak' fared even better. On the strength of the latter the duo were invited by David Arnold to participate in his album of *James Bond* theme remakes, and their contribution, 'On Her Majesty's Secret Service', became their first Top 10 hit. As a result, they recorded some of the incidental music for the movie *Tomorrow Never Dies*. 'OHMSS' was successfully followed by the UK Top 20 hit single 'History Repeating' (featuring Shirley Bassey) and *Decksandrumsandrockandroll*. Since its release the duo have been involved in projects with the Jungle Brothers and De La Soul. The main components of their characteristic blend of hip-hop, grungey rock and 60s kitsch can be heard in tracks such as 'Spybreak', which features chunky riffs and prominent drumbeats with various effects, Hammond organ melodies and *Mission Impossible*-style bongos. 'Bang On!' and 'Better?' offered slightly different versions of the same idea. While the duo claim that their music is not complex and is primarily dance music-orientated, after a few listens they begin to sound rather one-dimensional, relying on tired hip-hop and acid jazz clichés.
● ALBUMS: *Decksandrumsandrockandroll* (Wall Of Sound 1997)★★★.

Puff Daddy
(see Combs, Sean 'Puffy')

Pulp
UK pop troupe headed up by the inimitable Jarvis Cocker. Based in Sheffield, England, Cocker actually put the first version of Pulp together while still at school, recording a sole John Peel radio session in November 1981. That line-up boasted Cocker (vocals/guitar), Peter Dalton (keyboards), Jamie Pinchbeck (bass) and Wayne Furniss (drums). Bullied as a child for his angular, National Health-bespectacled looks, Cocker went on to work in a nursery for deaf children. Certainly his Pulp project could hardly be described as an overnight success. After the mini-album *It*, the first real evidence of Cocker's abilities as a lyricist arrived with 'Little Girl (With Blue Eyes)' ('There's a hole in your heart and one between your legs, you'll never have to wonder which one he's going to fill despite what he says'). Though singles like this and the subsequent 'Dogs Are Everywhere' and 'They Suffocate At Night' should have broken the band, it took a third chapter in their history, and a new line-up, to provide the impetus. Cocker's desire for success was always explicit: 'Until I've been on *Top Of The Pops* I will always consider myself a failure' (in fact, by 1994 he was to be seen presenting an edition). By 1993, the band had coalesced to a steady line-up, featuring Russell Senior (guitar/violin), Candida Doyle (keyboards), Stephen Mackey (bass) and Nicholas Banks (drums) and signed a deal with Island Records. The band's early 1994 single, 'Do You Remember The First Time?', was accompanied by a short film in which famous celebrities were quizzed on this very subject (the loss of their virginity). The *Sunday Times* described such songs as being like 'Mike Leigh set to music', which was ironic, given that the mother of Pulp member Doyle had previously appeared in two Leigh films. She had also, more famously, played posh employer to Hilda Ogden's cleaning lady in *Coronation Street*. The song appeared on their major-label debut, *His 'N' Hers*. The album, which also contained minor hits in 'Lipgloss' and 'Babies', was later nominated for the 1994 Mercury Music Prize. *Different Class*, with production supervised by Ed Buller, offered a supreme evocation of

the 'behind the net curtains' sexual mores of working-class Britons. Island offered the record with a choice of 12 different covers; fortunately the music within was better than the hype, with the sardonic hit single 'Common People' becoming one of the anthems of the year. Cocker became the darling of the music press in 1995, and, at the height of Britpop, successfully managed to detach himself from the Blur versus Oasis media hype. During the BRIT Awards in February 1996, Cocker found the stage display by Michael Jackson sickening, and during Jackson's heavily choreographed act, was seen mocking the superstar onstage. Cocker was arrested and later there was a spurious charge of actual bodily harm; it was claimed that he had deliberately hit one of the small children surrounding the godlike Jackson. Both camps were incensed, and a war of words ensued between Epic and Island. All charges were eventually dropped when sense prevailed and the accusers realized that Cocker was not a child-beater. Russell Senior left the band in February 1997 (later forming Venini), and in November of that year, Pulp returned with a new single, 'Help The Aged'. It was followed by the sexually-charged *This Is Hardcore*, a difficult album that alienated some of the band's new fans and suffered commercially as a result. Nevertheless, Cocker's mocking humour and cantankerous nature helped establish Pulp as one of the most interesting and original UK bands of the 90s.
● ALBUMS: *It* mini-album (Red Rhino 1983)★★, *Freaks* (Fire 1986)★★, *Separations* 1989 recording (Fire 1992)★★★, *His 'N' Hers* (Island 1994)★★★★, *Different Class* (Island 1995)★★★★, *This Is Hardcore* (Island 1998)★★★.
● COMPILATIONS: *Pulpintro: The Gift Recordings* (Island 1993)★★, *Masters Of The Universe: Pulp On Fire 1985-86* (Fire 1995)★★★, *Countdown 1992-83* (Nectar 1996)★★, *Primal ... The Best Of The Fire Years 1983-1992* (Music Club 1998)★★★, *Pulped 83-92* 4-CD box set (Cooking Vinyl 1999)★★★.
● VIDEOS: *Pulp - Sorted For Films And Vids* (VVL 1995), *Pulp - A Feeling Called Love* (VVL 1996), *The Park Is Mine* (VVL 1998).
● FURTHER READING: *Pulp*, Martin Aston.

Puressence
From Oldham, Lancashire, England, Puressence made their debut in May 1992 with the *Petrol Skin* EP for Northern 2 Damn Loud Records. Led by the affecting tenor of Jamie Mudriczki, it earned the band, comprising Neil McDonald (guitar), Kevin Matthews (bass) and Tony Szuminski (drums), significant early exposure. It was followed in 1993 by a second release, which coincided with an outing on the Rough Trade Records Singles Club. At this stage there was still a lack of focus and musical integrity within their guitar rock platform, but Toby Chalmers of Island Records evidently saw enough potential to offer them a recording contract. Support slots to local favourites Marion introduced them to new supporters, before their first Island single, 'I Suppose', was released in May 1995. Afterwards the band moved on to sessions for their debut album with Clive Martin. The result was *Puressence*, with Mudriczki's vocals particularly effective on tracks such as 'Casting Lazy Shadows'. *Only Forever* refined the band's style, reaching intense peaks on stand-out tracks 'It Doesn't Matter Anymore' and 'Sharpen Up Your Knives'.
● ALBUMS: *Puressence* (Island 1996)★★★, *Only Forever* (Island 1998)★★★.

Quaye, Finley

b. 25 March 1974, Edinburgh, Scotland. Quaye comes from a musical background with Ghanaian lineage - his father is the jazz composer Cab Quaye, while his brother Caleb Quaye played guitar for Hookfoot and Elton John in the 70s, followed by a stint with Hall And Oates in the 80s. Quaye was raised in Manchester and on leaving school he returned to Edinburgh, where he worked as a paint sprayer, and often drove to Newcastle to attend gigs by artists such as 808 State and Soft Cell. Moving back to Manchester, he embarked on a BTEC course in music and sound engineering, but did not complete his tuition. He briefly relocated to London where he joined the Donga Tribe and practised drumming. His aspirations towards a singing career began when he returned to Manchester, where he voiced a track for A Guy Called Gerald in one take. Shortly after the session, he returned to Edinburgh, where he unexpectedly heard the track on the radio, and subsequently began listening to dub music. His initial inspiration came from an unorthodox source, the New York-based avant-gardist John Zorn's 'Black Hole Dub', although he was later inspired by more conventional performers. Quaye recorded his first solo outing on a four-track tape, singing and playing drums, bass and guitar. In March 1997, he released the *Ultra Stimulation* EP which demonstrated his diverse influences, including Charles Mingus, Jimi Hendrix and Bob Marley. He also embarked on the live circuit, debuting at Bristol's Malcolm X centre, where he supported Luciano. In June, he released 'Sunday Shining', which gave a nod to Bob Marley's 'Sun Is Shining', as well as other reggae hits including Dennis Brown's 'Money In My Pocket'. The song, delivered in a style similar to that of a young Burning Spear, became his first UK chart hit and Quaye's unique approach was much lauded by the critics. The promotional wheels were set in motion with appearances at the major summer festivals, including the Essential Roots Day alongside Everton Blender, Cocoa Tea and Anthony B. in Finsbury Park, London, and the release of his debut album. Further chart success followed with the singles 'Even After All', 'It's Great When We're Together' and 'Your Love Gets Sweeter', and he was voted Best Male Singer at the 1998 BRIT Awards.

● ALBUMS: *Maverick A Strike* (Epic/550 1997)★★★★.

Queen Latifah

b. Dana Owens, 18 March 1970, East Orange, New Jersey, USA. Acknowledged as the first lady of hip-hop, Queen Latifah, broke through in the late 80s with a style that picked selectively from jazz and soul traditions. The former Burger King employee maintained her early commitment to answer the misogynist armoury of her male counterparts, and at the same time impart musical good times to all genders. After working as the human beatbox alongside female rapping crew Ladies Fresh, she was just 18 years old when she released her debut single, 'Wrath Of My Madness', in 1988. A year later her debut long-player enjoyed fevered reviews: an old, wise head was evident on the top of her young shoulders. Production expertise from Daddy-O, KRS-One, DJ Mark The 45 King and members of De La Soul doubtlessly helped as well. By the time of her third album she had moved from Tommy Boy Records to a new home, Motown Records, and revealed a shift from the soul and ragga tones of *Nature Of A Sista* to sophisticated, sassy hip-hop. She subsequently embarked on a career as an actor, notably in the hit streetwise black comedy, *Living Single*, where she played magazine boss Khadijah James. Her movie credits already include *Juice*, *Jungle Fever* and *House Party 2*. She additionally set up her own Flavor Unit record label and management company in 1993, as an outlet for new rap acts as well as her own recordings. The first release on it, 'Roll Wit Tha Flava', featured an all-star cast including Naughty By Nature's Treach, Fu-Schnickens' Chip-Fu, Black Sheep's Dres and D-Nice. She also guested on the Shabba Ranks single, 'Watcha Gonna Do'. Previous collaborations had included those with De La Soul ('Mama Gave Birth To The Soul Children', in that band's infancy) and Monie Love (the agenda-setting 'Ladies First'). Queen Latifah represents an intelligent cross-section of hip-hop influences. Although she is a forthright advocate of her race's struggle, she is also the daughter of and brother to policemen. *Black Reign*, in fact, is dedicated to the death of that same brother: 'I see both sides. I've seen the abuse and I've been the victim of police who abuse their authority. On the other side you've got cops getting shot all the time, you got people who don't respect them at all'. While a little too strident to live up to the Arabic meaning of her name (Latifah equates to delicate and sensitive), Queen Latifah remains one of the most positive role models for young black women (and men) in hip-hop culture: 'Aspire to be a doctor or a lawyer, but not a gangster'. As one of the singles lifted from *Black Reign* advocated: 'UNITY (Who You Calling A Bitch?)'. Following a lengthy hiatus owing to acting commitments, Latifah returned to recording with 1998's *Order In The Court*.

● ALBUMS: *All Hail The Queen* (Tommy Boy 1989)★★★★, *Nature Of A Sista* (Tommy Boy 1991)★★★, *Black Reign* (Motown 1993)★★★, *Order In The Court* (Flavor Unit 1998)★★★.

● FILMS: *Jungle Fever* (1991), *House Party 2* (1991), *Juice* (1992), *Who's The Man* (1993), *My Life* (1993), *Set It Off* (1996), *Hoodlum* (1997), *The Wizard Of Oz* (1998), *Living Out Loud* (1998), *Sphere* (1998), *The Bone Collector* (1999).

Quireboys

After violent incidents at early live shows, this UK band altered their name from Queerboys to Quireboys, to avoid further trouble. Comprising Spike Gray (vocals), Nigel Mogg (bass, brother of Phil Mogg of UFO), Chris Johnstone (keyboards), Guy Bailey (guitar), Ginger (b. 12 December 1964, South Shields, Tyne & Wear, England; guitar) and Coze (drums), they were all originally drinking buddies in London pubs. Drawing musical inspiration from the Faces, Rolling Stones and Mott The Hoople, they specialized in barroom boogie, beer-soaked blues and infectious raunch 'n' roll. Gray's rough-as-a-gravel-path vocal style, closely resembling Rod Stewart's, added fuel to accusations of the band being little more than Faces copyists. After releasing two independent singles they signed to EMI Records and immediately underwent a line-up reshuffle. Coze and Ginger (who went on to form the Wildhearts) were removed and replaced by Ian Wallace and Guy Griffin, respectively. They recorded *A Bit Of What You Fancy* in Los Angeles, under the production eye of Jim Cregan (former Rod Stewart guitarist). It was an immediate success, entering the UK album charts at number 2 in February 1990. 'Hey You', lifted as a single, also met with similar success, peaking at number 14 in January 1990. An eight-track live album followed, which duplicated most of the numbers from their first album, as a stop-gap measure to bridge the long period between successive studio releases. However, when *Bitter Sweet & Twisted* failed to ignite, Gray left to form his own band, God's Hotel, denying rumours that he had been invited to replace Axl Rose in Guns N'Roses (after having contributed to Slash's [Snakepit] solo album). The Quireboys had come to a natural conclusion, or, as Gray preferred to put it, 'we were past our sell-by-date'. Bass player Nigel Mogg put together his own project, the Nancy Boys, in New York.

● ALBUMS: *A Bit Of What You Fancy* (Parlophone 1989)★★★, *Live Around The World* (Parlophone 1990)★★★, *Bitter Sweet & Twisted* (Parlophone 1992)★★.

● COMPILATIONS: *From Tooting To Barking* (Castle 1994)★★★.

● VIDEOS: *A Bit Of What You Fancy* (PMI/EMI 1990).

R.E.M.

R.E.M. played their first concert in Athens, Georgia, USA, on 19 April 1980. Their line-up consisted of four drop-outs from the University of Georgia; Michael Stipe (b. 4 January 1960, Decatur, Georgia, USA; vocals), Peter Buck (b. 6 December 1956, Berkeley, California, USA; guitar), Mike Mills (b. 17 December 1958, Orange County, California, USA; bass) and Bill Berry (b. 31 July 1958, Duluth, Minnesota, USA; drums). Without the charisma of Stipe and his eccentric onstage behaviour, hurling himself about with abandon in-between mumbling into the microphone, they could easily have been overlooked as just another bar band, relying on the harmonious guitar sound of the Byrds for their inspiration. Acquiring a healthy following among the college fraternity in their hometown, it was not long before they entered the

studio to record their debut single, 'Radio Free Europe', to be released independently on Hibtone Records. This was greeted with considerable praise by critics who conceded that the band amounted to more than the sum of their influences. Their country/folk sound was contradicted by a driving bassline and an urgency that put the listener more in mind of the Who in their early mod phase. Add to this the distinctive voice of Stipe and his, on the whole, inaudible, perhaps even non-existent, lyrics, and R.E.M. sounded quite unlike any other band in the USA in the post-punk era of the early 80s. Newly signed to IRS Records, they gained further favourable notices for August 1982's mini-album, *Chronic Town*, produced by Mitch Easter. Their eagerly awaited full-length debut arrived in April 1983. With production duties handled by Easter and Don Dixon, *Murmur* surpassed all expectations, and was eventually made Album Of The Year by *Rolling Stone* magazine. As in the USA, the band earned a devoted cult following in Europe, largely comprised of college students. *Reckoning* appeared the following year and was permeated by a reckless spontaneity that had been missing from their earlier work. Recorded in only 12 days, the tracks varied in mood from frustration, as on 'So. Central Rain (I'm Sorry)', to the tongue-in-cheek sing along '(Don't Go Back To) Rockville'. The songs were accessible enough but, as would be the case for most of the 80s, the singles culled from R.E.M.'s albums were generally deemed uncommercial by mainstream radio programmers. However, their cult reputation benefited from a series of flop singles on both sides of the Atlantic. Although received enthusiastically by critics, the Joe Boyd-produced *Fables Of The Reconstruction* was a stark, morose album that mirrored a period of despondency within the band. Peter Buck summed it up in the 90s - 'If we were to record those songs again, they would be very different'. *Lifes Rich Pageant*, produced by Don Gehman, showed the first signs of a politicization within the band that would come to a head and coincide with their commercial breakthrough in the late 80s. Stipe's lyrics began to dwell increasingly on the prevailing amorality in the USA and question its inherited ethics, while retaining their much vaunted obliqueness. Tracks such as 'These Days' and 'Cuyahoga' were rallying cries to the young and disaffected; although the lyrics were reflective and almost bitter, the music was the most joyous and uplifting the band had recorded to date. This ironic approach to songwriting was typified by 'It's The End Of The World As We Know It (And I Feel Fine)', from 1987's equally impressive *Document*, which intentionally trivialized its subject matter with a witty and up-tempo infectiousness. In a similar vein was 'The One I Love', a deliberately cold and detached dismissal of an ex-lover that was, nevertheless, completely misinterpreted as romantic by countless record-buyers who pushed the single up to number 9 on the *Billboard* Hot 100 chart. The album was produced by Scott Litt, who would continue to work with the band over the next few years. Their major label debut *Green* arrived the following year and sold slowly but steadily in the USA. The attendant single 'Stand' reached US number 6 in January 1989, while 'Orange Crush' entered the UK Top 30 the same June. Apart from demonstrating their environmental awareness, particularly on 'You Are The Everything', the album laid more emphasis on Stipe's vocals and lyrics. This, to the singer's dismay, led to his elevation as 'spokesman for a generation', particularly with the apparent self-revelation of 'World Leader Pretend'. Already hero-worshipped by adoring long-term fans who saw him as both pin-up and creative genius, Stipe insisted: 'Rock 'n' roll is a joke, people who take it seriously are the butt of the joke'. The world tour that coincided with the album's release saw R.E.M. making a smooth transition from medium-size venues to the stadium circuit, owing as much to Stipe's individual choreography as to the elaborate, projected backdrops. After a break of two years, during which Berry, Buck and Mills collaborated with singer Warren Zevon as the Hindu Love Gods, the band re-emerged with *Out Of Time*. Their previous use of horns and mandolins to embroider songs did not prepare their audience for the deployment of an entire string section, nor were the contributions from B-52's singer Kate Pierson and Boogie Down Productions' KRS-One expected. Ostensibly the band's first album to contain 'love' songs, it was unanimously hailed as a masterpiece and topped both the US and UK album charts. The accompanying singles from the album, 'Losing My Religion' (US number 4/UK number 19), 'Shiny Happy People' (US number 10/UK number 6), 'Near Wild Heaven' (UK number 27) and 'Radio Song' (UK number 28), gave them further hits. *Automatic For The People* was released in October 1992 to universal favour, reaching the top of the charts in the UK and USA. The album produced a number of memorable singles including the moody 'Drive' (US number 28/UK number 11), the joyous Andy Kaufman tribute 'Man On The Moon' (US number 30/UK number 18) with its classic Elvis Presley vocal inflections from Stipe and an award-winning accompanying monochrome video, 'The Sidewinder Sleeps Tonite' (UK number 17) and 'Everybody Hurts' (US number 29/UK number 7). *Monster* showed the band in grunge-like mode. 'What's The Frequency, Kenneth?' (UK number 9) started a run of hit singles taken from the album and further awards were heaped upon them. Following the collapse of Bill Berry in Switzerland while on a major tour in 1995, the band were forced to rest. Berry was operated on for a ruptured aneurysm and made a full recovery. In August 1996, the band re-signed with Warner Brothers Records for the largest recording contract advance in history: $80 million was guaranteed for a five-album contract. *New Adventures In Hi-Fi* was released in September. Recorded mostly during soundchecks during the ill-fated *Monster* tour, it was nevertheless another excellent collection. From the epic chord changes of 'Be Mine' to the cool understated calm of 'How The West Was Won And Where It Got Us', it showed the band's remarkable creative depth. 'E-Bow The Letter', featuring Patti Smith, also provided the band with a UK Top 5 single. In October 1997, Bill Berry shocked the music world by announcing his intention to leave R.E.M. after 17 years with the band; the remaining members were quick to confirm that they would be continuing without him, using the adage 'a three-legged dog can still walk'. Although there was no official replacement on drums, with the rest of the band electing to continue R.E.M. as a three-piece, ex-Screaming Trees drummer Barrett Martin contributed to sessions for 1998's *Up*, which also featured new producer Pat McCarthy. Introduced by the single 'Daysleeper' (a UK Top 10 hit), this album was the band's most adventurous recording since the mid-80s. The following year they provided the soundtrack for the Andy Kaufman biopic *Man On The Moon*, which included the excellent new track, 'The Great Beyond'. The critical praise heaped upon R.E.M. has been monumental, but despite all the attention they have remained painfully modest and reasonably unaffected, and, despite the loss of Berry, still appear united. They are one of the most important and popular bands to appear over the past three decades, and although their commercial heyday appears to have passed they still retain massive credibility.

● ALBUMS: *Chronic Town* mini-album (IRS 1982)★★★, *Murmur* (IRS 1983)★★★★, *Reckoning* (IRS 1984)★★★★, *Fables Of The Reconstruction* (IRS 1985)★★★, *Lifes Rich Pageant* (IRS 1986)★★★★, *Document* (IRS 1987)★★★, *Green* (Warners 1988)★★★★, *Out Of Time* (Warners 1991)★★★★, *Automatic For The People* (Warners 1992)★★★★★, *Monster* (Warners 1994)★★★, *New Adventures In Hi-Fi* (Warners 1996)★★★★★, *Up* (Warners 1998)★★★.

● COMPILATIONS: *Dead Letter Office* (IRS 1987)★★★, *Eponymous* (IRS 1988)★★★★, *The Best Of R.E.M.* (IRS 1991)★★★, *In The Attic: Alternative Recordings 1985-1989* (Capitol/EMI 1997)★★★.

● VIDEOS: *Athens, Ga - Inside/Out* (A&M Video 1987), *Succumbs* (A&M Video 1987), *Pop Screen* (Warner Reprise Video 1990), *Tourfilm* (Warner Reprise Video 1990), *This Film Is On* (Warner Reprise Video 1991), *Parallel* (Warner Reprise Video 1995), *Roadmovie* (Warner Reprise Video 1996).

● FURTHER READING: *REMarks: The Story Of R.E.M.*, Tony Fletcher. *R.E.M.: Behind The Mask*, Jim Greer. *R.E.M.: File Under Water, The Definitive Guide To 12 Years Of Recordings And Concerts*, Jon Storey. *REMnants: The R.E.M. Collector's Handbook*, Gary Nabors. *It Crawled From The South: An R.E.M. Companion*, Marcus Gray. *Talk About The Passion: R.E.M. An Oral History*, Denise Sullivan. *R.E.M. The 'Rolling Stone' Files: The Ultimate Compendium Of Interviews*, no editor listed. *R.E.M. Documental*, Dave Bowler and Bryan Dray. *R.E.M. Inside Out*, Craig Rosen. *The R.E.M. Companion*, John Platt (ed.).

Radar Brothers

This Los Angeles, California, USA-based trio, who blend the melodic ache of Lemonheads-styled pop with the sparsity of country rock, first attracted attention with the release of a six-track mini-album debut for Fingerpaint Records in 1995. It was quickly followed by a full-length debut of the same title on Restless Records. The band's songs are written by the doleful Jim Putnam (b. 30 September 1967, Hollywood, California, USA), a veteran of both Medicine and Maids Of Gravity. In the mid-90s, he recruited bass player Senon Williams and drummer Steve Goodfriend and set about recording his own songs, based on ideas that had been in his head for some time. The intimate, deeply personalized results were much admired in the press, particularly for their temperate emotional pacing, one of the Radar Brothers' most distinctive qualities. The band were subsequently dropped by Restless and disappeared for a while to concentrate on writing songs. They returned in 1999 with a new record deal and *The Singing Hatchet*, another masterpiece of emotional and musical restraint.

● ALBUMS: *Radar Brothers* mini-album (Fingerpaint 1995)★★★, *Radar Brothers* (Restless 1996)★★★★, *The Singing Hatchet* (Seethru Broadcasting/Chemikal Underground 1999)★★★★.

Radio Tarifa

This roots ensemble was formed in Madrid, Spain, in 1992, by Rafael 'Fain' Sánchez Dueñas (b. 12 November 1951, Spain; percussion), Benjamín Escoriza (b. 20 December 1953, Spain; vocals) and Vincent Molino Cook (b. 1 October 1958, France; flute). Dueñas and Cook had been playing a mixture of flamenco, Arabic and medieval music as Ars Antiqua Musicalis since the early 80s. Following a trip to Morocco, Radio Tarifa was formed to explore further these Spanish and North African musical styles. The trio recorded *Rumba Argelina*, in Dueñas' one-track home studio, over-dubbing a diverse range of instruments, including Spanish guitar, bagpipes, bazouki accordion and Arabic flute, to obtain a truly multicultural sound. Intended as a document of the trio's musical research and explorations, *Rumba Argelina* was released on the tiny local Sin Fin label in 1993, by which time Dueñas had moved to Germany to work as a architect (all three members of the band still had day jobs at this point). On his return to Spain a year later, Dueñas put together the full eight-piece line-up of Radio Tarifa to per-form live concerts following much interest in the album's haunting and understated sound. *Rumba Argelina* was released internationally in 1996 following a demand created by the enthusiasm of world music writers and DJs. The band, comprising Sebastian Rubio Caballero (b. 26 January 1964, Spain; percussion), Juan Ramiro Amusategui Prado (b. 26 July 1963, Spain; guitars), Pedro Pablo Oteo Aguilar (b. 18 March 1966, Spain; bass), El Wafir Shaikheldin Gibril (b. 4 April 1964, Sudan; percussion), and Jaime Muela Quesada (b. 3 February 1957, Spain; flute/saxophone), toured across Europe and Japan in the same year to promote the album. Their live concerts featured a flamenco dancer performing with the band. Their sound was fuller and livelier than on their debut album and this was reflected in *Temporal*, the follow-up, which took the basic formula of *Rumba Argelina* a stage further by adding Sephardic Jewish and seventh-cen-tury French music to the Spanish-Arabic fusion. Following a tour to promote *Temporal*, Gibril left the band in December 1997 and was replaced by Eduardo Laguillo Menendez.

● ALBUMS: *Rumba Argelina* (World Circuit 1996)★★★★, *Temporal* (World Circuit 1997)★★★★.

Radiohead

The five members of Radiohead first met at a private boys school in Abingdon, a small, picturesque town on the out-skirts of Oxford. Thom Yorke (b. 7 October 1968, Wellingborough, Northamptonshire, England; vocals/guitar) had been given his first instrument, a Spanish guitar, at the age of eight by his mother. He formed his first band two years later, then joined an existing school punk band, TNT. Singing for the first time, he realized he would require more sympathetic band members and formed what would become Radiohead with school friends Ed O'Brien (b. 15 April 1968, Oxford, Oxfordshire, England; guitar), 'who looked cool', and Colin Greenwood (b. 26 June 1969, Oxford, Oxfordshire, England; bass) 'because he was in my year and we always ended up at the same parties'. They shared an interest in Joy Division and the Smiths and Greenwood earned Yorke's sympathy for joining TNT after him. Mild-mannered drummer Phil Selway (b. 23 May 1967, Hemmingford Grey, England; drums) bound the new band, titled On A Friday, together. The addition of Colin's brother and jazz fanatic, Jonny Greenwood (b. 5 November 1971, Oxford, Oxfordshire, England; guitar/keyboards) completed the line-up, originally on harmonica, after he pestered his elder brother and friends continually to let him join. In 1987, a week after his first rehearsal with the band, On A Friday played their debut gig at the now defunct Jericho Tavern in

Oxford. With a musical canon resembling a youthful Talking Heads, they added two saxophone-playing sisters to fill out the line-up. However, the band were then put on hold while the members pursued their academic careers, in an effort to appease already frantic parents (Jonny finished his schooling). Colin became entertainments officer at Peterhouse College, Cambridge University, and helped get his friends together for occasional gigs there. At Exeter University, Yorke played guitar in a techno band, Flickernoise, while Selway drummed for various theatrical productions (*Blood Brothers, Return To The Forbidden Planet*) while studying at Liverpool Polytechnic. The band finally regrouped in Oxford in the summer of 1991, but without the brass section. They recorded two demos and gained a deal with EMI Records before changing their name to Radiohead (after a Talking Heads song). Their first commercial broad-cast followed when 'Prove Yourself', from the *Drill* EP, was voted Gary Davies' 'Happening Track Of The Week' on BBC Radio 1. Two minor hit singles were followed by 'Creep', *the* alternative rock song of 1993, with a self-loathing lyric ('I'm a creep, I'm a weirdo, I don't belong here') stretched over driven guitars that at one point simply explode. Ignored when it was first released in September 1992, its re-release sparked enormous interest as the band toured with Kingmaker and James. Taking the band into the UK Top 10 and the US Top 40, it also announced a Top 30 debut album, *Pablo Honey*. Unlike other celebrated UK indie hopefuls such as Suede, Radiohead also translated well to international tastes, from the USA to Egypt. Two years of promotional activity followed, before the release of *The Bends* in March 1995. With the pressure on following the plaudits, the recording process was not easy. With hardly a note recorded over two months, producer John Leckie ordered all bar Yorke out of the studio and told the singer to 'just fucking play it'. The songs came, and he and the rest of the band relo-cated to Abbey Road Studios to finish off the album in a mere three weeks. *The Bends* did not disappoint, with a vibrant mood range encouraging Yorke's prosaic yet affecting lyrics: 'When your insides fall to pieces, You just sit there wishing you could still make love'. Notable tracks included the hyp-notic 'High And Dry' and 'Fake Plastic Trees', and the UK Top 5 single 'Street Spirit (Fade Out)'. By the end of 1995 *The Bends* had been universally acclaimed, enough to win them a BRIT Awards nomination as the best band of the year. Two years later, they unveiled the follow-up, *OK Computer*, which received the most spectacular reviews of any rock album in recent memory, and won the band a Grammy Award in 1998 for Best Alternative Rock Performance.

● ALBUMS: *Pablo Honey* (Parlophone/Capitol 1993)★★★, *The Bends* (Parlophone / Capitol 1995)★★★★★, *OK Computer* (Parlophone / Capitol 1997)★★★★★.

● VIDEOS: *27/5/94 The Astoria London Live* (PMI 1995), *7 Television Commercials* (Parlophone 1998), *Meeting People Is Easy* (Parlophone 1998).

● FURTHER READING: *Radiohead: An Illustrated Biography*, Nick Johnstone. *Coming Up For Air*, Steve Malins. *From A Great Height*, Jonathan Hale. *Radiohead: Hysterical And Useless*, Martin Clarke.

Raekwon

b. Corey Woods, New York, USA. Raekwon is a long-standing member of the Wu-Tang Clan, Staten Island's seminal hip-hop crew. Following the release of their 1993 debut *Enter*

The Wu-Tang (36 Chambers), several of the members released solo projects. Raekwon's *Only Built 4 Cuban Linx ...* followed albums by Method Man (*Tical*) and Ol' Dirty Bastard (*Return To The 36 Chambers: The Dirty Version*). The album was produced, like most Wu-Tang Clan releases, by RZA, and featured notable contributions from fellow members Ghostface Killah (credited on the album cover under the Tony Starks pseudonym) and Method Man. The album celebrated the 'gambino' lifestyle of New York gangstas, and incorporated the teachings of the 5% Nation Muslim set. The harsh rhyming and vicious rhetoric isolated it from the 'family vibe' of other Wu-Tang releases, although it proved popular with their fans, debuting at number 4 on the *Billboard* album chart in August 1995. The following year, Raekwon (who is also known as the Chef) received second billing on Ghostface Killah's *Ironman*. His sophomore album, *Immobilarity*, was released in November 1999, and attracted strong praise for its highly individual take on the Wu-Tang Clan sound.

● ALBUMS: *Only Built 4 Cuban Linx ...* (Loud/RCA 1995)★★★★, *Immobilarity* (Loud/RCA 1999)★★★.
● FILMS: *The Show* (1995), *Rhyme & Reason* (1997), *Black And White* (1999).

Rage Against The Machine

The name says everything about Rage Against The Machine. The aggressive musical blend of metal guitar and hip-hop rhythms is an appropriate background to the rap-styled delivery of angry, confrontational, political lyrics, addressing concerns over inner city deprivation, racism, censorship, propaganda, the plight of Native Americans and many other issues as the band strive to offer more than mere entertainment. Formed in Los Angeles, California, USA, in 1991 by Tom Morello (b. New York, USA; guitar, ex-Lock Up) and Zack de la Rocha (b. Long Beach, California, USA; vocals, ex-Inside Out), with Tim Commerford (bass) and Brad Wilk (b. Portland, Oregon, USA; drums), Rage Against The Machine signed a major record contract with, importantly, creative control on the strength of a self-released tape and some impressive early live shows. Further live work with Pearl Jam, Body Count, Tool and Suicidal Tendencies ensued, with the band encountering trouble with the French government during the Suicidal tour over T-shirts that showed a genuine CIA instructional cartoon on how to make a Molotov cocktail, taken from documents made for the Nicaraguan Contra rebels. The T-shirts were confiscated and destroyed by French Customs. The band subsequently released a self-titled debut, containing several tracks from their earlier cassette, with a stunning cover photograph of a Buddhist monk burning himself to death in protest at the Vietnam War, and rose rapidly to fame, Henry Rollins describing them as 'the most happening band in the US'. The album was a hit on both sides of the Atlantic, and Rage Against The Machine enjoyed single success with 'Killing In The Name', although de la Rocha was distinctly unhappy with a radio edit that removed all expletives and 'completely shut down the whole purpose of that song'. A sell-out UK tour in 1993 was followed by a silent protest against the P-M-R-C on the Philadelphia leg of the Lollapalooza festival tour. *Evil Empire* was another successful album, reaching number 1 in the USA. Tracks such as the highly political 'Vietnow' and 'Down Rodeo' showed the band at their potent best, while the incendiary 'Bulls On Parade' provided them with a transatlantic hit single. Beyond the swearing lay some of the most honest and powerful lyrical statements to be made during the 90s. After another long hiatus, the band returned in November 1999 with *The Battle Of Los Angeles*. Hardly deviating from the blueprint of their previous two records, the album was warmly received by their supporters but dismissed by detractors who felt the band had nothing new left to say.

● ALBUMS: *Rage Against The Machine* (Epic 1992)★★★★, *Evil Empire* (Epic 1996)★★★★, *The Battle Of Los Angeles* (Epic 1999)★★★.
● VIDEOS: *Rage Against The Machine* (Epic Music Video 1997).

Railroad Jerk

Practitioners of a style that combines herky-jerky, post-new wave rhythms with blues and folk, Railroad Jerk came together on the lower east side of New York City, and their music reflects the grittiness and urgency of that area. Marcellus Hall (b. Great Bluff, Minnesota, USA; vocals/guitar), who also worked as a cartoonist for New York Perspectives, met Tony Lee (b. Cherry Point, North Carolina, USA; bass) in Trenton, New Jersey, and the two began a musical partnership. With Jes Aspinall (b. Essex, England; drums) and Phillip (b. Belgium; guitar) they formed Railroad Jerk in the spring of 1989. By the end of that year, Phillip had left and Chris Mueller joined on guitar. The band's repertoire at the time consisted of songs with off-kilter, slap-happy drum beats, skewed, angular guitar lines and Hall's inspired yelping and absurdist lyrics. These tunes were augmented by twisted cover versions of songs by everyone from Aretha Franklin to Donovan. Reminiscent of a more urban Pavement (perhaps owing to the Fall influence), they were signed by Matador Records, who released the band's self-titled debut in 1990. After Steve Cerio replaced Aspinall, the band recorded *Raise The Plow*, an album that increased the weirdness quotient both musically and lyrically, but still represented a step forward. A considerable amount of turbulence followed, as Mueller and Cerio were replaced by Alec Stephen and Dave Varenka, respectively. This line-up, which has proved to be the most stable and successful, recorded the excellent *One Track Mind*, on which the band's vision finally emerged fully realized. The album is full of catchy, almost anthemic tunes, including the mock-egotistical 'The Ballad Of Railroad Jerk', but the left-field touches that are the band's trademark are still firmly in place. The album brought the band attention on an international level, and MTV exposure and more extensive worldwide tours followed. When commercial success failed to materialize, Hall began to busy himself with side projects, releasing several singles both under aliases and his own name. After the dust settled, the band gathered their collective breath and recorded *The Third Rail*. This album expanded on the sound of their previous effort; the witty lyrics were funnier and more biting and the band's instrumental attack more clearly focused on oddly syncopated, vaguely blues-based rockers, with fewer ballad detours. Stand-out tunes such as 'Sweet Librarian' and 'Natalie' are both deliciously arch and impossibly infectious.

● ALBUMS: *Railroad Jerk* (Matador 1990)★★★, *Raise The Plow* (Matador 1992)★★★, *One Track Mind* (Matador 1995)★★★★, *The Third Rail* (Matador 1996)★★★★.

Rainer

b. Rainer Ptacek, 7 June 1951, East Berlin, Germany, d. 12 November 1997, Tucson, Arizona, USA. A taste for seclusion and a penchant for unstructured, imaginative slide guitar playing made Rainer something of a cult figure before his records became generally available. His parents fled to West Berlin three years after his birth and in 1956 the family emigrated to America and settled in Chicago. While studying at the Saint Rita High School, Rainer heard blues players such as Muddy Waters, Paul Butterfield and Charlie Musselwhite at the Aragon Ballroom and the Electric Circus. He moved west in 1972 and settled in Tucson. For the next 20 years, his principal employment was as a guitar repairman after periods as a cab driver, janitor and cabinet maker. He was also a founding member of bands such as Giant Sand and the Band Of Blacky Ranchette, and formed Das Combo with Nick Augustine and Ralph Gilmore in 1984. Their initial cassette release, *The Mush Mind Blues*, was followed in 1986 by *Barefoot Rock With ...*, which was only released in England. Rainer's next release, 1992's *Worried Spirits*, was a solo effort recorded in two days direct to DAT, incorporating natural sounds and effects machinery. *The Texas Tapes*, credited to Das Combo, was a long-standing project with ZZ Top guitarist Billy Gibbons. Rainer also recorded several times with Robert Plant, who returned the favour on *The Inner Flame* tribute album in 1997, which helped raise money for Rainer's medical bills following the diagnosis of an inoperable brain tumour.

● ALBUMS: with Das Combo *Barefoot Rock With ...* (Making Waves 1986)★★★, *Worried Spirits* (Demon 1992)★★★, with Das Combo *The Texas Tapes* (Demon 1993)★★★, *Nocturnes (The Instrumentals)* (Glitterhouse 1995)★★★, various artists *The Inner Flame* (Atlantic 1997)★★★.

Rakim

b. William Griffin Jnr., Long Island, New York, USA. Between 1987 and 1992, Rakim released four influential albums in partnership with Eric B that have accorded him the status of one of rap's greatest figureheads. His complex, cross-referencing lyrics and relaxed delivery style inspired a new generation of hip-hop artists in the 90s, including the hugely successful Wu-Tang Clan, Nas and Dr. Dre. Following the duo's split in 1992, Rakim worked on the soundtrack to *Gunmen* before disappearing into seclusion for five years. He returned in 1997 with the long-awaited *The 18th Letter*, a smooth soulful album that earned praise for Rakim's imaginative and intelligent rhyming on tracks such as 'The 18th Letter' ('Nobody's been this long-awaited since Jesus/I heard the word on the street is/I'm still one of the deepest on the mike since Adidas') and 'The Mystery (Who Is God)'. The album also came with a greatest hits bonus CD, *The Book Of Life*, a compelling selection of the music which made Rakim the legendary figure he is today. His sophomore set, *The Master*, was released in November 1999. Falling short of both his work with Eric B and *The 18th Letter*, the album failed to distinguish itself from any other hip-hop album released in the late 90s, which, for a MC of Rakim's quality, was little short of a crime.

● ALBUMS: *The 18th Letter/The Book Of Life* (Universal 1997)★★★★, *The Master* (Universal 1999)★★★.

Rammstein

Formed in 1993 in East Berlin, Germany, this confrontational alternative rock band first came to international prominence when film and television director David Lynch (*Twin Peaks*) declared his admiration and commissioned them to work with him. By this time, Rammstein's explosive, unhinged live shows had already made them famous throughout mainland Europe. The band comprises Till Lindemann (vocals), Richard Kruspe (guitar), Paul Landers (guitar), Christoph Schneider (drums), Oliver Riedel (bass) and Flake Lorenz (keyboards). Their pyrotechnics earned them comparisons to Kiss, but their frenzied industrial metal sound and dubious lyrics were less obviously commercial. Those lyrics, touching on subjects including child molestation and natural and man-made catastrophes, at first saw them attract a right-wing audience - although the band strenuously deny that this was their intention. Rammstein, allegedly named after the 1988 air show disaster that killed 80, made their debut in October 1995 with *Herzeleid*, produced in Sweden by Jacob Hellner (previously a veteran of work with Clawfinger) on a modest budget. Nevertheless, the record sold in excess of half a million copies in Germany alone, and established the band as a potent commercial force. By the time *Sehnsucht* followed in 1997, they had extended their popularity via a clutch of headlining appearances at European festivals. Following Lynch's inclusion of two Rammstein songs on the soundtrack to his 1996 movie *Lost Highway*, US gore-metal fans, who followed controversial acts such as Marilyn Manson and KMFDM, were also won over. Although they sing in German, all the band's lyrics are translated in accompanying CD liner notes, adding to their growing international appeal.

● ALBUMS: *Herzeleid* (Motor Music/Eureka 1995)★★★, *Sehnsucht* (Motor Music/Slash 1997)★★★★, *Live Aus Berlin* (Motor Music/PolyGram 1999)★★★.

● VIDEOS: *Rammstein: Live Aus Berlin* (Universal/Island 1999).

Rampling, Danny

b. 15 July 1961, Streatham, London, England. One of the originators of the acid house scene in the UK, Rampling was pre-eminent in the Balearic movement of the late 80s, and has successfully negotiated dozens of shifts in dance music's climate since. DJing since the age of 18, he was a pivotal figure in importing the acid sound after an inspirational visit to the island of Ibiza in 1987 with friends Paul Oakenfold and Nicky Holloway. His 'Shoom' nights at south London's Fitness Centre, which he opened with his wife Jenny in 1988, are now part of clubland folklore. Though only short-lived, Shoom introduced many of the 'Phuture' tracks imported from Chicago, although Rampling, who came from a soul background, mixed them with other dance sounds. He waited some time before releasing his first record, Sound Of Shoom's 'I Hate Hate' in 1990, a cover version of an obscure track from Razzy Bailey sung by Steven Eusebe. In the meantime, he had remixed for the B-52's, the Beloved, Erasure and the James Taylor Quartet, among many others. He went on to run the club night 'Pure' and form the Millionaire Hippies, who released several strong singles on the hip Deconstruction Records label, including 'I Am The Music, Hear Me!', featuring the vocals of Das Strachen and Gwen Dupree, with remixes from Farley And Heller. Rampling was signed to the UK's Radio One in 1994 and began broadcasting his Saturday night 'Love Groove Dance Party' in November 1994, featuring a mixture of soulful, vocal house and garage (several mix sets were released). He remains a popular and respected DJ and producer and in October 1998, received the UK's *Muzik* magazine's award for his Outstanding Contribution To Dance Music. Among the many clubs he can be found playing at are: The Gallery, Heaven, The Manor, Slinky, Brighton's Zap, Miss Moneypenny's and Chuff Chuff. His first single for new label Distance Records, 'Community Of The Spirit' was released in early 1999, followed by 'Rhythms Of The World'. A retrospective compilation based on his career was released by Virgin Records in May of the same year.

● COMPILATIONS: *Love Groove Dance Party, Vols. 1 & 2* (Metropole 1996)★★★, *Love Groove Dance Party, Vols. 3 & 4* (Metropole 1996)★★★, *Love Groove Dance Party, Vols. 5 & 6* (Metropole 1997)★★★, *Decade Of Dance* (Virgin 1999)★★★★.

Rancid

Lars Frederiksen (guitar), Brett Reed (drums), Matt Freeman (bass) and Tim 'Lint' Armstrong (vocals/guitar) provide street-level punk with their ideas informed and inspired by a youth of blue-collar poverty in Albany, California, USA. Armstrong and Freeman (often under the alias Matt McCall) had formed their first band, Operation Ivy, in 1987 with Dave Mello (drums) and Jesse Michaels (vocals). When that band split up in 1989, Freeman, Armstrong and Reed became Rancid. They made their debut in 1992 with a five-track 7-inch single, 'I'm Not The Only One'. After flirting with the idea of using Green Day's Billie Joe Armstrong as a second guitarist, Rancid were contacted by Brett Gurewitz's Epitaph Records, with a view to recording their debut album. During these sessions Reed met Frederiksen (guitar, ex-Slip, UK Subs), and invited him to join the band. He did so, and Rancid's self-titled debut was released in April 1993, featuring more variety and composure than their debut single. In September, they began their first national tour, followed by an extended European trek in November. Frederiksen made his debut at the beginning of the following year on the 'Radio' single, co-written with Green Day's Armstrong and released on Fat Wreck Chords, the label run by Fat Mike of No FX. February saw sessions begin on their next album, *Let's Go*. Comprising 23 songs, including the single 'Salvation', it saw the band, and Armstrong in particular, compared favourably with the early Clash sound, albeit taken at a more frenetic pace. The album quickly achieved gold then platinum status, alerting the major labels to Rancid's presence. An offer was made by Madonna's Maverick Records, allegedly accompanied by a nude picture of the singer, but was declined. More tempting was a one and a half million dollar advance contract from Epic Records (the Clash's US label) but this too was turned down in favour of staying 'with friends' at Epitaph. Rancid were now a very bankable attraction for a band whose visual image had never strayed from bondage trousers and mohawks. They returned to the studio after touring in March 1995, with *... And Out Come The Wolves* the result. Returning to a punk/ska sound reminiscent of Operation Ivy at their peak and the Clash by their third album, as ever, the lyrics were written from earthy personal experience. Once again, it was a major seller, featuring the two radio hits, 'Time Bomb' and 'Ruby Soho'. The ska theme continued on 1998's *Life Won't Wait*,

with two tracks recorded in Jamaica. The album featured a collaboration with Mighty Mighty Bosstones vocalist Dicky Barrett on 'Cash, Culture And Violence'.

● ALBUMS: *Rancid* (Epitaph 1993)★★★, *Let's Go* (Epitaph 1994)★★★, *... And Out Come The Wolves* (Epitaph 1995)★★★, *Life Won't Wait* (Epitaph 1998)★★★.

Rankin Family

Canadian folk quintet built around Rankin family members John Morris (b. 28 April 1959, Mabou, Nova Scotia, Canada, d. 16 January 2000), Raylene (b. 15 September 1960, Mabou, Nova Scotia, Canada), Jimmy (b. 28 May 1964, Mabou, Nova Scotia, Canada), Cookie (b. 4 May 1965, Mabou, Nova Scotia, Canada) and Heather (b. 24 October 1967, Mabou, Nova Scotia, Canada). They formed when each gave up their respective careers to concentrate on music in the autumn of 1989. With instruments including guitar, bass, piano, synthesizer, violin, mandolin and percussion, the Rankin Family produce a blend of traditional and contemporary music that is dominated by the sweet vocals of the family sisters. Indeed, the 'wholesome' image of the band was supported by an appearance at the 1993 Cambridge Folk Festival in which they offered two sets, one of which was specifically for children. Their first album emerged independently in 1989, and was followed by *Fare Thee Well Love* a year later. Both albums were eventually repressed by EMI Records. *North Country* was released by the same company in September 1993 in an attempt to launch the band internationally. Their growing domestic profile was rewarded with no less than four Canadian JUNO Awards; Single Of The Year, Canadian Entertainer Of The Year, Best Group and Best Country Group, at the 1993 ceremony. However, despite strong-selling domestic fare in the shape of *Endless Seasons*, the Rankins were still finding it difficult to break out of the Canadian market. Heather, Cookie and Raylene recorded a Christmas album in 1997, following which the newly named Rankins spent an unprecedented six months recording 1998's slick *Uprooted*, with production from George Massenburg. The album was dedicated to band mother Kathleen 'Kaye' Rankin, who died in December 1997 from breast cancer. Further tragedy followed for the family in January 2000 when John Morris Rankin was killed in a car accident in Cape Breton, Nova Scotia.

● ALBUMS: *The Rankin Family* (Independent 1989)★★★, *Fare Thee Well Love* (Independent 1990)★★★, *North Country* (EMI Canada/Guardian 1993)★★★★, *Endless Seasons* (EMI Canada 1995)★★★, as the Rankins *Uprooted* (EMI Canada 1998)★★★.

● COMPILATIONS: *The Rankin Family Collection* (EMI Canada 1996)★★★★.

Ranks, Shabba

b. Rexton Rawlston Gordon, 17 January 1966, St. Ann's, Jamaica, West Indies. Ranks' family moved from a country parish to Kingston when he was eight. By the age of 12 he was learning from DJs such as General Echo, Brigadier Jerry, Yellowman and Josey Wales. Ranks served his apprenticeship with the Roots Melody sound system under Admiral Bailey, and recorded his debut, 'Heat Under Sufferers Feet', in 1985. Josey Wales took him to King Jammy, for whom Ranks recorded 1986's 'Original Fresh' and the *Rough And Rugged* collaboration with Chaka Demus. His reputation for 'slackness' began with 'Needle Eye Punany', recorded for

Wittys while in New York in 1988. He joined Bobby Digital's new label and Heatwave sound system shortly after this, and had considerable success with 'Mama Man', 'Peanie Peanie' and 'Wicked In Bed'. The special partnership between Digital and Ranks began at this time, although Digital, formerly the engineer at Jammy's, had known Ranks since the age of 15. 'Who She Love' and 'Stop Spreading Rumours' were collaborations with Cocoa Tea and his vocal group, Home T4, with whom Mike 'Home T' Bennett had teamed Ranks. Gussie Clarke later produced this combination for *Holding On*, which generated the big hits 'Pirates Anthem', 'Twice My Age' (with Krystal) and 'Mr Loverman' (with Deborahe Glasgow). Although he used few producers outside Bobby Digital and Gussie Clarke, Ranks became a dominating force in reggae music during 1989 and also began to attract interest from the hip-hop scene. Epic Records took the plunge and signed Ranks to a major label contract in late 1990. Their faith was rewarded when remixed versions of 'Mr Loverman' and 'Housecall', the latter a duet with Maxi Priest, and 'Slow And Sexy', became major crossover hits during the 90s. Ranks' first album for Epic, *As Raw As Ever*, used top Jamaican producers to forge a reggae-rap fusion that proved highly popular and earned him a US Grammy. The follow-up, *X-Tra Naked*, saw Ranks become the first DJ to win two consecutive Grammy Awards. He released further successful singles before 'Shine And Criss' and 'Respect' marked a return to the dancehall-style, delighting his loyal reggae fans. He was back in loverman mode for the single 'Let's Get It On', which preceded 1995's *A Mi Shabba*.

● ALBUMS: with Chaka Demus *Rough And Rugged* (Jammys 1988)★★★, *Best Baby Father* (Blue Mountain 1989)★★★★, with Home T, Cocoa Tea *Holding On* (Greensleeves 1989)★★★, *Just Reality* (Blue Mountain 1990)★★★, *Star Of The 90s* (Jammys 1990)★★★★, *Golden Touch* (Two Friends/Greensleeves 1990)★★★★, *As Raw As Ever* (Epic 1991)★★★, *Rough & Ready Vol. 1* (Epic 1992)★★★★, *X-Tra Naked* (Epic 1992)★★★, *Rough & Ready Vol. 2* (Epic 1993)★★★, *A Mi Shabba* (Epic 1995)★★★, *Get Up Stand Up* (Artists Only 1998)★★★.

● COMPILATIONS: *Rappin' With The Ladies* (Greensleeves 1990)★★★, *Mr Maximum* (Greensleeves 1992)★★★, *King of Dancehall* (Celluloid 1998)★★★, *Shabba Ranks And Friends* (Epic 1999)★★★★.

Reader, Eddi

b. Sadenia Reader, 28 August 1959, Glasgow, Scotland. Formerly lead singer of Fairground Attraction, Reader has enjoyed an acclaimed solo career throughout the 90s, always taking care to select complementary musicians and material, partly as a result of her previous chastening experience of the music industry. Having spent eight years as a session singer (nicknamed 'Ever Ready' because of her willingness to accept any offer of work, ranging from Gang Of Four and the Eurythmics to Tesco adverts), Reader eventually reached number 1 in the UK charts with Fairground Attraction's 'Perfect' in May 1988. The band broke up after only one album (*The First Of A Million Kisses*) because of internal tensions between the band and songwriter Mark Nevin. Reader appeared in John Byrne's BBC drama series *Your Cheatin' Heart* before embarking on a solo career at the turn of the decade. She relocated to Kilmarnock with Fairground Attraction drummer Roy Dodds, and set about recording material at the Trash Can Sinatras' studio. The two of them took the demos down to London, where they met guitarist

Neill MacColl (son of Ewan MacColl and half-brother of Kirsty MacColl). With the addition of bass player Phil Steriopulos, Reader's new 'backing' band, the Patron Saints Of Imperfection, was complete. RCA Records invested heavily in the artist, resulting in several expensive sessions, including stints at Jools Holland's studio in Greenwich, London. Guests included Holland, multi-instrumentalist Calum MacColl and fiddler Aly Bain. When the album eventually emerged after several re-recordings, it was given impetus by a strong suite of cover versions, including Loudon Wainwright III's 'The Swimming Song', Fred Neil's 'Dolphins', Steve Earle's 'My Old Friend The Blues' and John Prine's 'Hello In There'. Its title, *Mirmama*, was taken from the Yugoslavian word for peace, 'mir', and arose because of a story Reader had encountered about a speaking Madonna which had appeared in Herzegovena. However, sales failed to match RCA's expectations, with the album just scraping into the UK Top 40. Afterwards Reader appeared live with the Trash Can Sinatras, sang at 1993's Virago Women's Day celebration, and presented a BBC2 Scottish music television series. She also appeared in a London theatre production of *The Trick Is To Keep Breathing*. A second, self-titled album, on the Warner Brothers Records' subsidiary Blanco y Negro, followed in June 1994. Produced by Greg Penny (the man behind k.d. lang's *Ingenué*), the album debuted at UK number 4 and included the Top 40 hit 'Patience Of Angels', one of several compositions by Boo Hewerdine. Other credits included three songs co-written with Teddy Borowiecki, and four from Mark Nevin of Fairground Attraction, now the two parties had buried their past. The only retained musician was Roy Dodds, who joined Dean Parks (guitar), Nevin (guitar) and Borowiecki (accordion). In 1996, a change of image revealed a 50s glamour queen. Following her recording of Gene Pitney's 'Town Without Pity', which broke into the UK Top 30, Reader confessed 'I'm really into the torch stuff, Marlene Dietrich, Gilda with Rita Hayworth - there's something really attractive about it'. She returned to a more straightforward style for 1998's *Angels & Electricity*, which included superb readings of Hewerdine's 'Bell, Book And Candle' and Ron Sexsmith's 'On A Whim'. Reader left Blanco y Negro shortly after completing a promotional tour.

● ALBUMS: with the Patron Saints Of Imperfection *Mirmama* (RCA 1992)★★★, *Eddi Reader* (Blanco y Negro/Reprise 1994)★★★★, *Candyfloss And Medicine* (Blanco y Negro/Reprise 1996)★★, *Angels & Electricity* (Blanco y Negro 1998)★★★.

Rebel MC

b. Michael Alec Anthony West, 27 August 1965, Tottenham, London, England. After leaving his Double Trouble partners (Michael Menson and Leigh Guest), famed for 1989's UK Top 5 bubblegum ska hit 'Street Tuff', London-based former electronics student Rebel MC forged a successful career as a solo artist. Double Trouble scored minor hits with 'Love Don't Live Here Anymore' and 'Rub-A-Dub', without their former leader. Originally considered the UK's answer to M.C. Hammer, the Rebel's sound mutated into a dark hybrid of techno beats, ragga rhymes and roots harmonics that predicted the subsequent rise of jungle. Heartfelt music with a solid Rastafarian message, it was learned, no doubt, from his earlier stints on the live reggae circuit, having set up the Beat Freak sound system with jungle innovator DJ Ron. On

Black Meaning Good he was joined by Tenor Fly, Barrington Levy, P.P. Arnold, and Dennis Brown, the more political agenda emphasized by its sleeve dedication to: 'scapegoats of the British judicial system'. Several UK hit singles followed, including 'Wickedest Sound' and 'Tribal Base'. 'Rebel Music', meanwhile, was remixed by Pasemaster Mace of De La Soul. Recorded with Little T, 'Rich Ah Getting Richer' was an excellent social commentary rant with dub synchronized, orchestral mixes. The son of a semi-pro cricketer, West helped start the People Against Poverty And Oppression Movement, and joined with Musicians Against The War in the days of the Gulf conflict. More lastingly, he helped establish his own Tribal Bass label, working with home-grown UK rap talent including the Demon Boyz and others. His own recorded output, meanwhile, moved ever further towards jungle.

● ALBUMS: with Double Trouble *21 Mixes* (Desire 1990)★★, *Rebel Music* (Desire 1990)★★★, *Black Meaning Good* (Desire 1991)★★★★, *Word, Sound And Prayer* (Desire 1992)★★★.

Red Hot Chili Peppers

These engaging Hollywood ruffians' mixture of funk, punk and grunge encouraged a legion of other bands to regurgitate the formula. Led by 'Antwan The Swan' (b. Anthony Kiedis, 1 November 1962, Grand Rapids, Michigan, USA; vocals), the band's original line-up also featured 'Flea' (b. Michael Balzary, 16 October 1962, Melbourne, Australia; bass), Hillel Slovak (b. 31 March 1962, Israel, d. 25 June 1988; guitar) and Jack Irons (b. California, USA; drums). They began life as garage band Anthem before Balzary departed for seminal 80s punks Fear. When Irons and Slovak moved on to join the less notable What Is This?, the nails appeared to be firmly in place on the Anthem coffin. However, under their new name, the Red Hot Chili Peppers, with Flea back on board, acquired a speculative recording contract with EMI Records America. Unfortunately, as Irons and Slovak were under contract with their new band, their debut album had to be recorded by Kiedis and Balzary with Jack Sherman on guitar and Cliff Martinez (ex-Captain Beefheart, Weirdos) on drums. Production was handled, somewhat surprisingly, by the Gang Of Four's Andy Gill. The band set about building their considerable reputation as a live outfit, much of which was fuelled by their penchant for appearing semi-naked or worse. Slovak returned to guitar for the second album, this time produced by George Clinton. Also featured was a horn section comprising Maceo Parker and Fred Wesley, veterans of James Brown, among others. Martinez returned shortly afterwards to reinstate the original Anthem line-up, and their third album saw a shift back to rock from the soul infatuation of its predecessors. In 1988, they released the *Abbey Road* EP, featuring a pastiche of the famous Beatles album pose on the cover (the band were totally naked save for socks covering their genitalia). However, the mood was darkened when Slovak took an accidental heroin overdose and died in June. Deeply upset, Irons left, while the band recruited John Frusciante (guitar) and Chad Smith (b. 25 October 1962, St. Paul, Minnesota, USA; drums). After the release of *Mother's Milk*, the single 'Knock Me Down' was released as a tribute to Slovak. For the commercially successful *Blood Sugar Sex Magik* they accurately diagnosed their motivation, and much of their attraction: 'Just recognizing that I was a freak, but knowing that was a cool place

to be.' Producer Rick Rubin, usually associated with the harder end of the metal and rap spectrum (Slayer, Danzig), nevertheless brought out the band's first ballads, including the classic US number 2 hit single 'Under The Bridge'. Such sensitivity did little to deter the vanguard of critics who raged at what they saw as the band's innate sexism. Frusciante left in May 1992 and was replaced by a succession of guitarists, before Dave Navarro (b. 7 June 1967, Santa Monica, California, USA; ex-Jane's Addiction) joined in time to participate in the recording of *One Hot Minute*, released in 1995. The band enjoyed another transatlantic hit two years later with 'Love Rollercoaster', taken from the soundtrack of *Beavis And Butt-Head Do America*. Navarro left the band in 1998 and was replaced by ex-member John Frusciante. Having endured various personal upheavals, it was encouraging to hear the band in such good shape on 1999's US/UK Top 5 album, *Californication*, featuring stand-out tracks such as 'Scar Tissue' (a US Top 10 single), 'Parallel Universe', and 'Easily'.

● ALBUMS: *The Red Hot Chili Peppers* (EMI America 1984)★★★★, *Freaky Styley* (EMI America 1985)★★★, *The Uplift Mofo Party Plan* (EMI Manhattan 1987)★★★, *Mother's Milk* (EMI America 1989)★★★, *Blood Sugar Sex Magik* (Warners 1991)★★★★, *One Hot Minute* (Warners 1995)★★★, *Californication* (Warners 1999)★★★★.

● COMPILATIONS: *What Hits!?* (EMI 1992)★★★, *Plasma Shaft* (Warners 1994)★★★, *Out In L.A.* (EMI 1994)★, *Greatest Hits* (CEMA/EMI 1995)★★★, *Essential Red Hot Chili Peppers: Under The Covers* (EMI 1998)★★.

● VIDEOS: *Funky Monks* (Warner Music Vision 1991), *What Hits!?* (EMI Video 1992).

● FURTHER READING: *True Men Don't Kill Coyotes*, Dave Thompson. *Sugar And Spice*, Chris Watts. *The Complete Story*, Spike Harvey. *Body Parts: On The Road With The Red Hot Chili Peppers*, Grier Govorko.

Red House Painters

Once described by the *New Musical Express* as 'the most intensely sad and beautiful new band of 1992', this American indie band's carefully sculpted, highly impressive work has hardly been over-publicized. Band leader Mark Kozelek hates to do interviews, and is even less fond of having his picture taken, despite which he has continually basked in critical adoration. Addicted to drugs at the age of 10, he was admitted to a rehabilitation centre at 14. His way out of this misery was music, though he still remained an outsider in whatever community he lived, spending most of his time in his bedroom. He had previously formed his first band, God Forbid, in Massilon, Ohio, USA, before moving to Atlanta. There he met drummer Anthony Koutsos and formed the Red House Painters. When they relocated to San Francisco together, the band was fleshed out with the addition of Gordon Mack (guitar) and Jerry Vessel (bass). Via the intervention of American Music Club's Mark Eitzel, a tape of demos recorded between 1989 and 1990 was passed on to 4AD Records, who promptly signed the band. Six of the demo cuts were remixed and released on a mini-album as *Down Colorful Hill* in September 1992. By November they had played their first UK gig at London's Borderline club with Earwig. Given an outlet for his work, there then came a flood of Kozelek's meandering guitar and introspective travelogue lyrics on the double album *Red House Painters*, which, confusingly, was followed by a single album of the same title. In the wake of these two albums, and despite his reluctance to talk to them, Kozelek became venerated by UK critics, one describing his band's style as 'desolate music that's fragile but oddly warming'. Songs such as 'Summer Dress' on *Ocean Beach* saw a reflective, earnest delivery, allied to the familiar aching song structures. With Kozelek now at loggerheads with 4AD the band left the label and signed to the Island Records' imprint, Supreme Recordings. The semi-acoustic *Songs For A Blue Guitar* was effectively a Kozelek solo album although it was released under the Red House Painters name. Cover versions of Yes' 'Long Distance Runaround' and Wings' 'Silly Love Songs' indicated that Kozelek had not lost his sense of humour. Although Kozelek has reportedly completed another album the only new official release to date has been 1999's compilation set.

● ALBUMS: *Down Colorful Hill* mini-album (4AD 1992)★★★, *Red House Painters* (4AD 1993)★★★, *Red House Painters* (4AD 1993)★★★, *Ocean Beach* (4AD 1995)★★★★, *Songs For A Blue Guitar* (Supreme/Island 1996)★★★.

● COMPILATIONS: *Retrospective* (4AD 1999)★★★.

Red Snapper

Red Snapper are one of a number of bands who in the mid-90s began creating instrumental music from textures and beats after the rise of ambient, dance music and hip-hop. The American David Ayers (guitar), Ali Friend (double bass) and Richard Thair (drums) formed the band in London in 1993 after a varied musical background that included working in a number of jazz and rock outfits in the 80s. The three were on occasion joined by the saxophonists Allan Riding and Ollie Moore and the singer Beth Orton. Friend and Thair played with Dean Thatcher in the Aloof, before Thair and Thatcher formed the Flaw Records label in 1993 and produced a series of breakbeat tracks. The *Snapper* EP was released on Flaw the next year and followed by live performances including an appearance at the Glastonbury Festival. After two more EPs the band signed to Warp Records who in 1995 collected the first three releases on *Reeled And Skinned*. The *Mooking* and *Loopascoopa* EPs accompanied their debut album *Prince Blimey* in 1996. The follow-up, *Making Bones*, was recorded with engineer Luke Gordon and featured contributions from rapper MC Det, vocalist Alison David and trumpeter Byron Wallen. Red Snapper have also undertaken remix projects for such artists as Garbage and Ken Ishii, and have themselves been remixed by DJ Food and Squarepusher among others. As is the way with imaginative, intelligent bands such as Red Snapper, many bizarre terms have been used to describe their music, particularly trip-hop and jazz. Their jazz flavour comes not from the upright bass and saxophone but from their aesthetic of experimentation and improvisation in absolute music, creating sounds that do not necessarily adhere to any formulas, following the tradition of such innovators as Charles Mingus and Miles Davis. Hip-hop and jungle rhythms, twangy 50s guitar and overblown saxophone can be heard in the music, yet they are merely flavours in Red Snapper's own abstract soundtracks. Where they meet with dance music is not so much in the sounds used but the concept of rhythmical structureless textures which house and techno brought to the popular conscience.

● ALBUMS: *Prince Blimey* (Warp 1996)★★★★, *Making Bones* (Warp 1998)★★★.

● COMPILATIONS: *Reeled And Skinned* (Warp 1995)★★★★.

Redman

b. Reggie Noble, Newark, New Jersey, USA. Inventive and witty rapper whose 1992 debut *Whut? Thee Album* broke into the US Top 50, although it failed to get a UK release until much later in the year. Enshrining the new ethos of cannabis as the drug of choice ('How To Roll A Blunt'), there was also room for the traditional braggadocio ('Day Of Sooperman Lover', 'I'm A Bad'). As superb an album as it was, from the cover shot of the artist up to his elbows in blood onwards, many critics also noted it was a little close to the sound of EPMD. Not surprising considering that he was a member of their Hit Squad, alongside K-Solo and Das-EFX, and that Erick Sermon produced *Whut? Thee Album*. In fact, Redman had spent two years living with the latter when both his parents chucked him out of their respective homes. Redman was voted the top rap artist of 1993 by *The Source* magazine, while subsequent albums saw him developing into the complete article, earning a reputation as one of rap's leading lyricists. By the time of 1998's stylish *Doc's Da Name 2000*, Redman was emulating several of his contemporaries by becoming involved in all aspects of a project, from co-production duties to marketing and A&R. The following year he collaborated with Method Man on *Blackout!* They had previously recorded 1995's US Top 20 single 'How High' together.

● ALBUMS: *Whut? Thee Album* (RAL 1992)★★★, *Dare Iz A Darkside* (RAL/Def Jam 1994)★★★, *Muddy Waters* (Def Jam 1996)★★★★, *Doc's Da Name 2000* (Def Jam 1998)★★★★, with Method Man *Blackout!* (Def Jam 1999)★★★.

● FILMS: *Rhyme & Reason* (1997), *Ride* (1998), *P.I.G.S.* (1999).

Reef

The members of this UK rock band had played together in several west country-based outfits before several members relocated to London to study music at the West London Institute. Kenwyn House (b. 1 August 1970, Tiverton, Devon, England; guitar), Gary Stringer (b. 18 June 1973, Litchfield, Staffordshire, England; vocals), Dominic Greensmith (b. 2 June 1970, Denby, Derbyshire, England; drums) and Jack Bessant (b. 19 March 1971, Wells, Somerset, England; bass) subsequently formed Naked. After signing to Sony Records' subsidiary S2, the band changed their name to Reef. They rose to fame via an advert for the Sony Mini-Disc portable stereo system. This depicted them as a heavy metal band touting for a contract, presenting their self-titled song, 'Naked', to an unimpressed A&R man, who throws the offending demo out of the window only for it to be retrieved and played by a passing skateboarder. It falsely gave the impression of them being a US band (the video was filmed in New York). The band were keen not to be seen as a one-song wonder and to this end initially declined to offer 'Naked' as a single release, often refusing to play it live. Their first single was 'Good Feeling' in March 1995, but when 'Naked' was eventually released it climbed to number 11 in the UK charts. Their debut album was also well received, although comparisons to bands such as the Black Crowes and Free were widespread. Produced by George Drakoulias, *Glow* put them in the spotlight as a major act, helped by the UK Top 10 chart success of the anthemic singles 'Place Your Hands' and 'Come Back Brighter'. The band returned in April 1999 with the UK Top 5 album, *Rides*.

● ALBUMS: *Replenish* (Sony 1995)★★★, *Glow* (Sony 1996)★★★★, *Rides* (Sony 1999)★★★.

Reel 2 Real

This crossover dance music act featured the antics of the Mad Stuntman (b. Mark Quashie, Trinidad, West Indies), whose ragga-style vocals towered over their breakthrough hit, 'I Like To Move It'. A resident of Brooklyn, New York, since the age of nine, Stuntman took his name from the Lee Majors' television series *The Fall Guy*. He met prolific US producer Erick Morillo through a friend and the two combined on tracks for Strictly Rhythm Records which they never envisioned to be crossover material. They were proved emphatically wrong in 1994 by the sustained sales of 'I Like To Move It', a huge club hit the previous year. Licensed to Positiva Records in the UK, its chart life was an erratic one, running a sequence of weekly positions which read 10, 12, 12, 10, 9, 7, 5, 8, 7, 7, boosted by a 40-date club tour. That and the fact that at no stage was it play-listed by Radio 1 DJs. They followed up with the Top 10 hit, 'Go On Move', and the Top 20 hits 'Can You Feel It' and 'Raise Your Hands'. Reel 2 Real returned to the UK Top 10 in 1996, minus the Mad Stuntman, with 'Jazz It Up'. *Are You Ready For Some More?* attempted a more eclectic fusion of Latin and Afro-Caribbean music with house beats. Morillo has subsequently concentrated on other projects.

● ALBUMS: *Move It!* (Strictly Rhythm/Positiva 1994)★★★, *Reel 2 Remixed* (Strictly Rhythm/Positiva 1995)★★, *Are You Ready For Some More?* (Strictly Rhythm/Positiva 1996)★★★.

Reid, L.A.

(see L.A. And Babyface)

Reid, Vernon

Formerly the lead singer and guitarist with US rock band Living Colour, Reid (b. 22 August 1958, London, England) founded a new solo venture, titled Masque, in 1996. His debut solo album, *Mistaken Identity*, featured the full Masque band, while the bizarre choice of co-producers included hip-hop guru Prince Paul and jazz legend Teo Macero. The album represented his artistic rebirth after 10 years on the road with Living Colour, who disbanded in 1995. As Reid told *Rolling Stone*, 'Doing this album represents freedom for me. But freedom, as we know, is a responsibility. And part of what that responsibility calls me to do is not edit out what I'm feeling and thinking - and not to let anxiety and worry and market concerns infect the process.' Among the best tracks on view on this highly eclectic album were 'Lightnin'', a tribute to Lightnin' Hopkins, and the dancehall reggae of 'Freshwater Coconut'.

● ALBUMS: *Mistaken Identity* (Sony/550 1996)★★★.

Rembrandts

The Rembrandts, a Los Angeles, California, USA-based duo comprising Danny Wilde and Phil Solem (b. Duluth, Minnesota, USA), rose to prominence when 'I'll Be There For You', their theme song to the highly popular NBC-TV comedy series *Friends*, became a major radio hit in 1995. The duo, who had played together in Great Buildings, had previously scored significant success with 1990's self-titled debut, which included a US Top 20 hit in the sparkling 'Just The Way It Is, Baby'. The album itself peaked at number 88 in the US charts, and brought the Rembrandts a significant following for their gritty AOR. Among those attracted to the band's multi-layered songs was television producer Kevin Bright. He asked the band to write and record the theme for his proposed new series about the young clientele of a New York coffee house. Wilde and Solem cut a 42-second version of 'I'll Be There For You' on a single Saturday, mixing it in the same session for delivery on the following Monday. Radio demand for the song escalated, long before a full version of the song had been completed. A full-length version was finally added during recording sessions for the band's third album, *L.P.* (some copies of the record were shipped without the song being mentioned on the track-listing). The song continued to generate healthy radio response, partly due to a hastily convened video featuring the cast of the television show playing various instruments. 'I'll Be There For You' enjoyed most success in the UK where it was twice a Top 5 hit, in 1995 and 1997 respectively. Solem subsequently broke up the partnership to concentrate on his new project, Thrush. Wilde recorded 1998's *Spin This* as Danny Wilde And The Rembrandts, hiring Van Dyke Parks to provide some typically lush arrangements for 'Summertime' and 'Shakespeare's Tragedy'.

● ALBUMS: *Rembrandts* (Atco 1990)★★★, *Untitled* (Atco 1992)★★, *L.P.* (East West 1995)★★★, as Danny Wilde And The Rembrandts *Spin This* (Elektra 1998)★★★.

Renaissance (club)

Renaissance started its life in March 1992 with a manifesto of bringing quality to the UK dance music scene in terms of its imagery, venues and music. Along with the Ministry Of Sound and Cream, it pioneered the concept of the 'super-club'. Geoff Oakes first staged the Renaissance nights at Venue 44 in Mansfield, using high-profile DJs every week, including Sasha and the then relatively unknown John Digweed. It established a reputation for stylish, upmarket clubbing with much effort put into the look of the club itself and a strict dress code policy. The club was partly responsible for the move away from the crusty days of outdoor raves and festivals to a more image-conscious form of club culture. Initially, the club's use of Italian Renaissance art for its advertising campaigns and CD compilation sleeves attracted the interest of both the media and public. In October 1994, *Renaissance - The Mix Collection* mixed by Sasha and Digweed was released. It was a true reflection of the sound of the club, filling three CDs but costing the same as a double album. It achieved gold status within 16 weeks and went on to pass 150,000 copies. The album became the prototype for the club-based mix compilation but has rarely been bettered in terms of demonstrating how the DJs actually played at the club events. For several years in the mid-to-late 90s, Renaissance did not have a 'home venue' and instead toured various venues around the UK and the world. Perversely, this peripatetic approach worked in the club's favour, spreading its reputation for unsurpassed production values far and wide. Renaissance's insistence on a quality experience for the clubber remained and they used a professional design team to make over each venue - usually on a particular theme, such as the Orient, for example. This tradition continued for the club's special events outdoors, at stately homes and abroad. Renaissance's new home venue in Nottingham, England opened in June 1999, but in the intervening period the club had established itself as a world famous name in club culture and, unsurprisingly, a big business. It stages club nights and large-scale events all over the world and has a summer residency at Pacha in Ibiza. In association with electronics firm, Pioneer, the club has established its own record label and continues to release highly successful DJ-mixed compilation albums under the banners Renaissance Worldwide and Renaissance Presents.

● COMPILATIONS: *Renaissance - The Mix Collection* (Network 1994)★★★★, *Renaissance 2 – Mixed By John Digweed* (Network 1995)★★★★, *Renaissance 3 – Mixed By Fathers Of Sound* (Network 1996)★★★, *Renaissance 4 – Mixed By Dave Seaman & Ian Ossia* (Avex 1996)★★★, *Worldwide – London – Mixed By Dave Seaman & Robert Miles* (Passion 1997)★★★★, *Renaissance Presents ... Nigel Dawson & Ian Ossia* (Passion 1998)★★★, *Renaissance Worldwide – Singapore – Mixed By David Morales, Dave Seaman, BT* (Passion 1998)★★★, *Renaissance Presents ... Antony Pappa & Rennie Pilgrem* (Passion 1999)★★★.

Renegade Soundwave

London, England born and bred dance music trio whose esoteric recordings were variously described as 'Dance-Noise-Terror' and 'Chas And Dave with a beatbox'. Comprising the multi-faceted instrumentalists, Danny Briotett (ex-Mass), Carl Bonnie and Gary Asquith (ex-Mass), the trio claimed: 'We're a by-product of punk. It forged the way we think, though the sound is nothing to do with it.' Their first single, 1987's 'Kray Twins', emerged on Rhythm King Records, and featured the sound of a television documentary set to a throbbing bass undertow. After the equally notorious 'Cocaine Sex' (packaged in a coke envelope) they switched to Mute Records because of the greater eclecticism of their catalogue. A series of dancefloor singles such as 'Biting My Nails' and 'Probably A Robbery' prefaced a debut album that included an unlikely cover version of 'Can't Get Used To Losing You'. Their aggressive dancefloor attack was continued the same year with *In Dub*, on which 'Holgertron' made use of the theme music to BBC Television's *Doctor Who*. Bonnie left for a solo career shortly afterwards. Despite creative differences, Briotett and Asquith re-emerged in 1994 with *Howyoudoin?*, announcing on 'Last Freedom Fighter' that 'We've all been asleep for a very long time'. Another dub collection followed in May 1995. Briotett also worked alongside his wife, Linda X, as half of Planet X (who recorded the James Bond tribute 'I Won't Dance', and 'Once Upon A Dancefloor').

● ALBUMS: *Soundclash* (Mute 1990)★★★★, *In Dub* (Mute 1990)★★★, *Howyoudoin?* (Mute 1994)★★★, *The Next Chapter Of Dub* (Mute 1995)★★★.

● COMPILATIONS: *RSW 1987-1995* (Mute 1996)★★★.

Rentals

Formed by Matt Sharp (b. 22 September 1969, Arlington, Virginia, USA; vocals/bass/Moog synthesizer), Cherielynn Westrich (vocals/Moog synthesizer), Petra Haden (violin/vocals), Rod Cervera (guitar), Patrick Wilson (drums) and Jim Richards (keyboards), the Rentals were inaugurated as a spin-off project from Sharp and Wilson's better-known Weezer. An attempt to escape some of the preconceptions that surround that band's output, Sharp summarized the reason for the Rentals' creation thus: 'If you spend too much time sitting around doing nothing, you end up falling in the shitter. It makes life less boring to be busy.' The band were formed at the end of 1994 with friends from the local Los Angeles, California, USA music scene (Haden played with

That Dog). As well as the expected punk pop guitar, *Return Of The Rentals* also featured rudimentary keyboard playing that reminded many of the early 80s New York new wave scene. It was promoted by support slots on tours with Garbage and Blur. Sharp returned, post-Weezer, with *Seven More Minutes*, on which he was joined by Cervera, Richards, vocalist Maya Rudolph and bass player Justin Fischer.

● ALBUMS: *Return Of The Rentals* (Maverick/Reprise 1995)★★★, *Seven More Minutes* (Maverick/Reprise 1999)★★★.

Reprazent

(see Size, Roni)

Republica

This crossover pop outfit began to take shape in London in 1994 when Tim Dorney (keyboards, ex-Flowered Up), teamed up with engineer Andy Todd (keyboards/bass). They found Saffron (b. Nigeria; vocals) performing as part of the Prodigy's stage act and began creating a sound that gave club rhythms a radio-friendly, adult pop sheen. Adding drummer David Barbarossa (b. Mauritius; ex-Bow Wow Wow) and guitarist Johnny Male (ex-Soul Family Sensation) did nothing to shake off the accusation that they were a crew of refugees from second-rate 80s pop acts, jumping onto the dance music bandwagon. However, the doubters reckoned without the more forgiving US market, which pounced upon the 1996 single 'Ready To Go' and thus paved the way for the transatlantic encroachment of more purist UK dance acts such as the Prodigy and the Chemical Brothers. The single was eventually a bigger hit back in the UK but the media still could not forgive them for 'bastardizing' dance music, being too old, having an attractive female singer and (most heinous of all) cracking the USA before they had 'paid their dues' back home. The band, meanwhile, showed few signs of caring, releasing their debut album in 1997 and enjoying a UK Top 10 hit with 'Drop Dead Gorgeous'. Musical differences led to the departure of Todd the same year. *Speed Ballads* was recorded with the band's first permanent drummer, Pete Riley, with Clive Langer and Alan Winstanley handling the bulk of the production. While it contained trademark pop songs such as the debut single 'From Rush Hour With Love' (UK number 20), the album also indicated a general maturing of the band's songwriting talents.

● ALBUMS: *Republica* (Deconstruction/RCA 1997)★★★, *Speed Ballads* (Deconstruction 1998)★★★.

Rialto

Based in London, England, Rialto were formed in January 1997 following the break-up of mod revivalists Kinky Machine. Nevertheless, the new outfit formed by Louis Elliot (vocals) and Johnny Bull (guitar) rapidly won over hostile critics after they signed to East West Records. East West had originally signed Elliot and Bull as Kinky Machine, but after the release of a final single, A&R manager Ian Stanley suggested the core duo 'go away and come up with something different'. They returned with an accomplished 16-track demo tape, and new band members Julian Taylor (bass, ex-Paint), Pete Cuthbert (drums) and Toby Hounsham (keyboards). With management from David Jaymes also in place, the band's feisty pop was unveiled on two attractive and ambitious 1997 singles - 'When We're Together' and

'Monday Morning 5:19'. Both featured solid pop songwriting, partnered with the adventurous use of electronic sound. The best of these early releases was January 1998's 'Untouchable', a UK Top 20 single which revealed Elliot's maturing, but always downbeat, lyricism ('I'll soak my skin in alcohol/Until I feel untouchable'). Their debut album followed shortly afterwards. Having parted company with their original label, Rialto signed to China thus earning the distinction of releasing the same album with two different covers on two labels. Further quality singles were released including 'Summer's Over', a Beatlesque pop song. Indeed, Louis Elliot has definite shades of John Lennon in his vocals, his physical looks and his onstage stance.

● ALBUMS: *Rialto* (East West/China 1998)★★★★.

Rich, Tony, Project

b. Detroit, Michigan, USA. Influenced in his youth by a wide range of music from Madonna and Bruce Springsteen to the Gap Band, Funkadelic and Motown Records, multi-instrumentalist Rich grew up in the video age and modelled himself after its more expansive performers. Born to a musical father, it was not long before he began writing his own songs on a keyboard borrowed from his brother. By his early teens he was playing in local R&B and jazz fusion bands. He also worked with several gospel outfits and choirs while collaborating with local songwriters and helping them to produce demos. He might well have continued to neglect his own material had it not been for the input of John Salley, later the star of basketball team Miami Heat, but at that time a member of the Detroit Pistons and a well-known member of the local music community. He encouraged Rich to pursue a solo career, and also put him in touch with several local rappers who used his production and writing expertise. This employment helped him to purchase his own studio equipment, but more importantly, while in Salley's studio he was offered the chance to meet pop svengali Babyface. Rich then contributed several songs to an album by Pebbles, which in turn led to a meeting in Atlanta with her husband L.A. Reid. Reid listened with enthusiasm to his four-track demos and immediately offered him a contract with LaFace Records. Rich moved to Atlanta full-time in 1993. Among his first production commitments was a session with Elton John and the Sounds Of Blackness on a tribute record to Curtis Mayfield. He produced half an album for Savvy Records' 4.0 and 'I Sit Away' for the multi-platinum-selling Boyz II Men. He also produced for Johnny Gill and conducted remixes on material by Toni Braxton ('You Mean The World To Me') and TLC ('Red Light Special'). In 1994, he began work in earnest on his own debut. *Words* was a sophisticated blend of R&B and soul with some unusual elements - including a country song, 'Billy Goat'. The first single, 'Nobody Knows', included a guest role for brother Joe - whose keyboard Rich had originally purloined at the inception of his career many years previously. Although its success in US markets was widely anticipated (eventually reaching number 2 in the main pop charts), the single also broke through in the UK, reaching the Top 5 in summer 1996. A second single, 'Like A Woman', was a minor transatlantic hit. *Birdseye* was a brave but flawed follow-up, with Rich overreaching himself in an attempt to broaden his musical base.

● ALBUMS: *Words* (LaFace/Arista 1995)★★★★, *Birdseye* (LaFace/Arista 1998)★★★.

Richey, Kim

b. 1 December 1956, Zanesville, Ohio, USA. Country singer-songwriter Kim Richey has established an enviable reputation for the quality of her writing, earning credits for her work with Radney Foster ('Nobody Wins'), George Ducas ('Those Words We Said') and Trisha Yearwood ('Believe Me Baby (I Lied)'. Her own recording career began in earnest with a superbly observed, self-titled song cycle for Mercury Records in 1995. Richey grew up singing in the Greenmont-Oak Park Community Church, thereafter forming a folk trio she named Blue Monday. They became the house act at the local Steak and Ale restaurant, before Richey took up studies at first Kentucky then Ohio University. The first song she wrote was for the short-lived Southern Star, shortly before she graduated with a degree in environmental education. She was working with injured birds of prey when a friend persuaded her to move to Nashville in 1988. She sang on demo sessions for Radney Foster before securing a songwriting/publishing contract with Clearwater Music. The first time one of her songs was recorded, 'I Saw You Look At Her', it was by the Swedish country artist Inger Nordstrom. Richey soon established her reputation as a writer but remained keen to progress with her own material. The contract with Mercury has resulted in albums of rare simplicity but ample emotive power. As Timothy White declared in *Billboard* magazine in 1997, 'Richey entices you with sad and unembellished music that reveals an original spirit - and then she ensnares you for keeps by making you consider all the noiseless sensations that no songs can ever contain.' By 1999, Richey seemed poised for major success - as she states in 'Can't Lose Them All' from *Glimmer*; 'when I reach my full potential, when somebody gets my drift, all the stars are gonna line up, and the tides are gonna shift'.

● ALBUMS: *Kim Richey* (Mercury Nashville 1995)★★★★, *Bitter Sweet* (Mercury Nashville 1997)★★★, *Glimmer* (Mercury Nashville 1999)★★★★.

Ride

Formed at art school in Oxfordshire, England, in 1988 by Mark Gardener (vocals/guitar), Andy Bell (guitar/vocals), Stephan Queralt (bass) and Laurence Colbert (drums), Ride had a rapid impact on the alternative music scene. Initially described as 'the House Of Love with chainsaws', within a year the quartet's serrated guitar melodies were attracting unusual amounts of attention. At the start of 1990 their debut EP for Creation Records reached number 71 in the UK charts. By the end of the spring, Ride had transcended their independent parameters and entered the Top 40 of the UK chart with the *Play* EP, helped by their youthful good looks and large-scale touring (the two EPs were repackaged as *Smile* for the US market). Their debut *Nowhere* was also successful, breaking into the UK Top 20 before the close of the year. Tours of Japan, Australia and America showed just how impressively swift the band's rise had been. Their success was sealed by a headlining appearance at 1991's Slough Music Festival in front of 8,000 fans. In 1992, Ride consolidated their position as one of the most interesting new bands with the excellent *Going Blank Again* and the hypnotic UK Top 10 single 'Leave Them All Behind'. *Carnival Of Light*, released just as the Britpop scene was about to explode, became the victim of the attendant backlash in the UK music press against the 'shoegazing' scene. It didn't help that the band appeared to have stalled artistically, seemingly lacking the ideas that had come so quickly at their inception. *Tarantula* was recorded in London with producer Richard 'Digby' Smith, a veteran of work with Bob Marley and Free. However, immediately following its release Ride confirmed to the press that the band was no more, a decision aggravated by Gardener's decision to move to America in 1995 (according to Bell), or Bell's increasingly dominating position within the band and his marriage to fellow Creation Records artist Idha (according to Gardener). Bell went on to enjoy moderate success with Hurricane #1 before joining Oasis at the end of 1999.

● ALBUMS: *Smile* US only (Sire/Reprise 1990)★★★, *Nowhere* (Creation/Sire 1990)★★★, *Going Blank Again* (Creation/Sire 1992)★★★★, *Carnival Of Light* (Creation/Sire 1994)★★, *Live Light* 1994 recording (Mutiny 1995)★★★, *Tarantula* (Creation/Sire 1996)★★★.

Right Said Fred

This camp UK pop trio comprises the bald pated Fairbrass brothers Richard (b. 22 September 1953, East Grinstead, Sussex, England) and Fred (b. Christopher Abbott Bernard Fairbrass, 2 November 1956, East Grinstead, Sussex, England), plus Rob Manzoli (b. 29 January 1954, West London, England). Fred, who failed trials for Chelsea and Fulham football clubs, had formerly toured with Bob Dylan and played with Then Jerico in 1989. He had also appeared in Dylan's much derided movie, *Hearts Of Fire*. Lead vocalist Richard was originally a bass player who had served time with several prominent artists. Following their divergent paths, the brothers came together to form their own band in the late 80s. By 1988, they were back in London working as a duo. They eventually met up with collaborator Manzoli, a seasoned session guitarist and a qualified chef. To raise money for their first recording foray, the band had to secure a £100 loan from their bank manager. They lied, stating they were about to purchase a car. Initial names for the band included Trash Flash And Money, the Actors and the Volunteers. They finally settled on Right Said Fred after the novelty 1962 Bernard Cribbins hit of the same name. With the help of producer Tommy D. their initial success was embedded in the slow-burning kitsch classic 'I'm Too Sexy' (UK number 2/US number 1), with equally lascivious follow-ups 'Don't Talk Just Kiss' (UK number 3) and 'Deeply Dippy' (UK number 1). Almost overnight Right Said Fred had become the coolest pop band in the UK, cornering the pop market while adult audiences found them impossible to dislike. In 1991, they sold more singles than any other artist in the UK, (excluding Bryan Adams), and 'I'm Too Sexy' topped the charts in 26 countries. They were heavily involved in the 1993 Comic Relief fund-raising effort 'Stick It Out' (UK number 4) with the help of several celebrities. The failure of their second album effectively ended their brief period in the limelight. The brothers formed their own Happy Valley record label in 1995, releasing *Smashing!* the following year. They have continued to tour before Richard Fairbrass has become a media personality, appearing on various UK game shows and co-hosting BBC2's *Gaytime TV*.

● ALBUMS: *Up* (Tug/Charisma 1992)★★★, *Sex And Travel* (Tug/Charisma 1993)★★★, *Smashing!* (Happy Valley 1996)★★.

● VIDEOS: *Up The Video* (Tug 1992).

● FURTHER READING: *The Official Right Said Annual*.

Riley, Teddy

b. Edward Theodore Riley, 8 October 1967, Harlem, New York, USA. Widely regarded as not only the originator, but the motivating force behind 'new jack swing', Riley remains arguably the most successful and revered producer in modern soul music. Riley's origins were in the R&B group Kids At Work, and his stepfather was Gene Griffin, who released one of the earliest rap tracks with Trickeration's 'Rap, Bounce, Rollerskate'. 'New jack swing', or swingbeat as it is also called, represented a fusion of hip-hop beats and soul vocals which together created a more upfront-style of R&B. Riley revolutionised the R&B charts in the late 80s through his work with pioneering swingbeat artists such as Keith Sweat, Bobby Brown and his own trio, Guy, although the genre soon attracted ridicule as more and more major-label clones clogged up the charts. Riley's remixing and production credits have also included work with Jodeci, Mary J. Blige, DJ Jazzy Jeff And The Fresh Prince, Wreckx-N-Effect, James Ingram and Michael Jackson, and he has completed soundtrack work on prominent movies such as *New Jack City* and *Do The Right Thing*. He returned to the band format in 1994 with the highly successful BLACKstreet, which also boasted Chauncey 'Black' Hannibal, Levi Little (bass/guitar/keyboards) and David Hollister. The band hit a commercial and creative high point in 1996 with the Grammy-award winning single, 'No Diggity'.

Rimes, LeAnn

b. Margaret LeAnn Rimes, 28 August 1982, Jackson, Mississippi, USA. Rimes' father, Wilbur, was a part-time guitarist and, with his encouragement, LeAnn was singing and tap-dancing when aged only two and winning talent contests when five. The family moved to Texas and she sang 'The Star-Spangled Banner' at various sports events and the National Cutting Horse Championships in Fort Worth. Her parents recorded an album to sell at gigs when she was seven, and four years later she recorded *All That*, produced by her father, at Norman Petty's studio in Clovis, New Mexico. One track, an aching ballad, 'Blue', had been written by Bill Mack for Patsy Cline, who had died before it could be recorded. Roy Drusky and Kenny Roberts subsequently cut the song, but Bill Mack felt that it was ideal for Rimes. While listening to tapes on holiday, record executive Mike Curb heard Rimes' voice, rushed to a phone and offered her a contract with his nationally distributed label. On her debut album for Curb, she reworked 'Blue' and sang a duet with 78-year-old Eddy Arnold of his hit 'Cattle Call'. The new version of 'Blue' was an instant US hit, climbing high on the pop chart and topping the country chart. Her second country number 1 came with the up-tempo 'One Way Ticket (Because I Can)' with its Searchers-like guitars. *Blue* also topped the country albums chart - 22 weeks at the top and multi-platinum sales. She was the youngest ever nominee at the 1996 CMA Awards, although it was not until the 1997 event that she picked up the Horizon Award. At the 1997 Grammy Awards, Rimes won Best New Artist, Best Female Country and Best Country Song for 'Blue', and at the same year's *Billboard* Awards she won another six honours, including Artist Of The Year. By sticking to good, commercial material Rimes was able to enjoy the same level of success as other country child stars such as Brenda Lee and Tanya Tucker. Like them, she sounded and, with fashioned hair, Lolita sunglasses, AIDS ribbon and figure-hugging clothes, looked much older than her age (15), and was given adult material to perform - on 'My Baby' she sang the words, 'My baby is a full-time lover, My baby is a full grown man.' That aside, she does possess an extraordinarily rich voice for such a young singer, and she seems to be handling her incredible success with great maturity. Her excellent 1997 revival of 'Unchained Melody' gave an indication, however, that her management was having difficulty finding appropriate material, which was confirmed by the remixed reissue of old songs on *Unchained Melody/The Early Years* (although the album did debut at number 1 on the US album chart) and the release of the stop-gap *You Light Up My Life/Inspirational Songs*. That album indicated a move towards the AOR market, which was confirmed by the international success of the single 'How Do I Live' and *Sittin' On Top Of The World*, an album firmly in the Celine Dion mould. In October 1998, 'How Do I Live' became the most successful US single of all-time completing 69 straight weeks on the *Billboard* chart (with a peak position of number 2). It also stayed in the UK Top 40 for 30 weeks. 'Looking Through Your Eyes' provided her with another bestselling US Top 20 hit single in the same year. Rimes returned to her country roots on the following year's *LeAnn*, which featured six tracks associated with Cline and only one new song, the closing 'Big Deal'.

● ALBUMS: *All That* (Nor Va Jak 1993)★★, *Blue* (Curb 1996)★★★★, *Unchained Melody/The Early Years* (Curb 1997)★★, *You Light Up My Life/Inspirational Songs* (Curb 1997)★★★, *Sittin' On Top Of The World* (Curb 1998)★★★★, *LeAnn* (Curb 1999)★★★.

● FILMS: *Dill Scallion* (1999).

Roachford

This UK soul/funk band is led by Andrew Roachford (vocals/keyboards/percussion), and also features Chris Taylor (drums), Hawi Gondwe (guitars) and Derrick Taylor (bass). Andrew Roachford performed from the age of 14 when he played in London's Soho jazz clubs. The band was assembled in 1987, and by early 1988 were touring with Terence Trent D'Arby and the Christians, gaining a reputation for excellent live shows. Strong live support was instrumental to their breakthrough and CBS Records beat many other labels to sign the band. Two singles and an album came out in late 1988, but it was not until early 1989 that 'Cuddly Toy' was re-released to become a UK Top 5 hit. It was closely followed by the minor hit, 'Family Man'. The self-titled album was also rediscovered and the band started to make inroads into the American market, with 'Cuddly Toy' breaking into the Top 30. Sessions for their second album took place in Britain and at Prince's Paisley Park studios. None of the singles released from 1994's *Permanent Shade Of Blue* managed to break into the UK Top 20, but the album was an acclaimed fusion of blues and funk stylings. After a three-year hiatus Roachford returned with the more mainstream-orientated *Feel*, to mixed reviews.

● ALBUMS: *Roachford* (Columbia 1988)★★★, *Get Ready!* (Columbia 1991)★★★, *Permanent Shade Of Blue* (Columbia 1994)★★★★, *Feel* (Columbia 1997)★★.

Roberts, Juliet

The term house diva does not fully cover the career or capabilities of Roberts, who is in addition a proficient singer-songwriter, and a veteran of the early days of British soul.

Unlike many in the field, she did not learn her craft at the church choir, having instead been brought up in the more restrained Catholic faith. However, music was still in her blood. Her father was formerly a member of the calypso band the Nightingales, and took her to various concerts. Her first performances came as a member of reggae band Black Jade, before she signed solo to Bluebird Records in 1980, a label set up by her local record shop in Paddington, north London. Two tracks, a cover version of the Police's 'The Bed's Too Big Without You' and 'Fool For You', emerged, while she was still engaged in her day job as a sports tutor. They were enough to attract the attention of fellow Londoners the Funk Masters. She appeared as lead singer on the band's 1983 UK Top 10 hit, 'It's Over'. After a year's sabbatical in the USA she embarked on her music career proper, and, within a week of returning to British shores, was enlisted as singer for Latin jazz band Working Week. After leaving this band in 1988 she signed to Cooltempo Records as a solo artist, enjoying a string of UK Top 30 singles in the mid-90s including 'Free Love' (number 25, 1993), 'Caught In The Middle' (number 14, 1994) and 'I Want You' (number 28, 1994), the latter her first US chart entry. Firmly established as a house diva, but struggling to crossover into the mainstream market, Roberts bounced back on the Delirious label in January 1998 when 'So Good'/'Free Love 98' reached UK number 15. Her cover version of Donna Summer's 'Bad Girls' also broke into the UK Top 20 the following January.

● ALBUMS: *Natural Thing* (Cooltempo 1994)★★★.

Robson And Jerome

UK actors Robson Green (b. 18 December 1964, Hexam, Northumberland, England) and Jerome Flynn (b. 16 March 1963, England) originally teamed up as leading characters (Fusilier Dave Tucker and Corporal Paddy Garvey) in ITV's hit television series, *Soldier, Soldier*. In one episode of that programme, transmitted early in 1995, they sang a version of the Righteous Brothers' 'Unchained Melody' at a military social event. The following day record shops were said to be 'inundated' with enquiries as to where they could purchase the single. The duo subsequently signed a contract with RCA Records and 'Unchained Melody' was released on 8 May 1995, backed by a version of the traditional 'White Cliffs Of Dover', and immediately shot to number 1 in the UK charts. Staying on top for seven weeks, it sold nearly two million copies, making it at the time the bestselling UK single of the 90s. Another coupling of standards, 'I Believe'/'Up On The Roof', followed on 30 October and debuted at number 1. The combined sales of both their singles (nearly three million) duly registered the highest ever achieved by an act in its debut year. They also became the first act to have two singles in the year's Top 3 sellers since Adam And The Ants in 1981. The ensuing self-titled debut album was released on 13 November and again went straight to number 1, selling over a quarter of a million copies in its first week of release alone. Spending a further seven weeks at the top of the chart, by the end of the year it had achieved total sales of two million - breaking another record by dint of being the fastest to reach that mark in UK chart history. Strictly a UK phenomenon, the duo were dismissed by most music critics who attributed their impressive sales to the fact that their records were often bought on impulse as gifts. The formula was repeated with sickening opportunism the following year, ready for the

Christmas market. A cover version of Jimmy Ruffin's 'What Becomes Of The Brokenhearted', backed by versions of 'Saturday Night At The Movies' and 'You'll Never Walk Alone', debuted at number 1 and preceded the album *Take Two*. Although they returned to the studio to record five new tracks for 1997's compilation album, both men have subsequently concentrated on their successful acting careers.

● ALBUMS: *Robson & Jerome* (RCA 1995)★★, *Take Two* (RCA 1996)★.

● COMPILATIONS: *Happy Days: The Best Of Robson & Jerome* (RCA 1997)★★.

● VIDEOS: *So Far So Good* (RCA/BMG 1995), *Joking Apart* (RCA/BMG 1996).

● FURTHER READING: *The Story Of Robson & Jerome*, Bob Ogley. *Just The Beginning*, Robson Green and Deborah Holder.

Rock, Pete

One of rap music's most respected producers, Mount Vernon, New York-based Pete Rock was introduced to the world via Marley Marl's WBLS show in 1989. He has since gone on to work with everyone from forerunners Heavy D (his cousin), Slick Rick, EPMD and Run DMC (including their first single, 'Down With The King'), to newer talents including Lords Of The Underground (offering vocals on their 'Flow On'), Nas and K-Solo. Other projects include his soundtrack work on *Who's The Man* and *Menace II Society*. His remix roster is almost as impressive, with engagements with Brand Nubian, Public Enemy, House Of Pain, Das EFX, Father and non-rap artists like Shabba Ranks and Johnny Gill. He also put together the Untouchables producer network/umbrella organisation for the activities of himself and co-conspirators Eddie F, Dave Hall and Nevelle Hodge. Rock also recorded with rapper C.L. Smooth (b. Corey Penn), debuting with 1991's acclaimed *All Souled Out* EP. Rock's impeccable production skills were again to the fore on *Mecca And The Soul Brother*, which included the superb US Top 60 hit single 'They Reminisce Over You (T.R.O.Y.)'. Their second album tilted towards the mainstream on smooth R&B cuts such as 'Searching' and 'Take You There', but with the rise of gangsta rap challenging their old school-style the duo called it a day shortly afterwards. Rock returned to the studio for 1998's *Soul Survivor*, which featured a long guest list including members of the Wu-Tang Clan, Noreaga, Beenie Man, and his old partner Smooth. Rock's mellow, soul-influenced style provided a surprisingly effective backing to the abrasive MCing of most of the guest rappers.

● ALBUMS: with C.L. Smooth *Mecca And The Soul Brother* (Elektra 1992)★★★★, with C.L. Smooth *The Main Ingredient* (Elektra 1994)★★★, *Soul Survivor* (Loud/RCA 1998)★★★★.

● FILMS: *Who's The Man?* (1993).

Rocket From The Crypt

With a visual image denoted by 50s silk shirts, tattoos and sideburns, Rocket From The Crypt formed in 1990 in San Diego, California, USA. Led by John 'Speedo' Reis (vocals/guitar), who had played with hardcore outfit Pitchfork, the original band comprised Reis, Petey X (bass), N.D. (guitar), Sean (drums) and Elaina (backing vocals). This line-up released *Paint As A Fragance* and then fell apart. Reis, N.D. and Petey X were then joined by Atom (drums) and Apollo 9 (saxophone), and proceeded to build their reputation as a back-to-basics rock 'n' roll band supporting such incongruous artists as the Misfits and James Brown, and also

several west coast dates on the final Sun Ra tour. After a series of low-key recordings the band signed a deal with Interscope Records and then took a break to concentrate on Reis' punk side project, Drive Like Jehu, just as Rocket From The Crypt were being tipped as one of the bands 'most likely to' follow Nirvana's international breakthrough. Augmented by trumpeter JC 2000 the band's most productive phase began in 1995. In April, they released *The State Of Art Is On Fire*, a six-song vinyl-only 10-inch record for Sympathy For The Record Industry. In September, they toured the USA to perform free shows for fans - an expedition that resulted in them having to sell their tour van and equipment to cover the costs. Accordingly, 'Speedo' renamed the band the Ambassadors Of Very Good Will for the occasion. In October 1995, *Hot Charity*, a nine-song vinyl-only album with a limited pressing of 2,000 copies, was released on their own Perfect Sounds label. By January 1996, the band had completed the recording of their major label debut, *Scream, Dracula, Scream!*. Produced by 'Speedo', this utilized old tape machines and microphones to ensure an authentic, live-sounding recording, and was completed at Gold Star Studios (previously used by both Phil Spector and Elvis Presley). Employing an 11-string instrumental section, the album included typically blustering three minute songs such as 'Born In '69' and 'On A Rope' (a surprise UK Top 20 hit). Kevin Shirley (Aerosmith, Silverchair) took over production for *RFTC*, which opted for a more old-fashioned sound than the garage rock of *Scream, Dracula, Scream!*

● ALBUMS: *Paint As A Fragrance* (Headhunter 1991)★★, *Circa: Now!* (Headhunter 1992)★★★, *The State Of Art Is On Fire* mini-album (Sympathy For The Record Industry 1995)★★★, *Hot Charity* mini-album (Perfect Sound/Elemental 1995)★★, *Scream, Dracula, Scream!* (Interscope/Elemental 1996)★★★★, *RFTC* (Interscope/Elemental 1998)★★★.

● COMPILATIONS: *All Systems Go!* (Toy's Factory/Headhunter 1993)★★★, *All Systems Go 2* (Swami 1999)★★★.

Rodgers, Paul

b. 17 December 1949, Middlesbrough, Cleveland, England. The former Bad Company and Firm vocalist originally came to prominence as the frontman of the 70s blues rock band Free, but his solo career got off to a poor start with 1983's *Cut Loose*. Other ventures included a collaboration with former Small Faces/Who drummer Kenny Jones as the Law, but until the mid-90s Rodgers' solo career had never raised his profile above cult status, although few would deny he possessed one of the most powerful and recognizable voices in post-60s rock music. He finally broke through with 1993's *Muddy Water Blues*, a sensitive tribute album demonstrating Rodgers' strong natural feeling for the blues. He also released a live tribute to the music of Jimi Hendrix in collaboration with Journey guitarist Neil Schon. *Now*, co-produced by Eddie Kramer, was released to excellent reviews and healthy enough sales to maintain his new found commercial profile. Another well-received collection, *Electric*, was released in 1999. Although he will be requested to sing 'All Right Now' and 'Can't Get Enough of Your Love' for the rest of his performing life, Rodgers has now established himself as a credible solo artist.

● ALBUMS: *Cut Loose* (Atlantic 1983)★★, *Muddy Water Blues* (Victory 1993)★★★★, *The Hendrix Set* (Victory 1993)★★★, *Live* (SPV 1996)★★★, *Now* (SPV 1997)★★★, *Electric* (SPV 1999)★★★.

Roots

This Philadelphia, USA-based rap crew comprises rappers Black Thought (aka Tariq Trotter) and Malik B. (b. Malik Abdul Basit), bass player Hub (b. Leonard Nelson Hubbard) and drummer ?uestlove (b. Ahmir-Khalib Thompson). Specialising in old school freestyling, many comparisons to Digable Planets or Gang Starr's jazz-flavoured hip-hop followed the release of their debut mini-album. However, like Stetsasonic, the Roots are more of a self-contained musical unit, relying on their own talents rather than samples or session musicians. The band was started in 1987 when Trotter and Thompson were students at Philadelphia High School For The Performing Arts. They learned and earned on the busking circuit, hooking up with Hubbard and Basit. They attracted interest on the underground circuit, but made their breakthrough after performing a German showcase concert. An album recorded to sell at shows was released on Remedy Records, and they were spotted by Geffen Records who signed the crew for the USA (Talkin' Loud Records taking responsibility for the UK). Their major label debut, 1995's *Do You Want More?!!!??!*, eschewed samples and featured top jazz guests plus the Roots' own rap protégés, the Foreign Objects. The Roots appeared at Lollapalooza and the Montreux International Jazz Festival the same year, and added human beatbox Rahzel The Godfather Of Noyze and Scott Storch (aka Kamal) to the line-up. *illadelph halflife* found a greater rap audience than the previous set, and included samples taken from their jam sessions. The follow-up, *Things Fall Apart*, was another critical success and broke into the US Top 5.
● ALBUMS: *Organix* mini-album (Remedy 1993)★★★, *Do You Want More?!!!??!* (DGC 1995)★★★★, *illadelph halflife* (DGC 1996)★★★, *Things Fall Apart* (MCA 1999)★★★★.

Roxette

Sweden's first pop export of the 90s, Marie Fredriksson (b. 30 May 1958, Östra-Ljungby, Sweden) and Per Gessle (b. 12 January 1959, Halmstad, Sweden) enjoyed international success thanks to a highly commercial combination of a striking image and catchy pop/rock melodies. Gessle became a solo artist in the early 80s having previously played in the new wave band Gyllene Tider. He was 'discovered' by former Abba manager Thomas Johannson who was looking for songs for a Frida album. Meanwhile Fredriksson had released three popular solo albums. Johannson teamed them up in 1985 and they became Roxette. Recording at Gessle's studio in Halmstad, the band released their debut set the following year. They soon conquered Sweden, with 1988's *Look Sharp!* becoming the second bestselling album in Swedish history. They broke through in the USA in February 1989 with the number 1 single 'The Look', which also reached UK number 7 in April. Subsequent singles 'Dressed For Success' (US number 14, May 1989), 'Listen To Your Heart' (US number 1, August 1989) and 'Dangerous' (US number 2, December 1989) continued the band's phenomenal success. The ballad 'It Must Have Been Love', which was used on the soundtrack of the Richard Gere/Julia Roberts movie *Pretty Woman*, became the band's third US chart-topper in April 1990, and also reached UK number 3. 'Joyride' topped the US chart in March 1991, was a number 1 single throughout mainland Europe, and reached number 4 in the UK. 'Fading Like A

Flower (Every Time You Leave)' stalled at US number 2 in June, and signalled the end of the band's run of US Top 10 singles. 'Almost Unreal' reached UK number 7 in July 1993, and was followed into the Top 10 in September by a reissue of 'It Must Have Been Love', but subsequent singles failed to match the band's early 90s purple patch. Four new tracks were included on their greatest hits package in 1995. After a five-year absence, the band returned in February 1999 with the single 'Wish I Could Fly' and a respectable new album.
● ALBUMS: *Pearls Of Passion* (EMI Sweden 1986)★★, *Dance Passion* (EMI Sweden 1987)★★, *Look Sharp!* (EMI 1988)★★★, *Joyride* (EMI 1991)★★, *Tourism* (EMI 1992)★★★, *Crash! Boom! Bang!* (EMI 1994)★★★, *Baladas En Espanol* (EMI 1996)★★, *Have A Nice Day* (EMI 1999)★★★.
Solo: Marie Fredrikkson *MaMas Barn: Barn Som Barn* (WEA 1982)★★, *Het Vind* (EMI 1984)★★, *Den Sjunde Vågen* (EMI 1985)★★, ... *Efter Stormen* (EMI 1987)★★★, *Den Ständiga Resan* (EMI 1992)★★★. Per Gessle *Per Gessle* (EMI 1983)★★★, *Scener* (EMI 1985)★★, *På Väg* 3-CD box set (EMI 1992)★★★.
● COMPILATIONS: *Roxette Rarities* (EMI 1995)★★, *Don't Bore Us - Get To The Chorus! Roxette's Greatest Hits* (EMI 1995)★★★★.
● VIDEOS: *Look Sharp Live* (EMI 1989), *Roxette: The Videos* (EMI 1991), *Live-Ism* (EMI 1992), *Don't Bore Us - Get To The Chorus! Roxette's Greatest Video Hits* (EMI 1995).

Royal Trux

Neil Hagerty (vocals/guitar) and Jennifer Herrema (vocals/sundry instruments) specialize in a drug-addled, chemically-fuelled dirty rock habit. Royal Trux was formed in 1985 while Hagerty was still playing guitar in Pussy Galore. He was responsible for the latter's idea to cover the Rolling Stones' *Exile On Main Street* in its entirety. The duo debuted with an untitled 1988 album, and a declared ambition of retracing the US noise scene back to its primal roots (MC5, etc.). Descriptions such as 'garage psychobilly punk' proliferated in the press. The *Twin Infinitives* double set saw songs based on the works of science fiction writer Philip K. Dick, alongside the riffs of Led Zeppelin, Rolling Stones and AC/DC, music that had dominated their youth. Recorded in three months in a deserted warehouse, the touring schedule that ensued saw them physically and aurally confront their audience. In truth, Hagerty and Herrema were both heavily dependent on heroin. A third album, also untitled, was released in 1992, and largely essayed their heroin fixation/trials. One result of their ordeals saw them relocate to Washington DC, having found the ethos of New York a little destructive. Their fourth album, and the first to see them garner serious UK and European press, was recorded in a Virginian country home in 1993. Their major label debut, *Thank You*, saw them backed by a more permanent band, and also featured the help of producer David Briggs, a celebrated partner of Neil Young. It included the single 'Map Of The City', as well as confident R&B and rock numbers such as 'Shadow Of The Wasp' and 'Night To Remember'. *Sweet Sixteen* was another credible album, even though the subject matter continued to be dubious, including excretion and bestiality, and succeeded in getting the band removed from their Virgin Records contract. Flush with Virgin's money, they returned to independent status in the late 90s with two elegantly wasted masterpieces, *Accelerator* and *Veterans Of Disorder*.
● ALBUMS: *Royal Trux* (Royal 1988)★★, *Twin Infinitives* (Drag City

1990)★★, *Royal Trux* (Drag City 1992)★★★, *Cats And Dogs* (Drag City 1993)★★★, *Thank You* (Hut/Virgin 1995)★★★, *Sweet Sixteen* (Virgin 1997)★★★, *Accelerator* (Drag City 1998)★★★★, *Veterans Of Disorder* (Drag City 1999)★★★.

● COMPILATIONS: *Singles Live Unreleased* (Drag City 1997)★★.

Runrig

This premier Scottish band has emerged from a folk background to enjoy a strong commercial profile in the pop charts, and is arguably the most popular act north of Carlisle. By combining national and cultural pride with stadium rock appeal, Runrig have helped alert the world to Scottish popular music and traditions without a hint of compromise. The band made its debut - as the Run Rig Dance Band - at the Kelvin Hall, Glasgow in 1973. Initially a trio comprising of brothers Rory MacDonald (b. 27 July 1949, Dornoch, Sutherland, Scotland; guitar, bass, vocals, ex-Skyevers), Calum MacDonald (b. 12 November 1953, Lochmaddy, North Uist, Scotland; drums, percussion, vocals) and Blair Douglas (accordion), the band was viewed as a part-time venture, 'Something to do during the holidays,' as Calum later stated. Donnie Munroe (b. 2 August 1953, Uig, Isle Of Skye, Scotland; vocals, guitar) joined the following year as the band took on a more serious perspective. At this point their repertoire comprised of cover versions - Creedence Clearwater Revival was a particular favourite - and traditional material played in a folk/rock manner, reminiscent of Horslips and Fairport Convention. Although the MacDonald siblings were writing material, Runrig demurred from playing them live until 1978 and the release of *Play Gaelic*. Issued on the Scottish Lismor Records label, this pastoral set introduced newcomer Robert MacDonald (no relation) who had replaced Blair Douglas. A higher profile ensued and, with the extra credibility of an album behind them, the band set up their own label, Ridge Records. Malcolm Jones (b. 12 July 1959, Inverness, Scotland; guitar, mandolin, accordion) replaced Robert MacDonald who was unwilling to turn professional (sadly, he died of cancer in 1986). *Highland Connection* introduced a greater emphasis on electric styles and in 1980 Iain Bayne (b. 22 January 1960, St. Andrews, Fife, Scotland) took over as the drummer, freeing Calum to concentrate on vocals and percussion. By the release of *Recovery*, produced by Robert Bell of the Blue Nile, it was clear the band was more than just another folk/rock act. The music still retained its rural feel and traditions, with many songs being sung in Gaelic, but the sound took Runrig outside the narrow bounds of the traditional arena. English keyboard player Richard Cherns joined the band for its first European tour, but left following the release of *Heartland*. He was replaced by Peter Wishart (b. 9 March 1962, Dunfermline, Fife, Scotland; ex-Big Country). Runrig performed successful concerts in Canada and East Berlin in 1987 and played support to U2 at Murrayfield, Edinburgh, Scotland. After the release of *The Cutter & The Clan*, the band signed to Chrysalis Records, who immediately re-released the album. Chart success followed in 1989 with *Searchlight* almost making the Top 10 in the UK charts. Constant touring - the secret of Runrig's appeal - ensued and in 1990 the *Capture The Heart* EP entered the UK Top 50. A television broadcast of a live performance elicited huge response from viewers to the extent that five concerts at Glasgow's Royal Concert Hall sold out. A subsequent video,

City Of Lights, reached the Top 10-selling videos in the UK. The highly acclaimed *The Big Wheel* reached number 4 in the UK charts and an open-air concert at Loch Lomond was attended by 45,000 people. The *Hearthammer* EP broached the UK Top 30 in September 1991, followed by the Top 50 single 'Flower Of The West' and *Amazing Things*, which confirmed their crossover appeal by reaching number 2 in the UK album charts. The band were also to be found performing the singles 'Wonderful' and 'The Greatest Flame' on BBC Television's *Top Of The Pops*. Following an extensive tour the band bounced back into the pop charts when 'An Ubhal As Airde (The Highest Apple)', which was used as the music for a Carlsberg television advertisement, reached number 18 in the UK charts in May 1995. Donnie Munro stood as a Labour candidate in the 1997 General Election, and subsequently left the band to pursue a political career. The band celebrated their 25th anniversary in 1998 by releasing a collection of their Gaelic material. Later in the year Bruce Guthro (b. 31 August 1961, Cape Breton, Nova Scotia, Canada) was recruited as the band's new vocalist. He made his recording debut on the following year's *In Search Of Angels*.

● ALBUMS: *Play Gaelic* (Neptune/Lismor 1978)★★★, *Highland Connection* (Ridge 1979)★★★, *Recovery* (Ridge 1981)★★★, *Heartland* (Ridge 1985)★★★, *The Cutter & The Clan* (Ridge 1987)★★★, *Once In A Lifetime* (Chrysalis 1988)★★★, *Searchlight* (Chrysalis 1989)★★★, *The Big Wheel* (Chrysalis 1991)★★★★, *Amazing Things* (Chrysalis 1993)★★★, *Transmitting Live* (Chrysalis 1994)★★★, *Mara* (Chrysalis 1995)★★, *In Search Of Angels* (Ridge 1999)★★★.

● COMPILATIONS: *Long Distance: The Best Of Runrig* (Chrysalis 1996)★★★★, *Beat The Drum* (EMI 1998)★★★★, *The Gaelic Collection 1973-1998* (Ridge 1998)★★★, *BBC Session And Live At The Royal Concert Hall, Glasgow '96* (EMI 1999)★★★.

● VIDEOS: *City Of Lights* (PolyGram Video 1990), *Wheel In Motion* (PolyGram Video 1992), *Runrig Live At Stirling Castle: Donnie Munro's Farewell* (PolyGram Video 1997), *Live In Bonn* (2000).

● FURTHER READING: *Going Home: The Runrig Story*, Tom Morton.

Rusby, Kate

b. 1 December 1973, Barnsley, Yorkshire, England. Rusby's warmth and authenticity have won her fans beyond the folk scene. Despite frequent comparisons with other young female folk musicians such as Eliza Carthy, she scorns the catch-all label of 'folk babe'. Rusby's genre-defying popularity is due in great part to her distinctive clarity and maturity as a singer. Growing up in a musical family, Rusby sang and played fiddle and guitar with her sister and parents in their own ceilidh band, making her solo debut at the age of 15 at the Holmfirth Festival. After a stint with Kathryn Roberts which produced an award-winning album of duets and their brief collaboration with Equation, Rusby left to pursue her own direction with a commitment to keep her particular brand of music uncommercial and authentic. The result was the bestselling *Hourglass*, produced on her own label Pure Records, which she manages together with her parents. The album featured Rusby's own compositions, such as 'A Rose In April', as well as uncluttered renditions of classics such as 'As I Roved Out' and 'Drowned Lovers'. Mentor Dave Burland provided guest vocals. Rusby combined her solo work with membership of acclaimed female quartet, the Poozies, appearing on their 1998 release *Infinite Blue* and touring with them until October 1999. Further evidence of her songwriting talent came the same year with the follow-up album *Sleepless*, which included her song 'The Sleepless Sailor' and a cover version of Iris DeMent's 'Our Town'. Throughout, Rusby's unselfconscious Yorkshire accent combined with a stark simplicity of style confirmed her status as a unique talent. Admirable support was provided by her backing band, which includes regulars John McCusker (fiddles), Ian Carr (guitar), Michael McGoldrick (flute/whistles) and Conrad Ivitsky (double bass).

● ALBUMS: *Hourglass* (Pure 1997)★★★★, *Sleepless* (Pure 1999)★★★★.

RZA

b. Robert Diggs, New York, USA. Diggs was born in Brooklyn, but as a young child spent a brief period in North Carolina before returning to New York. He first recorded as a member of All In Together Now, alongside his cousins and future Wu-Tang Clan members Ol' Dirty Bastard and the Genius (aka GZA). He recorded one solo EP as Prince Rakeem for Tommy Boy Records, before forming the Wu-Tang Clan with his cousins. Considered by many to be rap's most proficient producer since Dr. Dre, RZA balances a solo career alongside work with the Wu-Tang Clan and Gravediggaz (as Prince Rakeem). Unlike Dre, whose reliance on George Clinton samples prefigured a myriad of artists employing ritual G-funk backing, RZA's minimalist approach recalls the work of Public Enemy's Bomb Squad. While Public Enemy's work is more politicised, RZA and his colleagues prefer to draw on religious elements, martial arts and inter-gang rivalry. As manager as well as producer of the Wu-Tang Clan, and instigator of the Razor Sharp imprint, RZA has effectively set this agenda, writing and recording at a furious pace from his own basement studio. As a producer he made a massive impact with his work on the Wu-Tang Clan's landmark 1993 debut *Enter The Wu-Tang Clan: 36 Chambers*, before producing the numerous solo projects from members of the posse, including Method Man's *Tical* and Raekwon's *Only Built 4 Cuban Linx ....* He has also worked with Wu-Tang Clan affiliates including Shyheim, Cappadonna and Killah Priest, and produced tracks for Tricky, Cypress Hill and Shaquille O'Neal, as well as remixes for Supercat and SWV. At the end of 1995 he combined with Genius on *Liquid Swords*, a superb album which broke into the US Top 10. RZA finally made his full-length debut in 1998, adopting the lover man/pimp persona of Bobby Digital on a witty and intelligent album dominated by his endlessly inventive backing tracks.

● ALBUMS: *RZA As Bobby Digital In Stereo* (Gee Street 1998)★★★★.

● COMPILATIONS: *The RZA Hits* (Epic 1999)★★★★.

● FILMS: *Rhyme & Reason* (1997).

S Club 7

S Club 7 evoked mixed reactions when they burst onto the UK music scene in 1999. Highly popular with their teenage fanbase, but the nadir of pre-packaged pop for others, the group was conceived, created and ruthlessly marketed as a multi-media entity. The highly photogenic mixed gender line-up comprises Bradley McIntosh (b. 8 August 1981), Hannah Spearritt (b. 1 April 1981), Jon Lee (b. 26 April 1982), Jo O'Meara (b. 26 April 1979), Paul Cattermole (b. 7 March 1977), Rachel Stevens (b. 9 April 1978), and Tina Barrett (b. 16 September 1976). Polydor Records were no doubt highly satisfied when the troupe's debut single, 'Bring It All Back', debuted at UK number 1 in June. 'S Club Party' narrowly failed to repeat the debut single's success, stalling at number 2 in September. For anyone who had temporarily forgotten who the singers were, the single included a handy segment where each member was introduced by the others. Another setback occurred in December when S Club 7's Christmas single, 'Two In A Million'/'You're My Number One', was given a good old fashioned mauling on the sales chart by Westlife's 'I Have A Dream'/'Seasons In The Sun'.

● ALBUMS: *S Club 7* (Polydor 1999)★★.

S*M*A*S*H

Formed in Welwyn Garden City, Hertfordshire, England, this trio, comprising Ed Borrie (vocals/guitar), Rob Haigh (drums) and Salvador Alessi (bass), actually dates back to 1984, when the UK miners' strike was in progress and irrevocably altered Ed and Sal's political ideals (although both were still schoolboys). Recruiting Rob from a nearby squat, Sal moved over from singing to playing bass when the original bass player failed to turn up for rehearsals. To this day Sal still plays the instrument 'wrong side up'. Their first gig did not take place until early 1992, and by the following year the *New Musical Express* had decided they sounded like 'the Stone Roses on PCP', while two singles, 'Real Surreal'/'Drugs Again' and 'Shame'/'Lady Love Your Cunt' were released on their own Le Disques De Popcor Records. The second single was Single Of The Week in both the *NME* and *Melody Maker*. Its b-side was a repetition of Germaine Greer's celebrated feminist remark. Showcases such as the 100 Club's New Art Riot gig in December 1993 and the *NME*'s On Into 94 event placed them within the New Wave Of The New Wave movement, a description that the band considered 'bollocks'. In truth, their reputation was built on tireless touring, and their popularity was enhanced by a cheap entry price policy. The 'buzz' attracted such admirers as Billy Corgan (Smashing Pumpkins) and Joe Strummer, while the American label Sub Pop Records, responsible for much of the grunge movement that S*M*A*S*H detested, tried to sign them. Instead they moved to Hi-Rise Records, releasing a mini-album six weeks

later (compiling the first two 7-inch singles). A Top 30 hit, it saw them appear on BBC Television's *Top Of The Pops*, and the band later played the London Anti-Nazi Carnival on the back of a float with Billy Bragg. Censorship proved a problem over July's '(I Want To) Kill Somebody', which reached the Top 30 despite being on sale for only one day. Its impact was scuppered by BBC Radio 1 (the song included a hit list of Conservative MPs, and was independently edited by the corporation to avoid offence). Their debut album was produced by Chris Allison (Wedding Present) in September 1994, but by June 1995 the band had been dropped by Hi-Rise after a series of poorly received live performances. Haigh left shortly afterwards, and, following the 'Rest Of My Life' single, the remaining members decided to split-up.
● ALBUMS: *S*M*A*S*H* mini-album (Hi-Rise 1994)★★★, *Self Abused* (Hi-Rise 1994)★★★.

Sabres Of Paradise

Andy Weatherall's favoured UK dance music emporium, whose releases included 'Smokebelch', arguably *the* techno anthem of the early 90s. In addition to Weatherall, famed for his groundbreaking work on Primal Scream's 1991 indie/dance classic *Screamadelica*, the company centred around Nina Walsh, Jagz Kooner and Gary Burns. Walsh was a regular at Weatherall's 'Shoom' evenings during the heady days of 1988's acid house scene. She in turn worked for the Boy's Own stable. Before joining the Sabres she also worked with Youth's WAU/Butterfly recordings. The duo set up their own label under the Sabres name, and released work from artists including, SYT, Blue, Secret Knowledge, Musical Science, Waxworth Industries, Jack O' Swords and the Corridor. The label operation eventually became known as Sabrettes. Typically, despite the otherworldly grandeur of their music, their studio was located above a Tandoori restaurant in West Hounslow. There was also a club (based in a brick-dust cellar under London Bridge), titled Sabresonic, as was their debut album. This seamless collection of post-Orb, dreamscape dance, with a vaguely industrial edge, increased the avalanche of plaudits that usually accompany Weatherall's best work. Together with assistants Burns and Kooner, Weatherall turned the Sabres Of Paradise into one of the UK's premier remix teams, working with everyone of note on the UK dance scene. The team also contributed one track, 'Sabres Theme', to the movie *Shopping*, and released another quirky album for Warp Records before splitting up to work on solo projects, the most prominent of which has been Weatherall's Two Lone Swordsmen.
● ALBUMS: *Sabresonic* (Warp 1993)★★★, *Haunted Dancehall* (Warp 1994)★★★.
● COMPILATIONS: *Septic Cuts* (Warp 1994)★★★★.

Saint Etienne

By far the most dextrous of those bands cursed with the 'indie-dance' label, and one of the few to maintain genuine support in both camps. Pete Wiggs (b. 15 May 1966, Reigate, Surrey, England) and music journalist Bob Stanley (b. 25 December 1964, Horsham, Sussex, England) grew up together in Croydon, Surrey, England. In the early 80s, the pair began to experiment with party tapes, but did not make any serious inroads into the music business until forming Saint Etienne in 1988, taking their name from the renowned French football team. Relocating to Camden in north London, the pair recruited Moira Lambert of Faith Over Reason for a reggae-inflected cover version of Neil Young's 'Only Love Can Break Your Heart'. Issued in May 1990 on the aspiring Heavenly Records label, the single fared well in the nightclubs and surfaced on a magazine flexi-disc remixed by labelmates Flowered Up (who appeared on the b-side) in July. Another cover version, indie guitar band the Field Mice's 'Kiss And Make Up', was given a similar dance music overhaul for Saint Etienne's second single, fronted this time by New Zealand vocalist Donna Savage of Dead Famous People. Then came the infectious, northern soul-tinged 'Nothing Can Stop Us' in May 1991. Its strong European feel reflected both their name, which helped attract strong support in France, and their logo (based on the European flag). It also benefited from Sarah Cracknell's (b. 12 April 1967, Chelmsford, Essex, England) dreamy vocals, which dominated Saint Etienne's debut, *Foxbase Alpha*, released in the autumn. Cracknell had formerly recorded with Prime Time. 'Only Love Can Break Your Heart' was reissued alongside the album, and provided them with a minor chart hit. Throughout the 90s the only critical barb that seemed to stick to Saint Etienne with any justification or regularity was that they were simply 'too clever for their own good', a criticism that Stanley clearly could not abide: 'The image that the media has built up of us as manipulators really makes us laugh'. *So Tough* revealed a rich appreciation of the vital signs of British pop, paying homage to their forerunners without ever indulging in false flattery. *Tiger Bay*, toted as a folk album, transcended a variety of musical genres with the sense of ease and propriety that Saint Etienne had essentially patented. The medieval folk/trance ballad 'Western Wind', and the instrumental 'Urban Clearway', redolent of, but not traceable to, a dozen prime-time television themes, were just two of the bookends surrounding one of the greatest albums of that year. It was followed by a fan club-only release, *I Love To Paint*, limited to 500 copies. Their biggest UK hit, 'He's On The Phone' (number 11), promoted the excellent compilation set *Too Young To Die*. In 1997, Sarah Cracknell released a solo album, having previously recorded a duet with Tim Burgess of the Charlatans, 'I Was Born On Christmas Day', released at the end of 1993 in a failed attempt to mug the Christmas singles market. The band recorded their comeback, *Good Humor*, in Sweden. Despite being another quality release the album met with an indifferent commercial response. They returned in late 1999 with the vinyl only EP, *Places To Visit*.
● ALBUMS: *Foxbase Alpha* (Heavenly 1991)★★★, *So Tough* (Heavenly 1993)★★★, *Tiger Bay* (Heavenly 1994)★★★★, *Good Humor* (Creation 1998)★★★.
● COMPILATIONS: *You Need A Mess Of Help To Stand Alone* (Heavenly 1993)★★★, *Too Young To Die - The Singles* (Heavenly 1995)★★★★, *Casino Classics* (Heavenly 1996)★★★.
● VIDEOS: *Too Young To Die* (Wienerworld 1995).

Salad

Fronted by ex-MTV presenter Marijne van der Vlugt, UK indie band Salad first took shape when she started writing songs with guitarist Paul Kennedy while working as a photographic fashion model. Signed to Island Records' indie offshoot label Red, Salad offer a sparse sound that contrasts with the dense narratives of their lyrics. Both Vlugt and Kennedy, at one time romantically linked, are ex-film students. Kennedy's work includes *The Yoghurt Laugh*, while Vlugt used her own revolving, naked torso as the subject of her film project. Kennedy also worked for a design company, painting betting shop windows, before signing up with the band full-time. It was through Vlugt's original band, Merry Babes, that she was offered the MTV job, being asked to audition after attempting to press the group's videos onto a member of staff. The songwriting on their debut album, *Drink Me*, was split three ways, with Kennedy writing half the songs, Vlugt four and drummer Rob Wakeman (ex-Colenso Parade) three. Bass player Peter Brown is the final, non-writing member of the band. Following 'Your Ma', which explored illicit sexual desires *à la* the movie *The Graduate*, 'Elixir', penned by Wakeman, gripped the charts in early 1995, portraying the destructiveness of the youth and beauty aesthetic associated with the world of fashion and advertising. Their 1997 follow-up album, *Ice Cream*, was another refreshing burst of indie adventurism in an increasingly pedestrian music scene, but sadly it proved to be the band's final album.

● ALBUMS: *Drink Me* (Red 1995)★★★, *Ice Cream* (Island 1997)★★★.

Salt-N-Pepa

Cheryl 'Salt' James (b. 8 March 1964, Brooklyn, New York, USA) and Sandra 'Pepa' Denton (b. 9 November 1969, Kingston, Jamaica, West Indies) grew up in the Queens district of New York City. They became telephone sales girls and envisioned a career in nursing until fellow colleague and part-time producer Hurby 'Luv Bug' Azor stepped in. He asked them to rap for his group the Super Lovers (credited on record as Supernature) on the answer record to Doug E. Fresh's 'The Show'. They started recording as Salt 'N' Pepa (correctly printed as Salt-N-Pepa) which was adapted from the Super Nature recording 'Showstopper'. At that time they were under Azor's guidance, and released singles such as 'I'll Take Your Man', 'It's My Beat' and 'Tramp', the latter a clever revision of the old Otis Redding/Carla Thomas duet. They also used the female DJ Spinderella aka Dee Dee Roper (b. Deidre Roper, 3 August 1971, New York, USA), backing singers and male erotic dancers to complete their act. Their big break came in 1988 when a reissue of 'Push It' reached the UK number 2 spot and was also a US Top 20 hit. Later that year a remake of the Isley Brothers' 'Twist And Shout' also went into the UK Top 5. Between those two they released 'Shake Your Thang' (once again, a take on an Isley Brothers track, 'It's Your Thing'), which featured the instrumental group EU. Nominated for the first ever Rap Grammy in 1989, they refused to attend the ceremony when it was discovered that the presentation of that particular bauble would not be televised - withdrawing to show solidarity with hip-hop's growing status. Their most confrontational release was the 1991 'Let's Talk About Sex' manifesto (UK number 2/US number 13), something of a change of approach after the overtly erotic 'Push It'. 'Do You Want Me' was similarly successful, encouraging the record company to put out *A Blitz Of Salt 'N' Pepa Hits*, a collection of remixes, in their absence. Both Salt and Pepa were otherwise engaged having babies (Pepa in 1990, Salt in 1991; DJ Spinderella would make it a hat-trick of single mothers in the group a short time later). In the interim they could content themselves with not only being the first female rap troupe to go gold, but also the most commercially successful of all-time. They sub-

sequently enjoyed an invitation to appear at President Clinton's inauguration party. In 1994, they returned to the charts with the US Top 5 hit 'Shoop' and the highly successful collaboration with En Vogue, 'Whatta Man'. It was a return to their 'naughty but nice' personas, typically suggestive and salacious. After a lengthy absence, during which they contributed tracks to several soundtracks, they returned with *Brand New*, which saw the trio struggling to assert themselves against the brasher style of the new rap queens Foxy Brown and Lil' Kim.

● ALBUMS: *Hot Cool & Vicious* (Next Plateau 1987)★★★, *A Salt With A Deadly Pepa* (Next Plateau 1988)★★★, *Blacks' Magic* (Next Plateau 1990)★★★, *Rapped In Remixes* (Next Plateau 1992)★★★, *Very Necessary* (Next Plateau/London 1993)★★★★, *Brand New* (London/Red Ant 1997)★★★.

● COMPILATIONS: *A Blitz Of Salt 'N' Pepa Hits* (Next Plateau 1991)★★, *The Greatest Hits* (London 1991)★★★★.

Sanchez, Roger

b. 1 June 1967, New York City, USA. With countless remixes, productions and releases to his name, Sanchez deserves his reputation as one of the most hard-working and skilled DJ-producers, and received official recognition by being nominated for a 1999 Grammy Award. Sanchez's career began behind the decks while he was studying architecture at the Pratt Institute in New York City and, despite his success in the studio, DJing remains Sanchez's first love. However, his first recorded success was with the single 'Luv Dancin'' in 1990, released under the name Underground Solution on the pioneering New York label Strictly Rhythm Records. With it, he established a sound that has become his trademark: a dense, syncopated bassline and simple, contagious melody. One of his first remix projects, 'Take Me Back To Love Again' by Kathy Sledge proved that he could handle quite a difficult project, turning the sultry R&B ditty into a full-throttle, gospel-tinged dancefloor stomper. In the early 90s, he became an in-demand remixer and, under the name Roger S, worked on singles by artists such as Juliet Roberts, M People, Brand New Heavies and Michael Jackson ('Don't Stop Till You Get Enough', 'Jam', 'Dangerous'). Sanchez formed One Records with Eddie Colon in 1992. His *Secret Weapons Vol. 1* was released on the label in 1994, and reaffirmed his commitment to the underground house sound at a time when his remixing and production clients were becoming a major success. One Records became known for pioneering releases by Sanchez and other underground luminaries. In 1994, he formed Narcotic Records and early releases on the label included work by Ashley Beedle, Deep Dish and DJ Disciple. Narcotic's reputation for quality was emphasized with a bimonthly release schedule, including work by Junior Sanchez and the Rhythm Masters. In 1997, he collaborated with Junior Vasquez and DJ Sneak in the dance supergroup S-Men. In 1998, Narcotic signed an important production and distribution deal with Strictly Rhythm. During the week of 21 March 1998, Sanchez had an unprecedented three remixes in the Top 30 of the *Billboard* chart. His DJ schedule also remains very busy, playing events such as Tribal Gathering in the UK and regular slots at the UK's superclubs, Ministry Of Sound and Cream. He also still 'spins' regularly at New York's Spy Bar and Life when he is not touring and, as a solo artist, is signed to Sony Records. Despite this Renaissance man's diversification, DJing is still where it all begins: 'To me, spinning records can be just as creative as producing and remixing. A great DJ can take a record and give it an entirely new sound or vibe, by the way they deal with the beats or chord progressions.' After the closure of Narcotic, Sanchez launched R-Senal Records in June 1999. He was also voted number 9 in the UK's *DJ* magazine's Top 100 DJs in the world.

● COMPILATIONS: *Secret Weapons Vol. 1* (One 1994)★★★, *Hard Times - The Album* (Narcotic/Hard Times 1995)★★★, *Mixmag Live!* (Mixmag 1995)★★★, *S-Man Classics: Essential Mixes* (Narcotic 1998)★★★★.

Sash!

b. Sascha Lappessen, Wuppertal, Germany. Created in a studio on an industrial estate in Düsseldorf, Germany, Sash!'s brand of easy-listening dance music became a huge international crossover pop success during the late 90s. Lappessen began recording music in his spare time, while working in a record store, before teaming up with producer DJ Thomas Lüdke and engineer/producer Ralf Kappmeier. The team's working practice of sending out an uncredited final cut of a track to club DJs to gauge dancefloor reaction enabled them to build up club and radio support, ensuring strong demand for their official releases on the Telstar offshoot, Multiply. Three bestselling singles in 1997 followed a successful blueprint of featuring a guest vocalist over a dancefloor friendly backing track. 'Encore Une Fois' (featuring Sabine Ohmes), 'Ecuador' (featuring Adrian Rodriguez) and 'Stay' (featuring Frankie La Trec) went Top 10 all over Europe, with all three reaching number 2 in the UK charts. *It's My Life* re-entered the UK charts in November on the back of the singles' success, eventually climbing to number 7. Despite carping critics accusing Sash! of purveying a lightweight version of the Faithless sound, the DJ earned a 1998 BRIT nomination for Best International Male Solo Artist. His run of UK chart hits continued into 1998, with 'La Primavera' (number 3 in February), 'Mysterious Times' (featuring Tina Cousins) (number 2 in August) and 'Move Mania' (featuring Shannon) (number 8 in November). A new album, *Life Goes On*, debuted at UK number 5 in September. The team also undertook remixing work for a wide range of artists, including Kylie Minogue, Dario G. and OMD. A new single, 'Colour The World', debuted at number 15 in March 1999. Sash! bounced back in February 2000 with the number 2 hit, 'Adelante'.

● ALBUMS: *It's My Life* (Multiply 1997)★★★, *Life Goes On* (Multiply 1998)★★★.

Sasha

b. Alexander Coe, 4 September 1969, Bangor, Wales. 'The First DJ Pin-up' (*Mixmag*) whose regular nights included Renaissance and La Cotta (Birmingham). A former fish-farm worker and grade 8 pianist, he moved from Wales to Manchester in the late 80s and began religiously attending the legendary Haçienda. He bluffed his way into his first DJ bookings and, via some of Blackburn's largest rave parties, soon became resident at Shelley's in Stoke, where he earned a formidable reputation. *Mixmag* even put him on the magazine cover with the words, 'The Son Of God'. After pioneering Italian house in 1989 and 1990 he made his name with a jazzy, garage-style as a remixer on projects such as Mr. Fingers' 'Closer' and Urban Soul's 'He's Always' and

'Alright'. Sasha moved to Deconstruction Records in 1993 in a three-album contract. Most had expected him to sign with Virgin Records following the success of his BM:Ex (Barry Manilow Experience) cut, 'Appolonia', a double-pack 12-inch with a running time of over an hour, released on their Union City Recordings subsidiary. 'Appolonia' originally emerged as an obscure Italian white label promo, and was a record Sasha played regularly at the end of his sets at Shelley's in Stoke without ever being able to discover the identity of its originators. As nobody could find out any further details he decided to re-record it himself. The first result of the liaison with Deconstruction was 'Higher Ground', recorded with production partner Tom Frederikse and vocalist Sam Mollison. He also provided a single, 'Quat', for Cowboy Records. Sasha also signed a publishing deal with PolyGram Records in 1993, indicating that at last dance music songwriters were beginning to be taken seriously by the industry, rather than simply being regarded as short-term recording artists. As Sasha himself expounded: 'I've plans for bigger things. I don't want to be restricted by the dancefloor. That's where my inspiration is, but I want to do something with a little more longevity than the latest number 1 on the Buzz chart'. Subsequent crossover UK chart successes included 'Higher Ground' (number 19, February 1994), 'Magic' (number 32, August 1994) and 'Be As One' (number 17, March 1996). Among his many other remix/production clients have been Ce Ce Rogers, Unique 3 ('No More') and soundtrack composer Barrington Pheloung. His association with Renaissance led to a long-standing partnership with John Digweed and they can often be found DJing together, both live and on compilation mix albums, under the banner Northern Exposure. Since 1997, they have maintained a monthly Friday night residency at New York City's Twilo club (formerly the famous Sound Factory). Sasha has also worked closely with BT, remixing his tracks and collaborating as Two Phat Cunts on Deep Dish's Yoshitoshi label. They also worked together on a remix of Madonna's 'Drowned World', although Sasha remixed the tracks 'Ray Of Light' and 'Sky Fits Heaven' on his own. These remixes came about through Sasha's friendship with William Orbit, who produced Madonna's acclaimed *Ray Of Light*. Sasha remains one of the world's highest-profile DJ/producers, fulfilling numerous bookings around the world. He has recently launched his own DJ and artist management company, Tyrant. In 1999, he was voted number 3 in the UK's *DJ* magazine's Top 100 DJs in the world. He also released the highly acclaimed mix set, *013 Ibiza*.

● COMPILATIONS: *The QAT Collection* (Deconstruction 1994)★★★, with John Digweed *Northern Exposure - Sasha & John Digweed* (MOS 1996)★★★, with Digweed *Northern Exposure 2 - Sasha & John Digweed* (MOS 1997)★★★★, *013 Ibiza* (Boxed 1999)★★★★.

Savage Garden

Australian pop duo Savage Garden formed in Brisbane at the end of 1996, their name inspired by fantasy author Anne Rice's term for the savage and isolated world of vampires. Within nine months of formation they had attained two domestic hit singles ('I Want You' and 'Halfway To The Moon'). This achievement came without the benefit of any live performances or even promotional interviews. Their sudden popularity became a global phenomenon when 'I Want You', officially the biggest-selling Australian single of

1996, became an international bestseller later in the year. The duo, singer Darren Hayes and multi-instrumentalist Englishman Daniel Jones, met while playing in bar bands in Queensland in 1994. However, they elected to form a band more suited to their personal tastes - an amalgamation of influences including XTC and Peter Gabriel. A demo was sent to veteran manager John Woodruff (associated with Australian success stories including the Angels, Baby Animals and Diesel). He immediately signed them to his JDM record label. Their self-titled debut album was recorded in Sydney in June 1996, with Hoodoo Gurus and Air Supply producer Charles Fischer at the helm. 'I Want You' climbed to US number 4 in May 1997, and they enjoyed a huge transatlantic hit during the early months of 1998 with 'Truly Madly Deeply', the single topping the US charts and spending several weeks in the UK Top 10. On the back of their singles success, *Savage Garden* rose to number 3 on the US album chart in April. The follow-up single, 'To The Moon And Back', peaked at US number 24 in August 1998, but climbed to number 3 in the UK chart. The song had originally stalled at number 55 in February. The duo's follow-up, *Affirmation*, was recorded in the luxurious studios of San Francisco, and included the huge US chart-topper, 'I Knew I Loved You'.

● ALBUMS: *Savage Garden* (JDM 1996)★★★, *Affirmation* (Columbia 1999)★★★.

● VIDEOS: *The Video Collection* (SMV 1998).

Saw Doctors

Originating in Tuam, County Galway, Eire, the Saw Doctors continue the practice of rock reacquainting itself with traditional Gaelic music. Inspired by the madcap antics of the Pogues, *et al*, the medium is a furious medley of traditional and modern instruments, meshing together in boozy sing alongs or sombre ballads that are best experienced live. They signed to WEA Records in 1992 for *All The Way From Tuam*, but they had made their mark with an independent debut featuring 'I Useta Love Her'. The latter would become Eire's biggest-selling single of all time, topping the singles chart for nine weeks. Previously Leo Moran (vocals) had been playing guitar with local reggae-folk outfit Too Much For The White Man. Fellow Tuam 'sham' singer Davy Carton (guitar) was recruited - or perhaps brought out of retirement might be a more accurate description, the father of three having served time some years previously with local punk force Blase X. The duo next recruited mandolin player and traditional singer John 'Turps' Burke. Science student Pearse Doherty came in as bass player, the rhythm section filled out by the presence of ex-footballer John Donnelly. The startling success of 'I Useta Love Her' brought a re-release of debut single 'N17', and the band, fresh from supports to the Waterboys, were selling out venues on both sides of the Irish sea in their own right. They had been joined at this juncture by Tony Lambert (keyboards, piano accordion, ex-Racing Cars). Media assertions that these were 'designer bogmen' were enhanced by the choice of producer Phil Tennant (Levellers). However, support slots for bands such as Genesis at Knebworth demonstrated their appeal. They were also featured in a Channel 4 documentary, *Sing A Powerful Song*. The band subsequently formed their own Shamtown label, and broke into the UK Top 30 with the *Small Bit Of Love* EP. Even more success followed with the

Top 20 hit 'World Of Good', and the Top 10 album *Same Oul' Town*. They also remain a huge concert draw in the US, a recognition of their status as the ultimate 'people's band'. A compilation set was followed in 1998 by *Songs From Sun Street*, their first album of all-new material to be released in America.

● ALBUMS: *If This Is Rock 'n' Roll I Want My Old Job Back* (Solid 1991)★★★, *All The Way From Tuam* (Solid/Grapevine 1992)★★★★, *Same Oul' Town* (Shamtown 1996)★★, *Songs From Sun Street* (Shamtown 1998)★★★.

● COMPILATIONS: *Sing A Powerful Song* (Paradigm 1997)★★★.

Sawhney, Nitin

b. England. One of a new wave of Asian acts achieving mainstream acceptance in the UK music industry - following the pioneering work of Apache Indian, Kaliphz and Babylon Zoo - Nitin Sawhney has developed an eclectic mix of Indian music elements with the innovations and techniques of British jazz, dance music and rock styles. A Hindu Punjabi, Sawhney was born in England just a year after his parents relocated there from Delhi. As well as listening to traditional Indian music at home, he quickly adopted to a number of instruments, including piano and flamenco guitar. He then formed his first jazz group, the Jazztones, before graduating to playing guitar with the James Taylor Quartet in 1988. Afterwards he returned to traditional music by forming the Tihai Trio with percussionist Talvin Singh (later a collaborator with Björk and Massive Attack). By the early 90s he was spending much of his time recording music for film, television and theatre, and also released his debut solo album, *Spirit Dance*. This was recorded for World Circuit Records with the aid of an Arts Council grant following an extensive search for music industry backing. As was the case with the follow-up collection, *Migration*, the album combined Western instruments such as flamenco and jazz guitar with drum and bass loops, electronica and classically inspired Indian singing. As he told the press, 'The whole thing I'm trying to do is show there are no barriers, it's just about checking other cultures and finding where they meet up.' For his second outing he moved to Outcaste Records, a division of PR agency Media Village. The album was then given widespread radio exposure by the patronage of Gilles Peterson on Kiss 100 FM and Jazz FM. One of its tracks, 'Ranjha', was subsequently included on the high-profile *Rebirth Of Cool* compilation album. *Displacing The Priest* was promoted by the successful club single, 'Into The Mind', and confirmed the growing audience for Sawhney's evocative Anglo-Indian hybrid. The follow-up *Beyond Skin* confirmed his reputation as one of the most interesting artists on the UK dance scene in the late 90s.

● ALBUMS: *Spirit Dance* (World Circuit 1991)★★★, *Migration* (Outcaste 1994)★★★, *Displacing The Priest* (Outcaste 1996)★★★★, *Beyond Skin* (Outcaste 1999)★★★★.

Sawyer Brown

The members of the country band Sawyer Brown come from different parts of the USA: Mark Miller (b. Dayton, Ohio, USA; vocals) and Gregg Hubbard (keyboards) were school friends in Apopka, Florida; Bobby Randall (b. Midland, Michigan, USA; guitar), Jim Scholten (b. Michigan, USA; bass) and Joe Smyth (drums) were part of the Maine Symphony Orchestra. They all went to Nashville around

1980 and took varying roles in singer Don King's band. In 1983 they decided to work together without King, first as Savanna and then as Sawyer Brown, taking their name from a street in Nashville. In 1983, they took part in a US television talent show, *Star Search*. They won the first prize of $100,000 and a recording contract. Their first single, 'Leona', was a US country hit and they toured with Kenny Rogers and Dolly Parton. Miller wrote their second single, a country number 1 hit, 'Step That Step' (1985), about the perseverance needed in the music business. To this end, they have established themselves as a goodtime country band, enjoying a string of hit singles in the late 80s with 'Used To Blue', 'Betty's Bein' Bad', 'This Missin' You Heart Of Mine' and a remake of George Jones' 'The Race Is On'. 'My Baby's Gone' made number 11 on the country charts in 1988 and, despite losing some of their impetus, they returned with two Top 5 hits from 1992's highly successful *The Dirt Road*. The band have achieved a consistent string of Top 10 hits since then, establishing themselves as one of the most successful and long-running country acts on the scene. They won the Vocal Group Award at the 32nd Academy Of Country Music Awards.

● ALBUMS: *Sawyer Brown* (Capitol/Curb 1985)★★★, *Shakin'* (Capitol/Curb 1985)★★★, *Out Goin' Cattin'* (Capitol/Curb 1986)★★★, *Somewhere In The Night* (Capitol/Curb 1987)★★★, *Wide Open* (Capitol/Curb 1988)★★★, *The Boys Are Back* (Capitol/Curb 1989)★★★, *Buick* (Curb 1991)★★★, *The Dirt Road* (Curb 1992)★★★, *Cafe On The Corner* (Curb 1992)★★★, *Outskirts Of Town* (Curb 1993)★★, *This Thing Called Wantin' And Havin' It All* (Curb 1995)★★, *Six Days On The Road* (Curb 1997)★★★, *Hallelujah He Is Born* (Curb 1997)★★, *Drive Me Wild* (Curb 1999)★★.

● COMPILATIONS: *Greatest Hits* (Curb 1990)★★★, *Greatest Hits 1990-1995* (Curb 1995)★★★★.

● VIDEOS: *Greatest Video Hits: Vol. 2* (1993), *This Time* (Curb 1994), *Outskirts Of Town* (High Five 1994), *I Don't Believe In Goodbye* (Curb 1995).

Schoolly D

b. Jesse B. Weaver Jnr., Baltimore, Philadelphia, USA. Posturing street rapper who, together with his DJ Code Money (b. Lance Allen, USA), was an early pioneer of gangsta rap, a format that featured an abundance of violence and vendettas, and the glorification of the MC's personal armoury. Allied to the usual sexual declamation, it was a limited world view but a partially effective one. Following 1984 singles 'Maniac' and 'Gangster Boogie', Schoolly D released an independent, eponymous album that was notable for the track 'PSK - What Does It Mean'. PSK transpired to be an acronym for Park Side Killers, a gang of Schoolly's acquaintance in Philadelphia. Though this breakthrough album will ensure Schoolly D's name remains hallowed in the annals of gangsta rap, he has done little since that would otherwise justify his inclusion. Whereas greater intellects explored gang violence as a means of illustrating the big picture, Schoolly D proved happy merely to indulge in often horrific reportage. Song titles such as 'Mr Big Dick' and 'Where's My Bitches' spoke volumes about the lyrical insight displayed on the vast majority of his output. The first light at the end of the tunnel came with *Am I Black Enough For You?*, which incorporated a few more socio-political concerns, with cuts such as 'Black Jesus' opening up new, potentially much more interesting, avenues of provocation.

The title track, too, was more insightful than previous fare led us to expect: 'All I need is my blackness, Some others seem to lack this'. By the time of his 'comeback' album of 1994, released by Philadelphia's Ruffhouse Records, Schoolly had progressed further still. Renouncing the basic samples that had underscored most of his career, he now employed a full live hardcore band, including Chuck Treece (bass) and Mary Harris (drums) from the Ruffhouse house band. The record was co-produced by the label's Joe 'The Butcher' Nicolo and Mike Tyler. The following year's self-released *Reservoir Dog* reverted to the stripped-down style of his earlier records. In the late 90s Schoolly D made contributions to the soundtracks of *The King Of New York* and *The Blackout*.

● ALBUMS: *Schoolly D* (Schoolly-D 1986)★★★, *Saturday Night! - The Album* (Schoolly-D 1987)★★, *Smoke Some Kill* (Jive 1988)★★, *Am I Black Enough For You?* (Jive/RCA 1989)★★★★, *How A Black Man Feels* (Capitol 1991)★★★, *Welcome To America* (Ruffhouse/Columbia 1994)★★★, *Reservoir Dog* (Contract/PSK 1995)★★★.

● COMPILATIONS: *The Adventures Of Schoolly D* (Rykodisc 1987)★★★, *The Jive Collection Series Vol. 3* (Jive/RCA 1995)★★★.

Science, Chico

b. Francisco de Assis Franca, 1967, Recife, Brazil, d. 2 February 1997, Olinda, Brazil. In an expanding market for contemporary popular music, Chico Science was one of South America's fastest-rising stars. Born in the northeastern Brazilian city of Recife, he was initially inspired by the local traditions of fast drum rhythms and dances known as 'frevo', 'embolada', 'coco de roda' and 'maractu'. Science merged these elements with hard rock riffs and punk, funk and rap references to produce 'mangue' - or mangrove beat - titled after the local vegetation. In the early 80s, while living in the Rio Doce suburbs, Science was introduced to the burgeoning US rap scene spearheaded by Grandmaster Flash. In tribute, in 1984 he formed a neighbourhood street band, the Hip Hop Legion. Subsequently, he was drawn more towards conventional rock, an influence he acknowledged in his next band, Orla Orbe. By the end of the 80s he was leading another rock band, Loustal, named in tribute to the French comic illustrator of the same name. He would continue to bring new influences to bear on his music, in justification of his adoption of the stage name Chico Science (he spoke of becoming a 'scientist of sound'). It was with Nação Zumbi (Nation Of Zumbi) that he achieved widespread fame. This group paired percussionists from the local Lamento Negro group with his rock-playing colleagues and derived its name from the leader of a nineteenth-century slave revolt. The group's first album, *Da Lama Ao Caos* (From Mud To Chaos), paid tribute to other rebel leaders including Zapata and America's Black Panther movement. In its wake Science undertook successful tours of Europe and the USA and wrote songs for popular Brazilian singers such as Maria Bethania. A second album continued to mine what Science portrayed as his own personal cultural model, *Afrociberdelia*, from which it took its title. The album sleeve notes analogized the term as a 'creative mixture of tribal and high-tech elements', a word built as a compound of 'Africa', 'Cybernetics' and 'Psychedelia'. He was booked for an appearance as the headliner of the Recife carnival in 1997 when he was involved in a fatal car accident in Olinda.

● ALBUMS: with Nacao Zumbi *Da Lama Ao Caos* (1994)★★, *Afrociberdelia* (1996)★★★.

Seal

Screaming Trees

Hard-drinking rock band from the rural community of Ellensburg, near Seattle, USA. The Screaming Trees blend 60s music (the Beach Boys being an obvious reference point) with psychotic, pure punk rage. Not to be confused with the Sheffield, England synthesizer band of the same name who were also operational in the mid-80s, brothers Gary Lee Conner (b. 22 August 1962, Fort Irwin, California, USA; guitar) and Van Conner (b. 17 March 1967, Apple Valley, California, USA; bass) are among the largest men in rock, rivalled in their girth only by fellow Seattle heavyweights Poison Idea. The rest of the line-up comprises Mark Lanegan (vocals) and Barrett Martin (b. 14 April 1967, Olympia, Washington, USA; drums - replacing original incumbent Mark Pickerell in 1991). *Even If And Especially When*, the best of three strong albums for SST Records, included notable compositions such as the live favourite 'Transfiguration', which typified the band's blend of punk aggression and 60s mysticism. Major label debut *Uncle Anaesthesia* brought production from Terry Date and Soundgarden's Chris Cornell. By the time Screaming Trees moved to Epic Records they had embraced what one *Melody Maker* journalist called 'unashamed 70s Yankee rock', straddled by bursts of punk spite. Lanegan had by now released a solo, largely acoustic album, *The Winding Sheet*, for Sub Pop Records in 1990. This affecting, intensely personal collection included a cover version of Lead Belly's 'Where Did You Sleep Last Night', which Kurt Cobain would later employ as the trump card in Nirvana's *MTV Unplugged* session. Other extra-curricular activities included Gary Lee Conner's Purple Outside project, and his brother Van fronted Solomon Grundy (one album each in 1990). After four years they returned with *Dust*, a comparatively mellow and highly commercial album. The mellowness was induced by Lanegan's friendship with the late Kurt Cobain, and reflected in the lethargic 'Look At You', although the album's mantric 'All I Know' and 'Make My Mind' dispelled any accusation of wallowing in self-pity. Lanegan has subsequently concentrated on his increasingly successful solo career.

● ALBUMS: *Clairvoyance* (Velvetone 1986)★★, *Even If And Especially When* (SST 1987)★★★, *Invisible Lantern* (SST 1988)★★★, *Buzz Factory* (SST 1989)★★, *Uncle Anaesthesia* (Epic 1991)★★★, *Sweet Oblivion* (Epic 1992)★★★, *Change Has Come* mini-album (Epic 1993)★★★, *Dust* (Epic 1996)★★★★.
Solo: Mark Lanegan *The Winding Sheet* (Sub Pop 1990)★★★, *Whiskey For The Holy Ghost* (Sub Pop 1994)★★★★, *Scraps At Midnight* (Sub Pop 1998)★★★★, *I'll Take Care Of You* (Sub Pop 1999)★★.
● COMPILATIONS: *Anthology: SST Years 1985-1989* (SST 1995)★★★.

Seahorses

When John Squire (b. 24 November 1962, Broadheath, Greater Manchester, England; guitar) announced his departure from the Stone Roses in March 1996, inevitable press speculation followed regarding what he would do next. The usually taciturn Squire stated: 'I've always been into the idea of a group . . . I don't want to be a solo artist, I want to contribute to a band.' Still contracted to Geffen Records, Squire chose three unknown musicians to join him in what constituted a fresh start after the friction of his final months in the Stone Roses. Chris Helme (b. 22 July 1971, York, England; vocals/acoustic guitar) was approached while he was busking outside his local Woolworths, while Stuart Fletcher

(b. 1976, York, England; bass) was standing in on bass for local band the Blueflies, when Squire happened to be drinking in the pub where they were playing that night. Squire, Helme and Fletcher rehearsed for several months before recruiting Andy Watts (b. 1970, London, England; drums/vocals) to complete the line-up. After playing a low-key debut performance in Scotland, the band decamped to Los Angeles to record their debut album with Tony Visconti (David Bowie, T. Rex). Featuring songs by both Squire and Helme, *Do It Yourself* was released in May 1997 on the back of an excellent Top 10 single, 'Love Is The Law'. The album eschewed the sub-Led Zeppelin riffing that weighed down the Stone Roses' *The Second Coming*, opting for a more melodic and playful style of Britpop. Helme's folk-influenced vocals were a welcome contrast to Squire's distinctive guitar work, while his string-laden ballad 'Blinded By The Sun' stood out as one of the album's highlights. Diverse enough to appeal to both old Stone Roses fans and new listeners, *Do It Yourself* justified Squire's faith in his new band by entering the UK album charts at number 2. Watts left the band in September 1997 and was replaced by Toby Drummond (b. 1976, Hastings, Sussex, England). Expectations for a second album were quashed when the band announced they were splitting-up in early 1999.
● ALBUMS: *Do It Yourself* (Geffen 1997)★★★.

Seal

b. Sealhenry Samuel, 19 February 1963, London, England. Singer-songwriter Seal established himself at the forefront of a British soul revival in the 90s, enjoying transatlantic success with his first two albums. The second eldest of six brothers, his ancestry mixed Nigerian, Brazilian and Afro-Caribbean blood. Seal's first performance was at school at the age of 11, but it would be much later before his tentative musical plans came to fruition. Despite making many demos, he found it difficult to break into the music industry. After six months in Asia, he returned to England to find it entrenched in the Summer Of Love House Explosion. As the result of a chance encounter with rap artist Chester he was introduced to techno wizard Adamski. Seal happily contributed lyrics to his embryonic dance track, 'Killer', which eventually took the UK's dance floors by storm. However, the partnership did not last and Seal released his debut solo single, 'Crazy'. The first thing he had ventured to write on the guitar, the lyrics were imbued with the sort of new age mysticism given vent by 90s dance music culture. With production handled by ZTT Records' Trevor Horn, Seal went on to record a magnificent debut album in Los Angeles with Wendy And Lisa which proved a huge commercial success (three and a half million copies worldwide). This was compounded when 1992's BRIT Awards saw him walk away with nearly every conceivable category. The high-profile campaign launched by WEA Records for his excellent second album in 1994, once again an eponymous affair, and once again a worldwide success (five million copies sold). The following year proved that Seal was no flash in the pan, with the heart stopping ballad 'Kiss From A Rose' used as the soundtrack theme for the movie *Batman Forever*. At the Grammy Awards in 1996 he gathered an armful of awards including, Record Of The Year, Song Of The Year and Best Pop Vocal Performance. He ended that year with a major US hit, a version of Steve Miller's 'Fly Like An Eagle'. Despite

343

being recorded over a period of three years, *Human Being* was another polished collection of material, although it lacked any of the dramatic highlights found on the previous two albums. The record's commercial performance, failing to break into the US Top 20, also saw a dramatic downturn from the success of those sets.

● ALBUMS: *Seal* i (WEA 1991)★★★★, *Seal* ii (WEA 1994)★★★★, *Human Being* (Warners 1998)★★★.

Seam

Seam were formed in Chicago, Illinois, USA, by singer/guitarist Sooyoung Park, who had formerly led local punk act Bitch Magnet. The original line-up, which convened in 1990 for the release of the band's debut 7-inch single 'Days Of Thunder', also included Ralph 'Mac' McCaughan of Superchunk and bass player Lexi Mitchell. Since their inception the membership of the band has been fluid, although Park has always remained Seam's principal songwriter. In the process the band have evolved a musical style which some critics have dubbed 'slowcore' - a marriage of reflective acoustic passages with raucous noise inserts approximating the abrasiveness of local legends Big Black. This has led to comparisons with Slint (produced by Big Black alumnus Steve Albini) and Codeine's bass-dominated sound. After *Are You Driving Me Crazy?* Park took the band on the Ear Of The Dragon tour, to draw attention to the underexposed Asian influence in alternative music. At the same time the band turned down a series of major label offers following the modest success of their third album. By 1998 and *The Pace Is Glacial*, Seam had acquired a more stable line-up with William Shin (bass), Reg Shrader (guitar) and Chris Manfrin (drums) joining Park.

● ALBUMS: *Headsparks* (Homestead 1992)★★★, *The Problem With Me* (Touch & Go 1993)★★★, *Are You Driving Me Crazy?* (Touch & Go 1995)★★★, *The Pace Is Glacial* (Touch & Go 1998)★★★.

Seaman, Dave

b. 29 April 1968, Wakefield, Yorkshire, England. Seaman is one half of the respected remixing and production team, Brothers In Rhythm, but has established his own credentials as a sought-after house DJ and producer. He has been involved with the famous UK club Renaissance since its earliest days and has DJed at most of the major clubs in the world. Seaman's DJing style and his work with Brothers In Rhythm became linked with what the music press labelled epic house, with DJs such as Sasha and John Digweed at the forefront of the style. Seaman grew up listening to his parents' Carpenters and Barry White records but became interested in electro, New Order and dance music in his teens. After appearing in the DMC mixing championships in the late 80s, he was asked to appear at the New Music Seminar in New York and was eventually offered a job at DMC. As Brothers In Rhythm with Steve Anderson, Seaman has produced artists such as Kylie Minogue, Take That and Pet Shop Boys. The team have also remixed tracks by some of the most high-profile artists of recent years such as M People, Sasha, Michael Jackson, Janet Jackson, Seal, Sting, Placebo, Garbage, Bruce Hornsby, Eurythmics, New Order, Blur and Pulp. Seaman was for a time, a key figure behind the DMC/Stress Records organisation, making all the major A&R decisions. He also turned DMC's paper newsletter into the 'bible' of clubland, *Mixmag*. Known for his obsessive

interest in sports shoes and his love of travel, Seaman now has his own management company, Therapy, and continues to DJ all over the world. He spent much of 1999 in the USA, DJing at clubs as part of a Renaissance US tour. He also recorded a mix compilation, reflecting his DJ sets in Argentina - *Global Underground 12: Buenos Aries*.

● COMPILATIONS: *DJ Culture Volume 2: Stress Records* (Moonshine Music 1994)★★★, *Mixmag Live Volume 1* (Mixmag Live 1996)★★★, *Mixmag Live Volume 10* (Mixmag Live)★★★, *DJ Culture* (Stress 1996)★★★, *Renaissance 4 – Mixed By Dave Seaman & Ian Ossia* (Avex 1996)★★★, *Renaissance Worldwide – Singapore – Mixed By David Morales, Dave Seaman, BT* (Passion 1998)★★★, *Back To Mine* (DMC 1999)★★★★, *Global Underground 12: Buenos Aries* (Boxed 1999)★★★★.

Sebadoh

Based in Boston, Massachusetts, USA, Sebadoh are led by Lou Barlow (vocals/guitar). Before his well-publicized partnership with J. Mascis in Dinosaur Jr, Barlow had also played guitar to Mascis' drums in primal Boston hardcore group Deep Wound. However, as Dinosaur Jr worked their way out of the alternative/college rock circuit and into the mainstream, friendships within the band began to fray. The break came in 1989 when Barlow mistakenly let his bass feedback after missing his cue. Mascis' response was to walk over and hit Barlow over the head with his guitar, thereby irrevocably damaging their relationship. Afterwards Barlow was fired, and admitted to being 'just kind of lost, for a whole year'. When he eventually regrouped he began to record four-track demos with drumming friend Eric Gaffney. Sebadoh's early recordings led to them being heralded as kings of the US 'lo-fi' scene, which also encompassed Pavement and Guided By Voices. These cassette releases, untutored but full of the pop hooks with which Barlow became identified, were dwarfed by the impact of 1991's *Sebadoh III*, at which time the duo was expanded with the addition of bass player/vocalist Jason Loewenstein. Seen by many as the ultimate 90s college rock album, *Sebadoh III* was composed of irony-laden indie folk rock with continually surprising pop twists. It remains the band's most enduring achievement. The UK-issued *Rockin The Forest* included the tongue-in-cheek 'Gimme Indie Rock' single and saw the band adopt a comparatively professional rock/pop sound. *Sebadoh Vs Helmet* included two Nick Drake cover versions as well as a revisited version of 'Brand New Love', originally issued on *Freed Weed* and recently released as a cover version by Superchunk. The band then joined Sub Pop Records for the deftly titled *Smash Your Head On The Punk Rock*, which was issued in the wake of Nirvana's global breakthrough. Their prolific output of albums continued, forcing critics to reassess perceived notions of Barlow as a minor figure in Dinosaur Jr's success, and as a genuine talent in his own right. With Sebadoh now a band proper, Barlow still found time to write solo material which was credited to Sentridoh, and collaborate with John Davis as the Folk Implosion. In 1994, Eric Gaffney left the band, to be replaced by Bob Fay, although Gaffney had 'sort of' quit and been replaced at least three times previously. *Bakesale* was the band's first album to benefit from production at the celebrated Fort Apache Studios in Cambridge, Massachusetts. The greater depth of sound allowed the listener better access to the Sebadoh ethos, with Barlow's voice having developed a real empathetic edge on songs such as 'Careful' and Dreams'. As Barlow maintained: 'What's really important are the words. We play guitars so you can actually hear the texture of the music. As a songwriter, if you have anything to give at all, it's what your words are.' In 1996, Barlow made a surprise entry into the US Top 40 with a song written with his Folk Implosion partner John Davis. 'Natural One' was issued as a single after being featured on the soundtrack to the controversial movie, *Kids*. The new Sebadoh album *Harmacy* seemed like an unintentional bid for pop stardom and was peppered with catchy riffs. A new drummer, Russ Pollard, was brought into the line-up on 1998's *The Sebadoh*.

● ALBUMS: *Freed Man* (Homestead 1989)★★★, *Weed Forestin* (Homestead 1990)★★★, *Sebadoh III* (Homestead 1991)★★★, *Rockin The Forest* (20/20 1992)★★, *Sebadoh Vs Helmet* (20/20 1992)★★★, *Smash Your Head On The Punk Rock* (Sub Pop 1992)★★★, *Bubble And Scrape* (Sub Pop 1993)★★★, *4-Songs* (Domino 1994)★★, *Bakesale* (Sub Pop/Domino 1994)★★★★, *... In Tokyo* (Bolide 1995)★★, *Harmacy* (Sub Pop 1996)★★★★, *The Sebadoh* (Domino 1998)★★★.

● COMPILATIONS: *Freed Weed* (Homestead 1990)★★★.

Sebestyén, Márta

b. Budapest, Hungary. Widely celebrated as one of the world's finest female vocalists, Sebestyén has recorded as a solo artist and also as an intrinsic part of Hungarian folk group Muszikás. She grew up in Budapest surrounded by music, her mother having studied under renowned composer and folk song collector Zoltan Kodaly. Sebestyén had begun singing at concerts and on television performances while still a child. She soon graduated to Budapest 'dance houses', a movement which rebelled against the uniformity of culture under the Communist regime. She joined the Sebö And Halmos group in 1975 before enlisting in Hungary's best-known folk group, Muszikás, in 1980. She also spent several years collaborating with another popular Hungarian group, Vujicsics. In the 80s, most of her energies were spent, however, touring Europe with Muszikás. In 1984, she sang a folk musical based on the life of Hungary's former king Stephen, and in 1991 was awarded the title Female Singer Of The Year. Later she became the first Hungarian singer to be given the Liszt Award. In 1992, she released her debut solo album, *Apocrypha*, featuring a repertoire of Romanian, Slovak, Bulgarian and Serbian songs, which brought international recognition. In 1995, she recorded *Kismet*, alongside multi-instrumentalist producer Nikola Parov, the leader of Budapest group Zsarotnok. Other musicians included Zoltan Lanton (violin), Kornel Horvath (percussion), Péter Éri (mandola) and András Berecz (vocals). This time the songs drew on her widespread travels rather than relying simply on indigenous Hungarian music. It was also her first album to be sung entirely in English. Many of the songs were based on Irish tradition, including 'The Shores Of Loch Bran' and 'On Leaving Derry'.

● ALBUMS: *Apocrypha* (Hannibal 1992)★★★, *Kismet* (Hannibal 1995)★★★★.

● COMPILATIONS: *The Best Of Márta Sebestyén* (Hannibal 1997)★★★★.

Secada, Jon

b. Juan Secada, 4 October 1961, Cuba. This romantic balladeer enjoyed several transatlantic hit singles in the early 90s, aided in no small part by the production work of Emilio Estefan Jnr., Clay Oswald and Jorge Casas. They had previously shaped the career of Gloria Estefan And Miami Sound Machine, with whom Secada had previously co-written songs and toured as a backing vocalist. The similarities do not end there; as well as the distinctive Latin rhythm, Secada is likewise of Latin American descent, and he has become a fixture on the Latin charts throughout the decade. A string of crossover hits in 1992/93, each formulaic but successful expositions of romantic pop, included 'Just Another Day' (US number 5/UK number 5), 'Do You Believe In Us' and 'Angel'. Secada also enjoyed widespread acclaim for the Spanish language album *Otro Dia Mas Sin Verte*, which won the Grammy Award for Best Latin Pop album. *Amor* was a smooth Latin/jazz inspired outing which demonstrated his strong roots in the genre (he holds a master's degree in jazz from the University Of Miami). His duet with Shanice 'If I Never Knew You' was featured in 1995's hugely successful Walt Disney movie, *Pocahontas*. The Spanish version, 'Si No Te Conociera', appeared on *Amor*. The English language follow-up, *Secada*, was another superbly recorded collection of contemporary adult pop.

● ALBUMS: *Jon Secada* (SBK 1992)★★★★, *Otro Dia Mas Sin Verte* (Capitol 1992)★★★★, *Si Te Vas* (EMI Latin 1994)★★★, *Heart, Soul & A Voice* (SBK 1994)★★★, *Amor* (SBK 1995)★★★, *Secada* (EMI 1997)★★★.

● COMPILATIONS: *The Greatest Hits* (EMI 1999)★★★, *Grandes Exitos* (EMI 1999)★★★.

Seefeel

An intriguing combination of introspective ambient textures (though they abhorred the term) and propulsive guitars distinguished Seefeel's career. Guitarist and songwriter Mark Clifford answered an advert that Justin Fletcher (drums) had placed on a noticeboard at Goldsmith's College, London. They added Darren 'Delores Throb' Seymour (bass) and set about auditioning over 70 hopefuls for the singer's job. In the end Clifford responded to another ad: 'Wanting to join or form band into My Bloody Valentine and Sonic Youth', and called ex-animation student Sarah Peacock, who had placed it. As her tastes reflected Seefeel's personal creed, a distillation of My Bloody Valentine's guitar abuse with ambient's drone, she was immediately taken on board. They made their recording debut with the *More Like Space* EP, an Aphex Twin-inspired outing which confused BBC Radio 1 disc jockey John Peel as to whether to play it at 33rpm or 45rpm. Two EPs and an album for Too Pure Records quickly followed, with 'Pure, Impure' featuring a spectral Aphex Twin remix. They also collaborated and toured with heroes the Cocteau Twins (the question Clifford asked Peacock when he telephoned her was whether or not she liked them). Another EP in 1994, *Starethrough*, was their first for Warp Records, and again provoked interest, coinciding with and reflecting a move from indie to dance music coverage in the UK music weeklies. *Succour* was another bold album, but coincided with Clifford starting work on a solo project, Disjecta. Fletcher, Seymour and Peacock reconvened with Mark Van Hoen (aka Locust) as Scala. Seefeel reunited briefly for 1996's *Ch-Vox*, but the members have subsequently concentrated on their various solo projects.

● ALBUMS: *Quique* (Too Pure/Astralwerks 1993)★★★★, *Succour* (Warp 1995)★★★, *Ch-Vox* (Rephlex 1996)★★★.

● COMPILATIONS: *Polyfusia* (Astralwerks 1994)★★★.

Selena

b. Selena Quintanilla-Pérez, 1971, Lake Jackson, Texas, USA, d. 31 March 1995. In her short and tragic career Selena became the popular figurehead for the growth in popularity of Tejano and Latino music. Her father was a renowned vocalist with Tejano combo Los Dinos, who in 1980 opened his own restaurant in Lake Jackson. It was here that Selena first performed in public, singing to diners with her brother and sister. She made her first record when she was only 14, and in 1986 was voted Best Female and Performer Of The Year at the Tejano Awards in San Antonio. She signed a major recording contract with EMI Latin in 1990. She was rapidly embraced by Hispanic communities the world over for her singing talent and endearing personality (she was hailed as a 'goodwill ambassador' by the critics). She recorded several albums, of which two (*Entre A Mi Mundo* and *Amor Prohibido*) had earned gold awards, the third (*Live!*) securing platinum sales. She was awarded a Grammy for the latter. Her success in the singles charts (especially *Billboard*'s Hot Latin Tracks) was considerable too, with 'Tú Solo Tú' and 'I Could Fall In Love' among her many hits. She made her acting debut appearing in the romantic comedy *Don Juan De Marco*. The singer was recording her first English language album when she was shot by the president of her fan club. However, she achieved a major landmark when *Dreaming Of You* raced to number 1 on the *Billboard* chart in July 1995, a huge achievement given that it was sung predominantly in Spanish. In the process it became the bestselling chart debut by a female artist and among the 10 bestselling debuts of all time. Following her death it was announced that Hollywood intended to make a major commercial movie out of her life story. The biopic *Selena*, starring Jennifer Lopez, eventually appeared in 1997. Joe Nick Patoski's book is already the standard work, amidst a plethora of tabloid-style publications.

● ALBUMS: *Entre A Mi Mundo* (EMI Latin 1992)★★★, *Live!* (EMI Latin 1993)★★★, *Amor Prohibido* (EMI Latin 1994)★★★, *Dreaming Of You* (EMI Latin 1995)★★★, *Siempre Selena* (EMI Latin 1996)★★★.

● COMPILATIONS: *Anthology* (EMI Latin 1998)★★★★.

● VIDEOS: *Selena Remembered* (EMI Latin 1995).

● FURTHER READING: *Selena: Como La Flor*, Joe Nick Patoski.

Semisonic

Formed in Minnesota, Minneapolis, USA, Semisonic comprise Jacob Slichter (drums), John Munson (bass) and Dan Wilson (guitar/vocals, ex-Trip Shakespeare). It was Wilson's harrowing lyrics, reinforced by innovative guitar samples and superb production, that dominated the band's 1996 debut, *Great Divide*. One of the singles extracted from it, 'E.N.T.', featured on the soundtrack to the hit movie *The Long Kiss Goodnight*. The follow-up collection, *Feeling Strangely Fine*, broke into the US Top 50. It was a quieter, less strained effort, described by Wilson himself as 'an after hours record'. The lead-off single, fittingly titled 'Closing Time', featured piano (played by Munson) and strings (arranged by Slichter). Another single, the wistful 'Secret Smile', provided the band with a surprise transatlantic hit.

● ALBUMS: *Great Divide* (MCA 1996)★★★, *Feeling Strangely Fine* (MCA 1998)★★★★.

Senseless Things

The Senseless Things formed around the enduring musical partnership of songwriter Mark Keds (vocals/guitar) and Morgan Nicholls (bass), who as 11-year-old schoolboys in Twickenham, London, England, put together Wild Division in the early 80s. With the addition of Cass 'Cade' Browne (drums) they became the Psychotics, playing various venues in their local area despite still being at school. Their first gig together as the Senseless Things followed at the subsequently demolished Clarendon in Hammersmith, London, in October 1986. The definitive Senseless Things line-up evolved in summer 1987 with new recruit, former BBC clerk Ben Harding (b. 31 January 1965, Stoke-On-Trent, England), acquiring the vacant guitarist's role. Taking their musical cue from the Ramones and the Dickies, and their spiritual lead from fellow guitar outfit Mega City Four, the quartet embarked upon a hectic touring schedule that unveiled their roguish charm and obvious potential. Their youthful zest initially outshone their musical achievements, which were first aired for public consideration on a 7-inch compilation single given away with issue 6 of London fanzine *Sniffin' Rock*. By March 1988, the band had attracted the attention of BBC disc jockey John Peel, who invited them to record the first of two sessions for his programme. Following another fanzine release, three tracks headed by 'I'm Moving', they released 'Up And Coming' and 'Girlfriend'/'Standing In The Rain' for Way Cool Records. The musical imbalance that had seen them sacrifice melody for speed had, by that time, been thoroughly redressed. The band's debut mini-album, entitled *Postcard C.V.*, arrived in November 1989. It comprised 22 minutes of scratchy, boisterous punk pop now imbued with more shading and subtlety. Continuing to trawl the independent wasteland, the band joined What Goes On Records just as it collapsed, but the situation was rescued by Vinyl Solution subsidiary Decoy Records, who released the four-track EP *Is It Too Late?*, in May 1990. The band stayed with Decoy for 'Can't Do Anything', which prefaced an appearance at the Reading Festival, but the groundswell of live support eventually saw them snapped up by Epic Records at the start of 1991. The subsequent *The First Of Too Many* introduced acoustic guitars and gentler moods to the punky blitzes of yore, and 'Got It At The Delmar' scuttled into the Top 60 of the UK singles chart. Two further Top 20 singles followed in 1992, 'Easy To Smile' and 'Hold It Down'. The first single from 1993's *Empire Of The Senseless*, 'Homophobic Asshole', was a brave statement but one that ultimately alienated radio programmers. Despite continuing to write high-quality songs (becoming more reminiscent of the Replacements as time passed by), the momentum had been irretrievably lost. Rumours circulated in March 1995 of the band's impending collapse, having been dropped by their record company. Keds moved on to Jolt, the band he formed in early 1996, Harding joined 3 Colours Red, Nicholls recorded as M Organ, and Browne formed the acclaimed Delakota with Des Murphy.

● ALBUMS: *Postcard C.V.* mini-album (Way Cool 1989)★★★, *The First Of Too Many* (Epic 1992)★★★, *Empire Of The Senseless* (Epic 1993)★★★, *Taking Care Of Business* (Epic 1995)★★★★.

● COMPILATIONS: *Peel Sessions* (Strange Fruit 1994)★★★.

Senser

This multi-ethnic, seven-piece south London, England band was conceived in 1987. Their *métier* is the synthesis of numerous styles of music into a format that at once stimulates both the feet and grey matter. Fronted by Heitham Al-Sayed (raps/vocals/percussion), Senser proved the only band of their generation to see features in magazines dedicated to heavy metal, hip-hop and indie music - and few were in any way grudging. The other members of the band included Nick Michaelson (guitar), Andy 'Awe' (a DJ who once held the national high score on the Asteroids video game), Haggis (engineer), James Barrett (bass), John Morgan (drums) and Kersten Haigh (vocals/flute). This line-up was cemented in 1992, as they began the first of two tours supporting Ozric Tentacles, plus low-key squat and benefit gigs. The first seeds of the band were sown when Michaelson and Barrett met at a guitarist competition at the Forum, in London. Ex-school friend Haigh fronted the band from 1988 onwards, before the Senser name had been invoked, bringing vocals inspired from her journeys in India. Wimbledon resident Al-Sayed joined in 1991 as a drummer, but soon progressed to rapping duties as the band attempted to tackle their own version of Public Enemy's 'She Watch Channel Zero'. Their 1993 singles, 'Eject' and 'The Key', brought rave reviews across dance music and indie periodicals, with their ferocious musical clatter evading categorization. 'Switch', entering the UK Top 40, in turn announced a Top 5 debut album, *Stacked Up*, and a widely applauded appearance at the 1994 Glastonbury Festival. Al-Sayed, meanwhile, was particularly vocal in espousing the cause of the travelling community, under threat in 1994 from a new Criminal Justice bill. Although his throat problems prevented the band from building on their impact for much of 1994, *Stacked Up* went on to achieve over 80,000 sales. Al-Sayed, Morgan and Haggis all left the band early in 1996 to form Lodestar. Now fronted by just Haigh, the band returned in 1998 with a long overdue follow-up, *Asylum*.
● ALBUMS: *Stacked Up* (Ultimate 1994)★★★, *Asylum* (Ultimate 1998)★★★★.
● VIDEOS: *States Of Mind* (Ultimate 1995).

Sepultura

Formed in Belo Horizonte, Brazil, in 1984 by brothers Igor (b. 24 September 1970, Brazil; drums) and Max Cavalera (b. 4 August 1969, Brazil; vocals/guitar), with Paulo Jnr. (b. 30 April 1969, Brazil; bass) and guitarist Jairo T, who was replaced in April 1987 by Andreas Kisser (b. 24 August 1968) of fellow Brazilian metal act Pestilence. Sepultura is the Portuguese word for grave, and this is a strong clue as to the nature of a music that deals with themes of death and destruction, originally influenced by bands such as Slayer and Venom. In 1985, Sepultura recorded an album with Brazilian band Overdose (whom Sepultura had supported on their first gig), but this debut, *Bestial Devastation*, was of poor quality and had limited circulation. Their first solo effort, *Morbid Visions*, was released in 1986, followed a year later by *Schizophrenia*. The music on both was typified by speed, aggression and anger, much of which stemmed from the band's preoccupations with the poor social conditions in their native land. It was Monte Conner of Roadrunner Records who brought the band to international notice in 1989 when they released *Beneath The Remains*, which had

been recorded in Rio with Scott Burns as producer. In 1990 Sepultura played at the Dynamo Festival in Holland where they met Gloria Bujnowski, manager of Sacred Reich; their relationship with her led to the re-release of *Schizophrenia*. Despite European and American success, Sepultura have not deserted Brazil, and they played at the Rock In Rio festival in 1990. *Arise*, released in 1991, proved the bestselling album in the history of Roadrunner Records. The sessions for *Chaos A.D.* saw the band strip down their music in a more minimalist approach, which mirrored the punk ethos, especially evident on a cover version of New Model Army's 'The Hunt' (they had previously cut the Dead Kennedys' 'Drug Me' for an Alternative Tentacles compilation). In 1994, Cavalera branched out to release the *Point Blank* CD, working alongside Fudge Tunnel's Alex Newport under the name Nailbomb. *Roots* was seen as their peak and an album that allowed them to create rather than imitate. Brazilian themes were explored, notably with the pulsating 'Ratamahatta' and the tribal 'Itsari'. Having hit a peak in 1996 it came as a shock when Cavalera left to form Soulfly. His replacement in Sepultura was American Derrick Green, who featured prominently on 1998's *Against*.
● ALBUMS: *Bestial Devastation* with Overdose (Cogumelo 1985)★★★, *Morbid Visions* (Cogumelo 1986)★★★, *Schizophrenia* (Cogumelo 1987)★★★, *Beneath The Remains* (Roadrunner 1989)★★★, *Arise* (Roadracer 1991)★★★, *Chaos A.D.* (Roadrunner 1993)★★★. Max Cavalera in Nailbomb *Point Blank* (Roadrunner 1994)★★★, *Roots* (Roadrunner 1996)★★★★, *Against* (Roadrunner 1998)★★★.
● COMPILATIONS: *Blood-Rooted* (Roadrunner 1997)★★★.
● VIDEOS: *Third World Chaos* (Roadrunner 1995), *We Are What We Are* (Roadrunner 1997).

702

A vocal R&B trio named after its Las Vegas, Nevada, USA home area code, 702 made their long-playing debut for Michael Bivins in 1996. Bivins first became acquainted with the trio (which was originally a quartet) after they improvised an audition piece for him at the music industry's Jack The Rapper convention. Comprising sisters Irish and LeMisha Grinstead and Kameelah Williams, the group members were only aged between 11 and 13 when they took this momentous step. However, it was five years before they released *No Doubt*, an album that made strong use of their elegant harmonies and their varied musical influences, ranging from gospel to blues, jazz and hip-hop. In the interim, Grinstead sang on the 1995 hit 'This Lil' Game We Play', by fellow Biv 10 recording artists, Subway. 702's first single, 'Steelo', utilized a slang expression for 'personal style and attitude', and made a strong impression on regional R&B stations. It was followed by a second single, 'Get It Together', in December 1996. Their sophomore effort, released in summer 1999, was premiered by the US number 4 single 'Where My Girls At?'. The single featured the production skills of Missy 'Misdemeanor' Elliott.
● ALBUMS: *No Doubt* (Biv 10/Motown 1996)★★★, *702* (Motown 1999)★★★★.

Sevendust

Formed in Atlanta, Georgia, USA, in 1994, extreme metal band Sevendust comprises Lajon Witherspoon (vocals), Morgan Rose (drums), Vince Hornsby (bass) and Clint Lowery (guitar, brother of Corey Lowery of Stuck Mojo) and

John Connolly (guitar). All were previously members of sundry local rock outfits, with Witherspoon recruited from a local bar blues/funk rock outfit, Said Rose. The quintet first became Rumblefish then Sevendust, recruiting former Twisted Sister member Jay Jay French as manager and signing to TVT Records (formerly home to Nine Inch Nails). A self-titled debut album followed. Buoyed by strong radio play and an intensive touring schedule throughout America, it hit the number 1 spot in the US metal charts and stayed there for 12 weeks. A small tour of England, sponsored by *Kerrang!* magazine, ensued. The follow-up was another highly impressive burst of intense metal, featuring a duet between Witherspoon and Skunk Anansie's Skin on 'Licking Cream'.

● ALBUMS: *Sevendust* (TVT 1998)★★★, *Home* (TVT 1999)★★★.

Sexsmith, Ron

b. St. Catherine's, Ontario, Canada. Formerly a motorcycle messenger, Toronto resident Sexsmith was first inspired by the music of Tim Hardin and other 60s singer-songwriters. By the age of 17 he was singing cover versions in local bars. Embarking on his own song cycles, he released 1991's cassette only *Grand Opera Lane*. Four years lapsed before Sexsmith teamed up with producer Mitchell Froom to record a proper debut, dedicated to the recently deceased Nilsson, which achieved almost universal press acclaim. Elvis Costello called it the best album of the year, and many others were attracted to the nakedness and intimacy of Sexsmith's songwriting. Largely comprising basic percussion, minimal keyboards, acoustic guitar and Sexsmith's fragile, understated voice, it proved a winning formula despite moderate sales. Sexsmith was subsequently able to heighten his profile by supporting Richard Thompson on tour. The follow-up, 1997's *Other Songs*, proffered another suite of strangely hesitant, downbeat narratives, the stand-out songs including 'Child Star' and 'Pretty Little Cemetery'. *Whereabouts* received excellent reviews and was his most assured recording. This time around his Tim Hardin influence came to the fore. On a number of the tracks the tone and delivery is chillingly similar.

● ALBUMS: *Grand Opera Lane* cassette only (1991)★★★, *Ron Sexsmith* (Interscope/Atlantic 1995)★★★★, *Other Songs* (Interscope/Atlantic 1997)★★★, *Whereabouts* (Geffen 1999)★★★★.

Shack

Formed in 1986 by brothers Michael (b. 28 November 1961, Liverpool, England) and John Head (b. 4 October 1965, England), Shack emerged from the ashes of the Pale Fountains. Having had their fingers burnt by the major record companies - the Pale Fountains reached number 46 in the UK charts with 'Thank You', but were generally misunderstood by their employers - Shack joined up with independent label the Ghetto Recording Company. Experts at the cleverly understated melodic guitar pop song, 1988 saw the release of their acclaimed debut album, *Zilch*, which was produced by Ian Broudie. Yet instead of persevering with their commercial instincts, Shack laid low until reappearing with a single in 1991. A planned second album was finally issued in 1995, after the master tapes had been destroyed in a studio fire and the DAT of the sessions went missing. Bass player Pete Wilkinson joined Cast while the Heads went on to back ex-Love singer Arthur Lee. They resurfaced in 1997

with *The Magical World Of The Strands*, a superb collection of downbeat, melodic indie pop recorded as the Strands. Having been barely credited for their originality at the time (much of what Shack were doing in 1990 could be heard in the wave of mid-90s guitar-based indie bands), the Head brothers received some much deserved critical support when they returned in 1999 with the wondrous Shack album, *HMS Fable*.

● ALBUMS: *Zilch* (Ghetto 1988)★★★, *Water Pistol* (Marina 1995)★★★★, *HMS Fable* (London 1999)★★★★.

Shaggy

b. Orville Richard Burrell, 22 October 1968, Kingston, Jamaica, West Indies. Shaggy is, effectively, the man who put New York reggae on the map, thanks to his worldwide hit, 'Oh Carolina'. The same record helped to start the ragga boom of 1993, an explosion that also carried artists such as Shabba Ranks, Chaka Demus And Pliers and Snow into the international pop charts. An amusing vocal stylist who can be rude without ever descending into a leer, Shaggy learned his trade on Brooklyn's Gibraltar Musik sound system. He had moved to America with his parents at the age of 18, and at 19 joined the Marines, based at Lejeune, North Carolina. Following active service in the Gulf War, Shaggy began to record singles for a variety of labels, among them 'Man A Me Yard'/'Bullet Proof Baddie' for Don One, and 'Big Hood'/'Duppy Or Uglyman' for Spiderman. A chance meeting with Sting, a radio DJ at KISS-FM/WNNK, led to Shaggy's first New York reggae chart number 1, 'Mampie', a version of the 'Drum Song' rhythm, produced by Sting for New York reggae ruler Phillip Smart's Tan-Yah label. His next single, 'Big Up', released on Sting International and recorded in tandem with singer Rayvon, also hit number 1, as did 'Oh Carolina'. A mighty cover version of the Folkes Brothers classic, replete with samples of the original, the record became a huge hit on import charts wherever reggae was sold. At the time, Shaggy was still in the Marines, and was forced to make an 18-hour round trip to Brooklyn for dates and studio sessions. At the end of 1992, Greensleeves Records picked up 'Oh Carolina' for UK release, and by spring 1993 Shaggy had achieved a pop chart hit all over Europe, with the song reaching number 1 in the UK and several other countries. His next single, the slow, raucous 'Soon Be Done' failed, however, to capitalize on his success. Apparently unruffled by this, a liaison with Maxi Priest for 'One More Chance' led to a Virgin Records contract, and the *Pure Pleasure* album. A third single from the LP, 'Nice And Lovely', again failed to repeat the sales of 'Oh Carolina' (which, by that time, had made it onto the soundtrack of the Sharon Stone movie, *Sliver*), but it was a fine, light-hearted record in its own right. The album also contained a version of his earlier 'Duppy Or Uglyman' cut, restyled as 'Fraid To Ask'. He returned to the pop charts in 1995 with the UK number 5 single 'In The Summertime' (featuring Rayvon) and 'Boombastic', which topped the UK and US singles charts following frequent exposure (in England) as the soundtrack to an animated television advertisement for Levis jeans. An album followed, produced by the New York team of Robert Livingstone and Shaun 'Sting' Pizzonia for Big Yard Productions, along with Jamaican Tony Kelly as guest producer on two tracks, 'Something Different' and 'How Much More'. Another song, 'Why You Treat Me So Bad' (UK number 11), was conducted in alliance with rapper Grand Puba. *Boombastic* quickly went gold in America where Shaggy launched an extensive tour. He won a Grammy in February 1996 for Best Reggae Album (*Boombastic*). *Midnite Lover* was a lesser album, although the featured duet with Marsha, 'Piece Of My Heart', became another crossover hit.

● ALBUMS: *Pure Pleasure* (Virgin 1993)★★★, *Boombastic* (Virgin 1995)★★★★, *Midnite Lover* (Virgin 1997)★★★.

Shakespears Sister

Formed by Siobhan Marie Deidre Fahey-Stewart (b. 10 September 1958, Dublin, Eire) who was better known simply as Siobhan Fahey, and Marcella Detroit (b. Marcella Levy, 21 June 1959, Detroit, Michigan, USA) with producer and writer Richard Feldman keeping a low profile as third member. Siobhan, who had left Ireland for the UK to become a press officer at Decca Records, was a member of the top 80s female band Bananarama. She left in early 1988, although Detroit, too, had previously released solo material and worked as songwriter to Al Jarreau and Chaka Khan (having co-penned 'Lay Down Sally' with Eric Clapton while touring as his backing singer). Taking their name from a Smiths' song and keeping the spelling mistake made by a designer, one of their first gigs took place in Leningrad, USSR, in January 1989. Their debut, 'Break My Heart (You Really)', was not a hit. However, 'You're History' reached the UK Top 10, while the debut album made number 9. The follow-up, *Hormonally Yours*, was recorded while both participants were pregnant: 'It's self-deprecating but yet its very female without being militant or apologetic. Its just . . . what we are.' The band recorded in Los Angeles where Fahey lived with husband David A. Stewart. In February 1992, Shakespears Sister achieved a spectacular UK number 1 coup with 'Stay' (remaining there for eight weeks, ostensibly through a powerful, melodramatic hookline and video) and followed it with 'I Don't Care' (number 7), a reissued 'Goodbye Cruel World' (number 32) and 'Hello (Turn Your Radio On)' (number 14). Seemingly destined for great things, the band was nevertheless disbanded by Fahey, without warning to Detroit, live on stage at an awards ceremony in 1993. Detroit (reportedly 'not bitter') was the first to launch a solo career.

● ALBUMS: *Sacred Heart* (London 1989)★★★, *Hormonally Yours* (London 1991)★★★.

Shakur, Tupac

(see 2Pac)

Shamen

From the ashes of the moderately successful Alone Again Or in 1986, the Shamen had a profound effect upon contemporary pop music over the next half decade. Formed in Aberdeen by Colin Angus (b. 24 August 1961, Aberdeen, Scotland; bass), Peter Stephenson (b. 1 March 1962, Ayrshire, Scotland), Keith McKenzie (b. 30 August 1961, Aberdeen, Scotland) and Derek McKenzie (b. 27 February 1964, Aberdeen, Scotland; guitar), the Shamen's formative stage relied heavily on crushing, psychedelic rock played by a relatively orthodox line-up. Their debut album, *Drop*, captured a sense of their colourful live shows and sealed the first chapter of the band's career. Soon after, Colin Angus became fascinated by the nascent underground hip-hop

movement. Derek McKenzie was rather less enamoured with the hardcore dance music explosion and departed, allowing Will Sinnott (b. William Sinnott, 23 December 1960, Glasgow, Scotland, d. 23 May 1991; bass) to join the ranks and further encourage the Shamen's move towards the dancefloor. In 1988, their hard-edged blend of rhythms, guitars, samples, sexually explicit slide shows and furious rhetoric drew anger from feminists, politicians and - after the scathing 'Jesus Loves Amerika' single - religious groups. That same year the band relocated to London, slimmed down to the duo of Angus and Sinnott who concentrated on exploring the areas of altered states with mind-expanding psychedelics. By 1990, the Shamen's influence - albeit unwitting - was vividly realized as the much-touted indie/dance crossover saw bands fuse musical cultures, with artists such as Jesus Jones openly admitting the Shamen's groundbreaking lead. By this time the Shamen themselves had taken to touring with the 'Synergy' show, a unique four-hour extravaganza featuring rappers and designed to take the band even further away from their rock roots. After four years of such imaginative adventures into sound, 1991 promised a huge breakthrough for the Shamen and their fluctuating creative entourage. Unfortunately, just as they inexorably toppled towards commercial riches, Will Sinnott drowned off the coast of Gomera, one of the Canary Islands, on the 23 May 1991. With the support of Sinnott's family, the Shamen persevered with a remix of 'Move Any Mountain (Pro Gen '91)' which climbed into the Top 10 of the UK chart, a fitting farewell to the loss of such a creative force. Mr C (b. Richard West), a cockney rapper, DJ and head of the Plink Plonk record label, had joined the band for a section of 'Move Any Mountain (Pro Gen '91)'. Although many found his patois ill-fitting, his rhymes founded the springboard for UK chart success with 'LSI' and the number 1 hit, 'Ebeneezer Goode' - which was accused in many quarters for extolling the virtues of the drug Ecstasy ('E's Are Good, E's Are Good, E's Ebeneezer Goode'). The Shamen denied all, and moved on with the release of *Boss Drum*.. Its title track provided a deeply affecting dance single, complete with lyrics returning the band to their original, shamanic ethos of universal rhythms. Placed next to the teen-pop of 'LSI' and 'Ebeneezer Goode', such innovative work reinforced the Shamen's position as the wild cards of the UK dance music scene, although later recordings suffered from a lack of fresh ideas or even any further hit singles. The Shamen finally bowed out with 1998's *UV*.

● ALBUMS: *Drop* (Moshka 1987)★★★, *In Gorbachev We Trust* (Demon 1989)★★★, *Phorward* (Moshka 1989)★★★, *En-Tact* (One Little Indian 1990)★★★, *En-Tek* (One Little Indian 1990)★★★, *Progeny* (One Little Indian 1991)★★★, *Boss Drum* (One Little Indian 1992)★★★★, *Different Drum* (One Little Indian 1992)★★★, *The Shamen On Air* (Band Of Joy 1993)★★, *Axis Mutatis* (One Little Indian 1995)★★, *Hempton Manor* (One Little Indian 1996)★★, *UV* (Moksha 1998)★★★.

● COMPILATIONS: *Collection* (One Little Indian 1997)★★★, *The Remix Collection (Stars On 45)* (One Little Indian 1997)★★★.

Shampoo

Adorned in ra-ra skirts, pigtails and dayglo T-shirts, Shampoo's arrival on the 1994 UK pop scene brought kitsch back to centre stage with a bang. 'The Kylie and Dannii of Baby Tears Punk Rock Pop', as the *New Musical Express* decreed, Jacqui Blake and Carrie Askew arrived fresh from school in Plumstead, London. The duo's early endeavours included writing a fanzine, *Last Exit*, about the Manic Street Preachers, appearing in one of their videos and earning a reputation for being 'around town'. They then met Saint Etienne's Bob Stanley at a party and talked him into giving them a contract on his Icerink label. The resultant single, 'Blisters & Bruises', earned a *Melody Maker* Single Of The Week award for its naïve, spunky charm. They wrote the lyrics, while Lawrence of Felt/Denim wrote the music and produced. Shampoo were fully launched with the release of the delinquent 'Trouble' and hopelessly amateur 'Viva La Megababes', the latter a cheap and unruly take on the Voodoo Queens' 'Supermodel': 'Riot girls, diet girls, who really gives a fuck'. 'Trouble', meanwhile, was bizarrely used by BBC Television to publicize a Frank Bruno boxing match, and sold over 150,000 copies. Fabulously popular in Japan, their lyrical concerns for their debut album had expanded to encompass video games, throwing up after dodgy kebabs and sentimental love songs. Their success was eclipsed and their girl-power crowns grabbed in one fell swoop by the Spice Girls in late 1996.

● ALBUMS: *We Are Shampoo* (Food 1994)★★★, *Girl Power* (Food 1996)★★.

Shanice

b. Shanice Wilson, 14 May 1973, McKees Rocks, Pittsburgh, Pennsylvania, but raised in Los Angeles, California, USA. Shanice began singing on stage with her mother Crystal and her aunt Penni, who now jointly oversee her career. Afterwards, she found her way into the modelling industry, appearing in television commercials, including one with Ella Fitzgerald, and performing in local musicals before reaching her teens. One particular performance in *Get Happy* led to her first recording contract when she was just 11-years old, with A&M Records. By 1990 she had been signed to Motown Records by president Jheryl Busby. Partnered with producer Narada Michael Walden, the resulting chemistry produced a 1992 gold-certified album, *Inner Child*, which featured the international hit single 'I Love Your Smile'. Two other US Top 10 hits were also featured: 'Silent Prayer' (which saw accompaniment from label-mate Johnny Gill) and 'I'm Crying'. Nominated for a Grammy as Best R&B Female Vocalist in her own country and awarded the Golden Lion Award as Best International Artist in Germany, Shanice built on the breakthrough with extensive international touring. Meanwhile, she found time to collaborate with Kenny Loggins on his *Live From The Redwoods* album and contributed to three film soundtracks, *Beverley Hills 90210* (which gave Shanice another Top 5 US hit with 'Saving Forever For You'), the Eddie Murphy film *Boomerang* ('Don't Wanna Love You') and *Meteor Man* (which included her US R&B number 1 'It's For You'). *21 Ways ... To Grow* moved to a more up-tempo style, with harder grooves inspired by hip-hop and the usual array of soulful ballads. If featured another hit single in 'I Like', with remixes from Kenny 'Dope' Gonzalez, while the album's production team included Jermaine Dupri (Kris Kross, Xscape) and Chris Stokes. She duetted with Jon Secada in 1995 on 'If I Never Knew You' from the highly successful Walt Disney movie *Pocahontas*. Following a stint on Broadway in *Les Misérables*, Shanice worked on an abortive project for Arista Records. Appearances on albums by Babyface and Usher followed,

before Shanice returned in 1999 with a solo album on the LaFace label. *Shanice* included the US Top 20 single, 'When I Close My Eyes'.

● ALBUMS: as Shanice Wilson *Discovery* (A&M 1987)★★, *Inner Child* (Motown 1992)★★★, *21 Ways ... To Grow* (Motown 1994)★★★, *Shanice* (LaFace 1999)★★★.

Shannon, Mem

b. New Orleans, USA. Shannon moved to New Orleans, Missouri, USA, in 1959. As an amateur blues singer he discovered plenty of musical opportunities in the region, occasionally adding guitar and sometimes clarinet accompaniment to impromptu bar-room sessions. The city's music circuit of that time demanded singers capable of copycat renditions of standards such as 'Hoochie Coochie Man' and 'Dust My Broom' rather than contemporary interpreters, but Shannon happily performed this function in bar bands and the occasional gospel group for several years while nurturing his own songwriting in private. However, when his father (also named Mem) died in 1981, Shannon was suddenly expected to become the household breadwinner. He put aside his music for nearly a decade while supporting the family as a taxi driver. Eventually, in 1990, he established his own group around a collective of musicians known as the Membership. Contributors included Peter Carter (bass), Barry Thomas (drums), Jackie Banks (keyboards) and Lance Ellis and Tim Green on saxophones. In 1991 they appeared in the Jazz Search contest organized by a New Orleans television station, before travelling to California to appear at the Long Beach Blues Festival. Later, saxophone player Green introduced Shannon to producer Mark Bingham. Together they recorded 10 songs, linked by studio dialogue, as the basis for *A Cab Driver's Blues*. Ranging from the comic domestic conflict of 'My Baby's Been Watching TV' to the incessant funk of 'Boogie Man', it was an inspirational achievement. Due to have been released on Bingham's regional label Gert Town, it was eventually housed on Joe Boyd's Hannibal Records. The title wryly reflected Shannon's long spell in the musical wilderness, which, given the evidence of his songwriting, was a substantial loss to the blues idiom. *Mem Shannon's 2nd Blues Album* was released in 1997, and built on the first by embracing southern soul alongside regular blues. Shannon's gorgeously fruity voice is exquisite, with shades of Brook Benton and Billy Eckstine - further confirmation of an immense vocal, guitar and songwriting talent. His third album was released by Shanachie Records in February 1999.

● ALBUMS: *A Cab Driver's Blues* (Hannibal 1996)★★★, *Mem Shannon's 2nd Blues Album* (Hannibal 1997)★★★★, *Spend Some Time With Me* (Shanachie 1999)★★★.

Shannon, Sharon

b. 8 June 1968, Corrofin, County Clare, Eire. A solo performer on accordion and fiddle, both Shannon's parents were dancers, and her brothers and sisters all played musical instruments. Initially she played local clubs with them. While still in her teens she joined Disirt Tola, with her sister Mary, the group then heading to the USA for live engagements. Shannon was asked to provide the music for Brendan Behan's play, *The Hostage*, at the Druid Theatre. She later joined Arcady, along with Frances Black, James Delaney, Patsy Broderick and Ringo McDonagh (formerly with De Dannan). Shannon remained with them for about a year, and in 1989 went to the Glastonbury Festival, as a guest of Mike Scott of the Waterboys, as their accordion player. She remained with the band for 18 months, recording and touring worldwide in the process. On leaving the Waterboys she commenced a solo tour with Christy Moore. Finally, she released her long awaited debut album, *Sharon Shannon*. The album was well-received, and featured a number of respected musicians, including Donal Lunny, Mike Scott and Adam Clayton (U2). Although largely a solo performer, her current band includes former Waterboys member Trevor Hutchinson (bass), Mary Custy (fiddle) and Gerry O'Beirne (guitar/ukulele). As a performer she has quickly captured the imagination of the folk scene, with subsequent albums making bold forays into reggae and world music styles.

● ALBUMS: *Sharon Shannon* (Solid 1991)★★★, *Out The Gap* (Solid 1994)★★★, *Each Little Thing* (Grapevine 1997)★★★.

● COMPILATIONS: *Spellbound: The Best Of Sharon Shannon* (Grapevine 1998)★★★.

Sharp Boys

The Sharp Boys is a UK-based DJing and production duo comprising George Sharp Michell (b. 11 November 1962, Scotland) and Steven Docherty (b. 8 March 1972, Londonderry, Northern Ireland). They have completed more than 100 remixes and established their own record label, Sharp Recordings, as one of the most respected UK house music labels. They also hold a Saturday night residency at London's famous gay club Trade at Turnmills in Farringdon, where they play a blend of US underground house and garage. Among the high-profile artists they have remixed are Aretha Franklin, Madonna, Backstreet Boys, George Michael, M People, All Saints, Britney Spears, Geri Halliwell, DJ Rap and Diana Ross. Former journalist Michell's DJing career began at the famous London club, Heaven, while Docherty's work as an A&R man for React Music led to his being known as Steven React for some time. They met on the DJing circuit and found a common interest in quality house music with an American influence and 'tribal' overtones. Founded in December 1994, Sharp Recordings first release was 1995's 'Krazy Noise' by Numerical Value. It was remixed by Malcolm Duffy and Nelly K., who also released their debut 'Come And Get My Good T'ings' on the label. The label's third release, Sara Parker's 'My Love Is Deep' (featuring a remix by Armand Van Helden), was licensed from Vestry, a subsidiary of the famous US label, Strictly Rhythm Records. Further singles came from artists such as East Anglia ('Unmanageable') and Cool Jack ('Jus' Come'), the latter remixed by Ralph Rosario and DJ Sneak. In 1998 they released tracks by Hip Hoperation featuring Kenny C., Joe T. Vanelli and Blend. Blend's 'Rise Of Tonight' was a huge club hit and featured on Pete Tong's *Spring Essential Mix, House Nation 6*, mixed by Brandon Block and 'Tall' Paul Newman for the Ministry Of Sound and the Kiss FM compilation *Clublife*. The Sharp Boys continue to DJ all over Europe and in South Africa, the USA and the Far East. They host a weekly radio show on London's Kiss 100 FM.

● COMPILATIONS: *Sharp Vs Sharp* (React Music 1999)★★★.

Shed Seven

This much maligned indie band from York, England comprises Rick Witter (lead vocals), Tom Gladwin (bass), Paul Banks (guitar) and Alan Leach (drums). Together they brought a flash of domesticity and anti-glamour to the independent scene of the mid-90s - their interests including slot machines, bad television (Banks allegedly writes songs while watching *Prisoner Cell Block H*) and cheap alcohol. There was a refreshingly parochial atmosphere to their profile - best symbolized by the fact that Leach is the boyfriend of Witter's sister - despite the fact that their primary influences included Happy Mondays and Stone Roses. The only hint of celebrity, aside from Witter once coming second in a karaoke competition in Cyprus, involved their vocalist's dalliance with Donna Matthews from Elastica. However, as their recorded output demonstrated, and many critics suggested, it remained a thin line between level-headedness and mundanity. To their credit, Shed Seven were unconcerned with the trappings of cool, happily signing to a major, Polydor Records, and making their debut with 'Mark': 'We chose to put Polydor on the middle of our records - like the Who and the Jam, two of the best British bands ever. That's what we aspire to, not to some crap indie credibility'. After playing the *New Musical Express*' On Into 94 gig, they made two appearances on BBC Television's *Top Of The Pops*, and achieved two Top 30 singles and a Top 20 album. The band was clearly at their best live, however, and their 1994 sell-out tours cemented a strong following. The band's second album, including their Top 15 UK hit 'Getting Better', was released in April 1996 to mixed reviews. They returned to the post-Britpop music scene in March 1998 with the defiantly brash single 'She Left Me On A Friday' and *Let It Ride*, another slice of retro indie-pop. The 1999 compilation set marked the end of their association with Polydor.

● ALBUMS: *Change Giver* (Polydor 1994)★★★, *A Maximum High* (Polydor 1996)★★★★, *Let It Ride* (Polydor 1998)★★★.

● COMPILATIONS: *Going For Gold: The Best Of* (Polydor 1999)★★★.

● VIDEOS: *Go And Get Stuffed* (PolyGram Music Video 1997).

Sheik, Duncan

b. South Carolina, USA. Sheik grew up in South Carolina and New Jersey, learning to play the piano and guitar. He played with Lisa Loeb while studying at Brown University, and later appeared with His Boy Elroy on a 1993 album for Epic Records. Sheik recorded his debut Atlantic Records album in 1996 - a suite of songs that was dominated by the recent ending of a personal relationship. The first single to be lifted from the self-titled album, the huge radio hit 'Barely Breathing', was typical of its contents, eschewing any distinctive pop content in its determinedly downbeat observations. Despite the absence of any quantifiable mass appeal, the debut album quickly gained a foothold in the *Billboard* Top 100, buoyed by the inclusion of Sheik's song, 'In The Absence Of Sun', on the soundtrack to *The Saint*. Appearances on the *David Letterman Show* and support dates with Frenté and Jars Of Clay further heightened his profile. In 1998, Sheik worked on the soundtrack to the remake of *Great Expectations*, and recorded his sophomore album *Humming*.

● ALBUMS: *Duncan Sheik* (Atlantic 1996)★★★, *Humming* (Atlantic 1998)★★★.

Shellac

Rock *enfant terrible* Steve Albini (ex-Big Black/Rapeman) formed this trio on an informal basis in 1993. Buoyed by the attention garnered in the wake of his producing *In Utero* for Nirvana, Albini (velocity), Bob Weston (mass) and Todd Trainer (time) issued 'The Rude Gesture A Pictorial History', the first of two limited-issue singles to appear on the trio's own label. It offered all the trademarks of Albini's previous bands - awkward time changes, thundering basslines, screaming guitar and frantic vocals. Weston was ex-Volcano Suns, while Trainer had worked with Rifle Sport and Breaking Circus. 'Uranus' followed in similar, exciting fashion. A third single, 'The Admiral', came in a sleeve still showing Albini's caustic remarks referring to how it should be designed. A different version of the a-side appeared on *Shellac At Action Park*, which developed Albini's distinctive style without subverting its power. His work remained as challenging as ever on the follow-up, *Terraform*, which was recorded in 1996 but not released until two years later.
● ALBUMS: *Shellac At Action Park* (Touch & Go 1994)★★★, *Terraform* (Touch & Go 1998)★★★.

Shepard, Vonda

b. 7 July 1963, New York City, New York, USA. Shepard relocated to California with her family as a child, and studied voice and piano from an early age. She began working in local clubs as a teenager, and before she was 20 had landed slots as a backing singer for Jackson Browne and Rickie Lee Jones (she has also worked with Al Jarreau, Julia Fordham, and Chaka Khan over the course of her career). Shepard signed a solo deal with Reprise Records in 1987, and two years later released an anodyne rock collection that muted her distinctive bluesy voice. *The Radical Light*, benefited from a more sympathetic production, but Shepard was dropped by Reprise shortly after its release. She retired to the Los Angeles club circuit, building up a loyal following in the process and releasing an excellent, independently released album in 1996. Her big break came when producer David E. Kelley and his wife, Michelle Pfeiffer, spotted her at a club. Kelley was developing the television series *Ally McBeal*, and cast Shepard as the resident singer in the local bar frequented by the star of the show and her legal co-workers. Shepard's 'Searchin' My Soul', which originally appeared on her second album, was used as the theme tune to the show. An album of songs from the series climbed to number 7 on the US album chart in May 1998 and sold over one and a half million copies. The album also broke into the UK Top 5, while 'Searchin' My Soul' reached number 10 in the singles chart in December 1998. Despite its success, the album was a rather stilted mixture of cover versions ('Walk Away Renee', 'It's In His Kiss (Shoop Shoop Song)', 'I Only Want To Be With You', 'The End Of The World') and Shepard originals. The following year's *By 7:30*, which appeared on Jacket Records, was a far more satisfactory overview of Shepard's talents, and included a reworking of a track from her debut album, 'Baby, Don't You Break My Heart Slow', recorded with Emily Saliers of the Indigo Girls. In November, a second collection of *Ally McBeal* songs was released.
● ALBUMS: *Vonda Shepard* (Reprise 1989)★★, *The Radical Light* (Reprise 1992)★★★, *It's Good Eve* (Vesperally 1996)★★★★, *Songs From Ally McBeal Featuring Vonda Shepard* (550 Music/Epic 1998)★★, *By 7:30* (Jacket 1999)★★★, *Heart And Soul: New Songs From Ally McBeal Featuring Vonda Shepard* (550 Music/Epic 1999)★★.

Shepherd, Kenny Wayne

b. USA. A classically-styled blues rock guitarist, Shepherd recorded his debut album for Revolution Records in 1995 with the aid of singer Corey Sterling. Extracted from the album, 'Déjà Voodoo' became a hit on mainstream rock radio and reached an audience beyond blues purists, though they too were impressed with the guitarist's skill - the album stayed at the top of *Billboard*'s Blues chart for 20 weeks. As a result, Shepherd was able to play dates with his heroes, B.B. King and Buddy Guy. Later he toured with celebrated rock guitarists including Steve Vai and Joe Satriani. By April 1997 and his second collection, Sterling had been replaced by fellow blues aficionado Noah Hunt. Shepherd again wrote all the lyrics, though this time his record label paired him with Talking Heads' alumni Jerry Harrison as producer. This unusual, seemingly incongruous partnership gelled immediately, resulting in a clean, reflective sound, augmented by the guest contributions of Chris Layton (Double Trouble), Tommy Shannon, Reese Wynans and James Cotton. As well as original material, the set included cover versions of Jimi Hendrix's 'I Don't Live Today' and 'Voodoo Chile', and Bob Dylan's 'Everything Is Broken'. *Trouble Is ...* proved to be immensely successful, spending months at the top of the US Blues Album chart.
● ALBUMS: *Ledbetter Heights* (Revolution 1995)★★★, *Trouble Is ...* (Revolution 1997)★★★★, *Live On* (Giant/Reprise 1999)★★★★.

Sherwood, Adrian

A pioneering force in UK reggae, Sherwood's first attempts to set up labels in the late 70s were disastrous, and cost him a great deal of money in the process. Despite such misadventures, he persevered, and set up the On U Sound label to house ex-Pop Group singer Mark Stewart's New Age Steppers project. Hundreds of albums and singles have subsequently been released, including music by Bim Sherman, Dub Syndicate and Mothmen (an embryonic Simply Red). Sherwood styled On U Sound after the reggae model of 'house bands' (Revolutionaries, Soul Syndicate, etc.). The label/organization also played out as a sound system, in a similar fashion to its Jamaican counterparts. Among the notable long-term protagonists at On U Sound have been Bonjo (African Head Charge), Bim Sherman and Skip McDonald, Doug Wimbush and Keith LeBlanc (Tackhead). However, Sherwood is equally renowned for his production skills, which he learned at first hand from Prince Far I and Dr Pablo. The Fall, Depeche Mode and Ministry have been among his notable clients. On U Sound came to the attention of the public outside reggae circles when self-styled 'white toaster' Gary Clail entered the UK charts in 1991 with 'Human Nature'. However, neither this, nor any other individual release, can be described as representative of the rock-reggae-dance fusion that On U Sound have fostered. On U Sound's eclecticism remains rampant, but as Sherwood himself concedes: 'I'm first and foremost a passionate fan of reggae music'.
● COMPILATIONS: *On-U-Sound Present Pay It All Back Volume 4* (On U Sound 1993)★★★, *Reggae Archive Volumes 1 & 2* (On U Sound)★★★, *Various Discoplates Collection Part 1* (On U Sound 1998)★★★★

Shooglenifty

Formed in Edinburgh, Scotland, Shooglenifty began life with a residency at the La Belle Angele pub and quickly drew a strong fanbase for their energised, contemporary roots material. Comprising Iain Macleod (b. 4 April 1962, Strathy Point, Scotland; mandolin), Angus R. Grant (b. 14 February 1967, Fort William, Scotland; fiddle), Garry Finlayson (b. 24 September 1952, Kirkwall, Scotland; banjax), Malcolm James Crosbie (b. 25 May 1960, Edinburgh, Scotland; guitar/whistling), Conrad Ivitsky (b. 28 October 1968, Edinburgh, Scotland; bass) and James MacKintosh (b. 11 August 1966, Fort William, Scotland; percussion), the band members' previous experiences had included stints with Capercaillie, the House Band, Mouth Music and Miro. All bar Macleod had also been part of the Edinburgh 'psychobilly' act, Swamptrash. By 1995 Shooglenifty were playing at the Hogmanay celebrations in Princes Street Gardens in Edinburgh in front of an audience of 250,000, before supporting Capercaillie at Glasgow's Celtic Connections Festival. They have also toured widely internationally, including performances in Poland, Spain and Kuala Lumpur. UK festival appearances included sets at the Bracknell, Sidmouth and WOMAD Festivals. These were universally well-received, despite the fact that the band's influences are much wider than the average Celtic revivalists, including mentions for Captain Beefheart, the Fall and modern ambient/techno artists (they have also released club remixes of some of their material). This had led to some amusing self-descriptions of their sound - including 'hypnofolkadelia' and 'acid croft'. Their debut album, *Venus In Tweeds*, which featured all originals bar one track, won BBC Radio Scotland's Best Folk Album Of The Year category. Grant also appeared as a musician in the movie *Rob Roy*, as the band returned to the studio to record *A Whisky Kiss*. That album managed to put the band on the map (as far as mainstream critics were concerned) and broadened their following beyond folk music circles. With *A Whisky Kiss*, Shooglenifty demonstrated that they are one of the most refreshing and uplifting roots bands of the 90s. Additionally their records should be prescribed by general practitioners as a drug-free cure for all forms of depression.

● ALBUMS: *Venus In Tweeds* (Greentrax 1995)★★★, *A Whisky Kiss* (Greentrax 1996)★★★★.

Sick Of It All

Sick Of It All are long-standing members of the infamous hardcore community bred in New York City, New York, USA, in the late 80s. Even in a genre noted for its uncompromising aggression, they earned both rave notices and suspicion for what many perceived as the sheer hatefulness of their songwriting. Despite the criticism, they continue to stand by the ethos of their theme song, 'We Stand Alone'. They were also committed to the popular US abstention movement dubbed 'straight edge' (no drugs, cigarettes or alcohol). The band was formed by brothers Lou (vocals) and Pete Kola (guitar), who released their 1989 debut album with Arman Majidi (drums, from New York hardcore band, Rest In Pieces) and Rich Cipriano (bass). This featured a spoken-word introduction by rapper KRS-One and punishing, primal punk rock music. Recorded with a new bass player and drummer, *We Stand Alone* featured one side of studio recordings and one live, including a cover version of Minor

Threat's 'Betray' (interesting not least because Minor Threat had popularized the straight edge phenomenon). The original line-up was reunited for 1992's self-produced *Just Look Around*. In 1994, the band were snapped up by a major label, Atlantic Records, with Craig Setari (later known as Craig Ahead) introduced as the new bass player. A single lifted from their debut for the label included another tell-tale choice of cover version, Sham 69's 'Borstal Breakout'. In 1995, they contributed a track, 'Just A Patsy', to an album pieced together by Corrosion Of Conformity's Reed Mullin dedicated to ending the imprisonment of Native American Leonard Peltier. They were also the victims of a concerted attack by baseball bat-wielding thugs while on tour in Manchester, England, allegedly orchestrated by bootleg T-shirt vendors. The band returned to their indie roots in 1998, signing up to No FX main man Fat Mike's Fat Wreck Chords' label.

● ALBUMS: *Blood, Sweat, And No Tears* (In-Effect 1989)★★★, *We Stand Alone* mini-album (In-Effect 1991)★★, *Just Look Around* (Relativity 1992)★★★, *Scratch The Surface* (East West 1994)★★★, *Live In A World Full Of Hate* (Lost & Found 1995)★★★, *Built To Last* (Elektra 1997)★★★, *Call To Arms* (Fat Wreck Chords 1998)★★★.

● COMPILATIONS: *Spreading The Hardcore Reality* (Lost & Found 1995)★★, *Sick Of It All* (Revelation 1997)★★★.

Sierra Maestra

Contemporary Cuban son and salsa band Sierra Maestra take their name from the mountain range to the east of the island. They formed in 1976 to play traditional son music, using the historic instrumental line-up of tres, trumpet, bongo and claves which had been all but forsaken by new generations. Playing acoustically, they depend on potent harmonies and punchy rhythms to win over audiences, which have grown consistently since their inception. They are led by founder member Juan de Marcos González, musical director and tres player, supervising a circle of friends who had grown up together before studying music. Their early repertoire was 'trova' or protest music. However, González's father, an original sonero or son player, suggested they play in the old style but maintain their modern clothing and appearance so as to appeal to the country's youth. His suggestion was adopted, beginning with concerts at various university locations. In 1978, they entered a television competition entitled *Todo El Mundo Canta* (Everybody Sings) and won. As a result they recorded their debut single in 1980, a traditional song updated as 'Sierra Maestra Ilego Con El Guanajo Rellenon', which achieved platinum sales. That set the pattern for future releases, with the members updating traditional arrangements but also writing original material or heavily adapting the originals: 'We've never wanted to be fashionable, we prefer to be established and respected. We stick to the canons of traditional son. For us, it's the essence of Cuban dance music - we want it to be a living thing, played by living artists.' Rather than incorporate the barrio slang of contemporary groups such as NG La Banda, the group stick to tried and tested subject matter, occasionally tackling an issue such as racism. This has made them easily digestible in polite society where they are very popular, but they have failed to attract the youth following associated with NG. Nevertheless they are musically peerless, prompting one *Folk Roots* reviewer to note of their 1994 album for World Circuit Records: '(they) have produced an album of such distinction it'll be immediately accepted as a modern classic. Erotic and emotional in the same moment - the tender vibrato in the voices knocks your knees away.' Trumpet-player Jesús Alemañy left the group to form ¡Cubanismo! in 1995.

● ALBUMS: *Son Highlights From Cuba* (Wergo 1992)★★★, *¡Dudndunbanza!* (World Circuit 1994)★★★★, *Tibiri Tabara* (World Circuit 1997)★★★.

Silk, Garnett

b. Garnett Smith, Manchester, Jamaica, West Indies, d. 9 December 1994, Mandeville, Jamaica, West Indies. Silk began his career in music at the age of 12 as a DJ under the name Little Bimbo. He spent his early years on sound systems such as Destiny Outernational, Pepper's Disco, Stereophonic and Soul Remembrance. His first recording, 'Problem Everywhere' for Delroy 'Callo' Collins, followed in 1987. He moved to Kingston in 1988 and recorded one song for Sugar Minott's Youth Promotion label, 'No Disrespect'. He recorded sessions with King Tubby, King Jammy's and Penthouse Records before signing a two-year contract with Steely And Clevie. He recorded an album's worth of material with them but only 'We Could Be Together', a duet with Chevelle Franklin, was released. He returned to the country parish where he was raised and concentrated on songwriting, collaborating with his childhood friend Anthony Rochester. He was introduced to Courtney Cole by Tony Rebel. Cole owned Roof International studio, based in Ocho Rios, and many of Silk's hits were cut here. 'I Can See Clearly Now', a duet with dub poet Yasus Afari, and 'Seven Spanish Angels' were among the most popular. During 1992 he recorded material for Bobby Digital who produced his debut set *It's Growing*, released at the end of the year. The album was declared a masterpiece of roots music and showed an original and profound lyricist. Comparisons were made with Bob Marley, owing to his emphasis on cultural themes ('I Am Vexed', 'The Rod' and the title song) and a vocal style that gave his music a quasi-religious atmosphere. Signed to Atlantic Records in mid-1993, he saw many of his past recordings reissued or released for the first time. These included tracks for Roof, Steely And Clevie, Danny Browne, Black Scorpio, Phillip Smart, Top Rank, Jahmento, Star Trail (for whom 'Hello Africa' reached number 1 on the UK reggae charts), and Sly And Robbie. In 1994, Garnett took a six-month break from recording but this did not affect his popularity, and he even developed an international following which was boosted by shining performances at 1994's Sunsplash and Sunfest festivals. He also signed to a major US label. Considering the pacifist themes of some of his lyrics, it is somewhat ironic that a gun was involved in his death. According to some of the Jamaican media, he had borrowed two guns from his lawyer, following a burglary at his home. Someone was showing Silk how to use one of the guns when it went off. The bullet hit a gas tank and the resulting explosion killed Silk and his mother, and severely burned two of his brothers.

● ALBUMS: *It's Growing* (Blue Mountain/VP 1992)★★★, *Gold* (Charm 1993)★★★, *100% Silk* (VP 1993)★★★, *In A Dancehall Conference* (Heartbeat 1994)★★★, *Love Is The Answer* (VP 1994)★★★, *Lord Watch Over Our Shoulders* (VP 1995)★★★, *Nothing Can Divide Us* (VP 1995)★★★, *Silky Mood* (VP 1995)★★★, *Journey* (VP 1998)★★★.

● COMPILATIONS: *Reggae Max* (1995)★★★

Silkk The Shocker

b. Vyshonne Miller, Louisiana, New Orleans, USA. Miller, recording as Silkk The Shocker, is arguably the most popular rapper on the hugely successful No Limit Records, the underground hip-hop label founded by his brother Master P. Miller began rapping as a teenager and was a member of several gangsta crews, including the Down South Hustlers. Originally known as Silk (without the additional k), he was a member of Tru alongside Master P and his other brother C-Murder. In keeping with No Limit's highly nepotistic approach to record promotion, he appeared as a guest rapper on label compilations and albums by several other No Limit artists. He released his debut set, *The Shocker*, in 1996, and soon afterwards adopted The Shocker as his given moniker. Like most other No Limit releases the album became a big underground hit, although there was nothing groundbreaking or remotely original about its clichéd gangsta rap. However, Silkk was easily the most marketable of No Limit's artists, with his imposing physique and youthful good looks. In 1997, he appeared on numerous No Limit releases, including the soundtrack for *I'm Bout It*, Tru's *Tru 2 Da Game*, Mia X's *Unlady Like*, Mystikal's *Unpredictable* and Master P's breakthrough chart-topper, *Ghetto D*. Silkk's sophomore effort, *Charge It 2 Da Game*, consolidated No Limit's commercial status. The album debuted at US number 3 in March 1998, while Silkk's duet with R&B singer Mya on 'Movin' On' became a big radio hit. *Made Man* was his most accomplished set to date, and debuted at US number 1 in February 1999. It quickly went platinum like its predecessor.

● ALBUMS: *The Shocker* (No Limit 1996)★★, *Charge It 2 Da Game* (No Limit 1998)★★★, *Made Man* (No Limit 1999)★★★.

● FILMS: *Hot Boyz* (1999), *Corrupt* (1999).

Silver Jews

Silver Jews started off as essentially a vehicle for poet David Berman (b. Virginia, USA), with the backing of co-writers Steve Malkmus and Bob Nastanovich from Pavement. The trio had first played together while studying at the University Of Virginia. The lo-fi ambience of two EPS, *Dime Map Of The Reef* (1990) and *The Arizona Record* (1992), preceded the band's debut long-player, *Starlite Walker*. This was a more fully realized recording which attracted admiring glances throughout the underground community for it's experimental mixture of angular pop and acoustic balladry, garnering comparisons to the Palace Brothers and Violent Femmes despite its billing as a concept album. Fans of Pavement's askew narratives would certainly not be disappointed with the track selection - ranging from improvisational pieces such as 'The Moon Is The Number 18' to charming, anecdotal dioramas 'Advice To The Graduate' and 'Trains Across The Sea'. Berman chose not to record with Malkmus and Nastanovich on the follow-up, 1996's *The Natural Bridge*. He proved his point with this remarkably confident and mature set, which earned critical accolades across the board. Malkmus returned to add lead guitar to Berman's most fully-realized album to date, 1998's *American Water*, with stand-out tracks 'We Are Real' and 'People' encapsulating Berman's sardonic world view.

● ALBUMS: *Starlite Walker* (Drag City/Domino 1994)★★★, *The Natural Bridge* (Drag City/Domino 1996)★★★, *American Water* (Drag City/Domino 1998)★★★★.

Silver Sun

Formed in London, England, in the mid-90s, Silver Sun (then titled merely Sun) numbered among a phalanx of young power pop bands signed by Polydor Records in the aftermath of Cast and Shed Seven's chart breakthrough. The band comprises James Broad (guitar/vocals), Richard Kane (bass), Paul Smith (guitar), Richard Sayce (drums). Their sound blends an aggressive melodic attack with tightly-wound harmonies, with an added 'wacky' strain along the lines of American bands such as Weezer. After their initial demo tape failed to generate interest, they were signed by Polydor A&R executive Paul Adam on the basis of their second tape. The song that convinced him to invest in the band was 'Lava', which was eventually released as their second single. Their debut came with the July 1996 EP *There Will Never Be Another Me*. This showcased songwriter, singer and guitarist James Broad's penchant for guitar-pop noise. Their debut EP was accompanied by a tour in support of Whipping Boy and Strangelove. The band changed their name to Silver Sun in Autumn 1996 and their debut album was released the following May. They reached number 20 in June 1998 with the *Too Much, Too Little, Too Late* EP, which featured four cover versions, including the Johnny Mathis and Deniece Williams title track. *Neo Wave* followed shortly afterwards. Sayce left the band in February 1999.

● ALBUMS: *Silver Sun* (Polydor 1997)★★★, *Neo Wave* (Polydor 1998)★★★.

Silverchair

When Australian rock trio Silverchair arrived in Europe in 1995, their press coverage concentrated firmly on the fact that each member was just 15 years old. However, Chris Joannou (b. 1979; bass), Daniel Johns (b. 1979; vocals/guitar) and Ben Gillies (b. 1979; drums) seemed quite capable of producing a noise in the best adult traditions of their primary influences, Pearl Jam and Nirvana. They actually formed in 1992 as Innocent Criminals. Covers of material by Led Zeppelin, Kiss and Deep Purple soon evolved into a set of original songs. A few hesitant concerts later they entered and won a national Talent Quest contest, which allowed them to record a more polished demo and a promotional video. The single they chose to record, 'Tomorrow', was released by Sony Records and quickly became a national number 1. When Hole and Ministry toured Australasia, Silverchair were booked as support, further bolstering their reputation. Johns' lyrics were a naive trawl through social dilemmas informed by their author's viewing of documentaries on the SBS channel. Despite this, *frogstomp* quickly achieved double platinum status in Australia, and even hardened critics found it difficult to completely ignore the band's enthusiasm. In the USA, where the album sold over two million, they were often thought to be another band from Seattle. Their Kurt Cobain-influenced lyrics of negativity and death were cited during a 1996 murder trial as two teenagers were accused of a family murder. Tracks from *frogstomp* were quoted during the trial. In an unlikely development, the band collaborated with classical pianist David Hefgott on a track called 'Emotion Sickness', taken from 1999's *Neon Ballroom*.

● ALBUMS: *frogstomp* (Murmur/Epic 1995)★★★, *Freak Show* (Epic 1997)★★★★, *Neon Ballroom* (Columbia 1999)★★★.

● FURTHER READING: *Silverchair*, Matthew Reid

Simply Red

This soul-influenced UK band revolves around the central figure of vocalist Mick Hucknall (b. 8 June 1960, Denton, Greater Manchester, England). Hucknall's first musical outing was with the punk-inspired Frantic Elevators, who recorded a handful of singles, including the impressive ballad, 'Holding Back The Years'. When they split up in 1983, the vocalist formed Simply Red with a fluid line-up that included Ojo, Mog, Dave Fryman and Eddie Sherwood. After signing to Elektra Records the band had a more settled line-up featuring Hucknall, Tony Bowers (bass), Fritz McIntyre (b. 2 September 1958; keyboards), Tim Kellett (brass), Sylvan Richardson (guitar) and Chris Joyce (drums). Their debut *Picture Book* climbed to number 2 in the UK charts, while their enticing cover version of the Valentine Brothers' 'Money's Too Tight To Mention' was a Top 20 hit. Although the band registered a lowly number 66 with the follow-up 'Come To My Aid', they rediscovered the hit formula with a sterling re-recording of the minor classic 'Holding Back The Years', which peaked at UK number 2. The song went on to top the US charts, ushering in a period of international success. Their next album, *Men And Women*, included collaborations between Hucknall and former Motown Records composer Lamont Dozier. Further hits followed with 'The Right Thing', 'Infidelity' and a reworking of the Cole Porter standard, 'Ev'ry Time We Say Goodbye'. Having twice reached number 2 in the album charts, Simply Red finally scaled the summit in 1989 with the accomplished *A New Flame*. The album coincided with another hit, 'It's Only Love', which was followed by a splendid reworking of Harold Melvin And The Blue Notes' 'If You Don't Know Me By Now', which climbed to number 2 in the UK and topped the US chart. Since then, Simply Red (now effectively Hucknall and various backing musicians) have consolidated their position as one of the most accomplished blue-eyed soul outfits to emerge from the UK in recent years. The 1991 album *Stars* pursued hip-hop-inspired rhythms, alongside their usual soul style. It topped the UK charts over a period of months, outselling much-hyped efforts by Michael Jackson, U2, Dire Straits and Guns N'Roses. The follow-up *Life* was also a bestseller, although it showed little sign of creative development. The album did feature the wonderful 'Fairground', however, which provided Hucknall with his first ever UK chart-topping single. The band returned to the charts in 1996 and 1997 with cover versions of Aretha Franklin's 'Angel' and Gregory Isaacs' 'Night Nurse'. Their fifth consecutive UK number 1 album, *Blue*, featured several other covers (including two takes of the Hollies' 'The Air That I Breathe') and marked a return to the smooth soul style of *A New Flame*. The disappointing *Love And The Russian Winter*, which was pilloried in the press, also broke the band's run of UK chart-toppers.

● ALBUMS: *Picture Book* (Elektra 1985)★★★★, *Men And Women* (Warners 1987)★★, *A New Flame* (Warners 1989)★★★, *Stars* (East West 1991)★★★★, *Life* (East West 1995)★★★, *Blue* (East West 1998)★★★, *Love And The Russian Winter* (East West 1999)★★.

● COMPILATIONS: *Greatest Hits* (East West 1996)★★★.

● VIDEOS: *Greatest Video Hits* (Warner Music Vision 1996), *Simply Red: Live At The Lyceum* (Warner Music Vision 1998).

● FURTHER READING: *Simply Mick: Mick Hucknall Of Simply Red. The Inside Story*, Robin McGibbon and Rob McGibbon. *The First Fully Illustrated Biography*, Mark Hodkinson

Singh, Talvin

b. 1970, London, England. Talvin Singh is one of the first artists to help bring traditional Indian tabla music to the mainstream, combining it with the rhythmic surges of drum 'n' bass. By 1997, he was able to speak in an assured fashion about the historic place and function of traditional Indian music: 'This has been happening for 15 years. But there's a different agenda for us now than saying, "Let's cash in on the Asian sound for the Western scene." It's about bringing music to people's attention which they've probably never heard before.' Head of the Omni Records label, based in south London, Singh is a virtuoso tabla player and an accomplished composer and arranger. As a child he travelled to India's Punjab region to study percussion with his uncle and grandfather, before becoming immersed in the acid house scene in the late '80s. The arrival of ambient and drum 'n' bass music in the early '90s inspired Singh to begin producing material, and in 1996 he released the ultra-rare *Calcutta Cyber Cafe* disc. By his early 20s Singh was also a veteran of recording sessions with Björk, Sun Ra and Future Sound Of London. Through projects such as the compilation album *Anokha: Soundz Of The Asian Underground*, he helped establish other Asian artists, including Osmani Soundz, Amar and Milky Bar Kid, and defined the vibrant Asian club scene. Anokha, meaning 'unique' in Urdu, is the weekly club night Singh hosts at the Blue Note club in London's East End. Both the club and his recording projects reflect an interest in the sounds and styles of Britain as well as affection for the Indian musical tradition. As he told *Rolling Stone* magazine: 'I love Indian culture, and I love my music, but we now live on a planet which is very small. It's a mixed culture, mixed vibes. You just have to study and respect certain traditions, then bring your character across in what you do.' Before launching his solo career in 1997, Singh found time to produce a percussion-based album, *One World, One Drum*, and appeared on Björk's world tour. His major label debut was an adventurous and vibrant work that fulfilled Singh's vow to challenge and re-define traditional musical categories. He was rewarded the following September when the album won the Mercury Music Prize.

● ALBUMS: *OK* (Island/Omni 1998)★★★.

● COMPILATIONS: *Talvin Singh Presents Anokha: Soundz Of The Asian Underground* (Mango 1997)★★★★.

Sixpence None The Richer

This band's melodic indie pop shot into the mainstream on the back of 1999's bestselling single 'Kiss Me'. The band, whose name was inspired by a passage of text in C.S. Lewis' *Mere Christianity*, was founded by vocalist Leigh Nash (b. Leigh Bingham, New Braunfels, Texas, USA) and guitarist and songwriter Matt Slocum (b. New Braunfels, Texas, USA). Bingham and Slocum first met at a church meeting in their native New Braunfels in the late 80s. They formed Sixpence None The Richer, although Slocum continued to play guitar with another Texas-based band, Love Coma. The duo recorded a four-track demo with bass player T.J. Behling, which led to a deal with REX Music. Their debut, *The Fatherless And The Widow*, was recorded with the help of Behling and Love Coma drummer Chris Dodds, and drew acclaim for Slocum's highly literate, quasi-religious lyrics and Bingham's expressive vocals. The following year the band toured extensively throughout Europe and America

with new drummer Dale Baker and rhythm guitarist Tess Wiley (ex-Nothing In Return), including a prestigious opening slot for 10,000 Maniacs. Bass player J.J. Plasencio joined in 1995 to help record *This Beautiful Mess* and the EP *Tickets For A Prayer Wheel*. A move to Nashville followed, although the collapse of REX Music and the departure of Wiley and Plasencio delayed sessions for a new album. Leigh Bingham became Leigh Nash after marrying in May 1996. Nash, Slocum and Baker eventually found a home on producer Steve Taylor's Squint Entertainment label, releasing their self-titled third album in November 1997. A version featuring three new mixes by Bob Clearmountain was released the following February. Bass player Justin Cary and guitarist Sean Kelly were added to the line-up for live shows, which included appearances with the Wallflowers and Abra Moore. Their major breakthrough came when 'Kiss Me' started being heavily rotated on national radio and television, and was promoted as the featured single from the movie *She's All That*. As a result 'Kiss Me' climbed steadily up the national charts, eventually reaching number 2 in May 1999. The song also reached UK number 4 later in the month. An anaemic cover version of the La's 'There She Goes' was released as the second single. The album also included two ambitious song suites and 'Puedo Escribir', a musical interpretation of poet Pablo Neruda's 'Tonight I Can Write ...'

● ALBUMS: *The Fatherless And The Widow* (REX 1993)★★★★, *This Beautiful Mess* (REX 1995)★★★, *Sixpence None The Richer* (Squint 1997)★★★.

● COMPILATIONS: *Collage: Portrait Of Their Best* (Flying Tart 1999)★★★.

16 Horsepower

Denver, Colarado, USA-based trio whose brooding, god-fearingly religious songs are reminiscent of the gothic tones of Nick Cave and Gun Club. Vocalist and lyricist David Eugene Edwards sings his tales of sin and redemption against a stripped down but powerful acoustic backdrop. The grandson of a travelling Nazarene preacher and a committed Christian, Edwards grew up listening to Old Testament tales of damnation and hellfire, and formed 16 Horsepower in 1992 to explore his fascination with these religious demons. He had previously played with the Denver Gentlemen, before a chance meeting with Jean Yves Tola, drummer with exiled French alternative rockers Passion Fodder, and his bandmate Pascal Humbert, led to the birth of 16 Horsepower. Briefly based in Los Angeles, California, Humbert left the band when Edwards and Tola returned to Denver, and was replaced by double bass player Keven Soll. The *Haw* EP was released in November 1995, the title track a doom-laden blues characteristic of Edwards' apocalyptic obsessions. The acclaimed debut *Sackcloth 'N' Ashes* was originally released in America in February 1996. The album featured the fiddle-playing of Edwards' soulmate, Gordon Gano of the Violent Femmes, which, alongside the band's deliberately old-fashioned instrumentation (bandonion, banjos, double bass, accordions), reinforced the archaic nature of Edwards' lyrics. The album was released in the UK in 1997 with 'Haw' added to the track listing, as the band toured their powerful live show around Europe and America. A new line-up was announced, with the return of Humbert on bass and Jeffrey Paul Norlander (ex-Denver Gentlemen) on guitar and fiddle. Their follow-up album was produced by John Parish (PJ Harvey collaborator), with tracks of the calibre of 'Brimstone Rock' and 'For Heaven's Sake' providing further testament to Edwards' powerful vision.

● ALBUMS: *Sackcloth 'N' Ashes* (A&M 1996)★★★, *Low Estate* (A&M 1997)★★★★.

60 Foot Dolls

This primal mid-90s UK rock trio comprises Carl Bevan (drums) and songwriters Richard Parfitt (vocals/guitar) and Mike Cole (vocals/bass). The latter pair spent 10 years on income support in Newport, Gwent, Wales, before starting the band in 1993, using the time industriously by investing in a four-track tape recorder. Their first performance came at Newport's TJ's venue, preparing the ground for a number of local bands, many later documented on the *I Was A Teenage Gwent Boy* compilation album, which quickly became a focal point for a resurgence of interest in Welsh rock. After supporting Oasis, Elastica and Dinosaur Jr they released their debut single, 'Happy Shopper', on their manager's Townhill Records label. After their subsequent appearance at 1994's In The City festival they were signed to Rough Trade Records (Geffen Records in the USA). In January 1995 they joined several others on the *New Musical Express*' Brat Bus tour, before a second single, the double a-side 'White Knuckle Ride'/'No.1 Pure Alcohol'. This was completed just before Rough Trade again entered a cycle of financial problems, leading to a move to Indolent Records. Their first single for their new label was 'Stay', released in January 1996, shortly after completing a nationwide UK tour with labelmates Sleeper. 'Talk To Me' then brought the group to the UK Top 40, preceding the release of their debut album, *The Big 3*, which was produced by Pixies/Boo Radleys veteran Al Clay. The follow-up *Joya Magica* (translating as 'little jewel' in Spanish) revealed a quieter and more melodic side to the band.

● ALBUMS: *The Big 3* (Indolent 1996)★★★, *Joya Magica* (Indolent 1998)★★★.

Size, Roni

Reprazent, a Bristol, England drum 'n' bass collective, came to national prominence in 1997 when its founder and leader, Roni Size (b. England), was awarded that year's Mercury Prize. Much of the acclaim centred around Size's melding of the new with the old - the propulsive jungle beats accompanied by live drums and double bass. The band - Size (compositions/programming), DJ Krust, Onallee (vocals), MC Dynamite and rapper Bahmadia (a former protégé of Gang Starr) - came together on Bristol's highly fertile and disparate club scene. As a result, Reprazent's sleek, highly musical take on drum 'n' bass is equally informed by hip-hop, funk, soul and house. Size was expelled from school at the age of 16, and starting attending house parties run by Bristol mavericks the Wild Bunch (later Massive Attack). His future partner, Krust, enjoyed an early dalliance with fame as part of the Fresh 4, whose 'Wishing On A Star' reached the UK Top 10 in late 1989. Reprazent's debut album, *New Forms*, was released on Full Cycle Records, which Size runs in partnership with DJ Krust. Size was keen to describe the mélange of influences as intuitive: 'If Krust walks into the studio and his head is nodding, that's enough. I know I've got a result there. He doesn't need to touch a button or tell

us what he thinks, 'cos we already know what he's thinking.' In consolidation of their mainstream breakthrough (the most significant for jungle since Goldie's debut), Reprazent set out to become the summer sound of 1997 with a series of festival appearances (including Tribal Gathering). Subsequently, Size teamed up with DJ Die and Leonie Laws in Breakbeat Era.

● ALBUMS: *New Forms* (Full Cycle/Talkin' Loud 1997)★★★★.

Sizzla

b. Miguel Collins, Jamaica, West Indies. Sizzla served his musical apprenticeship on the Caveman Hi Fi sound system, and in 1995 he released his debut through Zagalou before joining the Firehouse crew. He released a number of singles in Jamaica, notably 'Judgement Morning', 'Lifes Road', 'Blaspheme' and a combination with Shadow Man, 'The Gun'. His achievements earned him a Rockers nomination for Best New Artist. Sizzla quickly established an uncompromising attitude to his songwriting, similar to artists such as Peter Tosh and Mutabaruka. Although he continued their legacy, Sizzla was also able to appeal to a younger audience, empathizing with the struggles and experiences of the Jamaican youth. In 1996, as part of the Firehouse crew, he toured the globe alongside Luciano and Mikey General. In the middle of his hectic touring schedule, Sizzla recorded 'Ins And Outs' with Louie Culture, and 'Love Amongst My Brethren', 'No Other Like Jah' and 'Did You Ever', produced by Philip 'Fatis' Burrell. In 1997, Sizzla began working with Bobby Digital; the recording sessions featured Sly Dunbar, Robbie Shakespeare and Dean Fraser, whose saxophone graced the hit 'Black Woman And Child', a song that has since become an anthem. It subsequently featured as the title track of Sizzla's first album with Bobby Digital. He maintained a high profile in the singles market, releasing 'Like Mountain', 'Babylon A Listen' and a combination with Luciano, 'Build A Better World'. Sizzla has rightly been hailed as an integral part of the 90s cultural revolution, particularly with the enlightening albums *Black Woman And Child* and *Be I Strong*. Sizzla sported controversy when he made public endorsements at the 1998 Reggae Sumfest Festival in Montego Bay. During his performance he agitated his audience, and in particular the world press, after denouncing Queen Elizabeth II, homosexuals, and even the Sumfest Festival. He saved his most controversial racist diatribe for the finale when he stated, 'Burn all white people in Jamaica'. This led to a stunned silence from the multi-racial crowd. His attempts to win approval failed, which resulted in a talented performer being regarded as an embarrassment to Jamaican music.

● ALBUMS: *Burning Up* (RAS 1995)★★★, *Praise Ye Jah* (Xterminator 1997)★★★★, *Black Woman And Child* (Greensleeves 1997)★★★★, *Kalonji* (Xterminator/Jet Star 1998)★★★, with Anthony B. *2 Strong* (Star Trail 1999)★★★★, *Royal Son Of Ethiopia* (Greensleeves 1999)★★★, *Good Ways* (Jet Star 1999)★★★, *Be I Strong* (Xterminator 1999)★★★★.

● COMPILATIONS: *Reggae Max* (Jet Star 1998)★★★.

Skid Row

Skid Row were formed in New Jersey, USA, in 1986 by Dave 'The Snake' Sabo (b. 16 September 1964; guitar) and Rachel Bolan (b. 9 February 1964; bass). Sebastian 'Bach' Bierk (b. 3 April 1968, Freeport, Bahamas; vocals, ex-Madam X), Scott

Hill (b. 31 May 1964; guitar) and Rob Affuso (b. I March 1963; drums) completed the line-up. Influenced by Kiss, Sex Pistols, Ratt and Mötley Crüe, the band's rise to fame was remarkably rapid. The break came when they were picked up by Bon Jovi's management (Sabo was an old friend of Jon Bon Jovi) and offered the support slot on their US stadium tour of 1989. Bach's wild and provocative stage antics established the band's live reputation. Signed to Atlantic Records, they released their self-titled debut album to widespread critical acclaim the same year. It peaked at number 6 on the *Billboard* album chart and spawned two US Top 10 singles with '18 And Life' and 'I Remember You'. *Slave To The Grind* surpassed all expectations, debuting at number 1 in the US charts. Their commercial approach had been transformed into an abrasive and uncompromising barrage of metallic rock 'n' roll, delivered with punk-like arrogance. Afterwards, however, progress was halted by squabbling that broke the band apart following 1994's desultory *Subhuman Race*.

● ALBUMS: *Skid Row* (Atlantic 1989)★★, *Slave To The Grind* (Atlantic 1991)★★★, *B-Side Ourselves* mini-album (Atlantic 1992)★★, *Subhuman Race* (Atlantic 1994)★★.

● COMPILATIONS: *40 Seasons: The Best Of Skid Row* (Atlantic 1998)★★★.

● VIDEOS: *Oh Say Can You Scream?* (Atlantic 1991), *No Frills Video* (Atlantic 1993), *Roadkill* (Atlantic 1993).

Skint Records

This label was set up as a subsidiary of Loaded Records in 1995 by Damian Harris (aka Midfield General) and played an important role in the development of the sound known as big beat. Skint emerged from a scene in Brighton based around the 'Big Beat Boutique', from which the movement took its name, where Fatboy Slim was a resident DJ. Their first release was Fatboy Slim's 'Santa Cruz' in 1995, which was followed by a series of singles including Hip Optimist's 'Anafey' and Midfield General's 'Worlds/Bung'. The next year their compilation album, *Brassic Beats Volume One* (1996), featured tracks by these artists and others, notably Bentley Rhythm Ace, Cut Le Roc, Leuroj and Req. The label has since achieved widespread success and recognition, notably through Fatboy Slim hits such as 'Everybody Needs A 303', 'Gangster Trippin'', and 'Praise You', and the hugely popular albums *Better Living Through Chemistry* and *You've Come A Long Way, Baby*. They also enjoyed success with Bentley Rhythm Ace's 1997 debut, as well as the second and third volumes of the *Brassic Beats* series (released in 1997 and 1998, respectively). Subsequent album releases include the Lo-Fidelity Allstars' *How To Operate With A Blown Mind* (1998) and Req's *One* (1997) and *Frequency Jams* (1998). Although there is a notable difference between many of their acts, much of Skint's music is characterized by funky breakbeats and catchy riffs, and blends rock instrumentation with the sounds and approach of dance music. At the same time it often has a rough edge and purveys a sense of kitsch, reflecting the label's light-hearted attitude and willingness not to take themselves too seriously. In January 1998, after approaches from a number of major labels, Harris signed a contract with Sony Records that allowed to him to remain in control of Skint's output.

● COMPILATIONS: *Brassic Beats Volume 1* (Skint 1996)★★★, *Brassic Beats Volume 2* (Skint 1997)★★★, *Brassic Beats Volume 3* (Skint 1998)★★★

Skunk Anansie

This London, England-based quartet, formed in 1994, are led by the stunning singer Skin (b. Deborah Dyer, Brixton, London, England). After attending a furniture design course at Teeside Polytechnic in Middlesborough, she returned to the capital and started meeting musicians on the local circuit. Her original band was shelved for being too 'rockist', but she retained the services of bass player Richard 'Cass' Lewis and in January 1994 began rehearsing with Skunk Anansie, alongside guitarist Martin 'Ace' Kent and drummer Robbie French. After signing to One Little Indian Records they released their debut single, 'Little Baby Swastikkka', available only through mail order from BBC Radio 1's *Evening Session* programme. March 1995's controversial 'Selling Jesus' single was followed by work on labelmate Björk's 'Army Of Me' single. The band's debut album contained the predicted brew of agit prop and funk metal, while Skin's lyrics remained forceful, but over the course of a full album, it was clear that there was a lack of development in style and in terms of the issue-led subject matter. The singles 'I Can Dream' and 'Charity' skirted the fringes of the UK Top 40 in June and September respectively. The band toured with Therapy? and Senser and as part of the *New Musical Express*' Bratbus coalition, and appeared on the first edition of Channel 4's *The White Room* television programme. Featuring new drummer Mark Richardson (ex-Little Angels), *Stoosh* was a harder-edged collection, characterized by metal-edged guitar and Skin spitting out her lyrics. Controversial lyrics can sometimes sound deliberately contrived, but on this collection, Skin sounded as though she meant it. Her anger on the excellent opening track, 'Yes It's Fucking Political', was almost tangible. The band also reaped the rewards with four UK Top 30 singles in 1996, 'Weak' (number 20), a reissue of 'Charity' (number 20), 'All I Want' (number 14) and 'Twisted (Everyday Hurts)' (number 26). The band parted company with One Little Indian shortly afterwards, signing a worldwide deal with Virgin Records. *Post Orgasmic Chill* was premiered by the thunderous clatter of UK Top 20 single, 'Charlie Big Potato'.

● ALBUMS: *Paranoid And Sunburnt* (One Little Indian 1995)★★★, *Stoosh* (One Little Indian 1996)★★★★, *Post Orgasmic Chill* (Virgin 1999)★★★.

● FURTHER READING: *Skunk Anansie: Skin I'm In*, Steve Malins.

Sky Cries Mary

Though they are from Seattle, USA, Sky Cries Mary's sound has often been described as sponge, as opposed to grunge. Inspired by an Einsturzende Neubaten concert, Roderick Romero formed Grinder Crease with Ken Stringfellow and John Auer, before a deal with French label New Rose led to a name change. Their debut was an experimental industrial record, and included one of the band's most popular songs 'When The Fear Stops'. By 1990 Stringfellow and Auer had left to form the Posies, and Romero released the transitional *Don't Eat The Dirt* EP. His new band became infamous for their chaotic live shows, incorporating costumes and stage props. A compilation video featuring live footage was responsible for getting the band a deal with the World Domination label in 1992, but Romero had by then decided to end the band's industrial/experimental phase. The new line-up featured Romero's future wife Anisa on vocals, Todd Robbins aka DJ Fallout (ambient mix/turntables), Bennett

James (drums), Gordon Raphael (keyboards), Ivan Kral (guitar), Joseph E. Howard (bass/sitar/mellotron), this unit preferring a softer mantric approach, quite unlike their obvious Hendrixisms. With Marc Olsen replacing Kral on guitar, and new bass player Juano, the band released a creative and original debut. *A Return To The Inner Experience* contained mystic lyrics and tribal rhythms, together with interestingly different versions of Iggy Pop's 'We Will Fall' and the Rolling Stones' '2000 Light Years'. Recruiting Michael Cozzi (ex-Shriekback) on guitar, the band released the prog-rock orientated *This Timeless Turning* in 1994. Signing to Warner Brothers Records in 1995, the band's major label debut was an impressively diverse album that experimented with ambient and trance grooves.

● ALBUMS: *Until The Grinders Crease* (New Rose 1988)★★, *Return To The Inner Experience* (World Domination 1993)★★★, *This Timeless Turning* (World Domination 1994)★★★, *Moonbathing On Sleeping Leaves* (Warners 1996)★★★.

● COMPILATIONS: *Fresh Fruits For The Revolution* (World Domination 1998)★★★.

Slater, Luke

b. St. Albans, Hertfordshire, England. Turned on to music via early experiments with sounds and noises on his father's old reel-to-reel, rather than by any affinity to a particular musical subculture, Slater set about defining his vision during 1989 on the fledgling label Jelly Jam, an offshoot of the Brighton record shop of the same name where he was working at the time. A batch of Detroit-influenced tracks were spat out at an alarming rate, and a contract with D-Jax Records soon followed that saw Slater adopting the guise of Clementine. However, it was not until his link-up with Peacefrog Records in 1993, and another change of name to Planetary Assault Systems, that Slater's name became widely known and praised. He became heralded as the UK torchbearer for the Detroit techno sound, managing to capture the essence of that city's musical qualities, whether recording pounding, abrasive sounds as Planetary Assault Systems for Peacefrog, or alluding instead to classical textures as the 7th Plain for GPR. However, Slater's furious output during 1993/4 soon started to take its toll: 'I began to realise you can't do everything, I was beginning to lose focus on what I originally intended to do in the first place.' Taking time out from a hectic studio and DJing schedule, Slater returned in 1997, with *Freek Funk*, recorded in his home studio in Crawley, Sussex. With *Freek Funk*, Slater achieved what so many aspire to - a highly accomplished and highly variable album, unique and accessible, that pushed musical boundaries more than most. The follow-up *Wireless* experimented with electro and breakbeats to great effect.

● ALBUMS: *X-Tront - Volume 1* (Peacefrog 1993)★★★, *X-Tront - Volume 2* (Peacefrog 1993)★★★, as Morganistic *Fluids Amniotic* (Input Neuron Musique 1994)★★★★, as 7th Plain *Four Cornered Room* (GPR 1994)★★★★, as 7th Plain *My Yellow Wise Rug* (GPR 1994)★★★, *Freek Funk* (Novamute 1997)★★★★, *Wireless* (Mute 1999)★★★.

● COMPILATIONS: Planetary Assault Systems *Archives* (Peacefrog 1996)★★★★.

Sleater-Kinney

Potent feminist punk rock band Sleater-Kinney were formed in 1994 in Olympia, Washington, by Carrie Brownstein (b. 1975; guitar/vocals) and Corin Tucker (b. 1973; guitar/vocals). Tucker had previously played in the Heavens To Betsy, who only released one album but were an integral part of the radical feminist 'riot-grrrl' movement of the 90s. She met Brownstein while enquiring about the grass-roots feminist network in Olympia after a local show. Brownstein formed her own band, Excuse 17, before becoming Tucker's short-term lover and forming Sleater-Kinney (naming the band after a nearby road). Their edgy twin-guitar sound was, ironically, picked up by archetypal male rock critics Greil Marcus and Robert Christgau, bringing the band to the attention of an American music press still championing the 'riot-grrrl' movement. Having established themselves as an explosive live act, the band recorded two albums (with drummers Lora McFarlane and Toni Gogin) that explored the struggle of women to establish their identity in a male-dominated culture. They then gained a certain notoriety for a series of tempestuous performances in support of the Jon Spencer Blues Explosion. At one set in Portland, Brownstein kicked a microphone stand into the face of a persistent heckler, while at another performance Tucker issued the following, much-quoted agenda-setting remark: 'We just want to say that we're not here to fuck the band. We are the band.' The highly praised *Dig Me Out* was recorded with new drummer Janet Weiss. Maintaining the raw emotional range of its predecessor and the core duo's ferocious vocal style, these trademarks were now allied to greater musical complexity in a wholly engaging marriage of pop and punk. Less overtly preachy, the album was a highly personal expression of female desire and frustration that cemented the band's progress.

● ALBUMS: *Sleater-Kinney* (Kill Rock Stars 1995)★★★, *Call The Doctor* (Kill Rock Stars 1996)★★★, *Dig Me Out* (Kill Rock Stars 1997)★★★★, *The Hot Rock* (Matador 1999)★★★

Sleeper

The provocative sexual/politically incorrect statements of Louise Wener (b. 30 July 1966, Ilford, Essex, England; vocals/guitar) first launched Sleeper into the mainstream in 1994. Such was her 'rent-a-quote' status that it initially eclipsed the contribution of fellow members Jon Stewart (guitar), Andy McClure (drums) and Diid (pronounced Deed) Osman (b. Somalia, Africa; bass). The latter pair were recruited by the creative axis of Wener and Stewart, who had arrived in London from Manchester, where they had studied degrees in politics and had also gone out with one another. Their first gigs were played in October 1992, and they eventually signed to the new indie label Indolent Records the following year. Their debut EP, *Alice In Vain*, was recorded with Boo Radleys/My Bloody Valentine producer Anjeli Dutt. This set the band's agenda, Wener expressing her disenchantment with the austerity of feminism: 'Really women are as shitty and horrible and vindictive as men are.' Sleeper's musical perspective revealed urgent, stop-go punk pop close in construction to Elastica. February 1994 saw the release of *Swallow*, with a third EP, *Delicious*, following in May. 'Inbetweener' finally broke them into the UK Top 20 the following year when it climbed to number 16. Their debut album continued the fascination with matters anatomical; 'Swallow' and 'Delicious', which both reappeared, hardly required further exposition. Two further singles, 'Vegas' (number 33) and 'What Do I Do Now?' (number 14), also rose high in the UK charts, before extensive touring preceded sessions for a second album in autumn 1995, this time produced by Stephen Street. The band enjoyed three further UK Top 20 singles in 1996 with 'Sale Of The Century', 'Nice Guy Eddie' and 'Statuesque'. By now Wener had become a media star. In addition to her good looks, she was articulate and deliberately outspoken. Future success seemed assured as long as Wener stayed at the helm, but the critical backlash that greeted 'She's A Good Girl' and the disappointing third album *Pleased To Meet You* appeared to knock the singer off her stride. Dan Kaufman joined as replacement for Osman in October 1997, but by the following year the band had ceased working together.

● ALBUMS: *Smart* (Indolent 1995)★★★, *The It Girl* (Indolent 1996)★★★★, *Pleased To Meet You* (Indolent 1997)★★.

Slint

Formed in Louisville, Kentucky, USA, Slint comprised former members of local legends Squirrel Bait - Brian McMahan (vocals/guitar), Ethan Buckler (bass) and Britt Walford (drums) - plus David Pajo (guitar). Informed by a typically brutal Steve Albini production, the band's 1989 debut (later re-released on Touch & Go Records) featured loud guitar-playing and muted vocals, each track named after band members' parents and pets. The abrasive edge was toned down somewhat for 1991's *Spiderland*, which saw a number of changes. Buckler had left to form King Kong while producer Brian Paulson engendered a more sympathetic sound while maintaining the twin-guitar bite of the earlier recording. Rather than simple noise, *Spiderland* incorporated fully developed songwriting that made the album a popular item within the American alternative rock scene. However, afterwards progress stalled, and only one further desultory single was issued in 1994. By this time Walford and McMahan had joined the Palace Brothers.

● ALBUMS: *Tweez* (Jennifer Hartman 1989)★★★, *Spiderland* (Touch & Go 1991)★★★★.

Slipknot

This highly provocative, Des Moines, Iowa, USA-based alternative metal outfit, whose shock rock values are masked by their anonymous stage wear of matching jump suits and horror masks, was founded by Shawn Crahan (percussion) and Paul Grey (bass). The early line-up of Slipknot released the independently recorded and distributed *Mate. Feed. Kill. Repeat* in 1996. Although the band was struggling to make ends meet, their big break arrived when they were signed to leading metal label Roadrunner Records. The band, comprising nine members, subsequently adopted a lucky number to wear on their jump suits. Alongside Crahan (number 6) and Grey (number 2), was number 8 Corey Taylor (vocals), number 7 Mick Thompson (guitar), number 5 Craig Jones (samples), number 4 James Root (guitar), number 3 Chris Fehn (percussion), number 1 Joey Jordison (drums), and number 0 Sid Wilson (DJ). They recorded their self-titled second album at Indigo Ranch Studios in Los Angeles, California. The production work of Ross Robinson was a marked improvement on their messy debut, but failed to disguise the sub-Korn metal of tracks such as 'Eyeless' and 'Wait And Bleed'.

● ALBUMS: *Mate. Feed. Kill. Repeat* (Independent 1996)★★, *Slipknot* (Roadrunner 1999)★★.

Sloan

This Canadian alternative rock band originated at the Nova Scotia College Of Art in Halifax, where Andrew Scott (drums) and Chris Murphy (bass) linked with Patrick Pentland (b. Northern Ireland; guitar) and Jay Ferguson (guitar/vocals). Sloan developed their own sound from a mixture of hardcore and grunge influences, producing a guitar-fuelled battery of short, sharp songs, releasing 1992's *Peppermint* EP, recorded at a friend's house in Halifax, through their own Murderecords label. A lively performance at Canada's East Coast Music Conference brought the band to the attention of Geffen Records, who liked the EP and promptly signed Sloan. *Smeared* impressed reviewers and public alike, with the pop songwriting and vocal melodies counterpointed by Pentland's raw, aggressive guitar work. In spite of a low-key promotional approach, the record performed well as North American college radio picked up on 'Underwhelmed', which was released on a four-track EP. *Twice Removed* toned down the noise levels to positive effect, focusing attention on the band's melodic guitar pop, which rose to shimmering heights on 'Snowsuit Sound'. The band then broke up for a while and were dropped by their record company. The members reunited in 1996, issuing the sparkling power pop collection *One Chord To Another* locally on Murderecords. It was later released on EMI Records throughout the rest of the world, and established the band as one of the leading Canadian exports of the late 90s. Their reputation has been enhanced by two more collections of power pop gems, *Navy Blues* and *Between The Bridges*.

● ALBUMS: *Smeared* (DGC 1993)★★★, *Twice Removed* (DGC 1994)★★★★, *One Chord To Another* (Murderecords/Enclave 1996)★★★★, *Navy Blues* (Enclave 1998)★★★, *4 Nights At The Palais Royale* (Murderecords 1999)★★★, *Between The Bridges* (Murderecords 1999)★★★.

Slowdive

Thames Valley indie band formed in 1989 by Rachel Goswell (b. 16 May 1971, Hampshire, England; vocals/guitar), Neil Halstead (b. 7 October 1970, Luton, Bedfordshire, England; vocals/guitar), Brook Christian Savill (b. 6 December 1977, Bury, Lancashire, England; guitar), Nicholas Chaplin (b. 23 December 1970, Slough, Berkshire, England; bass) and Adrian Sell (drums), who departed after six months to go to university. His replacement was Neil Carter, who also played with local Reading band the Colour Mary, until Simon Scott (b. 3 March 1971, Cambridge, England) joined permanently, having drummed for the Charlottes. While this was happening, Slowdive were creating a dreamy sound that frequently escaped analysis, but the main ingredients were floating harmonies and ripples of guitar effects within a traditional three-minute pop framework. Signed by a revitalized Creation Records on the basis of one demo tape, Slowdive made a surprising number of friends with what seemed to be a blatantly esoteric sound; indeed, by the summer of 1991 they had reached number 52 in the UK charts with the *Holding Our Breath* EP. However, something of a press backlash ensued over the following two years, as the 'Thames Valley' scene and 'shoegazing', a name invoked to describe the motionless, effects pedal-driven dreamy pop of a welter of bands, fell from fashion. Contrary to expectations, Slowdive's second album, *Souvlaki*, was named after a Jerky Boys sketch in which a hotel receptionist is enrolled

in an imaginary *ménage à trois*. Despite this, and Brian Eno's production of three tracks, Slowdive remained widely perceived to be perennial Cocteau Twins apprentices. Scott was lost at the end of 1993 because 'he got into acid jazz'. *Pygmalion*, created at Halstead's home studio, saw the band move into ambient soundscapes, including two tracks ('I Believe' and 'Like Up') for an American art house movie. The band collapsed during 1995 after being dropped by Creation. Halstead and Goswell had reunited in Mojave 3 by the end of the year.
● ALBUMS: *Just For A Day* (Creation 1991)★★, *Souvlaki* (Creation 1993)★★★, *Pygmalion* (Creation 1995)★★★.

Smash Mouth

Formed in San Jose, California, USA, alternative rock band Smash Mouth first came to public prominence when 'Nervous In The Alley', a track from their first professionally produced demo tape, was played frequently during April 1996 on local rock station KOME. A support slot to No Doubt and Beck at the KOME music festival followed, along with press and record label interest. Despite their meteoric rise, all four members of the band had spent time in other ventures. Singer Steve Harwell came from the most unusual background, having previously led the House Of Pain-inspired hip-hop group F.O.S. (Freedom Of Speech). The other members are Greg Camp (guitar), Paul De Lisle (bass) and Kevin Coleman (drums). Smash Mouth were given a further boost by the success of 'Walkin' On The Sun', the first single to be extracted from 1997's *Fush Yu Mang*. It was originally designed as a drumming 'exercise track' for Coleman, until he persuaded the rest of the band of its melodic possibilities. In truth, this light-hearted pop ditty was wholly unrepresentative of the rest of the band's canon of acerbic punk songs. *Fush Yu Mang* also included a cover version of War's 'Why Can't We Be Friends?', and climbed to number 41 in the *Billboard* charts. The far more accessible follow-up, *Astro Lounge*, broke into the US Top 10, bolstered by the Top 5 success of the highly catchy 'All Star'.
● ALBUMS: *Fush Yu Mang* (Interscope 1997)★★★, *Astro Lounge* (Interscope 1999)★★★★.

Smashing Pumpkins

Once widely viewed as poor relations to Nirvana's major label alternative rock, Chicago, USA's Smashing Pumpkins, led by Billy Corgan (b. 17 March 1967, Chicago, Illinois, USA; vocals/guitar) have persevered to gradually increasing commercial acceptance and press veneration. Corgan's inspirations, the Beatles, Led Zeppelin, Doors and Black Sabbath, as well as a professional jazz musician father, add up to a powerful musical cocktail over which his lyrics, which frequently cross the threshold of normality and even sanity, float unsettlingly. The rest of the band comprised D'Arcy Wretzky (b. 1 May 1968, South Haven, Michigan, USA; bass), James Iha (b. 6 March 1968, Elk Grove, Illinois, USA; guitar) and Jimmy Chamberlain (b. 10 June 1964, Joliet, Illinois, USA; drums). Smashing Pumpkins made their official debut with a drum machine at the Avalon club in Chicago. Chamberlain was then drafted in from a 10-piece show band (JP And The Cats) to fill the percussion vacancy (Corgan had previously played in another local band, the Marked). The band made its recording debut in early 1990 with the release of 'I Am The One' on local label Limited Potential Records.

Previously they had included two tracks on a Chicago compilation, *Light Into Dark*. This brought the band to the attention of influential Seattle label Sub Pop Records, with whom they released 'Tristessa'/'La Dolly Vita' in September 1990, before moving to Caroline Records. *Gish*, produced by Butch Vig, announced the group to both indie and metal audiences, and went to number 1 on the influential Rockpool College Radio Chart. Ironically, given the Nirvana comparisons, this came before Vig had produced *Nevermind*. However, it was *Siamese Dream* that launched the band to centre stage with its twisted metaphors and skewed rhythms. A Top 10 success in the US *Billboard* charts, it saw them joined by mellotron, cello and violin accompaniment to give the sound extra depth. However, these remained secondary to the pop hooks and rock atmospherics that have defined the band's sound. *Mellon Collie And The Infinite Sadness* was a bold project (the double CD contained 28 songs), yet the band managed to pull it off. With swirling strings, angst-ridden vocals and some beautifully spiteful guitar the album was a major achievement artistically and commercially. Their touring keyboard player, Jonathan Melvoin (b. 6 December 1961, Los Angeles, California, USA, d. 12 July 1996; ex-Dickies) died of a heroin overdose in July 1996. At the same time the band sacked their drummer Chamberlain after his continuing drug abuse. His replacement was Matt Walker (ex-Filter), but he departed in late 1997 to form his own band. During frenetic preparations for the new Smashing Pumpkins album, Iha found time to release a surprisingly mellow solo set. *Adore* debuted at number 2 on the US *Billboard* album chart in June 1998. Wretzky left the band during recording sessions for the follow-up, and was replaced by Melissa Auf der Maur (bass, ex-Hole).
● ALBUMS: *Gish* (Caroline 1991)★★★, *Siamese Dream* (Virgin 1993)★★★★, *Mellon Collie And The Infinite Sadness* (Virgin 1995)★★★★, *Zero* (Hut 1996)★★, *Adore* (Hut 1998)★★★★, *Machina - The Machines Of God* (Hut 2000)★★★.
Solo: James Iha *Let It Come Down* (Hut 1998)★★★.
● COMPILATIONS: *Pisces Iscariot* (Virgin 1994)★★, *The Aeroplane Flies High* 5 CD-box set (Virgin 1996)★★★.
● VIDEOS: *Vieuphoria* (Virgin Music Video 1994).
● FURTHER READING: *Smashing Pumpkins*, Nick Wise.

Smith, Elliott

b. Dallas, Texas, USA. Raised in a musical family, acclaimed singer-songwriter Smith first recorded with Portland, Oregon-based alternative rockers Heatmiser. Despite achieving a modicum of success with this band's generic Fugazi-inspired hard rock, Smith felt happier recording acoustic material on his home four-track set-up. His solo career began after he mailed a tape to local independent label Cavity Search. His debut set, *Roman Candle*, appeared in 1994. The album introduced Smith's sparse folky style and introspective lyricism, redolent of the work of English singer Nick Drake. Later releases appeared on Californian independent label Kill Rock Stars, as Smith balanced his solo career with his continuing involvement in Heatmiser. By 1997's *Either/Or*, however, Heatmiser had split and Smith relocated to Brooklyn. His big break came about when cult film director and long-time fan Gus Van Sant used six of Smith's songs on the soundtrack to his acclaimed *Good Will Hunting*. The stand-out track 'Miss Misery' was nominated for an Oscar for Best Original Song, leading to the memorable sight of a dour Smith performing at March 1998's Academy Award ceremony. Smith had already taken the plunge earlier in the year and signed to the DreamWorks label. Any worries that a major label would choke his independent spirit and songwriting skills were dispelled when the superb *XO* was released in August. Produced (like *Either/Or*) by Tom Rothrock and Rob Schnapf of Bong Load, the album confirmed that Smith had developed into one of the finest songwriters of the 90s. His old albums were also re-released by Domino.

● ALBUMS: *Roman Candle* (Cavity Search 1994)★★★, *Elliott Smith* (Kill Rock Stars 1995)★★★, *Either/Or* (Kill Rock Stars 1997)★★★★, *XO* (DreamWorks 1998)★★★★.

● VIDEOS *Strange Parallel* (DreamWorks 1998).

Smith, Will

b. 25 September 1968, Philadelphia, Pennsylvania, USA. Rap music's most successful crossover artist, Smith started his career as one half of DJ Jazzy Jeff And The Fresh Prince. Although it was lightweight in comparison with the threatening 'street' style of Public Enemy and NWA, the duo's inoffensive, bubblegum rap made them a crossover success, with 1988's *He's The DJ, I'm The Rapper* going double-platinum and 'Parents Just Don't Understand' winning the duo a Grammy. Smith's inventive and charming rapping style brought him to the attention of NBC, who cast him in the starring role of *The Fresh Prince Of Bel-Air*. Smith shone as the streetwise tough suffering culture shock in affluent Beverly Hills, and the situation comedy went on to become one of the station's most successful series, running until 1996. Movie stardom beckoned, with Smith making his debut in 1992's *Where The Day Takes You*. He gained further acclaim for his role in 1993's *Six Degrees Of Separation*. The same year he released his final album with DJ Jazzy Jeff, topping the UK charts with 'Boom! Shake The Room'. A string of acting roles followed which pushed Smith into the superstar league, beginning with 1995's *Bad Boys* and culminating in *Independence Day* (1996) and *Men In Black* (1997), two of the most successful movies ever made. Smith also recorded under his own name for the first time, topping the US and UK charts with the infectious theme tune from *Men In Black*. He also found the time to release his solo debut, *Big Willie Style*, a smooth pop-rap production which featured 'Gettin' Jiggy Wit It', another catchy hit single which topped the US Hot 100 chart. The album took up a long residency at the top end of the US charts. Further hits followed in 1998 with 'Just The Two Of Us' (UK number 2/US number 20) and 'Miami' (UK number 3/US number 17). In July 1999, the theme tune from Smith's new movie *Wild Wild West*, based around Stevie Wonder's 'I Wish' and featuring vocal contributions from Dru Hill, topped the US charts. Released, predictably enough, at the end of the millennium, 'Will 2K' and *Willennium*, whose titles took some beating for sheer chutzpah, were also huge US and UK successes.

● ALBUMS: *Big Willie Style* (Columbia 1997)★★★, *Willennium* (Columbia 1999)★★★.

● VIDEOS: *The Will Smith Story* (MVP Home Video 1999), *The Will Smith Music Video Collection* (Sony 1999).

● FILMS: *Where The Day Takes You* (1992), *Six Degrees Of Separation* (1993), *Bad Boys* (1995), *Independence Day* (1996), *Men In Black* (1997), *Enemy Of The State* (1998), *Wild Wild West* (1999)

Smither, Chris

b. 11 November 1944, Miami, Florida, USA. Smither began his music career during the 60s, performing in the coffee houses and clubs of New Orleans, where he had lived from the age of two. His first real blues influence was a Lightnin' Hopkins recording, *Blues In My Bottle*, which he heard when he was 17. He moved to Boston, Massachusetts, in 1966, where he continued playing the lucrative coffee house/folk circuit, and began associating with artists such as Bonnie Raitt, John Hammond and Mississippi Fred MacDowell. After a promising start, with two albums on Poppy Records, the label folded. He recorded *Honeysuckle Dog* for United Artists Records, which featured Raitt, but this album was never released. He enjoyed greater success with cover versions of his songs by numerous performers, including Raitt, who included his 'Love Me Like A Man' and 'I Feel The Same' on two of her albums, and John Mayall, who recorded 'Mail Order Mystics'. He has performed at various times with many musicians including Nanci Griffith, Jackson Browne, Van Morrison, and also at numerous major festivals throughout the USA. Having fought off the demon alcohol, Smither faced the 90s as a survivor, fresh and enthusiastic towards his work. The live *Another Way To Find You* was recorded over two nights in a studio with an invited audience. *Happier Blue* shows the artist truly coming into his own. This excellent set included cover versions of Lowell George's 'Rock And Roll Doctor' and J.J. Cale's 'Magnolia', in addition to the original title track. The powerful lyric of the latter is but one example of his emotional talent: 'I was sad and then I loved you, it took my breath, now I think you love me and it scares me to death, cause now I lie awake and wonder, I worry I think about losing you, I don't care what you say, maybe I was happier blue'. Smither's smooth, lyrical guitar style encompasses elements of folk, blues, country and rock (Bonnie Raitt calls him 'her Eric Clapton'), and he plays in a fluid, busy style that is as breathtaking as it is effortless. His voice is another asset, capable of sounding soft one minute and gruff the next, with his floor-rumbling bass resonance perfectly demonstrated on an interpretation of Jesse Winchester's 'Thanks To You'. *Drives You Home Again* was a disappointing follow-up.

● ALBUMS: *I'm A Stranger Too* (Poppy 1970)★★, *Don't It Drag On* (Poppy 1972)★★, *It Ain't Easy* (1984)★★★, *Another Way To Find You* (Flying Fish 1991)★★★, *Happier Blue* (1993)★★★★, *Up On The Lowdown* (Hightone 1995)★★, *Small Revelations* (Hightone 1997)★★★★, *Drives You Home Again* (Hightone 1999)★★.

Smog

The creation of Bill Callahan (b. Silver Springs, Maryland, USA) and an ever-changing cast of musicians, Smog are important pioneers of the lo-fi movement in American independent music, influencing acts as diverse as Pavement and Will Oldham's Palace. Callahan's albums are characterized by their sparse, often discordant instrumentation, and his self-absorbed and intimately revealing lyrics. Basing himself in Georgia, his early cassette-only releases were self-produced, largely instrumental soundscapes, with just Callahan and his guitar alone in the studio. Moving to California and Drag City Records Callahan then released the more song-orientated *Forgotten Foundation*, which was quickly followed by the excellent *Julius Caesar*, an album whose tone was set by the gloom-laden 'Your Wedding'. The *Burning Kingdom* mini-album featured Callahan's fullest production to date, although the lyrical mood was still relentlessly downbeat (sample lyric: 'I'm crawling through the desert without water or love'). The inexorable pessimism was almost overwhelming on *Wild Love*, the stand-out track proving to be the reflective 'Prince Alone In The Studio'. Other musicians appearing on these albums included underground legend Jim O'Rourke and Callahan's girlfriend and occasional songwriting partner Cynthia Dall. In contrast, *The Doctor Came At Dawn* featured Callahan alone in the studio. The following year's *Red Apple Falls* fleshed out the instrumentation with pedal steel and French horn, but it was still Callahan's eerily detached guitar and vocals that provided the album's emotional core. *Knock Knock* was not one of Callahan's finest albums, although it still received polite reviews from critics enamoured of his low-key charm.

● ALBUMS: *Macramé Gunplay* cassette only (Disaster 1988)★★, *Cow* cassette only (Disaster 1989)★★, *A Table Setting* cassette only (Disaster 1990)★★, *Tired Machine* cassette only (Disaster 1990)★★, *Sewn To The Sky* (Disaster 1990)★★★, *Forgotten Foundation* (Drag City 1992)★★★, *Julius Caesar* (Drag City 1993)★★★★, *Burning Kingdom* mini-album (Drag City 1994)★★★, *Wild Love* (Drag City 1995)★★, *The Doctor Came At Dawn* (Drag City 1996)★★★★, *Red Apple Falls* (Drag City 1997)★★★, *Knock Knock* (Drag City 1999)★★★.

Smoke City

This UK band from London comprising Nina Miranda (vocals), Marc Brown (programming/turntables) and Chris Franck (guitar/keyboards), shot into the public eye when their atmospheric track 'Underwater Love' was used as the soundtrack to a risqué Levis television advert in April 1997. Brown, a part-time DJ and apprentice engineer, constructed the looped backing track in the studio, over which the half-Brazilian Miranda added her distinctive half-sung, half-spoken multi-lingual vocals. Originally released in February 1995 the track gained encouraging airplay on independent radio, and was included on the influential compilation, *Rebirth Of The Cool, Volume Six*. With the addition of guitarist Franck, the trio signed a contract with Jive Records and recorded their debut *Flying Away*, a wondrous mix of trip-hop rhythms, Brazilian adventure and soulful vocals. Unfortunately, the release of the album was overshadowed by the attendant success of 'Underwater Love', which reached the UK Top 5 and charted throughout Europe. The follow-up featured another impressively diverse range of musical styles.

● ALBUMS: *Flying Away* (Jive 1997)★★★★, *Jug* (Jive 1999)★★★.

Snakefarm

Snakefarm is the new moniker employed by veteran Tokyo, Japan-born *avant garde* musician Anna Domino, in consort with her romantic and musical partner, Belgian guitarist Michel Delory. Over the course of four albums and two EPs (compiled on 1996's *Favorite Songs From The Twilight Years*), Domino had created a cult audience for her releases on the fashionable Belgian imprint Les Disques Du Crepuscule. In 1999 she took her new creation to RCA Records' subsidiary, Kneeling Elephant. Snakefarm's elegantly titled debut album, *Songs From My Funeral*, saw them explore a number of traditional folk songs and compositions, including 'Banks Of The Ohio' and 'Laredo'. More unusually it employed a pleasing array of contemporary beats, loops and arrange-

ments. In a concept similar to Nick Cave's *Murder Ballads*, all the songs dealt with death and mortality, but the music's vibrancy gave the project more vitality than its subject matter may have suggested. Promotion of the record was completed with the aid of a touring band incorporating Paul Dugan (bass) and Stephen Ulrich (guitar).

● ALBUMS: *Songs From My Funeral* (Kneeling Elephant/RCA 1999)★★★★.

Snap!

Durron Butler (b. Maurice Durron Butler, 30 April 1967, Pittsburgh, Pennsylvania, USA) was initially a drummer with a heavy metal band in his hometown. Later he joined the army and was posted to Germany where he became a bomb disposal expert. While there he teamed up with Rico Sparx and Moses P. for several musical projects. After his discharge he returned to the USA but went back to Germany to tour with the Fat Boys. Germany-based producers Benito Benites (b. Michael Munzing) and John Garrett Virgo III (b. Luca Anzilotti), operating under pseudonyms, had put together a project they would call Snap!, after a function on a sequencing programme. Previously the producers had recorded widely in their Frankfurt studio, for their own label, Logic Records (whose former A&R man, Mark Spoon, is now half of Jam And Spoon). They also ran their own club, Omen. Notable successes prior to Snap! included the 16-Bit Project ('Where Are You' and 'High Score') and Off's 'Electric Salsa', which featured Sven Vath as singer. They then recorded a song called 'The Power' which was built from samples of New York rapper Chill Rob G (Robert Frazier)'s 'Let The Rhythm Flow'. They added the powerful female backing vocals of Penny Ford, who had previously worked with George Clinton, Chaka Khan and Mica Paris, among others. Jackie Harris (b. Jaqueline Arlissa Harris, Pittsburgh, USA) was also credited for providing 'guide' vocals, and appeared in press interviews. The record was first released on the Wild Pitch Records label in America with the credit 'Snap featuring Chill Rob G'. However, after the first 30,000 sales problems with Chill began to manifest themselves and they sought a replacement. They chose Butler, who was now renamed Turbo B. He had already recorded for Logic as back-up rapper for Moses P. Chill was allowed to release his own version of 'The Power' in America. Around the rest of the world a new version, featuring Turbo B, topped the charts. To promote the record he and Ford toured widely, before the latter embarked on a solo career. She was replaced by Thea Austin. Throughout Benites and Garrett utilised Turbo B as the public face of Snap!, remaining shadowy figures back in their Frankfurt studio, which was now a hugely impressive complex. Though they continued to score colossal hits with 'Oops Up', 'Cult Of Snap' and 'Mary Had A Little Boy', dissent had set in. Turbo wanted more artistic input, and hated 'Rhythm Is A Dancer' the projected lead-off single for the band's second album. When a substitute, 'The Colour Of Love', crashed, the duo went ahead without his agreement. Their judgement was proved correct when 'Rhythm Is A Dancer' became another international smash (the biggest selling UK single of 1992). But by now the rift between the parties was irreconcilable. Turbo had signed up for a solo career (debuting with 'I'm Not Dead' on Polydor Records) while the Snap! single was still climbing in several territories. Austin too found herself a solo contract. The producers proved that they could survive without a frontman when 'Exterminate!', the first record not to feature Turbo, became another million-seller. Austin was replaced by Niki Harris, formerly backing singer to Madonna, on 'Exterminate!' and 'Do You See The Light (Looking For)', but by the advent of 1994's *Welcome To Tomorrow* Snap!'s new singer was 'Summer'. A former dancer on the *Fame* television series, she had also worked as an actor in Spike Lee's *School Daze* and the Arnold Schwarzenegger vehicle *The Running Man*. Her singing background included sessions with Janet Jackson, Patti LaBelle and Snoop Doggy Dogg. Her vocals presided over further Snap! hits with 'Welcome To Tomorrow' (their ninth successive UK Top 10 hit) and 'The First, The Last Eternity'. Subsequent singles in 1996, featuring Rukmani and Einstein, failed to break into the UK Top 40.

● ALBUMS: *World Power* (Arista 1990)★★★, *The Madman's Return* (Arista 1992)★★★, *Welcome To Tomorrow* (Arista 1994)★★★.

● VIDEOS: *World Power* (BMG Video 1990).

Sneaker Pimps

One of the most unusual and potentially exciting bands to emerge out of the alternative rock milieu of the mid-90s, the Sneaker Pimps were immediately signed up by One Little Indian Records in the UK, a contract with Virgin Records in the USA being brokered shortly thereafter. The band's elegant fusion of dance music, indie and electronic sounds is dependent on the collaborative work of keyboard player Liam Howe, famed for regularly displaying his first ever purchase, a £20 Casio synthesizer, at the band's live shows, and guitarist Chris Corner. The pair had grown up together in Hartlepool, England, before relocating to London. Prior to Sneaker Pimps, both had spent several years working on the fringes of the electronic and experimental dance scenes as FRISK and then Line Of Flight. Anglo-Indonesian vocalist Kelly Dayton, formerly of London indie outfit the Lumieres, was brought in for their new project, broadening the horizons of the previously studio-bound Howe and Corner, as the trio began playing low-profile gigs with a live rhythm section. The band made its debut in April 1996 with 'Tesko Suicide', which incorporated elements of folk among the trip-hop beats and attracted strong critical praise. Much of *Becoming X*, their debut album released in August that year, was informed by a budget-mentality, the recording taking place at Howe's father's house in his tiny bedroom. Dayton reportedly sang the album's vocals while sitting in a nearby cupboard due to the lack of space. Despite this, the Sneaker Pimps fermented a sound that encouraged very different perceptions of the environment in which it was created - the instrumentalists' lightness of touch combined with an aura of rhythmic space to offset the claustrophobia evident in the vocals. '6 Underground', was included on the soundtrack to *The Saint*. The band appeared regularly on evening radio and charmed critics with their fresh, unsullied approach both to music-making and the media. They also made inroads into the fickle American market. Howe subsequently began working on remix projects, including a new version of the Shamen's 'Move Any Mountain'. Corner took over as vocalist when Dayton left the band at the start of 1998, featuring on the excellent follow-up *Splinter*.

● ALBUMS: *Becoming X* (One Little Indian 1996)★★★, *Splinter* (Clean Up 1999)★★★.

Snoop Doggy Dogg

b. Calvin Broadus, 20 October 1972, Long Beach, California, USA. Snoop Doggy Dogg's commercial rise in 1993 was acutely timed, riding a surge in hardcore rap's popularity, and smashing previous records in any genre. *Doggystyle* was the most eagerly anticipated album in rap history, and the first debut album to enter the *Billboard* chart at number 1. With advance orders of over one and a half million, media speculators were predicting its importance long before a release date. As was *de rigueur* for gangsta rappers, Broadus' criminal past cast a long, somewhat romanticized shadow over his achievements. He was busted for drugs after leaving high school in Long Beach, and spent three years in and out of jail. He first appeared in 1991 when helping out Dr. Dre on a track called 'Deep Cover', from the movie of the same title. Dogg was also ubiquitous on Dr. Dre's 1992 breakthrough, *The Chronic*, particularly on the hit single 'Nuthin' But A 'G' Thang', which he wrote and on which he co-rapped. After presenting a gong to En Vogue in September 1993 at the MTV video awards, Dogg surrendered himself to police custody after the show, on murder charges. This was over his alleged involvement in a driveby shooting. Inevitably, as news spread of Dogg's involvement, interest in his vinyl product accelerated, and this played no small part in the eventual sales of his debut album. Critics noted how closely *Doggystyle* was modelled on George Clinton's *Atomic Dog* project. Many also attacked the abusive imagery of women Dogg employed, particularly on the lurid 'Ain't No Fun'. His justification: 'I'm not prejudiced in my rap, I just kick the rhymes'. If the US press were hostile to him they were no match for the sensationalism of the English tabloids. During touring commitments to support the album and single, 'Gin And Juice', he made the front page of the *Daily Star* with the headline: 'Kick This Evil Bastard Out!'. It was vaguely reminiscent of the spleen vented at the Sex Pistols in their heyday, and doubtless a good sign. He was asked to leave his hotel in Milestone, Kensington on arrival. A more serious impediment to his career was the trial on charges of accessory to the murder of Phillip Woldermariam, shot by his bodyguard McKinley Lee. The trial was underway in November 1995 and attracted a great deal of media attention, due in part to Dogg's defence attorney being Johnnie Cochran, O.J. Simpson's successful defender. During the trial the rapper's bail was set at $1 million. The verdict on 20 February 1996 acquitted Dogg and McKinley Lee of both murder charges and the manslaughter cases were dropped in April. The trial had not overtly damaged his record sales, with his debut topping seven million copies worldwide, and the follow-up *Tha Doggfather* entering the US album chart at number 1, although it ultimately failed to match the commercial success of *Doggystyle*. A subsequent falling out with the ailing Death Row Records saw Dogg transferring to Master P's highly successful gangsta label, No Limit Records. Now going under the name Snoop Dogg, he released *Da Game Is To Be Sold, Not To Be Told* in August 1998. Repeating the success of his first two albums, it debuted at US number 1. 'Still A G Thang' climbed to number 19 the following month. Snoop Dogg released another new set, *No Limit Top Dogg*, in May 1999, although he was held off the top of the charts this time by Latino heart-throb Ricky Martin.

● ALBUMS: *Doggystyle* (Death Row 1993)★★★★, *Tha Doggfather*

(Death Row 1996)★★★, *Da Game Is To Be Sold, Not To Be Told* (No Limit 1998)★★★, *No Limit Top Dogg* (No Limit 1999)★★.

● VIDEOS: *Murder Was The Case* (Warners 1994), *Game Of Life* (Priority Video 1998).

● FILMS: *The Show* (1995), *The Wizard Of Oz* (1998), *Half Baked* (1998), *Caught Up* (1998), *Ride* (1998), *I Got The Hook Up* (1998), *Urban Menace* (1999), *Hot Boyz* (1999), *Bones* (1999), *Whiteboys* (1999).

Snowpony

Partly because of their past associations with bands such as Quickspace, Stereolab, Supersport and My Bloody Valentine, but equally because of the excellence of their debut single, 'Easy Way Down', Snowpony found it easy to attract early media interest when they arrived at the end of 1996. The trio comprises Katherine Gifford (vocals/keyboards), Max Corradi (drums) and Debbie Googe (bass). Gifford, formerly keyboard player for Stereolab, had abandoned the first incarnation of Snowpony to tour as replacement vocalist for Moonshake during 1996. She left a tape behind with Googe, who had left My Bloody Valentine just a few months earlier. Googe wrote new basslines and helped Gifford recruit Corradi, who left Quickspace, after 'business disagreements'. The group made its debut at the Garage in London shortly thereafter. 'Easy Way Down' was released on their own See No Evil label, and was followed by *The Little Girls Understand* EP, for the Rough Trade Records Singles Club. Two years later their brooding and atmospheric debut album, recorded with John McEntire of Tortoise, finally appeared.

● ALBUMS: *The Slow-Motion World Of Snowpony* (Radioactive 1998)★★★.

Son Volt

Led by singer and guitarist Jay Farrar, Son Volt are a contemporary US country rock band who have been widely applauded for their irreverent but clearly fond approach to the tradition. Additionally comprising bass player Jim Boquist, brother and multi-instrumentalist Dave Boquist and drummer Mike Heidorn, the group made its debut in 1996 with *Trace*, which took as its central influences the Byrds, Louvin Brothers and Creedence Clearwater Revival. Farrar and Heidorn were both previously members of Uncle Tupelo, rated by many as a seminal influence on the emergence of the alternative country movement of the 90s (when they split, Farrar's former bandmate Jeff Tweedy went on to form the acclaimed Wilco). Uncle Tupelo were frequently compared to the longer-established Jayhawks, with much of the critical attention surrounding Farrar's lyrics, which drew heavily on his experiences growing up in Illinois, working on a farm and in his mother's second-hand bookshop during his adolescent years. Son Volt seem set on pursuing a similar strategy, judged on the contents of *Trace*, which featured 11 Farrar originals written in New Orleans where he settled after the break-up of Uncle Tupelo. The relentlessly gloomy *Straightaways* confirmed Farrar's reputation as the flip-side to the goodtime vibe of Tweedy's Wilco, his songs chronicling the small-town angst of modern America. Farrar and his cohorts stuck to the same formula on the following year's *Wide Swing Tremelo*.

● ALBUMS: *Trace* (Warners 1995)★★★, *Straightaways* (Warners 1997)★★★★, *Wide Swing Tremelo* (Warners 1998)★★★.

Sonia

b. 13 February 1971, Liverpool, Merseyside, England. Another Stock, Aitken And Waterman (SAW) pop protégée, Sonia had been singing around Liverpool clubs since leaving school and was a well known starlet in Merseyside having appeared as Adrian Boswell's girlfriend in the hit UK television situation comedy *Bread*. She also regularly hosted the *Stars Of The Future Show* at the Liverpool Empire in aid of underprivileged children. In her bid to make it as a singer she cajoled Waterman in to allowing her to sing live on his regular *Radio City* programme. He was impressed enough to get her on his television show *The Hitman And Her* and shortly afterwards she recorded her debut single, 'You'll Never Stop Me Loving You'. Written and produced by the entire SAW team it was a UK number 1 in June 1989. Follow-up UK chart singles included 'Can't Forget You' (number 17), 'Listen To Your Heart' (number 10). The following year she recorded a Top 20 version of James Taylor's 'You've Got A Friend' with new SAW heroes Big Fun, and covered the Skeeter Davis hit 'End Of The World' (number 18, August 1990). A change of labels resulted in another hit, when 'Only Fools (Never Fall In Love)' reached number 10 in June 1991. 'You To Me Are Everything' reached number 13 the same November. In 1993, Sonia represented Britain in the Eurovision Song Contest, with 'Better The Devil You Know', but was beaten to the number one position by the Irish entry. Released as a single, the song reached UK number 15 in May 1993. She has since concentrated on live theatre work, appearing alongside Shane Richie in the West End revival of *Grease*, and touring the musical show *What A Feeling*.

● ALBUMS: *Everybody Knows* (Chrysalis 1990)★★, *Sonia* (IQ 1991)★★, *Better The Devil You Know* (Arista 1993)★★.

Sonic Boom

b. Peter Kember, 19 November 1965. UK-based Sonic Boom's solo project was originally planned as an aside for his main love, the Spacemen 3. Signing to the Silvertone label, Sonic issued 'Angel' (a drug-related tale not dissimilar both lyrically and musically to the Velvet Underground's 'Heroin') in 1989. This was followed by *Spectrum*, on which Sonic was assisted by fellow Spaceman Will Carruthers, plus the Jazz Butcher and the Perfect Disaster's Phil Parfitt. *Spectrum*'s hypnotic blend of repetitive guitar riffs and keyboard runs betrayed his love of New York duo Suicide, but nevertheless possessed a definite if quiet charm. It even sported a psychedelic, gatefold revolving sleeve. Early buyers could send away for an orange vinyl 10-inch, 'Octaves'/'Tremeloes', which featured two elongated, synthesized notes! Unfortunately, after recruiting Mark Refoy the Spacemen 3 split in Kember's wake to form Spiritualized, although their swan-song appeared later, ironically charting. Boom re-emerged in the summer of 1991 with a low-key instrumental demo single, '(I Love You) To The Moon And Back', distributed free at gigs. He has subsequently released albums as part of the band Spectrum; their music has become progressively more experimental, with Boom moving away from conventional song formats in his explorations of pure sound. He has also collaborated with Eddie Prévost (AAM) and Kevin Shields (My Bloody Valentine) as Experimental Audio Research.

● ALBUMS: as Sonic Boom *Spectrum* (Silvertone 1990)★★★. As

Spectrum *Soul Kiss (Glide Divine)* (Silvertone 1991)★★★, *Highs, Lows And Heavenly Blows* (Silvertone 1994)★★★, with Jessamine *A Pox On You* (Space Age 1996)★★★, *Songs For Owsley* (Birdman 1996)★★★, *Forever Alien* (1997)★★★, with Silver Apples *A Lake Of Teardrops* (Space Age 1999)★★★.

Soul Asylum

Originally a Minneapolis, Minnesota, USA garage hardcore band, Soul Asylum spent their early years under the yoke of comparisons with the more fêted Replacements and Hüsker Dü. Indeed, Bob Mould has been known fondly to describe Soul Asylum as 'our little brothers', and was on hand as producer for their first two long-playing sets. Their roots in hardcore are betrayed by their original choice of name, Loud Fast Rules. Their first formation in 1981 centred around the abiding creative nucleus of Dave Pirner (b. 16 April 1964, Green Bay, Wisconsin, USA; vocals/guitar) and Dan Murphy (b. 12 July 1962, Duluth, Minnesota, USA; guitar), alongside Karl Mueller (b. 27 July 1963, Minneapolis, USA; bass) and Pat Morley (drums). Together they specialized in sharp lyrical observations and poppy punk. Morley left in December 1984 to be replaced, eventually, by Grant Young (b. 5 January 1964, Iowa City, Iowa, USA), who arrived in time for *Made To Be Broken*. As their music progressed it became easier to trace back their heritage to the 60s rather than 70s. *Hang Time*, their third album proper, was their first for a major. It saw them move into the hands of a new production team (Ed Stasium and Lenny Kaye), with a very apparent display of studio polish. The mini-album that was meant to have preceded it (but ultimately did not), *Clam Dip And Other Delights*, included their dismantling of a Foreigner song, 'Jukebox Hero', and a riotous reading of Janis Joplin's 'Move Over'. When playing live they have been known to inflict their renditions of Barry Manilow's 'Mandy' and Glen Campbell's 'Rhinestone Cowboy' on an audience. Though *The Horse They Rode In On* was another splendid album, the idea of Soul Asylum breaking into the big league was becoming a progressively fantastic one (indeed, band members had to pursue alternative employment in 1990, during which time Pirner suffered a nervous breakdown). However, largely thanks to the MTV rotation of 'Somebody To Shove', the situation was about to change. In its aftermath they gained a prestigious slot on the *David Letterman Show* before support billing to Bob Dylan and Guns N'Roses, plus a joint headlining package with Screaming Trees and the Spin Doctors on the three-month Alternative Nation Tour. Soon they were appearing in front of a worldwide audience of 400 million at the 1993 MTV Awards ceremony, where they were joined by R.E.M.'s Peter Buck and Victoria Williams for a jam of their follow-up hit, 'Runaway Train'. With Pirner dating film starlet Winona Ryder, the profile of a band who seemed destined for critical reverence and public indifference could not have been more unexpectedly high, and *Grave Dancers Union* was a major success. However, in 1995 the band announced that their next studio sessions would avoid the overt commercial textures of their previous album, although subsequent reviews of *Let Your Dim Light Shine* were mixed. They also recruited their fourth drummer, Stirling Campbell, to replace Grant Young; however, Campbell left the band in 1997. Pirner and Murphy's side project is Golden Smog, together with the Jayhawks' Gary Louris (guitar) and Marc Perlman (bass). They reconvened

Soul Asylum for 1998's *Candy From A Stranger*, their most relaxed and intimate recording to date.

● ALBUMS: *Say What You Will* (Twin Tone 1984)★★★, *Made To Be Broken* (Twin Tone 1986)★★★, *While You Were Out* (Twin Tone 1986)★★★, *Hang Time* (Twin Tone/A&M 1988)★★★, *Clam Dip And Other Delights* mini-album (What Goes On 1989)★★★, *Soul Asylum And The Horse They Rode In On* (Twin Tone/A&M 1990)★★★★, *Grave Dancers Union* (A&M 1993)★★★, *Let Your Dim Light Shine* (A&M 1995)★★★, *Candy From A Stranger* (Columbia 1998)★★★.

● COMPILATIONS: *Time's Incinerator* cassette only (Twin Tone 1984)★★★, *Say What You Will Clarence, Karl Sold The Truck* (Twin Tone 1989)★★★.

Soul Coughing

Formed in New York City, New York, USA, Soul Coughing comprise M. Doughty (guitar/vocals/lyrics), composer Mark de Gli Antoni (keyboards/samples), Sebastian Steinberg (double bass, ex-Marc Ribot) and Yuval Gabay (b. Israel; drums). Their origins can be traced back to 1993 when Doughty was working on the door at the New York *avant garde* jazz club the Knitting Factory. There he gradually recruited the band's members from the club's clientele, and together they set out on a path of 'shared musical adventure'. Their debut album, *Ruby Vroom*, received universal critical acclaim, and preceded their first major touring commitments. It is in the live arena that they are best observed - in performance they regularly adopt and adapt the jazz predilection for extended improvisation. *Irresistible Bliss* was another successful marriage of hip-hop beats, mechanical noise and expansive musicianship, with each of the 12 songs thematically linked to day-to-day life in New York. Produced by Tony Bennett associate David Kahne and Steve Fisk, it was recorded in the same sessions that saw the band complete compositions for the *Blue In The Face* and *X-Files* film soundtracks. The band's third set, *El Oso*, proved to be their most successful fusion of lo-fi experimentalism and straightahead rock.

● ALBUMS: *Ruby Vroom* (Slash/London 1994)★★★★, *Irresistible Bliss* (Slash/London 1996)★★★, *El Oso* (Slash 1998)★★★★.

Soul II Soul

This highly successful UK rap, soul and R&B outfit originally consisted of Jazzie B (b. Beresford Romeo, 26 January 1963, London, England; rapper), Nellee Hooper (musical arranger) and Philip 'Daddae' Harvey (multi-instrumentalist). The early definition of the group was uncomplicated: 'It's a sound system, an organisation (which) came together to build upon making careers for people who had been less fortunate within the musical and artistic realms'. The name Soul II Soul was first used to describe Jazzie B and Harvey's company supplying disc jockeys and PA systems to dance music acts. They also held a number of warehouse raves, particularly at Paddington Dome, near Kings Cross, London, before setting up their own venue. There they met Hooper, formerly of Bristol's Wild Bunch sound system which evolved into Massive Attack. Joining forces, they took up a residency at Covent Garden's African Centre before signing to Virgin Records' subsidiary Ten Records. Following the release of two singles, 'Fairplay' and 'Feel Free', the band's profile grew with the aid of fashion T-shirts, two shops and Jazzie B's slot on the then pirate Kiss FM radio station. However, their next release would break not only them but vocalist Caron Wheeler, when 'Keep On Movin'' reached number 5 in the UK charts in 1989. The follow-up, 'Back To Life (However Do You Want Me)', once more featured Wheeler, topped the UK charts in the summer. The song was taken from their inspired debut *Club Classics Vol. One*. The ranks of the Soul II Soul collective had swelled to incorporate a myriad of musicians, whose input was evident in the variety of styles employed. Wheeler soon left to pursue a solo career, but the band's momentum was kept intact by 'Keep On Movin'' penetrating the US clubs and the album scaling the top of the UK charts. 'Get A Life' was a further expansion on the influential, much copied stuttering rhythms that the band had employed on previous singles, but Jazzie B and Hooper's arrangement of Sinead O'Connor's UK number 1, 'Nothing Compares 2 You', was a poignant contrast. Other artists who sought their services included Fine Young Cannibals and Neneh Cherry. The early part of 1990 was spent in what amounted to business expansion, with a film company, a talent agency and an embryonic record label. The band's second album duly arrived halfway through the year, including Courtney Pine and Kym Mazelle in its star-studded cast. However, despite entering the charts at number 1 it was given a frosty reception by some critics who saw it as comparatively conservative. Mazelle would also feature on the single 'Missing You', as Jazzie B unveiled his (ill-fated) new label Funki Dred, backed by Motown Records. Although *Volume III, Just Right* made its debut at number 3 in the UK album charts, it proffered no substantial singles successes, with both 'Move Me No Mountain' and 'Just Right' stalling outside the Top 30. Jazzie B would spend the early months of 1993 co-producing James Brown's first album of the 90s, *Universal James*, and Virgin issued a stop-gap singles compilation at the end of the year. Soul II Soul's fourth studio album was not available until July 1995, as Caron Wheeler returned to the fold. However, the accompanying hit single, 'Love Enuff', was sung by ex-Snap! singer Penny Ford. The band was dropped by Virgin in April 1996, but signed up to Island Records for the release of *Time For Change*. In 1999, Virgin Records released a 10th anniversary special edition of *Club Classics Vol. One*.

● ALBUMS: *Club Classics Vol. I* (Ten 1989)★★★★, *Volume II: 1990 A New Decade* (Ten 1990)★★★, *Volume III, Just Right* (Ten 1992)★★★, *Volume V - Believe* (Virgin 1995)★★★, *Time For Change* (Island 1997)★★★.

● COMPILATIONS: *Volume IV - The Classic Singles 88-93* (Virgin 1993)★★★★.

Soulfly

Formed in Los Angeles, California, USA, in 1997, by singer Max Cavalera (b. 4 August 1969, Brazil; ex-Sepultura). Soulfly additionally comprises guitarist Jackson Bandeira aka Lucio (previously played with Chico Science), drummer Roy Mayorga (ex-Agnostic Front, Shelter, Nausea) and bass player Marcello D Rapp. Marcello was formerly part of Sepultura's road crew, and had his own band, Mist, who recorded three albums between 1987 and 1992. Soulfly's debut single, 'Bleed', released in 1998, dealt with the death of Cavalera's stepson Dana Wells in a gang-related car crash. The rest of the self-titled album that accompanied its release also touched on the illness of Cavalera's two children and his conversion to Christianity. The band is managed by Cavalera's wife Gloria. Produced by Ross Robinson, *Soulfly*

featured a number of high-profile guest appearances - Chino Moreno of the Deftones ('First Commandment'), Christian Wolbers of Fear Factory ('Bumba' and 'No'), Fred Durst of Limp Bizkit (who co-wrote 'Bleed') and Benji from Dub War ('Prejudice' and 'Quicombo').

● ALBUMS: *Soulfly* (Roadrunner 1998)★★★★.

Soundgarden

This Seattle-based US quartet fused influences as diverse as Led Zeppelin, the Stooges, Velvet Underground and, most particularly, early UK and US punk bands into a dirty, sweaty, sexually explicit and decidedly fresh take on rock 'n' roll. The group, Chris Cornell (b. 20 July 1964, Seattle, Washington, USA; vocals/guitar), Kim Thayil (b. 4 September 1960, Seattle, Washington, USA; guitar), Hiro Yamamoto (b. 20 September 1968, Okinawa, Japan; bass) and Matt Cameron (b. 28 November 1962, San Diego, USA; drums), proffered a sound characterized by heavy-duty, bass-laden metallic riffs, which swung between dark melancholia and *avant garde* minimalism. Cornell's ranting vocal style and articulate lyrics completed the effect. The band's first recording, 1987's six-song *Screaming Life* EP, was the second release on the hugely influential Sub Pop Records label, and marked out their territory. Indeed, Thayil had brought together the label's owners Bruce Pavitt and Jonathan Poneman in the first place. Following the *Fopp* EP, the band became the first of the Sub Pop generation to sign to a major when they attracted the attention of A&M Records, although their debut set, *Ultramega OK*, was released through SST Records in order to maintain their indie credibility. A&M eventually released *Louder Than Love*, one of the most underrated and offbeat rock albums of 1989. After its release Cameron and Cornell also participated in the two million-selling Temple Of The Dog album, that co-featured future Pearl Jam members Stone Gossard and Jeff Ament laying tribute at the door of deceased Mother Love Bone singer Andrew Wood. However, following the recording sessions for *Louder Than Love*, Yamamoto was replaced by Jason Everman (ex-Nirvana), though he played on only one track, a cover version of the Beatles' 'Come Together', before departing for Mindfunk via Skunk. His eventual replacement was band friend Ben 'Hunter' Shepherd. *Badmotorfinger* built on the band's successful formula but added insistent riffs, the grinding but melodious guitar sound that would come to define the grunge genre, and their own perspectives on politics, religion and society. Among its many absorbing moments was the MTV-friendly single 'Jesus Christ Pose'. Landing the support slot on Guns N'Roses' US Illusions tour deservedly opened up Soundgarden to a much wider audience. *Superunknown* capitalized on this, and debuted at number 1 on the *Billboard* chart on 19 March 1994. Produced by Michael Beinhorn (Soul Asylum, Red Hot Chili Peppers) and the band themselves, it was a magnum opus, clocking in at more than 70 minutes and featuring 15 songs. Eventually selling over three million copies, it was promoted by an Australasian tour in January 1994, headlining the 'Big Day Out' festival package above the Ramones, Smashing Pumpkins and Teenage Fanclub, before moving on to Japan. *Down On The Upside* was another fine album, recorded during Cornell's allegedly serious drug problems; the record belied the band's internal strife with intense but highly melodic heavy rock.

Continuing unrest in the camp led to the band's split in April 1997, with Cameron moving on to Pearl Jam and Cornell embarking on a solo career.

● ALBUMS: *Ultramega OK* (SST 1988)★★★, *Louder Than Love* (A&M 1989)★★★, *Screaming Life/Fopp* (Sub Pop 1990)★★, *Badmotorfinger* (A&M 1991)★★★★, *Superunknown* (A&M 1994)★★★★, *Down On The Upside* (A&M 1996)★★★.

● COMPILATIONS: *A-sides* (A&M 1997)★★★★.

● VIDEOS: *Motorvision* (A&M 1993).

● FURTHER READING: *Soundgarden: New Metal Crown*, Chris Nickson.

Sounds Of Blackness

Led by bodybuilder Gary Hines, a former Mr Minnesota, Sounds Of Blackness are a US gospel/soul 40-piece choir whose work also crossed over to the R&B and dance music charts. Stranger still, perhaps, was the fact that they broke through so late in their career. They were 20 years old as an outfit when they came to prominence in 1991. Hines took them over from their original incarnation as the Malcalaster College Black Choir in January 1971, running the group on a strict ethical code of professional practices. The rule book is sustained by the long waiting-list of aspiring members, and Hines' self-appointed role as 'benevolent dictator'. They first made the charts under the aegis of Jimmy Jam And Terry Lewis, who had spotted the group and used them for backing vocals on their productions for Alexander O'Neal. The celebrated production duo, who had been advised to sign the choir on the advice of their major client Janet Jackson, used Sounds Of Blackness to launch their new record label, Perspective Records, succeeding almost immediately with 'Optimistic'. Released in 1990, it single-handedly sparked off a revival in the fortunes of gospel music. The album that accompanied it subsequently won a Grammy award, as 'The Pressure' and 'Testify' also charted. Subsequent singles were also successful, and included remixes from noted dance music producers such as Sasha. The distinctive, emotive vocals from Ann Bennett-Nesby proved extremely popular in the secular arena of the club scene. Hines was pleased with this exposure, insisting that their message could permeate people's consciences regardless of the environment. Sounds Of Blackness sang 'Gloryland', alongside Daryl Hall, as the official theme to the 1994 World Cup soccer tournament. They have also appeared on the soundtracks to the movies *Posse* and *Demolition Man*, and have recorded with John Mellencamp, Elton John and Stevie Wonder.

● ALBUMS: *The Evolution Of Gospel* (Perspective/A&M 1990)★★★★, *The Night Before Christmas: A Musical Fantasy* (Perspective/A&M 1992)★★★, *Africa To America* (Perspective/A&M 1994)★★★★, *Time For Healing* (A&M 1997)★★★.

Soup Dragons

The Soup Dragons emerged from Glasgow, Scotland, as one of a clutch of bands championed by the *New Musical Express* via their *C86* project. The band evolved around Sean Dickson (vocals/guitar/songwriter). In early 1985, he met up with Jim McCulloch (guitar), Ross A. Sinclair (drums) and Sushil K. Dade (bass), the collective taking their name from a character in the cult children's television programme *The Clangers*. A flexi-disc, 'If You Were The Only Girl In The World', emerged at the end of the year, by which time the band were circulating a demonstration tape, *You Have Some Too*. The Subway Organisation label issued the Soup Dragons' first single, 'Whole Wide World' (1986), a tight, exciting slab of Buzzcocks-styled pop, performed at breakneck pace. This attracted ex-Wham! manager Jazz Summers, who set up a new label for them, Raw TV Products, in time for 'Hang-Ten!' In the meantime, Dickson and later McCulloch had left another band with whom they were serving time, the BMX Bandits. 'Head Gone Astray' in 1987 revealed a marked change away from new wave towards 60s rock. 'Can't Take No More' and 'Soft As Your Face' fared well commercially but the latter's serene sound was at odds with the band's direction. 'The Majestic Head' lured Sire Records into a contract in 1988, but the next single, 'Kingdom Chairs', flopped. A subsequent debut album, *This Is Our Art*, emerged without fanfare. The Stooges-influenced 'Backwards Dog' and 'Crotch Deep Trash', introduced a rockier feel and this was followed by the dance-orientated 'Mother Universe' in 1990. Hinging around a Marc Bolan riff, the single was typical of the tracks on *Lovegod*, the band's second album. By this time, Sinclair had been replaced by new drummer Paul Quinn. After discovering an obscure Rolling Stones track from their 1965 *Out Of Our Heads* collection, the Soup Dragons teamed up with reggae singer Junior Reid and DJ/remixer Terry Farley (of Farley And Heller) to create a formidable crossover between white indie rock and dance music. The single 'I'm Free' was a UK number 5 hit in summer 1990, something that had previously eluded the band. *Lovegod* was re-promoted and a remixed 'Mother Universe' was reissued, giving them further chart success. They also enjoyed surprising success in America, with *Hotwired* selling well on the back of a Top 40 single 'Divine Thing'. As the 90s progressed, however, diminishing returns became the order of the day, and eventual dissolution with it. Dickson was left to record 1995's *Hydrophonic* with hired session musicians. Quinn would go on to replace Brendan O'Hare in Teenage Fanclub, while Jim McCulloch joined Superstar. Sushil played with the BMX Bandits and Telstar Ponies, and later recorded as Future Pilot AKA.

● ALBUMS: *This Is Our Art* (Sire 1988)★★, *Lovegod* (Raw TV 1990)★★★, *Hotwired* (Big Life 1992)★★★, *Hydrophonic* (Phonogram 1995)★★.

Space

The mid-90s Britpop phenomenon churned out numerous bands who seemed incapable of creating anything beyond variations on a single riff (usually stolen from George Harrison), but Liverpudlian quartet Space seemed to reinvent themselves single by single. The band came together around 1993 when childhood pals Tommy Scott (b. 18 February 1967, Liverpool, England; vocals, bass) and Andy Parle (drums) recruited 17-year-old singer/guitarist and Cypress Hill devotee Jamie Murphy. Kraftwerk fan Franny Griffiths (keyboards) joined soon afterwards and it was the Catholic mix of tastes (Scott admits to liking little apart from Tricky and film soundtracks) that lifted Space above their guitar-wielding contemporaries. The sound of their singles lurched from the sparse ska and sociopathic lyrics of 'Neighbourhood' to the stylish MOR noir crypto-misogyny in 'The Female Of The Species' and on to the (almost) conventional pop tune 'Me And You Against The World'. Their ability to touch any number of musical bases was further demonstrated by their live shows, supporting acts as diverse as Credit To The Nation, Catatonia and Dodgy. *Spiders*, released in September 1996, showed they were capable of sustaining their eclecticism across a whole album and making it commercially viable as well, entering the UK charts at number 5 and placing highly in music press end-of-year polls - a god-send for critics fed up with writing clichés about clichés. Guitarist Murphy briefly left the band following a breakdown, returning for the release of *Tin Planet*, while Parle was replaced by Leon Caffrey. Another highly eclectic collection, the album featured the Top 10 singles 'Avenging Angels' and 'The Ballad Of Tom Jones' (with Cerys Matthews of Catatonia), their biggest UK hits to date.

● ALBUMS: *Spiders* (Gut 1996)★★★, *Tin Planet* (Gut 1998)★★★★.

● COMPILATIONS: *Invasion Of The Spiders - Remixed & Unreleased Tracks* (Gut 1997)★★★.

● VIDEOS: *Tin Planet Live* (Warner Vision 1998).

Space Brothers

This UK-based duo of Ricky Simmonds (b. London, England) and Stephen Jones (b. London, England) has been responsible for several well-received and successful house and trance singles, and numerous remixes. They also record under several other pseudonyms, including Lustral, Chakra and Ascension and have released material on 10 different labels, including Jackpot, Hooj Choons and Paul Oakenfold's Perfecto Records. As the Space Brothers, they are now signed to Manifesto Records. Their single 'Shine' was a club-land favourite in 1997 with the support of many high-profile DJs, including Oakenfold and Judge Jules. As Lustral, their single 'Every Time', an ambient drum 'n' bass track, received an excellent remix from Nalin And Kane, which allowed it to cross over to the house dancefloors and onto many club-based compilation albums, including Renaissance's *Worldwide - London*. Their next release for Manifesto was 'Forgiven', which, although successful, did not gain the same reception as 'Shine'. In 1999, they released two singles 'Legacy' and 'Heaven Will Come' - with remixes by trance Renaissance man, Matt Darey and Lange. In September 1999, they released their debut *Shine*, which featured a bonus disc of dance music remixes of the album, in a seamless mix by Oakenfold. The Space Brothers' excellent credentials and the style of their music puts them at the forefront of tuneful, accessible trance in the late 90s.

● ALBUMS: *Shine* (Manifesto 1999)★★★★.

Spacehog

Comprising Royston Langdon (lead vocals/bass), Antony Langdon (guitar/vocals), Richard Steel (lead guitar) and Jonny Cragg (drums), the origins of Spacehog can be traced back to early 1994 when Antony Langdon met Cragg at a seedy espresso bar where he was employed killing rodents. After recruiting brother Royston and guitarist Steel, the group began to cultivate their reputation in the fertile East Village music scene of New York, USA. Despite their origins in New York, in actuality the members of the band are all drawn from Leeds, Yorkshire, England. They supported Tripping Daisy through their 1995 autumn dates before signing to WEA Records subsidiary Hi Fi Recordings. Their original name Grass was changed to Spacehog when Supergrass made their breakthrough in the UK. They subse-

quently entered the studio and made their major label bow with the single 'In The Meantime'. It was followed by a 13-track debut album, *Resident Alien*, released in April 1996, which highlighted the group's affection for the 70s sounds of T. Rex, Mott The Hoople and David Bowie, replete with space travel references such as 'Starside' and 'Space Is The Place'. A one-off showcase performance at London's Paramount City club was their first UK appearance The album topped the US *Billboard* Heatseekers chart as further live appearances saw the group sell out venues such as New York's Irving Plaza before setting out as support to the Red Hot Chili Peppers in the spring of 1996. *The Chinese Album*, released in 1998, featured a guest appearance from R.E.M. vocalist Michael Stipe.

● ALBUMS: *Resident Alien* (WEA 1996)★★★, *The Chinese Album* (Sire 1998)★★★.

Sparklehorse

Mark Linkous first came to record under the band identity of Sparklehorse thanks to the munificence of David Lowery, who left his eight-track recording equipment at Linkous' Richmond, Virginia, USA home for two years while his band, Cracker, went on tour. Linkous recorded many of the instrumental parts for his debut album himself, with occasional assistance from local musicians including multi-instrumentalist David Charles. The powerful single 'Someday I Will Treat You Good' attracted media interest, although many of Linkous' songs were more reflective and country-influenced, bearing comparison to the quieter moments of Pavement, Sebadoh and early Neil Young. Sparklehorse's brand of acoustic alienation began to impress critics in the UK and it was after a London gig that Linkous mixed his prescription drugs and collapsed in his hotel bathroom, trapping his legs beneath his body. He was only found 12 hours later, by which time he had suffered a heart attack and caused bad damage to his leg muscles. He made a steady recovery, performing from a wheelchair with his touring band of Paul Watson (guitar/banjo/mandolin), Scott Fitzsimmons (double bass) and Scott Minor (drums). A quantum leap was made with their excellent second album.

● ALBUMS: *Vivadixiesubmarinetransmissionplot* (Parlophone 1996)★★★, *Good Morning Spider* (Parlophone 1998)★★★★.

Spears, Britney

b. 2 December 1981, Kentwood, Louisiana, USA. One of the last teenage superstars of the millennium, Spears enjoyed her breakthrough success at the end of 1998. She appeared in local dance revues and church choirs as a young girl, and at the age of eight auditioned for *The Mickey Mouse Club*. Although she was too young to join the series, a producer on the show gave her an introduction to a New York agent. She subsequently spent three summers at the Professional Performing Arts School Center. She appeared in a number of off-Broadway productions as a child actor, including *Ruthless* (1991). She returned to the [Walt] Disney Channel for a spot on *The Mickey Mouse Club*, where she was featured for two years between the ages of 11 and 13. She began to audition for pop bands in the New York area, her demo tapes eventually landing on the desk of Jive Records' Jeff Fenster. 'Her vocal ability and commercial appeal caught me right away,' he recalls. She was expensively groomed by Jive, who put her in the studio with Eric Foster White (producer and writer for Boyzone, Whitney Houston and others). They employed top R&B writer Max Martin (of Backstreet Boys fame) to produce her debut single, '... Baby, One More Time', and an album of the same title. They also set up a promotional free phone number where fans could listen to Spears' music and interviews throughout the summer of 1998. She toured American venues for a series of concerts sponsored by US teen magazines, eventually joining 'N Sync on tour. The careful planning paid off when her debut album and single went on to top the American charts at the start of 1999. The album and single enjoyed similar success in the UK and Europe. The ballad 'Sometimes' and the funky '(You Drive Me) Crazy' were also substantial transatlantic hits. 'Born To Make You Happy' topped the UK charts in January 2000.

● ALBUMS: ... *Baby, One More Time* (Jive 1999)★★★.

● VIDEOS: *The Britney Spears Story: Unauthorised* (Creative Media 1999), *Time Out With Britney Spears* (Zomba 1999).

Spectrum
(see Sonic Boom)

Spencer, Jon, Blues Explosion

When Washington, DC, noiseniks Pussy Galore ended their five-year reign of terror, singer/guitarist Jon Spencer (b. Hanover, New Hampshire, USA) realigned with Russell Simins (drums, ex-Honeymoon Killers) and Judah Bauer (guitar) to form a trio that would bend the rules of alternative rock while demonstrating an obvious devotion to the music's basic R&B roots. On early recordings the group's minimalist, bass-free sound (occasionally augmented by Spencer's doodles on the Theremin) resembled little more than a trimmed-down variant on Spencer's earlier group, but each successive album added new elements of blues, soul and rockabilly. *Orange* blended a string section reminiscent of Isaac Hayes with hip-hop touches, including a bizarre rap by Beck. The slacker minstrel was also involved in the interesting but ultimately unsatisfying remix EP, along with Mike D of the Beastie Boys, Genius of Wu-Tang Clan and Moby. Parallel with JSBE work, Spencer was playing in the more conventionally alt-rock Boss Hog with fellow Pussy Galore survivor Cristina Martinez and drummer Charlie Ondras, and the whole Explosion backed blues legend R.L. Burnside on his groundbreaking *A Ass Pocket O' Whiskey*, a project compared by some to John Lee Hooker's work with Canned Heat. A move to London-based Mute Records was predicted by some to herald a tailing-off of the band's R&B experiments but *Now I Got Worry* featured 'Chicken Dog', a collaboration with the seminal Rufus Thomas. *Acme* was recorded with Steve Albini, and featured an extensive guest list including Alec Empire, Jim Dickinson and Calvin Johnson. They remain part of a select coterie, alongside Beck, the Beastie Boys and few others, who can fuse roots and indie sounds to the satisfaction of both camps.

● ALBUMS: *Crypt Style* (Crypt 1992)★★, *The Jon Spencer Blues Explosion* (Caroline 1992)★★, *Extra Width* (Matador 1993)★★, *Mo Width* (Au-Go-Go 1994)★★, *Orange* (Matador 1994)★★★, *Remixes* (Matador 1995)★★, *Now I Got Worry* (Mute 1996)★★★★, *Acme* (Mute 1998)★★★★, with Dub Narcotic Sound System *Sideways Soul* (K 1999)★★★.

● COMPILATIONS: *Acme-Plus* (Mute 1999)★★★.

Spice Girls

When Take That abdicated as monarchs of the UK teen band scene in February 1996, there were several pretenders lining up, but few could have predicted that a female quintet would have more success in the *Smash Hits*-reading market than Boyzone or Peter Andre. The Spice Girls - Victoria Adams aka Posh Spice (b. 17 April 1975, Goff's Oak, Hertfordshire, England), Melanie Janine Brown aka Mel B/Scary Spice (b. 29 May 1975, Leeds, Yorkshire, England), Emma Lee Bunton aka Baby Spice (b. 21 January 1976, Barnet, England), Melanie Jayne Chisholm aka Mel C/Sporty Spice (b. 12 January 1974, Liverpool, Merseyside, England) and Geraldine Halliwell aka Geri/Ginger Spice (b. 6 August 1972, Watford, Hertfordshire, England - this birthdate is the matter of some conjecture) - met at various unsuccessful auditions for film and dance jobs and the five ended up sharing a house in Maidenhead, Berkshire, in late 1993. They started writing and demoing songs, until manager Simon Fuller took them on in May 1995. A record deal with Virgin Records followed and by June 1996, the single 'Wannabe', an expression of the 'girl power' philosophy, with a deliciously silly rap interlude, was on its way to number 1 in the UK. The Spice success story was down to a number of factors. Most importantly, they managed to add post-feminist attitude to a commercial pop package - the boys could fancy them, although their first loyalty was to each other and their fellow females. However, they also had a set of highly hummable pop ditties, so that female bonding and the arcane mysteries of the 'zigazig-ha' never got in the way of the pure disco thrill. 'Wannabe' and the follow-up, 'Say You'll Be There', had all the glorious catchiness of Take That or Wham! at their commercial peaks. Things began to get out of hand by the end of 1996, when Halliwell's past as a nude model was splashed over the tabloid press, and an ill-advised interview with *The Spectator* magazine revealed her and Adams to be unlikely supporters of Conservative Prime Minister John Major. Nevertheless, nothing could stop the Spice Trail; as the lush ballad '2 Become 1' grabbed the coveted Christmas number 1 berth, boy bands wondered what had hit them and the Girls prepared to ravish the USA. By February 1997 their mission was completed with ease when 'Wannabe' effortlessly made number 1 in the *Billboard* singles chart, after only four weeks. Shortly afterwards, the album also topped the US chart and they became the first UK act ever to reach the top of the chart with their debut album. Phenomenal success continued all over the world throughout 1997 with some well-chosen sponsorship deals, and the quintet's faces were published as regularly as the Beatles in their peak media year of 1964. *Spiceworld* was another slice of highly commercial pop music, featuring the UK number 1s 'Spice Up Your Life' and 'Too Much'. Although the album debuted at number 1 in six countries its sales were nowhere near as high as expected, and it stalled at number 3 in the US. To put their sales into perspective, however, *Spice* and *Spiceworld* were easily the most commercially successful albums released by a UK act in the 90s. Towards the end of 1997 they unceremoniously dumped their svengali manager, Simon Fuller. The repercussions to this bold 'go it alone' mission were watched with interest as many felt that this could be their first wrong move. The commercial success of their debut movie *Spiceworld - The Movie*, premiered on 26 December 1997, indicated otherwise. Their third single, the Motown-pastiche 'Stop', only reached number 2 in the UK charts, breaking the group's run of chart-toppers. A potentially terminal threat to the future of the Spice Girls came at the end of May 1998, when Geri Halliwell, their de facto leader and undisputed driving force, announced she had left the group. Nevertheless, 'Viva Forever', the first single issued since Halliwell's departure (although her vocals appeared on the single), proved that the Spice phenomenon lived on when it entered the UK charts at number 1 in August 1998. A month later, Mel B collaborated with hip-hop artist Missy 'Misdemeanor' Elliott on the one-off single, 'I Want You Back', which debuted at number 1 in the UK charts. The group then became the first artists to enjoy three consecutive UK number 1 Christmas singles since the Beatles, when 'Goodbye' emulated the success of 'Too Much' and '2 Become 1'. Mel C's duet with Canadian rock singer Bryan Adams, 'When You're Gone', climbed to number 3 in the UK charts in December 1998. Mel B, now known as Mel G following her marriage to the group's Dutch dancer Jimmy Gulzar (the couple have since split-up), released a cover version of Cameo's 'Word Up'. The single was the first notable failure associated with the Spice Girls, stalling at UK number 14 in July 1999. Melanie C. also reinvented herself as a rock singer, touring as a solo act and releasing the *Northern Star* album. Later in the year, Emma Bunton's dull cover version of Edie Brickell's 'What I Am' lost a highly publicised 'battle of the singles' with her former bandmate Halliwell's 'Lift Me Up'.

● ALBUMS: *Spice* (Virgin 1996)★★★★, *Spiceworld* (Virgin 1997)★★★.
● VIDEOS: *Spice Power* (Visual). *Spice - Official Video Volume 1* (Virgin Video 1997). *One Hour Of Girl Power* (Warner Home Video 1997), *Spice Exposed: Too Hot!* (Quantum Leap 1998), *Spiceworld - The Movie* (PolyGram Music Video 1998), *Girl Power! Live In Istanbul* (Virgin Music Video 1998), *Spice Girls Live At Wembley Stadium* (Virgin Music Video 1998), *Spice Girls In America: A Tour Story* (Virgin Music Video 1999).
● FURTHER READING: *Girl Power*, Spice Girls. *Spice Power: The Inside Story*, Rob McGibbon. *Spiceworld: The Official Book Of The Movie*, Dean Freeman (photographer). *Spiced Up! My Mad Year With The Spice Girls*, Muff Fitzgerald.
● FILMS: *Spiceworld - The Movie* (1997).

Spin Doctors

This four-piece band came together in 1989 when Christopher Barron (b. 5 February 1968, Hawaii; vocals) and Eric Schenkman (b. 12 December 1963, Massachusetts, USA; guitar) met Aaron Comess (b. 24 April 1968, Arizona, USA; drums) at the New School of Jazz in New York. With the line-up completed by Mark White (b. 7 July 1962, New York, USA; bass), the band signed a recording contract the following year. *Pocket Full Of Kryptonite* was a varied collection of well-crafted, tuneful rock songs flavoured with funk rhythms and witty, intelligent lyrics. It also displayed the band's considerable musical ability, playing in a wide range of styles from the light, jazzy feel of the softer numbers to hard funk reminiscent of the Red Hot Chili Peppers, with almost nonchalant ease, while retaining a recognizable sound of their own. Undeterred by the album's lack of initial success, the Spin Doctors took to the road in the USA, touring to the point of physical and financial exhaustion. When a Vermont radio station began to plug the album heavily, others soon followed, and the band's popularity spi-

ralled upwards. *Pocket Full Of Kryptonite* became a major hit, producing a US Top 10 single in 'Little Miss Can't Be Wrong', despite the small storm caused by the track's opening line, 'Been a whole lot easier since the bitch left town' (the lyric was in fact aimed satirically at Barron's former stepmother rather than an exercise in rock misogyny). A live set, *Homebelly Groove*, was released to satisfy the new demand. By this time, comparisons were being drawn between the rise of the Spin Doctors and that of Nirvana, both being the people's choice, but the band simply stayed on the road, maintaining their impressive live reputation, while another single, 'Two Princes', led to worldwide success. However, late 1994 saw their first major setback, when news filtered through that guitarist Eric Shenkman had been ousted in favour of Anthony Krizan (b. New Jersey, USA). *Turn It Upside Down* was but a pale shadow of the multi-million-selling *Pocket Full Of Kryptonite*. There were a few highlights ('Cleopatra's Cat, 'Mary Jane' and 'You Let Your Heart Go Too Fast') and perhaps the band had been pressured to follow-up quickly. After such a superb debut, it was a bitter disappointment and would-be purchasers stayed away in their millions. Such success seems to have counted for nothing, and they have apparently ceased to be a commercial proposition. News that Barron was allegedly suffering from vocal problems did not help their cause.

● ALBUMS: *Pocket Full Of Kryptonite* (Epic 1991)★★★★, *Homebelly Groove* (Epic 1992)★★, *Turn It Upside Down* (Epic 1994)★★, *You've Got To Believe In Something* (Epic 1996)★★.

Spinanes

A duo of Rebecca Gates (vocals/guitar) and Scott Plouf (drums) based in Portland, Oregon, USA, the Spinanes made a mighty impact in 1993 with the release of *Monos* - the first record released on the acclaimed Sub Pop Records label to top the college radio charts. The harrowing, acutely detailed lyrical narratives penned by Gates made for difficult listening, though more than enough consumers and critics were won over by the band. Gates had met Plouf through the former's college radio show. Previously, she had also played one set at Olympia's Fringe Festival in 1990, as part of a 'thrown-together' group called the Cradle Robbers. There was a long delay before a follow-up Spinanes collection emerged, though the reason for the delay was partly explained by a new suite of lyrics detailing in minute detail the emotional turmoil and mishaps undergone by Gates in the intervening period. It was also much less bombastic than their debut, the mood being redolent of Big Star - unsurprising, perhaps, as it was recorded in that band's home city of Memphis. Plouf later played with the critically acclaimed Built To Spill. After relocating to Chicago, Gates continued the Spinanes as a solo project, releasing the imaginative and accessible *Arches And Aisles* in 1998.

● ALBUMS: *Monos* (Sub Pop 1993)★★★, *Strand* (Sub Pop 1996)★★★, *Arches And Aisles* (Sub Pop 1998)★★★★.

Spiritualized

This dark, neo-psychedelic band, who sometimes use the sub-title Electric Mainline, was formed by Jason Pierce (b. 19 November 1965, Rugby, Warwickshire, England; vocals/guitar) after his messy break-up from former writing partner and Spacemen 3 cohort Pete 'Sonic Boom' Kember. Based in Rugby, they were actually inaugurated while

Spacemen 3 were still officially active. Pierce took the remnants of that band with him (Mark Refoy (guitar), Will Carruthers (bass)and John Mattock (drums)) and added his girlfriend Kate Radley (organ). Their first release was a sensitive cover version of the Troggs' 'Anyway That You Want Me', then 'Feel So Sad', a sonic opera lasting 13 minutes and 20 seconds. Headliners at ICA's Irn Bru Rock Week, their familiar Velvet Underground guitar noise/dream pop found favour with old Spacemen 3 fans as well as new converts, and their debut album, *Lazer Guided Melodies*, was widely regarded as one of the best of 1992. Singles such as 'Why Don't You Smile', however, were something of a departure from Pierce's morbid and moribund legacy. Notoriously shy and reticent in interviews, he had a preference for sitting down while playing gigs, which an impressionable audience eagerly imitated. A mail-order live album arrived in 1993, after which sessions began on a second album proper. In the meantime Pierce discovered an affinity with some of the 90s ambient house artists, working on remixes for LFO, Global Communications and others. With the core of the band reduced down to Pierce, Radley and new bass player Sean Cook, *Pure Phase* finally arrived in 1995 to the usual critical fanfare, going some way to accommodate its protagonist's assertion that he wanted to make 'a record so beautiful it brings a tear to your eye'. The best example of this approach to creating elegiac pop was 'All Of My Tears', with strings provided by the Balanescu Quartet. The line-up by late 1997 featured Mike Mooney (guitar), Tim Jeffries (keyboards), Damon Reece (drums) and Ray Dickaty (saxophone). The aptly-titled *Ladies And Gentlemen We Are Floating In Space* was Pierce's finest distillation yet of his wide range of styles, an ambitious sonic experiment that even found room for the piano work of Dr. John on the epic closing track 'Cop Shoot Cop'. The album was crammed full of influences that sounded refreshing rather than plagiarist. From the *Smiley Smile*-period Beach Boys on the title track to the Primal Scream groove on 'Come Together', *Ladies And Gentlemen We Are Floating In Space* was one of the musical highlights of 1997, and also featured one of the most original and cleverly designed album sleeves in recent years. Following the release of a live album, the notoriously fickle Pierce dismissed most of his former bandmates and returned to the recording studio.

● ALBUMS: *Lazer Guided Melodies* (Dedicated 1992)★★★★, *Fucked Up Inside* (Dedicated 1993)★★, *Pure Phase* (Dedicated 1995)★★★, *Ladies And Gentlemen We Are Floating In Space* (Dedicated 1997)★★★★, *Live At The Royal Albert Hall: October 10 1997* (Deconstruction 1998)★★★★.

Squarepusher

In the mid-90s, Tom Jenkinson was one of a number of artists who attempted to create more integrated dance music in the midst of a splintering scene. He began playing the bass guitar and drums as a teenager, inspired by his father's collection of dub records. From there he became interested in 70s jazz fusion artists such as Stanley Clarke, Weather Report and Chick Corea, and later, the music of Miles Davis, Charlie Parker and Dizzy Gillespie. When he was 15 he switched on to electronic music having heard LFO's 'LFO' (1990) and the music of Carl Craig. As the Duke Of Harringay he released a number of tracks on the Zoom Records spin-off Spymania, including the *Conumber* EP and

'Alroy Road Tracks'. The latter set the tone for Squarepusher's style, which blended virtuosic bass guitar, electronic sounds and complex jungle, jazz and funk drum grooves, often structured with chord sequences. A remix of DJ Food's 'Scratch Yer Head' (1996) was followed by interest from such labels as Ninja Tune Records, Warp Records and R&S Records; however, as a result of his friendship with Richard James (aka Aphex Twin), his first album, *Feed Me Wierd Things*, was released on Rephlex Records. He signed to Warp in 1996 and released the *Port Rhombus* EP in July, followed the next year by the album *Hard Normal Daddy* and two further EPs, *Vic Acid* and *Big Loada*. The *Burning'n Tree* collection featured his pre-Warp material gathered together. He has had an enthusiastic, if occasionally somewhat hysterical, response from the press. Squarepusher is best when he successfully integrates his diverse influences with his musical skill. 'Papalon', from *Hard Normal Daddy*, presents various understated jazz and jungle rhythms, with a number of subtle textures created from bubbling bass guitar and bass clarinet, as well as floating, oscillating chords, while the remix of DJ Food's 'Scratch Yer Head', after an onslaught of coarse drums, settles into a relaxed chord sequence that frames Jenkinson's tasteful melodic basslines. However, there is sometimes a tendency to become boring when his drum programming becomes over-intricate and fidgety, and he develops an Aphex Twin-style nastiness-for-the-sake-of-it attitude. There is also a feeling on *Hard Normal Daddy* that he has created a number of interesting pastiches – 'Cooper's World' (70s television cop theme), 'Papalon' (Miles Davis' *Bitches Brew*), 'E8 Boogie' (an indulgent jazz rock trio), 'Fat Controller' (big beat) – mingled with mediocre electronic and jungle tunes, rather than producing a coherent whole. His prolific output also means that quality control sometimes goes awry, with the impact of 1998's dark fusion classic *Music Is Rotted One Note* lessened by the subsequent clutch of experimental mini-albums including the warped electronica of *Budakhan Mindphone* and *Selection Sixteen*.

● ALBUMS: *Feed Me Wierd Things* (Rephlex 1996)★★★, *Hard Normal Daddy* (Warp 1997)★★★, *Burning'n Tree* (Warp 1997)★★★, *Music Is Rotted One Note* (Warp 1998)★★★★, *Budakhan Mindphone* mini-album (Warp 1999)★★★, *Selection Sixteen* (Warp 1999)★★.

Squirrel Nut Zippers

A throwback to the world of big band jazz and swing bands, the Squirrel Nut Zippers are a seven-piece outfit formed in Chapel Hill, North Carolina, USA. The original line-up comprised Jim 'Jimbo' Mathus (vocals, guitar, trombone; ex-Metal Flake Mother), Katharine Whalen (vocals, banjo), Ken Mosher (vocals, guitar, reeds), Chris Phillips (drums), Tom Maxwell (vocals, guitar, saxophone), Stu Cole (bass) and Je Widenhouse (trumpet). Taking their name from a peanut-flavour confectionery manufacturer from Massachusetts, they began life in 1992 entertaining a wide range of audiences with their mix of swing, hot jazz and calypso. Their bookings have included everything from nightclub sets to festivals, weddings, wine-tastings and even a fireman's ball. They subsequently signed with Mammoth Records, making their debut with *The Inevitable* in 1995. Though this sold less than 20,000 copies, it did include 'Anything But Love', later featured in the Ben Stiller movie, *Flirting With Disaster*, where it was covered by Dr. John. The follow-up collection, *Hot*, was promoted by a limited-edition 7-inch single and the

Squirrel Nut Zippers' own blend of coffee, which was made available in cafés in the North Carolina region. Recorded at Daniel Lanois' Kingsway Studios in New Orleans, it featured a guest spot from local trumpet player Duke Heitger to add some regional flavour. With everything recorded in two or three takes, it captured the Squirrel Nut Zippers' lucid sound more succinctly than their debut and saw the band rise in prominence within alternative rock circles, though many radio programmers were bemused at the impact a contemporary 'showband' were making on their listeners. In August 1998, *Perennial Favorites* debuted at number 18 on the *Billboard* Top 200 album chart. Whalen released a solo set the following May.

● ALBUMS: *The Inevitable* (Mammoth 1995)★★★, *Hot* (Mammoth 1996)★★★, *Sold Out EP* (Mammoth 1997)★★, *Perennial Favorites* (Mammoth 1998)★★★★, *Christmas Caravan* (Mammoth 1998)★★.

Staind

The line-up of this US alternative metal act, comprising Aaron Lewis (vocals), Mike Mushok (guitar), Johnny April (bass) and Jon Wyscoki (drums), came together in February 1995. The following year, having established themselves as a leading live draw, the band recorded and distributed their debut, *Tormented*. The album went on to sell over 4,000 copies by word of mouth, and also gained them a high-profile support slot for Limp Bizkit's Connecticut show in October 1997. An initial misunderstanding about *Tormented*'s satanic cover art almost saw them coming to blows with Fred Durst, but Limp Bizkit's lead vocalist was impressed enough to invite the band to record demos for his production company. A deal with Flip Records ensued in early 1998, and the band decamped to Pearl Jam's studio in Seattle to record their major-label debut with producer Terry Date. A reworking of Public Enemy's 'Bring The Noise', featuring Durst, was left off the final track listing. This proved to be a good choice, as the songs on *Dysfunction* eschewed the overt hip-hop influence of Limp Bizkit for a more traditional style of hard rock rooted in the early 90s sound of Alice In Chains.

● ALBUMS: *Dysfunction* (Flip/Elektra 1999)★★★★.

Stansfield, Lisa

b. 11 April 1966, Rochdale, Greater Manchester, England. Stansfield started her musical career singing in her early teens, entering and winning several talent contests. She gained valuable experience presenting the Granada television children's programme, *Razzamatazz* in the early 80s. After quitting the programme Stansfield teamed up with former school friends and budding songwriters Andy Morris and (Lisa's boyfriend) Ian Devaney to form the white-soul group, Blue Zone in 1983. With backing from Arista Records, they released 1986's *Big Thing*, and several singles on the Rockin' Horse label but achieved little success outside the club circuit. In 1989, the trio were invited by the dance music production team, Coldcut (Matt Black and Jonathon Moore) to record the single 'People Hold On'. The single reached the UK Top 20 and prompted former Blue Zone/Wham! manager Jazz Summers to sign Stansfield as a solo act while retaining Morris and Devaney in the capacity as composers (with Stansfield), musicians and producers. The first single, on Arista, 'This Is The Right Time' reached number 13 in the UK chart while the follow-up, 'All Around The World' emerged as one of best singles of 1989, hitting

the UK number 1 spot and becoming an international hit. Her debut *Affection*, reached number 2, eventually selling five million copies worldwide. Stansfield, with her infectious smile, a disarmingly broad Lancastrian/Rochdale accent, down-to-earth nature and kiss-curled hair emerging from a collection of hats, became one of the top pop personalities of the year and collected a variety of awards including the Best British Newcomer at the 1990 BRIT Awards. That same year, the Blue Zone songwriting team of Stansfield, Morris and Devaney were also acknowledged by being presented the prestigious Ivor Novello Award for their number 1 hit as Best Contemporary Song. While 'Live Together' was peaking at number 10 in the UK singles chart, plans were afoot to break into the US chart. 'All Around The World' then reached number 3 and topped the *Billboard* R&B listing, while *Affection* reached the US Top 10. Her success in the US was followed by 'You Can't Deny It' (number 14) and 'This Is The Right Time' (number 21). The following years' BRIT Awards were notable for Stansfield winning the Best British Female Artist award. She also succeeded in offending organizer Jonathan King, by speaking out against the Gulf War. *Real Love*, which allowed Stansfield free rein to express herself, won over previously reticent admirers and promoted a more mature image. She had further UK hits in late 1991 with 'Change' (number 10) and 'All Woman' (number 20), although both singles failed to break into the Top 25 in America. 'In All The Right Places' put Stansfield back into the UK Top 10 (number 8) in June 1993, but by her own admission *So Natural* was a self-indulgent mistake. After a long break she returned with *Lisa Stansfield* in 1997, which featured 'Never, Never Gonna Give You Up', a song originally recorded by her musical hero Barry White. In 1999, Stansfield starred in the movie *Swing*, a romantic comedy following the exploits of a swing band formed in Liverpool, England. She gave a convincing performance, demonstrating a natural flair for acting.

● ALBUMS: *Affection* (Arista 1989)★★★, *Real Love* (Arista 1991)★★★, *So Natural* (Arista 1993)★★, *Lisa Stansfield* (Arista 1997)★★★, *The Number 1 Remixes* mini-album (Arista 1998)★★★.

● VIDEOS: *Lisa Live* (PMI 1993).

● FILMS: *Swing* (1999).

Stegall, Keith

b. 1 November 1954, Wichita Falls, Texas, USA. Keith is the son of Bob Stegall, who played steel guitar for Johnny Horton. He made his stage debut when only eight years old and performed in a variety of folk and country groups during his adolescence. He formed his own band, the Pacesetters, when only 12 and toured overseas with the folk group the Cheerful Givers. Stegall then moved to Nashville and became a staff writer for CBASS. He wrote 'Sexy Eyes' (Dr Hook), 'We're In This Love Together' (Al Jarreau) and 'Hurricane' (Leon Everette). He had a few minor US country hits with Capitol Records but had more success with Epic, making the Top 10 with 'Pretty Lady' and a further hit with 'California'. Stegall co-produced all of Alan Jackson's albums including the landmark *Here In The Real World*, and also sang harmony vocals on it. He has produced many other albums including those for Tracy Byrd, Terri Clark, Shenandoah, Randy Travis and Aaron Neville. He writes with Alan and Roger Murrah and their songs have included 'Blue Blooded Woman', 'Dallas' (Alan Jackson) and 'If I

Could Make A Living' (Clay Walker). Additionally he became vice-president of A&R with Mercury Records. He returned to singing on his own projects again in 1995 after deciding the new songs on *Passages* suited his own voice better than others. He produced George Jones' outstanding *Cold Hard Truth* in 1999.

● ALBUMS: *Keith Stegall* (Epic 1985)★★★, *Passages* (Mercury 1996)★★★.

Steps

A collaboration between Pete Waterman and promotions veteran Steve Jenkins that produced one of the UK pop sensations of the late 90s. The five members of Steps were recruited through an advertisement placed in *Stage* in 1997 by manager Tim Byrne. Lisa Scott-Lee was a graduate of London's Italia Conti stage school and had toured as a professional singer/dancer, while Faye Tozer had gained experience working in a cabaret band at the Hilton in London. The other female member Claire Richards had previously appeared with girl band TSD. Lee Latchford, after turning down the opportunity to become a professional football player, had toured in various theatre productions, while Ian Watkins previously worked as a children's holiday-camp entertainer. The group's dancing backgrounds were reflected in their tightly choreographed performances, augmenting the appeal of Waterman's effortless pop productions. Inspired by the concurrent line-dancing fad, '5,6,7,8' was released in November 1997, spending 17 weeks in the UK Top 40 and reaching a peak position of 14, making it the biggest-selling single of the 90s to fail to enter the Top 10. For the follow-up single, Waterman revived an old Bananarama single, 'Last Thing On My Mind', which climbed to number 6 in May 1998 and was memorably described by Waterman as 'Abba on speed'. The group's debut album entered the UK album chart at number 2 in September, buoyed by the success of 'One For Sorrow', a number 2 single in the same month. 'Heartbeat/Tragedy', originally recorded for a Bee Gees tribute album, debuted at number 2 in November. The song climbed back to UK number 1 in January 1999, eventually spending an impressive 15 weeks in the Top 10. 'Better Best Forgotten' debuted at number 2 in March, having failed to dislodge Boyzone from the top slot. 'Love's Got A Hold On My Heart' provided the group with their third UK number 2 single in July 1999, but the failure of the insipid 'After The Love Has Gone' to climb higher than number 5 indicated that some of their appeal might be waning. This did not stop the follow-up album, *Steptacular*, topping the UK chart in October.

● ALBUMS: *Step One* (Jive 1998)★★★, *Steptacular* (Jive 1999)★★.

● VIDEOS: *The Video* (Zoo 1998), *The Steps Story: Unauthorised* (Visual Entertainment 1999).

Stereo MC's

This UK crossover outfit's commercial breakthrough in the early 90s was the result of both sustained hard work and an original talent. Their line-up revolved around three women and three men: Rob Birch (b. Robert Charles Birch, 11 June 1961, Ruddington, Nottinghamshire, England; vocals), Nick 'The Head' Hallam (b. 11 June 1962, Nottingham, England; synthesizers/computers/scratching), and Owen If (b. Ian Frederick Rossiter, 20 March 1959, Newport, Wales; percussion, ex-Bourbonese Qualk), plus Cath Coffey (b. Catherine

Muthomi Coffey, Kenya - 'I can't tell you my real age because I act and tell different casting directions various different ages), Andrea Bedassie (b. 7 November 1957, London, England), and Verona Davis (b. 18 February 1952, London, England) on backing vocals. Hallam and Birch had been friends in Nottingham since the age of six. There they formed a rock duo titled Dogman And Head, before moving to London in 1985. Together they started recording rap music, though keeping intact their original love of soul, and set up their own label Gee Street Records with John Baker and DJ Richie Rich, from their base in Clapham. They were given a cash windfall when they were each handed £7,000 by a property developer to move out of their adjacent flats. This allowed them to establish the Gee St studio in a basement on the London street of the same name. The Stereo MC's first recording was 'Move It', released before the duo recruited Italian-British DJ Cesare, and formed their alter-ego remix team, Ultimatum. In the meantime, Island Records signed up Gee St for distribution, re-releasing 'Move It' in March 1988. Their first remix as Ultimatum arrived shortly afterwards (Jungle Brothers' 'Black Is Black'). Cesare left after a tour supporting Jesus Jones, stating that he was unhappy with the band's direction and financial arrangements. He went on to produce in his own right. Hallam and Birch continued, recording, *Supernatural*, with Baby Bam of the Jungle Brothers. They also recruited Owen If, originally for live percussion, who had previously been employed at Pinewood Studios as a special effects trainee, working on films like *Batman* and *Full Metal Jacket*. A support tour with Living Colour turned out to be a disaster, however. They enjoyed their first crossover hit with 1991's 'Lost In Music', based on the Ultimatum remix of the Jungle Brothers' 'Doin' Your Own Dang'. Their remixes have since encompassed artists like Aswad ('Warrior Re-Charge'), Definition Of Sound ('Wear Your Love Like Heaven'), Disposable Heroes Of Hiphoprisy ('Television - The Drug Of The Nation', 'Language Of Violence'), Dreams Warriors ('Follow Me Not'), Electronic ('Idiot Country Two'), Mica Paris ('Stand Up', 'Contribution'), Monie Love ('It's A Shame', 'Monie In The Middle'), P.M. Dawn ('Reality Used To Be A Friend Of Mine'), Queen Latifah ('Dance 4 Me') and U2 ('Mysterious Ways'). Coffey was added to the line-up for 'Elevate My Mind', her two female compatriots joining shortly after. She enjoys a concurrent career as an actor and dancer. She was even in the famed Broadway flop version of *Carrie*. 'Elevate My Mind' actually gave them a US Top 40 hit in 1991 - a first for a UK hip-hop outfit. The powerful *Connected* was released in September 1992 to mounting acclaim; previous albums had all been well received, but this was comfortably their most rounded and spirited effort. However, it was not until the title track and the exquisite rhythms of 'Step It Up' hit the UK charts that it was brought to the wider audience it richly deserved. 'Connected' also broke into the US Top 20. In its wake the Stereo MC's collared the Best Group category at the 1994 BRIT Awards ceremony, which celebrated the band's pre-eminence within the commercial dance music field to the detriment of their hip-hop roots. The band's failure to release a follow-up proved to be one of the biggest disappointments of the decade.

● ALBUMS: *33, 45,78* (4th & Broadway 1989)★★★, *Supernatural* (4th & Broadway 1990)★★★, *Connected* (4th & Broadway 1992)★★★★.

● VIDEOS: *Connected* (4th & Broadway 1993).

Stereolab

From south London, England, Stereolab have within a short time-span amassed an impressive body of work. The principal mover is Tim Gane (b. 12 July 1964, Barking, Essex, England; ex-McCarthy), who was at first joined by his girlfriend Laetitia Sadier (b. 1968, Paris, France), Martin Kean (ex-Chills) and Th' Faith Healers' drummer Joe Dilworth, also a *Melody Maker* photographer. Gane gave the band its name, after an obscure offshoot of 60s folk label Vanguard Records (it has also been stated that the title was taken from a hi-fi testing label). At their early gigs they were joined by Russell Yates (Moose) on guitar and Gina Morris (*New Musical Express* journalist) on vocals. Too Pure signed them, allowing them to keep their own Duophonic imprint. By the time of the release of the 'Low-Fi' 10-inch in September 1992, Mary Hansen had arrived to lend keyboard and vocal support, and Andy Ramsay replaced Dilworth on drums. 'John Cage Bubblegum', which some critics have noted as an adequate description of their sound, was released in the USA only, on Slumberland, via a limited edition version containing a stick of gum. By the time *The Groop Played Space Age Bachelor Pad Music* was released in March 1993, further line-up changes had occurred, with Duncan Brown joining on bass and ex-Microdisney guitarist Sean O'Hagan also guesting. This set was the closest to ambient soundscapes, *à la* Martin Denny or Arthur Lyman, that they had yet come. The group left Too Pure for Elektra Records at the end of 1993, once again retaining the Duophonic Ultra High Frequency Disks imprint for their domestic releases. Duophonic would also issue material by Arcwelder and Herzfeld, the latter featuring another former McCarthy member, Malcolm Eden. The double LP *Transient Random Noise-Bursts With Announcements* straddled both indie and dance music markets. This was more minimalist than ambient, and maintained their reputation not only as a competent rock outfit, but also as an important fixture of the experimental dance axis. The addictive *Music For The Amorphous Body Study Centre* continued to embrace subjects outside of pop music convention, on this occasion acting as a soundtrack to the work of artist Charles Long for an exhibition at New York's Tanya Bonakdar Gallery. *Emperor Tomato Ketchup* (the title was taken from a Japanese cult movie) was another mix of melodies that crept under the skin. Stereolab, with all their influences, from the sparse sounds of Moondog to the gentle side of Nico's Velvet Underground, remain hauntingly original and one of the most rewarding acts of the 90s. Ever prolific, they have subsequently released the dance-orientated *Dots And Loops* and *Cobra And Phases Group Play Voltage In The Milky Night*, indicating a willingness to experiment with their established sound. Gane also collaborated with O'Hagan as Turn On.

● ALBUMS: *Peng!* (Too Pure 1992)★★★, *The Groop Played Space Age Bachelor Pad Music* mini-album (Too Pure 1993)★★★★, *Transient Random Noise-Bursts With Announcements* (Duophonic 1993)★★★, *Mars Audiac Quintet* (Duophonic 1994)★★★★, *Music For The Amorphous Body Study Centre* mini-album (Duophonic 1995)★★★, *Emperor Tomato Ketchup* (Duophonic 1996)★★★★, *Dots And Loops* (Duophonic 1997)★★★★, *Cobra And Phases Group Play Voltage In The Milky Night* (Duophonic 1999)★★★★.

● COMPILATIONS: *Switched On* (Too Pure 1992)★★★, *Refried Ectoplasm (Switched On Volume 2)* (Duophonic 1995)★★★, *Aluminium Tunes (Switched On Volume 3)* (Duophonic 1998)★★★.

Stereophonics

Famed for being the first ever signings to Richard Branson's new music label, V2 Records, the Stereophonics are a three-piece Welsh rock/pop band who created an enormous buzz around the UK's A&R departments before finally electing to join V2 in August 1996. Indeed, Branson was reported to have taken a personal hand in their signing. Dovetailing 60s-inspired pop melodicism with 90s technology and the innovations of the dance music era, the Newport-based band were first spotted by V2's A&R head Ronnie Gurr via a tip-off. However, they were keen to distance themselves from Newport's recent press designation as 'the Seattle of the 90s', refusing to acknowledge any kinship with bands such as the 60 Foot Dolls or the Welsh-language movement. The band comprises three friends: songwriter Kelly Jones (guitar/vocals), Richard Jones (bass) and Stuart Cable (drums), grew up with each other in the small Welsh village of Cwmaman. Kelly Jones and Stuart Cable played together in various covers bands, before bringing in Richard Jones in 1991 to replace original bass player Mark Everett. Adopting the name Tragic Love Company, and recruiting the first of various rhythm guitarists, they set about making an impression on the local rock circuit. Changing their name to Stereophonics in 1996, and reverting to a trio, the band signed to V2 and supported several leading bands, including the in vogue Manic Street Preachers. The debut album, released in August 1997, confirmed their promise, attracting strong reviews, with Jones' character-driven songwriting on tracks such as 'Local Boy In The Photograph' and 'A Thousand Trees' winning particular praise. Their reward was a UK Top 10 album and a 1998 BRITS Award for Best Newcomer. Their new single, 'The Bartender And The Thief', debuted at number 3 in the UK charts in November the same year. 'Just Looking' reached number 4 the following March, and was followed by the chart-topping *Performance And Cocktails*. The band enjoyed their third consecutive UK Top 5 single when 'Pick A Part That's New' debuted at number 3 in May. It would seem that the band have passed the 'difficult second album' phase with great ease.

● ALBUMS: *Word Gets Around* (V2 1997)★★★★, *Performance And Cocktails* (V2 1999)★★★★.

● VIDEOS: *Word Gets Around* (PAL 1998), *Cwmaman Feel The Noize: Live At Cardiff Castle* (Visual Entertainment 1999), *Performance And Cocktails Live At Morfa Stadium* (Visual Entertainment 1999).

● FURTHER READING: *High Times & Headlines: The Story Of Stereophonics*, Mike Black.

Stewart, David A.

b. 9 September 1952, Sunderland, Tyne & Wear, England. At the age of 15, the fledgling guitarist Stewart introduced himself to the world of rock music by stowing away in the back of Amazing Blondel's tour van, after the band had given a performance in Stewart's home town of Newcastle. He later teamed up with guitarist Brian Harrison to form a duo, which after releasing *Deep December* went on to form Longdancer on Elton John's Rocket label in 1973. During this time, Stewart had met ex-Royal Academy of Music student Annie Lennox in London, where the couple co-habited. In 1977, together with friend Peter Coombes, they first recorded as a trio, the Catch, which developed into the Tourists. After establishing a following on the European continent, the Tourists achieved fame in the UK with minor hit singles, culminating in the number 4 hit cover version of Dusty Springfield's 1979 'I Only Want To Be With You' and 'So Good To Be Back Home Again'. This popularity with the public, however, was at odds with the particularly virulent and antagonistic attitude of the popular music press who viewed the band as 'old wave' cashing in on the 'new wave'. When the band split in late 1980, Stewart and Lennox, who had now ended their romantic relationship, continued working together and formed the Eurythmics. After a spell spent shaking off their reputation left over from the Tourists, the duo gradually won favourable reviews to eventually emerge as one of the world's major pop acts of the 80s. They were awarded the Ivor Novello Award for Songwriter Of The Year in 1984 and Stewart received the Best British Producer award at the BRIT Awards ceremony in 1986. He increased his role and reputation as a producer by working with, among others, Bob Dylan, Feargal Sharkey and Mick Jagger. A flurry of awards followed the next year for songwriting and production and in August, Stewart married Siobhan Fahey of Bananarama. In 1989, Boris Grebenshikov, the first Russian rock artist to record and perform in the West, travelled to the USA and UK to record *Radio Silence* with Stewart. After the recording of the Eurythmics' *We Too Are One*, the band's activities were put on hold while the duo allowed themselves time to rest and indulge in other projects. For Stewart, this included forming his own record label, Anxious, working with saxophonist Candy Dulfer on the UK Top 10 hit 'Lily Was Here' (1990), and the formation of his new band the Spiritual Cowboys, who achieved a minor UK chart placing for 'Jack Talking' (1990). Comprising Martin Chambers (drums, ex-Pretenders), John Turbull (guitar) and Chris James (bass), the band toured and recorded as a full-time project, and their debut album reached the UK Top 40. Stewart is now regarded as one of the major figures of the pop establishment, and despite attacks of a personal and artistic nature from the more radical quarters of the UK press, it can be said that he has been responsible for some of the finest pop music produced in the latter part of the 20th century. For his 1994 solo outing he enlisted the services of a wide range of artists including Carly Simon, Lou Reed, Bootsy Collins, David Sanborn and Laurie Anderson. Following an excellent reunion performance at the 1999 BRIT Awards, Stewart and Lennox announced dates for an Eurythmics tour. Stewart also devoted a lot of time to his innovative Sly-Fi web page, which launched an album of the same name.

● ALBUMS: *Lily Was Here* film soundtrack (AnXious 1990)★★, with the Spiritual Cowboys *Dave Stewart And The Spiritual Cowboys* (RCA 1990)★★★, with the Spiritual Cowboys *Honest* (RCA 1991)★★, *Greetings From The Gutter* (East West 1994)★★, *Sly-Fi* (Edel 1999)★★.

Stigers, Curtis

b. Boise, Idaho, USA. Stigers originally started out playing in punk and blues bands in his local music community. However, his classical training was in clarinet, before he decided to switch to saxophone in high school. It was then he took the decision to move to New York in search of rock 'n' roll. There, he moved back to familiar waters: 'When I got there I started out in the Blues scene. I wanted to play with other people and they had the best jams!' Despite having worked hard to attract record company interest on the club

circuit, it was in the unfamiliar world of jazz he would be discovered. He was playing saxophone and singing in a jazz-influenced trio with piano and bass, when spotted by the son of record company mogul Clive Davis (Arista Records' head): 'I could have gone to other companies and had unfettered freedom. But I wanted the guidance. I had to learn to collaborate'. Stigers quickly became an MOR airwaves favourite, likened disparagingly to Michael Bolton, but with his true influences Ray Charles and Otis Redding. Transatlantic hits in 1992 with 'I Wonder Why' and 'You're All That Matters To Me', if not delineating a bold new talent, marked him as an adequate commercial balladeer. His subsequent career has failed to reproduce the success of these early hit singles.

● ALBUMS: *Curtis Stigers* (Arista 1992)★★, *Time Was* (Arista 1995)★★, *Brighter Days* (Columbia 1999)★★★.
● VIDEOS: *Live In Concert* (BMG 1993).

Stiltskin

Authors of the most distinctive riff of 1994, few knew who Stiltskin were at the time, yet millions recognized the instrumental section of 'Inside' that accompanied a lavish Levis television advertisement. Picked up by the jeans manufacturer when it was overheard playing at the band's publishers, 'Inside' shot to number 1 in the UK charts when finally released as a single in the summer of 1994. The band had actually formed in 1989 when Peter Lawlor (guitar) and James Finnigan (bass) met for the first time in London. Finnigan had previously spent two years working alongside the Kane brothers in Hue And Cry, before electing to pursue a rockier direction. His new partner, meanwhile, had just returned from New York, dismayed with the dominance of dance music and rap. The duo began working on songs together in Lawlor's demo studio, recruiting an old friend of Finnigan's, Ross McFarlane, as drummer. However, unable to find a suitable singer or arouse record company interest, McFarlane relocated to Glasgow to drum with several bands, including Slide and Fireball. There were few further developments until the summer of 1993, when Lawlor and Finnigan were driving along the M8 between Edinburgh and Glasgow and passed a figure 'frantically retrieving objects which resembled guitars from a van engulfed in flames on the motorway's hard shoulder'. That distressed figure was Ray Wilson, who accepted an offer of a lift from the pair in order to make the gig he was playing that night. When he walked offstage, Lawlor and Finnigan offered him the job as Stiltskin vocalist. The new formation persuaded McFarlane to return to the fold, shortly after which they were approached to use 'Inside'. Their management team set up White Water records to house their releases, with a second single, 'Footsteps', also charting, before a debut album appeared in late 1994. Forever overshadowed by their albatross, 'Inside', Stiltskin joined a long list of one-hit wonders. Wilson went on to become lead singer with Genesis following Phil Collins' departure.

● ALBUMS: *The Mind's Eye* (White Water 1994)★★★.

Stone Roses

A classic case of an overnight success stretched over half a decade, the UK band Stone Roses evolved through a motley collection of Manchester-based non-starters such as the Mill, the Patrol and English Rose before settling down as Stone

Roses in 1985. Acclaimed for their early warehouse gigs, at this time the line-up consisted of Ian Brown (b. Ian George Brown, 20 February 1963, Ancoats, Gt. Manchester, England; vocals), John Squire (b. 24 November 1962, Broadheath, Gt. Manchester, England; guitar), Reni (b. Alan John Wren, 10 April 1964, Manchester, England; drums), Andy Couzens (guitar) and Pete Garner (bass). In their home-town, at least, the band had little trouble in working up a following, in spite of their predilection for juxtaposing leather trousers with elegant melodies. In 1987, guitarist Andy Couzens left, later to form the High, and Pete Garner followed soon after, allowing Gary 'Mani' Mounfield (b. 16 November 1962, Crumpsall, Gt. Manchester, England) to take over bass guitar. By this time the band had already made a low-key recording debut with the ephemeral 45, 'So Young'. By the end of the year the reconstituted foursome were packing out venues in Manchester, but finding it difficult to attract attention in the rest of the country. A contract with the Silvertone Records label in 1988 produced 'Elephant Stone', and showed its makers to have grasped the essence of classic 60s pop. A year later they had carried it over the threshold of the independent scene and into the nation's living rooms. When the follow-up, 'Made Of Stone', attracted media attention, the Stone Roses' ball started rolling at a phenomenal pace. Their debut album was hailed in all quarters as a guitar/pop classic, and as the Manchester 'baggy' scene infiltrated Britain's consciousness, Stone Roses - alongside the funkier, grubbier Happy Mondays - were perceived to be leaders of the flare-wearing pack. By the close of 1989, the Roses had moved from half-filling London's dingiest clubs to playing to 7,500 people at Alexandra Palace. Having achieved such incredible success so quickly, when the band vanished to work on new material, the rumour-mongers inevitably came out in force. In 1990, 'One Love' reached the UK Top 10, but aside from this singular vinyl artefact, the media was mainly concerned with the Roses' rows with a previous record company, who had reissued old material accompanied by a video made without the band's permission. This resulted in the band vandalizing the company's property, which in turn led to a much-publicized court case. As if this was not enough, Stone Roses were back in court when they tried to leave Silvertone, who took an injunction out against their valuable protégés. This prevented any further Stone Roses material from being released, even though the band eventually won their case and signed to Geffen Records for a reported $4 million. At the end of 1991, their eagerly awaited new product was still stuck somewhere in the pipeline while, in true Stone Roses fashion, after their live extravaganzas at Spike Island, Glasgow, London and Blackpool, plans were afoot for a massive open-air comeback gig the following spring. It never happened that year, nor the next. In fact, the Stone Roses' absence from the limelight - initially through contractual problems with Silvertone and management squabbles - then seemingly through pure apathy, became something of an industry standing joke. Had their debut album not had such a huge impact on the public consciousness they would surely have been forgotten. Painstaking sessions with a series of producers finally saw the immodestly titled *Second Coming* released in 1995. It was announced in an exclusive interview given to *The Big Issue*, the UK magazine dedicated to helping the homeless, much to the chagrin of a slavering British music press. Almost

inevitably, it failed to meet expectations, despite the fact that the US market was now opening up for the band. They also lost drummer Reni, who was replaced within weeks of its release by Robbie Maddix, who had previously played with Manchester rapper Rebel MC. Promotional gigs seemed less natural and relaxed than had previously been the case, while Silvertone milked the last gasp out of the band's legacy with them to compile a second compilation album (from only one original studio set). The tour they undertook in late 1995 dispelled any further gossip about loss of form or break-ups and nudged them back into the minds of critics who were beginning to see the band in a less than favourable light. In interview, it was clear that Squire was becoming disenchanted; he would not always show a united front, admitting that they had lost much by having such a gap between releases. It was, therefore, not too great a shock when he announced his departure in April 1996. Squire's carefully worded official statement read: 'It is with great regret that I feel compelled to announce my decision to leave. I believe all concerned will benefit from a parting of the ways at this point and I see this as the inevitable conclusion to the gradual social and musical separation we have undergone in the past few years. I wish them every success and hope they go on to greater things'. This left Ian Brown and company faced with deciding on a concrete plan of action or becoming another memorable rock legend. They chose the former and only commented on Squire's departure at the 1996 Reading Festival, where they were headlining. Speaking positively, Brown said that Squire had been a barrier for the band playing live. With new members Aziz Ibrahim (guitar) and Nigel Ippinson (keyboards), they planned to be much more active. The press reports were a different matter. Most sources confirmed that Brown's vocals were so off-key it was excruciating to have to listen. They made the right decision in October 1996 by announcing their demise. Mani joined Primal Scream full-time and ex-guitarist John Squire was retained by their record company Geffen, going on to form the Seahorses. Brown, meanwhile, embarked on a solo career. Too much was against them to survive together either creatively or socially.

● ALBUMS: *The Stone Roses* (Silvertone 1989)★★★★, *Second Coming* (Geffen 1995)★★★.

● COMPILATIONS: *Turns Into Stone* (Silvertone 1992)★★★, *The Complete Stone Roses* (Silvertone 1995)★★★, *Garage Flower* (Silvertone 1996)★★.

● VIDEOS: *The Complete Stone Roses* (Wienerworld 1995).

● FURTHER READING: *The Stone Roses And The Resurrection Of British Pop*, John Robb. *Breaking Into Heaven: The Rise And Fall Of The Stone Roses*, Mick Middles.

Stone Temple Pilots

The Stone Temple Pilots are the result of a chance meeting between Weiland (b. Scott Weiland, 27 October 1967, Santa Cruz, California, USA; vocals) and Robert DeLeo (b. 2 February 1966, New Jersey, USA; bass) at one of Black Flag's final shows in Los Angeles. After discovering that they both went out with the same girl, a songwriting partnership led to the formation of a full band, originally known as Mighty Joe Young, and later renamed Stone Temple Pilots, with Eric Kretz (b. 7 June 1966, Santa Cruz, California, USA; drums) and DeLeo's brother Dean (b. 23 August 1961, New Jersey, USA; guitar) joining the duo. Moving away from the Guns

N'Roses-crazed Los Angeles scene of the time to San Diego, the band were able to play club shows and develop hard rock material given an alternative edge by their varied influences. Although the sound of the band brought many others to mind, from Led Zeppelin to Seattle bands such as Pearl Jam and Alice In Chains, and Weiland's deep voice bore a passing resemblance to that of Eddie Vedder, it was very much Stone Temple Pilots' own sound, and there was no denying the quality of *Core*. The dense wall of muscular guitar over a tight, precise rhythm section provided a powerful setting for Weiland's emotive vocals and challenging lyrics. 'Sex Type Thing', perhaps the band's best-known song, deals with sexual harassment from the viewpoint of a particularly brutish male, and the singer was initially concerned that the message would be misinterpreted. His fears proved unfounded and, helped by heavy touring, *Core* reached the US Top 20 by the summer of 1993, eventually selling over four million copies in the USA. The follow-up, *Purple*, debuted at number 1 in the US album charts, staying there for three weeks. This time the band purposely avoided any material that could be construed as derivative of Pearl Jam, having tired of the unfair criticism. Their second effort proved to be an atmospheric and rewarding experience, as STP produced a quasi-psychedelic sound that confirmed their own identity and considerable talents. In May 1995, Weiland was arrested in Pasadena, California, and was charged with possession of heroin and cocaine, a misdemeanour that carried with it a possible four-year jail sentence. In early 1996, their best album to date was released amid rumours of serious drug abuse during the recording sessions. *Tiny Music ... Songs From The Vatican Gift Shop* was indeed a powerful record, but its success was tainted by Weiland being ordered by the courts to be confined to a drug rehabilitation centre. To have this happen at such a crucial time in the band's career (when the new album was still in the US Top 20) was a severe blow and raised serious questions about the band's future. However, by the end of 1996, Weiland had been cleared of the drugs charges and the band were back on the road. In 1998, Weiland released his solo debut and announced the band would record another album. Shortly afterwards, however, he was arrested in New York and charged with heroin possession, leading to a jail sentence. Despite their singer's incarceration, the band went ahead and released *No. 4* the following year.

● ALBUMS: *Core* (Atlantic 1992)★★★, *Purple* (Atlantic 1994)★★★, *Tiny Music ... Songs From The Vatican Gift Shop* (Atlantic 1996)★★★, *No. 4* (Atlantic 1999)★★★.

Solo: Scott Weiland *12 Bar Blues* (East West 1998)★★★.

● FURTHER READING: *Stone Temple Pilots*, Mike Wall and Malcolm Dome.

Strangelove

UK indie band Strangelove played their first set at Bath Moles Club on 9 October 1991, their line-up having evolved from an earlier incarnation as Words And Pictures. Comprising Patrick Duff (vocals), Alex Lee (guitar/keyboards), Julian Pransky-Poole (guitar), Joe Allen (bass) and John Langley (drums), they played sporadic gigs thereafter. These early shows were distinguished by the 40 or more songs (with lyrics always written by Duff) on which the band drew, all of them possessing one word titles. Their first release was a four-track EP, *Visionary*, released on the independent label Sermon Records in 1992. A growing profile in the industry weeklies was cemented when 1993's 'Hysteria Unknown' became one of the most popular singles of the year, although in interview the band remained cold and aloof. Duff's drunken stage performances also ignited considerable interest. David Balfe headed off a bidding war to sign the band to his Food Records label later that year. In 1994, they released their debut album, *Time For The Rest Of Your Life*, which paired them with longstanding collaborator and producer Paul Corkett for the first time. Their supporters in the music industry now included Suede, with whom they toured through the early part of 1995, including a set at London's Royal Albert Hall. A follow-up album, *Love And Other Demons*, was recorded in 1995, but before its release Duff was forced to attend a rehabilitation clinic to confront his alcohol problems. He and Strangelove made their comeback with a performance of frightening intensity at London's Camden Monarch venue in April 1996. The album was then released, and while many of their earlier supporters had moved on, there was no doubting Duff's power as a writer and lyricist. The self-titled third album was Duff's first without alcohol as a prop. A far more commercial set, the band's continued failure in the singles chart cast an unfortunate shadow on an excellent album.

● ALBUMS: *Time For The Rest Of Your Life* (Food 1994)★★★, *Love And Other Demons* (Food 1996)★★★, *Strangelove* (Food 1997)★★★.

Strapping Fieldhands

Underground enough to make some of their lo-fi peers seem like publicity hounds, Philadelphia's Strapping Fieldhands pursue a resolutely uncommercial brand of alternative rock that has won them a small but dogged group of fans in the USA and UK. In the mid-90s, when indie darlings Guided By Voices were being heralded by hipsters as the next Pavement, Strapping Fieldhands were already being touted as the next Guided By Voices. Led by Bob Malloy, the band, which has displayed a marked dislike for personnel credits, occasionally deigning to include their first names on their album sleeves (Jacy, Bob, Sky and Jeff), creates a heady mixture of punk, psychedelia, noise, 60s Britpop and general strangeness, featuring elliptical, absurd lyrics. They favour the kind of stop-start, cut-and-paste dynamics of the aforementioned bands, and the recording process is approached with a casualness that occasionally verges on the (delightfully) shambolic. Beginning as a trio of Philadelphia baby boomers/record store employees, the Strapping Fieldhands played their first show in 1991, opening for the equally unusual Frogs. Later that year, they began releasing limited-pressing 7-inch singles (including a split single with Mudhoney). By 1994, the band had gathered up enough steam to sustain a 10-inch EP (eventually reissued on CD), *In The Pineys*, containing a highly memorable desecration of Melanie's 60s hit 'Lay Down (Candles In The Rain).' 1996 was a banner year for the band, who by now had swelled to a quartet. The band began to receive international acclaim, and released *Wattle And Daub*, which solidified their position as kings of the lo-fi hill. One admiring critic was moved to comment 'one of the weirdest bands I know. Bob Malloy must be an absolute freak. Their music is strange as hell'. The gloriously indefinable racket of their debut album earned them a place on many writers' Top 10 lists for that year. The same year, they made it easier for their fans to acquire their pre-album canon by releasing *Gobs On The Midway*. This album was a comprehensive collection of the various blasts of twisted psych pop the band had previously committed only to vinyl.

● ALBUMS: *In The Pineys* (Siltbreeze 1995)★★★★, *Wattle & Daub* (Shangri-La 1996)★★★★.

● COMPILATIONS: *Gobs On The Midway: Singles 1991-1995* (Siltbreeze 1996)★★★.

Suede

This hugely promoted UK band broke through in 1993 by merging the lyrical perspective of Morrissey with the posturings of David Bowie and the glam set. Brett Anderson (b. 29 September 1967, Haywards Heath, England; lead vocals) quickly established a rare gift for brilliantly evocative mood swings and monochrome dioramas. Just as much was made of Bernard Butler (b. 1970, Leyton, London, England; guitar) and his similarity to indie guitar hero Johnny Marr (Smiths, Electronic). The rhythm section of the band comprises Matt Osman (b. 9 October 1967, Welwyn Garden City, England; bass) and Simon Gilbert (b. 1965, Stratford-Upon-Avon, Warwickshire, England; drums), a position for which Mike Joyce (ex-Smiths) originally tried out. Anderson and Osman had originally met at Haywards Heath Sixth Form College, playing together in various bands including Geoff, Bruiser and Suave And Elegant. The pair both decamped to London in the late 80s, where they met up with Justine Frischmann. The future Elastica singer became Anderson's partner and played with and helped promote the band in their early days. She left shortly after Gilbert joined Anderson, Osman and Butler in June 1991. The band began to generate a strong word-of-mouth reputation, and won Gary Crowley's demo clash on GLR Radio for five weeks running. Anderson's arrogant wit and seedy, sexually ambivalent narratives fascinated the press at a time when the music scene was dominated by American grunge and the UK's 'Madchester' bands. They signed a two-single contract with Nude Records in February 1992. Their first release, 'The Drowners', arrived in March 1992, and 'My Insatiable One', on the b-side, was a brooding low-life London tale of 'shitting paracetamol on the escalator', which so impressed Morrissey he would later cover it live. By this time, the mainstream music media, starved of an adequate figurehead for the 90s, had latched onto the band in a quite disconcerting manner. Q magazine put them on a front cover before the release of their debut album, a previously unthinkable concession. Their second single, 'Metal Mickey', broke into the UK Top 20 in September, following which they signed with Sony Music worldwide (while remaining loyal to Nude in the UK). Their appearance at February 1993's televised BRIT Awards gave them massive exposure, and their third single, 'Animal Nitrate', broke into the UK Top 10. On the back of this high profile their debut album went straight to number 1 in the UK charts, going gold on the second day of release. Again, much of the lyrical imagery was deliberately homoerotic, reflected in the sleeve artwork. The picture of two androgynous figures kissing, taken by Tee Corrine, was cut to head and shoulders to hide the identity of the two disabled women involved. The band proceeded to go from strength to strength, winning the Mercury Music Prize in September. All seemed rosy in the garden until the eve of their second album in 1994, when it was announced that Butler had left the band (recent interviews had hinted at rancour between Anderson and the guitarist). He would be replaced by a 17-year-old unknown Richard Oakes (b. 1 October 1976, Perivale, London, England). However, as the writing for *Dog Man Star* (which emerged to mixed reviews) had already been completed, there was little immediate evidence on which to gauge the reshuffled Suede until 1995. Chart returns, on the other hand, suggested that the band's chart thunder may have been stolen by Blur and Oasis. The album stayed at the top of the UK album charts for three weeks, but was quickly deposed by the latter's *Definitely Maybe*. Butler, meanwhile, went on to write well-regarded new material with David McAlmont and later embarked on a solo career. In early 1996, Neil Codling (b. 1973, Stratford-Upon-Avon, Warwickshire, England; keyboards), cousin of drummer Simon Gilbert, became the band's official fifth member. Great pressure was on the band for their third album, a lengthy gap between releases and the fickle music public being major factors. Any fears were dispelled by *Coming Up*, as it was a stunning collection of crafted, concise songs, epitomised by July's UK number 3 single 'Trash'. The album became the band's third successive UK chart-topper. The following year's *Sci-Fi Lullabies* collected together their consistently excellent b-sides. In 1999, the band premiered their new album with April's UK number 5 single 'Electricity'. The following month *Head Music* entered the UK album chart at number 1, although it soon dropped down, leaving pundits to agree that Suede's commercial star had faded.

● ALBUMS: *Suede* (Nude 1993)★★★★, *Dog Man Star* (Nude 1994)★★★, *Coming Up* (Nude 1996)★★★★, *Head Music* (Nude 1999)★★★.

● COMPILATIONS: *Sci-Fi Lullabies* (Nude 1997)★★★★.

● VIDEOS: *Love & Poison* (1993), *Bootleg 1* (1993), *Introducing The Band* (1995).

● FURTHER READING: *Suede: The Illustrated Biography*, York Membrey.

Sugar Ray

One of an increasing number of US bands in the 90s to combine hip-hop beats with heavy metal riffs following Rage Against The Machine's breakthrough, Orange County, California-based Sugar Ray comprise Mark McGrath (vocals), Rodney Sheppard (guitar), Murphy Karges (bass), Stan Frazier (drums) and DJ Homicide (b. Craig Bullock; turntables). Their lyrical concerns can be gauged by the fact that their debut album's title was based on an advertisement in a pornographic magazine. Or, as McGrath put it: 'We're meat-eating, beer-drinking pigs from America.' Heavily promoted by their record company on both sides of the ocean, their songs were undoubtedly punchy and charismatic in a grubby, Beastie Boys-styled fashion, but beyond its effortless vulgarity there was little musical innovation to distinguish it from their peers. The band have gone on to great success, however, charting with the memorable Top 40 radio hit 'Fly' and two best-selling albums, 1997's *Floored* and 1999's *14:59*. The latter included April's US number 3 hit, 'Every Morning', and the follow-up Top 10 single, 'Someday'.

● ALBUMS: *Lemonade And Brownies* (Atlantic 1995)★★, *Floored* (Atlantic 1997)★★★, *14:59* (Atlantic 1999)★★★.

Suggs

Former Madness singer Suggs McPherson (b. Graham McPherson, 13 January 1961, Hastings, Sussex, England) had toyed with various reformations of that hugely successful UK pop band before launching his solo career in 1995. The success of the band's 'Madstock' shows in Finsbury Park, London, in 1993, had reawakened public affection for the engaging singer. Suggs explained the delay thus: 'When I left Madness, I didn't want to stay in the music industry as a performer.' Instead he managed the Farm, co-producing their first album, and worked on his own show on satellite television (the ill-fated BSB). He began to write his own songs again in 1991, with the co-operation of former Madness colleague Mike Barson. When he decided to undertake a belated solo career in 1994 he found a willing aid in the shape of Warner Music chairman Rob Dickins, who had arranged Madness' publishing and originally lent the band the £200 necessary to record their first single, 'The Prince'. However, sessions for Suggs' self-produced solo release were delayed until Dickens suggested that Sly And Robbie, the reggae production/rhythm team, were available. Their input revitalised the sessions, along with the contributions of Jamaican saxophonist Rico Rodriguez, bass maestro Jah Wobble and Aswad's brass section. The first release was in August 1995 with the double a-side, 'Off On Holiday' and 'I'm Only Sleeping', followed by 'Camden Town'. Its offbeat celebration of the hip north London district was immediately recognisable to fans of Madness, far too much so for some critics. The reception afforded *The Lone Ranger*, which fell down the charts rather ominously after an initially high placing, was similarly muted. Few did not celebrate the return of one of Britain's most accessible songwriters, though more enthusiasm greeted the news that Suggs was also scheduled for December 1995 dates leading a re-formed Madness. A second major hit was culled from the album in the shape of 'Cecilia', the former Simon And Garfunkel hit and now a fixture of 'gold' radio stations. A second collection, *The Three Pyramid Club*, failed to build on the success of his earlier singles. On UK television he also hosts Channel 5's wonderfully trashy celebrity karaoke show, *Night Fever*.
● ALBUMS: *The Lone Ranger* (WEA 1995)★★★, *The Three Pyramid Club* (WEA 1998)★★★.

Suicidal Tendencies

Mike Muir (vocals) formed Suicidal Tendencies in the early 80s in the Venice Beach area of Los Angeles, California, USA, enlisting Grant Estes (guitar), Louiche Mayorga (bass) and Amery Smith (drums). Despite an inauspicious start, being voted 'worst band and biggest assholes' in *Flipside* magazine's 1982 polls, the band produced a hardcore classic in *Suicidal Tendencies*, and although they initially fell between hardcore punk and thrash stools, MTV's support of 'Institutionalized' helped the group take off. *Join The Army* was recorded with respected guitarist Rocky George and drummer R.J. Herrera replacing Estes and Smith, and the skateboarding anthem, 'Possessed To Skate', kept the group in the ascendancy. *How Will I Laugh Tomorrow ... When I Can't Even Smile Today?* marked the debut of Mike Clark (rhythm guitar) as the band's sound exploded, extending from a ballad title track to the furious 'Trip At The Brain'. This progression continued on *Controlled By Hatred/Feel Like Shit ... Deja Vu*, but as the band's stature increased, so did

their problems. Their name and image were easy targets for both the PMRC and the California police, with the former blaming teenage suicides on a band who were unable to play near their home-town due to performance permit refusals from the police, who feared Suicidal Tendencies were an LA gang. Naturally, the outspoken Muir fought vehemently against these bizarre accusations and treatment. Talented bass player Robert Trujillo, with whom Muir formed Infectious Grooves in tandem with Suicidal, made his debut on the excellent *Lights ... Cameras ... Revolution*, which produced hits in the defiant 'You Can't Bring Me Down' and 'Send Me Your Money', a vitriolic attack on television evangelist preachers. The band also re-recorded their debut during these sessions for release as *Still Cyco After All These Years*. The Peter Collins-produced *The Art Of Rebellion*, with new drummer Josh Freece, was a more ambitious, diverse work, and rather more lightweight than previous albums. Any fears that the band was mellowing were dispelled by furious live shows. *Suicidal For Life*, with Jimmy DeGrasso (ex-White Lion, Y&T) replacing Freece, emphasized the point as the band returned in fast-paced and profanity-peppered style, while continuing to extend individual talents to the full. Shortly after its release, in 1995 news filtered through that the band were no more. However, in 1997, Muir returned with new material and a revamped line-up, featuring Mike Clark and Dean Pleasants (guitars), Josh Paul (bass) and Brooks Wackerman (drums).
● ALBUMS: *Suicidal Tendencies* (Frontier 1983)★★★★, *Join The Army* (Caroline/Virgin 1987)★★★, *How Will I Laugh Tomorrow ... When I Can't Even Smile Today* (Epic 1988)★★★, *Controlled By Hatred/Feel Like Shit ... Deja Vu* (Epic 1989)★★, *Lights ... Camera ... Revolution* (Epic 1990)★★★, *The Art Of Rebellion* (Epic 1992)★★★, *Still Cyco After All These Years* (Epic 1993)★★★, *Suicidal For Life* (Epic 1994)★★★, *Six The Hard Way* mini-album (Suicidal 1999)★★★, *Freedumb* (Radiation 1999)★★★.
● COMPILATIONS: *FNG* (Virgin 1992)★★★, *Prime Cuts* (Epic 1997)★★★.

Sultans Of Ping FC

Formed in 1989 in Cork, Eire, and titled after the Dire Straits song of similar title, the Sultans Of Ping FC built up a rabid live following for their cross-dressing antics and tales of the totally unexpected. They chose their name in mock admiration of Mark Knopfler's outfit, being virulently anti-stadium rock 'n' roll 'baloney'. The band comprises Niall O'Flaherty (vocals), Paddy O'Connell (guitar), Morty McCarthy (drums) and Dat (b. Alan McFeely; bass). Their gigs quickly became legend after a local affair in which the promoter asked the crowd to sit down. The band joined them in solidarity, leading to audience participation of a bizarre nature: a series of floor gymnastics, with kicks to the air from a prone position. The gig that launched them nationally came when taking part in an Irish rock open, where they were the token local Cork entrants. Home support pushed them into the winner's enclosure. The first single endorsed this lunacy: 'Where's Me Jumper' on Rhythm King Records, revolved around the tale of O'Flaherty having his jumper pinched at a dance. In the best traditions of Serious Drinking and Half Man Half Biscuit, the Sultans are a band sharing the esoteric conviction of fellow Cork residents the Frank And Walters. However, their debut album was more than a barrage of jokes; with string and harmonica arrangements backing the strange lyrical observations. These included songs about Jesus' second coming (in a track suit), and a pole-vaulter unhindered by arms, legs or head. Titles such as 'Give Him A Ball And A Yard Of Grass' and 'Riot At The Sheepdog Trials' still gave a fairly strong indication of which planet in the pop universe the Sultans pinged from. *Teenage Drug* emerged to less flattering reviews, but was ultimately no less endearing in its humour, a strain that is often more complex than has been portrayed in some sections of the media. Modifying their name to the Sultans did not rescue their 1996 comeback album from obscurity.

● ALBUMS: *Casual Sex In The Cineplex* (Rhythm King 1992)★★★, as the Sultans Of Ping   *Teenage Drug* (Rhythm King 1993)★★★, as the Sultans *Good Year For Trouble* (Rhythm King 1996)★★.

Sundays

This UK indie band was formed in London, England, in the summer of 1987, by songwriters David Gavurin (b. 4 April 1963, England; guitar) and Harriet Wheeler (b. 26 June 1963, England; vocals), who had already gained prior singing experience in a band called Jim Jiminee. Later joined by the rhythm section of Paul Brindley (b. 6 November 1963, England; bass) and Patrick Hannan (b. 4 March 1966, England; drums), the Sundays' debut live performance at the seminal Falcon 'Vertigo Club' in Camden Town, London, in August 1988, sparked off abnormally excessive interest from both media and record business circles. Playing what many perceived to be a delicate, flawless mix of the Smiths' guitars and the Cocteau Twins' vocal acrobatics, the band's high profile ensured a Top 50 place in the UK pop charts for their debut single, 'Can't Be Sure', in early 1989. The song topped the independent charts for two months. Despite this dramatic arrival, the Sundays did not capitalize on their success until exactly a year later, when *Reading, Writing And Arithmetic* took everyone by surprise by entering the UK pop chart at number 4. Despite these rapid advances, the Sundays are notorious for being slow songwriters - legend has it that their label, Rough Trade Records, wanted to release a single from the album but the band did not have any other material for a b-side. This was to be their last release for two years, as touring commitments took the quartet to Europe, Japan and the equally reverential America, where *Rolling Stone* magazine had voted the Sundays Best Foreign Newcomer and their debut album had broken into the Top 40. Financial difficulties at their label also held-up proceedings. They sought a new record contract, eventually signing to Parlophone Records in January 1992. A second album was not completed until October of that year, and reactions, though not unkind, lacked the fervour that had greeted their debut (reissued on Parlophone Records in 1996). After an even longer sabbatical the band returned in 1997 with a surprise hit single, 'Summertime', and *Static And Silence*, which showed little sign of any musical progress. Wheeler's vocals still floated effortlessly over the music, but critical reaction saw the band as an anachronism. A cover version of the band's 'Here's Where The Story Ends' by UK dance music act Tin Tin Out, featuring the vocals of Shelley Nelson, reached UK number 7 in March 1998.

● ALBUMS: *Reading, Writing And Arithmetic* (Rough Trade 1990)★★★, *Blind* (Parlophone 1992)★★★, *Static And Silence* (Parlophone 1997)★★.

Sunhouse

This Nottingham-based outfit were grouped with other English bands of the late 90s, including Gomez, the Unbelievable Truth and Witness, due to their perceived musical and lyrical earnestness. This serious image gained them the rather derogatory and unrepresentative 'stool rock' tag. Songwriter Gavin Clarke originally met film director Shane Meadows when both were working in dead-end jobs at the Alton Towers leisure park. Several years later, Meadows contacted Clarke to provide songs for the soundtrack to his acclaimed low-budget film, *Small Time*. Clarke quickly formed a band for the work, recruiting guitarist Paul Bacon and two former members of late-80s indie band the Telescopes, bass player Robert Brooks (b. 11 April 1969, Burton-upon-Trent, Staffordshire, England) and drummer Dominic Dillon (b. 26 September 1964, Bolton, Lancashire, England). The band signed a deal with Independiente Records and completed further soundtrack work for Meadows' feature-length debut, *Twenty-Four Seven*. The limited edition *Small Time* EP and single 'Monkey Dread' introduced the band's full-length debut, *Crazy On The Weekend*. Working with producer John Reynolds (Sinead O'Connor), the band continued their practice of recording outside a studio environment. Their acoustic-based songs were augmented by washes of strings and organ, earning comparisons to Nick Drake, Tom Waits and Beth Orton. Clarke's cinema verité style lyrics, meanwhile, soared above their soundtrack origins.

● ALBUMS: *Crazy On The Weekend* (Independiente 1998)★★★★.

Sunny Day Real Estate

Formed in Seattle during 1992, this rock quartet was yet another excellent hopeful from this fertile area of the west coast. The band comprised Dan Hoerner (b. 13 May 1969, Seattle, Washington, USA; guitar/vocals), Jeremy Enigk (b. 16 July 1974, Seattle, Washington, USA; guitar/vocals), Nate Mendel (b. 2 December 1968, Seattle, Washington, USA; bass) and William Goldsmith (b. 4 July 1972, Seattle, Washington, USA; drums). They financed a debut single, 'Song Number 8/Song Number 9', on their own One Day I Stopped Breathing label and eventually signed with Sub Pop Records in 1994. Their debut, *Diary*, was locally acclaimed but shortly after its release Mendel and Goldsmith defected to form the Foo Fighters and the band effectively collapsed. In October 1995, a self-titled belated second album was released with a minimalist cover design that seemed to deliberately discourage any sales. The ghastly plain pink cover had the band's name printed in minuscule type. Inside, apart from the track listing, was a small picture of a fly. The music, however, was quite excellent, blending Seattle grunge with melodic pop. Enigk released his solo debut, *Return Of The Frog Queen*, the following year. In 1997, Goldsmith returned to the re-formed Sunny Day Real Estate, with Mendel replaced by Jeff Palmer. The rejuvenated band carried on where they left off with the passionate *How It Feels To Be Something On*.

● ALBUMS: *Diary* (Sub Pop 1994)★★★, *Sunny Day Real Estate* (Sub Pop 1995)★★★★, *How It Feels To Be Something On* (Sub Pop 1998)★★★.

Sunz Of Man

Originating from Brooklyn, New York, USA, the Sunz Of Man comprise rappers Killah Priest (b. Walter Reed, New York, USA), 60 Second Assassin, Prodigal Sunn and Hell Razah. Closely affiliated with Staten Island's Wu-Tang Clan, the Sunz crew worked on their debut album for three years while contributing to numerous Wu-Tang associated releases. After working on Ol' Dirty Bastard's 1995 set *Return To The 36 Chambers: The Dirty Version*, the Sunz Of Man released their debut single 'Soldiers Of Darkness'/'Five Arch Angels' on the Wu-Tang label. The single also marked the production debut of their associate 4th Disciple, and featured vocal contributions from future stars Killarmy. The fifth arch angel referred to on the b-side was Shabazz The Disciple, recording under the pseudonym of Holy Psychiatrist, although contrary to rumour he never joined the crew. The single became an underground hit, and was followed by an appearance on 'Wicked Wayz' from the *One Million Strong* compilation. Killah Priest also contributed to 'Where Ya At?' on the same album. His high-profile contribution to the Genius' *Liquid Swords* attracted further attention to the Sunz Of Man, who released a second single 'No Love Without Hate'. A switch to Red Ant Records enabled them to finally complete work on their much delayed album. The stellar cast list on *The Last Shall Be First* included cameo appearances from Wu-Tang Clan members Method Man, Raekwon, U-God, Masta Killa and Ol' Dirty Bastard, with the majority of the production work shared by RZA and 4th Disciple. Additional production input came from True Master, Supreme and Mathematics, with Fugees star Wyclef Jean overseeing a superb collaboration with Earth, Wind And Fire on a reworking of their 'Shining Star'. The remainder of the album offered up the usual heady brew, peppered with some inspired lyrical barbs from the four rappers.

● ALBUMS: *The Last Shall Be First* (Red Ant 1998)★★★★.

Super Furry Animals

Founded in Cardiff, Wales, this offbeat indie pop band comprise Gruff Rhys (b. 18 July 1970, Haverford West; vocals/guitar), Dafydd Ieuan (b. 1 March 1969, Bangor, North Wales; drums), Cian Ciaran (b. 16 June 1976, Bangor, North Wales; electronics), Guto Pryce (b. 4 September 1972, Cardiff, Wales; bass) and Huw 'Bunf' Bunford (b. 15 September 1967, Bath, Avon; guitar/vocals). Each member had worked in a series of underachieving bands before forming Super Furry Animals in 1993, although Ieuan was in the original line-up of future Welsh pop stars Catatonia. The next two years were spent writing and rehearsing original material. The first evidence of the band's distinctive, scabrous pop came with the release of the *Welsh Concept* EP for Cardiff independent Ankst Records in June 1995. Fully-titled *Llanfairpwllgwyngyllgogerchwyrndrobwllantysiliogo-goy-ocynygofod (In Space)*, the EP was a shameless attempt to get the band listed in the *Guinness Book Of Records*. The follow-up EP, *Moog Droog*, drew further praise. Occasional London shows now brought the band to the attention of the media and, more significantly, Creation Records. Invited to submit some of their English-language material in demo form, the result was a long-term development contract with the noted English independent (the contract included a proviso that the band would never be forced to work on St. David's Day).

Of course, their decision to sing in English attracted criticism from some of their former peers, but Rhys commented to the press: 'The Welsh language music scene is very insular. There is no room for ambition and the environment can be very stifling. Although our language is very important to us we don't want to limit ourselves or our audience by singing entirely in Welsh.' The band's debut album, *Fuzzy Logic*, was recorded at Rockfield Studios in Monmouth, Wales, and showcased their ambitions to 'push technology to the limit'. It included their debut single for Creation, 'Hometown Unicorn' (the story of a French barrow-boy who was allegedly abducted by aliens in 1979) and the album's second single, 'God! Show Me Magic'. Subsequent singles 'Something 4 The Weekend' and 'If You Don't Want Me To Destroy You' broke the band into the UK Top 20. Critical approval as well as a growing fanbase confirmed their breakthrough, and proved that 60s retro-pop can still sound fresh. In the meantime the band continued to agitate the Welsh mainstream media - causing uproar at the Welsh BAFTA Awards and denouncing Tory Party agent Elwyn Jones as a 'neo-fascist' live on the *I-Dot* youth programme. Their Christmas single, 'The Man Don't Give A F**k', used a Steely Dan sample which resulted in the song, not surprisingly, being banned from the airwaves. Further late 60s shenanigans were apparent with the lighter *Radiator*. This was their equivalent of the Beach Boys' *Friends* album - an understated but ultimately rewarding collection. The band released the *Ice Hockey Hair* EP in May 1998, and a compilation of b-sides a few months later. The reggae-styled 'Northern Lites' provided the band with their biggest UK chart hit so far in May 1999, and it was followed by the excellent *Guerilla* the following month. Super Furry Animals presently show no sign of running out of ideas. Their originality is a refreshing change in an area of music that is soaked with Oasis soundalikes.

● ALBUMS: *Fuzzy Logic* (Creation 1996)★★★★, *Radiator* (Creation 1997)★★★★, *Guerilla* (Creation 1999)★★★★.

● COMPILATIONS: *Out Spaced* (Creation 1998)★★★.

Superchunk

Superchunk, formed in North Carolina, USA, are an energetic, prolific pop punk band who faced first acclaim and then derision as a reaction to the number of Hüsker Dü-influenced outfits of that time. Laura Ballance (b. 22 February 1968; bass), Jim Wilbur (b. 22 December 1966, New London, Connecticut, USA; guitar), John Wurster (31 October 1966; drums) and Ralph 'Mac' McCaughan (b. 12 July 1967; vocals/guitar), formed the band in Chapel Hill. Ballance and McCaughan were romantic partners who established their own label, Merge Records, at the same time. The band, known initially as Chunk, released their first single, 'What Do I'/'Train From Kansas City', in 1989. They were forced to add a prefix after another band in New York claimed prior usage. Merge's first release had been a cassette compilation of North Carolina's Bricks, one of many bands (Wax, Slushpuppies, etc.) in which McCaughan had played prior to Superchunk. Later he would also drum for Seam and add guitar to an album by fIREHOSE. Superchunk's career took off with the recording of 'Slack Motherfucker'. Based on work experience at Kinko's Copy Shop in their home-town, it made their name in the US underground rock firmament, and became a fixture on college radio. A self-titled debut album, full of feisty, abbreviated punk rock, followed for the newly established Matador Records. Their second album, *No Pocky For Kitty*, was promoted with a tour alongside Mudhoney, while in England they were pictured alongside their national flag on an ill-advised cover of the *New Musical Express*. Their disparate releases were then compiled on the excellent *Tossing Seeds* compilation, which included their second classic single to date, 'Cool'. *On The Mouth* largely prompted disappointment on its release in 1993, lacking any discernible musical progression and failing to produce the winning hooks of previous albums. *Foolish*, which followed a McCaughan solo venture (the much quieter Portastatic), largely restored their reputation with a return to their frontman's strength. *Here's Where The Strings Come In* was not quite as strong, although it included the vintage 'Hyper Enough'. Subsequent albums *Indoor Living* and *Come Pick Me Up* continued to mine the band's well-worn pop punk seam to little effect.

● ALBUMS: *Superchunk* (Matador 1990)★★★, *No Pocky For Kitty* (Matador 1991)★★, *On The Mouth* (Matador 1993)★★, *Foolish* (Merge 1994)★★★, *Here's Where The Strings Come In* (Merge 1995)★★★, *Indoor Living* (Merge 1997)★★, *Come Pick Me Up* (Merge 1999)★★★. Solo: Ralph McCaughan as Portastatic *I Hope Your Heart Is Not Brittle* (Merge 1994)★★★.

● COMPILATIONS: *Tossing Seeds (Singles '89-'91)* (Merge 1992)★★★, *Incidental Music 1991-1995* (Merge 1995)★★★.

Supergrass

Initially regarded as new entrants in the UK's indie guitar band movement of the mid-90s, Oxford's Supergrass suddenly found themselves thrust into the rock mainstream. The band comprises Danny Goffey (drums), Gary Coombes (vocals/guitar) and Mickey Quinn (bass). Previously Goffey and Coombes had been part of Ride-influenced upstarts the Jennifers, who recorded one single for Suede's label, Nude Records. With the addition of Quinn, rehearsals took place in early 1994, inspired by the Pixies, Sonic Youth and Buzzcocks. They eventually worked their way up to a ramshackle half-hour live set that made up in enthusiasm what it lacked in musical accomplishment. Their debut single, 'Caught By The Fuzz', about being arrested by the police for cannabis possession, brought them to much wider attention, though not before it had been released on three separate occasions. Bedroom label Backbeat first supplied 250 copies in the summer of 1994. Fierce Panda then included it as part of a six-track EP of various teenage bands on the advent of Supergrass signing to Parlophone Records. Re-released by the major in October, it climbed to number 42 in the UK charts, and by the close of the year it was voted number 5 in disc jockey John Peel's Festive 50 selection. They also toured with Shed Seven and supported Blur at their Alexandra Palace gig, before the release of a second single, 'Man Size Rooster', in early 1995. Their debut album was produced at Sawmills Studios, Golant, with Mystics singer Sam Williams, while the band also contributed to the Sub Pop Records Singles Club with 'Lose It'. However, all was eclipsed by the astonishing success of 'Alright' (b/w 'Time'). An updated Monkees-styled summer hit, accompanied by a video filmed in Portmeirion (the town immortalized in the cult 60s television series *The Prisoner*), 'Alright' shot to number 2 in the UK charts and made instant celebrities of the band. The resultant interest in Supergrass pushed *I*

Should Coco to number 1 in the UK album chart and it remained on the play-list for the best part of 1996. In 1997, the band rose to the pressure of producing a follow-up with the magnificent *In It For The Money*, confirming their standing as one of the country's brightest new talents. The album displayed a heartening collection of good, melodic hooks, each song flowing into the next with assured energy. The opening title track was followed by the hard rock/surfin' 'Richard III', which is how the Beach Boys might have sounded if they had plugged in their guitars. 'Tonight' utilised a delicate coating of brass, while 'Late In The Day' brought to mind piano-inspired Beatles. Derivative it may have been, but the album represented a highlight of the musical year, with the band hitting an early peak on an outstanding, polished pop collection. They returned in May 1999 with a punchy new single, 'Pumping On Your Stereo', taken from their self-titled third album.

● ALBUMS: *I Should Coco* (Parlophone 1995)★★★★, *In It For The Money* (Parlophone 1997)★★★★, *Supergrass* (Parlophone 1999)★★★★.

● FURTHER READING: *Supergrass*, Linda Holorny.

Supernaturals

Described as 'the future of Scotpop' by the UK music weekly *New Musical Express* in 1996, Glaswegian band the Supernaturals comprise James McColl (vocals/guitar), Derek McManus (guitar/vocals), Ken McAlpine (keyboards/tambourine), Mark Guthrie (bass) and Alan Tilston (drums). Though employing a visual image that was conclusively anti-fashion, and favouring the 60s pop dynamics of outfits such as Dodgy or Cast, what immediately distinguished the Supernaturals was their emphatic live performances. As McColl told the press: 'We learnt our trade playing in small pubs trying to get people's attention. I used to wear a full sailor's suit with these enormous sailor flares. It was so amusing to watch people's reactions. I like that Queen thing where everything's really outrageous.' The band soon built a substantial local following, enhanced by a series of privately distributed tape recordings, before they were signed by Andy Ross to Food Records in 1996 after he saw their second London date. Their happily cynical debut hit single, 'Smile', with the opening line, 'every silver lining has a cloud', followed shortly afterwards (the song was later nominated for an Ivor Novello songwriting award). Their excellent debut album was an assured mix of 60s retro and melodic 90s pop. It was one of the 'indie guitar band' highlights of the year, and generated three further UK Top 40 hits. The follow-up album, which debuted at number 21 in August 1998, was premiered by the highly addictive 'I Wasn't Built To Get Up', which received extensive radio play and debuted at number 25 in the UK singles chart.

● ALBUMS: *It Doesn't Matter Anymore* (Food 1997)★★★★, *A Tune A Day* (Food 1998)★★★.

Supernaw, Doug

b. 26 September 1960, Houston, Texas, USA. It surprises many to find that Supernaw, which he claims is of French/Native American extraction, is his real name. His mother was a coal miner's daughter and a fanatical country music fan, while his father was a scientist who only liked classical music. He learned to play guitar and grew up heavily influenced by fellow Texans George Jones, Gene

Watson and Joe Ely. Supernaw briefly attended college on a golf scholarship but dropped out in 1979. He worked on an oil rig before playing with a local band and acting as a local theatre promoter booking country acts. In 1987, he relocated to Nashville, where he worked as a songwriter for four years, before tiring of Music City and returning to Texas. He formed his own band, Texas Steel, and built a reputation playing a residency in Tyler. In 1993, a scout for RCA Records was impressed and sent him back to Nashville, where RCA assigned him to their BNA label. Three singles from his debut, *Red And Rio Grande*, provided the breakthrough that he needed. After 'Honky Tonkin' Fool' charted at number 50, 'Reno' (a number 4) quickly followed, before the catchy 'I Don't Call Him Daddy' gave him his first number 1. The album's title track also charted but during this time, Supernaw encountered more than his fair share of bad luck. At the time of his chart success, he first suffered a broken neck surfing, followed by being involved in a head-on car crash. Soon afterwards, all his band's instruments and equipment were stolen from the tour bus. Finally, he suffered a severe case of food poisoning, which saw him rushed to hospital after collapsing in the street in Richmond. When his follow-up album failed to live up to the high standards of his first, he moved label to Giant, still with Richard Landis as his producer. In January 1996, 'Not Enough Hours In The Night' re-established Supernaw as a commercial force.

● ALBUMS: *Red And Rio Grande* (BNA 1993)★★, *Deep Thoughts From A Shallow Mind* (BNA 1994)★★★, *You've Still Got Me* (Giant 1995)★★★★.

● VIDEOS: *She Never Looks Back* (Giant 1996).

Superstar

This talented singer/songwriter and multi-instrumentalist Joe McAlinden formed Superstar in 1992 when he left seminal Scottish indie-pop band BMX Bandits. Nellie Grant and Raymond Prior completed the original line-up. The band released an EP of demos confidently called *Greatest Hits Volume One* on Creation Records. However, a potentially lucrative contract with SBK America led to a disastrous US college tour supporting Barney The Singing Dinosaur, and the band's excellent debut was sadly buried by their label. After finally escaping the SBK contract McAlinden put together Superstar Mark II, retaining guitarist Jim McCulloch (ex-Soup Dragons) and recruiting drummer Quentin McAfee and bass player Alan Hutchison. This new line-up signed to former Go! Discs A&R director Jona Cox's Camp Fabulous label in November 1996. Showing great faith in his own potential, McAlinden turned down an offer to work with Brian Wilson to work on the *18 Carat* mini-album, which was released in spring 1997. 'Everyday I Fall Apart' was released to great acclaim in January 1998. The follow-up single 'Superstar' reached UK number 49 in April, but gained wider exposure when it was covered by Rod Stewart on *When We Were The New Boys*. The band's new album, *Palm Tree*, was also released in April, and provided the most compelling evidence to date of McAlinden's mastery of Jimmy Webb-styled pop arrangements. The band released the five-track *Superstar Vs Alan Warner* EP in August 1998, a collaboration with the cult Scottish author.

● ALBUMS: *Greatest Hits Volume One* mini-album (Creation 1992)★★★, *Superstar* (SBK 1994)★★★, *Palm Tree* (Camp Fabulous 1998)★★★★.

Sweet, Matthew

b. 6 October 1964, Lincoln, Nebraska, USA. Before the success of his third album, *Girlfriend*, Matthew Sweet had been best known for his work in the late 80s with the Golden Palominos. Before that, in the early 80s, he had recorded under the name Buzz Of Delight, based in Athens, Georgia, issuing a mini-album entitled *Sound Castles* which was produced by Don Dixon. Two further albums of 'keyboard doodlings' were never released. His partner on the first of these albums was Dave Pierce. Both also performed with Oh-OK, the Athens band featuring Linda Stipe (sister of R.E.M.'s Michael Stipe), which later evolved into Magnapop. *Inside*, his debut solo album under his own name, followed in 1986, and featured contributions from the Bangles and Chris Stamey. Included in the production credits was Alan Tarney, who produced Cliff Richard's 'Devil Woman', as well as material by Dream Syndicate. On *Girlfriend* Sweet was accompanied by New York musicians including Fred Maher (of Material), Robert Quine (ex-Lou Reed; Richard Hell And The Voidoids) and Richard Lloyd (ex-Television), plus the UK's Lloyd Cole and the Velvet Crush drummer Ric Menck (Lloyd, Menck and Quine had first appeared on *Earth*). The mature rock of *Girlfriend*, which went on to sell over half a million copies in the USA, was compared by some to Neil Young and Big Star, despite its shoestring recording budget. *Son Of Altered Beast* remixed the best track from *Altered Beast*, 'Devil With The Green Eyes', and added five live tracks recorded with Lloyd, Menck and Quine in October 1993 and January 1994. For *100% Fun* that trio were joined by Greg Leisz (formerly with k.d. lang) on pedal steel and mandolin, with Brendan O'Brien (Pearl Jam, Bob Dylan, Soundgarden) producing. In acknowledgement of his popularity in the Far East, it was accompanied by a comic that featured Sweet. The touring band for 1995 added Tony Marsico (bass) and Stuart Johnson (drums). *Blue Sky On Mars* was crammed with appealing hooks, nifty breaks and snappy songs - all with high commercial potential but none with the mark of 'a truly great pop song'. *In Reverse* was a sumptuous follow-up that many believed was his finest album since *Girlfriend*. Sweet has oodles of talent spread over numerous songs, but despite this the 'classic' monster composition still eludes him.

● ALBUMS: as Buzz Of Delight *Sound Castles* mini-album (DB 1984)★★, *Inside* (Columbia 1986)★★, *Earth* (A&M 1989)★★★, *Girlfriend* (Zoo 1992)★★★★, *Altered Beast* (Zoo 1993)★★★, *Son Of Altered Beast* mini-album (Zoo 1994)★★, *100% Fun* (Zoo 1995)★★★, *Blue Sky On Mars* (Zoo 1997)★★★, *In Reverse* (Zomba 1999)★★★★.

SWV

Acronym for Sisters With Voices, these 'ghetto sisters' from Brooklyn and the Bronx, New York, comprised the talents of Coko (b. Cheryl Gamble), Taj (b. Tamara Johnson) and Lelee (b. Leanne Lyons). Shaped by swingbeat producer Teddy Riley to reflect streetwise dress and attitude, the trio's sound was somewhat harder than that which might be expected of 'new jill swingers'. On tracks like 'Downtown' they revealed themselves happy to engage in intimate details of the sex wars. Their 1993 debut also encompassed both rap and *a cappella* vocal stylings, and included three massive crossover US hit singles, 'I'm So Into You' (number 6), the chart-topping 'Weak' and 'Right Here/Human Nature' (number 2). The latter also provided the trio with a UK number 3 hit single. Nominated for a Grammy in 1995 they returned in 1996 with the equally slick *A New Beginning*, and repeated the formula in 1997 with *Release Some Tension*. More sexual innuendo recorded to perfection, but too smooth for some people's taste in urban R&B. The group broke up in 1998, with Coko releasing her solo debut the following year.

● ALBUMS: *It's About Time* (RCA 1993)★★★, *A New Beginning* (RCA 1996)★★★, *Release Some Tension* (RCA 1997)★★.

● COMPILATIONS: *Greatest Hits* (RCA 1999)★★★.

Symposium

London, England-based Symposium were at the forefront of the wave of adolescent power pop bands signed up on the back of Ash's success. Formed at school in Kensington, West London, the band comprise ex-choirboys Wojtek Godzizsz (bass), Ross Cummins (vocals), Joe Birch (drums), Will McGonacle (guitar) and Hagop Tehaparian (guitar). Originally known as the Jump Puppets, they built up an exciting live reputation on the strength of a few gigs, selling out the 100 Club in July 1996 barely a month after they had finished their education. Support slots for Ash and Bis followed, along with several bans on account of their fans' tendency to vandalize venues. After signing to Ash's label, Infectious, they released their debut single, 'Farewell To Twilight', followed by the euphoric 'Drink The Sunshine'. Despite suffering the setback of having Andrew Lloyd Webber declare them his favourite pop group, the band continued to be championed by the music press, and played on the *New Musical Express*' Brats tour in January 1997. Following their third top 40 single, 'The Answer To Why I Hate You', Cummins managed to break his leg during an overly energetic performance. The release of their debut mini-album in November 1997 ensured more glowing press coverage. With production by Clive Langer and Alan Winstanley (Madness, Morrissey, Elvis Costello), the eight-song set captured the raw vigour and youthful enthusiasm of their live shows in all its noisy, tuneful glory. Their debut full-length album was more refined, indicating that the band were beginning to mature musically. Following the release of the follow-up, *On The Outside*, the band left Infectious and set-up their own Sympomania label.

● ALBUMS: *One Day At A Time* mini-album (Infectious 1997)★★★, *On The Outside* (Infectious 1998)★★★.

System 7

Ambient dance music duo featuring Miquette Giraudy (b. 9 February 1953, Nice, France; synthesizers/samples) and the more celebrated Steve Hillage (b. Stephen Simpson Hillage, 2 August 1951, Walthamstow, London, England; guitars/samplers/synthesizers). Giraudy is a former film maker from the south of France, where she met up with Hillage's band, the cult synth prog-rockers Gong. Her films had included *More* and *La Vallee*, both of which featured Pink Floyd on their soundtracks. Fascinated by synthesizers, she became a self-taught musician and in the current format writes most of the material before Hillage adds a layer of guitar work. Hillage enjoys his own cult following through his work with Kevin Ayers, Gong and the Steve Hillage Group, and had become enveloped in the ambient house explosion via the work of Spooky, the Drum Club, Orbital, Black Dog Productions and Fluke, before collaborating with another listening favourite, the Orb. In turn System 7 have been joined

on vinyl by a host of rock, pop and dance stars; Alex Paterson (Orb), Youth (Killing Joke), Mick McNeil (Simple Minds) Paul Oakenfold, Carl Craig and Derrick May. Their recording career started in August 1991 with 'Miracle' on Ten Records, after which they moved to Big Life Records and their own Weird & Unconventional imprint. The Top 40 *777*, and singles of the quality of 'Freedom Fighters' and 'Sinbad', have helped them garner a considerable reputation among both their peers and late-night ravers searching for the perfect chill-out tune. *Point 3* was released in two versions, *The Fire Album* and *The Water Album*, the latter comprising drumless mixes of the former's tracks. *The Power Of Seven* introduced a harder techno edge, thanks to the input of leading Detroit mixers Craig and May.

● ALBUMS: *System 7* (Ten 1991)★★★, *777* (Weird & Unconventional/Big Life 1993)★★★★, *Point 3* (Big Life 1994)★★★, *Power Of Seven* (Butterfly 1996)★★★, *Golden Section* (Butterfly 1997)★★★.

● COMPILATIONS: *System Express* (Butterfly 1996)★★★.

System Of A Down

This Los Angeles, California, USA-based alternative metal band comprises three members of Armenian heritage, Serj Tankian (vocals), Daron Malakian (guitar) and Shavo Odadjian (bass), and John Dolmayan (drums). Tankian, Malakian and Odadjian first played together in 1993 as Soil, renaming themselves System Of A Down, from a poem by Malakian, in 1995. Recruiting drummer Dolmayan they built up a following on the southern California circuit with their explosive live act. Rick Rubin, who, in September 1997, made the band the first new act on his American Recordings label, spotted them playing at Hollywood's Viper Room. Their debut album, released in June 1998, was recorded at the Sound City studios with Rubin and Dave Sardy acting as producers. The band's heady fusion of alternative metal and programmed beats was augmented by subtle Eastern European influences, earning them comparisons to contemporary metal bands such as Korn and the Deftones. The band's political agenda raised their aggro-metal to another level, however, with songs such as 'P.L.U.C.K.' ('Politically, Lying, Unholy, Cowardly Killers') and live favourite 'War?' refusing to draw a veil over atrocities committed in their homeland. The band subsequently enjoyed high-profile touring slots with Slayer and on summer 1998's Ozzfest.

● ALBUMS: *System Of A Down* (American 1998)★★★★.

Taff, Russ

b. 11 November 1955. Grammy–winning US Christian singer-songwriter Taff was the fourth of five sons of a Pentecostal preacher and gospel-loving mother. After relocating to Arkansas as a teenager, he formed his own group, the Sounds Of Joy, but he found wider acclaim when he joined the Imperials in 1976. Taff was instrumental in helping the famous southern gospel group modernise their sound on albums such as *Sail On*, but after five years with the group he left to embark on a solo career. His debut set, 1983's *Walls Of Glass*, featured an enduring classic, 'We Will Stand', but it was the highly popular follow-up, *Medals*, which confirmed Taff as one of the leading artists in contemporary Christian music. A self-titled set and 1989's *The Way Home* brought further acclaim for Taff's songwriting skills and his powerful voice. Although these albums remained true to Taff's Christian roots, they also demonstrated his willingness to experiment outside the genre. At the start of the 90s, Taff released two contrasting sets, the traditional gospel outing, *Under Their Influence, Vol. 1*, and the mainstream-orientated *A Christmas Song*. During the mid-90s he recorded three albums worth of material for the country market, although only 1995's *Winds Of Change* saw the light of day. He returned to more familiar territory on 1999's *Right Here Right Now*, which included several songs exploring his troubled relationship with his father, who had died in 1997.

● ALBUMS: *Walls Of Glass* (Myrrh 1983)★★★, *Medals* (Myrrh 1985)★★★, *Russ Taff* (Myrrh 1987)★★★★, *The Way Home* (Word/Epic 1989)★★★★, *Under Their Influence, Vol. 1* (Word/Epic 1991)★★★, *A Christmas Song* (Sparrow 1992)★★, *Winds Of Change* (Reprise 1995)★★★, *Right Here Right Now* (Benson 1999)★★★★.

● COMPILATIONS: *We Will Stand: Yesterday And Today* (Word/Epic 1994)★★★★.

Take 6

Initially a quartet known as the Sounds Of Distinction then the Alliance, this *a cappella* gospel group of breathtaking ability first formed at Oakwood College, Huntsville, Alabama, USA, in 1980. The group evolved into a six-piece comprising Alvin Chea, Cedric Dent, David Thomas, Mervyn Warren, Mark Kibble and Claude V. McKnight. The combination of their Seventh-day Adventist beliefs and their appreciation of jazz and R&B styles enabled them to make inroads into both record-buying markets, winning Grammies for best Soul Gospel and best Jazz Vocal categories. Their 1990 appearance with k.d. lang in the movie *Dick Tracy* singing 'Ridin' The Rails' also gave them further valuable exposure. Additionally they have recorded with artists including Dianne Reeves, Quincy Jones and Joe Sample. *Join The Band* marked a new direction for the group as it incorporated live musicians including Greg Phillinganes, Gerald Albright and Herbie Hancock. It also featured lead vocals from Ray Charles, Stevie Wonder and a rap from Queen Latifah. In 1998 they returned to their roots with the predominantly *a cappella So Cool*. Music writer David Okamota aptly described Take 6 as 'winning over a loyal congregation of secular fans with a soothing, uplifting sound that stirs the soul without twisting the arm', and the singles 'I L-O-V-E U', 'Biggest Part Of Me' and 'All I Need (Is A Chance)' all charted on the *Billboard* R&B Hot 100, the latter peaking at number 7.

● ALBUMS: *Take 6* (Reprise 1988)★★★, *So Much 2 Say* (Reprise 1990)★★★★, *He Is Christmas* (Reprise 1991)★★, *Join The Band* (Reprise 1994)★★★, *Brothers* (Reprise 1997)★★★, *So Cool* (Reprise 1998)★★★★.

Take That

Formed in Manchester, England, this vocal group arguably came closest to emulating the Beatles' legacy of phenomenal mass popularity. Teen pop can be a fickle career, but one similarity they displayed in common with their Liverpool cousins was the rare ability to unite both young and middle-aged music fans. The group was led by lead vocalist Gary Barlow (b. 20 January 1971, Frodsham, Cheshire, England), with Mark Owen (b. Mark Anthony Owen, 27 January 1972, Oldham, Lancashire, England), Howard Paul Donald (b. 28 April 1968, Droylsden, Manchester, England), Jason Thomas Orange (b. 10 July 1970, Manchester, England) and Robbie Williams (b. Robert Peter Williams, 13 February 1974, Stoke on Trent, England). As a child Barlow was a talented musician, and backed Ken Dodd shows on the organ by the time he was 14. His first break came when he submitted a song, 'Let's Pray For Christmas', which was short-listed and played on the 'A Song For Christmas' competition on BBC Television's *Pebble Mill*. Owen had failed soccer trials for Manchester United before taking work at an Oldham bank, while Orange was a former breakdancer brought up as a Mormon. Williams' mother was a singer and his father a comedian and prior to the commencement of Take That he had a small role in Channel 4's *Brookside*. Donald's parents, too, had a musical background, before he took up work in a garage and joined Orange in a breakdancing unit, Street Beat. Barlow, Owen and Williams were formerly part of the Cutest Rush. Take That released their debut single, 'Do What U Like', on their own Dance U.K. label in July 1991. Much of the publicity they initially attracted surrounded the risqué video that accompanied it, featuring the band revealing their buttocks. The furore helped to make up the minds of RCA Records, who signed the band in September, and 'Promises' reached number 38 in the UK charts two months later. In February 1992, 'Once You've Tasted Love' reached number 47, coinciding with a 'Safe Sex' club tour undertaken with the support of the Family Planning Association, before June brought their UK chart break-through with a cover version of the Tavares' 'It Only Takes A Minute'. By the time it reached number 7 in the UK charts the country's pop press swooped on them for their clean-cut (with the exception of the bearded Orange) good looks, dance routines and simple, catchy songs. Barlow also stepped up his reputation as a songwriter for the ensuing *Take That And Party*, which debuted at number 5 in the UK album charts. October's *A Million Love Songs* EP, led off by its powerful title ballad (originally written by Barlow aged 16), also reached number 7. Their popularity was confirmed by the receipt of seven trophies at the *Smash Hits* Poll Winners Party Awards in December, as effective a barometer as any of the prevailing tastes of the UK's youth. By the following year the fortunes of the group's debut album were resuscitated as it climbed to number 2 in the UK charts, following the number 3 success of their cover version of Barry Manilow's 'Could It Be Magic'. This also won them a BRIT Award for Best British Single in February, before 'Why Can't I Wake Up With You' rose to number 2 at the end of the same month. By April the group's debut album and 'It Only Takes A Minute' had been launched in the USA, with the help of a Take That cereal box, but initial forays into the American market proved unsuccessful. 'Pray' became their first UK number 1 in July 1993, a feat repeated with 'Relight My Fire', featuring a guest appearance from Lulu, in October. In the meantime the band were concentrating on recording their second album, and when *Everything Changes* emerged on 23 October 1993 it debuted at number 1 in the UK charts. Proving that their popularity was not impinging on their prolific release schedule, 'Babe' became a third successive UK number 1 in December, though it eventually lost the coveted Christmas number 1 spot to Mr Blobby. The band's success continued throughout 1994 and into 1995, when 'Everything Changes', 'Sure', 'Back For Good' and 'Never Forget' earned them four more UK number 1 placings. 'Back For Good' demonstrated much more substance than their usual lightweight pop, and was also a US Top 10 hit. There were strong signs that Take That were finally being accepted by the music critics. Fans were shocked when Williams announced his departure for a solo career in mid-1995 - although the writing had been on the wall for some time - his participation in *Nobody Else* had been minimal. Further disaster ensued when, after weeks of rumours, it was confirmed at a press conference in February 1996 that the band members were going their separate ways, and they bowed out with a chart-topping cover version of the Bee Gees' 'How Deep Is Your Love' in June. Barlow, Owen and Williams all embarked on solo careers, with the latter's proving the most spectacular.

● ALBUMS: *Take That And Party* (RCA 1992)★★★, *Everything Changes* (RCA 1993)★★★, *Nobody Else* (RCA 1995)★★★.
● COMPILATIONS: *Greatest Hits* (RCA 1996)★★★.
● VIDEOS: *Take That And Party* (BMG 1992), *Take That: The Party-Live At Wembley* (BMG 1993), *Greatest Hits* (BMG 1995), *From Zeros To Heroes* (Wienerworld 1995), *Everything Changes* (BMG 1995), *Hometown: Live At Manchester G-Mex* (BMG 1995), *Berlin* (BMG 1995), *Nobody Else: The Movie* (BMG 1996).
● FURTHER READING: *Take That: Our Story*, Piers Morgan. *The Unofficial Biography*, Mick St. Michael. *Everything Changes*, Take That. *Talk Back*, Luke Taylor.

Tansads

Formed around the songwriting of guitarist John Kettle and members of his family, the Tansads dispensed a mixture of English folk and pop influences, with a dash of funk. Coming together in 1989, Kettle, his long-term partner Janet Anderton (vocals), his brother Robert (harmonica/guitar/mandolin), Ed Jones (bass), Bug (drums) and Shrub (keyboards) formed the nucleus of the band. When younger brother, Andrew, was recruited in early 1990, the twin lead

vocal sound reminded some of the 70s folk/rock giants. With Dominic Lowe on accordion and brass and percussionist Cudo, the band recorded the self-financed *Shandyland* in 1991. Lyrically homespun, and tongue-in-cheek, *Folk North West* wrote: 'They are our future . . . and they are absolutely brilliant'. The album attracted the attention of producer Phil Tennant, and the band was signed to French company Musidisc (who had released the Levellers first album). Subsequent sessions resulted in 'Brian Kant' and *Up The Shirkers*, followed by the recruitment of former Railway Children drummer Guy Keegan. Follow-up single 'Up The Revolution' received national airplay and reached the independent and folk charts. By then the sound was harder, and the lyrics contemporary, but still humorous. Extensive touring followed, along with BBC Radio 1 sessions, and further singles 'English Rover' and 'Camelot'. The double A-side 'Iron Man/A Band On The Rainbow' was released before the band were signed by Castle Communications on the relaunched Transatlantic Records. The band recorded *Flock* and released 'I Know I Can', but were unable to gain a breakthrough hit. The live *Drag Down The Moon* was their last release for Castle, following which the band fragmented, with only Kettle and Anderton remaining from the original line-up.

● ALBUMS: *Shandyland* (1991)★★★, *Up The Shirkers* (Musidisc 1993)★★★, *Flock* (Transatlantic 1994)★★★, *Drag Down The Moon* (Transatlantic 1995)★★.
● FURTHER READING: *This Is Pop*, Ed Jones.

Taylor, Lewis

The first artist ever to be signed by Island Records solely on the strength of a demo tape received through the post, R&B singer-songwriter Taylor then spent three years working on his debut album. As sessions progressed, it was immediately obvious that Taylor was not a standard soul revisionist, claiming influences as varied as Yes, Killing Joke, Tim Buckley and Miles Davis. As he stated, 'I'm very, very interested in atmospherics. I tend to conjure up an atmosphere that harks back to some experience I might have had or some other piece of music I've heard'. His background was also varied, having once played guitar in the Edgar Broughton Band. His debut solo album was originally released in a promotional pressing of 500 copies, and distributed without a press release or photograph, ensuring swathes of interest among R&B and dance music writers. The first official release was a single, 'Lucky', which incorporated a Joe Meek sample as well as strings, piano and a guitar motif. The self-titled album it accompanied was similarly eclectic, and featured Taylor playing all the instruments.

● ALBUMS: *Lewis Taylor* (Island 1996)★★★★.

Tedeschi, Susan

b. 7 November 1970, Boston, Massachusetts, USA. A blues singer/guitarist who draws adroitly from other musical traditions, including rock and reggae, Tedeschi's literate songs are informed by writers such as Massachusetts poet Emily Dickinson. She grew up the youngest of three children in the Boston suburb of Norwell, immersing herself in her father's blues and folk records and writing her first song, 'Somebody Watches', at the age of 14. She also sang in churches before taking a degree in jazz and rock at the

Berklee College Of Music. After graduation in 1991, she became a regular at local blues jams held at Boston venues such as Wally's. She made her recording debut in 1995 with *Better Days*, a record whose songwriting authority and skill belied its low-budget recording. Tracks such as 'Love Never Treats Me Right' and 'Gonna Write Him A Letter' attracted critical plaudits and precipitated a move to a major label for the follow-up collection, 1998's *Just Won't Burn*. This time the outstanding songs included 'It Hurt So Bad' and the single, 'You Need To Be With Me'. A firm believer in the values of live performance, Tedeschi set out to promote it on blues bills alongside B.B. King and Buddy Guy, but also more rock-orientated acts such as Rusted Root, New Radicals and John Hiatt.

● ALBUMS: as the Susan Tedeschi Band *Better Days* (Oarfin 1995)★★★, *Just Won't Burn* (Tone-Cool/Rounder 1998)★★★.

Teenage Fanclub

Formerly the bulk of infamous Glaswegian band the Boy Hairdressers, Teenage Fanclub, a more sober sobriquet than the original suggestion of 'Teenage Fanny', came into being after Norman Blake (b. 20 October 1965, Bellshill, Scotland; guitar/vocals), Raymond McGinley (b. 3 January 1964, Glasgow, Scotland; guitar/vocals) and Francis MacDonald (b. 21 November 1970, Bellshill, Scotland; drums) moved on from that pseudo-punk combo and linked up with Gerard Love (b. 31 August 1967, Motherwell, Scotland; bass/vocals). During 1989 the quartet recorded an entire album - completed three months before the band had even played live - until MacDonald (later to join the Pastels) made way for Brendan O'Hare (b. 16 January 1970, Bellshill, Scotland). As well as the historical connection with the Boy Hairdressers, members of Teenage Fanclub also had dealings with fellow Scots outfit BMX Bandits. Thus brought up on a diet of fun, loud guitars and irreverence, Teenage Fanclub stamped their mark on 1990 with a series of drunken live shows and the erratic but highly promising Americanized rock debut *A Catholic Education*. In October, the band paid tribute to John Lennon by covering his 'Ballad Of John And Yoko', releasing and deleting the record on the same day. A year on and supplemented by the support of a vociferous music press, Teenage Fanclub toned down their sound, allowing the melodies to come through more forcefully in a manner that self-consciously recalled the 70s guitar sound of Big Star and Neil Young (they became fundamental in instigating the former band's revival in the early 90s). Inevitably, 'Starsign' - with a cover version of Madonna's 'Like A Virgin' on the b-side - threatened the UK charts on the back of the band's new impetus. *Bandwagonesque* arrived at the end of 1991 and became one of the year's most memorable albums. Laced with chiming guitar and irresistible melody, it suggested a band ready to outgrow their humble independent origins. A sense of huge disappointment accompanied the release of *Thirteen*, completed in eight months after touring on the back of the better-received *Bandwagonesque* (which sold 70,000 copies in the UK and 150,000 in the USA, where the band are signed to Geffen Records). This resulted in a concerted effort to make the band's fifth studio album, *Grand Prix*, an exceptional return to form. The songs were rehearsed for three months before entering the studio, where everything was fine-tuned over a five-week period at the Manor in Oxford with producer Dave Bianco (formerly

Black Crowes producer George Dracoulias' engineer). It also saw the introduction of new drummer Paul Quinn, formerly of the Soup Dragons. O'Hare, meanwhile, formed the Telstar Ponies with ex-Creation guitarist David Keenan. Reassuringly, the opening singles from these sessions, 'Mellow Doubt' and 'Sparky's Dream', showed them still to be writing basic, heroically romantic and happy guitar pop songs. *Songs From Northern Britain* continued the theme, showing further shades of the 60s with strong Beatles and Byrds influences present. Although the pace was lighter, this record contained some of their finest moments, with the jewel being Blake's glorious 'I Don't Want Control Of You'. Gene Clark would have doffed his cap to this magnificent slice of lilting pop. Ex-BMX Bandits keyboard player Finlay McDonald joined the band full-time at the end of 1997.

● ALBUMS: *A Catholic Education* (Paperhouse 1990)★★, *The King* (Creation 1991)★★, *Bandwagonesque* (Creation 1991)★★★★, *Thirteen* (Creation 1993)★★, *Grand Prix* (Creation 1995)★★★★, *Songs From Northern Britain* (Creation 1997)★★★★.

● COMPILATIONS: *Deep Fried Fanclub* (Paperhouse/Fire 1995)★★.

Telstar Ponies

Telstar Ponies have their roots and their original influences in the rich field of Scottish indie rock; however, in the space of two years they had developed their sound in directions most guitar bands never dream of. David Keenan (guitar/vocals), formerly of 18 Wheeler (the band that will always be remembered for topping the bill the night Alan McGee first saw Oasis) teamed up with ex-Teenage Fanclub drummer Brendan O'Hare in the autumn of 1994, but it was not until early the following year that Rachel Devine (guitar/piano/vocals) and Gavin Laird (bass) arrived to form Telstar Ponies. Their brooding debut, highlighted by Devine's beautiful 'The Moon Is Not A Shadow', elicited ecstatic comparisons with everyone from Sonic Youth to Popol Vuh but even these challenging benchmarks were not enough for Keenan's vision. The follow-up, fleshed out by the addition of Richard Youngs (organ, piano), strayed even further from rock 'n' roll as most of us know it, with Keenan name-checking the free jazz experimentation of Albert Ayler and any number of obscure Japanese noise bands. The band did have time for the droll Nick Cave pastiche 'Sail Her On' but their new sound was best exemplified by the intense 13-minute epic 'Does Your Heart Have Wings?'. This wilful eclecticism led O'Hare and Laird to decamp in late 1996, forming the 'kraut rock'-influenced Macrocosmica and leaving Keenan and Devine to briefly push the boundaries of guitar rock even further. O'Hare joined Mogwai in 1997.

● ALBUMS: *In The Space Of A Few Minutes* (Fire 1995)★★★★, *Voices From The New Music* (Fire 1996)★★★.

Tenaglia, Danny

Italian-American Tenaglia has, together with keyboard player Peter Dauo, played host to an impressive slew of garage/house cuts emanating from New York in the 90s. He first turned to dance music when hearing a mix tape for the first time, subsequently selling them for the artist concerned. He was a keen enthusiast in the early disco boom, and played his first gig at a local club in Bayside, Queens, New York, when he was still 14. From there he picked up on musical trends as they occurred, being particularly influenced by the early innovations of David Morales and Kevin

Saunderson. His productions of cuts like 'Glammer Girl' by the Look (a Jon Waters tribute), and the techno-jazz innovations of his partner Dauo, built an enviable reputation, as his profile grew alongside that of fellow New Yorkers DJ Duke and Junior Vasquez. He also held high-profile residencies at New York clubs including Twilo and the Tunnel. Naturally this helped bring in the remix projects, including Right Said Fred and Yothu Yindi, and the hugely influential 1993 version of Dauo's 'Surrender Yourself'. His popularity in New York is matched in Europe and even the Orient. In the UK his reputation has been franked by performances at the musically sympathetic Ministry Of Sound club nights. In 1999, Tenaglia was voted number 8 in the UK's *DJ* magazine's Top 100 DJs in the world.

● ALBUMS: *Hard & Soul* (Capitol 1995)★★★, *Tourism* (MCA 1998)★★★★.
● COMPILATIONS: *Gag Me With A Tune* (MCA 1996)★★★, *Color Me Danny: A Collection Of Best Remixes* (MCA 1997)★★★, *Back To Mine* (DMC 1999)★★★, *Global Underground: Athens* (Global Underground 1999)★★★★.

Tenor Fly

b. Jonathan Sutter, Brixton, London, England. Tenor Fly began his career with Lloyd Coxsone's International Sound System, working alongside such dignitaries as Jah Screechy and Blacker Dread. In 1989 his debut release, 'Roughneck Fashion', topped the UK reggae chart, and was swiftly followed by the equally successful 'Inner Cities'. His growing reputation led to collaborations with the Ragga Twins (under the guise of Demon Rocker), the highly acclaimed DJ Top Cat, and seasoned vocalist Nerious Joseph. He has also enjoyed crossover success, having three consecutive Top 40 hits with the Rebel MC, 'Tribal Bass', 'Wickedest Sound' and 'Coming On Strong'. In 1994 his satirical interpretation of the Monty Python *Life Of Brian* chant, 'Bright Side Of Life', over a sample of Nina Simone's 'My Baby Just Cares For Me', rewarded him with a UK Top 50 hit. His success was followed by the Big Orange duet, 'Let's Play', reuniting the DJ with Nerious Joseph. In 1996 Tenor Fly toured Japan, appearing alongside Top Cat and Sweetie Irie at the annual Japan Splash Festival. On his return he was invited to perform on the Louchie Lou And Michie One album, *Danger Us*, for the track 'Before The Night Is Over'. In 1997, he embarked on recording sessions for his long-awaited debut, to be released by his advocate Top Cat on the DJ's own Nine Lives label.

Terrorvision

This quartet from Bradford, England formed in 1986 as Spoilt Bratz, and quickly fused rock, funk and thrash influences into an infectiously upbeat pop metal style. Tony Wright (b. 6 May 1968, Yorkshire, England; vocals), Mark Yates (b. 4 April 1968, Bradford, Yorkshire, England; guitar), Leigh Marklew (b. 10 August 1968, England; bass), and Shutty (b. 20 March 1967, England; drums) were signed by EMI Records on the strength of their 'Pump Action Sunshine' demo, and negotiated the formation of their own label name, Total Vegas. Two remixed demo tracks, 'Urban Space Crime' and 'Jason', appeared on the *Thrive* EP as Terrorvision followed a hectic touring schedule prior to the release of *Formaldehyde*. The debut produced minor hits in 'American TV' and 'New Policy One', and was backed by UK

and European tours with the Ramones and Motörhead, respectively, while Def Leppard frontman Joe Elliott was sufficiently impressed to invite Terrorvision to open Leppard's 1993 show at Sheffield's Don Valley Stadium. 1994 proved to be quite a year for Terrorvision, beginning with their UK Top 30 breakthrough with 'My House'. *How To Make Friends And Influence People* emerged to rave reviews and entered the UK Top 20, bringing the band their first silver disc, and produced four more Top 30 singles in 'Oblivion', 'Middleman', 'Pretend Best Friend' and 'Alice, What's The Matter?'. They also played both the Reading and Donington Festivals, in addition to two sold-out UK tours and a series of European dates, before moving on to work on a new album in 1995. Major critical acclaim and healthy sales accompanied their most commercial and assured work to date with *Regular Urban Survivors*. Exactly 10 years after they were formed as the Spoilt Bratz, Terrorvision finally made the big screen. They maintained their commercial momentum with *Shaving Peaches*, and their highest-charting UK single, 'Tequila', which reached number 2 in January 1999. Shortly afterwards, however, they left long-standing label EMI.

● ALBUMS: *Formaldehyde* (Total Vegas 1992)★★★, *How To Make Friends And Influence People* (Total Vegas 1994)★★★★, *Regular Urban Survivors* (Total Vegas 1996)★★★★, *Shaving Peaches* (Total Vegas 1998)★★★★.
● VIDEOS: *Fired Up And Lairy* (PMI 1995).

Terry, Todd

Terry is a US house production innovator and expert with a reputation second to none (in fact, some journalists from specialist magazines took to nicknaming him 'God' for easy reference). An established producer and DJ, he learned his trade playing early house and hip-hop at parties in New York. 'Bongo (To The Batmobile)', a major signpost in the development of acid house, and further singles like 'Can You Party?' and 'A Day In The Life Of A Black Riot' were credited to the Todd Terry Project alias. In addition to an album and singles on Champion (including the mighty 'Put Your Hands Together'), he also cut records for Strictly Rhythm, Nervous and Freeze Records (SAX's 'This Will Be Mine'). His distinctive use of samples underpins all his production and remix work: 'What I try to do is to make an art out of the samples'. This often involves multi-layers of creative theft without allowing a given example to offer its 'signature' to the listener. His remix clients have included Bizarre Inc. ('I'm Gonna Get You') and Snap!, and he also collaborated with old friend Tony Humphries to remix Alison Limerick's 'Make It On My Own'. 'Whenever I do a remix I strip the vocal right down and use just a little bit. That's why I don't do many remixes, they are a long way from the original'. A good example was the magic he worked on P.M. Dawn's 'From A Watcher's Point Of View' and Everything But The Girl's 'Missing', the latter resurrecting the indie duo's career and re-establishing Terry's name as a leading remixer. He owns his own home-studio, the Loudhouse, in his native Brooklyn, and released a new album in 1997. The following year he had further crossover success with remix work for the Corrs ('Dreams'), Sash! ('Mysterious Times') and the Rolling Stones ('Saint Of Me'). In 1999, *Resolutions* signalled a change in direction, comprising mainly drum 'n' bass and breakbeats. It received a mainly positive critical reception.

● ALBUMS: *This Is The New Todd Terry Project Album* (Champion

1992)★★★, *A Day In The Life - Todd Terry* (MOS 1994)★★★, *Sessions 8 - Todd Terry* (MOS 1997)★★★, *Ready For A New Day* (Manifesto 1997)★★★, *Resolutions* (Innocent 1999)★★★.

Tesh, John

b. 9 July 1952, New York City, New York, USA. One of the most prolific and successful composers of the 90s, Tesh is a fixture on the Top 10 New Age bestsellers list, where his easy listening blend of classical, pop and jazz has endeared him to thousands of devoted fans. Tesh was raised in the Garden City suburb of New York. Thanks to a classical music education he learnt to play piano and trumpet before he was 10 years old, although he later played in local rock bands during his teenage years. He attended North Carolina State University, graduating in 1975 with a degree in communications. Tesh's early career was spent working as an investigative reporter on local television in places as diverse as Nashville, Raleigh and Orlando, before he landed a job at the WCBS station in New York. He joined CBS Sports as a commentator in 1981. Employed to cover the following year's Tour De France, Tesh jumped at the opportunity to compose music to go with the coverage. A healthy viewer response resulted in Tesh selling several thousand homemade tapes out of his garage, which in turn led to further commissions. He won his first Emmy in 1983, collecting the award for Best Musical Composition for his Pan-American Games theme. His big break came as a presenter, however, when in 1986 he was offered the co-host slot on the nightly *Entertainment Tonight* show. Tesh continued to compose music for sporting events, and in 1987 won a second Emmy for his Tour De France theme. His albums, including his debut *Tour De France* and the following year's *Garden City*, also proved to be strong sellers on the new age lists. Tesh won another Emmy in 1991 for the Best Opening Music for NBC Sports' World Track And Field Championships. The following year Tesh set up his own GTS label, releasing his soundtrack work for the Barcelona Olympic Games and the gold-selling *A Romantic Christmas*. His breakthrough as a musician came with the hugely successful fund-raising concert, *Live At Red Rocks*, which was broadcast on PBS in 1995. The attendant album went gold, the video reached double platinum sales, and Tesh was being fêted as one of the leading stars of adult contemporary music. He left the security of *Entertainment Tonight* in 1996 to concentrate on writing and recording music. He has subsequently released albums as a solo artist and with the John Tesh Project, an informal gathering of musicians offering smooth interpretations of modern songs, with Tesh acting as executive producer and contributing musician. His second PBS special, 1997's *The Avalon Concert*, was another major success. The following year's *Grand Passion* was nominated for a Grammy. Tesh's most ambitious project to date, the *One World* special broadcast on PBS in March 1999, featured footage of the composer recording with local musicians in several countries. The project included the adult contemporary radio hit 'Forever More (I'll Be The One)', featuring soul singer James Ingram.

● ALBUMS: *Tour De France* (Private 1988)★★★, *Garden City* (Cypress 1989)★★★, *Tour De France ... The Early Years* (Private 1990)★★★, *The Games* (GTS 1992)★★★, *Ironman Triathlon* (GTS 1992)★★, *A Romantic Christmas* (GTS 1992)★★★, *Winter Song* (GTS 1993)★★★, with the John Tesh Project *Sax By The Fire* (GTS 1994)★★★, *A Family Christmas* (GTS 1994)★★★, with the Colorado Symphony Orchestra *Live At Red Rocks* (GTS 1995)★★★★, with the John Tesh Project *Sax On The Beach* (GTS 1995)★★★, with the John Tesh Project *Discovery* (GTS 1996)★★★, *John Tesh Presents The Choirs Of Christmas* (GTS 1996)★★, *Avalon* (GTS 1997)★★★, with the John Tesh Project *Sax All Night* (GTS 1997)★★★, with the John Tesh Project *Guitar By The Fire* (GTS 1998)★★★, with the John Tesh Project *Pure Movies* (GTS 1998)★★, *Grand Passion* (GTS 1998)★★, *One World* (GTS 1999)★★★.

● COMPILATIONS: *Monterey Nights* (GTS 1993)★★★, *The Holiday Collection* (GTS 1996)★★★, *Victory: The Sports Collection* (GTS 1997)★★★, *A Windham Hill Retrospective* (Windham Hill 1997)★★★★, *Songs From The Road* (BMG 1998)★★★.

● VIDEOS: *A Romantic Christmas* (GTS 1993), *Live At Red Rocks* (GTS 1995), *The Avalon Concert* (PolyGram Video 1997), *One World* (PolyGram Video 1999).

Texas

The Scottish guitar pop band with the American name originally consisted of Italian-descended Sharleen Spiteri (b. Glasgow, Scotland; vocals/guitar), Ally McErlaine (guitar), Johnny McElhone (bass) and Stuart Kerr (drums, ex-Love And Money). The band were formed in 1986 around McElhone who formerly played bass in Altered Images and Hipsway, though Spiteri and McErlaine quickly became the focal point, partly owing to McErlaine's fluent guitar playing and their joint mastery of Ry Cooder-inspired slide guitar. It was the latter style that distinguished February 1989's UK number 8 single, 'I Don't Want A Lover', the very first song main songwriters Spiteri and McElhone had written together. It helped to break them nationwide as one of a clutch of Scottish bands occupying a slightly awkward space between commercial rock and pop. The band had made its live debut at Dundee University in March 1988, signing to Phonogram subsidiary Vertigo Records through McElhone's former connections with Hipsway. Their first album, 1989's *Southside*, continued to explore the theme of doomed relationships, though the original sessions with Chic's Bernard Edwards were abandoned as 'too heavy handed'. When eventually released it sold over two million copies worldwide, peaking at number 3 in the UK album charts. Richard Hynd replaced Kerr on drums in 1991 and the band was also augmented by the presence of Eddie Campbell on keyboards. *Mother's Heaven* failed to repeat the success of their debut, though by now the band had established itself as a strong concert attraction throughout Europe. The band achieved their second Top 20 hit in April 1992 when a version of Al Green's 'Tired Of Being Alone' reached number 19. *Rick's Road* was completed with new producer Paul Fox after the band stated their fondness for his work with 10,000 Maniacs and the Wallflowers. It included backing vocals from Rose Stone, sister of Sly Stone, and was recorded at Bearsville Studios in Woodstock. In 1997, after another lengthy hiatus, they returned in style with the UK Top 10 hit 'Say What You Want'. Their dramatic comeback continued with the remarkable UK success of *White On Blonde*, an album which demonstrated the band's mastery of a number of musical styles. The oriental-styled 'In Our Lifetime' debuted at UK number 4 in April 1999, and was followed by the chart-topping *The Hush*, another bestselling collection of note-perfect white soul. Mykie Wilson replaced Hynd shortly afterwards.

● ALBUMS: *Southside* (Mercury 1989)★★★, *Mother's Heaven* (Mercury 1991)★★, *Rick's Road* (Vertigo 1993)★★★, *White On Blonde* (Mercury 1997)★★★★, *The Hush* (Mercury 1999)★★★★.

Tha Dogg Pound

The release of Tha Dogg Pound's debut album in 1995 came at a time when their mentor and the best-known member of the Death Row Records/Dr. Dre enclave, Snoop Doggy Dogg, had just gone on trial charged with murder. The Los Angeles, California-based duo of Dat Nigga Daz (b. Delmar Arnaud) and Kurupt Tha Kingpin (b. Ricardo Brown, Philadelphia, Pennsylvania, USA) made their debut on Dogg's multi-platinum *Doggystyle*, and were largely responsible for 1994's *Murder Was The Case* movie soundtrack, which introduced a sound that used Dre's patented G-funk formula as a launching pad. The duo largely steered clear of gangsta rhetoric on their debut album, but with guests including Snoop Doggy Dogg himself, Nate Dogg, Lady Of Rage and Michel'le, *Dogg Food* was bound to attract interest from hardcore rap fans. The album also revealed a comparative deftness of touch and a penchant for self-parody largely lacking in their more esteemed colleagues. However, the sexually explicit content was rumoured to be still strong enough to end Warner Brothers Records' alliance with Interscope Records, Death Row's distributors, even though the album sold a million copies in the USA alone.
● ALBUMS: *Dogg Food* (Death Row/Interscope 1995)★★★.

That Dog

Formed in 1992 in Los Angeles, California, USA, that dog (their name usually omits capitalization) comprised several music business 'offspring'. Anna Waronker (b. 10 July 1972, Los Angeles, California, USA; vocals/guitar) is the daughter of record producer and Warner Brothers Records label-head Lenny Waronker, and Rachel Haden (b. 11 October 1971, Manhattan, New York, USA; bass) and Petra Haden (b. 11 October 1971, Manhattan, New York, USA; violin) are daughters of jazz bass player/composer Charlie Haden. Petra Haden also appeared with Matt Sharp's Rentals. Along with Tony Maxwell (b. 3 June 1968, Paris, France; drums), that dog carved out a fine niche in the indie-rock scene, punk-pop division. The band joined gently surging, subtly quirky, immediate and catchy songs (easiest comparisons would be Redd Kross and Wednesday Week) with wry slice-of-life tales of young love/lust and sexual variation, best demonstrated by 'He's Kissing Christian' (*Totally Crushed Out!*) and 'Gagged And Tied' (*Retreat From The Sun*). The band broke up shortly after the release of the latter album. Waronker's genially bratty singing and the entire band's thoughtful yet terse playing endeared them to those whom Redd Kross, early Blondie, Dolly Mixture and the Buzzcocks remain standard bearers of dreamy pop-with-attitude.
● ALBUMS: *That Dog* (DGC 1994)★★★, *Totally Crushed Out!* (DGC 1995)★★★★, *Retreat From The Sun* (DGC 1997)★★★★.

Theaudience

Comprising Sophie Ellis Bextor (b. 10 April 1979, Middlesex, England; vocals), Billy Reeves (guitar), Dee Molle (guitar), Patrick Hannan (b. 4 March 1966, England; drums), Kerin Smith (bass) and Nyge Butler (keyboards). Theaudience initially attracted press interest due to the fact that Bextor's mother was Janet Ellis, presenter of the UK's long-running television children's programme *Blue Peter*. Music veteran Reeves had previously worked as a press officer at Fire Records, and released an album in 1994 as the Congregation. He met Bextor and the other members of the band at his Uncle Bob's Wedding Reception club night in Highbury, London. Bextor had no previous musical experience, but impressed Reeves with a demo tape comprising cover versions of Oasis songs. Two of the other members boasted impressive musical pedigrees, Hannan having played with the Sundays and Butler sitting in for the Charlatans in 1992 while Rob Collins served a prison sentence. Despite a 14-year age difference, Reeves and Bextor forged a productive writing partnership characterized by a zeitgeist-tapping lyrical slant. The band signed to Mercury Records in June 1997 but retained the rights to release material through their own eLLeFFe label (named after Leo Finlay, the late A&R editor of *Music Week*). They released their first single, 'I've Got The Wherewithal', in October 1997. Follow-up releases confirmed the band's penchant for epigrammatic titles, including 'If You Can't Do It When You're Young, When Can You Do It?' and the Top 30 hits 'A Pessimist Is Never Disappointed' and 'I Know Enough (I Don't Get Enough)'. The latter reached number 25 in August 1998, the same month their debut album was released. Bextor's haughty indie sneer was somewhat wearing over the course of a whole album, but was redeemed by the band's pop nous. Reeves left the band in December.
● ALBUMS: *Theaudience* (Mercury/eLLeFFe 1998)★★★.

Thee Headcoats

Formed in 1989, Thee Headcoats was one of a number of bands fronted by Billy Childish, formerly of the Milkshakes and Thee Mighty Caesars. Featuring either John Agnew or Allan Crockford (from the Prisoners) on bass, and drummer Bruce Brand, *Headcoats Down!* echoed its predecessors with a blend of US garage band styles, punk and, for good measure, country blues. *The Earls Of Suavedom* was similarly derivative, but *The Kids Are All Square - This Is Hip!* represented a new departure with memorable, and contrasting, pop songs. Members of the Delmonas, redubbed Thee Headcoatees, and new bass player Ollie Dollar, enlivened the content considerably, and for once, Childish seemed more concerned with quality rather than haste. By comparison, *Heavens To Murgatroyd, Even! It's Thee Headcoats (Already)* was a disappointment, consisting of new versions of previously recorded songs, cover versions and new material. Nevertheless, the fact that the CD was mastered 'directly from vinyl' reveals much about the group's and Childish's spirit. Childish 'retired' from the music business in 1995, but returned with Thee Headcoats in 1998 for the uncompromising *The Messerschmitt Pilot's Severed Head*.
● ALBUMS: *Headcoats Down!* (Hangman 1989)★★★, *The Earls Of Suavedom* (Crypt 1990)★★★, *The Kids Are All Square - This Is Hip!* (Hangman 1990)★★★, *Heavens To Murgatroyd, Even! It's Thee Headcoats (Already)* (Sub Pop 1990)★★, *The Knights Of The Baskerville* (Birdman 1996)★★★, *The Messerschmitt Pilot's Severed Head* (Damaged Goods 1998)★★.
● COMPILATIONS: *Beach Bums Must Die* (Crypt 1990)★★★.
● VIDEOS: *Live At The Picket* (Visionary 1994).
● FURTHER READING: *17%: Hendrix Was Not The Only Musician!!*.

Therapy?

Northern Irish hard rock/indie metal trio comprising Andy Cairns (guitar, vocals), Michael McKeegan (b. Belfast; bass) and Fyfe Ewing (drums). Cairns and Ewing first met by chance at a charity concert in the late 80s. At that time both

were playing in covers bands, but decided to begin writing together. McKeegan was drafted in for live support (having originally lent his bass to the duo's bedroom sessions) and the enduring Therapy? line-up was in place. They played their first gig supporting Decadence Within at Connor Art College in the summer of 1989, by which time they had already composed some 30 songs. After two demos failed to ignite attention from suitable labels, the band released their debut single, 'Meat Abstract'/'Punishment Kiss', on their own Multifuckingnational imprint. Following approving plays from John Peel the group found their way on to Wiiija Records, via the intervention of Silverfish's Leslie Rankine. Their debut single was then added to new material for a mini-album, *Baby Teeth*. This was followed in short order by a second abbreviated set, *Pleasure Death*. Both these collections went to number 1 in the UK indie charts, but the band remained hamstrung by lack of finance from their record company. Therapy? signed to A&M Records in 1992, and collected a much bigger budget for a new album, *Nurse*, and touring. However, at best the press were neutral about the record, which featured more complex arrangements and themes than the punk-descended speed burn-outs of earlier releases. The band's career was revitalized in March 1993 when 'Screamager' made the UK Top 10. Almost a year later *Troublegum* was unveiled, which returned to more familiar Therapy? elements - buzz-saw guitar, harsh but persistent melodies and musical adrenaline - aided by a cleaner, leaner production than had previously been the case. Nominated for the Mercury Music Prize - alongside the Prodigy, easily the most extreme record to be offered as a candidate - it enshrined Therapy?'s progress as the most commercially successful UK band working in their territory. In 1995, *Infernal Love* offered a significant departure. Alongside the trademark grinding hardcore sound came ballads, string quartets and upbeat lyrics, indicating a band able to shed their old skins musically and lyrically, where it might have been easier to retread former glories. Ewing left the band in January 1996 and was eventually replaced by Graham Hopkins (b. 1976; ex-My Little Funhouse). The band was further augmented by cellist Martin McCarrick. After a protracted absence they released *Semi-Detached*, an excellent album that returned the band to their roots. Following the collapse of the UK's A&M operation, the band returned to their independent label roots for *Suicide Pact - You First*, another powerful collection of old school metal.
● ALBUMS: *Baby Teeth* mini-album (Wiiija 1991)★★, *Pleasure Death* mini-album (Wiiija 1992)★★★, *Nurse* (A&M 1992)★★★, *Troublegum* (A&M 1994)★★★★, *Infernal Love* (A&M 1995)★★, *Semi-Detached* (A&M 1998)★★★, *Suicide Pact - You First* (Ark 21 1999)★★★.

These Animal Men

Essential but nevertheless relatively aged participants in the media-led New Wave Of The New Wave movement, These Animal Men's debut single was 'Speeed King', a tribute to the power of amphetamines. It arrived in a cover with a bowl of white powder and four straws, prompting Brighton MP Andrew Bowden to criticize their attitude to drugs as 'appalling'. The local council of Plymouth banned them full stop. Like an even more ill-mannered Manic Street Preachers, elsewhere their 10 commandments included such errant nonsense as 'Get A Catholic Education' and 'Love's Good, But Not As Good As Wanking'. The latter state-

ment caused trouble when they offered to demonstrate its advantages live on a youth television show. The band was formed in Brighton by Hooligan (b. Julian; guitar) and Patrick (b. Liverpool, Merseyside, England; bass), who knew each other from nursery school. They added additional members Boag (vocals) and Stevie (drums), following 'Speeed King' with 'You're Not My Babylon'. A stopgap release compiled both with a live version of the title track 'Too Sussed', recorded live for the last ever edition of BBC Radio 5's *Vibe* programme. Breaking the UK Top 40, it also brought the band to BBC Television's *Top Of The Pops* stage. A full album, produced by Dave Eringa, was available before the end of the year, and replicated the punk-pop approach of the debut with some particularly virulent lyrics ('Flawed Is Beautiful' and 'Sitting Tenant', in particular). Following the stop-gap *Taxi* mini-album and the loss of Stevie, the band released the frenetic *Accident And Emergency*, which showed no signs of bowing to either fashion or musical conformity.
● ALBUMS: *Too Sussed* mini-album (Hi-Rise 1994)★★, *(Come On, Join) The High Society* (Hi-Rise 1994)★★★, *Taxi For These Animal Men* mini-album (Hi-Rise 1995)★★★, *Accident And Emergency* (Hut 1997)★★★.

They Might Be Giants

John Flansburgh and John Linnell formed this New York, USA-based duo in 1984 after an initial meeting in Massachusetts. The band took their name from a 1972 George C. Scott movie. Their original intention to recruit a full band was abandoned, but Linnell learned the accordion and Flansburgh mastered the guitar. Following Linnell's broken wrist which decimated their early tour dates, they devised the 'Dial-A-Song Service', which still operates today, premiering their intelligent pop skills. A self-titled debut album collated many of these early songwriting ventures, gaining the band a considerable cult reputation. MTV picked up on their quirky visual appeal, and *Lincoln* became the biggest-selling independent album of 1989 in the USA. With wry and perverse lyrics such as 'I can't help but feel jealous each time she climbs on his knee' ('Santa's Beard') they struck an immediate chord with college radio. The UK independent label One Little Indian Records released the album before the group finalized a major contract with Elektra Records. *Flood* showcased their obtuse lyrical approach, contrasting influences as diverse as the Ramones and Love. The UK hit single 'Birdhouse In Your Soul' was a beautifully crafted pop song highlighting the band's affection for the naïve charm of the 60s ballad. While *Apollo 18* brought minor hits in 'The Statue Got Me High' and 'The Guitar (The Lion Sleeps Tonight)', *John Henry* saw them introduce a full band for the first time, including Brian Doherty (drums, ex-Silos), Tony Maimone (bass, ex-Pere Ubu, Bob Mould), Kurt Hoffman (saxophone/keyboards, ex-Ordinaires, Band Of Weeds) and Steven Bernstein (trumpet, ex-Spanish Fly). In 1995, the band made an unlikely appearance, with the track 'Sensurround', on the soundtrack to the children's movie *Mighty Morphin Power Rangers*. Doherty, Graham Maby (bass) and Eric Schermerhorn (guitar) joined Flansburgh and Linnell on the following year's *Factory Showroom*, their last album for Elektra. In 1999, they attracted media attention by making their new album, *The Long Tall Weekend*, available exclusively via the Internet as an MP3 file.
● ALBUMS: *They Might Be Giants* self-released cassette (TMB Music 1985), *They Might Be Giants* (Bar/None 1986)★★★, *Lincoln* (Bar/None

1989)★★★, *Don't Let's Start* (Elektra 1989)★★★, *Flood* (Elektra 1990)★★, *Apollo 18* (Elektra 1992)★★, *John Henry* (Elektra 1994)★★, *Factory Showroom* (Elektra 1996)★★★, *Severe Tire Damage* (Cooking Vinyl 1998)★★, *The Long Tall Weekend* (GoodNoise 1999)★★★.

● COMPILATIONS: *Don't Let's Start* (One Little Indian 1989)★★★, *Miscellaneous T* (Bar/None 1991)★★★, *Then: The Earlier Years* (Restless 1997)★★★.

● VIDEOS: *They Might Be Giants* (Warner Music Video 1991).

Third Eye Blind

Formed in the Bay area of San Francisco, California, USA, contemporary rock band Third Eye Blind are led by singer-songwriter Stephan Jenkins (b. USA). Said to be influenced equally by the Geto Boys and Joy Division, they began to attract a following through a series of high-profile performances, including a support slot to Oasis in San Francisco, before they were signed. They also took over the headliners' billing when Tim Booth of James was forced to cancel a series of concerts because of illness. Their first single, 'Semi-Charmed Life', duly reached number 1 on *Billboard*'s Modern Rock chart, and number 4 on the Hot 100 singles chart. It was a typical effort, in that, beneath the slick-surface pop sound, the lyrics portrayed 'a storm brewing'. Their self-titled debut album, produced by Jenkins and Eric Valentine, reached the US Top 100 following its release in April 1997, peaking at number 25 the following March. The band enjoyed further mainstream success when 'How's It Going To Be' reached US number 9 in February 1998, and 'Jumper' climbed to number 5 the following January. *Blue* failed to capture the imagination of the public, and after initial strong sales quickly faded from view.

● ALBUMS: *Third Eye Blind* (Elektra 1997)★★★★, *Blue* (Elektra 1999)★★★.

3 Colours Red

Formed in London, England, in 1994, uninhibited hard rock band 3 Colours Red earned immediate comparisons to the Wildhearts, whom they duly supported through 1995. Comprising Pete Vuckovic (b. 16 February 1971, Tiverton, Devon, England; vocals/bass), Chris McCormack (b. 21 June 1973, South Shields, Tyne & Wear, England; guitar, and brother of Danny McCormack of the Wildhearts), Ben Harding (b. 31 January 1965, Stoke-On-Trent, England; guitar, ex-Senseless Things) and Keith Baxter (b. 19 February 1971, Morecombe, Lancashire, England; drums), their early stage show combined the earnest ferocity of the best garage rock with memorable pop hooklines. Despite this, the group were not quite as fresh to the rock scene as many had assumed - Vuckovic was formerly a member of the ground-breaking Diamond Head in their later period. Backed by a major management company, the group found themselves a further notable support slot in 1996 as 'first on the bill' to the Sex Pistols at the latter's re-formation concert at Finsbury Park, London. Doubtless this came as a result of McCormack and Baxter's work on Glen Matlock's 1996 solo album, *Who's He Think He Is When He's At Home?* At the same time their debut single, 'This Is My Hollywood', was released on *New Musical Express* journalist Simon Price's Fierce Panda label. Creation Records signed the band in late 1996 and Alan McGee was suitably modest when he claimed '3 Colours Red are the second best band in UK' (after Oasis). The debut

album, *Pure*, attempted to consolidate on the modest showing of their chart singles, debuting at number 16 in the album chart. They returned in October 1998 with the *Paralyse* EP, and finally achieved mainstream success in January 1999 when the powerful ballad 'Beautiful Day' debuted at UK number 11. On the back of the single's success, *Revolt* became a considerable success. Surprisingly, the band then announced they were splitting-up, citing musical differences.

● ALBUMS: *Pure* (Creation 1997)★★★, *Revolt* (Creation 1999)★★★.

311

Formed at high school in Omaha, Nebraska, USA in 1990, hip-hop/rock crossover band 311 recorded three independent albums before relocating to Los Angeles in 1992. Named after the local police code for indecent exposure, the band comprises Nick Hexum (b. 12 April 1970, Madison, Wisconsin, USA; vocals/guitar), Tim Mahoney (b. 17 February 1970, Omaha, Nebraska, USA; guitar), P-Nut (b. Aaron Wills, 5 June 1974, Indianapolis, Indiana, USA; bass), SA Martinez (b. Douglas Martinez, 29 November 1970, Omaha, Nebraska, USA; vocals/turntables) and Chad Sexton (b. 7 September 1970, Lexington, Kentucky, USA; drums). With the Red Hot Chili Peppers and Rage Against The Machine having popularized a cross-genre rock hybrid, 311 seemed to be a ripe commercial prospect, and they were quickly signed to Capricorn Records. Unfortunately, neither of their initial album releases provided them with any commercial reward. Instead they concentrated on live work, playing with bands as diverse as Kiss and Cypress Hill and building a loyal fanbase. Their fortunes were transformed when 'Down' was released as a single in 1995 and was given rotation play on MTV. The single was housed on the band's self-titled third album, which as a consequence went on to sell over three million copies and break into the US Top 20. The home video *Enlarged To Show Detail* preceded 1997's sprawling double set, *Transistor*. The following year's live album was a welcome release for the band's loyal fans. Hugh Padgham was recruited to help regular producer Scotch Ralston on the band's new album, *Soundsystem*, which was regarded by fans and critics alike as their best since *311*.

● ALBUMS: *Music* (Capricorn 1993)★★, *Grassroots* (Capricorn 1994)★★★, *311* (Capricorn 1995)★★★★, *Transistor* (Capricorn 1997)★★★, *311 Live* (Capricorn 1998)★★★, *Soundsystem* (Capricorn 1999)★★★.

● COMPILATIONS: *Omaha Sessions* (What Have You 1999)★★★.

● VIDEOS: *Enlarged To Show Detail* (Capricorn Video 1996).

3T

Comprising three brothers - Tariano Adaryll 'Taj' (b. 4 August 1973), Taryll Adren (b. 8 August 1975), and Tito Joe 'TJ' Jackson (b. 16 July 1978) - 3T are the latest additions to the extraordinary Jackson family (Michael Jackson, Janet Jackson, Jackson Five, etc.). They are sons of original Jackson Five member Tito Jackson, who co-manages their career. The connections were heavily promoted - their aunt Janet was seen wearing their merchandise throughout 1995. They are also signed to Michael Jackson's own label, MJJ, a joint venture with Sony Records. He produced several tracks on their debut album, *Brotherhood*, and sung on one of its tracks, 'Why', written by Babyface. This was the second single to be taken from the album after the huge hit,

'Anything'. Both were typical of the smooth R&B pop of the album, which became a success in both the UK and the USA. The trio had actually made its debut in 1993 with the inclusion of a track, 'Didn't Mean To Hurt You', on the *Free Willy* soundtrack album. The trio returned in 1997 with another transatlantic smash, 'Gotta Be You', although loyal fans are still waiting for their long-delayed sophomore album.

● ALBUMS: *Brotherhood* (MJJ/Sony 1995)★★★.

Throwing Muses

Formed in Providence, Rhode Island, USA, by Kristin Hersh (b. Atlanta, Georgia, USA; vocals/guitar), Tanya Donelly (b. 14 August 1966, Newport, Rhode Island, USA; vocals/guitar), Elaine Adamedes (bass) and David Narcizo (drums), Throwing Muses added an entirely new perspective to the pop model of the late 80s. The band was formed by step-sisters (who had previously been best friends) Hersh and Donelly, though Hersh was the primary influence: 'The band was totally my idea. We were 14, and I was a pain in the ass about it, Tanya didn't even want to play anything for a year'. The duo picked up the services of Narcizo in their junior year in high school after he invited them to play a set at his parents' house. Previously he had only played marching drums, while the cymbal-less set-up of his kit was the result of borrowing from a friend who had mislaid them, rather than any great conceptual plan. The band's first bass player, Adamedes, departed while Donelly was still playing a Casio placed on an ironing board. Dreadlocked vegetarian Leslie Langston arrived in Adamedes' stead and the band relocated to Boston, Massachusetts. Seemingly unaware of conventional constraints, the quartet went on to peddle an off-kilter brand of guitar noise that accentuated the female self-expression implicit rather than explicit in their songs. Nevertheless, instead of becoming too awkward for their own commercial good, the band were picked up by Britain's 4AD Records and thrust into the European limelight alongside local contemporaries the Pixies. Over the next five years and five albums, the media made much of singer Hersh's psychological disorders, drawing parallels between her state of mind and the music's unsettling idiosyncrasies. Langston departed to be replaced by bass player Fred Abong for *The Real Ramona*, and more problems were to manifest themselves by the end of the decade as Throwing Muses became embroiled in a series of legal disputes with their manager (Ken Goes), the Musicians' Union and over personal aspects of individual band members' lives. During the recording of *The Real Ramona*, guitarist Tanya Donelly - who had also moonlighted in the Breeders - announced her permanent departure from the Muses, although she stayed on for the subsequent tour before forming Belly. The amicable split had come about because, instead of wishing to contribute her usual one or two songs to the new album, Donelly had written seven, and there was no room to accommodate these in the final selection. This left the Throwing Muses' picture in a decidedly muddled state by the close of 1991. By the following year the core of the band comprised the trio of Hersh, Narcizo and Bernard Georges (bass). This line-up recorded the critically acclaimed *Red Heaven*, but the band all but broke up the following year. Hersh attempted to retreat to Newport to concentrate on her family, but the 'muse' would not leave her, and the band regrouped in 1994 following her well-received solo album *Hips And Makers*. In

1995, *University* served to remind doubters of what had made Throwing Muses so unique in the first place - a wilfully adventurous approach to songwriting, though this time there were also more songs of potential commercial import. However, the poor sales of this album and 1997's follow-up *Limbo* convinced Hersh to finally leave the band and concentrate on her solo career. Narcizo recorded ambient electronica as Lakuna.

● ALBUMS: *Throwing Muses* (4AD 1986)★★★, *The Fat Skier* mini-album (Sire/4AD 1987)★★★, *House Tornado* (Sire/4AD 1988)★★★, *Hunkpapa* (Sire/4AD 1989)★★, *The Real Ramona* (Sire/4AD 1991)★★★★, *Red Heaven* (Sire/4AD 1992)★★★ *University* (Sire/4AD 1995)★★★★, *Limbo* (4AD 1996)★★★.

● COMPILATIONS: *In A Doghouse* (4AD 1998)★★★.

Thunder

This UK hard rock quintet was heavily influenced by Bad Company and the Rolling Stones. Thunder evolved from the ashes of Terraplane, with the surviving nucleus of Danny Bowes (vocals), Luke Morley (guitar) and Gary James (drums) recruiting Mark Luckhurst (bass) and Ben Matthews (guitar) to complete the line-up. Moving away from the melodic power pop of their former incarnation, they teamed up with producer Andy Taylor (ex-Duran Duran) to record *Backstreet Symphony*, a stunning album of bluesy rockers and atmospheric ballads, which received widespread critical acclaim. Their style is characterized by a dual guitar attack of alternating riffs and lead breaks, with Bowes' gritty and emotional vocals adding charisma and distinction. Live, the icing on the cake is drummer Gary James' erratic behaviour, which has included appearing in a tutu or offering impromptu Frank Sinatra impersonations. They landed the opening slot at the Donington Festival in 1990 and were the surprise success of the day. In 1991, they concentrated on the American market, touring extensively in an attempt to make the all-important breakthrough. However, though another strong collection, *Laughing On Judgement Day* was not the album to do it. Luckhurst (who would go on to join the David Coverdale/Jimmy Page touring band) departed in acrimony in 1993 to be replaced by Mikael Hoglund (ex-Great King Rat). The title of their excellent third album, *Behind Closed Doors*, proved appropriate as the group had spent over 12 months recording the set in the USA with the aid of Aerosmith/AC/DC producer Mike Fraser. Thunder have retained the spirit of great hard rock bands of the 60s and 70s (Free, Bad Company) without sounding remotely dated. They are arguably the present leaders of the pack.

● ALBUMS: *Back Street Symphony* (EMI 1990)★★, *Laughing On Judgement Day* (EMI 1992)★★★, *Behind Closed Doors* (EMI 1995)★★★★, *Live Circuit* (EMI 1995)★★, *The Thrill Of It All* (B. Lucky Music 1996)★★★★, *Thunder Live In England* (Eagle 1998)★★★, *Giving The Game Away* (Eagle 1999)★★.

● COMPILATIONS: *Their Finest Hour (And A Bit): The Best Of Thunder* (EMI 1995)★★★, *The Rare, The Raw And The Rest ...* (EMI 1999)★★★.

● VIDEOS: *Back Street Symphony: The Videos* (PMI 1990), *Live* (Eagle Rock Entertainment 1998).

Tiger

Based in London, England, Tiger became the subject of major press scrutiny in 1996 with only a handful of gigs and no releases behind them. So meteoric was the quintet's rise that they had played only three times before they were signed by Island Records subsidiary Trade 2 and EMI Music Publishing. Representatives of both companies had seen the band at London's Dublin Castle venue by chance and a contract with both was completed by May. However, the band's first single was actually released on music journalist Simon Price's Fierce Panda Records. This drew early comparisons with left-field mavericks such as Jonathan Richman and the Fall, with singer and songwriter Dan Laidler's reserved persona and Julie Sims' guitar work (usually played through the amplification medium of a ghetto blaster) attracting special plaudits. The band were included on the *New Musical Express' C-96* compilation cassette, as further critical praise followed their every move. The debut album confirmed their position as champions of the anti-Britrock backlash. After a lengthy absence, and the loss of Sims, the band returned in August 1998 with the single 'Friends', a taster for the following year's *Rosaria*.

● ALBUMS: *We Are Puppets* (Trade 2 1996)★★★★, *Rosaria* (Tugboat 1999)★★★.

Tillis, Pam

b. 24 July 1957, Plant City, Florida, USA. The eldest of the five children of country singer Mel Tillis, Pam did not have the happiest childhood. Mel spent much of his time touring, her parents eventually parted and she grew up often looking after her siblings. Initially, she had no wish to follow in her father's country footsteps, although she had ambitions to sing and write songs. After her education at the University of Tennessee, she relocated to San Francisco where, for a time, she worked on a show with a jazz group. She married Rick Mason, moved back to Nashville and worked as a writer with Sawgrass Publishing. Around 1974, a few weeks after the birth of her son, Ben, she and Mason parted. She gradually became more active in music and sang and wrote in styles that varied from jazz and rock, to R&B and pop, without achieving any major success in any genre. In the early 80s, she spent some time in Britain but on her return to Nashville, moving more towards new country, she spent most of her time singing demos and advertising jingles. After joining Warner Brothers Records, for whom she recorded what has often been described as a pop album, she gained her first country chart success in 1984, with 'Goodbye Highway'. In 1986/7, she managed four more minor hits, including 'Those Memories Of You', but later described the late 80s as 'years of languishing in obscurity', although she did attract attention in 1986, when she performed a mock-country show she called *Twang Night*. In 1990, still seeking to establish her own identity and reluctant to be known as 'Mel Tillis' daughter', she joined Arista Records. Her first single for the label, 'Don't Tell Me What To Do', became a Top 5 country hit and finally launched her career. 'One Of Those Things', originally released five years earlier on Warner, quickly followed and peaked at number 6. During the next two years, further Top 5 hits followed with 'Maybe It Was Memphis', 'Shake The Sugar Tree' and 'Let The Pony Run'. Her own compositions accounted for more than half of the songs on her first two Arista albums and included the autobiographical 'Melancholy Child' and 'Homeward Looking Angel', which she co-wrote with new husband Bob DiPiero. Her rocking number 11 hit, 'Cleopatra, Queen Of Denial', also proved a popular video. In 1994, she registered further hits that included 'Spilled Perfume', her

version of Jackie DeShannon's 'When You Walk In The Room' and her own 1995 number 1, 'Mi Vida Loca' (My Crazy Life). She has never been afraid to dress in an unusual manner and has appeared in hats that could have come from Minnie Pearl's wardrobe. An American magazine once described her as 'a failed punk rocker, one-time hell on wheels, reincarnated as a drop-dead country singer'. Her powerful vocal styling may not suit everybody; one reviewer commenting on an album wrote 'if strident-voiced females are your thing, this should suit you nicely'. Her songs are recorded by other artists but it still remains to be seen whether she can really establish herself with the hardline country traditionalists. She still has a long way to go to equal her father's tally of chart hits, but she has made a promising start.

● ALBUMS: *Above & Beyond The Call Of Cutey* (Warners 1983)★★★, *Put Yourself In My Place* (Arista 1991)★★★★, *Homeward Looking Angel* (Arista 1992)★★★★, *Sweetheart's Dance* (Arista 1994)★★★, *All Of This Love* (Arista 1995)★★★, *Every Time* (Arista 1998)★★★.

● COMPILATIONS: *Pam Tillis Collection* (Warners 1994)★★★, *Greatest Hits* (Arista 1997)★★★, *Super Hits* (Arista 1999)★★★.

● VIDEOS: *When You Walk In The Room* (Arista 1994).

● FURTHER READING: *Pam Tillis: Out Of Her Father's Shadows*, Ace Collins.

Timbaland

b. Tim Mosley, 10 March 1971, Norfolk, Virginia, USA. Timbaland has rapidly established himself as one of the hottest producers of the 90s thanks to his highly acclaimed work with hip-hop and R&B artists including Aaliyah, Missy 'Misdemeanor' Elliott and Ginuwine. Since the late 80s he has worked on and off with rapper Magoo, a fellow Virginian. Timbaland's concerted efforts to break into the music business bore its first fruits on Jodeci's *Diary Of A Mad Band* and *The Show, The After-Party, The Hotel*, co-writing the latter's 'Bring On Da Funk'. His real breakthrough came in autumn 1996, when he worked on Aaliyah's *One In A Million*, the follow-up to her R. Kelly-produced debut. Timbaland worked his magic touch on standout tracks such as 'If Your Girl Only Knew', '4 Page Letter' and 'One In A Million'. On a roll, he then wrote and produced hits for Ginuwine ('Pony') and SWV ('Can We'), before hooking up with Elliott, his other long-term musical partner. Timbaland and Magoo's major contributions to Elliott's *Supa Dupa Fly* introduced a new sound to the record-buying public. The funky syncopated beats on the hugely popular single 'Rain (Supa Dupa Fly)' confirmed the arrival of a new southern dynamic to rival the traditional east coast/west coast hip-hop axis. Timbaland built on his success with October 1997's *Welcome To Our World*, a joint effort with Magoo that was hailed as one of the year's key albums. It was premiered by 'Up Jumps Da' Boogie', a Top 10 R&B/number 12 Hot 100 hit in September. The following May's 'Clock Strikes' single sampled the theme to *Knight Rider*, and reached number 37 on the *Billboard* Hot 100. By now Timbaland was heavily in-demand as a producer, and the soundtracks for *Can't Hardly Wait* and *Dr. Dolittle* included his remixes of Elliott's 'Hit 'Em Wit Da' Hee', Busta Rhymes' 'Turn It Up/Fire It Up', Aaliyah's 'Are You That Somebody' and All Saints' 'Lady Marmalade'. He then worked with Elliott's protégée Nicole on her August 1998 breakthrough, *Make It Hot*, and collaborated with Elliott on the soundtrack to *Why Do Fools Fall In Love*, which included Destiny Child's 'Get On The Bus', Coko's 'He Be Back', Total's 'What The Dealio', and the Missy Elliott collaborations with Busta Rhymes ('Get Contact') and Mel B. of the Spice Girls ('I Want You Back'). Timbaland also contributed to Jay-Z's chart-topping *Vol. 2 ... Hard Knock Life* ('Ni*** What, Ni*** Who', 'Paper Chase'), and, in November, released his debut set *Tim's Bio*, the soundtrack to a purported movie about his life and music. The following March saw the release of Ginuwine's eagerly awaited new set, *100% Ginuwine*, and in June Elliott's sophomore set *Da Real World* received excellent reviews.

● ALBUMS: with Magoo *Welcome To Our World* (Blackground/Atlantic 1997)★★★★, *Tim's Bio: From The Motion Picture: Life From Da Bassment* (Blackground/Atlantic 1998)★★★.

Tin Machine

Following a creative nadir in the mid-80s, David Bowie launched a new 'back to basics' band in May 1989. The twin guitars, bass, and drum-driven Tin Machine consisted of Bowie (vocals/guitar), Reeves Gabrels (b. Boston, Massachusetts, USA; guitar), and Tony and Hunt Sales in the rhythm section. The band proved to be much more blues- and rock-orientated than Bowie had been for a considerable time. Tony and Hunt Sales' father was US children's television host Soupy Sales, whose television series *The Soupy Sales Show* ran for several years in the late 50s and early 60s. In addition, he hosted a teenage dance programme called *Soupy's Soda Shop*. His sons started out playing in bands in the 60s, notably Tony And The Tigers. They then became an in-demand rhythm section either together or with other partners, playing with artists/bands including Todd Rundgren, Utopia, Chequered Past, but more significantly they both played alongside David Bowie on Iggy Pop's *Lust For Life*; thus, a prototype Tin Machine was tested as early as 1977. Gabrels had previously played with Bowie in 1988 (having met him when both were working with the dance group La La La Human) and before that had spells with Life On Earth, Rubber Rodeo, the Bent Men, and the Atom Said, and performed session work for David Lynch, the Mission and Deaf School. Tin Machine made its live debut on 31 May 1989 at the International Music Awards in New York. After an initial tour and album (which reached the UK Top 5), they were put on hold while Bowie embarked on The Sound And Vision World Tour 1990, which he claimed would be his last. Tin Machine were then resurrected for a second stab with a considerable promotional push, which seemed to have failed just as convincingly as before. The project fizzled out with the release of a posthumous concert recording. Bowie returned to his own career, while Gabrels began work on his debut solo project, *The Sacred Squall Of Now*.

● ALBUMS: *Tin Machine* (EMI 1989)★★★, *Tin Machine II* (London/Victory 1991)★★★, *Live: Oy Vey, Baby* (London/Victory 1992)★★.

Tin Tin Out

UK dance music outfit comprising Darren Stokes and Lyndsey Edwards. The group was formed in 1993 when Stokes, also a renowned DJ, was A&R Director for Pulse 8 Records (responsible for signing, among others, Gloworm's 'I Lift My Cup' and Urban Cookie Collective's 'The Key: The Secret'). He met Edwards, an acclaimed keyboard player and musical technician, on a session for the label. Adopting the name Tin Tin Out they undertook a burgeoning repertoire of remixes, including Jon Pleased Wimmin ('Passion'), Lisa Moorish ('That's The Way It Is') and Michelle Gayle ('Freedom'). In their own right they reached the UK charts in August 1994 with 'The Feeling', which featured rapper Sweet Tee, and the following March with a memorable version of 'Always Something There To Remind Me' featuring Espiritu singer Vanessa Quinnones (the Top 20 hit was later used on UK television's football programme *Endsleigh League Extra*). They signed to VC Recordings in 1995, releasing *Always* later in the year. They enjoyed their first UK Top 10 hit in March 1998 when a version of the Sundays' 'Here's Where The Story Ends', featuring the vocals of Shelley Nelson, reached number 7. The follow-up single, 'Sometimes', stalled at number 20 in September. The following year's collaboration with Emma Bunton of the Spice Girls, a lame cover version of Edie Brickell's 'What I Am', reached UK number 2 in November.

● ALBUMS: *Always* (VC 1995)★★★, *Eleven To Fly* (Virgin 1999)★★.

Tindersticks

Formed in Nottingham, England, and previously known as the Asphalt Ribbons, Tindersticks revolve around the melancholic tones of singer Stuart Staples. Dickon Hinchcliffe (violin) and Dave Boulter (keyboards) joined him in a new act, which was completed by Neil Fraser (guitar), Mark Colwill (bass) and Al McCauley (drums). The sextet made its debut in November 1992 with 'Patchwork', released on their own Tippy Toe label. A second single, 'Marbles', presaged 'A Marriage Made In Heaven', a collaboration with Niki Sin of Huggy Bear issued on Rough Trade Records. Having then completed the *Unwired* EP, the Tindersticks were signed by Andrew Lauder for his newly formed This Way Up company. *Tindersticks* was well received, *Melody Maker* magazine citing it as their album of the year. It also earned them a top three placing in *Rolling Stone*'s best new band poll. Centring on Staples' lugubrious vocals, which are part Scott Walker, part Ian Curtis (Joy Division) and part Lee Hazlewood, its atmosphere of late-night disenchantment was matched by haunting melodies and beautiful instrumentation. Critical comparisons to Nick Cave's work were further encouraged by a series of support dates with that artist. Ensuing releases included a version of 'We Have All The Time In The World', written by John Barry for the James Bond movie *On Her Majesty's Secret Service* and a live collection. The *Kathleen* EP then gave the band its first UK chart hit, reaching number 61 in January 1994. The band's second studio album was released in 1995, recorded at Conny Plank's studio in Cologne, Germany, and London's Abbey Road, with Ian Caple again co-producing. Again the preoccupations were doomed romance and life on the edge, with a guest appearance from the like-minded Terry Edwards of Gallon Drunk on saxophone and trumpet, and the Walkabouts' Carla Torgerson on the duet 'Travelling Light'. Once more the reaction was overwhelmingly positive, as the group consolidated progress to date with further European touring and a second live album, this time recorded with a full 28-piece orchestra. The band also contributed two songs to the Chris And Carla (Walkabouts) solo album. The stable line-up remained for the excellent *Curtains*, beautifully laid-back, doom-laden and heavily orchestral, which sometimes masks the ironic humour of several of the songs. Staples' voice is both enticing and relaxing, and although he has often been compared to Nick Cave and Tim Hardin, the most striking vocal similarity is to Moby Grape's Peter Lewis.

● ALBUMS: *Tindersticks* (This Way Up 1993)★★★★, *Amsterdam February '94* 10-inch album (This Way Up 1994)★★, *The Second Tindersticks Album* (This Way Up 1995)★★★★, *The Bloomsbury Theatre 12.3.95* 10-inch album (This Way Up 1995)★★, *Nénette Et Boni* film soundtrack (This Way Up 1996)★★★, *Curtains* (This Way Up 1997)★★★★, *Simple Pleasure* (Island 1999)★★★.

● COMPILATIONS: *Donkeys '92-'97* (Island 1998)★★★★.

TLC

This spirited, sassy female trio from Atlanta, Georgia, USA, comprise Lisa 'Left Eye' Lopes, Rozanda 'Chilli' Thomas and T-Boz (b. Tionne Watkins). They initially worked under the tutelage of manager Pebbles, scoring immediate chart success with fresh, funky material such as 'Ain't 2 Proud 2 Beg' (US number 5), 'Baby-Baby-Baby' (number 2) and 'What About Your Friends' (number 7). They also took to adorning themselves in barrier contraceptives to advocate safe sex, before moving on to work with celebrated dance/soul producers Dallas Austin and Babyface. Primarily conducted in 'new jill swing' mode, their debut album addressed the joys of womanhood, with staunch advice on how to treat errant boyfriends. As with the gangsta rappers, it became evident that TLC meant every word when Lopes was jailed for burning down the mansion of Andre Rison, her Atlanta Falcons' football star boyfriend. She also trashed his cars in a drunken rage, and was later admitted to an alcohol rehabilitation clinic, becoming one of America's top news stories in the process. Luckily for TLC her sentence was commuted to probation and probably helped rather than hindered their career. A third album repeated the group's original formula, albeit with slightly more sophisticated, less strident material. The concept behind it was 'TLC's way of saying 'I'm Every Woman' - you know, every woman is crazy, sexy and cool, though on some days she might be more one than the other. Certainly we're all three, though if there is a dominant side Left Eye is crazy, I'm sexy and T-Boz is the cool one.' With beats provided by Jermaine Dupri and Sean 'Puffy' Combs in addition to Austin, *CrazySexyCool* subdued some of Lopes' rapping in favour of more ensemble singing, with the hip-hop quotient maintained largely through the urban rhythms. The best example was the US number 1, 'Creep', a sensuous groove embossed by lively funk flourishes. Elsewhere a Prince cover, 'If I Was Your Girlfriend', proved secondary to the group's own street articulate material. *CrazySexyCool* soon went quadruple platinum in America, but nevertheless the group was forced to file for bankruptcy in 1995 with liabilities of $3.5 million. $1.3 million of this sum was owed to Lloyd's Of London Insurance, and related to an unpaid insurance claim on Rison's house destroyed by Lopes. Further complications arose over the group's management. LaFace Records and Pebbitone, their record label and production company, the former run by L.A. Reid and the latter by his estranged wife Pebbles, entered a financial dispute. Pebbles claimed that each member of TLC owed her company $566,434. She also accused LaFace and parent company Arista Records of attempting to entice TLC away from Pebbitone, and undermining the trio's obligation to

return $500,000 in advances and their obligation to record at least six albums for her company. The band were able to put all this behind them when their year of success was reflected in picking up two Grammies at the 1996 ceremony. They won Best R&B Performance By A Duo Or Group With Vocal for 'Creep' and best R&B album for *CrazySexyCool*. At the same time their album passed 10 million copies in the USA alone and their debut passed four million units in June 1996. Ongoing contractual negotiations ensured a lengthy delay before the release of March 1999's American chart-topper *Fan Mail*. The glorious single 'No Scrubs' climbed to the top of the US Hot 100, and spent several weeks in the UK Top 10, peaking at number 3 in May. 'Unpretty' followed it to the top of the US charts in September.

● ALBUMS: *Oooooooohhh ... On The TLC Tip* (LaFace/Arista 1992)★★, *TLC* (LaFace/Arista 1993)★★★★, *CrazySexyCool* (LaFace/Arista 1995)★★★★, *Fan Mail* (Arista 1999)★★★★.

● VIDEOS: *Crazy Video Cool* (BMG Video 1995).

Toad The Wet Sprocket

This US rock band was formed in the mid-80s at high school in Santa Barbara, California, by friends Dean Dinning (bass, backing vocals, keyboards), Randy Guss (drums), Todd Nichols (guitar, vocals) and Glen Phillips (vocals, guitar, keyboards). The unconventional name came from British television's cult comedy series *Rutland Weekend Television*, notably their brilliant satire of *The Old Grey Whistle Test*. By the time they had established their reputation on the local Santa Barbara club circuit, none of the band had even reached the legal drinking age required for entrance. Despite the irreverence of their name, the band's lyrics were delivered with intelligence and poise, and addressed social issues and personal relationships. With a budget of just $650, their debut album was recorded in a cramped living room, but still caught the immediacy of their live show. Sold at local stores and gigs, it allowed them to finance the release of a second set, before the major record labels began to notice their local popularity. The band signed to Columbia Records in 1988, who agreed to re-release both albums in their original form. As Phillips recalls, 'We got signed in the summer after what was going to be our last year together. When the summer ended I was supposed to go off to college.' What they did instead was to depart on support tours with the B-52's, Debbie Harry and Michael Penn. Their major label debut, *Fear*, followed in August 1991. With 'Hold Her Down' receiving widespread airplay, the 100,000 sales return of the album satisfied both artist and record company. Then, quite unexpectedly, Toad The Wet Sprocket took a giant commercial leap forward. 'All I Want' entered the US Top 40, as did its follow-up, 'Walk On The Ocean'. With nearly 300 shows played in 18 months across North America and Europe, *Fear* acquired platinum status. When they finally came off the road the band returned to the studio, this time the Site in Marin County, California, with the express intention of rediscovering the organic writing process that had produced their earliest songs (in interviews they expressed the collective view that *Fear* was too 'manicured'). Produced with Gavin MacKillop, *Dulcinea* took its title from the story of Don Quixote, specifically the love of his life. The idea of unattainable perfection was central to the album's concept, further explored in opening single 'Fall Down': 'She hates her life, she hates her skin/She even hates her friends/Tries to hold on to all the reputations/She can't mend'. Alternating lead vocals from Nichols and Phillips added further musical contrast to a selection of songs that drew heavily on folk and country as well as rock traditions, paying homage to Nanci Griffith and Loretta Lynn on 'Nanci'. On 1997's *Coil* Toad The Wet Sprocket abandoned their pop format and went for a harder-edged sound with deeper lyrics. The following year they announced they were splitting up.

● ALBUMS: *Bread And Circus* (Abe's 1986)★★★, *Pale* (Abe's 1988)★★, *Fear* (Columbia 1991)★★, *Dulcinea* (Columbia 1994)★★★, *In Light Syrup* (Columbia 1995)★★, *Coil* (Columbia 1997)★★★.

Tong, Pete

b. Dartford, Kent, England. Certainly one of the most high-profile personalities in UK dance music, Tong has been described by some as the most powerful. This is perhaps because of the range of activities in which he is involved – head of ffrr Records, among the world's top 10 club DJs and host of the hugely popular *Essential Selection* show on the UK's BBC Radio 1. This gives him tremendous influence in determining which tracks transfer from the club scene to the national charts and often international success. He also runs his own imprint, Essential Recordings, and releases mix compilations for the Ministry Of Sound and Cream. His distinctive tones and streetwise turns of phrase represent the popular voice of commercial dance music.

Tong grew up listening to funk and soul artists such as Funkadelic, James Brown and Evelyn 'Champagne' King and played his first gig as a DJ at the age of 15 at a wedding. Naturally entrepreneurial, he began promoting local bands, booking gigs and DJing at local clubs. After leaving school, he set up his own mobile sound system and would transport it from gig to gig in a Ford van. In 1979, he began to write for the magazine *Blues And Soul* and was features editor between 1980 and 1983. Simultaneously, he DJed for regional radio stations, such as BBC Radio Medway and Radio London. An important break came when he presented a regular 15-minute dance 'magazine' feature on Peter Powell's Radio 1 show. In 1983, he was appointed A&R manager at the newly-founded independent label, London Records. While overseeing the career of pop chart acts such as Bananarama, he continued his radio career on Kent's regional station, Invicta, before returning to Radio London. Almost immediately, Tong was lured by Capital Radio, where his weekly soul and dance show became hugely popular with London clubbers. By 1988, with the explosion of acid house in the UK and the beginning of the dance music revolution that followed, Tong had launched the ffrr Records imprint through London Records, with the aim of promoting Detroit techno and Chicago house, alongside his first love, black soul and disco. The label began with club/chart crossover successes such as 'Bass (How Low Can You Go?)' by Simon Harris and rappers Salt-N-Pepa's 'Push It' and continued throughout the 80s and 90s with influential hits from artists such as Steve Hurley, D-Mob, Smith And Mighty, Cookie Crew, Lil' Louis, Brand New Heavies, Orbital and Goldie.

By 1991, club culture was booming in the UK and Tong left Capital Radio to present *The Essential Selection* on national BBC Radio 1. House-based but championing all forms of dance music, it has become a club culture institution,

attracting a million and-a-half listeners in the UK and a significant audience in continental Europe. Tong was instrumental in reinventing the station in the mid-90s to reflect the new clubbing generation. Since then, much of the station's output has become dance-orientated, notably at the weekend. Other DJs on the station from dance music backgrounds now include Danny Rampling, Judge Jules, Fabio and Grooverider. With his role at ffrr Records, his radio and club DJing, mix compilations, advertising voice-over work and his radio production company, Tong's wealth is estimated to be more than £2 million.

● COMPILATIONS: with Boy George *The Annual* (MOS 1995)★★★, with Boy George *Dance Nation 2* (MOS 1996)★★★, with Boy George *The Annual II* (MOS 1996)★★★★, with Judge Jules *Dance Nation 3* (MOS 1997)★★★★, with Boy George *Dance Nation 4* (MOS 1997)★★★, with Boy George *Dance Nation 5* (MOS 1998)★★★, with Judge Jules *Clubbers Guide* (MOS 1998)★★★, with Judge Jules *Ibiza Annual* (MOS 1998)★★★, with Boy George *The Annual IV* (MOS 1998)★★★★, with Fatboy Slim, Paul Oakenfold *Essential Millennium* (ffrr 1999)★★★★.

Tony! Toni! Toné!

This swingbeat trio from Oakland, California, comprises brothers Dwayne (b. 14 February 1963, Oakland, California, USA; lead vocals/guitar) and Raphael Wiggins (b. 14 May 1966, Oakland, California, USA; lead vocals/bass), and their cousin Timothy Christian (b. 10 December 1965, Oakland, California, USA; drums). They arrived with 'Little Walter' in 1988, a US R&B number 1 hit, which combined the best traditions of soul with new-age rap. They remain at their most successful when moving, unceremoniously, from tight, gospel-tinged harmonics to assured, laconic hip-hop, as on 1990's hit, 'It Never Rains In Southern California'. Despite their high profile (notably as support on Janet Jackson's 1993 US tour), they retain a sense of propriety and musical history. Christian still plays for his church when at home, while Raphael made his public debut at age seven playing bass with his father's semi-professional blues band. Their name (pronounced 'Tony' on each of the three occurrences) was taken from a character they invented when they went out shopping to buy vintage clothing.

● ALBUMS: *Who?* (Wing 1988)★★★, *The Revival* (Wing/Mercury 1990)★★★, *Sons Of Soul* (Wing/Mercury 1993)★★★, *House Of Music* (Mercury 1996)★★★★.

● COMPILATIONS: *Hits* (Mercury 1997)★★★★.

Tool

One of the leading new heavy metal acts of the 90s, Tool were formed in Los Angeles, USA, in 1990 by Adam Jones (guitar), Maynard James Keenan (vocals), Paul D'Amour (bass) and Danny Carey (drums). The mini-album, *Opiate*, was a powerful introduction to Tool's densely rhythmic style, with 'Hush' helping establish a buzz for the band; the accompanying video graphically displayed the song's anti-censorship slant of 'I can't say what I want to/Even if I'm not serious' as the band appeared naked with their mouths taped shut. European dates with friends Rage Against The Machine and a US tour with the Rollins Band helped to sharpen Tool's live performances. Their increased confidence was evident on *Undertow*, which featured a guest vocal from Henry Rollins on 'Bottom'. While the band retained their angry intensity and penchant for difficult lyrical subjects, their songwriting became more adventurous, culminating in the experimental ambient closer, 'Disgustipated' - lyrically, however, the track displayed a sense of humour that belied Tool's miserable image by protesting about a carrot's right to life, satirizing the politically correct movement. *Undertow* reached platinum status as the band toured extensively, including a stint on the 1993 Lollapalooza tour. *Aenima* was their most assured and most successful album, narrowly missing the top of the *Billboard* album chart in November 1996.

● ALBUMS: *Opiate* (Zoo 1992)★★, *Undertow* (Zoo 1993)★★★, *Aenima* (RCA 1996)★★★★.

Top Cat

b. Anthony Codrington, Manchester, England. Codrington's nickname came from his schooldays, when he was likened to the roguish cartoon cat. Moving to south London resulted in Anthony completing his education in Lewisham, home of the renowned Saxon sound system. His father was influential in inspiring his love of music, which was further fuelled when visiting relatives in Jamaica. In the early 80s he chatted on various sound systems, but was unable to make a living from this and pursued a career outside of music. However, he perpetually performed on the microphone at dances and in 1988 he recorded 'Love Mi Sess', an ode to marijuana that rocketed to the number 1 position in the reggae chart. His success led to a career in music and following the release of *Sensemilla Man*, he embarked on an international promotional tour, making personal appearances on sound systems throughout Europe and America. Fashion Records realized Top Cat's potential and a number of tunes were recorded at the A Class studio, including 'Request The Style' and 'Shot A Batty Boy', which failed to attract media attention. Top Cat's 1992 release, 'Over You Body', held the number 1 spot in the reggae chart for nine weeks, ironically on his own 9 Lives label. The label released a number of recordings from Anthony Red Rose, Simpleton, Mike Anthony, Prento Youth and Poison Chang. The follow-up, 'Push Up Your Lighter', was equally successful and, when remixed for the 'junglist posse', topped the chart representing this genre. Accolades from the media were bestowed upon Top Cat and his success continued with the chart-topping 1994 Christmas hit, 'Wine Up You Body', along with *Nine Lives Of The Cat*. A visit to Jamaica found Top Cat recording with Poison Chang, resulting in the third clash album of Jamaican and English DJs, the two previous ones being Papa San versus Tippa Irie and Johnny Ringo versus Asher Senator. In 1995, 'Sweetest Thing' with its Jackson Five riff, an appearance on BBC Television's *The Vibe*, and a duet with General Levy on 'Girls Dem', maintained his high profile.

● ALBUMS: *Sensemilla Man* (1989)★★★, *Request The Style* (1992)★★, *Nine Lives Of The Cat* (Nine Lives 1995)★★★, with Poison Chang *JA To UK MC Clash Part Three - Top Cat Meets Poison Chang* (Fashion 1995)★★★, with General Levy *Rumble In The Jungle* (Glamma 1995)★★★★, *Cat O' Nine Tails* (Nine Lives 1996)★★★.

Tortoise

Formed in Chicago, Illinois, USA, in 1990, Tortoise are an instrumental band founded by Douglas McCombs (bass, of Eleventh Dream Day) and John Herndon (drums) as an experiment. By 1994, they had recruited John McEntire (drums/vibraphone, also Gastr Del Sol, Red Crayola), Bundy K. Brown (bass, also Gastr Del Sol) and Dan Bitney (percussion), and set about work on their self-titled debut album. A richly formulated collection of atmospheric collages, combining dub reggae bass, electronic, jazz, ambient and classical movements, it saw them become the toast of a number of US and UK magazines. *Rhythms, Resolutions & Clusters*, a remix project drawing principally on the debut, was released the following year. Leading alternative engineers such as Steve Albini, Jim O'Rourke and Brad Wood essentially used each track as *carte blanche* for their sonic experiments. David Pajo (ex-Slint) replaced Brown for the band's second album, *Millions Now Living Will Never Die*. Released early in 1996, the album fairly exploded with audacious ideas and daring experiments with song structures, epitomised by the 20-minute plus 'Djed'. The band were also celebrated in novel form in *Low Fidelity*, author Timothy White vividly narrating his protagonist's trip to London to find every record by Tortoise he could. *TNT* was less experimental, concentrating on meandering jazz-fusion complete with suitably pretentious song titles, including 'In Sarah, Menchen, Christ And Beethoven There Were Women And Men' and 'I Set My Face To The Hillside'.

● ALBUMS: *Tortoise* (Thrill Jockey/City Slang 1994)★★★, *Rhythms, Resolutions & Clusters* (Thrill Jockey/City Slang 1995)★★★, *Millions Now Living Will Never Die* (Thrill Jockey/City Slang 1996)★★★★, *TNT* (Thrill Jockey/City Slang 1998)★★★.

Total

This New Jersey, USA-based female trio's sound is commonly described as 'new jill flava', shorthand for a smooth mix of soul, hip-hop and funk closely modelled on the swingbeat style of Mary J. Blige and male counterparts Jodeci. Comprising singers Kima Raynor, Pam Long and Keisha Spivey, the trio have enjoyed a string of gold and platinum-selling singles in the mid-to-late 90s. They were originally discovered by Sean 'Puffy' Combs, who signed the trio to his newly formed Bad Boy Entertainment. They shot to attention in late 1994 backing Notorious B.I.G on his US Top 30 single 'Juicy'. A remix of the rapper's 'One More Chance' was even more successful, reaching number 2 in July 1995. Notorious B.I.G. returned the complement on Total's debut hit single, 'Can't You See'. Taken from the soundtrack to the movie *New Jersey Drive*, this song peaked at US number 13 June 1995. Another US Top 30 hit, 'No One Else' (number 22, February 1996) was followed by their self-titled debut. Combs shared production duties with Raphael Saadiq (Tony! Toni! Toné!) on a confident and upbeat set, showcasing the trio's strong harmonies. The album debuted at US number 23 and went gold. Another Top 20 single, 'Kissin' You' (number 12, July 1996), and cameo appearances on tracks by Tevin Campbell ('You Don't Have To Worry') and LL Cool J ('Loungin'') maintained their profile during a quiet period. The trio bounced back when the Timbaland/Missy 'Misdemeanor' Elliott collaboration 'What About Us', taken from the double platinum soundtrack to the Bad Boy movie *Soul Food*, reached number 16 in November 1997. Concert appearances alongside Dru Hill, Mase, Jay-Z and Lil' Kim preceded a collaboration with Mase on the international hit single 'What You Want' (US number 6, March 1998), taken from his highly acclaimed *Harlem World*. Featuring an all-star production cast of Combs, Missy Elliott and Diane Warren, *Kima, Keisha & Pam* debuted at number 39 in November 1998. The stand-out track, Missy Elliott's hypnotic 'Trippin'', reached US number 7 in January 1999. The trio also appeared on Foxy Brown's chart-topping *Chyna Doll*.

● ALBUMS: *Total* (Bad Boy 1996)★★★, *Kima, Keisha & Pam* (Bad Boy 1998)★★★.

TQ

b. Terrence Quaites, Mobile, Alabama, USA. Combining the streetwise lyrical slant of hip-hop with the smooth vocal inflections of urban R&B, TQ scored a big chart hit in 1998 with his tribute single 'Westside'. When he was still young Quaites' family relocated to the notorious Compton area of Los Angles, California. He sang in the church choir as a teenager, but at the same time was running into problems on the streets. He was sent to live in Atlanta with his aunt when he was 16 after his mother found a gun in his bedroom, an action the singer acknowledges probably saved his life. He worked as an intern at A&M Records before joining a group called Coming Of Age as lead singer. Signed to Zoo Entertainment, they scored a Top 40 R&B single in 1993 with 'Coming Home To Love', before TQ left to pursue a solo career on Atlantic Records. He relocated to Sony Records when Atlantic asked him to water down his lyrics. 'Westside' was dedicated to Eazy-E and 2Pac, and climbed to US number 12 in November 1998 and UK number 4 the following January. *They Never Saw Me Coming* was produced by Mike Mosley of Steady Mobbin Productions, and featured guest appearances from established rappers Too Short and E-40. Besides the stand-out hit single, the album featured further hard-hitting lyrical observations of street life such as 'Remember Melinda' and the linked narratives of 'Bye Bye Baby' and 'The Comeback'.

● ALBUMS: *They Never Saw Me Coming* (Sony 1998)★★★★.

Tractors

The 90s country roots band the Tractors were formed in Tulsa, Oklahoma, USA. Leader Steve Ripley started playing in Oklahoma honky tonks while still in his teens. Building up a reputation as a leading session musician, his credits include appearances with Leon Russell and J.J. Cale, and he was Bob Dylan's lead guitarist on 1981's *Shot Of Love*. He also invented a guitar that can be recorded in stereo and which has been used by J.J. Cale, Eddie Van Halen and Ry Cooder. All the band members can boast strong musical backgrounds. Walt Richmond (keyboards/co-producer) toured with Bonnie Raitt, Ron Getman (electric and steel guitar) played with Janis Ian and Leonard Cohen, Casey Van Beek (bass) toured with the Righteous Brothers and Linda Ronstadt, and Jamie Oldaker (drums) played with Eric Clapton. *The Tractors*, which was recorded (as was their second album) at Leon Russell's Church Studios in Tulsa, featured Ry Cooder and James Burton, and sold two million copies in the USA. They reworked the single 'Baby Likes To Rock It' as 'Santa Claus Is Comin' (In A Boogie Woogie Choo Choo Train)' for their Christmas album. Steve Ripley has said of their approach to music: 'We're doing music the way people did it before it was so specifically categorized - rock 'n' roll, rockabilly, country, country-rock. Back then no-one knew what it was - they just did what they felt.' They belatedly followed-up their debut set with 1998's *Farmers In A Changing World*, which wisely did not tamper with a winning formula.

● ALBUMS: *The Tractors* (Arista 1994)★★★★, *Have Yourself A Tractors Christmas* (Arista 1995)★★, *Farmers In A Changing World* (Arista 1998)★★★.

Trade

Trade, based at Turnmills, Farringdon, London, has become one of the most famous and influential clubs in the world since it first opened its doors as an underground gay venue in 1988. It was launched by entrepreneur and club promoter, Laurence Malice and was inspired by the attitude to nightlife of Ibiza, Barcelona and US cities such as New York and San Francisco. It became famous for its unusual opening hours (4 am until 12 noon on a Sunday morning) and the up-tempo, fierce house and techno played there. It was the training ground for DJs who later became internationally renowned, including, 'Tall' Paul Newman, Pete Wardman and a name almost synonymous with the club, Tony De Vit. The club is *the* place for London's youthful, good-looking gay crowd but also attracts a substantial 'straight' contingent, purely on the strength of its pounding, up-lifting house music and its unique, anything-goes atmosphere. The club has released several compilation albums which provide an insight into the music if not the entire experience.

Transglobal Underground

Formed in west London, England in 1991 as a loose collective of DJs and musicians around the nucleus of Alex Kasiek (b. Tim Whelan, 15 September 1958, London, England; keyboards/programming), and Hamid Mantu (b. Hamilton Lee, 7 May 1958, London, England; drums/programming), Transglobal Underground released 'Templehead', their debut single, in June of that year. Its mix of pounding house rhythms with sampled Tibetan chants introduced a dance music/world fusion explored in greater depth two years later on their debut album, *Dream Of 100 Nations*, which added the extraordinary silk and spice vocals of Natacha Atlas, various rappers and a diverse assortment of sampled Eastern, African and Caribbean voices and instruments to the cross-culture stew. Now regulars on the festival circuit and godparents to a growing global dance music subculture of bands, DJs and record labels, the band released *International Times* in October 1994. While offering no radical departures from the 'ethno techno' sound of its predecessor, the album featured fewer samples, relying more on live musicians including Egyptian violinist Essam Rachad, tabla player Satin Singh and free jazz guitarist Billy Jenkins. Following an album of remixes, the band's third album proper, *Psychic Karaoke*, featured a string section, slower tempos and an atmosphere of experimentation. A genuinely mature piece of work, it used regular band collaborators such as bass player Count Dubulah and clarinettist and keyboard player Larry Whelan to remodel the basic sound of previous albums into something darker and more hypnotic. There were echoes of dub reggae, film scores and even European art rockers such as Can in places. In the summer of 1996, advertising companies suddenly seemed to recognise the potential for the band's music as a soundtrack. 'Templehead' was used in a worldwide Coca Cola campaign, while the title track of *International Times* featured in a North American campaign for Levis jeans. In 1998, *Rejoice*

Rejoice featured Transglobal Underground's broadest musical mix yet, with Hungarian gypsy bands and an Indian drum troupe guesting on different tracks.

● ALBUMS: *Dream Of 100 Nations* (Nation 1993)★★★★, *International Times* (Nation 1994)★★★, *Interplanetary Meltdown* (Nation 1995)★★★, *Psychic Karaoke* (Nation 1996)★★★, *Rejoice Rejoice* (Nation 1998)★★★.

● COMPILATIONS: *Backpacking On The Graves Of Our Ancestors* (Nation 1999)★★★★.

Trash Can Sinatras

Despite a name that suggests a garage rock band, the Trash Can Sinatras, from Kilmarnock, Scotland, were more similar to the Glasgow independent pop of Orange Juice and Josef K. They consisted of John Douglas (guitar/vocals), George McDaid (bass), Frank Read (vocals/guitar; brother of Eddi Reader), Stephen Douglas (drums) and Paul Livingston (guitar), and following acclaimed demo tapes the band resisted the overtures of several major record labels to sign with Andy McDonald at Go! Discs. The band's first two singles, the plaintive 'Obscurity Knocks' and the similarly caustic 'Only Tongue Can Tell', were acclaimed. Their debut, produced by John Leckie and Roger Bechirian, was an exercise in well-crafted pop music, with considerable melody and impressive harmonies. It sold over 100,000 copies in America, primarily through its extensive profile on college radio. The follow-up album arrived two and a half years later, produced by Ray Schulman (Sugarcubes/Ian McCulloch) at the band's own Shabby Road Studios. Beginning with the haughty 'comeback' single 'Hayfever', the Sinatras' lyrics offered stylish visions of relationships such as 'Easy Read' and 'Bloodrush'. The release of *A Happy Pocket* in 1996 saw the band still pursuing their increasingly outdated brand of jangly pop, and they have subsequently faded from view.

● ALBUMS: *Cake* (Go! Discs 1990)★★★, *I've Seen Everything* (Go! Discs 1993)★★★, *A Happy Pocket* (Go! Discs 1996)★★.

Travis

One of Travis' chief claims to fame when they launched their career in 1997 was the fact that they were the first band to be signed to Independiente Records, the new label started by Andy McDonald following his departure from Go! Discs. Heavily influenced by classic rock acts such as Neil Young, Travis were formed in Glasgow, Scotland from the ashes of local act Glass Onion. The line-up comprises Francis Healy (vocals), Neil Primrose (drums), Andy Dunlop (guitar) and Dougie Payne (bass), the latter the last to join in 1996. McDonald had been keen to sign the band while still at Go! Discs, but was unable to do so due to difficulties with parent company PolyGram Records. However, the band were an intrinsic part of his plans when he elected to set up Independiente, and his label paid for them to relocate to London. Independiente also found the band a manager (Ian McAndrew, manager of Brand New Heavies) and encouraged songwriter Healy to sign a publishing contract with Sony/ATV Music. By this time the band had released their debut single, 'All I Want To Do Is Rock', on their own Red Telephone label. A support slot for Oasis heralded a debut album, on which Healy's dramatic and often Lennonesque vocals drew attention away from their average songwriting. The excellent *The Man Who* built on the band's reputation as

a charismatic live act. Released in May 1999 it proved to be one of the summer's surprise hit records, with 'Why Does It Always Rain On Me?' providing the band with a UK Top 10 single in August. A surge in sales following a hugely successful performance at the UK's V99 festival resulted in *The Man Who* finally topping the album charts andpassing the million sales mark.

● ALBUMS: *Good Feeling* (Independiente 1997)★★★, *The Man Who* (Independiente 1999)★★★★.

Tresvant, Ralph

b. 16 May 1968, Boston, Massachusetts, USA. Following the success of Bell Biv DeVoe, Bobby Brown and Johnny Gill, Tresvant became the final former member of New Edition to record a solo album in 1990. Released on MCA Records and featuring moderate swingbeat numbers such as 'Rated R', *Ralph Tresvant* did little to remove the impression that this artist was technically the most gifted but least inspired of the band. Even so, the album achieved platinum status and produced a number 1 US single, 'Sensitivity'. Tresvant was also the beneficiary of a song written especially for him by Michael Jackson, 'Alright Now'. A follow-up set featured more traditionally-inclined R&B songs. Though predictably seamless and well-produced, *It's Goin's Down* lacked excitement or attack.

● ALBUMS: *Ralph Tresvant* (MCA 1990)★★★, *It's Goin' Down* (MCA 1994)★★.

Tricky

b. Adrian Thaws, Knowle West, Bristol, Avon, England. One of the leading exponents of the trip-hop genre, Tricky began his musical career in the late 80s as a member of an informal crew of MCs, DJs and singers based in Bristol and known as the Wild Bunch. This collective eventually mutated into the pioneering Massive Attack, with Tricky contributing guest raps to 'Daydreaming' and 'Five Man Army' on the band's brilliant 1991 debut, *Blue Lines*. Although he worked on two tracks for the follow-up *Protection* (eventually released in 1994), Tricky expressed dissatisfaction with his colleagues' musical direction and moved to London to concentrate on his solo career. In late 1993, he released his first single, the trippy 'Aftermath', which arose from informal sessions with Mark Stewart (ex-Pop Group) on a four-track mobile. Tricky employed the services of local schoolgirl Martine (the song was recorded when she was only 15) on vocals, releasing it on his own Naive label. Despite its strong critical reception, Tricky was, in the best traditions of Massive Attack, reticent about his abilities: 'I don't really consider myself to be a rapper. I'm more of a lyricist really'. The subsequent *Maxinquaye* was one of the critical favourites of 1995, and a surprising commercial success despite being an atmospheric and unsettling record that explored the darker recesses of its creator's mind on tracks such as 'Hell Is Round The Corner' and 'Feed Me'. Stylistically, the album ranged from a dramatic hard rock cover version of Public Enemy's 'Black Steel In The Hour Of Chaos' to the mock soul of 'Abbaon Fat Tracks'. The album's murky, claustrophobic sound had roots in both the hip-hop and ambient genres, and was dubbed 'trip-hop' by critics struggling to define what would become known as the 'Bristol sound'. Later in the year Tricky collaborated with horrorcore rap crew Gravediggaz on the *The Hell* EP, and set-up his Durban Poison production company. The following year's *Nearly God* was a compelling side-project that saw Tricky collaborating with guest vocalists including Björk, Neneh Cherry and Terry Hall. After moving to New York City he continued to pursue a busy remixing schedule while writing tracks for his second album. *Pre-Millennium Tension* made for even more uneasy listening, with tracks such as 'Tricky Kid' and 'Lyrics Of Fury' being both threatening and paranoid in turn. By 1998's *Angels With Dirty Faces*, however, Tricky had begun to sound like a pastiche of himself as song after song stooped further into dark isolation against a relentlessly droning musical backdrop. In 1999, *Juxtapose*, a collaboration with DJ Muggs (Cypress Hill) and DMX producer Grease, was a timely return to form. It proved to be his last release on Island Records, with whom the artist parted company at the end of the year.

● ALBUMS: *Maxinquaye* (4th & Broadway 1995)★★★★★, as Nearly God *Nearly God* (Durban Poison 1996)★★★★, *Pre-Millennium Tension* (Island 1996)★★★, *Angels With Dirty Faces* (Island 1998)★★, with DJ Muggs and Grease *Juxtapose* (Island 1999)★★★.

● FILMS: *The Fifth Element* (1997).

Tripping Daisy

Comprising Tim DeLaughter (vocals), Wes Berggren (d. 27 October 1999, Dallas, Texas, USA; guitar), Mark Pirro (bass) and Bryan Wakeland (drums/percussion), Tripping Daisy were formed in Dallas, Texas, USA, in 1991. Their 1992 debut *Bill* produced somewhat misleading comparisons to the Smashing Pumpkins - the wistful lyrics and the pop punk construction of many of the songs lacking that band's intensity. It was reissued when the band signed a deal with Island Records. Though largely ignored in the UK and Europe, the band became a major attraction on the US college rock circuit, boosted by several appearances on MTV. Their increasing popularity was confirmed by the sales of 1995's *i am an ELASTIC FIRECRACKER*, which featured the single 'I Got A Girl', which again secured regular showings on MTV through its innovative 'Wright brothers' flying-machine video. A three-year hiatus followed before a revamped five-man line-up returned with *Jesus Hits Like The Atom Bomb*. The album was an artistic success, but following a slump in sales the band was dropped by Island. They released a self-titled album in 1999, but their future was put in doubt when Berggren was found dead at his Dallas home in October.

● ALBUMS: *Bill* (Dragon Street/Island 1992)★★★, *i am an ELASTIC FIRECRACKER* (Island 1995)★★★, *Jesus Hits Like The Atom Bomb* (Island 1998)★★★★.

Tritt, Travis

b. 8 February 1963, Marietta, Georgia, USA. He started writing songs and playing honky tonks and beer joints when he was about 14 years old. One of Tritt's songs is called 'Son Of The New South', and his US country hit 'Put Some Drive Into Your Country' includes the lines, 'I made myself a promise when I was just a kid/I'd mix Southern rock and country and that's just what I did.' In other words, Tritt is where Merle Haggard meets Lynyrd Skynyrd. Although the title track of his debut album presented him as a honky tonk revivalist, Tritt's music reflects his childhood love for the classic country of George Jones and the southern rock of the Allman Brothers Band. He reached superstar status in 1991 with the first single from *It's All About To Change* - a wonderful bar-room ballad of love betrayed, 'Here's A Quarter

(Call Someone Who Cares)'. The follow-up, 'Anymore', proved his credentials as a balladeer, while his acting in the award-winning video clip for the song won him several offers of film work. After two magnificent albums, *T-R-O-U-B-L-E* was something of a holding operation, though it contained at least one classic, the traditional-sounding 'Lord Have Mercy On The Working Man'. Tritt further extended the boundaries of modern country with a nine-minute workout on Buddy Guy's blues standard, 'Leave My Woman Alone'. He combined with Marty Stuart for two hit singles and a series of concerts playfully titled The No-Hats Tour in honour of the duo's full heads of hair. Only some outspoken criticism of Billy Ray Cyrus in the summer of 1992, and the decision to issue a sentimental album of Christmas favourites later in the year, threatened his relentless progress to the top. He continued on his path to American icon status by giving a half-time performance at the 1993 Super Bowl in Atlanta's Georgiadome. *Ten Foot Tall And Bulletproof* was as much southern rock as it was country, and included guest appearances from Waylon Jennings and Hank Williams Jnr. The power-charged title track was helped by a fine video and Tritt's incredible rise continued with the hugely successful *Greatest Hits*, which contained an astonishing 10 country number 1 singles. He contributed Jackson Browne's 'Take It Easy' to *Common Thread: The Songs Of The Eagles*, and 'Lawdy Miss Clawdy' to *It's Now Or Never - The Tribute To Elvis*. In 1996, he sang the main song, a revival of the Platters' 'Only You (And You Alone)', for the Steve Martin movie *Sgt. Bilko*. *The Restless Kind*, produced by Don Was, was a pure honky-tonk country album, with no rock drum timings or hard guitar. An accomplished songwriter and performer, with one of the most distinctive voices in country music, he is a major talent who is set to encompass every branch of country music.

● ALBUMS: *Country Club* (Warners 1990)★★★, *It's All About To Change* (Warners 1991)★★★, *T-R-O-U-B-L-E* (Warners 1992)★★★, *A Travis Tritt Christmas - Loving Time Of The Year* (Warners 1992)★★, *Ten Feet Tall And Bullet Proof* (Warners 1994)★★★, *The Restless Kind* (Warners 1996)★★★, *No More Looking Over My Shoulder* (Warners 1998)★★★★.

● COMPILATIONS: *Greatest Hits, From The Beginning* (Warners 1995)★★★★.

● VIDEOS: *A Celebration* (Warner Reprise 1993), *Ten Feet Tall And Bulletproof* (Warner Reprise 1994), *It's All About To Change* (Warner Reprise 1994), *From The Beginning* (Warner Reprise 1995).

Trout, Walter, Band

b. 6 March 1951, Atlantic City, New Jersey, USA. This highly talented and experienced blues guitarist finally formed and recorded with his own band in 1989 after a lengthy spell with John Mayall and Canned Heat. With a line-up of Jim Trapp (bass), Leroy Larson (drums) and Dan Abrams (keyboards), he debuted with *Life In The Jungle* in 1990. This showcased Trout's remarkable feel and dexterity and courted Jimi Hendrix, Robin Trower and Gary Moore comparisons. Klas Anderhill took over on drums for *Prisoner Of A Dream*, on which the band moved into a more commercial mainstream rock direction. Much of the soulful passion was replaced for a heavier approach more akin to bands such as Europe, Whitesnake and Bon Jovi. Trout moved away from his blues roots with *Transition*, although his remarkable ability as a guitarist shone through an album of patchy songs. Following a live album Trout moved to Silvertone Records, presumably in the hope of expanding his market to a wider audience. *Tellin' Stories* was an exciting set of crisply recorded rock/blues yet surprisingly it was not the anticipated commercial success. A year later he was back with Provogue, having now replaced Larson and Abrams with Bernard Pershey and Martin Gerschwitz, respectively. *Breaking The Rules* was a quieter and more introspective album, with Trout's contentment with life seemingly apparent from the lyrics. *Positively Beale Street* mixed together all of Trout's previous styles and on this collection his guitar playing was exemplary. The slow, gospel-influenced ballad 'Let Me Be The One', written by Dave Williams and Mick Parker, was the album's highlight. A self-titled collection followed in 1998.

● ALBUMS: *Life In The Jungle* (Provogue 1990)★★★★, *Prisoner Of A Dream* (Provogue 1991)★★★, *Transition* (Provogue 1992)★★, *Live, No More Fish Jokes* (Provogue 1992)★★, *Tellin' Stories* (Silvertone 1994)★★★, *Breaking The Rules* (Provogue 1995)★★★, *Positively Beale Street* (Provogue 1997)★★★, *Walter Trout* (Ruf/A&M 1998)★★★.

Tru

Hip-hop trio formed by No Limit Records supremo Master P with his younger brothers Silkk The Shocker and C-Murder. Tru helped establish No Limit as one of the leading underground hip-hop labels, and set the standard for their promotional practices, with lack of mainstream press compensated for by strong word-of-mouth sales. *True* reached number 25 in the R&B charts in September 1995. By 1997's follow-up, *Tru 2 Da Game*, No Limit releases had begun to make a national impact. The album debuted at number 2 on the R&B charts in March, and number 8 on the *Billboard* Hot 200. From a creative point of view *Tru 2 Da Game* was barely distinguishable from other No Limit product, with the predictable G-funk rhythms and hardcore gangsta lyrics slavishly adhering to the label's highly popular formula.

● ALBUMS: *True* (No Limit 1995)★★★, *Tru 2 Da Game* (No Limit 1997)★★★, *Da Crime Family* (No Limit 1999)★★★.

Tsunami

From Arlington, Virginia, USA, Tsunami remained true to the 'street level activism' credo of punk, though their music was more pop-orientated than that categorization implied. Comprising Jenny Toomey (guitar/vocals), Kristin Thomson (guitar/vocals), Andrew Webster (bass/vocals) and John Palmer (drums), they once invited the press to 'try to prove we're not punk rock'. They rose to prominence in the 90s through a series of 7-inch singles released on their own Simple Machines Records (other artists featured included Nation Of Ulysees, Velocity Girl, Unrest, Superchunk and Scrawl, as well as Toomey's 'other bands' - Choke and Geek). Their debut release was 1991's *Headringer* EP. Later they recorded for the renowned Sub Pop Records Singles Club. Though committed to the continuation of the 7-inch single, they also favoured elaborate packaging. January 1993's 'Diner', for example, was accompanied by a menu, while 'Matchbox' was packaged as a huge box of matches. A series of cassettes, the 'Simple Machines Tool Set', was also released, as was an album titled *Fortune Cookie Prize: A Tribute To Beat Happening*, which included a booklet on how to self-release records. Their first full length album, *Deep End*, was finally released in June 1993. It saw them com-

pared to the emergent 'riot grrrl' scene, Toomey commenting to the press that 'A lot of the lyrics deal with the girl's perspective.' It also included a series of asinine taped answerphone messages left by A&R executives keen to sign the band. Afterwards they supported PJ Harvey on her US tour before joining the Lollapalooza mobile festival (they played over 200 shows in 1993 alone). They then released a second studio album, *The Heart's Tremelo*, followed by a compilation of their singles and b-sides, *World Tour And Other Destinations*. Toomey and Thomson dissolved the band and Simple Machines in 1998.

● ALBUMS: *Deep End* (Simple Machines 1993)★★★, *The Heart's Tremelo* (Simple Machines 1994)★★★.

● COMPILATIONS: *World Tour And Other Destinations* (Simple Machines 1994)★★★.

Tuatara

A quixotic, obtuse experiment in the use of exotic instruments and styles, Tuatara was formed in 1996 as a side-project for several household-name musicians who wished to escape the more restrictive aspects of working in a modern rock group. The band features Barrett Martin (Screaming Trees), Peter Buck (R.E.M.), Justin Harwood (Luna) and Sherik (Critters Buggin). Some of the instruments employed on *Breaking The Ether*, the band's 1997 debut album for Epic Records, included Tibetan horns, tablas, a bull-roarer and steel drums. The range of mood and styles evoked by the record included jazz and world music. What was obvious was that this was an attempt to be as distant as possible from the certainties of contemporary rock music. Other guests for the recording included Mike McCready (Pearl Jam), Steve Berlin (Los Lobos) and Scott McCaughey (Young Fresh Fellows). Martin explained the band's ethos to *Billboard* magazine in 1997: 'We have that jazz bebop influence that is coming from a Miles Davis-[Charles] Mingus-[John] Coltrane-Thelonious Monk influence. The record itself is the kind of thing that you can put on and get into if you want to, or it can just be there and you can enjoy it, but you don't have some screaming angst-ridden vocalist overpowering everything. At the same time there isn't any one lead instrument, so it is not a barrage of saxophone-driven bebop. It's a lot of different things.' A series of low-key gigs at venues such as Seattle's Crocodile Cafe followed, as well as the announcement of a package tour with Mark Eitzel.

● ALBUMS: *Breaking The Ether* (Epic 1997)★★★, *Trading With The Enemy* (Epic 1998)★★★★.

Tuff Jam

Tuff Jam is the UK's leading garage DJing and production team comprising Matt 'Jam' Lamont and Karl 'Tuff Enuff' Brown. They began their partnership at the end of 1995 and have since completed numerous remixes and productions and achieved success and a high profile on both sides of the Atlantic. Their name was associated with the UK's 'speed garage' movement, although the term is something despised and rejected by the partnership. Rather, they wish to stand for quality UK garage music that draws influences from the USA but has a sound that is undeniably British. The duo have compiled an impressive portfolio of remix work, including both UK and US artists: Rosie Gaines ('Closer Than Close'), Tina Moore ('Never Gonna Let You Go'), En Vogue, Boyz II Men, Usher and Coolio. The duo also host their own radio show on Saturday evenings on the UK's Kiss 100 FM and they have a club night, 'Underground Frequencies', that is held at the Cross in London. As a DJing team, they are able to tour internationally, including bookings in Ibiza (for the Ministry Of Sound, Kiss 100 FM and Garage City), Germany, Japan, Singapore, Hong Kong, Switzerland, France and the USA. Their productions and remixes frequently appear on dance music compilations all over the world. In 1997, Tuff Jam launched their own label, Unda-Vybe Music. Tuff Jam are truly a grass roots outfit, who have built their career and following by remaining devoted to the underground scene and a style of music that they love - fashionable or not.

● COMPILATIONS: *Havin' It Stateside Volume 2* (DWA 1996)★★★, *Tuff Jam's Underground Frequencies - Volume 1* (Satellite/BMG 1997)★★★, *Tuff Jam's Underground Frequencies - Volume 2* (Satellite/BMG 1998)★★★.

Twain, Shania

b. Eilleen Regina Edwards, 28 August 1965, Windsor, Ontario, Canada. This glamorous Canadian country/pop star (her first name is pronounced 'Shu-nye-ah') grew up in the mining town of Timmins. Before her musical career began she planted trees with her Native American stepfather as part of a forest crew. Poor even by rural Canadian standards, her family made great sacrifices to support her embryonic career. She took a job at the Deerhurst resort in northern Ontario as the headline vocalist in a variety of musical productions. Afterwards she concentrated on country music, employing her friend and former performer Mary Bailey as her manager. Bailey put her in contact with attorney Dick Frank in 1991, leading to a demo tape recorded in Nashville with songwriter and producer Norro Wilson and Buddy Cannon, Mercury Records' A&R manager. Both the tragedy of her parents' death (they were both killed in an automobile accident in November 1987) and their musical legacy were explored on her debut, with songs written by Mike Reid and Kent Robbins. The album's best song, 'God Ain't Gonna Get You For That', was the only one part-composed by the artist, pointing the way to future artistic growth. Elsewhere the single 'Dance With The One That Brought You', a staple of Country MTV, directed by Sean Penn, provoked comparisons with Trisha Yearwood. The follow-up album saw a rare non-rock outing for her producer, songwriting partner and husband Robert 'Mutt' Lange (Def Leppard, Foreigner), who spent much of 1994 working on sessions with Twain in Nashville. *The Woman In Me* was an extraordinary crossover success in the USA, not only when it was first released, but over a year later, when it went back to the top of the album charts for another six months. Sales of this album had topped 10 million by 1998 and yielded four Top 10 country hits. During that eventful year she won most of the country music awards, including the Entertainer Of The Year trophy, and released her follow-up album, *Come On Over*. This was predominantly a pop collection, with Twain's country roots buried beneath Lange's glossy production. 'You're Still The One' was a crossover hit, peaking at number 2 on the *Billboard* Hot 100 in May, and the album became a permanent fixture in both the US and UK Top 10. Another huge US hit, 'From This Moment On', was the single which broke Twain in the UK, debuting at number 9 in November. 'That Don't Impress Me Much' and

'Man! I Feel Like A Woman' were also huge US/UK hit singles the following year. By altering her musical course slightly, Twain has done much to popularize country music to a wider US audience and to reinvent herself in the UK as a pop singer.

● ALBUMS: *Shania Twain* (Mercury 1993)★★★, *The Woman In Me* (Mercury 1995)★★★★, *Come On Over* (Mercury 1997)★★★★, with Mariah Carey, Celine Dion, Gloria Estefan, Aretha Franklin *Divas Live* (Epic 1998)★★.

● VIDEOS: *Any Man Of Mine* (Mercury 1995), *The Complete Woman In Me* (PolyGram Music Video 1996), with Mariah Carey, Celine Dion, Gloria Estefan, Aretha Franklin *Divas Live* (Sony Music Video 1998), *Live* (USA Home Entertainment/Universal 1999).

2 Live Crew

These rap headline-makers from Miami, Florida (via California) became unlikely figures in a media censorship debate when, in June 1990, *As Nasty As They Wanna Be* was passed sentence on by a judge in Broward County, Florida. In the process it became the first record in America to be deemed legally obscene (a Georgia appeal court overturned the decision in May 1992). Their right to free speech saw them defended by sources as diverse as Sinead O'Connor, Bruce Springsteen and Mötley Crüe, but the overbearing impression remained that 2 Live Crew was a third-rate rap outfit earning first division kudos by little more than circumstance.

In 1985, the California-based trio Chris Wong Won ('Fresh Kid-Ice'), DJ David Hobbs ('Mr. Mixx'), and rapper Amazing V released the debut 2 Live Crew single, 'Revelation'. After moving to Miami and replacing Amazing V with New Yorker Mark Ross ('Brother Marquis'), the trio signed with Luke Skyywalker Records, the new label set up by their manager/promoter Luther Campbell (b. 22 December 1960, Miami, Florida, USA). (The label's name was later shortened to Luke Records when film-maker George Lucas, who created the Luke Skywalker character in the movie *Star Wars*, filed suit.) The new line-up assembled a single together, 'Throw The D', based on a new dance move, and recorded it in front of Campbell's mother's house. Their debut set, recorded before Campbell became an actual member, marked out the group's territory. To this end, 2 Live Crew several times expressed themselves to be an adult comedy troupe in the best traditions of crude party records by Blowfly and others. Hence, 'We Want Some Pussy' and other, inconsequential, mildly offensive tracks. Their music was underpinned by the familiar 'Miami Bass' sound of synthesized, deep backbeats. *As Nasty As They Wanna Be*, replete with 87 references to oral sex alone, included the notorious 'Me So Horny', built around a sample from Stanley Kubrick's *Full Metal Jacket*. It was an unquestionably offensive lyric, but no more so than those by the Geto Boys or others. There are probably worse examples within the 2 Live Crew's own songbook - 'The Fuck Shop', which samples Guns N'Roses guitar lines, or 'Head Booty And Cock' which became almost a battle-cry, notably when repeated by chanting fans on the Phoenix, Arizona-recorded live album. Advocates of record stickering such as the Parents Music Resource Center (PMRC) and Florida attorney/evangelist Jack Thompson, argued strongly that the group's records should not be available for sale to minors. A retail record store owner arrested for selling a copy of the album- albeit to an adult - was later acquitted. The group itself was then arrested for performing music from *As Nasty As They Wanna Be* in an adults-only club, sparking charges by anti-censorship groups that the law enforcement officials were becoming over-zealous. There is not much doubt that this was true - Miami has one of the biggest pornography industries in the country, and it was obvious the moguls behind it were not being pursued with equal vigour, if they were being pursued at all. The group attempted to exploit the commercial advantages of such notoriety by signing a distribution deal with Atlantic Records for *Banned In The U.S.A.*, which was followed by the lame *Sports Weekend (As Nasty As They Wanna Be Part II)*. The latter even included an AIDS awareness ditty, 'Who's Fuckin' Who', and the group also promoted safe sex with their own brand of Homeboy Condoms, one of their more acceptable acts of misogynist titillation. The original line-up had disbanded by the time Luther Campbell attempted to stoke up further controversy on the CBS network television show *A Current Affair* by claiming that he had oral sex on stage with female fans in Japan. In early 1994, Campbell became a legal ground-breaker again, this time over 2 Live Crew's 1989 parody of Roy Orbison's 'Oh Pretty Woman'. Acuff-Rose Music, who had refused a license for the song, had sued on the grounds that the cover version tarnished the image of the original. Although a Nashville court had ruled against Acuff-Rose in 1991, a successful appeal was brought to the Supreme Court, who finally ruled in favour of Campbell. On top of all the heat Campbell began a solo career. As the scandal surrounding the group abated, Campbell assembled the New 2 Live Crew comprising himself, Won and MC Larry 'Verb' Dobson for 1994's *Back At Your Ass For The Nine-4*. The original line-up reunited briefly for soundtrack work, but Campbell, who filed for bankruptcy in 1995, was gone by the time Won, Ross and Hobbs signed a new deal with Lil' Joe Records. Only Won and Ross remained for 1998's *The Real One*.

● ALBUMS: *The 2 Live Crew "Is What We Are"* (Luke Skyywalker 1986)★★★, *Move Somethin'* (Luke Skyywalker 1987)★★, *As Nasty As They Wanna Be* (Luke Skyywalker 1989)★★, *As Clean As They Wanna Be* (Luke Skyywalker 1989)★, as Luther Campbell Featuring The 2 Live Crew *Banned In The U.S.A.* (Luke/Atlantic 1990)★★★, *Live In Concert* (Effect 1990)★★, *Sports Weekend (As Nasty As They Wanna Be Part II)* (Luke 1991)★★★, *Sports Weekend (As Clean As They Wanna Be Part II)* (Luke 1991)★★, as the New 2 Live Crew *Back At Your Ass For The Nine-4* (Luke 1994)★★, *Shake A Lil' Somethin'* (Lil' Joe 1996)★★, *The Real One* (Lil' Joe 1998)★★.

● COMPILATIONS: *Greatest Hits* (Luke 1992)★★★, *Goes To The Movies: A Decade Of Hits* (Lil' Joe 1997)★★★, *Greatest Hits Vol. 2* (Lil' Joe 1999)★★★.

● VIDEOS: *Banned In The U.S.A.* (Luke 1990).

Two Lone Swordsmen

This outfit is a partnership between Keith Tenniswood and one of the best known names on the UK's dance music scene, Andy Weatherall. Tenniswood worked with Weatherall in the Sabres Of Paradise and continued to work with him after the demise of that project. They released their first album as Two Lone Swordsmen in 1996, *The Fifth Mission - Return To The Flightpath Estate* on Weatherall's own Emissions imprint. They have also released singles under aliases such as Rude Solo and Lino Squares and have remixed tracks for clients including Etienne De Crecy,

Texas, Sneaker Pimps, Primal Scream, Beth Orton and Spiritualized. They released a second album, *Stay Down* in October 1998. Tenniswood has also worked with David Holmes on his acclaimed album *Let's Get Killed* as well as working with Aloof and Red Snapper. The sound of Two Lone Swordsmen is in the same area as their labelmate, Aphex Twin and is perhaps best described as experimental techno. Down-tempo and ambient in feel, it is based around collages of sound, texture and percussion.

● ALBUMS: *The Fifth Mission - Return To The Flightpath Estate* (Emissions 1996)★★★, *Swimming Not Skimming* remix album (Emissions 1996)★★★, *Stay Down* (Warp 1998)★★★.

2Pac

b. Tupac Amaru Shakur, 16 June 1971, Brooklyn, New York, USA, d. 13 September 1996, Las Vegas, Nevada, USA. The controversy-laced gangsta rapper '2Pac' was the son of two Black Panther members, and his mother was actually pregnant with her son while being held in a New York prison. As a teenager Shakur studied at the Baltimore School Of Arts, before he moved to Marin City, California with his family and began hustling on the streets. His first appearance on the hip-hop scene came with a brief spell as part of Digital Underground, but it was with his 1991 debut *2Pacalypse Now* that he announced himself as one of rap's newest talents, while gaining censure from various quarters for the album's explicit lyrical content. He gained his first crossover success in July 1993 with 'I Get Around'. The platinum-selling album which housed it, *Strictly 4 My N.I.G.G.A.Z. ...* offered a rare degree of insight, with glints of wisdom like 'Last Wordz' - 'United we stand, divided we fall, they can shoot one nigga, but they can't shoot us all'. To further his views he ran the Underground Railroad network for troubled teenagers in his native Oakland, California.

In 1994, Shakur collaborated with his older brother Mopreme, Syke, Macadoshis and the Rated R on the short-lived Thug Life project, releasing the morbid and violent *Volume 1*. By this time his acting career was also burgeoning, following a memorable performance as Bishop in Ernest Dickerson's *Juice*. After appearing in director John Singleton's movie *Poetic Justice*, alongside Janet Jackson, he was dropped from the same director's *Higher Learning*. Shakur took things into his own hands when he was also removed from the set of Allen Hughes' *Menace II Society* when he attacked the director, for which he received a 15 day jail sentence in February 1994. He did however, make it on to the final cut of the basketball movie *Above The Rim*. Shakur's run-ins with the police had escalated in line with his profile as a prominent black artist. He was arrested in 1992 when a fight he was involved in resulted in the accidental death of a six-year-old boy, although the charges were later dismissed. He was accused in October 1993 of involvement in the shooting of two plain clothes policemen (later dismissed), and one count of forceful sodomy of a female fan. He was already on bail for an outstanding battery charge for allegedly striking a woman who asked for his autograph, and had also been arrested in Los Angeles for carrying a concealed weapon and assaulting a driver. Further controversy followed when a tape of *2Pacalypse Now* was found in the possession of a man arrested for murder. Shakur was found guilty of the sexual assault in November 1994, but the following day (30 November) was shot and robbed in the lobby of Quad Studios in New York's Times Square. Shakur later accused Biggie Smalls (Notorious B.I.G.), Andre Harrell and Sean 'Puffy' Combs of involvement in the shooting, directly leading to the east coast/west coast feud that would eventually result in the deaths of both Notorious B.I.G. and Shakur himself. Following the shooting incident, Shakur was sentenced to four and a half years in jail on February 7 1995. The epic *Me Against The World* was released while he was serving his sentence, but still debuted at number 1 in the US charts. Meanwhile, Marion 'Suge' Knight, president of hip-hop's most successful label Death Row Records, had arranged parole for Shakur, who eventually served only eight months of his sentence. Newly signed to Death Row, Shakur released 1996's sprawling double set *All Eyez On Me*, which entered the main *Billboard* US chart at number 1. The reviews were both supportive and outstandingly good, and the album sold over six million in its first year, and generated a huge hit single with the Dr. Dre duet 'California Love'. During the same year, Shakur began concentrating on his acting career again, appearing in *Bullet* and *Gridlock'd* (opposite Tim Roth). Further drama came when he was gunned down in Las Vegas on 8 September after watching the Mike Tyson-Bruce Seldon fight at the MGM Grand, and died five days later. Various explanations were given, including the theory that Notorious B.I.G. arranged the shooting after Shakur had bragged about sleeping with his wife, Faith Evans. The east coast/west coast rivalry continued after his death, leading to Notorious B.I.G.'s murder in similar circumstances six months later. In a further twist, Orlando Anderson, the chief suspect in Shakur's murder, was shot dead on 29 May 1998. Since his death Shakur's recorded legacy has generated several posthumous releases and hit singles, amid ugly squabblings over his estate. *R U Still Down? (Remember Me)* (released on his mother's new Amaru label) collects unreleased material from 1992-1994.

● ALBUMS: *2Pacalypse Now* (TNT/Interscope 1991)★★★, *Strictly 4 My N.I.G.G.A.Z.* (TNT/Interscope 1993)★★★, *Me Against The World* (Out Da Gutta/Interscope 1995)★★★★, *All Eyez On Me* (Death Row/Interscope 1996)★★★★, as Makaveli *The Don Killuminati: The 7 Day Theory* (Death Row/Interscope 1996)★★, *In His Own Words* (Mecca 1998)★★, with Outlawz *Still I Rise* (Interscope 1999)★★★.

● COMPILATIONS: *R U Still Down? (Remember Me)* (Amaru 1997)★★★, *Greatest Hits* (Interscope 1998)★★★★.

● VIDEOS: *Thug Immortal - The Tupac Shakur Story* (Xenon Entertainment 1998), *Words Never Die* (IMC/Scimitar 1998).

● FURTHER READING: *Tupac Shakur*, editors of Vibe. *Rebel For The Hell Of It: The Life Of Tupac Shakur*, Armond White. *Got Your Back: Life As Tupac Shakur's Bodyguard In The Hardcore World Of Gangsta Rap*, Frank Alexander with Heidi Siegmund Cuda.

● FILMS: *Nothing But Trouble* (1991), *Juice* (1992), *Poetic Justice* (1993), *Above The Rim* (1994), *Bullet* (1996), *Gridlock'd* (1997), *Rhyme & Reason* (1997), *Gang Related* (1997).

2 Unlimited

This cod-house act from Holland enjoyed a string of UK chart hits in the 90s. They epitomised the style with the irritating chart-topping 'No Limits', which featured Anita Dels' diva vocals and Ray Slijngaard's hilarity-inducing chorus of 'Techno! Techno! Techno! Techno!'. An album of the same name contained further variations on the formula, though arguably of an even lower quality threshold. Slijngaard was previously a chef at Amsterdam airport, while Dels previ-

ously worked as a secretary, singing part-time with the Trouble Girls. The men behind the group were Jean-Paul De Coster and Phil Wilde, of Byte Records (who previously tasted success with Bizz Nizz's 'Don't Miss The Party Line'). Their philosophy was redolent of the Euro-techno axis, but anathema to traditional British views of artistic input. They readily admitted to creating music to satiate a market rather than attempting to build a fanbase around any creative vision. The statistics, while not exonerating them, did prove them to be entirely correct in their supposition - in 1993 2 Unlimited sold over a million singles in Britain alone. 'No Limits' was also the biggest-selling European record of the year, while their second album sold nearly three million copies. Earlier success had included the arguably more interesting 'Get Ready For This' (UK number 2, October 1991), 'Twilight Zone' (UK number 2, January 1992), 'Workaholic' (UK number 4, May 1992) and 'The Magic Friend' (UK number 11, August 1992). A further run of UK Top 10 hit singles included 'Tribal Dance' (number 4, May 1993), 'Faces' (number 8, September 1993), 'Let The Beat Control Your Body' (number 6, February 1994) and 'The Real Thing' (number 6, May 1994). Subsequent singles were not as successful, but still broke into the UK Top 20. They returned in July 1998 with a new line-up on a different label (Big Life Records), but 'Wanna Get Up' made a disappointing debut at number 38.

● ALBUMS: *Get Ready* (PWL 1992)★★★, *No Limits* (PWL 1992)★★★, *Real Things* (PWL 1994)★★.

● VIDEOS: *No Limits* (PWL 1993).

Type O Negative

From the carcass of controversial nihilist New York act Carnivore, vocalist and bass guitarist Peter Steele formed Type O Negative in 1988. Fusing elements of heavy metal, gothic rock, industrial music and psychedelia, Type O Negative are a four-piece that explore the darker edges of the human soul with caustic irony. Their second release, *The Origin Of The Feces*, was a typical act of media terrorism. Mixed by the band to sound like a live recording from hell, it features chants of 'You Suck' and slow-handclapping from the audience, while Steele cynically drawls to the band 'Let's get this over with'. The sleeve featured a close up of a sphincter, while the band photos inside each have a 'turd' lovingly laid upon them. Despite such truculence, success beckoned as Type O Negative secured tours with influential bands such as Nine Inch Nails, Jackyl, Danzig and Mötley Crüe. *Bloody Kisses* proved a surprise success, with its effective blend of musical velvet and razor blades, leading to the re-release of *Origin Of The Feces* (in less offensive packaging). Steele subsequently hit the headlines in 1995 when he posed naked in *Playgirl* magazine. The following year's *October Rust* indicated a further mellowing of Steele's musical vision. The current line-up comprises Peter Steele (vocals/bass), Josh Silver (keyboards), Kenny Hickey (guitar) and Johnny Kelly (drums).

● ALBUMS: *Slow, Deep, Hard* (Roadrunner 1991)★★★, *Origin Of The Feces* (Roadrunner 1992)★★, *Bloody Kisses* (Roadrunner 1993)★★★★, *October Rust* (Roadrunner 1996)★★★, *World Coming Down* (Roadrunner 1999)★★.

● VIDEOS: *After Dark* (Roadrunner Video 1998).

U.N.K.L.E.

U.N.K.L.E. is the recording name used by James Lavelle and DJ Shadow of leading UK hip-hop label, Mo' Wax Records. Their *Psyence Fiction* set was released amid a blaze of hype and publicity in September 1998, debuting at number 4 on the UK album chart. Three years in the making, the album featured the talents of Richard Ashcroft of the Verve, Mike D of the Beastie Boys, Thom Yorke of Radiohead and members of Badly Drawn Boy. It embraced a range of styles from brooding, orchestrated trip-hop to breakbeat and rap. A brave project, it received mixed critical responses and was felt by some to have suffered from over-ambitiousness. The tour supporting the album caused some controversy when fans discovered that it did not feature any of the celebrity guests on the album or DJ Shadow, and was effectively a 'James Lavelle Live With The Scratch Perverts' experience. A single, 'Be There' was released in February 1999. It was a reworking of the track 'Unreal' from the album and vocals were provided by Ian Brown (ex-Stone Roses). The single broke into the UK Top 10 and received excellent reviews from the music press.
● ALBUMS: *Psyence Fiction* (Mo' Wax 1998)★★★.

Ugly Kid Joe

Formed in Isla Vista, California, USA, in 1989 by Whitfield Crane (vocals), later joined by guitarist Klaus Eichstadt, drummer Mark Davis, second guitarist Roger Lahr and bass player Cordell Crockett (whose father owned *Guitar Player* magazine), the band flirted with several names before settling on Ugly Kid Joe, coined for a support slot in order to satirize headliners Pretty Boy Floyd. The band made their debut with a mini-album, *As Ugly As They Wanna Be*, which was an almost instant success, selling over two million copies in the USA on the back of the poppy Top 10 hit 'Everything About You', a humorous number featured in the enormously popular movie, *Wayne's World*. The song, which also reached number 3 in the UK, rather belied the true musical nature of the band, in reality much heavier with funk influences, drawing comparisons with both Mötley Crüe and Faith No More from reviewers. Shannon Larkin (drums; ex-Wrathchild America) and Dave Fortman (ex-Sugartooth) were brought in for *America's Least Wanted*, which produced further hits in the shape of 'Neighbor' and 'Cats In The Cradle', which reached number 6 in early 1993. Given a powerful sound by Mark Dodson, the album established the band's credibility without sacrificing their sense of humour, and live shows, including a support slot on Ozzy Osbourne's farewell US tour, further helped the band to shake off their novelty tag. Sessions for a second album proper began in 1994 at a rented house in Santa Ynez,

California. The release of *Menace To Sobriety*, was preceded by a series of AIDS benefits on a tour of US ski resorts, and another offbeat single, 'Milkman's Son'. However, there was also a concerted effort by their management and label to market the band as serious rock artists - including an 'approved photographs only' contract not seen since Guns N'Roses were at the height of their collective paranoia. The band returned to independent status when they released 1996's *Motel California* on their own Evilution label, but split-up shortly afterwards. Whitfield Crane briefly fronted Life Of Agony.
● ALBUMS: *As Ugly As They Wanna Be* mini-album (Stardog 1992)★★, *America's Least Wanted* (Stardog 1992)★★★, *Menace To Sobriety* (Mercury 1995)★★★, *Motel California* (Evilution 1996)★★.
● COMPILATIONS: *As Ugly As It Gets: The Very Best Of* (Mercury 1998)★★★.

Ultra Naté

b. Baltimore, Maryland, USA. Dance music diva, who first rose to fame via the club hit, 'It's Over Now'. Ultra Naté (which is her real name) is a former trainee psychotherapist. She was originally spotted by the Basement Boys in 1989, going on to sing backing vocals on Monie Love's debut album. The Basement Boys then persuaded her to step into the spotlight, leading to a deal with WEA Records. Reminiscent of a souped up Philly soul singer, or Donna Summer, Ultra Naté has all the correct stylings down to a tee, measuring jazz, funk and gospel within her compass. All are made distinctive by her slightly unconventional, and highly arresting, vocal phrasing. And for once, a garage vocalist with lyrics which, taken in isolation, were not an embarrassment. Her second, wildly diffuse, album for WEA, *One Woman's Insanity*, broke her internationally, and included duets with childhood hero Boy George (who wrote the song, 'I Specialize In Loneliness' for her), as well as D-Influence, Nellee Hooper, Ten City and the omnipresent Basement Boys. In the late 90s she enjoyed massive international hits with the club anthems 'Free' and 'Found A Cure', and also released the bestselling *Situation: Critical*.
● ALBUMS: *Blue Notes In The Basement* (WEA 1991)★★★, *One Woman's Insanity* (WEA 1993)★★★★, *Situation: Critical* (AM:PM 1998)★★★.

Ultramarine

A London, England-based progressive dance music duo comprising Paul John Hammond (b. 12 December 1965, Chelmsford, Essex, England; bass/keyboards) and Ian Harvey Cooper (b. 15 August 1966, Derby, England; programming/guitars). They took their name from an album by A Primary Industry, who in turn had first seen it used for a Mexican brand of Mescal. Both members of Ultramarine were veterans of the latter band, Hammond having also played with God And The Rest. Previously, both had worked in a variety of professions, Hammond as an orchard worker and in publishing, Cooper as a furniture salesman and insurance clerk. Influenced by the Canterbury Scene (Kevin Ayers, Robert Wyatt) and modern dance music (Massive Attack, Orbital, Spooky), Ultramarine made their recording debut in 1989 with 'Wyndham Lewis', on Belgian label Les Disques Du Crepescule. After a further single, 'Folk', in 1990, Ultramarine moved on to Brainiak, then Rough Trade Records, before winding up on Blanco y Negro. Their debut album, *Every Man And Woman Is A Star*, was based on an imaginary canoe journey across America. Song structures were embossed by a dub-heavy backbeat and strong, resonant melodies. By the time of its follow-up, *United Kingdoms*, their Canterbury influences were beginning to show, and Robert Wyatt was invited to join them in a rendition of a 100-year-old weaver's folk song, 'Kingdom', and 'Happy Land'. Wyatt's old sparring partner Ayers also wrote Ultramarine's double EP, *Hymn*. *Bel Air* took as its theme paranoia and anxieties about the approaching millennium, though this time the musical terrain encompassed Latin jazz and ethnic pop without ever being grand or pompous. Song titles such as 'Schmaltz' revealed that the band had not lost their self-deprecating sense of humour. Ultramarine made a welcome return to independent label status for the follow-up, *A User's Guide*.

● ALBUMS: *Every Man And Woman Is A Star* (Rough Trade 1992)★★★, *Every Man And Woman Is A Star - Expanded* (Rough Trade 1992)★★★★, *United Kingdoms* (Blanco y Negro 1993)★★★, *Bel Air* (Blanco y Negro 1995)★★★, *A User's Guide* (New Electronica 1997)★★★.

Ultrasound

Originally a quartet from London, England, Ultrasound first attracted media and music industry interest during a series of *New Musical Express* 'Brat' showcases in January 1997. They contributed a song, 'Stay Young', to a CD for London Music Week, while their accompanying live performances won them rave reviews. Early singles 'Same Band', backed by 'Floodlite World' and 'Over There', built on the foundations of their live work, exhibiting a combination of musical prowess, surprisingly deft arrangements and lyrical obtuseness. The band's fulcrum was 20-stone singer and writer Andy 'Tiny' Wood (b. Birkenhead, England), a veteran of several 80s bands including Step TLV. When Step TLV failed to secure a contract, Wood attended Wakefield Music College to study modern music. There, he made the acquaintance of future Ultrasound members guitarist Richard Green and drummer Andy Peace. The trio went on to study at Newcastle, where they met bass player Vanessa West. In the interim, however, Wood and Green both served as members of Newcastle's Sleepy People (whose singer, Paul Hope, was a former member of Step TLV). Following the release of their debut single, a fifth member, keyboard player and programmer Matt Jones, was recruited to embellish their already ambitious sound. Further acclaimed releases during 1998 included 'Best Wishes', 'Stay Young' (UK number 30) and 'I'll Show You Mine'. The 16 tracks on the following year's debut album had a running time of 88 minutes, either foolhardy or inspired depending on reaction to their prog-rock inspired sound. Before the end of the year, however, the various members of the band announced they were returning to solo projects.

● ALBUMS: *Everything Picture* (Nude 1999)★★★.

Unbelievable Truth

Taking their name and their pervading art school image from a Hal Hartley movie, this UK indie band is based in Oxford, England and was formed by Andy Yorke and old school friends Nigel Powell (drums) and Jason Moulster (bass). Powell and Moulster had worked as a rhythm section for hire on the Oxford musical scene, while Yorke, brother of

Thom Yorke of Radiohead, studied Russian Language & Literature in Russia and worked as a translator for the Greenpeace organization. Yorke's return to Moscow in 1994 resulted in the band putting on hold a proposed publishing deal. After regrouping they released a limited edition single on an Oxford independent label Shifty Disco, before signing to Virgin Records in 1997. The *Stone* EP was followed by 'Higher Than Reason', which broke into the UK Top 40. A second single, 'Solved', was released in April 1998. Their atmospheric debut, *Almost Here*, evoked obvious comparisons to other exponents of the newly christened 'stool rock' genre, including Radiohead, Sunhouse and Witness.

● ALBUMS: *Almost Here* (Virgin 1998)★★★.

Uncle Tupelo

Formed in Belleville, Illinois, USA in 1987, Uncle Tupelo were built around childhood friends and songwriters Jeff Tweedy and Jay Farrar. Primarily influenced by punk, then the blue-collar folk and country of Gram Parsons and John Prine, they specialized in grizzled bar-room laments to unforgiving or unforgiven lovers at a time when the grunge rock of Nirvana and Pearl Jam dominated the alternative music scene. They released two independent albums before a Sire/Reprise Records contract arrived in 1992. Peter Buck of R.E.M. produced *March 16-20, 1992*, which reinforced the good impressions critics held of their earlier material, and sustained Tweedy's belief that 'You can find the same things in punk records as in Hank Williams records. There's no difference, it's the communication factor.' *Anodyne* was a further classic example of country rock, with cranked-up rock blow-outs alternating with Gram Parsons-styled laments. Sadly, the band broke up in 1994 just as their marriage of bluegrass and pop was being to be recognized as a touchstone in the re-emergence of roots rock, with their first album giving its name to the alternative country movement of the late 90s. Tweedy teamed up with his fellow Uncle Tupelo travellers John Stirratt, Ken Coomer and Max Johnson to form Wilco. Another veteran of Uncle Tupelo, drummer Mike Heidorn, teamed with Farrar to become Son Volt. Their debut album, like that of Wilco, was produced by Brian Paulson, who had worked on *Anodyne*. Meanwhile, the band's roadie and occasional guitarist Brian Henneman formed Bottle Rockets, who secured a contract with East Side Digital Records when both Farrar and Tweedy backed him on a demo tape of original songs.

● ALBUMS: *No Depression* (Rockville 1990)★★★★, *Still Feel Gone* (Rockville 1991)★★★, *March 16-20, 1992* (Sire 1992)★★★★, *Anodyne* (Sire 1993)★★★★.

Underworld

Based in Romford, Essex, England, Underworld arose from the ashes of Freur in the late 80s. Their debut album as Underworld, a funk rock affair produced by Tom Bailey of the Thompson Twins, found some success, particularly in the USA. A second album followed, before key members Karl Hyde (guitar/vocals) and Rick Smith (keyboards) brought this line-up to an abrupt end during a 1990 tour supporting the Eurythmics. Hyde worked with Deborah Harry, before returning to England to reform Underworld as a predominantly dance music-orientated band with Smith and DJ Darren Emerson. Their first releases were the privately distributed 'The Hump' and 'Dirty', the latter released as

Lemon Interrupt. They had their first success as Underworld in early 1993 with 'Mmm Skyscraper ... I Love You' and later that year with 'Rez', both of which became popular with the dance fraternity. While the latter was a straightforward dance track that arranged a few analogue riffs, regular four-on-the-floor drums as well as more busy tribal-sounding percussion, into various build-ups and break-downs, 'Mmm Skyscraper ... I Love You' was a more varied and carefully structured track which introduced Hyde's vocals into a rich, psychedelic techno sound. During this time the band gained respect in wider circles by performing live at various events including Megadog and the MIDI Circus and achieved further recognition and popularity in 1994 when they released the album *Dubnobasswithmyheadman*. Building on the same kind of diversity as 'Mmm Skyscraper ...' the album featured a broad ranging techno style which was at times deep and psychedelic, and other moments melodic and almost pop-like, and was always characterized by Hyde's fragmented lyrics. Mixing elements of what were unreconcilable styles including ambient, house, techno and dub with pop sensibilities, it appealed to a broad audience and was hailed by some of the rock press as the most important dance album of the time, while purists had reservations about them diluting their techno sound. Much of the sound from this innovative album continued to have resonance in music produced into the late 90s. In June 1995, they received an enthusiastic response when they played a number of dates in America with the Chemical Brothers, the Orb and Orbital. In the same year they released a single 'Born Slippy', which gained mass exposure on the soundtrack to the ultra-hip movie, *Trainspotting* and was subsequently re-issued in 1996 when it became a chart hit. *Second Toughest In The Infants*, which introduced breakbeats and elements of drum 'n' bass into the sound, was even more successful than its predecessor, despite being a darker and sometimes more claustrophobic set. That year they also headlined a number of dance and rock festivals, including Reading and Tribal Gathering's Big Love. Underworld have remixed a number of artists including Björk, Simply Red and Orbital, and continue to DJ around the UK. At the same time Hyde and Smith have been involved with the art and design collective Tomato which has experimented with various innovative multi-media projects, as well as various commercial projects including advertising and promo videos. In 1998, Underworld and Tomato combined in a series of performances aimed at blurring the lines between bands and visual artists. In March 1999, *Beaucoup Fish* was released to rave reviews and became a major success.

● ALBUMS: *Underneath The Radar* (Sire 1988)★★, *Change The Weather* (Sire 1989)★★★, *Dubnobasswithmyheadman* (Junior Boy's Own 1994)★★★★, *Second Toughest In The Infants* (Junior Boy's Own 1996)★★★★, *Beaucoup Fish* (V2 1999)★★★★.

Urban Cookie Collective

Urban Cookie Collective achieved a major breakthrough in 1993 with 'The Key: The Secret', one of the most riveting dance music tracks of the season. Comprising Rohan Heath (keyboards), Diane Charlemagne (vocals, ex-Nomad Soul), Marty (MC) and DJ Pete (DJ), the project was masterminded by Heath, who had formerly worked with Yargo and A Guy Called Gerald. He had learned classical piano as a child,

going electric in time to perform with the latter two outfits. He had decided on music after abandoning a PhD at Vermont University. After a tour of Japan supporting the Happy Mondays, he left A Guy Called Gerald to release 'Hardcore Uproar' as Together, which made number 12 in the UK charts in August 1990. After a brief stint with Eek A Mouse, he elected to concentrate on solo work, and inaugurated Urban Cookie Collective. 'The Key: The Secret' was originally a track written at home by Heath, in a soul/hip-hop vein, produced by Chapter And The Verse on the tiny Unheard Records imprint. However, after a remix provoked a massive club response it was picked up by Pulse 8 Records, and climbed to number 2 in the UK singles chart. A follow-up single, 'Feels Like Heaven', also reached the UK Top 5 later in the year. Of their subsequent singles, only the following February's 'Sail Away' managed to break into the Top 20.

● ALBUMS: *High On A Happy Vibe* (Pulse 8 1993)★★★.

Urban Shakedown
(see Aphrodite)

Urban Species

Since their formation in Tottenham, London, England, in the late 80s, Urban Species were widely tipped as the next potential breakthrough in UK hip-hop. They originally comprised lead rapper Mint (b. Peter Akinrinola) and DJ Renegade (b. Winston Small), whose partnership principally involved messing about in their north London bedrooms, since when they have added the services of toaster Slim (b. Rodney Green). The trio started to produce small runs of white labels, distributing them under the names of either Mint or Renegade. This earned them a reputation among both the pirate radio stations and clubs, where they would be invited to appear. Even the hip New York stations Kiss and WBLS picked up on one of their tracks, 'It's My Thing', but they were hamstrung by finances and unable to capitalize. Their next cut, 'Got To Have It', was the one that brought them to the attention of Talkin' Loud Records boss Gilles Peterson. By 1991 he had their signatures. Their eclectic blend of ragga, dub, and even acoustic folk rumblings saw them placed in several musical categories, from soul to rap and jazz fusion, and comparisons to Arrested Development arose. Their second single as Urban Species, 'Listen', shared its title with their first LP, and featured 'fourth' member Lynette Bracewaite, alongside live guest musicians such as Galliano and Incognito. Guest vocalists have also included MC Solaar (a fellow-traveller on the Talkin' Loud roster) and Maysa Leak, and Urban Species have built their reputation as much on the back of impressive live appearances as much as their studio touch. *Blanket* finally appeared at the start of 1999, and featured guest vocals from US funk/soul artist Terry Callier.

● ALBUMS: *Listen* (Talkin' Loud 1993)★★★, *Blanket* (Talkin' Loud 1999)★★★.

Urge Overkill

Formed in 1986 in Chicago, Illinois, USA, Urge Overkill are led by National 'Nash' Kato (b. 31 December 1965, Grand Forks, North Dakota, USA; vocals) and Blackie 'Black Caesar' Onassis (b. Johnny Rowan, 27 August 1967, Chicago, Illinois, USA; vocals/drums). The line-up is completed by Eddie

'King' Roeser (b. 17 June 1969, Litchfield, Minnesota, USA; bass). They took their name from an old Funkadelic song, and combined the upfront rock riffs of AC/DC with the pop of the Raspberries and Cheap Trick. After releasing a lack-lustre debut 12-inch, the *Strange, I...* EP, Urge Overkill went on to record four albums for seminal Chicago punk label Touch & Go Records, and supported Nirvana. With producers that included Steve Albini and Butch Vig, no one could contest their punk rock credentials. However, such product placement proved misleading They covered Neil Diamond's 'Girl, You'll Be A Woman Soon', stating that he was more important to their development than any late 70s band. As they revealed, 'We come from the fine tradition of James Brown and the soul bands, for whom looking good was paramount.' As if to confirm their lack of sympathy for the growing punk movement Urge Overkill took delight in wearing outlandish ethnic clothes, touring Chicago in an open-top car, with chilled champagne nestling in the boot. They also flew in the face of grunge fashion by filming videos about picnics, yachting and their second most-favoured form of transport - the horse-drawn carriage. Such behaviour won them few friends within the tightly knit Chicago scene, the most public demonstration of their rejection coming from Steve Albini (he cited them as 'freakish attention-starved megalomaniacs'). *The Supersonic Storybook* saw the band trade in overblown images of Americana, resenting the new austerity that had swept the nation and deprived its teenagers of opportunities for excess - in particular, the band's favoured drug, the hallucinogenic artane. *Stull* was inspired by a visit to the ghost town of the same name, situated exactly at the mid-point of the USA, 40 miles away from Kansas. *Saturation*, their debut record for major label Geffen Records, was produced by hip-hop duo the Butcher Brothers, once again revealing a much more gaudy, vaudeville and escapist outlook than other Chicago bands. *Exit The Dragon* was an equally impressive follow-up. Their cover version of 'Girl, You'll Be A Woman Soon' became a chart hit in 1994 as a result of its use on the soundtrack to Quentin Tarantino's *Pulp Fiction*. Roeser, who had grown increasingly dismayed by Onassis' drug problems, left the band and was replaced by Nils St. Cyr at the end of 1996. The new line-up signed a deal with 550 Music, but with the label rejecting Kato's new material the band's future looks extremely doubtful.
● ALBUMS: *Jesus Urge Superstar* (Touch & Go 1989)★★, *Americruiser* (Touch & Go 1990)★★, *The Supersonic Storybook* (Touch & Go 1991)★★★, *Stull* mini-album (Touch & Go 1992)★★, *Saturation* (Geffen 1993)★★★★, *Exit The Dragon* (Geffen 1995)★★★★.

Urusei Yatsura

When they achieved critical recognition in early 1996, Glaswegian quartet Urusei Yatsura were lumped together with other so-called 'lo-fi' teen bands, such as Bis and Dweeb, but they owe as much to US bands such as Sonic Youth and Weezer. Lyricists Graham Kemp (b. 3 December 1968; vocals/guitar) and Fergus Lawrie (b. 23 January 1968; vocals/guitars), with the sibling rhythm section of Elaine (b. 16 June 1970; bass) and Ian Graham (b. 19 October 1972; drums), fuse 'geeky' concerns such as *Star Trek* and pinball with a feedback-drenched wall of guitar sound that Kemp describes as 'horrible, fucked-up bubblegum'. An extra sonic ingredient is the band's deployment of toy ray guns and

other childhood ephemera. A rollicking John Peel session and gigs highlighted by some particularly sadistic guitar abuse helped them to a contract with east London's Ché Records and a reputation as leaders of a Glasgow scene that, as far as outsiders could tell, came from nowhere. The band's name, incidentally, is borrowed from a Japanese comic book and translates approximately as 'Those Pesky Female Aliens'. The appropriation resulted in legal threats from the comic's publishers and outside the UK the band are known simply as Yatsura. The row did not stop the band's debut album topping the UK indie charts and making the *New Musical Express'* Top 50 for 1996; their first offering of 1997, the 'Strategic Hamlets' single, seemed to be making a bid for more commercial success. The 1998 album, *Slain By Urusei Yastsura* made a further concession to accessibility, with some winning pop melodies shining through the lo-fi murkiness.
● ALBUMS: *We Are Urusei Yatsura* (Ché 1996)★★★★, *Slain By Urusei Yatsura* (Ché 1998)★★★★.

Usher

b. Usher Raymond, Chattanooga, Tennessee, USA. Drawn from LaFace Records' seemingly inexhaustible wellspring of young R&B acts, Usher is one of the few who can boast of real star quality. Indeed, after the release of his self-titled debut in 1994, there seemed to be a danger that he would become better known as a face rather than a musical talent. He appeared on the *Oprah Winfrey Show* and also performed at the American Music Awards as part of the all-star recording collaboration Black Men United. However, sales of his Sean 'Puffy' Combs-produced debut were a little disappointing at just over a quarter of a million, though it did spawn the hit single 'Think Of You'. As a consequence, he took creative control over the production of the US Top 10 follow-up *My Way*, although he did enlist Jermaine Dupri, Teddy Riley and Babyface as co-writers and co-producers. The first single to be taken from the album, 'You Make Me Wanna', was typical of the smooth ballads on offer. More unusual was the experimental, hip-hop-styled 'Nice 'N' Slow', a US chart-topper in March 1998. The album also included a remake of Midnight Star's 'Slow Jam', featuring fellow teenage R&B star Monica. The title track climbed to US number 2 in August 1998.
● ALBUMS: *Usher* (LaFace 1994)★★★, *My Way* (LaFace 1997)★★★, *Live* (LaFace 1999)★★★.

Utah Saints

Formed in Leeds, Yorkshire, England, Utah Saints comprises Jez Willis (b. 14 August 1963, Brampton, Cumbria, England; ex-Cassandra Complex) and Tim Garbutt (b. 6 January 1969, London, England; also a DJ at the Bliss club in Leeds). Both were formerly members of MDMA, who practised an unlikely and unappetizing hybrid of electro-gothic dance music. They released five 12-inch singles on their own Ecstatic Product label, the band name taken from the chemical description for the 'Ecstasy' drug, though they initially claimed never to have actually used it. However, both were more than familiar with developments in the club scene. After MDMA Willis drifted into DJing, specializing in 70s disco evenings (Garbutt had already performed widely in such a role from the late 80s onwards). Together they established their name at their own 'Mile High Club' nights at The

Gallery in Leeds; these were such a success that corresponding events also transferred to York and then London. They then returned to recording, taking the Utah Saints name from the Nicolas Cage movie, *Raising Arizona* (it had previously been employed on a MDMA b-side). The duo's move to house music, using samples and a driving backbeat, proved much more successful than the efforts of their former incarnation. After acclimatizing to the charts with 1991's UK Top 10 hit 'What Can You Do For Me' (featuring a Eurythmics sample), they produced the Top 5 hit 'Something Good'. This was built around a Kate Bush sample (the line 'I just know that something good is going to happen') from 'Cloudbusting', but it had other strengths too. As Willis elaborated: 'We're trying to get a bit of rock 'n' roll into rave.' They later backed Neneh Cherry on a version of the Rolling Stones' 'Gimme Shelter' for the *Putting Our House In Order* campaign for the homeless in 1993, one of several acts to release the song. Their own follow-up was the Top 10 hit 'Believe In Me', this time featuring a sample of Philip Oakey of the Human League singing 'Love Action'. Other steals, meanwhile, are less obvious, and include heavy metal Satanists Slayer and industrial funk band Front 242. *Utah Saints* sold over a quarter of a million copies in the USA (where it was released first) in addition to its UK success. This was compounded by international touring with a wide range of bands. In just two weeks in 1993 they supported East 17, Take That and U2 at Wembley Stadium, then joined Moby and the Prodigy in Europe before returning to Leeds to support the Mission and Sisters Of Mercy. In contrast to their debut (recorded in six weeks) their second album was the result of a year in the studio, aided by co-producer Mark 'Spike' Kent (previously mixer to Depeche Mode and KLF). Their first release in over a year, 'Ohio', arrived in August 1995. This utilized a Jocelyn Brown sample (her 1984 hit 'Somebody Else's Guy'), but was atypical of the album as a whole where the sampling was now downplayed. Despite this, their playful instincts continue to offer an accessible bridge between rock audiences and the house movement, although their work ethic remains almost non-existent. Garbutt's busy DJing schedule took in a stint at New York's The Tunnel, while Willis continued to tinker in the studio. Remixing work for Alabama 3, Nina Hagen, Simple Minds, Hawkwind and the Osmonds was followed, in January 2000, by a rare new Utah Saints track, 'Love Song'.

● ALBUMS: *Utah Saints* (London/ffrr 1992)★★★★.

Van Dyk, Paul

b. 16 December 1971, Eisenhuttenstadt, Germany. Van Dyk has risen to prominence as one of Europe's most popular DJs, artists and remixers in only a few years. As a teenager, he listened to the rather sombre UK indie sounds of the Smiths, Depeche Mode and New Order but he was taken with the thriving club scene in Berlin and began DJing in 1988. He secured his first gig at Turbine and made such an impression on his debut that he soon became a popular DJ on the booming Berlin dance music scene. He went on to become the long-standing resident at 'Dubmission' at the E-Werk club in Berlin. He released his first 12-inch single, 'Perfect Day', under the name Visions Of Shiva in 1992 on the German label MFS. He has since gone on to release a number of albums and several successful singles. He has earned a highly-respected name as a remixer and has worked on tracks for artists including New Order, Inspiral Carpets, Sven Vath, Secret Knowledge, BT, Tori Amos, Dina Carroll, Amen, Qattara, Tilt, Age Of Love, Curve and, in the late 90s Binary Finary and Faithless. As a DJ, Van Dyk has a huge following in Europe and he has played at every major club in the world. Like Sasha, John Digweed and Carl Cox, he presently has a bimonthly residency at Twilo in New York City. He has established his UK popularity at Sheffield's Gatecrasher club with a blend of melodic, uplifting trance and pumping house, a sound that he pioneered and popularized. His own singles have been massively popular with clubbing audiences, most notably 'Words' and a reworking of a track from his first album, 'For An Angel 98'. The latter was one of 1998's most popular club tracks, a number 1 in the UK dance charts and appeared in many DJs' lists of their Top 10 tunes of the year. It is typical of Van Dyk's style: a pounding kick-drum, layered with a beautifully melodic riff and a hands-in-the-air breakdown. In 1998, a three-CD collection of his remixes, *Vorsprung Dyk Technik* was released to critical acclaim and commercial success. It demonstrated the versatility and skill of an artist/producer at the peak of his ability. His remix of Humate's 'Love Stimulation' was a UK Top 20 hit in early 1999. Later in the year, Van Dyk was voted number 5 in the UK's *DJ* magazine's Top 100 DJs in the world.

● ALBUMS: *45 RPM* (Deviant 1994)★★★, *Seven Ways* (Deviant 1997)★★★★.

● COMPILATIONS: *Vorsprung Dyk Technik* (Deviant 1998)★★★★.

Van Helden, Armand

b. New York, USA. Based in Times Square in New York, USA, Van Helden had, by the mid-90s, supplanted Masters At Work as the most in-demand remixer in the music industry. However, Van Helden himself was troubled by this reputation. As he told the *New Musical Express*: 'The perception in the UK is that I'm rolling in cash, but I could make a lot more money if I was a real entrepreneur and said yes to every remix I got offered.' As a testament to this, he claimed to have turned down offers to work with Mick Jagger and Janet Jackson in the same week in 1997. His childhood consisted of several foreign postings (his father was in the service of the US armed forces), though he eventually settled in Boston, losing much of his youth to cocaine addiction. Although he was a high-profile DJ on the American and continental European circuit for several years thereafter, his breakthrough in Britain came in 1996 with his house remix of Tori Amos' 'Professional Widow', which topped the UK charts. Previously he had recorded 'Witchdocktor', an underground club favourite that regularly accompanied Alexander McQueen's fashion shows. Though a veteran of several different styles of house - including the techno, trance and tribal variations - his solo debut album was rooted in hip-hop (vocal samples included the Wu-Tang Clan and KRS-1). At the end of January 1999 Van Helden topped the UK singles chart with 'You Don't Know Me', featuring vocalist Duane Harden. Later in the year he took part in a well-publicised battle of the DJs with Fatboy Slim in Brixton, London.

● ALBUMS: *Sampleslaya ... Enter The Meat Market* (ZYX 1997)★★★★, *2Future4U* (ffrr 1999)★★★★.

Vanilla Ice

b. Robert Van Winkle, 31 October 1968, Miami Lakes, Florida, USA. Controversial white rapper who borrowed liberally from M.C. Hammer's blueprint for commercial success, and scored a UK/US number 1 with 'Ice Ice Baby' (15 million worldwide sales). Just as Hammer utilized easily recognisable rock/pop classics to underpin his rhymes, Ice used the same technique in reshaping 'Under Pressure', 'Satisfaction' and 'Play That Funky Music' for his repertoire. Winkle was raised by his mother in a poor area of Miami, and never knew his father. He spent his teenage years hanging out on the street. However, the later claims to the press about being stabbed five times were erroneous - in fact he had been slashed across his bottom on a singular occasion. Contrary to his new image he actually sang in church choir until he was 15 and had a stepfather who owned a Chevrolet dealership, before he was first discovered playing the City Lights in Dallas, Texas. His debut album covered all bases, the ballad-rap 'I Love You' sitting alongside the gangsta-inclined 'Go III' and dance pop of 'Dancin''. While rap aficionados held up their hands in horror at what they loudly decried as a phoney, Vanilla Ice responded by telling his detractors they could 'Kiss My White Ass' at an MTV Awards ceremony. An obvious reference to contentions that rap was an intrinsically black music, his comments did little to pacify angry factions in the genre. Ironically, Public Enemy had originally encouraged their producer, Hank Shocklee, to sign him to their label, based on his good looks and snappy dance routines. However, following his huge success he fell foul of a management that wished to pigeonhole him within the teen-market. It took several years before he fully extricated himself from the deal. Whether this, adverse press or a lack of genuine talent called a halt to Vanilla Ice's meteoric rise is a worthy debate. He certainly did little to bring the jury to a favourable verdict with his comeback album. In a desperate attempt to catch up with the gangsta set, *Mindblowing* made frequent references to 'blunts', while the music sampled James Brown and, predictably, George Clinton. It was a blueprint hardcore rap album, but one with fewer convictions, in both senses, than Ice-T or Snoop Doggy Dogg. Ice disappeared from the music scene for several years before returning with 1998's *Hard To Swallow*, produced by Korn associate Ross Robinson.

● ALBUMS: *To The Extreme* (SBK 1990)★★★, *Extremely Live* (SBK 1991)★★, *Mindblowing* (SBK 1994)★★, *Hard To Swallow* (Republic/Universal 1998)★★★.

Värttinä

Mari Kaasinen (b. 6 December 1971, Raakkyla, Finland; vocals), Sari Kaasinen (b. Raakkyla, Finland), Kirsi Kahkonen (b. 30 June 1970, Raakkyla, Finland; vocals), Susan Aho (b. 5 March 1974, Espoo, Finland; vocals/accordion), Janne Lappalainen (b. 21 April 1974, Raakkyla, Finland; bouzouki/saxophones), Antto Varilo (b. 9 August 1966, Helsinki, Finland; guitar/banjo/kantele), Kari 'Reiska' Reiman (b. 31 January 1955, Helsinki, Finland; violin/kantele), Sirpa Reiman (b. 16 July 1966, Ostrobothnia, Finland; vocals), Pekka Lehti (b. 23 January 1965, Joensuu, Finland; bass), Marko Timonen (b. 7 September 1966, Helsinki, Finland; drums/percussion). Formed in 1983 by sisters Sari and Mari Kaasinen in the village of Raakkyla in Kaarelia, the south-east region of Finland, Värttinä was originally a youth folk group who recited Kaarelian poetry, sang and played the kantele (a multi-stringed zither that is Finland's national instrument). The group expanded to 21 members (15 female vocalists backed by six men on various instruments). This line-up recorded two albums for the local market, *Värttinä* and *Musta Lindu*. By 1989 most of the original members had left the group. The remaining core membership of the Kaasinen sisters, Janne Lappalainen and Kirsi Kahkonen recruited a new set of backing musicians. This 11-piece line-up incorporated rock influences and introduced original material into their repertoire. At the same time, they also delved deeper into their Kaarelian cultural roots and started to seriously explore other Finno-Ugric traditions. In 1991, *Oi Dai*, the first release by the new line-up, introduced their new sound, best described as breakneck Scandinavian folk-rock. *Seleniko*, the follow-up, was released a year later and went straight to number 1 in the European World Music Charts, where it remained for three months. In the same year the group toured extensively in Europe and the USA. *Aitara* was their first release to feature a drummer. In the same year they appeared alongside Baaba Maal and Angelique Kidjo at Prize Of Europe (MTV's anti-racism video competition), performed at festivals in the USA and Europe and played on albums by Hector Zazov and Maggie Reilly. In 1996, they released *Kokko*, their most varied and accomplished album to date, establishing their position as international ambassadors of Finnish music. They also continued to tour, including support slots for Björk and Joan Armatrading. *Vihma* (1998), their first release for Wicklow Records (the label set up by Paddy Moloney of the Chieftains), continued their high standard of releases with guest appearances from Finland's JPP and members of the Tuvan group Yat-Kha. In the same year Värttinä celebrated their 15th anniversary with a concert at the Kihaus Festival in their home village of Raakkyla.

● ALBUMS: *Värttinä* (Mipu 1987)★★★, *Musta Lindu* (Olarin

1989)★★★, *Oi Dai* (PolyGram/Xenophile 1991)★★★, *Seleniko* (PolyGram/Xenophile 1992)★★★, *Aitara* (Xenophile 1995)★★★, *Kokko* (Nonesuch 1996)★★★★, *Vihma* (Wicklow 1998)★★★.

Vasquez, Junior

Junior Vasquez (not his real name, he is in fact a German-American from Philadelphia, but declines to provide further details) found his induction into the world of dance music as a (reluctant) dancer at Larry Levan's Paradise Garage. He soon decided the life of a DJ was for him. He applied himself to his apprenticeship, working his way up the ladder via shops (working at Downstairs Records in the early 80s where he first met friends such as Shep Pettibone), clubs and house parties (notably the Kiss FM bashes), until he had built his own following. This allowed him to put together his own clubs - starting with the 'Hearthrob' nights at the Funhouse, then the Basline, and finally the Sound Factory club (owned by Christian Visca). One of New York's premier nights, it quickly saw Vasquez's reputation as a fiercely hot turntable operator soar. Innovating live by playing backwards and forwards, alternating rhythms and throwing in live samples, he offered a total aural experience. There was a visual dimension too, with Vasquez stepping out from behind the desks to present his adoring public with flowers. His reputation spread to the point at which Madonna was spotted at the Sound Factory on several occasions (he also DJed at her party to celebrate the launch of her erotica collection, *Sex*). As a recording artist Vasquez provides Tribal Records with the majority of his labours, including cuts like 'X', 'Get Your Hands Off My Man' and 'Nervaas'. He has also written for artists including Lisa Lisa and Cyndi Lauper and remixed for many others, ranging from Eat Static ('Gulf Breeze') to Ce Ce Peniston ('I'm In The Mood'). In 1998, he helped add a modern spin to Cher's hugely successful *Believe*.

● COMPILATIONS: *Future Sound Of New York: Junior Vasquez* (MOS 1994)★★★, *Junior Vasquez Live Vol. 1* (Pagoda 1997)★★★.

VAST

The creation of one man, Jon Crosby (b. 25 July 1976, Los Angeles, California, USA), the VAST (Visual Audio Sensory Theater) project was one of the most ambitious alternative rock recordings of the late 90s. Crosby grew up in the rural communities of Humboldt and Sonoma Counties in Northern California. His precocious talent was recognised when, having completed a demo for Shrapnel Records, he was featured in *Guitar Player* magazine at the age of 13. Having completed his education at home, Crosby immersed himself, hermit-like, in his home studio. The art-house rock creation VAST gradually took shape in the form of demo tapes, before Crosby signed a lucrative deal with Elektra Records. The resulting album, released in April 1998, was a stunning fusion of ambient electronica and alternative rock, utilising a full orchestra and a diverse range of samples that included a choir of Benedictine monks and Bulgarian folk music singers. Having received uniformly ecstatic reviews, Crosby took VAST on the road with Thomas Froggatt (b. 19 January 1979, Byron Bay, Australia; bass), Steve Clark (drums), and Rowan Robertson (b. 22 November 1971, Cambridge, England; guitar, ex-Dio).

● ALBUMS: *Visual Audio Sensory Theater* (Elektra 1998)★★★★.

Vath, Sven

Frankfurt, Germany-based Vath (pronounced to rhyme with Fate) first DJed at his father's bar, the Queens Pub, playing old disco and Barry White records. He started his recording career as frontman for the Off, whose 'Electric Salsa' was a big European hit and one of the first for Michael Munzing and Luca Anzilotti, the duo behind Snap!. Vath grew up listening to various kinds of electronica – Tangerine Dream, Ryûichi Sakamoto, Holger Czukay and Jean-Michel Jarre – and was further inspired by the house explosion of the 80s. During the early 90s he became involved with trance, founding the pioneering labels Harthouse Records, Eye Q and the environmentally pleasing Recycle Or Die (whose CD-only issues use biodegradable cardboard packaging). Following a spell in India Vath wrote *Accident In Paradise*, recognized as a masterpiece in the techno world, and an important part of the early trance sound. However, the follow-up, *The Harlequin, The Robot And The Ballet Dancer*, did not fare so well; one commentator described it as 'overblown . . . self important . . . Wagner meets Tangerine Dream over a 909 beat'. In the mid-90s, after various other projects had not gone his way, Vath left the ailing Eye-Q and Harthouse which soon went bankrupt. However with 1998's *Fusion* Vath ditched the techno sound and produced a more melodic, funky, eclectic album that presented impressionistic washes over a mixture of textures, including samba rhythms ('Fusion') and relaxed breakbeats ('Sensual Enjoyments' and 'Trippy Moonshine'), sometimes touching on funky house ('Face It') and dark techno ('Schubduse').

● ALBUMS: *Accident In Paradise* (Eye Q 1993)★★★★★, *The Harlequin, The Robot And The Ballet Dancer* (Eye Q 1994)★★, *Fusion* (Virgin 1998)★★★.

Vega, Little Louie

A New York, USA-based DJ, Vega's career began at high school at the age of 18, after watching his friends spin records. He played high school parties before eventually establishing his own label. He went on to DJ at the Devil's Nest (regarded as the birthplace of the New York 'freestyle' approach, alongside TKA and Sa-Fire), then Hearthrob and 1018. By the time he had reached the 4,000 capacity Studio 54 Todd Terry passed Vega his new mixes to try out on the crowd. His first remix job was 'Running' by Information Society, then Noel's 'Silent Morning'. He even worked Debbie Gibson's first record. He began his own-name productions with the instrumental 'Don't Tell Me' for SBK Records in 1989 and 'Keep On Pumpin' It Up' (as Freestyle Orchestra), before signing to CBS Records' subsidiary WTG Records with Latin singer Marc Anthony. He had previously been commissioned to write songs for the movie *East Side Story*, where he first met the singer. Together they hooked up for a Latin R&B flavoured album and single, 'Ride On The Rhythm', a huge club hit. He also worked with India, his girlfriend, and Todd Terry for the latter's 'Todd's Message'. Together with Barbara Tucker, Vega instigated the Underground Network Club in New York (he has also produced 'Beautiful People' for Tucker). Despite this background as an established house star, he is probably best known now for his work alongside Kenny 'Dope' Gonzalez as half of the Masters At Work remix team. He is not to be confused with Chicago house veteran Lil' Louis, or, with the Louie Vega who remixed for Lakim Shabazz, despite the fact

that both shared the same management. Vega's most recent remix clients include Juliet Roberts and Urban Species.
● ALBUMS: with Marc Anthony *When The Night Is Over* (Atlantic 1991)★★★.

Velocity Girl

An alternative rock pop quintet from Washington, USA, Sub Pop Records stalwarts Velocity Girl comprised Archie Moore (b. 3 June 1968, Washington, USA; guitar/bass/vocals), Brian Nelson (b. 2 November 1967, Washington, USA; guitar), Kelly Riles (b. 22 March 1967, Encino, California, USA; guitar/bass), Sarah Shannon (b. 7 October 1969, Washington, USA; vocals) and Jim Spellman (b. 5 November 1967, Washington, USA; drums). Formed from the remnants of a university band put together by Riles and Moore in 1988, they took on a permanent footing a year later. However, despite their emergence on *the* 'grunge' label, Velocity Girl took their name from a (much lauded) Primal Scream b-side, and played songs similar to mid-80s shambling bands such as June Brides or Loft. Indeed, the band were all self-confessed anglophiles. Several compilation and 7-inch appearances preceded the arrival of 'My Forgotten Favorite' on Slumberland Records, which earned a degree of press attention. Shortly after its release, the band recorded a split-single for Sub Pop's celebrated singles club. Signing to the label shortly thereafter, they completed their first full-length album with the assistance of Sebadoh producer Bob Weston. It was Sub Pop's biggest seller since Nirvana's *Bleach*. For the follow-up, John Porter (Roxy Music, Smiths) stepped in to produce a more polished sound, and one even more closely aligned with English pop semantics. The lead-off single, 'I Can't Stop Smiling', with its carefree, jangling guitar, even recalled the restrained dynamic of the Sarah Records roster. *Gilded Stars And Zealous Hearts* contained songs with further gorgeous riffs and infectious hooks, revealing gentle pop at its best ('Formula 1 Throwaway'), yet with enough heavy guitar ('Finest Hour') to sustain the grunge connections.
● ALBUMS: *Copacetic* (Sub Pop 1993)★★★, *!Simpatico!* (Sub Pop 1994)★★★, *Gilded Stars And Zealous Hearts* (Sub Pop 1996)★★★.

Velvet Crush

Formed in Rhode Island, USA, in 1989, Velvet Crush comprises Paul Chastain (vocals/bass), Ric Menck (drums) and Jeffrey Borchardt (guitar). Growing up in Illinois, Chastain and Menck were obsessed with Big Star and the Raspberries, and Menck started his own Picture Book label. They also released singles as solo performers and under the band names Springfields, Paint Set, Bag O'Shells and Choo Choo Train. Meanwhile, Borchardt was running his band, the White Sisters, in Milwaukee, but corresponding regularly with Menck, who was releasing White Sisters material on Picture Book. When Borchardt moved to Providence in 1988, he encouraged Menck and Chastain to follow, which they did. Their energetic live shows, sometimes augmented by Matthew Sweet or members of the Gigolo Aunts, brought an enthusiastic following, widened by increasing college radio play. A debut album, *In The Presence Of Greatness*, appeared in 1992, and secured a place in the *New Musical Express*' Top 50 of the year. The second album, *Teenage Symphonies To God*, using R.E.M. producer Mitch Easter against the wishes of Alan McGee of Creation Records, appeared in 1994 on American Independence Day (4 July). Soon afterwards,

Velvet Crush became support band to Roger McGuinn for a one-off gig at an Epic Records publicist's wedding reception. In 1998, they signed to the UK's Cooking Vinyl Records.
● ALBUMS: *In The Presence Of Greatness* (Creation 1992)★★★, *Teenage Symphonies To God* (Creation 1994)★★★★, *Heavy Changes* (Cooking Vinyl 1998)★★★.

Vengaboys

The Netherlands-based Vengaboys became an almost permanent fixture on singles charts throughout Europe during the late 90s with their banal brand of lightweight euro house. Reclusive Dutch DJs Danski and Delmundo, who had already built up a name for themselves on the Balearic club circuit, masterminded the group. They hired four Dutch singers/dancers, Kim, Roy, Denice, and Robin, and created the Vengaboys, and invented exotic birthplaces such as Brazil, Venezuela, Trinidad and Hungary to enliven their biographies. Their singles were initially released in Holland, and then licensed to various independent labels in different countries. A succession of huge European hits ensued, including 'Up & Down', 'We Like To Party! (The Vengabus)'), 'Boom, Boom, Boom, Boom!', 'We're Going To Ibiza!', and 'Kiss (When The Sun Don't Shine)'. A successful album was released under various titles throughout Europe. Certainly not regarded as credible artists by dance music cognoscenti, the Vengaboys produce a pop/dance hybrid that speaks to a teenage audience as well as less discerning clubbers.
● ALBUMS: *The Party Album!* UK release (Positiva 1999)★★.

Veruca Salt

Chicago, USA quartet formed in 1992 around singer/guitarists Nina Gordon and Louise Post, eventually joined by Steve Lack (bass) and Jim Shapiro (drums, Gordon's brother). 'We started off playing acoustic together and our songs tended to be slower. When we switched to electric and playing distorted guitar they were still kind of slow and we thought of ourselves as dreamy and ethereal with a heavy bottom. Then Steve added a lot of depth to the songs and Jim turned us into a rock band'. Playing their first tentative gigs in September 1993, they went on to release a single, 'Seether', on Jim Powers' Minty Fresh Records. This impressed the flock of A&R personnel descending on the Midwest following the success of the Smashing Pumpkins, Liz Phair and Urge Overkill. After a bidding war between Virgin and Geffen Records, the band opted to stay on the Minty Fresh label for their first album. The ensuing debut, released in September 1994, was named after a line in AC/DC's 'You Shook Me All Night Long', and became an instant favourite among MTV viewers and followers of literate US rock. The following month Veruca Salt signed a contract with Geffen Records, which had by now also signed up Powers for A&R, along with his label. Joining new labelmates Hole on their 1994 tour helped generate further interest, the band's appeal also spreading quickly to the UK. Central to the Veruca Salt attraction is the space with which they allow ideas to develop - despite a full sound, there is a scarcity to their instrumentation that distinguishes them musically. Indeed, some commentators noted how Veruca Salt represented the first post-grunge pop band - similar to the way that Blondie in the late 70s and the heavier side of the Bangles in the 80s represented post-punk pop. Shapiro was replaced by Stacy Jones towards the end of 1996. Using the original title for the Beatles' second film *Help*, the band returned with *Eight Arms To Hold You* in 1997. The record contained rich harmonies and feisty guitar, with some outstanding middle eight hooks on tracks such as 'Volcano Girls', 'The Morning Sad' and 'Shutterbug'.

● ALBUMS: *American Thighs* (Minty Fresh 1994)★★, *Blow It Out Your Ass It's Veruca Salt* mini-album (Minty Fresh/DGC 1996)★★★, *Eight Arms To Hold You* (Outpost/DGC 1997)★★★★.

Verve

UK indie rock band Verve released their first record, 'All In The Mind', in March 1992, although they had already been in existence for several years, having made their live debut at Winstanley College, Wigan, in the Autumn of 1989 (three of the band members studied there). The Verve comprised Peter Salisbury (b. Peter Anthony Salisbury, 24 September 1971, Bath, Avon, England; drums), Richard Ashcroft (b. Richard Paul Ashcroft, 11 September 1971, Billinge, Wigan, Lancashire; vocals), Simon Jones (b. 29 July 1972, Liverpool, Merseyside, England; bass) and Nick McCabe (b. 14 July 1971, St Helens, Lancashire, England; guitar). After a run of singles that covered '(She's A) Superstar', 'Gravity Grave' and 'Blue' (all released on Virgin Records' 'indie' subsidiary Hut), their debut album arrived in June 1993. Surprisingly, the hits were omitted in favour of new material that saw further comparisons to artists as diverse as T. Rex and the Stone Roses. On the back of this rise to prominence the band had come to the attention of the Verve Records jazz label, who insisted on copyright of the name. Failing to accept a compromise 'Verv' spelling, after a two-year battle the band were re-christened The Verve. They then embarked on 1994's Lollapalooza tour, before joining with Oasis for a double-headed package later that year. Progress in 1995 was interrupted when McCabe broke his finger during an attack by a bouncer at the Paris Bataclan venue on April 20, from which litigation ensued. However, they had the consolation of an overwhelming press response to 1995's *A Northern Soul*, which included Oasis' Noel Gallagher, who added handclaps to one track, 'History', and cited the record as the 'third best album of the year'. Ashcroft left the band during 1995 to form his own version of the Verve and the band officially broke up in August, only to announce in early 1997 that they had re-formed. Richard Ashcroft had no doubts as to why they re-formed, he told the *New Musical Express*: 'It's the power of the music that drew the Verve back together. It's the addictive quality of being in the greatest rock 'n' roll band in the world'. The break had rejuvenating qualities for their career; in addition to the considerable media coverage and favourable reappraisal, their new material stormed the bestsellers in the UK. Accompanied by a memorable promotional video, 'Bitter Sweet Symphony' made the UK Top 5, despite legal wranglings over the use of a Rolling Stones instrumental sample (the Verve were obliged to hand over the single's royalties to Allen Klein and credit Keith Richards and Mick Jagger as songwriters). The song also broke the band in the USA, reaching number 12 in April 1998. 'The Drugs Don't Work' reached UK number 1 on the week of release. *Urban Hymns* then received rave critical reviews and entered the UK album chart at number 1, knocking Oasis off the top in the process and remaining at the top for seven weeks. The band won Best Group and Best Album at the 1998 BRIT Awards. McCabe opted out of subsequent live

work, however, hinting at new tensions between the members. This was confirmed in April 1999 when the band announced they were splitting-up. Ashcroft then entered the studio to record tracks for a projected solo album.

● ALBUMS: *Storm In Heaven* (Hut 1993)★★★, *A Northern Soul* (Hut 1995)★★★★, *Urban Hymns* (Hut 1997)★★★★.
● COMPILATIONS: *No Come Down* (Virgin 1994)★★★.
● VIDEOS: *Some Bitter - Some Sweet: Unauthorised Biography* (Talking Heads Video 1998), *The Verve: The Video 96-98* (Hut 1999).
● FURTHER READING: *The Verve: Bitter Sweet*, Peter Wilding. *The Verve: Crazed Highs + Horrible Lows*, Martin Clarke. *The Verve: Star Sail*, Sean Egan.

Voice Of The Beehive

Formed by sisters Tracey Bryn (b. 17 May 1962, Encino, California, USA) and Melissa Brooke Belland (b. 6 February 1966, Los Angeles, California, USA), this unusual indie pop band had a strong pedigree. The girls' father was Bruce Belland, a former member of the Four Preps. Following a showbusiness childhood, in which they acted in various television commercials, the female duo decided to move to England and start a band. They soon infiltrated rock circles and after appearing on Bill Drummond's solo album, they formed Voice Of The Beehive, the name drawn from a Bette Davis movie. With Mike Jones (guitar), the band began recording various demos. Their line-up was soon expanded following the recruitment of Dan Woodgate (b. 19 October 1960, London, England; drums) and Mark Bedford (b. 24 August 1961, London, England; bass, ex-Madness). After signing with David Balfe's Food label, they appeared on an EMI Records' compilation album and subsequently recorded for London Records. Their early singles, 'Just A City', 'I Say Nothing' and 'I Walk The Earth', encouraged comparisons with the Bangles and Blondie. Bedford, meanwhile, had left to form Butterfield 8 and was replaced by Martin Brett, who assisted with the band's debut album. *Let It Bee* was a pleasant, witty pop confectionery, which included the UK Top 20 single 'Don't Call Me Baby'. The appealing pop of Voice Of The Beehive continued on the punningly titled *Honey Lingers*, which climaxed in the heat of the summer of 1991 with a series of live appearances in London, which, tongue in cheek, were entitled Orgy Under The Underworld. *Sex & Misery* (on new label East West Records) demonstrated how quickly the music scene changes. The new mature Voices, reduced to a duo of Bryn and Belland, had lost the pop edge and gained a large spoonful of saccharine; this dichotomy placed them in a musical netherworld, and shortly afterwards the band quietly broke up.

● ALBUMS: *Let It Bee* (London 1988)★★★, *Honey Lingers* (London 1991)★★★★, *Sex & Misery* (East West 1995)★★.

Vulgar Boatmen

The Vulgar Boatmen were founded in 1982 by Robert Ray (b. Memphis, Tennessee, USA), professor of English at the University of Florida. The rest of the line-up comprised three of Ray's students (one of whom was future Silos founder Walter Salas-Humara), but he gained a more long-standing collaborator in the Indianapolis-based Dale Kirkland (aka Dale Lawrence; ex-Gizmos). With Kirkland he embarked on a series of songwriting projects based on regular postal tape exchanges. Since those early days, the Vulgar Boatmen have largely continued as two separate enti-

ties, with their songwriting repertoire delivered by both partners in their respective locales with their own sets of musicians. Salas-Humara returned to guest on and produce the Vulgar Boatmen's first album, *You And Your Sister*, after two cassette-only efforts. Immediately the clarity of the band's songwriting shone through on a set resplendent in blissful, unpretentious pop. The follow-up set was also lovingly received, with critics sketching comparisons ranging from the Feelies to Buddy Holly. However, in the 90s Ray found himself limited by his teaching and writing responsibilities, so the Florida version of the Vulgar Boatmen was disbanded. Ray continued to write with Kirkland instead, also appearing with his Gainsville-based version of the band when they played in his home state. In 1995, *Opposite Sex* was released on their new label, East West Records, and was another striking collection of songs that received high critical praise.
● ALBUMS: *You And Your Sister* (Record Collect 1989)★★★, *Please Panic* (Rough Trade 1992)★★★★, *Opposite Sex* (East West 1995)★★★★.

Walker, Clay

b. 19 August 1969, Beaumont, Texas, USA. From the same city and similar strand of country music as Tracy Byrd and Mark Chesnutt, the 90s US country singer Clay Walker owes much of his vocal style to George Strait. He was taught guitar by his father at a young age and started to write songs as soon as he knew enough chords. Walker was no overnight success, and toured throughout the USA and Canada, playing bars and small clubs, building a reputation and desperately trying to attract attention. He finally secured a contract with Giant Records in Nashville. His debut single in 1993, 'What's It To You', was a US country number 1. The debut album, *Clay Walker*, did well on the US country charts and the single 'Live Until I Die' reached number 3. Walker's other hit singles have included 'If I Could Make A Living', 'Who Needs You Baby', 'This Woman And This Man' 'Hypnotize The Moon', and another number 1 in 1997 with 'Rumor Has It'. Walker was reported to be suffering from multiple sclerosis the same year.
● ALBUMS: *Clay Walker* (Giant 1993)★★★, *If I Could Make A Living* (Giant 1994)★★★★, *Hypnotize The Moon* (Giant 1995)★★★, *Rumor Has It* (Giant 1997)★★★★, *Live, Laugh, Love* (Giant 1999)★★.
● COMPILATIONS: *Greatest Hits* (Giant 1998)★★★★.
● VIDEOS: *If I Could Make A Living* (1994).

Walker, Hezekiah

b. New York, USA. Since joining a major record label in the early 90s, Hezekiah Walker has become one of the undoubted stars of the gospel world, his powerful voice recognised throughout America and beyond. Growing up in the Fort Greene housing projects of Brooklyn, New York, Walker formed his first gospel group, the Love Fellowship Crusade Choir (LFCC) in his early twenties - as an extension of his activities as the ordained Pentecostal minister of the Love Fellowship in Brooklyn. That group released albums for independent labels in 1987 and 1990, before Walker judged the time was right to launch his solo career. His first album, 1992's *Focus On Glory*, was well-received by the gospel music press. However, it was the following year's *Live In Toronto* that really provided him with his breakthrough, rising to the top of the gospel charts. None of his subsequent efforts have quite reproduced that level of sales, though all have done well, particularly *Live In Atlanta At Morehouse College*, which won a Grammy Award for Best Gospel Album By A Choir Or Chorus. In the process Walker has committed to posterity a canon of excellent songs - particularly 'Clean Inside' and '99 And A Half'. His efforts have been widely credited with increasing the interest of young people in gospel, while the LFCC have maintained a healthy profile of their own, backing Whitney Houston at the 1996 Grammy Awards and playing a sold-out show with Hootie And The Blowfish at New York's Apollo.
● ALBUMS: *Focus On Glory* (Benson 1992)★★★★, *Live In Toronto* (Benson 1993)★★★, *Live In Atlanta At Morehouse College* (Benson 1994)★★, *Live In New York/By Any Means* (Benson 1995)★★, with Fred Hammond, Yolanda Adams *Shakin' The House ... Live In L.A.* (Benson 1996)★★★, *Live In London* (Benson 1997)★★.

Walker, Joe Louis

b. 26 December 1949, San Francisco, California, USA. Although born in the city and raised during the era of 'flower power', Joe Louis had a strong and realized sense of the blues tradition. He was also a guitarist of considerable accomplishment. His albums are superior examples of modern blues, generally consisting of songs that are fluent and witty and sacrifice none of their 'bluesiness' in their awareness of contemporary trends. Formal musical training allows him to write and arrange his own material, including the horn charts. He usually produces lyrics alone or in various combinations made up from the impressive team of Amy and (Dennis) Walker and Henry Oden. On one of his finest songs, 'I'll Get To Heaven On My Own', he performs solo, accompanying himself with some delta-styled slide guitar. Yet even this number, which has the pure feel and power of the early blues, does not take refuge in recycling traditional verses. In an interview with M.K. Aldin he expressed his ideas about other people's material: 'I don't do cover songs (on recordings). I do some of them live. I have a real theory about 'em. I can't do 'em any better than they've been done but . . . I change them'. Another statement: 'And my style is not all playing 90 miles-an-hour,' indicates another reason why, in the heavily rock-influenced modern scene, Joe Louis Walker is a man to watch. *Blues Of The Month Club* or *Great Guitars* would make an excellent starting point, although the latter features other major artists, who tend to overcrowd the star of the show.
● ALBUMS: *Cold Is The Night* (Ace 1987)★★, *The Gift* (Ace

1988)★★★, *Blue Soul* (Demon 1989)★★★★, *Live At Slim's* (Demon 1991)★★, *Live At Slims, Volume Two* (Demon 1992)★★, *Blues Survivor* (Verve 1993)★★★, *JLW* (Verve 1994)★★★, *Blues Of The Month Club* (Verve 1995)★★★★, *Great Guitars* (Verve 1997)★★★, *Preacher And The President* (Verve 1998)★★★, *Silvertone Blues* (Blue Thumb 1999)★★★.

Wall, Chris

b. Los Angeles, California, USA. Wall grew up in southern California but spent his summers on his uncle's ranch in Montana. After gaining a degree in history, he decided on a career in music, working as a bartender in Jackson Hole, Wyoming while he established himself. He jammed with Pinto Bennett and the Famous Motel Cowboys and he and Bennett later wrote 'No Sweat'. Wall's talent was recognized by Jerry Jeff Walker, who suggested he move to Austin to further his career. He was signed to Walker's own Tried And True label and he wrote and played skilfully worded but very danceable honky tonk music. He penned 'I Feel Like Hank Williams Tonight' for Walker, who also made the US country charts with a cover version of 'Trashy Woman'. The song went on to become a substantial hit for Confederate Railroad in 1993, and remains his most popular song. Wall's debut album was full of wry, cynical material, such as 'I Wish John Stetson Made A Heart' ('Mine's been stomped and stole and stepped on and damn near tore apart/Lord, I wish John Stetson made a heart'), 'Entourage' ('I want an entourage/I got a big old ego and I need to get that sucker massaged'), and 'Something To Shoot' ('We got deer, we got elk, we got old owls that hoot/And when I killed them all, there are yankees to shoot'). Wall set up his own Cold Spring Records label in 1994 allowing him complete creative control over his own recordings, a move vindicated by the artistic success of the studio sets *Cowboy Nation* and *'Tainted Angel*, the latter his first self-production.

● ALBUMS: *Honky Tonk Heart* (Tried And True/Rykodisc 1989)★★★★, *No Sweat* (Tried And True/Rykodisc 1991)★★★, *Cowboy Nation* (Cold Spring 1994)★★★★, *Any Saturday Night In Texas* (Cold Spring 1997)★★★, *Tainted Angel* (Cold Spring 1998)★★★★.

Wallflowers

The vast majority of the initial attention surrounding US alternative rock band the Wallflowers concerned the fact that one Jakob Dylan (b. 1970, New York, USA), the son of Bob Dylan, was their songwriter, singer and guitarist. Interest in his career was only natural, though on the evidence of the Wallflowers' self-titled debut for Virgin Records in 1992, there was more to the band than simple nepotism. However, despite good reviews, the album failed to translate critical approval into sales. At that point Virgin's management changed and the Wallflowers found themselves without a label. 'We'd been on the road awhile after the first album, got home, and then there was the big company mix-up and all the people we were connected with disappeared.' They subsequently signed to Interscope Records, with Dylan reassembling a new line-up around founding members Rami Jaffe (keyboards) and Greg Richling (bass), with the addition of Michael Ward (guitar) and Mario Calire (drums). In contrast to their debut, which took only four weeks to record, *Bringing Down The Horse* was completed over eight months, with T-Bone Burnett producing. Guests included Michael Penn, Sam Phillips, Gary Louris (ex-Jayhawks) and mem-

bers of Counting Crows. It was a much better record and elevated the band following its success in the USA. The younger Dylan has proved to be articulate and interesting in interviews. To his credit he refuses to use his father's name and fame as a buffer for his own career.

● ALBUMS: *The Wallflowers* (Virgin 1992)★★, *Bringing Down The Horse* (Interscope 1996)★★★★.

Wamdue Project

The recording name of Chris Brann (b. 1974, Atlanta, Georgia, USA), the Wamdue Project is a successful and respected vehicle for Brann's funky house productions. Wamdue Project had already achieved excellent critical receptions for two albums when a remix by the Italian remixer Roy Malone (aka Walterino) of 'King Of My Castle' struck gold for them in November 1999. Featuring the Argentinean vocalist Victoria Foigerio, it reached number 1 in the UK national charts and kept Cliff Richard's 'Millennium Prayer' from the number 1 spot, if only for a week. It was originally released in the UK in 1998 but failed to enter the charts, despite being a club and Ibiza favourite. However, during 1999, the single was a Top 3 hit in Italy, France, the Netherlands, Belgium and Germany, where it sold more than 600,000 copies. In addition to the Malone mix, the UK release featured those by Armin Van Buuren, Bini And Martini and Roger Sanchez. As a teenager, Brann had listened to *avant garde* electronic music by artists including Steve Reich, Cabaret Voltaire, Ryûichi Sakamoto and Kraftwerk. He became involved in the Atlanta dance music scene in the early 90s and staged illegal warehouse parties before teaming up with the house DJ-producers Deep C (b. Chris Clark) and Udoh (b. Chris Udoh) in 1994. With the help of the Detroit techno producer K-Hand, their first single 'Higher' as Wamdue appeared in 1995 followed by releases for various dance labels including Studio !K7, Jus' Trax, Peacefrog and Multiply. Their pseudonyms were variations on a theme: Wamdue Kidz, Wambonix and Wamdue Project. In 1996, the Wamdue Kidz mixed a compilation for Studio !K7 and released their debut *Resource Toolbook Vol. 1* on the highly respected New York City-based label, Strictly Rhythm Records. The album received many plaudits and was regarded by some critics as a landmark in the development of truly sophisticated dance music. The following year saw a Wamdue Kidz album and *Deepfall* as the Project, both on the Peacefrog label. *Program Yourself* was released in mid-1998 and featured the soulful vocals of the New York-based singer Gaelle on several tracks. Although essentially a house-based sound, the album also touched on drum 'n' bass, dub and urban R&B. The single 'Where Do We Go?' included a remix by Armand Van Helden but did not make the commercial impact that 'King Of My Castle' had a year later.

● ALBUMS: *Resource Toolbox Vol. 1* (Strictly Rhythm 1996)★★★★, *Deepfall* (Peacefrog 1997)★★★, *Program Yourself* (Eruption 1999)★★★★.

Wannadies

Comprising Par Wicksten (vocals/guitar), Fredrik Schonfeldt (bass) and brother Stefan Schonfeldt (guitar), Sweden's Wannadies came from mixed vocations - Wicksten and Fredrik worked as gravediggers, while Stefan played semi-professional football (for MBSK Skelleftea). Formed in 1990, the band enjoyed domestic success with their first two albums before bursting onto the international scene. Their 1995 releases garnered lavish praise in the UK - particularly the single 'You And Me Song'. This was described by the *New Musical Express* as 'the best single of the entire summer', while *Melody Maker* took hyperbole further still in its praise: '(the Wannadies are) the best band in the whole world ever'. A second single, the appropriately titled 'Might Be Stars', followed in November, accompanied by cover versions of the Go-Betweens' 'Lee Remick' and Depeche Mode's 'New Life', two handy pop references for the band's uncomplicated, emotionally direct music. Afterwards they returned to Sweden to concentrate on writing the material for *Bagsy Me*, an album that confirmed the Wannadies as a reliable if somewhat passionless indie-rock band.

● ALBUMS: *The Wannadies* (Snap 1990)★★, *Aquanautic* (Snap 1992)★★★, *Be A Girl* (Indolent 1995)★★★★, *Bagsy Me* (Indolent 1997)★★★, *Yeah* (RCA 2000)★★★.

Wardman, Pete

Wardman is a versatile and respected figure on the European hard house scene. He is a DJ, producer and remixer, a resident at the club Trade and presents a show on the UK's leading dance music radio station, Kiss 100 FM. He has been DJing since the age of 17, when his talent was spotted by an agency and he was signed to their books. In 1988, he set up a small radio station in Hampshire, England, that focused on a somewhat neglected youth audience. Its popularity flourished and it was later bought by the Capital Radio group. In 1992, Wardman was 'head-hunted' by Kiss 100 FM and hired to present the weekday breakfast show before moving to an afternoon slot. The show helped increase his popularity and Wardman became an in-demand name in clubland. He currently presents his *House Nation* show on Thursday evenings. In early 1997, he was signed as the new weekly resident at Trade and mixed their compilation *Trade - Volume 4*. It was here that he confirmed his reputation as one of the leading exponents of hard house and nu-energy as practised by his contemporary and fellow Trade resident, Tony De Vit. Wardman was one of the DJs to take Trade on its first 'world tour' to Australia and South Africa as well as on a comprehensive tour of the UK. In 1998, Wardman completed remixes of Jocelyn Brown's 'Love Is ...' and 99th Floor Elevator's 'Hooked On Love'. An EP of Trade's resident DJs' recording work was also released in 1998, featuring the Trade DJs, Alan Thompson, Malcolm Duffy, Steve Thomas, Ian M and Tony De Vit. Sadly, the De Vit track was the last that he recorded before his premature death. Wardman also signed a deal with Tripoli Trax in 1998 and his debut single 'The Lizard Queen'/'Tragically Glamorous' was their best-selling release of the year. Wardman is now able to tour independently with clubs in the USA, Canada, Israel, Europe, South Africa and the Far East. He was rated number 41 in the chart of The World's Top 100 DJs in the UK's *DJ* magazine. In 1999, Wardman completed further singles for Tripoli Trax, mixed further compilation albums and collaborated with Baby Doc.

● COMPILATIONS: *Sherbet* (React Music 1995)★★★, *Sound Of The Hoover* (Tec 1997)★★★, *Trade - Volume 4* (Feverpitch/EMI 1997)★★★.

Warp Records

Since its foundation in Sheffield, England in 1989 by Rob Mitchell and Steve Beckett as an offshoot from their record shop Warp has played an important role in the development of dance music in the UK. Mitchell and Beckett had played together in an indie band, but on opening Warp they found themselves inadvertently cast into the flourishing acid house and techno scene of the late 80s. Their first release was the Forgemasters 'Track With No Name' (pressed with the help of an Enterprise Allowance grant) and heralded the emergence of a Chicago and Detroit inspired minimal techno sound dubbed 'bleep'. This was followed by Nightmare On Wax's 'Dextrous' and early the following year Sweet Exorcist's bleep anthem 'Testone'. Such was the response to this new sound that in the summer of 1990 both LFO and Tricky Disco's eponymous debuts reached the Top 20. As the rave scene developed Warp changed their ethos and began to promote more listenable, experimental electronic music 'to re-educate people who bought dance records to sit down and pay attention'. This approach was crystalised by the first *Artificial Intelligence* compilation which included tracks by the Diceman (Aphex Twin), Autechre and Alex Paterson (of the Orb) and had a more reflective, cerebral feeling with links to artists such as Brian Eno, Kraftwerk and even Pink Floyd. The series was extended and Warp released individual albums by several of the participants including Polygon Window (Aphex Twin), Black Dog Productions, B12, FUSE (Ritchie Hawtin) and Speedy J. This so called 'ambient techno' resonated throughout the UK's dance music scene, and its sound was reflected in the rise of drum 'n' bass in the mid-90s. It developed substantial interest among the public and the media such that Aphex Twin was one of the most talked about artists in 1993 and his *Selected Ambient Works Vol. 2* most eagerly awaited. While continuing to release pure electronic material, Warp have begun to sign artists with more diverse styles, notably Sabres Of Paradise, Squarepusher, Red Snapper, and Jimi Tenor. The *Blech* compilation (1996) confirmed this change of tack where electronic sounds were blended with hip-hop beats, jazzy textures, drum 'n' bass grooves and snatches of dialogue creating a fragmented electric style similar in concept to that of Ninja Tune Records. Although the sounds have moved on it seems the idea of listenable dance music is still very much at the heart of Warp. They celebrated their 10th anniversary in 1999 with the release of the *Warp 10* collection.

● COMPILATIONS: *Pioneers Of The Hypnotic Groove* (Warp 1991)★★★★, *Evolution Of The Groove* (Warp 1992)★★★★, *Artificial Intelligence* (Warp 1992)★★★★★, *Tequila Slammers And The Jump Jump Groove Generation* (Warp 1993)★★★, *Artificial Intelligence II* (Warp 1994)★★★, *Blech* (Warp 1996)★★★★, *We Are Reasonable People* (Warp 1998)★★★★, *Warp 10 + 1: Influences* (Warp 1999)★★★, *Warp 10 + 2: Classics 89-92* (Warp 1999)★★★★, *Warp 10 + 3: Remixes* (Warp 1999)★★★.

Warren, Diane

b. Van Nuys, California, USA. With songs performed by Aretha Franklin, Cheap Trick, Cher, Chicago, Cyndi Lauper, Dusty Springfield, Elton John, Four Tops, Gladys Knight, Gloria Estefan, Joan Jett, John Waite, Joe Cocker, Heart, Roy Orbison, Celine Dion, the Jacksons, Tom Jones and Ziggy Marley, among well over 100 others, 'Valley Girl' Warren is one of the most successful, gifted and prolific songwriters in the music industry. This despite her guitar teacher having originally pronounced her tone deaf after her father brought home her first guitar, purchased in Tijuana, Mexico. Even as a child she maintained a constant output of compositions, until her family grew so weary of their constant repetition they erected a metal shed in the back yard for her to practice in. Having gleaned her interest in music from radio and her sisters' record collections, throughout she restrained any ambitions to perform her songs, electing instead to give them to a vast and grateful army of interpreters. Warren did struggle initially however, only making songwriting a viable living by the time she was 24. She has less than fond memories of her initial attempts to enter the music industry: 'I got a lot of stupid advice. I remember one publisher looking at a verse of one of my songs and saying, "You have nine lines in this verse, you can only have eight lines. It has to be even."' However, always in place was the dedication which has hallmarked her career: 'I've written songs on Kotex, lyrics on the palm of my hand. If I don't have a tape recorder, I'll call home and sing into my answering machine'. She legendarily works over 12 hours a day, often seven days a week, ensconced in a tiny office cum studio. Before she became the hottest songwriting property in the contemporary US market she was also just as determined to see her work used - one anecdote concerns her falling on her knees to persuade Cher to sing 'If I Could Turn Back Time'. It became the artist's biggest hit for 15 years, and nowadays she has no need for such powers of persuasion. Her first major break had come when Laura Branigan recorded 'Solitaire', an MOR staple. By 1985 DeBarge had taken the altogether different 'Rhythm Of The Night' to number 3 in the *Billboard* charts and Warren was established as a major songwriting source to artists from almost every genre of popular music. She formed Realsongs in 1985 in response to contractual difficulties she experienced with former manager, and Laura Branigan producer, Jack White. Realsongs is administered by business colleague Doreen Dorion, who together with Ken Philips takes responsibility for placing Warren's songs with prospective artists. By now the hits were flowing freely, after the DeBarge hit had opened up a lucrative market to her. Some of her greatest compositions, such as 'Look Away' (Chicago), 'When I See You Smile' (Bad English), 'Blame It On The Rain' (Milli Vanilli), 'Love Will Lead You Back' (Taylor Dayne), 'Nothing's Gonna Stop Us Now' (Starship), 'I Get Weak' (Belinda Carlisle) and 'We're Not Making Love Anymore' (Barbra Streisand), were written between then and 1989. Her profile quickly earned her nicknames such as 'industry powerhouse' and 'hit machine'. Though she professes not to customise her material for such diverse artists, it is a source of considerable pleasure to her that critics have been unable to discern any 'house style'. Which is why she has been able to work with artists as diverse as Bette Midler and Bon Jovi. *Billboard* subsequently named Realsongs the top singles publisher of 1990. The flood of awards snowballed throughout the 90s. She received several Songwriter Of The Year awards from ASCAP and *Billboard*, and was voted Songwriter Of The Year in the Los Angeles Music Awards in 1991. Realsongs has also remained in the Top 6 Publishing Corporations assessed by *Billboard* since 1990. By the end of the 90s Warren had over 100 million unit sales to her name, and numerous Top 10 US hits (including, at one point, holding the number 1 and 2 posi-

tions in the US singles chart via two separate artists). By now she had also moved heavily into movies, seeing her material aired on soundtracks including *Golden Child*, *Ghostbusters*, *License To Kill*, *White Men Can't Jump*, *Karate Kid III* and *Neverending Story III*. A *Billboard* special feature celebrated her achievements, interviewing several of the artists who had recorded her songs. One who regularly returns to her for his repertoire is Michael Bolton: 'She is destined to achieve her appropriate status as one of the greatest songwriters in the history of music.' Grace Slick offered a more personal tribute: 'I've never met anybody who is rolling around in that much fame and money who is that real, honest and funny.' One of the few writers qualified to assess her impact on the music scene as a genuine peer was Lamont Dozier: 'She's not only a gifted songwriter, but she seems to have a sixth sense about what music lowers want to hear.' Despite her multi-millionaire status and phenomenal success, Warren still maintains her stoic resistance to any interruption in her daunting work schedule.

Warren, Nick
b. Bristol, Avon, England. Warren worked in various part-time jobs before pursuing his DJing career, initially at Bristol clubs Most Excellent and Venus in the mid-80s. It was here that he caught the ear of fellow Bristolians, Massive Attack, who liked his musical eclecticism and invited him to support them on a US tour. He also remixed a bestselling Les Negresses Vertes track when Massive Attack were unable to do it, helping to establish his name as a skilled DJ producer. In collaboration with Jody Wisternoff, he was signed by Cream's James Barton to Deconstruction Records. As Way Out West they have released a string of acclaimed and commercially successful singles, including 'Ajare', 'Domination', 'The Gift' and 'Blue', and an album, 1997's *Way Out West*. Warren's residency at the Cream club in Liverpool, alongside Paul Oakenfold, helped him establish his DJing credentials as a purveyor of intelligent, funky trance. Since then, he has continued to DJ all over the world and, with Jon Carter, was the first British DJ to visit Taiwan. His mix albums, notably *Live In Prague*, *Brazil* and *Back To Mine*, have all received praise from critics and achieved respectable sales. Warren is a DJ who has achieved a sometimes rare thing in dance music: he has retained his musical integrity without losing his immense popularity with clubbers and colleagues.
● COMPILATIONS: *Live In Prague* (Boxed 1996)★★★★, *Brazil* (Boxed 1998)★★★★, *Back To Mine* (DMC 1999)★★★.

Waterson, Lal, And Oliver Knight
Lal Waterson (b. Elaine Waterson, 15 February 1943, England, d. 4 September 1998) and her son Oliver Knight (b. Hull, North Humberside, England) were already renowned figures within the UK folk community when they launched their joint 1996 album, *Once In A Blue Moon*. Lal Waterson originally trained as a painter and weaver, and worked for seven years as an heraldic artist before beginning her singing career in 1961 as a member of the Watersons. This band enjoyed massive popularity as pioneers of English traditional music until their temporary retirement in 1968. Lal continued to collaborate with brother Mike Waterson, writing songs and poetry which eventually culminated in the release of the acclaimed *Bright Phoebus* album, featuring contributions from Richard Thompson, Martin Carthy and

Ashley Hutchings. Together with her daughter Maria and niece Eliza Carthy she also toured with the Waterdaughters, but retired from public performances in later years.

Oliver Knight, having lived in the family 'folk commune' in Robin Hood's Bay in Yorkshire from the age of seven, had plenty of opportunity to develop his skills. After taking up guitar at the age of 13 he joined several rock and blues bands before forming Tannteka with Jo Freya, Andy Cutting and Alice Kinloch. Trained as a studio engineer, he also recorded and engineered Eliza Carthy's 1996 album, *Heat, Light & Sound*. The mother and son duo first recorded together for a sampler album for the No Master's Voice Co-operative, performing the track 'Midnight Feast'. It led to their collaboration on the 1996 Topic Records' album *Once In A Blue Moon*, which attracted a great deal of critical praise for the unusual arrangements made possible by Oliver's inventive guitar playing and his mother's distinctive voice. Sadly, Lal Waterson died of cancer two years later. Another fine collection, *A Bed Of Roses*, was completed shortly before her death, and gained a posthumous release the following year.
● ALBUMS: *Once In A Blue Moon* (Topic 1996)★★★★, *A Bed Of Roses* (Topic 1999)★★★.

Waterson, Norma

b. Norma Christine Waterson, 15 August 1939, Kingston Upon Hull, East Riding, Yorkshire, England. Both sides of Waterson's family were musical, her father playing guitar and piano, her mother the piano. Almost all of her extended family were accomplished musicians on one instrument or another. However, she was orphaned at an early age and raised, alongside her sister Elaine (Lal Waterson) and brother Mike, by her grandmother. They formed their first informal band together in the late 50s, singing around local tea houses and friends' homes. Later they opened one of the first folk clubs in Yorkshire, which still exists today. In the early 60s Lal, Mike and Norma formed the Watersons, alongside their cousin, John Harrison. One of the most influential harmony vocals bands on the English folk scene of that time, they toured widely before their break-up in 1968. They reformed in 1972, at which time Harrison's place was taken first by Bernie Vickers then Martin Carthy, who married Norma in the same year (their daughter, Eliza Carthy, is currently the darling of the new generation of contemporary UK folk singers). The Watersons have continued to appear together sporadically ever since, though each member has also concentrated on solo activities. Norma's first extra-curricular recording was a collaboration with sister Lal, 1977's *A True Hearted Girl*. She was also a prominent member of the Waterdaughters, a band comprising the female members of the Watersons family. In 1996, a year after recording an acclaimed set with her daughter and husband, *Waterson: Carthy*, Norma made her solo debut proper. It came as a result of a performance with Lal at the McCabes club in Los Angeles two years previously. Lal was taken ill leading to an improvised solo spot for Norma. Club organiser John Chelew, a record producer in his own right, was so taken with Norma's voice he implored her to record a solo album. Joe Boyd backed the project and the resulting self-titled collection saw her record a number of contemporary compositions; including songs by Billy Bragg ('St. Swithin's Day'), Elvis Costello ('The Birds Will Still Be Singing'), Jerry Garcia ('Black Muddy River') and Ben Harper ('Pleasure And Pain')

alongside more traditional English folk songs. Her backing band included Richard Thompson (guitar), Danny Thompson (bass) and family members Martin Carthy (guitar) and Eliza Carthy (violin). The album was a masterpiece of controlled and effortless beauty. Her voice has the rich patina of age and as she sings each lyric the listener is aware that she *has* been there. Whatever the subject, you feel that Waterson has shared the experience. A late developer as a solo artist, but one of the decade's folk highlights. The album was nominated for the Mercury Music Prize, but was beaten by Pulp's *Different Class*. An album of similarly eclectic choice followed in 1999, with sensitive interpretations of songs by Nick Drake and John Martyn.
● ALBUMS: with Lal Waterson *A True Hearted Girl* (Topic 1977)★★★, with Eliza Carthy, Martin Carthy *Waterson: Carthy* (Topic 1995)★★★★, *Norma Waterson* (Hannibal 1996)★★★★, *The Very Thought Of You* (Hannibal 1999)★★★, with Eliza Carthy, Martin Carthy *Broken Ground* (Topic 1999)★★★★.

Watley, Jody

b. 30 January 1959, Chicago, Illinois, USA. Formerly one third of Shalamar between 1977 and 1984, a hugely successful group of the disco era, Watley's first professional experience had come as a dancer on the television show *Soul Train*. After Shalamar disbanded she made the progression to solo artist, working in a contemporary soul/urban R&B vein. Her self-titled debut album, released in 1987, became a million-seller and included three US Top 10 hits - 'Looking For A New Love', 'Don't You Want Me' and 'Some Kind Of Lover'. It brought her a Grammy award for best new artist of 1987. The subsequent *Larger Than Life* achieved gold status, and included the US number 2 hit 'Real Love', as well as further hits 'Everything' and 'Friends', a collaboration with Eric B And Rakim and Whodini. 'Precious Love' (1990) was remixed by Soul II Soul's Simon Law and 'I'm The One You Need' by David Morales and Drizabone as part of the remix project, *You Wanna Dance With Me?*. Though not replicating the scale of earlier successes, the release of *Affairs Of The Heart* and *Intimacy* consolidated her position as one of the most energetic and able contemporary soul singers, readily adaptable to changes in R&B such as the swingbeat movement. She moved to Avitone Records in 1995 for *Affection* On *Flower* she collaborated with artists including Rakim, Masters At Work, Rahsaan Patterson and Changing Faces.
● ALBUMS: *Jody Watley* (MCA 1987)★★★, *Larger Than Life* (MCA 1989)★★★, *You Wanna Dance With Me?* (MCA 1989)★★, *Affairs Of The Heart* (MCA 1991)★★★, *Intimacy* (MCA 1994)★★★, *Affection* (Avitone 1995)★★★, *Flower* (Atlantic 1998)★★★.

Way Out West

This eclectic dance music duo was formed in Bristol, England by Jody Wisternoff and Nick Warren. The latter was a veteran DJ of the Liverpool club Cream and had also previously collaborated with Massive Attack and Smith And Mighty. The duo originally released two independent singles as Echo in the early 90s and as Way Out West continued to record independently, releasing a brace of singles for Peace Of The Action. In 1994, they were signed by James Barton (the organizer of Cream) to Deconstruction Records and achieved immediate success with 'Ajare', released at the end of 1994. Following the success in the clubs of the single 'Domination' they achieved more widespread success when their atmospheric single 'The Gift' reached the UK Top 20 in the summer of 1996. Rather than issue a quick follow-up, Wisternoff and Warren became involved with remix and production work with Dubstar, Fluke and the Orb. With the proceeds from this work they were able to overhaul and upgrade their existing studio. Their self-titled debut album was branded by some sections of the dance community as the 'sunrise sound', reflecting the warm, dreamlike qualities of such songs as 'Blue', the album's first single. Way Out West have remixed a number of other artists including Saint Etienne and Reprazent.

● ALBUMS: *Way Out West* (Deconstruction 1997)★★★.

Weatherall, Andy

b. 6 April 1963. Dance music magnate Weatherall began the 80s working on building sites and film sets before picking up DJ work. His career proper began with residencies at the Shoom and Spectrum clubs in the acid house boom of 1988. Afterwards he founded the *Boy's Own* fanzine with Terry Farley (of Farley And Heller) and Steve Mayes, which concentrated on club music, fashion and football. When Boy's Own became a record label, he also appeared, as a guest vocalist, on a Bocca Juniors' track. He made his name, however, by remixing Primal Scream's 'Loaded'. Artists including James, Happy Mondays, That Petrol Emotion, Saint Etienne, Grid, Meat Beat Manifesto, Big Hard Excellent Fish, S'Express, the Orb, Finitribe, A Man Called Adam, Jah Wobble, Future Sound Of London, Moody Boyz, One Dove, Throbbing Gristle, Galliano, Flowered Up, Björk, Espiritu, Yello, Stereo MC's and New Order followed. His landmark achievement, however, remains his supervising role on old friend's Primal Scream's *Screamadelica* - the album which effectively forged a new musical genre, the indie/dance crossover album. He also enjoyed a stint as DJ on Kiss 100 FM, before his eclectic, anarchic tastes proved too much for programmers. 'My background is rock 'n' roll. The Clash are still the best band in the world'. His recording methodology has been compared to that of Joe Meek: sampling strange sounds such as answerphones and dustbin lids for percussion. He subsequently set up a further label, recording and remix operation under the title Sabres Of Paradise, which proved hugely successful. Weatherall continued to play out regularly at Sabresonic club nights, and in 1993 signed a major publishing deal with MCA Music. His most recent project is an ongoing collaboration with Keith Tenniswood as the Two Lone Swordsmen.

Ween

This prolific duo from New Hope, Pennsylvania, USA, are as out of step with everything that surrounds them as a modern rock band could ever hope to be. They have their own religion, led by demon god Boognish, and delight in lyrical and musical mischief-making. The core of the band is Gene (b. Aaron Freeman) and Dean Ween (b. Micky Melchiondo). They have been compared to everyone from Prince to Captain Beefheart. They started their career in elaborate style with a double album that opened with a menacing track called 'You Fucked Up'. From there on *God Ween Satan - The Oneness* floated in and out of a collage of cheerfully artless songs, sampling reggae ('Nicole'), space metal ('Mushroom Festival In Hell'), Flamenco ('El Camino') and blues ('I Gots A Weasel'). It was surprisingly enjoyable, and

included parodies of Bruce Springsteen, the Beastie Boys and other members of pop's aristocracy. As they said at the time, '99% of our lyrics are written from personal experience and focus on our own lives. We're very honest in that respect.' They also insist that, essentially, every new Ween album is a 'greatest hits' collection, spanning two years' work, with hundreds of hours kept in the can at any given time. Following an even more bizarre follow-up, *The Pod*, many were surprised when Elektra Records signed such a left-field concern. *Pure Guava* showed the band had lost none of their idiosyncrasies (memorable song titles this time included 'Hey Fat Boy (Asshole)' and 'Poop Ship Destroyer'). The band became Flying Nun Records' first non-New Zealand signings in 1994, for European distribution. *Chocolate And Cheese* saw the introduction of a permanent rhythm section for the first time, in the shape of Andrew Weiss (ex-Henry Rollins Band), who had previously produced for the band, and Claude Coleman, and it came with a dedication to the comedian/actor John Candy. It confirmed their sick sense of humour in tracks such as 'Spinal Meningitis' and 'Mister Won't You Please Help My Pony', although there seemed to be little attempt to extend their appeal. *12 Golden Country Greats* featured the legendary Jordanaires on harmonies, a coup which was ignored in a series of harsh reviews. The following year's *The Mollusk* restored their musical pastiches to more traditional territory.

● ALBUMS: *God Ween Satan - The Oneness* (Twin/Tone 1990)★★★, *The Pod* (Shimmy-Disc 1991)★★, *Pure Guava* (Elektra 1992)★★★, *Chocolate And Cheese* (Elektra 1994)★★, *12 Golden Country Greats* (Elektra/Flying Nun 1996)★★, *The Mollusk* (Mushroom 1997)★★★.

● COMPILATIONS: *Paintin' The Town Brown: Ween Live '90-'98* (Mushroom 1999)★★★.

Weezer

'Post-slacker' US guitar pop artisans from Los Angeles, California, USA, comprising Rivers Cuomo (b. Connecticut, USA; vocals/guitar), Brian Bell (b. Tennessee, USA; guitar), Matt Sharp (bass) and Patrick Wilson (b. Buffalo, New York State, USA; drums). Cuomo grew up in rural Connecticut before deciding to move to Los Angeles at the age of 18 to form a band. It was to little immediate success, but, tortured by the sundering of a relationship, he began to write his own songs. Sharp brought the unlikely influences of Talk Talk and Gary Numan to the bass player's role. Bell first learnt guitar in Tennessee by playing along to television shows such as *Hee Haw*, picking on a ukulele his grandmother won at a bingo game. Wilson was introduced to the other members via fellow Buffalo citizen Pat Fin (of Winkler). The four protagonists had met as strangers who found themselves abroad in Los Angeles, and decided to form a band together. The official date of formation was 14 February 1992, signing to DGC Records in June of the following year. On the back of offbeat singles, 'Undone - The Sweater Song' and 'Buddy Holly' (a tale of high school prom rejection featuring a memorable *Happy Days* pastiche video), and seven months' touring their native country, their self-titled debut album, produced by Ric Ocasek of the Cars and Chris Shaw in New York, went on to sell nearly a million copies. Their preference for goofy garage aesthetics soon distinguished them, and, with fuzzboxes and falsetto harmonies (from Sharp) to the fore, comparisons to They Might Be Giants hardly delineated their musical compass, despite helping to pinpoint their humour. The participants, meanwhile, remained awestruck at the depth of their appeal: 'We've sold all these albums when, honestly speaking, we're a super straight-ahead American guitar garage rock band'. The title of their 1996 album infuriated the security company Pinkerton Service, and they issued legal proceedings shortly after its release. Wilson and Sharp also recorded with the Rentals; the latter left Weezer in 1998 to concentrate on this new outfit.

● ALBUMS: *Weezer* (DGC 1994)★★★★, *Pinkerton* (DGC 1996)★★★.

Welch, Gillian

b. California, USA. Welch's debut album drew strong acclaim for its revival of Appalachian musical styles and the lyrical evocation of Depression-era rural America. The daughter of Hollywood television composers, Welch attended the Berklee College Of Music in Boston, where she met her musical and songwriting partner David Rawlings. They began playing bluegrass clubs as a duo, gradually incorporating original material into a set consisting of traditional country songs. Moving to Nashville in 1993, they gained a writing contract at Almo-Irving, before Welch signed as a solo artist to Almo Sounds. Produced by T-Bone Burnett, *Revival* (marketed under Welch's name, but essentially a duo album with Rawlings) featured a stellar list of session men including James Burton, Roy Huskey Jnr., Buddy Harmon and Jim Keltner. Beautifully melodic and brutally moral, the songs ranged from the dirty, rockabilly groove of 'Pass You By' to the sparse gospel of 'By The Mark', a surprise favourite on American alternative radio. Though often seen as part of the 'alternative country' scene, Welch and Rawlings have supported more mainstream artists such as Mark Knopfler and Emmylou Harris. The latter had provided Welch with her first success when she covered 'Orphan Girl' on her acclaimed *Wrecking Ball*. Burnett was again hired to record 1998's critically acclaimed *Hell Among The Yearlings*, which featured just Welch and Rawlings on a collection of songs marked by their melancholic beauty.

● ALBUMS: *Revival* (Almo 1996)★★★★, *Hell Among The Yearlings* (Almo 1998)★★★★.

Weller, Paul

b. John William Weller, 25 May 1958, Woking, Surrey, England. The rise and fall from critical grace, and subsequent rise of vocalist and guitarist Paul Weller could occupy a small chapter in any book on UK rock music of the 70s, 80s and 90s. The recipient of almost universal acclaim and 'spokesman for a generation' accolades with the Jam, after the release of the Style Council's second album his relationship with the press became one of almost total antipathy, some might argue with good reason; the thread of soul-stirring passion that had always seen Weller at his most affecting had been squandered in a less earnest quest for dry musical sophistication. The fact that he was now married (to Style Council backing vocalist D.C. Lee) and a father of two children contributed to what he later admitted was a lack of thirst for music. By 1990, he found himself without either a band or a recording contract for the first time in 13 years. This period saw him reacquaint himself with some of his old influences, the omnipresent Small Faces/Steve Marriott fixation, as well as discover new ones such as house and acid jazz, as well as Traffic, Spooky Tooth, Tim Hardin and Tim Buckley. Inspired enough to write new material, despite his

recent travails with the Style Council having drained him of confidence, he began to set up a new band in the autumn. Comprising Paul Francis (bass), Max Beesley (keyboards/vibraphone), Jacko Peake (saxophone/flute), Joe Becket (percussion), Damon Brown (trumpet/flügelhorn), Chris Lawrence (trombone) as well as Jam biographer and 'best friend' Paulo Hewitt (DJ) and Style Council drummer Steve White, the band was christened the Paul Weller Movement. They made their live debut on UK tours in November and December, with a second spree in April 1991. These served to renew Weller's previously unimpeachable self-belief and test new songs like 'Round And Round' and 'Kosmos'. The line-up now saw Henry Thomas (formerly of music education television programme *Rock School*) on bass, with the brass section reduced to Gerard Prescencer (trumpet/flügelhorn), with Zeta Massiah and Lina Duggan on backing vocals.

Weller released his first solo single, 'Into Tomorrow', on his own Freedom High label in May, before contributing seven compositions to D.C. Lee's Slam Slam project. However, he was still refining his muse and the vast majority of the Movement and the name itself were dispensed with, leaving a kernel of White and Peake with guests including Robert Howard (aka Dr. Robert of the Blow Monkeys), Marco Nelson of the Young Disciples, Style Council bass player Camille Hinds and singer Carleen Anderson. However the debut album was delayed for almost a year while he searched for a suitable label. It was initially released on Pony Canyon in Japan, where Weller maintained a formidable personal popularity, six months before a UK issue on Go! Discs. *Paul Weller* was strangely overlooked by the UK press, who at this stage seemed resistant to the artist's revival, despite the presence of fine songs in 'Clues' and 'Strange Museum'. Further line-up changes accrued during the quiet early months of 1992, with Orange Juice drummer Zeke Manyika joining, as did former Style Council compatriot Helen Turner (organ). The subject of second single 'Uh Huh, Oh Yeh' was Weller's Woking youth, and its Top 20 UK status kindled a prodigal-son welcome from the UK press. This was confirmed in 1993 with the release of 'Sunflower', a breezy, Traffic-inspired folk rock enterprise, and *Wild Wood*, arguably the finest collection of songs Weller had written since the Jam's *All Mod Cons*. With a fresh, natural production from Brendan Lynch, and multitudinous musical accompaniment from White, Turner, Beesley and Howard plus Mick Talbot (Weller's former Style Council songwriting collaborator), D.C. Lee, Simon Fowler and Steve Cradock (Ocean Colour Scene), the set was nevertheless firmly located in the classic English singer-songwriter pantheon. Live favourites 'The Weaver' and 'Hung Up' again reached the charts as Weller was at last able to shake off the albatross of his previous musical ventures. He was joined on tour in Japan by new bass player Yolanda Charles in October, while early 1994 saw him jamming on stage with Kenny Jones (Faces), James Taylor and Mother Earth for the filming of *The History Of Acid Jazz*. The summer of that year saw euphoric performances at the Glastonbury and Phoenix Festival stages, before a 1994 double live album drawn from four different sets between late 1993 and mid-1994. For the first time in a decade Weller had cultivated a new set of fans, rather than dragging existing followers with him, and this fact drew evident satisfaction. *Stanley Road* was titled after the street in which Weller grew up, and featured Oasis' Noel Gallagher on a cover version of Dr. John's 'Walk On Gilded Splinters'. Of more enduring interest were the Weller originals, however, which spanned a wide range of musical styles unified by the 'live' approach to recording. The follow-up *Heavy Soul* showed Weller to be at the peak of his musical powers, and, for the time being, still retaining the support of the majority of the music press.

● ALBUMS: *Paul Weller* (Go! Discs 1992)★★, *Wild Wood* (Go! Discs 1994)★★★★, *Live Wood* (Go! Discs 1994)★★★, *Stanley Road* (Go! Discs 1995)★★★★, *Heavy Soul* (Island 1997)★★★★.

● COMPILATIONS: *Modern Classics* (Island 1998)★★★★.

● VIDEOS: *The Paul Weller Movement Live* (Video Collection 1991), *Highlights And Hang Ups* (PolyGram Music Video 1994), *Live Wood* (PolyGram Music Video 1994).

● FURTHER READING: *Days Lose Their Names And Time Slips Away: Paul Weller 1992-95*, Lawrence Watson and Paulo Hewitt. *Paul Weller: My Ever Changing Moods*, John Reed. *The Unauthorised Biography*, Steve Malins. *Paul Weller: In His Own Words*, Michael Heatley.

Wemba, Papa

b. Shungu Wembiado, 1952, Kasai, Zaire. Wemba's musical roots can be traced to 1969 when he formed Zaiko Langa Langa. The idea was to update traditional African sounds with the imported rhythms and melodies of the West, including rock and R&B. Zaiko Langa Langa was an experimental concern, using multitudinous singers to produce harmonies and chants, with electric instruments and drum kits brought home by Zairean students living in Belgium. He left in 1970 to form Isifi Lokole, then Yoka Lokole and, in 1977, Viva La Musica. On leaving Zaiko Langa Langa, he kept up the ragged, streetwise sound, the 'beau desordre', associated with the group, his voice adding a high wailing tone that cut through two decades of sweet Kinshasa harmonies. Kinshasa's Radio Trottoir first fastened on to Wemba during his Isifi Lokole days, when he was accused of an illicit affair with a young girl and spent a few days in jail. Viva La Musica took its name from a 'charanga' song by Johnny Pacheco. He also re-introduced a traditional instrument to the music, the lokolé, a hollow tree trunk played with two sticks like a drum, which was conventionally used to pass messages between neighbouring villages. In Zaire, Brussels and Paris, Wemba's followers, and those of other great fashion leaders, are known as 'Sapeurs', members of the Societe Des Ambianceurs et des Personnes Elegantes. The hallmarks are the same: expensive clothes, bearing the most prestigious of designer labels from Giorgio Armani to Cardin and Jimmy Weston. One particular song, 'Matebu', has become the Sapeurs' hymn. During the course of such songs, Wemba has been known to balance his shoes, doubtless Westons, on his head and turn round his vest to show off the labels. Overseas, Wemba has also made an impact - with 'La Firenze', which praises Florence, Paris, Tokyo and other style centres, introducing electro handclaps and a beat-box into a straight, sharper soukous style. For the true, exuberant Wemba, though, it is necessary to listen to albums like *La Vie Comme Elle Va Bola* (1984), with its electric-saw vocals rising above echoing guitars and a wall of ragged harmonies that seem to have come straight off a night-time Kinshasa street. His debut solo album, recorded in collaboration with producer Martin Messonier, was released in 1988. Genuine acclaim, though, arrived with *Le Voyageur*, which saw him

make his debut on Real World Records. Here he risked alienating African purists by forging an international style which was both distinct and innovative. Even more cosmopolitan was 1995's *Emotion*, overseen in the studio by Pet Shop Boys/Erasure producer Stephen Hague. Just as important was the contribution of keyboard player Jean-Philippe Rykiel (a collaborator with Salif Keita and Youssou N'Dour), Papa Noel (bass) and Christian Polloni (guitar), though regular backing vocalists Reddy Amisi and Stino had been replaced by female accompanists. Of many notable tracks perhaps the most interesting was a cover version of Otis Redding's 'Fa-Fa-Fa-Fa-Fa (Sad Song)', Wemba's favourite singer. Despite his obvious desire to seek international success, elsewhere his impressive vocals remained rooted in his own native Lingala language, helping to offset accusations that he had turned his back on the continent of his birth. He also maintains a separate, 20-piece soukous orchestra for 'real African music fans', as further evidence of this commitment. His third album for Real World was co-produced by noted English producer, John Leckie (Fall, Radiohead), and proved to be a more vibrant collection than previous albums.

● ALBUMS: *Papa Wemba* (Stern's 1988)★★★, *La Vie Est Belle* (Stern's 1988)★★★, *Le Voyageur* (Real World 1992)★★★, *Foridolis* (Viva La Musica 1994)★★★, *Kershaw Sessions* (Strange Roots 1994)★★★, *Emotion* (Real World 1995)★★, *Molokai* (Real World 1998)★★★★.

Westerberg, Paul

b. 31 December 1960, Minneapolis, Minnesota, USA. Westerberg had been planning a solo project even before his band, the Replacements, imploded in 1991, but his first work under his own name comprised two tracks on the soundtrack of the 1992 'slacker' movie *Singles*. This was followed by *14 Songs*, perceived by some critics to be a return to the punked-up glory days of Bob Stinson-era Replacements, and including 'World Class Fad', a warning to the fast-living likes of Nirvana's Kurt Cobain. By 1996, however, Westerberg appeared to be ready to leave his punk days behind. *Eventually* was more overtly influenced by 60s pop and soul, and even offered tinges of folk rock, with acoustic guitars given more prominence than feedback-heavy riffing. The lyrics again provided rueful reflection on past excesses: 'Decided not to raise some mixed-up kid/Just like my mama and daddy did' could almost be a mantra for the redeemed hell raiser. The album also saw a reunion with Replacements bass player Tommy Stinson on 'Trumpet Clip', although the track owed more to the Kinks than to their original band. Westerberg ended his association with Warner Brothers Records shortly afterwards, releasing a single and an EP under the Grandpaboy name in 1997. After signing to Capitol Records in America, Westerberg recorded most of his third album in his own basement studio. Producer Don Was concurred with the singer about leaving the songs on *Suicaine Gratification* in their raw, unembellished state.

● ALBUMS: *14 Songs* (Sire/Reprise 1993)★★, *Eventually* (Reprise 1996)★★★, *Grandpaboy* mini-album (Monolyth/Soundproof 1997)★★★, *Suicaine Gratification* (EMI/Chrysalis 1999)★★★★.

Westlife

This Irish boy band, originally known as Westside, emerged in the late 90s as the highly successful protégés of Ronan Keating of Boyzone. The three founding members, Kian Egan (b. 29 April 1980, Sligo, Eire), Shane Filan (b. 5 July

1979, Sligo, Eire) and Mark Feehily (28 May 1980, Sligo, Ireland), came together in a local Sligo production of *Grease*. They formed IOU with three fellow actors after friends encouraged them to continue singing, and began performing cover versions in local clubs. A demo tape of a track written by Filan and Feehily, 'Together Girl Forever', found its way to Boyzone manager Louis Walsh. Suitably impressed, Walsh hired them to support US boy band Backstreet Boys when they visited Dublin. A change of line-up ensued, with three of the original members making way for ex-soccer player Nicky Byrne (b. 9 October 1978, Dublin, Eire) and Bryan McFadden (b. 12 April 1980, Dublin, Eire). Keating became involved with the band as co-manager in April 1998. After a showcase appearance at London's Café de Paris in February 1999, the band changed their name to Westlife after learning of the existence of several American acts performing as Westside. Groomed as natural successors to Boyzone, the quartet's debut single 'Swear It Again', was a highly predictable Irish and UK chart-topper in May. The follow-up, 'If I Let You Go', repeated the feat when it entered the UK singles chart at number 1 in August. 'Flying Without Wings' made it three number 1s in a row in October. Their status as the most popular boy band of the moment was underlined when their lame double a-side, featuring cover versions of Abba's 'I Have A Dream' and Terry Jacks' 'Seasons In The Sun', topped the charts for four weeks over Christmas and the new year.

● ALBUMS: *Westlife* (RCA 1999)★★★.

Westside Connection

A three-way collaboration between rappers Ice Cube (b. O'Shea Jackson, 15 June 1969, Crenshaw, South Central Los Angeles, California, USA), Mack 10 (b. D. Rolison, 9 August 1971, Inglewood, California, USA) and W.C., Westside Connection was started as a riposte to what the participants saw as 'dissing' by their east coast colleagues. The tone of 1996's *Bow Down* was one of outright hostility, particularly on tracks such as 'King Of The Hill', Ice Cube's vindictive attack on the main protagonists in Cypress Hill. 'Sen Dog you can't rap from the guts/And B-Real sounding like he got baby nuts/Comin' with voice high-pitched/The B in B-Real must stand for bitch'. More discerning hip-hop commentators reacted with dismay at one of the most vicious albums in gangsta rap's already controversial history. In truth, the album was also a musical disappointment, displaying an over-reliance on repetitive, stripped-down funk to underpin its bleak lyrical narratives.

● ALBUMS: *Bow Down* (Priority 1996)★★.

Whale

The outlandish rock band Whale, from Stockholm, Sweden, are led by vocalist Cia Berg, famed for delivering songs such as 'Young, Dumb 'n' Full Of Cum' without a trace of self-consciousness. She formed the band in the early 90s in collusion with guitarist, semi-professional comedian and one-time fiancé Henrik Schyffert. They first met when Schyffert, a veteran of several punk bands such as Ubangi, was producing a Swedish pop show, *Topp E Pop*. He invited Berg to become the show's host. Also part of the new team was hip-hop producer and bass player Gordon Cyrus, who originally provided the show with its background music. Their initial intention, in addition to writing radio jingles together, was to

release just one single as Whale. However, when MTV began to play the resultant artefact, the typically salacious 'Hobo Humpin' Slobo Babe' (concerning a rich girl who 'gets off' on sleeping with tramps), their career change was made permanent. The following singles, 'Pay For Me' and 'I'll Do Ya', were also heavily endorsed by MTV. Live, the combination of conventional heavy metal (they cite old-school rockers Saxon and Judas Priest as a major influence) was skewered on Cyrus' hip-hop beats and funk grooves, providing a platform for Berg's animated, sexually-themed vocals. *We Care*, which included a guest appearance from Tricky on two tracks, provided a more restrained, yet still vibrant version of that sound. It was recorded in a small studio in the Spanish countryside owned by manager Cameron McVey, who lives there with his wife Neneh Cherry. In 1998, augmented by three new members, the band released the vibrant *All Disco Dance Must End In Broken Bones*.

● ALBUMS: *We Care* (Hut 1995)★★★, *All Disco Dance Must End In Broken Bones* (Hut 1998)★★★.

Wheat

Formed in Taughton, Massachusetts, USA in 1995 by college friends Scott Levesque (guitar/vocals) and Brendan Harney (drums), with the line-up completed by Ricky Brennan (guitar) and Kenny Madaras (bass). The band signed to the newly formed Chicago-based independent label, Sugar Free Records, shortly afterwards. *Medeiros*, a country-influenced alternative rock collection, drew comparisons to venerable bands such as Sebadoh and Pavement, and newer arrivals Sparklehorse and Smog, with Levesque's evocative songwriting reaching an early creative peak on 'Karmic Episodes' and 'Summer'. Reduced to a trio following the departure of Madaras, the band recorded *Hope And Adams* with producer David Fridmann. The Mercury Rev associate polished off the rough edges of the band's sound while still retaining their ramshackle charm. The subtle embellishments added new depths to the downbeat sentiments of songs such as 'Don't I Hold You', 'Who's The One' and 'No One Ever Told Me'. Kevin Camarce was recruited as the band's new bass player shortly afterwards.

● ALBUMS: *Medeiros* (Sugar Free 1997)★★★, *Hope And Adams* (City Slang 1999)★★★★.

Whigfield

b. Sannie Charlotte Carlson, Denmark. Whigfield, her stage-name derived from the surname of a former music teacher, made her debut in 1994 with 'Saturday Night', a repetitive example of Europop which became a huge international seller on release in September of that year, reaching the top of the UK charts and selling over 750,000 copies in its first week of release. It was the Barcelona-based former model's debut single, though it had originally been released in Italy in 1992. Though purists saw it as the antithesis of art, Whigfield herself merely lapped up the attention: 'The greatest satisfaction was hearing cameramen and technicians on *Top Of The Pops* saying that they hated it, then afterwards hearing them all humming it.' She appeared widely on television with her distinctive braided hair to support the single, but several commentators questioned the authenticity of the product. They pointed instead to the involvement of producer Larry Pignagnoli (formerly behind Ivana Spagna) and writer David River. The follow-up single,

'Another Day', adopted a similar approach to reduced effect, although it still reached the UK Top 10. Before Whigfield, Carlson had spent several years playing in a jazz-based duo, the Whigfield Project, with her brother in Denmark (her brother publicly disowned her after the success of 'Saturday Night'). A third UK Top 10 hit single, 'Think Of You', accompanied the release of her debut album. In 1995, Whigfield presented an edition of BBC Television's *Top Of The Pops*, and drew a series of complaints for the revealing costume she wore. Later attempts to revive her career have failed.
● ALBUMS: *Whigfield* (Systematic 1995)★★.

Whiskeytown

Raleigh, North Carolina-based alternative country band led by songwriter David Ryan Adams (vocals/guitar/banjo). Adams was raised in Jacksonville, North Carolina, and formed high school punk band the Patty Duke Syndrome in his teens. He reverted to more traditional musical forms with Whiskeytown, formed in 1994 with Phil Wandscher (guitar/vocals), Caitlin Cary (violin/vocals), Eric 'Skillet' Gilmore (drums/vocals) and Steve Grothman (bass). The band issued the *Angels* EP on North Carolina independent Mood Food Records the same year. They contributed a cover version of Richard Hell's 'Blank Generation' to a tribute compilation in 1995, before embarking on sessions for their debut album. Recorded in The Funny Farm studio in the tiny hamlet of Apex, *Faithless Street* appeared in January 1996. The album's mix of George Jones/Gram Parsons-styled emotional country songs ('Drank Like A River', 'Black Arrow, Bleeding Heart') and rough punkish rock 'n' roll ('Top Dollar') followed in the footsteps of alternative country pioneers Uncle Tupelo. Adams' abrasive and reckless vocal style was reminiscent of Paul Westerberg of the Replacements, although Cary contributed the album's most affecting vocal on 'Matrimony'. The band attracted the interest of several majors on the strength of some highly praised live appearances, subsequently signing to the Outpost label, a subsidiary of Geffen Records. Adams, Wandscher, Cary, Jeff Rice and new drummer Steve Terry recorded the material for the Jim Scott-produced *Strangers Almanac*, although Wandscher left shortly afterwards. Released in June 1997, the album progressed from the gentle, acoustic harmonies of 'Inn Town' and '16 Days' to the aggressive foot to the floor stomp of tracks such as 'Yesterday's News' and 'Waiting To Derail'. Adams songwriting attracted particular praise, showing a marked progression from *Faithless Street*. *Rural Free Delivery* was a collection of older material put together by their former label. Chris Stamey (ex-dB's) and Tim Harper (who had worked with another Raleigh band, the Connells) were hired by Outpost to work on a re-engineered and expanded version of *Faithless Street*, which contained material from 1996's Baseball Park Sessions. The current line-up of the band comprises Adams, Cary, Ed Crawford (guitar/vocals, ex-fIREHOSE), Mike Daly (keyboards/guitar), Jenni Snyder (bass), with founder member Gilmore returning on drums.
● ALBUMS: *Faithless Street* (Mood Food 1996)★★★, *Strangers Almanac* (Outpost 1997)★★★★, *Faithless Street* expanded/remastered version (Outpost 1998)★★★.
● COMPILATIONS: *Rural Free Delivery* (Mood Food 1997)★★★.

Whisky Priests

Strongly influenced by the Pogues and The Men They Couldn't Hang, the Whisky Priests evolved as a five-piece in the late 80s around the nucleus of twins Gary and Glenn Miller, and Bill Bulmer. Their repertoire consisted of lively mixture of the traditional, and their own material, delivered in strong north east England dialect. Two 1988 EPs, *No Chance* and *Grandfatha's Fatha*, indicated their future direction. The lyrics are based on their experience of growing up in County Durham. After the two EPs, they worked briefly as a trio, before expanding to include Pete French (Northumbrian pipes/fiddle), Mick Tyas (bass) and Steve Green (drums), and recorded their debut, *Nee Gud Luck*, in 1989. The style remained uncompromising, and the power of the songs undiluted, but it was their last release for three years. A compilation of earlier recordings, and the new *Timeless Street*, heralded a resurgence in 1992. This was followed by extensive touring, and *Bloody Well Live*, a good example of their finely-honed punk-folk. *Life's Tapestry* saw Gary Miller coming to the forefront as a fine songwriter.
● ALBUMS: *Nee Gud Luck* (1989)★★★, *Timeless Street* (1992)★★★★, *Bloody Well Live* (1993)★★, *Bleeding Sketches* (Whippet 1995)★★★, *Life's Tapestry* (Whippet 1996)★★★, *Think Positive* (Whippet 1998)★★★, *Here Come The Ranting Lads - Live* (Whippet 1999)★★★.
● COMPILATIONS: *The First Few Drops* (1992)★★★.
● VIDEOS: *Here Come The Ranting Lads - Live* (Whippet 1999).

White Town

Jyoti Mishra (b. 30 July 1966, Rourkela, India) appears to embody a number of peculiar trends in 90s pop: the bedroom one-man band; the self-sufficient indie scene; the unexpected marriage of wildly different musical styles and traditions; and, so far at least, the 'unknown' act that leaps to number 1, apparently from nowhere, then disappears from sight. His family moved to Derby, England in 1969 and Mishra's first brush with fame was playing keyboards with local band Daryl And The Chaperones. He then began touring the clubs as a solo synthesiser act, performing covers of Buzzcocks songs, before, under the influence of the Wedding Present and the Pixies, he formed White Town as a guitar band. He began releasing singles on his own Satya Records, at the same time producing other bands and DJing in indie clubs. Five more limited edition singles followed before the debut album came together, by which time the other band members had fallen away and White Town was, effectively, Mishra. A portly Asian on a scene that favours skinny white kids, he was something of a local character in the Midlands but it was not until Radio 1 disc jockey Mark Radcliffe began to play 'Your Woman', a bizarre fusion of dance-beats and sampled 30s jazz trumpet (Nat Gonella's introducion to Lew Stone's 'My Woman'), cobbled together on Mishra's eight-track home studio, that White Town finally went overground. Re-released by Chrysalis Records, it went straight to the top of the UK charts in early 1997, despite Mishra's refusal to make a video or appear on BBC Television's *Top Of The Pops*. He went down well with music journalists, revealing a delightfully anorak knowledge of acts as diverse as the Rah Band, Michael Nesmith, Landscape and the Merseys but his first album on a major label was not really strong enough to justify the original promise.
● ALBUMS: *Socialism, Sexism and Sexuality* (Parasol 1994)★★★, *Women In Technology* (Chrysalis 1997)★★.

White Zombie

This theatrical metal band was formed in 1985 in the Lower East Side of New York City, New York, USA, and were named after a horror movie. Led by Rob 'Zombie' Straker and female bass player Sean Yseult, with drummer Ivan DePlume and guitarist Tom Guay, White Zombie released two albums of noisy metal on their own label while they played chaotic shows around local clubs to increasing acclaim from the underground press. John Ricci replaced Guay on guitar for *Make Them Die Slowly*, and the band's more focused approach helped rid them of the art-noise label that had been placed upon their earlier albums. However, Bill Laswell's production still failed to capture the band's raw onstage power. Musical differences meant that Ricci was replaced by Jay Yuenger, who made his debut on the *God Of Thunder* EP, a cover of the Kiss classic (rumoured legal action from Gene Simmons over the use of his copyrighted make-up image on the sleeve never materialized). The Andy Wallace production on their major label debut, *La Sexorcisto: Devil Music Vol. 1*, finally did White Zombie justice, with Rob Zombie sounding positively demonic as he roared his bizarre stream-of-consciousness lyrics against a monstrous instrumental barrage punctuated by sampled B-movie dialogue. This also proved to be their breakthrough album as White Zombie toured the USA ceaselessly, extending their tours continually as MTV played 'Thunder Kiss 65' and 'Black Sunshine' regularly, with further support coming from cartoon critics *Beavis And Butthead*. As *La Sexorcisto* took off, Philo replaced DePlume, only to be sacked as the touring finally ended, reinstated, and then replaced by ex-Exodus/Testament drummer John Tempesta as White Zombie returned to the studio. The long-delayed *Astro Creep 2000* was greeted with enthusiasm in the American rock community, selling over a million copies in a few weeks. The single, 'More Human Than Human', also became a major hit, with plays on mainstream radio stations that had previously shunned the band. They continued to tour widely, now with a Rob Zombie-designed stage set designed as a replica of a junkyard. Yuenger also involved himself in two notable collaborative projects. The first, with bandmate Yseult, was work with Dave Navarro (Red Hot Chili Peppers), Keith Morris (Circle Jerks) and Greg Rogers (ex-Obsessed), masquerading as Zombie All Stars for a Germs tribute album. He also formed a punk-inspired side project, Bull Taco, with Morris, Navarro, Chad Smith (Red Hot Chili Peppers) and Zander Schloss (Circle Jerks). *Supersexy Swingin' Sounds* in 1996 was very well received, although as a marketing tool the 60s easy listening hammock style cover was a total contradiction to the music within. Rob Zombie released his solo debut, *Hellbilly Deluxe*, in 1998, retaining Tempesta on drums. The album debuted at US number 5 in September, shortly before White Zombie announced they were splitting-up.

● ALBUMS: *Psycho-Head Blowout* (Silent Explosion 1986)★★, *Soul Crusher* (Silent Explosion 1987)★★★, *Make Them Die Slowly* (Caroline 1989)★★★, *La Sexorcisto: Devil Music Vol. 1* (Geffen 1992)★★★★, *Astro Creep 2000: Songs Of Love, Destruction And Other Synthetic Delusions Of The Electric Head* (Geffen 1995)★★★★, *Supersexy Swingin' Sounds* (Geffen 1996)★★★.

Whitley, Chris

b. USA. Whitley is a blues rock guitarist, who plays slide guitar to his own romantic compositions. In his youth he was influenced by John Lee Hooker, Johnny Winters, Howlin' Wolf and Muddy Waters. Afterwards he began busking on the streets of New York, before 'trying to sound like Gary Numan with a dobro' for most of the 80s. He then relocated to Belgium where he formed a band entitled A Noh Radio, in which he played guitar synthesizer. Eventually he returned to America and back to the busking circuit. However, with blues having come back into fashion, Whitley took up residency at the Exterminator Chili, a Mexican club, which resulted in management, publishing and record deals. He recorded his debut at Daniel Lanois' nineteenth-century mansion in New Orleans with Lanois' regular sideman, Malcolm Burn. However, although the album won approval from artists including Bonnie Raitt and Bob Dylan (who invited Whitley to open for him on European dates), it did not entirely satisfy the artist. 'The songs on that album came from years of working in a factory and not having any money. They were written for solo acoustic and I always wanted a band.' This was exactly what he achieved for *Din Of Ecstasy*, plus a rawer more rock-orientated sound. In concert he is as likely to cover Jesus And Mary Chain as any traditional blues standard. *Dirt Floor* was an acoustic album recorded in one day through one microphone, returning to the spirit of his debut.

● ALBUMS: *Living With The Law* (Columbia 1991)★★★★, *Din Of Ecstasy* (Columbia 1995)★★★★, *Terra Incognita* (Columbia 1997)★★, *Dirt Floor* (Messenger 1998)★★★★.

Widespread Panic

An Allman Brothers Band for the 90s, Athens, Georgia, USA-based Widespread Panic were formed at the University of Georgia in the mid-80s by college friends John Bell (vocals/guitar), Michael Houser (guitar) and Dave Schools (bass). This trio recorded a single, 'Coconut Image', before Todd Nance (drums) joined in February 1986, and with the addition of temporary member Domingo Ortiz (percussion), the new line-up toured extensively, inspiring a devoted loyal live following. A poorly recorded debut album appeared on the independent Landslide label in September 1988, but they were subsequently signed to Capricorn Records. Tee Lavitz (ex-Dixie Dregs) stood in as keyboard player for live dates and appeared on their self-titled Capricorn debut. The band's final line-up came about when Ortiz joined full time and John 'JoJo' Herman replaced Lavitz. The band gained a higher profile with their appearances on the first two HORDE tours (Horizons Of Rock Developing Everywhere), a roots-orientated package founded by themselves and Blues Traveler in 1992 as an antidote to Lollapalooza. Their Capricorn albums have faithfully replicated their loose, jamming live sound, and songs such as 'Airplane' and 'Can't Get High', from 1994's *Ain't Life Grand*, were successful radio hits. In 1995, they recorded *Brute: Nine High A Pallet* with fellow Athens songwriter Vic Chesnutt. Their 1999 collection, *'Til The Medicine Takes*, attempted to cut out the jams in favour of a more song-orientated approach, but with limited success.

● ALBUMS: *Space Wrangler* (Landslide 1988)★★, *Widespread Panic* (Capricorn 1991)★★★, *Everyday* (Capricorn 1993)★★★, *Ain't Life Grand* (Capricorn 1994)★★★, with Vic Chesnutt *Brute: Nine High A*

Pallet (Capricorn 1995)★★, *Bombs & Butterflies* (Capricorn 1997)★★★, *Panic In The Streets* (Capricorn 1998)★★★, *Light Fuse, Get Away* (Capricorn 1998)★★★, *'Til The Medicine Takes* (Capricorn 1999)★★★.
● VIDEOS: *Live From The Georgia Theatre* (Capricorn 1992).

Widowmaker

Not to be confused with the UK band of same name, this Widowmaker were formed in 1991 by Dee Snider (vocals, ex-Twisted Sister). Between 1983 and 1987, Twisted Sister sold over eight million albums, and Snider became one of metal's most distinctive and easily recognizable figureheads. Widowmaker sought to blend 90s innovations with 'classic' 80s rock-style, Snider bringing along experienced musicians Joe Franco (drums), Al Pitrelli (guitar) and Marc Russell (b. London, England; bass). Their debut album, *Blood And Bullets*, was released on an independent label before the band signed to CMC International (Music For Nations in the UK). A second set, *Stand By For Pain*, evidently caught the 90s bug for writing about serial killers ('Killing Time'), with other stand-out tracks such as 'Protect And Serve' lambasting corruption in the legal system. Though Snider had hardly been away since the death of Twisted Sister, devising and presenting MTV's *Heavy Metal Mania* (now *Headbanger's Ball*) and hosting *Metal Nation* on radio station WRCN, it was reassuring to have him back as his former fans knew and loved him - fronting a thoroughly rock 'n' roll rock 'n' roll band.
● ALBUMS: *Blood And Bullets* (Music For Nations 1991)★★★, *Stand By For Pain* (CMC International 1995)★★★.

Wilco

This US quintet was initially viewed as part of the 'No Depression' movement of neo-country rock acts in the early 90s - one of a clutch of bands eschewing the melancholia and sentimentality associated with the genre but retaining its musical traditions. The band was formed from the ashes of Uncle Tupelo, a unit with similar musical inclinations and one that also accrued significant critical respect during its lifetime. Jeff Tweedy (vocals/guitar) is the creative engine behind both bands (in Uncle Tupelo's case with Jay Farrar, who enjoyed subsequent success heading Son Volt), his songs regularly attaining a universality and intimacy that has reminded some of Sebadoh. Wilco was formed with fellow Uncle Tupelo members John Stirratt (bass), Ken Coomer (drums) and multi-instrumentalist Max Johnson. *A.M.* was a continuation of Uncle Tupelo's sound, but sold modestly. Johnson was replaced by the less traditional Jay Bennett for the follow-up, *Being There*. The band agreed to take a cut in their royalties in order to facilitate the release of a double album, and Tweedy was rewarded with further critical plaudits, including several comparing the album favourably to the Rolling Stones' *Exile On Main Street*. This time much of the material was informed by the birth of his son, Spencer Miller Tweedy. As he told *Billboard* magazine in 1996: 'It was actually really healthy to understand what real life is about for the first time.' The ever productive Tweedy has also recorded two albums with Golden Smog, a side project involving, among others, members of the Jayhawks and Soul Asylum. In 1998, the whole band worked with English singer-songwriter Billy Bragg on the acclaimed *Mermaid Avenue* project, adding music to lyrics bequeathed by American folk legend Woody Guthrie. In contrast, *Summer*

Teeth was an album swimming in the lush pop sounds of synthesizers, mellotrons and brass.
● ALBUMS: *A.M.* (Reprise 1995)★★★, *Being There* (Reprise 1996)★★★, with Billy Bragg *Mermaid Avenue* (East West 1998)★★★★, *Summer Teeth* (Reprise 1999)★★★★.
● VIDEOS: with Billy Bragg *Man In The Sand* (Union Productions 1999).

Wildhearts

Following his sacking from the Quireboys and a brief tenure with the Throbs, UK guitarist/songwriter Ginger (b. 12 December 1964, South Shields, Tyne & Wear, England) set about forming the Wildhearts around the nucleus of himself plus ex-Tattooed Love Boys guitarist Chris 'CJ' Jagdhar, with the duo taking vocal duties after the departure of ex-Torbruk frontman Snake. The line-up stabilized with the recruitment of Bam Bam (drums, ex-Dogs D'Amour) and Danny McCormack (bass, ex-Energetic Krusher), and the quartet signed to East West Records in late 1989. Contractual difficulties meant that the Wildhearts' debut EP, *Mondo Akimbo A-Go-Go*, was delayed until early 1992, but the poor production could not obscure the quality of the songs or the band's original style, mixing pop melodies with aggressive, heavy riffing. A Terry Date-remixed version was released as a double-pack with the *Don't Be Happy ... Just Worry* EP (later reissued as a single album). This had much greater impact, and the band's following increased as they undertook a succession of support tours. Bam rejoined his old band during this period, with his predecessor Andrew 'Stidi' Stidolph filling the gap. *Earth Vs The Wildhearts* was recorded in a mere seven days, but turned out to be one of the best British rock albums for years, mixing metal, punk and pop into an adrenalized collection of songs, with their commercial appeal tempered only by the liberal use of expletives in the song titles. Stidolph was ousted shortly afterwards in favour of ex-Radio Moscow drummer Ritch Battersby, and following an acclaimed tour with the Almighty, the band broke into the UK Top 40 in February 1994 with 'Caffeine Bomb'. Subsequent headline dates saw the sound augmented by the keyboards of ex-Grip frontman Willie Dowling, while the summer of 1994 saw guitarist Jagdhar ousted. He would later re-emerge with a new band, Honeycrack, which also featured Dowling. Later that year an exclusive 40-minute mini-album, available only through the Wildhearts' fan club, was released (still featuring CJ on guitar). *Fishing For Luckies* revealed new dimensions to the Wildhearts, stretching even to Pogues influences on 'Geordie In Wonderland', and the commercially available single, 'If Life Is Like A Love Bank I Want An Overdraft', brought a UK number 31 hit in January 1995, but the band delayed their second album proper until their line-up was restored to a quartet. Auditions for a replacement were held in November, after using Steve Vai guitarist Devin Townsend as a stand-in. Despite the unsettling lack of a second guitarist, *P.H.U.Q.* was widely applauded as their strongest collection to date, with Ginger maturing as a lyricist and the band producing a much more accessible sound. Jagdhar was eventually replaced by Jeff Streatfield. They countered accusations of pandering to a new audience with typically uncomplicated statements to the media such as: 'There's nothing wrong with playing a short snappy song that's got a chorus you can sing along to. What's accessible mean?'. This was justified by 'I Wanna Go

Where The People Go' reaching UK number 16 in May 1995. Media speculation that Senseless Things guitarist Mark Keds would be recruited permanently was confirmed in 1995, but when he joined his former band for dates in Japan and failed to return in time for the Wildhearts' appearance at the Phoenix Festival, the venture soured into acrimony on both sides. By July they were still auditioning for a new singer and guitarist, despite the release of 'Just In Lust' (UK number 28), with Keds making his sole Wildhearts appearance on the b-side. Confusion was rife during the autumn of 1995: had the band broken up or not? They attempted to qualify the rumour by saying that they would break up if they failed to secure a new recording contract. They were in dispute with East West over the re-release of an expanded *Fishing For Luckies*, and when the record company released *Fishing For More Luckies* the band made a great deal of noise in opposing it and urged fans not to buy it. Ironically, it was an excellent album and one that fans were keen to own. The following year the restless band achieved their highest charting single, when 'Sick Of Drugs' (on Round Records) reached number 14 in April. The band signed a new contract with Mushroom Records in April 1997, releasing the lacklustre *Endless, Nameless* later that year amid more rumours of a split. The departed McCormack formed the Yo-Yo's in 1998, while Ginger worked with Alex Kane as Clam Abuse.

● ALBUMS: *Earth Versus The Wildhearts* (East West 1993)★★★★, *Don't Be Happy ... Just Worry* (East West 1994)★★★, *Fishing For Luckies* mini-album (Fan Club 1994)★★★★, *P.H.U.Q.* (East West 1995)★★★★, *Fishing For More Luckies* (East West 1995)★★★★, *Fishing For Luckies* (Round Records 1996)★★★★, *Endless, Nameless* (Mushroom 1997)★★★, *Anarchic Airwaves: The Wildhearts At The BBC* (Kuro Neko 1998)★★★.

● COMPILATIONS: *The Best Of The Wildhearts* (East West 1996)★★★, *Landmines & Pantomines: The Last Of The Wildhearts ...?* (Kuro Neko 1998)★★★.

Willard Grant Conspiracy

Based around vocalist Robert Fisher, this Boston, USA-based ensemble work with a fluctuating cast of musicians. Fisher and Paul Austin (guitar) had played together in several outfits, before forming the Flower Tamers with three accomplished musicians, James Apt (Six Finger Satellite), Malcolm Travis (ex-Sugar) and Dana Hallowell. The Willard Grant Conspiracy came about when Hallowell invited Austin and Fisher to try out his new recording studio. The informal sessions proved highly productive, providing enough finished material to release *3 am Sunday @ Fortune Otto's*. An intimate and atmospheric recording, the album crossed the alternative country sound of Lambchop and the Scud Mountain Boys, with a distinctly European sense of melancholia reminiscent of the UK's Tindersticks. Stand-out tracks included a cover version of the Silos' 'The Only Story I Tell' and 'Morning Is The End Of The Day'. The band built up a stronger following in Europe, touring with Chris and Carla from the Walkabouts, with whom they released the 'Wake Me When I'm Under' single. A fluid membership policy introduced an improvisatory feel to both their live and studio work, with guest members including Come guitarist Chris Brokaw, Silos' frontman Walter Salas-Humara, Hallowell and Travis. More permanent members include Fisher, Austin, Apt, David Curry (violin), Eric Groat (mandolin), Matt Griffin (bass) and Sean O'Brien (guitar). The

sophomore effort, *Flying Low*, was released in Europe before America. Superbly realised songs such as 'Evening Mass' and 'House Is Not A Home (Palmdale, CA)' indicated the twin influences of Nick Cave and Mark Eitzel respectively, filtered through Fisher's own distinctive vision.

● ALBUMS: *3 am Sunday @ Fortune Otto's* (Dahlia 1996)★★★★, *Flying Low* (Slow River/Rykodisc 1998)★★★★, *Weevils In The Captain's Biscuit* (Return To Sender 1998)★★★, *Mojave* (Slow River/Rykodisc 1999)★★★★.

Williams, Dar

b. Mount Kisco, Massachusetts, USA. Singer-songwriter Dar Williams first gained exposure by playing tiny church halls and cramped coffee houses on the small-town Massachusetts folk circuit. Her debut album, *The Honesty Room*, was released by Grapevine Records in 1995 and attracted immediate critical acclaim. *Billboard* magazine featured Williams on its cover and ran a story concerning the 'redefinition' of the folk genre. The songs on *The Honesty Room* which inspired the media glare balanced lyrical poise with musical accessibility. The album was quickly followed by the release of *Mortal City* in 1996, a collection recorded in her own bedroom and produced by Steven Miller (a Jane Siberry, Marianne Faithfull, Juliana Hatfield and Suzanne Vega collaborator). Some critics noted that Miller's resumé also quite accurately pinpointed Williams influences, though some of the song titles, such as 'The Pointless, Yet Poignant Crisis Of A Co-Ed' and 'Southern California Wants To Be Western New York', were entirely her own. Other contributors included John Prine and Eileen Ivers. Though some considered that the songs lacked the immediacy of her debut, critical reaction was once again complimentary. *End Of The Summer* fleshed out her acoustic musings with electric instrumentation, and saw the singer moving away from the oppressive personal confessions of her previous sets. A joint set with fellow singer-songwriters Lucy Kaplansky and Richard Shindell followed in 1999.

● ALBUMS: *The Honesty Room* (Grapevine 1995)★★★, *Mortal City* (Razor & Tie/Grapevine 1996)★★★, *End Of The Summer* (Razor & Tie 1997)★★★, with Lucy Kaplansky, Richard Shindell *Cry Cry Cry* (Razor & Tie 1999)★★★.

Williams, Lucinda

b. 26 January 1953, Lake Charles, Louisiana, USA. Her father, Miller Williams, is a professor of literature and a professional poet, but it was her mother, a music graduate, who influenced Lucinda the most. After a period spent travelling in the early 70s, Williams concentrated on playing folk clubs in Texas, mixing traditional blues and folk songs with original material. She recorded two albums for Folkways Records, with *Happy Woman Blues* comprising her own material. Her career failed to take off until she moved to Los Angeles some years later, but she was further stymied by an abortive development contract with CBS Records in the mid-80s. Her self-titled album for Rough Trade Records in 1988 moved closer into rock 'n' roll territory, and re-established Williams as a songwriting force with its attendant strong press. *Sweet Old World* provided darker subject matter than most folk-country albums, with the title track and 'Pineola' exploring suicide (Williams describes songwriting as 'like writing a journal but I don't want it to sound self-indulgent'). It included a cover version of Nick Drake's 'Which Will', with musical backing by Benmont Tench, Bryce Berline and Doug Atwell. Williams has also performed on tribute albums to Merle Haggard (*Tulare Dust*) and Victoria Williams (*Sweet Relief*), and Mary-Chapin Carpenter earned a major US country hit with her 'Passionate Kisses'. In 1998, Williams broke a long recording silence when she contributed 'Still I Long For Your Kiss' to the soundtrack of Robert Redford's adaptation of *The Horse Whisperer*, and released the superb *Car Wheels On A Gravel Road*.

● ALBUMS: *Ramblin' On My Mind* (Folkways 1979)★★★, *Happy Woman Blues* (Folkways 1980)★★★, *Lucinda Williams* (Rough Trade 1988)★★★★, *Sweet Old World* (Chameleon 1992)★★★, *Car Wheels On A Gravel Road* (Mercury 1998)★★★★.

Williams, Robbie

b. 13 February 1974, Stoke-on-Trent, Staffordshire, England. Williams was the cheeky chappie in hugely successful boy band Take That, and at the time appeared to be the only one who could be badly behaved (or normal). When Take That broke up the predictions were that Mark Owen (the nice one) and Gary Barlow (the voice and marketability) would succeed. Little hope was given to Williams, who immediately set about stirring up the media with anti-Barlow tales. While Barlow was being groomed as the UK's new George Michael, Williams caused mayhem. He partied, he overindulged (drink and drugs) and he seemed to pay little attention to the music. Fittingly, August 1996's debut single was a cover version of Michael's 'Freedom'. Following a spell in a clinic for detoxification, a seemingly wiser Williams stepped out into the glare of the sunshine, blinked, and set about recording an excellent album that eclipsed Barlow's debut both musically and critically. *Life Thru A Lens*, was a joy throughout and contained the symbolic 'Old Before I Die', which followed 'Freedom' to number 2 in the UK charts. The comparative failure of follow-up singles 'Lazy Days' and 'South Of The Border' cast doubt on Williams' staying power, before the Christmas single 'Angels' almost single-handedly revived his ailing career. His album, which had slumped, entered the UK Top 10 for the first time and eventually climbed to number one 28 weeks after it was first released. Never before had so many pundits and critics been proved so wrong. His renaissance continued with 'Millennium' entering the UK singles chart at number 1 in September 1998, and *I've Been Expecting You* topping the album chart two months later. Williams was also announced to be the biggest selling album artist of 1998. Featuring backing vocals by Neil Tennant (Pet Shop Boys) and Neil Hannon (Divine Comedy), 'No Regrets', one of Williams' finest songs to date, surprisingly stalled at number 4 in December. The wonderfully self-deprecating 'Strong' debuted at the same position in March. In 1999, Williams set about trying to woo America, touring in support of *The Ego Has Landed*, a selection of the best tracks from both albums. In November, he returned to the top of the UK charts with the double a-side, 'She's The One'/'It's Only Us'.

● ALBUMS: *Life Thru A Lens* (EMI 1997)★★★★, *I've Been Expecting You* (Chrysalis 1998)★★★★, *The Ego Has Landed* US only (EMI 1999)★★★★.

● VIDEOS: *Live In Your Living Room* (Chrysalis 1998).

● FURTHER READING: *Robbie Williams: Let Me Entertain You*, Jim Parton.

Williams, Vanessa

b. 18 March 1963, New York, USA. Williams grew up in a household surrounded by musical influences from Broadway shows, before she attended Syracuse University to major in musical theatre. A mother of three and actress as well as singer, she has come a long way since becoming embroiled in a minor scandal over her appearance in *Penthouse* magazine (after becoming the first black woman to win the Miss USA pageant). Four years later Williams began to pursue a recording contract, and found a sympathetic ear in Ed Eckstine at Wing Records (a Mercury Records subsidiary). Her husband, Ramon Hervey, took over her management. Williams' talents have nevertheless been inadequately displayed on her albums. Her musical career began in 1989 with *The Right Stuff*, which provided a US number 8 single in 'Dreamin'', a song recognized by ASCAP as one of the most frequently played singles of 1989 (it also contained the minor hit 'Darling I'). It brought her the NAACP Image Award, which she won once again for the US chart-topping ballad, 'Save The Best For Last'. The album which accompanied that single, *The Comfort Zone*, achieved double platinum status. The following year Williams enjoyed a US Top 5 single duetting with Brian McKnight on 'Love Is', which was taken from the television series *Beverly Hills, 90210*. There was more invention and ambition displayed on a third collection, *The Sweetest Days*, delayed for three years while she gave birth and raised her third child, Devin, and moved back to New York from Los Angeles. This featured vocals that were pleasant rather than striking, hovering over gentle jazz, soul or Latin arrangements. The stronger material, like the warm, sensuous 'Higher Ground', was deprived of its potential stature by disappointments like 'Moonlight Over Paris' or the joyless Sting cover, 'Sister Moon' (with Toots Thielemans on harmonica). Sting also produced, alongside other big names like Babyface and Roy Ayers. Wendy Waldman, Jon Lind, Phil Galdston and producer Keith Thomas, the team responsible for 'Save The Best For Last', wrote the title track. The album was released while Williams was also the toast of Broadway in her role in *Kiss Of The Spiderwoman*. She has also appeared widely in film and television, including the Emmy Award winning *Motown Returns To The Apollo*, *The Boy Who Loved Christmas* and *Stompin' At The Savoy*. Earlier she had starred alongside Richard Pryor and Gene Wilder in *Another You* and Micky Rourke and Don Johnson in *Harley Davidson And The Marlboro Man*. She has also hosted her own contemporary R&B television show, *The Soul Of VH-1*. In January 1996, Williams sung the national anthem at Super Bowl XXX in Phoenix, Arizona.

● ALBUMS: *The Right Stuff* (Wing 1989)★★★, *The Comfort Zone* (Wing 1991)★★★★, *The Sweetest Days* (Wing 1995)★★, *Star Bright* (Mercury 1996)★★.

Williams, Victoria

b. 23 December 1958, Shreveport, Louisiana, USA. This talented singer-songwriter had her career disrupted by the onset of multiple sclerosis, which was diagnosed in the spring of 1992. At that time she was touring with Neil Young and receiving plaudits as a promising newcomer. She made her recording debut in 1987 (at that time still married to Peter Case), with an album produced by Anton Fier and Stephen Soles that surrounded her compositions with a varied background, including a sitar, strings and horns. The most notable accompaniment came from an award-winning Donn Pennebaker video. Williams' second set was a considerable improvement and revealed her to be a writer of depth by removing some of the extraneous instrumentation. Instead, co-producer Michael Blair (multi-instrumentalist with Elvis Costello and Tom Waits) focused on Williams' childlike, rural spirit and inspired lyrics with simple, effective song constructions. Her rise had already been noted in the film world, and she made her acting debut in Gus Van Sant's movie Even Cowgirls Get The Blues. However, once her illness had been diagnosed, Williams' hospital bills soared, and guest musicians played a series of benefit concerts throughout 1992. This culminated in a core of friends and admirers putting together the cast for Sweet Relief - The Songs Of Victoria Williams, where 14 artists contributed cover versions of her songs. Soul Asylum's version of 'Summer Of Drugs' began the set, while other contributions included Lou Reed ('Tarbelly & Feather Foot'), Jayhawks ('Lights'), Waterboys ('Why Look At The Moon'), Giant Sand ('Big Fish'), Lucinda Williams ('Main Road'), Evan Dando of the Lemonheads ('Frying Pan'), Michelle Shocked ('Opelousas (Sweet Relief)'), and Maria McKee ('Holy Spirit'). The lyrics to 'Main Road' were perfectly apt: 'I never knew I had so many friends'. By 1994 Williams reasserted her own strength as a performer with the release of Loose, sustaining herself on stage with little evidence of her illness, with husband Mark Olson of the Jayhawks joining her for a duet of 'When We Sing Together' and Peter Buck and Mike Mills of R.E.M. on hand to support a new collection of supremely simple but deeply affecting songs. She continued her rich rein of form on 1998's Musings Of A Creekdipper, a typically left-field and engaging collection dominated by Williams' eerie vocals.

● ALBUMS: Happy Come Home (Geffen 1987)★★★, Swing The Statue! (Mammoth 1990)★★★★, Loose (Mammoth/Atlantic 1994)★★★, This Moment In Toronto With Victoria Williams And The Loose Band (Mammoth/Atlantic 1996)★★★, Musings Of A Creekdipper (East West 1998)★★★★.

● COMPILATIONS: various artists Sweet Relief - The Songs Of Victoria Williams (Thirsty Ear/Columbia 1993)★★★.

Willis, Kelly

b. 1 October 1968, Annandale, Oklahoma, USA. An Austin, Texas-based singer-songwriter, Kelly Willis was signed by MCA Records' country division in 1990 and widely embraced by critics as a torchbearer for 'new traditionalism'. Willis played in her first band when aged 16, performing with her future husband Mas Palermo. Her raucous vocals proved immediately popular, so much so that the band was renamed Kelly And The Fireballs in her honour. Willis and Palermo relocated to Austin after graduation and established a new band, Radio Ranch. The band impressed Nanci Griffith, who arranged an audition at MCA Records. Their debut album was marketed under Willis' name in an attempt to capitalise on her striking looks. Willis has often been compared to another MCA artist, Brenda Lee, because her records suggest the same blend of rockabilly, rock 'n' roll and ballads, updated for the 90s. The title track of Bang Bang, for example, was an obscure title from rock 'n' roller Janis Martin. The songwriting credits on her albums are always interesting. 'Sincerely' was written by Steve Earle and Robert Earl Keen, and the Don Was-produced third

album included songs co-written with John Leventhal and Paul Kennerley. She also duetted with Kevin Welch on 'That'll Be Me' and took time out to add background harmonies to Chris Wall's Cowboy Nation. She sang the Paul Kennerley song 'I Don't Want To Love You (But I Do)' on the movie soundtrack of Thelma And Louise, and appeared as Clarissa Flan in Tim Robbins' political satire movie Bob Roberts. Willis was dropped by MCA in 1993, and remained quiet until she returned to recording with 1996's Fading Fast EP. A new album appeared on Rykodisc Records in 1998 and the critics really started noticing her as an important 'new' talent. What I Deserve was a beautifully constructed album which veers away from her straight country style. The guitar-rich tracks feature Max Butler and the distinctive tones of Chuck Prophet, with stand-out songs including 'Wrapped', 'Cradle Of Love' and a superb version of Nick Drake's 'Time Has Told Me'.

● ALBUMS: Well Travelled Love (MCA 1990)★★★, Bang Bang (MCA 1991)★★★, Kelly Willis (MCA 1993)★★★, What I Deserve (Rykodisc 1998)★★★★.

● FILMS: Bob Roberts (1992).

Wilson Phillips

The daughters of Beach Boys leader Brian Wilson and his ex-wife Marilyn (formerly of the Honeys) and John Phillips and Michelle Phillips of the Mamas And The Papas, this trio proved that they were up to the task of following those famous footsteps by scoring three number 1 singles in the US charts, with 'Hold On', 'Release Me' and 'You're In Love', plus a US number 2 album at their first attempt. The girls, Chynna Phillips (b. Chynna Gilliam Phillips, 12 February 1968, Los Angeles, California, USA) and the Wilson sisters, Wendy (b. 16 October 1969, Los Angeles, California, USA) and Carnie (b. 29 April 1968, Los Angeles, California, USA), were all in their early twenties when they released their self-titled debut album on the newly-formed SBK Records in early 1990, although they had known each other and even sung together since early childhood. While they received moral support from their parents, the trio deliberately shied away from asking for musical assistance. Their debut was hugely successful, going on to sell in excess of five million copies. The follow-up, Shadows And Light, shot into the US bestsellers list in the first week of release. Featuring a tougher sounding production, the album addressed the problems suffered by the girls as children, citing the stress caused by their respective fathers' over-indulgences. Both Brian Wilson and John Phillips could benefit from listening to the lyrics 'Flesh And Blood' and 'Would You Fly All The Way From New York'. The unit broke up towards the end of 1992. As Carnie And Wendy Wilson, the sisters released the dreadful Hey Santa! late in 1993 while Phillips started a solo career. The Wilson sisters patched up relationships with their estranged father, to the extent that he participated with a 1997 album recorded as the Wilsons.

● ALBUMS: Wilson Phillips (SBK 1990)★★★★, Shadows And Light (SBK 1992)★★★.

● VIDEOS: So Far (PMI 1993).

Winans, BeBe

b. Benjamin Winans, 17 September 1962, Detroit, Michigan, USA. The seventh child of the Winans gospel family, BeBe enjoyed crossover success performing with his sister CeCe.

The duo recorded two gold albums and 1991's platinum-selling *Different Lifestyles*, and won several R&B and gospel awards. In 1989, BeBe won a Grammy for Best Soul Gospel Performance, Male for his contribution to 'Abundant Life', a track on his brother Ronald's *Family & Friends Choir*. He also contributed as a producer to the Grammy-winning soundtrack for the Whitney Houston/Kevin Costner movie *The Bodyguard*. Additional production work for Gladys Knight, Bobby Brown and Stephanie Mills followed as his recording career with his sister was put on hold. He co-starred with Mills in a 1996 run of *Your Arms Too Short To Box With God*, before making a long-awaited return to recording with his solo debut in 1997. Released in October, the star-studded affair utilised leading producers including Rhett Lawrence, Arif Mardin and Keith Andes in an obvious attempt to capture the modern soul market. BeBe's voice cut above the occasionally bland backing music, particularly on a standout collaboration with Hezekiah Walker's Love Fellowship Crusade Choir on 'Oh Happy Day'. The video for opening track 'In Harm's Way', a song inspired by brother Ronald's recovery from heart disease, was directed by actor Denzel Washington.

● ALBUMS: *BeBe Winans* (Atlantic 1997)★★★.

Winans, BeBe And CeCe

Brother and sister BeBe (b. Benjamin Winans) and CeCe (b. Priscilla Winans) are the most successful members of America's premier gospel group, the Winans. During 10 years together as recording artists the duo were garlanded with awards, including two Grammy successes. More impressively they also crossed over into the contemporary R&B market while retaining their large Christian following. The two originally worked together in the PTL Singers, before recording their first album as a duo in 1987. This self-titled effort was produced by Keith Thomas, and contained the R&B crossover hits 'I.O.U. Me' and 'For Always'. Their second album *Heaven* went gold, and not only reached the Top 10 on *Billboard*'s R&B chart but broke into the Top 100 on the pop chart. Both BeBe and CeCe were awarded Grammys for their vocal performances. *Different Lifestyles* was an even bigger breakthrough, reaching number 74 on the pop charts, going platinum and winning a further Grammy for Best Contemporary Soul Gospel Album. The singles 'I'll Take You There' and 'Addicted Love' both topped the R&B charts, with the former also breaking into the Top 100 of the pop charts. The seasonal *First Christmas* was released in 1993. The following year's *Relationships* was the duo's first recording without long-term producer Keith Thomas. Instead they drafted in big name producers Arif Mardin, David Foster and Cedric Caldwell. Mardin also oversaw their contribution to the following year's Carole King tribute album. With CeCe having embarked on a solo career, and BeBe enjoying an increasingly busy production schedule, the duo put their career on hold. A *Greatest Hits* collection in 1996 included several new tracks.

● ALBUMS: *BeBe & CeCe Winans* (Capitol 1986)★★★, *Heaven* (Capitol 1988)★★★, *Different Lifestyles* (Capitol 1991)★★★, *First Christmas* (Capitol 1993)★★, *Relationships* (Capitol 1994)★★★.
● COMPILATIONS: *BeBe & CeCe Winans Greatest Hits* (EMI 1996)★★★.

Winans, CeCe

b. Priscilla Winans, Detroit, Michigan, USA. Part of the famous Winans gospel clan, CeCe was the eighth of 10 children. She worked with her brother BeBe in the PTL Singers, before recording with him as the Grammy award-winning duo BeBe And CeCe Winans. The duo became highly influential figures in modern gospel, their blend of soulful vocals and modern swingbeat rhythms also proving popular in the R&B and pop markets. Two albums went gold, and 1991's *Different Lifestyles* went platinum. Following the release of 1994's *Relationships*, the duo put their career on hold while CeCe concentrated on recording her solo debut. Released in 1995, *Alone In His Presence* established CeCe as a solo star. The album won a Grammy for Best Contemporary Soul Gospel Album, achieved gold sales and narrowly failed to enter the *Billboard* Hot 200 album chart. Her duet with Whitney Houston on 'Count On Me', taken from the *Waiting To Exhale* soundtrack, reached number 8 on the *Billboard* Hot 100 in May 1996, and was also nominated for a Grammy. CeCe's sophomore set, *Everlasting Love*, featured a stellar production/writing cast, including Tony Rich, Lauryn Hill, Keith Crouch and Darryl Simmons. In contrast to her debut album, the songs were aimed directly at the R&B/soul market, with Hill's 'On That Day' surprisingly the most gospel-orientated track. A Christmas record, *His Gift*, followed. Winans launched her own Wellspring Gospel Records label in October 1999.

● ALBUMS: *Alone In His Presence* (Sparrow 1995)★★★, *Everlasting Love* (Atlantic 1998)★★★, *His Gift* (Atlantic 1998)★★★, *Alabaster Box* (Wellspring Gospel 1999)★★★★.

Winans, Mario

b. USA. One of the younger members of the extensively recorded Winans musical family, in the mid-90s, after over a decade of work in gospel music, Mario moved into contemporary R&B. He produced R. Kelly's multi-platinum self-titled album of 1995, and followed this with his own effort, *Story Of My Heart*. He made his reasons clear: 'There's a gospel audience, but much more people buy R&B and pop than gospel, and for my songs to be heard, I knew it had to be done.' Apparently, the switch caused friction with his parents, Vicky and Marvin Winans, but they withdrew their objections on the condition that Winans' new R&B material did not contain anything 'offensive'. Winans began as a gospel producer at the age of 14, and has maintained his commitment to the church. As he told *Billboard* magazine in 1997, 'I know in my heart it's not bad to write a love song, because the best example of love is God.' *Story Of My Heart* was preceded by a single, 'Don't Know', which included a guest appearance from Ma$e, a rapper from Sean 'Puffy' Combs' Bad Boy Entertainment stable.

● ALBUMS: *Story Of My Heart* (Motown 1997)★★★.

Wink, Josh

b. Philadelphia, Pennsylvania, USA. The techno artist Josh Wink combines a number of influences, from deep house to acid jazz and more experimental electronic music. His musical taste came from his family's record collection that included Philip Glass, Stevie Wonder, Kraftwerk, Steely Dan and James Brown. He began DJing in 1987 in underground Philadelphia clubs. In 1990, he released 'Tribal Confusion', on Strictly Rhythm Records, an acclaimed single produced with King Britt and credited to E-Culture that was later sampled by Future Sound Of London. The reaction enabled Britt and Wink to establish their own production company, WinKing Productions, in Philadelphia. Over the next five years they remixed over 20 tracks, including Rozalla's 'Are You Ready To Fly?', Digital Orgasm's 'Running Out Of Time' and Book Of Love's 'Boy Pop'. In 1993, when King went on tour as the Digable Planets' DJ, Wink continued as a solo artist, using a variety of names, including Wink, Winx, Winc, Winks and the Crusher. The records were released on a variety of labels such as Vinyl Solution, Strictly Rhythm, Nervous Records, Limbo Records and R&S Records. He also recorded 30-second musical compositions for television advertisements, as well as launching his own underground dance music label, Ovum Recordings, in October 1994. In 1995, he was signed to Virgin Records in the USA and Mercury Records in the UK, releasing (as Winx) the Top 10 hit 'Higher State Of Consciousness'.

● ALBUMS: *Profound Secrets Vol. 1* (Incredible 1999)★★★.

Wiseguys

UK hip-hop and big beat outfit the Wiseguys started as a duo, but is now one man, Touché, aka Theo Keating. Hip-hop obsessives, Touché and Regal met while at college in Clerkenwell, London. Regal was working with the Direct Current MCs and Touché joined through a mutual friend. They released an independent single, 'Keep In Step' in 1990 and began to assemble primitive pieces from the breakbeat tracks they had collected, using record decks and a tape recorder. In 1992, Regal and Touché began to work on tracks for Solo E, who was managed by Rene Gelston, head of the Blackmarket International label. Gelston liked what he heard and asked them to record for the label. In 1994, as the Wiseguys, they released the EP *Ladies Say Ow!*. It received support from high profile DJs on London's booming acid jazz/hip-hop scene, such as Gilles Peterson and Patrick Forge. The newly-formed label, Wall Of Sound licensed 'The Real Vibes' for its first *Give 'Em Enough Dope* compilation, and released the double a-side, 'Nil By Mouth'/'Too Easy', in April 1995. An old friend of Touché's, New York City-based rapper, Sense Live, provided rhymes for the Wiseguys' second album *The Antidote*, released in August 1998. Touché is a popular DJ on the big beat scene in Europe, usually working as part of the Wall Of Sound collective of DJs/artists. He has also supported labelmates Propellerheads on tour, and enjoyed commercial success in May 1999 with the UK number 2 single 'Ooh La La'. The song originally peaked outside the Top 50 in summer 1998, but was picked up second time around thanks to its extensive use in a television advertisement for Budweiser lager.

● ALBUMS: *Executive Suite* (Wall Of Sound 1996)★★★, *The Antidote* (Wall Of Sound 1998)★★★.

Witness

This Wigan, Greater Manchester, England-based band was formed by long time friends Gerard Starkie (vocals) and Ray Chan (guitar). The two men attended art college with the Verve's future guitarist Nick McCabe, and struggled around the local music scene in various bands, including Siren and High Mountain Jag. Witness was formed when the latter split-up, with guitarist Dylan Keeton switching to bass. The new line-up adopted a more positive approach to their music

career and began recording demos in late 1997. One tape came to the attention of the Verve's PR company and a deal with Island Records followed shortly afterwards. John Langley (drums, ex-Strangelove) completed the line-up for the band's debut single, 'Quarantine', which was released in November 1998. *Before The Calm* was recorded with producer Phil Vinall at Rockfield Studios in South Wales. The album was released to positive reviews in July 1999, and was promoted by a strong set at the following month's Glastonbury Festival. The album's melancholic soundscapes evoked memories of early R.E.M. and American Music Club, although the delicate nuances of tracks such as 'Freezing Over Morning' and 'My Own Old Song' earned comparisons to the 'stool rock' sound of contemporaries Unbelievable Truth and Radiohead.

● ALBUMS: *Before The Calm* (Island 1999)★★★★.

Wolfsbane

This UK quartet from Tamworth, Staffordshire, England, employed a strong biker image to augment their incendiary heavy metal anthems. Featuring Blaze Bayley (b. Birmingham, West Midlands, England; vocals), Jason Edwards (guitar), Steve 'Danger' Ellet (drums) and Jeff Hately (bass), they incorporated elements of Van Halen, Iron Maiden and Zodiac Mindwarp into their own high-energy and, at times, chaotic style. Picked up by Rick Rubin's Def American label, they released *Live Fast, Die Fast* as an opening philosophical statement. The album failed to match the manic intensity of their live shows and was let down by weak production. Their next two releases saw some development on the songwriting front, with the addition of sci-fi and B-movie imagery, to supplement the well-worn themes of sex, booze and rock 'n' roll. After three albums their style remained loud, aggressive and, to a degree, derivative. In 1993, they separated both from P Grant Management and Def American, and by the following year Bayley quit to replace Bruce Dickinson in Iron Maiden. The remaining members soon abandoned their former name to become Stretch, signing with Cottage Industry Records in the summer of 1995.

● ALBUMS: *Live Fast, Die Fast* (Def American 1989)★★, *All Hell's Breaking Loose Down At Little Kathy Wilson's Place* (Def American 1990)★★★, *Down Fall The Good Guys* (Def American 1991)★★★, *Massive Noise Injection* (Bronze 1993)★★★.

Womack, Lee Ann

b. Jacksonville, Texas, USA. A contemporary country artist fired by traditional songwriting virtues, Womack earned widespread praise in the late 90s for her fidelity to country music of a bygone era. Her material's resemblance to early works by Tammy Wynette and Dolly Parton was remarked upon by many, and acknowledged in print by the artist herself. Her interest in music came from a disc jockey father, who would regularly take his daughter to bookings After graduation she attended college in Levelland, Texas, one of the first schools to offer degrees in country and bluegrass music. She joined the college band, Country Caravan, and travelled alongside the group until she undertook a music business course at Belmont University in Nashville. She subsequently became an intern at MCA Records' A&R department, eventually joining Tree Publishing after a showcase in 1995. There she co-wrote material for Ed Hill, Bill Anderson and Sam Hogin. A year later she signed to Decca Records as a solo artist. Her 1997 debut album was produced by Mark Wright (with whom she had co-written at Tree Publishing) and resulted in two nominations at that year's CMA Awards. It was followed by another Wright-supervised set, *Some Things I Know*, which many judged to be the superior work. Womack contributed two songs herself in collaboration with ex-husband Jason Sellers ('If You're Ever Down In Dallas') and Billy Lawson and Dale Dodson ('The Man Who Made My Mama Cry'). It was promoted via shows in late 1998 before the birth of Womack's second child in January 1999.

● ALBUMS: *Lee Ann Womack* (Decca 1998)★★★, *Some Things I Know* (Decca 1998)★★★★.

Wondermints

The epic struggle of this dynamic force in US power pop to gain commercial release in their own country attests to the virtue of persistence and to the good taste of Japanese music lovers. The Wondermints began in Los Angeles, California as a partnership between Nick Walusko (b. USA; guitars/vocals) and Darian Sahanaja (b. USA; keyboards/vocals). In the early 90s, they embarked on a series of home-made, self-distributed cassettes, each colour-coded according to the cover. Despite echoes of retro influences endemic in 90s pop, the Wondermints' blend of disarming hook-lines with complex instrumentation managed to transcend many of their contemporaries' rather more insipid efforts. However, record contracts continued to elude them. By 1993, the band had become a four-piece with the addition of Brian Kassan (b. USA; bass) and Mike D'Amico (b. USA; drums). Growing prominence on the LA underground scene led to a demo contract with Epic Records although no album ensued. Kassan left to be replaced by Jim Mills (b. USA), who in turn was replaced a year later by Probyn Gregory (b. USA). They continued to be active on the gig circuit performing a mix of original songs and cover versions. Their profile was given a boost in spring 1995 when they were hired as Brian Wilson's backing band. Reportedly, the former Beach Boy stated that had he had the support of the Wondermints back in 1967 he would have taken the abortive *Smile* on the road. A cult following abroad led to the Japanese Toy's Factory label releasing a critically acclaimed selection from their first three cassettes. Despite a belated US release of the album through indie label Big Deal, the Wondermints' success continued only in Japan with an album of cover versions (plus one original composition), entitled *Wonderful World Of Wondermints*. The band attracted the interest of actor/director Mike Myers, who used the Wondermints' track 'Austin Powers' in the soundtrack of his James Bond-parody movie, *Austin Powers*, although the song did not feature as the theme as had been originally planned. In 1998, the band released *Bali*, a showcase for their rich but accessible sound. This impressive album finally gained a well-deserved domestic release in summer 1999.

● ALBUMS: *Wondermints* (Toy's Factory 1995/Big Deal 1996)★★★, *Wonderful World Of Wondermints* (Toy's Factory 1996)★★★, *Bali* (Sony NeOSITE 1998)★★★★.

World Party

Founded on the talents of ex-Waterboy Karl Wallinger (b. 19 October 1957, Prestatyn, Wales), World Party have worked hard to shrug off comparisons with his former band. This is a little unjust, bearing in mind Wallinger's quite separate, but in many ways equal, songwriting abilities. Wallinger was born the son of an architect father and housewife mother. He was brought up in North Wales on a diet of 60s ephemera, from the Supremes, through the Spencer Davis Group, to Merseybeat. His first musical experience arrived in 1976 with Quasimodo, who would eventually lose their hump to become the Alarm. Later he moved to London to become a clerk for ATV/Northern Songs, who counted the Beatles' catalogue among their acquisitions. He delved back into performance in his own time, eventually going on to become musical director of *The Rocky Horror Show* in the West End of London. A short residency with funk band the Out overlapped his liaison with the Waterboys. After he split amicably from Mike Scott, Wallinger set out on a solo career that would see him sign to Prince's management. He also helped Sinead O'Connor on her *Lion And The Cobra* set. Wallinger recorded the first two World Party albums practically single-handed, though 1993's *Bang!* saw him joined by Chris Sharrock (drums, ex-Icicle Works) and Dave Catlin-Birch (guitars/keyboards). The minor UK hit single 'Ship Of Fools' (from 1987) showcased Wallinger's muse, a relaxed and melancholic performance reminiscent of mid-period Beatles. This has not so much been updated as revitalized on his subsequent, sterling work, although a minor breakthrough was made with 1993's *Bang!*, which featured Wallinger's only UK Top 20 hit to date, 'Is It Like Today'. Some of the reviews for *Egyptology* were unnecessarily cruel (especially the *New Musical Express*). It was by his standards another good album, which, although still locked into the Beatles' sound (this time *circa* the *White Album* period), has some great moments, notably the gentle 'She's The One' and the meatier 'Curse Of The Mummy's Tomb'. The former indirectly gave Wallinger a chart-topping single, when Robbie Williams' cover version reached number 1 in November 1999.

● ALBUMS: *Private Revolution* (Ensign 1987)★★, *Goodbye Jumbo* (Ensign 1990)★★★★, *Thank You World* mini-album (Ensign 1991)★★★, *Bang!* (Ensign 1993)★★★, *Egyptology* (Chrysalis 1997)★★★★.

Wu-Tang Clan

This chess-playing hip-hop crew, whose ranks originally comprised the Genius aka GZA (b. Gary Grice, New York, USA), RZA aka Prince Rakeem (b. Robert Diggs, New York, USA), Ol' Dirty Bastard (b. Russell Jones, 15 November 1968, Brooklyn, New York, USA), Raekwon (b. Corey Woods, New York, USA), Method Man (b. Clifford Smith, 1 April 1971, Staten Island, New York, USA), Ghostface Killah (b. Dennis Coles, 9 May 1970, USA), Inspectah Deck aka Rebel INS (b. Jason Hunter, New York, USA) and U-God, based themselves in the Staten Island district of New York City. The roots of the Wu-Tang Clan lay in the earlier crew All In Together Now, formed by cousins Rakeem, the Genius and Ol' Dirty Bastard. Both Rakeem and the Genius had released solo records prior to their involvement with the Wu-Tang Clan, for Tommy Boy Records and Cold Chillin' Records respectively, both of which sank without trace and instilled a hatred of record labels in the founder members. Each of the team boasted keen martial arts knowledge, and their debut album was divided into two sides, Shaolin and Wu-Tang Sword, to symbolise the combat-like disciplines applied to their rapping. An independently released single 'Protect Ya Neck' became an underground hit, leading to major label interest. When the Wu-Tang Clan as a whole signed with Loud/RCA Records, provision for each member to work as solo artists was enshrined in the contract. The Genius joined his third record company, Geffen Records, Method Man linked to Def Jam Records, Ol' Dirty Bastard with Elektra Records, and Raekwon stayed with Loud/RCA. RZA also worked alongside Prince Paul and Fruitkwan (ex-Stetsasonic) as part of the Gravediggaz, as well overseeing the production of all Wu-Tang Clan product and later setting up his own Razor Sharp imprint.

Wu-Tang Clan's musical armoury centres around old school rhyming and trickery, which with multi-contributors offers ample opportunity for quick fire wise-cracking and playing off each other. The musical backing is one of stripped down beats, with samples culled from kung-fu movies. Such appropriation of martial culture was a theme which has occupied rap music from the days of Grandmaster Flash onwards. Their debut set *Enter The Wu-Tang (36 Chambers)* was recorded in their own studio, its '36 Chambers' suffix alluding to the number of critical points on the body as disclosed by Shaolin theology. RZA's production work, all spare beats and minimal samples, rapidly became one of the most recognisable and influential sounds in hip-hop and set the underground scene alight. The album eventually notched gold status, although it only debuted at US number 41 in November 1993. The belated success of the 'C.R.E.A.M.' single helped to spread the word, making the crew one of the hottest tickets in rap. However, all was not well in 1994. U-God's two-year old, Dante Hawkins, was hit in a gun battle crossfire as he played outside his baby-sitter's house on 13 March. The bullet destroyed one of his kidneys and damaged his hand. Just a day later a member of their inner circle of friends was killed in a separate incident.

The ranks of the Wu-Tang Clan have been swelled with the addition of the ninth and tenth official members, Masta Killa and Cappadonna, and an ever-expanding list of associates, including Shyheim, Killah Priest, Shabazz The Disciple, Killarmy and the Sunz Of Man, have all released acclaimed albums. The crew regrouped for 1997's *Wu-Tang Forever*, a long sprawling record that rarely matched the quality of their debut or GZA's exceptional solo collection, *Liquid Swords*. The album, nonetheless, was one the most eagerly anticipated hip-hop releases ever and entered the US charts at number 1 in June. Recent releases from the Wu-Tang Clan stable have included Killah Priest's excellent *Heavy Mental*, and Cappadonna's bestselling *The Pillage*.

● ALBUMS: *Enter The Wu-Tang (36 Chambers)* (Loud/RCA 1993)★★★★, *Wu-Tang Forever* (Loud/RCA 1997)★★★.
● COMPILATIONS: *Wu-Chronicles* (Priority 1999)★★★.
● VIDEOS: *Da Mystery Of Kung-Fu* (MIA 1998).

Wynonna

b. Christina Ciminella, 30 May 1964, Ashland, Kentucky, USA. The mother-and-daughter duo the Judds was one of the most successful country acts of the 80s. After contracting chronic hepatitis, Naomi Judd decided to retire owing to ill health but, having announced this, they undertook a farewell world tour of 100 concerts. With her lead vocals and rhythm guitar, Wynonna had become the dominant part of the Judds and, indeed, their final album, *Love*

Can Build A Bridge, is virtually Wynonna's solo debut. The Judds played their final concert in December 1991 and the following month Wynonna performed on her own at the American music awards in Los Angeles with her mother in the audience. Her solo album, *Wynonna*, led to three US country number 1s, 'She Is His Only Need', 'I Saw The Light' and 'No One Else On Earth' (which, with its synthesizer effects, was far removed from traditional country music). The album touched many musical bases and Wynonna's role model was Bonnie Raitt. By the mid-90s the sales had topped four million. *Tell Me Why* was an equally assured album; opening with the breezy title track, written by Karla Bonoff, there was rarely a dull moment. Songs by Jesse Winchester, Sheryl Crow and Mary-Chapin Carpenter enabled Wynonna to cross over into the AOR market. After contributing an excellent version of Lynyrd Skynyrd's 'Freebird' for the *Skynyrd Friends* album, she came off the road when she became pregnant with her son Elijah. It was a particularly emotional time because she also broke up with her manager and discovered the real identity of her father. She said that making *Revelations* kept her sane, and during the recording she married Nashville businessman Arch Kelley III (Elijah's father). This album and the following year's *The Other Side* provided a further indication of her move away from country, with strong rock and blues influences. Wynonna's position is now far removed from the cosy American family unit of the Reagan era, one that the Judds espoused.

● ALBUMS: *Wynonna* (Curb 1992)★★★, *Tell Me Why* (Curb 1994)★★★★, *Revelations* (Curb 1996)★★★★, *The Other Side* (Curb 1997)★★★, *New Day Dawning* (Curb 2000)★★★.
● COMPILATIONS: *Collection* (Curb 1997)★★★★.

X-ecutioners

These US turntablists, formerly known as the X-Men, officially became the X-ecutioners when they made the leap from battle-DJs to recording artists in their own right. Founded in 1989 with the stated intention of dethroning the reigning battle-DJs of the moment, Clark Kent's Supermen, the crew saw several changes of membership between its inception and its debut to the general listening audience. The eventual line-up comprised Roc Raida (b. Anthony Williams, 17 May 1972), Total Eclipse (b. Keith Bailey, 26 January 1977), Mista Sinista (b. Joel Wright, 27 October 1970) and Rob Swift (b. Rob Aguilar, 14 May 1972), who collectively signed a deal with Asphodel Records that resulted in 1997's *X-pressions*. These four New York natives can count themselves among a select handful of DJs (including their west coast peers the Invisibl Skratch Piklz) who spearheaded the turntablist movement, by taking the classic hip-hop techniques of mixing and cutting into a whole new realm of musical improvisation. In particular, they made their reputation with the technique of beat-juggling; manually alternating between individual kick and snare sounds to create original drum patterns in real-time. This method was pioneered by X-Men founding member Steve Dee circa 1990. He in turn was inspired by the 'beat-making' of Barry Bee, a member of Doug E. Fresh's Get Fresh Crew, and taken to its full potential by Swift and Roc Raida. Raida, who began DJing at the tender age of 10 (having been introduced to the various aspects of hip-hop culture by his father, a member of the Sugarhill Records-signed act Mean Machine), is the only founding X-Men who remains active with the X-ecutioners. Rob Swift was inducted into the crew by Steve Dee after facing him in competition at the 1991 north-east DMC finals. Sinista was mentored in the art of battling by another longtime member (Dr. Butcher), and Total Eclipse, although long acquainted with various members of the crew through the New York battle circuit, was not officially inducted until he took the ITF world championship in July 1996. Individually, and as a crew, the four have contributed beats and scratches for some of the most notable hip-hop artists of their generation, including Common, Organized Konfusion, Jungle Brothers, and Beatnuts, in addition to numerous appearances on compilations such as Bill Laswell's *Altered Beats*. Rob Swift became the first X-ecutioner to release a solo effort with *The Ablist* in 1999, roughly concurrent with their switch to Loud Records to begin work on a second full-length release.

● ALBUMS: *X-pressions* (Asphodel 1997)★★★★.

Xscape

An initially rather laboured attempt at emulating the swing-beat success of SWV and their ilk, this four-piece was assembled in Atlanta, Georgia, USA, by writer/producer Jermaine Dupri, who was previously the force behind Kriss Kross' chart success. However, there was an important difference. While acts such as TLC (another band overseen by Dupri) had been closely identified with provocative sexuality, Xscape had roots in the gospel tradition and eschewed such salacious themes. Xscape comprises sisters LaTocha 'Juicy' Scott, Tamika 'Meatball' Scott, Kandi Burruss and Tameka 'Tiny' Cottle. The intention was to offer a female Jodeci, and they certainly achieved commercial recognition with their 'Just Kickin' It' debut single, which made number 2 on the *Billboard* Hot 100. *Hummin' Comin' At Cha'*, also achieved mainstream success alongside a second single, 'Who's That Man', which was included on the soundtrack to the movie *The Mask*. Their second album, *Off The Hook*, also charted in the Top 3 of the US R&B Albums chart and went platinum. It featured more expansive song arrangements, including electric guitar and acoustic piano. 'The Arms Of The One Who Loves You' was a US number 7 hit in May 1998, and was followed in October by another Top 10 hit, 'My Little Secret'.

● ALBUMS: *Hummin' Comin' At Cha'* (Columbia 1994)★★★, *Off The Hook* (Columbia 1995)★★★★, *Traces Of My Lipstick* (Columbia 1998)★★★.

Yanni

b. Yanni Chryssomalis, Kalamata, Greece. One of modern instrumental music's most distinctive and popular composers, Yanni moved to the USA in 1972 where he attended the University of Minnesota, pursuing a degree in psychology while also playing with prog-rock band Chameleon. However, he is now a naturalized US citizen based in Los Angeles, California, leaving behind his academic studies to concentrate on richly orchestrated and complex keyboard compositions - he was already a self-taught musician with perfect pitch in Greece, as well as a one-time national swimming champion, though to this day he insists he cannot 'read' music. His statement of intent: 'My goal is to connect with people emotionally. I take life's experiences and translate them into music', though perhaps a little pompous, has resulted in albums that have developed a huge following in his adopted homeland. The best example of this, and something of a career summation, was *Yanni Live At The Acropolis*. Planned over two years, this concert in front of 2,000 people in September 1993 (the first time Yanni had played live in his own country) developed an astonishing chart life when released as a double album, reaching platinum status several times over. One of the most phenomenal bestsellers of the mid-90s, it saw Yanni joined by his own band as well as the Royal Philharmonic Concert Orchestra. British Airways' use of 'Aria' as part of their advertising campaign furthered his mainstream appeal, while his relationship with actress Linda Evans brought him fame in the US tabloids. *Yanni: Live At The Acropolis* refreshed memories of some of the artist's most memorable compositions, including new versions of 'Keys To Imagination', 'Nostalgia', 'The Rain Must Fall' and 'Reflections Of Passion', the latter the title track to 1990's platinum-selling album. The rationale behind the orchestral accompaniment ran thus: 'Symphonies can generate a tremendous amount of sound, beauty and emotion. That is part of their human feel and sweetness. Keyboards . . . give us access to millions of sounds. When I put the two together, the result is unique, and it's not only pleasing to the ear, but produces emotional responses that neither can achieve on their own.' The event was broadcast throughout the USA in March 1994, a visual *tour de force* directed by six-times Emmy-winning director, George Veras. With an international crew of more than 200 lighting, sound technicians and cameramen, it gave the whole production a visual might not seen since Jean-Michel Jarre's populist Parisian spectacles. Afterwards Yanni confirmed his position as one of the few artists within the new age sphere with a rock band's appetite for touring. In 1997, he signed with Virgin Records who released *Tribute*, a live album recorded in India and China, the following year.

● ALBUMS: *Keys To Imagination* (Private 1986)★★★, *Out Of Silence*

(Private 1987)★★★, *Chameleon Days* (Private 1988)★★★, *Nini Nana* (Private 1989)★★★, *Reflections Of Passion* (Private 1990)★★★, *In Celebration Of Life* (Private 1991)★★★, *Dare To Dream* (Private 1991)★★★, *In My Time* (Private 1992)★★★★, *Yanni: Live At The Acropolis* (Private 1993)★★, *In The Mirror* (Private 1997)★★★, *Port Of Mystery* (Windham Hill 1997)★★★, *Nightbird* (BMG 1997)★★, *Tribute* (Virgin 1998)★★★.
● COMPILATIONS: *Devotion: The Best Of Yanni* (Private Music 1997)★★★★.
● VIDEOS: *Live At The Acropolis* (Private Music 1994), *Tribute* (Virgin 1997).

Yearwood, Trisha
b. 19 September 1964, Monticello, Georgia, USA. In 1985, Yearwood started working as a session singer in Nashville. She was discovered by Garth Brooks and sang backing vocals on his album *No Fences*. She was the opening act on his 1991 tour and became the first female singer to top the US country charts with her sparkling debut single, 'She's In Love With The Boy'. Further singles such as 'Like We Never Had A Broken Heart', 'That's What I Like About You', 'The Woman Before Me' and 'Wrong Side Of Memphis' quickly established her as a major new talent in contemporary country music. By 1994 she had accomplished major headlining tours, placed albums in the national charts and published her (ghosted) autobiography. Yearwood became a figurehead of the new wave of highly creative female country singers, including Suzy Bogguss, Kathy Mattea and Mary-Chapin Carpenter. Together they have breathed exciting new life into an old formula. Her mid-90s album, *Thinkin' Bout You*, contained irresistible light rockers such as the Berg/Randall composition 'XXX's And OOO's' (with apologies to Richard Thompson's 'I Feel So Good'). Her choice of material is one of her great strengths; her use of contemporary songwriters, and her country-tinged interpretations of their songs, is inspiring. Melissa Etheridge's 'You Can Sleep While I Drive' benefited greatly from the Yearwood treatment, as did James Taylor's 'Bartender Blues'. Married to the Mavericks' bass player Robert Reynolds in 1995, she is at present riding a peak of popularity and won the CMA Award in September 1997 for Best Female Artist.
● ALBUMS: *Trisha Yearwood* (MCA 1991)★★★, *Hearts In Armor* (MCA 1992)★★★, *The Song Remembers When* (MCA 1993)★★★★, *The Sweetest Gift* (MCA 1994)★★★, *Thinkin' Bout You* (MCA 1995)★★★★, *Everybody Knows* (MCA 1996)★★★, *Where Your Road Leads* (MCA 1998)★★★★.
● COMPILATIONS: *Songbook: A Collection Of Hits* (MCA 1997)★★★★.
● FURTHER READING: *Get Hot Or Go Home: The Making Of A Nashville Star*, Lisa Rebecca Gubernick.

Yo La Tengo
New Jersey, USA band who have crafted a formidable reputation within the US alternative rock community with their succulent, Velvet Underground-inspired melodicism. Comprising central duo Ira Kaplan (vocals/guitar) and Georgia Hubley (drums/vocals), plus various associates who in the 90s included James McNew (bass), the band have built a strong reputation with critics worldwide. Yo La Tengo took their name from the cry of a Spanish-speaking baseball outfielder (strictly translating as 'I Got It'), and had their debut album produced by Mission Of Burma bass player Clint Conley. With guest guitar from Dave Schramm, the set

included a cover version of Ray Davies' 'Big Sky'. The oft-stated comparisons between Kaplan's vocals and those of Lou Reed were further endorsed by a version of the latter's 'It's Alright (The Way That You Live)' on the subsequent *New Wave Hot Dogs* collection. Two live songs from a CBGB's set were included on the band's best early recording, 1989's *President Yo La Tengo*. This saw the introduction of bass player Gene Holder, who also produced, on an esoteric set that included two versions of Kaplan's famed composition 'The Evil That Men Do'. Schramm returned alongside double bass player Al Greller for *Fakebook*, primarily a collection of cover versions drawn from the canons of the Kinks, the Flying Burrito Brothers, John Cale and Cat Stevens. Schramm also worked with Greller as Schramms the band - who recorded *Walk To Delphi* for OKra Records in 1990. McNew joined up in time for 1992's *May I Sing With Me*, which also featured lead vocals from Hubley. *Painful* contained the usual assortment of beautiful pop moments, notably 'Nowhere Near' and 'The Whole Of The Law'. Kaplan joined Dave Grohl onstage for his post-Nirvana return as Foo Fighters in 1995. The same year's *Electr-O-Pura*, their seventh album, saw the band picking up UK press for the first time, following a London gig performed under the title Sleeping Pill. Both *I Can Hear The Heart Beating As One* and the follow-up, *And Then Nothing Turned Itself Inside-Out*, gained the band some excellent reviews.
● ALBUMS: *Ride The Tiger* (Coyote/Twin Tone 1986)★★★, *New Wave Hot Dogs* (Coyote/Twin Tone 1987)★★, *President Yo La Tengo* (Coyote 1989)★★★, *Fakebook* (Bar/None 1990)★★★, *May I Sing With Me* (Alias 1992)★★★, *Painful* (City Slang 1993)★★★★, *Electr-O-Pura* (City Slang 1995)★★★, *I Can Hear The Heart Beating As One* (Matador 1997)★★★★, with Jad Fair *Strange But True* (Matador 1998)★★★, *And Then Nothing Turned Itself Inside-Out* (Matador 2000)★★★★.
● COMPILATIONS: *Genius + Love = Yo La Tengo* (Matador 1996)★★★.

Yo Yo
b. Yolanda Whitaker, 4 August 1971, Los Angeles, California, USA. A protégé of Ice Cube, Yo Yo made her name as a female rapper who likes to play it as rough and dirty as her male gangsta brethren. Raised in the South Central district of Los Angeles, her big break came when she appeared on Ice Cube's 1990 debut, *AmeriKKKa's Most Wanted*, duetting on 'It's A Man's World', representing her gender in admirable style. Her own long-playing debut introduced her combative attitude, with frequent interjections from Ice Cube's Lench Mob posse. However, amid the assertive, abrasive lyrics lurked a sophistication that might not have been envisaged by the casual buyer. That album's torch song was 'Sisterland', a rallying call for her fellow female MCs. Yo Yo's insight was later confirmed by her leading role in the formation of the Intelligent Black Woman's Coalition. The following year's *Black Pearl* confirmed her role as a self-styled guru of female dignity and pride in the male dominated world of rap. Keen not to be pigeonholed, Yo Yo largely eschewed the social issues for hardcore reportage on 1993's *You Better Ask Somebody*, which included stand-out tracks 'Girls Got A Gun', and her duet with Ice Cube, 'The Bonnie And Clyde Theme'. Better still, she managed to invert the usual gangsta trappings by acting as a female pimp on 'Macktress'. Following the release of the album Yo Yo concentrated on her acting career, appearing in several movies

including the Hughes brothers acclaimed *Menace II Society*, while continuing to play an active role in community projects. She returned to recording with the lacklustre *Total Control*, on which the lifeless grooves blunted her still impressive rapping skills. *Ebony* was a more effective attempt at updating her sound to match the new generation of female rappers led by Foxy Brown and Lil' Kim. The album included combative collaborations with Missy 'Misdemeanor' Elliott ('I Would If I Could') and Lil' Shawn ('Fantasy').

● ALBUMS: *Make Way For The Motherlode* (East West 1991)★★★, *Black Pearl* (East West 1992)★★★, *You Better Ask Somebody* (East West 1993)★★★, *Total Control* (East West 1996)★★, *Ebony* (East West 1998)★★★.

● FILMS: *Boyz N The Hood* (1991), *Menace II Society* (1993).

Young Disciples

Although their roots were in the rave scene, this UK band's debut single, 1990's 'Get Yourself Together', combined hip-hop with jazz inflections, and featured the voice of Carleen Anderson and MC Mell 'O' on either side. Formed by Mark 'O' and Femi, the Young Disciples would win much of their notoriety through Anderson's vocal attributes. It was she who wrote and sang on many of their best recordings, including 'Apparently Nothin'', which entered the UK Top 20 when it was reissued in autumn 1991. Her final release with the Young Disciples was *Dusky Sappho*, a limited edition EP, after which she concentrated on her solo career. Femi and Mark 'O' continued to use the Young Disciples banner, though the former would also undertake remix work for Xscape ('Just Kickin'') and others.

● ALBUMS: *Road To Freedom* (Talkin' Loud 1991)★★★.

Youth

b. Martin Glover, 27 December 1960, Africa. This highly respected and versatile UK-based producer and remixer is the former bass player from seminal post-punk band Killing Joke. He has produced or remixed for a diverse range of artists, including the Verve, Embrace, Crowded House, P.M. Dawn, the Orb, U2, Bananarama, INXS, James, Wet Wet Wet, the Shamen, Texas and even Tom Jones. He is able to turn his skills to almost any musical style including folk, rock, dance music and straightforward pop. Glover began producing while still with Killing Joke and left the band in 1982 to pursue solo projects, the first of which was the band Brilliant – which included contributions from Jimmy Cauty, later of the KLF. He then worked with the successful dance act Blue Pearl before producing and helping to write the Orb's first two albums. More dance-orientated productions followed in the form of work with Transglobal Underground and P.M. Dawn. In 1991, he also formed Butterfly and Dragonfly Records, groundbreaking labels for ambient and trance recordings. In 1994, Youth resumed work with Killing Joke and they released the well-received *Pandemonium* and *Democracy*. His most significant recent production work has been on the Verve's hugely successful *Urban Hymns*, which topped the UK album charts for several weeks and included the UK number 1 single 'The Drugs Don't Work' and the UK Top 10 hits 'Bitter Sweet Symphony' and 'Lucky Man'. The album won the UK's 1998 BRIT Award for Best Album, while Youth won the Producer Of The Year award.

Zhané

This east coast urban R&B duo comprises Renee Neufville (b. Brooklyn, New York, USA) and Jean Norris (b. Moorestown, New Jersey, USA), who started singing together while studying at Philadelphia Temple University, and were discovered at a talent show by DJ Jazzy Jeff And The Fresh Prince. They went on to contribute backing vocals to the latter's 1991 single, 'Ring My Bell', before linking with another prominent rapper, Queen Latifah, as part of her Flavor Unit collective. Their debut, 'Hey Mr DJ', was first featured on the compilation album, *Roll Wit Tha Flava*, before subsequent release as a single saw it reach the Top 5 in the USA. Like Latifah, they signed with Motown Records, enjoying further success with the follow-up single 'Groove Thang'. Both hits were produced in association with DJ Kay Gee of Naughty By Nature fame, and prefaced a similarly successful debut album, the title of which offered instruction as to the pronunciation of Zhané's name. The follow-up, *Saturday Night*, was another excellent collection, but proved less of a commercial success.

● ALBUMS: *Pronounced Jah-Nay* (Illtown/Motown 1994)★★★, *Saturday Night* (Illtown/Motown 1997)★★★★.

Zion Train

Formed in 1990, the UK's Zion Train have proved to be innovators in the revolutionary new wave of dub. While many other bands preferred a revivalist stance, the north London-based co-operative established an enviable reputation. The cross-cultural line-up consists of Molora (vocals/percussion), Neil (DJ/beats/bass), Colin C (melodica), Dave Hake (trumpet, also part of the Tassilli Players) and Chris Hetter (trombone). Influenced by Jah Shaka, Lee Perry and other dub masters, their dub/roots equation was first unveiled on the sequential singles 'Power One' and 'Power Two'. As well as recording dub sounds, the collective also run the Universal Egg label, the Bass Odyssey club and their own sound system, produce their own magazine, *The Wobbler*, and released the first promotional dub video, *Get Ready*, and a CD-ROM to accompany *Homegrown Fantasy*, their debut release for China Records. One of their most effective and highly regarded works was the 'Follow Like Wolves' single, a fertile cross between dub and house music, with samples drawn from the Specials' back-catalogue. In a departure from usual reggae practice, they subsequently instigated the (no copyright) Soundpool, allowing free sampling, and thus dispensing with the need for acquisitive lawyers. They have also worked with Junior Reid, Maxi Priest, Studio One veteran Devon Russell and the Dub Syndicate, as well as Indian tabla players and Brazilian drummers. In 1996, they ventured into ambient dub territory, performing with artists including the Shamen, New Model Army and Gary Clail, and instigated the re-formation of Ruts DC for a collaboration on a live session for BBC Radio. The release of *Grow Together* featured Dave Ruffy, the Ruts' drummer, and a revival of the band's 1979 hit 'Babylon's Burning'. That single was followed by 'Rise', with which they achieved their first exposure on national daytime radio. Extensive touring and major festival appearances have secured the band international popularity. They later released 'Stand Up And Fight', featuring Kate Cameron on lead vocals and a 19-minute soulful reggae remix. *Love Revolutionaries* marked a return to their own Universal Egg label.

● ALBUMS: *Passage To Indica* (Zion 1994)★★★★, *Great Sporting Moments In Dub* (Zion 1994)★★★, *Natural Wonders Of The World* (Universal Egg 1994)★★★, *Siren* (Universal Egg 1995)★★★, *Homegrown Fantasy* (China 1995)★★★, *Grow Together* (China 1996)★★★★, *Single Minded And Alive* (China 1997)★★★, *Love Revolutionaries* (Universal Egg 1999)★★★.

● COMPILATIONS: *Forward Roots* cassette only (Zion 1993)★★★.

Zoe

b. Zoe Pollock, Peckham, London, England. Zoe made a huge impact in 1991 with the release of her debut single, 'Sunshine On A Rainy Day', a perfect Europop cover version that went to number 4 in the UK charts. It had originally been released a year earlier when it reached the Top 60. However, subsequent efforts 'Lightning' and 'Holy Days' fared poorly. When her solo debut also flopped, she found herself in conflict with her label bosses over the extensive personal appearances she was required to perform at tawdry discos throughout Europe, and the relationship almost collapsed. Pollock had joined her first band, the soul outfit Cacique, after leaving stage school aged 16. She eventually regrouped in 1995 and began working on new tracks with her partner Youth, whom she first met while auditioning for Brilliant at his Butterfly Studios in Brixton. When she presented these to her record company M&G Records, new A&R director Jack Steven was impressed, and arranged for a concurrent US release of the album by RCA Records. Most of the instruments on *Hammer* were played by Youth, though the duo's emotional relationship had sundered during the sessions - leaving Youth doubtlessly wondering at whom some of the more pointed lyrics were aimed. Rather than the slightly sickly pop of her debut, *Hammer* comprised a number of bittersweet lyrics and harsh vignettes, typified by 'Love Is The Beast' and the title track. Zoe's interest in the ethnic music of Ireland and India was also well represented in the Buddhist mantra 'R.A.M' and 'Down The Mountain'. 'The Lion Roars', meanwhile, was written in tandem with Anthony Thistlewaite, formerly of the Waterboys, and co-produced by revered Irish producer Donal Lunny in Dublin with Davy Spillane contributing uilleann pipes.

● ALBUMS: *Scarlet Red And Blue* (M&G 1992)★★, *Hammer* (RCA/M&G 1996)★★★.

Zombie, Rob

b. Robert Straker, 1966, USA. The lead vocalist of controversial hard rock band White Zombie delivered his US Top 5 debut in August 1998. Co-produced with Nine Inch Nails and Metallica alumnus Scott Humphrey, the contents would have proved no surprise to Zombie's existing fans, with horror and gore-inspired lyrics predominating and abrasive hard rock the dominant musical motif. Indeed, among the collaborators on the project were White Zombie's drummer John Tempesta. The album's subtitle, *Tales Of Cadaverous Cavorting Inside The Spookshow International*, was illustrative of the subject matter. Songs like 'Living Dead Girl' and 'Return Of The Phantom Monster' said much about the depth of the writer's vision, though some of the more entertaining moments came from the album's employment of old movie dialogue and specially-created spoken word sections. For some, however, Zombie's 50s B-movie fixations had been made redundant by the remorseless rise of Marilyn Manson. Probably the most distinctive feature of the album was the packaging, with illustrations from noted comic artists Basil Gogos, Dan Brereton and Gene Colon. The album was remixed the following year by various members of Nine Inch Nails, Rammstein and Limp Bizkit, by which time White Zombie had split-up.

● ALBUMS: *Hellbilly Deluxe* (Geffen 1998)★★★★, *American Made Music To Strip By* remix album (Geffen 1999)★★★.

Index

Index

Index

Index

Index

Index